A Gale Ready Reference Handbook

Gale's Guide to Genealogical & Historical Research

ISSN 1526-6796

A Gale Ready Reference Handbook

Gale's Guide
to Genealogical
& Historical
Research

Dawn Conzett DesJardins, editor

GALE GROUP

Detroit
San Francisco
London
Boston
Woodbridge, CT

Gale's Guide to Genealogical and Historical Research
A Gale
Ready Reference
Handbook

Dawn Conzett DesJardins
Editor

Carolyn A. Fischer, *Contributing Editor*

Kristin Mallegg, Erin Nagel, Annette Novallo, Amy L. Rance,
and Jeff Sumner *Contributors*

Kathleen Lopez Nolan, *Managing Editor*

Theresa Rocklin, *Manager, Technical Support Services*
Richard Antonowicz, Charles Beaumont, Dan Bono, Magdalena Cureton,
Venus Little, and Natasha Mikheyeva, *Programmers*

Dorothy Maki, *Manufacturing Manager*
Wendy Blurton, *Senior Buyer*

Mary Beth Trimper, *Composition Manager*
Evi Seoud, *Assistant Production Manager*

Cindy Baldwin, *Product Design Manager*
Pamela A. E. Galbreath, *Senior Art Director*

ISBN 0-7876-3955-9

ISSN 1526-6796

Printed in the United States of America

Table of Contents

A series of books designed to quickly answer questions on a number of subjects, the *Gale Ready Reference Handbooks* are a great addition to any library. The *Gale Ready Reference Handbooks* feature six industry-targeted sourcebooks which contain a comprehensive cross-section of data, including information on associations, libraries, publishers, research centers, directories, newsletters, periodicals, CD-ROMs, databases and online services. Indexed geographically and by keyword for ease-of-use. Also featured in this series are four task-specific references containing high-quality data, including essays, overviews, and contact information.

Gale's Guide to Genealogical and Historical Research

Gale's Guide to Genealogical and Historical Research (GGGHR) contains over 4,200 genealogy and family history-related sources. So whether you're just starting to research your family tree or you've hit a dead end, you can rely on *GGGHR* to point you in the right direction.

Gale's Guide to Nonprofits

Featuring over 4,600 entries covering all aspects of the world of nonprofits from associations that are involved in nonprofit activities to directories that list nonprofit corporations. Make *Gale's Guide to Nonprofits (GGNP)* the first place you turn to when you need to find this information.

Coming Soon

Gale's Guide to the Arts
Gale's Guide to the Government
Gale's Guide to Industry
Gale's Guide to the Media

Related Titles

Fast Answers to Common Questions (FACQ)
Presented in a question and answer format, *FACQ* contains answers to 4,500 commonly asked ready-reference questions on a variety of subjects.

Fast Help for Major Medical Conditions (FHMMC)
Features essays about 100 common medical diseases and conditions, including an explanation of the disease/condition, symptoms, treatment, prognosis, prevention, and alternative treatments.

First Stop for Jobs and Industries (FSJI)
With information on more than 500 jobs and 1,100 industries, *FSJI* is a great source for job seekers, career counselors, investors, and entrepreneurs alike.

Where to Go/Who to Ask (WGWA)
Contains contact information for approximately 4,900 associations, 8,600 publications, 1,600 databases, and 3,200 agencies, research centers and organizations. Arranged in a yellow pages-type format by keyword.

Gale's Guide to Genealogical and Historical Research is a handy directory to grab when you want to locate points of contact for associations, libraries, publishers, research centers, directories, newsletters, periodicals, and databases covering all aspects of genealogy and family historical research. This useful product contains names, addresses, phone/fax numbers, and e-mail addresses/URLs for more than 4,200 listings. Also included are detailed descriptions of the organizations, publications, and databases with other pertinent details.

Content and Arrangement

The information in this product is arranged by type of data (organizations, publications, and databases) for ease of use. There is also a title and keyword index which lists the names of all entries as well as important keywords within each name, and a geographic index that includes the names of all entries sorted by state/province then city which offers convenient access to resources in a particular community.

Descriptive Listings

Divided into three chapters (organizations, publications, and databases), *Gale's Guide to Genealogical and Historical Research* further specifies what type of information is included in each.

- Organizations: Associations, Libraries, Publishers, and Research Centers;
- Publications: Directories, Newsletters, and Periodicals;
- Databases: CD-ROMs, Online, and Other Formats.

Geographic Index

This index provides a geographical listing of all entry names by country (USA, then Canada), then by state/province, and finally by city. The number following the index citations refer to book entry numbers rather than page numbers.

Master Index

This index contains an alphabetical listing of all entry names and important keywords mentioned within entry names. The numbers following the index citations refer to book entry numbers (rather than page numbers) on which the word or phrase can be found.

Method of Compilation

Gale's Guide to Genealogical and Historical Research is compiled from a vast array of important reference sources. Information was carefully selected from many core Gale Group directories which cover sources relevant to genealogy and family historical research. Specific source information can be found in the User's Guide section following this introduction.

Acknowledgments

The staff of *Gale's Guide to Genealogical and Historical Research* would like to thank Lisa DeShantz-Cook, Late Dinner, for her contributions to this book.

Comments and Suggestions

We invite comments and suggestions for improvement. Please contact:

Gale Group Inc.
27500 Drake Rd.
Farmington Hills, MI 48331-3535

Telephone: (248)699-4253
Toll-free: 800-347-4253
Fax: (248)699-8070

Gale's Guide to Genealogical and Historical Research comprises descriptive listings of more than 4,200 organizations, publications, and databases, as well as a geographic and keyword index. Each is fully explained below.

Descriptive Listings

- **Associations**
  - **Content and selection criteria:** Can include the following elements: name of the association; address; phone, fax, and toll-free numbers; e-mail address; URL; names and titles of key personnel; and a brief description, founded date, and number of members.
    - **Source:** *Encyclopedia of Associations* (includes *National Organizations of the U.S.*; *Regional, State, and Local Organizations*; and *International Organizations*)

- **Libraries**
  - **Content and selection criteria:** Can include the following elements: name of the library; address; phone, fax, and toll-free numbers; e-mail address; URL; names and titles of key personnel; and a brief description listing services, subjects covered, and holdings.
    - **Source:** *Directory of Special Libraries*

- **Publishers**
  - **Content and selection criteria:** Can include the following elements: name of the publisher; address; phone, fax, and toll-free numbers; e-mail address; URL; names and titles of key personnel; and a brief description.
    - **Source:** *Publishers Directory*

- **Research centers**
  - **Content and selection criteria:** May contain the following elements: name of the center; name of the organization which heads up the center; phone, fax, and toll-free numbers; e-mail address; URL; names and titles of key personnel; and a brief description including type of research conducted.
    - **Source:** *Research Centers Directory*

- **Directories**
  - **Content and selection criteria:** May include the following elements: directory title; publishing company's name; address; phone, fax, and toll-free numbers; e-mail address; URL; names and titles of key personnel; and a brief description including fre-quency of publication, price, online availability, and alternate formats.
    - **Source:** *Directories in Print*

- **Newsletters**
  - **Content and selection criteria:** May contain the following elements: newsletter title; publishing company's name; address; phone, fax, and toll-free numbers; e-mail address; URL; names and titles of key personnel; and a brief description including frequency of publication, price, online availability, and alternate formats.
    - **Source:** *Newsletters in Print*

- **Periodicals**
  - **Content and selection criteria:** May contain the following elements: periodical title; publishing company's name; address; phone, fax, and toll-free numbers; e-mail address; URL; names and titles of key personnel; alternate contact information; and a brief description including frequency of publication, price, online availability, and alternate formats.
    - **Source:** *Gale Directory of Publications and Broadcast Media*

- **CD-ROMs**
  - **Content and selection criteria:** May contain the following elements: CD-ROM name; producer's name, address; phone, fax, and toll-free numbers; e-mail address; URL; names and titles of key personnel; and a brief description including database type.
    - **Source:** *Gale Directory of Databases*

- **Online**
  - **Content and selection criteria:** May contain the following elements: name of the database; vendor name, address; phone, fax, and toll-free numbers; e-mail address; URL; names and titles of key personnel; and a brief description including database type.
    - **Source:** *Gale Directory of Databases* and *Gale Guide to Internet Databases*

- **Other Formats**
  - **Content and selection criteria:** May contain the following elements: name of the database; name of the company; address; phone, fax, and toll-free numbers; e-mail address; URL; names and titles of key personnel; and a brief description including the type of format it's produced in and database type.
    - **Source:** *Gale Directory of Databases*

Geographic Index

This index provides a geographical listing of all entry names. Sorted by country (USA, then Canada), then by state/province, and finally by city (city name is listed in parentheses following the entry name). Index references are to book entry numbers rather than page numbers.

Master Index

This index offers alphabetical access by title and important keywords within titles to all entries included in the book. Index references are to book entry numbers rather than page numbers.

On occasion, the same entry may be listed more than once with different book entry numbers. Please note that although quite frequently these may appear to be duplicate entries, these entries are most likely not duplicates. Rather, one entry may be a periodical while the other entry of the same name is a database. (For example, the Dayton Daily News contains some of the same material but not all of the same material in its database form as it does in its print form.) Although these two entries may have the same name and the same basic contact information, more often than not there will be differences in what type of information each contains or what products or services each has to offer. Therefore, this book lists all of the different descriptions of a product, to ensure that you find what you need.

Were there standard cautions to start one on a quest for familial heritage, such a warning might begin like this: "Take heed. You are about to embark on a journey that could take you very far. You might unearth great surprises and uncover startling secrets. You might learn of romance, crime or tragedy. You may find yourself transported to long ago ages. You may find your everyday life taking a backseat to the treasures you uncover."

Of course, a less romantic warning might simply inform you that your search will be frustrating at times as some of your hottest leads end up to be dead ends, and that it might take years, even decades of your life. Both "warnings" are true. Whatever our reasons—romantic, historical, legal, just for fun, or some combination thereof—we dig into our past to make sense of our own present and enlighten our future.

Another truth: genealogy is one of the most popular hobbies in America. We are interested in our histories, not just to know where it is we came from, but to know whom we came from and to have a story to tell about it. A tallying of the family scorecard at the start of a new century tidies things up a bit. A jumping off point, if you will, for later generations, your own children, your children's children, their cousins. And, while some of our family histories really do read more like a fantastic novel, with mystery, intrigue, crime and redemption, most are simply filled with the stuff of everyday lives, everyday people doing what needed to be done to get through the times. Perhaps not as glamorous or romantic as we'd hoped, but keys to our own lives, nonetheless.

Delving into family history is an individual journey, a process that begins by moving backwards, to your own parents, your parents' parents and beyond. Through this research, you weave a rich tapestry of ancestors, history, heritage, events and happenings, much like the tapestry of an old quilt handed down through the generations. And while the quest is yours alone, there are tools and procedures that anyone can use to make the process less daunting. The book you hold now will help guide you as you journey into the lives of your own ancestors.

The Basics

Simply put, genealogy is the search for one's own heritage through the study of ancestors. It involves searching public records mainly for names and dates. Family history research, while not totally synonymous with genealogy, is similar, yet delves further. Research

in this direction aims to produce a documented narrative that describes not just when or where family members lived, but how they lived as well as surrounding historical events. Together, the two modes of study can combine to create as thorough a picture of lineage as the researcher is willing (or has the time) to realize. While genealogical research may divulge the names and pertinent dates of ancestors, family history research brings about the more interesting details, like criminal or social records. You may find your lineage includes famous, or likewise infamous, members.

Whether you plan on digging for the bare bones of genealogical detail, or intend to create a full picture for future generations by including family history, you may be boggled by the myriad of sources of information and approaches to getting that information. Regardless, the best way to begin is with a how-to book or some basic beginner's tips. Your local library may have tip sheets as well as forms that you can fill out as you research so that you can keep track of sources you've checked. The next step is to begin interviewing living family members, and looking through old family mementos such as journals, letters, photo albums, newspaper clippings, memorial cards, school or medical records and anything else that's been kept or handed down. Once you've passed what's readily available around you (parents, grandparents, aunts, uncles, cousins), you'll branch out to the library or courthouse to find available birth, marriage, death, school, census, cemetery, and church records, to name a few. *Gale's Guide to Genealogical and Historical Research*, as well as the Internet and your local library (and its employees) will be indispensable in helping you locate sources for vital information.

The Internet as a Tool

Where people wishing to dig up family history and genealogical details once had only city or court offices, church records and living relatives to glean details from, now the sources for this information have become innumerable. Likewise, computers now join libraries and genealogical societies as tools of the genealogical trade. Still, even the newest sources will lead you back to the "old fashioned" ways of finding genealogical and historical information, i.e. public records and local newspapers. These primary sources are the main tools of the trade and are still the best ways to uncover information. Before current technology, though, you'd have had to spend long hours at the library searching index after index. Or, you'd have had to make trips to distant libraries in search of details. Now, much of this preliminary searching can be done right from your own computer.

With the explosion of computer technology comes new sources, as well as interesting new challenges. The Internet and family tree-type software programs can make your journey easier and head off some of the dead-ends you may have found with only traditional sources. Online indexes, published genealogies, genealogical societies and forums are all a huge boon to the researcher. They're available to you anytime you sit down in front of your computer and log onto the Internet. However, the reliability of every Internet source may not be proven, which is why experts and experienced researchers strongly suggest crosschecking and verifying all references. If you find a name or date in an index on the Internet, get a copy of the original record for verification. And while research on the Internet may provide new clues and open up new avenues in your research, remember that for every cemetery index, death record, census report, marriage record and published genealogy on the Internet, there are countless more in archives, courthouses, museums and libraries. Use the Internet as you use everything else in your search: as one tool to filling in the holes of your heritage. The use of a guide such *Gale's Guide to Genealogical and Historical Research*, as well as the tools current technology has made available, can help eliminate some unnecessary footwork.

Getting Started

The Internet has thus far changed the way people do many different kinds of research, and the same can be said for genealogical and historical research. Currently, any Internet search for "genealogy" will turn up hundreds of sites for everything from basic information and how-to's, to someone's own web site publishing their genealogy, to sites that will do some of the work for you for a fee, none guaranteed to give you the results you need in your own journey. While you may or may not find information about your own family online, some very good articles exist there about the necessities of record-keeping, double-checking your sources, tips for preserving old documents, and organizing and compiling your information.

At this book's publishing time, countless online sites offer not only useful tips for beginners and advanced genealogists, but convenient, online searches of public records, death notices, newspapers, library indexes and more, as well as downloadable tip sheets and forms for recording your research. You'll also find online genealogical and family history forums, where beginning and experienced researchers offer support, advice, and perhaps even their help in your search. Added to your list of sources for general information as well as pointed searches, the Internet is indeed a valuable tool. And while much can be done online, you still must do the real work of the project offline to assure yourself that the genealogy you're creating for future ancestors is accurate.

Another technological avenue to travel on your journey is the growing array of software titles, some relatively inexpensive, that can help you create your family tree. Some of these titles will make easier work of organizing your data; others provide tools to help you research; some even provide a means of documenting your findings, along with places to add photographs or other family mementos in your documents. You'll find many listed in these pages, and you'll find discussion or reviews about them on various Internet sites.

Gale's Guide to Genealogical and Historical Research

Genealogy is vast, yet personal. There are no rights or wrongs, and no sole guidebook that works for each individual's journey. But the many tools available can help you create as much detail as you want in the picture of your heritage. Your own search may not turn up what you expect. You may find unsavory characters in the story of your heritage or events that you find disagreeable. Take heart, these are in the past. Your documentation will serve as interesting research and perhaps an exciting read for future generations.

More tools are available for genealogical and family research every day. A trip to the library or several hours searching the Internet may make the task at hand seem daunting or overwhelming at times, but a focused effort will pay off with rich and accurate details.

Gale's Guide to Genealogical and Historical Research lists the best organizations, publications, and databases in the U.S. and Canada to help you create a full picture of your ancestry. It's arranged to help you easily find the information you need, so if you're looking for newsletters, libraries, or CD-ROMs, you'll find them quickly.

Associations

1 ▪ A. D. Johnson Family Association
930 W. Long Ave.   Ph: (814)371-2532
Du Bois, PA 15801-1737   Fax: (814)371-2532
E-mail: rbt@lindbergcomputer.com

Contact: John S. Walker, Family Historian/Pres.

Desc: Individuals related to the families of A. D. Johnson, Sarah Dillon Johnson, Dennison Johnson, Wealthy Johnson Hoover, and Edward and Esther Wheaton Johnson of Branford, CT, and Edward Johnson of Canterbury, England, founder of Woburn, MA. *Founded:* 1981. *Members:* 100.

2 ▪ Abbott Family
123 A Park Ln.   Ph: (803)761-4904
Moncks Corner, SC 29461-8049

Contact: Victor Paul Mertrud, Contact.

Desc: Abbott family members. Promotes interest in, and study of, Abbott family history and genealogy. *Founded:* 1980.

3 ▪ Abbs Surname Organization
1404 N St   Ph: (541)747-9799
Springfield, OR 97477
E-mail: barbaras@rio.com

Contact: Barbara Abbs Stockwell, Exec. Officer.

Desc: Individuals interested in researching the Abbs surname and Abbs descendents in the U.S. Conducts genealogical research. *Founded:* 1993.

4 ▪ Acadian Cultural Society
PO Box 2304   Ph: (978)342-7173
Fitchburg, MA 01420-0015

Contact: P.J. LeBlanc, Pres.

Desc: Works to preserve and promote Acadian heritage among people of Acadian descent. *Founded:* 1985. *Members:* 800.

5 ▪ Acomb Reunion
10498 County Rd. 46   Ph: (716)335-5173
Dansville, NY 14437

Contact: Alice Acomb, Historian.

Desc: Descendants of Joseph and Elizabeth Acomb. Promotes and facilitates social interaction among members. *Founded:* 1913.

6 ▪ Adair County Genealogical Society
PO Box 613
Columbia, KY 42728

Contact: Debora J. Nobles, Pres.

Desc: Individuals interested in genealogy. Conducts research and educational programs; provides assistance to beginning genealogists. Gathers, restores, and donates genealogical materials to local libraries. *Members:* 200.

7 ▪ Adam Hawkes Family Association
3600 Lester Ct.   Ph: (770)985-9285
Lilburn, GA 30047   Fax: (770)985-5792

Contact: Susan Hawkes Cook, Registrar/Historian.

Desc: Lineal descendants of Adam Hawkes (1605-1672) of Saugus, MA, and of John and Matthew Hawkes, who arrived in America before 1635; spouses of lineal descendants. Unrelated persons interested in the Hawkes/Hawks family line may join as subscribing (nonvoting) members. Seeks to publish Hawkes family genealogies and histories. *Founded:* 1876. *Members:* 250.

8 ▪ Adams Family Association
946 Morgan Ave.   Ph: (850)663-4507
Chattahoochee, FL 32324

Contact: Emily S. Hart, Secretary.

Desc: Descendants of Jesse Allen Adams (1791-1866) and Elizabeth Bryant (1792-1832); other interested individuals. Facilitates communication among members of the Adams family. *Founded:* 1979. *Members:* 1251.

9 ▪ Addington Association
12407 Millstream Dr.   Ph: (301)464-0435
Bowie, MD 20715   Fax: (301)352-3869
E-mail: jerysox@erols.com

Contact: Jerry Sue Bowersox, Exec. Officer.

Desc: Individuals interested in the genealogy and family history of people with the surname Addington. Promotes genealogical and historical study and interest. *Founded:* 1988. *Members:* 100.

10 ▪ Adoptees' Birthparents' Association
2027 Finch Ct.   Ph: (805)482-8667
Simi Valley, CA 93063   Fax: (805)583-4160
E-mail: mygrandkidsrgr8@juno.com

Contact: Alberta F. Sorensen, Contact.

Desc: Adoptees, birthparents, and interested others. *Founded:* 1984. *Members:* 50.

11 ▪ Adoptees and Natural Parents Organization
949 Lacon Dr.   Ph: (757)874-9091
Newport News, VA 23608

Contact: Billie Quigley, Pres.

Desc: Adoptees over the age of 18; birth parents of adult adoptees. Provides search assistance and support services for individuals interested in locating their biological families. Search services are generally limited to individuals who were adopted in or have lived in Virginia. *Founded:* 1965.

12 ▪ Adoption Identity Movement
PO Box 9783   Ph: (616)531-1380
Grand Rapids, MI 49509   Fax: (616)532-5589

Contact: Peg Richer, Dir.

Desc: Birthparents, adoptive parents, and adoptees; others affected by or interested in adoption. Promotes the opening of sealed adoption records for adoptees and birth parents searching for their biological families. *Founded:* 1977.

13 ▪ Advocating Legislation for Adoption Reform Movement
162 SW 48th St.
Cape Coral, FL 33914

Contact: Sandra Musser, Exec Dir.

Desc: Birthparents, adoptive parents, adoptees, mental health professionals, and others interested in reforming the adoption process in the U.S. Promotes open adoption, in which adult adoptees have free access to their birth certificates and other records. Functions as a grass roots lobbying organization for humane and constructive change in the adoption system. Works for repeal of current state laws denying adoptees access to their genealogical records; opposes falsification of adoptees' genealogical records; seeks to rectify current procedures which effectively deny government assistance to adoptees who were born in one state, adopted in another, and living in still another state. Provides referral service and search assistance for individuals searching for their birth relatives; conducts research. Operates speakers' bureau; compiles statistics. *Founded:* 1987. *Members:* 750.

14 ▪ Afghan Women Counselling and Integration Community Support Organization
2333 Dundas St. W, Ste. 205   Ph: (416)588-3585
Toronto, ON, Canada M6R   Fax: (416)588-4552
  3A6
E-mail: aniazi@afghan_women.org

Contact: Adeena Niazi, Pres.

Desc: Individuals and organizations. Seeks to insure the successful integration of Afghan women into Canadian society.

15 ▪ African-Atlantic Genealogical Society
PO Box 7385
Freeport, NY 11520-0757

Contact: Julius O. Pearse, Contact.

16 ■ African and Caribbean Immigrant Resource Center

600 Cleveland Ave.
Plainfield, NJ 07060-1727

Contact: Joy A. Wilson, Contact.

17 ■ Afro-American Historical and Genealogical Society, Chicago Chapter

PO Box 438652   Ph: (773)821-6473
Chicago, IL 60643
E-mail: seldridge@sandc.com

Contact: Thelma S. Eldridge, Pres.

Desc: Promotes scholarly research, projects, writing and publishing which further the study of African-American genealogy, history, and culture. Collects yearbooks, programs (all types), family histories, church histories, Bible records. *Founded:* 1989. *Members:* 137.

18 ■ Afro-American Historical and Genealogical Society

PO Box 73086   Ph: (202)234-5350
Washington, DC 20056   Fax: (202)829-9280
E-mail: badbdw@aol.com
URL: http://www.rootsweb.com/mdaahgs

Contact: Barbara Dodson Walker, Pres.

Desc: Individuals, libraries, and archives. Encourages scholarly research in Afro-American history and genealogy as it relates to American history and culture. *Founded:* 1977. *Members:* 800.

19 ■ Agnew Association of America

1920 Highland Ave.   Ph: (724)864-5625
Irwin, PA 15642   Fax: (724)864-9358

Contact: Thomas I. Agnew, Convener.

Desc: Individuals and descendants of Scotch-Irish heritage with the surname Agnew. Promotes the study of and interest in members' lineage. *Founded:* 1984. *Members:* 165.

20 ■ Aiken-Barnwell Genealogical Society

PO Box 415   Ph: (803)649-9273
Aiken, SC 29802-0415
E-mail: lhutto@ifx.net
URL: http://www.ifx.net/lhutto/page2.html

Contact: Albert H. Peters, III, Pres.

Desc: Interested persons organized to promote genealogical research and preserve genealogical information in Aiken County, S.C. and old Barnwell District, S.C. *Founded:* 1984. *Members:* 230.

21 ■ Akert Family Geneaology Research Organization

3784 Grove Ave.
Palo Alto, CA 94303

Desc: Promotes research and study of the Akert family name.

22 ■ Alachua County Genealogical Society

PO Box 12078   Ph: (904)378-8092
Gainesville, FL 32604

Contact: Jack B. Wood, Pres.

Desc: Conducts genealogical research and educational programs. *Founded:* 1980. *Members:* 140.

23 ■ Alaska Historical Society

PO Box 100299   Ph: (907)276-1596
Anchorage, AK 99510-0299

Contact: Kay Shelton, Pres.

Desc: Individuals interested in preserving the history of Alaska. *Founded:* 1967. *Members:* 460.

24 ■ Albert Andrew Bahr Family Organization

529 West 1600 South   Ph: (801)224-2297
Orem, UT 84058-7319

Contact: Leona Rowley, Pres.

Desc: Descendants and relatives of Albert Andrew Bahr. Collects and preserves important history and genealogical records of the Bahr family. *Founded:* 1977. *Members:* 100.

25 ■ Albison Family History Association

4065 Berrywood Dr.   Ph: (541)461-4473
Eugene, OR 97404-4061

Contact: James R. Brann, Pres./Historian.

Desc: Collects, preserves, and disseminates information on all persons with the surnames Albison and Albiston from England to Maine. *Founded:* 1989. *Members:* 10.

26 ■ Alden Kindred of America

105 Alden St.   Ph: (781)934-9092
PO Box 2754
Duxbury, MA 02331-2754
E-mail: director@alden.org
URL: http://www.alden.org

Contact: Robert A. Edmunds, Dir.

Desc: Descendants of John Alden and Priscilla Mullins Alden. Promotes interest in Alden family history and genealogy. *Founded:* 1901. *Members:* 1500.

27 ■ Alderson Cousins

127 Topaz Way
San Francisco, CA 94131-2535
URL: http://www.slip.net/dgf/Alderson

Contact: David Fridley, Contact.

Desc: Individuals with the surname Alderson and its variants; others with an interest in the Alderson family. Promotes study of, and interest in, Alderson family history and genealogy. *Founded:* 1989. *Members:* 100.

28 ■ Alexander Hamilton Hutton, Sr., Family Organization

6945 South 3420 West   Ph: (801)966-6585
West Jordan, UT 84084

Contact: Gerald W. Hutton, Contact.

Desc: Works to further the history of the Alexander H. Hutton family. Traces the family history from Hutton's 1842 departure from Ireland and arrival in New York City. *Founded:* 1980.

29 ■ Alford American Family Association

PO Box 1586   Ph: (314)831-8648
Florissant, MO 63031
E-mail: 72154.1610@compuserve.com
URL: http://www.alford.com/alford/aafa/
       homepage.html

Contact: Gil Alford, Jr., Pres.

Desc: Works to collect, record, and preserve biographical data on Alfords (and other spelling variations) and their ancestors. *Founded:* 1987. *Members:* 1000.

30 ■ Allen County Genealogical Society of Indiana

PO Box 12003
Fort Wayne, IN 46862
URL: http://www.cvax.ipfw.indiana.edu/www/depts/
       history/historgs/acgsi.htm

Contact: Linda Churchward, Pres.

Desc: To collect and preserve genealogical information about Allen County, IN families. Encourages genealogical research. *Founded:* 1976. *Members:* 350.

31 ■ Allgood Ancestry

3709 S. Mission Pky.   Ph: (303)693-0175
Aurora, CO 80013-2405
E-mail: ljcurtis@aol.com

Contact: Linda Curtis, Editor.

Desc: Conducts genealogical research of the surname Allgood. Disseminates information. Presently inactive. *Founded:* 1988.

32 ■ Allison Family Association

<c/o> Sandy Allison   Ph: (314)341-3549
10095 County Rd. 5120   Fax: (314)364-5310
Rolla, MO 65401
E-mail: sandy@rollenet.org

Contact: Sandy Allison, Pres.

Desc: Individuals with the surname Allison; interested members of other family lines. Conducts genealogical research; sponsors history seminars. Provides indexing service; operates speakers' bureau; compiles statistics. *Founded:* 1969. *Members:* 12532.

33 ■ Alloway Family Association

855 Greenway Ct.   Ph: (316)788-3090
Derby, KS 67037

Contact: H. Jay Alloway, Contact.

Desc: Individuals interested in the genealogy of the Alloway family from the lineage of John Alloway Strange (1727-1811) of Fluvanna County, VA. Promotes fellowship between persons with the Alloway surname. Compiles, maintains, and exchanges genealogical research and data on the history of the Alloway family. *Founded:* 1982.

34 ■ Allton, Alton, Aulton Family Association

15510 Laurel Ridge Rd.   Ph: (703)670-4842
Dumfries, VA 22026
E-mail: ccalton@aol.com
URL: http://members.aol.com/altonnews/aaaafn.htm

Contact: Cecil C. Aulton, Publisher.

Desc: Individuals interested in the family history and genealogy of people with the surname Alton and its variant spellings. Promotes genealogical study. *Founded:* 1992. *Members:* 110.

35 ■ ALMA Society - Adoptees' Liberty Movement Association

PO Box 727, Radio City Sta.   Ph: (212)581-1568
New York, NY 10101-0727   Fax: (212)765-2861
E-mail: almainfo@aol.com

Contact: Florence Anna Fisher, Founder & Pres.

Desc: Adults (persons over 18) who were adopted or foster children, natural parents who have given children up for adoption, adoptive parents, and individuals separated by adoption. Seeks to increase public awareness of what the group feels is the injustice of laws that seal birth and adoption records from adoptees, and is preparing a lawsuit challenging such laws. Provides mutual assistance to members searching for their natural parents or children. Conducts encounter groups, research projects, and classes in genealogical research. Sponsors educational programs as an aid to adoptive parents in understanding the adoptee's search for "identity." *Founded:* 1971.

36 ■ Alma Wesley Millet Family Organization

Millet Heritage Enterprises   Ph: (602)964-1613
MHE Heritage
433 S Hobson St.
Mesa, AZ 85204

Contact: Alma W. Millet, Jr., Pres.

Desc: Individuals with the surname Millet or its variant spellings; others with an interest in the descendants of Alma Wesley Millet. Promotes study of Millet family history and genealogy; facilitates communication among family members. *Founded:* 1966. *Members:* 100.

37 ■ Alternate Roots
1083 Austin Ave., NE   Ph: (404)577-1079
Atlanta, GA 30307   Fax: (404)577-7991
E-mail: altrootsl@earthlink.net

Contact: Gregory Carraway, Managing Dir.

Founded: 1976. *Members:* 252.

38 ■ Amelia Island Genealogical Society
Box 6005
Fernandina Beach, FL 32035-6005

39 ■ Amenia Historical Society
Rt. 22   Ph: (914)373-9376
PO Box 22
Amenia, NY 12501

Contact: Kenneth L. Hoadley, Pres.

Desc: Individuals interested in preserving the history of Amenia, NY. Provides information for genealogy research. *Founded:* 1968. *Members:* 20.

40 ■ American Archives
433 E 100 S
Provo, UT 84606-4748

41 ■ American Baptist Historical Society
PO Box 851   Ph: (610)768-2378
Valley Forge, PA 19482-0851 Fax: (610)768-2266

Contact: Deborah VanBroekhoven, Exec. Dir.

Desc: Promotes the study of Baptist history and theology; collects Baptist historical documents and printed records. Operates the American Baptist Archives Center at Valley Forge, PA, and the Samuel Colgate-American Baptist Historical Library in Rochester, NY. *Founded:* 1853. *Members:* 270.

42 ■ American Biographical Institute Research Association
5126 Bur Oak Cir.   Ph: (919)781-8710
PO Box 31226   Fax: (919)781-8712
Raleigh, NC 27622

Contact: Janet Mills Evans, Chwm.

Desc: Professional men and women who are listed in "Who's Who" publications united to share contacts, ideas, and talents. Fosters correspondence and organizes tours. Conducts educational programs. *Founded:* 1979. *Members:* 2000.

43 ■ American-Canadian Genealogical Society
PO Box 6478   Ph: (603)622-1554
Manchester, NH 03108   Fax: (603)626-9812
URL: http://www.acgs.org

Contact: Albert Hamel, Pres.

Desc: Genealogists interested in ancestries of French-Canadian origin. Serves as resource center for the collection, preservation, and dissemination of American-Canadian and Franco-American genealogical information. Acquires and purchases repertories, genealogies, notarial records, indexes, histories, biographies, journals, census records, and other pertinent data. Encourages the gathering of personal and public data such as is found in Bibles, newspapers, directories, histories, and photographs. Promotes the gathering of civil and church records for publication

and/or genealogical research. Encourages individual members to research their family lineage and contribute a copy of their findings. *Founded:* 1973. *Members:* 3000.

44 ■ American Clan Gregor Society
114 S. Lake Shore Dr.   Ph: (910)949-3119
Whispering Pines, NC 28327   Fax: (910)949-2089
E-mail: jtichy@mindspring.com

Contact: Mr. Malcolm G. MacGregor, Chieftain.

Desc: Traces historical and genealogical material relating to the MacGregor clan. *Founded:* 1909. *Members:* 600.

45 ■ American College of Heraldry
PO Box 710
Cottondale, AL 35453

Contact: Dr. David Pittman Johnson, Pres.

Desc: Persons having coats of arms or who are interested in heraldry. *Founded:* 1972. *Members:* 1329.

46 ■ American Family Records Association
PO Box 15505   Ph: (816)252-0950
Kansas City, MO 64106   Fax: (816)254-7114
E-mail: amfamrecrd@aol.com

Contact: Elizabeth Ergovitch, Pres.

Desc: Institutes and individuals including genealogists, historians, and adoptologists seeking to improve education and availability of information in the fields of family history, genealogy, local history, and adoptive relationships. *Founded:* 1978. *Members:* 300.

47 ■ American-French Genealogical Society
Box 2113   Ph: (401)765-6141
Pawtucket, RI 02861   Fax: (401)765-6141
E-mail: afgs@ids.net

Contact: Roger Beaudry, Pres.

Desc: Seeks to study and preserve Franco-American heritage and French-Canadian culture in the U.S. by assisting members in researching their ancestors and the events that shaped their lives. *Founded:* 1978. *Members:* 2000.

48 ■ American Legion Auxiliary
777 N. Meridian St., 3rd Fl. Ph: (317)630-1263
Indianapolis, IN 46204   Fax: (317)237-9891
E-mail: sshort@iquest.net
URL: http://www.legion.org/auxil.htm

Contact: Peggy Sappenfield, National Secretary.

Desc: Mothers, wives, sisters, daughters, grandmothers, granddaughters, and great granddaughters of members of the American Legion or of men and women who were in the U.S. Armed Forces during World War I or II, the Korean War, the Vietnam War, Grenada/Lebanon, Panama, or Persian Gulf and lost their lives in war service or died after honorable discharge; women who served in the armed forces during these periods of hostility. *Founded:* 1919. *Members:* 1000000.

49 ■ American/Schleswig-Holstein Heritage Society
PO Box 313   Fax: (319)843-2867
Davenport, IA 52805-0313

Contact: Jack Schinckel, Pres.

Desc: Works to promote the heritage of Schleswig-Holstein, Germany and the immigrants from Schleswig-Holstein to America. *Founded:* 1989. *Members:* 800.

50 ■ American Society of Genealogists
PO Box 1515
Derry, NH 03038-1515

Desc: Specialists in genealogy and heraldry chosen on the basis of their published work in these fields; membership limited to 50 fellows. Promotes scientific methods of genealogical research through publication of articles in genealogical and historical periodicals and through instructorships at genealogical institutes, seminars, and conferences. *Founded:* 1940. *Members:* 50.

51 ■ Amsbaugh Family Association
2787 335th   Ph: (515)524-5110
Menlo, IA 50164

Contact: Sherry Foresman, Exec. Officer.

Desc: Members of the Amsbaugh family; interested others. Gathers and disseminates information related to the Amsbaugh family. *Founded:* 1966.

52 ■ Ancestral Family Association of Andrew Elton Williams
30596 Caribbean Blvd.
Spanish Fort, AL 36527-9302

53 ■ Ancestry Research Club
PO Box 476   Ph: (801)531-1790
Salt Lake City, UT 84110   Free: 800-531-1790
                             Fax: (801)531-1798
URL: http://www.ancestry.com

Contact: John Tolman, Contact.

Desc: Genealogists and family and local history researchers. Works to increase knowledge of resources available to and the purchasing power of researchers of local and family history. Provides product announcements, and special offers and discounts from suppliers of genealogical materials. *Founded:* 1985. *Members:* 7000.

54 ■ Anderson County Genealogical Society
PO Box 194
Garnett, KS 66032-0194

Contact: Robert A. Meliza, Contact.

55 ■ Andlauer Family Association
3929 Milton Dr.   Ph: (816)373-5309
Independence, MO 64055-4043
E-mail: groversar@aol.com

Contact: Robert L. Grover, Pres.

Desc: Exchanges information among family members. *Founded:* 1963. *Members:* 30.

56 ■ Angele Fernande Daniel Family Organization
24 Reynolds Dr.   Ph: (732)542-0770
Eatontown, NJ 07724-2324

Contact: Jacqueline F. Fernandez, Exec. Officer.

Desc: Individuals interested in the genealogy of Angele Fernande Daniel. Promotes discussion and investigation of Daniel and Fernande family histories. *Founded:* 1975. *Members:* 4.

57 ■ Anne Arundel Genealogical Society
PO Box 221   Ph: (410)760-9679
Pasadena, MD 21123-0221

58 ■ Anneke Jans and Everardus Bogardus Descendants Association
1121 Linnof Rd.   Ph: (937)382-3803
Wilmington, OH 45177-2917

Contact: William Brower Bogardus, Founder.

Desc: Descendants of Anneke Jans and Everardus Bogardus. Promotes interest in family history and genealogy. *Founded:* 1978. *Members:* 1000.

59 ■ Ansley Family Association

1800 Forest Dr. Ph: (803)432-8075
Camden, SC 29020-2020 Fax: (803)432-8075
E-mail: bba@ansley-family-assn.org
URL: http://www.ansley-family-assn.org

Contact: Roger Spafford, Chair.

Desc: Individuals with the surname Ansley or its variants and others related to the Ansley family through marriage or adoption. Promotes interest in Ansley family genealogy. *Founded:* 1978. *Members:* 200.

60 ■ Anthony Sharp and Rachael Ellison Family Organization

<c/o> Frances Sharp Watson
19 Hickory Hills Dr.
Springfield, IL 62707-9688

Contact: Frances Sharp Watson, Contact.

Desc: Members of the Sharp family and interested others. Promotes genealogical research. *Founded:* 1981.

61 ■ Appanoose County Genealogical Society

1020 Shamrock Ln., Apt. 107
Centerville, IA 52544

Contact: Pam Milani, Treas.

Desc: Individuals interested in the history and genealogy of Appanoose County, IA. Gathers, preserves, and disseminates information; assists researchers. *Members:* 60.

62 ■ Arbuckle Exchange

42 West 100 North Ph: (801)623-4532
Nephi, UT 84648 Fax: (801)623-7117
E-mail: drhooker@sisna.com

Contact: Darrell R. Hooker, Pres.

Desc: Descendants of the Arbuckle family. *Founded:* 1988.

63 ■ Archer Association

PO Box 6233 Ph: (703)264-1372
Mc Lean, VA 22106
E-mail: garcher@bix.com

Contact: George W. Archer, Pres.

Desc: Genealogists and family historians. Collects, preserves, and disseminates information on persons in the U.S. and Canada with the surname Archer and its variants. Offers research service. *Founded:* 1982. *Members:* 100.

64 ■ Archuleta County Genealogical Society

PO Box 1611 Ph: (303)264-2645
Pagosa Springs, CO 81147

Contact: Janice M. O'Hare, Pres.

65 ■ Arizona State Genealogical Society

PO Box 42075 Ph: (520)513-ASGS
Tucson, AZ 85733-2075
URL: http://www.rootsweb.com/asgs

Contact: Donald Gerzetic, Pres.

Desc: Conducts research of genealogical records. Sponsors classes, seminars, and research trips. Participates in the Arizona Pioneer Descendant Certification Program. *Founded:* 1965. *Members:* 330.

66 ■ Ark/LA/Tex Genealogical Association

PO Box 4462 Ph: (318)868-1681
Shreveport, LA 71134-0462
E-mail: aga@softdisk.com

Contact: Ray Allan Barlow, Jr., Pres.

Desc: Genealogists whose interests lie in the South, especially in the states of Arkansas, Louisiana, and Texas. Purposes are: to collect, preserve, and make available genealogical materials, documents, and records; to encourage

interest in genealogy and to sponsor educational programs for its development; to promote and publicize the city of Shreveport, LA, as a major genealogical research center for genealogists and historians interested in records of the entire state of Louisiana and the Ark-La-Tex area; to cooperate with and assist all other genealogical-historical societies and libraries in furtherance of these purposes. Supports and contributes to the Genealogy Room of the Shreve Memorial Library in Shreveport, LA. *Founded:* 1955. *Members:* 300.

67 ■ Ark-La-Tex Genealogical Association

PO Box 4462 Ph: (318)868-1681
Shreveport, LA 71134-0462

Contact: R. Allan Barlow, Jr., Pres.

Desc: Genealogists whose interests lie in the South, especially in the states of Arkansas, Louisiana, and Texas. Collects, preserves, and makes available genealogical materials, documents, and records and encourages interest in genealogy and to sponsor educational programs for its development. Promotes and publicizes the city of Shreveport, LA, as a major genealogical research center for genealogists and historians interested in records of the entire state of Louisiana and the Ark-La-Tex area. *Founded:* 1955. *Members:* 300.

68 ■ Arkansas Genealogical Society

PO Box 908 Ph: (501)262-4513
Hot Springs, AR 71902 Fax: (501)262-4513

Contact: Margaret Harrison Hubbard, Editor.

Desc: Provides primary and secondary source materials to researchers of family history. Conducts educational programs. *Founded:* 1962. *Members:* 1000.

69 ■ Ashcroft Family Heritage Society

9982 Summit View Dr.
Sandy, UT 84092-4286

Contact: Craig T. Ashcroft, Contact.

70 ■ Ashland and Bayfield Counties, Wisconsin, Genealogical Society

Rte. 1, Box 139 Ph: (715)765-4597
Mason, WI 54856
E-mail: cjwilson@win.bright.net
URL: http://www.win.bright.net/cjwilson

Desc: Individuals with an interest in local history and genealogy. Gathers cemetery records and other historical genealogical information.

71 ■ Ashley County Genealogical Society

PO Drawer R Ph: (501)364-2885
Crossett, AR 71635

Contact: Mary F. Spainhour, Pres.

Founded: 1986. *Members:* 90.

72 ■ Association of Catholic Diocesan Archivists

Archives and Records Center Ph: (312)831-0711
711 W Monroe St. Fax: (312)831-0610
Chicago, IL 60661-3515
E-mail: heidy@mcs.net

Contact: Dr. Charles Nolan, Pres.

Desc: Archivists responsible for the maintenance of diocesan records, archives, and historical materials. Promotes and fosters professional care of diocesan records through meetings and archival theory workshops. Works to establish archival programs in local dioceses; acts as a channel for personal discussions and exchanges among archivists;

represents the profession before Catholic associations and laity. Develops guidelines designed to standardize archival procedures and practices. *Founded:* 1981. *Members:* 180.

73 ■ Association for the Development of Religious Information Systems

PO Box 210735 Ph: (615)662-5189
Nashville, TN 37221-0735 Fax: (615)662-5251
E-mail: adris@firestormcom.com

Contact: Dr. David O. Moberg, Coord.

Desc: Faculty members in colleges, universities, and theological seminaries; administrative agencies of religious bodies; bibliographical and indexing services for publications related to religion; libraries, social agencies, commercial organizations and interested individuals. Purpose is to promote coordination and cooperation among bibliographic and other information systems and services pertinent to religion by sharing relevant information, identifying needs, discussing mutual interests, exploring the feasibility of proposed projects, and developing cooperative ventures. Activities reflect educational, scientific, and administrative needs. *Founded:* 1971.

74 ■ Association of the German Nobility in North America

1101 W. 2nd St. Ph: (707)745-1605
Benicia, CA 94510
E-mail: gvonstud@aol.com

Contact: Gilbert von Studnitz, Pres.

Desc: Individuals belonging to noble families in German-speaking areas and who now reside in North America. Seeks to unify and further the cultural ties of individuals belonging to the historical German nobility. Sponsors genealogical studies; compiles statistics on the number of German nobles in North America. *Founded:* 1980. *Members:* 48.

75 ■ Association Houde International

Box 82
Glencoe, IL 60022

Contact: John (Jean-Louis) Houde, Contact.

Desc: Serves as a clearinghouse for information on the lineage of the Houde family and related family names. *Founded:* 1990.

76 ■ Association of Jewish Genealogical Society, Orange County Chapter

2370 1-D Via Mariposa W. Ph: (949)855-4692
Laguna Hills, CA 92653
E-mail: dkohansk@net-star.net

Contact: Dorothy Kohanski, Founder.

Desc: Jewish people interested in their genealogy. Assists individuals wishing to begin research into their lineage. *Founded:* 1983. *Members:* 100.

77 ■ Association of One-Name Studies

589 Cocopan Dr.
Altadena, CA 91001-4012

Contact: George P. Coulter, Contact.

78 ■ Association of Personal Historians

<c/o> Robert Joyce Free: 800-449-7483
1509 S. Raitt St., No. C Fax: (714)545-2799
Santa Ana, CA 92704
URL: http://www.personalhistorians.com

Contact: Robert D. Joyce, Pres.

Desc: Seeks to "help people preserve their life stories and memories". Advances the efforts of personal historians through networking and training. Encourages personal history activities and projects. Conducts classes in memoir writing, the organization of memoribilia, lifewriting and presentations. *Founded:* 1994. *Members:* 250.

79 ∎ Association of Professional Genealogists

PO Box 40393
Denver, CO 80204-0393
E-mail: apg-admin@genealogy.org

Contact: Kathleen W. Hinckley, Exec. Sec.

Desc: Genealogists, libraries, businesses, and interested individuals. Promotes awareness, interest, and education in genealogy, family history, and local history; cooperates with record repositories to ensure access to records for professional use. Encourages professional genealogists to maintain high standards of ethics, research techniques, and business practices. *Founded:* 1979. *Members:* 1200.

80 ∎ Atchley/Harden Family Association

<c/o> Wayne D. Atchley   Ph: (806)359-6479
6709 Hurst   Fax: (806)359-0721
Amarillo, TX 79109
E-mail: match61125@aol.com

Contact: Wayne D. Atchley, Contact.

Desc: Descendants of John and Jane (Harden) Atchley. *Founded:* 1989.

81 ∎ Athy Tribe of Galway

3834 Overbrook Ln.   Ph: (713)622-1480
Houston, TX 77027

Contact: Lawrence F. Athy, Jr., Chieftain.

Desc: Descendants of Captain George Athy of Galway, Ireland, and Maryland; persons with the surnames Athy, Athey, Atha, Athan, Athon, Athen. Assists members with genealogical research. *Founded:* 1987. *Members:* 400.

82 ∎ Audrain County Area Genealogical Society

305 W. Jackson St.   Ph: (573)581-4939
Mexico, MO 65265-2789

Contact: Linda Kable, Pres.

Founded: 1986. *Members:* 130.

83 ∎ Augustan Society

PO Box 75
Daggett, CA 92327-0075

Contact: Dr. Robert Cleve, Pres.

Desc: Persons interested in the fields of genealogy, heraldry, monarchy, and chivalry; members of chivalric orders; herald artists; authors. *Founded:* 1957. *Members:* 4195.

84 ∎ Aurand - Aurant - Aurandt Family Association

921 Trailwood Dr.   Ph: (919)851-6782
Raleigh, NC 27606
E-mail: eaurand@juno.com

Contact: Marlin Aurand, Contact.

Desc: Individuals with the surname Aurand or its variants; others with an interest in Aurand family genealogy. Promotes study of, and interest in, Aurand family genealogy and history. *Founded:* 1988. *Members:* 175.

85 ∎ Austin Genealogical Society

PO Box 1507
Austin, TX 78767-1507
URL: http://www.main.org/ags/

Contact: John C. Miller, Pres.

Desc: Promotes the investigation, collection, recording, and publishing of genealogical material in Austin, TX. *Founded:* 1960. *Members:* 300.

86 ∎ Austins of America Genealogical Society

23 Allen Farm Ln.   Ph: (978)369-8591
Concord, MA 01742   Fax: (603)843-1486
E-mail: aoags@alum.mit.edu
URL: http://www.aoags.org

Contact: Dr. Michael E. Austin, Contact.

Desc: Exchanges Austin information. Specializes in Austin histories and genealogies. *Founded:* 1979. *Members:* 433.

87 ∎ Autry Family Association

416 Candler St. NE
Atlanta, GA 30307-2036

Contact: Phillip J. Autrey, Editor.

Desc: Works to document and preserve Autry, Autrey, Autery, (and approximately 40 other spellings) family history. Fosters genealogical research. Compiles statistics. *Founded:* 1986. *Members:* 420.

88 ∎ Auxiliary to Sons of Union Veterans of the Civil War

2449 Center Ave.   Ph: (330)823-6919
Alliance, OH 44601-4531

Contact: Beatrice Greenwalt, Historian.

Desc: Women relatives of descendants of Union veterans of the Civil War. Promotes patriotism; presents American flags; supports veterans' hospitals. *Founded:* 1883. *Members:* 3172.

89 ∎ Baker Family International

326 Panhorst
Staunton, IL 62088

Contact: Crystal Jensen, Genealogist.

Desc: Seeks to preserve research on all branches of the Baker family. Fosters exchange among researchers working on the Baker family. Collaborates with genealogical libraries. *Founded:* 1987. *Members:* 277.

90 ∎ Baldwin County Genealogical Society

PO Box 108
Foley, AL 36536-0108

Contact: Herman Baumann, Pres.

Desc: Individuals interested in genealogy and family history. Conducts research and educational programs. Gathers, preserves, and disseminates genealogical information. *Founded:* 1987. *Members:* 96.

91 ∎ Ballew Family Association of America

2711 Leslie Dr. NE   Ph: (770)491-0664
PO Box 450684   Fax: (770)723-9220
Atlanta, GA 31145

Contact: Thomas M. Ballew, Pres.

Desc: Descendants of the Ballew family; interested others. Conducts genealogical research; studies the history of families related to the Ballew name. *Founded:* 1981. *Members:* 225.

92 ∎ Baltimore County Genealogical Society

PO Box 10085   Ph: (410)750-9315
Towson, MD 21285
URL: http://www.serve.com/bcgs/bcgs.html

Contact: Robert Barnes, Pres.

Desc: Works to help individuals interested in tracing their family histories. Gathers and disseminates genealogical information. *Founded:* 1977. *Members:* 429.

93 ∎ Barney Family Historical Association

7503 Ridgebook Dr.   Ph: (703)451-3916
Springfield, VA 22153-1981   Fax: (703)451-2814
E-mail: bfha@aol.com

URL: http://www.barneyfamily.org

Contact: William C. Barney, Pres.

Desc: Collects information on the Barney family history. *Founded:* 1979. *Members:* 425.

94 ∎ Baronial Order of Magna Charta

625 S. Bethlehem Pike   Ph: (215)628-2349
Ambler, PA 19002   Fax: (215)628-9865
E-mail: gtvaughan@nni.com

Contact: G. Tully Vaughan, II, Marshall.

Desc: Lineal descendants of the 25 earls and barons and five nonsurety supporters who forced England's King John to seal the Magna Charta and were elected to be the first official guardians of adherence to the charter by the Magna Charta Earls and Barons in 1215. (The original Magna Charta, or Magna Carta, was a definitive statement of feudal law and general charter of liberties. It became a symbol of protection against oppression and was adopted, in part, into succeeding charters of England and other English colonies; it is an integral part of U.S. constitutional law and legislation.) Promotes literary study and social intercourse among members and fosters admiration and respect for related principles of constitutional government. Promotes awareness of the Magna Charta's history and perpetuates the memory of the 25 earls and barons and five supporters of the Magna Charta; observes June 15 as the anniversary of the granting of the charter. Holds annual commemorative events. Conducts research, educational and charitable programs. Maintains speakers' bureau and collection of heraldic banners. *Founded:* 1898. *Members:* 425.

95 ∎ Barry County Genealogical and Historical Society

PO Box 291
Cassville, MO 65625

Contact: Iva J. Roller, Pres.

Founded: 1990. *Members:* 125.

96 ∎ Barry County Genealogical and Historical Society

Rte. 1, Box 322
Purdy, MO 65734-9785

97 ∎ Bartow County Genealogical Society

PO Box 993   Ph: (770)606-0706
Cartersville, GA 30120-0993
E-mail: jbelew@bellsouth.net
URL: http://www.geocities.com/heartland/park/9465/
     bartowcoga.html

Contact: Jean Belew, Pres.

Desc: Individuals in the Bartow County, Georgia area interested in collecting and preserving the history of their ancestors. *Founded:* 1992. *Members:* 250.

98 ∎ Bater Surname Organization

1820 W. 600 North   Ph: (219)562-3066
Howe, IN 46746

Contact: A.L. Bowerman, Historian.

Desc: Works to record and publish descendants of the Bater surname and its variants, Batter and Batt. *Founded:* 1894. *Members:* 150.

99 ∎ Bautz Descendants

1313 W Paradise Ct.
Milwaukee, WI 53209

Contact: Elynn Lee Bautz, Founder.

Desc: Descendants of Werdelin Bautz (1803-89), who came to the United States in 1854. Seeks to locate Bautz descendants worldwide. *Founded:* 1968. *Members:* 1500.

100 ▪ Bay Area Genealogical Society

PO Box 283   Ph: (414)494-9286
Green Bay, WI 54305-0283

Contact: Myra Michaletz, Treas.

Desc: Individuals and organizations interested in tracing histories of ancestors who lived in northeastern Wisconsin. Provides assistance with genealogical research. *Founded:* 1975. *Members:* 245.

101 ▪ Bay County Genealogical Society

PO Box 27   Ph: (517)892-5951
Essexville, MI 48732
E-mail: ddolsen@concentric.net

Contact: Bill Harrington, Sr., Pres.

Desc: Individuals interested in the study of genealogy. *Founded:* 1968. *Members:* 97.

102 ▪ Beall Family Association

135 NE 74th Ave.
Portland, OR 97213-5649

Contact: Robert Clair Beall, Pub.

Desc: Individuals interested in researching the surname Beall and its variants, Beale, Beal, Beals, Bale, and Bell. Works to consolidate information relating to the Beall families. *Founded:* 1991. *Members:* 130.

103 ▪ Beaudet Surname Organization

2071 Quailwood Ln.   Ph: (352)686-0537
Spring Hill, FL 34606
E-mail: jboud@innet.com

Contact: John E. Boudette, Pres.

Desc: Individuals with the surname Beaudet or its variant spellings; others with an interest in Beaudet family history and genealogy. Promotes genealogical and historical research on the Beaudet family. *Founded:* 1982. *Members:* 100.

104 ▪ Beaufort County Genealogical Society

PO Box 1089   Ph: (919)946-4212
Washington, NC 27889

Contact: Louise Cowell, Treas.

Desc: Individuals interested in genealogy. Gathers and disseminates information. *Founded:* 1985. *Members:* 222.

105 ▪ Beaver County Genealogical Society

3225 Dutch Ridge Rd.
Beaver, PA 15009
E-mail: bcgs@timesnet.net
URL: http://www.rootsweb.com/pabecgs

Contact: W. Martin Ruckert, Pres.

Desc: Promotes study of the history and demographics of Beaver County, PA. Conducts educational programs; assists individuals wishing to research their family histories.

106 ▪ Bedford Family Registry

4845 Castle Rd.   Ph: (818)248-6553
La Canada, CA 91011-1305
E-mail: lkirker@juno.com
URL: http://www.myfamily.com

Contact: Luetta Bedford Kirker, Contact.

Desc: Promotes study of, and interest in, the history and genealogy of people bearing the surname Bedford and its variants. *Founded:* 1991.

107 ▪ Bell County Historical Society

PO Box 1344   Ph: (606)248-4812
Middlesboro, KY 40965
E-mail: allagreen@aol.com

Contact: Virginia Green, Corr.Sec.

Desc: Individuals interested in preserving the history of Bell County, KY. Collects genealogical records. *Founded:* 1982. *Members:* 250.

108 ▪ Bell Family Association of the United States

3102 Lakeshore Blvd.   Ph: (904)387-4669
Jacksonville, FL 32210   Free: 800-332-1072
      Fax: (904)389-1161

Contact: Grace B. Rogers, VP.

Desc: Scottish descendants and friends of Family/Clan Bell. Studies Bell family and Scottish genealogy and history. *Founded:* 1985. *Members:* 575.

109 ▪ Bend Genealogical Society

PO Box 8254
Bend, OR 97708-8254

110 ▪ Benjamin Franklin Johnson Family Organization

1230 N Cottonwood Circle
Heber City, UT 84032-1144

Contact: Homer McKay Lebaron, Contact.

111 ▪ Benton County Genealogical Society

1505 4th Ave.
Belle Plaine, IA 52208-1421

Contact: Kathryn Daily, Contact.

112 ▪ Berry Surname Organization

Highway 87 North   Ph: (409)565-4751
PO Box 340
Burkeville, TX 75932

Contact: Helen Rogers Skelton, Contact.

Desc: Conducts ancestor searches. *Founded:* 1980. *Members:* 154.

113 ▪ Big Horn County Genealogical Society

Box 51
Hardin, MT 59034

Members: 10.

114 ▪ Bigelow Society

PO Box 4115   Ph: (810)239-0276
Flint, MI 48504

Contact: Helena Roth, Treas.

Desc: Members of the Bigelow family. Studies the Bigelow family name. *Founded:* 1976. *Members:* 450.

115 ▪ Bishop Hill Heritage Association

103 N. Bishop Hill St.   Ph: (309)927-3899
PO Box 1853   Fax: (309)927-3010
Bishop Hill, IL 61419-0092

Contact: Morris Nelson, Pres.

Desc: Seeks to preserve Bishop Hill as a living community and restore and maintain historical properties. *Founded:* 1962. *Members:* 350.

116 ▪ Black Archives of Mid America

2033 Vine St.   Ph: (816)483-1300
Kansas City, MO 64108   Fax: (816)483-1341
URL: http://www.blackarchives.org

Contact: Pamela Ross, Exec.Dir.

Desc: Dedicated to the acquisition, preservation, study, display and interpretation of regional African-American history and culture. *Founded:* 1974. *Members:* 200.

117 ▪ Black Women in Church and Society

700 Martin Luther King Dr.   Ph: (404)527-7740
Atlanta, GA 30314   Fax: (404)527-0901
E-mail: jgraut@itc.edu

Contact: Jacquelyn Grant, Ph.D., Dir.

Desc: Women in ministry, both ordained and laity. Seeks to provide: structured activities and support systems for black women whose goals include participating in leadership roles in church and society; a platform for communication between laywomen and clergywomen. Conducts research into questions and issues pivotal to black women in church and society. Compiles statistics. Maintains a research/resource center and a library with subject matter pertaining to liberation and black theology, feminism, and womanist movements. *Founded:* 1982.

118 ▪ Blackburn Family Association

449 Garfield St.   Ph: (303)377-1678
Denver, CO 80206-4511
E-mail: khowley@aol.com

Contact: Kevin R. Howley, Sec.Treas.

Desc: Families and individuals, especially descendants of John Blackburn (born in County Armagh, Ireland in the 17th century), interested in studying and preserving the Blackburn heritage. Supports historic preservation and research projects including restoration of Quaker cemeteries. Erects monuments in memory of early U.S. settlers. Provides genealogical and historical information to libraries. *Founded:* 1985. *Members:* 400.

119 ▪ Blair County Genealogical Society

431 Scotch Valley Rd.   Ph: (814)696-3492
Hollidaysburg, PA 16648

Contact: Jack Speece, Pres.

Desc: Individuals interested in the genealogy of Blair County, PA. Promotes genealogical study and collects data; does seminars. *Founded:* 1979. *Members:* 500.

120 ▪ Blair Society for Genealogical Research

1006 Cambria Ave.   Ph: (814)467-9695
Windber, PA 15963-1516
URL: http://www.blairsociety.org

Contact: Charlotte Blair Stewart, Contact.

Desc: Individuals with the surname Blair and its variants; others with an interest in Blair family genealogy. Promotes interest in, and study of, Blair family genealogy; seeks to preserve family records and artifacts. *Founded:* 1983. *Members:* 400.

121 ▪ Blencowe Families Association

550 N Darlington St.   Ph: (626)280-2506
South San Gabriel, CA
  91770-4312
E-mail: gwwf20@prodigy.com
URL: http://www.geocities.com/Heartland/5088

Contact: Helen Bimcoe Simpson, Sec.

Desc: Individuals with the surname Blencowe or its variant spellings; others with an interest in family history and genealogy. Promotes study of Blencowe family history and genealogy. *Founded:* 1985. *Members:* 200.

122 ▪ Bloss-Pyles-Ross-Sellards Family

4031 Grand Ave.   Ph: (904)985-4046
Deland, FL 32720
E-mail: hsellard@bellsouth.net

Contact: Harry L. Sellards, Jr., Contact.

Desc: Promotes genealogical research and study. *Founded:* 1975.

123 ■ Blunden Family History Association
7052 Fallbrook Ct.   Ph: (727)376-4619
New Port Richey, FL
34655-4204
E-mail: americaab@aol.com

Contact: Mrs. America M. Carlson, Contact.

Desc: Individuals with an interest in the history and genealogy of the Blunden family. Promotes research and study of Blunden family genealogy. *Founded:* 1984.

124 ■ B'Man Family Association
607 E. Market   Ph: (501)268-3179
Searcy, AR 72143

Contact: Ruth E. Browning, Editor.

Desc: Individuals with any form of the B'Man surname. Fosters communication and exchange among members. Accepts queries from non-members free of charge. *Founded:* 1977. *Members:* 50.

125 ■ Board for Certification of Genealogists
PO Box 14291
Washington, DC 20044
URL: http://www.genealogy.org/bcg/

Contact: Helen F.M. Leary, Pres.

Desc: Works to formulate and administer standards of professional genealogical research. Grants certification in classifications of Certified Genealogical Record Specialists, Certified American Lineage Specialists, Certified American Indian Lineage Specialists, Certified Genealogists, Certified Genealogical Lecturers, and Certified Genealogical Instructors. *Founded:* 1964. *Members:* 375.

126 ■ Board for Certification of Genealogists
PO Box 14291
Washington, DC 20044-4291

127 ■ Boggess Family Association
1410 Lamar Dr.   Ph: (281)341-5257
Richmond, TX 77469   Fax: (713)988-6643
E-mail: boffess@sage-engineering-inc.com

Contact: Ronald Lee Boggess, Exec. Officer.

Desc: Members of the Boggess and related families. Seeks to unite Boggess family members. *Founded:* 1988. *Members:* 100.

128 ■ Bolling Family Association
Box 835490   Ph: (972)239-7353
Richardson, TX 75083-5490   Fax: (214)239-9613
E-mail: abo122@airmail.net
URL: http://www.bolling.net

Contact: Alexander R. Bolling, Jr., Pres.

Desc: Descendants of the Bolling/Bowling/Bowlin/Bolen immigrants to the American continent. Promotes the maintenance of family ties and the preservation of family records. *Founded:* 1991. *Members:* 920.

129 ■ Bondurant Family Association
170 Windsor Ct.   Ph: (706)549-1264
Athens, GA 30606

Contact: Mary Bondurant Warren, Editor.

Desc: Conducts research on ancestors and descendants of Jean-Pierre Bondurant (1677-1734), who was born in France and died in Virginia. *Founded:* 1987. *Members:* 210.

130 ■ The Boone Society, Inc.
23 Nord Circle Rd.   Ph: (651)482-0194
North Oaks, MN 55127-6515
E-mail: prpete@aol.com

Contact: Peter N. Holste, Co-Chr.

Desc: Works to identify and preserve Boone sites, artifacts and history. *Founded:* 1996. *Members:* 500.

131 ■ Born Young
<c/o> Vicki Young Albu   Ph: (612)455-3626
347 12th Ave. N   Fax: (612)455-2897
South St. Paul, MN 55075-1957
E-mail: valbu@postoffice.worldnet.att.net

Contact: Vicki Young Albu, Editor.

Desc: Individuals interested in preserving the history of the Young family. *Founded:* 1983. *Members:* 200.

132 ■ Bowman County Historical and Genealogical Society
PO Box 13
Bowman, ND 58623-0013

133 ■ Boyt/e - Boyet/t/e Association
1060 Magnolia Ave.   Ph: (714)993-1168
Placentia, CA 92870-4423   Fax: (714)278-2101
E-mail: welliot@exchange.fullerton.edu

Contact: Wendy Bebout Elliott, Pres.

Desc: Individuals with the surnames Boyt or Boyet or their variant spellings; others with an interest in the families' history and genealogy. Promotes interest in family history and genealogy. *Founded:* 1981. *Members:* 25.

134 ■ Bradley County Genealogical Society
PO Box 837
Warren, AR 71671-0837
URL: http://www.rootsweb.com/arbradle

Contact: Peggy Bowman, Contact.

Desc: To publish, distribute info on history of Bradley County as well as publish genealogical information. Volumes of info in courthouse as well as private sources. To add research books to libraries as funds become available. *Founded:* 1990. *Members:* 140.

135 ■ Brainard-Brainerd-Braynard Family Association
813 SW Alder St., No. 700   Ph: (503)243-2652
Portland, OR 97205-3115

Contact: Richard D. Brainard, Contact.

Desc: Individuals with the surname Brainard and its variants; others with an interest in Brainard family history and genealogy. Promotes study of Brainard family genealogy. *Founded:* 1988. *Members:* 200.

136 ■ Brancheau-Branchaud Family Association
27909 Youngberry Dr.   Ph: (805)296-8740
Santa Clarita, CA 91350-1757
E-mail: djmill@earthlink.net
URL: http://www.home.earthlink.net/djmill/

Contact: Douglas J. Miller, Pres.

Desc: Individuals with the surname Brancheau and its variants; others with an interest in the Brancheau family. Promotes study of, and interest in, Brancheau family history and genealogy. *Founded:* 1984. *Members:* 150.

137 ■ Brann-Brawn Family History Association
Family History Association   Ph: (541)461-4473
4065 Berrywood Dr.
Eugene, OR 97404-4061

Contact: James R. Brann, Pres.

Desc: Collects, preserves, and disseminates information on all persons with the surname Brann and Brawn and its variants. *Founded:* 1988. *Members:* 200.

138 ■ Brantley Association of America
5245 Moon Rd.   Ph: (770)943-4677
Powder Springs, GA 30127
E-mail: brantleyassoc@mindspring.com
URL: http://members.tripod.com/BrantleyAssociation

Contact: John Kenneth Brantley, Founder.

Desc: Conducts genealogical research on the Brantly and Brantley surname. Seeks to connnect the various Brantley lines to the common ancestor, Edward Brantley, who immigrated to the state of Virginia in 1638. *Founded:* 1987. *Members:* 373.

139 ■ Brittenburg Surname Organization
6750 E Main St., No. 106   Ph: (602)833-2165
Mesa, AZ 85205-9049   Fax: (602)396-9778

Contact: Warren D. Steffey, Pres.

Desc: Individuals with the surname Brittenburg or its variant spellings; others with an interest in the Brittenburg family. Promotes study of Brittenburg family history and genealogy. *Founded:* 1975.

140 ■ Brookfield Township Historical Society
Box 143   Ph: (315)899-5893
Brookfield, NY 13314

Contact: Caroline Keith, Pres.

Desc: Individuals interested in the history and genealogy of Brookfield Township, NY. *Founded:* 1971. *Members:* 200.

141 ■ Brough-Malkin/Nielsen/Wilson/Willson Family Organization
87 Cedarwood Ave.   Ph: (626)359-3575
Duarte, CA 91010   Fax: (626)359-2026

Contact: Faye B. Nielsen, Contact.

Desc: Conducts genealogical research. *Founded:* 1978. *Members:* 1.

142 ■ Brown County Genealogical Society
PO Box 1202   Ph: (812)336-6146
Nashville, IN 47448
E-mail: sclevenger@iquest.com

Contact: Dr. Sarah Clevenger, Pres.

Founded: 1986. *Members:* 164.

143 ■ Buchannan County Genealogical Society
PO Box 4   Ph: (319)334-9333
Independence, IA 50644-0004

Contact: Ann Gitsch, Pres.

Desc: Works to assist people in finding a missing link to their past, an unknown bit of information about their family, or the last piece of fact that is necessary to bring it all together. *Founded:* 1980. *Members:* 64.

144 ■ Bucks County Genealogical Society
PO Box 1092   Ph: (215)230-9410
Doylestown, PA 18901

Contact: Audrey J. Wolfinger, Pres.

Desc: Individuals and libraries interested in the genealogy of Bucks County, PA. Conducts educational programs; provides genealogical and historical information; sponsors library projects. Conducts charitable activities. Sponsors Family Ancestry Fair. *Founded:* 1981. *Members:* 740.

145 ■ Bullitt County Genealogical Society
PO Box 960   Ph: (502)538-6428
Shepherdsville, KY 40165   Fax: (502)538-8743
E-mail: dcox36@bullitt.net

Desc: Promotes the study of genealogy in Bullitt County, KY. *Founded:* 1988. *Members:* 175.

146 ■ Bunker Family Association of America
9 Sommerset Rd.   Ph: (609)589-6140
Turnersville, NJ 08012-2122
E-mail: gilbunker@snip.net
URL: http://www.bunkerfamilyassn.org/index.html

Contact: Gil Bunker, Pres.

Desc: Collects, preserves, and publishes Bunker surname genealogical & general information. *Founded:* 1913. *Members:* 500.

147 ■ Burleson Family Association
10555 Le Mans Dr.
Dallas, TX 75238-3667

Contact: Helen Burleson Kelso, Editor.

Desc: Members of the Burleson family and interested others. Facilitates tracing the Burleson lineage. Works to preserve Burleson family history. *Founded:* 1981. *Members:* 950.

148 ■ Burnett Family Genealogy Association
3891 Commander Dr.   Ph: (770)455-6445
Chamblee, GA 30341-0016
E-mail: tburnett@usa.net
URL: http://www.mindspring.com/tburnett/bfgoa.html

Contact: Thomas R. Burnett, Pres.

Desc: Strives to acquire information on the genealogy of the Burnett family. Maintains speakers' bureau. *Founded:* 1980. *Members:* 100.

149 ■ Burton Family Organization (Burten/ Burtin/Berton)
4216 Saint Paul Way Apt. 101
Concord, CA 94518-1872

Contact: A. Maxim Coppage, Editor.

Desc: Provides original research from members. Includes Bible records, family histories, pictures, and group sheets. *Founded:* 1967. *Members:* 100.

150 ■ Cabbage/Cabage Surname Organization
Rte. 2, Box 97A   Ph: (423)497-2287
Washburn, TN 37888   Fax: (423)497-2287
E-mail: jv-ma-cabage@worldnet.att.net

Contact: John V. Cabage, Pres.

Desc: Individuals with the surname Cabbage or its variants; others with an interest in Cabbage family history and genealogy. Promotes study of Cabbage family genealogy. *Founded:* 1976. *Members:* 600.

151 ■ Cadenhead Family Association
3301 Brook Glen Dr.
Garland, TX 75044
E-mail: rogers@prefect.com

Contact: Rogers Cadenhead, Pres.

Desc: Individuals with the surname Cadenhead and their relatives. Dedicated to researching the history of the Cadenhead family, which originated in 15th century Scotland. Seeks to link current generations of the Cadenhead family. *Founded:* 1991.

152 ■ Cahill Cooperative
2050 Cedar Johnson Rd.   Ph: (319)643-2829
West Branch, IA 52358
E-mail: xptz80a@prodigy.com

Contact: Jim Cahill, Partner.

Desc: Newsletter promotes awarness of Cahills of today and the past, as well as conditions in Ireland. *Founded:* 1987. *Members:* 100.

153 ■ Calhoun County Genealogical Society
PO Box 777   Ph: (616)962-3498
Marshall, MI 49068

Contact: Sandy Redmond, Pres.

Desc: Gathers and preserves genealogical information, aids genealogists, publishes and promotes genealogical materials of Calhoun County and other areas. *Founded:* 1988. *Members:* 200.

154 ■ Calvert County Genealogy Society
PO Box 9   Ph: (410)535-0839
Sunderland, MD 20689

Contact: Mildred Bowen O'Brien, Contact.

Founded: 1986. *Members:* 200.

155 ■ Calvert County Historical Society
30 Duke St.   Ph: (410)535-2452
PO Box 358
Prince Frederick, MD 20678
URL: http://www.somd.lib.md.us/calv.cchs

Contact: R. Michael Holland, Pres.

Desc: Individuals interested in the history and genealogy of Calvert County, MD. Maintains official genealogical records. Disseminates information relative to the County's history. *Founded:* 1953. *Members:* 400.

156 ■ Campbell Contacts in America
416JF Townline Rd.   Ph: (608)756-2495
Janesville, WI 53545

Contact: Chris Campbell, Editor.

Desc: Campbell family members and others with an interest in Campbell familiy genealogy. Promotes genealogical study. *Founded:* 1984.

157 ■ Canadian Association of Professional Heritage Consultants
PO Box 1023, Sta. F
Toronto, ON, Canada M4Y 2T7
URL: http://www.caphc.ca

Contact: Barbara MacPhail, Pres.

Desc: Professional heritage consultants. Promotes high standards of practice and ethics within the field of heritage consultancy. *Members:* 190.

158 ■ Canadian Council of Archives
344 Wellington St. W,   Ph: (613)995-2373
  Rm. 1009   Fax: (613)947-6662
Ottawa, ON, Canada K1A 0N3
E-mail: mhoude@archives.ca
URL: http://www.cdncouncilarchives.ca/

Contact: Michel Houde, Exec.Dir.

Desc: Archives and archivists. Promotes preservation of, and free public access to, archival materials. *Founded:* 1985. *Members:* 18.

159 ■ Canadian County Genealogical Society
PO Box 866   Ph: (405)262-2409
El Reno, OK 73036
E-mail: elreno@oltn.odl.state.ok.us
URL: http://www.rootsweb.com/okcanadi/okcanad.htm

Contact: Nelson Stout, Pres.

Founded: 1978. *Members:* 28.

160 ■ Canadian Federation of Genealogical and Family History Societies
227 Parkville Bay   Ph: (204)256-6176
Winnipeg, MB, Canada R2M 2J6

Contact: Cecile Alarie-Skene, Sec.

Desc: Genealogical and family history societies in Canada. Promotes study and interest in genealogy and family history.

161 ■ Canadian Friends of the Judaica Archive
320 Crichton St., Ste. 204   Ph: (613)746-4075
Ottawa, ON, Canada K1M 1W5

Contact: Walter A. Cole, Pres.

Desc: Supporters of the Judaica Archive and its projects. Promotes preservation of Judaic archival materials.

162 ■ Canadian Immigration Historical Society
PO Box 9502   Ph: (613)256-1033
Ottawa, ON, Canada K1G 3V2

Contact: J. Aldard Gunn, Contact.

Desc: Historians, genealogists, and other individuals with an interest in the history of immigration to Canada. Promotes research and study of immigration to Canada and related studies.

163 ■ Canfield Family Association
1144 N. Gordon   Ph: (316)942-7120
Wichita, KS 67203-6611

Contact: Genevieve (Canfield) Martinson, Editor.

Desc: Individuals interested in, or engaged in research of, the names Canfield, Camfield, or Campfield. Seeks to help members trace their ancestry. *Founded:* 1982. *Members:* 130.

164 ■ Capital District Genealogical Society
PO Box 2175, Empire State   Ph: (518)482-9374
  Plaza Sta.
Albany, NY 12220-0175

Contact: Harry Taylor, Contact.

Desc: Individuals, libraries, and genealogical societies interested in the genealogy of Albany, Rensselaer, Schenectady, Schoharie, and Greene counties, NY. Holds genealogy education programs. Maintains local records, conducts research, and disseminates information. Operates Volunteer Desk at the New York State Library. *Founded:* 1981. *Members:* 300.

165 ■ Caret Family History Association
4065 Berrywood Dr.   Ph: (541)461-4473
Eugene, OR 97404-4061

Contact: James R. Brann, President and Historian.

Desc: Collects, preserves, and disseminates information on all persons with the surnames Caret and Carette from France to Quebec to Maine. *Founded:* 1989. *Members:* 15.

166 ■ Carlton/Reed/Ashley/Williams/ Bradford/ McGoffier/Mattews/Reade Family Organization
1132 N. Tela Dr.   Ph: (405)789-2842
Oklahoma City, OK 73127-4308
E-mail: famhistnut@aol.com

Contact: Pauline Carlton Fletcher, Sec.

Desc: Descendants of Albert Hardeway Carlton and Cynthia Belle Reed Carlton. Promotes the preservation of the family heritage. Compiles statistics and maintains register of all family members. Provides resources and information related to the family. *Founded:* 1950. *Members:* 258.

167 ■ Carn Surname Organization
803 Bel Mar Dr.
Ogden, UT 84403

Contact: Eunice R. Carn, Pres.

Desc: Individuals with the surname Carn and its variants; others with an interest in the Carn family. Promotes interest in, and study of, Carn family genealogy and history. *Founded:* 1985.

168 ▪ Carnegie Clan Society

48739 Far Cry Rd.   Ph: (301)863-6972
Lexington Park, MD
  20653-3055

Contact: W. Richard Lomax, Sec.

Desc: Individuals with the surname Carnegie or its variant spellings. Seeks to locate all Carnegie clan members worldwide; promotes study of Carnegie clan history and genealogy. *Founded:* 1968.

169 ▪ Carolinas Black Family Reunion

PO Box 560125
Charlotte, NC 28256-0125

170 ▪ Carper Family Association

4918 Sudley Rd.   Ph: (703)754-2665
Catharpin, VA 20143

Contact: Janice M. Carper, Historian.

Desc: Members of the Carper family and others with an interest in Carper family history and genealogy. Serves as a clearinghouse on the Carper family and its history.

171 ▪ Carroll County Genealogical Society

PO Box 354   Ph: (815)273-3707
Savanna, IL 61074

Contact: Jean Marken, Pres.

Founded: 1975. *Members:* 80.

172 ▪ Carroll County Genealogical Society

Box 1752   Ph: (410)876-1552
Westminster, MD 21158
E-mail: ccgs@ccpl.carr.lib.md.us
URL: http://www.carr.lib.md.us/ccgs/ccgs.html

Contact: Harold Robertson, Treas.

Founded: 1981. *Members:* 230.

173 ▪ Carroll County Historical Society

640 N. Main St.   Ph: (901)352-3510
McKenzie, TN 38201   Fax: (901)352-3456
E-mail: grbrowning@mailexcite.com
URL: http://www.carroll.aeneas.net/gbm/

Contact: Patricia J. Clark, Exec.Dir.

Desc: Individuals interested in preserving the history of Carroll County, TN. Maintains the Governor Gordon Browning Museum and the County Genealogical Library. *Founded:* 1973. *Members:* 104.

174 ▪ Carruthers Clan Society

<c/o> Richard A. Crothers   Ph: (410)392-2216
76 Old Elm Rd.
North East, MD 21901

Contact: Richard A. Crothers, Exec. Officer.

Desc: Descendants of the Carruthers family or any family bearing one of Carruthers' variant spellings. Conducts genealogical research; collects and disseminates information.

175 ▪ Cass County Genealogical Society

PO Box 880   Ph: (903)796-2107
Atlanta, TX 75551
E-mail: fourpines@juno.com
URL: http://www.rootsweb.com/txcass/

Contact: Patsy R. Livingston, Pres.

Desc: Works to preserve Cass County, TX genealogical records and cemeteries. Maintains genealogy section of the Atlanta, TX public library. *Founded:* 1974. *Members:* 200.

176 ▪ Caster Association of America

1559 Moffett Dr.
Winchester, VA 22601-3183

Contact: Hal G. Ferguson, Pres.

Desc: Persons interested in researching the surnames Caster, Castor, Custer, Kester and other variants. Works to collect and preserve family history. *Members:* 400.

177 ▪ Catholic War Veterans Auxiliary of the U.S.A.

441 N. Lee St.   Ph: (703)549-3622
Alexandria, VA 22314   Fax: (703)684-5196

Contact: Linda M. Torreyson, Exec. Asst.

Desc: Mothers, widows, sisters, daughters, granddaughters, and nieces of living and deceased members of the Catholic War Veterans of the U.S.A. *Founded:* 1949. *Members:* 10000.

178 ▪ Catlow/Whitney Family Organization

222 Frances Ln.   Ph: (847)382-2621
Barrington, IL 60010

Contact: Gloria Heramb, Historian.

Desc: Descendants of Joseph Goodman Catlow, Clara Permelia Whitney, and their ancestors. Conducts genealogical research. *Founded:* 1976. *Members:* 500.

179 ▪ Caton Family Association

212 Sunset Pl.   Ph: (505)327-9501
Farmington, NM 87401
E-mail: bmc@cyberport.com

Contact: Barbara Caton, Contact.

Desc: Individuals with the surname Caton, other members of the Caton family, and other interested individuals. Promotes study of, and interest in, the family of Thomas Caton and his descendants in Virginia, Missouri, Oklahoma, and New Mexico. *Founded:* 1988. *Members:* 50.

180 ▪ Central New York Genealogical Society

PO Box 104, Colvin Sta.
Syracuse, NY 13205

Contact: Ron Kruhl, Chm.

Desc: Libraries, archives, genealogists, and historians. Promotes the study of the genealogy of upstate New York counties. *Founded:* 1961. *Members:* 850.

181 ▪ Centre County Genealogical Society

PO Box 1135   Ph: (814)446-2246
State College, PA 16804
E-mail: ellencopperfec3@psu.edu
URL: http://www.rootswet.com/pacentre/centre.htm

Contact: Elizabeth Dutton, Secretary.

Desc: Promotes interest in the genealogy of local families. Conducts educational programs; maintains catalog of Centre County, PA cemetery records and members' surnames and interests. *Founded:* 1975. *Members:* 200.

182 ▪ Century Association Archives Foundation

7 W 43rd St.
New York, NY 10036-7402

Contact: Lansing Lamont, Contact.

183 ▪ Champe Surname Organization

333 Center St.   Ph: (307)789-2893
Evanston, WY 82930

Contact: Harry L. Bodine, Contact.

Desc: Conducts genealogy and family history research. Family names covered include Bodine, Bogart, Van Sant, Tueller, Kunz, Millspaugh, Bergen, Lubbertson, Rogers, Shepherd, and Walker.

184 ▪ Chapman Family Association

770 S. Post Oak Ln., Ste. 435   Ph: (713)877-8333
Houston, TX 77056-1913   Fax: (713)877-1547
E-mail: sonfield@flash.net

Contact: Bernard Shapiro, Exec.Sec.

Desc: Collection, preservation, and dissemination of the genealogy and history of the Chapman Family. *Founded:* 1994. *Members:* 254.

185 ▪ Charlebois/Shalibo Family Association

712 NW 95th Terr.   Ph: (352)332-2065
Gainesville, FL 32607

Contact: Mitchell E. Sapp, Rep.

Desc: Works to collect family data and history. *Founded:* 1991. *Members:* 20.

186 ▪ Charlotte County Genealogical Society

PO Box 2682   Ph: (941)637-6208
Port Charlotte, FL 33949-2682
E-mail: genie@nut-n-but.net

Contact: Gene Dudley, Pres.

Desc: Individuals interested in the history and genealogy of Charlotte County, FL. Compiles and preserves local historic demographic records. *Founded:* 1975. *Members:* 240.

187 ▪ Chartier Family Association

13095 SW Glenn Cr.   Ph: (503)646-8186
Beaverton, OR 97008-5664   Fax: (503)646-8186
E-mail: vlchartier@transport.com

Contact: Vernon L. Chartier, Chm.

Desc: Individuals who have purchased or subscribe to Chartier family publications. Conducts genealogical research on the Chartier family in Europe and North America. *Founded:* 1992. *Members:* 200.

188 ▪ Chaves County Genealogical Society

PO Box 51
Roswell, NM 88201

189 ▪ Cheboygan County Genealogical Society

PO Box 51   Ph: (616)347-3806
Cheboygan, MI 49721

Contact: Julia Hinds, Pres.

Desc: Individuals interested in the genealogy of Cheboygan County, MI. *Founded:* 1979. *Members:* 70.

190 ▪ Cherokee County Genealogical Society

PO Box 1332   Ph: (409)824-2485
Jacksonville, TX 75766
E-mail: gordonbe@e-tex.com
URL: http://www.e-tex.com/gordonbe/index.htm

Contact: R.L. McGuire, Pres.

Desc: Individuals with an interest in genealogy and family history. Facilitates exchange of information among members. Conducts research; gathers genealogical and historical records for donation to local libraries. *Founded:* 1975. *Members:* 150.

191 ▪ Cherokee County Kansas Genealogical-Historical Society

100 S. Tennessee   Ph: (316)429-2992
PO Box 33
Columbus, KS 66725

Contact: Winona Goedeke, Pres.

Desc: Individuals interested in preserving the history of Cherokee County, KS. Gathers, preserves, and disseminates historical and genealogical information. *Founded:* 1980. *Members:* 166.

192 ■ Chester District Genealogical Society
PO Box 336
Richburg, SC 29729

Contact: George H. Moore, Pres.

Founded: 1978. *Members:* 850.

193 ■ Cheyenne County Genealogical Society
PO Box 802   Ph: (308)254-2325
Sidney, NE 69162

Contact: Lorraine Lafler, Pres.

Desc: Persons interested in genealogy and being a constructive part of the community by gathering and preserving history as well as being of assistance to others who are tracing family history are encouraged to join Cheyenne County Genealogical Society. Present membership is 25. Members transcribe historical records and answer queries, conduct workshops. *Founded:* 1979. *Members:* 28.

194 ■ Children of the Confederacy
328 North Blvd.   Ph: (804)355-1636
Richmond, VA 23220-4057   Fax: (804)353-1396

Contact: Marion H. Giannasi, Exec.Sec.

Desc: Boys and girls from infancy to age 18 who are lineal or collateral descendants of men and women who served honorably in the Confederate Army, Navy, or civil service; children who are lineal or collateral descendants of members of the United Daughters of the Confederacy and the Sons of Confederate Veterans (see separate entries). Members are affiliated through state or local groups where there are no divisions. *Founded:* 1954. *Members:* 3926.

195 ■ Chippewa County Genealogical Society
1427 Hilltop Blvd.   Ph: (715)723-3715
Chippewa Falls, WI 54729
E-mail: aek54729@aol.com

Contact: Anne Keller, Newsletter Editor.

Desc: Individuals interested in the history and genealogy of Chippewa County, WI. *Founded:* 1980. *Members:* 200.

196 ■ Chisago County Historical Society
PO Box 146   Ph: (651)257-5310
Lindstrom, MN 55045

Contact: Shery Stirling, Exec.Dir.

Desc: Works to collect, preserve and disseminate historical information on Chisago County. *Founded:* 1963. *Members:* 750.

197 ■ Chittenden Family Association
2 Buxton Ave.   Ph: (802)235-2302
Middletown Springs, VT 05757

Contact: Frances B. Krouse, Ed. and Officer-in-Charge.

Desc: Individuals with the surname Chittenden and their descendants who are interested in their heritage, and their lineal connection to the first governor of the state of Vermont. *Founded:* 1985. *Members:* 300.

198 ■ Christian County Genealogical Society
1101 Bethel St.   Ph: (502)886-9155
Hopkinsville, KY 42240

Contact: Jeanne Lancaster, Pres.

Members: 77.

199 ■ Chula Vista Genealogy Society
PO Box 3024
Chula Vista, CA 91909-3024

200 ■ Cibrowski Family Foundation
6059 S Quebec St., Ste. 202   Ph: (303)740-9497
Englewood, CO 80111-0000   Fax: (303)740-9593

201 ■ Citrus County Genealogical Society
PO Box 2211   Ph: (352)746-0021
Inverness, FL 34451-2211
E-mail: bernieoh@citrus.infi.net

Contact: Bernie O'Neil, Pres.

Founded: 1980. *Members:* 277.

202 ■ Civil War Sons
1725 Farmer Ave.   Ph: (602)967-5405
Tempe, AZ 85281

Contact: Stan Schirmacher, Dir.

Desc: All Civil War veteran's descendants and buffs of this era. Provides sources for photocopies of Civil War veterans' records. *Founded:* 1991. *Members:* 100.

203 ■ Clackamas County Family History Society
211 Tumwater Dr.   Ph: (503)682-1531
PO Box 995
Oregon City, OR 97045

Contact: Sandy McGuire, Pres.

Founded: 1988. *Members:* 150.

204 ■ Clallam County Genealogical Society
PO Box 1327   Ph: (360)417-2384
Port Angeles, WA 98362-0244
E-mail: ccgs@olypen.com

Contact: Ron Foss, Pres.

Desc: Fosters, stimulates, and shares ideas, information, methods, and practices in family research; collects, preserves and makes available to interested persons, books and material for furthering genealogical research; and encourages officials in charge of public records and genealogical collections to preserve them and make them accessible to interested persons. *Founded:* 1981. *Members:* 195.

205 ■ Clan Archibald Family Association
8 Westwood Ln.   Ph: (727)586-4287
Belleair, FL 33756-1619

Contact: Elbert L. Archibald, Pres.

Desc: Individuals with the surname Archibald and its variant spellings; others with an interest in the Archibald family. Promotes study of, and interest in, Archibald family history and genealogy. *Founded:* 1980. *Members:* 125.

206 ■ Clan Brodie International
PO Box 372   Ph: (705)887-9863
Fenelon Falls, ON, Canada   Fax: (705)887-9373
  K0M 1N0

Contact: Craig H. Brodie, Pres.

Desc: Descendants of the Scottish Brodie clan bearing the name Brodie, Brody, Byrde, De Brothe, or Byrdie. Conducts genealogical research on the Brodie clan; facilitates contact among members. Seeks worldwide Brodie or kin. *Founded:* 1978.

207 ■ Clan Buchan Association
155 Marine Dr.   Ph: (250)743-8084
Arbutus Ridge   Fax: (250)743-8095
Cobble Hill, BC, Canada V0R
  1L1

E-mail: buchan@seaside.net

Contact: Dr. W.R. Buchan, Contact.

Desc: Descendants of the Scottish Buchan clan. Conducts genealogical research on the Buchan clan; facilitates contact among members. *Founded:* 1960.

208 ■ Clan Campbell Society, North America
6412 Newcastle Rd.   Ph: (910)864-4231
Fayetteville, NC 28303-2137
E-mail: wjcfaync@aol.com
URL: http://www.ccsna.org

Contact: David R. Campbell, Pres.

Desc: Disseminates information about Clan Campbell and its members. *Founded:* 1971. *Members:* 3150.

209 ■ Clan Carmichael U.S.A.
2591 Rocky Springs Dr.
Marietta, GA 30062
E-mail: alanacarmichael@carmichael.org
URL: http://www.carmichael.org

Contact: Alana Carmichael Nigro, Sec.-Treas.

Desc: Individuals with the surname Carmichael or its variants; others with an interest in the Carmichael clan. Promotes interest in, and study of, Carmichael clan history and genealogy. *Founded:* 1993. *Members:* 250.

210 ■ Clan Chisholm Society - United States Branch
PO Box 1091   Ph: (603)357-5003
Keene, NH 03431   Fax: (603)352-3316
E-mail: ccsusb@top.monad.net
URL: http://www.geocities.com/Paris/4111/
  chisholm.html

Contact: Mrs. Val Chisholm Perry, Chairman.

Desc: Clan Chisholm is an ancient Highland Clan dating back to at least 1249. Clan lands extended through the fertile valley of Strathglass, Invernesshire, Scotland. The Clan Society binds together those whose ancestors had wandered afar. *Founded:* 1950. *Members:* 250.

211 ■ Clan Colquhoun Society of North America
2984 Mike Dr.   Ph: (770)425-3647
Marietta, GA 30064
E-mail: ealachann@aol.com

Contact: Skeets Calhoun, Pres.

Desc: Individuals with the surname Colquhoun or Calhoun and their variant spellings. Seeks to identify clan members; promotes genealogical research. *Founded:* 1981. *Members:* 410.

212 ■ Clan Cunning Association
3121 36th St.   Fax: (515)255-1371
Des Moines, IA 50310-4612

Contact: Willis Cunning, KTJ, Pres.

Desc: Descendants of 12th century Scottish clan Cunning, including spelling variants Coning, Conand, Conan, etc. Has resurrected clan history and works with Scottish authorities to restore the clan identity. Promotes awareness of the correct historical connections between surnames. Conducts educational and historical programs. Answers genealogical inquiries; provides referrals. *Founded:* 1977. *Members:* 500.

213 ■ Clan Cunningham Society of America
4471B SW 54th Ct.   Ph: (954)587-8919
Fort Lauderdale, FL 33314

Contact: Rev. James David Cunningham, Sec.

Desc: Members of the Cunningham clan. Promotes interest in Cunningham family history and genealogy, and in Scottish history and culture. Seeks to identify and unite members of the Cunningham clan in America. *Founded:* 1984. *Members:* 178.

214 ∎ Clan Currie Society

PO Box 541   Ph: (908)273-3509
Summit, NJ 07902-0541   Fax: (908)273-4342

Contact: Robert Currie, Pres.

Desc: Individuals of Scottish/Irish descent who have the surname Currie, Curry, Currey, Corey, MacCurrie, Mac-Curry, MacCorey, or MacMhuirrich. Promotes the history and accomplishments of the Currie family. *Founded:* 1991. *Members:* 100.

215 ∎ Clan Davidson Society

5650 Harmony Bend   Ph: (770)967-6317
Braselton, GA 30517

Contact: Richard Davis Halliley, Pres.

Desc: Seeks to assist Davidsons with a common heritage and background to associate themselves together. *Founded:* 1981. *Members:* 525.

216 ∎ Clan Farquharson Association of Canada

PO Box 23045, DSC RPO   Ph: (902)463-6277
Dartmouth, NS, Canada B3A
4S9

Contact: Robert M. Findlay, Pres.

Desc: Descendants of the Scottish Farquharson clan. Conducts genealogical research on the Farquharson clan; facilitates contact among members. *Founded:* 1984. *Members:* 203.

217 ∎ Clan Forrester Society

3070 Georgia Hwy. 81 SW
Loganville, GA 30249

Contact: E. Jerald Forrester, Pres.

Desc: Descendants of the Forrester, Forester, Forrister, Foster family. *Founded:* 1963. *Members:* 150.

218 ∎ Clan Forsyth Society of Canada

170 Sloane Ave.   Ph: (416)751-6517
North York, ON, Canada M4A   Fax: (416)489-2570
2C3

Contact: Neil Forsyth, Pres.

Desc: Descendants of the Forsyth clan. Conducts genealogical research on the Forsyth clan; facilitates contact among members. *Founded:* 1990. *Members:* 150.

219 ∎ Clan Fraser Society of Canada

71 Charles St. E, Ste. 1101   Ph: (416)920-6851
Toronto, ON, Canada M4Y   Fax: (416)920-1275
2T3
E-mail: cdnexplorer@msn.com

Contact: W. Nell Fraser, Chm.

Desc: Descendants of the Scottish Fraser clan. Conducts genealogical and historical research on the Fraser clan; facilitates contact among members. *Founded:* 1868. *Members:* 300.

220 ∎ Clan Graham Society

1228 Kensington Dr.   Ph: (336)885-5789
High Point, NC 27262
E-mail: rhunthoward@hotmail.com

Contact: Richard Graham, Pres.

Desc: Members of the Clan Graham. Promotes the "general interests of the clan;" seeks to "cultivate the spirit of

kinship, fellowship, and social intercourse among the Clan members throughout the United States and Canada." *Founded:* 1975. *Members:* 1500.

221 ∎ Clan Grant Society

9619 Concession 9   Ph: (905)850-9299
Rural Route 2   Fax: (905)850-9244
Beeton, ON, Canada L0G 1A0
E-mail: jrantscot@aol.com

Contact: Jim Grant, Convenor.

Desc: Descendants of the Scottish Grant clan and its septs. Conducts genealogical research on the Grant clan; facilitates contact among members. *Founded:* 1982.

222 ∎ Clan Gregor Society of Canada

4086 Blue Grass Ct.   Ph: (905)897-2024
Mississauga, ON, Canada L5C   Fax: (416)586-5807
3Y4
E-mail: ianm@rom.on.ca

Contact: Ian McGregor, Pres.

Desc: Descendants of the Scottish MacGregor clan with the surname MacGregor or any of its 100 variants. Conducts genealogical research; facilitates contact among members. Special focus on members of the clan in Canada. *Founded:* 1980. *Members:* 100.

223 ∎ Clan Gregor Society Pacific Northwest Chapter

PO Box 3267
Federal Way, WA 98063-3267

224 ∎ Clan Irwin Association

226 1750th Ave.   Ph: (217)792 5226
Mount Pulaski, IL 62548-6635
E-mail: cia_chairman@juno.com

Contact: Guy C. Irvin, Chm.

Desc: Members of the Irwin family. Promotes interest in family history and genealogy and Scottish history and culture. Seeks to identify and unite members of the Irwin clan. *Founded:* 1976. *Members:* 950.

225 ∎ Clan Johnston(e) in America

<c/o> Stephen Johnston   Ph: (919)541-5885
215 SE Maynard   Fax: (919)541-6683
Cary, NC 27511

Contact: Stephen Johnston, Contact.

Desc: Descendants of the Johnstone, Johnston, or Johnson families who emigrated to the U.S. from Scotland. Collects, preserves, and disseminates information on the families; promotes interest in genealogical research. Awards scholarships and grants. Conducts charitable programs; participates in Scottish highland games and other festivals. Maintains biographical archives and library. *Founded:* 1976. *Members:* 475.

226 ∎ Clan Leslie Society

612 N Maple Ave.
Ridgway, PA 15853

Desc: Descendants of Scotland's Clan Leslie. Seeks to identify and gather members of the Leslie Clan worldwide. *Founded:* 1978. *Members:* 550.

227 ∎ Clan Lockhart

716 Robin Hood Hill
Sherwood Forest, MD 21405-2020

Contact: Dolly E. Baker, Contact.

228 ∎ Clan MacArthur Society of Canada

252 Kananaskis Green   Ph: (780)987-2602
Devon, AB, Canada T9G 1Y8

E-mail: mcartld@telusplanet.net

Contact: Lloyd K. McArthur, Contact.

Desc: Descendants of the Scottish MacArthur clan. Conducts genealogical research on the MacArthur clan; facilitates contact among members. *Founded:* 1986. *Members:* 100.

229 ∎ Clan MaCarthy Society

Mp 672, Hwy. 200
PO Box 69
Plains, MT 59859-0069

Contact: William M. McCarty, MD, Contact.

230 ∎ Clan MacDuff Society of America

5901 Walden Trail
Arlington, TX 76016-2726

231 ∎ Clan MacDuff Society of America

3524 Slade Blvd.   Ph: (817)244-4071
Fort Worth, TX 76116-6910
E-mail: mwardrop@worldnct.att.nct
URL: http://www.tartans.com/official/MacDuff/usa

Contact: Milton Wardrop, Chm.

Desc: Descendants of the MacDuff clan. Promotes interest in the history and genealogy of the MacDuff clan; encourages communication and good fellowship among members. *Founded:* 1974. *Members:* 750.

232 ∎ Clan MacInnes Society

8232 Kay Ct.   Ph: (703)560-4371
Annandale, VA 22003   Fax: (703)560-2080
E-mail: maryfaulk@juno.com

Contact: Mary A. Faulk, Sec.-Treas.

Desc: Members of the MacInnes family. Promotes interest in family history and genealogy, and in Scottish history, music, dance, and culture. *Founded:* 1970. *Members:* 500.

233 ∎ Clan Mackay Association of Canada

3665 Autumn Leaf Cr.   Ph: (905)820-5715
Mississauga, ON, Canada L5L   Fax: (905)820-5715
1K7

Contact: Mora Cairns, Pres.

Desc: Descendants of the Scottish Mackay clan. Conducts genealogical research on the Mackay clan; facilitates contact among members. *Founded:* 1980. *Members:* 140.

234 ∎ Clan MacKenzie Society in the Americas

1065 S Lakemont Cir. No. 206   Ph: (407)622-2153
Winter Park, FL 32792
E-mail: dorjohn@juno.com
URL: http://www.clanmackenzie.com

Contact: John D. Mackenzie, Sec.

Desc: Fosters fellowship among members. *Founded:* 1974. *Members:* 694.

235 ∎ Clan Mackenzie Society in the Americas - Canada

580 Rebecca St.   Ph: (905)842-2106
Oakville, ON, Canada L6K 3N9
E-mail: alanmck@cqocable.net
URL: http://www.clanmackenzie.com

Contact: Alan McKenzie, Commissioner.

Desc: Descendants of the Scottish Mackenzie clan. Conducts genealogical research on the Mackenzie clan; facilitates contact among members and those interested in Scottish history. History and heritage. Attend highland games. *Founded:* 1986. *Members:* 400.

236 ▪ Clan MacLennan Association, U.S.A.
Willtown Bluff
Adams Run, SC 29426-0360
E-mail: tntz22a@prodigy.com
URL: http://www.usa.maclennan.com

Contact: M. W. Baumeister, Nat.Sec.

Desc: Family association for persons of MacLennan descent and associated septs. Conducts research, educational, and charitible programs. *Founded:* 1971. *Members:* 367.

237 ▪ Clan MacLennan, Central Ontario Branch
<c/o> Mr. David R. MacLennan   Ph:(905)627-0811
70 Pleasant Ave.
Dundas, ON, Canada L9H 3T4

Contact: David R. MacLennan, President.

Desc: Descendants of the Scottish MacLennan clan. Facilitates contact among members. *Founded:* 1971. *Members:* 80.

238 ▪ Clan Macneil Association of America
1824 Stoneyridge Dr.   Ph: (704)399-1134
Charlotte, NC 28214-8341

Contact: Doris Byrd McNeill, Sec.

Desc: Individuals with the surname Macneil, O'Neill, Mcneil, Mcneill, Neal, MacNeally, MacNealedge, MacKneale, and other variations. Promotes interest in the heritage of descendants of the Macneil Clan. *Founded:* 1921. *Members:* 1200.

239 ▪ Clan MacRae Society of North America
306 Surrey Rd.
Savannah, GA 31410-4407

Desc: Individuals with the surname MacRae and its variant spellings. Promotes interest in the history and genealogy of the MacRae clan, and in the history and culture of Scotland.

240 ▪ Clan Maitland Society of North America
108 Lawson Rd.   Ph: (781)545-2637
Scituate, MA 02066-2546

Contact: Clint Lauderdale, Pres.

Desc: Families and individuals who are descendants or relatives of the Maitland and Lauderdale surname. *Founded:* 1970. *Members:* 125.

241 ▪ Clan Matheson Society
PO Box 307
The Plains, VA 20198-0307   Ph: (703)771-7171
    Fax: (703)777-3608
E-mail: clanmathsn@aol.com

Contact: Malcolm Matheson, Chief Lieutenant.

Desc: Members of the Matheson family. Promotes study of family history and genealogy; encourages interest in Scottish culture. *Members:* 240.

242 ▪ Clan McKay Society
93 Killam Hill Rd.
Boxford, MA 01921

Desc: Individuals with the surname McKay and its variant spellings. Promotes appreciation of Scottish history and culture; facilitates communication among members of the McKay clan.

243 ▪ Clan McLaren Association of North America
3322 Old Hwy. 68   Ph: (423)442-2161
Madisonville, TN 37354
E-mail: fhlowry@icx.net
URL: http://members.aol.com/rapmack/maclaren.html

Contact: F. Houston Lowry, Pres.

Desc: Members of the McLaren family. Promotes interest in McLaren family history and genealogy; encourages appreciation of Scottish history and culture. *Founded:* 1983. *Members:* 325.

244 ▪ Clan Menzies Society, North American Branch
323 Rough Water Pt.   Ph: (828)648-4255
Canton, NC 28716
E-mail: mathewes@primeline.com
URL: http://www.menzies.org

Contact: David Mathewes, Convener.

Desc: Members of the Menzies family. Promotes interest in Menzies clan history and genealogy, and in Scottish history and culture. *Founded:* 1984. *Members:* 210.

245 ▪ Clan Munro Association of Canada
100 City Centre Dr.   Ph: (905)607-1439
PO Box 2084
Mississauga, ON, Canada L5B 3C6

Contact: Ian M. Munro, Pres.

Desc: Descendants of the Scottish Munro clan. Conducts genealogical research; facilitates contact among members. Supports Highland music. *Founded:* 1975. *Members:* 106.

246 ▪ Clan Murray Society, North American Branch
803 Evergreen Dr.   Ph: (610)670-1433
Wyomissing, PA 19610
E-mail: murrayrw@aol.com

Contact: Mr. R.W. Murray, Chm.

Desc: Descendants of the Scottish Murray clan and its septs. Conducts genealogical research; facilitates contact among memebers. *Founded:* 1969. *Members:* 350.

247 ▪ Clan Napier in North America
Kilmahew Rte. 2   Ph: (334)281-0505
Box 614
Ramer, AL 36069-9245

Contact: Brig.Gen. John H. Napier, III, Lieutenant to the Chief.

Desc: Napiers by birth, descent, or adoption living on the North American continent. (Variant surnames include Napper, Nappier, Nipper, and, according to some sources, Leper, Raper, and Rapier.). Promotes pride and camaraderie among all Napiers. *Founded:* 1985. *Members:* 300.

248 ▪ Clan Pollock
12712 St. Clair Dr.   Ph: (502)245-0091
Middletown, KY 40243-1037
E-mail: dickpoll@aol.com

Contact: Richard H. Pollock, Pres.

Desc: Families sharing common surnames and Scottish ancestry. Fosters the study of Scottish heritage with emphasis on the Pollock clan. *Founded:* 1979. *Members:* 560.

249 ▪ Clan Ramsey of North America
434 Skinner Blvd.   Ph: (813)734-7020
Dunedin, FL 34698-4738   Fax: (813)734-7392

Contact: David F. Ramsey, Membership Sec.

Desc: Participates at the Highland Games throughout U.S. and Canada. *Founded:* 1977. *Members:* 420.

250 ▪ Clan Rose Society of America
629 Mohican Tr.   Ph: (910)395-5697
Wilmington, NC 28409   Fax: (910)395-5697
E-mail: kirkrose@aol.com

Contact: Kirk D. Rose, Contact.

Desc: North American descendants of the Scottish Rose family. Works to preserve the family heritage and Tradition of Kilravock in North America and to unite the American descendants of the Scottish Roses. *Founded:* 1970. *Members:* 235.

251 ▪ Clan Ross Association of the United States
5430 S. 5th St.   Ph: (703)671-5210
Arlington, VA 22204
URL: http://www.ClanRossAssociation.org

Contact: Marilyn Ross, Membership Sec.

Desc: Persons of Ross ancestry or family names connected with Ross. *Founded:* 1975. *Members:* 650.

252 ▪ Clan Scott Society
PO Box 13021
Austin, TX 78711-3021
E-mail: clanscott@aol.com
URL: http://www.clanscott.org

Contact: David M. Scott, Membership Sec.

Desc: Individuals bearing the surname Scott, or one of the following septs, however spelled: Buccleuch, Geddes, Laidlaw, Langlands, and their descendants and spouses. Fosters cultural, historical, and genealogical studies. *Founded:* 1978. *Members:* 550.

253 ▪ Clan Shaw Society
3031 Appoxmattox Ave. Apt. 102
Olney, MD 20832-1498

Contact: Mr. Meredith L. Shaw, Pres.

Desc: Persons bearing the surname Shaw and/or descendants of a Shaw or one of the septs of the clan, including relationships by marriage. The septs of Clan Shaw include: Ayson (New Zealand), Adamson, Esson, MacAy, MacHay, Sheach, Shiach, Sheath, Seith, Seth, Scaith, Skaith, and Shay, with variant spellings of each. (Clan Shaw is based principally on the Scottish Clan Shaw heritage, but welcomes all Shaws regardless of believed national origin.). Seeks to provide opportunities for communication between and socializing among members, to further genealogical research on the Shaw lineage, and to bring credit to Clan Shaw and the family name. *Founded:* 1983. *Members:* 1000.

254 ▪ Clan Shaw Society
3031 Appomattox Ave Apt 102
Olney, MD 20832-1498

255 ▪ Clan Sinclair Association of Canada
133 Major St.   Ph: (416)966-1523
Toronto, ON, Canada M5S   Fax: (416)966-1587
2K9

Contact: Rory Sinclair, Sec.

Desc: Descendants of the Scottish Sinclair clan. To promote restoration of Sinclair landmarks in Scotland and historical research into the clan's history; facilitates contact among members in North America and Scotland. *Founded:* 1972. *Members:* 500.

256 ▪ Clan Sinclair Association U.S.A.
3211 Big Woods Rd.   Ph: (919)542-2795
Chapel Hill, NC 27514
E-mail: sinclaire@mindspring.com

Contact: Bradley Sinclair Barker, Pres.

Desc: Families (300) and individuals (300) who are descendants of or related to the Sinclair family. Encourages a closer relationship among members through the continuation of traditions. *Founded:* 1978. *Members:* 600.

257 ■ Clan Sutherland Society of North America
1509 21st Ave.   Ph: (309)786-5777
Rock Island, IL 61201
E-mail: hwtv90a@prodigy.com

Contact: E. Kenneth White, Pres.

Desc: Persons of Sutherland lineage (variant spellings accepted) and of the Septs, Cheyne, Duffus, Federith, Gray, Keith, Mowat, and Oliphant ancestries. Seeks to foster a spirit of kinship by providing a focal point for expression of clan sentiment and encouraging communication between members. Promotes friendship and loyalty among members. Seeks to promote public knowledge of and interest in the history and traditions of the Sutherland name. Encourages deeper understanding of the cultural background of the clan by publishing scholarly articles on the historical and social aspects of the Sutherland name. Attempts to establish family connections between members. Maintains genealogical records. *Founded:* 1976. *Members:* 300.

258 ■ Clan Watson Society of Canada
485 Cobequid Rd.   Ph: (902)864-8335
Lower Sackville, NS, Canada
B4C 3Y7

Contact: Andrew P. Watson, President.

Desc: Society researching in Scotland, old clan estates and past chiefs. Promoting the learning of Scottish history and culture in schools. Provides genealogy of member families and donates scottish books to schools. *Founded:* 1988. *Members:* 90.

259 ■ Clan Young
4402 Brandeis Ave.
Orlando, FL 32839-1468

Contact: Edward A. Young, Contact.

260 ■ Clark County Genealogical Society
PO Box 2728
Vancouver, WA 98668

Contact: Jerri St. John, Pres.

Desc: Provides information, direction, and assistance to researchers of Clark County, WA history and genealogy. Conducts educational programs.

261 ■ Clark County Nevada Genealogical Society
PO Box 1929   Ph: (702)225-5838
Las Vegas, NV 89125-1929   Fax: (702)258-4099
E-mail: ccngs@juno.com
URL: http://www.lvrj.com/communitylink/ccngs/

Contact: Rose E. Turner, Pres.

Desc: Individuals interested in genealogical research. *Founded:* 1976. *Members:* 210.

262 ■ Clay County Genealogical and Historical Society
361 W. Main St.   Ph: (501)598-3666
Piggott, AR 72454   Fax: (501)598-3666

Contact: Gerald Runyon, Pres.

Desc: Individuals interested in preserving the history of Clay County, AR. Locates, restores, and preserves historical and genealogical records. *Founded:* 1985. *Members:* 140.

263 ■ Clinton County Genealogical Society
Frankfort Community   Ph: (765)654-8746
  Public Library   Fax: (765)654-8747
208 W. Clinton St.
Frankfort, IN 46041

E-mail: fcpl@accs.net

Contact: Karen Timmons Patchett, Pres.

Desc: Works to improve the genealogical collection of the Frankfort Community Public Library. *Founded:* 1991. *Members:* 80.

264 ■ Cloud Family Association
508 Crestwood Dr.   Ph: (256)881-2578
Eastland, TX 76448
URL: http://genweb.net/cloud

Contact: Linda Boose, Sec.-Treas.

Desc: Individuals interested in researching the Cloud surname. Acts as a clearinghouse for Cloud family history and genealogy. *Founded:* 1978. *Members:* 150.

265 ■ Coal County Genealogical Society
PO Box 436
Coalgate, OK 74538-0436

266 ■ Coatney/Courtney Family Association
809 S Walnut
Freeman, SD 57029
E-mail: kosankc@gwtc.net

Contact: Carol Peterson, A.G., Contact.

Desc: Individuals interested in the history and genealogy of people with the surname Coatney and its variant spellings. Promotes increased interest in, and study of, family history and genealogy. *Founded:* 1984.

267 ■ Cobb County Genealogical Society
PO Box 1413   Ph: (770)434-0507
Marietta, GA 30061-1413
URL: http://www.rootsweb.com/gecobb2/cobbgen.htm

Contact: Joe F. Tillman, Sr., Pres.

Desc: Individuals interested in genealogy. Conducts historical research; operates historical preservation programs. Sponsors educational programs. *Founded:* 1979. *Members:* 200.

268 ■ Coffey County Genealogical Society
712 Sanders   Ph: (316)364-8795
Burlington, KS 66839-1656

Contact: Della Meyer, Pres.

269 ■ Cogswell Family Association
1479 Great Plain Ave.   Ph: (781)444-0852
Needham, MA 02192   Fax: (781)444-0902
E-mail: cogs6@aol.com

Contact: John H. Cogswell, Treas.

Desc: Individuals with an interest in the family history and genealogy of people with the surname Cogswell and its variant spellings. Promotes historical and genealogical interest and study. *Founded:* 1986. *Members:* 250.

270 ■ Colonial Dames of America
421 E. 61st St.   Ph: (212)838-5489
New York, NY 10021   Fax: (212)688-1389

Contact: Diedre Bay, Exec.Dir.

Desc: Women whose ancestors served an armed forces commission for or held public office in one of the 13 North American colonies. Collects and preserves educational resources, including manuscripts, relics, and mementos of the colonial period in American history; commemorates the important colonial events of the U.S. and of the 13 colonies. Seeks to disseminate information about and create popular interest in colonial history. Maintains Abigail Adams Smith Museum in New York City. Provides educational programs. *Founded:* 1890. *Members:* 2000.

271 ■ Colonial Order of the Acorn
20 MacKenzie Glen   Ph: (203)661-3993
Greenwich, CT 06830   Fax: (203)661-3992

Contact: John Badman, III, Chancellor.

Desc: Male descendants of residents of the North American colonies, which became the 13 original states. Members are primarily from NY, NJ, CT, PA, though COA has 60% of its members from other parts of the U.S. Acorn signifies the members of the 13 colonies who were the "Acorns from which grew the Tall Oak of the U.S." Cherishes and perpetuates American traditions and associations; promote patriotism and loyalty to American national institutions; encourages social intercourse among the descendants of the nation's founders; stimulates vigilance and united action in the preservation and promotion of political theories and principles of America's forefathers without regard to political party divisions or ecclesiastical denominations. Collects and preserves records of colonial incidents; encourages preparation and study of historical and patriotic papers and history. *Founded:* 1894. *Members:* 185.

272 ■ Colorado Council of Genealogical Societies
PO Box 24379   Ph: (303)642-7262
Denver, CO 80224-0379   Fax: (303)642-3646
E-mail: pakemper@aol.com
URL: http://www.rootsweb.com/coccgs/index.html

Contact: Patricia A. Kemper, Pres.

Desc: Coordinates genealogical societies throughout Colorado. Provides information to genealogical societies about education, membership, and community service. Conducts outreach projects. *Founded:* 1979. *Members:* 2500.

273 ■ Colorado Genealogical Society
PO Box 9218   Ph: (303)571-1535
Denver, CO 80209-0218
URL: http://www.cogensoc.org/cgs/cgs-home.htm

Contact: Sandra Carter Duff, Pres.

Desc: Promotes genealogy in Colorado. Seeks to locate, preserve, and index historical records; assists and supports state libraries. Sponsors Black Sheep Writing Contest. Purchases books and periodicals for Genealogy Collection, Denver Public Library. *Founded:* 1924. *Members:* 471.

274 ■ Colorado Springs Registry
PO Box 62357
Colorado Springs, CO 80962-2357

275 ■ Colrain Historical Society
91 E Catamount Hill Rd   Ph: (413)624-3710
Colrain, MA 01340-9514

Contact: Phillips B. Sherburne, Pres.

Desc: Individuals interested in preserving the history of Colrain, MA. Promotes genealogical study. *Founded:* 1957. *Members:* 60.

276 ■ Comal County Genealogy Society
PO Box 310160   Ph: (210)625-8766
New Braunfels, TX 78131-0160

Contact: Mrs. Ethel Canion, Pres.

Desc: Individuals interested in local history and genealogy. Gathers, restores, and preserves historical demographic records; donates materials to the Sophienburg Archives Research Library. *Founded:* 1981. *Members:* 150.

277 ■ Comite des Archives de la Louisiane
PO Box 44370   Ph: (504)387-4264
Baton Rouge, LA 70804
E-mail: judy.riffel@cajunelectric.com

URL: http://www.sec.state.la.us/arch-1.htm

Contact: Damon Veach, Pres.

Desc: Promotes the maintaining of archives, historic preservation, and genealogical research in Louisiana. Provides materials for the Louisiana State Archives. *Founded:* 1978. *Members:* 550.

278 ▪ Concordia Historical Institute

801 DeMun Ave.　　　　　Ph: (314)505-7900
St. Louis, MO 63105　　　Fax: (314)505-7901
E-mail: chi@chilcms.org

Contact: Daniel Preus, Dir.

Desc: Serves as information bureau and research center on all phases of Lutheranism in America. Locates, collects, and preserves items of historical value for Lutheranism in America. *Founded:* 1847. *Members:* 1500.

279 ▪ Confessing Synod Ministries

East Liberty Lutheran Church　Ph: (412)362-1712
5707 Penn Ave.
Pittsburgh, PA 15206

Contact: Pastor Philip Long, Contact.

Desc: Six congregations in the Pittsburgh, PA area; interested institutional leaders throughout the U.S. Teaches and practices the prophetic ministry based on scriptural models. (Prophetic means to speak and act out in order to address problems without trying to achieve a consensus.) Instructs pastors and institutional leaders on acting prophetically. Promotes prophetic ministry model in the U.S. Believes numerous denominations accomodate big business, politics, and the state instead of challenging the culture and the state and serving the "true Biblical Jesus." Addresses problems such as family addictions/dysfunction, unemployment, and community deterioration. Maintains speakers' bureau, library, and archives; conducts research programs. *Founded:* 1982.

280 ▪ Contra Costa County Genealogical Society

PO Box 910　　　　　　Ph: (510)235-7707
Concord, CA 94522-0910
E-mail: weebteddys@worldnet.att.net
URL: http://www.geocities.com/heartland/plains/4335/
　　cccgs.html

Contact: Joyce Gutridge, Treas.

Desc: Individuals interested in local history and genealogy. Conducts educational programs and seminars. Provides classes, work/study group. *Founded:* 1975. *Members:* 260.

281 ▪ Cooley Family Association of America

1106 N. Eagle Lake Dr.　　Ph: (616)375-0343
Kalamazoo, MI 49009-8428

Contact: Edna L. Farthing, Contact.

Desc: Persons named or descended from a Cooley, Cowley, Coley, or other variants of the surname Cooley; interested individuals. To further research and gather records on the Cooley name and its variants. Plans to establish a permanent storage place for all records on the surname. Sponsors genealogical search service. *Founded:* 1936. *Members:* 350.

282 ▪ Coordinating Committee for Ellis Island

3003 Van Ness St. NW,　　Ph: (202)244-2834
　　Apt. W727
Washington, DC 20008

Contact: Eleanor Sreb, Founder.

Desc: Conducts Americans All, an educational program designed to support and motivate students from diverse cultural backgrounds. Offers training for teachers involved with culturally diverse student populations, specialized teaching materials, and volunteer and support staff. Sponsored an exhibit of sculptures, photographs, and drawings reflecting the immigrant experience at Ellis Island, which served as the entrance point to the U.S. for 12,000,000 immigrants from 1892 to 1954.

283 ▪ Coosa River Valley Historical and Genealogical Society

RFD 5, Box 109　　　　Ph: (205)447-2939
Piedmont, AL 36272

Contact: Mrs. Frank Ross Stewart, Pres.

Desc: Individuals interested in genealogical and historical research of the Coosa River valley area of Alabama and Georgia.

284 ▪ Copeland/Sewell Family Organization

1132 N. Tela Dr.　　　　Ph: (405)789-2842
Oklahoma City, OK 73127-4308
E-mail: famhist@aol.com

Contact: Pauline Carlton Fletcher, Family Genealogist.

Desc: Descendants of William Felix Copeland and his wife Samantha Ellen (Sewell) Copeland. Registers known descendants and is compiling family genealogy. Conducts annual genealogical research training session. *Founded:* 1918.

285 ▪ Corbin Genealogical Society

PO Box 353　　　　　　Ph: (606)878-8074
Corbin, KY 40702

Contact: Carol Pace, Pres.

Desc: Individuals interested in collecting, researching, and preserving family histories and records in Knox, Laurel, and Whitley counties, KY. *Founded:* 1980. *Members:* 90.

286 ▪ Corbin Research

10315 Lagrange Rd.　　　Ph: (502)245-7317
Louisville, KY 40223
E-mail: kcorbin1@compuserve.com

Contact: Kenneth C. Corbin, Recorder.

Desc: Records information on persons with the surname Corbin in their family tree. Conducts genealogical research. Compiles statistics. *Founded:* 1972.

287 ▪ Cornerstone Genealogical Society

PO Box 547　　　　　　Ph: (412)627-5653
Waynesburg, PA 15370

Contact: Laurine Schneck Williams, Pres.

Desc: Libraries and individuals in Greene County, PA with an interest in genealogy and genealogical records. *Founded:* 1975. *Members:* 725.

288 ▪ Corson/Colson Family History Association

2300 Cedarfield Pkwy., No. 476　Ph: (804)747-8180
Richmond, VA 23233-1947

Contact: Mrs. Iverne Corson Rinehart, Corr.Sec.

Desc: Descendants or individuals interested in Corson or Colson ancestry. Collects and shares information on the origins and descent of individuals with the surname Corson and its variants. Works to maintain communication among descendants. *Founded:* 1987. *Members:* 175.

289 ▪ Coshocton County Genealogical Society

PO Box 128　　　　　　Ph: (614)622-4706
Coshocton, OH 43812-0128
E-mail: gkiwkade@sota-oh.com
URL: http://www.cu.soltec.com/photo/coshocton.html

Contact: Glenn E. Kinkade, Pres.

Desc: Individuals interested in the genealogy of Coshocton County, OH. Offers genealogy course. *Founded:* 1977. *Members:* 200.

290 ▪ Council of Jewish Organizations - Immigrants from the Former Soviet Union

62-54 97th Pl., Ste. 4i
Rego Park, NY 11374-1350

291 ▪ Covert Family Association

303 W. Violet St.　　　　Ph: (813)238-3816
Tampa, FL 33603
E-mail: tracingfam@aol.com

Contact: Diane Covert Broderick, Editor.

Desc: Promotes genealogical research into the Covert surname and the history of the Coverts and related families. Collects and distributes data and assists researchers. Compares family group sheets and attempts to connect families and researchers. (The Covert Family Association was active in the late 1800s and early 1900s, became inactive due to lack of interest, and was revived in 1987.). *Founded:* 1987. *Members:* 40.

292 ▪ Coward Family Organization

2140 Marion St.　　　　Ph: (205)822-2446
Birmingham, AL 35226-3012

Contact: Trudy Adams, Editor.

Desc: Members of the Coward, Cowart, or Cowherd families; interested others. Promotes the history and genealogy of the families. *Founded:* 1891.

293 ▪ Coweta County Genealogical Society

PO Box 1014　　　　　Ph: (770)251-2877
Newnan, GA 30264-1014

Contact: Norma Gunby, Pres.

Desc: Individuals and businesses dedicated to the research, recording, and preservation of historical and genealogical records. *Founded:* 1981. *Members:* 660.

294 ▪ Cowles Family Association

1717 S Angeline St.　　　Ph: (206)763-3289
Seattle, WA 98108

Desc: Individuals with the surname Cowles and its variant spellings. Promotes study of, and interest in, Cowles family history and genealogy. *Founded:* 1935.

295 ▪ Cowley County Genealogical Society

1518 E. 12th St.　　　　Ph: (316)221-4591
Winfield, KS 67156

Contact: Claire Utt, Sec.-Treas.

Desc: Collecting compiling and recording Cowley county history and genealogical material. *Founded:* 1979. *Members:* 26.

296 ▪ Crandall Family Association

PO Box 1472　　　　　Fax: (815)328-2866
Westerly, RI 02891
E-mail: eperry@cfa.net
URL: http://www.cfa.net/cfa/contents.html

Contact: Earl P. Crandall, Genealogist.

Desc: Descendants and friends of Elder John Crandall of Rhode Island. *Founded:* 1986. *Members:* 350.

297 ▪ Crawford County Genealogical Society

PO Box 120
Robinson, IL 62454

Contact: Burl Rich, Pres.

Members: 125.

298 ▪ Crawford County Genealogical Society
848 N. Main St.
Meadville, PA 16335

Contact: William B. Moore, Pres.

Desc: Individuals interested in the genealogy of Crawford County, PA. Collects, preserves, and publishes genealogical data. *Founded:* 1977. *Members:* 200.

299 ▪ Crawford County Historical and Genealogical Society
PO Box 133   Ph: (812)739-2358
Leavenworth, IN 47137
E-mail: rockman@disknet.com

Contact: Sharon Morris, Treas.

300 ▪ Creekmore Family Association
15502 MacArthur
Redford, MI 48239

Contact: Don L. White, Pres.

Desc: Members of the Creekmore family. Promotes communication and good fellowship among members; facilitates family historical and genealogical research.

301 ▪ Crispell Family Association
PO Box 35   Ph: (570)226-4721
Tafton, PA 18461   Fax: (570)226-4721
E-mail: 73130.30@compuserve.com

Contact: Sharon S. Robinson, Tres.

Desc: Preserves Huguenot Heritage in New Poltz, NY. Maintains genealogy of Antoine Crispell. *Founded:* 1969. *Members:* 150.

302 ▪ Crittenden County Genealogical Society
PO Box 61
Marion, KY 42064

Contact: Fay Carol Crider, Pres.

Founded: 1991. *Members:* 75.

303 ▪ Croatian Genealogical Society
2527 San Carlos Ave.
San Carlos, CA 94070
E-mail: croatians@aol.com

Contact: Adam S. Eterovich, Dir.

Desc: Individuals, libraries, and ethnic organizations. Encourages Croatian genealogical and heraldic research. *Founded:* 1978. *Members:* 537.

304 ▪ Crook County Genealogical Society
246 N. Main St.   Ph: (503)447-3715
Prineville, OR 97754

Contact: Ruth Cholin, Pres.

Desc: Genealogists. Gathers and disseminates information. *Founded:* 1994. *Members:* 33.

305 ▪ Crotty Family Organization
48 Coventry Ln.   Ph: (540)992-1292
Daleville, VA 24083
E-mail: crottyg@aol.com

Contact: A. E. Crotty, Exec. Officer.

Desc: Individuals interested in the history and genealogy of people with the surname Crotty and its variant spellings. Promotes genealogical and historical study and research. *Founded:* 1953. *Members:* 100.

306 ▪ Crow Wing County Genealogical Society
2103 Graydon Ave.   Ph: (218)829-9738
Brainerd, MN 56401
E-mail: lkirk@brainerd.net

Contact: Lucille Kirkeby, Pres.

Desc: Individuals interested in preserving the history of central Minnesota and its people. Conducts genealogical research. *Founded:* 1973. *Members:* 35.

307 ▪ Crowl Name Association
9603 Bel Glade St.   Ph: (703)281-9562
Fairfax, VA 22031-1105
E-mail: gkomar@eroes.com

Contact: Gail Komar, Chm.

Desc: Individuals and institutions with an interest in the family history and genealogy of people with the surname Crowl and its variant spellings. Promotes genealogical and historical research and study. *Founded:* 1985. *Members:* 105.

308 ▪ Czechoslovak Genealogical Society International
PO Box 16225   Ph: (651)739-7543
St. Paul, MN 55116   Fax: (651)426-0969
E-mail: cgsi@aol.com
URL: http://www.cgsi.org

Contact: Dave Pavelka, Pres.

Desc: Individuals of Bohemian, Moravian, Silesian, Carpatho-Rusyn, Slovakian, German, or Jewish descent. Promotes research and interest in Czechoslovakian culture and genealogy. *Founded:* 1988. *Members:* 3970.

309 ▪ Dakota County Genealogical Society
PO Box 74   Ph: (651)455-1530
South St. Paul, MN 55075
E-mail: valbu@worldnct.att.net
URL: http://www.geocities.com/heartland/flats/9284/

Contact: Vicki Young Albu, Pres.

Desc: Promotes interest in the people and history of Dakota County, MN. Operates library. *Founded:* 1987. *Members:* 130.

310 ▪ Dallas County Genealogical Society
S. Hwy. 65, HC 85 Box 291 B6   Ph: (417)345-7297
Buffalo, MO 65622

Contact: Leni Howe.

311 ▪ Dameron Family Association
<c/o> Mary Dameron Shearholdt   Ph: (417)862-7121
203 E. Portland
Springfield, MO 65807

Contact: Mary Dameron Shearholdt, Sec.

Desc: Individuals with the surname Dameron or Damron. Collects and disseminates genealogical information on family descendents. *Founded:* 1981. *Members:* 200.

312 ▪ Dames of the Loyal Legion of the United States of America
1805 Pine St.
Philadelphia, PA 19103
E-mail: ohiomollus@aol.com
URL: http://www.usmo.com/momollus/dollus.htm

Contact: Mrs. Lowell V. Hammer, National Pres.

Desc: Lineal and collateral female descendants of commissioned officers of the regular and volunteer forces of the United States during the Civil War; mothers, wives, and widows of companions of the Military Order of the Loyal Legion of the U.S. *Founded:* 1899. *Members:* 230.

313 ▪ Daniel Boone and Frontier Families Research Association
1770 Little Bay Rd.
Hermann, MO 65041

Contact: Ken Kamper, Pres.

Desc: Individuals with an interest in the history of the American frontier, Daniel Boone, and the genealogy of frontier families. Promotes study of, and interest in, frontier history and genealogy. Seeks to discover historical and genealogical materials pertaining to the settlement of the West. *Founded:* 1996. *Members:* 240.

314 ▪ Darnall Family Association
8177 Turn Loop Rd.   Ph: (410)247-9297
Glen Burnie, MD 21061-1113

Contact: Avlyn Conley, Contact.

Desc: Individuals researching the surnames Darnall and Darnell and their variant spellings. Acts as clearinghouse for genealogical information.

315 ▪ Daubenspeck-Doverspike Family Exchange
51 Forbus St.   Ph: (914)473-3757
Poughkeepsie, NY 12603

Contact: Christine Crawford-Oppenheimer, Coord.

Desc: Individuals involved in genealogical research on the Daubenspeck and Doverspike families. Works to assist genealogical research on this family. Promotes cooperation among family members and researchers. *Founded:* 1980. *Members:* 80.

316 ▪ Daughters of the Cincinnati
122 E. 58th St.   Ph: (212)319-6915
New York, NY 10022

Contact: Rolly Woodyatt, Exec.Dir.

Desc: Women descendants of the officers of George Washington's Continental Army or Navy. *Founded:* 1894. *Members:* 550.

317 ▪ Daughters of the Republic of Texas
510 E. Anderson Ln.   Ph: (512)339-1997
Austin, TX 78752   Fax: (512)339-1998
E-mail: drt@onr.com

Contact: Tookie Dempsey Walthall, Pres.Gen.

Desc: Women over age 16 who are lineal descendants of men or women who lived in Texas during the time of the Republic. Members are custodians of the Alamo, San Antonio, TX, the French Legation, Austin, TX, and the Republic of Texas Museum, Austin, TX. *Founded:* 1891. *Members:* 6470.

318 ▪ Daughters of Union Veterans of the Civil War, 1861-1865
503 S. Walnut St.   Ph: (217)544-0616
Springfield, IL 62704-1932
E-mail: duvcw@aol.com

Contact: Beverly Goodenough, Natl Pres.

Desc: Lineal descendants of Union veterans of the U.S. Civil War. Objectives are to perpetuate the memories of veterans of the U.S. Civil War, their loyalty to the Union, and their sacrifices for its preservation. Seeks to: keep alive the history of those who participated in the struggle for the maintenance of our free government; aid the descendants of Union veterans of the Civil War; assist those who are worthy and needy; cooperate in movements relating to veterans, civic, and welfare projects; inculcate a love of country and patriotism; promote equal rights and universal liberty; honor Union veterans of the Civil War by placing flowers on graves on Memorial Day. Conducts genealogical projects. Supports and maintains public museum in Springfield, IL. Conducts volunteer work in veterans' hospitals. Supports local historical societies.

Takes part in patriotic ceremonial programs and holiday observances. Conducts specialized education programs. *Founded:* 1885. *Members:* 4000.

319 ▪ David Family Organization

8810 Lagrima de Oro Rd. NE   Ph: (505)298-5050
Albuquerque, NM 87111
E-mail: fredhaury@juno.com

Contact: Frederick W. Haury, Contact.

Founded: 1986. *Members:* 1200.

320 ▪ David Hutchinson and Agnus Nish Family Organization

1538 W 860 S   Ph: (801)226-0227
Orem, UT 84058
E-mail: jnsorensen@aol.com

Contact: Vickie Wheeler Wilson, Sec.

Desc: Descendants of David Hutchinson and Agnus Nish; other individuals with an interest in Hutchinson and Nish family history. Promotes study of, and interest in, Hutchinson and Nish family history and genealogy. *Founded:* 1990. *Members:* 30.

321 ▪ Davis County Genealogy Society

PO Box 94   Ph: (515)664-2223
Bloomfield, IA 52537

Contact: D. Sue Spilman, Pres.

Desc: Individuals in the Davis County, IA area interested in tracing their family histories. Conducts workshops and seminars. *Founded:* 1973. *Members:* 100.

322 ▪ Dawson County Tree Branches, A Genealogical Society

203 Mulberry Dr.   Ph: (406)365-2026
PO Box 1275
Glendive, MT 59330
E-mail: wyldrose@midrivers.com
URL: http://www.men.net/hmscook/dawson/
    dwsgers.htm

Contact: Betty Hagen, Treas.

Desc: Educational organization promoting interest in genealogy. Gathers and disseminates historic genealogical information. *Founded:* 1985. *Members:* 25.

323 ▪ Dawson Family Organization

11845 Newsom Dr.
Baton Rouge, LA 70811-1160
E-mail: spatin@eatil.net
URL: http://www.familytreemaker.com/users/p/a/t/
    salliem.patin/index.html

Desc: Members of the Dawson family. Seeks to identify and united Dawson family members; promotes interest in family history and genealogy. *Founded:* 1950.

324 ▪ De Kalb County Historical-Genealogical Society

PO Box 295   Ph: (815)758-5983
Sycamore, IL 60178

Contact: Robert Hutcheson, Pres.

Founded: 1975. *Members:* 180.

325 ▪ Dearborn Genealogical Society

PO Box 1112   Ph: (313)728-7833
Dearborn, MI 48121

Contact: Tom Barrett, Contact.

Desc: Promotes genealogical research in Dearborn, MI. *Founded:* 1966. *Members:* 85.

326 ▪ Defiance County Chapter of the Ohio Genealogical Society

PO Box 7006   Ph: (419)658-2483
Defiance, OH 43512-7006

Contact: Bev Hohenberger, Presidnet.

Desc: Gathering together to share and learn how to trace our family lineage. *Founded:* 1977. *Members:* 110.

327 ▪ Delaware County Genealogical Society

300 N. Franklin
Manchester, IA 52057

328 ▪ Delaware County Historical Alliance

120 E. Washington St.   Ph: (765)282-1550
Muncie, IN 47305-1734   Fax: (765)282-1058
E-mail: dcha@iquest.net
URL: http://www.iquest.net/dcha/

Contact: Joyce Mattingly, Exec.Dir.

Founded: 1987. *Members:* 420.

329 ▪ Delaware Genealogical Society

505 N. Market St.   Ph: (302)655-7161
Wilmington, DE 19801-3091   Fax: (302)652-8615
E-mail: tdoherty@magpage.com
URL: http://www.delgensoc.org

Contact: Johelene W. Thompson, Pres.

Desc: Encourages and supports genealogical research. Primary focus is Delaware, but also provides educational programs to assist members with family research in general. *Founded:* 1977. *Members:* 600.

330 ▪ Delta County Genealogical Society

PO Box 442
Escanaba, MI 49829-0442
URL: http://hometown.aol.com/DeltaIMi4/home.html

Contact: Nancy Polishak, Pres.

Desc: Assists in genealogical research and the compilation of local records. *Founded:* 1980. *Members:* 75.

331 ▪ Denison Society

120 Pequotsepos Rd.   Ph: (860)536-9248
PO Box 42   Fax: (860)536-9248
Mystic, CT 06355-0042

Contact: Wayne Denison, Pres.

Desc: Descendants of Captain George Denison, who settled in what is now Stonington, CT in 1654. Promotes interest in Denison family history and genealogy, and the history of colonial America. *Founded:* 1930. *Members:* 1100.

332 ▪ Denton County Genealogical Society

PO Box 424707, TWU Station   Ph: (940)382-0464
Denton, TX 76204
E-mail: fordham@lglobal.net

Contact: Ms. Willie Malone, Pres.

Desc: Individuals with an interest in genealogy. Assists genealogical researchers; supports collections of the Denton Public Library; locates, preserves, and disseminates local genealogical information and records. *Founded:* 1979. *Members:* 66.

333 ▪ Descendants of Daniel Cole Society

PO Box 367
Mahopac Falls, NY 10542

Contact: J. Phillip Huntingdon, Pres.

Desc: Descendants of Daniel Cole. *Founded:* 1987. *Members:* 48.

334 ▪ Dichtl Surname Organization

41 Pineview Ln.   Ph: (303)442-3032
Boulder, CO 80302-9414

Contact: Rudolph J. Dichtl, Researcher.

Desc: Conducts research relative to indicated surnames throughout the U.S. and Europe from 1600 to present. *Founded:* 1960. *Members:* 112.

335 ▪ Dick Family Association

<c/o> Nani M. Neal   Ph: (602)788-7041
18002 N. 12th St., No. 30
Phoenix, AZ 85022
E-mail: nneal1840@aol.com

Contact: Nani M. Neal, Editor.

Desc: Libraries; genealogists and researchers interested in surnames containing the word Dick. Facilitates exchange of information among members; compiles genealogical records using census, birth, marriage, and death data obtained from primary sources. *Founded:* 1987. *Members:* 118.

336 ▪ Dickinson County Genealogical Society

401 Iron Mountain St.   Ph: (906)774-1218
Iron Mountain, MI 49801

Contact: John Alquist, Pres.

Desc: Individuals united to gather and preserve the genealogical records of Dickinson County, MI. *Founded:* 1978. *Members:* 60.

337 ▪ Disciples of Christ Historical Society

1101 19th Ave. S   Ph: (615)327-1444
Nashville, TN 37212   Fax: (615)327-1445
E-mail: dishistsoc@aol.com
URL: http://members.aol.com/dishistsoc

Contact: Peter M. Morgan, Pres.

Desc: Works to maintain and further interest in the religious heritage, background, origins, development, and general history of Christian Church (Disciples of Christ), the Christian Churches and Churches of Christ, and Churches of Christ. *Founded:* 1941. *Members:* 1450.

338 ▪ Doane Family Association of America

1044 S Ironwood Rd.   Ph: (703)430-2255
Sterling, VA 20164-5111   Fax: (703)406-2474
E-mail: kblairk@aol.com

Contact: Dorothy Doan Baker, Pres.

Desc: Descendants of Deacon John Doane (1590-1685), who emigrated from England to Plymouth, MA in 1629. Seeks to "create interest in the history and welfare of Deacon John Doane." *Founded:* 1911. *Members:* 1200.

339 ▪ Dodge and Allied Family Surname Organization

PO Box 1452
Las Vegas, NV 89125

Desc: Members of the Dodge family; interested others. Encourages the study of and interest in Dodge lineage and history. Facilitates communication among members. Maintains museum and biographical archives; compiles statistics; conducts research. *Founded:* 1986. *Members:* 350.

340 ▪ Dodge County Genealogical Society

PO Box 683
Dodge Center, MN 55927

Contact: Idella Conwell, Researcher.

Founded: 1988. *Members:* 20.

341 ■ Dodge Family Association
16168 Beach Blvd., Ste. 200   Ph: (303)237-4947
Huntington Beach, CA 92647   Fax: (303)233-2099
E-mail: barbdodge@dodgefamily.org
URL: http://www.dodgefamily.org

Contact: Everett J. Dodge, Pres.

Desc: Members of the Dodge family. Promotes goodwill and fellowship among members; promotes family genealogical and historical research. *Founded:* 1981. *Members:* 625.

342 ■ Dominican Institute of Genealogy
EPS A306   Ph: (809)686-8849
PO Box 52-4121   Fax: (809)687-0027
Miami, FL 33184
E-mail: idg.rd@codetel.net.do

Contact: Luis Jose Prieto Novel.

Desc: Historians, academics, and genealogy researchers. Encourages the study and practice of genealogy in the Dominican Republic. Identifies the ancestors of Dominican families and constructs family trees. Compiles statistics. *Founded:* 1983. *Members:* 28.

343 ■ Donley County Genealogical Society
PO Box 1152
Clarendon, TX 79226-1152

344 ■ Donohoe Clan Society
2160 Leavenworth St., Apt. 401
San Francisco, CA 94133-0000

345 ■ Douglas County Genealogical Society
PO Box 3664
Lawrence, KS 66044-0664

Contact: Shelley Hickman Clark, Pres.

346 ■ Douglas County Genealogical Society
PO Box 505   Ph: (320)763-3896
Alexandria, MN 56308   Fax: (320)763-3896
E-mail: swarvol@att.com

Contact: Ginny Swartz, Pres.

Founded: 1982. *Members:* 35.

347 ■ Douglas County Historical and Genealogical Society
PO Box 986   Ph: (417)683-5799
Ava, MO 65608

Contact: Sharon Sanders, Pres.

Desc: Individuals interested in the history and genealogy of Douglas County, MO. Conducts charitable activities. *Founded:* 1984. *Members:* 150.

348 ■ Downriver Genealogical Society
PO Box 476   Ph: (313)381-0507
Lincoln Park, MI 48146
E-mail: langes@mail.wcresa.k12.mi.us
URL: http://www.rootsweb.com/midrgs/drgs.htm

Contact: Sarah Lange, Pres.

Desc: Individuals interested in researching and preserving the history and genealogy of their ancestors. Objectives are: to encourage and assist members in genealogical research; to compile and preserve history; to sponsor educational courses and activities in genealogy and history. *Founded:* 1980. *Members:* 360.

349 ■ Dripps-Drips Family Association
<c/o> Allen Dripps
7000 Y St.
Lincoln, NE 68505-2101
E-mail: Adripps@Unlinfo.unl.edu

Contact: Allen Dripps, Exec. Officer.

Desc: Genealogical organization researching the surnames Drips and Dripps.

350 ■ Dubuque County-Key City Genealogical Society
PO Box 13
Dubuque, IA 52004-0013

Contact: Deanna Asleson, Pres.

Desc: Individuals interested in researching family roots. Promotes further research and knowledge in family research. Researches and publishes pertinent genealogical records and materials in Dubuque Co. *Founded:* 1975. *Members:* 150.

351 ■ Duncan Surname Association
5938 SE 45th   Ph: (913)379-5585
Tecumseh, KS 66542-9743
E-mail: wad@sound.net
URL: http://www.networksplus.net/wad/dsa/dsa.htm

Contact: W. A. Duncan, Treas.

Desc: Individuals sharing research on the Duncan surname. Wishes to identify all Duncans in the United States prior to 1850 and tie the family histories together. *Founded:* 1989. *Members:* 625.

352 ■ Dunlop - Dunlap Family Society
3985 Radcliff Ave.   Ph: (303)798-7799
Denver, CO 80236
E-mail: joann@insightcolo.com

Contact: Elizabeth W. Girard, Exec.Dir.

Desc: Individuals with the surname Dunlop and its variant spellings; other members of the Dunlop family. Promotes interest in Scottish history and culture and the Dunlop family and its history. *Founded:* 1980. *Members:* 318.

353 ■ Dunnavant/Donavant Family Association
3929 S. Milton Dr.   Ph: (816)373-5309
Independence, MO 64055-4043
E-mail: grover@aol.com

Contact: Robert L. Grover, Pres.

Desc: Persons with the surname Dunnavant or Donavant. Seeks to share family and genealogical information among members. *Founded:* 1963. *Members:* 200.

354 ■ Durham-Orange Genealogical Society
PO Box 4703
Chapel Hill, NC 27515-4703
E-mail: dogs@rtpnet.org
URL: http://www.rtpnet.org/dogs

Contact: Linda Skinner, Pres.

Desc: Genealogical research in Durham and Orange, North Carolina. *Founded:* 1989. *Members:* 210.

355 ■ Dutch Family Heritage Society
2463 Ledgewood Dr.   Ph: (801)967-8400
West Jordan, UT 84084   Fax: (801)963-4604
E-mail: spijkerman@aol.com

Contact: Mary Lynn Spijkerman Parker, Pres.

Desc: Libraries; historical and genealogical societies; interested individuals. Gathers and disseminates information on Dutch history, culture, and genealogy in the U.S., Canada, and Netherlands. *Founded:* 1987. *Members:* 400.

356 ■ Dutys in America
70 W Lawrence Circle, Apt. 507   Ph: (407)841-1310
Orlando, FL 32801

Contact: Clifton D. Duty, Facilitator.

Desc: Members of the Duty and related families. Promotes study of Duty and related family histories and genealogies. *Founded:* 1978.

357 ■ East Ascension Genealogical and Historical Society
PO Box 1006   Ph: (504)644-1869
Gonzales, LA 70707-1006
E-mail: dpowers@eatel.net

Contact: David Powers, Pres./Ed.

Desc: Collects and preserves genealogical and historical material. *Founded:* 1981. *Members:* 1981.

358 ■ East Bay Genealogical Society
PO Box 20417   Ph: (510)482-2479
Oakland, CA 94620-0417
URL: http://www.katpher.com/EBGS/EBGS.html

Contact: Barbara J. Parkin, Pres.

Desc: Individuals interested in genealogy. *Founded:* 1979. *Members:* 150.

359 ■ East Bell County Genealogical Society
2613 Forest Tr.
Temple, TX 76502

Contact: Anice Vance, Pres.

Desc: Promotes interest in genealogy and local history. *Founded:* 1991. *Members:* 70.

360 ■ Easterling Family Genealogical Society
1126 Pearl Valley Rd.   Ph: (601)894-2642
Wesson, MS 39191-9311   Fax: (601)894-2642
URL: http://www.easterling.org

Contact: Letson E. Easterling, Sr., Pres.

Desc: Lateral and collateral members and relatives of the Easterling family. Compiles and preserves the history and artifacts of the family; conducts genealogical and historical research and prepares genealogies for members. Assists members in locating historical records of their descendants. *Founded:* 1985. *Members:* 500.

361 ■ Eaton County Genealogical Society
100 Lawrence Ave.   Ph: (517)543-8792
PO Box 337   Fax: (517)543-6999
Charlotte, MI 48813-0337
E-mail: ecgsoc@juno.com
URL: http://www.userdata.acd.net/mmgs

Contact: Drouscella Halsey, Corr.Sec.

Desc: Seeks to aid the general public in the pursuit of their ancestry and learning about the history of Eaton County. *Founded:* 1988. *Members:* 140.

362 ■ Eddy Family Association
Box 354   Ph: (781)934-6058
Duxbury, MA 02331

Contact: Sylvia T. Breck, Exec.Sec. VP.

Desc: Individuals descended from, or interested in, John and Samuel Eddy, pioneer settlers of Massachusetts who came from England in 1630 on the ship Handmaid. Works to preserve family history. Locates and records information about ancestors and descendants. Compiles statistics. Contributes to St. Dunstan's Church, in England, where William Eddy was vicar 1587-1616. Maintains 1600s Eddy Burying Ground, Swansea, MA. *Founded:* 1920. *Members:* 800.

363 ■ Edgar County, Illinois Genealogical Society
PO Box 304   Ph: (217)463-4209
Paris, IL 61944-0304   Fax: (217)463-4209
URL: http://www.tigerpaw.com/ecg1/

Contact: Fred Delap, Pres.

Desc: Preservation of local archives, dissemination of genealogical and historical information, education of interested persons (including children and adults) acquisition of pertinent materials for Edgar County Genealogy Library and staffing of same. *Founded:* 1984.

364 ▪ Effingham County Genealogical Society

PO Box 1166   Ph: (217)342-2210
Effingham, IL 62401-1166

Contact: Arnetia Osborn, Pres.

Desc: Individuals interested in genealogy. *Founded:* 1980. *Members:* 280.

365 ▪ Elder Brewster Society

PO Box 1245
East Orleans, MA 02643-1245

Contact: Michael J. L. Greene, Pres.

Desc: Descendants of William Brewster who have had their Brewster lineage approved by the Historian General of the Society of Mayflower Descendants. Honors the memory of Elder William Brewster; encourages camaraderie among Brewster cousins; collects, preserves, and shares lineage data relating to descendants; assists non-members in Brewster lineages; encourages and assists with membership in the society of Mayflower Descendants. *Founded:* 1978. *Members:* 500.

366 ▪ Elijah Gillespie Family Organization

7650 Fairview Rd.   Ph: (503)842-6036
Tillamook, OR 97141   Fax: (503)842-6036

Contact: Orella Chadwick, Contact.

Desc: Descendants of Elijah Gillespie and Mary Rabun. Promotes genealogical study of the Gillespie and Rabun families and collateral lines. *Founded:* 1980. *Members:* 42.

367 ▪ Elkhart County Genealogical Society

51585 Winding Waters Ln. N
Elkhart, IN 46514-0000

368 ▪ Eller Family Association

42 28th St. N.W.   Ph: (404)351-4304
Atlanta, GA 30309-1806
E-mail: dcr6@juno.com

Contact: Lynn Eller, Contact.

Desc: Researches, compiles, and publishes Eller genealogy and family history. *Founded:* 1987. *Members:* 300.

369 ▪ Elsey Family Association

1 E. 8th St.   Ph: (219)942-4089
Hobart, IN 46342-5143

Contact: Carol Elsey, VP.

Desc: Individuals, families, societies, and libraries. Obtains, records, publishes, and disseminates genealogical and historical information about the Elsey (and its various spellings) and related families. Seeks to preserve genealogical knowledge for future generations. *Founded:* 1985. *Members:* 70.

370 ▪ Elswick Family Association

Rte. 2, Box 302A   Ph: (703)337-4101
Staunton, VA 24401

Contact: Rev. Albert Elswick, Genealogist.

Desc: Descendants of John Elswick I (d. 1759). Promotes fellowship among family members and assembles, preserves, and publishes family records. *Founded:* 1970. *Members:* 250.

371 ▪ Emanuel Family Genealogy

213 Mill Stream Dr.   Ph: (205)837-7487
Huntsville, AL 35806-1247
E-mail: emanuelg@ro.com

Contact: Garvin R. Emanuel, Exec.Sec.

Desc: Clearinghouse for genealogical information on the surnames Emanuel, Emmanuel, and Manuel. *Founded:* 1966.

372 ▪ Emerald Isle Immigration Center

5926 Woodside Ave., 2nd Fl.   Ph: (718)478-5502
Woodside, NY 11377   Fax: (718)446-3727
E-mail: cryan@eiic.org
URL: http://www.eiic.org

Contact: Carolyn Ryan, Exec.Dir.

Desc: Immigrants, including Irish immigrants, and U.S. citizens of Irish descent. Provides immigration counseling and citizenship application advice and assistance. Provides employment and education advice and assistance, including computer training. *Founded:* 1987.

373 ▪ Erastus Snow Family Organization

1847 Oak Ln.
Provo, UT 84604-2140

374 ▪ Eskridge Family Association

6627 Summer Darby Ln.   Ph: (704)366-0215
Charlotte, NC 28270

Contact: Cyndee Eskridge, Sec.

Desc: Descendants of Colonel George Eskridge and others interested in genealogy, historical preservation, and ecological conservation, especially of the Chesapeake Bay and its tributaries. *Founded:* 1937. *Members:* 703.

375 ▪ Essex Society of Genealogists

PO Box 313   Ph: (978)664-9279
Lynnfield, MA 01940
E-mail: essexsoc@aol.com

Contact: Nancy C. Hayward, Exec.Sec.

Desc: Libraries, organizations, and individuals interested in the genealogy of Essex County, MA. *Founded:* 1981. *Members:* 800.

376 ▪ Etchingham Family Tree

PO Box 260170   Ph: (303)985-3508
Lakewood, CO 80226-0170   Fax: (303)985-7872
E-mail: jogeo10709@aol.com

Contact: George Van Trump, Jr., Pres.

Desc: Persons researching the surname Etchingham. *Founded:* 1980. *Members:* 50.

377 ▪ Ethington Family Organization

9802 Chylene Dr.   Ph: (801)942-0918
Sandy, UT 84092

Contact: Harold D. Ethington, Contact.

Desc: Persons of Ethington descent. *Founded:* 1955. *Members:* 3000.

378 ▪ Etling Clearinghouse

1605 Holly   Ph: (308)436-5617
Gering, NE 69341
E-mail: jweihing@prairieweb.com

Contact: S. Weihing, Contact.

Desc: Persons researching the surname Etling.

379 ▪ Evangelical and Reformed Historical Society

555 W. James St.   Ph: (717)290-8711
Lancaster, PA 17603

E-mail: erhs@lts.org
URL: http://www.lts.org/erhs/erhs.htm

Contact: Richard Berg, Archivist.

Desc: Seeks to: stimulate interest in the heritage of the Reformed Church in the United States, the Evangelical Synod of North America, and the Evangelical and Reformed Church; collect and preserve historical material of the churches and to make it available to all who are interested. Maintains official archival depositories in the Philip Schaff Library, Lancaster Theological Seminary, Lancaster, PA and in the Eden Theological Seminary Library, Webster Groves, MO. *Founded:* 1863. *Members:* 300.

380 ▪ Evangeline Genealogical and Historical Society

PO Box 664   Ph: (318)457-0324
Ville Platte, LA 70586
E-mail: jconway@centuryinter.net

Contact: James Reed, Pres.

Desc: Individuals interested in local genealogical research and history of south central Louisiana. *Founded:* 1980. *Members:* 265.

381 ▪ Fagan Family Association

<c/o> Nancy Ragsdale
7 Pleasant Ct.
Kirkwood, MO 63122-3936

Contact: Nancy Ragsdale, Exec. Officer.

Desc: Persons researching the surnames Fagan, Fagin, Fagon, and Feagin. *Founded:* 1967.

382 ▪ Family History Department of the Church of Jesus Christ of Latter-Day Saints

50 E. North Temple   Ph: (801)240-2331
Salt Lake City, UT 84150   Fax: (801)240-5551
E-mail: fhl@ldschurch.org
URL: http://www.lds.org

Contact: Richard E. Turley, Jr., Mng. Dir.

Desc: A department of the Church of Jesus Christ of Latter-day Saints Promotes local and family history (genealogical) research; microfilms and preserves genealogical data, genealogical researchers. Maintains 3000 family history centers in 64 countries. *Founded:* 1894.

383 ▪ Family Setzekorn Association

PO Box 706   Ph: (530)622-5886
Somerset, CA 95684   Fax: (530)644-5107
E-mail: baronsetz@aol.com

Contact: William D. Setzekorn, Exec. Officer.

Desc: Members and relatives of the family Setzekorn and its variant spellings. *Founded:* 1979. *Members:* 105.

384 ▪ Farmington Genealogical Society

23500 Liberty   Ph: (248)474-7770
Farmington, MI 48335
URL: http://metronet.lib.mi.us/fcl/gensoc.html

Contact: Sue Cromwell, Pres.

Desc: Individuals interested in genealogy. *Founded:* 1973. *Members:* 75.

385 ▪ Fayette County Genealogical and Historical Society

PO Box 177   Ph: (618)283-0484
Vandalia, IL 62471-0177

Contact: Steven Durbin, Pres.

Founded: 1971. *Members:* 300.

386 ▪ Fayette County Genealogical Society
PO Box 8113
Lexington, KY 40533-8113   Ph: (606)278-9966
E-mail: mehurst@prodigy.net
URL: http://www.rootsweb.com/kyfayett/
   faycogensoc.htm

Contact: Melvin E. Hurst, Treas.

Founded: 1985. *Members:* 210.

387 ▪ Fayette County Genealogical Society
PO Box 342
Washington Court House, OH   Ph: (740)335-6060
   43160

Contact: Bettie Kerr Gray, Pres.

Desc: Genealogists with ancestors from Fayette County, OH. Promotes research and education in genealogy and works for publication of research materials pertaining to the region and its history. *Founded:* 1981. *Members:* 136.

388 ▪ Fayette County Genealogical Society
24 Jefferson St.
Uniontown, PA 15401-3602

Contact: Sonia Cesarino, Sec.

389 ▪ Fearing Surname Organization
558 Little Piney Island Dr.
Fernandina Beach, FL 32034   Ph: (904)277-3536
E-mail: jamesgen@aol.com

Contact: Jeri James, Contact.

Desc: Works to promote research on the Fearing surname.
Founded: 1980. *Members:* 50.

390 ▪ Federation of East European Family History Societies
PO Box 510898
Salt Lake City, UT 84151-0898   Ph: (801)284-5917
    Fax: (801)485-5745
E-mail: feefhs@feefhs.org
URL: http://www.feefhs.org

Contact: John Movius, Pres.

Desc: Genealogists and genealogical societies specializing in east European family history. Promotes the international language of Esperanto as a viable tool for east European family research. Collects and disseminates information on conducting family history research in eastern Europe. Maintains speakers' bureau; compiles statistics. *Members:* 130.

391 ▪ Federation of French War Veterans
18 E. 41st St., No. 401
New York, NY 10017-6222

Contact: Bruce Boeglin, Chm.

Desc: Veterans of the World Wars and other conflicts who are of French origin or descent. *Founded:* 1919. *Members:* 150.

392 ▪ Federation of Genealogical Societies
PO Box 200940   Ph: (512)336-2731
Austin, TX 78720   Fax: (512)336-2732
E-mail: fgs-office@fgs.org
URL: http://www.fgs.org

Contact: David Rencher, Pres.

Desc: Genealogical societies, genealogical libraries, historical societies, family associations, and other organizations dealing with genealogy and family history. Objectives are to: stimulate the activities of state and local organizations interested in genealogy and family history; collect, preserve, and disseminate information with reference to genealogical and historical data; promote careful documenta-

tion and scholarly genealogical writing and publication; avoid duplication of effort; promote interest in genealogy and family history. *Founded:* 1975. *Members:* 530.

393 ▪ Felton Family Association
7791 MacLeay Rd. SE   Ph: (503)370-9028
Salem, OR 97301
E-mail: felton96@aol.com

Contact: Cora Felton Anderson, Pres.

Desc: Members of the Felton family. Facilitates communication and good fellowship among members. *Founded:* 1988. *Members:* 240.

394 ▪ Ferry/Ferrie Family History Association
4065 Berrywood Dr.   Ph: (541)461-4473
Eugene, OR 97404-4061

Contact: James R. Brann, President and Historian.

Desc: Collects, preserves, and disseminates information on all persons with the surnames Ferry and Ferrie from County Clare, Ireland to New York City to Maine. *Founded:* 1989. *Members:* 5.

395 ▪ Filipino American National Historical Society
810 18th Ave., Rm. 100   Ph: (206)322-0203
Seattle, WA 98122   Fax: (206)461-4879

Contact: Dorothy Cordova, Dir.

Desc: Gathers, maintains, and disseminates Filipino American history. *Founded:* 1982. *Members:* 1000.

396 ▪ Finney County Genealogical Society
PO Box 592
Garden City, KS 67846

Contact: Ruth M. Dunlap, Treas.

Desc: Individuals interested in genealogy. Gathers, preserves, and disseminates historical and genealogical information. *Founded:* 1967. *Members:* 65.

397 ▪ First Families of Georgia 1733-1797
15 Watson Dr.
Newnan, GA 30263

Contact: Hardwick Smith Johnson, Jr., Gov.Gen.

Desc: Individuals that are able to substantiate lineal descent from an ancestor who settled in Georgia between 1733 and 1797. Promotes interest in and study of the history, culture, and traditions of Georgia. *Founded:* 1986. *Members:* 250.

398 ▪ Flagon and Trencher
850-A Thornhill Ct.   Ph: (732)920-3279
Lakewood, NJ 08701-6661
E-mail: bsmith@aol.com

Contact: Barbara Carver Smith, Exec. Officer.

Desc: Descendants of persons operating a tavern, inn, or other type of hostelry on, or prior to, July 4, 1776. *Founded:* 1962. *Members:* 875.

399 ▪ Flint Hills Genealogical Society
PO Box 555   Ph: (316)343-2719
Emporia, KS 66801

Contact: Carol Mlynar, Pres.

Desc: Individuals interested in genealogy. Assists Lyon County Historical Museum and Emporia Public Library in researching local history. *Founded:* 1978. *Members:* 50.

400 ▪ Flippin Family Association
12206 Brisbane Ave.   Ph: (972)241-2739
Dallas, TX 75234-6528   Fax: (972)620-1416
E-mail: lemstar@juno.com

URL: http://www.homestead.com/flippinfiles/

Contact: Nova A. Lemons, Editor & Founder.

Desc: Persons researching the surnames Flippin Flippen, Flipping and their families. Collects information and identifies ancestors. *Founded:* 1987. *Members:* 65.

401 ▪ Forby Family Historical Society
12550 W. Idaho Dr.
Lakewood, CO 80228

Contact: George W. Forby, Exec. Officer.

Desc: Persons with the surnames Forby and its variant spelling Forbey. Collects and disseminates genealogical and historical information. *Founded:* 1987.

402 ▪ Forsyth County Genealogical Society
PO Box 5715   Ph: (919)724-0714
Winston-Salem, NC 27113
URL: http://www.erols.com/fmoran/gensoc/
   gensoc.html

Contact: Cleo McBride, Treas.

Desc: Genealogists. Conducts research and educational programs. Gathers and disseminates information; provides research assistance.

403 ▪ Ft. Bend County Genealogical Society
PO Box 274   Ph: (281)341-2608
Richmond, TX 77469
URL: http://www.intertex.net/fbclib/lib.html

Desc: Genealogists. Conducts research and educational programs. *Founded:* 1965. *Members:* 30.

404 ▪ Franklin County Genealogical Society
PO Box 44309   Ph: (614)469-1300
Columbus, OH 43204-0309
E-mail: fcgs@freewweb.com
URL: http://genweb.net/fcghs

Contact: Kenneth Poling, Pres.

Desc: Genealogical researchers and historians. Collects, preserves, and promotes genealogical and historical materials. Conducts seminars and ten lectures per year. Sponsors essay contests. Maintains Computer Interest Group and African-American Genealogy Interest Group. *Founded:* 1970. *Members:* 550.

405 ▪ Frawley Family History Association
4065 Berrywood Dr.   Ph: (541)461-4473
Eugene, OR 97404-4061

Contact: James R. Brann, President and Historian.

Desc: Collects, preserves, and disseminates information on all persons with the surname Frawley from County Clare, Ireland to Maine. *Founded:* 1989. *Members:* 5.

406 ▪ Frederick County Genealogy Society
PO Box 234   Ph: (301)831-5781
Monrovia, MD 21770

Contact: Pepper Scotto, Pres.

Desc: Works to increase public interest in history and genealogy; encourages genealogical research and provides assistance to beginning genealogists; preserves and disseminates genealogical information. *Founded:* 1970. *Members:* 150.

407 ▪ Frederick Wilhelm Haury Family Organization
8810 Lagrima de Oro Rd. NE   Ph: (505)298-5050
Albuquerque, NM 87111
E-mail: fredhaury@juno.com

Contact: Frederick Wilhelm Haury, Jr., Contact.

Founded: 1986. *Members:* 700.

408 ■ Freeborn County Genealogical Society
1033 Bridge Ave.
Albert Lea, MN 56007-2205
E-mail: bvstorlie@deskmedia.com

Contact: Vickie Storlie, Recording Sec.

Desc: Individuals interested in the genealogy of Freeborn County, MN. *Founded:* 1979. *Members:* 75.

409 ■ Fremont County Genealogical Society
1330 W. Park Ave.   Ph: (307)856-5310
Riverton, WY 82501
E-mail: jtanner@rmisp.com

Contact: Jeanie Tanner, Pres.

Founded: 1979. *Members:* 25.

410 ■ Fremont County Historical Society
PO Box 671   Ph: (712)374-2335
Sidney, IA 51652

Contact: Emily Bengston, Pres.

Founded: 1962. *Members:* 300.

411 ■ French Canadian-Acadian Genealogists of Wisconsin
PO Box 414   Ph: (414)284-5636
Hales Corners, WI 53130-0414

Contact: Tom Glassel, Pres.

Desc: Members are genealogists researching French Canadian and Acadian Lines with ties to Wisconsin. Objectives are to foster and encourage interest and research in French Canadian and Acadian genealogy, heritage, and culture. *Founded:* 1982. *Members:* 150.

412 ■ French-Canadian Genealogical Society
CP 335, succursale   Ph: (514)729-8366
  Place d'Armes   Fax: (514)729-1180
Montreal, PQ, Canada H2Y
  3H1
URL: http://www.sgcf.com

Contact: Normand Robert, Pres.

Desc: Individuals with an interest in French-Canadian genealogy. Promotes genealogical research and study. *Founded:* 1943. *Members:* 3750.

413 ■ French Family Association
521 River View Dr.   Ph: (408)227-4411
San Jose, CA 95111
E-mail: mara@cadence.com

Contact: Mara French, Editor.

Desc: Individuals with the surname French and genealogical and historical researchers. Seeks to unite the French family and related families; promote interest and scholarly research in genealogy, heraldry, and French family history. Answers genealogical queries. Collects books, photographs, tapes, stories and cemetery registries. Currently compiling genealogical charts. *Founded:* 1984. *Members:* 700.

414 ■ Fretz Family Association
R.M.C. Apt. 263   Ph: (215)257-4635
3250 State Rd.
Sellersville, PA 18960

Contact: J. Franklin Fretz, Pres.

Desc: Descendants of John and Christian Fretz. Seeks to preserve family history. *Founded:* 1888.

415 ■ Friend Family Association of America
1st and Maple Sts.   Ph: (301)746-5615
PO Box 96
Friendsville, MD 21531

Contact: Ina Hicks, Librarian.

Desc: Works to promote historical and genealogical research. *Founded:* 1976. *Members:* 400.

416 ■ Friends of Arizona Archives
PO Box 64532
Phoenix, AZ 85082-4532

417 ■ Friends of the Jasper County Archives Museum
600 Olive St.
Jasper, TX 75951-3541

418 ■ Friends of the Oklahoma Historical Society Archives
PO Box 18781
Oklahoma City, OK 73154-0781

419 ■ Frisbie - Frisbee Family Association of America
45982 180th Ave.
Lake Mills, IA 50450-7498

Contact: Ruth Cope, Pres.

Desc: Descendants of Edward Frisbie (1621-1690). *Founded:* 1950. *Members:* 300.

420 ■ Fullam Family Organization
PO Box 1525
Mi Wuk Village, CA 95346

Contact: Marilyn Fullam, Exec. Officer.

Desc: Descendants of Philip Fullam and Ellen Kennedy. *Founded:* 1986.

421 ■ Fuller Society
HCR 69, Box 666   Ph: (207)832-7298
Friendship, ME 04547
E-mail: pjs568@expaol.com
URL: http://www.redrock.sedona.net/fullersociety

Contact: Mary Lee Merrill, Contact.

Desc: Descendants of the Mayflower Pilgrims Dr. Samuel Fuller and Edward Fuller. Promotes genealogical research and social gatherings of descendants of Samual and Edward Fuller. *Founded:* 1992. *Members:* 480.

422 ■ Fulton County Genealogical Society
PO Box 1031   Fax: (502)472-6241
Fulton, KY 42041
E-mail: eallen@apex.net

Contact: Elaine Allen, Pres.

Desc: Individuals in Fulton and Hickman counties, KY interested in genealogy. Seeks to gather and publish local genealogical records. Donates research books to library. *Founded:* 1972. *Members:* 124.

423 ■ Fulton County Historical and Genealogical Society
45 N. Park Dr.   Ph: (309)647-0771
Canton, IL 61520
E-mail: mbordner@netins.net

Contact: Marjorie R. Bordner, Pres.

Desc: Individuals, school libraries, and other genealogical societies in western Illinois. Seeks to preserve the heritage, historic landmarks, and records of the area. *Founded:* 1967. *Members:* 350.

424 ■ Fuqua(y) Family Association
PO Box 24092   Ph: (606)273-7814
Lexington, KY 40524-4092

Contact: Mary Louise Fuqua McAskill, Pres.

Desc: Individuals with the surname Fuqua or Fuquay and variations such as Feuquay and Faqua. Collects, researches, and disseminates genealogical data on the Fuqua(y) family name. *Founded:* 1987. *Members:* 100.

425 ■ Gable Family Association
PO Box 547   Ph: (903)379-2001
Talco, TX 75487-0547

Contact: Bertha L. Gable, Historian.

Desc: Descendants of Arthur Barnabas Gabriel Gable and his wives, Permelia Sims and Margaret Elizabeth Greene. Collects, exchanges, and preserves genealogical and historical information; purchases and places tombstones on unmarked graves.

426 ■ Gabler Family Association
470 Acoma Blvd.   Ph: (520)855-2392
Lake Havasu City, AZ 86406

Contact: David Gabler, Contact.

Desc: Descendants of Michael Gabler. Promotes study of, and interest in, Gabler family history and genealogy. *Founded:* 1982. *Members:* 75.

427 ■ Gafford Family of America Association
PO Box 1416   Ph: (601)234-7602
Oxford, MS 38655
E-mail: gafford@dixie/net.com

Contact: Gerald Gafford, Chm.-Board.

Desc: Seeks to unite individuals with the Gafford (or related) surname, including variations. Exchanges and preserves research, photos, and records. Gathers cemetery records, and conducts historical research of the Gafford name. *Founded:* 1994. *Members:* 98.

428 ■ Garner Family History Association
4065 Berrywood Dr.   Ph: (541)461-4473
Eugene, OR 97404-4061

Contact: James R. Brann, President and Historian.

Desc: Collects, preserves, and disseminates information on all persons with the surname Garner from England to Maine. *Founded:* 1989. *Members:* 12.

429 ■ Gaylord Family Organization
3275 Blue Ridge Cir.   Ph: (209)477-7216
Stockton, CA 95219-3502
E-mail: bcwood@worldnet.att.net

Contact: Barry C. Wood, Contact.

Desc: Conducts genealogical research on descendants of William Gaylord (1590-1673) in the United States. Acts as a clearinghouse for genealogical information. *Founded:* 1978. *Members:* 200.

430 ■ Geauga County Genealogical Society
110 E. Park St.   Ph: (440)285-7601
Chardon, OH 44024

431 ■ Genealogical Association of English-Speaking Researchers in Europe
HQ USAREUR
CMR 420, Box 142
APO New York, NY 09063
E-mail: whit@thepentagon.com

Contact: Lu Hays, Pres.

Desc: Professional genealogists, researchers, American and Canadian and German servicepeople, and interested others in Europe involved in tracing family histories. Promotes the science of genealogy. Seeks to develop cooperation among family historians in Europe; encourages careful documentation of genealogical research. Conducts educational programs with an emphasis on European records and archives. Maintains speakers' bureau; operates microfilm rental program. Maintains library of reference material. *Founded:* 1988. *Members:* 201.

432 ■ Genealogical Club of the Montgomery County Historical Society
Beall-Dawson House   Ph: (301)340-2974
103 W. Montgomery Ave.   Fax: (301)340-2871
Rockville, MD 20850
E-mail: mchistory@mindspring.com
URL: http://www.montgomeryhistory.com

Contact: Mary Kay Harper, Exec.Dir.

Founded: 1944. *Members:* 1300.

433 ■ Genealogical and Historical Society of Caldwell County
215 S. Pecan Ave.   Ph: (210)875-9466
Luling, TX 78648-2607
E-mail: ccg&hsoc@bcsnet.net

Contact: Eva L. Wilson, Editor.

Desc: Collects, preserves and disseminates local historical and geneaological information. *Founded:* 1983. *Members:* 400.

434 ■ Genealogical Institute
PO Box 124   Ph: 800-377-6058
Tremonton, UT 84337   Free: 800-377-6058
     Fax: (801)250-6717
E-mail: genealogy@utahlinx.com

Contact: Arlene H. Eakle, Ph.D., CEO & Pres.

Desc: Conducts training activities and client research. *Founded:* 1972.

435 ■ Genealogical Research Institute of Virginia
PO Box 29178
Richmond, VA 23242-0178
URL: http://www.cvco.org/sig/genealogy/

Contact: Jean B. Robinson, Pres.

436 ■ Genealogical Research Society of New Orleans
PO Box 51791   Ph: (504)581-3153
New Orleans, LA 70151
E-mail: jab05@gnofn.org

Contact: Jack Belsom, Past Pres.

Desc: Individuals, libraries, and universities promoting the study of genealogy in the Mississippi Gulf Coast region of the U.S. *Founded:* 1960. *Members:* 500.

437 ■ Genealogical Research Society of Northeastern Pennsylvania
PO Box 1
Olyphant, PA 18447-0001

438 ■ Genealogical Society of Allegany County
PO Box 3103
Lavale, MD 21504-3103

Contact: Lucy G. Wagner, Pres.

Founded: 1977.

439 ■ Genealogical Society of Bergen County
PO Box 432   Fax: (201)447-0140
Midland Park, NJ 07432
E-mail: las1087@aol.com
URL: http://www.geocities/heartland/9759

Contact: Lucille Siebold, Pres.

Desc: Individuals in Bergen County, NJ interested in genealogy. Provides research assistance. Sponsors adult education course in beginning genealogy. *Founded:* 1973. *Members:* 300.

440 ■ Genealogical Society of Broward County
PO Box 485   Ph: (954)463-8834
Ft. Lauderdale, FL 33302
E-mail: thalass1@ix.netcom.com
URL: http://www.rootsweb.com/flgsbc

Contact: Charles Vollman, Pres.

Founded: 1977. *Members:* 138.

441 ■ Genealogical Society of Butler County, Missouri
PO Box 426
Poplar Bluff, MO 63901

442 ■ Genealogical Society of Cecil County
Box 11   Ph: (410)658-6062
Charlestown, MD 21914
E-mail: dmccall@dol.net

Contact: Joanne Daly, Pres.

Desc: Promotes genealogical interest in the community. *Founded:* 1977. *Members:* 64.

443 ■ Genealogical Society of Citrus County
PO Box 2211   Ph: (352)726-3130
Inverness, FL 34451   Fax: (352)637-6482

Contact: Dolly Silva, Pres.

Desc: Individuals interested in genealogical research. *Founded:* 1979. *Members:* 90.

444 ■ Genealogical Society of Clarke County, Iowa
300 S. Fillmore
Osceola, IA 50213

Contact: Diane Shough, Pres.

Desc: Gathers and disseminates genealogical information pertaining to Clarke County, IA. *Founded:* 1992. *Members:* 60.

445 ■ Genealogical Society of Collier County
PO Box 7933   Ph: (941)348-3535
Naples, FL 34101   Fax: (941)348-3536
E-mail: helecko@aol.com

Contact: Helen E. Eckhardt, Pres.

Founded: 1984. *Members:* 206.

446 ■ Genealogical Society of Dunklin County
226 N. Main St.
Kennett, MO 63857

447 ■ Genealogical Society of Flemish Americans
18740 13 Mile Rd.   Ph: (810)776-9579
Roseville, MI 48066

Contact: Margaret Roets, Corr.Sec.

Desc: People of Flemish or Dutch ancestry residing in the U.S., Canada, or Belgium. Seeks to promote interest in and preserve Belgian culture and history. Assists in genealogical research; assists members with translations. Sponsors programs for the genealogical and historical societies. Conducts oral history and educational programs, including lacemaking and a demonstration of Christmas customs. *Founded:* 1976. *Members:* 225.

448 ■ Genealogical Society of Hancock County
Old Courthouse   Ph: (502)927-8095
Hawesville, KY 42348
E-mail: archives@juno.com

Contact: George Gibbs, Sr., Ed.

Desc: Provides complete list of marriages, divorces, wills, chancery, and equity cases of Hancock County. *Founded:* 1984. *Members:* 178.

449 ■ Genealogical Society of Henry and Clayton Counties
71 Macon St.   Ph: (770)954-1456
PO Box 1296
McDonough, GA 30253

Contact: Roy Swann, Pres.

Desc: Individuals interested in local history and genealogy. Gathers genealogical and historical data relating to Henry and Clayton counties and their surrounding areas. *Members:* 250.

450 ■ Genealogical Society of Hispanic American
PO Box 9606   Ph: (719)561-0585
Denver, CO 80209-0606
E-mail: wmartinez2@compuserve.com

Contact: Wilfred Martinez, Exec. Officer.

Desc: Hispanic family researchers, genealogists, historians, libraries. *Founded:* 1988. *Members:* 700.

451 ■ Genealogical Society of Kendall County
PO Box 623
Boerne, TX 78006-0623

Founded: 1981. *Members:* 80.

452 ■ Genealogical Society of Monroe County, Michigan
PO Box 1428
Monroe, MI 48161

Contact: Rick Grimsley, Pres.

Desc: Works to preserve and improve access to genealogical records. Sponsors information booth at Old Frenchtown Days celebration. *Founded:* 1976. *Members:* 200.

453 ■ Genealogical Society of Morongo Basin
PO Box 234   Ph: (760)365-9201
Yucca Valley, CA 92286-0234
URL: http://www.cci-29palms.com/gsmb

Contact: Gordon Barkley, Pres.

Desc: Promotes genealogical study of families. *Founded:* 1979. *Members:* 70.

454 ■ Genealogical Society of Okaloosa County
PO Drawer 1175   Ph: (850)243-4589
Ft. Walton Beach, FL 32549
E-mail: flembeck@aol.com

Founded: 1977. *Members:* 100.

455 ■ Genealogical Society of Page County, Virginia
PO Box 734   Ph: (540)743-6867
Luray, VA 22835
URL: http://www.rootsweb.com/vagspc/pcgs.htm

Contact: Vicki G. Cyphert, Pres.

Desc: Individuals whose ancestors lived in Page County, VA. Gathers, preserves, and disseminates genealogical records; assists researchers. *Founded:* 1990. *Members:* 200.

456 ■ Genealogical Society of Pennsylvania

1305 Locust St.   Ph: (215)545-0391
Philadelphia, PA 19107   Fax: (215)545-0936

Contact: Jane Adams Clarke, Exec.Dir.

Desc: Genealogical researchers in Pennsylvania and the Delaware Valley area of Delaware and New Jersey. Collects and preserves genealogical records. Conducts abstracting, indexing, and microfilming of newspapers and records. *Founded:* 1892. *Members:* 1500.

457 ■ Genealogical Society of Rowan County

PO Box 4305
Salisbury, NC 28145-4305

Contact: James B. Lloyd, Pres.

Founded: 1987. *Members:* 425.

458 ■ Genealogical Society of Santa Cruz County

PO Box 72   Ph: (408)429-3530
Santa Cruz, CA 95063
URL: http://www.compuology.com/scruzcty.htm

Contact: W. Dean Reynolds, Pres.

Desc: Seeks to provide a library through the on-going acquistion of genealogical books, periodicals, microfilm, and microfiche. Provides instruction on genealogical research. *Founded:* 1971. *Members:* 225.

459 ■ Genealogical Society of Siskiyou County

PO Box 225   Ph: (530)842-6018
Yreka, CA 96097   Fax: (530)842-6018

Contact: Sharon Youngs, Pres.

Desc: Print-genealogy pertaining to the history of Siskiyou Co. Also provides workshops and speakers. *Members:* 60.

460 ■ Genealogical Society of Southwestern Pennsylvania

PO Box 894
Washington, PA 15301-0894

Contact: Betty Jane Hiles, Pres.

Desc: Individuals interested in preserving the genealogy of southwestern Pennsylvania . Conducts genealogical research. *Founded:* 1971. *Members:* 1000.

461 ■ Genealogical Society of Washtenaw County

PO Box 7155   Ph: (734)483-2799
Ann Arbor, MI 48107-7155
URL: http://www.hvcn.org/info/gswc

Contact: Marcia McCrary, Pres.

Desc: Individuals interested in Washtenaw County, MI interested in local history and genealogy. Promotes study of history and genealogy. Assists genealogical research efforts. *Founded:* 1974. *Members:* 350.

462 ■ Genealogical Society of the West Fields

Westfield Memorial Library   Ph: (908)789-4090
550 E. Broad St.
Westfield, NJ 07090
E-mail: gswf@westfieldnj.com

Contact: Frederick Bollinger, Pres.

Desc: Genealogists in central New Jersey. Preserves and disseminates records and resources. *Founded:* 1979. *Members:* 140.

463 ■ General Society of Colonial Wars

1316 7th St.   Ph: (504)895-5013
New Orleans, LA 70115-3319   Fax: (504)899-7086

Contact: Howard Kent Soper, Lieutenant Governor Gen.

Desc: Male descendants of men who rendered military or civil service to the colonies between 1607 (settlement of Jamestown, VA) and 1775 (battle of Lexington). *Founded:* 1892. *Members:* 4250.

464 ■ General Society of Mayflower Descendants

PO Box 3297   Ph: (508)746-3188
Plymouth, MA 02361   Fax: (508)746-2488

Contact: Caroline L. Kardell, Historian Gen.

Desc: Descendants of passengers of the Mayflower, the vessel that transported the Pilgrims from England to Plymouth, MA in 1620. Conducts research into descendants of the Mayflower Pilgrims through the fifth generation. *Founded:* 1897. *Members:* 22000.

465 ■ General Society, Sons of the Revolution

Fraunces Tavern Museum   Ph: (212)425-1776
54 Pearl St.   Fax: (212)509-3467
New York, NY 10004
E-mail: gssr1776@worldnet.att.net

Contact: Thomas C. Etter, Jr., Gen.Pres.

Desc: Descendants, on either parent's side, of veterans of the American forces who served in the Revolution of 1776, or of American officials whose activities made them liable to charges of treason under British law. Fraunces Tavern, the oldest building in Manhattan, serves as a public museum. *Founded:* 1876. *Members:* 5800.

466 ■ General Society of the War of 1812

Box 106   Ph: (610)444-8492
Mendenhall, PA 19357

Contact: Dr. Forrest R. Schaeffer, Sec.Gen.

Desc: Male descendants of veterans of the War of 1812. "Perpetuates the memory and victories of the War of 1812; encourages research and publication of historical data; and cherishes, maintains, and extends the institution of American freedom and fosters true patriotism and love of country." *Founded:* 1814. *Members:* 1600.

467 ■ George McCleave Family Organization

29 E Portland Ave.   Ph: (812)882-9371
Vincennes, IN 47591

Contact: Richard Carl Rodgers, Jr., Contact.

Desc: Descendants of George McCleave, who immigrated to Delaware, PA in the mid-seventeenth century. Promotes study of McCleave and related family history and genealogy; facilitates communication among members. *Founded:* 1982. *Members:* 568.

468 ■ George Wadsworth Family Organization

PO Box 4267   Ph: (760)775-4943
Palm Desert, CA 92261   Fax: (760)775-4943
E-mail: kerrworks@bigfoot.com
URL: http://www.bigfoot.com/kerrworks

Contact: LaRae Free Kerr, Pres.

Desc: Descendants of George Allen Wadsworth. Promotes study of Wadsworth family history and genealogy; seeks to identify and unite Wadsworth family members. *Founded:* 1981.

469 ■ Georgia Genealogical Society

PO Box 54575   Ph: (770)971-1173
Atlanta, GA 30308-0575   Fax: (770)971-9945
E-mail: mulng45@worldnet.att.net

Contact: Esther Barnes Mulling, Pres.

Founded: 1964. *Members:* 1024.

470 ■ German Genealogical Society of America

2125 Wright Ave, C-9   Ph: (909)593-0509
La Verne, CA 91750-0517
E-mail: btoeppe@wdc.net

Contact: Francis Ferrier Hanks, Pres.

Desc: Individuals and libraries interested in German genealogy. Encourages and assists individuals in the study of German genealogy and the history of the German-speaking areas of Europe. Provides translation and research services and access to foreign telephone directories, family files, and surname index. *Founded:* 1986. *Members:* 600.

471 ■ German Research Association

PO Box 711600
San Diego, CA 92171-1600
URL: http://www.feefhs.org/gra/frg-gra.html

Contact: Leona N. Chaffee, Contact.

Desc: Persons interested in genealogical research focused on German-language areas of Europe. *Founded:* 1977. *Members:* 600.

472 ■ Germroth Family Association International

PO Box 20652   Ph: (703)660-9246
Alexandria, VA 22320-1652
E-mail: germroth@aol.com

Contact: David S. Germroth, Dir.

Desc: Persons interested in German genealogy particularly the history of the Germroth surname and all its various spellings. Collects German genealogical records and records of the Germroth family name. Works to document the Germroth family name and decendents of the Germroth family name living in the U.S., Canada, and the German-speaking nations of Europe. Works to advance German-American studies, to promote German-American understanding, and to study German-Americana. *Founded:* 1980. *Members:* 2036.

473 ■ Geshkewich Surname Organization

PO Box 2594
Rancho Cucamonga, CA 91729

Desc: Individuals with the surname Geshkewich and its variant spellings; other members of the Geshkewich family. Promotes study of Geshkewich family history and genealogy.

474 ■ Gideon Family Association

160 W. Dunedin Rd.   Ph: (614)263-4232
Columbus, OH 43214

Contact: Mark R. Gideon, Sec.

Desc: Individuals interested in researching the surname Gideon. *Founded:* 1987.

475 ■ Gilberth Haws and Hannah Whitcomb Family Organization

448 Barlow   Ph: (801)776-2551
Clearfield, UT 84015

Contact: Richard L. Scott, Pres.

Desc: Descendants of Gilberth Haws and Hannah Whitcomb. Seeks to identify and unite family members; promotes interest in family history and genealogy. *Founded:* 1948.

476 ■ Gildea Family History Association

4065 Berrywood Dr.   Ph: (541)461-4473
Eugene, OR 97404-4061

Contact: James R. Brann, President and Historian.

Desc: Collects, preserves, and disseminates information on all persons with the surnames Gildea and Gilday from County Clare, Ireland to Maine. *Founded:* 1989. *Members:* 5.

477 ■ Gillie - Gilley Family Organization
1480 Edison St.   Ph: (801)485-0976
Salt Lake City, UT 84115
E-mail: carsonpam@uswest.net

Contact: Pamela Gillie Carson, Contact.

Desc: Individuals with the surname Gillie and its variant spellings; other members of the Gillie family. Promotes study of Gillie family history and genealogy; seeks to identify and unite Gillie family members. *Founded:* 1969.

478 ■ Gilmer County Genealogical Society
15 Dalton St.
Ellijay, GA 30540-1008

Contact: Ernest L. Partridge, Pres.

479 ■ Gilstrap Family Association
1921 N Harrison   Ph: (915)949-0792
San Angelo, TX 76901
E-mail: marcusg100@aol.com
URL: http://www.familytreemaker.com/users/g/i/l/
    marcus-d-gilstrap/index.html

Contact: Marcus D. Gilstrap, Contact.

Desc: Members of the Gilstrap family. Promotes study of Gilstrap family history and genealogy. *Founded:* 1991.

480 ■ Goff/Gough Family Association
8624 Wimbledon Dr.   Ph: (423)690-2432
Knoxville, TN 37923
E-mail: bbgoff@aol.com

Contact: Bob B. Goff, Newsletter Ed.

Desc: Persons with the surnames Goff or Gough; descendants of a Goff/Gough family; anyone who endorses the purposes of the association. Seeks to stimulate an interest in the history of the Goff/Gough families and their descendants, especially those living in the United States. *Founded:* 1982. *Members:* 209.

481 ■ Goodenow Family Association
65 Glenhurst Dr.   Ph: (440)775-4652
Lima, OH 44074
E-mail: petetree@ix.netcom.com
URL: http://users.ilnk.com/ejcornell/goodenow.htm

Contact: Kristin L. Peterson, Corr.Sec.

Desc: Collects information on descendents of persons with the surnames Goodenow, Goodenough, Goodnow, and Goodno; seeks to locate members of those families. Conducts research programs. *Founded:* 1988. *Members:* 200.

482 ■ Goodwin Family Organization
39 Lost Tr.   Ph: (505)625-0961
Roswell, NM 88201-9509
E-mail: tdcshard@roswell.net

Contact: Alice B. Sharp, Pres.

Desc: Promotes genealogical research. *Founded:* 1978. *Members:* 200.

483 ■ Gospel Truth Association
PO Box 239
Peru, IL 61354

Contact: James E. Kurtz, Pres.

Desc: Presents studies, reports, and lectures on theology, philosophy, and sociology. Conducts research, educational, and charitable programs. *Founded:* 1951. *Members:* 435.

484 ■ Gosselin Family Association
1647 Chemin Royal   Ph: (418)829-2874
St.-Laurent, PQ, Canada G0A   Fax: (418)829-3138
   3Z0

Contact: Denise Gosselin, Pres.

Desc: Individuals with the surname Gosselin and others with an interest in Gosselin family history and genealogy. Promotes historical and genealogical research on the Gosselin family.

485 ■ Gottscheer Heritage and Genealogy Association
174 S Hoover Ave.   Fax: (303)665-4898
Louisville, CO 80027-2130
E-mail: anthro@privatei.com
URL: http://www.gottschee.org/ghga/ghga.htm

Contact: Elizabeth Nick, Pres.

Desc: Preserve the ancestral heritage, culture, history and family records of Gottsheers. *Founded:* 1993. *Members:* 350.

486 ■ Gottscheer Heritage and Genealogy Association
PO Box 725
Louisville, CO 80027
E-mail: thegenie@inreach.com
URL: http://www.gottschee.org/ghga/ghga.htm

Contact: Kate Loschke, Treas.

Desc: Descendants of the Gottschee Region of Slovenia, which was inhabited by German-speaking people from the 14th century until 1941, when they were relocated to Untersteiermark (lower Syria) and the Gottschee Region was transferred to Italian rule. Gottschee is now a part of Slovenia. Seeks to preserve the history of the Gottschee region and its German-speaking inhabitants. *Founded:* 1993. *Members:* 425.

487 ■ Graham Family Association
118 Yosemite   Ph: (210)494-2772
San Antonio, TX 78232
E-mail: edg32130@aol.com

Contact: Edward A. Graham, Exec. Officer.

Desc: Clearing house for persons researching the surname Graham. *Founded:* 1973.

488 ■ Grant County Genealogical Society
PO Box 281   Ph: (608)568-3124
Dickeyville, WI 53808-0281   Fax: (608)568-3573
E-mail: reese@mwci.net

Contact: Karen Reese, Pres.

Desc: Works to create and foster interest in genealogy and family history and to preserve the same. *Members:* 365.

489 ■ Grant/Lee Association
607 N. Logan St.   Ph: (618)993-5439
Marion, IL 62959

Contact: Alice L. Grant, Contact.

Desc: Descendants of Wyatt Grant, born in North Carolina, and Henry Toggle Lee, born in Virginia. Conducts genealogical reasearch and seeks to unite family members. Maintains biographical archives. *Founded:* 1924. *Members:* 100.

490 ■ Gratiot County Historical and Genealogical Society
228 W. Center   Ph: (517)875-4240
PO Box 73
Ithaca, MI 48847
URL: http://www.rootsweb.com/migratio/gch&gs.html

Contact: Georgiana Peet Miller, Chair, Gen. Group.

Desc: Individuals interested in the history and genealogy of Gratiot County, MI. Locates and marks historic sites; conducts research on county families and their histories. *Founded:* 1978. *Members:* 125.

491 ■ Graves Family Association
2 Binney Cir.   Ph: (508)384-8084
Wrentham, MA 02093
E-mail: ken.graves@gravesfa.org
URL: http://www.gravesfa.org

Contact: Kenneth V. Graves, Pres.

Desc: Descendants of a Graves, Greaves, or Grave family worldwide; anyone interested in the family name. Works to collect, preserve, and publish all information on the Graves, Greaves, or Grave family name. *Founded:* 1976. *Members:* 650.

492 ■ Grawunder and Graffunder Connection
13108 Penn Ave.   Ph: (612)890-3240
Burnsville, MN 55337

Contact: Gladys Grovender, Co-Editor.

Desc: Conducts genealogical research on the surnames Grawunder and Graffunder and on variations of spellings of these surnames. *Founded:* 1987.

493 ■ Greene County Genealogical Society
PO Box 133   Ph: (515)386-8111
Jefferson, IA 55129-0133
E-mail: darlynem@netins.net
URL: http://www.rootsweb.com/iagreene/index.htm

Contact: Janet Owen, Pres.

Desc: Individuals in Greene County, IA, or with Greene county roots, interested in gathering, preserving, and sharing local genealogical information. *Founded:* 1978. *Members:* 120.

494 ■ Greene County Historical and Genealogical Society
120 N. 12th St.   Ph: (870)739-4878
Paragould, AR 72450

Contact: Frances A. Morris, Pres.

Desc: Individuals interested in preserving the history of Greene County, AR. Gathers, preserves, and disseminates historical and genealogical information. *Founded:* 1987. *Members:* 250.

495 ■ Greenway Family Association
10 Munroe Rd.   Ph: (781)862-6528
Lexington, MA 02173

Contact: Robert C. S. Greenway, Pres.

Desc: Individuals with the surnames Greenaway and Greenway and their relatives. Seeks to trace origins of family in England. *Founded:* 1960.

496 ■ Griesemer Family Association
PO Box 814   Ph: (805)736-9637
Lompoc, CA 93438-0814
E-mail: ack@utech.net

Contact: Albert C. Hardy, Jr., V.Pres.

Desc: Griesemer family members. Seeks to "perpetuate the family name in all its 26 spellings." *Founded:* 1927. *Members:* 544.

497 ■ Grinnell Family Association
1623 16th Lane   Ph: (561)439-8519
Greenacres, FL 33463
E-mail: grinnell@gate.net
URL: http://www.gate.net/grinnell

Contact: Lawrence J. Grinnell, Pres.

Desc: Descendants of Matthew Grinnell, who emigrated to America circa 1635. Works to continue research on the Grinnell name and share this information with other interested parties. *Founded:* 1980. *Members:* 300.

498 ■ Groberg - Holbrook Genealogical Organization
1605 S Woodruff   Ph: (208)522-3185
Idaho Falls, ID 83404   Fax: (208)522-3060
E-mail: dvgroberg@aol.com

Contact: Mary Jane Fritzen, Coordinator.

Desc: Members of the Groberg and Holbrook families; other interested individuals. Seeks to strengthen family ties and foster and encourage family genealogical research. *Founded:* 1985. *Members:* 50.

499 ■ Grover Family Organization
3929 Milton Dr.   Ph: (816)373-5309
Independence, MO 64055-4043
E-mail: groversar@aol.com

Contact: Robert L. Grover, Pres.

Desc: Persons with the surname Grover. Seeks to share family and genealogical information among members. *Founded:* 1961. *Members:* 2000.

500 ■ Hacker's Creek Pioneer Descendants
PO Box 56
Horner, WV 26372-0056
E-mail: hcpd.lewisco@westvirginia.com
URL: http://www.westvirginia.com/hcpd

Contact: Joy Stalnaker, Exec.Dir.

Desc: Amateur and professional genealogists interested in Central West Virginia. To further the study of genealogy and history. Preserves and maintains pioneer cemeteries. *Founded:* 1982. *Members:* 850.

501 ■ Hadley - Hawthorne - Dickey - Walden Family Reunion Association
6407 NE 25th Ave.
Portland, OR 97211-6045

Contact: Matthew Barnett, Contact.

502 ■ Hales Family History Society
5990 N. Calle Kino   Ph: (520)888-9199
Tucson, AZ 85704-1704
E-mail: hales@primenet.com
URL: http://www.primenet.com/hales

Contact: Kenneth Glyn Hales, CEO & Founder.

Desc: Preserves and shares history of the Hales family, including varient spellings. *Founded:* 1970. *Members:* 3100.

503 ■ Halferty Family Registry
408 Countryside Ln.   Ph: (716)689-9371
Williamsville, NY 14221

Contact: Patrick J. Halferty, Exec. Officer.

Desc: Genealogical organization for the surname Halferty. *Founded:* 1990.

504 ■ Hallam Association
300 Greenglade Ave.   Ph: (614)888-1236
Worthington, OH 43085-2223
E-mail: henriettan@aol.com

Contact: Henrietta Nichols, Contact.

Desc: Traces all bracnhes of the Hallam family from early England to the present day. *Founded:* 1995.

505 ■ Hallockville Museum Farm
6038 Sound Ave.   Ph: (516)298-5292
Riverhead, NY 11901
E-mail: hallockville@ieaccess.net

Contact: John Eilertsen, Exec Dir.

Desc: Promotes, preserves, and interprets the 1765 Hallock Farm, and the rural and agricultural history of the North Fork of Long Island. Locates, restores, and preserves local historical and genealogical artifacts. Conducts educational programs. *Founded:* 1974. *Members:* 700.

506 ■ Hamilton County Genealogical Society
209 W. Henry   Ph: (817)386-4566
Hamilton, TX 76531   Free: 800-460-2847

Contact: Carlian Pittman, Pres.

Desc: Individuals interested in genealogy and local history. Plans to operate library and research center. *Founded:* 1992. *Members:* 600.

507 ■ Hamilton National Genealogical Society
215 SW 20th Terr.   Ph: (816)690-7768
Oak Grove, MO 64075
E-mail: hamgen@qni.com

Contact: Ann B. Hamilton, Dir. of Oper.

Desc: Persons interested in genealogical research and preservation of records. Works to collect information on the surname Hamilton and its variations, including Hamelton, Hamleton, Hambelton, and Hambleton. *Founded:* 1978. *Members:* 425.

508 ■ Haney Family Association
717 Pahaquarry St.   Ph: (908)475-2942
Belvidere, NJ 07823-2013

Contact: Grace M. Sassaman, Historian.

Desc: Persons with the surname Haney and their relatives. Conducts genealogical research; promotes family fellowship. *Founded:* 1910. *Members:* 150.

509 ■ Hans/Henry Segrist Family Organization
145 New Haven Dr.   Ph: (937)653-6500
Urbana, OH 43078

Contact: Arlene J. Secrist, Contact.

Desc: Individuals with the surname Segrist and its variant spellings. Seeks to locate and unite family members. *Founded:* 1987. *Members:* 25.

510 ■ Harden - Hardin - Harding Family Association
2500 Winningham Rd.   Ph: (804)645-8595
Crewe, VA 23930
E-mail: oranhj@nottwayez.net

Contact: James Oran Harding, Contact.

Desc: Individuals with the surname Harden and its variant spellings; other members of the Harden family. Promotes study of family history and genealogy. *Founded:* 1983. *Members:* 1423.

511 ■ Hardin County Chapter, Ohio Genealogical Society
PO Box 520   Ph: (419)675-6230
Kenton, OH 43326-0520
E-mail: laubis@kenton.com
URL: http://www.kenton.com/users/chuck/index.htm

Contact: Jeanne A. Bostater, Pres.

Founded: 1983. *Members:* 300.

512 ■ Hardin County Historical and Genealogical Society
PO Box 72   Ph: (618)287-2361
Elizabethtown, IL 62931

Contact: Noel E. Hurford, Pres.

Founded: 1985. *Members:* 15.

513 ■ Harless Family Association
595 Camellia Way   Ph: (415)948-0477
Los Altos, CA 94024

Contact: Carol and William Harless, Editors & Publishers.

Desc: Descendants of Johan Philip Harless and Margaretha (Preiss) Harless, German immigrants who settled in the Western Virginia frontier area in the 1750s. Collects and preserves genealogical and historical information. *Founded:* 1963. *Members:* 200.

514 ■ Harper County Genealogical Society
1002 Oak   Ph: (316)896-2959
Harper, KS 67058
URL: http://www.pe.net/_lucindaw/kansas/genalog/has.htm

Contact: Gail Bellar, Pres.

Desc: Individuals interested in local history and genealogy. Fosters exchange of information among members. *Members:* 43.

515 ■ Harrison County Genealogical Society
2810 190th Trail   Ph: (712)647-2593
Woodbine, IA 51579-4063
E-mail: hcgs51579@aol.com
URL: http://www.rootsweb.com/iaharris

Contact: Jeanette Lager, Pres.

Founded: 1984. *Members:* 75.

516 ■ Harrison County Genealogical Society
2307 Central St.   Ph: (660)425-2459
Bethany, MO 64424
E-mail: pejames@netins.net

Contact: Maudene Bennum, Pres.

Desc: Individuals with an interest in the genealogical records and history of Harrison County, MO. Gathers and disseminates information on local history and genealogy. *Founded:* 1978. *Members:* 175.

517 ■ Harrison Family Association
5243 Carpell Ave.   Ph: (801)964-2825
PO Box 18044   Fax: (801)964-0551
Salt Lake City, UT 84118-8044
E-mail: asiamarketing@worldnet.att.net

Contact: George M. McCune, Contact.

Desc: Descendants of William Henry Harrison, who was born in North Carolina in 1834. Promotes study of Harrison family history and genealogy. *Founded:* 1994.

518 ■ Hart County Historical Society
PO Box 606   Ph: (502)524-0101
Munfordville, KY 42765-0606
URL: http://www.ovnet.com/userpages/feenerty/history.html

Contact: David Hawkins, Pres.

Desc: Genealogists and others interested in the history of Hart County, KY. Seeks to collect and preserve historical manuscripts and artifacts. Recently received grants to preserve a local civil war battlefield. *Founded:* 1968. *Members:* 556.

519 ■ Harting Family Association
1135 Washington Ave.   Ph: (510)524-1410
Albany, CA 94706-1625
E-mail: hartingp@sirius.com

Contact: Paul W. Harting, Pres.

Desc: Descendants of the Harting family, which emigrated from Germany to the United States in 1854. Seeks to identify and unite family members; promotes study of Harting family history and genealogy. *Founded:* 1988. *Members:* 200.

520 ■ Hartshorn Family Association
1204 4th Street Dr. SE   Ph: (704)464-4981
Conover, NC 28613
E-mail: derick@twave.net

Contact: Derick S. Hartshorn, Pres.

Desc: Researches the surnames Hartshorn, Hartshorne, Hartson, and related family lines. *Founded:* 1983. *Members:* 384.

521 ■ Hathaway Family Association
3102 Royal Troon
Woodstock, GA 30189-6894
E-mail: wkeightley@aol.com

Contact: Edward Vernon Hathaway, Pres.

Desc: Members of the Hathaway family. Seeks to identify and unite family members; promotes study of Hathaway family history and genealogy. *Founded:* 1911. *Members:* 411.

522 ■ Haviland Family Organization
19662 Westover Ave.   Ph: (440)331-6444
Rocky River, OH 44116

Desc: Members of the Haviland family. Encourages study of Haviland family history and genealogy. *Founded:* 1985.

523 ■ Hawaii Times Photo Archives Foundation
567 S King St., Ste. 110
Honolulu, HI 96813-3036

Contact: Dennis M. Ogawa, Contact.

524 ■ Hawkins Association (Descendants of Robert and Mary of Massachusetts, Zachariah Hawkins of New York, and Joseph Hawkins of Connecticut)
PO Box 2392
Setauket, NY 11733-0742

Desc: Conducts genealogical research on Robert, Mary, Zachariah, and Joseph Hawkins and their descendants. *Founded:* 1935. *Members:* 200.

525 ■ Haymore Family Organization
241 N. Vine St., No. 1104E   Ph: (801)355-0919
Salt Lake City, UT 84103-1945   Fax: (801)355-0935
E-mail: r-mcoleman@prodigy.com

Contact: Ronald Coleman, Contact.

Desc: Conducts research on the Haymore family. Works to maintain Haymore homes and cemeteries. Conducts research and charitable programs; compiles statistics. Maintains museum. Has published 2 books. *Founded:* 1970. *Members:* 800.

526 ■ Hazelbaker Families
PO Box 450154   Ph: (918)786-2360
Grove, OK 74345-0154
E-mail: imogene@greencio.net

Contact: Imogene Sawvell Davis, Exec. Officer.

Desc: Persons with the surname Hazelbaker and their relatives. Collects family and historical data.

527 ■ Heald Family Association
250 Robinson Rd.   Ph: (541)592-3203
Cave Junction, OR 97523-9719

Contact: Jack Heald, Pres.

Desc: Heald family members and other interested individuals. Promotes study of Heald family history and genealogy. *Founded:* 1967. *Members:* 500.

528 ■ Heiney Family Tree
PO Box 260170   Ph: (303)985-3508
Lakewood, CO 80226-0170   Fax: (303)985-7872
E-mail: jogeo10709@aol.com

Contact: George Van Trump, Jr., Pres.

Desc: Persons interested in researching the surnames Heiney and Heiny. *Founded:* 1980. *Members:* 160.

529 ■ Hempstead County Genealogical Society
202 W. Ave. C. St.   Ph: (870)777-1278
Hope, AR 71801

Contact: Doris Millican, Pres.

530 ■ Henderson County Genealogical and Historical Society
400 N. Main St.   Ph: (704)693-1531
Hendersonville, NC 28793-2616

Contact: Evelyn Jones, Pres.

Founded: 1983. *Members:* 370.

531 ■ Hendricks County Genealogical Society
101 S. Indiana St.   Ph: (317)745-2604
Danville, IN 46122   Fax: (317)745-0756
E-mail: dplind@in-motion.net

532 ■ Henlein/Heinlein Family Association
<c/o> Enid I. Beihold   Ph: (317)823-2376
11502 Grace Ter.
Indianapolis, IN 46236

Contact: Enid I. Beihold, Founder.

Desc: Persons researching the surname Heinline and its variant spellings. Promotes genealogical research and seeks to preserve family history. Produces indices. Compiles statistics. *Founded:* 1985.

533 ■ Henry County Genealogical Society
PO Box 346   Ph: (309)853-2648
Kewanee, IL 61443

Contact: Alice Neirynck, Exec. Officer.

Desc: Individuals interested in the genealogy of Henry County, IL. Promotes the preservation of genealogical material. *Founded:* 1983. *Members:* 190.

534 ■ Henry Historical and Genealogical Society
610 N. St.   Ph: (309)364-3272
Henry, IL 61537

Contact: Connie Swanson, Pres.

535 ■ Hereditary Order of the Descendants of Colonial Governors
21 Claremont Ave.
New York, NY 10027

Contact: Mrs. Hans Bielenstein, Gov.Gen.

Desc: Lineal descendants of a governor of one of the American colonies. Objectives are to perpetuate the memory of colonial governors and chief executive officers in the colonies before July 4, 1776, and to foster interest in genealogy and colonial history. *Founded:* 1896. *Members:* 810.

536 ■ Hereditary Order of Descendants of the Loyalists and Patriots of the American Revolution
608 S. Overlook Dr.
Coffeyville, KS 67337-1108

Contact: Mr. Thomas Clifton Etter, Jr.Esq, Governor General.

Desc: Persons having both a loyalist and a patriot ancestor; associate members are those having only a patriot or a loyalist ancestor. Works to replace lost or destroyed historical records of members, many of which were burned during the Revolutionary War period; records lineage of members, but does not trace lineage for the public. Visits graves on Memorial Day; commemorates the Fourth of July. Maintains speakers' bureau. *Founded:* 1972. *Members:* 300.

537 ■ Heritage and Genealogical Society of Montgomery County
Railroad St.   Ph: (518)853-8186
PO Box 1500   Fax: (518)853-8392
Fonda, NY 12068-1500
E-mail: histarch@superior.net

Contact: Jacqueline Murphy.

Desc: The Department of History and Archives has one of the largest genealogical and historical collections in the state of New York. (The Heritage & Genealogical Society is a friendly society to this municipal county department.). *Founded:* 1976. *Members:* 70.

538 ■ Higdon Family Association
PO Box 26008   Ph: (703)683-3900
Alexandria, VA 22313-6008   Fax: (703)548-7207

Contact: Frank B. Higdon, Treas.

Desc: Individuals with the surname of Higdon. Promotes communication among members of the Higdon family. Provides historical and genealogical information. Conducts educational activities. *Founded:* 1975.

539 ■ Hinman Family Association
7769 E. Lemon St.   Ph: (602)890-2817
Mesa, AZ 85213-2260
E-mail: mittonh1@juno.com

Contact: William I. Mooso, Pres.

Desc: Promotes genealogical research on the Hinman family. *Founded:* 1972. *Members:* 200.

540 ■ Historic Ocala/Marion County Genealogical Society
PO Box 1206
Ocala, FL 34478-1206

Contact: Norm Perry, Pres.

Desc: Members try to locate and obtain information on past family members. Activities consist mainly in assisting members to find information and inform them of what is available in the library and show video tapes on computer use. *Founded:* 1991. *Members:* 65.

541 ■ Historical Committee of the Mennonite Church
1700 S. Main St.   Ph: (219)535-7477
Goshen, IN 46526   Fax: (219)535-7293
E-mail: johnes@goshen.edu
URL: http://www.goshen.edu/mcarchives

Contact: John E. Sharp, Dir.

Desc: Coordinates the Mennonite Church program of historical interpretation. Studies are centered in the 16th century Anabaptist period and the post-16th century Mennonite and Peace church areas. Seeks to ensure chronicling of the church history in an ongoing manner and interpretation of church heritage for new generations. *Founded:* 1911. *Members:* 8.

542 ■ Historical and Genealogical Society of Panola County
210 Kyle St.   Ph: (601)563-7287
Batesville, MS 38606
Founded: 1972. *Members:* 96.

543 ■ Historical Society of the Episcopal Church
PO Box 2247   Ph: (512)282-3234
Austin, TX 78768
Contact: May Lofgreen, Bus.Editor.
Desc: Promotes historical research on the Episcopal church. *Founded:* 1910. *Members:* 1500.

544 ■ Historical Society of the United Methodist Church
PO Box 127   Ph: (973)408-3189
Madison, NJ 07940   Fax: (973)408-3909
E-mail: cyrigoyen@gcah.org
URL: http://www.gcah.org
Contact: John E. Sims, Pres.
Desc: Individuals interested in the history of the United Methodist church. Promotes the study, preservation, and dissemination of information on the history of the United Methodist church and its antecedent bodies. Serves as a forum for exchange of information among members; monitors research projects involving United Methodist Church history. Assists in expanding the archival collections of the General Commission on Archives and History of the United Methodist Church. Makes available to members discounts on publications and admissions to convocations and meetings. *Founded:* 1988. *Members:* 800.

545 ■ Hodgeman County Genealogical Society
PO Box 441   Ph: (316)357-6594
Jetmore, KS 67854
Contact: Twila Smidt, Pres.
Founded: 1984. *Members:* 11.

546 ■ Hoefler Family Association
1039 Hwy. W   Ph: (314)456-4610
Warrenton, MO 63383
E-mail: dorjour@mocty.com
Contact: Dorey Schrick, Contact.
Desc: Members of the Hoefler family and other interested individuals. Promotes study of Hoefler family history and genealogy. *Founded:* 1992. *Members:* 60.

547 ■ Hogg Family Genealogical Society
1601 Verna St   Ph: (409)384-3995
Jasper, TX 75951-3303   Fax: (409)384-3935
E-mail: bitsy@jas.net
Contact: Mary Doris, Admin.
Desc: Decendants of any branch of the Hogg/Hoge/Hoag/Hogue families or other persons interested in the history and genealogy of such families. *Founded:* 1993. *Members:* 150.

548 ■ Hoggatt - Hockett Family Association
12390 SW North Dakota St.   Ph: (503)590-2348
Tigard, OR 97223-3299
E-mail: kenhoggatt@aol.com
Contact: Ken Hoggatt, Founder.

Desc: Individuals with the surname Hoggatt or its variant spellings; other members of the Hoggatt family. Promotes family historical and genealogical research. *Founded:* 1994. *Members:* 50.

549 ■ Holland Society of New York
122 E. 58th St.   Ph: (212)758-1675
New York, NY 10022   Fax: (212)758-2232
Contact: Annette Van Rooy, Exec.Sec.
Desc: Descendants in the direct male line of settlers in the Dutch Colonies in North America prior to 1675. Collects and preserves data on the early history of the Dutch Colonies and the genealogy of descendants of early settlers. Has translated baptismal, marriage, and death records of early Dutch churches. Conducts research and historical publications programs. *Founded:* 1885. *Members:* 1000.

550 ■ Holloway - Ralston Family Association
7650 Fairview Rd.   Ph: (503)842-6036
Tillamook, OR 97141   Fax: (503)842-6036
Contact: Orella Chadwick, Contact.
Desc: Members of the Ralston and Holloway families. Seeks to identify and unite Ralston and Holloway family members; promotes interest in family history and genealogy. *Founded:* 1953. *Members:* 60.

551 ■ Holmes-Greatorex Family Organization
1869 S. Fairway Dr.   Ph: (208)232-5777
Pocatello, ID 83201
Contact: Brent Michael Holmes, Family Historian.
Desc: Descendants of Robert Holmes and Mary Hannah Greatorex Holmes, Mormon converts in Great Britian in 1892. Strives to share genealogical information with and among the family members. *Founded:* 1965. *Members:* 1000.

552 ■ Hood County Genealogical Society
109 Ewell St.   Ph: (817)573-2557
PO Box 1623
Granbury, TX 76048-8623
E-mail: ancestor@hcnews.com
URL: http://www.genealogy.org/granbury
Contact: Wayne Moyers, Pres.
Desc: Preserve and disseminate information on the history and settlers of Hood County, TX. *Founded:* 1982. *Members:* 88.

553 ■ Hood's Texas Brigade Association
Box 619   Ph: (254)582-2256
Hillsboro, TX 76645
Contact: Dr. B. D. Patterson, Sec. Treas.
Desc: Direct and collateral descendants of members of Hood's Texas Brigade of the Civil War. The Brigade fought with Robert E. Lee for 4 years. Maintains Confederate Research Center and Museum. *Founded:* 1966. *Members:* 1000.

554 ■ Hooker County Genealogical Society
PO Box 280   Ph: (308)546-2458
Mullen, NE 69152
Contact: Betty Brown, Pres.
Desc: Individuals interested in genealogy. Promotes the art and practice of genealogical research; works to locate, collect, and preserve archival materials pertaining to genealogy and demographics. *Founded:* 1977. *Members:* 16.

555 ■ Hopkins County Genealogical Society
PO Box 51
Madisonville, KY 42431

Contact: Wanda Adams, Editor.
Desc: Individuals interested in genealogical research in Hopkins County, KY. *Founded:* 1969.

556 ■ House of Boyd Society
PO Box 2400, Sta. D   Ph: (613)333-5140
Ottawa, ON, Canada K1P 5W5
E-mail: 106111.647@compuserve.com
Contact: James Boyd, Contact.
Desc: Descendants of the Scottish and Irish Boyd clan. Conducts genealogical research on the Boyd clan; facilitates contact among members. *Founded:* 1987. *Members:* 325.

557 ■ House of Boyd Society
5 Little Creek Lane
Fredericksburg, VA 22405-3643
Contact: Diane Boyd Nolan, Contact.
Desc: Studies the history of the Boyds of Scotland and Ireland; promotes the exchange of genealogical information; increases the appreciation of the unique values of Scottish and Celtic culture; and participates in Scottish and Celtic Festivals and other educational programs. *Founded:* 1988. *Members:* 400.

558 ■ House of Gordon - Canada
10 Elmer Ave.e.   Ph: (613)687-2921
Petawawa, ON, Canada K8H 2M2
Contact: Iain A. Mills.
Desc: Descendants of the Scottish clan Gordon and any of its septs. Conducts genealogical research; facilitates contact among members. *Founded:* 1985. *Members:* 300.

559 ■ Houston County Historical Commission
Houston County Courthouse,   Ph: (409)544-3255
1st Fl.   Fax: (409)544-8053
Crockett, TX 75835
Contact: Eliza H. Bishop, Chm./Marker Committee.
Desc: Interested persons organized to provide genealogical research assistance and to preserve genealogical records. Conducts programs. Encourages interest in and preservation of area heritage. Locates sites and establishes official Texas Historical Markers. *Founded:* 1961. *Members:* 12.

560 ■ Howard County Genealogical Society
PO Box 274   Ph: (410)465-6696
Columbia, MD 21045
Contact: L. Duane Smith, Pres.
Desc: Promotes interest in genealogy. Sponsors research programs; gathers and publishes local cemetry and Bible records. *Founded:* 1976. *Members:* 160.

561 ■ Howard County Genealogical Society
PO Box 2
Oakford, IN 46965
URL: http://www.rootsweb.com/inhoward/gensoc.html
Contact: Dahl Perry, Pres.
Desc: Individuals interested in genealogy. Gathers and disseminates information. *Founded:* 1972. *Members:* 150.

562 ■ Howard-Winneshiek Genealogy Society
PO Box 362   Ph: (319)547-4278
Cresco, IA 52136
E-mail: djsowers@sbtek.net
URL: http://www.netins.net/showcase/winter/genweb/howard.htm
Contact: Janice Sowers, Pres.
Founded: 1994.

563 ■ Hoyt Family Association
360 Watson Rd.   Ph: (502)898-8168
Paducah, KY 42003-8978
E-mail: barbwolson@aol.com

Contact: Roy F. Olson, Jr., Founder.

Desc: Individuals with the surname Hoyt or its variant spellings. Seeks to identify and unite Hoyt family descendants. *Founded:* 1983.

564 ■ Hubbell Family Historical Society
2051 E. McDaniel St.
PO Box 3813 GS
Springfield, MO 65808-3813
URL: http://www.hubbell.org

Contact: Jack J. Hubbell, Dir.

Desc: Gathers information on the history of the Hubbell family. *Founded:* 1980. *Members:* 500.

565 ■ Hudson Genealogical Study Group
Hudson Library and Historical   Ph: (330)653-6658
  Society, Dept. G
22 Aurora St.
Hudson, OH 44236
E-mail: hgsg1@juno.com
URL: http://www.rootsweb.com/ohhudogs/hudson.htm

Contact: Douglas A. Henderson, Pres.

Desc: Individuals interested in genealogy. Works to promote interest in genealogical research. Provides support to the archives of the Hudson Library and Historical Society. Conducts educational activities, including professional training in research techniques. *Founded:* 1990. *Members:* 120.

566 ■ Huebotter Family Organization
2634 Associated Rd., Apt. A110   Ph: (714)990-5946
Fullerton, CA 92835
E-mail: nhuebotter@msmail2.hac.com

Contact: Nancy M. Huebotter, Pres.

Desc: Collects, preserves, and maintains Huebotter family genealogical and historical information. *Founded:* 1984. *Members:* 150.

567 ■ Humboldt County Genealogical Society
2336 G St.
Eureka, CA 95501

568 ■ Hunt County Genealogical Society
PO Box 398   Ph: (903)886-8690
Greenville, TX 75403-0398

Contact: Dorothy Wood Moore, Corresponding Sec./ Publications Chm.

Members: 12.

569 ■ Hutchinson County Genealogical Society
625 Weatherly St.   Ph: (806)274-3530
Borger, TX 79007

Contact: Charles Howell, Pres.

Desc: Individuals with an interest in genealogy. Assists the research of amateur genealogists. Maintains genealogical collection at the Borger Public Library.

570 ■ Hyde County Historical and Genealogical Society
PO Box 392   Ph: (605)852-3103
113 Iowa South
Highmore, SD 57345-0392
E-mail: sgrable@sullybuttes.net

Contact: Ms. Suzanne Grable, Pres.

Desc: Individuals interested in the genealogy and history of the Hyde County, SD area. *Founded:* 1973. *Members:* 30.

571 ■ Idaho Genealogical Society
4620 Overland Rd., No. 204   Ph: (208)384-0542
Boise, ID 83705

Contact: Jane Walls Golden, Pres.

Desc: Compiles and preserves historical and genealogical records pertaining to Idaho. Conducts genealogical research and educational programs. *Founded:* 1961. *Members:* 425.

572 ■ Illiana Jewish Genealogical Society
PO Box 384   Ph: (708)957-9457
Flossmoor, IL 60422-0384
E-mail: ijgs@lincolnnet.net
URL: http://www.lincolnnet.net/ijgs

Contact: Trudy Barch, Pres.

Desc: Promotes general and Jewish genealogy in southern Chicago suburbs and northwestern Indiana. Holds summer BBQ's. *Founded:* 1984. *Members:* 40.

573 ■ Immigrant Genealogical Society
1310B Magnolia Blvd.   Ph: (818)848-3122
PO Box 7369   Fax: (818)716-6300
Burbank, CA 91510-7369
URL: http://www.fcchs.org/igs/frg-igs.html

Contact: Marilyn Deatherage, Treas.

Desc: Individuals interested in genealogy. Works to trace foreign ancestors, particularly from German-speaking areas of Europe. *Founded:* 1982. *Members:* 700.

574 ■ Indiana Genealogical Society
PO Box 10507
Fort Wayne, IN 46852-0507
URL: http://www.indgensoc.org

Contact: Dawne Slater-Putt, Pres.

Desc: Members may be individuals, or organizations. The purpose of the society is to promote genealogical and historical research and education; preserve and safeguard manuscripts, books, cemeteries, and memorabilia relating to Indiana and its people; and assist in the publication of materials about the people, place, institutions, and organizations of Indiana. *Founded:* 1988. *Members:* 900.

575 ■ Innes Clan Society
1709 Crooked Ln.
Fort Worth, TX 76112

Contact: Myrna Peterjohn, Pres.

Desc: Descendants of or individuals related to the Innes clan; individuals interested in Scottish heritage. Seeks to strengthen relations within the Innes clan and encourage Scottish kinship. Conducts research; and collects literary, historical, and genealogical records, documents, and relics relating to Clan Innes and Scottish cultural heritage. Maintains genealogical archives. *Founded:* 1984. *Members:* 250.

576 ■ International Association of Jewish Genealogical Societies
104 Franklin Ave.   Ph: (914)963-1059
Yonkers, NY 10705-2808
E-mail: khsmus@aol.com
URL: http://www.jewishgen.org/ajgs/

Contact: Karen S. Franklin, Pres.

Desc: Coordinates efforts to advance the work of members. *Founded:* 1987. *Members:* 70.

577 ■ International Association of the Skubinna Family
16 3rd St. NE   Ph: (202)675-6685
Washington, DC 20002-7312
E-mail: iasf@hotmail.com

Contact: Martin L. Skubinna, Pres.

Desc: Conducts genealogical research on the Skubinna family. Sponsors charitable programs. *Founded:* 1990. *Members:* 175.

578 ■ International Genealogy and Heraldry Fellowship of Rotarians
10 Fox Tail Ln.   Ph: (203)775-2854
Brookfield, CT 06804   Fax: (203)775-0180

Contact: James High, Sec.

Desc: Rotarians and others interested in recreational, avocational, or vocational genealogy activities. Promotes increased understanding and goodwill through the exchange of genealogical backgrounds. *Founded:* 1980. *Members:* 300.

579 ■ International Institute of Flint
515 Stevens St.   Ph: (810)767-0720
Flint, MI 48502   Fax: (810)767-0724
URL: http://www.gfn.org/iif

Contact: Pamela Bakken, Exec.Dir.

Desc: Associations and individuals interested in helping foreign-born residents and their descendants. Assists foreign born individuals with their integration into the community. Works to educate the community about other cultures. Facilitates international exchange; makes available translation and language instruction services. *Founded:* 1922. *Members:* 540.

580 ■ International Molyneux Family Association
PO Box 10306   Ph: (206)842-6636
Bainbridge Island, WA 98110   Fax: (206)842-6639
E-mail: mxworld_us@halcyon.com
URL: http://www2.crosswinds.net/st-paul/lyndy/
  molyneux/home.html

Contact: Betty Molyneux Brown, Pres.

Desc: Members of the Molyneux family. Encourages family historical and genealogical research; facilitates communication among members. *Founded:* 1986. *Members:* 300.

581 ■ International Society for British Genealogy and Family History
PO Box 3115   Ph: (801)272-2178
Salt Lake City, UT 84110-3115
URL: http://www.homestart.com/isbgfh/

Contact: Anne Wuehler, Pres.

Desc: Professional and amateur genealogists with an interest in the genealogy and family history of persons of British descent. *Founded:* 1979. *Members:* 1000.

582 ■ International Society Daughters of Utah Pioneers
300 N. Main St.   Ph: (801)538-1050
Salt Lake City, UT 84103-1699   Fax: (801)535-1119

Contact: Mary A. Johnson, Pres.

Desc: Descendants of Utah pioneers. *Founded:* 1901. *Members:* 24000.

583 ■ International Soundex Reunion Registry
PO Box 2312   Ph: (775)882-7755
Carson City, NV 89702-2312

Contact: Anthony S. Vilardi, Registrar.

Desc: A central reunion registry for adults (18 years or older) who were adopted, orphaned, or separated from their parents by war or divorce, or were foundlings, foster children, or wards of the state, and their blood relatives. Provides a free mutual consent registry system for matching persons who desire contact with their next of kin-by-birth. If data matches and the ISRR registrar determines a relationship exists, both parties will be notified immediately. This registry does not perform a search or provide search advice. Conducts surveys; compiles statistics. *Founded:* 1975.

584 ■ Iowa City Genealogical Society/Johnson County Chapter
PO Box 822
Iowa City, IA 52244

Contact: Peter J. Seaba, Pres.

Founded: 1967. *Members:* 130.

585 ■ Iowa Genealogical Society
PO Box 7735   Ph: (515)276-0287
Des Moines, IA 50322-7735
E-mail: igs@digiserve.com
URL: http://www.digiserve.com/igs/igs.htm

Contact: Rhonda G. Riordan, Exec.Dir.

Desc: Persons interested in genealogy. Seeks to preserve Iowa records for genealogists and to make them available to researchers. *Founded:* 1965. *Members:* 3000.

586 ■ Iowa Genealogical Society, Carroll County Chapter
PO Box 21   Ph: (712)659-3033
Carroll, IA 51401
URL: http://www.rootsweb.com/iacarroll/carroll.html

Contact: Stan Dalhoff, Pres.

Desc: Seeks to preserve Carroll County heritage. Sponsors research on individual families. Transcribes all of the Carroll County cemeteries and is working on publishing the complete collection. Working on copying naturalization list of Carroll Co. and Census records. *Founded:* 1989. *Members:* 120.

587 ■ Iowa Genealogical Society, Cherokee County Chapter
PO Box 247   Ph: (712)436-2624
Cleghorn, IA 51014

Contact: Pat Behrens, Chr.

Desc: Preserves, collects, and organizes genealogical records of Cherokee County, IA.

588 ■ Iowa Genealogical Society, Clinton County/Gateway Genealogical Society
618 14th Ave.   Ph: (319)259-1285
Camanche, IA 52730
E-mail: erevans@clinton.net

Contact: Ruth Evans, Pres.

Founded: 1977.

589 ■ Iowa Genealogical Society, Des Moines County Chapter
PO Box 493
Burlington, IA 52601

Contact: Beth Schwenker, Pres.

Desc: Individuals interested in genealogy. Locates, restores, preserves, and disseminates genealogical information pertaining to Des Moines County, IA residents. Conducts research and educational programs. Maintains genealogical collection at the Burlington, IA public library. *Founded:* 1972. *Members:* 216.

590 ■ Iowa Genealogical Society, Henry County Chapter
PO Box 81
Mt. Pleasant, IA 52641

591 ■ Iowa Genealogical Society, Humboldt County Chapter
30 6th St. N.   Ph: (515)332-2155
Humboldt, IA 50548
E-mail: bolson@trvnet.net

Contact: Marilyn Hundertmark, Contact.

Desc: Seeks to establish a genealogical research library. Holds meetings with speakers. Publishes an annual calendar with pictures of Humboldt County. *Founded:* 1987. *Members:* 60.

592 ■ Iowa Genealogical Society, Jackson County Chapter
PO Box 1065   Ph: (319)652-5020
Maquoketa, IA 52060
E-mail: eedleman@sanasys.com

Contact: Lucille E. Sorensen, Pres.

Desc: Seeks to share information on research problems & successes; to seek out information on individual members' family history; to write and publish family histories; to help those who come to do their family research. *Founded:* 1976. *Members:* 297.

593 ■ Iowa Genealogical Society, Jefferson County Chapter
2791-240th St.   Ph: (515)472-4667
Fairfield, IA 52556-8518

Contact: Verda Baird, Corresp.Sec.

Desc: Genealogists. Preserves historical and genealogical data. Donates materials to the Fairfield Public Library. *Founded:* 1972. *Members:* 28.

594 ■ Iowa Genealogical Society, Jones County Chapter
PO Box 174   Ph: (319)462-4101
Anamosa, IA 52205

Contact: Jo Ann Walters, Pres.

Desc: Assists people in finding their ancestors from Jones County, IA. Houses information on family histories and cemetery records. Publishes many books on families. *Founded:* 1985. *Members:* 50.

595 ■ Iowa Genealogical Society, Keo Mah County Chapter
Keo-Mah Library   Ph: (515)673-6507
Penn Central Mall
Oskaloosa, IA 52577-0616
E-mail: mabgenank@lisco.net
URL: http://www.geocities.com/Heartland/Acres/2263/

Contact: Mabel Daniels, Corr.Sec./Libr.

Desc: Promotes interest in genealogy. Conducts research; assists beginning genealogists. *Founded:* 1981. *Members:* 190.

596 ■ Iowa Genealogical Society, Lucas County Chapter
Family History Rm.   Ph: (515)774-5514
803 Braden
Chariton, IA 50049-1742
E-mail: lucasgene@hotmail.com

Contact: Betty Cross, Corr.Sec.

Desc: Collects, preserves, and disseminates genealogical and historical information. *Founded:* 1976. *Members:* 150.

597 ■ Iowa Genealogical Society, Monona County Chapter
901 12th St., Box 16   Ph: (712)423-2075
Onawa, IA 51040

Contact: Emma Lou Stanislaw, Sec.

Desc: To help one another. *Founded:* 1977. *Members:* 14.

598 ■ Iowa Genealogical Society, Monroe County Chapter
203 Benton Ave. E.   Ph: (515)932-2726
Albia, IA 52531-9803
E-mail: hindman@cknet.net

Contact: Twila Chidester, Pres.

Founded: 1976. *Members:* 150.

599 ■ Iowa Genealogical Society, Ringgold County Chapter
204 W. Jefferson
Mt. Ayr, IA 50854

600 ■ Iowa Genealogical Society, Sac County Chapter
PO Box 54   Ph: (712)662-4094
Sac City, IA 50583

Contact: Janice Larsen, Pres.

Desc: Persons interested in genealogy and local history. Compiles information from county cemeteries and other data. *Members:* 25.

601 ■ Iowa Genealogical Society, Tama County Tracers Chapter
200 N. Broadway St.   Ph: (515)484-6767
Toledo, IA 52342

Contact: Wilma Parizek, Sec.

Founded: 1976. *Members:* 190.

602 ■ Iowa Genealogical Society, Taylor County Chapter
Box 8   Ph: (712)537-2475
Gravity, IA 50848

Contact: Helen Janson, Pres.

Founded: 1974.

603 ■ Iowa Genealogical Society, Tree Shakers Chapter
1009 Woodland Ridge Ct.
Louisville, KY 40245-5209

604 ■ Iowa Genealogical Society, Union County Chapter
Creston Public Library   Ph: (515)782-2277
310 N. Maple
Creston, IA 50801

Contact: Dorothy Eyberg, Pres.

Desc: Encourages an interest in genealogy. Assists in compiling genealogies. Preserves Union County historical and genealogical information.

605 ■ Iowa Genealogical Society, Warren County Chapter
306 W. Salem Ave.   Ph: (515)961-4409
Indianola, IA 50125-2438

606 ■ Iowa Genealogical Society, Washington County Chapter
PO Box 446   Ph: (319)653-2726
Washington, IA 52353

Contact: Cindy Juhl, Pres.

Desc: Gathers and disseminates genealogical information; assists genealogical researchers. *Founded:* 1983. *Members:* 100.

607 ▪ Iowa Genealogical Society, Wayne County Chapter

110 S. Franklin   Ph: (515)872-1621
Corydon, IA 50060-1518
E-mail: lecompte@netins.net
URL: http://www.swirls.lib.ia.us/libspages/Corydon/libhome.htm

Contact: Roberta Amdor, Pres.

Desc: Provide resources for genealogical research. *Founded:* 1976. *Members:* 95.

608 ▪ Iowa Genealogical Society, Webster County Chapter

PO Box 1584
Ft. Dodge, IA 50501

Contact: Charles Tigner, Pres.

Founded: 1976. *Members:* 95.

609 ▪ Iowa Genealogical Society, Winneshiek County Chapter

PO Box 344   Ph: (319)382-3421
Decorah, IA 52101
URL: http://www.netins.net/showcase/winter/wineshek.htm

Contact: George Pfister, Pres.

Founded: 1986. *Members:* 63.

610 ▪ Iowa Genealogical Society, Woodbury County Chapter

PO Box 624
Sioux City, IA 51102

Founded: 1977. *Members:* 120.

611 ▪ Iowa Genealogy Society, Van Buren County Chapter

PO Box 158   Ph: (319)293-5766
Keosauqua, IA 52565   Fax: (319)293-3766
E-mail: keolib@worf.netins.net
URL: http://www.netins.net/showcase/vbciowa/vbcgs/vbcfs.htm

Contact: Melva Jane Workman, Pres.

Desc: Promotes genealogical research in Van Buren County, IA. Gathers, restores, and preserves local historical and demographic records.

612 ▪ Irish-American Archival Society

100 Federal Plaza E, Ste. 514
Youngstown, OH 44503-1810

613 ▪ Irish-American Archives Society

3701 Mayfield Rd.
Cleveland Heights, OH 44121-1764

614 ▪ Irish Family Names Society

PO Box 861656
Plano, TX 75086-1656

Contact: William P. Durning, Dir.

Desc: Individuals researching the origins of their Irish family names. Promotes research and education concerning Irish genealogy. Members conduct their own research; the society serves as clearinghouse for exchange of information. Encourages members to visit Ireland. *Founded:* 1979.

615 ▪ Irish Genealogical Foundation

PO Box 7575   Ph: (816)454-2410
Kansas City, MO 64116   Fax: (816)454-2410
E-mail: mike@irishroots.com
URL: http://www.irishroots.com

Contact: Michael C. O'Laughlin, Contact.

Desc: Genealogists, historians, rare book collectors, and Irish-American enthusiasts. Promotes Irish cultural preservation. Seeks to assist researchers in Irish family history and genealogy. Offers audiocassette programs. Operates speakers' bureau. *Founded:* 1978. *Members:* 7000.

616 ▪ Isaac Garrison Family Association

5567 Ecton Rd.   Ph: (606)842-3028
Winchester, KY 40391
E-mail: edwanna@meginc.com

Contact: Edwanna Garrison Chenault, Exec.Sec.

Desc: Descendants of Issac Garrison. *Founded:* 1960. *Members:* 500.

617 ▪ Israel Barlow Family Association

PO Box 723   Ph: (801)546-1445
Kaysville, UT 84037-0723
E-mail: gbarlow@aros.net

Contact: Glenn Barlow, Pres.

Desc: Families tracing their roots to Israel Barlow. *Founded:* 1955. *Members:* 1900.

618 ▪ Italian Genealogical Society of America

PO Box 8571
Cranston, RI 02920-0571

619 ▪ Italian Genealogy Group

PO Box 626
Bethpage, NY 11714
URL: http://www.italiangen.org

Contact: Gene Capobianco, Pres.

Desc: Individuals of Italian descent. Promotes study of Italian family history and genealogy. *Founded:* 1993. *Members:* 530.

620 ▪ Ivory Family Association

7409 S Balboa Dr.   Ph: (801)233-9142
Midvale, UT 84047-2283   Fax: (801)268-1022
E-mail: rutnut@burgoyne.com

Contact: George Ivory, Pres.

Desc: Members of the Ivory family and other interested individuals. Encourages interest in, and study of, Ivory family history and genealogy. *Founded:* 1978. *Members:* 200.

621 ▪ Jackson County Genealogical Society

415 1/2 S. Poplar St.   Ph: (812)358-2118
Brownstown, IN 47220-1939

Contact: Lynn Hinnefeld, Pres.

Desc: Surveys, researches, and compiles genealogical data in Jackson County, IN. *Founded:* 1982. *Members:* 280.

622 ▪ Jackson County Genealogical Society

244 W. Michigan   Ph: (517)787-8105
Jackson, MI 49201

Contact: Wanda Worthington, Pres.

Desc: To preserve and make available the genealogical records of Jackson County, MI. Encourages the study of family history. Issues publications. *Founded:* 1977. *Members:* 140.

623 ▪ Jacob Hochstetler Family Association

1102 S 13th St.   Ph: (219)533-7819
Goshen, IN 46526
E-mail: dhochstetler@compuserve.com

Contact: Daniel E. Hochstetler, V.Pres.

Desc: Descendans of Jacob Hochstetler, who emigrated from Switzerland to North America in 1738. Promotes appreciation of the heritage shared by Hochstetler family members. *Founded:* 1988. *Members:* 700.

624 ▪ Jacob Horning Family Organization

1665 Hartland Woods Dr.   Ph: (810)632-5763
Howell, MI 48843-9044   Fax: (810)632-5427

Contact: Kathleen Horning, Contact.

Desc: Maintains genealogical records tracing all Horning family members back to Germany. Fosters communication and exchange among genealogical researchers. *Founded:* 1975. *Members:* 250.

625 ▪ Jacob More Society

391 Taylor Dr.
Claremont, CA 91711-4136

Contact: Hugh P. Moore, Pres.

Desc: Aids the study of Scottish history both in the U.S. and abroad; studies the part immigrant Scots, especially Campbells, have played in the development of the U.S. Society is named for Jacob More, a Scottish immigrant who came to the U.S. in 1701. Is interested in the history of the families who lived in Argyllshire and the western Highlands. Maintains collection of rare and unusual books on Scottish history. *Founded:* 1975. *Members:* 1000.

626 ▪ James Happy Family Organization

1161/ Gravelly Lake Dr.   Ph: (253)588-2585
Tacoma, WA 98499-1407
E-mail: rhappy@scanet.com

Contact: Cyrus Happy, III, Contact.

Desc: Descendants of James Happy, who married Mary Burgin in Delaware in 1775 and died in Kentucky in 1814. Seeks to unite members; promotes interest in the Happy family and its history.

627 ▪ James Leonard Williams Family Organization

29 E Portland Ave.   Ph: (812)882-9371
Vincennes, IN 47591

Contact: Richard Carl Rogers, Contact.

Desc: Descendants of James Leonard Williams, Ohio businessman who was born around 1823 in Perry County, IN, and related families including the Bicknell family of Rhode Island. Promotes study of Williams family history and genealogy. *Founded:* 1982. *Members:* 369.

628 ▪ James Redman Miller Family Organization

29 E Portland Ave.   Ph: (812)882-9371
Vincennes, IN 47591

Contact: Richard Carl Rogers, Contact.

Desc: Descendants of James Redman Miller, who was born near the end of the 18th century in Lincoln County, KY, and Jacob Miller, who immigrated the the United States from Germany in the early 19th century; other individuals with an interest in the Miller family and its history. Promotes study of Miller family history and genealogy. *Founded:* 1982. *Members:* 286.

629 ▪ Jamestowne Society

PO Box 17426   Ph: (804)673-6006
Richmond, VA 23226   Fax: (804)285-0394
URL: http://www.jamestowne.org

Contact: Mrs. Judith Hart, Exec.Dir.

Desc: Lineal descendants of early settlers of Jamestown, VA. *Founded:* 1936. *Members:* 5500.

630 ■ Jefferson County Genealogical Society
210 Madison
Port Townsend, WA 98368
Ph: (360)385-1003

Contact: Beverly Brice, Pres.

Founded: 1983. *Members:* 67.

631 ■ Jefferson County Genealogical Society
2791 240th St.
Fairfield, IA 52556-8518
Ph: (515)472-4667

Contact: Verda Baird, Corresponding Sec.

Desc: Donate all materials to Fairfield Library including 78 county cemeteries, 1839-1990 (added maiden names where possible.) Just finished copying 1921-1940 death records at courthouse for new volume. Fairfield Library has collection of 6,114 family sheets, 201 published genealogies. *Founded:* 1972. *Members:* 28.

632 ■ Jefferson County Historical and Genealogical Society
PO Box 51
Brookville, PA 15825
Ph: (814)849-0077

Contact: Randon Bartley, Pres.

Founded: 1967. *Members:* 200.

633 ■ Jefferson Genealogical Society
PO Box 961
Metairie, LA 70004-0961
E-mail: madbro@delphi.com
URL: http://www.gnofn.org/jgs
Ph: (504)466-4711

Contact: Dwight Duplessis, Pres.

Desc: Genealogists united to collect, preserve, and disseminate genealogical records. Assists researchers. *Founded:* 1985. *Members:* 390.

634 ■ Jeremiah Greene Family Organization
6002 Tolmie Dr. NE
Olympia, WA 98516

Contact: Linnen R. Brewer, Contact.

Desc: Descendants of Jeremiah Greene. Seeks to identify and unite all Greene family members; promotes interest in family history and genealogy. *Founded:* 1982.

635 ■ Jett Set Family Association
2776 County Rd. 27
Bellevue, OH 44811

Contact: Kate Jett, Contact.

Desc: Maintains a central repository on Jett family data and shares information among members. *Founded:* 1986. *Members:* 80.

636 ■ Jewish Genealogical Society
PO Box 6398
New York, NY 10128
E-mail: jgsny@aol.com
URL: http://members.aol.com/jgsny/main.htm
Ph: (212)330-8257
Fax: (212)787-9552

Contact: Estelle M. Guzik, Pres.

Desc: Individuals seeking information about their Jewish ancestry. Although the group does not conduct research for individuals, it does offer advice, assistance, and sources to members searching for genealogical information. Organizes field trips. *Founded:* 1977. *Members:* 1100.

637 ■ Jewish Genealogical Society of Cleveland
996 Eastlawn Dr.
Highland Heights, OH 44143
E-mail: abr2326@aol.com
Ph: (216)449-2326
Fax: (216)621-7560

Contact: Arlene Blank Rich, Pres.

Desc: Promotes genealogical research and new techniques; keeps count of Jewish cemeteries in the area. *Founded:* 1983. *Members:* 150.

638 ■ Jewish Genealogical Society of Illinois
PO Box 515
Northbrook, IL 60065
E-mail: se-meyer@nwu.edu
Ph: (312)666-0100

Contact: Lawrence R. Hamilton, Pres.

Desc: Provides forum to share experiences and research methods and learn new techniques and sources in tracing their Jewish ancestry. *Founded:* 1981. *Members:* 200.

639 ■ Jewish Genealogical Society of Los Angeles
PO Box 55443
Sherman Oaks, CA 91413-0443
E-mail: sgroll@ix.netcom.com
URL: http://www.jewishgen.org/jgsla
Ph: (818)771-5554

Desc: Individuals promoting Jewish family history research. *Founded:* 1979. *Members:* 500.

640 ■ Jewish Genealogical Society of Philadelphia
1279 June Rd.
Huntingdon Valley, PA 19006
E-mail: jlspector@aol.com
URL: http://www.jewishgen.org/jgsp
Ph: (609)667-0532

Contact: Joel L. Spector, Pres.

Desc: Individuals interested in Jewish genealogy. Conducts activities and projects and provides forum for exchange of information. *Founded:* 1979. *Members:* 380.

641 ■ Jewish Genealogical Society of Pittsburgh
2127-31 5th Ave.
Pittsburgh, PA 15219
E-mail: julfalk@aol.com
Ph: (412)471-0772
Fax: (412)471-1004

Contact: Julian Falk, Chm.

Desc: Individuals interested in recording and researching Jewish family histories. Promotes genealogical education and holds lectures. *Founded:* 1980. *Members:* 40.

642 ■ Jewish Genealogical Society of Southern Nevada
PO Box 29342
Las Vegas, NV 89126
E-mail: carmont7@juno.com
Ph: (702)871-9773
Fax: (702)646-3323

Contact: Carole Montello, Founder.

Desc: Individuals interested in promoting the study of Jewish genealogy. *Founded:* 1986. *Members:* 50.

643 ■ Jewish Genealogy Society of Greater Washington
PO Box 31122
Bethesda, MD 20824-1122
URL: http://www/jewishgen.org/jgsgw
Ph: (301)365-4546

Contact: Roberta Solit, Pres.

Desc: Individuals interested in genealogy. Preserves and disseminates information regarding Jewish genealogy. *Founded:* 1980. *Members:* 400.

644 ■ Jewish War Veterans of the U.S.A. - National Ladies Auxiliary
1811 R St. NW
Washington, DC 20009
Ph: (202)667-9061
Fax: (202)462-3192

Contact: Barbara Greenberg, Nat.Pres.

Desc: Sisters, wives, mothers, daughters, widows, and lineal descendants of Jewish veterans of wars of the United States. Sends gifts to servicemen overseas; conducts youth programs; provides service to hospitalized veterans. Has furnished a surgical wing at Chaim Sheba Medical Center in Israel and has contributed equipment to an amniotic laboratory there. Provides children's services; conducts charitable programs. *Founded:* 1928. *Members:* 15000.

645 ■ Johan Andreas Scheible Family Association
816 N. Chester
Monticello, AR 71655
Ph: (870)367-2348

Contact: Frieda S. Fischer, Family Genealogist.

Desc: Descendants of Johan Andreas Scheible. Promotes the research and history of the Scheible family. *Founded:* 1979. *Members:* 325.

646 ■ Johann Frederick Mouser Family Organization
29 E Portland Ave.
Vincennes, IN 47591
Ph: (812)882-9371

Contact: Richard Carl Rodgers, Jr., Contact.

Desc: Descendants of Johann Frederick Mouser, who was born in Germany in 1740 and died in North Carolina in 1799. Promotes and facilitates Mouser family historical and genealogical research. *Founded:* 1984. *Members:* 705.

647 ■ Johannes Schwalm Historical Association
PO Box 99
Pennsauken, NJ 08110
Ph: (609)663-8292

Contact: Richard C. Barth, Exec.Dir.

Desc: Individuals and associations. Purpose is to promote and perform research regarding Hessians who remained in America and their descendants. (Hessians were German auxiliaries to the British Crown in North America during the American Revolution.) Publishes, preserves, and disseminates information on Hessian art, culture, heritage, history, genealogy, and the economic, religious, and social practices of Americans whose ancestors came to the U.S. as Hessians during the Revolutionary War. Maintains biographical archives and depository. Operates speakers' bureau. JSHA began as a family organization named for Hessian soldier Private Johannes Schwalm, who, in 1776, was the first of the clan to come to the U.S. At the urging of other Hessian historians and genealogists, the group became a national historical association. *Founded:* 1979. *Members:* 425.

648 ■ John Bosher Family Organization
PO Box 1314
Chester, VA 23831-8314
Ph: (804)265-0618

Contact: Carson G. Bosher, Founder.

Desc: Seeks to exchange information on the Bosher family and others connected to the family, which came from England and Scotland in the 17th century. *Founded:* 1959.

649 ■ John Carver Family Organization
6602 W King Valley Rd.
West Valley City, UT 84128-4217
Ph: (801)250-9017

Contact: Jay G. Burrup, Genealogist.

Desc: Descendants of John Carver (1822-1912) and his wives. (Carver was born in Herefordshire, England, immigrated to the United States, and died in Plain City, UT.). Promotes study of family history and genealogy; encourages communication among Carvers' descendants.

650 ■ John Clough Genealogical Society
PO Box 239
Marshfield Hills, MA 02051

Contact: Sheila Anderson, Contact.

Desc: Strives to provide genealogical information to all members. *Founded:* 1941. *Members:* 300.

651 ■ John and Elizabeth Curtis/Curtiss Society
131 Lake Rd. Ph: (716)265-0621
Ontario, NY 14519-9311
E-mail: bcweaver@frontiernet.net
URL: http://www.curtis-curtiss.com

Contact: Barbara Curtis Weaver, Pres.

Desc: Individuals with an interest in the family history of people with the surname Curtis/Curtiss/Curtice and its variant spellings. Promotes interest genealogy. *Founded:* 1939. *Members:* 500.

652 ■ John Hall and Mary Bates Family Organization
2421 N 750 E Ph: (801)375-4390
Provo, UT 84604

Contact: Margaret Talbot, Sec.

Desc: Descendants of John Hall and Mary Bates; other individuals with an interest in Hall and Bates family history. Promotes study of, and interest in, Hall and Bates family history and genealogy. *Founded:* 1988. *Members:* 50.

653 ■ John More Association
9831 Sidehill Rd. Ph: (814)725-4915
North East, PA 16428
E-mail: jmaprez@erie.net

Contact: Eric More Marshall, Pres.

Desc: Direct descendants and spouses of Betty Taylor More (1738-1823), and John More (1745-1840). Works to preserve genealogical records of the More family and perpetuate the family ties. *Founded:* 1890. *Members:* 12000.

654 ■ John Morgan Evans of Merthyr Tydil
Rte. 1 Ph: (406)494-3066
260 Meadow View Dr.
Butte, MT 59701
E-mail: aalu@montana.com

Contact: Robert T. Evans, Exec. Officer.

Desc: Descendants of John Morgan Evans who lived in MerthyrTydil county borough in southern Wales. Compiles genealogical information. *Founded:* 1940. *Members:* 200.

655 ■ John Robinson - Ann Gregson Family Association
825 W 600 S Ph: (435)753-5108
Logan, UT 84321 Fax: (435)753-6511
E-mail: wayne@bridgenet.com

Contact: E. Wayne Robinson, Pres.

Desc: Descendants of John Robinson and Ann Gregson. Promotes interest in Robinson and Gregson family history and genealogy. *Founded:* 1998. *Members:* 100.

656 ■ John and Walter Cusick Family Association
9603 Bel Glade St. Ph: (703)281-9562
Fairfax, VA 22031-1105
E-mail: gkomar@erols.com

Contact: Gail Komar, VP.

Desc: Promotes interest in the genealogy and history of the Cusick family. *Founded:* 1987. *Members:* 400.

657 ■ Johnson County Genealogical and Historical Society
PO Box 1207
Vienna, IL 62995-1207

658 ■ Joseph Cox and Mary Rue Family Association
6703 Holdrege Ph: (402)466-1818
Lincoln, NE 68505

Contact: Ruth Anna Hicks, Exec. Officer.

Desc: Descendants of Joseph Cox and Mary Rue. Conducts genealogical research in an effort to locate as many descendants as possible. *Founded:* 1986.

659 ■ Joseph Goodbrake Montgomery Family Organization
PO Box 183 Ph: (608)759-2755
Benton, WI 53803

Contact: Glen Montgomery, Chariman.

Desc: Descendants or relatives by marriage of Joseph Montgomery. Social and genealogical organization; collects statistics. *Founded:* 1980. *Members:* 155.

660 ■ Joshua Gibbons Family Association
205 Elysian St. Ph: (412)362-8451
Pittsburgh, PA 15206
E-mail: don.gibbon@ecc.com

Contact: Donald Gibbon, Coordinator.

Desc: Descendants of Joshua Gibbons, the first record of whom emerged from the Currituck City, NC tax list of 1789. Gibbons is believed to have emigrated to America from Ireland. Promotes interest in Gibbons and related family histories and genealogies. *Founded:* 1984.

661 ■ Joyner Family Association
5243 Carpell Ave. Ph: (801)964-2825
PO Box 18044 Fax: (801)964-0551
Salt Lake City, UT 84118-8044
E-mail: asiamarketing@worldnet.att.net

Contact: George M. McCune, Contact.

Desc: Descendants of John Redman Joyner, who was born in North Carolina in 1875. Promotes study of Joyner family history and genealogy. *Founded:* 1994.

662 ■ Judkins Family Association
<c/o> Kathi Judkins Abendroth Ph: (206)784-3644
1538 NW 60th St. Fax: (206)781-4946
Seattle, WA 98107-2328
E-mail: genu13a@prodigy.com
URL: http://users.aol.com/judkinsfa/judkins.htm

Contact: Kathi Judkins Abendroth, Pres.

Desc: Descendants of Job, Samuel, Obediah, and Thomas Judkins; other interested individuals. Seeks to unite members of the Judkins family. Gathers and disseminates genealogical and historical information on the Judkins family. Assists in genealogical research. *Founded:* 1985. *Members:* 115.

663 ■ Julius William Hitchcock Family Organization
1056 E. Castle Rock Rd. Ph: (801)571-3545
Sandy, UT 84094 Fax: (801)571-9443

Contact: Ricardo G. Hitchcock, Pres.

Desc: Persons of Hitchcock descent. Conducts genealogical research on the Hitchcock family. Has traced the Hitchcock family back to Waterford, PA, (circa 1810 to 1820) and seeks information on earlier ancestors. *Founded:* 1970. *Members:* 100.

664 ■ Junkins Family Association
259 Cider Hill Rd. Ph: (207)363-6975
York, ME 03909-5303
E-mail: alnjunkins@aol.com
URL: http://www.morrisville.com/JFA

Contact: Alan D. Junkins, Pres.

Desc: Decendents of Robert Junkins (1621-1699) and interested individuals. Promotes and preserves the history and genealogical records of the surname Junkins. *Founded:* 1984. *Members:* 120.

665 ■ Kanawha Valley Genealogical Society
PO Box 8555 Ph: (304)776-1037
South Charleston, WV 25303
E-mail: dpeter15ba@aol.com
URL: http://www.rootsweb.com/wvkv65

Contact: Donald E. Peterson, Pres.

Desc: Individuals interested in the genealogy of the Kanawha County area of West Virginia. Provides assistance to local individuals searching for their ancestors. Conducts mini-workshops and bimonthly library research. *Founded:* 1977. *Members:* 350.

666 ■ Kansas Council of Genealogical Societies
PO Box 3858 Ph: (316)431-2125
Topeka, KS 66604-6858
E-mail: lkensett@chanuteks.com
URL: http://www.ukans.edu/kansas/seneca/kscoun/kscoun.htm

Contact: Lee Kensett, Pres.

Desc: Kansas State organization to promote and encourage preservation of manuscripts, books, and memorabilia relating to the people of KS, and serve as communications within the KS genealogical communities. *Founded:* 1974. *Members:* 240.

667 ■ Kansas Genealogical Society
Village Square Mall - Ph: (316)225-1951
2601 Central
PO Box 103
Dodge City, KS 67801
URL: http://www.dodgecity.net;kgs/

Contact: Mrs. Betty Herrman, Exec.Dir.

Desc: Individuals interested in genealogy. Works to locate, gather, restore, and preserve genealogical and historical documents and artifacts. *Founded:* 1958. *Members:* 525.

668 ■ Kaufman County Genealogical Society
PO Box 337
Terrell, TX 75160

Contact: Barbara Guynes Sloan, Pres.

Desc: Gathers, restores, preserves, and disseminates historic genealogical and demographic records. Conducts research and educational programs. *Founded:* 1981.

669 ■ Kelsey Kindred of America
113 Montoya Dr. Ph: (203)481-9804
Branford, CT 06405 Fax: (203)481-9804
E-mail: Kelsey@servetech.com
URL: http://www.servetech.com

Contact: Grace K. Benoit, Sec.

Desc: Descendants of William Kelsey, an early Puritan settler. Seeks to locate all descendants; promotes friendship and fellowship among members. *Founded:* 1928. *Members:* 900.

670 ■ Kentucky Genealogical Society

PO Box 153   Ph: (502)223-7541
Frankfort, KY 40602
E-mail: bdharney2@aol.com
URL: http://members.aol.com/bdharney2/bh3.htm

Contact: Roberta Padgett, Contact.

Desc: Individuals interested in the study of Kentucky genealogy. Maintains library. *Founded:* 1973. *Members:* 2100.

671 ■ Kerr Family Association of North America

3027 Leesburg Tr.   Fax: (770)591-4337
Woodstock, GA 30189

Contact: James Carr Gizzard, Jr., Contact.

Desc: Individuals and families interested in the history of the Kerr family history. Explores the history of the Kerr family surname back to the 12th century. *Founded:* 1979. *Members:* 400.

672 ■ Kerrville Genealogical Society

505 Water St.   Ph: (830)257-8422
Kerrville, TX 78028   Fax: (830)792-5552
URL: http://www.ktc.net/kgs

Desc: Members maintain the genealogy room. *Founded:* 1976. *Members:* 177.

673 ■ Kershner Family Association

PO Box 1131   Ph: (304)274-3104
Falling Waters, WV 25419-1131

Contact: Larry D. Kump, Pres.

Desc: Members of the Kershner family. Promotes study of Kershner family history and genealogy. *Founded:* 1991.

674 ■ Kidwell Family Association

5474 N. Capitol   Ph: (317)257-3833
Indianapolis, IN 46208
E-mail: skidwell@gateway.net

Contact: Sharon A. Kidwell, Pres.

Desc: Persons with the surname Kidwell and their relatives. Assists members in tracing their lineage and promotes the history of the Kidwell family. *Founded:* 1988. *Members:* 122.

675 ■ Kinseekers Genealogical Society

PO Box 492711   Ph: (352)787-3737
Leesburg, FL 34749-2711

Contact: Joyce Rorabaugh, Pres.

Desc: Sharing and helping genealogy objectives, purchase genealogy books for Leesburg City Library. *Founded:* 1960. *Members:* 170.

676 ■ Knox County Genealogical Society

PO Box 13   Ph: (309)483-6504
Galesburg, IL 61402-0013

Contact: Diane Bectler, VP.

Desc: Researching family history. *Founded:* 1971. *Members:* 220.

677 ■ Knox County Genealogical Society

PO Box 1098   Ph: (740)392-4745
Mt. Vernon, OH 43050   Fax: (740)392-4745

Contact: Russell E. Peffers, Sec.

Desc: Promotes genealogical study of local families. *Founded:* 1978. *Members:* 125.

678 ■ Kootenai County Genealogical Society

8385 N. Government Way   Ph: (208)772-5612
Hayden Lake, ID 83835
URL: http://usgenweb.com

Contact: Jeanne Venturino, Pres.

Desc: Members interested in or researching genealogy. Purpose is to introduce and assist in genealogy research. Maintaining society book collection located in Hayden Library, assisting members and the public in doing genealogy research, and monthly speaker on some type of genelogy research. *Founded:* 1979. *Members:* 35.

679 ■ Kump Family Association

PO Box 1131   Ph: (304)274-3104
Falling Waters, WV   Fax: (304)274-8906
  25419-1131

Contact: Larry D. Kump, Contact.

Desc: Individuals with the surname Kump and its variants; others with an interest in Kump family genealogy. Promotes interest in, and study of, Kump family genealogy. *Founded:* 1969. *Members:* 200.

680 ■ La Salle County Genealogy Guild

115 W. Glover St.   Ph: (815)433-5261
Ottawa, IL 61350
E-mail: dpc@mtco.com
URL: http://www.genealogy.org/-dpc

Contact: Margaret D. Clemens, Pres.

Desc: Preservation and dissemination of historical and genealogical records of LaSalle County, IL. *Founded:* 1979. *Members:* 937.

681 ■ Lackey Family Association

1708 Turtle Point Dr.   Ph: (972)296-2508
DeSoto, TX 75115-2746

Contact: Lynn B. Lackey, Sec.-Treas.

Desc: Dedicated to genealogical resesarch of the Lackey family name. Discusses research and publications by members; shares oral histories. Compiles statistics. *Founded:* 1989. *Members:* 226.

682 ■ Laclede County Genealogical Society

PO Box 350   Ph: (417)532-4069
Lebanon, MO 65536
E-mail: tknigh01@llion.org
URL: http://www.llion.org/molacled

Contact: Thomas Cayce Knight, Pres.

Desc: Promotes interest in genealogy and family history. Conducts genealogically related programs. *Founded:* 1989. *Members:* 60.

683 ■ Ladies Auxiliary, Military Order of the Purple Heart, United States of America

419 Franklin St.   Ph: (781)944-1844
Reading, MA 01867

Contact: Nancy C. Klare, Sec.

Desc: Female blood lineal descendants and adopted female descendants of veterans who have been wounded in combat and awarded the Purple Heart. *Founded:* 1932. *Members:* 4500.

684 ■ LaHaye Family History Association

4065 Berrywood Dr.   Ph: (541)461-4473
Eugene, OR 97404-4061

Contact: James R. Brann, President and Historian.

Desc: Collects, preserves, and disseminates information on all persons with the surnames LaHaye and Lepele from France to Quebec to Maine. *Founded:* 1989. *Members:* 5.

685 ■ Lake County Genealogical Society

184 Phelps St.   Ph: (216)352-3383
Painesville, OH 44077
E-mail: cynthia.turk@juno.com
URL: http://www.morleylibrary.org/genealogy/lcgs.html

Contact: Cynthia Turk, Pres.

Desc: Individuals interested in the genealogy of Lake County, OH. *Founded:* 1968. *Members:* 110.

686 ■ Lake County Genealogical Society

PO Box 1323   Ph: (707)263-4555
Lakeport, CA 95453-1323

687 ■ Lake County Genealogical Society

Dakota State University   Ph: (605)256-5203
Madison, SD 57042-1799   Fax: (605)256-5208
E-mail: olsonb@columbia.dsu.edu
URL: http://www.dsu.edu/

Contact: Bonnie Olson, Libr.Assoc.-Archives.

688 ■ Lake County Illinois Genealogical Society

PO Box 721   Ph: (847)336-7151
Libertyville, IL 60048-0721   Fax: (847)688-2745
E-mail: finance@gateway.net

Contact: Michael J. Wynn, Pres.

Desc: Individuals interested in the research and preservation of the genealogy of Lake County, IL. Offers research trips and programs; provides for indexing and printing of various records. *Founded:* 1978. *Members:* 215.

689 ■ Lamar County Genealogical Society

P.J.C. Box 187-2400 Clarksville   Ph: (903)782-0448
Paris, TX 75460
URL: http://gen.1starnet.com

Contact: Ron Brothers, Pres.

Founded: 1982. *Members:* 225.

690 ■ Lancaster Mennonite Historical Society

2215 Millstream Rd.   Ph: (717)393-9745
Lancaster, PA 17602-1499   Fax: (717)393-8751

Contact: Carolyn C. Wenger, Dir.

Desc: Individuals interested in the historical background, religious thought and expression, culture, and genealogy of Mennonite- and Amish-related groups originating in Pennsylvania. *Founded:* 1958. *Members:* 2850.

691 ■ Lapeer County Genealogical Society

Marguerite de Angeli Branch Library
921 W. Nepessing St.
Lapeer, MI 48446

Contact: Keitha Ver Planck, Libr./Newsletter Editor.

Desc: Individuals, librarians, and historical societies research the genealogical history of Lapeer County, MI. *Founded:* 1981. *Members:* 163.

692 ■ Lawrence County Genealogical Society

Rt. 1, Box 44   Ph: (618)945-7181
Bridgeport, IL 62417

Founded: 1976. *Members:* 50.

693 ■ Lawrence County Genealogical Society

204032 Plaza Dr. 309
Bedford, IN 47421

694 ■ Le Flore County Genealogists

RR 3 Box 55   Ph: (918)655-3126
Wister, OK 74966

Contact: GloryAnn Young, Contact.

Desc: Preserves records for public research.

695 ■ Leavenworth County Genealogical Society
PO Box 362   Ph: (913)651-4835
Leavenworth, KS 66048-0362
E-mail: greyink@idir.net

Contact: Debra Graden, Pres.

Desc: Works to preserve and pursue historical and family research from the area. Founded: 1984. Members: 100.

696 ■ Lee County Genealogical Society
PO Box 150153
Cape Coral, FL 33915
E-mail: bobbaechle@aol.com

Contact: Mr. G. Robert Baechle, 1st VP.

Desc: Dedicated to collecting, preserving and perpetuating the genealogical and historical records of our ancestors. Encourages and aids individuals in their family research. Founded: 1976. Members: 250.

697 ■ Lee County Genealogical Society (of Iowa)
PO Box 303   Ph: (319)524-2936
Keokuk, IA 52632-0303

Contact: Sharon Johnson, Pres.

Desc: Works to preserve genealogical and historical information in Lee County, IA. Promotes increased interest in local history and genealogy. Founded: 1964. Members: 68.

698 ■ Lewis and Clark County Genealogical Society
PO Box 5313   Ph: (406)442-2380
Helena, MT 59604
URL: http://www.mth.mtlib.org/lclhomepage/
    hoursservice/services/genealogicalsoc.html

Contact: Eloyce Kockler, Pres./Contact.

Desc: Individuals with an interest in local history and genealogy. Gathers and disseminates genealogical information, including primary source materials, and research queries. Founded: 1981. Members: 60.

699 ■ Licking County Genealogical Society
PO Box 4037   Ph: (614)345-3571
Newark, OH 43055
E-mail: lcgs1@juno.com

Contact: John J. Evans, Pres.

Desc: Individuals interested in the genealogy of the Licking County, OH area. Aids people who wish to trace their genealogy. Founded: 1972. Members: 600.

700 ■ Lillard Family Association
1669 Mountain View Rd.   Ph: (423)338-5777
Benton, TN 37307   Fax: (423)338-0332
E-mail: rlill55941@wingnet.net

Contact: Ralph Emerson Lillard, Sec.-Treas.

Desc: Members of the Lillard and related families. Promotes study of Lillard family history and genealogy; seeks to identify and unite Lillard family members. Founded: 1979. Members: 19000.

701 ■ Lincoln County Genealogical Society
1508 W. Washington St.   Ph: (615)433-5991
Fayetteville, TN 37334

Contact: Mabel A. Tucker, Treas.

Desc: Volunteer organization. Purpose is to accumulate and preserve records of Lincoln county families. Founded: 1976. Members: 460.

702 ■ Lincoln County Genealogical Society
Hamlin Public Library   Ph: (304)824-5481
7999 Lynn Ave.   Fax: (304)824-7014
Hamlin, WV 25523

Contact: Silces Begley, Pres.

Desc: To gather and preserve the history of Lincoln, CO, WV, and the family records of it's people. Founded: 1980. Members: 250.

703 ■ Lincoln Family Association
12 Smith Hill Rd.
Lincoln, MA 01773-1310

Contact: Robyn Laukien, Contact.

704 ■ Lincoln/Lancaster County Genealogical Society
PO Box 30055
Lincoln, NE 68503-0055

705 ■ Littlefield Family Newsletter
Box 817   Ph: (207)646-3753
Ogunquit, ME 03907   Fax: (207)646-3753

Contact: Charles Littlefield Seaman, Owner.

Desc: Compiles and disseminates information on the surname Littlefield. Founded: 1989.

706 ■ Litzenberger-Litzenberg Association
900 Mickley Rd., Ste. C2-3   Ph: (610)432-3034
Whitehall, PA 18052-5035
E-mail: litzassoc@aol.com
URL: http://www.litzenberg.org

Contact: Homer L. Litzenberg, Pres.

Desc: Descendants of people who used any surname recognized as derived from the German words Lutzel Burg, such as Lutzelburger, Litzenberger, Litsenberg, Litsinberger, Litchenburg, etc. Promotes genealogical research. Conducts social activities. Founded: 1991. Members: 68.

707 ■ Living Church Foundation
816 E. Juneau Ave.   Ph: (414)276-5420
PO Box 514096   Fax: (414)276-7483
Milwaukee, WI 53203
E-mail: livngchrch@aol.com

Contact: David A. Kalvelage, Editor & Gen.Mgr.

Desc: Clergy and laity. Operates publication and communication within the Episcopal church and the wider religious community. Conducts research. Founded: 1878. Members: 45.

708 ■ Livingston County Genealogical Society
PO Box 1073
Howell, MI 48844-1073

Desc: Individuals interested in preserving the history of Livingston County, MI.

709 ■ Livingston County Genealogical Society
PO Box 303
Nunda, NY 14517-0303

Contact: Kimberly Truax, Correspondence Sec.

Desc: Individuals with an interest in genealogy. Files ancestor charts for members; donates books and genealogical sources to local library. Founded: 1980.

710 ■ Livingston County Genealogical Society
450 Locust St.   Ph: (816)646-0547
Chillicothe, MO 64601   Fax: (816)646-5504
E-mail: travler1@aol.com
URL: http://www.greenhills.net/fwoods/

Contact: Nancy K. Hoyt, Pres.

Desc: Collects, maintains, and restores historical and genealogical artifacts of Livingston County, MO, including photos, documents, and books. Founded: 1986. Members: 100.

711 ■ Locke Surname Organization
7650 Fairview Rd.   Ph: (503)842-6036
Tillamook, OR 97141-9714 Fax: (503)842-6036

Contact: Orella Chadwick, Contact.

Desc: Individuals with the surname Locke and other Locke family members. Promotes genealogical research on the Locke family. Founded: 1978. Members: 60.

712 ■ Logan County Genealogical Society
406 E. Oklahoma   Ph: (405)282-8492
PO Box 1419
Guthrie, OK 73044-1419
E-mail: nalkadhimi@aol.com
URL: http://www.rootsweb.com/oklcgs/lcgsmain.htm

Contact: Martha Evans, Pres.

Desc: Logan county residents with genealogical interests who collect and preserve, through publication, records of genealogical value. Founded: 1981. Members: 50.

713 ■ Logan County Genealogical Society
PO Box 36   Ph: (937)593-7811
Bellefontaine, OH 43311-0036
E-mail: logan.county.ogs@logan.net

Contact: Ethel Buchenroth, VP.

Desc: Genealogists and others with an interest in the history of Logan County, OH. Catalogs and documents local cemetery records and other sources of genealogical information. Founded: 1979. Members: 400.

714 ■ Lorin Elias Bassett Family Organization
1055 E Hillcrest Dr.
Springville, UT 84663

Contact: Irvin Gene Bassett, Pres.

Desc: Descendants of Loren Elias Bassett, who arrived in the United States in 1809. Seeks to locate all Bassett descendants; encourages good fellowship among members. Founded: 1976. Members: 70.

715 ■ Los Californianos
PO Box 1693   Ph: (619)291-3966
San Leandro, CA 94577-0169
E-mail: mandmbandy@aol.com

Contact: Maurice Bandy, Pres.

Desc: Descendants of the Spanish who arrived in Alta (upper) California prior to Feb. 2, 1848; libraries, historical organizations, and schools are historical or corresponding members. Seeks to preserve the heritage of the early Spanish Californians in Alta California; provide authentic interpretation of Alta California's history via oral, written, pictorial, or other methods. Founded: 1969. Members: 725.

716 ■ Lucky Mee Family Association
Drawer 4487   Ph: (915)751-7233
El Paso, TX 79914   Fax: (915)751-7233
E-mail: joemee@juno.com

Contact: Joseph Mee, Historian.

Desc: Individuals with the Mee surname and related families. Maintains genealogical archives and library. Conducts research; compiles statistics; bestows awards. Founded: 1977. Members: 140.

717 ■ Luther Family Association
2027 Spyglass Ct.
Lakeland, FL 33810-6737

E-mail: luthergen@juno.com

Contact: George A. Luther, Exec.Sec./Genealogist.

Desc: Descendants of John Luther (1595-1645), an English ship's captain who emigrated to Massachussetts between 1630 and 1635 and was killed by Indians while on a trading venture near Delaware Bay in 1645. Seeks to preserve the history and genealogy of the family of Captain John Luther. *Founded:* 1936. *Members:* 1011.

718 ■ Lutheran Historical Conference

<c/o> James W. Albers	Ph: (219)464-5313
Department of Theology	Free: 888-GO-VALPO
Valparaiso University	Fax: (219)464-5381
Valparaiso, IN 46383	

E-mail: jim.albers@valpo.edu
URL: http://www.luthhist.org

Contact: James W. Albers, Pres.

Desc: Archivists and librarians from Lutheran churches and institutions; historians of American Lutheranism. Works to coordinate archival, library, research, and photo-duplication activities of Lutheran church bodies in the Americas; to provide forum for exchange of ideas and information among members; to disseminate information; and to encourage research and production of scholarly works in the history of Lutheranism in America. *Founded:* 1962. *Members:* 150.

719 ■ Lybarger Memorial Association

PO Box 611   Ph: (740)369-9093
Delaware, OH 43015-0611
E-mail: lybarger@midohio.net
URL: http://www.richnet.net/jllyb/

Contact: Lee H. Lybarger, Gen.Sec.

Desc: Individuals with the surname Lybarger and its variant spellings; other members of the Lybarger family. Promotes interest in Lybarger family history and genealogy; facilitates communication and cooperation among members. *Founded:* 1985. *Members:* 400.

720 ■ Lyman-Brule Genealogical Society

PO Box 555   Ph: (605)473-5391
Chamberlain, SD 57325   Fax: (605)734-5862

721 ■ MacCartney Clan Society

827 Continental Blvd.   Ph: (419)536-5690
Toledo, OH 43607-2254

Contact: Kenneth E. McCartney, Convenor.

Desc: Individuals interested in the history and genealogy of the MacCartney name and its variants. Maintains hall of fame. *Founded:* 1970. *Members:* 150.

722 ■ MacFaddien Family Society

General Delivery   Ph: (803)473-2643
Sardinia, SC 29143   Fax: (803)473-2643
E-mail: njmcfsr@sct-i.net

Contact: Norman J. McFaddien, Sr., Contact.

Desc: Strives to inform members of genealogical connections. *Founded:* 1936. *Members:* 200.

723 ■ MacLellan Clan in America

PO Box 640468
El Paso, TX 79404
E-mail: glaze55@dzn.com

Contact: Russell McClelland, Contact.

Desc: Members of the MacLellan family. Studies genealogy of the MacLellan clan. *Founded:* 1980. *Members:* 900.

724 ■ Macomb County Genealogy Group

150 Cass Ave.   Ph: (810)469-6200
Mt. Clemens, MI 48043   Fax: (810)469-6668

Contact: Nancy Burge, Exec. Officer.

Desc: Acts as a forum for persons interested in genealogy to exchange information. *Founded:* 1973. *Members:* 60.

725 ■ Macoupin County Genealogical Society

PO Box 95
Staunton, IL 62088
E-mail: smckenzi@midwest.net
URL: http://www.rootsweb.com/ilmacoupin/
macoupin.htm

Desc: Collect and share genealogy and history of Macoupin County, IL. *Founded:* 1980. *Members:* 250.

726 ■ Madison County Genealogical and Historical Society

PO Box 427   Ph: (501)738-6408
Huntsville, AR 72740

Contact: Virginia Hall, Pres.

Desc: Individuals interested in preserving the history of Madison County, AR. Gathers, preserves, and disseminates genealogical information. Assists researchers. *Founded:* 1982. *Members:* 740.

727 ■ Madison County Genealogical Society

PO Box 631   Ph: (618)656-2299
Edwardsville, IL 62025-0631

Founded: 1980. *Members:* 500.

728 ■ Madison County Historical Society

435 Main St.   Ph: (315)363-4136
PO Box 415
Oneida, NY 13421

Contact: Thomas J. Kernan, Exec.Dir.

Desc: Businesses, historical societies, teachers, and interested individuals. Individuals interested in preserving the history of Madison County, NY. Operates Cottage Lawn as a museum. Holds annual Traditional Craft Days and Victorian Christmas Celebration. Conducts crafts classes, genealogy series, lectures, workshops, and other educational programs. Holds historic house tours. Holds Madison County Hop. Festival. *Founded:* 1895. *Members:* 500.

729 ■ Magny Families Association

5 Fieldstone Ct.   Ph: (914)565-3638
Newburgh, NY 12550

Contact: Francis G. Coleman, Pres.

Desc: Individuals interested in the history and genealogy of the familys with the surname Magny or its variant spellings. Seeks to identify and united Magny family members; promotes accurate genealogical research. *Founded:* 1979. *Members:* 150.

730 ■ Major County Genealogical Society

PO Box 74
Fairview, OK 73737
E-mail: mayorcook@yahoo.com

Contact: Barbara Pannell, Pres.

Desc: Updates and locates lost and unused cemeteries. Conducts research on Oklahoma Territorial marriages, and Major County history. *Members:* 20.

731 ■ Maniak Surname Organization

PO Box 2594
Rancho Cucamonga, CA 91729

Desc: Individuals with the surname Maniak and its variant spellings; others Maniak family members. Promotes interest in Maniak family history and genealogy.

732 ■ Manning Family Club

15 Manning Rd.
North Franklin, CT 06254-1410

Contact: Thomas A. Manning, Contact.

733 ■ Mareen Duvall Descendants Society

3580 S. River Terr.   Ph: (410)798-4531
Edgewater, MD 21037-3245   Fax: (410)798-4883
E-mail: bmckown@web.aacpl.lib.md.us

Contact: Barrett L. McKown, Registrar.

Desc: Direct descendants of Mareen Duvall, a planter and merchant who emigrated from France to Maryland in 1655. Unites individuals and families who are offspring of Duvall's 12 children. *Founded:* 1926. *Members:* 624.

734 ■ Marion County Genealogical Society

PO Box 385   Ph: (515)842-5626
Knoxville, IA 50138
E-mail: jeanlee@harenet.net

Contact: Jean Leeper, VP.

Desc: Individuals interested in local history and genealogy. Works to locate and preserve historical demographic information. Conducts educational programs. *Founded:* 1975. *Members:* 150.

735 ■ Marley Family Association

8910 W. 62nd Terr.   Ph: (913)362-4600
Shawnee Mission, KS 66202   Free: 800-292-2273
                Fax: (913)362-4627
E-mail: eriworld@unicom.net

Contact: Michael Frost, PhD, Contact.

Founded: 1990. *Members:* 150.

736 ■ Marquette County Genealogical Society

217 N. Front St.   Ph: (906)225-8052
Marquette, MI 49855
E-mail: sherryew@aol.com

Contact: Sandy Caden, Pres.

Desc: Gathers, restores, preserves, and disseminates historic genealogical information. *Founded:* 1988. *Members:* 100.

737 ■ Marshall County Genealogical and Historical Society

Box 373   Ph: (502)527-4749
Benton, KY 42025

Contact: Clara A. Creason, Sec.

Desc: Individuals interested in preserving the history of Marshall County, KY. Promotes genealogical study. Compiles and preserves county records. Maintains archives. *Founded:* 1976. *Members:* 120.

738 ■ Mary Ellen Kinney Family Organization

8810 Lagrima de Oro Rd. NE   Ph: (505)298-5050
Albuquerque, NM 87111
E-mail: fredhaury@juno.com

Contact: Fred Haury, Dir.

Desc: Descendants of Mary Ellen Kinney. Seeks to identify and unite Kinney's descendants. *Founded:* 1978. *Members:* 175.

739 ■ Mason County Genealogical Society

PO Box 266   Ph: (606)759-7257
Maysville, KY 41056   Fax: (606)759-5370
E-mail: epryan@maysvilleky.campuswix.net

Contact: Edith Ryan, Corr.Sec.

Desc: Individuals interested in the genealogy and history of Mason County, KY. Records and collects cemetery, church, school, and other data. *Founded:* 1983. *Members:* 220.

740 ■ Massachusetts Genealogical Council

PO Box 5393   Ph: (781)784-5664
Cochituate, MA 01778

Contact: David C. Dearborn, Pres.

Desc: Serves as "frontline advocate to the genealogical community." Monitors legislation affecting public access to historical and current demographic records. *Founded:* 1980. *Members:* 100.

741 ■ Massachusetts Society of Genealogists, Middlesex Chapter

62 Tyler Terrace   Ph: (617)527-1312
Newton Centre, MA
02459-1814

Contact: Wheaton Wilbar, Pres.

Founded: 1976. *Members:* 250.

742 ■ Matagorda County Genealogical Society

PO Box 264   Ph: (409)245-6931
Bay City, TX 77404-0264

Contact: Joseph B. Cook, Pres.

Founded: 1901. *Members:* 120.

743 ■ Maxfield Family Organization

250 S 1st E   Ph: (435)245-6984
Hyrum, UT 84319

Contact: Dianne Pierson, Coordinator.

Desc: Individuals with the surname Maxfield or its variant spellings; other members of the Maxfield family. Promotes study of family history and genealogy. *Founded:* 1978.

744 ■ Maybee Society

10020 23rd Dr. SE   Ph: (425)337-1369
Everett, WA 98208

Contact: Belva Maybee Perry, Exec.Sec.

Desc: Members of the Maybee family. Seeks to find "the background history and genealogy of all the branches of the family, and making this material available for all members of the family, and to preserve the research that has been carried on by many dedicated researchers and students." *Founded:* 1986. *Members:* 262.

745 ■ Mazur Surname Organization

PO Box 2594
Rancho Cucamonga, CA 91729

Desc: Individuals with the surname Mazur and its variant spellings; other Mazur family members. Promotes interest in family history and genealogy.

746 ■ McAdams Historical Society

14018 Davana Ter.   Ph: (818)789-1086
Sherman Oaks, CA 91423
URL: http://www.jps.net/mcadams

Contact: Joe McAdams, Dir.

Desc: Family members and individuals interested in the MacAdam, McAdam, McAdams, and McCaddams allied families. Preserves the history of the MacAdam family. *Founded:* 1982. *Members:* 500.

747 ■ McAlpin(e) Family Association

8600 Hickory Hill Ln.   Ph: (256)881-4697
Huntsville, AL 35802

Contact: Doris McAlpin Russell, Pres.

Desc: Works to collect, compile, and preserve information on the history and genealogy of the surname McAlpin and its variants. *Founded:* 1975.

748 ■ Mcconnell and Related Family Clans

110 Embar Rd.
Gate City, VA 24251-3509

749 ■ McCullough/McCulloch Clan Society

PO Box 271759   Ph: (970)223-5874
Fort Collins, CO 80527

Contact: Betty K. Summers, Editor.

Desc: Collects and disseminates information on the McCullough/McCulloch families. *Founded:* 1978. *Members:* 150.

750 ■ McCuna Family Association

5243 Carpell Ave.   Ph: (801)964-2825
PO Box 18044   Fax: (801)964-0551
Salt Lake City, UT 84118-8044
E-mail: asiamarketing@worldnet.att.net

Contact: George M. McCune, Historian.

Desc: Descendants of Michael McCune, who was born on the Isle of Man in 1811 and died in Utah in 1889. Promotes study of McCune family history and genealogy. *Founded:* 1972. *Members:* 600.

751 ■ McGahen/McGhen/McGahn/McGahan Family Association

112 W. Main St.   Ph: (717)762-2011
Waynesboro, PA 17268   Fax: (717)762-2011

Contact: Joel McGahen, Pres.

Desc: Gathers for fellowship and to trace family origins. *Founded:* 1909. *Members:* 100.

752 ■ McGrath Family Association

57894 866th Rd.   Ph: (402)584-2407
Concord, NE 68728
E-mail: huskerette@hotmail.com

Contact: Marlys McGrath Rice, Contact.

Desc: Individuals with the surname McGrath and its variant spellings. Promotes interest in McGrath family history and genealogy. *Founded:* 1972. *Members:* 140.

753 ■ McGregor Family Association

2325 Ridge Dr.
Northbrook, IL 60062
E-mail: larrycxpl@aol.com

Contact: Larry L. McGregor, Treas.

Desc: McGregor family members. Promotes study of McGregor family history and genealogy; facilitates communication and good fellowship among members.

754 ■ McHenry County Illinois Genealogical Society

PO Box 184   Ph: (815)653-9459
Crystal Lake, IL 60039-0184
E-mail: mcigs@listserv.nslsilus.org

Contact: Kathy Bergan-Schmidt, Pres.

Desc: Individuals interested in the genealogy of McHenry County, IL. Provides instruction on methods and practices of family history research. *Founded:* 1981. *Members:* 310.

755 ■ McLean County Genealogical Society

PO Box 488   Ph: (309)827-0428
Normal, IL 61761-0488

Contact: Reva Merrick, Pres.

Desc: Preserving and publishing genealogical records and articles and assisting members and others with their research. *Founded:* 1966. *Members:* 395.

756 ■ Meader Family Association

158 Ashdown Rd.   Ph: (518)399-5013
Ballston Lake, NY 12019

Contact: Glenn S. Meader, Jr., Pres.

Desc: Members of the Meader family and other interested individuals. Promotes study of Meader family history and genealogy. *Founded:* 1974.

757 ■ Mecosta County Genealogical Society

PO Box 1068
Big Rapids, MI 49307-0968

Contact: Margaret Stimpson, Contact.

758 ■ Meigs County Genealogical Society

34465 Crew Rd.   Ph: (740)992-7874
Pomeroy, OH 45769

Contact: Patricia Cook, Pres.

Desc: Individuals interested in the genealogy of Meigs County, OH. Acquires and disseminates genealogical information. *Founded:* 1979. *Members:* 100.

759 ■ Melting Pot Genealogical Society

PO Box 936   Ph: (501)624-0229
Hot Springs, AR 71902

Contact: Ruby Duke, Pres.

Desc: Conducts genealogical research in Hot Springs, AR. Holds annual workshops. *Founded:* 1976. *Members:* 120.

760 ■ Memorial Foundation of Germanna Colonies in Virginia

PO Box 693   Ph: (540)825-1496
Culpeper, VA 22701   Fax: (540)825-6572
E-mail: office@germanna.org
URL: http://www.germanna.org

Contact: William Herndon Martin, Pres.

Desc: Seeks to preserve and make known the history of the Germanna Colonies in Virginia, their operations under the patronage of Governor Alexander Spotswood, and his residence and activities in Germanna and the surrounding areas. Aims to purchase and improve real estate that was part of the original Germanna tract. *Founded:* 1956. *Members:* 2000.

761 ■ Merced County Genealogical Society

PO Box 3061
Merced, CA 95340

Contact: Ron Lund, Pres.

Desc: Works for the preservation and research of genealogical and historical information. *Founded:* 1984. *Members:* 136.

762 ■ Mercer County Genealogical Society

PO Box 812   Ph: (412)346-5117
Sharon, PA 16146
E-mail: iorgen@infonline.net

Contact: Paul Corbett, Pres.

Desc: Individuals interested in promoting genealogical research in Mercer County, PA. Collects and preserves genealogical records. *Founded:* 1955. *Members:* 298.

763 ■ Merier-Gourley-Roark Family Organization

Gourley Hill   Ph: (912)384-1033
80 Ivy & N Bowen's Mill Rd.
Broxton, GA 31519

Desc: Members of the Merier, Gourley, and Roark families. Promotes interest in family history and genealogy.

764 ■ Miama County H. & G. Society, Chapter OGS

PO Box 305
Troy, OH 45373-0305
E-mail: vljbrown@bright.net
URL: http://www.tdn-net.com/mchgs

Contact: Arlene Rasor, Pres.

Desc: For persons interested in genealogical research, objective, finding our ancestors. *Founded:* 1952. *Members:* 250.

765 ■ Miami County Genealogical Society

PO Box 393   Ph: (913)294-4940
Paola, KS 66071

Contact: Helen Gilliland, Pres.

Desc: Individuals with Miami County, KS ancestors. Promotes and facilitates genealogical research; preserves historic demographic records.

766 ■ Mid-Cities Genealogical Society

PO Box 407   Ph: (817)868-0920
Bedford, TX 76095-0407
E-mail: nmhay@aol.com
URL: http://www.geocities.com/heartland/ranch/3825

Contact: Terri Bradshaw O'Neill, Pres.

Desc: Genealogical researchers throughout Dallas and Ft. Worth, TX. Provides assistance in the study of genealogy. Works to encourage libraries to obtain genealogical research materials. Conducts semiannual workshop. *Founded:* 1978. *Members:* 130.

767 ■ Mid-Michigan Genealogical Society

PO Box 16033   Ph: (517)641-4628
Lansing, MI 48901-6033
E-mail: watte@sojourn.com
URL: http://www.sojourn.com/mmgs

Contact: Earl Watt, Pres.

Desc: Seeks to preserve and increase the number of genealogical records of mid-Michigan available for research. Issues publications. *Founded:* 1967. *Members:* 300.

768 ■ Midwest Archives Conference

Ward M. Canaday Center   Ph: (419)530-2170
University of Toledo
Toledo, OH 43606

Contact: Barbara Floyd, Sec.

Desc: Archivists, genealogists, historians, librarians, local historical society and museum personnel, manuscript curators, oral historians, records managers, and related professionals (membership is international). Promotes cooperation and exchange of information among individuals and institutions interested in the preservation and use of archives and manuscript materials. Disseminates information on research materials and the methodology and theory in current archival practice. Provides a forum for discussion among members. Awards emeritus status to retired members who have made significant contributions to the profession or the organization. *Founded:* 1972. *Members:* 1100.

769 ■ Midwest Regional Chapter of Katyn Families Foundation

5813 Capri Ln.   Ph: (847)966-0788
Morton Grove, IL 60053-1573   Fax: (312)384-6197

Contact: Edward J. Kaminski, Pres.

Founded: 1994. *Members:* 70.

770 ■ Miles Merwin Association

1733 Blue Bell Rd.   Ph: (215)646-0231
Blue Bell, PA 19422-2117

Contact: Merwyn R. Buchanan, Contact.

Desc: Descendants of Miles Merwin (1623-97). Promotes study of Merwin family history and genealogy. *Founded:* 1957. *Members:* 450.

771 ■ Military Order of the Loyal Legion of the United States

1805 Pine St.   Ph: (215)546-2425
Philadelphia, PA 19103
URL: http://www.suvcw.org/mollus.htm

Contact: William A. Hamann, III, Recorder-in-Chief.

Desc: Male descendants of honorably discharged commissioned officers serving in the Union forces during the Civil War and descendants of the brothers or sisters of such officers. *Founded:* 1865. *Members:* 950.

772 ■ Miller County Historical Society

PO Box 343   Ph: (870)653-6011
Fouke, AR 71837-0343
E-mail: whalibrary@aol.com

Contact: Linda Rayburn, Exec. Officer.

Desc: Promotes interest in local history. *Founded:* 1985. *Members:* 50.

773 ■ Milliron - Millison - Muhleisen Family Exchange

51 Faubus St.   Ph: (914)473-3757
Poughkeepsie, NY 12603-2703

Desc: Works to assist genealogical research on this family. Promotes the cooperation among family members and researchers. *Founded:* 1980. *Members:* 70.

774 ■ Mills County Genealogical Society

Glenwood Public Library   Ph: (712)527-5252
109 N. Vine   Fax: (712)527-3619
Glenwood, IA 51534

Contact: Linda Rose, Pres.

Desc: Seeks to preserve local and county history and genealogical information. *Founded:* 1978. *Members:* 35.

775 ■ Milwaukee County Genealogical Society

PO Box 27326
Milwaukee, WI 53227-0326
E-mail: rrundel@juno.com

Contact: Richard and Mary Rundel, Editors.

Founded: 1935. *Members:* 1235.

776 ■ Mingo County Genealogical Society

PO Box 2581   Ph: (606)237-4646
Williamson, WV 25661

Contact: Robert Burris, Pres.

Desc: Disseminates local genealogical information, research, and publication materials. *Founded:* 1985.

777 ■ Missionary Church Historical Society

Bethel College   Ph: (219)257-2570
1001 W. McKinley   Fax: (219)257-3499
Mishawaka, IN 46545
E-mail: erdelt.@bethel-in.edu

Contact: Wayne Gerber, Pres.

Desc: Seeks to: gather the materials, documents, pictures, tapes, and artifacts of the Missionary Church and its anticedents; preserve church's historical documents and make them visible for study and display; encourage and sponsor research; publish and encourage the publication of literature dealing with Missionary Church history; and

promote interest in the history of the Missionary Church leading to a greater understanding and appreciation of its heritage. *Founded:* 1979. *Members:* 150.

778 ■ Mississippi County Genealogical Society

PO Box 5
Charleston, MO 63834

779 ■ Mitchell Kinship Program

900 W 5th
Box 1183
Mitchell, SD 57301-1710

Contact: Dana Weber, Contact.

780 ■ Monmouth County Genealogy Club

70 Court St.   Ph: (732)462-1466
Freehold, NJ 07728   Fax: (732)214-1666
E-mail: beahive@aol.com
URL: http://nj5.injersey.com/kishelly/mcgc.html

Contact: Bea Denman Howley.

Founded: 1988. *Members:* 550.

781 ■ Monroe County Genealogical Society

Albia Public Library   Ph: (515)932-5477
203 Benton Ave. E
Albia, IA 52531

Contact: Vivian Shelquist, Ed. & Treas.

Desc: Persons interested in genealogical and historical research in Monroe County, IA. *Founded:* 1976. *Members:* 145.

782 ■ Montgomery County Chapter, Ohio Genealogical Society

PO Box 1584   Ph: (937)434-1174
Dayton, OH 45401
E-mail: genejames@aol.com
URL: http://www.members.aol.com/ogsmont/

Contact: Trudy Reemelin, Treas.

Desc: Individuals interested in genealogy. Conducts public educational programs and lectures; holds trade days, ethnic days, and workshops. *Founded:* 1974. *Members:* 330.

783 ■ Montgomery County Genealogical Society

PO Box 867   Ph: (409)788-8363
Conroe, TX 77305-0867
URL: http://www.rootsweb.com/txmcghs/index.htm

Contact: Mel Westmoreland, Pres.

Desc: Persons interested in history and genealogy. Works to preserve county records. *Founded:* 1976. *Members:* 246.

784 ■ Montgomery County Genealogical Society

Box 444   Ph: (316)251-0716
Coffeyville, KS 67337

Contact: Carol Duvall, Pres.

Desc: Individuals interested in preserving the history of Montgomery County, KS. and helping others with Family Research. *Founded:* 1967. *Members:* 85.

785 ■ Moody Family Association

5243 Carpell Ave.   Ph: (801)964-2825
PO Box 18044   Fax: (801)964-0551
Salt Lake City, UT 84118-8044
E-mail: asiamarketing@worldnet.att.net

Contact: George M. McCune, Contact.

Desc: Descendants of Jonas Lunis Moody, who was born in North Carolina in 1874. Promotes study of Moody family history and genealogy. *Founded:* 1994.

786 ■ Moore County Historical and Genealogical Society
PO Box 408   Ph: (615)759-7763
Lynchburg, TN 37352-0408

Contact: Betty J. Robertson, Exec. Off.

Founded: 1990. *Members:* 75.

787 ■ Moravian Historical Society
214 E. Center St.   Ph: (610)759-5070
Nazareth, PA 18064   Fax: (610)759-5070

Contact: Susan M. Dreydoppel, Exec.Dir.

Desc: Maintains museum pertaining to Moravian Church history and American colonial life including religious paintings, musical instruments, household equipment, textiles, building materials, and Indian and foreign mission artifacts. Offers educational programs; maintains speakers' bureau. *Founded:* 1857. *Members:* 507.

788 ■ Morgan County Historical and Genealogical Society
PO Box 52   Ph: (304)258-2569
Berkeley Springs, WV 25411

Contact: Leonard Davis, Pres.

789 ■ Mormon Miner Family Organization
529 W 1600 S
Orem, UT 84058-7319

Contact: Eugene Jones, Contact.

Desc: Individuals with the surname Miner or its variant spellings; other Miner family members. Seeks to identify and unite Miner family members; promotes study of Miner family history and genealogy. *Founded:* 1940.

790 ■ Morse Society
5208 Mallory Dr   Ph: (516)627-3694
Ft. Worth, TX 76117   Fax: (516)627-4996
URL: http://www.morssweb.com/morse/

Contact: Dr. John R. Morse, Pres.

Desc: Individuals with an interest in the history and genealogy of the Morse and Morss families in North America. Promotes accurate historical and genealogical research. *Founded:* 1892. *Members:* 528.

791 ■ Moses Collins Family Organization
7902 Edgemoor   Ph: (713)774-7881
Houston, TX 77036

Contact: Dr. A. O. Collins, Contact.

Desc: Descendants of Moses Collins (1785-1858), who founded New Albany, MS in 1840, and other individuals with an interest in Collins family genealogy and local history. Promotes study of the history of the New Albany area; encourages Collins family genealogists. *Founded:* 1965.

792 ■ Motree Family Association
Rte. 5, Box 53
Laconia, NE 03246

Desc: Individuals with the surname Motree and its variant spellings. Promotes interest in Motree family history and genealogy.

793 ■ Mt. Vernon Genealogical Society
1500 Shenandoah Rd.
Alexandria, VA 22308-0000

794 ■ Mountain Press Research Center
PO Box 400   Ph: (423)886-6369
Signal Mountain, TN   Fax: (423)886-5312
  37377-0400

URL: http://www.mountainpress.com

Contact: James L. Douthat, Owner.

Desc: Promotes genealogical and historical research in the mid-Atlantic and Southeastern regions of the U.S. Provides research materials and information. Conducts training events. Arranges displays of genealogical and historical materials. *Founded:* 1980.

795 ■ Moursund Family History Association
4065 Berrywood Dr.   Ph: (541)461-4473
Eugene, OR 97404-4061

Contact: James R. Brann, President and Historian.

Desc: Collects, preserves, and disseminates information on all persons with the surnames Moursund and Mausund from Norway to America. *Founded:* 1994. *Members:* 10.

796 ■ Movius and Mevius Family Association
PO Box 20938   Ph: (801)284-5917
Reno, NV 89515-0938
E-mail: feefhs@feefhs.org

Contact: John Movius, Pres.

Desc: Individuals with the surname Movius and its variant spellings; other members of the Movius and related families. Promotes Movius family historical and genealogical research. *Founded:* 1989. *Members:* 800.

797 ■ Mower County Genealogical Society
PO Box 145
Austin, MN 55912

Contact: Collette Chaffee, Pres.

Founded: 1972. *Members:* 64.

798 ■ Muhlenberg County Genealogical Society
PO Box 758   Ph: (502)338-3713
Greenville, KY 42345

Contact: Carol Brown, Pres.

Founded: 1978.

799 ■ Mullee Irish Clan Society
7905 W Walker Dr.
Littleton, CO 80123-3547

Contact: John L. Butler, Contact.

800 ■ Mumford Family Association
3721 S Westnedge, Ste. 108   Ph: (616)833-8917
Kalamazoo, MI 49008
E-mail: sstyx@hotmail.com

Contact: Sherrie A. Styx, Contact.

Desc: Members of the Mumford family. Seeks to identify and unite Mumford family members; encourages study of Mumford family history and genealogy. *Founded:* 1995. *Members:* 382.

801 ■ Mumpower Family Association
614 N. Calvert   Ph: (765)288-1888
Muncie, IN 47303

Contact: Joe Mumpower, Contact.

Desc: Clearinghouse for genealogical information on the Mumpower family. *Founded:* 1978. *Members:* 400.

802 ■ Muskegon County Genealogical Society
Hackley Public Library   Ph: (616)722-7276
316 W. Webster
Muskegon, MI 49440

Contact: Sherry Schmuker, Pres.

Desc: Individuals interested in researching the genealogy of their families in Muskegon County, MI. *Founded:* 1972. *Members:* 112.

803 ■ Muskingum County Genealogical Society
PO Box 2427   Ph: (614)453-0391
Zanesville, OH 43702-2427
E-mail: dugmusk@y.city.net

Contact: R. Douglas Kreis, Pres.

Desc: Genealogy researchers and other individuals. Promotes the study of genealogy in Muskingum County, OH. Preserves local cemeteries. Holds annual genealogy week. *Founded:* 1975. *Members:* 450.

804 ■ Nassau County Historical Society
PO Box 207   Ph: (516)747-1141
Garden City, NY 11530

Contact: Denward W. Collins, Jr., Pres.

Desc: Individuals interested in preserving the history and researching the genealogy of Nassau County, NY. *Founded:* 1915. *Members:* 550.

805 ■ Natchez Trace Genealogical Society
PO Box 420
Florence, AL 35631-0420

Contact: L. Harold Judd, Pres.

Desc: Individuals interested in the genealogy of northwestern Alabama. Seeks to preserve local genealogical records; promotes programs for better genealogical research. Sponsors courses and workshops. *Founded:* 1980. *Members:* 251.

806 ■ Natchitoches Genealogical and Historical Association
PO Box 1349   Ph: (318)357-2235
Natchitoches, LA 71458-1349
E-mail: ngha@walt.net.k12.la.us

Contact: Bob Knipmeyer, Pres.

Founded: 1976. *Members:* 350.

807 ■ National Archives and Records Administration Volunteer Association
NWD-V, Rm. G-13   Ph: (202)501-5205
National Archives   Fax: (202)219-1250
8th at Pennsylvania NW
Washington, DC 20408
E-mail: rsexton@arch1.nara.gov

Contact: Jane M. Weldman, Pres.

Desc: Volunteers at the National Archives (U.S. government housing of public records and historical documents including papers, machine-readable records, motion pictures, sound recordings, still pictures, and maps). Purpose is to provide information, administrative service, and public awareness of the National Archives through volunteer participation in: tours of specified areas and exhib its for the public, school groups, and congressional constituencies; outreach programs for senior citizens, nursing homes, community groups, and classrooms, assistance in genealogical research; assisting the staff working on archival projects. *Founded:* 1976. *Members:* 328.

808 ■ National Association of Government Archives and Records Administrators
48 Howard St.   Ph: (518)463-8644
Albany, NY 12207   Fax: (518)463-8656
E-mail: nagara@caphill.com
URL: http://www.nagara.org

Contact: Bruce Dearstyne, Exec.Dir.

Desc: Purposes are to improve the administration of government records and archives and to raise public awareness and increase understanding of government archives and records management programs. Goals are to: act as forum for members and foster exchange among government archives and records management agencies in order to improve their programs and services; promote research, development, and use of archival management methods; encourage research and examination of problems in the administration and preservation of government records; create and implement professional standards of administration of archival and government records. Develops and disseminates publications and program guidelines for state and local programs; reports on issues concerning federal records programs; works with local government associations and other organizations towards solving the special problems of county, municipal, and government records. Represents the government records community in national issues affecting records management and archival programs. A member of the Council of State Governments. *Founded:* 1974. *Members:* 250.

809 ▪ National Association of the Van Valkenburg Family

121 Cardinal Rd.   Ph: (919)847-5088
White, GA 30184

Contact: Mary E. VanValkenburgh, Membership Coord.

Desc: Descendants of Lambert Van Valkenburg. Preserves and advances the Van Valkenburg family heritage. Fosters the ideals of honor, integrity, independence, and loyalty. Assembles and publishes the Van Valkenburg genealogy; serves as a central repository for family records and artifacts. Sponsors social events. *Founded:* 1970. *Members:* 800.

810 ▪ National Coordinating Committee for the Promotion of History

400 A St. SE   Ph: (202)544-2422
Washington, DC 20003   Fax: (202)544-8307

Contact: Dr. Page Putnam Miller, Dir.

Desc: Archival and historical organizations such as: American Historical Association; Organization of American Historians; Phi Alpha Theta; Society of American Archivists; Western History Association (see separate entries). Seeks to protect historians' interests with regard to federal policy. Serves as central advocacy office and information clearinghouse for government agencies, legislative aides, and professional history and archival associations; develops network of constituent contacts in districts and states; testifies before congressional committees; monitors employment opportunities. *Founded:* 1977. *Members:* 50.

811 ▪ National Genealogical Society

4527 17th St. N.   Ph: (703)525-0050
Arlington, VA 22207-2399   Free: 800-473-0060
      Fax: (703)525-0052

E-mail: ngs@ngsgenealogy.org
URL: http://www.ngsgenealogy.org

Contact: Francis Shane, Exec.Dir.

Desc: Individuals, families, societies and organizations. Promotes genealogical research and education; stimulates and fosters preservation and publication of records of genealogical interest including national, state, county, township, city, town, church, cemetery, Bible, and family records. *Founded:* 1903. *Members:* 17500.

812 ▪ National Grigsby Family Society

<c/o> Margaret G. Mottley   Ph: (713)789-5766
10138 Valley Forge
Houston, TX 77042
E-mail: mmottley@aol.com
URL: http://www.grigsby.org

Contact: Margaret G. Mottley, Admin.

Desc: Descendents of John and Jane Prosser Grigsby and others with the surname Grigsby; libraries and genealogical and historical societies. Promotes communication and friendship among members. *Founded:* 1981. *Members:* 380.

813 ▪ National Society of the Children of the American Revolution

1776 D St. NW   Ph: (202)638-3153
Washington, DC 20006   Fax: (202)737-3162
E-mail: nscar@nscar.org
URL: http://www.nscar.org

Desc: "Lineal descendants of patriots of the American Revolution from birth to 22 years of age." Supports several mountain schools in the South. *Founded:* 1895. *Members:* 10000.

814 ▪ National Society of the Colonial Dames of America

2715 Q St. NW   Ph: (202)337-0972
Washington, DC 20007   Fax: (202)337-0348

Contact: A. Corkorin Nimick, Pres.

Desc: No further information was available for this edition.

815 ▪ National Society Colonial Dames XVII Century

1300 New Hampshire Ave. NW   Ph: (202)293-1700
Washington, DC 20036-1595   Fax: (202)466-6099

Contact: Mrs. Dougas Swanson, Pres.Gen.

Desc: American women who are lineal descendants of persons who lived and served prior to 1701 in one of the Original Colonies in the geographical area of the present United States of America. *Founded:* 1915. *Members:* 14000.

816 ▪ National Society, Daughters of the American Colonists

2205 Massachusetts Ave. NW   Ph: (202)667-3076
Washington, DC 20008

Contact: Mrs. Harold N. Ottaway, Pres.

Desc: Women descended from men and women who gave civil or military service to the Colonies prior to the Revolutionary War. *Founded:* 1921. *Members:* 10700.

817 ▪ National Society, Daughters of the American Revolution

1776 D St. NW   Ph: (202)628-1776
Washington, DC 20006-5392   Fax: (202)879-3252

Contact: Mrs. Dale K. Love, Pres.Gen.

Desc: Women descendants of Revolutionary War patriots. Conducts historical, educational, and patriotic activities. *Founded:* 1890. *Members:* 188000.

818 ▪ National Society Daughters of Founders and Patriots of America

Park Lane Bldg., Ste. 300-05   Ph: (202)833-1558
2025 Eye St. NW
Washington, DC 20006-2813

Contact: Mrs. Jarvis A. Collins, Pres.

Desc: Women who are lineal descendants, in the male line of either parent, from an ancestor who settled in any of the colonies between May 13, 1607 and May 13, 1687, and whose intermediate ancestors in the same line gave military service or assistance to the colonies during the American Revolution. *Founded:* 1898. *Members:* 2250.

819 ▪ National Society Descendants of Early Quakers

3917 Heritage Hills Dr., No. 104   Ph: (612)893-9747
Bloomington, MN 55437

Contact: Arthur L. Sinnell, Contact.

Desc: Lineal and collateral descendants of early members of the Religious Society of Friends, commonly known as Quakers. Promotes appreciation for and preservation of historical and genealogical information regarding Quakers. Sponsors educational programs; maintains library and biographical archives. *Founded:* 1980. *Members:* 265.

820 ▪ National Society, Sons of the American Revolution

1000 S. 4th St.   Ph: (502)589-1776
Louisville, KY 40203   Fax: (502)589-1671
URL: http://www.sar.org

Contact: Wayne Wideman, Exec.Dir.

Desc: Descendants of men and women who served the patriot cause in the Revolutionary War. Sponsors competitions; operates museum. *Founded:* 1889. *Members:* 26000.

821 ▪ National Society Sons and Daughters of the Pilgrims

3917 Heritage Hills Dr., No. 104   Ph: (612)893-9747
Bloomington, MN 55437
E-mail: alfinnell@compuserve.com
URL: http://www.nssdp.org

Contact: Arthur Louis Finnell, Reg.Gen.

Desc: Adults (age 18 years and older) and juniors (under age 18) who can prove descent from an ancestor who settled in the U.S. prior to 1700; associate members are husbands or wives of members in good standing. Objectives are to: perpetuate the memory and promote the principles and virtues of the pilgrims; publicly commemorate principal events in the history of the pilgrims and erect durable memorials of historic men and events; foster and establish departments of study and organizations to promote social rights, civic virtues, industrial freedom, political equality, supremacy of just laws, the value and sacredness of the ballot, the purity of the home, temperate and godly living, and the independence of individuals, communities, and states. Encourages study and research of pilgrim history. *Founded:* 1908. *Members:* 2000.

822 ▪ National Society of the Sons of Utah Pioneers

3301 East 2920 South   Ph: (801)484-4441
Salt Lake City, UT 84109   Fax: (801)484-4442

Contact: John Anderson, Pres.

Desc: Men age 18 or older who are interested in preserving the history and names of the pioneers who settled the West. Sponsors historical treks, promotes pageants, and conducts other historical activities. Participates in Pioneer Village, Farmington, UT, and in museums of life in the pioneer West. Conducts research. Maintains Pioneer Historical Gallery. *Founded:* 1933. *Members:* 2700.

823 ▪ National Society, United States Daughters of 1812

1461 Rhode Island Ave. NW   Ph: (202)745-1812
Washington, DC 20005-5402

Contact: Mrs. Frank C. Stewart, Jr., Pres.Natl.

Desc: Women descendants of those who rendered civil, military, or naval service during the years 1784-1815. Promotes patriotism and seeks to increase knowledge of American history by preserving documents and relics, marking historic spots, recording family histories and traditions, and celebrating patriotic anniversaries. *Founded:* 1892. *Members:* 3800.

824 ▪ National Society Women Descendants of the Ancient and Honorable Artillery Company

<c/o> Mrs. George W. Hallgren   Ph: (410)515-1824
PO Box 453
Abingdon, MD 21009-0453

Contact: Mrs. George W. Hallgren, Natl.Pres.

Desc: Women of lineal descent from members of the Ancient and Honorable ArtilleryCompany (1637-1774), or from the clergy who preached on the Drumhead Election Day (1638-1774) or of the General Court (Boston) of 1638. *Founded:* 1927. *Members:* 1400.

825 ■ Naval Order of the United States
4404 Anderson Ave.   Ph: (510)531-6797
Oakland, CA 94619   Fax: (510)482-3946

Contact: Captain J. Armstrong, Recorder Gen.

Desc: Persons who have served as commissioned officers in the U.S. Navy, Marine Corps, or Coast Guard, and their descendants over 18 years of age; other maritime military servicemen of the U.S. and its allies. Seeks to transmit to posterity the names and memories of the great naval commanders, their companion officers, and their subordinates in the wars of the United States. Encourages research and publication of literature pertaining to naval history and science. Establishes libraries to preserve all documents, rolls, books, portraits, and relics relating to the Navy and its heroes of all times. *Founded:* 1890. *Members:* 1600.

826 ■ Neal Dougan-Theodorus Scowden Family Organization
165-4th St.   Ph: (724)726-5653
Aultman, PA 15713-9500

Contact: Richard F. Dougan, Historian.

Desc: Members of the Dougan and Scowden families. Conducts research and provides family history to all branches of the families. *Founded:* 1983. *Members:* 200.

827 ■ Nebraska State Genealogical Society
PO Box 5608
Lincoln, NE 68505

Members: 900.

828 ■ Neighborhood Bible Studies
56 Main St.   Ph: (914)693-3273
Dobbs Ferry, NY 10522   Fax: (914)693-1915

E-mail: nbstudies@aol.com
URL: http://www.nbstudy.org

Contact: Shirley Jacobs, Dir.

Desc: Encourages and assists churches and individuals in the formation of adult Bible study groups as a means of sharing the Gospel and teaching spiritual leadership. Advocates an "inductive" approach in Bible study, which entails first presenting the context and meaning of biblical scriptures before relating those scriptures to religious doctrine. *Founded:* 1960.

829 ■ Nesbitt/Nisbet Society: A Worldwide Clan Society
1443 Dorothy Dr.
Glendale, CA 91202
E-mail: nizbabe@aol.com
URL: http://www.ibydeit.com

Contact: Stuart Nisbet, Pres.

Desc: Members of the Nesbitt or Nisbet clan. Shares genealogical information and family history. *Founded:* 1980. *Members:* 400.

830 ■ New Canaan Historical Society
13 Oenoke Ridge   Ph: (203)966-1776
New Canaan, CT 06840   Fax: (203)972-5917
E-mail: newcanaan.historical@snet.net
URL: http://www.nchistory.org

Contact: Janet Lindstrom, Exec.Dir.

Desc: Individuals interested in the history of New Canaan, CT. Seeks to "bring together and arrange the historical events of the town of New Canaan and the genealogies of the families who have lived in town." *Founded:* 1889. *Members:* 860.

831 ■ New England Historic Genealogical Society
101 Newbury St.   Ph: (617)536-5740
Boston, MA 02116-3007   Free: 888-906-3447
                            Fax: (617)536-7307
E-mail: membership@nehgs.org
URL: http://www.nehgs.org

Contact: Ralph J. Crandall, Exec.Dir.

Desc: Collects and preserves materials relating to family history and local history. Conducts lectures on local and national levels. *Founded:* 1845. *Members:* 18000.

832 ■ New Hampshire Historical Society
30 Park St.   Ph: (603)225-3381
Concord, NH 03301   Fax: (603)224-0463
E-mail: NHHSadmin@aol.com
URL: http://newww.com/org/nhhs

Contact: John L. Frisbee, CEO.

Desc: Individuals interested in preserving the history of New Hampshire. Operates museum and library. *Founded:* 1823. *Members:* 3000.

833 ■ New York Genealogical and Biographical Society
122 E. 58th St.   Ph: (212)755-8532
New York, NY 10022-1939   Fax: (212)754-4218

Contact: William P. Johns, Exec.Dir.

Desc: To discover, procure, preserve, and perpetuate information and items relating to genealogy, biography, and local history, especially of New York state. Publishes compiled genealogy and source material for genealogists and historians. *Founded:* 1869. *Members:* 2100.

834 ■ New York Genealogical and Biographical Society
122 E. 58th St.   Ph: (212)755-8532
New York, NY 10022-1939   Fax: (212)754-4218
URL: http://www.nygbs.org

Contact: William P. Johns, Exec.Dir.

Desc: To collect, preserve, and make available to the public information relating to genealogy, biography, and history, especially of the state of New York. *Founded:* 1869. *Members:* 2500.

835 ■ Niagara County Genealogical Society
215 Niagara St.   Ph: (716)433-1033
Lockport, NY 14094-2605

Contact: Douglas V. Farley, Dir. & Bd.Cmn.

Desc: Individuals interested in promoting genealogical research. *Founded:* 1979. *Members:* 500.

836 ■ Nicholas County Historical and Genealogical Society
PO Box 443   Ph: (304)872-2478
Summersville, WV 26651

Contact: Belinda Bennett, Pres.

Desc: Promotes historic preservation and genealogical research. *Founded:* 1982. *Members:* 265.

837 ■ Nicholas Thomas Pittenger Family Organization
4840 Wyandot
Denver, CO 80221

Contact: Mary E. Ludder, Sec.

Desc: Individuals with the surname Pittenger and its variant spellings. Promotes interest in, and study of, Pittenger family history and genealogy. *Founded:* 1962.

838 ■ Nims Family Association
PO Box 99   Ph: (310)530-6263
Deerfield, MA 01342-0099   Fax: (310)530-3994
E-mail: wnims10372@aol.com

Contact: William Nims, Pres.

Desc: Individuals with the surname Nims. *Founded:* 1979. *Members:* 485.

839 ■ Nishihara Sakota Family Organization
PO Box 163
Rexburg, ID 83440-0163

840 ■ Nishnabotna Genealogical Society - Shelby County
1103 Rd. M56   Ph: (712)799-4285
Harlan, IA 51537-6022

Desc: A small group where each member is to preserve his or her family history. Helps others to research their history in the local area.

841 ■ Nixon Family Association
5817 144th St. E   Ph: (253)537-8288
Puyallup, WA 98375-5221
E-mail: janetgb@worldnet.att.net

Contact: Janet Nixon Baccus, Pres.

Desc: Collects and disseminates information on the surname Nixon. *Founded:* 1980.

842 ■ Noble County Genealogical Society
813 E. Main St.   Ph: (219)636-7197
Albion, IN 46701   Fax: (219)636-3321

Contact: Linda J. Shultz, Pres.

Desc: Amateur and professional genealogists and libraries interested in the genealogy of northeastern Indiana. Provides assistance to individuals researching their own genealogy. *Founded:* 1980. *Members:* 75.

843 ■ Nodaway County Genealogical Society
110 N. Walnut St.   Ph: (816)582-3254
Maryville, MO 64468

Contact: Joan Eital, Treas.

Desc: Genealogists and other individuals with an interest in genealogy and local history. Conducts research and educational programs. Gathers and disseminates historic demographic records.

844 ■ Norbert Barrie Family Organization
PO Box 45   Ph: (605)897-6528
Turton, SD 57477
E-mail: rlbfrogg@nvc.net

Contact: Richard L. Barrie, Contact.

Desc: Individuals with the surname Barrie or its variant spellings; others with an interest in family history and genealogy. Promotes study of Barrie family genealogy and history; encourages communication and good fellowship among members. *Founded:* 1970. *Members:* 1000.

845 ■ North Carolina Genealogical Society
PO Box 1492   Ph: (252)551-3727
Raleigh, NC 27602
E-mail: ncgs@earthlink.net
URL: http://www.ncgenealogy.org

Contact: Crestena Oakley, Sec.

Desc: Interested persons. Promotes genealogical research and the collection, preservation, and use of archival material. Provides network for the exchange of information. Bestows awards; conducts workshops. *Founded:* 1974. *Members:* 2268.

846 ■ Northampton County Historical and Genealogical Society

107 S. 4th St.   Ph: (610)253-1222
Easton, PA 18042   Fax: (610)253-1222

Contact: Paul A. Goudy, Exec.Dir.

Desc: Individuals interested in the history and genealogy of Northampton County, PA. Provides library service. Sponsors lectures and exhibits. Holds area festival. Conducts county wide historic resource survey and research by mail for a fee. *Founded:* 1906. *Members:* 411.

847 ■ Northern Antelope County Genealogical Society

PO Box 56   Ph: (402)893-4565
Orchard, NE 68764

Contact: Dorothy Zimmerman, Contact.

Desc: Genealogists united to gather, preserve, and disseminate genealogical and demographic information pertaining to northern Antelope County, NE.

848 ■ Northern Gila County Genealogical Society

PO Box 952   Ph: (520)474-2139
Payson, AZ 85547

Contact: Robert B. Biggs, Pres.

Desc: Promotes increased public interest in genealogy. Gathers, preserves, and disseminates genealogical information. *Founded:* 1980. *Members:* 77.

849 ■ Northern New York American-Canadian Genealogical Society

PO Box 1256   Ph: (518)834-5401
Plattsburgh, NY 12901-0120
E-mail: grcp@juno.com

Contact: Barbara Seguin, Pres.

Desc: Historians and genealogical researchers in northern New York, the New England states and Quebec, Canada. *Founded:* 1983. *Members:* 350.

850 ■ Northwest Arkansas Genealogical Society

PO Box 796   Ph: (501)273-3890
Rogers, AR 72757-0796

Contact: Marjorie Caskey, Pres.

Desc: Promotes research in genealogy and helps preserve historical records. *Founded:* 1971. *Members:* 320.

851 ■ Northwest Georgia Historical and Genealogical Society

PO Box 5063   Ph: (706)234-2110
Rome, GA 30162-5063
E-mail: pmillic@aol.com
URL: http://www.rootsweb.com/ganwhags/index.html

Contact: Jacqueline D. Kinzer, Sec.

Desc: Individuals interested in the genealogy and history of northwestern Georgia. Sponsors lectures and annual genealogy workshop. *Founded:* 1966. *Members:* 345.

852 ■ Northwest Territory Genealogical Society

Lewis Historical Library-LRC 22   Ph: (812)888-4330
Vincennes University   Fax: (812)888-5471
Vincennes, IN 47591

Contact: Donna Beeson, Editor.

Desc: Persons involved in genealogical research. Seeks to advance research in area records, preserve historical documents, and make such information more accessible to the public. *Founded:* 1980. *Members:* 215.

853 ■ Norton County Genealogical Society

One Washington Square   Ph: (913)877-2481
Norton, KS 67654

854 ■ Norvell Family Organization

26925 Cougar Pass Rd.   Ph: (619)749-9077
Rte. 6
Escondido, CA 92026

Contact: Wanda Norvell, Corr.Sec.

Desc: Persons researching the surnames Norvell, Norval, Norvil, Norville, and Nowell. Collects and disseminates information; maintains biographical archives and library. *Founded:* 1980. *Members:* 150.

855 ■ Obion County Historical Society

PO Box 241   Ph: (901)885-2322
Union City, TN 38281

Contact: Martha Clendenin, Corr.Sec.

Desc: Individuals interested in preserving the history of Obion County, TN. Promotes increased public interest in local history and genealogy.

856 ■ Oblinger/Oplinger Family Association

1008 N. Poplar St.   Ph: (610)437-2566
Whitehall, PA 18052

Contact: Don Oplinger, Pres.

Desc: Preserves the family history associated with the Oblinger, Uplinger, Oplinger, and derivative names. *Founded:* 1914. *Members:* 400.

857 ■ O'Carragher Clan Association: Caraher Family History Society

142 Rexford St.   Ph: (304)652-2009
Sistersville, WV 26175

Contact: D. Caraher Manning, Sec.-Editor.

Desc: Individuals and their descendants with the surname Carragher and its various spellings in the U.S., Australia, the United Kingdom, and Ireland. *Founded:* 1979.

858 ■ Oceana County Historical Genealogical Society

114 Dryden St.   Ph: (616)873-2600
Hart, MI 49420

Contact: Edwin Johnson, Pres.

Desc: Mission is to collect, preserve and disseiminate knowledge of the history of Oceana Co. *Founded:* 1967. *Members:* 200.

859 ■ Odell Family Association

718 Summerland Dr.
Henderson, NV 89015-8135
E-mail: stvhans@ix.netcom.com

Contact: James R. O'Dell, Pres.

Desc: Members of the Odell family. Promotes research and study of Odell family history and genealogy. *Founded:* 1992. *Members:* 200.

860 ■ O'Hare Family Association

9190 Oak Leaf Way   Ph: (916)791-0405
Granite Bay, CA 95746-8913
E-mail: dewald@prenticenet.com

Contact: Joe Dewald, Contact.

Desc: O'Hare family members and other interested individuals. Promotes study of O'Hare family history and genealogy.

861 ■ Ohio Genealogical Society

713 S. Main St.   Ph: (419)756-7294
Mansfield, OH 44907-1644   Fax: (419)756-8681
E-mail: ogs@ogs.org
URL: http://www.ogs.org

Contact: Fred E. Mayer, Pres.

Desc: Genealogists, historians, and individuals across the United States with interests in Ohio. Preserves genealogical and historical material regarding Ohio families and places. Conducts charitable activities. *Founded:* 1959. *Members:* 6600.

862 ■ Ohio Genealogical Society

713 S. Main St.   Ph: (419)756-7294
Mansfield, OH 44907-1644   Fax: (419)756-8681
E-mail: ogs@ogs.org
URL: http://www.ogs.org

Contact: Fred E. Mayer, Pres.

Desc: Genealogists, historians, libraries, and other interested individuals from throughout the U.S. Promotes genealogical research and the preservation of historical records in Ohio. *Founded:* 1959. *Members:* 6550.

863 ■ Ohio Genealogical Society, Ashland County Chapter

PO Box 681
Ashland, OH 44805-0681

Contact: Rita Kopp, Libn.

Founded: 1970. *Members:* 280.

864 ■ Ohio Genealogical Society, Athens County Chapter

65 N. Court St.
Athens, OH 45701-2506

865 ■ Ohio Genealogical Society, Auglaize County Chapter

PO Box 2021
Wapakoneta, OH 45895-0521
E-mail: acgsogs@geocities.com

Contact: Dan A. Bennett, Pres.

866 ■ Ohio Genealogical Society, Belmont County Chapter

PO Box 285   Ph: (614)484-4416
Barnesville, OH 43713-0285

Founded: 1978.

867 ■ Ohio Genealogical Society, Brown County Chapter

PO Box 83   Ph: (513)379-1519
Georgetown, OH 45121-0083

Contact: Barbara Dean, Contact.

Desc: Individuals engaged in genealogical research. Works to preserve Brown County, OH history and family records in order to help those searching for their ancestors. Holds annual seminar; operates library. Sponsors annual Heritage Harvest programs. *Founded:* 1977. *Members:* 300.

868 ■ Ohio Genealogical Society, Butler County Chapter

PO Box 2011   Ph: (513)422-1490
Middletown, OH 45044-2011

Contact: Charles Menke, Pres.

Founded: 1977. *Members:* 150.

869 ▪ Ohio Genealogical Society, Carroll County Chapter
59 3rd Street, NE.
Carrollton, OH 44615-1205   Ph: (216)627-2094

Contact: Emma McMannamy, Pres.

Desc: To promote and assist genealogists with their family history research. Mann a genealogy room containing wills, etc., in the courthouse. Publish "Carroll Cousins" six times a year. *Founded:* 1976. *Members:* 400.

870 ▪ Ohio Genealogical Society, Clermont County CHA
PO Box 394   Ph: (513)522-8458
Batavia, OH 45103-0394

Contact: Debra Geesner, Pres.

Founded: 1979.

871 ▪ Ohio Genealogical Society, Clinton County Chapter
PO Box 529   Ph: (513)382-4684
Wilmington, OH 45177

Contact: David Holmes, Pres.

Desc: Individuals interested in genealogy. Gathers, restores, and preserves historical demographic records. *Members:* 120.

872 ▪ Ohio Genealogical Society, Columbiana County Chapter
PO Box 861   Ph: (216)525-7540
Salem, OH 44460-0861

Contact: Pat McArtor, Pres.

Founded: 1976. *Members:* 200.

873 ▪ Ohio Genealogical Society, Crawford County Chapter
PO Box 92
Galion, OH 44833-0092

Contact: Winnie Kleinknecht, Contact.

Members: 500.

874 ▪ Ohio Genealogical Society, Darke County Chapter
PO Box 908
Greenville, OH 45331-0908

875 ▪ Ohio Genealogical Society, Delaware County Chapter
PO Box 1126   Ph: (614)369-3831
Delaware, OH 43015-8126

876 ▪ Ohio Genealogical Society, East Cuyahoga Chapter
PO Box 24182
Lyndhurst, OH 44124-0182

Contact: Lucinda Newton, Pres.

Founded: 1972. *Members:* 163.

877 ▪ Ohio Genealogical Society, Erie County Chapter
PO Box 1301
Sandusky, OH 44871-1301

Contact: Liz Proudfoot, Pres.

Founded: 1975. *Members:* 70.

878 ▪ Ohio Genealogical Society, Fairfield County Chapter
PO Box 1470   Ph: (740)653-2745
Lancaster, OH 43130-0570

E-mail: chapter@fairfieldgenealogy.org
URL: http://www.fairfieldgenealogy.org/

Contact: Patsy M. Kishler, Pres.

Desc: Individuals with an interest in local history and genealogy. Maintains genealogical collection at Fairfield County District Library; conducts educational programs. *Founded:* 1978. *Members:* 375.

879 ▪ Ohio Genealogical Society, Fulton County Chapter
PO Box 337   Ph: (419)825-5437
Swanton, OH 43558-0337
URL: http://www.rootsweb.com/ohfulton

Contact: Jana Sloan Broglin, Co.-Pres.

Founded: 1980.

880 ▪ Ohio Genealogical Society, Gallia County Chapter
PO Box 295   Ph: (740)446-7200
430 Second Ave.
Gallipolis, OH 45631-0295
E-mail: histsoc@zoomnet.net
URL: http://www.zoomnet/histsoc

Contact: Henrietta Evans, Corr.Sec.

Desc: Individuals with an interest in genealogy. Locates, restores, and preserves historic genealogical and demographic records. *Founded:* 1983. *Members:* 500.

881 ▪ Ohio Genealogical Society, Greene County Chapter
PO Box 706   Ph: (937)676-3711
Xenia, OH 45385

Contact: Gene Hollingsworth, Pres.

Desc: Individuals interested in genealogical research. Provides assistance to genealogists. Donates materials to Greene County Room, Xenia Public Library. *Founded:* 1980. *Members:* 200.

882 ▪ Ohio Genealogical Society, Hamilton County Chapter
PO Box 15865   Ph: (513)956-7078
Cincinnati, OH 45215-0865
URL: http://members.aol.com/ogshc

Contact: Kenny R. Burck, Pres.

Desc: Works to provide programs and resources for members to increase their knowledge of geneaology and family history. *Founded:* 1973. *Members:* 1250.

883 ▪ Ohio Genealogical Society, Hancock County Chapter
PO Box 672   Ph: (419)422-1737
Findlay, OH 45840-0672

884 ▪ Ohio Genealogical Society, Henry County Chapter
PO Box 231   Ph: (419)278-3616
Deshler, OH 43516

Desc: Works to encourage Henry County Ohio genealogical research and help preserve the family information that is available in Henry County.

885 ▪ Ohio Genealogical Society, Hocking County Chapter
PO Box 115   Ph: (740)385-6512
Rockbridge, OH 43149

Contact: Debbie Angle, Pres.

Desc: Individuals interested in the study of genealogy. Gathers and publishes census, birth, death, marriage, and cemetery records of interest to genealogists. *Founded:* 1989. *Members:* 150.

886 ▪ Ohio Genealogical Society, Holmes County Chapter
PO Box 136   Ph: (513)674-3741
Millersburg, OH 44654

Desc: Individuals interested in preserving the history of Holmes County, OH. Donates books and genealogical records to local libraries. *Members:* 400.

887 ▪ Ohio Genealogical Society, Huron County Chapter
PO Box 923   Ph: (419)668-1415
Norwalk, OH 44857-0923

888 ▪ Ohio Genealogical Society, Lorain County Chapter
PO Box 865   Ph: (216)458-4495
Elyria, OH 44036-0865

Contact: Barbara A. Reining, Pres.

Founded: 1983.

889 ▪ Ohio Genealogical Society, Lucas County Chapter
325 N. Michigan St.
Toledo, OH 43624-1614
URL: http://www.utoledo.edu/gried/lcogs.htm

Contact: Dorothy R. McHenry, Pres.

Desc: Persons interested in genealogy and in preserving historical and genealogical materials in Lucas County, OH. *Founded:* 1976. *Members:* 120.

890 ▪ Ohio Genealogical Society, Mahoning County Chapter
PO Box 9333
Boardman, OH 44513-9333

Contact: Jocelyn Wilms, Contact.

Desc: Gathers and disseminates genealogical data. Assists local and out-of-town members in their research. *Founded:* 1972. *Members:* 260.

891 ▪ Ohio Genealogical Society, Medina County Chapter
PO Box 804   Ph: (330)723-3877
Medina, OH 44258-0804

Contact: Julia L. Hach, Pres.

Desc: Individuals interested in genealogy and local history. Conducts research; assists beginning genealogists. *Founded:* 1976. *Members:* 75.

892 ▪ Ohio Genealogical Society, Morgan County Chapter
PO Box 418
McConnelsville, OH 43756-0418

Founded: 1981. *Members:* 200.

893 ▪ Ohio Genealogical Society, Morrow County Chapter
PO Box 401   Ph: (419)946-8910
Mt. Gilead, OH 43338-0401
E-mail: patron@bright.net
URL: http://www.rootsweb.com/ohmorrow

Contact: Betty Meier, Pres.

Desc: Persons interested in genealogy. Compiles cemetery books, conducts speaker meetings, donates materials to library. *Founded:* 1976. *Members:* 120.

894 ■ Ohio Genealogical Society, Noble County Chapter
PO Box 0174
Caldwell, OH 43724-0174

Contact: Susan K. Radcliff, Corresponding Sec.

895 ■ Ohio Genealogical Society, Ottawa County Chapter
PO Box 193   Ph: (419)732-2051
Port Clinton, OH 43452-0193

Contact: Wayne Dreier, Pres.

Founded: 1969. *Members:* 200.

896 ■ Ohio Genealogical Society, Parma Cuyahoga Chapter
PO Box 29509
Parma, OH 44129-0509

Contact: Rose C. Wolf, Pres.

Founded: 1981. *Members:* 40.

897 ■ Ohio Genealogical Society, Perry County Chapter
PO Box 275   Ph: (740)987-7646
Junction City, OH 43748-0275

Contact: Sue Saylor, Librarian and Corresponding Sec.

Desc: Promote and preserve genealogical research and materials. *Founded:* 1983. *Members:* 175.

898 ■ Ohio Genealogical Society, Pike County Chapter
PO Box 224   Ph: (614)226-2412
Waverly, OH 45690-0224

Contact: Opal McCracken, Co.Pres.

Founded: 1966.

899 ■ Ohio Genealogical Society, Seneca County Chapter
PO Box 157   Ph: (419)457-8082
Tiffin, OH 44883
E-mail: donrogier@aol.com

Contact: Donald J Rogier, Pres.

Desc: Genealogists united to gather, preserve, and disseminate genealogical and historical information pertaining to Seneca County, OH. *Founded:* 1981. *Members:* 385.

900 ■ Ohio Genealogical Society, Southwest Cuyahoga Chapter
13305 Pearl   Ph: (216)238-7644
Strongsville, OH 44136-7621

Contact: Louise Varisco, Pres.

Founded: 1981. *Members:* 54.

901 ■ Ohio Genealogical Society, Stark County Chapter
7300 Woodcrest, NE   Ph: (330)494-9574
North Canton, OH 44721

Contact: Wendell K. Edwards, Contact.

Desc: Individuals interested in genealogy. Gathers, preserves, and disseminates genealogical information. Assists researchers. *Founded:* 1973. *Members:* 350.

902 ■ Ohio Genealogical Society, Trumbull County Chapter
PO Box 309
Warren, OH 44482-0309

903 ■ Ohio Genealogical Society, Tuscarawas County Chapter
PO Box 141   Ph: (614)269-2602
New Philadelphia, OH
    44663-0141

Contact: Ketih Schaar, Pres.

Founded: 1968. *Members:* 650.

904 ■ Ohio Genealogical Society, Warren County Chapter
300 E. Silver St.   Ph: (513)695-1144
Lebanon, OH 45036

Contact: H. Robert Mehl, Pres.

Desc: Genealogists and others with an interest in family history in Warren County, OH. Gathers and publishes local birth, marriage, court, death, and cemetery records. *Founded:* 1981. *Members:* 165.

905 ■ Ohio Genealogical Society, Washington County Chapter
PO Box 2174   Ph: (740)373-1641
Marietta, OH 45750-7174

Contact: Sharon Cory Gardner, Pres.

Desc: Individuals interested in the genealogy and history of Washington County, OH. Collects tomb stone information for books. Prints books for genealogical research. Operates local genealogy and history room at the Washington County Public Library. *Founded:* 1983. *Members:* 230.

906 ■ Ohio Genealogical Society, Wood County Chapter
PO Box 722
Bowling Green, OH 43402-0722

Contact: Steve Charter, Pres.

Desc: Assists in family research, provides information for tracing ancestors. *Founded:* 1980. *Members:* 500.

907 ■ Ohio Genealogy Society, Jefferson County Chapter
PO Box 4712
Steubenville, OH 43952-8712
E-mail: fkrutill@weir.net
URL: http://www.rootsweb.com/ohjefogs

Contact: Julia A. Krutilla, Pres.

Desc: To promote and educate about family history through monthly meetings. We have for sale, various Jefferson County genealogy books to promote advancement of our goals. *Founded:* 1986. *Members:* 200.

908 ■ Okanogan County Genealogical Society
263 Old Riverside Hwy.   Ph: (509)826-1686
Omak, WA 98841

Contact: Lola Power, Exec. Officer.

Desc: Supports and promotes the genealogy in Okanogan County, WA. *Founded:* 1979. *Members:* 25.

909 ■ Oklahoma Confederate Archives
6626 S 76th E Ave.
Tulsa, OK 74133-0000

910 ■ Oklahoma Genealogical Society
PO Box 12986
Oklahoma City, OK 73157

Founded: 1955.

911 ■ Olmsted Archive Foundation
3700 E Alameda Ave., Ste. 500
Denver, CO 80209-3172

Contact: Susan Franki, Contact.

912 ■ Olmsted County Genealogical Society
PO Box 6411   Ph: (507)282-9447
Rochester, MN 55903

Founded: 1978. *Members:* 115.

913 ■ Onslow County Genealogical Society
PO Box 1739   Ph: (910)347-5287
Jacksonville, NC 28541-1739   Fax: (910)455-9796

Contact: JoAnn Becker, Pres.

Desc: Opens to all interested in genealogical research, the objectives are to stimulate the interest and support of genealogy, serve as a medium of exchange of research material, and to promote educational programs, publications, and workshops of genealogical study. *Founded:* 1989. *Members:* 85.

914 ■ Orange County California Genealogical Society
PO Box 1587
Orange, CA 92856-1587
URL: http://occgs.com

Contact: Pat Cohen, Pres.

Desc: To promote genealogical research and to assist members with family history research. *Founded:* 1963. *Members:* 850.

915 ■ Orange County Genealogical Society
PO Box 344   Ph: (812)723-3437
Paoli, IN 47454

Contact: Wilma Davis, Interim Pres.

Desc: Aides other genealogists and preserves the genealogy of the area. Educates those aspiring to do genealogy. *Founded:* 1982. *Members:* 200.

916 ■ Orangeburgh German Swiss Genealogical Society
PO Box 974   Ph: (803)534-1227
Orangeburg, SC 29116

Contact: Rev. Harold W. Syfrett, Contact.

Desc: Descendents of settlers of Orangeburg, SC from 1735-1800; others interested in Orangeburgh genealogy. *Founded:* 1981. *Members:* 700.

917 ■ Order of Americans of Armorial Ancestry
408 Sassafras Ct.   Ph: (410)515-1824
Bel Air, MD 21015-6022

Contact: Mr. George W. Hallgren, Sr., Pres.Gen.

Desc: Descendants of immigrants who were settlers in one of the 48 conteguous states and of the U.S. or descendants of those who had a proved right to bear coat of armor in their original countries. Objectives are to promote genealogical, biographical, and historical research on the ancestry of American families of armorial descent, and to print the research results. Membership is by invitation only. *Founded:* 1903. *Members:* 600.

918 ■ Order of the First Families of Mississippi 1699-1817
PO Box 821   Ph: (601)442-0018
Natchez, MS 39121-0821

Contact: A.K. Jones, Governor General.

Desc: Must be able to prove lineal descent from a native or resident of the territory now the State of Mississippi. Purpose is to perpetuate the memory of founders, preserve records relating to history and genealogy of Mississippi. Patriotic, literary and social as well as educational, historic and genealogical. *Founded:* 1968. *Members:* 750.

919 ■ Order of the Founders and Patriots of America

3892 College Ave.   Ph: (410)461-9591
Ellicott City, MD 21043   Fax: (410)461-9591
E-mail: wehland@erols.com

Contact: Joseph Kilbourn, Gov.Gen.

Desc: Men who are lineal descendants, in the male line of either parent, of an ancestor who settled in any of the colonies now included in the U.S. prior to May 13, 1657, and whose intermediate ancestors in the same line served the patriot cause during the American Revolution. Promotes discovery, collection, and preservation of records, documents, manuscripts, monuments, and history relating to the first colonists, and their ancestors and descendants. Maintains lineage papers of members. *Founded:* 1896. *Members:* 1200.

920 ■ Oregon County Genealogical Society

PO Box 324
Alton, MO 65606

Contact: Reva Baker, Pres.

Desc: Assists genealogical researchers who wish to check county records or library holdings. Conducts research. *Founded:* 1981.

921 ■ Oregon Genealogical Society

PO Box 10306   Ph: (503)746-7924
Eugene, OR 97440-2306

922 ■ Oregon Mennonite Historical and Genealogical Society

5326 Briar Knob Loop NE   Ph: (503)873-6406
Scotts Mills, OR 97375-9615

Contact: Jerry Barkman, Pres.

Desc: Individuals interested in preserving the history of the Mennonite community in Oregon. Conducts genealogical research. *Founded:* 1988.

923 ■ Orphan Train Heritage Society of America

614 E. Emma Ave., No. 115   Ph: (501)756-2780
Springdale, AR 72764-4634 Fax: (501)756-0769
E-mail: mej102339@aol.com

Contact: Mary Ellen Johnson, Dir.

Desc: Orphan train riders and their descendants, genealogists, and others interested in the orphan trains. (Orphan trains were used by the New York Children's Aid Society and other charitable institutions from 1854 to the early 1930's to relocate inner-city orphans to sparsely-populated rural areas where they were more likely to find adoptive homes.). Seeks to gather and disseminate information concerning orphan train riders and their biological families. *Founded:* 1986. *Members:* 510.

924 ■ Osborne County Genealogical and Historical Society

929 N. 2nd St   Ph: (785)346-2418
Osborne, KS 67473-1629

Contact: Lillian Zvolanek, Pres.

Desc: Seeks to pressure Osborne Co. history, answer queries. Working to preserve the vacated carnegie Library as research library. Seeks to update all the cemeteries in the County. *Founded:* 1975. *Members:* 61.

925 ■ Ottawa County Genealogical Society

PO Box 1383   Ph: (918)542-8550
Miami, OK 74355

Contact: Marjorie Patton, Pres.

Desc: Gathers and preserves Ottawa County, OK records of historical or genealogical interest. Conducts research. *Members:* 100.

926 ■ Otter Tail County Genealogical Society

1110 W. Lincoln Ave.   Ph: (218)736-6038
Fergus Falls, MN 56537

927 ■ Ouderkerk Family Genealogical Association

700 Atlanta Country Club Dr.   Ph: (770)956-9565
Marietta, GA 30067

Contact: H. John Ouderkirk, Pres.

Desc: Persons of Ouderkerk, Ouderkirk, Odekirk, and Oderkirk descent. Conducts genealogical research. *Founded:* 1981. *Members:* 450.

928 ■ Ouellette Family Association

13 rue Garant   Ph: (418)835-1254
Levis, PQ, Canada G6W 1N6 Fax: (418)835-3175
E-mail: ouelletj@icr.dl.net
URL: http://www3.sympatico.ca/jeannine.ouellet

Contact: Alphonse Ouellet, Dir.Gen.

Desc: Individuals with the surname Ouellet or Ouellette. Promotes interest in family history and genealogy. *Founded:* 1966. *Members:* 450.

929 ■ Owen Family Association

5213 Twinkle Dr.
Louisville, KY 40258
E-mail: ezacsia@prodigy.com
URL: http://www.geocities.com/Heartland/ridge/1402/

Contact: Arnold C. Owen, Pres.

Desc: Individuals interested in researching the Owen surname. *Founded:* 1985. *Members:* 205.

930 ■ Owsley Family Historical Society

916 Northridge Dr.   Ph: (706)324-7237
Columbus, GA 31904
E-mail: rbodine996@aol.com

Contact: Ronny O. Bodine, Pres.

Desc: Seeks to collect, preserve, and disseminate knowledge and information of a genealogical, historical, and biographic nature of the Owsley family, including Ousley and Housley family members. Promotes interest in accurate research in the fields of genealogy, history, and biography. *Founded:* 1978. *Members:* 250.

931 ■ Ozark County Genealogical and Historical Society

PO Box 4
Gainesville, MO 65655

Contact: Theresa Strong, Pres.

Founded: 1986. *Members:* 150.

932 ■ Pacific County Genealogical Society

PO Box 843   Ph: (360)665-6293
Ocean Park, WA 98640
E-mail: mjtaylor@aone.com

Contact: Ed Manning.

Founded: 1982. *Members:* 20.

933 ■ Paisley Family Society

2715 170th St.   Ph: (712)662-4140
Newell, IA 50568-7502
E-mail: emvogel@goodnet.com

Contact: Duncan W. Paisley of Westerlea, Chieftain.

Desc: Nonsectarian, nonpolitical family association for anyone with the surnames Paisley, Pasley, Pasly, or other variants most commonly originating in southwest Scotland and Ireland. Aims to promotes a spirit of kinship among members and stimulate interest in the surname Paisley and its variants by conducting genealogical and historical research programs. *Founded:* 1988. *Members:* 800.

934 ■ Palatines to America

Capital University   Ph: (614)236-8281
Box 101
Columbus, OH 43209-2394
E-mail: pal-am@juno.com
URL: http://www.PalAm.org

Contact: Beth A. Kroehler, Pres.

Desc: Researchers and other individuals interested in the migration of German-speaking people from Europe to America. Promotes interest in and study of German immigration; facilitates information exchange on the social and historical backgrounds of German-speaking immigrants. *Founded:* 1975. *Members:* 3290.

935 ■ Palm Beach County Genealogical Society

PO Box 1746   Ph: (407)832-3279
West Palm Beach, FL 33402

Contact: Dahrl E. Moore, Pres.

Desc: Individuals in Palm Beach County, FL interested in genealogical research. Maintains two rooms in local library. Holds two workshops per year. *Founded:* 1964. *Members:* 275.

936 ■ Palo Alto County Genealogical Society

Geneology Room, Smith   Ph: (712)842-4009
  Wellness/Library Center Fax: (712)852-4009
707 N. Superior
Emmetsburg, IA 50536
E-mail: meleners@ilcc.cc.ia.us

Contact: Vickie Kesler, Sec.

Desc: Gathers and disseminates historical and genealogical information pertaining to Palo Alto County, IA. Assist genealogical researchers. *Founded:* 1985. *Members:* 52.

937 ■ Pan-American Indian Association

8335 Sevigny   Ph: (941)731-7029
Fort Myers, FL 33917
E-mail: whitebear10@juno.com
URL: http://www.netonecom.net/shaman/
  membapp.htm

Contact: Chief Cindy Barnard, Contact.

Desc: Americans of Native American descent; students and other interested individuals. Assists persons with Native American heritage in researching their tribal roots. *Founded:* 1984. *Members:* 4100.

938 ■ Parenteau Family Association

3569 Gershwin Ln.
Oakdale, MN 55128-2931

939 ■ Park County Genealogy Society

PO Box 3056
Cody, WY 82414

940 ■ Parke Society

PO Box 590   Ph: (414)332-9984
Milwaukee, WI 53201
E-mail: 70741.2122@compuserve.com
URL: http://www.parke.org/

Contact: Theodore Edward Parks, Exec. Coordinator & Historian.

Desc: Persons interested in Parke ancestry. Includes immigrants and their descendants of Parke surname variations, whose origin was in the British Isles. Emphasizes research of Park(e)(s) genealogy. Serves as a clearinghouse of biographical and historical records. *Founded:* 1963. *Members:* 1100.

941 ■ Parker County Genealogical Society

1214 Charles   Ph: (817)598-4156
Weatherford, TX 76086

Contact: W. E. Bedinger, Pres.

Desc: Promotes genealogical research in the Parker County, TX area. *Founded:* 1969. *Members:* 175.

942 ■ Patt Family Association

172 Schoosett St.   Ph: (781)826-8032
Pembroke, MA 02359
E-mail: pattp300@aol.com

Contact: Robert M. Patt, Contact.

Desc: Individuals with the surname Patt and its variant spellings, including Patts, Pett, and Petts; other family members. Promotes study of Patt family history and genealogy.

943 ■ Pea River Historical and Genealogical Society

PO Box 628   Ph: (334)393-2901
Enterprise, AL 36331

Contact: Charles E. Hundley, Pres.

Desc: Individuals interested in the history and genealogy of southeastern AL. Operates Welcome Center, historical museum, and gift shop and Little Red Schoolhouse. *Founded:* 1970. *Members:* 238.

944 ■ Pellien/Jaeger/Loretan/Steiner/Ross Society

10435 W Concordia Ave.   Ph: (414)259-1315
Milwaukee, WI 53222   Fax: (414)771-8827
E-mail: pellien@execpc.com

Contact: Paul L. Pellien, Contact.

Desc: Individuals with an interest in the Pellien, Jaeger, Loretan, Steiner, and Ross families. Seeks to facilitate study of family history and genealogy. *Founded:* 1987.

945 ■ The Pennsylvania German Society

PO Box 244   Ph: (610)894-9551
212 S. Whiteoak St.   Fax: (610)894-9808
Kutztown, PA 19530-0244
URL: http://www.pgs.org

Contact: Robert M. Kline, Pres.

Desc: Descendants of German, Swiss, and Alsatian pioneers who settled in Pennsylvania and other states; others interested in collecting and preserving landmarks and records of the culture, language, and history of the Pennsylvania Germans (sometimes referred to as Pennsylvania Dutch). Maintains collection of PGS publications. Conducts workshops for educators. *Founded:* 1891. *Members:* 1100.

946 ■ Phelps Family Association of America

1002 Queen St.   Ph: (803)432-8432
Camden, SC 29020-3113
E-mail: phelps1953@yahoo.com

Contact: Dallas Leroy Phelps, Pres.

Desc: Disperses family news. *Founded:* 1987. *Members:* 150.

947 ■ Phillipe du Trieux Descendants Association

5602 Kingsway W
Cincinnati, OH 45215

Desc: Descendants of Phillipe du Trieux and his offspring. Promotes interest in, and study of, du Trieux family history and genealogy.

948 ■ Phillips County Genealogical Society

PO Box 114   Ph: (913)543-5325
Phillipsburg, KS 67661   Fax: (913)543-5374

Contact: Darlene Rumbaugh, Pres.

Desc: Individuals with an interest in genealogy. Provides research support to members.

949 ■ Pickens County Genealogical Society

PO Box 38
Gordo, AL 35466

950 ■ Pierre Bowdoin/Baudoin Family Association

903 Chatsworth Cir.   Ph: (512)442-7932
Austin, TX 78704

Contact: Jack R. Sodke, Contact.

Desc: Compiles and disseminates research reports and information on Pierre Bowdoin/Baudoin and his descendants. Maintains pedigree charts, family group sheets, descendancy charts, individual notes, and 15,000 names of kin. *Founded:* 1982.

951 ■ Pierre Chastain Family Association

Route 2, Box 289-J3   Ph: (601)289-9675
Kosciusko, MS 39090

Contact: William "Bill" J. Chastain, Pres.

Desc: Individuals and families interested in the Chastain family history. Dedicated to the preservation of Chastain records and information. Includes families with the surnames of Chastain, Chasteen, Chastaine, Shasteen, Shastine, Chasten, Castine, and Shastid as descendants of Dr. Pierre Chastain, a French Huguenot who migrated to America in 1700. *Founded:* 1975. *Members:* 400.

952 ■ Pilgrim Society

Pilgrim Hall Museum   Ph: (508)746-1620
75 Court St.   Fax: (508)747-4228
Plymouth, MA 02360
URL: http://www.pilgrimhall.org

Contact: Peggy M. Baker, Dir.

Desc: Seeks to collect, preserve, and display artifacts and written and photographic records relating to the pilgrims, Plymouth Colony, and the Town of Plymouth; encourages research in these areas; maintains Forefathers Monument and Pilgrim Hall. Operates museum. Conducts research and educational programs. *Founded:* 1820. *Members:* 1100.

953 ■ Pilgrims of the United States

122 E 58th St., 2nd Fl.
New York, NY 10022-1909

Contact: Hugh Bullock, G.B.E., Pres.

Desc: Promotes goodwill and understanding in Anglo-American relations by organizing speeches of prominent English and American citizens to clarify problems arising between the two countries. An incoming British ambassador to the United States has, traditionally, made his first speech at a United States Pilgrim dinner. *Founded:* 1903. *Members:* 1000.

954 ■ Pinellas Genealogy Society

PO Box 1614   Ph: (813)586-7410
Largo, FL 33779-1614

Contact: Marjory Hazel, Contact.

Desc: Individuals interested in genealogy. Gathers and disseminates information; assists researchers. Maintains genealogy collection at the Largo Public Library. *Founded:* 1972. *Members:* 150.

955 ■ Pipestone County Historical Society

113 S. Hiawatha Ave.   Ph: (507)825-2563
Pipestone, MN 56164
E-mail: pipctymu@rconnect.com
URL: http://www.pipestone.mn.us/museum/homepa.htm

Contact: Chris Roelfsema-Hummel, Dir.

Desc: Objectives are the discovery, preservation, and dissemination of knowledge about the history of Pipestone County, discovery and collection of materials which illustrate this history and conducting and fostering of historical research for the county and region. The society maintains a history museum, one-room school house, research materials and facilities, and provides programming for local and area schools, community groups, and other interested parties. *Founded:* 1880. *Members:* 450.

956 ■ Piscataqua Pioneers

314 High St.   Ph: (603)882-3949
Hampton, NH 03842-4004

Contact: Mr. William Drew, Registrar.

Desc: Direct descendants of those who settled prior to July 1776 in the Piscataqua Valley, location of the first settlement in New Hampshire. Works to secure and preserve the records of the Piscataqua Valley pioneers and their descendants. *Founded:* 1905. *Members:* 700.

957 ■ Pittsburg County Genealogical and Historical Society

113 E. Carl Albert Pkwy.   Ph: (918)426-0388
McAlester, OK 74501-5039
E-mail: tobucksy@050-ext.pittsburg.ok.us
URL: http://oso-ext.pittsburg.ok.us/tobucksy

Contact: Thurman Shuller, M.D.

Desc: Individuals interested in local history and genealogy. Conducts research; gathers and disseminates information. *Founded:* 1979. *Members:* 200.

958 ■ Placer County Genealogical Society

PO Box 7385   Ph: (530)887-2646
Auburn, CA 95604-7385
URL: http://www.webcom.com/gunruh/pcgs.html

Contact: Barbara E. Leak, Pres.

Desc: Persons with an interest in genealogy. Provides education in genealogy research techniques; sponsors genealogy section at Auburn-Placer County Library. *Founded:* 1980. *Members:* 240.

959 ■ Platt Family Association

132 Platt Ln.   Ph: (203)878-6094
Milford, CT 06460
E-mail: rnplatt@ix.netcom.com

Contact: Richard N. Platt, Jr., Pres.

Desc: Members of the Platt family. Promotes interest in family history and genealogy; identifies and unites Platt family members. *Founded:* 1982. *Members:* 150.

960 ■ Platte County Genealogical Society

PO Box 103   Ph: (816)858-3599
Platte City, MO 64079

Contact: Betty N. Soper, Exec.Sec.

Desc: Works to preserve the history, architecture, and genealogy of Platte County, MO. Maintains historic building and museum. *Founded:* 1945. *Members:* 700.

961 ■ Plymouth County Genealogists
PO Box 7025   Ph: (508)588-2253
Brockton, MA 02301-7025
E-mail: mkxj92a@prodigy.com
URL: http://www.rootsweb.com/maplymou/
pcgsmain.htm

Contact: Diane Gusciora, Pres.

Founded: 1975. *Members:* 180.

962 ■ Polish Genealogical Society of America
984 N. Milwaukee Ave.
Chicago, IL 60622
E-mail: pgsamerica@aol.com
URL: http://www.pgsa.org

Contact: Paul S. Valasek, DDS, Pres.

Desc: Family tree hobbyists involved in researching ancestors from Poland (including Lithuanians and Jews and
Rusyns) and areas formerly associated with Poland. Promotes Polish genealogical study and establishes communication among researchers. Informs members of new
sources of information. Maintains ancestor index card
file, accessible to all researchers. *Founded:* 1978. *Members:* 2000.

**963 ■ Polish Genealogical Society of
Connecticut**
8 Lyle Rd.   Ph: (860)223-5596
New Britain, CT 06053-2104
E-mail: pgsne2@aol.com
URL: http://www.members.aol.com/pgsne2

Contact: Jonathan D. Shea, Pres.

Desc: Individuals of Polish origin compiling family histories. Promotes the study of Polish-American genealogy
through publications, lectures, and seminars. Collects archival materials. Maintains resource center. Sponsors genealogical research tours to Eastern Europe. *Founded:*
1984. *Members:* 450.

964 ■ Pontius Family Association
2009 Garden Dr.   Ph: (518)374-1965
Niskayuna, NY 12309-2309   Fax: (518)374-4453
E-mail: pontiusjw@aol.com

Contact: James W. Pontius, Archivist.

Desc: Individuals with the surnames Pontius, Pontious,
Punches, Pontzius, Poncy, and Pounrious; descendants of
individuals with these surnames. Gathers and disseminates
information on the Pontius family and its activities; fosters
genealogical research. Maintains Pontius family registry.
Founded: 1968. *Members:* 390.

**965 ■ Pottawattamie County Genealogical
Society**
Box 394   Ph: (712)322-4051
Council Bluffs, IA 51502
E-mail: geniebuff1@novia.net
URL: http://www.rootsweb.com/iapottaw/

Contact: Marsha Pilger, Pres.

Desc: Individuals interested in genealogy. Gathers, preserves, and disseminates genealogical information; provides research assistance. *Founded:* 1992. *Members:* 220.

966 ■ Prall Family Association
14104 Piedras Rd. NE   Ph: (505)299-8386
Albuquerque, NM 87123-2323

Contact: Dan Thomas, Pres.

Desc: Individuals interested in the history and genealogy
of the Prall and related families. Promotes historical and
genealogical research and study. Seeks to identify and
unite Prall family members. *Founded:* 1986. *Members:*
140.

967 ■ Preble County Genealogical Society
450 S. Barron St.   Ph: (937)456-4250
Eaton, OH 45320   Fax: (937)456-6092
E-mail: pcroom@intinet.com
URL: http://www.pcdl.lib.atsoh.us

Contact: Barbara Cox, Pres.

Desc: Individuals with ancestry in Preble County, Ohio;
interested others. Promotes genealogical and historical
research. Provides materials and instruction in genealogy
matters. *Founded:* 1986. *Members:* 175.

**968 ■ Predmore - Pridmore - Pridemore -
Pregmore Association**
545 Jefferson   Ph: (208)423-4293
Kimberly, ID 83341
E-mail: how@micron.net

Contact: Howard Johnston, Contact.

Desc: Individuals with the surname Predmore and its
variant spellings; other Predmore family members. Encourages study of Predmore family history and genealogy.
Founded: 1985. *Members:* 40.

969 ■ Premm Family Association
9190 Oak Leaf Way   Ph: (916)791-0405
Granite Bay, CA 95746-8913
E-mail: dewald@prenticenet.com

Contact: Joe Dewald, Contact.

Desc: Individuals with the surname Premm and other
Premm family members. Promotes Premm family genealogical research.

970 ■ Presbyterian Women
100 Witherspoon St.   Ph: (502)569-5365
Louisville, KY 40202   Free: 800-872-3283
                              Fax: (502)569-8026

Contact: Gladys Strachan, Exec.Dir.

Desc: Purposes are to promote the Presbyterian church
and its teachings and to provide a forum for Presbyterian
women. Administers to the needs of individuals through
missions worldwide; defends the rights of those who are
economically and politically powerless; makes political
and social commitments to issues involving justice, peace,
freedom, and world hunger; examines topics such as apart-
heid, child abandonment, rape, divorce, and displaced
women. Participates in Presbyterian educational ministry
and the training of church leaders. Offers economic justice
consultations; organizes overseas study seminars and leadership and training events; conducts local, regional, and
national workshops. Maintains speakers' bureau, biographical archives, and library; offers charitable program;
compiles statistics. *Founded:* 1988. *Members:* 400000.

971 ■ Presidential Families of America
7011 Spring Briar St.   Ph: (407)896-4531
San Antonio, TX 78209-4283

Contact: Dr. Lawrence Kent, Founder.

Desc: Persons who share direct or collateral kinship with
any American president. Encourages research regarding
family histories of presidents of the United States of
America. *Founded:* 1995.

**972 ■ Prince Georges County Genealogical
Society**
PO Box 819   Ph: (301)262-4869
Bowie, MD 20718

Contact: Carole Begenwald, Corr.Sec.

Desc: Individuals interested in genealogy. Conducts research and educational programs. Maintains research
center.

**973 ■ Prince William County Genealogical
Society**
PO Box 2019   Ph: (703)361-0173
Manassas, VA 20108-0812
E-mail: takelley@erois.com
URL: http://www.rootsweb.com/takelley/pwcgshtm

Desc: Genealogists. Gathers, preserves, and disseminates
historical and genealogical information pertaining to
Prince William County, VA. *Members:* 200.

974 ■ Progenitor Genealogical Society
PO Box 345   Ph: (435)245-9386
Paradise, UT 84328

Contact: Ronald Allan Bremer, Pres.

Founded: 1985. *Members:* 12.

975 ■ Prowers County Genealogical Society
PO Box 928   Ph: (719)336-4507
Lamar, CO 81052-0928

Contact: Donita Price, Pres.

Members: 21.

976 ■ Pruitt/Prewitt Family Association
1800 NW 81st St.
Des Moines, IA 50325
E-mail: rprewitt1@juno.com

Contact: Richard A. Prewitt, Contact.

Desc: Formed as a central depository for all Prewitt/Pruitt/
Pruett family information. *Founded:* 1964. *Members:* 250.

977 ■ Puget Sound Genealogical Society
1026 Sidney Ave., Ste. 110
Port Orchard, WA 98366-4298

978 ■ Purcell Family of America
3929 Southview Ave.   Ph: (937)426-0460
Dayton, OH 45432-2121

Contact: Alice Crist Purcell, Editor/Sec.

Desc: Shares news of Purcell/Pursell/Pursley family.
Founded: 1972. *Members:* 350.

**979 ■ Purser - Storer Family History
Association**
103 Riggins Ct.
Folsom, CA 95630-5222

Contact: David A. Storer, Contact.

980 ■ Pursuing Our Italian Names Together
PO Box 2977   Ph: (310)832-4041
Palos Verdes, CA 90274
E-mail: POINTER01@AOL.com

Contact: Thomas Militello, M.D., Editor.

Desc: Individuals of Italian descent. Promotes genealogical
and historical research into Italian ancestry. *Founded:*
1987. *Members:* 4000.

981 ■ Putnam County Genealogical Society
PO Box 403   Ph: (419)523-3747
Ottawa, OH 45875-0403

Contact: Linda Hermiller, Corr.Sec.

Desc: Individuals interested in the history and genealogy
of Putnam County, OH. Gathers, preserves, and disseminates genealogical and historical information. *Founded:*
1984. *Members:* 190.

982 ■ Rader Association
2633 Gilbert Way   Ph: (916)366-6833
Rancho Cordova, CA 95670

E-mail: jim@rader.org
URL: http://www.rader.org

Contact: Jim Rader, Contact.

Desc: Persons researching the surnames Rader, Rotter, Roder, and Raeder. *Founded:* 1991.

983 ■ Ralph Shepard Family Organization
1672 Forests Ct. NE   Ph: (770)457-6644
Atlanta, GA 30341

Contact: Joseph E. Shepard, Contact.

Desc: Descendants of Ralph Shepard, who arrived in North America in 1635. Promotes communication and exchange of information among Shepard family historians and genealogists.

984 ■ Randolph County Genealogical Society
PO Box 4394   Ph: (910)318-6815
Asheboro, NC 27204

Desc: Individuals interested in genealogy and local history. Locates, collects, restores, and preserves historic demographic records and historical artifacts.

985 ■ Randolph County Historical Genealogical Society
2212 E. Greenville Pike   Ph: (765)584-4323
Winchester, IN 47394-9429

Contact: Monisa Wisener, Contact.

Desc: Collects and preserves family and local historical artifacts for use by genealogical researchers and museum visitors. *Founded:* 1979. *Members:* 200.

986 ■ Rawlin(g)s-Rollin(g)s Family History Association
4918 Kenneth Ave.   Ph: (916)482-8261
Carmichael, CA 95608

Contact: Katherine Rawlings, Editor.

Desc: Persons interested in genealogical and historical information related to the Rawlin(g)s, Rollin(g)s, and Rollens families. Traces these and other spellings of the name. *Founded:* 1988. *Members:* 195.

987 ■ Rawlins County Genealogical Society
102 S. 6th St.   Ph: (913)626-3805
PO Box 203
Atwood, KS 67730

Contact: Mrs. Wayne Harper, Pres.

Desc: Works to stimulate interest in genealogy and gather and preserve historical and genealogical data. Conducts educational programs; plans to operate library. *Founded:* 1980.

988 ■ Ray County Genealogical Association
901 W. Royle St.   Ph: (816)776-2305
Richmond, MO 64085
E-mail: kproffitt@raycounty.net

Contact: Carol Proffitt, Pres.

Desc: Individuals with an interest in genealogy. Works to locate and preserve historical demographic records. *Founded:* 1989. *Members:* 275.

989 ■ Reed-Reid Clearinghouse
207 Auburn Dr.   Ph: (706)278-1504
Dalton, GA 30720

Contact: Joseph W. Reid, Contact.

Desc: Provides family history information for those with the surname Reid, its variants, and the names Carter, Bagley, Daniel, Pryor, Garder, Glawson, Wilson, Bailey, Brown, Suggs. Serves as a clearinghouse for genealogical data. *Founded:* 1980.

990 ■ Reimer Genealogy Center Worldwide
Fawn Ridge Rd.   Ph: (518)494-3347
Box 121
Warrensburg, NY 12885-0121
E-mail: rgcw@juno.com

Contact: Arthur A. Reimer, Dir.

Desc: Individuals interested in the Reimer genealogy and family history. Includes variations of the German surname. Variations include the surnames Remer, Rymer, Reemer, Riemer, Raemiser, Raimarus, Raimer, Ramer, Rammer, Reamer, Reymor, Reymar, and Reymer. Exchanges genealogical records. *Founded:* 1953. *Members:* 5000.

991 ■ Reno County Genealogical Society
PO Box 5   Ph: (316)663-2804
Hutchinson, KS 67504-0005

992 ■ Renville County Genealogical Society
PO Box 331   Ph: (320)329-3215
Renville, MN 56284

Contact: Denise O. Connor, Pres.

Desc: Maintains Renville County history. Conducts own research and assists others in research. *Founded:* 1985. *Members:* 168.

993 ■ Research Foundation for Jewish Immigration
570 7th Ave., 11th Fl.   Ph: (212)921-3871
New York, NY 10018   Fax: (212)575-1918

Contact: Herbert A. Strauss, Sec. & Coor.

Desc: Educational foundation established for the preparation, research, writing, and editing of the history of German-speaking immigrants of the Nazi period and their world-wide resettlement and acculturation. Holds jointly with the Institut fur Zeitgeschichte in Munich, Federal Republic of Germany, archives of 25,000 biographies of outstanding emigres of the Nazi period. *Founded:* 1971.

994 ■ Reynolds County Genealogy and Historical Society
PO Box 281   Ph: (573)663-3233
Ellington, MO 63638-0281

Contact: Lee Sylcox, Pres.

Desc: Individuals interested in preserving the history of Reynolds County, MO. *Founded:* 1983. *Members:* 300.

995 ■ Reynolds Family Association
274 Fairview Ave.
Painted Post, NY 14870
E-mail: reynoldsml@corning.com

Contact: Melody L. Reynolds, Contact.

Desc: Individuals interested in the history and genealogy of Reynolds families who settled in colonial America and Canada. Collects and maintains a permanent record of Reynolds family history; also studies variant spellings of the surname. Assists in genealogical research for members. Works to establish acquaintance and continued communication among Reynolds families; fosters recognition of a common ancestry. Maintains library. *Founded:* 1892. *Members:* 500.

996 ■ Rhode Island Genealogical Society
PO Box 433
Greenville, RI 02828-0433

Members: 800.

997 ■ Rich Family Association
16 Braddock Ln.   Ph: (508)432-2883
Harwyck Port, MA 02648

Contact: Robert L. Park, Pres.

Desc: Persons descended from the Rich family. Assists members in tracing their ancestry. *Founded:* 1872. *Members:* 600.

998 ■ Richard "Rock" Taylor Descendants
2776 County Rd. 27   Ph: (419)483-2363
Bellevue, OH 44811

Contact: Kate Griffin Jett, Contact.

Desc: Seeks to accumulate and share information on the descendants of Richard "Rock" Taylor and his wife, Ruth Burgess, beginning circa 1650 and continuing to the present. *Founded:* 1990.

999 ■ Richland County Genealogical and Historical Society
PO Box 202   Ph: (618)869-2425
Olney, IL 62450

Contact: Jan Doan, Pres.

Desc: Collects genealogical and historical material for Richland County, IL, and the surrounding area. *Founded:* 1977. *Members:* 275.

1000 ■ Richmond Area Historical and Genealogical Society
PO Box 68   Ph: (810)727-3001
Richmond, MI 48062-0068   Fax: (810)727-5817
E-mail: ubatrans@gte.net

Contact: Laurel A. Emerson, Contact.

Desc: Individuals committed to the preservation of Richmond, MI and neighboring townships. *Founded:* 1990. *Members:* 69.

1001 ■ Rickey Family Association
235 15th St. NE   Ph: (503)363-4389
Salem, OR 97301-4228
E-mail: rickeyroot@aol.com

Contact: Stanton M. Rickey, Pres.

Desc: Descendants of the Rickey or Rickeys surname. Works to preserve the Rickey family heritage. *Founded:* 1989. *Members:* 1100.

1002 ■ Riley County Genealogical Society
2005 Claflin Road   Ph: (785)565-6495
Manhattan, KS 66502
E-mail: rcgs@flinthills.com
URL: http://www.flinthills.com/regs

Contact: M. Jane Brown, Brd.Chm.

Desc: Anyone interested in preserving family and community records is invited. Objectives: to create and foster an interest in genealogy, to preserve genealogical data, to preserve early records through publication and to aid members in compiling genealogies. Holds classes, workshops, and regular meetings. *Founded:* 1963. *Members:* 230.

1003 ■ Risley Family Association
PO Box 552   Ph: (716)637-6419
Clarkson, NY 14430
URL: http://members.aol.com/RisleyFA/index.html

Contact: Roy Goold, Pres.

Desc: Families whose members are descendants of Richard Risley, Sr., and members of the Wrisley, Rizley, and Riseley families in America. Makes available to members genealogical, historical, and biographical data about the Risley family in the U.S. and England. *Founded:* 1889. *Members:* 711.

1004 ▪ Roane County Genealogical Society
PO Box 297   Ph: (423)376-9905
Kingston, TN 37763

Contact: Denise May, Pres.

Desc: Individuals with an interest in genealogy. Collects and preserves demographic records. *Founded:* 1984. *Members:* 250.

1005 ▪ Robert Bruce Bradley Family Organization
PO Box 183   Ph: (608)759-2755
Benton, WI 53803

Contact: Lynne Bradley Montgomery, Chair.

Desc: Promotes family name. *Founded:* 1990. *Members:* 60.

1006 ▪ Robert Shankland Family Organization
2048 Forest Park Dr.
Jackson, MS 49201

Contact: Ron Shankland, Contact.

Desc: Members of the Shankland family. Seeks to identify and unite Shankland family members; encourages interest in family history and genealogy. *Founded:* 1990.

1007 ▪ Rochester Genealogical Society
PO Box 10501   Ph: (716)234-2584
Rochester, NY 14610
E-mail: thurston@frontiernet.net
URL: http://home.cznet.net/halsey/rqs.html

Contact: Roy Thurston, Pres.

Founded: 1939. *Members:* 400.

1008 ▪ Rockafellow Family Association
1425 Watersmeet Lake Rd.
Eagle River, WI 54521-8916
E-mail: maxrock@newnorth.net

Contact: Max E. Rockafellow, Contact.

Desc: Members of the Rockafellow family. Seeks to identify and unite Rockafellow family members. *Founded:* 1990.

1009 ▪ Rockingham Society of Genealogists
PO Box 81   Ph: (603)436-5824
Exeter, NH 03833-0081
E-mail: path3242@aol.com

Contact: Maynard Waltz, Contact.

Desc: Conducts genealogical research and aiding in the search for ancestry. *Founded:* 1976. *Members:* 120.

1010 ▪ Rockwood Area Historical and Genealogical Society
358 Market St.
Rockwood, PA 15557-1125

1011 ▪ Rogers Clan
Hwy. 87 N.   Ph: (409)565-4751
PO Box 340
Burkeville, TX 75932

Contact: Helen Rogers Skelton, Genealogist.

Desc: Descendants of the Rogers and Skelton families. Promotes and researches family history. *Founded:* 1975. *Members:* 152.

1012 ▪ Roots and Gold Dust Genealogical Society
PO Box 1354
Diamond Springs, CA 95619-1354

Contact: Lynette Mizell, Contact.

1013 ▪ Rose Family Association
1474 Montelegre Dr.   Ph: (408)268-2137
San Jose, CA 95120-4831   Fax: (408)268-2165
E-mail: christiner@compuserve.com
URL: http://ourworld.compuserve.com/homepages/
        ChristineR

Contact: Christine Rose, Contact.

Desc: Members of the Rose family and other interested individuals. Promotes study of Rose family history and genealogy. *Founded:* 1966. *Members:* 700.

1014 ▪ Ross County Genealogical Society
444 Douglas Ave.   Ph: (740)773-2715
PO Box 6352
Chillicothe, OH 45601-6352

Contact: Caroline L. Whitten, Pres.

Desc: Works to collect, preserve, and make available genealogical and historical records. Promotes historical education. *Founded:* 1973. *Members:* 600.

1015 ▪ Rudd Family Research Association
3340 Del Sol Blvd. No. 214   Ph: (619)690-9690
San Diego, CA 92154
E-mail: ruddfamres@aol.com

Contact: Norman N. Rudd, Founder.

Desc: Primarily descendants of the nine children of Gordon Arthur Rudd and Alicia Wellwood Rudd, both born in the Irish midlands in the late 1700s, and other Rudd descendants of Irish and English ancestry interested in their family history. Promotes social activities for members, genealogical research, and information exchanges. *Founded:* 1983. *Members:* 2000.

1016 ▪ Runkle Family Association
PO Box 14   Ph: (609)294-0597
Ringoes, NJ 08551

Contact: Audrey McCaffrey, Pres.

Desc: Individuals with the surname Runkle or its variant spellings. Promotes study of Runkle family history and genealogy. *Founded:* 1990. *Members:* 35.

1017 ▪ Russian Nobility Association in America
971 1st Ave.   Ph: (212)755-7528
New York, NY 10022

Contact: Alexis Scherbatow, Pres.

Desc: Persons listed in nobility archives of the former Russian Imperial Senate. Compiles immigration records of former Russian nobles in America. Provides assistance to the needy. Maintains biographical archives and library of 2000 volumes of historical and genealogical material. *Founded:* 1938. *Members:* 90.

1018 ▪ Sabin Association
13380 S Hwy. 211   Ph: (503)829-7444
PO Box 577
Molalla, OR 97038
E-mail: ptorsen@molalla.net

Contact: Patricia Torsen, Contact.

Desc: Members of the Sabin and related families. Seeks to identify and unite Sabin family members; promotes study of Sabin family history and genealogy. *Founded:* 1992. *Members:* 167.

1019 ▪ Saginaw Genealogical Society
Saginaw Public Library   Ph: (517)755-0904
505 Janes
Saginaw, MI 48607

Contact: Connie Snyder, Pres.

Desc: Individuals interested in the genealogy of Saginaw, MI. *Founded:* 1971. *Members:* 259.

1020 ▪ St. Andrew's Society of the State of New York
3 W. 51st St.   Ph: (212)807-1730
New York, NY 10019   Fax: (212)807-1877

Contact: Victor Stewart, Esq., CNT.

Desc: Men of Scottish birth or descent. Sponsors scholarships and an Almoner's program which helps Scottish natives or persons of Scottish descent who are in distress. *Founded:* 1756. *Members:* 950.

1021 ▪ St. Bernard Genealogical Society
PO Box 271   Ph: (504)271-0896
Chalmette, LA 70044   Fax: (504)271-0896

Contact: Virginia McElroy, Pres.

Desc: Individuals with an interest in history and genealogy. *Founded:* 1977. *Members:* 200.

1022 ▪ St. Charles County Genealogical Society
PO Box 715   Ph: (314)724-6668
St. Charles, MO 63302
URL: http://www.rootsweb.com/mosccgs/

Contact: Marva Lee Roellig, Pres.

Founded: 1974. *Members:* 91.

1023 ▪ St. David's Society of the State of New York
3 W. 51st. St.   Ph: (212)397-1346
New York, NY 10019-6909   Fax: (212)422-5480

Contact: James Thomas, Hon.Sec.

Desc: Welshmen, their descendants, and those connected with them. Collects and preserves information on Wales, its people, and their descendants in the U.S.; cultivates knowledge of the history of Wales and of the Welsh language and literature; aids distressed Welshmen and their descendants. Sponsors festival. *Founded:* 1801. *Members:* 311.

1024 ▪ St. George's Society of New York
175 9th Ave.   Ph: (212)924-1434
New York, NY 10011-4977   Fax: (212)727-1566
E-mail: stgeony@aol.com

Contact: John Shannon, Exec.Dir.

Desc: Serves families and individuals of British or Commonwealth birth or descent. Engages solely in charitable activities. *Founded:* 1770. *Members:* 700.

1025 ▪ St. Marys Genealogical Society
PO Box 1109   Ph: (301)373-5764
Leonardtown, MD 20650

Contact: Julia P. Palmer, Pres.

Desc: Individuals interested in genealogical research. *Founded:* 1977. *Members:* 300.

1026 ▪ St. Nicholas Society of the City of New York
122 E. 58th St.   Ph: (212)753-7175
New York, NY 10022

Desc: Membership limited to male descendants of persons living in New York City or New York State prior to 1785. Founded by author Washington Irving to preserve the historical heritage of New York City and to sustain its future. *Founded:* 1835. *Members:* 510.

1027 ▪ Saint Nicholas Society of the City of New York

122 E. 58th St. Ph: (212)753-7175
New York, NY 10022 Fax: (212)980-0769

Contact: Mrs. Edward S. Jones, Exec.Dir.

Desc: Membership by invitation restricted to male descendants of persons living in New York State prior to 1785. Founded by author Washington Irving to preserve the historical heritage of New York City and to sustain its future. *Founded:* 1835. *Members:* 500.

1028 ▪ Saline County Genealogical Society

PO Box 24
Crete, NE 68333

Contact: Tom Harrison, Pres.

Desc: Individuals interested in preserving the history of Saline County, NE. Gathers, preserves, and disseminates genealogical and historical information. Conducts research and educational programs. *Founded:* 1992. *Members:* 70.

1029 ▪ Saline County Genealogical Society

PO Box 4 Ph: (618)252-1216
Harrisburg, IL 62946
E-mail: kstill@midamer.net

Contact: Charles Hankins, Pres.

Desc: Preserves and records records. *Founded:* 1986. *Members:* 275.

1030 ▪ San Angelo Genealogical and Historical Society

PO Box 3453 Ph: (915)949-3223
San Angelo, TX 76902 Fax: (915)942-7035

Contact: Harold T. Chandler, Pres.

Desc: Individuals interested in preserving the history of San Angelo, TX and surrounding areas. Conducts educational activities. *Founded:* 1974. *Members:* 200.

1031 ▪ San Diego African-American Genealogy Research Group

PO Box 740240 Ph: (619)566-7566
San Diego, CA 92174-0240 Fax: (619)566-1083
E-mail: marvh@prodigy.net

Contact: Milton Hines, Pres.

Desc: Works to encourage, teach, enable family history research and genealogy. *Founded:* 1996. *Members:* 30.

1032 ▪ San Diego County Genealogical Association

PO Box 422 Ph: (619)789-2534
Ramona, CA 92065

Contact: Jacqueline Beck, Pres.

1033 ▪ San Diego Geneological Society

1050 Pioneer Way, Ste. E Ph: (619)588-0065
El Cajon, CA 92020 Fax: (619)588-0056
URL: http://www.genealogy.org/sdgs/welcome.html

Contact: Phyllis B. Hoke, Pres.

Founded: 1947. *Members:* 640.

1034 ▪ San Francisco Bay Area Jewish Genealogical Society

PO Box 471616 Ph: (415)666-0188
San Francisco, CA 94147
E-mail: eandr@ix.netcom.com
URL: http://www.jewishgen.org/sfbajgs

Contact: Rodger Rosenberg, Pres.

Desc: Open to individuals interested in Jewish genealogy. Dedicated to the development, preservation, and distribution of Jewish genealogical knowledge and material, and the sharing of techniques and tools with others who may be searching their Jewish roots. Provides assistance to families researching their genealogy. Donates to local archives and libraries. *Founded:* 1978. *Members:* 260.

1035 ▪ San Marcos/Hays County Genealogical Society

PO Box 503
San Marcos, TX 78666

Contact: Ella Smith, Pres.

Founded: 1990.

1036 ▪ Santa Barbara County Genealogical Society, Inc.

PO Box 1303 Ph: (805)884-9909
Goleta, CA 93116-1303
E-mail: sbcgs@juno.com
URL: http://www.compuology.com/sbarbara

Contact: Emily Aasted, Pres.

Desc: Works to promote interest in genealogy research, to publish genealogical materials, to provide genealogical educational opportunities, and to maintain a genealogical library. *Founded:* 1972. *Members:* 475.

1037 ▪ Santa Clara County Historical and Genealogical Society

2635 Homestead Road Ph: (408)615-2986
Santa Clara, CA 95051-5387
URL: http://www.catpher.com/scchgs/

Contact: Charlotte Scoble, VP.

Desc: Individuals interested in genealogy. Conducts research and educational programs; provides assistance to beginning genealogists. Gathers, restores, and donates genealogical materials to local libraries. *Founded:* 1957. *Members:* 275.

1038 ▪ Sapp Family Association

712 NW 95th Terr. Ph: (352)332-2065
Gainesville, FL 32607
E-mail: sapp@gru.net

Contact: Mitchell E. Sapp, Contact.

Desc: Individuals interested in researching the surname Sapp and its variant spellings, such as Zapp and Zapft. *Founded:* 1988. *Members:* 130.

1039 ▪ Savannah Area Genealogical Association

PO Box 15385 Ph: (912)354-2708
Savannah, GA 31416
E-mail: savsaga@aol.com

Contact: Yancey Watkins, Pres.

Desc: Genealogists, historians, archaeologists, and writers. Seeks to: preserve and protect historical and genealogical documents; educate the public; and assist genealogical researchers. Indexing 1820 Chatham County census and other genealogical material. Conducts workshops. *Founded:* 1983. *Members:* 110.

1040 ▪ Sawin Society

82 Humiston Drive Extension Ph: (203)393-0657
Bethany, CT 06524-3174 Fax: (203)393-0622

Contact: Beverly S. Davie, Contact.

Desc: Descendants and related family members of John Sawin, who immigrated to the U.S. about 1650. Promotes genealogical research of the Sawin surname; conducts social activities. Maintains biographical archives. *Founded:* 1977. *Members:* 170.

1041 ▪ Schreckengost Family Exchange

51 Forbus St. Ph: (914)473-3757
Poughkeepsie, NY 12603

Desc: Provides assistance for genealogical research on the Schreckengost family (all spellings). Promotes cooperation among family members and researchers. Maintains computerized database on the family. *Founded:* 1980. *Members:* 77.

1042 ▪ Schuyler County Historical Museum and Genealogical Center

200 S. Congress Ph: (217)322-6975
Rushville, IL 62681

Contact: Evelyn Eifert, Contact.

Founded: 1968. *Members:* 411.

1043 ▪ Scotch-Irish Foundation

Box 181 Ph: (610)527-1818
Bryn Mawr, PA 19010 Fax: (610)527-1818

Contact: James Mackie, Pres.

Desc: Individuals with maternal or paternal Scotch-Irish ancestry. Sole purpose is the compilation of biographical archives and library containing books, documents, and historical materials relating to the Scotch-Irish people in Scotland and Ireland and their immigration to the U.S. *Founded:* 1949. *Members:* 230.

1044 ▪ Scotch-Irish Society of the United States of America

Box 181
Bryn Mawr, PA 19010

Contact: Eric Newell, Pres.

Desc: Individuals of Scotch-Irish descent through one or both parents. "To broaden, deepen, and enlarge the principles from which our nation has drawn the sustaining power for its development by recalling past achievements, remembrances, and associations." Encourages communication among Ireland, Scotland, and the U.S. to promote better understanding of the Scotch-Irish heritage. Collects books relating to Scotch-Irish history from the date of the original Ulster Plantation under James I of England, and the transportation of the planters and their descendants to the American colonies; also collects family registrations and histories including letters, journals, and other documents. Sponsors the Scotch-Irish Foundation. *Founded:* 1890. *Members:* 350.

1045 ▪ Scott County Iowa Genealogical Society

PO Box 3132
Davenport, IA 52808-3132

Contact: Sandra Luse, Pres.

Desc: To foster interest in genealogy and family history. Collects and preserves records. Provides assistance to researchers. Supports microfilming of county records; conducts workshops. *Founded:* 1973. *Members:* 210.

1046 ▪ Scripps Family Association

350 County Rd. 175 Ph: (205)447-2939
Piedmont, AL 36272

Contact: Mrs. Frank Ross Stewart, Founder & Pres.

Desc: Collects, researches, and disseminates research on the family name Scripps.

1047 ▪ Scruggs Family Association

Rte 1, Box 154 Ph: (918)542-5772
Miami, OK 74354 Fax: (918)542-5415
E-mail: miamit6@onenet.net

Contact: Patricia Scruggs Trolinger, Sec.

Desc: Individuals with the surname of Scruggs or its variants and allied lines, and others interested in genealogy. Seeks to gather information on the history and genealogy of the Scruggs family and allied lines. *Founded:* 1981. *Members:* 135.

1048 ▪ Scully-Greene-Dunn Family Association
57 Westwood Lane
Middletown, CT 06457-1964

Contact: James P. Laban, Contact.

1049 ▪ Sears Family Association
PO Box 127   Ph: (508)420-6548
Osterville, MA 02655-0127
E-mail: lrsears@capecod.net
URL: http://www.emcee.com/lrsears

Contact: L. Ray Sears, III, Exec. Officer.

Desc: Descendants of Richard Sears, who landed at Plymouth, MA in 1632. Promotes genealogical research. *Founded:* 1976. *Members:* 220.

1050 ▪ Seeley Genealogy Society
17800 Langois Rd., No. 508   Ph: (760)329-0422
Desert Hot Springs, CA 92441
E-mail: seeleydan@prodigy.net

Contact: Daniel Parsons Seeley, Contact.

Desc: Descendants of the Seeley family and its variants (Seely, Seelye, Seela, Sealey, Cilley, Seale, Ceely, Seily); individuals interested in genealogy, history, or biography. Seeks to maintain and provide genealogical information on all Seeley ancestors. Encourages study of family history; promotes exchange of information. *Founded:* 1960. *Members:* 450.

1051 ▪ Seth and Della Cummings Family Association
928 N Humboldt Ave.   Ph: (909)395-0661
Ontario, CA 91764-3024

Contact: Helen A. Lynch, Pres.

Desc: Descendants of Seth and Della Cummings. Promotes family unity; seeks to identify and preserve artifacts and sites pertaining to Cummings family history. *Founded:* 1984.

1052 ▪ Seventh Day Baptist Historical Society
3120 Kennedy Rd.   Ph: (608)752-5055
PO Box 1678   Fax: (608)752-7711
Janesville, WI 53545-0225
E-mail: sdbgen@inwave.com
URL: http://www.seventhdaybaptist.org

Contact: Don A. Sanford, Historian.

Desc: Investigates the history of religious organizations and related subjects, especially those pertaining to Seventh Day Baptists (a group that originated in England and organized in Rhode Island in 1671, which observes Saturday as the Sabbath). Provides reference service for denominational agencies and leaders; compiles statistics. Conducts family research for those with Seventh Day Baptist Roots. *Founded:* 1916. *Members:* 120.

1053 ▪ Seward County Genealogical Society
PO Box 72   Ph: (402)532-7635
Seward, NE 68434-0072
E-mail: pc00520@havix.net

Contact: Trish Collister, Treas.

Desc: Residents of Seward County, NE with an interest in genealogy and local history. Gathers, preserves, and disseminates genealogical information. Conducts research and educational programs. *Founded:* 1982. *Members:* 45.

1054 ▪ Shanks Family Association
4085 Pleasant Valley Rd.   Ph: (414)644-6562
West Bend, WI 53095
E-mail: shanks@piketech.com

Contact: Dennis A. Shanks, Pres.

Desc: Doctors, attorneys, teachers, laborers, and housewives. Conducts genealogical research on the Shank family throughout the United States to establish the family line. Works to determine the origin of the name. *Founded:* 1980.

1055 ▪ Shasta County Genealogical Society
PO Box 994652   Ph: (530)241-4540
Redding, CA 96099-4652
E-mail: magister@c-zone.net

Contact: Dave Homewood, Pres.

Founded: 1968. *Members:* 85.

1056 ▪ Sheboygan County Genealogical Society
518 Water St.   Ph: (414)467-4667
Sheboygan Falls, WI 53085-1455

Contact: Nancy Luckow, Pres.

Desc: Individuals interested in the genealogy of residents of the Sheboygan County, WI area. *Founded:* 1980.

1057 ▪ Shelby County Genealogical Society
17755 St. Rt. 47   Ph: (937)492-0071
Sidney, OH 45365

Contact: Betty Bevans, Editor.

Desc: Individuals interested in genealogy. Conducts genealogical research. *Founded:* 1976. *Members:* 200.

1058 ▪ Shelby County Historical Society
1854 Old Courthouse   Ph: (205)669-3912
PO Box 457
Columbiana, AL 35051

Contact: Ken Penhale, Pres.

Desc: Individuals interested in preserving the history of Shelby County, AL. Sponsors outreach program to schools and organizations; maintains museum. *Founded:* 1974. *Members:* 300.

1059 ▪ Sherman County Historical Society
PO Box 684   Ph: (913)899-5461
Goodland, KS 67735

Contact: Gennifer House, Pres.

Desc: Individuals interested in preserving the history of Sherman County, KS. *Founded:* 1975. *Members:* 302.

1060 ▪ Shiawassee County Genealogical Society
PO Box 841   Ph: (517)725-8549
Owosso, MI 48867
E-mail: wilma4@shianet.org

Contact: Susan Bettys, Pres.

Desc: Individuals interested in genealogy; helps individuals trace their family history. *Founded:* 1968. *Members:* 150.

1061 ▪ Shirley Association
10256 Glencoe Dr.   Ph: (408)255-8511
Cupertino, CA 95014
E-mail: shirleyl@ricochet.net
URL: http://www.shirleyassociation.com

Contact: Betty Shirley, Contact.

Desc: Individuals interested in preserving the history of the Shirley family. Seeks to unite Shirley descendants; provides research assistance to members; makes available census records. *Founded:* 1978. *Members:* 400.

1062 ▪ Shomers/Schomers Family Organization
4240 NW 36 Way
Fort Lauderdale, FL 33309

Contact: David W. Shomers, Pres.

Desc: Persons with the surnames Shomers or Schomers. Promotes genealogical and biographical research. Encourages erection of memorials, gravemarkers, and other historical markers. Offers educational programs; maintains speakers' bureau. *Founded:* 1986. *Members:* 1400.

1063 ▪ Shropshire Society
1181 Hill Rd.
Paris, KY 40361-9739

Contact: Kenney Shropshire Roseberry, Pres.

Desc: Collateral and lineal descendants of Oliver Shropshire (1624-67) of Marlborough, England. Objectives are to: conduct genealogical research of the Shropshire family; disseminate genealogical and anecdotal information; support the marking, restoration, and maintenance of buildings and monuments related to family history; collect and preserve artifacts and manuscripts that contribute to genealogical history. *Founded:* 1984. *Members:* 102.

1064 ▪ Sierra Vista Genealogical Society
PO Box 1084   Ph: (520)458-8122
Sierra Vista, AZ 85636-1084
E-mail: tjm@primenet.com

Contact: Mrs. T.J. Martin, Pres.

Founded: 1975. *Members:* 45.

1065 ▪ Skinner Surname Organization
PO Box 2594
Rancho Cucamonga, CA 91729-2594
E-mail: skinner.kinsmen@usa.net

Contact: Greg Legurki, Contact.

Desc: Individuals with the surname Skinner; other Skinner family members and interested individuals. Promotes interest in family history and genealogy. *Founded:* 1984. *Members:* 200.

1066 ▪ Smith-Hedrick Family Association
4553 Hwy. 158 S   Ph: (870)237-8104
Lake City, AR 72437-8562
E-mail: dalemc@insolwwb.net
URL: http://www.familytreemaker.com/users/m/c/m/dale-h-mcmasters/

Contact: Dale McMasters, Contact.

Desc: Persons interested in the surname Smith or Hedrick. Researches, publishes, and preserves the surnames Smith and Hedrick. *Founded:* 1964. *Members:* 200.

1067 ▪ Snodgrass Clan Society
8221 Stonewall Dr.   Ph: (703)560-6631
Vienna, VA 22180-6947   Fax: (703)560-0462
E-mail: search4u@msn.com

Contact: Paul D. Snodgrass, Contact.

Desc: Individuals interested in Snodgrass family history and genealogy. Promotes genealogical research; facilitates communication and cooperation among members. *Founded:* 1977. *Members:* 230.

1068 ▪ Society of American Archivists
527 S. Wells, 5th Fl.   Ph: (312)922-0140
Chicago, IL 60607   Fax: (312)347-1452
E-mail: info@archivists.org
URL: http://www.archivists.org

Contact: Susan E. Fox, Exec.Dir.

Desc: Individuals and institutions concerned with the identification, preservation, and use of records of historical value. *Founded:* 1936. *Members:* 3400.

1069 ■ Society of the Ark and the Dove

<c/o> The Maryland   Ph: (410)685-3750
  Historical Society
201 W. Monument St.
Baltimore, MD 21201

Contact: William T. Conkling, Gov.

Desc: Direct descendants of Sir George Calvert (Baron of Baltimore); persons with ancestors who came in 1633, under the command of Governor Leonard Calvert, in the ships The Ark or The Dove to settle the Province of Maryland. *Founded:* 1909. *Members:* 207.

1070 ■ Society of California Archivists

ASUC Store Box 605
Berkeley, CA 94720-0001

1071 ■ Society of California Pioneers

300 4th St.   Ph: (415)957-1849
San Francisco, CA 94107-1272   Fax: (415)957-9858

Contact: Mercedes Devine, Admin.Dir.

Desc: Direct descendants of pioneers who arrived in California before 1850. Sponsors cultural and historical programs. Maintains museum of California history and art. *Founded:* 1850. *Members:* 1000.

1072 ■ Society of the Cincinnati

2118 Massachusetts Ave. NW   Ph: (202)785-2040
Washington, DC 20008   Fax: (202)785-0729

Contact: Mrs. Sandra Prucher, Exec.Dir.

Desc: Male descendants of officers commissioned in the Continental Army and Navy in the American Revolution who gave the required length of service, of certain officers in the French Army and Navy, and of other foreign officers (only 1 person may represent an officer). State societies (13) represent the original colonies. Society also exists in France. Maintains Anderson House in Washington, DC, an archive and library of 30,000 volumes on the society, the American Revolution, the art of war, and the decorative arts. Bestows triennial Society of the Cincinnati Prize to an author of a distinguished work on any aspect of American history from the Revolution through the end of the Washington presidency. The society was named after Lucius Quinctius Cincinnatus, a hero of the fifth century B.C. who saved Rome from threatened hostile invasions and returned to his farm without thought of personal reward. The city of Cincinnati, OH was named in honor of the society by the first governor of the Northwest Territory, Major General Arthur St. Clair, an original member of the society. *Founded:* 1783. *Members:* 3500.

1073 ■ Society of Daughters of Holland Dames

620 Park Ave.   Ph: (212)249-4949
New York, NY 10021   Fax: (212)410-3554

Contact: Mrs. Alexander O. Vietor, Directress General.

Desc: Female descendants of settlers of New Netherland (New York) prior to 1674. Promotes the principles of Dutch ancestors; collects genealogical and historical documents relating to the Dutch in America. *Founded:* 1895. *Members:* 150.

1074 ■ Society of the Descendants of the Colonial Clergy

Deputy Secretary General
17 Lowell Mason Rd.
Medfield, MA 02052-1709

Contact: Mrs. Smith, Contact.

Desc: Lineal descendants of clergymen regularly ordained, installed, or settled over any Christian church in the thirteen colonies prior to July 4, 1776. Created "to cherish the memory of the lives and works of the colonial clergy in America; to collect and preserve documents, histories, biographical sketches, and memorials pertaining to the colonial clergy of America and the parishes they served." *Founded:* 1933. *Members:* 1400.

1075 ■ Society of the Descendants of Washington's Army at Valley Forge

PO Box 915   Ph: (610)647-5532
Valley Forge, PA 19482

Contact: Betty Brown-Miller, Commander-in-Chief.

Desc: Descendants of officers and men serving in the Continental Army under the command of General George Washington at Valley Forge from Dec. 19, 1777 through June 19, 1778. Purpose is to compile rolls of all the soldiers at Valley Forge to preserve their names and honor for posterity and to discover, compile, preserve, and publish the incidents of the encampment. Compiles statistics. *Founded:* 1976. *Members:* 900.

1076 ■ Society of the Friendly Sons of St. Patrick in the City of New York

80 Wall St., Rm. 712   Ph: (212)269-1770
New York, NY 10005   Fax: (212)344-8966

Contact: Raymond C. Teatum, Contact.

Desc: Men of Irish descent in the New York City area. Conducts charitable activities. *Founded:* 1784. *Members:* 1500.

1077 ■ Society of Indiana Pioneers

315 W. Ohio St.   Ph: (317)233-6588
Indianapolis, IN 46202

Contact: Colleen Ridlen, Genealogist/Office Sec.

Desc: Individuals having at least one ancestor who was a resident of Indiana during the pioneer period, lasting from 1825-1850. Seeks to honor the memory of Indiana pioneers and their work, which opened Indiana to settlement. Works with other historical agencies to disseminate information on the history of Indiana, its leadrs, and its residents. Sponsors trips for members within Indiana or to adjoining states. *Founded:* 1916. *Members:* 1650.

1078 ■ Society of Richmond County Descendants

PO Box 848   Ph: (910)997-6641
Rockingham, NC 28380

Contact: Joe M. McLaurin, Pres.

Desc: Descendants of one or more persons who lived in or are living in Richmond County, NC; interested individuals. Works to collect and preserve historical and genealogical information on Richmond County and its people. Supports the Richmond County Historical Collection. *Founded:* 1988. *Members:* 500.

1079 ■ Society of Richmond County, North Carolina Descendants

PO Box 848   Ph: (919)997-6641
Rockingham, NC 28380

Contact: Joe M. McLaurin, Pres.

Desc: Descendants of Richmond County, NC past or present residents organized to exchange historical and genealogical information. *Members:* 300.

1080 ■ Society of Rocky Mountain Archivists

1313 Sherman St., Rm. 1B20
Denver, CO 80203

Desc: Unites those who champion the acquisitions and preservation of the evolving historical record and promote access to records for present and future generations. *Founded:* 1982.

1081 ■ Society of Stukely Westcott Descendants of America

2145 Richvale Rd.
Nashport, OH 43830-9478
E-mail: betw@prodigy.net

Desc: Descendants of Stukeley Westcott. Seeks to identify and unite family members. *Founded:* 1934.

1082 ■ Society of Tennessee Archivists

403 7th Ave. North   Ph: (615)741-2561
Nashville, TN 37243-0312   Fax: (615)741-6471
E-mail: dsowell@datatek.com
URL: http://www.arkay.net/tnarchivist

Contact: Doris Rivers-Martinson, CA, Pres.

Desc: Promotes the preservation, description, use, administration, and accessibility of archives and manuscripts according to accepted archival principles. Promotes according to professional standards, the education and training of archivists, manuscripts curators, and other interested individuals. Promotes the exchange of information among archival institutions both within and outside Tennessee. *Founded:* 1977. *Members:* 130.

1083 ■ Sofene Family Association

4710 Bethesda Ave., Ste. 1217
Bethesda, MD 20814-5216

1084 ■ Solano County Genealogical Society

PO Box 2494   Ph: (707)446-6869
Fairfield, CA 94533

Contact: Nancy Mahoney, Pres.

Desc: Provides assistance to people researching their family history. *Founded:* 1981. *Members:* 200.

1085 ■ Sonoma County Genealogical Society

PO Box 2273   Ph: (707)838-1311
Santa Rosa, CA 95405-0273   Fax: (707)838-3635
E-mail: chuckadoo@aol.com
URL: http://www.com/hwmiller/genealogy/scgs.htm

Contact: Charles H. Warner, Pres.

Desc: Encourages interest in genealogy and family history research. Maintains local history and genealogy collection at the Sonoma County Library. *Founded:* 1967. *Members:* 370.

1086 ■ Sons of the American Legion

PO Box 1055   Ph: (317)630-1204
Indianapolis, IN 46206   Fax: (317)630-1369
E-mail: tal@legion.org
URL: http://www.legion.org

Contact: John W. Kerestan, Liaison.

Desc: Male descendants, stepsons, and adopted sons of members of The American Legion (see separate entry) or of deceased veterans of wartime military service who were eligible for Legion membership. Supports the principles of the AL and conducts patriotic activities. Operates charitable program. *Founded:* 1932. *Members:* 211000.

1087 ■ Sons of Confederate Veterans

PO Box 59   Ph: (615)380-1844
Columbia, TN 38401   Free: 800-697-6884
                             Fax: (615)381-6712

E-mail: exedir@scv.org
URL: http://www.scv.org

Contact: Maitland O. Westbrook, III, Exec.Dir.

Desc: Lineal and collateral descendants of Confederate Civil War veterans. *Founded:* 1896. *Members:* 25500.

1088 ▪ Sons and Daughters of the First Settlers of Newbury, Massachusetts
PO Box 444
Newburyport, MA 01950

Contact: David Ladd, Contact.

Desc: Descendents of the first European settlers of Newbury, MA. Seeks to preserve the history of the people and events surrounding the settling of Newbury. *Founded:* 1927. *Members:* 825.

1089 ▪ Sons and Daughters of Oregon Pioneers
PO Box 6685
Portland, OR 97228
E-mail: mpmiller@pop3eoni.com

Contact: Merle G. Miller, Pres.

Desc: Lineal descendants of pioneers who arrived in the Oregon country prior to Feb. 14, 1859, the day Oregon became a state. Objectives are to pursue social and literary activities and to preserve historic sites. Strives to perpetuate the memory of Oregon pioneers. Holds four history study programs annually; annual membership meetings; statehood banquet; annual picnic; and other social and history related events. *Founded:* 1901. *Members:* 1100.

1090 ▪ Sons and Daughters of Pioneer Rivermen
126 Seneca Dr.   Ph: (740)373-7829
Marietta, OH 45750

Contact: J. W. Rutter, Pres.

Desc: Sponsors permanent exhibits in the River Museum, Marietta, OH. Provides material for the Inland Rivers Library, Cincinnati, OH. Not a reference for family genealogy research. *Founded:* 1939. *Members:* 2000.

1091 ▪ Sons of Union Veterans of the Civil War
440 Clark Dr.   Ph: (609)567-7527
Hammonton, NJ 08047-1011
E-mail: jmw1200vi@aol.com
URL: http://www.suvcw.org

Contact: David Hann, Natl.Sec.

Desc: Male descendants of veterans of the Union Army, Navy, or Marine Corps of the Civil War. *Founded:* 1881. *Members:* 6000.

1092 ▪ Sophus Frederick Hansen Family Organization
8686 Beauxart Circle   Ph: (916)689-4644
Sacramento, CA 95828-4661

Contact: Donna Hansen Glasser, Pres.

Desc: Descendants of Sophus Frederick Hansen. Promotes study of Hansen family history and genealogy.

1093 ▪ South Carolina Genealogical Society, Old Edgefield District Chapter
104 Courthouse Sq.   Ph: (803)637-4010
PO Box 546
Edgefield, SC 29824

Contact: Annette Burton, Pres.

Founded: 1985. *Members:* 455.

1094 ▪ South King County Genealogical Society
PO Box 3174   Ph: (206)226-8956
Kent, WA 98032-0203

Contact: Susan Coles, Pres.

Desc: Individuals with an interest in genealogy. Works to compile, preserve, and perpetuate family and genealogical records. *Founded:* 1984. *Members:* 300.

1095 ▪ South Plains Genealogical Society
PO Box 6607   Ph: (806)747-1319
Lubbock, TX 79493-6607
URL: http://www.door.net/spgs

Contact: Yvonne Spence Perkins, Pres.

Desc: Promotes the study and interest in genealogy in the Lubbock County and South Plains area of Texas. *Founded:* 1961. *Members:* 336.

1096 ▪ Southeast Michigan Census Council
17321 Telegraph Rd., Ste. 204   Ph: (313)535-2077
Detroit, MI 48219   Fax: (313)535-3556
E-mail: pbecker@umich.edu

Contact: Patricia C. Becker, Exec.Dir.

Desc: Organizations and agencies in Michigan using census and/or other demographic and related regularly. Represents state interests to Census Bureau and provides information and education to the public. *Founded:* 1946. *Members:* 90.

1097 ▪ Southern Baptist Hisorical Library and Archives
901 Commerce St., Ste. 400   Ph: (615)244-0344
Nashville, TN 37203-3630   Fax: (615)242-2153
E-mail: bsumners@edge.net

Contact: Slayden Yarbrough, Exec.Dir.

Desc: Commissioners elected by Southern Baptist Convention. Assists Baptist churches, associations, conventions, and institutions in recording, preserving, and utilizing historical materials. Aids in procuring and preserving printed and manuscript materials by or about Baptists; operates microfilming program. *Founded:* 1951. *Members:* 30.

1098 ▪ Southern Genealogist's Exchange Society
PO Box 2801   Ph: (904)387-9142
Jacksonville, FL 32203

Contact: Richard B. Cardell, Pres.

Desc: Individuals interested in genealogy. Conducts seminars and teaches classes. *Founded:* 1964. *Members:* 500.

1099 ▪ Southern Kentucky Genealogical Society
PO Box 1782   Ph: (502)843-9452
Bowling Green, KY 42102-1782
E-mail: betty.lyne@bgamug.org

Contact: Betty Lyne, Sec.

Desc: Individuals interested in family history and preserving genealogical materials. Makes contributions to Western Kentucky University Library and Museum. Conducts charitable activities; volunteers at Warren County Courthouse and Western Kentucky University's Kentucky Library. *Founded:* 1977. *Members:* 200.

1100 ▪ Southern Society of Genealogists
RFD 5, Box 109   Ph: (205)447-2939
Piedmont, AL 36272

Contact: Mrs. Frank Stewart, Dir.

Desc: Genealogists; other individuals interested in southern families. Seeks to encourage genealogical research. Conducts seminars. *Founded:* 1962. *Members:* 50.

1101 ▪ Southwest Georgia Genealogical Society
PO Box 4672   Ph: (912)435-9659
Albany, GA 31706   Fax: (912)435-9659

Contact: Bobbie Meyer von Bremen, Pres.

Desc: Individuals in southwest Georgia interested in tracing family histories. *Founded:* 1968. *Members:* 300.

1102 ▪ Southwest Louisiana Genealogical Society
PO Box 5652   Ph: (318)477-3087
Lake Charles, LA 70606-5652

Contact: Mrs. Pat Huffaker, Pres.

Desc: Promotes genealogical research. *Founded:* 1973. *Members:* 483.

1103 ▪ Sparks Family Association
1709 Cherokee Rd.   Ph: (734)662-5080
Ann Arbor, MI 48104-4498

Contact: Russell E. Bidlack, Sec.-Treas.

Desc: Members of the Sparks and related families and other individuals with an interest in genealogy. Seeks to identify and preserve historical artifacts and genealogical information pertaining to the Sparks family. *Founded:* 1953. *Members:* 1000.

1104 ▪ Spencer Historical and Genealogical Society
123 Vail St.
Michigan City, IN 46360

Contact: Janet Lautenschlager, Contact.

Desc: Historians, genealogists, and other individuals with an interest in the Spencer family. Promotes "accurate and permanent recording of family history, vital statistics, and individual accomplishments of direct family descendants and others related to or otherwise associated with the Spencer line." *Founded:* 1978.

1105 ▪ Sprayberry/Spraberry/Sprabary Family Association
PO Box 1204   Ph: (806)872-8326
Lamesa, TX 79331   Fax: (806)872-3598
E-mail: dccs@pics.net

Contact: John P. Spraberry, Pres.

Desc: Works to gather genealogical information on the surname Sprayberry and its variations.

1106 ▪ Spurlock Family Association
PO Box 567   Ph: (423)323-1356
Blountville, TN 37617-0567
E-mail: patelder@preferred.com
URL: http://www.geocities.com/Heartland/hills/4411

Contact: Pat Spurlock Elder, Pres.

Desc: Individuals with the surname Spurlock or a variant. Preserves family history; acts as a clearinghouse for genealogical information. Compiles statistics. *Founded:* 1987. *Members:* 85.

1107 ▪ Stafford County Historical and Genealogical Society
100 S. Main   Ph: (316)234-5664
PO Box 249
Stafford, KS 67578

Contact: Ruth Shocklee, Exec.Sec.

Founded: 1976. *Members:* 185.

1108 ▪ Stanly County Genealogical Society
PO Box 31
Albemarle, NC 28002

Contact: Quentin G. Smith, Pres.

Desc: Individuals interested in genealogy. Works to preserve historic genealogical and demographic records.

1109 ■ Staples Family History Association

1009 Lakemont Cir   Ph: (407)599-5700
Winter Park, FL 32792-5048   Fax: (407)599-5700
E-mail: jcstaples@aol.com

Contact: James C. Staples, Pres.

Desc: Collects and publishes family history data on the Staple/Staples name. *Founded:* 1977. *Members:* 264.

1110 ■ Steere Family Association

300 Roseland Park Rd., Ste. 10
Woodstock, CT 06281

Contact: Randall Steele, Pres.

Desc: Members of the Steele family. Facilitates communication and good fellowship among members; promotes interest in family history and genealogy. *Members:* 2000.

1111 ■ Stephens County Genealogical Society

PO Box 350   Ph: (254)559-8471
Breckenridge, TX 76424

Contact: Freda Mitchell, Corr. Sec.

Desc: Research local member's families and area historical research and preservation. *Founded:* 1986. *Members:* 45.

1112 ■ Stephenson County Genealogical Society

PO Box 514
Freeport, IL 61032

Contact: Joseph Ginger, Pres.

Founded: 1967. *Members:* 130.

1113 ■ Stevens County Genealogical Society

102 East 6th St.
Morris, MN 56267

Contact: Jerry Kopacek, Pres.

Desc: Aid and promote genealogy and family histories, record cemeteries, funeral records, obituaries, and record vital statistics. *Founded:* 1984. *Members:* 70.

1114 ■ Stevens Point Area Genealogical Society

1001 Main St.   Ph: (715)341-3815
Stevens Point, WI 54481

Contact: Ruth Steffen, Pres.

Desc: Individuals interested in genealogy. Maintains obituary index and updates newspaper file in public library. *Founded:* 1975.

1115 ■ Stewart Family Association

350 County Rd., 175   Ph: (205)447-2939
Piedmont, AL 36272

Contact: Mrs. Frank Ross Stewart, Pres.

Desc: Individuals with the surname Stewart and their families. *Founded:* 1958.

1116 ■ Stires Family Association

19 Crash Road   Ph: (207)897-4222
Livermore, ME 04253-3014

Contact: W. Dennis Stires, Editor.

Desc: Promotes the history of the surname Stires and its variants (Styers, Stiers, Stire, Steyr, Steer, Steyer, Steiermark, Stoehr, Steirs, Steers, Steier, Steeres, Styer, Stehr, and Stohr). *Founded:* 1977. *Members:* 45.

1117 ■ Stovall Family Association

5000 Rock River Dr.   Ph: (817)457-5383
Fort Worth, TX 76103-1226
E-mail: stovalldata@c-gate.net

Contact: Lyle K. Williams, Sec.

Desc: Individuals with the Stovall/Stoval/Stoveall surname. Promotes interest in Stovall family history and heritage. *Founded:* 1989. *Members:* 550.

1118 ■ Strafford County Genealogical Society

PO Box 322   Ph: (603)742-6394
Dover, NH 03821-0322
E-mail: hgcb76d@prodigy.com

Contact: Beverly A. McCann, Pres.

Desc: Provides an interaction between people interested in genealogy, family history, and other pursuits. *Founded:* 1978. *Members:* 200.

1119 ■ Streeter Family Association

26 Fishermans Cove   Ph: (305)367-4013
Key Largo, FL 33037   Fax: (305)367-4565

Contact: Joan Vincunas, Sec.

Desc: Individuals and families with the surname Streeter or Streator; friends of Streeter families and interested others. Compiles and disseminates genealogical information to Streeters in the U.S. and Canada. Maintains biographical archives.

1120 ■ Strong Family Association of America

<c/o> Dianne Strong Runser   Ph: (412)372-2313
156 Maple Dr.
Trafford, PA 15085-1435
URL: http://www.geocities.com/Heartland/Prairie/4715

Contact: Dianne Strong Runser, Sec.

Desc: Individuals with the surname Strong or a variant. Promotes unity among family members and awareness of family heritage. *Founded:* 1975. *Members:* 850.

1121 ■ Studebaker Family National Association

6555 State St., Rte. 202   Ph: (937)667-4451
Tipp City, OH 45371-9444   Fax: (937)667-4798

Contact: Ruth E. Studebaker, Exec.Sec./Pres.

Desc: Promotes the genealogy and family history of the Studebaker family. *Founded:* 1964. *Members:* 1704.

1122 ■ Sullivan County Genealogical Society

PO Box 326   Ph: (812)268-6253
Sullivan, IN 47882   Fax: (812)268-4836
E-mail: imrzip@aol.com

Contact: Donna Adams, Pres.

Founded: 1974. *Members:* 558.

1123 ■ Sumner Family Association

62 Sandbury Dr.   Ph: (716)334-2989
Pittsford, NY 14534-2636   Fax: (716)334-2989
E-mail: charles.sumner@juno.com
URL: http://www.westchesterweb.com/sumner

Contact: Charles Hanson Sumner, Dir.

Desc: Individuals with the surname Sumner and its variants, and their families. Works to locate and maintain communication with Sumners around the world. *Founded:* 1982. *Members:* 350.

1124 ■ Sumter County Genealogical Society

219 W. Liberty St.   Ph: (803)773-9144
PO Box 2543
Sumter, SC 29150

Contact: Don Johnson, Contact.

Desc: Works to raise standards of genealogical research. Promotes preservation of demographic records of Sumter County and the state of South Carolina. Operates Genealogical and Historical Research Center. *Founded:* 1974. *Members:* 503.

1125 ■ Surry County Genealogical Society

PO Box 997   Ph: (910)786-7449
Dobson, NC 27017

Contact: Robert B. Holder, Pres.

Desc: Seeks to promote valid genealogical research and writing.

1126 ■ Suwannee Valley Genealogical Society

PO Box 967
Live Oak, FL 32064-0967

Contact: Donald L. Brim, Contact.

1127 ■ Swedish American Museum Association of Chicago

5211 N. Clark   Ph: (312)728-8111
Chicago, IL 60640   Fax: (312)728-8870
E-mail: mncnm@samac.org
URL: http://www.samac.org

Contact: Kerstin Lane, Exec.Dir.

Desc: Americans of Swedish descent; other interested Swedes. Group is national in scope, but membership is concentrated in the Chicago, IL area. Seeks to preserve the history and culture of Swedish Americans. Maintains speakers' bureau and Swedish Museum and Cultural Center; offers genealogy classes, craft lessons, and language instruction; provides children's services. Sponsors concerts; observes Swedish holidays; holds exhibits. *Founded:* 1976. *Members:* 1400.

1128 ■ Tackett Family Association

1830 Johnson Dr.   Ph: (510)680-0383
Concord, CA 94520   Fax: (510)686-0563
URL: http://www.jps.net/jtackitt/index.html

Contact: Jim W. Tackitt, Pres.

Desc: Descendants of Lewis Tacquett and those with related surnames. Collects, preserves, and disseminates genealogical information related to Tackett families in America. *Founded:* 1963. *Members:* 1107.

1129 ■ Taft Family Association

3119 Heatherwood   Ph: (508)362-7073
Yarmouth Port, MA 02675-1457
E-mail: rtaftm@capecod.net

Contact: Richard T. Messinger, Contact.

Desc: Descendants of Robert and Sarah Taft, who immigrated to the United States in 1675. Promotes study of Taft family history and genealogy. *Founded:* 1955. *Members:* 400.

1130 ■ Tarrant County Black Historical and Genealogical Society

1020 E. Humbolt   Ph: (817)332-6049
Ft. Worth, TX 76104

Contact: Lenora Rolla, Exec.Dir.

Desc: Individuals in Tarrant County, TX interested in studying the effects of black traditions on education, creativity, and politics. *Founded:* 1977. *Members:* 100.

1131 ■ Taylor County Historical and Genealogical Society

PO Box 522   Ph: (304)265-5549
Grafton, WV 26354

Contact: Thomas Dadisman, Pres.

Desc: Individuals interested in preserving the history of Grafton, WV. *Founded:* 1982. *Members:* 135.

1132 ▪ Tazewell County Genealogical Society

PO Box 312   Ph: (309)477-3044
Pekin, IL 61554

Contact: Margaret Bush, Pres.

Members: 300.

1133 ▪ Tea Family Organization

752 Gran Kaymen Way   Ph: (813)645-6562
Apollo Beach, FL 33572-2438
E-mail: srtea@aol.com

Contact: Charles L. Tea, Contact.

Desc: Conducts genealogical research on the surname Tea and descendants of the Tea family (including Tea, Boone, Bondurant, McClain, Munsell, Titt, and Tully). *Founded:* 1980.

1134 ▪ Templin Family Association

7411 Fairway Ln.   Ph: (972)317-4441
Parker, CO 80134-5922

Contact: Richard R. Templin, Pres.

Desc: Conducts genealogical research on Templin family ancestors using family Bible records; census, tax, marriage, birth, and death records in official files of city, county, and state bureaus; written histories, biographies, land files, and archives from various states, foreign countries, genealogical societies, and patriotic associations, including the Daughters of the American Revolution and the Sons of the American Revolution . Also researches family lines of members related by marriage. *Founded:* 1972. *Members:* 220.

1135 ▪ Tennessee Genealogical Society

PO Box 247   Ph: (901)381-1447
Brunswick, TN 38014-0247

Contact: Mary Ann Littley Bell, Pres.

Desc: Individuals with an interest in local genealogy. Promotes genealogical research, gathers genealogical materials for donation to local libraries and archives. *Founded:* 1954. *Members:* 1500.

1136 ▪ Tevebaugh - Teverbaugh Surname Organization

217 Grand Ave.   Ph: (616)842-6121
Grand Haven, MI 49417-2473
E-mail: jteveb6441@aol.com

Contact: John L. Tevebaugh, Dir.

Desc: Individuals with the surname Tevebaugh and its variant spellings; other members of the Tevebaugh family. Seeks to identify and unite Tevebaugh family members; promotes interest in family history and genealogy. *Founded:* 1990.

1137 ▪ Texas County Genealogical and Historical Society

PO Box 12   Ph: (417)967-2946
Houston, MO 65483

Contact: Shirley Wenger, Pres.

Desc: Seeks to preserve and perpetuate ancestral records for educational and historical purposes. *Founded:* 1980. *Members:* 250.

1138 ▪ Texas State Genealogical Society

3219 Meadow Oaks Dr.   Ph: (254)778-2073
Temple, TX 76502-1752

Contact: Wanda Donaldson, Pres.

Desc: Individuals interested in the genealogy of Texas. Conducts annual lecture series. Bestows writing awards. Issues Texas Pioneer and First Families of Texas certificates. *Founded:* 1960. *Members:* 800.

1139 ▪ Thayer County Genealogical Society

PO Box 387   Ph: (402)768-7313
Belvidere, NE 68315-0387
E-mail: kjwmson@navix.net

Contact: Jackie Williamson, Vice.Pres.

Desc: Collects information on Thayer Co. families and makes it available for research. Aids those looking for ancestors. Maintains abandoned cemeteries. *Founded:* 1986. *Members:* 12.

1140 ▪ Thomas Blair Family Organization

747 Lovell Ave.   Ph: (612)484-4178
Roseville, MN 55113

Contact: Florence H. Carr, Contact.

Desc: Descendants of Thomas and Agnes Blair of Scotland, who emigrated to Minnesota to establish a farm in 1856. Plans reunions and meets to exchange family news. *Founded:* 1985. *Members:* 200.

1141 ▪ Thomas Borland Family Organization

1 Kingsbridge Pl.   Ph: (719)542-2779
Pueblo, CO 81001

Contact: Mrs. John E. Chenoweth, Contact.

Desc: Conducts research on the genealogy and history of the Borland family. *Founded:* 1968.

1142 ▪ Thomas Glisson Family Organization

1599 Monaco Circle   Ph: (801)278-7708
Salt Lake City, UT 84121

Contact: Dr. Eldon B. Tucker, Jr., Contact.

Desc: Descendants of Thomas Glisson. Seeks to identify and unite Glisson family members; promotes interest in Glisson family history and genealogy. *Founded:* 1975.

1143 ▪ Thomas Guthrie Family Organization

39 S 300 E   Ph: (801)225-4161
Orem, UT 84058-5536
E-mail: bevans2@sisna.com

Contact: Robert E. Evans, Contact.

Desc: Members of the Guthrie family. Promotes study and preservation of Guthrie family history. *Founded:* 1980.

1144 ▪ Thomas Hall Family Organization

1599 Monaco Circle   Ph: (801)278-7708
Salt Lake City, UT 84121

Contact: Dr. Eldon B. Tucker, Jr., Contact.

Desc: Members of the Hall family and other interested individuals. Seeks to advance the study of Hall family history and genealogy. *Founded:* 1950.

1145 ▪ Thomas McDonough Family Organization

1599 Monaco Circle   Ph: (801)278-7708
Salt Lake City, UT 84121

Contact: Dr. Eldon B. Tucker, Jr., Contact.

Desc: Descendants of Thomas McDonough (1750-1820). Promotes study of McDonough family history and genealogy. *Founded:* 1995.

1146 ▪ Thomas Minor Family Society

815 N 300 W
Provo, UT 84604

Contact: O. Geral Wilde, Pres.

Desc: Descendants of Thomas Minor. Seeks to identify and unite members of the Minor family; promotes interest in family history and genealogy. *Founded:* 1979. *Members:* 500.

1147 ▪ Thomas Thorn and Mary Ann Downman Family Organization

2421 N 750 E   Ph: (801)375-4390
Provo, UT 84604

Contact: Jackie Leonard Lambson, Sec.

Desc: Descendants of Thomas Thorn and Mary Ann Downman; other individuals with an interest in Thorn and Downman family history. Promotes study of, and interest in, Thorn and Downman family history and genealogy. *Founded:* 1986. *Members:* 50.

1148 ▪ Tippah County Historical and Genealogical Society

308 N. Commerce St.   Ph: (601)837-7773
Ripley, MS 38663   Fax: (601)837-7773
URL: http://www2.dixie-net.com/tch/

Contact: Tommy Covington, Contact.

Desc: Genealogists. Collects, preserves, and disseminates historical and genealogical information. *Founded:* 1975.

1149 ▪ Tippecanoe County Historical Association/Tippecanoe County Area Genealogical Society

1001 South St.   Ph: (765)476-8420
Lafayette, IN 47901   Fax: (765)476-8414
E-mail: library@tcha.mus.in.us
URL: http://www.tcha.mus.in.us

Contact: Paul J. Schueler, Colls.Mgr.

Desc: Assists persons searching for ancestors in Tippecanoe County. *Founded:* 1970. *Members:* 150.

1150 ▪ Towns County Historical and Genealogical Society

PO Box 101   Ph: (404)379-3150
Young Harris, GA 30582
E-mail: jerrytaylor@juno.com

Contact: Jerry A. Taylor, Pres.

Desc: Individuals interested in preserving the history of Towns County, GA. *Founded:* 1981. *Members:* 25.

1151 ▪ Trahan Family Association

600 S Ave. D
Crowley, LA 70526-5606

1152 ▪ Tri-County Genealogical Society

PO Box 580   Ph: (501)829-2772
Marvell, AR 72366

Contact: Verneal Montgomery, Pres.

Desc: Persons interested in genealogy; maintains collection of books, periodicals, microfilm, and microfiche. *Founded:* 1985. *Members:* 328.

1153 ▪ Tripp Family Association

7536 Gladstone Ave.
White City, OR 97503-1724

Contact: Breffni Whelan, Pres.

Desc: Individuals with the surname Tripp and other Tripp family members. Promotes interest in Tripp family history and genealogy. *Founded:* 1996.

1154 ▪ Tulsa Genealogical Society

PO Box 585   Ph: (918)742-3893
Tulsa, OK 74101

Contact: Fran Frame, Pres.

Desc: Individuals, genealogical societies, city libraries, and others interested in researching and recording family genealogy. Seeks to educate members and the public regarding research methods and sources by conducting community education classes. Hosts State Fair Genealogy Booth. *Founded:* 1965. *Members:* 300.

1155 ■ Tuolumne County Genealogical Society

The Golden Roots of Ph: (209)532-1317
Mother Lode
PO Box 3956
Sonora, CA 95370

Contact: Phyllis Hembree, Pres.

Desc: Individuals interested in genealogy. Conducts research and educational programs. *Founded:* 1980. *Members:* 140.

1156 ■ Ulster County Genealogical Society

PO Box 536 Ph: (914)382-1932
Hurley, NY 12443
E-mail: jim_garde@prodigy.com

Contact: James Garde, Pres.

Desc: Genealogists. Gathers and disseminates information on Ulster County, NY history and genealogy. *Founded:* 1972. *Members:* 400.

1157 ■ Union County Genealogical Society

200 E. Fifth Ph: (870)863-5447
El Dorado, AR 71730-3897 Fax: (870)862-3944

Contact: Freddie Sligh, Pres.

Founded: 1976. *Members:* 200.

1158 ■ Unitarian Universalist Historical Society

Massachusetts Historical Society Ph: (617)536-1608
1154 Boylston St. Fax: (617)859-0074
Boston, MA 02215
E-mail: publications@masshist.org

Contact: Conrad E. Wright, Pres.

Desc: Persons interested in the history of liberal religion. *Founded:* 1978. *Members:* 350.

1159 ■ United Church Board for World Ministries

700 Prospect Ave. E., 6th Fl. Ph: (216)736-3200
Cleveland, OH 44115 Fax: (216)736-3259

Contact: Dale Bishop, Exec.VP.

Desc: Clergy and laypersons of the United Church of Christ. Purposes are to: work with Christians worldwide to bring people into "fellowship with Jesus Christ"; proclaim the gospel and be a witness to God's love in the world; support individuals working to strengthen their churches, improve their lives, and be witnesses in their communities; raise public conciousness of the effects that U.S. social, political, and economic policies have on other countries; encourage globally responsible actions by individuals and bureaucracies. Maintains library, speakers' bureau, and biographical archives; compiles statistics; places missionaries overseas. *Founded:* 1810. *Members:* 225.

1160 ■ United Daughters of the Confederacy

328 N Blvd. Ph: (804)355-1636
Richmond, VA 23220-4057 Fax: (804)359-1325

Contact: Ms. Marion Giannasi, Exec.Sec.

Desc: Women descendants of Confederate veterans of the Civil War. *Founded:* 1894. *Members:* 25000.

1161 ■ Urbain Baudreau Graveline Genealogical Association

PO Box 905 Ph: (413)283-8378
Palmer, MA 01069-0905 Free: 800-887-2878
Fax: (413)283-2556

Contact: Robert Graveline, Pres.

Desc: Works to collect genealogical and historical information. *Founded:* 1978. *Members:* 275.

1162 ■ Utah Genealogical Association

PO Box 1140 Ph: (801)240-1009
Salt Lake City, UT 84110-1144 Free: 888-463-6842

1163 ■ Vahey Family Association

<c/o> Jack Vahey Ph: (503)760-5512
6137 SE 128th Ave.
Portland, OR 97236-4627
E-mail: jasajoda@integrityonline.com
URL: http://www.integrityonline.com/vahey

Contact: Jack Vahey, Researcher.

Desc: Individuals with the Vahey surname. Promotes unity among all Vaheys. Conducts genealogical research. *Founded:* 1983.

1164 ■ Valley County Genealogical Society

PO Box 10
Cascade, ID 83611-0010

Contact: Patricia J. Turek, Contact.

Desc: Conducts genealogical research and preserves information and records. *Founded:* 1981.

1165 ■ Van Buren County Historical Society

PO Box 857 Ph: (615)946-7607
Spencer, TN 38585

Contact: Oliver A. Bayless, Sec.-Treas.

Desc: Individuals interested in preserving the history of Van Buren County, TN. Promotes genealogical research. *Founded:* 1980. *Members:* 180.

1166 ■ Vandenberg Genealogical Society

PO Box 81 Ph: (805)733-2965
Lompoc, CA 93438-0081

Contact: Richard Hunter, Pres.

Desc: Promotes the study of genealogy in Lompoc, CA. Provides assistance and classes for novice genealogists; offers consulting services. *Founded:* 1986. *Members:* 47.

1167 ■ Vawter - Vauter - Vaughter Family Association

4145 N 900 W Ph: (812)392-2149
Scipio, IN 47273 Fax: (812)346-1442
E-mail: bwelch@seidata.com

Contact: Bonita Welch, Contact.

Desc: Individuals with the surname Vawter and its variant spellings; other members of the Vawter and related families. Promotes study of Vawter family history and genealogy; facilitates communication among Vawter family members. *Founded:* 1978. *Members:* 300.

1168 ■ Veitch Historical Society

1325 NW 138th St. Ph: (405)752-9228
Edmond, OK 73013-1651
E-mail: wav1.kmox.tm@worldnet.att.net

Contact: William A. Veitch, V.Pres.

Desc: Individuals with the surname Veitch and its variant spellings; other members of the Veitch family. Promotes study of Veitch family history and genealogy; identifies and preserves historic properties and landmarks figuring in Veitch family history. *Founded:* 1976. *Members:* 400.

1169 ■ Venango County Genealogical Club

2 Central Ave
Oil City, PA 16301-2734

Contact: Gary Edwards, Contact.

Desc: Family genealogists, oil company news editors, oil historians, and individuals interested in the genealogy of northwestern Pennsylvania. Provides assistance with genealogical research. Participates in Oil Heritage Week in Oil City, PA. Has copied cemetery, Bible and church records, newspaper abstracts, and vital statistics. *Founded:* 1975. *Members:* 230.

1170 ■ Ventura County Genealogical Society

PO Box 24608 Ph: (805)985-7784
Ventura, CA 93002

Founded: 1977.

1171 ■ Vermazen/Vermason Family Organization

161 Delhi Rd. Ph: (319)927-2964
Manchester, IA 52057

Contact: John Vermazen, Contact.

Desc: Individuals with the surname Vermazen or Vermason and their families. Conducts search for others with the same surname. *Founded:* 1980. *Members:* 36.

1172 ■ Vermont French Canadian Genealogical Society

PO Box 65128
Burlington, VT 05406-5128
URL: http://members.aol.com/utfcgs/genealogy/
index.html

Contact: John Fisher, Contact.

Founded: 1996. *Members:* 225.

1173 ■ Vernon Historical and Genealogical Society

PO Drawer 159
Anacoco, LA 71403-0159

1174 ■ Vesterheim Genealogical Center and Naeseth Library

415 W. Main St. Ph: (608)255-2224
Madison, WI 53703 Fax: (608)255-6842

Contact: Blaine Hedberg, Dir.

Desc: Members of the Norwegian-American Museum interested in learning about their heritage. Promotes the study of Norwegian heritage and ethnic background; provides for searches of library and archival collections; serves as clearinghouse for inquiries. Assembles transcripts of cemetery, census, and church records with indexes; offers suggestions to researchers. *Founded:* 1975. *Members:* 1900.

1175 ■ Vier/Viers Family Organization

2817 Moulton Dr. Ph: (530)626-3090
Placerville, CA 95667-4333
E-mail: lhunt5@juno.com

Contact: Lester N. Hunt, Sec.Treas.

Desc: Vier and Viers family members (110) and libraries and genealogical organizations (18). Conducts research and catalog findings; compiles statistics. Maintains over 6900 individual member files. *Founded:* 1980. *Members:* 110.

1176 ■ Virginia Genealogical Society

5001 W. Braod St., No. 115 Ph: (804)285-8954
Richmond, VA 23230-3023 Fax: (804)285-0394

Contact: Bonnie Trainor, Admin.

Founded: 1960. *Members:* 3000.

1177 ■ Volusia County Genealogical and Historical Society
PO Box 2039
Daytona Beach, FL 32115

Contact: Leah Fetzlaff, Sec.

1178 ■ Wagon Train Descendants
1368 E Rosenoff Rd.
Ritzville, WA 99169-8708

Contact: Gerald E. Schoesler, Contact.

1179 ■ Walker County Genealogical Society
PO Box 1295   Ph: (409)294-9431
Huntsville, TX 77342   Fax: (409)295-3444
E-mail: vbanes@myriad.net
URL: http://personalwebs.myriad.net/jdickenson/wcgen.htm

Contact: Johnnie Jo Dickinson, Pres.

Desc: Individuals with an interest in genealogy. Maintains genealogical collection at the Huntsville City Library. *Founded:* 1968. *Members:* 107.

1180 ■ Walworth County Genealogical Society
POB 159   Ph: (608)752-8816
Delavan, WI 53115-0159
E-mail: pgleich@aol.com

Contact: Peggy Gleich, Pres.

Desc: Provides educational and resourceful workshops, preserves documents, publishes and reprints such items as atlases and cemetery records. Opened genealogical research library. Publications are for sale. *Founded:* 1988. *Members:* 180.

1181 ■ Ward County Genealogical Society
400 E. 4th St.   Ph: (915)943-6312
Monahans, TX 79756

Contact: Ms. Jackie Duncan Youngblood, Pres.

Desc: To enhance and extend the genealogy library, assist those researching ancestors, whether local persons, or people who come into the community to do research. *Founded:* 1996. *Members:* 32.

1182 ■ Wardner Family Historical Association
9305 N. Ivanhoe St.   Ph: (802)457-4938
Portland, OR 97203   Fax: (503)285-5464
E-mail: melbob@sover.net

Contact: Melanie Williams, Chairperson.

Desc: Individuals interested in the Wardner family history. Shares family data, photos, and genealogical information. *Founded:* 1976. *Members:* 90.

1183 ■ Warren County Illinois Genealogical Society
PO Box 761   Ph: (309)734-2763
Monmouth, IL 61462-0761
E-mail: warren.library@misslink.net

Contact: Elwida Osborn, Pres.

Founded: 1981. *Members:* 200.

1184 ■ Washington County Genealogical Society
RR 1, Box 382
Charlotte, ME 04666-9701

Contact: Sandra Standish-Bunnell, Contact.

1185 ■ Washington County Genealogical Society
210 S. 17th
Blair, NE 68008

Contact: Arlene Stork, Pres.

Desc: Assist in family research. Hold programs related to genealogy. *Founded:* 1975. *Members:* 20.

1186 ■ Watkins Family History Society
PO Box 1698
Douglas, GA 31534-7698

Contact: Bernard J. Watkins, Contact.

1187 ■ Waukesha County Genealogical Society
PO Box 1541
Waukesha, WI 53187-1541

Desc: Individuals interested in tracing their own family trees. *Founded:* 1967. *Members:* 135.

1188 ■ Wayland Area Tree Tracers Genealogical Society
129 Cedar St.   Ph: (616)792-6112
Wayland, MI 49348-1301

Contact: Donna L. Benedict, Corr.Sec.

Desc: Participants are genealogical researchers in the Allegan County, MI area. Promotes historical and genealogical research. *Founded:* 1975.

1189 ■ Wayne County Genealogical Society
Box 856
Wooster, OH 44691-0856

Contact: Lloyd Vandersall, Contact.

1190 ■ Wayne County Genealogical Society
PO Box 2599   Ph: (765)935-0614
Richmond, IN 47375

Contact: Arnold L. Dean, Pres.

Desc: Promotes genealogical research and education. Gathers and preserves historic genealogical information. Conducts research and publishes books of genealogical information. *Founded:* 1990. *Members:* 100.

1191 ■ Weakley County Genealogical Society
PO Box 894
Martin, TN 38237

Contact: Pansy Nanney Baker, Pres.

Desc: To collect, preserve, and transcribe Weakley County, TN genealogical and historical records and documents. *Founded:* 1976. *Members:* 200.

1192 ■ Webster County Historical and Genealogical Society
PO Box 215   Ph: (502)639-5170
Dixon, KY 42409
URL: http://www.dsenter.com/cpalmer/wchgapp.html

Contact: Betty J. Branson, Sec.-Treas.

Desc: Individuals interested in genealogy and history of Webster County, KY. *Founded:* 1980. *Members:* 175.

1193 ■ Weedman Family Organization
130 Berry Creek Dr.   Ph: (828)693-5300
Flat Rock, NC 28731-8531   Fax: (828)692-6194
E-mail: hnweedman@compuserve.com

Contact: Marianne Montgomery, Exec. Officer.

Desc: Relatives of Christian Weedman descendants. Strives to acquire information on the Weedman descendants and to trace the Weedman family history. Maintains biographical archives; compiles statistics. *Founded:* 1968. *Members:* 120.

1194 ■ Wefel Family Association
555 Freeman Rd., Ste. 91   Ph: (541)664-3622
Central Point, OR 97502
E-mail: ralph_m_wefel@compuserve.com

Contact: Ralph M. Wefel, Chm.

Desc: Individuals with the surname Wefel and its variant spellings; other Wefel family members. Seeks to identify and unite members of the Wefel family. *Founded:* 1990. *Members:* 200.

1195 ■ Weld County Genealogical Society
PO Box 278
Greeley, CO 80632
URL: http://www.rootsweb.com/cowcgs/

Founded: 1973. *Members:* 64.

1196 ■ Wells Family Research Association
PO Box 5427   Ph: (253)630-5296
Kent, WA 98064-5427   Fax: (253)639-2701
E-mail: orwells@bigfoot.com
URL: http://www.rootsweb.com/wellsfam/wfrahome.html

Contact: Orin R. Wells, Pres.

Desc: Open to anyone interested in genealogical research on Wells surname. Seeks to share research information and computerize Wells' information shared through the newsletter, website, and between members. *Founded:* 1988. *Members:* 500.

1197 ■ Welsh-American Genealogical Society
60 Norton Ave.
Poultney, VT 05764-1011
E-mail: wagsjan@sover.net
URL: http://www.ancestry.com/societyhall/pages/soehall-352

Contact: Janice B. Edwards, V.Pres. & Sec.

Desc: Promotes Welsh heritage and aiding Welsh researchers. *Founded:* 1990. *Members:* 800.

1198 ■ Wert Family History Association
PO Box 240   Ph: (717)436-8998
Port Royal, PA 17082-0240   Fax: (717)436-8938
E-mail: jwert@mid-wert.com
URL: http://www.mdi-wert.com

Contact: Dr. Jonathan M. Wert, Jr., Pres.

Desc: Individuals with the surname Wert and its variant spellings; others with an interest in Wert family history and genealogy. Promotes Wert family historical and genealogical scholarship. *Founded:* 1990. *Members:* 400.

1199 ■ West Baton Rouge Genealogical Society
PO Box 1126   Ph: (504)344-0518
Port Allen, LA 70767

Desc: Promotes interest in genealogy. Provides support and assistance to beginning genealogists. Locates, restores, and preserves historic genealogical materials.

1200 ■ West Virginia Genealogical Society and Library
PO Box 249   Ph: (304)965-1179
Elkview, WV 25071   Fax: (304)345-2394
E-mail: cafouty@aol.com

Contact: Harry Lynn, Pres.

Desc: Works to educate and assist genealogists. *Founded:* 1983.

1201 ■ Western Heraldry Organization
543 Main St. 2   Ph: (970)257-9602
Grand Junction, CO 81503
E-mail: ellie@mariah.com

URL: http://www.mariah.com

Contact: Ellie Young, Pres.

Desc: Assists amateur genealogists in researching surnames. *Founded:* 1974.

1202 ■ **Western Massachusetts Genealogical Society**
PO Box 80206, Forest Park Sta.
Springfield, MA 01108

Contact: Claudia Chicklas, Pres.

Desc: Individuals interested in genealogical research. *Founded:* 1972. *Members:* 171.

1203 ■ **Western New York Genealogical Society**
PO Box 338
Hamburg, NY 14075

Contact: Virginia Zugger, Pres.

Desc: Genealogists in western New York counties. Seeks to collect and preserve genealogical records of early settlers in western New York. *Founded:* 1974. *Members:* 800.

1204 ■ **Western Wayne County Genealogical Society**
PO Box 530063   Ph: (734)422-5725
Livonia, MI 48153-0063

Contact: John E. Lambert, Ed.

Desc: Individuals interested in genealogy and genealogical research. Serves as a forum for the exchange of information among members. *Founded:* 1976. *Members:* 160.

1205 ■ **Wetzel County Genealogical Society**
PO Box 464
New Martinsville, WV 26155
E-mail: dlneff@ovis.net

Contact: Carol Hassig, Corr.Sec.

Desc: Persons interested in genealogy in Wetzel County, WV. *Founded:* 1979. *Members:* 200.

1206 ■ **Whitman County Genealogical Society**
PO Box 393   Ph: (509)332-2386
Pullman, WA 99163-0393
URL: http://www.completebbs.com/simonsen/
      wcgsindex.html

Contact: Judy McMurray, Ed.

Founded: 1984. *Members:* 100.

1207 ■ **Whitworth Family Association**
6205 Woodlore Dr.   Ph: (770)429-0706
Acworth, GA 30103   Fax: (770)429-9656
E-mail: bubbles500@aol.com

Contact: Pat Reeser, Chair.

Desc: Individuals interested in the history and genealogy of the Whitworth family. Promotes genealogical and historical research and study. *Founded:* 1994. *Members:* 185.

1208 ■ **Wider Quaker Fellowship**
1506 Race St.   Ph: (215)241-7293
Philadelphia, PA 19102   Fax: (215)241-7285
E-mail: americas@fwcc.quaker.org

Contact: Joanne Spears, Clerk.

Desc: Nonsectarian, spiritual movement of persons, primarily members of other religious denominations, who wish to be in touch with the Religious Society of Friends (Quakers). Maintains fellowship primarily through mailing of literature and correspondence with staff. Includes Fellows in some 90 countries, although majority live in North America. *Founded:* 1936. *Members:* 3000.

1209 ■ **Wilkerson/Wilkinson Clearinghouse**
1605 Holly   Ph: (308)436-5617
Gering, NE 69341
E-mail: jweihing@prairieweb.com

Contact: S. Weihing, Contact.

Desc: Individuals with the surname Wilkerson or Wilkinson and its variants. Gathers information on the history and genealogy of the Wilkerson/Wilkinson family.

1210 ■ **Wilkes County Genealogical Society**
PO Box 1629
North Wilkesboro, NC 28659

Contact: Peggy Martin, Pres.

Desc: Gathers and disseminates genealogical information pertaining to Wilkes County, NC. *Members:* 600.

1211 ■ **William Armstrong and Mary Kirk Family Organization**
2421 N 750 E   Ph: (801)375-4390
Provo, UT 84604

Contact: Elizabeth Fletcher Hunter, Sec.

Desc: Descendants of William Armstrong and Mary Kirk; other individuals with an interest in Armstrong and Kirk family history. Promotes study of, and interest in, Armstrong and Kirk family history and genealogy. *Founded:* 1990. *Members:* 75.

1212 ■ **William Burrup Family Organization**
6602 W. King Valley Rd.   Ph: (801)250-9017
West Valley City, UT
   84128-4217

Contact: Jay G. Burrup, Genealogist.

Desc: Persons interested in the genealogy of the William and Hannah Maria Byington Burrup family. *Members:* 500.

1213 ■ **William Geddes Family Organization**
6602 W King Valley Rd.
West Valley City, UT 84128-4217

Contact: Jay G. Burrup, Contact.

Desc: Members of the Geddes family. Seeks to centralize and coordinate Geddes family historical and genealogical research. *Members:* 500.

1214 ■ **William Hutchinson and Jane Penman Family Organization**
2421 N 750 E   Ph: (801)375-4390
Provo, UT 84604

Contact: Elizabeth Fletcher Hunter, Sec.

Desc: Descendants of William Hutchinson and Jane Penman; other individuals with an interest in Hutchinson and Penman family history. Promotes study of, and interest in, Hutchinson and Penman family history and genealogy. *Founded:* 1990. *Members:* 50.

1215 ■ **William Jacob Heckman Family Organization**
200 Los Robles Way   Ph: (530)753-7376
Woodland, CA 95695

Contact: William Marble, Contact.

Desc: Descendants of William Jacob Heckmann. Promotes and facilitates historical and genealogical research pertaining to the Heckmann and related families. *Founded:* 1988.

1216 ■ **Williams County Genealogical Society**
PO Box 293   Ph: (419)636-3751
Bryan, OH 43506
URL: http://www.bright.net/-southpa/page2.html

Contact: Pamela S. Lash, Pres.

Desc: Individuals interested in preserving the history of Williams County, OH. Disseminates information. *Founded:* 1980. *Members:* 218.

1217 ■ **Williams Family Association**
91 Paddington Way   Ph: (210)829-5987
San Antonio, TX 78209-8301
E-mail: Hankwill@idworld.net

Contact: Henry Williams, Exec. Officer.

Desc: Individuals interested in researching the surname Williams. *Founded:* 1980. *Members:* 12.

1218 ■ **Williamson County Genealogical Society**
PO Box 585   Ph: (512)255-7057
Round Rock, TX 78664

Contact: Carol Verbeek, Pres.

Desc: Help members research family trees. Preserve genealogical records. *Members:* 150.

1219 ■ **Windsor Family Historical Association**
67 West Hill Rd.   Ph: (607)785-5785
Vestal, NY 13850-6101

Contact: N. Waterman, Contact.

Desc: Individuals interested in preserving the history of the Windsor Family. Conducts research. *Founded:* 1983. *Members:* 50.

1220 ■ **Windsor Historical Society**
96 Palisado Ave.   Ph: (860)688-3813
Windsor, CT 06095

Contact: Robert T. Silliman, Dir.

Desc: Individuals interested in the history and genealogy of Windsor, CT. Operates 1640 Lieutenant Walter Flyer House, 1765 Dr. Hezekiah Chaffee House, and museum. Sponsors educational programs. *Founded:* 1921. *Members:* 950.

1221 ■ **Wingfield Family Society**
301 Belleview Blvd.   Ph: (727)461-4187
Belleair, FL 33756   Fax: (727)461-1083
E-mail: 76612.603@compuserve.com
URL: http://www.wingfield.org

Contact: Vance Wingsfield, Pres.

Desc: Individuals with the surname Wingfield and their relatives or interested persons. *Founded:* 1987. *Members:* 900.

1222 ■ **Winnebago/Boone Counties Genealogical Society**
PO Box 10166   Ph: (815)226-4884
Rockford, IL 61131

Founded: 1986.

1223 ■ **Wisconsin State Genealogical Society**
2109 20th Ave.   Ph: (608)325-2609
Monroe, WI 53566-3426
E-mail: md2609@tds.net
URL: http://www.rootsweb/wsgs

Contact: J.A. Brissee, Pres.

Desc: Persons interested in Wisconsin genealogy; libraries and organizations with genealogical collections. *Founded:* 1939. *Members:* 1390.

1224 ■ **Woenne/Wonne/Winne Family Association**
12800 Briar Forest Dr. Ste. 83
Houston, TX 77077-2206

Contact: Bernice Mistrot, Sec.

Desc: Persons with the surname Woenne, Wonne or Winne. Records and preserves family history and genealogical records. *Founded:* 1979. *Members:* 75.

1225 ■ Wolfensberger Family Association
6400 N Ann Arbor Terrace   Ph: (405)721-4383
Oklahoma City, OK 73132
E-mail: wolfberg@icon.net
URL: http://www.icon.net/wolfberg/

Contact: Lawrence M. Jones, Contact.

Desc: Descendants of Knight Balderbert (1233-1259), who may have participated in the Third Crusade and founded Castle Wolfsburg near Baum, Switzerland. Promotes interest in the history and genealogy of the Wolfsberger family. *Founded:* 1994. *Members:* 350.

1226 ■ Womelsdorf Family Association
2727 N Wickham Rd.,   Ph: (407)253-9062
    Apt. 10-101
Melbourne, FL 32935

Contact: Donald Womelsdorf, Pres.

Desc: Descendants of Daniel Womelsdorf, who emigrated from Germany to North America in 1729. Seeks to identify and unite members of the Womelsdorf family. *Founded:* 1968. *Members:* 400.

1227 ■ Wood County Genealogical Society
PO Box 832   Ph: (903)763-4191
Quitman, TX 75783
E-mail: markreid@ballistic.com
URL: http://www.rootsweb.com/txwood/index.htm

Contact: R. Mark Reid, Pres.

Members: 100.

1228 ■ World Jewish Genealogy Organization
PO Box 420   Ph: (718)435-4400
Brooklyn, NY 11219   Fax: (718)633-7050

Contact: Rabbi Naftali Halberstam, Pres.

Desc: Researchers and scholars of Jewish genealogy. Encourages research and publication of Jewish biographies, bibliographies, and genealogies. *Founded:* 1980. *Members:* 295.

1229 ■ World Methodist Historical Society
PO Box 127   Ph: (973)408-3189
Madison, NJ 07940   Fax: (973)408-3909
E-mail: cyrigoye@drew.edu

Contact: Dr. Charles Yrigoyen, Jr., Exec.Sec.

Desc: Oversees the historical activities of world Methodism. *Founded:* 1911. *Members:* 200.

1230 ■ Wren Family Association
5809 Tautoga   Ph: (915)755-0083
El Paso, TX 79924

Contact: Ruth Wren, Editor.

Desc: Surname researchers dedicated to collecting documentation on kin of the Wren, Wrenn, Ren, Renn, Ran, and Rain families. Researches and preserves all records and information related to all spellings of the Wren family name. *Founded:* 1990. *Members:* 100.

1231 ■ Wyandot Tracers Chapter of the Ohio Genealogical Society
PO Box 414   Ph: (740)482-2559
Upper Sandusky, OH 43351
E-mail: corfmanjl@tkdyer.com
URL: http://www.udata.com/users/hsbaher/tracers.htm

Contact: James/Luella Corfman, Pres.

Desc: Works to create and build interest in preserving and collecting historical demographic materials. Gathers and disseminates genealogical information. *Founded:* 1982. *Members:* 300.

1232 ■ Wyckoff House and Association
PO Box 100376   Ph: (718)629-5400
Brooklyn, NY 11210   Fax: (718)629-5400

Contact: Diana Kraus, Dir.

Desc: Promotes interest in Wyckoff House Museum and in the history of the Pieter Claesen Wyckoff family. Disseminates materials and information on the museum and the Wyckoff descendants. *Founded:* 1937. *Members:* 1350.

1233 ■ Yates County Genealogical and Historical Society
200 Main St.   Ph: (315)536-7318
Penn Yan, NY 14527   Fax: (315)536-7318

Contact: John Mahaffy, Dir.

Desc: Individuals interested in preserving the history and genealogy of Yates County, NY. *Founded:* 1860. *Members:* 530.

1234 ■ York County Genealogical Society
PO Box 431   Ph: (207)439-4243
Eliot, ME 03903-0431

Contact: Theodore S. Bond, Ed.

Founded: 1985. *Members:* 150.

1235 ■ York County Genealogical Society
PO Box 431   Ph: (781)665-4664
Eliot, ME 03903

Contact: Theodore Bond, Ed.

Desc: Conducts limited research and makes available genealogical source data pertaining to York County, ME. *Founded:* 1985. *Members:* 175.

1236 ■ Young Surname Organization
347 12th Ave. N   Ph: (651)455-3626
South St. Paul, MN 55075-1957   Fax: (651)455-2897
E-mail: valbu@worldnet.att.net

Contact: Vicki Young Albu, Contact.

Desc: Individuals with the surname Young or Jung and other members of the Young and related families. Promotes study of Young family history and genealogy. *Founded:* 1985. *Members:* 200.

1237 ■ Your Genealogy Committee
1113 S Orem Blvd.
Orem, UT 84058-6931

Contact: John Whitaker, Contact.

1238 ■ Zang Family Organization
15186 Kelly St.   Ph: (616)798-1310
Spring Lake, MI 49456   Fax: (616)739-7200
E-mail: gzang@juno.com

Contact: Gary P. Zang, CPIM, Chm.

Desc: Persons with the surname Zang. Promotes and researches the history of the surname Zang. *Founded:* 1978.

1239 ■ Zartman Association of America
713 Quaint Acres   Ph: (301)622-5151
Silver Spring, MD 20904   Fax: (301)622-5151

Contact: I. William Zartman, Pres.

Desc: Families of American descendants of Alexander and Anna Zartman. Perpetuates the cultural heritage of and promotes contact among members. *Founded:* 1908. *Members:* 800.

Libraries

1240 ■ Adams County Genealogical Society Library
PO Box 231
West Union, OH 45693

Contact: Kathryn Miller, Libn.

Desc: Subject: Genealogy, family histories, Adams County. Holdings: Figures not available. Services: Copying; Library open to the public on a limited schedule.

1241 ■ Adams County Historical Society Archives
PO Box 102   Ph: (402)463-5838
Hastings, NE 68901
E-mail: achs@tcqcs.com

Contact: Catherine Renschler, Dir.

Desc: Subject: Local history, the Great Plains. Holdings: 400 books; 250 bound periodical volumes; 500 reels of microfilm of newspapers; 500 cassette tapes; 25 AV programs; 62 document cases of church records; 30 linear feet of school records; 150 maps; 100 document cases of other archival materials; inventory of county and city records, 1873 to present. Services: Copying; archives open to the public.

1242 ■ Adams County Historical Society Library
Schmucker Hall   Ph: (717)334-4723
Seminary Campus, Box 4325
Gettysburg, PA 17325

Contact: Dr. Charles H. Glatfelter, Dir.

Desc: Subject: Adams County history. Holdings: 1000 volumes; 240 VF drawers of records, manuscripts, clippings, newspapers, genealogical files. Services: Library and museum open to the public.

1243 ■ Adams State College Nielsen Library Special Collections
Edgemont & 1st   Ph: (719)587-7781
Alamosa, CO 81102   Fax: (719)587-7590
E-mail: dlmachad@adams.edu
URL: http://www.adams.edu

Contact: Dianne Machado, Dir.

Desc: Holdings: 146,154 books; 34,651 bound periodical volumes; 1600 archives; 626,541 microfiche; 12,204 microfilm. Services: Interlibrary loan; copying; Library open to the public.

1244 ■ Adath Jeshurun Congregation Jenny Gross Memorial Library
10500 Hillside Ln. W.   Ph: (612)545-2424
Minnetonka, MN 55305   Fax: (612)545-2913

Contact: Marilyn Burstein

Desc: Subject: Zionism, Bible, theology, Jewish history, liturgy, law and literature, modern Israel. Holdings: 5000 books. Services: Library open to the public.

1245 ■ Agudas Achim Congregation Stein Memorial Library
2767 E. Broad St.   Ph: (614)237-2747
Columbus, OH 43209   Fax: (614)237-3576

Desc: Subject: Judaica. Holdings: 3238 volumes. Services: Library not open to the public.

1246 ■ Agudath Achim Synagogue Abe and Esther Tenenbaum Library
9 Lee Blvd.   Ph: (912)352-4737
Savannah, GA 31405   Fax: (912)352-3477

Contact: Anne C. Siegel, Libn.

Desc: Subject: Jewish literature, authors, biographies, and children's books and other media. Holdings: 2000 books. Services: Library open to the public.

1247 ■ Agudath Israel Congregation
Malca Pass Library
1400 Coldrey Ave.   Ph: (613)722-3501
Ottawa, ON, Canada K1Z 7P9

Contact: Donna Guttman, Libn.

Desc: Subject: Judaism - religion, art, philosophy, biography; holocaust literature. Holdings: 6300 books; 100 videocassettes; 130 compact disks; 30 audiocassettes. Services: Library open to the public with restrictions.

1248 ■ Alabama State University
University Library & Learning Resources
Archives & Special Collections
Levi Watkins Learning Center   Ph: (334)229-4106
915 S. Jackson St.   Fax: (334)229-4940
Montgomery, AL 36104-5732
E-mail: davis@asunet.alasu.edu
URL: http://asu.alasu.edu/library/

Contact: Rubye Sullivan, Spec.Coll.Libn.

Desc: Subject: Afro-Americans. Holdings: 11,980 books; 600 bound periodical volumes; 384 reels of microfilm; 435 microfiche; 305 16mm films, cassettes, filmstripcassette sets; 2 vertical files of clippings; 200 phonograph records, slides, audiotapes; 1690 theses. Services: Copying; collections open to the public.

1249 ■ Alaska (State) Department of Labor
Research and Analysis Section
Census & Geographic Information Network
Box 25504   Fax: (907)465-4506
Juneau, AK 99802-5504
E-mail: kathryn-lizik@labor.state.ak.us

Contact: (907)465-2437

Desc: Subject: U.S. census and demographics, population trends. Holdings: 1752 publications and periodicals. Services: Copying; Library open to the public.

1250 ■ Albemarle County Historical Society
Charlottesville-Albemarle Historical Collection
McIntire Bldg.   Ph: (804)296-7294
200 2nd St., NE   Fax: (804)296-4576
Charlottesville, VA 22902
URL: http://www.monticello.avenue.gen.va.us/achs/

Contact: Margaret M. O'Bryant, Libn.

Desc: Subject: History and genealogy - Charlottesville, Albemarle County, Virginia. Holdings: 2900 books; 100 bound periodical volumes; 10 reels of microfilm; 2000 photographs; 1000 slides; 350 manuscripts; 7500 pamphlets; 82 cu. ft. of VF drawers; 300 maps. Services: Copying; Library open to the public.

1251 ■ Alberta Genealogical Society
Libraries
Prince of Wales Armouries   Ph: (780)484-4429
  Heritage Centre   Fax: (780)423-8980
10440 108 Ave., No. 116
Edmonton, AB, Canada T5H
  3Z9
E-mail: agsoffice@compusmart.ab.ca
URL: http://www.compusmart.ab.ca/abgensoc

Desc: Subject: Genealogy, history. Holdings: 4500 books; 1000 microfiche; microfilm; CD-ROMs. Services: Copying.

1252 ■ Albuquerque Public Library
Special Collections Branch
423 Central, N.E.   Ph: (505)848-1376
Albuquerque, NM 87102
URL: http://www.cabg.gov/rgvls

Contact: Joe Sabatini, Actg.Br.Mgr.

Desc: Subject: Genealogy, local and state history. Holdings: 19,500 books; 475 bound periodical volumes; 9000 reels of microfilm and microfiche. Services: Copying; collections open to the public.

1253 ■ Alex F. Weisberg Library
8500 Hillcrest Rd.   Ph: (214)706-0000
Temple Emanu-El   Fax: (214)706-0025
Dallas, TX 75225
URL: http://www.tedallas.org

Contact: Maureen Reister, Lib.Dir.

Desc: Subject: Judaica and related topics. Holdings: 12,000 books; 200 videotapes. Services: Library open to the public on a fee basis.

1254 ■ Alexandria Library
Special Collections at Lloyd House
220 Washington St.   Ph: (703)838-4577
Alexandria, VA 22314-2420   Fax: (703)706-3912
URL: http://www.alexandria.lib.va.us/lloyd.html

Contact: Joyce A. McMullin, Br.Libn.

Desc: Subject: History - Southern, Virginia, Alexandria; genealogy; Alexandria manuscripts. Holdings: 16,000 books; 1862 bound periodical volumes; 17,700 pamphlets; 950 boxes of manuscripts; 10,130 reels of microfilm; 26 linear feet of boxes of early city records. Services: Copying; Library open to the public with restrictions on circulation.

1255 ■ Allaire Village, Inc.
Allaire Research Library
PO Box 220   Ph: (732)938-2253
Allaire, NJ 07727   Fax: (732)938-3302
E-mail: allaire@bellatlantic.net

Contact: John C. Curtis, III, Exec.Dir

Desc: Subject: Ja Works (iron industry); history - Monmouth and Ocean Counties, and Allaire Village, New Jersey; social history (early to mid-1800s). Holdings: 300 books; 70 bound periodical volumes; 7 nonbook items; 60 manuscripts; deeds; letters; account books. Services: Copying; Library by reservation open to the public with restrictions.

1256 ■ Allen County Historical Society
Elizabeth M. MacDonell Memorial Library
620 W. Market St.   Ph: (419)222-9426
Lima, OH 45801-4604   Fax: (419)222-0649

Contact: Anna B. Selfridge, Cur., Archv. & Mss.

Desc: Subject: Local history and genealogy, Ohio history, railroading, American Indian. Holdings: 8271 books; 585 bound periodical volumes; Lima, Ohio newspapers, 1840s to present; Lima directories, 1876 to present; 1938 reels of microfilm of newspapers and census records. Services: Copying; Library open to the public.

1257 ■ Allen County Public Library
Fred J. Reynolds Historical Genealogy
Collection
900 Webster St.   Ph: (219)421-1225
PO Box 2270   Fax: (219)422-9688
Fort Wayne, IN 46802
URL: http://www.acpl.lib.in.us/genealogy/
   genealogy.html

Contact: Curt B. Witcher, Mgr.

Desc: Subject: North American genealogy and family history, Indiana history, heraldry. Holdings: 226,134 books; 17,003 bound periodical volumes; 500 vertical file materials and clippings; 272,149 microforms; 12 audiovisual programs; 157,000 clippings and pamphlets. Services: Copying; collection open to the public.

1258 ■ Amana Heritage Society
Research and Archive Library
PO Box 81   Ph: (319)622-3567
Amana, IA 52203   Fax: (319)622-6481
E-mail: amherit@juno.com

Contact: Lanny Haldy, Dir.

Desc: Subject: Immigration, travel, and settlement of the Amana people, 1714 to present, German Pietism, reigious communal societies. Holdings: 1000 books; 5000 photographs; diaries; letters; deeds; records; oral history tapes; videocassettes; local newspapers on microfilm, maps. Services: Archives open to the public by appointment.

1259 ■ Amarillo Genealogical Library
Amarillo Public Library   Ph: (806)378-4211
Box 2171   Fax: (806)378-9327
Amarillo, TX 79189
E-mail: library@ci.amarillo.tx.us
URL: http://www.ci.amarillo.tx.us/library

Contact: Mary Kay Snell, Dir., Lib.Svcs.

Desc: Subject: Family histories. Holdings: 9868 books; 1250 bound periodical volumes; 11,048 reels of microfilm; county resource material. Services: Interlibrary loan; copying; Library open to the public.

1260 ■ Amelia Historical Society
Amelia Historical Library
Jackson Bldg., Box 113   Ph: (804)561-3180
Amelia, VA 23002

Contact: Joseph O. Humphreys, Chm.

Desc: Subject: Genealogy, local artifacts and history. Holdings: 950 books. Services: Copying; library open to the public on a limited schedule.

1261 ■ American Antiquarian Society
Library
185 Salisbury St.   Ph: (508)755-5221
Worcester, MA 01609   Fax: (508)753-3311
E-mail: library@mwa.org
URL: http://MARK.MWA.ORG

Contact: Ellen S. Dunlap, Pres.

Desc: Subject: American history, literature, and culture through 1876. Holdings: 680,000 books; 150,000 bound periodical volumes and newspaper volumes; 2000 linear feet of manuscripts. Services: Copying; Library open to qualified researchers.

1262 ■ American-Canadian Genealogical
Society, Inc.
Library
4 Elm St.   Ph: (603)622-1554
PO Box 6478   Fax: (603)626-9812
Manchester, NH 03108-6478
E-mail: amperrault@aol.com
URL: http://www.acgs.org

Contact: Mary-Jeanne Colburn, Lib.Dir.

Desc: Subject: French-Canadian American materials, genealogy, history. Holdings: 4500 books; 3000 bound periodical volumes; family histories; town histories; marriage repertoires, Quebec and some U.S. - New England; archival resources; maps. Services: Research on payment of fee; Library open to the public Performs searches on fee basis.

1263 ■ American College
Oral History Center & Archives
270 Bryn Mawr Ave.   Ph: (610)526-1452
Bryn Mawr, PA 19010   Fax: (610)526-1322

Contact: Marjorie Amos Fletcher, Archv.

Desc: Subject: History - American College, life insurance business and education, women in life insurance as a profession, professional education. Holdings: 200 books; 70 cubic feet of records; museum display cases. Services: Copying; center open to the public (limited hours).

1264 ■ American College of Heraldry
Library
PO Box 11084
Tuscaloosa, AL 35486-0025

Contact: Dr. David P. Johnson, Pres.

Desc: Subject: Heraldry, chivalry, genealogy, names, flags. Holdings: 561 books; 251 bound periodical volumes. Services: Library not open to the public.

1265 ■ American Family Records Association
Library
PO Box 15505   Ph: (816)252-0950
Kansas City, MO 64106   Fax: (816)252-0950

Contact: Ann Reinhart, Libn.

Desc: Subject: Genealogy, history, adoptive relationships. Holdings: 5000 volumes. Services: Interlibrary loan; Library open to the public.

1266 ■ American-French Genealogical Society
Library
PO Box 2113   Ph: (401)765-6141
Pawtucket, RI 02861   Fax: (401)765-6141
E-mail: afgs@ids.net
URL: http://users.ids.net/afgs/afgshome.html

Contact: Janice Burkhart, Libn.

Desc: Subject: French-American genealogy, vital records from Quebec and United States, family history and biography. Holdings: 10,000 books; 1000 bound periodical volumes; microfilm; microfiche. Services: Library open to the public (5 fee per visit for non-members).

1267 ■ American Genealogical Lending Library
Heritage Quest
PO Box 329   Ph: (801)298-5446
Bountiful, UT 84011-0329   Fax: (801)298-5468
E-mail: sales@heritagequest.com
URL: http://www.heritagequest.com

Contact: Bradley W. Steuart, Pres.

Desc: Subject: Genealogy. Holdings: 250,000 reels of microfilm including census records, mortality schedules, ship passenger lists, military records, vital records, deeds, wills, tax lists, county and family histories. Services: Interlibrary loan; microfilming.

1268 ■ American Historical Society of Germans
from Russia
Library
631 D St.   Ph: (402)474-3363
Lincoln, NE 68502-1199   Fax: (402)474-7229
E-mail: ahsgr@aol.com
URL: http://www.ahsgr.org

Contact: Jan Traci Roth

Desc: Subject: Germans from Russia - culture, history, genealogy. Holdings: 5000 books; 175 yearbook and periodical titles; 40 AV programs; 125 nonbook items. Services: Interlibrary loan; copying; Library open to the public.

1269 ■ American Indian Research Project
South Dakota Oral History Center
Library
12 Dakota Hall   Ph: (605)677-5209
University of South Dakota   Fax: (605)677-6525
414 E. Clark St.
Vermillion, SD 57069
E-mail: iais@usd.edu
URL: http://www.usd.edu/iais

Contact: Leonard R. Bruguier, Dir., Inst. of American Indian

Desc: Subject: North American frontier, mining, South Dakota and Indian history. Holdings: 5000 audiotapes. Services: Copying; Library and archives open for scholarly research by appointment.

1270 ■ American International College
James J. Shea Memorial Library
Oral History Center
1000 State St.   Ph: (413)747-6225
Springfield, MA 01109-3189   Fax: (413)737-2803
URL: http://www.westmass.com/shea

Contact: Dr. F. Knowlton Utley, Dir. of Lib.

Desc: Holdings: 630 oral history tapes. Services: Interlibrary loan; copying; center open to the public with restrictions.

1271 ■ American Irish Historical Society
Library
991 5th Ave.   Ph: (212)288-2263
New York, NY 10028   Fax: (212)628-7927
URL: http://www.aihs.org

Contact: Paul Ruppert, Dir.

Desc: Subject: Irish in the American colonies and the United States, Irish history and literature. Holdings: 15,000 books; 200 linear feet of archives and manuscripts; 50 discontinued serial titles. Services: Library open to the public.

1272 ■ American Jewish Committee
Blaustein Library
165 E. 56th St.   Ph: (212)751-4000
New York, NY 10022   Fax: (212)751-4017
E-mail: research@ajc.org
URL: http://www.ajc.org

Contact: Cyma M. Horowitz, Lib.Dir.

Desc: Subject: Intergroup relations, Jewish community organization, contemporary Jewish problems, civil rights and liberties, ethnic groups, interreligious relations. Holdings: 30,000 books and pamphlets; 60 VF drawers; 1450 reels of microfilm. Services: Library open to qualified scholars for reference use only.

1273 ■ American Jewish Committee
Oral History Library
Dorot Jewish Division   Ph: (212)930-0603
New York Public Library   Fax: (212)642-0141
5th Ave. & 42nd St.
New York, NY 10018
E-mail: lgold@nypl.org
URL: http://www.nypl.org

Contact: Dr. Leonard Gold

Desc: Subject: All aspects of the "American Jewish Experience in the 20th Century." Holdings: 2500 taped interviews and transcripts. Services: Library open to accredited researchers.

1274 ■ American Jewish Historical Society
Library
2 Thornton Rd.   Ph: (781)891-8110
Waltham, MA 02453   Fax: (781)899-9208

E-mail: ajhs@ajhs.org
URL: http://www.ajhs.org

Contact: Michael Feldberg, Exec.Dir.

Desc: Subject: American Jewish history. Holdings: 50,000 books, 500,000 unbound periodicals; 7000 linear feet of manuscripts; 500 Yiddish theater posters; 2000 pieces of Yiddish sheet music; 75,000 synagogue and other Jewish institutional items. Services: Copying; Library open to the public with restrictions.

1275 ■ Amerind Foundation, Inc.
Fulton-Hayden Memorial Library
PO Box 400   Ph: (520)586-3666
Dragoon, AZ 85609-0400   Fax: (520)586-4679
E-mail: amerind@amerind.org
URL: http://amerind.org

Contact: Celia Skeeles, Libn.

Desc: Subject: Archeology, anthropology, Greater American Southwest, ethnology and history. Holdings: 28,000 books; 2260 pamphlets and reprints; 550 manuscripts; 250 maps; 12,000 slides and photographs; 2 VF drawers of clippings and translations. Services: Copying; Library open to serious researchers by appointment only and with written statement of intent.

1276 ■ Ames Public Library
Ames and Iowa History Collection
515 Douglas Ave.   Ph: (515)239-5656
Ames, IA 50010-6215   Fax: (515)232-4571
URL: http://www.ames.lib.ia.us

Contact: Gina J. Millsap

Desc: Subject: State and local history, genealogy. Holdings: Books; pamphlets; clippings; state and federal census data on microfilm, photographs; scrapbooks; telephone directories; city and county documents; publications of local organizations; yearbooks; atlases; genealogical materials. Services: Interlibrary loan; copying; collection open to the public.

1277 ■ Amistad Research Center
LibraryArchives
Tulane University   Ph: (504)865-5535
Tilton Hall   Fax: (504)865-5580
6823 St. Charles Ave.
New Orleans, LA 70118
E-mail: arc@mailhost.tcs.tulane.edu
URL: http://www.arc.tulane.edu

Contact: Dr. Donald E. DeVore, Exec.Dir.

Desc: Subject: Ethnic minorities of America, Afro-American history and culture, civil rights, Africa, abolitionism, United Church of Christ. Holdings: 22,000 books; 1600 bound periodical volumes; 25,000 pamphlets; 210 dissertations on microfilm; 3000 reels of microfilm; 1.5 million clippings. Services: Interlibrary loan; copying; Library open to the public.

1278 ■ Andover Historical Society
Caroline M. Underhill Research Library
97 Main St.   Ph: (978)475-2236
Andover, MA 01810   Fax: (978)470-2741
E-mail: andhists@ma.ultranet.com
URL: http://www.town.andover.ma.us/commun/society.htm

Contact: Barbara Thibault, Exec.Dir.

Desc: Subject: Local history, genealogy, architecture, decorative arts. Holdings: 3000 books; 16 VF drawers; 17,500 historical and contemporary photographs and negatives; 100 linear feet of manuscript materials; prints; drawings; maps; architectural plans. Services: Copying; Library open to the public; volunteer research committee available to respond to written inquires from researcher.

1279 ▪ Androscoggin Historical Society
Clarence E. March Library
County Bldg.   Ph: (207)784-0586
2 Turner St.
Auburn, ME 04210-5978
E-mail: itigapa@aol.com
URL: http://www.rootsweb.com/meandrhs

Contact: Michael Lord

Desc: Subject: History and genealogy of Androscoggin County and Maine. Holdings: 5000 books; 20 bound periodical volumes; 200 maps; 1900 documents and records; 5000 pages on microfilm. Services: Copying; Library open to the public for reference use only.

1280 ▪ Annie Halenbake Ross Library
Special Collections
232 W. Main St.   Ph: (717)748-3321
Lock Haven, PA 17745   Fax: (717)748-1050
E-mail: ross@oak.kcsd.k12.pa.us
URL: http://oak.kcsd.k12.pa.us/ross/library

Contact: Diane L. Whitaker, Exec.Dir.

Desc: Subject: Pennsylvania, genealogy. Holdings: 110,000 books; 85 bound periodical volumes; 825 reels of microfilm. Services: Interlibrary loan; copying; Library open to the public.

1281 ▪ Anoka County Historical Society
Library
1900 3rd Ave., S.   Ph: (612)421-0600
Anoka, MN 55303

Desc: Subject: Anoka County and Minnesota history; geneaology. Holdings: 6 VF drawers of manuscripts; 18 drawers of county birth, death, and marriage records, 1863-1920; 125 reels of microfilm; 50 oral history tapes and maps; newspapers; clippings; research reference books; family history books, photo collection, 5000 of Anoka Co. Services: Interlibrary loan (microfilm only); copying; Library open to the public for reference use only.

1282 ▪ Anshe Hesed Temple
Library
930 Liberty St.   Ph: (814)454-2426
Erie, PA 16502

Contact: Barbara Shapiro

Desc: Subject: Jewish fiction, literature, biography, history; Bible and Talmud; religion; art. Holdings: 3800 books. Services: Library open to the public by appointment.

1283 ▪ Appalachian State University
Belk Library
William L. Eury Appalachian Collection
       Ph: (828)262-4041
rs>Boone, NC 28608   Fax: (828)262-2553
E-mail: hayfj@appstate.edu
URL: http://www.library.appstate.edu/appcoll/

Contact: Dr. Fred J. Hay, Dir.

Desc: Subject: Appalachian region, folk culture, local history, ethnography, genealogy, music, tourism, Native Appalachia, African Appalachia. Holdings: 25,704 volumes; 14,530 reels of microfilm; 5300 microfiche; 2290 audiotapes; 2805 sound discs; 1000 linear feet of manuscripts; 680 slides; 150 photographs; 150 feet of clippings files; 827 videotapes and films; 21 CD-ROMs. Services: Interlibrary loan; copying; collection open to the public.

1284 ▪ Archelaus Smith Museum
Archives
PO Box 291   Ph: (902)745-3361
Clark's Harbour, NS, Canada
  B0W 1P0
E-mail: timkins@atcon.com

URL: http://www.bmhs.ednet.ns.ca/tourism/smith.htm

Contact: Heather Atkinson, Pres.

Desc: Subject: Genealogy, local history. Holdings: Figures not available. Services: Library open to the public.

1285 ▪ Arizona Historical Society
Library and Archives Departments
949 E. 2nd St.   Ph: (520)617-1157
Tucson, AZ 85719   Fax: (520)628-5695
E-mail: azhist@azstarnet.com

Contact: Deborah Shelton, Lib.Dir.

Desc: Subject: History of Arizona, The Southwest, and Northern Mexico, 1540 to the Present; mining; ranching; military; and Southwest Indian tribes. Holdings: 50,000 books; 5000 bound periodical volumes; 10,000 pamphlets; 5000 maps; 750,000 photographs; 1000 manuscripts; 1200 Oral Histories. Services: Copying; Library open to the public for reference use only (copies from the photograph collection are available for a fee).

1286 ▪ Arizona Historical Society Museum
LibraryArchives
1300 N. College Ave.   Ph: (602)929-0292
Tempe, AZ 85281   Fax: (602)967-5450
E-mail: ahs@ahs.lib.az.us
URL: http://www.tempe.com/AHS

Desc: Subject: Arizona and western history, preservation, 20th-century Phoenix history. Holdings: 1500 volumes; 20,000 historical photographs; 120 boxes of manuscript collections; 5000 films and videotape programs; 700 oral history tapes; 19,000 architectural drawings. Services: Copying; Library open to the public.

1287 ▪ Arizona (State) Department of Library,
Archives & Public Records
State Capitol, Rm. 200   Ph: (602)542-4035
1700 W. Washington   Fax: (602)542-4972
Phoenix, AZ 85007
E-mail: slrefde@dlapr.lib.az.us
URL: http://www.dlapr.lib.az.us

Contact: GladysAnn Wells, Dir.

Desc: Subject: Arizona and southwestern history, law, genealogy. Holdings: 1.1 million volumes; federal document depository; state document Center; public records center; state archives. Services: Interlibrary loan; Library open to the public for reference use only.

1288 ▪ Arizona State University
Department of Archives and Manuscripts
Hayden Library   Ph: (602)965-4932
Tempe, AZ 85287-1006   Fax: (602)965-0776
E-mail: rob.spindler@asu.edu
URL: http://www.asu.edu/lib/archives/dampage.htm

Contact: Robert P. Spindler, Hd., Archv. & Mss.

Desc: Subject: Arizona and Southwestern United States - history, politics, water, land use, peoples, Mexican-Americans; Arizona State University; visual literacy. Holdings: 29,238 books; 1120 bound periodical volumes; 11,094 linear feet of manuscripts; 906,199 photographic images; 28 drawers of microfilm; 60 map case drawers; biographical and general information files on Arizona history; 180 linear feet of ephemera. Services: Copying (limited); digital photo duplication service; collections open to the public.

1289 ▪ Arkansas (State) History Commission
Archives
One Capitol Mall   Ph: (501)682-6900
Little Rock, AR 72201

Contact: Dr. John L. Ferguson, State Hist.

Desc: Subject: Arkansas history, Civil War, genealogy, family history, the South, Ozarks, Arkansas folklore. Holdings: 20,000 books; 1000 bound periodical volumes; 100,000 reels of microfilm; 600 maps; 4000 photographs and paintings; 500 cubic feet of manuscript materials; 5000 pamphlets; 100 VF drawers of clippings; Arkansas newspaper files; county records; cemetery records; church records; Civil War records. Services: Copying; archives open to the public.

1290 ▪ Arlington County Central Library
Virginia Room
1015 N. Quincy St.   Ph: (703)228-5966
Arlington, VA 22201   Fax: (703)228-7720
URL: http://www.co.arlington.va.us/lib/

Contact: Judith Knudsen

Desc: Subject: Arlington County, Virginia; Washington Metropolitan Area, State of Virginia - history and current information. Holdings: 16,000 volumes; 800 unbound reports and documents; 32 VF drawers of clippings and ephemera; 100 linear feet of manuscripts; 6300 photographs; 400 maps; 700 videotapes. Services: Copying; room open to the public on a limited schedule and by appointment only.

1291 ▪ Arlington Historical Society
Smith Museum Archives
7 Jason St.   Ph: (781)648-4300
Arlington, MA 02476-1610
URL: http://www.ahs.org

Contact: Donna Lambrechts, Reg.

Desc: Subject: History, religion, fashion, Arlington. Holdings: 200 books; 75 bound periodical volumes; 500 documents. Services: Copying; Library open to the public under staff supervision.

1292 ▪ Asheboro Public Library
Randolph Room
Asheboro Public Library   Ph: (336)318-6815
201 Worth St.
Asheboro, NC 27203

Contact: Marsha F. Haithcock, Libn., Randolph Rm.

Desc: Subject: Genealogy. Holdings: 6000 books; 600 reels of microfilm; photographs; VF drawers of memorabilia; historical maps. Services: Copying; Library open to the public with restrictions.

1293 ▪ Ashland Avenue Baptist Church
Library
2001 Ashland Ave.   Ph: (419)243-3171
Toledo, OH 43620

Contact: Vivian Sollman

Desc: Subject: Religion, biblical topics, social issues, youth, current events, biographies. Holdings: Archives. Services: Library not open to the public.

1294 ▪ Ashland Historical Society
Library
2 Myrtle St.   Ph: (508)881-8183
Box 145
Ashland, MA 01721

Contact: Catherine G. Powers, Cur.

Desc: Subject: Local history and genealogy. Holdings: 300 books and pamphlets; manuscripts; clippings; ephemera; local newspapers, 1869-1915, on microfilm; photographs and portraits of town officials, 1850-1900; 400 slides. Services: Library open to the public by appointment.

1295 ▪ Ashville Area Heritage Society
Library
34 Long St. Ph: (740)983-9864
Ashville, OH 43103
URL: http://www.pickaway.com

Contact: Charles Morrison, Cur.

Desc: Subject: Local history. Holdings: Microfiche; microfilm. Services: Copying; Library open to the public.

1296 ▪ Aspen Historical Society
Library
620 W. Bleeker St. Ph: (970)925-3721
Aspen, CO 81611 Fax: (303)925-5347

Contact: Lisa Hancock, Collections Mgr.

Desc: Subject: Aspen area history, Colorado state. Holdings: 800 books; 120 bound periodical volumes; 10,000 photographs; 400 tapes; 2000 glass plates; 4 VF drawers of clippings; 40 16mm films; Aspen Times Newspaper, 1881 to present; 200 videotapes. Services: Copying; Library open to members, and on a fee basis to nonmembers.

1297 ▪ Association Museums New Brunswick
Library
503 Queen St. Ph: (506)452-2908
PO Box 116, Sta. A Fax: (506)459-0481
Fredericton, NB, Canada E3B
4Y2
E-mail: muse@nbnet.nb.ca
URL: http://www.amnb.nb.ca

Contact: G. Bourque, Exce.Dir.

Desc: Subject: Museums, heritage, nonprofit management, conservation. Holdings: 200 books; videotapes; slides. Services: Library open primarily to members only.

1298 ▪ Atascadero Historical Society
Museum
6500 Palma Ave Ph: (805)466-8341
Box 1047
Atascadero, CA 93423

Contact: Mike Lindsay, Cur.

Desc: Subject: Atascadero history, primarily of its colony days (1913-1924). Holdings: 300 volumes; 25 oral history tapes; ledgers; deeds; Atascadero newspapers; high school yearbooks. Services: Museum open to the public.

1299 ▪ Atchison County Kansas Genealogical
Society
Collection
Atchison Library Ph: (913)367-1902
401 Kansas Fax: (913)367-2717
Atchison, KS 66002

Contact: Cora Chambers, Pres.

Desc: Subject: Atchison County, Kansas, surrounding counties, Missouri, genealogy. Holdings: 100 books; 10 bound periodical volumes; 34 reports; 10 microfiche; 166 reels of microfilm. Services: Library open to the public for reference use only.

1300 ▪ Athens-Clarke County Library
Heritage Room
2025 Baxter St. Ph: (706)613-3650
Athens, GA 30606 Fax: (706)613-3660
URL: http://www.clarkc.public.lib.ga.us/public/arls/
heritageroom.html

Desc: Subject: Georgia history and genealogy; African Americans; War Between the States. Holdings: Books; maps; records; vertical files; county/state histories. Services: Interlibrary loan (limited); copying; room open to the public.

1301 ▪ Atlanta-Fulton Public Library
Genealogy and Georgia History Department
1 Margaret Mitchell Square Ph: (404)730-1700
Atlanta, GA 30303 Fax: (404)730-1989
URL: http://www.af.public.lib.ga.us

Contact: Joyce Burns, Mgr.

Desc: Subject: Genealogy, Georgia history and literature, oral history, Margaret Mitchell. Holdings: 14,300 books; 2300 bound periodical volumes; 3000 reels of microfilm; 11,000 microfiche; 300 audiocassettes; 790 other cataloged items. Services: Copying; department open to the public for reference use only.

1302 ▪ Atlanta History Center
Archives/Library
130 W. Paces Ferry Rd. Ph: (404)814-4040
Atlanta, GA 30305 Fax: (404)814-4175
E-mail: atla@hist.org
URL: http://www.atlhistory.org

Contact: Anne A. Salter, Dir., Lib. & Archv.

Desc: Subject: History of Atlanta and its environs, personalities, organizations, businesses; Civil War history. Holdings: 30,000 books; 152 newspaper titles; 203 periodical titles; 85,000 indexed photographs; 20,000 slides; 172 cubic feet of vertical files. Services: Copying; Library open to the public.

1303 ▪ Atlantic City Free Public Library
Special Collections
1 N. Tennessee Ave. Ph: (609)345-2269
Atlantic City, NJ 08401

Contact: Maureen Sherr Frank, Dir.

Desc: Subject: State and local history, genealogy. Holdings: 3500 books; 150 bound periodical volumes. Services: Copying; collections open to the public with valid identification.

1304 ▪ Atlantic County Historical Society
Library
907 Shore Rd. Ph: (609)927-5218
Box 301
Somers Point, NJ 08244

Contact: June Sheridan, Libn.

Desc: Subject: History, genealogy, and maritime history of Atlantic County and Southern New Jersey; Civil War. Holdings: 6000 books and bound periodical volumes; 36 VF drawers; 140 manuscript books; 100 family Bibles; 132 maps; Atlantic County census data on microfilm; photographs; lantern slides; postcards; deeds; letters; diaries; shiplogs; oral history tapes. Services: Copying; Library open to the public.

1305 ▪ Audrain County Historical Society
Graceland Library/American Saddle Horse
Museum
Library
501 S. Muldrow Ph: (573)581-3910
PO Box 398
Mexico, MO 65265

Contact: Kathryn Adams, Exec.Dir.

Desc: Subject: County history, saddle horses. Holdings: 500 books; magazines; newspapers; breeder manuals; genealogical records; cemetery records. Services: Copying; Library open to the public for reference use only on a limited schedule.

1306 ▪ Aurora History Museum
Library
15001 E. Alameda Dr. Ph: (303)739-6663
Aurora, CO 80012 Fax: (303)739-6657
E-mail: nrickey@ci.aurora.co.us

Contact: Nan Rickey, Presrv. & Archv.Adm.

Desc: Subject: Aurora and Colorado history. Holdings: 1500 books; 10 AV programs; 16,000 photographs; 200 cubic feet of documents and manuscripts. Services: Copying; Library open to the public by appointment for reference use only.

1307 ▪ Autry Museum of Western Heritage
Research Center
4700 Western Heritage Way Ph: (323)667-2000
Los Angeles, CA 90027-1462 Fax: (323)953-8735
E-mail: jhoskinson@autry-museum.org

Contact: Kevin Mulroy, Dir., Res.Ctr.

Desc: Subject: Mythical West, western history. Holdings: 50,000 books; 3000 bound periodical volumes; 300 government documents; 1000 cubic feet of archives; 300 cubic feet of motion pictures, TV shows, and sound recordings. Services: Interlibrary loan; copying; SDI; Library open to the public by application.

1308 ▪ Bad Axe Museum of Local History
Reference Collection
123 Hanselman Ph: (517)269-8325
Bad Axe, MI 48413

Contact: Cliff Willett, Pres.

Desc: Subject: Bad Axe area history. Holdings: 70 books; oral history materials. Services: Collection open to the public for reference use only.

1309 ▪ Balch Institute for Ethnic Studies
Library
18 S. 7th St. Ph: (215)925-8090
Philadelphia, PA 19106 Fax: (215)925-4392
E-mail: balchlib@balchinstitute.org
URL: http://www.balchinstitute.org

Desc: Subject: North American immigration and ethnic history. Holdings: 62,000 books and other printed items; 5000 linear feet of manuscripts; 200 sound recordings; 13,000 photographs; 100 broadsides; 6000 reels of microfilm. Services: Interlibrary loan; copying; Library open to the public.

1310 ▪ Baltimore County Historical Society
Library
9811 Van Buren Ln. Ph: (410)666-1876
Cockeysville, MD 21030

Contact: Elmer, R. Haile, Jr., Libn.

Desc: Subject: Baltimore County, Maryland - history, genealogy, cemeteries, roadside markers. Holdings: 1200 books; 10 manuscripts; 20 nonbook items; 60 VF drawers of clippings, pamphlets, circulars, letters, pictures, family charts, group sheets, Bible records, and family histories. Services: Copying; Library open to the public for reference use only.

1311 ▪ Bangor Historical Society
Library
159 Union St. Ph: (207)942-5766
Bangor, ME 04401 Fax: (207)941-0266
E-mail: bangorhistorical@juno.com
URL: http://www.bairnet.org

Desc: Subject: Bangor area history. Holdings: 900 books; 400 ledgers, scrapbooks, and recordbooks; 12 videotapes; 500 receipts, letters, ephemera; 650,000 linear feet of television film transferred to video (1953-1974); historic photographs. Services: Library open to the public by appointment.

1312 ■ Bartholomew County Historical Society
Cline-Keller Library
524 3rd St.　　　　　　Ph: (812)372-3541
Columbus, IN 47201　　　Fax: (812)372-3113
E-mail: bchs@hsonline.net

Desc: Subject: Local and state history, antiques, genealogy. Holdings: 500 books; 500 bound periodical volumes; 12 cubic feet of clippings and ephemera; 300 volumes of City of Columbus records; 57 volumes of city county directories; 90 volumes of high school year books; 800 family history files; cemetery records; naturalization records. Services: Copying; Library open to the public on a limited schedule.

1313 ■ Bartlesville Public Library
Special Collections
600 S. Johnstone　　　　Ph: (918)337-5353
Bartlesville, OK 74003　Fax: (918)337-5338
E-mail: jsanders@bartlesville.lib.ok.us

Contact: Jan Sanders, Dir.

Desc: Subject: State and local history and genealogy, Delaware Indians. Holdings: 89,000 books; 1900, 1910, and 1920 Oklahoma census records; tribal rolls and censuses; mortuary records. Services: Interlibrary loan; copying.

1314 ■ Barton County Historical Society
85 S. Hwy. 281　　　　　Ph: (316)793-5125
PO Box 1091　　　　　　Fax: (316)793-5125
Great Bend, KS 67530

Desc: Subject: Barton County, Kansas, genealogy. Holdings: Reports; manuscripts; archives. Services: Copying; Library open to the public with restrictions.

1315 ■ Baxter Springs Heritage Center and Museum
Library
PO Box 514　　　　　　Ph: (316)856-2385
Baxter Springs, KS 66713

Contact: Phyllis Abbott, Musm.Cur.

Desc: Subject: Local history, lead and zinc mining, Civil War. Holdings: 8 books; 15 bound periodical volumes; 100 reports; 1500 archival materials; maps; blueprints; photographs. Services: Copying; Library open to the public.

1316 ■ Beaumont Public Library System
Tyrrell Historical Library
695 Pearl St.　　　　　Ph: (409)833-2759
PO 3827　　　　　　　Fax: (409)833-5828
Beaumont, TX 77704

Contact: David E. Montgomery, Branch Mgr.

Desc: Subject: Texas history, local history, genealogy, art. Holdings: 19,200 books; 2300 bound periodical volumes; 250 cubic feet of archives; 9120 reels of microfilm; 12,550 microfiche; 105 linear feet of Texas documents; 30,000 photographs and negatives; 5000 stereoscopes; 120 compact discs. Services: Copying; photo-reproduction; Library open to the public.

1317 ■ Becker County Historical Society
Walter D. Bird Memorial Historical Library
PO Box 622　　　　　　Ph: (218)847-2938
Detroit Lakes, MN 56502　Fax: (218)847-5048
E-mail: bolerud@tekstar.com

Contact: Becky Olerud, Dir.

Desc: Subject: History - Northwest Area, Minnesota, Becker County. Holdings: 2500 volumes; 15 VF drawers of letters, manuscripts, clippings; 25 linear feet of township and school records; 8 VF drawers of photographs;

125,500 cards of county vital statistics records; Chippewa Indian artifacts. Services: Copying; Library open to the public with restrictions.

1318 ■ Bedford Historical Society
Library
2 Mudge Way　　　　　Ph: (781)275-7235
Bedford, MA 01730-2138

Contact: Lois Hamill, Archv.

Desc: Subject: Local history, Bedford flag, battles of Lexington and Concord, Rufus Porter. Holdings: 2000 deeds, wills, legal documents, receipts, school and church records, photographs; town annual reports, 1892 to present; newspaper columns, 1910-1929. Services: Library open to the public by appointment.

1319 ■ Bedford Historical Society
Library
30 S. Park St.　　　　　Ph: (440)232-0796
Box 46282　　　　　　Fax: (440)232-0796
Bedford, OH 44146

Contact: Richard J. Squire, Lib. Hd.

Desc: Subject: Ohio and local history, local government, 1876 centennial, Lincoln and Civil War, railroads and electric traction. Holdings: 6500 books; 150 bound periodical volumes; 190 ledgers, record books, scrapbooks, albums; 160 file boxes and drawers of manuscripts, archival materials, maps, other cataloged items. Services: Library open to the public.

1320 ■ Behringer-Crawford Museum
Lawrence Duba Research Library
PO Box 67　　　　　　Ph: (606)491-4003
Covington, KY 41012-0067

Contact: Laurie Risch, Dir.

Desc: Subject: Northern Kentucky archeology and history. Holdings: 1186 books; 296 bound periodical volumes; 400 documents; 555 photographs. Services: Copying; Library open to the public by appointment.

1321 ■ Bella Vista Historical Society
MuseumLibrary
1885 Bella Vista Way　　Ph: (501)855-2335
Bella Vista, AR 72714

Contact: Nancy Russell, Libn.

Desc: Subject: History, genealogy, archaeology. Holdings: 500 books; 700 bound periodical volumes; 4200 documents; 12 AV programs; 6 manuscripts; 9000 nonbook items. Services: Copying; Library open to the public for reference use only.

1322 ■ Belleville Public Library
Archives Collection
121 E. Washington St.　　Ph: (618)234-0441
Belleville, IL 62220　　　Fax: (618)234-9474

Contact: Lou Ann James, Archv.Libn.

Desc: Subject: Genealogy and history of Belleville, Illinois. Holdings: 136,000 items, including 2500 archival materials and 2000 microfiche. Services: Interlibrary loan; copying; archives open to the public.

1323 ■ Beloit Historical Society
Luebke Family Memorial Library
Lincoln Center　　　　　Ph: (608)365-7835
845 Hackett St.　　　　Fax: (608)365-5999
Beloit, WI 53511
E-mail: beloiths@ticon.net

Contact: Paul K. Kerr, Dir.

Desc: Subject: Local history, politics, education, religion, industry, home and family. Holdings: 500 books, diaries, journals; scrapbooks. Services: Library open to the public for reference use only.

1324 ■ Beltrami County Historical Society
Archives
7301 Frontage Rd. NW　Ph: (218)751-7824
PO Box 683　　　　　　Fax: (218)751-2234
Bemidji, MN 56619

Contact: Wanda Hoyum, Dir.

Desc: Subject: Beltrami County, lumber industry. Holdings: 500 books; 500 maps; 10,000 photographs; 100 linear feet and 200 volumes of manuscripts. Services: Copying; staff research; archives open to the public.

1325 ■ Bennington Museum
Genealogy Library
W. Main St.　　　　　　Ph: (802)447-1571
Bennington, VT 05201　Fax: (802)442-8305
E-mail: bennmuse@sover.net
URL: http://www.neinfo.net/

Contact: Tyler Resch, Libn.

Desc: Subject: Genealogy, regional and state history. Holdings: 4500 books; manuscripts; bound newspaper files; Vermont atlases; microfilmed newspapers, regional and state history; cemetery records; church records; census records; early maps and atlases; early town records; published histories and biographies relevant to the Vermont and Bennington region. Services: Copying; Library open to the public on fee basis.

1326 ■ Benton County Historical Society
LibraryArchives
Box 1034　　　　　　　Ph: (501)273-3890
Bentonville, AR 72712-1034

Contact: Judy Hughes, Pres.

Desc: Subject: Local history and genealogy. Holdings: 116 books and bound periodical volumes. Services: Library open to the public on a limited schedule.

1327 ■ Bergen County Historical Society
274 Main St.　　　　　Ph: (201)343-4169
Hackensack, NJ 07601　Fax: (201)457-1213
URL: http://www.carroll.com/bchs

Contact: Maureen Taffe, Lib.Dir.

Desc: Subject: State and local history, genealogy. Holdings: 2900 books; 30 VF drawers of pamphlets; 5 VF drawers of maps; 49 reels of microfilm of manuscripts; 68 reels of microfilm of newspapers. Services: Copying; Library open to the public.

1328 ■ Berrien County Historical Association
Library
1839 Courthouse Square　Ph: (616)471-1202
PO Box 261　　　　　　Fax: (616)471-7412
Berrien Springs, MI 49103
E-mail: info@berrienhistory.org

Contact: Robert C. Myers, Cur.

Desc: Subject: Berrien County history. Holdings: 200 books; 1000 manuscripts. Services: Copying; Library open to the public by appointment.

1329 ■ Bertha Historical Society
Museum Library
Box 307　　　　　　　Ph: (218)924-4095
Bertha, MN 56437

Contact: Laura Foster, Pres.

Desc: Subject: Local history. Holdings: Local newspapers (1901-1906, 1917-1926, 1928-1936, 1938 to present; all bound); list of all Bertha graduates, 1921-1998. Services: Library open to the public for reference use only on a limited schedule.

1330 ▪ Beth David Congregation
Harry Simono Library
2625 S.W. Third Ave.   Ph: (305)854-3911
Miami, FL 33129   Fax: (305)285-5841

Contact: Lillian S. Beer, Lib.Chm.

Desc: Subject: Judaica. Holdings: 7000 books; videotapes. Services: Library not open to the public.

1331 ▪ Beth David Reform Congregation
Jewel K. Markowitz Library
1130 Vaughans Ln.   Ph: (610)896-7485
Gladwyne, PA 19035   Fax: (610)642-5406

Desc: Subject: Judaica, Jewish literature. Holdings: 3500 books; synagogue archives; adult and children's collection. Services: Library not open to the public.

1332 ▪ Beth El Synagogue
Max Shapiro Library
5224 W. 26th St.   Ph: (612)920-3512
St. Louis Park, MN 55416   Fax: (612)920-8755

Contact: Marcia Olcisky, Libn.

Desc: Subject: Judaica, Jewish literature, religion, philosophy. Holdings: 3000 books. Services: Library open to the public.

1333 ▪ Beth El Temple Center
Carl Kales Memorial Library
2 Concord Ave.   Ph: (617)484-6668
Belmont, MA 02178   Fax: (617)484-6020

Contact: Leslie S. Lundberg, Libn.

Desc: Subject: Israel, Judaism, religion, philosophy, Bible, history, theology, customs. Holdings: 2370 books; 500 bound periodical volumes. Services: Interlibrary loan; Library open to the public for reference use only.

1334 ▪ Beth Emet, The Free Synagogue
Bruce Gordon Memorial Library
1224 Dempster   Ph: (847)869-4230
Evanston, IL 60202

Desc: Subject: Judaica and religion. Holdings: 8000 volumes. Services: Interlibrary loan; copying; Library open to synagogue members.

1335 ▪ Beth Israel Congregation
Beth Israel Community Library
1015 E. Park Ave.   Ph: (609)691-0852
Vineland, NJ 08362-0400

Contact: Ruth Greenblatt, Dir.

Desc: Subject: Judaism - customs, ceremonies, biography, literature, fiction; Hebrew language, music, art; history - biblical times to modern Israel; the Bible. Holdings: 6761 books; 4 VF drawers of pamphlets and other items; 186 audiotapes; 262 video cassettes. Services: Interlibrary loan (limited); copying; Library open to the public at librarian's discretion.

1336 ▪ Beth Shalom Congregation
Blanche and Ira Rosenblum Memorial Library
9400 Wornall Rd.   Ph: (816)361-2990
Kansas City, MO 64114   Fax: (816)361-4495
E-mail: franwolf@sky.net

Contact: Frances Wolf, Libn.

Desc: Subject: Judaica. Holdings: 10,000 books; 300 phonograph records; 150 filmstrips; 300 videotapes. Services: Library open to the public with restrictions.

1337 ▪ Beth Sholom Congregation
Joseph & Elizabeth Schwartz Library
Foxcroft & Old York Rd.   Ph: (215)887-1342
Elkins Park, PA 19027   Fax: (215)887-6605
URL: http://www.uscj.org/delvlly/epvsc

Contact: Cynthia Zimmerman, Libn.

Desc: Subject: Jewish music and Judaica. Holdings: 7500 volumes; 500 phonograph recordings. Services: Library open to the public at librarian's discretion.

1338 ▪ Beth Tzedec Congregation
Max & Beatrice Wolfe Library
1700 Bathurst St.   Ph: (416)781-3511
Toronto, ON, Canada M5P   Fax: (416)781-0150
3K3
E-mail: btlibrary@jcwishmail.com

Contact: Zina Glassman, Libn.

Desc: Subject: Judaism - history, religion, philosophy, art, literature; Israel; holocaust. Holdings: 18,000 books; VF drawers of pamphlets and documents. Services: Interlibrary loan; copying; Library open to the public for reference use only.

1339 ▪ Bethel Historical Society
Eva Bean Research Room
Dr. Moses Mason House   Ph: (207)824-2908
14 Broad St.   Fax: (207)824-0882
PO Box 12
Bethel, ME 04217-0012
E-mail: history@bdc.bethel.me.us
URL: http://www.orion.bdc.bethel.me.us/history

Contact: Stanley Russell Howe, Dir.

Desc: Subject: History - western Maine, White Mountain region of New Hampshire and Maine; western Maine genealogy. Holdings: 3000 books, 100 bound periodical volumes; 100 AV programs; 400 nonbook items; 1000 manuscripts; maps; photographs; pamphlets. Services: Copying; genealogical research by mail; room open to the public.

1340 ▪ Beverly Historical Society & Museum
Library and Archives
Cabot House   Ph: (508)922-1186
117 Cabot St.
Beverly, MA 01915

Contact: Fred Hammond, Chm.

Desc: Subject: Americana; history - local, general, maritime; genealogy. Holdings: 5000 books; 500 bound periodical volumes; 20,000 manuscripts; maps; broadsides. Services: Copying; Library open to the public with restrictions.

1341 ▪ Bibliotheque de Montreal
Collection Gagnon
1210 Sherbrooke St., E.   Ph: (514)872-1616
Montreal, PQ, Canada H2L 1L9 Fax: (514)872-1626
URL: http://ville.montreal.qc.ca/biblio/

Contact: Gilbert Lefebvre, Dept.Hd.

Desc: Subject: Canadian history, French Canadian genealogy, French and English Canadian literature, Canadian geography, French Canadian heritage, Americana. Holdings: 53,995 books; 13,933 pamphlets; 79,700 microfiche and microcards; 19,553 reels of microfilm; 10 maps, plans, and surveys; 3035 slides; 1629 rare books. Services: Interlibrary loan; copying; reference by telephone; bibliographic and information retrieval; collection open to the public.

1342 ▪ Birmingham Public Library
Linn-Henley Research Library
Department of Archives and Manuscripts
2100 Park Place   Ph: (205)226-3660
Birmingham, AL 35203   Fax: (205)226-3663

E-mail: jbaggett@bham.lib.al.us
URL: http://www.bham.lib.al.us

Contact: James L. Baggett, Archv.Cur., Mss.

Desc: Subject: Birmingham, Alabama - history, civil rights, economic development, politics and government, private utilities, industry, civic organizations, photographic history, women's history, sports history, church and religious history, labor movement. Holdings: 290 books; 415 bound periodical volumes; 11,000 linear feet of archives and manuscripts; 1002 reels of microfilm of archives and manuscripts; 2106 microfiche; 600 oral history cassette tapes; 215,000 photographic prints and negatives. Services: Copying; department open to the public for reference use only.

1343 ▪ Birmingham Public Library
Linn-Henley Research Library
Government Documents Department
2100 Park Place   Ph: (205)226-3620
Birmingham, AL 35203-2794   Fax: (205)226-3743
E-mail: gov@bham.lib.al.us
URL: http://www.bham.lib.al.us

Contact: Rebecca Scarborough, Hd., Gov.Doc.Dept.

Desc: Subject: Census, patents, statistics, federal, state and local legislation, laws and regulations. Holdings: 250,000 documents; 2500 shelves of federal documents; 6000 reels of microfilm; 670,500 microfiche. Services: Interlibrary loan; copying; SDI; department open to the public.

1344 ▪ Birmingham Public Library
Linn-Henley Research Library
Tutwiler Collection of Southern History and Literature
2100 Park Place   Ph: (205)226-3665
Birmingham, AL 35203   Fax: (205)226-3743
E-mail: sou@bham.lib.al.us
URL: http://www.bham.lib.al.us

Contact: Yvonne Crumpler, Dept.Hd.

Desc: Subject: Birmingham and Alabama history and literature; Southeastern genealogy; Civil War and Reconstruction history; black history. Holdings: 63,000 books; 7300 bound periodical volumes; 12,500 reels of microfilm; 1800 pamphlets; 6100 microforms; 154 VF drawers. Services: Collection open to the public for reference use only.

1345 ▪ Birmingham Temple
Library
28611 W. 12 Mile Rd.   Ph: (248)477-1410
Farmington Hills, MI 48334 Fax: (248)477-9014

Contact: Pera Kane, Libn.

Desc: Subject: Humanism, Judaism, philosophy. Holdings: 2000 books. Services: Interlibrary loan; Library open to the public by special request.

1346 ▪ Bisbee Mining and Historical Museum
Shattuck Memorial Library
Box 14   Ph: (602)432-7071
Bisbee, AZ 85603-0014   Fax: (602)432-7800
E-mail: bisbeemuseum@theriver.com

Contact: Judy Reis, Libn.

Desc: Subject: Copper mining, genealogy, Bisbee and Cochise County history, Mexican Revolution. Holdings: 850 books; 150 bound periodical volumes; 100 manuscript collections; 30,000 photographic prints and negatives. Services: Copying; Library open to the public.

1347 ▪ Blackford County Historical Society
Museum and Beeson Library
PO Box 264   Ph: (317)348-3103
Hartford City, IN 47348
E-mail: sacastelo@hotmail.com

URL: http://www.retired-usaf.com/historicalsociety.com

Contact: Sinuard Castelo, Pres.

Desc: Subject: Local history, genealogy. Holdings: 200 books; 100 bound periodical volumes; 100 Quaker records and 40 county records on microfilm; 83 genealogies. Services: Copying; Library open May-December with restrictions.

1348 ■ Blackhawk Genealogical Society of Rock Island and Mercer Counties Library

Box 3912   Ph: (309)786-5927
Rock Island, IL 61204-3912
E-mail: pamelam@prodigy.net

Contact: Pamela Langston

Desc: Subject: Genealogy. Holdings: 1200 books; 800 bound periodical volumes; 100 microfiche; 50 CD-ROMs. Services: Library open to the public.

1349 ■ Blair Society for Genealogical Research Hoenstine Rental Library

414 Montgomery St.   Ph: (814)695-0632
PO Box 208
Hollidaysburg, PA 16648
URL: http://www.blairsociety.org/library.htm

Contact: Barbara A. Hoenstine, MLS, Owner

Desc: Subject: Genealogical and historical research in central Pennsylvania. Holdings: Microfilm of personal letters; cemetery records; diaries.

1350 ■ Blue Earth County Historical Society Archives

Heritage Center   Ph: (507)345-5566
415 Cherry St.
Mankato, MN 56001

Contact: Carol Oney, Archv.

Desc: Subject: Blue Earth County history - agriculture, Indians, industries, genealogy, organizations. Holdings: 700 books; 250 daybooks, diaries, manuscript collections; 2500 other cataloged items; scrapbooks; atlases; maps; 2000 photographs; bound newspaper volumes; newspapers, church and cemetery records on microfilm. Services: Copying; archives open to the public.

1351 ■ Blue Ridge Regional Library System Bassett Branch Library

3964 Fairystone Park Hwy.   Ph: (540)629-2426
Bassett, VA 24055   Fax: (540)629-9840
E-mail: pross@vlinsvr.vsla.edu

Contact: Diane S. Adkins, Branch Libn.

Desc: Subject: Genealogy, Virginia. Holdings: 2611 books; 249 bound periodical volumes; 5114 manuscripts; 38 CD-ROMs; 4 microfiche; 412 reels of microfilm. Services: Interlibrary loan; copying; Library open to the public.

1352 ■ Blue Springs Historical Society Library

Box 762   Ph: (816)224-8979
Blue Springs, MO 64015

Contact: Karol Witthar, Archv.

Desc: Subject: Local history. Holdings: 50 books; 5 oral histories. Services: Library not open to the public.

1353 ■ B'nai Jeshurun Temple on the Heights Jacobson Library

27501 Fairmount Blvd.   Ph: (216)831-6555
Pepper Pike, OH 44124   Fax: (216)831-4599

Contact: Marcia Klein, Libn.

Desc: Subject: Judaica, Holocaust, juvenile Judaica, Israel. Holdings: 9000 volumes. Services: Library open to members only.

1354 ■ B'nai Zion Temple Memorial Library

245 Southfield Dr.   Ph: (318)861-2122
Shreveport, LA 71105   Fax: (318)861-7961

Contact: Judy Grunes, Libn.

Desc: Subject: Judaica - reference and teaching, history, philosophy, literature, language, arts, music. Holdings: 4016 books; 102 bound periodical volumes. Services: Library not open to the public.

1355 ■ Bonne Terre Memorial Library Vermont Collection

5 SW Main St.   Ph: (573)358-2260
Bonne Terre, MO 63628   Fax: (573)358-5941
E-mail: xbj000@mail.connect.more.net

Contact: Sharon Roberts, Libn.

Desc: Subject: Bonne Terre; Missouri - history, mining history, Masonic history, genealogy. Holdings: 21116 books; 2 microfilm. Services: Interlibrary loan; copying; faxing; archives open to the public by appointment.

1356 ■ Bonner County Historical Society, Inc. Research Library & Museum

611 S. Ella Ave.   Ph: (208)263-2344
Sandpoint, ID 83864-1100

Contact: Ms. Joy O'Donnell

Desc: Subject: Local history, biography. Holdings: 400 books; 8000 photographs; 50 maps; 5000 clippings; 120 oral history tapes; 3000 pieces of memorabilia; newspaper file (print and microfilm); obituary file. Services: Research; copying.

1357 ■ Boone County Genealogical Society Library

Boone Madison Public Library   Ph: (304)369-7842
PO Box 306
Madison, WV 25130

Desc: Subject: Genealogy. Holdings: 500 books; microfilm. Services: Copying; Library open to the public.

1358 ■ Boot Hill Museum Research LibraryArchives

Front St.   Ph: (316)227-8188
Dodge City, KS 67801   Fax: (316)227-7673

Contact: Susan Dame, Asst.Cur.

Desc: Subject: Dodge City history, 19th century social history, material culture, decorative arts. Holdings: 1167 books; 50 bound periodical volumes; 40,000 nonbook items; 20 manuscripts. Services: Copying; Library open to the public by appointment.

1359 ■ Boston College Social Work Library

McGuinn Hall, Rm. B 38   Ph: (617)552-3233
Chestnut Hill, MA 02167   Fax: (617)552-3199
URL: http://www.bc.edu/bc_org/aup/ulib/swlib/
      swlib.html

Desc: Subject: Clinical social work; child welfare and families, individuals, and groups; ethnic studies and special populations; gerontology; human behavior; mental health; social policy; administration and research; social planning. Holdings: 32,000 books; 5733 bound periodical volumes; 840 masters' theses; 800 doctoral dissertations in social work on microfiche; government documents. Services: Interlibrary loan; copying; library open to the public.

1360 ■ Boston Magazine Research Department Library

300 Massachusetts Ave.   Ph: (617)262-9700
Boston, MA 02115   Fax: (617)267-9700
E-mail: bosmag@aol.com

Contact: Tina Iyer, Res.Ed.

Desc: Subject: Boston history, politics, travel, sports, film, television. Holdings: 500 books. Services: Library not open to the public.

1361 ■ Boston Public Library Government Documents

Copley Square   Ph: (617)536-5400
PO Box 286   Fax: (617)536-7758
Boston, MA 02117
E-mail: government@bpl.org
URL: http://www.BPL.org

Contact: Gail Fithian, Cur.

Desc: Subject: The Government Documents Section serves as a depository for United Nations, Danube Commission, and U.S. Government Printing Office (1859 to present; regional, 1971 to present). Special strengths include U.S. congressional publications, censuses, publications of many international organizations, Current Urban Documents, 19th and early 20th century foreign and state publications, federal and Massachusetts laws and regulations, court decisions, Massachusetts and Boston documents, 18th-20th century British documents, and indexing services; member of Documents Expediting Project. Holdings: Figures not available. Services: Interlibrary loan; copying; section open to the public.

1362 ■ Boston Public Library MicrotextNewspaper Department

666 Boylston St.   Ph: (617)536-5400
Boston, MA 02117
URL: http://www.BPL.org

Contact: Charles Longley, Cur.

Desc: Subject: Newspapers, history, genealogy, literature. Holdings: 35,000 bound periodical volumes; 163,500 reels of microfilm; 2.4 million microfiche; 1.6 million other cataloged items. Services: Copying; Library open to the public.

1363 ■ Boston Public Library Social Sciences Department

Copley Square   Ph: (617)536-5400
700 Boylston St.
Boston, MA 02117
URL: http://www.BPL.org

Contact: Mary Frances O'Brien, Cur. of Social Sciences

Desc: Subject: History, business and economics, education, financial reporting services, geography and maps, genealogy and heraldry, political science, sports and games, travel. Holdings: College catalogs (microfiche); U.S., Canada, and major foreign city street maps; Family Search Database; annual reports for major U.S. corporations. Services: Interlibrary loan; copying; open to the public with courtesy card.

1364 ■ Boulder Public Library Carnegie Branch Library for Local History

1125 Pine St.   Ph: (303)441-3110
PO Drawer H   Fax: (303)441-3110
Boulder, CO 80306
E-mail: hallw@boulder.lib.co.us

Contact: Wendy Hall, Br.Mgr.

Desc: Subject: History - Colorado, Boulder, Boulder County. Holdings: 5000 books; 40 bound periodical volumes; 14 VF drawers of clippings; 200,000 historic photographs; 700,000 manuscript items; 300 linear feet of genealogical materials; 6 drawers of microfilm of archival materials; 240 historic maps; 60 videocassettes. Services: Copying; Library open to the public.

1365 ■ Branches and Twigs Genealogical Society Collection
Kingman Carnegie Library   Ph: (316)532-3061
455 N. Main   Fax: (316)532-2528
Kingman, KS 67068
E-mail: kingc1lb@websurf.net

Contact: Linda Slack, Lib.Dir.

Desc: Subject: Genealogy. Holdings: 312 books; 8000 microfiche; 210 reels of microfilm. Services: Interlibrary loan; copying; SDI; Library open to the public.

1366 ■ Brant County Museum Library
57 Charlotte St.   Ph: (519)752-2483
Brantford, ON, Canada N3T 2W6

Contact: Elizabeth Hunter, Dir.

Desc: Subject: Local history. Holdings: 500 books; 200 pamphlets; 200 documents; 5000 pictures; 400 files of clippings; 17 binders of historical articles. Services: Copying (limited); Library open to the public.

1367 ■ Brazoria County Historical Museum Museum Research Center - Adriance Library
100 E. Cedar   Ph: (409)849-5711
Angleton, TX 77515   Fax: (409)849-5711
E-mail: handy@bchm
URL: http://www.bchm.org

Contact: Jamie Murray, Res.Ctr.Info.Coord.

Desc: Subject: Brazoria County and Texas history. Holdings: 1200 books; 9 VF drawers of pamphlets, manuscripts, and clippings; 4 slidetape sets; videotapes. Services: Copying; center open to the public.

1368 ■ Bridgeport Public Library Historical Collections
925 Broad St.   Ph: (203)576-7417
Bridgeport, CT 06604   Fax: (203)576-8255
URL: http://bridgeport.lib.ct.us/bpl/

Contact: Mary K. Witkowski, Dept.Hd.

Desc: Subject: Local history, genealogy, circus, P.T. Barnum, labor and business history. Holdings: 13,500 books; 670 bound periodical volumes; 750 linear feet of manuscripts and archival materials; 420 linear feet of newspaper clipping files; 2800 photographs; U.S. Census; 5200 reels of microfilm; 250 maps. Services: Special Collections open to the public by appointment with archivist.

1369 ■ Bridgeton Public Library Special Collections
150 E. Commerce St.   Ph: (609)451-2620
Bridgeton, NJ 08302-2684   Fax: (609)455-1049

Contact: Gail S. Robinson, Lib.Dir.

Desc: Subject: Cumberland County history, local genealogy, Woodland Indians. Holdings: 2000 volumes, including newspapers, 1881 to present, bound and on microfilm; 20,000 Indian artifacts, 10,000 B.C. to circa 1700 A.D., collected within a 30-mile radius of the Library. Services: Interlibrary loan; copying; collections open to the public.

1370 ■ Bridgewater College Alexander Mack Memorial Library Special Collections
   Ph: (540)828-5410
rs>Bridgewater, VA 22812   Fax: (540)828-5482

E-mail: rgreenaw@bridgewater.edu
URL: http://www.bridgewater.edu/departments/library/ library.html

Contact: Ruth Greenawalt, Dir.

Desc: Holdings: 40,000 U.S. government documents. Services: Interlibrary loan; copying; collections open to the public with restrictions.

1371 ■ Brigham Young University Religion and History Division Library
4222 HBLL   Ph: (801)378-6118
Provo, UT 84602   Fax: (801)378-6708
E-mail: gary_gillum@byu.edu
URL: http://www.lib.byu.edu

Contact: Gary P. Gillum, Hist.Rel.Libn.Dept.Chm.

Desc: Subject: History, religion, genealogy, philosophy, geography, anthropology, archeology. Holdings: 500,000 books. Services: Interlibrary loan; copying; Library open to the public.

1372 ■ Brigham Young University Utah Valley Regional Family History Center and Microforms Department
Harold B. Lee Library,   Ph: (801)378-6200
Rm. 4386   Fax: (801)378-9233
Provo, UT 84602
E-mail: diane_parkinson@byu.edu
URL: http://www.lib.byu.edu/dept/uvrfhc/

Contact: Diane R. Parkinson, Dir.Microforms Libn.

Desc: Subject: Genealogy. Holdings: Genealogical Society of Salt Lake City Library Catalog; primary and secondary source material in microform; 35,000 journals, serials, and newspapers on microfilm. Services: Copying; center open to the public.

1373 ■ Bristol Historical Preservation Society Library
48 Court St.   Ph: (401)253-7223
Bristol, RI 02809   Fax: (401)253-7223

Contact: Reinhard Battcher, III, Libn.

Desc: Subject: Genealogy and local history. Holdings: 1500 volumes; 4 VF drawers of shipping papers; 12 VF drawers of local area clippings, obituaries, deeds, correspondence. Services: Copying; Library open to the public with fee for nonmembers.

1374 ■ Brome County Historical Society Archives
130 Lakeside   Ph: (514)243-6782
PO Box 690
Knowlton, PQ, Canada J0E 1V0

Contact: Marion L. Phelps, Archv.

Desc: Subject: Eastern Townships history; World War I. Holdings: 2012 volumes; 12 drawers of subject, personage, and genealogical files; census records to 1891; Protestant and Catholic church records for District of Bedford; directories; documents; local newspapers. Services: Interlibrary loan; copying; archives open to the public by appointment.

1375 ■ Bronx County Historical Society Research Library
3309 Bainbridge Ave.   Ph: (718)881-8900
Bronx, NY 10467   Fax: (718)881-4827
URL: http://www.bronxhistoricalsociety.org

Contact: Dr. Gary Hermalyn, Exec.Dir.

Desc: Subject: Bronx and New York City history. Holdings: 7000 books; 30,000 photographs; current Bronx newspapers; atlases; pamphlets; audio and video cassettes;

clipping files; postcards; maps; manuscripts; slides; microfilm. Services: Copying; photo and slide duplication; Library open to the public.

1376 ■ Brookfield Historical Society Library
8820-1/2 Brookfield Ave.   Ph: (708)485-3420
Brookfield, IL 60513-1670
URL: http://www.gv.net/gailla/bhs/bhsinfo.html<crs> memory

Desc: Subject: Brookfield, Illinois history and culture. Holdings: Figures not available.

1377 ■ Brooklyn Children's Museum Resource Center
145 Brooklyn Ave.   Ph: (718)735-4427
Brooklyn, NY 11213   Fax: (718)604-7442

Contact: Dina Sherman, Educ.Rsrcs.Mgr.

Desc: Subject: Anthropology, history, arts and crafts, sciences, natural history. Holdings: 7000 books; 260 bound periodical volumes; uncataloged pamphlets; maps; atlases; photographs. Services: Center open to the public by appointment.

1378 ■ Brooklyn Historical Society Library
128 Pierrepont St.   Ph: (718)624-0890
Brooklyn, NY 11201   Fax: (718)875-3869
E-mail: bhs@panix.com

Contact: Michell Hackwelder, Hd.Libn.

Desc: Subject: Brooklyn, Long Island, New York City, history, genealogy, biography. Holdings: 155,000 volumes; 1000 bound periodical volumes; 1700 linear feet of manuscripts; 90,000 photographs; 700 periodical titles; 350 local and regional newspapers; 750 maps and atlases; newspapers in microform. Services: Copying; Library open to the public.

1379 ■ Brooklyn Historical Society Library
4442 Ridge Rd.   Ph: (216)749-2804
Brooklyn, OH 44144

Contact: Edward Koschmann, VP

Desc: Subject: Brooklyn history, area history. Holdings: Reports; area yearbooks; photographs; records; newspaper clippings, 1948 to present. Services: Library open to the public with restrictions.

1380 ■ Brooks Memorial Library Vermont Collection
224 Main St.   Ph: (802)254-5290
Brattleboro, VT 05301   Fax: (802)257-2309
E-mail: brattlib@brooks.lib.vt.us
URL: http://www.state.vt.us/libraries/b733/ brookslibrary

Contact: Jerry Carbone

Desc: Subject: History and life in Vermont, New Hampshire, and Massachusetts; genealogy. Holdings: 1800 books; documents; maps; atlases; manuscripts; 3000 photographs; 10 videocassettes; 20 audiocassettes; 20 vertical files; microfilm. Services: Interlibrary loan; copying; Library open to the public.

1381 ■ Broome County Historical Society Josiah T. Newcomb Library
30 Front St.   Ph: (607)772-0660
Binghamton, NY 13905

Contact: Charles J. Browne, Lib.Mgr.

Desc: Subject: History of Broome County and New York State, genealogy. Holdings: 2500 books; 5000 documents;

30 VF drawers; personal letters; furnishings. Services: Copying; research; photo reproduction; Library open to the public.

1382 ■ Brown County Genealogy Society Library

PO Box 83   Ph: (513)444-3521
Georgetown, OH 45121

Contact: L'Vera Seipelt

Desc: Subject: Local history, genealogy. Holdings: 200 books; microfilm. Services: Copying; Library open to the public.

1383 ■ Brown County Historical Society Archives

2 N. Broadway   Ph: (507)354-2016
New Ulm, MN 56073   Fax: (507)354-1068

Contact: Darla Cordes Gebhard, Res.Libn.

Desc: Subject: Local and regional history. Holdings: 2000 books; Family Record Files for 5000 families; 7 journals; 594 reels of microfilm. Services: Copying; archives open to the public for reference use only.

1384 ■ Brown County Historical Society Genealogy Collection

PO Box 668   Ph: (812)988-4297
Nashville, IN 47448

Contact: Helen H. Reeve, Geneal.

Desc: Subject: Genealogy of Brown County. Holdings: 50 books, 15 reels of microfilm, microfiche. Services: Copying; Library open to the public.

1385 ■ Bruce Mines Museum and Archives

75 Taylor St.   Ph: (705)785-3426
P.O. Box 220   Fax: (705)785-3170
Bruce Mines, ON, Canada P0R
1C0

Contact: Bee Jackson

Desc: Subject: History, genealogy. Holdings: Mining manuscripts; pioneer artifacts; newspapers, 1901-1943, on microfilm, photographs, customs and store ledgers. Services: Archives open to the public.

1386 ■ Buchanan County Public Library Special Collections

Rte. 2, Box 3   Ph: (540)935-6581
Grundy, VA 24614   Fax: (540)935-6292
URL: http://www.mtinter.net/bcpl/

Contact: Patricia Hatfield, Libn.

Desc: Subject: Local history, genealogy. Holdings: 80,000 books; 150 bound periodical volumes; 5 microfiche; 100 reels of microfilm. Services: Interlibrary loan; copying; Library open to the public.

1387 ■ Bucks County Historical Society Spruance Library

84 S. Pine St.   Ph: (215)345-0210
Doylestown, PA 18901   Fax: (215)230-0823
URL: http://www.libertynet.org:80/bchs

Contact: Betsy Smith, Libn.

Desc: Subject: Bucks County history and genealogy, history of crafts and technology. Holdings: 25,000 volumes; 1500 cubic feet of Bucks County Archives. Services: Copying; Library open to the public.

1388 ■ Buffalo & Erie County Historical Society Library

25 Nottingham Ct.   Ph: (716)873-9612
Buffalo, NY 14216   Fax: (716)873-8754

Contact: Mary F. Bell, Dir., Lib. & Archv.

Desc: Subject: City of Buffalo, Erie County, Western New York, Niagara Frontier, War of 1812. Holdings: 20,000 bound volumes; 50,000 periodicals and ephemera; manuscript collections of 4500 linear ft.; iconographic collections of over 130,000 separate items; large clipping file; large scrapbook collection; local newspapers on microfilm. Services: Interlibrary loan; copying (both limited); limited staff research for appropriate inquiries; Library open to the public for reference use only.

1389 ■ Bukovina Society of the Americas Library

PO Box 81   Ph: (913)625-9492
Ellis, KS 67637
E-mail: owindholz@dailynews.net
URL: http://members.aol.com/LJensen/bukovina.html

Contact: Oren Windholz, Pres.

Desc: Subject: Bukovina history, genealogy. Holdings: 20 books; 10 reports; microfilm. Services: Copying; Library open to the public.

1390 ■ Burdick International Ancestry Library

2317 Riverbluff Pkwy., No. 249   Ph: (941)922-7931
Sarasota, FL 34231-5032

Contact: Frank P. Mueller, Exec.Dir.

Desc: Subject: Burdick family. Holdings: Historical records. Services: Library not open to the public.

1391 ■ Bureau County Historical Society Museum & Library

109 Park Ave., W.   Ph: (815)875-2184
Princeton, IL 61356-1927

Contact: Barbara Hansen, Dir.

Desc: Subject: Bureau County history, Civil War histories, local genealogies. Holdings: 500 books; bound periodical volumes of local newspapers; other cataloged items; files of manuscripts and clippings. Services: Library open to the public with restrictions.

1392 ■ Bureau de la Statistique du Quebec Centre d'Information et de Documentation

200, chemin Sainte-Foy - 3 etage   Ph: (418)691-2401
Quebec, PQ, Canada G1R 5T4   Free: 800-463-4090
    Fax: (418)643-4129

E-mail: cid@bsq.gouv.qc.ca
URL: http://www.bsq.gouv.qc.ca

Contact: Renaud Dugas, Coord., Comm.

Desc: Subject: Economics, agriculture, census information, demographics, social science, the environment. Holdings: 17,000 books; 350 bound periodical volumes. Services: Interlibrary loan; copying; center open to the public.

1393 ■ Burke County Public Library

North Carolina Room   Ph: (828)437-5638
204 S. King St.   Fax: (828)433-1914
Morganton, NC 28655-3535

Contact: Steve Farlow, Dir.

Desc: Subject: Genealogy, North Carolina history, Burke County history. Holdings: 1400 books; 400 bound periodical volumes; 200 reels of microfilm. Services: Copying; Library open to the public.

1394 ■ Burlingame Historical Society Archives

PO Box 144   Ph: (650)340-9960
Burlingame, CA 94011-0144

Desc: Subject: Burlingame and Hillsborough, California history and culture. Holdings: Printed materials; films; slides; photographs. Services: Archives open to the public by appointment.

1395 ■ Burlington County Historical Society Delia Biddle Pugh Library

457 High St.   Ph: (609)386-4773
Burlington, NJ 08016   Fax: (609)386-4828
E-mail: historyctr@juno.com

Contact: Joan Lanphear, Libn.

Desc: Subject: History of Burlington County and New Jersey; antiques; colonial arts and crafts; genealogy. Holdings: 3000 books; periodicals; deeds; photographs; slides; clippings; maps; prints; postcards; manuscripts; 250 reels of microfilm; 300 archival items. Services: Copying; Library open to the public on a limited schedule.

1396 ■ Burlington Public Library Burlington Collection

2331 New St.   Ph: (905)639-3611
Burlington, ON, Canada L7R   Fax: (905)681-7277
1J4
URL: http://www.hhpl.on.ca/library/bpl/
    collect.htm<crs>bur

Desc: Subject: Burlington history and culture. Holdings: Maps; plans; family biographies; architectural files; local newspapers; indexes; directories; gazetteers; records of local government, churches, cemeteries, schools, and societies.

1397 ■ Burt County Museum, Inc. Library

PO Box 125   Ph: (402)374-1505
Tekamah, NE 68061

Contact: Bonnie Newell, Cur.

Desc: Subject: Burt County history, genealogy. Holdings: Books; reports; genealogy. Services: Copying; Library open to the public on a limited schedule.

1398 ■ Butler County Historical and Genealogical Society Library

PO Box 247   Ph: (502)526-4722
Morgantown, KY 42261

Contact: Syble Givens, Hd.Libn.

Desc: Subject: History - local, family, surrounding counties and families. Holdings: 300 books; 25 nonbook items. Services: Copying; Library open to the public.

1399 ■ Butler County Historical Society Olive Clifford Stone Library

381 E. Central   Ph: (316)321-9333
Box 696
El Dorado, KS 67042

Contact: Anna Louise Borger, Libn.

Desc: Subject: Local history, genealogy, oil history. Holdings: 3400 books. Services: Copying; Library open to the public.

1400 ■ Butler County HistoricalGenealogical Society

PO Box 561   Ph: (334)383-9564
Greenville, AL 36037

Contact: Judy Taylor

Desc: Subject: History - family, Butler County, Alabama; photograph history. Holdings: 500 books; 15 bound periodical volumes; 46 microfilm; census; 200 family histories; 15 church records. Services: Copying; Library open to the public.

1401 ▪ Butterfield Memorial Research Library

321 Washington Ave.　　Ph: (517)893-5733
Bay City, MI 48708　　Fax: (517)893-5741

Contact: Ron Bloomfield, Cur. of Coll.Res.

Desc: Subject: History - Bay County and Bay City, Michigan, U.S.; Readi-cut House industry; shipbuilding; lumbering. Holdings: 3200 books; periodicals; 35 diaries; 120 scrapbooks; 50 albums containing 3000 photographs; 350 linear feet of archival materials; 100 linear feet of pamphlets and clippings; 40 map drawers of maps; blueprints and publications of Aladdin, Sterling, Lewis, and Liberty Homes. Services: Copying; Library open to the public on a limited schedule but staff member must be present.

1402 ▪ Buttonwood Library Genealogy Room

745 Rockdale Ave.　　Ph: (508)991-6276
New Bedford, MA 02740-6203

Contact: Paul Albert Cyr, Cur.

Desc: Subject: Genealogy of New England, Massachusetts town histories, history of New Bedford and vicinity, French-Canadian and Acadian genealogy. Holdings: 5000 books; 500 bound periodical volumes; 1250 reels of microfilm of New Bedford newspapers and city documents. Services: Interlibrary loan (microfilm only); copying; room open to the public for reference use only.

1403 ▪ Calhoun County Historical Museum Library

858 Lake St.　　Ph: (712)297-8139
Rockwell City, IA 50579

Contact: Judy Webb, Cur.

Desc: Subject: Local history, genealogy. Holdings: 3000 books; 400 genealogical records; 5000 county obituary notices; 80 scrapbooks; clippings; county and school records; telephone books; cemetery records. Services: Library open to public under supervision. The library is closed October through March.

1404 ▪ Calhoun County Museum Archives and Library

303 Butler St.　　Ph: (803)874-3964
St. Matthews, SC 29135　　Fax: (803)874-4790
E-mail: calmus@oburg.net

Contact: Debbie Roland, Dir.

Desc: Subject: Genealogy, local history, archeology, geology. Holdings: 430 books; 320 bound periodical volumes; 200 plats and grants; 100 private papers; 50 oral histories, 1952-1975. Services: Interlibrary loan; copying; Library open to the public.

1405 ▪ California Historical Society History Center

1120 Old Mill Rd.　　Ph: (626)449-5450
San Marino, CA 91108

Contact: Roy McJunkin, Photo.Cur.

Desc: Subject: Local and state history. Holdings: Figures not available. Services: Photographs available on order; center open to the public.

1406 ▪ California (State) Department of Finance - California State Census Data Center Library

915 L St., 8th Fl.　　Ph: (916)322-4651
Sacramento, CA 95814　　Fax: (916)327-0222
E-mail: ficalpop@dof.ca.gov
URL: http://www.dof.ca.gov

Contact: Richard Lovelady, Res.Prog.Spec.

Desc: Subject: Census, demography, housing, population. Holdings: 200 machine-readable files. Services: Copying; Library open to the public.

1407 ▪ California State Library

Library & Courts Bldg.　　Ph: (916)654-0183
914 Capitol Mall　　Fax: (916)654-0064
Box 942837
Sacramento, CA 95814
E-mail: csl_ill@library.ca.gov
URL: http://www.library.ca.gov/

Contact: Dr. Kevin Starr, State Libn.

Desc: Subject: General research collection in support of state government, Californiana, law, genealogy, business, education, applied science and technology, population, public administration, statistics, water resources. Holdings: 708,542 volumes; 780,449 documents; 2.6 million microforms; 74,700 maps and charts; 165 video recordings; 310,231 audio recordings; federal and state government document depository. Services: Interlibrary loan; copying; consultant service for public libraries; Library open to the public.

1408 ▪ California State Library Sutro Library

480 Winston Dr.　　Ph: (415)731-4477
San Francisco, CA 94132　　Fax: (415)557-9325

Contact: Clyde Janes, Dir.

Desc: Subject: American genealogy and local history, English history, history of science and technology, Americana, bibliography, voyages and travels, Mexican history, Hebraica, natural history. Holdings: 150,000 volumes; 20,000 manuscripts. Services: Interlibrary loan; copying; Library open to the public.

1409 ▪ California State University Desert Studies Center Library

PO Box 490　　Ph: (619)733-4266
Baker, CA 92309　　Fax: (619)733-4266
E-mail: DSC@FULLERTON.EDU

Contact: Robert Fulton, D.S.C. Mgr.

Desc: Subject: Natural sciences, Mojave Desert, desert literature, local history, local archeology, reference material, local research. Holdings: 590 books; 145 reports; 95 scientific reprints; 205 maps. Services: Library open to the public upon registration with Desert Studies Center manager.

1410 ▪ California State University at Dominguez Hills Library Special Collections

1000 E. Victoria St.　　Ph: (310)516-3895
Carson, CA 90747　　Fax: (310)516-4219
E-mail: kjhunt@dhvx20.csudh.edu
URL: http://archives.csudh.edu/

Contact: Karen Jean Hunt, Dir.

Desc: Subject: History - local, university, California State University; children's literature; historic best-sellers. Holdings: 3500 books; 125 bound periodical volumes. Services: Copying; Library open to the public for reference use only.

1411 ▪ California State University, %Fullerton Oral History Program Library

PO Box 6846　　Ph: (714)278-3580
Fullerton, CA 92834-6846　　Fax: (714)773-2439
E-mail: g.gutierrez@fullerton.edu

Contact: Gail Gutierrez, Archv.

Desc: Subject: Local, community, and family history; ethnic groups: Japanese Americans, Chinese Americans, African Americans, Native Americans, Mexican Americans, Swedish Americans; biography; political and university history; Philippine studies; Southeast Utah uranium; Mormon colony; women in military; World War II. Holdings: 825 volumes; 4000 interviews (audio); 19 masters' theses. Services: Program open to the public by appointment.

1412 ▪ California State University, Long Beach Special Collections Library

1250 Bellflower Blvd.　　Ph: (562)985-4087
Long Beach, CA 90840-1901　　Fax: (562)985-1703
E-mail: irene@lib.csulb.edu

Contact: Irene Still Meyer, Supv., Spec.Coll., Archv.

Desc: Subject: Political history, California literature, local history, music and the arts. Holdings: 16,000 books. Services: Library open to the public.

1413 ▪ California State University, %Northridge University Library's Urban Archives Center Special Collections and Archives

Oviatt Library, Rm. 4　　Ph: (818)677-2832
Northridge, CA 91330-8329　　Fax: (818)677-2676
E-mail: robert.marshall@csun.edu
URL: http://library.csun.edu/spcoll/urban_archives/hpuac.html

Desc: Subject: Los Angeles County and San Fernando Valley history, Chambers of Commerce, education, labor and guild history, political history, minority and ethnic groups, women's studies, social service organizations, environment, journalism. Holdings: 2900 linear feet of documents, minutes, labor newspapers, photographs; oral histories. Services: Copying; microfilming; center open to the public with restrictions on some collections.

1414 ▪ California University of Pennsylvania Louis L. Manderino Library Pennsylvania Collection

　　Ph: (412)938-4404
rs>California, PA 15419
URL: http://www.library.cup.edu/spec.html<crs>spc

Desc: Subject: Pennsylvania - history, genealogy, law, geology. Holdings: Books; pamphlets; maps; court records; reports. Services: Interlibrary loan; Library open to the public.

1415 ▪ Calvert County Historical Society Library

Prince Frederick Library Bldg.　　Ph: (410)535-2452
30 Duke St.
Prince Frederick, MD 20678
E-mail: lcollins@somd.lib.md.us
URL: http://www.somd.lib.md.us/CALV/cchs

Contact: Linda M. Collins, Cur.

Desc: Subject: Genealogy, history, Maryland, Maryland counties. Holdings: 2000 books, documents, photographs and objects. Services: Copying; Library open to the public.

1416 ▪ Cambria County Historical Society Museum & Library

615 N. Center St.　　Ph: (814)472-6674
Ebensburg, PA 15931

Contact: Leslie Conrad, Cur.

Desc: Subject: Genealogy, history of Cambria County, general history. Holdings: 2000 volumes. Services: Copying; Library open to the public for reference use only.

1417 ■ Cambridge Historical Society
Library
159 Brattle St.   Ph: (617)547-4252
Cambridge, MA 02138-3300   Fax: (617)661-1623

Contact: Aurore Eaton, Exec.Dir.

Desc: Subject: Local history. Holdings: 500 books; 250 other cataloged items. Services: Copying; Library open to the public on Tuesday and Thursday.

1418 ■ Camden Archives and Museum
1314 Broad St.   Ph: (803)425-6050
Camden, SC 29020-3535

Contact: Agnes B. Corbett, Dir.

Desc: Subject: History - local, state, national, military; genealogy. Holdings: 5000 books; 75 bound periodical volumes; 300 reels of microfilm; manuscripts; newspapers; maps; city records; photographic collections; records of community institutions; local artifacts. Services: Copying; archives open to the public for reference use only.

1419 ■ Camden County Historical Society
Library
Park Blvd. & Euclid Ave.   Ph: (609)964-3333
Camden, NJ 08103   Fax: (609)964-0378
URL: http://www.cyberenet.net/GSTEINER/CCHS/

Desc: Subject: History - Camden, Camden County, New Jersey, Pennsylvania, U.S.; decorative arts; Walt Whitman; genealogy; biography. Holdings: 20,000 books; 20 VF drawers; 587 reels of microfilm of newspapers; manuscripts; building contracts; maps; photographs; deeds. Services: Copying; Library open to the public on a fee basis.

1420 ■ Camden-Rockport Historical Society
Archives
Old Conway House and   Ph: (207)236-2257
  Cramer Museum
PO Box 747
Rockport, ME 04856
E-mail: chmuseum@mint.net
URL: http://www.mint.net/chmuseum

Contact: Marlene Hall, Exec.Dir.

Desc: Subject: History - Camden, Rockport. Holdings: 1000 archival materials including ships' logs and records, photographs, other historical materials. Services: Archives open to the public during the summer months or by appointment.

1421 ■ Cameron County Historical Society
Little Museum
102 W. 4th St.   Ph: (814)486-2162
Emporium, PA 15834

Contact: Sandra R. Hornung, Hist.

Desc: Subject: History of Cameron County, logging, early industry; genealogy. Holdings: Cameron County documents; maps; 3 VF drawers of newspaper clippings and documents; all tombstone inscriptions in 38 cemeteries and some church records on microfilm; early Cameron County newspapers on microfilm. Services: Museum open to the public on a limited schedule.

1422 ■ Campus Martius Museum
Library
601 Second St.   Ph: (740)373-3750
Marietta, OH 45750-2122   Fax: (740)373-3680
URL: http://www.ohiohistory.org/places/campus

Contact: John B. Briley, Mgr.

Desc: Subject: Area history and genealogy prior to 1830, river history. Holdings: 1000 books. Services: Copying; Library open to the public by appointment on a fee basis.

1423 ■ Canada
Canadian Heritage
Departmental Library, Hull Branch
15 Eddy St., 2nd Fl.   Ph: (819)997-3981
Hull, PQ, Canada K1A 0M5   Fax: (819)953-7988

Contact: Rejean Heroux, Chf.Libn.

Desc: Subject: Social sciences, Canadian identity, bilingualism, ethnic groups, human rights, Canadian history. Holdings: 50,000 books; 4000 departmental documents; 90 AV items; 5000 microfiche; 1000 linear feet of government documents. Services: Interlibrary loan; SDI; Library open to the public with restrictions on circulation.

1424 ■ Canada
Citizenship & Immigration
Library
Place du Portage   Ph: (819)953-9123
Phase IV, Level 1 140
Promenade du Portage
Hull, PQ, Canada K1A 1L1

Contact: Dawn Monroe, Mgr.Lib.Svcs.

Desc: Subject: Immigration; citizenship. Holdings: Figures not available.

1425 ■ Canada
Human Resources Development
Quebec Regional Library
200, boul Rene Levesque Ouest Ph: (514)283-4695
Tourouest 3C   Fax: (514)283-3874
Montreal, PQ, Canada H2Z
  1X4

Contact: Jacinthe Castonguay, Reg.Chf., Lib.Svc.

Desc: Subject: Manpower, immigration, unemployment insurance, counseling, employment, economics, management. Holdings: 14,000 books and government documents. Services: Interlibrary loan; copying; Library open to the public on a limited schedule.

1426 ■ Canada
Immigration Refugee Board
Documentation, Information and Research
Branch - Resource Center
344 Slater St., 11th Fl.   Ph: (613)996-0703
Ottawa, ON, Canada K1A 0K1 Fax: (613)992-4723
E-mail: n1640@netcom.ca
URL: http://www.irb.gc.ca

Contact: Dianne L. Parsonage, Rsrc.Ctr.Coord.

Desc: Subject: Human rights, immigration, refugees. Holdings: 4000 books. Services: Center open to the public for reference use only.

1427 ■ Canada - Employment & Immigration
Canada
Ontario Regional Library
4900 Yonge St., Ste. 700   Ph: (416)954-7682
North York, ON, Canada M2N Fax: (416)954-7537
  6A8

Contact: Flaka R. Hersom, Libn.

Desc: Subject: Immigration, employment. Holdings: 6000 books; clippings file. Services: Library open to the public by appointment.

1428 ■ Canada - National Library of Canada
Reference and Information Services Division
Government and Law Specialist
395 Wellington St.   Ph: (613)995-9481
Ottawa, ON, Canada K1A 0N4 Fax: (613)943-1112
URL: http://www.nlc-bnc.ca/services/egovdoc.htm

Contact: Claire Bourassa, Govt. & Law Spec.

Desc: Holdings: 2 million government documents in hardcopy and 2 million in microform from Canada, foreign countries, and international governmental organizations. Services: Reference, information, and referral services to libraries and individual researchers on site, by mail (conventional and electronic) and telephone; advisory service on bibliographic compilation; services available to researchers across Canada and other libraries.

1429 ■ Canadian Museum of Civilization
Library and Archives
100 Laurier St.   Ph: (819)776-7173
PO Box 3100, Sta. B   Fax: (819)776-8491
Hull, PQ, Canada J8X 4H2
E-mail: library@civilization.ca

Contact: Manon Guilbert, Dir.

Desc: Subject: Anthropology, archaeology, ethnology, history, material culture, folklore and culture studies. Holdings: 5900 linear feet of books and periodicals; 60,000 monographs; 48,000 periodical volumes; 500,000 photographs and slides; pamphlets; microforms; films; videotapes. Services: Interlibrary loan; copying; SDI; Library open to the public for reference use only.

1430 ■ Canton Historical Society
Library
11 Front St.   Ph: (860)693-2793
Collinsville, CT 06022

Contact: Cynthia Griggs, Asst.Libn.

Desc: Subject: Local and state history, Victoriana, Collins Manufacturing Company. Holdings: 250 books; 73 years of Annual reports; 30 deeds; 10 scrapbooks; 150 manuscripts; 50 unbound magazines of historical interest; 1000 photographs; census for Canton, CT, 1790-1920, on microfilm. Services: Library open to the public for reference use only.

1431 ■ Cape Ann Historical Association
Library
27 Pleasant St.   Ph: (978)283-0455
Gloucester, MA 01930

Contact: Ellen Nelson, Libn.Archiv.

Desc: Subject: Cape Ann - fishing industry, history, art history, genealogy. Holdings: 2500 books; 75 volumes of manuscripts and day books; 8 drawers of clippings; 4 drawers of Cape Ann Artists Archive. Services: Library open to the public for reference use only.

1432 ■ Cape May County Historical &
Genealogical Society
Robert Crozer Alexander Memorial Library
504 Rte. 9   Ph: (609)465-3535
Cape May Court House, NJ   Fax: (609)465-4274
  08210

Contact: Ione Williams, Libn.

Desc: Subject: Local history and genealogy. Holdings: 500 books; 20 bound periodical volumes; manuscripts; clippings; 31 volumes of New Jersey archives; Star and Wave newspapers, 1866-1971, on microfilm. Services: Copying; Library open to the public on a limited schedule and by appointment.

1433 ■ Carlsbad City Library
Genealogy and Local History Division
1250 Carlsbad Village Dr. Ph: (760)434-2931
Carlsbad, CA 92008   Fax: (760)729-2050

Contact: Mary Van Orsdol, Div.Hd.

Desc: Holdings: 19,000 volumes; 110,000 microfiche; 7300 reels of microfilm; 200 CD-ROMS. Services: Interlibrary loan; Library open to the public.

1434 ■ Carlton County Historical Society Library

406 Cloquet Ave.   Ph: (218)879-1938
Cloquet, MN 55720
E-mail: cchs@cpinternet.com

Contact: Marlene Wisuri, Dir.

Desc: Subject: Carlton County, logging and lumbering, Ojibwa Indians, settlements, railroads. Holdings: 600 books and pamphlets; 80 boxes of archival materials and maps; 8 AV programs; 11 VF drawers; newspapers (microfilm); census records (microfilm). Services: Copying; Library open to the public.

1435 ■ Carnegie Library of Pittsburgh Pennsylvania Department

4400 Forbes Ave.   Ph: (412)622-3154
Pittsburgh, PA 15213   Fax: (412)621-1267
E-mail: holtm@clpgh.org
URL: http://www.clpgh.org/clp/Pennsylvania

Contact: Marilyn C. Holt, Dept.Hd.

Desc: Subject: Pennsylvania history, biography, economics, and sociology, with emphasis on Pittsburgh and western Pennsylvania; genealogy; heraldry. Holdings: 30,000 volumes; 100 VF drawers of clippings and pamphlets; 57,000 photographs; 11,500 reels of microfilm. Services: Reference and reader's assistance; Library open to the public.

1436 ■ Carnegie Public Library of Clarksdale and Coahoma County Delta Blues Museum Collection

114 Delta Ave.   Ph: (601)627-8870
PO Box 280   Fax: (601)627-7263
Clarksdale, MS 38614
URL: http://www.deltabluesmuseum.org

Contact: Ronald H. Gorsegner, Dir.

Desc: Subject: Blues music; history - local, state, regional, black; genealogy. Holdings: 65,000 books, periodicals, phonograph records, photographs, videotapes. Services: Interlibrary loan; copying; collection open to the public with restrictions.

1437 ■ Caroline County Public Library Maryland and Caroline County Genealogy Collection

100 Market St.   Ph: (410)479-1343
Denton, MD 21629   Fax: (410)479-1443
E-mail: info@mail.caro.lib.md.us
URL: http://www.caro.lib.md.us/library

Desc: Subject: Maryland and the Eastern Shore - genealogy, government, history, authors. Holdings: Figures not available. Services: Interlibrary loan; copying; Library open to the public.

1438 ■ Carver County Historical Society, Inc. Library

555 W. 1st St.   Ph: (612)442-4234
Waconia, MN 55387-1203 Fax: (612)442-3025

Contact: Leanne Brown

Desc: Subject: Carver County history. Holdings: 500 books; 10,000 photographs; 400 reels of microfilm of newspapers; censuses. Services: Interlibrary loan (limited); copying; Library open to the public.

1439 ■ Casa Grande Valley Historical Society Museum Library

110 W. Florence Blvd.   Ph: (602)836-2223
Casa Grande, AZ 85222

Contact: Kay Benedict, Cur. of Coll.

Desc: Subject: Local history. Holdings: 500 volumes; manuscripts; artifacts. Services: Library open to the public for reference use only.

1440 ■ Cascade County Historical Society Archives and Information Center

1400 1st Ave., N.   Ph: (406)452-3462
Great Falls, MT 59401

Contact: Cindy Kittredge, Dir.

Desc: Subject: State and local history. Holdings: 2000 books; 700 bound newspapers; 12,000 photographs; 4 VF drawers of pamphlets; 4 VF drawers of clippings; 75 oral history tapes, library of period regional literature. Services: Copying; center open to the public with restrictions.

1441 ■ Casey County Public Library Genealogy Collection

238 Middleburg St.   Ph: (606)787-9381
Liberty, KY 42539   Fax: (606)787-7720
E-mail: caseylib@kih.net

Contact: Jan J. Banks, Dist.Libn.

Desc: Subject: Genealogy. Holdings: 845 books; 50 AV programs; 120 nonbook items; 200 reels of microfilm; 22 videocassettes; 350 VF; 86 audiotapes. Services: Copying; collection open to the public.

1442 ■ Casper College Library Special Collections

125 College Dr.   Ph: (307)268-2269
Casper, WY 82601   Fax: (307)268-2682
E-mail: kevinand@acad.cc.whecn.edu
URL: http://www.cc.whecn.edu/library/sc.htm

Contact: Lynnette Anderson, Dir.

Desc: Subject: History - Wyoming, Natrona county, Casper city. Holdings: 5302 books; 107 bound periodical volumes; 47 archival items; 9 microfiche; 54 videotapes; 22 audiocassettes; 2 sound recordings; 33 reels of microfilm; 218 maps. Services: Library open to the public.

1443 ■ Cass County Historical Society and Museum Library

1004 E. Market St.   Ph: (219)753-3866
Logansport, IN 46947 Fax: (219)753-3866

Contact: Bruce Stuart, Cur.

Desc: Subject: History - Cass County, general; genealogy. Holdings: 7500 books; 25 bound periodical volumes; 16 AV programs; 75 manuscripts. Services: Copying; Library open to the public with restrictions.

1444 ■ Cassia County Historical Society Reference Room

PO Box 331   Ph: (208)678-7172
Burley, ID 83318

Desc: Subject: Local history. Holdings: Books; yearbooks; journals; clippings; tapes; thesis. Services: Room open to the public for reference use only on a limited schedule.

1445 ■ Catawba County Historical Association Library

Box 73   Ph: (828)465-0383
Newton, NC 28658   Fax: (828)465-9813

Contact: Sidney Halma, Dir.

Desc: Subject: Local history, genealogy. Holdings: 1600 volumes; 860 bound periodical volumes; 2100 other cataloged items. Services: Copying; library open to the public for reference use only.

1446 ■ Cedar Falls Historical Society Donald & Alleen Howard Library

303 Franklin St.   Ph: (319)266-5149
Cedar Falls, IA 50613 Fax: (319)268-1812

Contact: Brian Collins, Exec.Dir.

Desc: Subject: Local, state, U.S. history; natural ice industry; 19th century agriculture. Holdings: 400 books; 250 bound periodical volumes; 300 oral history tapes; 65 scrapbooks; 324 issues of The Palimpsest magazine, 1950 to present; 18 linear feet of photographs; 54 linear feet of local and family history; videos.

1447 ■ Center for Migration Studies CMS Library

209 Flagg Place   Ph: (718)351-8800
Staten Island, NY 10304-1199 Fax: (718)667-4598
E-mail: cmslft@aol.com

Contact: Diana J. Zimmerman, Hd., CMS Lib.

Desc: Subject: International migration, refugees, ethnicity, ethnic groups in the U.S. Holdings: 24,913 volumes; 4493 reports; 285 reels of microfilm of archival material; 527 dissertations on microfilm; manuscripts. Services: Copying; center open to the public.

1448 ■ Central Arkansas Library System Reference Services Department Library

100 Rock St.   Ph: (501)918-3000
Little Rock, AR 72201-1624 Fax: (501)375-7451
URL: http://www.cals.lib.ar.us

Contact: Carol Y. Coffey, Ref.Svc.

Desc: Holdings: 130,000 federal documents; 25,000 state and local documents; 1600 maps. Services: Interlibrary loan; copying; department open to the public with restrictions.

1449 ■ Central Minnesota Historical Center Library

St. Cloud State University Ph: (320)255-3254
St. Cloud, MN 56301
E-mail: cmhc@stcloudstate.edu

Contact: Dr. Don L. Hofsommer, Dir.

Desc: Subject: Church history, business, Minnesota politics and government, oral history, railroad and labor history, World War II military history. Holdings: 230 linear feet of local history materials. Services: Copying; Library open to the public.

1450 ■ Central Nevada Historical Society Museum Library

PO Box 326   Ph: (702)482-9676
Logan Field Rd.   Fax: (702)482-5423
Tonopah, NV 89049

Contact: William J. Metscher, Dir.

Desc: Subject: Central Nevada history - Nye and Esmeralda Counties. Holdings: 2000 books; 50 AV programs; 250 microform and nonbook items; 15 manuscripts; 60,000 photographs; 600 maps; 140 oral histories (franchised). Services: Copying; Library open to the public for reference use only.

1451 ■ Central Presbyterian Church Library

12455 S.W. 104 St.
Miami, FL 33186

Desc: Subject: Religion, education, social sciences. Holdings: 880 books; 111 videotapes. Services: Library open to the Presbyterian community.

1452 ▪ Central Synagogue of Nassau County
Helen Blau Memorial Library
430 DeMott Ave.   Ph: (516)766-4300
Rockville Centre, NY 11570   Fax: (516)678-9832
Contact: Miriam Schonwald, Libn.

Desc: Subject: Religion, comparative religion, sociology, history, biography. Holdings: 5200 books; 200 bound periodical volumes; 200 filmstrips; maps; phonograph records; cassettes; slides. Services: Interlibrary loan; copying; Library open to the public.

1453 ▪ Central United Methodist Church
Library
616 Jackson St., S.E.   Ph: (205)353-6941
Decatur, AL 35601   Fax: (205)353-6945
Contact: Betty Tull

Desc: Subject: Bible, Methodist Church history, Bible history, devotional literature. Holdings: Books; 200 archival items; United Methodist women's reading list. Services: Library open to the public.

1454 ▪ Chaffey Communities Cultural Center
Cooper Regional History Museum
Library
PO Box 772   Ph: (909)982-8010
Upland, CA 91785-0772   Fax: (909)920-9292
E-mail: info@culturalcenter.org
URL: http://www.culturalcenter.org
Contact: Max van Balgooy, Cur.

Desc: Subject: Western San Bernandino county, citrus fruit industry, women's organizations, wine industry. Holdings: 500 books; archival items. Services: Copying; Library open to the public by appointment.

1455 ▪ Champaign County Historical Archives
The Urbana Free Library   Ph: (217)367-4025
201 S. Race St.   Fax: (217)367-4061
Urbana, IL 61801-3283
Contact: Jean Koch, Dir.

Desc: Subject: Champaign County history, genealogy of Illinois and the eastern United States. Holdings: 10,607 books; 2581 bound periodical volumes; 6003 reels of microfilm; 215 microfiche titles; 190 VF drawers of photographs, family information, clippings, manuscripts, documents, marriage records, chancery court records, probate records; guardianship records, appellate court records, and titles abstracts; 306 audiocassettes; 36 videos. Services: Copying; archives open to the public for reference use only; private researchers available.

1456 ▪ Chaparral Genealogical Society
Library
310 N. Live Oak   Ph: (281)255-9081
PO Box 606
Tomball, TX 77376
URL: http://www.rootsweb.com/txwaller/
Contact: Ella Louise Hill, Libn.

Desc: Subject: Genealogy, local history. Holdings: 3200 books; 675 bound periodical volumes; 340 reels of microfilm of census and county records; 2 VF drawers. Services: Interlibrary loan; copying; Library open to the public.

1457 ▪ Chapman Historical Museum
Archives
348 Glen St.   Ph: (518)793-2826
Glens Falls, NY 12801   Fax: (518)793-2831
Contact: Alexandra Mckee, Cur. of Coll.

Desc: Subject: Glen Falls and Queensbury history and social history; Adirondacks; Warren, Washington and Sar-

atoga counties. Holdings: 800 books; 20,000 photographs; 30,000 archives. Services: Copying; Library open to researchers by appointment.

1458 ▪ Charles A. Weyerhaeuser Memorial
Museum
Library
Box 239   Ph: (320)632-4007
2151 Lindbergh Dr. S   Fax: (320)632-8409
Little Falls, MN 56345
Contact: Jan Warner, Exec.Dir.

Desc: Subject: Local history of Morrison County. Holdings: 800 books; photographs. Services: Copying; Library open to the public for reference use only.

1459 ▪ Charleston County Library
South Carolina Room
68 Calhoun St.   Ph: (843)805-6956
Charleston, SC 29401   Fax: (843)727-6752
E-mail: scroom@ccpl.org
URL: http://www.ccpl.org/scr.html
Contact: Jan Buvinger, Dir.

Desc: Subject: South Carolina - history, genealogy. Holdings: 51,000 books; 480 bound periodical volumes; 13 sets microfiche; 300 microfilm. Services: Library open to the public.

1460 ▪ Charleston Library Society
164 King St.   Ph: (803)723-9912
Charleston, SC 29401
Contact: Catherine E. Sadler, Libn.

Desc: Subject: Genealogy, history, southern U.S. literature. Holdings: 95,000 volumes; 1600 reels of microfilm. Services: Interlibrary loan; copying; Library open to the public.

1461 ▪ Charlotte and Mecklenburg County
Public Library
Robinson-Spangler Carolina Room
310 N. Tryon St.   Ph: (704)336-2980
Charlotte, NC 28202-2176   Fax: (704)336-6236
E-mail: ncr@plcmc.lib.nc.us
URL: http://www.plcmc.lib.nc.us/branch/main/ncr
Contact: Chris A. Bates, Cur.Mgr.

Desc: Subject: Local and regional history, genealogy. Holdings: 23,000 books; 1776 bound periodical volumes; 120 VF drawers of clippings and genealogical materials; 4800 reels of microfilm of Federal Population Schedules; 2300 reels of microfilm of local newspapers; 400 reels of microfilm of county records; local and state documents. Services: Interlibrary loan; copying; room open to the public.

1462 ▪ Charlton County Historical Society
Library
PO Box 575   Ph: (912)496-4578
Folkston, GA 31537
Contact: Lois B. Mays, Pres.

Desc: Subject: Local history, genealogy. Holdings: 100 books. Services: Copying; Library open to the public by appointment.

1463 ▪ Chase County Historical Society
Library
301 Broadway   Ph: (316)273-8500
Cottonwood Falls, KS 66845
Contact: Pat Donelson, Cur.

Desc: Subject: Chase County history, genealogy. Holdings: 200 books; 85 reels of microfilm; Collectibles; pictures. Services: Copying; Library open to the public.

1464 ▪ Chatsworth Historical Society
Frank H. Schepler, Jr. Memorial Library
10385 Shadow Oak Dr.   Ph: (818)882-5614
Chatsworth, CA 91313
E-mail: chatsmimi@aol.com
Contact: Virginia Watson, Cur. & Libn.

Desc: Subject: History of Chatsworth, the San Fernando Valley, and California, Prehistoric to present. Holdings: 300 slides, photographs, oral history tapes, documents, and books. Services: Library open to the public by appointment for reference use only.

1465 ▪ Chattanooga-Hamilton County
Bicentennial Library
Local History and Genealogy Department
1001 Broad St.   Ph: (423)757-5317
Chattanooga, TN 37402
URL: http://www.lib.chattanooga.gov
Contact: Clara W. Swann, Dept.Hd.

Desc: Subject: Southeast U.S. genealogy; local and state history. Holdings: 28,778 books; 344 manuscript collections; 174 VF drawers of clippings and photographs; 12,884 reels of microfilm of county records and local newspapers; 8841 microfiche. Services: Copying; collections open to the public for reference use only.

1466 ▪ Chautauqua County Historical Society
Library
Village Park   Ph: (716)326-2977
Box 7
Westfield, NY 14787
Contact: Mrs. Derby-Cuadrado, Dir.

Desc: Subject: History of Chautauqua County. Holdings: 2000 books. Services: Library open to the public with restrictions.

1467 ▪ Chelmsford Historical Society
Barrett-Byam Homestead Library
40 Byam Rd.   Ph: (508)256-2311
Chelmsford, MA 01824
Contact: Donald Pattershall, Cur.

Desc: Subject: Chelmsford and Massachusetts history, Civil War and Revolution, early agriculture. Holdings: Reports; pamphlets; deeds. Services: Library open to the public on limited schedule, mid-April to mid-December.

1468 ▪ Chemung County Historical Society, Inc.
Mrs. Arthur W. Booth Library
415 E. Water St.   Ph: (607)734-4167
Elmira, NY 14901   Fax: (607)734-1565
Contact: Constance Barone, Dir.

Desc: Subject: New York State and local history, Mark Twain, U.S. military history. Holdings: 2000 volumes; 200 microfiche; 150 reels of microfilm; 30,000 archival items. Services: Copying; Library open to the public by appointment (fee charged).

1469 ▪ Cherokee County Genealogical-
Historical Society
Library
100 S. Tennessee   Ph: (316)429-2992
PO Box 33
Columbus, KS 66725-0033
Contact: Helen Kelley, Libn.

Desc: Subject: Genealogy - Cherokee County, Kansas. Holdings: 1153 books; 712 reels of microfilm. Services: Interlibrary loan; copying; Library open to the public.

1470 ■ Cherokee County Historical Society Research Center

Box 247　　　　　Ph: (712)436-2624
Cleghorn, IA 51014

Contact: Anne Wilberding, Pres.

Desc: Subject: Local history, genealogy. Holdings: Figures not available. Services: Center open to the public by appointment.

1471 ■ Cherokee National Historical Society, Inc.
Cherokee National Archives

Box 515　　　　　Ph: (918)456-6007
TSA-LA-GI　　　　Fax: (918)456-6165
Tahlequah, OK 74465

Contact: Tom Mooney, Archv.

Desc: Subject: Cherokee history. Holdings: 3000 books; 500 bound periodical volumes; 147 reels of microfilm; 5 VF drawers of pamphlets; 7 VF drawers of papers and committee minutes. Services: Copying; archives open to the public on request.

1472 ■ Cherokee Strip Land Rush Museum
Docking Research Center Archives Library

S. Summit Street Rd.　Ph: (316)442-6750
PO Box 778
Arkansas City, KS 67005
E-mail: museum@horizon.hit.net

Contact: Allen Goff, Pres.

Desc: Subject: Local history, genealogy, Cherokee Strip Run, Chilocco. Holdings: Books; bound periodical volumes; pamphlets on historical events; unbound reports; newspapers; maps; pictures; letters; manuscripts; clippings; 6 reels of microfilm; 10 tapes. Services: Copying; research upon request; Library open to the public for reference use only on fee basis.

1473 ■ Cherry County Historical Society

PO Box 284　　　　Ph: (402)376-2105
Valentine, NE 69201-0284

Contact: Mary E. Schroeder, Cur.

Desc: Subject: Genealogy. Holdings: 300 books; 200 bound periodical volumes; 500 archival materials; 150 reels of microfilm; photographs. Services: Copying.

1474 ■ Chester County Archives and Records Services

Government Service Center　Ph: (610)344-6760
601 Westtown Rd., Ste. 080　Fax: (610)692-4357
West Chester, PA 19382-4527
URL: http://www.chesco.com/cchs

Contact: Jeffrey Rollison, Dir.

Desc: Subject: Local history, county government and politics, genealogy. Holdings: 2000 cubic feet of historic county government records. Services: Copying; mail research services; archives open to the public.

1475 ■ Chester County Historical Society Library

225 N. High St.　　　Ph: (610)692-4800
West Chester, PA 19380　Fax: (610)692-4357
E-mail: cchs@chesco.com
URL: http://www.chesco.com

Contact: Diane Rofini, Libn.

Desc: Subject: Local history and politics, genealogy, decorative arts, church history. Holdings: Books; periodicals; 140 VF drawers of newspaper clippings; 250 reels of microfilm; 70,000 photographs; maps; manuscripts; letters; diaries; deeds. Services: Copying; research by mail services; Library open to nonmembers on fee basis.

1476 ■ Chesterfield Historical Society Library

PO Box 40　　　　Ph: (804)748-1026
Chesterfield, VA 23832

Contact: Lucille C. Mosley, Libn.

Desc: Subject: Chesterfield history and genealogy. Holdings: 1000 books; 20 bound periodical volumes; 300 manuscripts; letters; diaries; 200 maps; photographs. Services: Copying; Library open to the public for reference use only.

1477 ■ Chicago County Historical Society Library

Box 185　　　　　Ph: (651)465-6905
Taylor Falls Public Library
Taylors Falls, MN 55084

Contact: Marilyn Rimestad, Libn.

Desc: Subject: St. Croix Valley and Taylors Falls history. Holdings: 12,093 books. Services: Library open to the public on a limited schedule.

1478 ■ Chicago Historical Society Research Center

1601 N. Clark St. at North Ave.　Ph: (312)642-4600
Chicago, IL 60614　　　　Fax: (312)266-2077
URL: http://www.chicagohistory.org

Contact: Bernard F. Reilly, Dir.

Desc: Subject: History - Chicago, Illinois, Civil War, Lincoln. Holdings: 112,700 books and pamphlets; 10,000 bound periodical volumes; 3500 volumes of newspapers; 16,000 broadsides and posters; 9860 maps; 725 atlases; 37 VF drawers of clippings; 40,000 pieces of miscellanea; 11,000 reels of microfilm; 300,000 architectural drawings; 53,000 prints; 1.5 million photographs; 12,000 reels of newsfilm. Services: Copying; Library open to the public.

1479 ■ Chicago Public Library Central Library Social Sciences Division

Harold Washington　　Ph: (312)747-4600
　Library Center　　　Fax: (312)747-4646
400 S. State St.
Chicago, IL 60605
URL: http://www.chipublib.org

Contact: Diane Purtill, Div.Chf.

Desc: Subject: Sociology, history, education, religion, psychology, philosophy, political science, sports, anthropology, law, genealogy, travel. Holdings: 440,604 books, 45,055 bound periodical volumes; 711,046 microforms; 50 VF drawers of clippings and pamphlets; ARL spec kits; 4600 college catalogs on microfiche; 2645 maps; ERIC microfiche. Services: Interlibrary loan; copying; division open to the public.

1480 ■ Chicago Sinai Congregation Library

15 W. Delaware Pl.　　Ph: (312)867-7000
Chicago, IL 60610　　Fax: (312)867-7006
E-mail: sinai@interaccess.com

Contact: Sally J. Barnum, Libn.

Desc: Subject: Judaica, Reform Judaism. Holdings: 7000 books; 50 bound periodical volumes; 50 other cataloged items. Services: Library open to the public.

1481 ■ Chilliwack Archives

9291 Corbould St.　　Ph: (604)795-9255
Chilliwack, BC, Canada V2P　Fax: (604)795-5291
　4A6

Contact: Kelly Harms, Arch.

Desc: Subject: Local history and genealogy. Holdings: 1500 books; 200 sound recordings; 400 maps; 25,000

pictorial images; 50 paintings, drawings, and prints; 39 meters of government records; 65 meters of manuscript collections. Services: Copying; Library open to the public with restrictions.

1482 ■ Chinese Historical Society of America

644 Broadway St., No. 402　Ph: (415)391-1188
San Francisco, CA 94133　Fax: (415)391-1150
URL: http://www.chsa.org

Desc: Subject: Chinese in America, late 19th century to present. Holdings: Newspaper clippings; photographs; manuscripts.

1483 ■ Church of England Institute
Toronto Family History Library

95 Melbert Rd.　　　Ph: (416)621-4607
PO Box 247
Etobicoke, ON, Canada M9C
　4V3

Contact: Edward G. Lansitie, Libn.

Desc: Subject: Genealogy. Holdings: Figures not available.

1484 ■ Church of Jesus Christ of Latter-Day Saints
Albuquerque South Stake Family History Center

5709 Haines, NE　　　Ph: (505)266-4867
Albuquerque, NM 87110

Contact: John Hawk, Lib.Dir.

Desc: Subject: Genealogy, social history, heraldry, geography. Holdings: 950 books; 700 reels of microfilm of U.S. Census Records; 155 reels of microfilm of Boyd's Marriage Index; 600 reels of microfilm of U.S. records; microfilm of many New Mexico church records. Services: Copying, access to the microfilm collection of the main center in Salt Lake City; center open to the public.

1485 ■ Church of Jesus Christ of Latter-Day Saints
Bennington, Vermont
Family History Center

Houghton Ln.　　　Ph: (802)447-1983
Bennington, VT 05201

Desc: Subject: Genealogy; Vermont vital statistics. Holdings: Microfiche; microfilm; CD-ROMs. Services: Center open to the public.

1486 ■ Church of Jesus Christ of Latter-Day Saints
Boston Family History Center

PO Box 138　　　　Ph: (617)964-7584
150 Brown St.
Weston, MA 02193

Contact: Elizabeth Bentall, Dir.

Desc: Subject: Genealogy, family histories. Holdings: 500 books; 50 bound periodical volumes; 10 manuscripts; 81 million names on microfiche; microfilm. Services: Copying; access to the microfilm collection of the main center in Salt Lake City; center open to the public.

1487 ■ Church of Jesus Christ of Latter-Day Saints
Boulder City Family History Center

528 Hopi Pl.　　　　Ph: (702)293-3304
Boulder City, NV 89005-3059

Contact: Helen F. Reese, Dir.

Desc: Subject: Genealogy. Holdings: Books; microfilm; microfiche of holdings of Salt Lake City Family History Library. Services: Access to microfilm and microfiche collections of the main center in Salt Lake City, UT; center open to the public.

1488 ▪ Church of Jesus Christ of Latter-Day Saints
Cleveland, Ohio Stake Family History Center
c/o Rick Bublik   Ph: (440)777-1518
2500 Westwood Rd.
Westlake, OH 44145

Contact: Ira T. Myers, Hd.Libn.

Desc: Subject: Genealogy. Holdings: 265 reels of microfilm of U.S., British, Canadian collections; 112 reels of microfilm of non-English speaking countries (continental European, Afro-Asian, Latin American, Iberian Peninsula, Scandinavian Collections). Services: Access to the microfilm collection of the main center in Salt Lake City; center open to the public.

1489 ▪ Church of Jesus Christ of Latter-Day Saints
Detroit Family History Center
425 N. Woodward   Ph: (248)647-5671
Bloomfield, MI 48302

Contact: Ted Jenson, Dir.

Desc: Subject: Genealogy. Holdings: 165 books; 148 bound periodical volumes; International Genealogical Index (88 million names). Services: Interlibrary loan; copying; access to the microfilm collection of the main center in Salt Lake City; center open to the public.

1490 ▪ Church of Jesus Christ of Latter-Day Saints
El Paso Family History Center
11200 Ivan Hoe Dr.   Ph: (915)599-8565
El Paso, TX 79936   Fax: (915)599-8565

Contact: Michael B. Smith, Dir.

Desc: Subject: Genealogy. Holdings: 352 books. Services: Copying; access to the microfilm collection of the Family History Library in Salt Lake City; center open to the public.

1491 ▪ Church of Jesus Christ of Latter-Day Saints
Etobicoke Family History Library
95 Melbert Rd.   Ph: (416)621-4607
Box 1-STN A
Etobicoke, ON, Canada M9C
 4V2

Contact: Edward G. Lansitie, Libn.

Desc: Subject: Genealogy. Holdings: Microfiche; microfilm. Services: Library open to the public.

1492 ▪ Church of Jesus Christ of Latter-Day Saints
Eugene, Oregon Family History Center
3550 W. 18th Ave.   Ph: (541)343-3741
Eugene, OR 97402

Contact: Leon R. Barnwell, Libn.

Desc: Subject: Genealogy. Holdings: 2800 books; 400 bound periodical volumes; 5 VF drawers; 3 VF drawers of family histories; 3230 reels of microfilm; 200 maps. Services: Copying; access to the microfilm collection of the main center in Salt Lake City; center open to the public.

1493 ▪ Church of Jesus Christ of Latter-Day Saints
Eureka Ward Family History Center
3441 Edgewood Rd.   Ph: (707)443-7411
Eureka, CA 95501   Fax: (707)443-7411
E-mail: eurekafhc@juno.com

Contact: Alan S. Cookson, Dir.

Desc: Subject: Genealogy. Holdings: Books; bound periodical volumes; local obituaries; directories; microfiche. Services: Access to the microfilm collection of the main center in Salt Lake City, UT; center open to the public.

1494 ▪ Church of Jesus Christ of Latter-Day Saints
Family History Center
67 Chester St.   Ph: (508)852-7000
Worcester, MA 01602

Contact: Judy Kelder

Desc: Subject: Genealogy. Holdings: bound periodical volumes; microfiche; microfilm; CD-ROMS. Services: Copying; library open to the public with restrictions.

1495 ▪ Church of Jesus Christ of Latter-Day Saints
Family History Center
Genealogy Branch Library
PO Box 82202   Ph: (402)423-4561
Lincoln, NE 68501

Contact: Susan Randall, Dir.

Desc: Subject: Genealogy. Holdings: 400 books; 6000 microfiche; 1100 reels of microfilm. Services: Copying; Library open to the public.

1496 ▪ Church of Jesus Christ of Latter-Day Saints
Family History Library
1536 E. Cherokee Ln.
Safford, AZ 85546

Contact: Leven B. Ferrin

Desc: Subject: Genealogy. Holdings: 5000 books; 1087 bound periodical volumes; 3000 films; microfiche for genealogical research. Services: Interlibrary loan; copying; center open to the public.

1497 ▪ Church of Jesus Christ of Latter-Day Saints
Family History Library
35 NW Temple St.   Ph: (801)240-2331
Salt Lake City, UT 84150-3400   Fax: (801)240-5551
E-mail: fhl@ldschurch.org

Contact: Jimmy B. Parker, Mgr.

Desc: Subject: Genealogy, family history, church and civil records, local history. Holdings: 280,000 volumes; 3000 bound periodical volumes; 2 million reels of microfilm; 700,000 microfiche. Services: Copying; patron classes; Library open to the public.

1498 ▪ Church of Jesus Christ of Latter-Day Saints
Helena Family History Center
1610 E. 6th Ave.   Ph: (406)443-0716
Helena, MT 59601-0465

Contact: Jeanette Bingham, Co.-Dir.

Desc: Subject: Genealogy. Holdings: 140 books; 1200 reels of microfilm; accelerated indexing systems on microfiche; 2 drawers of microfiche. Services: Interlibrary loan; copying; access to the microfilm collection of the main center in Salt Lake City; center open to the public.

1499 ▪ Church of Jesus Christ of Latter-Day Saints
Jacksonville, Florida Family History Center
7665 Fort Caroline Rd.   Ph: (904)743-0527
Jacksonville, FL 32211-4065

Contact: Edie Mixon, Dir.

Desc: Subject: Genealogy, local history. Holdings: 671 volumes; 1203 reels of microfilm; 25 drawers of newspaper vital statistics. Services: Copying; center open to the public with restrictions.

1500 ▪ Church of Jesus Christ of Latter-Day Saints
Laie Family History Center
55-629A Iosepa St.   Ph: (808)293-2133
Laie, HI 96762

Desc: Subject: Genealogy. Holdings: 200 books; 1900, 1910, 1920 Hawaii Census; 1920 Census Soundex; Federal Index of Hawaii Delayed Births (online); 1300 reels of microfilm including 1890 Hawaii Census, 1881 Census of England and Wales, and 1881 Census of Scotland; church records. Services: Copying; access to the microfilm collection of the Family History Library in Salt Lake City; center open to the public.

1501 ▪ Church of Jesus Christ of Latter-Day Saints
Lansing (Mich.) Family History Center
431 E. Saginaw   Ph: (517)332-2932
PO Box 1610
East Lansing, MI 48826

Contact: Mary Griffes, Dir.

Desc: Subject: Genealogy. Services: Film and microfiche copying; access to microfilm and microfiche collection of the main Family History Library in Salt Lake City (rental charge for use); center open to the public.

1502 ▪ Church of Jesus Christ of Latter-Day Saints
Las Vegas Family History Center
509 S. 9th St.   Ph: (702)382-9695
Las Vegas, NV 89101-7010   Fax: (702)382-1597

Contact: Deon J Sanders, Dir.

Desc: Subject: Genealogy, county history. Holdings: 6000 books; 1200 bound periodical volumes; 15,000 reels of microfilm; 20,000 microfiche. Services: Copying; center open to the public.

1503 ▪ Church of Jesus Christ of Latter-Day Saints
Los Angeles Family History Center
10741 Santa Monica Blvd.   Ph: (310)474-9990
Los Angeles, CA 90025   Fax: (310)441-0066

Contact: Ross L. Birdsall, Dir.

Desc: Subject: Genealogy, local and county history. Holdings: 53,000 books; 4450 bound periodical volumes; 140,000 reels of microfilm; 62 VF drawers of U.S. gazetteer files; 40 index sets; 185,000 microfiche. Services: Copying; microfilm copying; member of the borrowing program of the Genealogical Society, Salt Lake City, UT; genealogical consultant services; center open to the public.

1504 ▪ Church of Jesus Christ of Latter-Day Saints
Lovell, Wyoming Family History Center
1618 Lane Ten   Ph: (307)548-2963
Lovell, WY 82431

Contact: Von Zeller, Libn.

Desc: Subject: Genealogy, history, biography. Holdings: 325 books; 200 bound periodical volumes; 20 unbound cemetery records; 1 set of unbound mortuary records; 10 folders of unbound obituary clippings; genealogy microforms. Services: Copying; center open to the public.

1505 ▪ Church of Jesus Christ of Latter-Day Saints
Philadelphia, Pennsylvania Stake
Family History Center
721 Paxon Hollow Rd.   Ph: (610)356-8507
Broomall, PA 19008

Contact: Martine Green, Dir.

Desc: Subject: Genealogy. Holdings: 1500 books; 42,000 microfiche; 500 reels of microfilm. Services: Access to microfilm and microfiche records of the main Library in Salt Lake City; Center open to the public.

1506 ▪ Church of Jesus Christ of Latter-Day Saints
Pompano Beach, Florida Family History Center
1099 SW 9th Ave.   Ph: (561)395-6644
Boca Raton, FL 33486   Fax: (561)395-8957

Contact: Donald W. Jennings, Jr., Dir.

Desc: Subject: Genealogical research. Holdings: 500 books; 4000 reels of microfilm; International Genealogical Index (IGI); catalog of Salt Lake Family History Library on microfiche; family registery; Social Security Index. Services: Copying; access to microfilm collection of the main center in Salt Lake City; Center open to the public on a limited schedule.

1507 ▪ Church of Jesus Christ of Latter-Day Saints
Richland Family History Center
400 Catskill   Ph: (509)946-6637
Richland, WA 99352
E-mail: rp_allen@oneworld.owt.com

Contact: Dr. Richard P. Allen, Dir.

Desc: Subject: Genealogy. Holdings: 1200 books; 500 bound periodical volumes; 5000 reels of microfilm; 20,000 microfiche. Services: Genealogical classes; copying; access to the microfilm collection of the main library in Salt Lake City; center open to the public.

1508 ▪ Church of Jesus Christ of Latter-Day Saints
Roswell Family History Center
39 Lost Trail Rd.   Ph: (505)623-4492
Roswell, NM 88201

Contact: Murray H. Sharp, Dir.

Desc: Subject: Genealogy, Roswell history. Holdings: 150 books; 150,000 microfiche; 300 microfilms. Services: Interlibrary loan; center open to the public.

1509 ▪ Church of Jesus Christ of Latter-Day Saints
St. George Family History Center
410 South 200 East   Ph: (801)673-4591
St. George, UT 84770

Contact: Norley Hall, Dir.

Desc: Subject: Genealogy and history. Holdings: 5000 volumes; 2300 reels of microfilm; 50,000 microfiche; 2000 research CD-ROMs. Services: Copying; center open to the public.

1510 ▪ Church of Jesus Christ of Latter-Day Saints
San Diego Family History Center
4195 Camino Del Rio S.   Ph: (619)584-7668
San Diego, CA 92108

Contact: Wm. Ross Konold, Dir.

Desc: Subject: Genealogy, local history. Holdings: 12,000 volumes; 12,500 reels of microfilm; 41,000 microfiche. Services: Copying; access to the microfilm collection of the main center in Salt Lake City; center open to the public.

1511 ▪ Church of Jesus Christ of Latter-Day Saints
Tacoma Branch Family History Center
5915 S. 12th   Ph: (253)564-1103
Tacoma, WA 98465

Contact: Gaylen Masters, Dir.

Desc: Subject: Genealogy and local history. Holdings: 600 volumes; 7400 reels of microfilm; 25 VF drawers of western Washington obituaries; 3 VF drawers of genealogical materials; hanging file of surnames; census records; films. Services: copying; access to the microfilm collection of the main center in Salt Lake City; center open to the public.

1512 ▪ Church of Jesus Christ of Latter-Day Saints
Tampa Stake Family History Center
4106 E. Flecther   Ph: (813)971-2869
Tampa, FL 33612

Contact: James B. Williams, Dir.

Desc: Subject: Local history, genealogy. Holdings: 2200 books; 9000 reels of microfilm; 1000 unbound periodicals; 2500 clippings, maps, manuscripts; 12 drawers of microfiche of the International Family History Index; U.S. census, 1790-1850, Heads of Household Index. Services: Copying; access to the microfilm collection of the main center in Salt Lake City; center open to the public.

1513 ▪ Church of Jesus Christ of Latter-Day Saints
Ventura Family History Center
3501 Loma Vista   Ph: (805)643-5607
Ventura, CA 93001

Contact: Dorothy Leeds, Dir.

Desc: Subject: Genealogy. Holdings: 600 books; 500 reels of microfilm; 20,000 microfiche. Services: Copying; microfiche‑microfilm copying; access to microfilm collection of the main center in Salt Lake City; center open to the public.

1514 ▪ Church of Jesus Christ of Latter-Day Saints
Visalia, California Stake Family History Center
825 W. Tulare Ave.   Ph: (209)732-3712
Visalia, CA 93277

Contact: Jessie M. Jones, Dir.

Desc: Subject: Genealogy. Holdings: Card Catalog of the Salt Lake Index (MCC) on microfilm; Genealogical Library Catalog (GLC) on microfiche; International Genealogical Index (IGI); Accelerated Index System to U.S. Census (AIS); Family Register; Sutro File. Services: Interlibrary loan; copying; Library open to the public.

1515 ▪ Church of the Lighted Window
Library
1200 Foothill Blvd.   Ph: (818)790-1185
La Canada, CA 91011

Contact: Roberta M. Parsons

Desc: Subject: Christian living, Bible, devotions, family, biography, poetry, literature. Holdings: 1500 books. Services: Library open to the public on a limited schedule.

1516 ▪ Churchill County
Museum & Archives
1050 S. Maine St.   Ph: (775)423-3677
Fallon, NV 89406   Fax: (775)423-3662
E-mail: ccmuseum@phonewave.net
URL: http://www.ccmuseum.org

Contact: Jane Pieplow, Dir.Cur.

Desc: Subject: Nevada history, local history. Holdings: 1000 books. Services: Copying; archives open to the public for reference use only.

1517 ▪ Cincinnati Historical Society
Library
1301 Western Ave.   Ph: (513)287-7000
Cincinnati, OH 45203-1129   Fax: (513)287-7095
URL: http://www.cincymuseum.org

Contact: Laura L. Chace, Dir.

Desc: Subject: Northwest Territory, Miami Purchase, Hamilton County and Cincinnati metropolitan area, genealogy. Holdings: 90,000 volumes; 20,000 cubic feet of manuscripts; 1,000,000 photographs; 3,000,000 feet of film; 14,000 slides; 2500 maps; 5000 reels of microfilm; 1300 broadsides; 350 linear feet of clippings. Services: Copying; Library open to the public for reference use only.

1518 ▪ Clarion County Historical Society
Library Museum
18 Grant St.   Ph: (814)226-4450
Clarion, PA 16214   Fax: (814)226-7106
URL: http://www.csonline.net/cchs

Contact: Lindsley A. Dunn, Dir.Cur.

Desc: Subject: Genealogy, Pennsylvania history. Holdings: 1500 books; bound newspapers, 1894-1929; pictures; pamphlets; documents; correspondence; church and cemetery records; 300 family trees; census indexes; archival material. Services: Copying, genealogical research, Library open to the public with restrictions.

1519 ▪ Clark County Historical Society
Library
Box 2157   Ph: (937)324-0657
Springfield, OH 45501-2157   Fax: (937)324-1992

Contact: Floyd A. Barmann, Dir.

Desc: Subject: Clark County and Ohio history. Holdings: 1000 books; 7500 archival materials. Services: Copying; Library open to the public.

1520 ▪ Clark County Historical Society
Pioneer-Krier Museum
Library
430 W. 4th   Ph: (316)635-2227
PO Box 862
Ashland, KS 67831

Contact: Floretta Rogers, Cur.

Desc: Subject: County and state history. Holdings: 10 VF drawers of manuscripts; Clark County newspapers, 1884 to present. Services: Library open to the public for reference use only.

1521 ▪ Clayton County Library
Local History Genealogy Collection
865 Battlecreek Rd.   Ph: (770)473-3850
Jonesboro, GA 30236
URL: http://www.clayton.public.lib.ga.us/

Desc: Subject: Georgia history and genealogy. Holdings: County histories; family histories; census data; microfilm. Services: Interlibrary loan.

1522 ▪ Clearwater Historical Society
Clearwater Public Library
Local History Collection
100 N. Osceola Ave.   Ph: (813)462-6800
Clearwater, FL 33755-4083   Fax: (813)462-6420
E-mail: library@public.lib.ci.clearwater.fl.us
URL: http://public.lib.ci.clearwater.fl.us/cpl/
     lochist.html

Desc: Subject: Clearwater history and genealogy. Holdings: Books; videocassettes; VF drawers; photographs. Services: Library open to the public.

1523 ▪ Clemson University
Special Collections
Strom Thurmond Institute Bldg.   Ph: (864)656-3031
Box 343001   Fax: (864)656-0233
Clemson, SC 29634-3001
E-mail: kohl@clemson.edu
URL: http://www.lib.clemson.edu/SpCol/schp.html

Contact: Michael Kohl, Hd. of Spec.Coll.

Desc: Subject: History - South Carolina, Clemson University, 20th-century politics, textiles, agriculture; National Park Service; genealogy. Holdings: Books; manuscripts; periodicals; papers; university publications; theses and dissertations; rare books and manuscripts. Services: Library open to the public.

1524 ▪ Cleveland Public Library
Government Documents Department
325 Superior Ave.   Ph: (216)623-2870
Cleveland, OH 44114-1271   Fax: (216)623-7030
E-mail: docmgr@library.cpl.org
URL: http://www.cpl.org

Contact: Siegfried Weinhold, Dept.Hd.

Desc: Subject: United States Government publications. Holdings: 803,000 volumes. Services: Interlibrary loan (limited); copying; collection open to the public.

1525 ▪ Cleveland Public Library
History and Geography Department
325 Superior Ave.   Ph: (216)623-2864
Cleveland, OH 44114-1271   Fax: (216)902-4978
E-mail: hist1@library.cpl.org
URL: http://www.cpl.org

Contact: JoAnn Petrello, Dept.Hd.

Desc: Subject: History - ancient, medieval, modern; archaeology; local history; genealogy; heraldry; geography; black history; African-American history; African-American exploration and travel; numismatics. Holdings: 217,682 volumes; 11,818 bound periodical volumes; 18,800 Cleveland pictures on microfiche; 1562 maps and brochures with current travel data; local history clipping file; Coat-of-Arms file; 1562 World Wars I and II posters; 1,200,000 photographs; 160,000 sheet maps; movie posters; 4859 microfiche. Services: Interlibrary loan; copying; department open to the public.

1526 ▪ Clinch Valley College
John Cook Wyllie Library
Archives and Special Collections
   Ph: (540)328-0150
rs>Wise, VA 24293   Fax: (540)328-0105
URL: http://book.clinch.edu/

Contact: Robin Benke, Dir.

Desc: Subject: Wise County, Virginia - history, genealogy, culture; Clinch Valley College history; Virginia; politics. Holdings: Books; microfilm; personal papers and letters; pamphlets; documents; scrapbooks; diaries; reports. Services: Copying; Library open to the public.

1527 ▪ Clinton County Historical Society
Archives
Box 23   Ph: (517)482-1291
St. Johns, MI 48879-0023

Desc: Subject: Clinton County - genealogy, history. Holdings: Archives; microfilm. Services: Copying; archives open to the public on a limited schedule.

1528 ▪ Clinton County Historical Society
Genealogy Library
149 E. Locust St., Box 529   Ph: (937)382-4684
Wilmington, OH 45177   Fax: (937)382-5634
URL: http://www.postcom/ccgshs

Desc: Subject: Clinton County history and family genealogy, local Quaker history, local author's works, Ohio history, Pennsylvania history, Virginia history. Holdings: 1500 books and periodicals; 200 reels of microfilm of courthouse records and census records. Services: Copying; Library open to the public.

1529 ▪ Cloud County Historical Society
Library
Cloud County   Ph: (785)243-2866
  Historical Museum
635 Broadway
Concordia, KS 66901

Contact: Brad J. Chapin, Cur.

Desc: Subject: Local history. Holdings: 900 books; 50 bound periodical volumes; 10 cubic feet of historical files; atlases; newspapers, 1884-1950; 9 drawers of birth, death, and marriage records; 3 drawers of unbound manuscripts. Services: Library open to the public for reference use only.

1530 ▪ Cohasset Historical Society
Burtram J. Pratt Memorial Library
14 Summer St.   Ph: (781)383-1434
Cohasset, MA 02025

Contact: David H. Wadsworth, Sr.Cur.

Desc: Subject: Cohasset area history; local and area maritime history; genealogy. Holdings: 800 books. Services: Library open to the public for reference use only.

1531 ▪ Colchester Historical Museum Archives
Library
29 Young St.   Ph: (902)895-6284
PO Box 412   Fax: (902)895-9530
Truro, NS, Canada B2N 5C5
E-mail: chmusarc@auracom.com
URL: http://www.shelburn.nscc.ns.ca

Contact: Nan Harvey, Archv.

Desc: Subject: Censuses, vital statistics, geneaology. Holdings: 1600 books; 350 bound periodical volumes; archival items; reels of microfilm. Services: Copying; Library open to the public.

1532 ▪ Cole County Historical Society
Museum and Library
109 Madison St.   Ph: (573)635-1850
Jefferson City, MO 65101

Desc: Subject: History - Cole County, Jefferson City; history; limited genealogy. Holdings: 600 books; 50 bound periodical volumes; 25 scrapbooks; 300 documents and manuscripts; 2000 pictures; 22 inaugural ball gowns of former Missouri governors' wives. Services: Library open to the public on a very limited basis.

1533 ▪ Colebrook Historical Society, Inc.
Library and Archives
Box 85   Ph: (860)379-3616
Colebrook, CT 06021

Contact: Bob Grigg, Cur.

Desc: Subject: Local history, local authors, genealogy, early settlers and industries. Holdings: 600 books; 70 linear feet of town and church records, account books, early maps, cemetery headstone information, photographs, pictures. Services: Collections open to the public for reference use only on a limited schedule, Memorial Day through Columbus Day; otherwise by appointment.

1534 ▪ College of St. Joseph
Vermont Collections
71 Clement Rd.   Ph: (802)773-5900
Rutland, VT 05701-3899
E-mail: coll_stjosph@dol.state.vt.us
URL: http://www.vermontelcomm/stjoeph

Contact: Doreen McCullough, (Librarian)

Desc: Subject: Vermont - society, culture, history, Rutland county; Ethan Allen; Calvin Coolidge; Julia Dorr. Holdings: Books; maps; films; videocassettes. Services: Copying; collection open to the public.

1535 ▪ Collegiate Reformed Dutch Church
Library
45 John St.   Ph: (212)233-1960
New York, NY 10038   Fax: (212)406-1856
E-mail: rhollenga@collegiatechurch.org
URL: http://www.collegiatechurch.org

Contact: Maria Hollenga, Libn.

Desc: Subject: Genealogical data, 1633 to present. Holdings: 45 books; archival materials; documents. Services: Library not open to the public.

1536 ▪ Collin County Genealogical Society
Library
PO Box 865052
Plano, TX 75086-5052

Desc: Subject: Collin County, Texas history and genealogy. Holdings: Figures not available. Services: Library open to the public with restrictions.

1537 ▪ Collingwood Library and Museum on
Americanism
8301 East Blvd. Dr.   Ph: (703)765-1652
Alexandria, VA 22308   Fax: (703)765-8390
E-mail: clma1@erols.com
URL: http://www.nels.com/sojoura/cwood.html

Contact: Norman Venzke

Desc: Subject: U.S. history, U.S. government, Masonic history and law, genealogy, world history. Holdings: 7000 books; 110 bound periodical volumes. Services: Copying; library open to the public.

1538 ▪ Collingwood Public Library
Local HistoryGenealogy Department
100 Second St.   Ph: (705)445-1571
Collingwood, ON, Canada L9Y   Fax: (705)445-3704
1E5
E-mail: clib@georgian.net
URL: http://www.georgian.net/clib/info.htm

Contact: Kerri Robinson, CEO

Desc: Subject: Collingwood history and genealogy. Holdings: Cemetery inscriptions; burial records; local history books; family histories. Services: Interlibrary loan; copying; Library open to the public.

1539 ▪ Colorado College
Charles Leaming Tutt Library
Special Collections
1021 N. Cascade   Ph: (719)389-6668
Colorado Springs, CO 80903   Fax: (719)389-6859
E-mail: VKIEFER@CC.Colorado.EDU
URL: http://www.coloradocollege.edu/library

Contact: Virginia R. Kiefer, Cur., Spec.Coll.Archv.

Desc: Subject: History - Colorado, Colorado College, 19th- and 20th-century American West, printing; Abraham Lincoln. Holdings: 30,000 books; 350 bound periodical volumes; 640 linear feet of manuscripts; 518 oral history tapes; 70,000 photographs; 70 feet of ephemera; 81 historical tapes. Services: Copying; collections open to the public with restrictions.

1540 ▪ Colorado Historical Society
Stephen H. Hart Library
Colorado History Museum   Ph: (303)866-2305
1300 Broadway   Fax: (303)866-4600
Denver, CO 80203
URL: http://erl_1.bcr.org

Contact: Rebecca Lintz, Dir.

Desc: Subject: Colorado and business history, railroads, mining, cattle industry, social and cultural movements. Holdings: 47,000 volumes; 1800 manuscript collections; 29,334 reels of microfilm; 2900 serial titles; 14,500 reels of television newsfilm; 1500 newspapers titles; 2500 maps and atlases; 600,000 photographs and negatives. Services: Copying; mail and phone reference service; Library open to the public.

1541 ▪ Colorado Springs Pioneers Museum
Starsmore Center For Local History
215 S. Tejon St.   Ph: (719)578-6650
Colorado Springs, CO 80903   Fax: (719)578-6718
E-mail: LWitherow@ci.colospgs.co.us
URL: http://www.colorado-springs.com/cultredu/museums.htm

Contact: Leah Davis Witherow, Archv.

Desc: Subject: History of the Pikes Peak region. Holdings: 9000 books; 50 bound periodical volumes. Services: Copying; center open to the public, appointment suggested.

1542 ▪ Columbia County Historical and Genealogical Society
Edwin M. Barton Library
225 Market St.   Ph: (570)784-1600
PO Box 360
Bloomsburg, PA 17815-0360

Contact: Bonnie Farver, Exec.Dir.

Desc: Subject: Columbia County history, local history and genealogy. Holdings: 1600 books; 50 bound periodical volumes; 200 bound manuscripts and 20 linear feet of unbound manuscripts; 50 scrapbooks; 12 linear feet of pamphlet files cataloged by subject and area; 3 linear feet of Works Progress Administration (WPA) files of mid-1930s historical and genealogical compilations; 1200 photographs and maps. Services: Copying; Library open to the public.

1543 ▪ Columbia County Historical Society
Columbia County Museum
5 Albany Ave.   Ph: (518)758-9265
PO Box 311   Fax: (518)758-2499
Kinderhook, NY 12106

Contact: Sharon S. Palmer, Exec.Dir.

Desc: Subject: Regional, county, American history; genealogy; art history; architecture; decorative arts. Holdings: 3000 books; antiques. Services: Copying; museum open to the public.

1544 ▪ Columbia County Historical Society
Museum
Old County Courthouse   Ph: (503)397-3868
P.O. Box 837
St. Helens, OR 97051
E-mail: cchsb@columbia-center.org

Contact: Billie S. Ivey, Cur.

Desc: Subject: History of Columbia County, genealogy, county cemetery records; marriage records (1850 to 1900). Holdings: 450 books; 150 bound periodical vol-

umes; deeds and contracts; maps; local pictures; magazines; newspapers; scrapbooks. Services: Copying; museum open to the public.

1545 ▪ Columbia University
Oral History Research Office
Butler Library   Ph: (212)854-2273
Box 20   Fax: (212)854-5378
New York, NY 10027
URL: http://www.columbia.edu/cu/library/indiv/oral/

Contact: Ronald J. Grele, Dir.

Desc: Subject: National affairs, New York history, international relations, culture and the arts, social welfare, business and labor, philanthropy, African-American community, law, medicine, education, journalism, religion. Holdings: 6500 volumes of edited transcript; 4000 reels and cassettes of tapes, 1963 to present; microforms of one third of the collection; supporting papers accompany some memoirs; data on other oral history holdings and centers worldwide. Services: Limited research service available; copying (limited); collection open to the public with restrictions. The office provides books on oral history - for sale.

1546 ▪ Comanche Crossing Museum
Library
Box 647   Ph: (303)622-4690
Strasburg, CO 80136   Fax: (303)622-4890

Contact: Sandy Miller, Cur.

Desc: Subject: Local history, transcontinental railroad history. Holdings: Books; government documents. Services: Library open to the public for reference use only.

1547 ▪ Congregation Adam Shalom Synagogue
Library
29901 Middlebelt Rd.   Ph: (248)851-5100
Farmington Hills, MI 48334

Desc: Subject: Judaica, Jewish theology and liturgy, Bible, Old Testament, cantorial liturgy, Jewish history. Holdings: 13,500 books; 80 records of liturgical music in Hebrew and Yiddish, 75 pamphlets. Services: Interlibrary loan; copying; Library open to the public.

1548 ▪ Congregation Agudas Achim
Joe Tills Library
16550 Huebner Rd.   Ph: (210)479-0307
San Antonio, TX 78248   Fax: (210)479-0295

Contact: Felice Feldman

Desc: Subject: Judaica. Holdings: 2000 volumes; magazines of Jewish content. Services: Copying; Library open to the public.

1549 ▪ Congregation Beth Am
Dorothy G. Feldman Library
3557 Washington Blvd.   Ph: (216)321-1000
Cleveland Heights, OH 44118   Fax: (216)321-4467

Contact: Dr. Ralph Simon, Libn.

Desc: Subject: Judaica. Holdings: 7000 volumes; records. Services: Interlibrary loan; Library open to the public.

1550 ▪ Congregation Beth Am
Library
26790 Arastradero Rd.   Ph: (415)493-4661
Los Altos Hills, CA 94022

Contact: Diane Rauchwerger, Libn.

Desc: Subject: Judaica. Holdings: 4000 books. Services: Library open to the public subject to approval.

1551 ▪ Congregation Beth-El Zedeck
Library
600 W. 70th St.   Ph: (317)253-3441
Indianapolis, IN 46260   Fax: (317)259-6849

Contact: Amy Abrams-Blakemore

Desc: Subject: Judaism, Jewish literature. Holdings: 3000 books. Services: Library open to the public.

1552 ▪ Congregation Beth Emeth
Judaica Library
100 Academy Rd.   Ph: (518)436-9761
Albany, NY 12208   Fax: (518)436-0476
E-mail: cbemeth@aol.com

Contact: Helene Adler, Libn.

Desc: Subject: Judaica. Holdings: 2000 Books; archival items. Services: Library open to the public.

1553 ▪ Congregation Beth Jacob-Beth Israel
Segal-Dion Family Library
850 Evesham Rd.
Cherry Hill, NJ 08003

Contact: Lester Hering, Rabbi

Desc: Subject: Judaica. Holdings: 5500 books. Services: Library open to the public.

1554 ▪ Congregation B'nai Israel
Isidore and Rose Bloch Memorial Library
4401 Indian School Rd., NE   Ph: (505)266-0155
Albuquerque, NM 87110

Contact: Elinor K. Sherry, Libn.

Desc: Subject: Judaica. Holdings: 3800 books; 38 videocassettes; audiocassettes; 250 classical compact discs. Services: Copying; Library open to the public with restrictions.

1555 ▪ Congregation Brith Sholom
Jewish Center
Morris P. Radov Library
3207 State St.   Ph: (814)454-2431
Erie, PA 16508   Fax: (814)452-0790

Contact: Freda Brown

Desc: Subject: Talmud, Bible, Judaica, Midrash, rabbinics, mysticism, Kabbalah, Chasidism. Holdings: 2500 books. Services: Interlibrary loan; copying; Library not open to the public.

1556 ▪ Congregation Emanu-El B'ne Jeshurun
Rabbi Dudley Weinberg Library
2419 E. Kenwood Blvd.   Ph: (414)964-4100
Milwaukee, WI 53211   Fax: (414)964-6136

Contact: Paula H. Fine, Libn.

Desc: Subject: Judaica, Talmud, Holocaust, the arts, general reference. Holdings: 8500 books and other cataloged items. Services: Interlibrary loan; copying; Library open to the public by recommendation with identification.

1557 ▪ Congregation Kins of West Rogers Park
Jordan E. Feuer Library
2800 W. North Shore   Ph: (312)761-4000
Chicago, IL 60645

Contact: Bee Greenstein, Libn.

Desc: Subject: Religion and Hebraica. Holdings: 4500 books; 60 filmstrips. Services: Library open to the public.

1558 ▪ Congregation Mishkan Israel
Library
785 Ridge Rd.   Ph: (203)288-3877
Hamden, CT 06517

Contact: Linda K. Cohen

Desc: Subject: Judaica. Holdings: 5000 books. Services: Interlibrary loan; Library open to the public by arrangement.

1559 ▪ Congregation Mishkan Tefila
Harry and Anna Feinberg Library
300 Hammond Pond Pkwy.   Ph: (617)332-7770
Chestnut Hill, MA 02167   Fax: (617)322-2871

Contact: Judith S. Greenblatt, Libn.

Desc: Subject: Judaica. Holdings: 4000 books. Services: Library open to the public by permission.

1560 ▪ Congregation Rodeph Shalom
Library
1338 Mount Vernon St.   Ph: (215)627-6747
Philadelphia, PA 19123   Fax: (215)627-1313
E-mail: rshalom@libertynet.org
URL: http://www.libertynet.org/rshalom

Contact: Elliot J. Rothschild

Desc: Subject: Judaica; Jewish history and religion, especially American. Holdings: 8720 books; 8 VF drawers of clippings and pamphlets. Services: Interlibrary loan; Library open to the public by appointment.

1561 ▪ Congregation Rodfei Zedek
J.S. Hoffman Memorial Library
5200 Hyde Park Blvd.   Ph: (773)752-2770
Chicago, IL 60615   Fax: (773)752-0330
URL: http://wwwuscj.org/midwest/chicagorz

Contact: Jonathan Krieger

Desc: Subject: Judaica, Americana, Lincolniana. Holdings: 8000 books; phonograph records. Services: Library open to the public.

1562 ▪ Congregation Shaarey Zedek
Library and Media Center
27375 Bell Rd.   Ph: (248)357-5544
Southfield, MI 48034   Fax: (248)357-0227

Contact: Sharon Cohen, Dir.

Desc: Subject: Hebraica and Judaica, children's literature. Holdings: 27,500 volumes; 20 VF drawers of pamphlets, clippings, pictures; 6 drawers of audio cassettes; 200 videocassettes; 200 phonograph records; educational and archival materials. Services: Copying; Library open to the public with restrictions.

1563 ▪ Congregation Shalom
Sherman Pastor Memorial Library
7630 N. Santa Monica Blvd.   Ph: (414)352-9288
Milwaukee, WI 53217   Fax: (414)352-1980
E-mail: marcadmin@aol.com

Contact: Elaine Friedman

Desc: Subject: Bible, Jewish history, Israel, Jewish biography and holidays. Holdings: 5900 books. Services: Interlibrary loan; copying; Library open to the public with restrictions.

1564 ▪ Congregation Shearith Israel
Spanish and Portuguese Synagogue
Sophie and Ivan Salomon Library Collection
8 W. 70th St.   Ph: (212)873-0300
New York, NY 10023   Fax: (212)724-6165

Desc: Subject: Judaica, Hebraica, sephardica. Holdings: 5500 books. Services: Library open to the public by appointment.

1565 ▪ Congregation Solel
Library
1301 Clavey Rd.   Ph: (847)433-3555
Highland Park, IL 60035   Fax: (847)433-3573

E-mail: congsolei@aol.com

Desc: Subject: Jewish history and philosophy, Bible, Talmud, Midrash, prophets, Israel. Holdings: 8000 books. Services: Library open to the public.

1566 ▪ Connecticut Historical Society
Library
1 Elizabeth St.   Ph: (860)236-5621
Hartford, CT 06105   Fax: (860)236-2664
E-mail: cthist@ix.netcom.com
URL: http://www.hartnet.org/chs/

Contact: Kelly Nolin, Actg.Hd.Libn.

Desc: Subject: New England and Connecticut history and genealogy, colonial sources. Holdings: 100,000 books; 400 bound periodical volumes; 3 million manuscripts; 1500 volumes of 18th and early 19th century newspapers. Services: Library open to the public.

1567 ▪ Connecticut Society of Genealogy
Library
175 Maple E. Hartford Ct.   Ph: (860)569-0002
PO Box 435
Glastonbury, CT 06033

Contact: Helen H. Hodge, Off.Mgr.

Desc: Subject: Genealogy. Holdings: Books; manuscripts; microfiche; CD-ROM. Services: Copying; Library open to the public.

1568 ▪ Connecticut State Library
231 Capitol Ave.   Ph: (860)566-4301
Hartford, CT 06106   Fax: (860)566-8940
E-mail: powens@csl.ctstateu.edu
URL: http://www.cslib.org

Contact: Kendall F. Wiggins, State Libn.

Desc: Subject: Connecticut, local history and genealogy, state and federal law, politics and government, legislative reference. Holdings: 948,924 volumes; 32,000 cubic feet of archival records; newspaper clipping files, 1927 to present; 26,000 reels of microfilm; 6000 maps; regional federal documents depository of 1.5 million documents; state documents depository of 50,000 state documents. Services: Interlibrary loan; copying; Library open to the public.

1569 ▪ Connecticut State Library
History and Genealogy Unit
231 Capitol Ave.   Ph: (860)566-3692
Hartford, CT 06106-1537   Fax: (860)566-2133
E-mail: ISref@cslib.org
URL: http://www.cslib.org/handg.htm

Contact: Kendall F. Wiggin

Desc: Subject: Genealogy, state history. Holdings: Books, bound periodical volumes, manuscripts, archives, microfiche, microfilm. Services: Library open to the public.

1570 ▪ Connecticut Valley Historical Museum
Library and Archives
220 State St.   Ph: (413)263-6800
Springfield, MA 01103   Fax: (413)263-6898

Contact: Margaret Humberston, Hd., Lib. & Archv.Coll.

Desc: Subject: Connecticut Valley history and genealogy, Springfield history (1636 to present), New England genealogy, Springfield business history. Holdings: 30,000 books; 2000 bound periodical volumes; 40,000 photographs; 3000 linear feet of archival records; 300 feet of vertical files, atlases, and maps; 5000 microform records. Services: Fee-based correspondence service; department open to the public.

1571 ▪ Contra Costa Historical Society
History Center
1700 Oak Park Blvd., Rm. C-5   Ph: (925)939-9180
Pleasant Hill, CA 94523   Fax: (925)939-4832
E-mail: cchistry@ix.netcom.com
URL: http://www.ccnet.com/xptom/cchs/frm-welcome.html

Contact: Betty Maffei

Desc: Subject: Northern California history. Holdings: Books; 39,000 photographs; periodicals; letters; documents; maps; memorabilia (40,000 items). Services: Copying; Library open to the public by appointment (fee).

1572 ▪ Cordova Historical Society, Inc.
Archives
Cordova Museum   Ph: (907)424-6665
Box 391   Fax: (907)424-6666
Cordova, AK 99574
E-mail: cdvmsm@ptialaska.net

Contact: Cathy Sherman, Musm.Dir.

Desc: Subject: Cordova history, early 1900s to present; the railroad era, fishing. Holdings: Manuscript maps and photographs of the Copper River, the Northwest Railway, Cordova; charts; technical drawings; aerial photographs; correspondence of state and local officials. Services: Archives open to the public when attendant is present.

1573 ▪ Corporation du Seminaire St-Joseph de Trois-Rivieres
Archives du Seminaire de Trois-Rivieres
858, rue Laviolette   Ph: (819)376-4459
Trois-Rivieres, PQ, Canada   Fax: (819)378-0607
  G9A 5S3

Contact: Suzanne Girard, Dir.

Desc: Subject: Local history and genealogy, Canadiana, medical, scolan books. Holdings: 12,000 books; 2000 bound periodical volumes; 12 microfiche; 65 reels of microfilm; 20 films; 230 audiotapes, 75,286 photographs. Services: Copying; photograph reproduction; archives open to the public.

1574 ▪ Corry Area Historical Society
Tiffany Archives
PO Box 107   Ph: (814)664-4749
Corry, PA 16407

Contact: Robert Lindsey, Libn.

Desc: Subject: Climax locomotives, local history, Corry authors. Holdings: 100 volumes; 200 old newspapers; city directories. Services: Copying; Library open to the public for reference use only.

1575 ▪ Cortland County Historical Society
Kellogg Memorial Research Library
25 Homer Ave.   Ph: (607)756-6071
Cortland, NY 13045

Contact: Mary Ann Kane, Soc.Dir.

Desc: Subject: Cortland County history and genealogy. Holdings: 3000 books; 91 bound periodical volumes; 310 reels of microfilm; 620 cubic feet of manuscripts; 100 linear feet of cemetery records and vital records; 225 journal and serial titles; 148 maps; 3000 photographs; 90 oral history tapes; 14,000 negatives and prints from Brockway Motor Trucks Company. Services: Copying; Library open to the public.

1576 ▪ Cottonwood County Historical Society
Library
812 4th Ave.   Ph: (507)831-1134
Windom, MN 56101
URL: http://www.mtn.org/mgs/othersoc/cottonwd.html

Contact: Linda Franson, Dir.

Desc: Subject: County history. Holdings: Family histories, clippings and pamphlets; 2 filing cases of obituaries and history; local newspapers on microfilm. Services: Copying; Library open to the public.

1577 ▪ Coweta County Genealogical and Historical Research Library
PO Box 1014
Newnan, GA 30264-1014

Contact: Norma Gunby, Pres.

Desc: Subject: Genealogy, state and local history. Holdings: Books; magazines; microfilm; family charts and sheets; newspapers and other genealogical material. Services: Copying; library open to the public.

1578 ▪ Cranbrook Institute of Science Library
1221 N. Woodward Ave.　　　Ph: (248)645-3255
PO Box 801　　　　　　　　Fax: (248)645-3050
Bloomfield Hills, MI
　48303-0801
E-mail: gretchen_young-weiner@cc.cranbrook.edu

Contact: Gretchen Young-Weiner, Libn.

Desc: Subject: Anthropology, ethnology, natural sciences, physics, astronomy. Holdings: 18,000 books; 21 VF drawers of pamphlets; 2000 maps. Services: Interlibrary loan; copying; Library open to the public.

1579 ▪ Cranford Historical Society Museum Library
38 Springfield Ave.　　　　Ph: (908)276-0082
Cranford, NJ 07016

Contact: Joanne Westcott

Desc: Subject: Local history, Indian artifacts, paintings. Holdings: Books; pictures; clippings; articles; maps; oral history tapes; scrapbooks. Services: Library open to the public for reference use only.

1580 ▪ Croatian Genealogical & Heraldic Society Library
2527 San Carlos Ave.　　　Ph: (415)592-1190
San Carlos, CA 94070　　　Fax: (615)592-1526
E-mail: croatians@aol.com
URL: http://www.modena-motors.com/croation.html

Contact: Adam S. Eterovich, Dir.

Desc: Subject: Genealogy, heraldry, census, Croatian history prior to 1900. Holdings: 2000 books; 20 bound periodical volumes; 20 drawers of index cards; 30 manuscripts. Services: Library open to the public by appointment.

1581 ▪ Crosswicks Public Library Local History Collection
Box 147　　　　　　　　　Ph: (609)298-6271
Crosswicks, NJ 08515
E-mail: abumbera@burlco.lib.nj.us

Contact: Alice Bumbera, Libn.

Desc: Subject: Local history and genealogy. Holdings: 10,000 books. Services: Interlibrary loan; collection open to the public with restrictions.

1582 ▪ Crow Wing County Historical Society Library
320 Laurel St.　　　　　　Ph: (218)829-3268
Box 722
Brainerd, MN 56401

Contact: Mary Lou Moudry, Exec.Dir.

Desc: Subject: Local history. Holdings: Maps; diaries; historical scrapbooks and photograph albums; oral history collection; county newspapers; Brainerd city directories, 1901-1996. Services: Copying; Library open to the public with restrictions.

1583 ▪ Crowley Ridge Regional Library Local History Collection
315 W. Oak　　　　　　　Ph: (501)935-5133
Jonesboro, AR 72401　　　Fax: (501)935-7987

Contact: Rusty Dancer, Ref.Libn.

Desc: Subject: Arkansas history, 1790 to present; genealogy of northeastern Arkansas, southeastern Missouri, western Tennessee. Holdings: 500 linear feet of area and family histories, census records, cemetery records, genealogical research materials. Services: Copying; collection open to the public.

1584 ▪ Cumberland County Historical Society Warren Lummis Genealogical and Historical Library
Box 16　　　　　　　　　Ph: (609)455-4055
Greenwich, NJ 08323

Desc: Subject: History and genealogy of New Jersey and Cumberland County. Holdings: 1500 books; 8 VF drawers of family genealogical data; 9 VF drawers of historical data; 2 VF drawers of maps and charts; 1 map case; deeds; family sheets; ledgers; Bible records; sheriff books. Services: Copying; Library open to the public March - November, Wednesday and Sundays.

1585 ▪ Cumberland County Historical Society & Hamilton Library
21 N. Pitt St.　　　　　　Ph: (717)249-7610
PO Box 626　　　　　　　Fax: (717)258-9332
Carlisle, PA 17013
E-mail: info@historicalsociety.com
URL: http://www.historicalsociety.com

Contact: Linda Witmer, Exec.Dir.

Desc: Subject: Cumberland County history, Pennsylvania history. Holdings: 20,000 books; 700 linear feet of Cumberland County documents including tax lists, 1750-1930; 200 linear feet of manuscripts; 270 maps; 1300 reels of microfilm; 35,000 photographs. Services: Copying; Library open to the public.

1586 ▪ Cummington Historical Commission Kingman Tavern Historical Museum Lyman Library
Main St.　　　　　　　　Ph: (413)634-5335
Cummington, MA 01026
E-mail: bergmann@cs.smith.edu

Contact: Merrie Bergmann, Ch.

Desc: Subject: Genealogy, local history. Holdings: 300 books; diaries; ledgers. Services: Copying; Library open to the public on a limited schedule.

1587 ▪ Custer County Historical Society Library
445 S. 9th　　　　　　　　Ph: (308)872-2203
PO Box 334
Broken Bow, NE 68822-0334
E-mail: custercountyhistory@navix.net
URL: http://www.rootsweb.com/custer

Contact: Mary Landkamer, Res.

Desc: Subject: History - state, local; genealogy. Holdings: 200 books; 110 volumes of bound newspapers; 700 photographs; 50 maps; 241 reels of microfilm; 24 VF drawers of obituaries and biographical materials. Services: Copying; Library open to the public.

1588 ▪ Dakota County Historical Society Research Center
130 3rd Ave., N.　　　　　Ph: (612)451-6260
South St. Paul, MN 55075

Contact: Rebecca Snyder, Libn.

Desc: Subject: State, county, and local history. Holdings: 1000 volumes; county newspapers and census on microfilm; photographs; maps. Services: Copying; center open to the public for reference use only.

1589 ▪ Dakota Wesleyan University Layne Library Jennewein Western Library Collection
1200 W. University　　　　Ph: (605)995-2618
Mitchell, SD 57301　　　　Fax: (605)995-2893
E-mail: kkenkel@dwu.edu
URL: http://www.dwu.edu/library/layne.htm

Contact: Kevin Kenkel, Dir.

Desc: Subject: Western history. Holdings: 4000 books. Services: Library open to the public.

1590 ▪ Dallas County Historical Society Historical and Genealogical Library
HC 85 Box 291B6　　　　　Ph: (417)345-7297
Buffalo, MO 65622

Contact: Leni Howe, Corresponding Sec.

Desc: Subject: Family and county history. Holdings: 200 books; 20 documents; 10 manuscripts. Services: Library open to the public by appointment.

1591 ▪ Dallas Historical Society G.B. Dealey Library
Hall of State, Fair Park　　　Ph: (214)421-4500
Box 150038　　　　　　　Fax: (214)421-7500
Dallas, TX 75315

Contact: Gaylon Polatts, Libn.Archv.

Desc: Subject: Dallas, Texas, Southwestern, and U.S. history. Holdings: 14,000 books; 10,000 bound periodical volumes; 2 million archival materials. Services: Copying; center open to the public.

1592 ▪ Dallas Public Library J. Erik Jonsson Central Library Genealogy Collection
1515 Young St.　　　　　　Ph: (214)670-1433
Dallas, TX 75201　　　　　Fax: (214)670-7839
URL: http://wwwlib.ci.dallas.tx.us

Contact: Lloyd DeWitt Bockstruck, Supv., Geneal.Sect.

Desc: Subject: Genealogy, heraldry, onomatology, local history. Holdings: 66,348 books; 30,401 reels of microfilm; 1237 microcards; 64,224 microfiche. Services: Copying; collection open to the public.

1593 ▪ Danbury Museum and Historical Society Library
43 Main St.　　　　　　　Ph: (203)743-5200
Danbury, CT 06810　　　　Fax: (203)743-1131
URL: http://www.danburyhistorical.org

Desc: Subject: Town and state history, genealogy, hat industry and other local industries. Holdings: 800 books; 50 bound periodical volumes; manuscripts; diaries; deeds; maps; negatives and prints of local scenes, 1875 to present. Services: Copying; Library open to the public with restrictions.

1594 ▪ Danville Public Library Archives
319 N. Vermilion St.　　　Ph: (217)477-5228
Danville, IL 61832　　　　Fax: (217)477-5230
E-mail: rallen@ltnet.ltls.org

URL: http://www.danville.lib.il.us/arch.html

Contact: Roberta D. Allen, Dir.Ref.Dir.Archv.

Desc: Subject: East Central Illinois and West Central Indiana genealogy; Vermilion County (Illinois) history. Holdings: 3300 books; 100 bound periodical volumes; 1500 unbound periodical volumes; 1418 reels of microfilm; 1140 microfiche; 1095 nonbook items. Services: Interlibrary loan; copying; archives open to the public for reference use only.

1595 ▪ Danville Public Library - Special Collections

511 Patton St.   Ph: (804)799-5195
Danville, VA 24541   Fax: (804)799-5221

Contact: Denise Johnson, Lib.Dir.

Desc: Subject: Local genealogy, local history. Holdings: 100,000 books; 56,179 microform. Services: Interlibrary loan; copying.

1596 ▪ Darien Historical Society Library

45 Old Kings Hwy., N.   Ph: (203)655-9233
Darien, CT 06820

Contact: Madeline Hart, Exec.Dir.

Desc: Subject: Local and regional history, genealogy, Connecticut architecture, decorative arts, biography. Holdings: 1750 books; 30 linear feet, 60 boxes, and 2 file cases of other cataloged items. Services: Copying; Library open to the public.

1597 ▪ Darke County Historical Society Library

205 N. Broadway St.   Ph: (937)548-5250
Greenville, OH 45331

Contact: Judy Logan, Dir.

Desc: Subject: Genealogy, Darke County history. Holdings: 1200 books; 20,000 microfiche. Services: Library open to the public for reference use only.

1598 ▪ Darlington County Historical Commission
Darlington County Archives

204 Hewitt St.   Ph: (803)398-4710
Darlington, SC 29532

Contact: Horace Fraser Rudisill, Hist.

Desc: Subject: Local history and genealogy. Holdings: Books; documents; pamphlets; journals; early county court records, newspapers. Services: Copying; Library open to the public with restrictions.

1599 ▪ Daughters of Charity Archives
West Central Province

7800 Natural Bridge Rd.   Ph: (314)382-2800
St. Louis, MO 63121   Fax: (314)382-8392
E-mail: mpharc@juno.com

Contact: Sr. Genevieve Keusenkothen, Archv.

Desc: Subject: Daughters of Charity - foundation, history, administration, personnel, spiritual life; healthcare; child care; education; social work; missions. Holdings: Documents; manuscripts; publications; articles; registers; photographs; slides; tapes; filmstrips; videocassettes; memorabilia. Services: Library open to researchers by appointment.

1600 ▪ Daviess County Public Library
Kentucky Room

450 Griffith Ave.   Ph: (502)684-0211
Owensboro, KY 42301   Fax: (502)624-0218

Contact: Shelia E. Heflin, Supv.

Desc: Subject: Kentucky history, local history, genealogy. Holdings: 7000 volumes; 10 VF drawers of family files 34 VF drawers of clippings and pamphlets; local newspapers and state census (microfilm); Kentucky county tax lists through 1875 on microfilm (limited); Ohio County. Kentucky circuit court equity record, 1800-1900 (microfilm); Kentucky Death Certificates, 1911-1948; various Daviess County courthouse records, 1815-1985 (microfilm); various McLean County court records, 1854-1985. Services: Copying; limited research; room open to the public with restrictions.

1601 ▪ Davis Friends Meeting Library

345 L. St.   Ph: (530)662-3364
Davis, CA 95616

Contact: Noel Peattie

Desc: Subject: Quaker studies, peace, social concerns. Holdings: 1450 books; 30 bound periodical volumes; audiocassettes; videotapes; globes. Services: Library open to the public after meeting for worship.

1602 ▪ Dawgwood Research Library

609 Oak at Ymbacion St.   Ph: (512)526-4406
Refugio, TX 78377

Desc: Subject: Texana, history, philosophy, genealogy, historical correspondence and maps. Holdings: 25,000 books, bound historical periodicals, magazines, bound and unbound manuscripts, documents; 42 book cases; 5 filing cabinets; map vault. Services: Library open to the public by appointment.

1603 ▪ Dearborn Historical Museum
Historical Records & Archives

915 S. Brady St.   Ph: (313)565-3000
Dearborn, MI 48124   Fax: (313)565-4848

Contact: William Gould McElhone, Cur. of Res.

Desc: Subject: Dearborn history. Holdings: 2600 books; 382 bound periodical volumes; 15 VF drawers and 16 storage cabinets of manuscripts; 50 VF drawers of clippings, pamphlets, photographs, maps; 15 storage cabinets of diaries, documents, archival materials; 424 reels of microfilm of local newspapers and records; 16,000 feet of tape of oral histories; several collections of local celebrities. Services: Copying; Library open to the public for reference use only.

1604 ▪ Decatur Genealogical Society Library

356 N. Main St.   Ph: (217)429-0135
Box 1548
Decatur, IL 62525-1548

Contact: Cheri Hunter

Desc: Subject: Genealogy. Holdings: 45,000 books; 15,000 bound periodical volumes; 5000 microfiche; census on microfilm; birth, marriage, court, and death and cemetery records; family histories. Services: Copying; Library open to the public on fee basis.

1605 ▪ Dedham Historical Society Library

612 High St.   Ph: (781)326-1385
PO Box 215   Fax: (781)326-5762
Dedham, MA 02027-0215
E-mail: dhs@dedham.com
URL: http://www.dedham.com/dhs

Contact: Ronald F. Frazier, Exec.Dir.C.E.O.

Desc: Subject: History of New England, particularly the Town of Dedham. Holdings: 10,000 volumes; diaries; account books; family papers; genealogies; Dedham town history and records; societies and associations records; Massachusetts local histories; records of firms; maps. Services: Copying; Library open to the public.

1606 ▪ Del Norte County Historical Society Museum

577 H St.   Ph: (707)464-3922
Crescent City, CA 95531

Desc: Subject: History of Del Norte County and California, local Indians, logging, lighthouses, fishing, mining, pioneers. Holdings: 1056 books; 2000 personal papers, diaries, other materials; historic photographs; Yurok and Tolowa Indian artifacts; newspapers. Services: Copying; research center open to the public for reference use only.

1607 ▪ Delaware County Historical Society Library

85 N. Malin Rd.   Ph: (610)359-1148
Broomall, PA 19008-1928   Fax: (610)359-4155

Contact: M. D. Squyres, Pres.

Desc: Subject: Delaware County history and genealogy. Holdings: 5000 books; 4500 files of clippings and pictures. Services: Copying; Library open to the public; Research-by-mail.

1608 ▪ Delaware Public Archives

Hall of Records   Ph: (302)739-5318
121 Duke of York St.   Fax: (302)739-2578
Dover, DE 19901
E-mail: archives@state.de.us
URL: http://www.lib.de.us/archives

Contact: Howard P. Lowell, State Archv.Rec.Adm.

Desc: Subject: Delaware history and government, county and city records. Holdings: 3000 books; 5000 maps and architectural drawings; 40,000 cubic feet of state and local records; 75,000 photographs and slides; 75,000 reels of microfilm. Services: Copying; archives open to the public.

1609 ▪ Denver Public Library
Western HistoryGenealogy Department
Genealogy Collection

10 W. 14th Ave. Pkwy.   Ph: (303)640-6200
Denver, CO 80204   Fax: (303)640-6298
URL: http://www.denver.lib.co.us/

Contact: Eleanor M. Gehres, Mgr.

Desc: Subject: County, state, town histories; census schedules, 1790-1920; genealogy; military rosters; heraldry. Holdings: 61,000 books; 3683 bound periodical volumes; 8471 reels of microfilm of census schedules and other material; 65,000 microcards and microfiche; vital records; census indexes; 7 VF drawers of Denver Tramway personnel records. Services: Interlibrary loan; copying; genealogical research.

1610 ▪ Des Plaines Historical Society
John Byrne Memorial Library

789 Pearson St.   Ph: (847)391-5399
Des Plaines, IL 60016   Fax: (847)297-1710
E-mail: dphslibrary@juno.com

Contact: Joy A. Matthiessen, Musm.Dir.

Desc: Subject: Local history. Holdings: 550 books; 12 VF drawers of clippings; 6000 photographs; 75 boxes of documents; microfilm; magnetic tapes; maps; Des Plaines and Maine Township archival materials; Maine Township census, 1840-1900 indexed, 1910 and 1920 indexed. Services: Copying; Library open to the public by appointment on weekdays only.

1611 ▪ Detroit Public Library
Burton Historical Collections
5201 Woodward Ave.   Ph: (313)833-1480
Detroit, MI 48202
URL: http://www.detroit.lib.mi.us

Contact: Janet B. Whitson, Mgr.

Desc: Subject: History - Detroit, Michigan, Old Northwest, local, Great Lakes; genealogy; rare books in all subject areas; autographs; the book arts, including binding and design; book collecting, selling, and values; calligraphy; conservation and preservation; cookery; first editions; illuminated manuscripts; presses and printers; printing and typography. Holdings: 300,000 volumes; 13,100 pamphlets; 4800 bound volumes of newspapers; 7000 feet of manuscripts and personal papers; 10,500 feet of archival materials; 30,000 reels of microfilm; 13,000 microfiche; 1100 microcards; 150,000 pictures; 4000 maps; 5000 glass negatives; 6800 scrapbooks; 1000 color transparencies; 260 literary manuscripts and letters; 9000 bookplates; 19,000 dealer catalogues. Services: Copying (limited); collection open to the public.

1612 ▪ Dewitt Historical Society of Tompkins County
ArchiveLibraryMuseum
401 E. State St.   Ph: (607)273-8284
Ithaca, NY 14850   Fax: (607)273-6107
E-mail: dhs@lakenet.org
URL: http://www.lakenet.org/dewitt

Contact: Lorraine S. Johnson, Dir.

Desc: Subject: Local history, genealogy. Holdings: 4000 books; 347 bound periodical volumes; 900 linear feet of archival materials and manuscripts; 1500 maps; 100,000 photographs; 12,000 glass plate negatives; 300 scrapbooks (indexed); genealogy letter files; microfilm. Services: Copying; photo printing available; library open to the public with restrictions.

1613 ▪ Dezign House
Library
Box 188   Ph: (440)294-2778
Jefferson, OH 44047

Contact: Ramon Jan Elias, Dir.

Desc: Subject: Art history, design, theater, mechanical music, family history. Holdings: 20,000 books. Services: Library not open to the public.

1614 ▪ Dighton Historical Society
Museum Library
1217 Williams St.   Ph: (508)669-5514
Dighton, MA 02715

Contact: Elaine Varley, Cur.

Desc: Subject: Local history - Bristol County, Dighton, Somerset, and Rehoboth, Massachusetts; genealogy. Holdings: Books; documents; scrapbooks; clipping files. Services: Library open to the public by appointment for reference use only.

1615 ▪ Disciples of Christ Historical Society
Library
1101 19th Ave., S.   Ph: (615)327-1444
Nashville, TN 37212   Fax: (615)327-1445
E-mail: dishistsoc@aol.com
URL: http://users.aol.com/dishistsoc/index.htm

Contact: David I. McWhirter, Dir.

Desc: Subject: Christian Church, Disciples of Christ, Churches of Christ. Holdings: 35,000 volumes; 200 record groups of archival materials; 2500 collections of personal papers; manuscripts; microfilm; phonograph records. Services: Interlibrary loan; copying; Library open to members.

1616 ▪ District of Columbia Public Library
Biography Division
Martin Luther King   Ph: (202)727-2079
  Memorial Library   Fax: (202)727-1129
901 G St., NW
Washington, DC 20001
E-mail: jzvonkin@capaccess.org
URL: http://www.dclibrary.org

Contact: Judith Zvonkin, Chf.

Desc: Subject: Biography, heraldry, genealogy. Holdings: 46,000 books; 90 VF drawers of pamphlets and clippings; 376 microfiche; 41 reels of microfilm. Services: Interlibrary loan.

1617 ▪ Dodge County Historical Society
Library
PO Box 433   Ph: (507)635-5508
Mantorville, MN 55955

Contact: Idella M. Conwell, Musm.Dir.

Desc: Subject: Minnesota and early American history, the military. Holdings: 2000 books; 200 manuscripts; documents; newspapers. Services: Copying; Library open to the public for reference use only.

1618 ▪ Dodge County Historical Society
May Museum - Library
PO Box 766   Ph: (402)721-4515
Fremont, NE 68025   Fax: (402)721-8354
E-mail: dchs-may@teknetwork.com
URL: http://connectfremont.org

Contact: Patty Manhart, Cur.

Desc: Subject: Dodge County history, historic preservation, Nebraska history, 19th-century decorative arts. Holdings: 1220 volumes; 1 VF drawer of maps; 12 file boxes of documents; 2 manuscripts. Services: Copying; library open to the public.

1619 ▪ Dorchester County Public Library
Dorchester County Historical Society Collection
303 Gay St.   Ph: (410)228-7331
Cambridge, MD 21613   Fax: (410)228-6513
E-mail: jdelsordo@dorchesterlibrary.com
URL: http://www.dorchesterlibrary.org

Contact: Jean Del Sordo, Dir.

Desc: Subject: Genealogy, local history, Maryland history. Holdings: 500 books; 90 microforms; Bibles; scrapbooks; ephemera; census records; local newspapers; fire insurance maps; family histories; other items. Services: Copying; collection open to the public.

1620 ▪ Dorchester Historical Society
Robinson-Lehane Library
195 Boston St.   Ph: (617)265-7802
Dorchester, MA 02125

Contact: Elaine Croce Happnie, Cur.

Desc: Subject: Local history, genealogy, architecture. Holdings: 1500 books; 5000 manuscripts; 100 newspapers and clippings. Services: Interlibrary loan; copying; Library open to the public by appointment.

1621 ▪ Douglas County Historical Society
Archives
906 E. Harbor View Pkwy.   Ph: (715)394-5712
Superior, WI 54880   Fax: (715)394-2043

Contact: Rachael E. Martin, Exec.Dir.

Desc: Subject: History of Superior, Douglas County, Lake Superior; political, economic, industrial, social, cultural aspects of the area. Holdings: 823 books; 16,500 photo-

graphs; 2500 maps of the area. Services: Copying (limited); copying of photographs; Library open to the public for reference use only.

1622 ▪ Downey Historical Society
Downey History Center
12540 Rives Ave.   Ph: (562)862-2777
Box 554
Downey, CA 90241

Contact: Barbara Callarman, Dir.

Desc: Subject: Local history, Governor John G. Downey, genealogy. Holdings: 800 books; records of Downey Cemetery with tombstone inscriptions; 10 VF drawers of records, clippings, photographs; 1850-1920 census on microfilm; Sanborn maps of Downey, 1887-1907, on microfilm; original Sanborn maps of Downey, 1925-1932; original records of Los Angeles County District Attorney's Registers of Arrest, 1883-1919; original records of Los Nietos and Downey Townships court dockets, 1871-1952. Services: Copying; center open to the public.

1623 ▪ Drew County Historical Society
Museum and Archives
404 S. Main St.   Ph: (870)367-7446
Monticello, AR 71655

Contact: Ruby Jeter, Archv.

Desc: Subject: History - Monticello, Drew County, Southeast Arkansas, Arkansas; genealogy. Holdings: 265 books; 60 bound periodical volumes; 286 cassette tapes; 16 VF drawers of clippings, pamphlets, letters; 45 reels of microfilm; 25 maps; family histories; original Goodspeeds; textile collection; quilts and looms; early printing press; Indian artifacts. Services: Copying; archives open to the public for reference use only.

1624 ▪ Duplin County Historical Society
Leora H. McEachorn Library of Local History
PO Box 130   Ph: (910)289-2430
Rose Hill, NC 28458
E-mail: history@duplinnet.com
URL: http://www.history.duplinnet.com

Contact: William Dallas Herring

Desc: Subject: Genealogy, local history. Holdings: Books; reports; archival materials; microfiche; microfilm; family correspondence files; 28 volumes of public record abstracts. Services: Copying; Library open to the public on a limited schedule.

1625 ▪ Dutchess County Genealogical Society
Library
PO Box 708   Ph: (914)462-2470
Poughkeepsie, NY 12602

Contact: Linda Koehler, Libn.

Desc: Subject: Genealogy, history, heraldry. Holdings: 269 books; 232 pamphlets; 3 reels of microfilm of 1790 census; 71 reels of microfilm of 1810 census; Dutchess county census of 1800-1910 (ten year intervals) on microfilm. Services: Library open to the public.

1626 ▪ East Bay Genealogical Society
Library
405 14th St., Terrace Level   Ph: (510)451-9599
Oakland, CA 94612

Contact: Lois J. Kline, Libn.

Desc: Subject: Genealogy. Holdings: 400 books; surname file; California Information file. Services: Library open to the public for reference use only.

1627 ▪ East Hampton Library
Long Island Collection
159 Main St.
East Hampton, NY 11937
Ph: (516)324-0222
Fax: (516)329-7184
E-mail: ehamlib@suffolk.li.ny.us

Contact: Beth Gray, Dir.

Desc: Subject: Long Island history, biography, genealogy; Long Island imprints; books by Long Island authors. Holdings: 3500 books; 300 bound periodical volumes; 112 VF drawers of reports, manuscripts, clippings, pamphlets, documents, maps; 126 reels of microfilm of Long Island newspapers, Whaling Log Books, Suffolk County Federal Census, 1820-1880 and 1900-1920. Services: Copying; collection open to the public.

1628 ▪ Eastchester Historical Society
Angelo H. Bianchi Library
Box 37
Eastchester, NY 10709
Ph: (914)793-1900

Contact: Madeline D. Schaeffer, Libn.

Desc: Subject: Juvenile literature, 1795-1905; local and general history. Holdings: 6000 books; manuscripts; diaries; maps. Services: Copying; Library open to the public with restrictions.

1629 ▪ Eastern Kentucky University
Libraries
Special Collections and Archives, Rm. 126
521 Lancaster Ave.
Richmond, KY 40475-3102
Ph: (606)622-1792
Fax: (606)622-1174
E-mail: ARCHIVE@EKU.EDU
URL: http://www.library.eku.edu/

Contact: Charles C. Hay, III, Univ.Archv.

Desc: Subject: History - university, local, leisure and athletics in Kentucky; environmental and conservation movements in Kentucky. Holdings: 1300 cubic feet of archival materials; 2688 cassettes and tapes; 1527 films and videotapes. Services: Copying; AV production facilities; archives open to the public with restrictions on the use of some collections.

1630 ▪ Eastern Mennonite University
Menno Simons Historical Library and Archives
Ph: (540)432-4178
rs>Harrisonburg, VA
22802-2462
Fax: (540)432-4977
E-mail: bowmanlb@emu.edu
URL: http://www.emu.edu/units/library/lib.htm

Contact: Lois B. Bowman, Libn.

Desc: Subject: Anabaptist and Mennonite history, German culture in Eastern United States, history of the Shenandoah Valley, genealogy. Holdings: 29,000 volumes; 375 reels of microfilm; 216 microfiche; 800 reels of magnetic tape; 815 linear feet of manuscript and archival material; 63 VF drawers and 45 linear feet of general files. Services: Interlibrary loan; copying (both limited); Library open to the public for reference use only.

1631 ▪ Eastern Nebraska Genealogical Society
Library
Box 541
Fremont, NE 68025-0541
Ph: (402)721-9553

Contact: Claire Mares, Ed.

Desc: Subject: Local history, genealogy. Holdings: 500 books; genealogies and pedigree sheets. Services: Library open to the public by appointment.

1632 ▪ Eastern Washington State Historical Society
Research Library and Special Collections
Cheney Cowles Museum
W. 2316 1st Ave.
Spokane, WA 99204
Ph: (509)456-3931
Fax: (509)456-7690

E-mail: karend.ccm@pacnw.com

Contact: Karen DeSeve, Cur. of Spec.Coll.

Desc: Subject: History of Eastern Washington, Spokane, the Inland Empire; Inland Empire mining; Eastern Washington social, agricultural, women's history; Spokane business history; Native American plateau cultures. Holdings: 8000 books; 135,000 historical photographs; 140 bound periodical volumes; 2795 linear feet of manuscripts; 75 VF drawers of newspaper clippings; Ephemera collection related to Spokane and Pacific Northwest (1889-date) (61 linear feet); 750 oral history tapes; 12 drawers of maps. Services: Copying (limited); Library open to the public by appointment.

1633 ▪ Eccles-Lesher Memorial Library
GenealogyLocal History Room
231 N. Main St.
PO Box 359
Rimersburg, PA 16248
Ph: (814)473-3800
Fax: (814)473-8200
E-mail: ecclesh@alpha.clarion-net.com
URL: http://www.csonline.net/ecclesh/

Contact: Joanne Hosey

Desc: Subject: Clarion County, Pennsylvania - genealogy, history, culture. Holdings: 22,000 books, 38 reels of microfilm. Services: Interlibrary loan; copying.

1634 ▪ Ector County Library
Southwest HistoryGenealogy Department
321 W. 5th St.
Odessa, TX 79761
Ph: (915)332-0633
Fax: (915)337-6502

Contact: Emil Ciallella, Lib.Dir.

Desc: Subject: Southwest history (Oklahoma, New Mexico, Arizona, Texas); United States and world genealogy; Texas city and county histories; Texas biographies. Holdings: 12,100 books; 1833 bound periodical volumes; 6302 reels of microfilm; 11,985 microfiche; 29,214 Texas state documents. Services: Copying; department open to the public.

1635 ▪ (Eden) Town Historian's Office
Library
PO Box 156
Eden, NY 14057-0156
Ph: (716)992-4422

Contact: Dorothea Hickman Meyer, Town Hist.

Desc: Subject: Local history and genealogy. Holdings: 300 books; 30 scrapbooks; 8 boxes of deeds, tax records, road warrants, tavern licenses, school district records; 10 photograph albums; 21 drawers of local history and genealogy files; 110 reels of microfilm. Services: Copying; Library open to the public by appointment.

1636 ▪ Edwards County Historical Society
Library
212 W. Main St.
Albion, IL 62806
Fax: (618)445-3969
E-mail: melrose@wworld.com

Contact: Terry L. Harper, Pres.

Desc: Subject: Genealogy, history. Holdings: 693 books; 37 nonbook items. Services: Copying; Library open to the public.

1637 ▪ El Paso Public Library
Genealogy Section
501 N. Oregon St.
El Paso, TX 79901
Ph: (915)543-5413
Fax: (915)543-5410
E-mail: annm@laguna.epcc.edu

Contact: Mary Kaye Donahue-Hooker, Dir. of Lib(s).

Desc: Subject: Genealogy. Holdings: 4700 books; 825 bound periodical volumes; 5 VF drawers; 650 reels of microfilm. Services: Interlibrary loan; copying; section open to the public.

1638 ▪ El Segundo Public Library
Special Collections
111 W. Mariposa
El Segundo, CA 90245
Ph: (310)322-4121
Fax: (310)322-4323
E-mail: Brighton@elsegundo.org

Contact: Debra Brighton, Interim Lib.Dir.

Desc: Subject: South Bay (California) history, genealogy, children's literature. Holdings: 130,490 books; 300 bound periodical volumes; 500 reports; 1000 archive items; 68,000 microforms. Services: Interlibrary loan; copying; faxing; mini-computers; Library open to the public.

1639 ▪ Ellen Payne Odom Genealogy Library
PO Box 1110
Moultrie, GA 31776-1110
Ph: (912)985-6540
Fax: (912)985-0936
URL: http://www.teleport.com/binder/famtree.shtml

Contact: Melody Jenkins, Dir.

Desc: Subject: Genealogy. Holdings: Figures not available. Services: Copying; Library open to the public.

1640 ▪ Ellis County Historical Society
Archives
100 W. 7th St.
Hays, KS 67601
Ph: (785)628-2624

Contact: Janet Johannes, Archv.

Desc: Subject: Local history, Volga-German migration. Holdings: 64,000 documents and photographs. Services: Copying; archives open to the public with restrictions.

1641 ▪ Ellsworth County Historical Society
Hodgden House Museum Complex
104 W. Main St.
PO Box 144
Ellsworth, KS 67439
Ph: (785)472-3059

Contact: Tyra Denny, Dir.

Desc: Subject: Ellsworth County. Holdings: 400 books; 500 photographs. Services: Copying; Archives open to the public by appointment.

1642 ▪ Emanuel Congregation
Joseph Taussig Memorial Library
5959 N. Sheridan Rd.
Chicago, IL 60660
Ph: (773)561-5173
Fax: (773)561-5420
E-mail: EmanCong@aol.com
URL: http://shamash.org.reform/uahc/congs/il/il004

Contact: Deborah Arendt

Desc: Subject: Judaica, Judaism, children's Jewish literature, theology. Holdings: 4000 books; 50 reports. Services: Library open to the public at librarian's discretion.

1643 ▪ Enoch Pratt Free Library
Business, Science and Technology Department
400 Cathedral St.
Baltimore, MD 21201
Ph: (410)396-5316
Fax: (410)396-1481
E-mail: bstcen@mail.pratt.lib.md.us
URL: http://www.pratt.lib.md.us/pratt/depts/bst/

Contact: Wesley Wilson, Dept.Hd.

Desc: Subject: Science, business, economics, health and nutrition, cookery, chemistry, physics, U.S. census, medicine, consumerism, small business. Holdings: 250,000 books; 140 VF drawers of pamphlets; 5000 shelves of U.S. documents; 220 drawers of U.S. documents on microfiche. Services: Interlibrary loan; copying; department open to the public; resources available via telephone, e-mail, fax or walk-in.

1644 ■ Enon Community Historical Society Library
PO Box 442
Enon, OH 45323
Ph: (937)864-7080
Fax: (937)864-7080
E-mail: echs@erinet.com

Contact: Charlot Wade, VP

Desc: Subject: Genealogy; Clark County, Ohio; local history. Holdings: 300 books; 150 archival materials; 4 sets of microfiche; 10 reels of microfilm. Services: Library open to the public for reference use only.

1645 ■ Erie County Historical Society Library & Archives
Erie History Ctr.
419 State St.
Erie, PA 16501
Ph: (814)454-1813
Fax: (814)452-1744
E-mail: echs@velocity.net

Contact: Annita Andrick, Libn. & Archv.

Desc: Subject: History - Erie County, history of northwestern Pennsylvania; Lake Erie region; genealogy; historic preservation; architecture; agriculture. Holdings: 4300 volumes; 105 bound periodical volumes; 650 maps and 2250 measured drawings; 350 reels of microfilm; 183 linear feet of newspaper clippings, typescripts, and reports; 115,000 photographic prints and negatives; 12,000 postcards, stereoviews, and slides; manuscripts and archival materials. Services: Copying; Library open to the public.

1646 ■ Essex County Historical Society Brewster Library
Court St.
PO Box 428
Elizabethtown, NY 12932
Ph: (518)873-6466

Desc: Subject: Adirondack history, folklore, literature, Essex County, New York. Holdings: 1500 books; 40 periodical titles; 600 pamphlets; 24 VF drawers of ephemera; 330 manuscripts; 32 reels of microfilm; 15 newspaper titles; 400 maps; 34 drawers of cemetery records. Services: Copying (limited); Library open to the public by appointment.

1647 ■ Ethel Miner Cooke Historical Library Academy Hall Museum Library
785 Old Main St.
Box 185
Rocky Hill, CT 06067
Ph: (860)563-6704

Contact: Mildred R. Sword, Libn.

Desc: Subject: Local history. Holdings: 1000 books; 20 magnetic tapes (some oral history); local news scrapbooks; 18th and 19th century school texts; local Indian artifacts. Services: Library open to the public by appointment.

1648 ■ Evans Memorial Library Historical Division
105 N. Long St.
Aberdeen, MS 39730
Ph: (601)369-4601
URL: http://www.ahs.aberdeen.k12.ms.us/netclub/evans.htm

Desc: Subject: Genealogy, Mississippi family histories, Mississippi literature. Holdings: Books; magazines; videotapes; audiocassettes; CD-ROMs.

1649 ■ Evanston Historical Society Charles Gates Dawes Home Research Room and Library
225 Greenwood St.
Evanston, IL 60201-4713
Ph: (847)475-3410
Fax: (847)475-3599

E-mail: evanstonhs@nwu.edu
URL: http://www.acns.nwu.edu/ev-chi/ehs/index.html

Contact: Eden Juron Pearlman, Coll.Mgr.

Desc: Subject: History of Evanston and Illinois. Holdings: 2500 books; 250 bound periodical volumes; 11,000 photographs; 2500 slides; clippings; local government documents and reports; Evanston newspapers, 1872 to present; oral history interviews. Services: Copying; Library open to the public.

1650 ■ Everest Community Historical Society Library
Ph: (913)548-7792
rs>Everest, KS 66424

Contact: Bob Smith, Pres.

Desc: Subject: Local history. Holdings: Figures not available. Services: Library open to the public on a limited schedule or by appointment.

1651 ■ Ezra Habonim (Niles Township) Jewish Congregation Hillman Library
4500 Dempster
Skokie, IL 60076
Ph: (847)675-4141
Fax: (847)675-0327

Contact: Janice B. Footlik, Libn.

Desc: Subject: Jewish children's literature, Judaica, Israel, Jewish history, American Jewish history. Holdings: 5300 books; 8 bound periodical volumes; unbound periodicals. Services: Interlibrary loan (limited); copying; Library open to the public.

1652 ■ Fairfax County Public Library Fairfax City Regional Library Virginia Room
3915 Chain Bridge Rd.
Fairfax, VA 22030
Ph: (703)246-2123
Fax: (703)385-1911
E-mail: va_room@fcpl.co.fairfax.va.us
URL: http://www.co.fairfax.va.us/library/

Contact: Suzanne S. Levy, Libn.

Desc: Subject: Virginia - history, government, genealogy. Holdings: 25,000 books; 1600 bound periodical volumes; 14 VF drawers of Historic Landmark Files; 1570 reels of microfilm; 165 boxes of manuscripts and scrapbooks; 16,100 photographs; 70,000 photographic negatives; 10,225 microfiche; 461 microcards; 35 VF drawers of clippings and pamphlets related to Virginia and local history. Services: Interlibrary loan; copying; room open to the public.

1653 ■ Fairfield Historical Society Library
636 Old Post Rd.
Fairfield, CT 06430
Ph: (203)259-1598
Fax: (203)255-2716

Contact: Barbara E. Austen, Libn.Archv.

Desc: Subject: Local and regional history, genealogy, decorative arts. Holdings: 10,000 books; 760 bound periodical volumes; 700 linear feet of manuscript material, including 17th-20th century family, court, cemetery, church, school, town, and shipping records, personal diaries, scrapbooks, account books and records of merchants, craftsmen, and organizations, local ephemera; maps; photographs; 28 VF drawers of local history and genealogy; almanacs; city directories; tapes and transcripts of oral history. Services: Copying; genealogical research on fee basis; Library open to the public for reference use only.

1654 ■ Fairleigh Dickinson University Weiner Library Government Documents Department
1000 River Rd.
Teaneck, NJ 07666
Ph: (201)692-2290
Fax: (201)692-9815

URL: http://www.fdu.edu/studentsvcs/teanecklibes.html

Contact: Richard Goerner, Hd., Govt.Docs.

Desc: Subject: Census, environment, energy, foreign affairs, education, business, health, labor and fair employment information, foreign affairs. Holdings: 96,000 paper documents; 134,000 documents on microfiche. Services: Interlibrary loan; copying.

1655 ■ Fairmount Temple Arthur J. Lelyveld Center for Jewish Learning
23737 Fairmount Blvd.
Cleveland, OH 44122
Ph: (216)464-1330
Fax: (216)464-3628
E-mail: ftemple@en.com

Contact: Julie A. Moss, Libn.

Desc: Subject: Judaica. Holdings: 27,000 books; 20 bound periodical titles. Services: Interlibrary loan; center open to the public.

1656 ■ Fairport Harbor Historical Society Library
129 2nd St.
Fairport Harbor, OH 44077
Ph: (440)354-4825
E-mail: fhlh@ncweb.com

Contact: Kathryn Popp

Desc: Subject: History - Great Lakes, Lake County, Fairport Harbor; lighthouses. Holdings: 1000 books; 500 bound periodical volumes; 25 reels of microfilm. Services: Copying; Library open to the public with restrictions.

1657 ■ Fall River Historical Society MuseumLibrary
451 Rock St.
Fall River, MA 02720
Ph: (508)679-1071

Contact: Michael Martins, Cur.

Desc: Subject: Fall River Line, cotton textile industry, local history and genealogy. Holdings: 3000 books; 200 bound periodical volumes; 5000 manuscripts; reports; Fall River Evening News, January 1890 to December 1925 (complete) and several more volumes. Services: Library open to the public by appointment for research.

1658 ■ Falls Village-Canaan Historical Society Library
PO Box 206
Main St.
Falls Village, CT 06031
Ph: (860)824-0707
Fax: (860)824-4506

Contact: Marion L. Stock, Cur.

Desc: Subject: Local history, ledgers and account books, Connecticut history, geneology. Holdings: 250 books. Services: Library open to the public for reference use only on limited schedule.

1659 ■ Falmouth Historical Society Resources Center History & Genealogy Archives
Palmer Ave. at the Village Green
PO Box 174
Falmouth, MA 02541
Ph: (508)548-4857
Fax: (508)548-4857
E-mail: rfitzpa24@aol.com
URL: http://members.aol.com/rfitzpa24/FHS/index.htm

Contact: Ann Sears, Exec.Dir.

Desc: Subject: Local history, genealogy. Holdings: 550 books; 30 ships logs, 1820 to present; church records; family genealogical files; 135 boxes of archival materials. Services: Archives open to the public on a limited schedule.

1660 ■ Fayette County Historical Society Library
195 Lee St. Ph: (404)487-2000
PO Box 421
Fayetteville, GA 30214

Contact: Carolyn Cary, County Hist.

Desc: Subject: Fayette County genealogy, the Civil War and Georgia. Holdings: 300 books; 100 bound periodical volumes; 20 manuscripts. Services: Library open to the public.

1661 ■ Fayette County Historical Society Library
100 N. Walnut Ph: (319)422-5797
West Union, IA 52175

Contact: Frances R. Graham

Desc: Subject: Genealogy, history. Holdings: 500 books; 40 land record documents; 56 VF drawers of family files; 90 reels of microfilm; school records; photographs. Services: Copying; Library open to the public. Performs historical and genealogical research in Fayette County.

1662 ■ Fayette County Public Library Genealogy and Local History
Indiana Room Ph: (765)827-0883
828 Grand Ave. Fax: (765)825-4592
Connersville, IN 47331
E-mail: libstaff@si-net.com
URL: http://www.fcplibrary.com/

Contact: Connie Lake, Dir.

Desc: Subject: Indiana history, genealogy, and culture. Holdings: Pamphlets; books; microfilm; microfiche; CD-ROMs; cemetery records; marriage records. Services: Interlibrary loan; copying; Library open to the public with restrictions.

1663 ■ Fenton Historical Society Museum and Library
67 Washington St. Ph: (716)664-6256
Jamestown, NY 14701 Fax: (716)483-7524

Contact: Karen E. Livsey, Cur.Mss.

Desc: Subject: Genealogy, local history, Civil War. Holdings: 4500 books; 100 bound periodical volumes; local daybooks, account books, town and school district records; 8 drawers of clippings and pamphlets; 15 shelves and 5 drawers of manuscripts. Services: Copying; Library open to the public on fee basis.

1664 ■ Fillmore County Historical Society Historical Center
202 County Rd., No. 8 Ph: (507)268-4449
Fountain, MN 55935

Contact: Jerry Henke, Exec.Dir.

Desc: Subject: History - Southeastern Minnesota, Southeastern Minnesota immigrants, agrarian history, agrarian machinery, Native American, rural lifestyles. Holdings: 3700 books; 2200 bound periodical volumes; 1100 documents; 2800 nonbook items; 67 manuscripts. Services: Copying; Library open to the public for reference use only.

1665 ■ Filson Club Historical Society Library
1310 S. 3rd St. Ph: (502)636-0471
Louisville, KY 40208 Fax: (502)635-5086
E-mail: filson@filsonclub.org
URL: http://www.filsonclub.org

Contact: Judith Partington, Hd.Libn.

Desc: Subject: Kentucky history and genealogy; Civil War history. Holdings: 50,000 volumes; 1.5 million manuscripts and private papers; 50,000 prints and photographs;

3700 scores; 1500 maps of Kentucky and the U.S.; broadsides and ephemera. Services: Copying (limited); Library open to the public (fee required for nonmembers).

1666 ■ Finney County Genealogical Society Library
PO Box 592 Ph: (316)275-6270
Garden City, KS 67846-0592

Contact: Loraine Taylor, Libn.

Desc: Subject: Genealogy. Holdings: 1025 books; 427 periodical volumes; 500 reports; 1500 microfiche; 85 microfilm. Services: Copying; Library open to the public.

1667 ■ Finnish American Historical Society of Michigan Archives
19885 Melrose
Southfield, MI 48075

Contact: Felix V. Jackonen, Pres.

Desc: Subject: Finnish history, culture, religion; books in Finnish. Holdings: 200 books; archival materials; clippings; pamphlets. Services: Archives not open to the public.

1668 ■ Firelands Historical Society Library
4 Case Ave. Ph: (419)663-0392
PO Box 572
Norwalk, OH 44857-0572

Contact: Henry Timman, Libn.

Desc: Subject: Genealogy, local history. Holdings: 5000 books; 10,000 archival materials; 50 reels of microfilm; photographs. Services: Copying; Library open to the public.

1669 ■ First Baptist Church Mattie D. Hall Library
Front St. Ph: (601)759-6378
Box 459
Rosedale, MS 38769

Contact: Beulah R. Lane, Media Dir.

Desc: Subject: Theology, Christian living. Holdings: 3919 books. Services: Library open to the public with restrictions.

1670 ■ First Baptist Church of Blanchard FBC Media Center
201 Attaway Ph: (318)929-4707
PO Box 65 Fax: (318)929-4680
Blanchard, LA 71009

Contact: Kevin Sandifer, Dir.

Desc: Subject: Religion, family, biography, psychology, hobbies and recreation, missions, fiction, history, geography, pure and applied science. Holdings: 2500 books; 150 bound periodical volumes; 4050 documents; 400 AV programs; 190 nonbook items; 5 manuscripts; 4200 photographs. Services: Interlibrary loan; copying; Library open to church members and their relatives; archives open to the public.

1671 ■ First Congregational Church Library
Walton Place Ph: (203)323-0200
Stamford, CT 06901

Contact: Barbara Arata

Desc: Subject: Children's books, adult fiction, biography, religion, church history. Holdings: 10,000 books. Services: Library open to the public.

1672 ■ First Presbyterian Church Library
500 Farragut Circle Ph: (619)442-2583
El Cajon, CA 92020 Fax: (619)442-2588

Desc: Subject: Bible, religion, congregational life, Christian life, biography, fiction. Holdings: 3400 books; 24 audiocassettes; 92 videocassettes. Services: Library open to the public with the permission of a pastor or librarian.

1673 ■ First Presbyterian Church Library
101 E. Foothill Ph: (626)358-3297
Monrovia, CA 91016 Fax: (626)358-5997

Contact: Dana Young

Desc: Subject: Bible study, history, family, biography, missions, church-related literature. Holdings: 2000 books; audiocassettes. Services: Library not open to the public.

1674 ■ First Reformed Church Johnson Library
8 N. Church St. Ph: (518)377-2201
Schenectady, NY 12305-1699

Contact: Joan W. Ipsen, Libn.

Desc: Subject: Religion, art, music, history, biography, personal development, literature. Holdings: 7500 books. Services: Library open to the public with restrictions on a limited schedule.

1675 ■ First United Methodist Church Library
411 Turner St. Ph: (813)446-5955
Clearwater, FL 33756-5328

Contact: Marjorie A. Kann, Libn.

Desc: Subject: Religion, literature, biography. Holdings: 4000 books; audio- and videotapes. Services: Library open to the public at librarian's discretion.

1676 ■ First United Methodist Church Library
1020 S. Granite Ph: (505)546-2791
Deming, NM 88030

Contact: Elizabeth K. Gottschalk, Libn.

Desc: Subject: Religion, biography, fiction. Holdings: 2600 books; 12 AV programs; 1 vertical file of nonbook items; 106 audiocassettes; 170 videotapes; games; 5 maps; phonograph records. Services: Library open to members and friends only.

1677 ■ Fisk University Special Collections Department Library
17th at Jackson St. Ph: (615)329-8646
Nashville, TN 37203 Fax: (615)329-8761

Contact: Ann Allen Shockley, Hd. of Spec.Coll.Univ.Archv.

Desc: Subject: African-American history and culture. Holdings: 64,000 books; 1565 bound periodical volumes; 3050 reels of microfilm of information by and about blacks; 2300 phonograph records; 4 VF drawers of pictures; 2 VF drawers of newspaper clippings; 4 VF drawers of biographical information by or about blacks; 878 Fisk University masters' theses; 100 archival and manuscript collections. Services: Copying; department open to the public with restrictions.

1678 ■ Fitchburg Historical Society Library
50 Grove St. Ph: (978)345-1157
PO Box 953
Fitchburg, MA 01420

Contact: Ruth Ann Penka, Exec.Dir.

Desc: Subject: Fitchburg history, genealogy, Civil War, Fitchburg authors. Holdings: Books; bound periodical volumes; documents; 15 AV programs; manuscripts; reports; town histories. Services: Copying; Library open to the public.

1679 ■ Flag Research Center
Library
Box 580   Ph: (781)729-9410
Winchester, MA 01890-0880   Fax: (781)721-4817
URL: http://www.vexillopolis.com

Contact: Whitney Smith, Dir.

Desc: Subject: Flags, heraldry, symbolism. Holdings: 13,000 books; 200,000 documents (correspondence, news clippings, pictures, pamphlets;) 1000 charts; 4500 periodicals; 20,000 cards of flag information; 2000 flags. Services: Copying; consultation; rental artwork; translation provided to organizations; Library open to those stating purpose of research by prior application.

1680 ■ Flagstaff City-Coconino County Public
Library
Genealogy Collection
300 W. Aspen Ave.   Ph: (520)779-7670
Flagstaff, AZ 86001

Contact: Kay Whitaker, Dir.

Desc: Subject: Arizona genealogy, U.S. genealogy. Holdings: 1350 books; 50 CD-ROMs. Services: Copying; Library open to the public.

1681 ■ Fletcher Free Library
Local History Collection
235 College St.   Ph: (802)865-7217
Burlington, VT 05401   Fax: (802)865-7227

Desc: Subject: History - Burlington, Vermont, Lake Champlain. Holdings: 1600 books; documents; maps; atlases; photographs; vertical files. Services: Library open to the public.

1682 ■ Flint Genealogical Society
Genealogical Society Collection
PO Box 1217   Ph: (810)760-1415
Flint, MI 48501-1213

Contact: David White, Cur. of Colls.

Desc: Subject: Genealogy. Holdings: 300 volumes; 250 notebooks. Services: Copying; collection open to the public on a limited schedule.

1683 ■ Flint Public Library
Local History and Genealogy Collections
1026 E. Kearsley St.   Ph: (810)232-7111
Flint, MI 48502   Fax: (810)767-6740

Contact: Cheryl Frounfelter, Ref.Libn.

Desc: Subject: Local history, Michigan history, genealogy. Holdings: 18,000 books; 67 VF drawers; 875 microcards; 3062 microfiche; 1670 reels of microfilm of census material; 318 drawers of surname-obituary indexes; Michigan document depository. Services: Interlibrary loan; copying; mail inquiries answered; room open to the public.

1684 ■ Florence-Lauderdale Public Library
Genealogy, Local History, & Civil War
Collection
218 N. Wood Ave.   Ph: (205)764-6564
Florence, AL 35630   Fax: (205)764-6629

Contact: Brent Stokesberry, Dir.

Desc: Subject: Genealogy, local history, Civil War. Holdings: 1700 books; 450 bound periodical volumes; 700

reels of microfilm; 9000 microfiche; 18 linear feet of manuscripts. Services: Copying; collection open to the public.

1685 ■ Florida History Center & Museum
Research Center
805 N. U.S. Hwy. One   Ph: (561)747-6639
Jupiter, FL 33477   Fax: (561)575-3292

Contact: Dr. Violet Magyar

Desc: Subject: General Florida cultural and natural history. Holdings: 600 books; 200 bound periodical volumes; 500 documents; 40 AV programs; professional journals; maps. Services: Copying; research assistance; Library open to the public by appointment with librarian.

1686 ■ Florida (State) Division of Libraries &
Information Services
Bureau of Archives & Records Management
Florida State Archives
R.A. Gray Bldg.   Ph: (850)487-2073
500 S. Bronough St.   Fax: (904)488-4894
Tallahassee, FL 32399-0250
URL: http://www.dos.state.fl.us/dlis/archives.html

Contact: Jim Berberich, Chf.

Desc: Subject: Florida history. Holdings: 25,000 cubic feet of state historical records, 1822 to present; 1250 cubic feet of manuscripts. Services: Copying; archives open to the public.

1687 ■ Florida State University
Center for the Study of Population
654 Bellamy Bldg.   Ph: (850)644-1762
Tallahassee, FL 32306-2240   Fax: (850)644-8818
E-mail: rmccann@coss.fsu.edu

Desc: Subject: Migration, urbanization, fertility, mortality, population education, family planning. Holdings: 9700 books; 3500 bound periodical volumes; 3200 vertical files. Services: Copying; SDI; center open to the public for reference use only.

1688 ■ Floyd County Historical Society Museum
Library
500 Gilbert St.   Ph: (515)228-1099
Charles City, IA 50616-2738   Fax: (515)228-1157
E-mail: fchs@fia.net

Contact: Franklin B. McKinney, Dir.

Desc: Subject: History - Floyd County, family, Charles City. Holdings: 500 books; 100 bound periodical volumes; manuscripts; 350 films. Services: Copying; Library open to the public with restrictions.

1689 ■ Fond du Lac County Historical Society
Historic Galloway House and Village
Adams House Resource Center
PO Box 1284   Ph: (920)922-1166
Fond du Lac, WI 54935   Fax: (414)922-9099
E-mail: mbetz@tcccom.net
URL: http://www.rootsweb.com/wifonddu/

Contact: John Ebert, Dir.

Desc: Subject: Wisconsin and Fond du Lac area history, 1836 to present. Holdings: Diaries; correspondence; photographs; genealogical records; vital statistics; land transfers; newspaper files; county histories; cemetery inscriptions; poll taxes; tax records. Services: Archives open to the public on a limited schedule and by appointment.

1690 ■ Forest Lambton Museum Inc.
Archives
59 Broadway St.   Ph: (519)786-5629
Box 707
Forest, ON, Canada N0N 1J0

Contact: Clarence Hodgson, Pres.

Desc: Subject: Genealogy; town histories; area businesses, schools, churches. Holdings: Historical records. Services: Archives open to the public with permission.

1691 ■ Fort Clark Historical Society
The Old Guardhouse Museum
Swanson Archives
Fort Clark Springs   Ph: (830)563-9150
Box 1061
Brackettville, TX 78832

Contact: Emet Huntsman

Desc: Subject: Fort Clark history, U.S. Army units, U.S. Cavalry. Holdings: 220 volumes; 20 reels of microfilm; manuscripts; Fort Clark Post Returns, 1852-1916. Services: Archives open to the public by appointment.

1692 ■ Fort Collins Public Library
Local History Collection
201 Peterson St.   Ph: (970)221-6688
Fort Collins, CO 80524   Fax: (970)221-6398
E-mail: massey@libsys.ci.fort-collins.co.us
URL: http://www.ci.fort-collins.co.us/

Contact: Rheba Massey, Local Hist.Libn.

Desc: Subject: Fort Collins and Larimer County history. Holdings: 130,000 photographs; 400 oral history interview tapes and transcripts; maps; clipping and pamphlet files. Services: Interlibrary loan; copying; collection open to the public.

1693 ■ Fort Frances Museum and Cultural
Centre
Library
259 Scott St.   Ph: (807)274-7891
Fort Frances, ON, Canada P9A   Fax: (807)274-4103
1G8

Desc: Subject: Rainy River district, Fort Frances, indigenous people, fur trade, pioneers, forest industries. Holdings: 5000 archival materials. Services: Copying; library open to the public.

1694 ■ Fort Larned Historical Society, Inc.
Santa Fe Trail Center Library
Rte. 3   Ph: (316)285-2054
Larned, KS 67550   Fax: (316)285-7491
E-mail: trailctr@larned.net
URL: http://www.larned.net/trailctr/

Contact: Betsy Crawford-Gore, Cur.

Desc: Subject: History of Santa Fe Trail and Kansas. Holdings: 3500 books; 100 bound periodical volumes; 11 boxes of W.P.A. county histories; 2 boxes of maps of the Santa Fe Trail; 100 pieces of historical sheet music; Pawnee County Archives; photographic collection; Civil War official records. Services: Copying; Library open to the public with restrictions.

1695 ■ Fort Lauderdale Historical Society
Library & Archives
219 S.W. 2nd Ave.   Ph: (954)463-4431
Fort Lauderdale, FL 33301   Fax: (954)463-4434

Contact: Susan Gillis, Cur.

Desc: Subject: Local and state history, historic preservation. Holdings: 2800 books; 450 bound periodical volumes; 120 feet of manuscripts; 250 oral history cassettes; 250,000 photographs and slides. Services: Copying; Library open to the public by appointment.

1696 ■ Fort Worth Public Library
Genealogy and Local History Department
300 Taylor St.   Ph: (817)871-7740
Fort Worth, TX 76102   Fax: (817)871-7734

URL: http://198.215.16.8:443/fortworth/FWPL

Contact: Ken Hopkins, Mgr.

Desc: Subject: Local history, genealogy. Holdings: 39,000 books; 8900 bound periodical volumes; 8500 reels of microfilm; 108,000 microcards; 8000 titles on microfiche; 50 lateral file drawers of pamphlets and clippings on local history; 2000 linear feet of miscellaneous manuscript material; 2000 photographs. Services: Copying.

1697 ▪ The Foxfire Fund, Inc.
Archives

PO Box 541   Ph: (706)746-5828
Mountain City, GA   Fax: (706)746-5829
  30562-0541
E-mail: foxfire@foxfire.org
URL: http://www.foxfire.org

Contact: Robert Murray

Desc: Subject: Cultural traditions in southern Appalachia (primarily northern Georgia and western North Carolina). Holdings: 1323 hours of taped interviews and oral histories; 30,000 negatives. Services: Archives open to the public.

1698 ▪ Framingham Public Library
Framingham Room

49 Lexington St.   Ph: (508)879-3570
Framingham, MA 01701 Fax: (508)820-7210
E-mail: fplref@mln.lib.ma.us
URL: http://www.mln.lib.ma.us

Contact: Tom Gilchrist

Desc: Subject: Framingham history and genealogy. Holdings: Maps; VF drawers of memorabilia, clippings, pamphlets, illustrations, photographs, uncataloged items; microfilm; annual town reports (1838 to present); vital records dating to 1850 and 1890-1908; New England Historical and Genealogical Register, 1847 to present; military records; 1790 Census. Services: Copying (limited); Library open to the public for reference use only.

1699 ▪ Franklin Area Historical Society
Library

302 Park Ave.   Ph: (513)746-8295
Franklin, OH 45005

Contact: Harriet Foley, Libn.

Desc: Subject: Franklin history, Warren County history, military history. Holdings: 940 books; 24 bound periodical volumes. Services: Library open to the public by appointment.

1700 ▪ Franklin County Genealogical Society
Library

PO Box 44309   Ph: (614)469-1300
Columbus, OH 43204-0309
E-mail: fcgs@juno.com

Desc: Subject: Franklin County, Ohio families, genealogy, Ohio counties. Holdings: 3000 books; 100 bound periodical volumes; 1300 microfiche; 70 reels of microfilm. Services: Copying; Library open to the public.

1701 ▪ Franklin County Historical Society
Archives

PO Box 145   Ph: (785)242-1232
Ottawa, KS 66067
E-mail: history@ott.net

Contact: Deborah Barker, Dir.

Desc: Subject: Franklin County - biography, history. Holdings: 500 books, Franklin County and City of Ottawa records. Services: Library open to the public.

1702 ▪ Franklin County Library
Gertrude C. Mann Local History Room

120 E. Court St.   Ph: (540)483-3098
Rocky Mount, VA 24151 Fax: (540)483-1568
E-mail: dbass@leo.usla.edu

Contact: David Bass, Dir.

Desc: Subject: Local history and genealogy. Holdings: 800 books; 70 tape recordings; 1000 photographs; 200 maps and charts; vertical file; clippings; newspapers. Services: Copying; room open to the public with restrictions.

1703 ▪ Frederic Remington Area Historical Society
Library

PO Box 133   Ph: (316)799-2123
Whitewater, KS 67154 Fax: (316)799-2943

Contact: Pam Harber

Desc: Subject: Local history, local family history. Holdings: 75 books; 100 manuscripts; 15 archive volumes; 600 slides; 101 reels of microfilm. Services: Library open to the public with restrictions.

1704 ▪ Freeborn County Historical Society
Library

1031 Bridge Ave.   Ph: (507)373-8003
Albert Lea, MN 56007-2205

Desc: Subject: History - Albert Lea, Freeborn County, Minnesota. Holdings: 500 books; 40 bound periodical volumes; 100 boxes of manuscripts; 2000 slides and photographs; 600 reels of microfilm. Services: Copying; Library open to the public for reference use only.

1705 ▪ French-Canadian Genealogical Society of Connecticut, Inc.
French-Canadian Genealogical Library

53 Tolland Green   Ph: (860)872-2597
PO Box 928
Tolland, CT 06084-0928
E-mail: fcgsc@juno.com
URL: http://home.att.net/rich.carpenter/fcgsc

Contact: Maryanne Roy LeGrow, Lib.Dir.

Desc: Subject: French-Canadian genealogy and history. Holdings: 2000 books; 500 bound periodical volumes; 550 other cataloged items; 10,000 index cards on Acadians; index to 10,000 births, deaths, and marriages of Franco-Americans in Connecticut; 5000 index cards on Worcester County, Massachusetts, area. Services: Copying; Library open to the public with restrictions.

1706 ▪ French-Canadian Heritage Society of Michigan
Library

PO Box 10028   Ph: (517)372-9707
Lansing, MI 48901-0028

Desc: Subject: French-Canadian history, genealogy. Holdings: 600 books; birth, death, marriage records; family genealogies. Services: Library open to the public.

1707 ▪ Fresno City and County Historical Society
Archives

PO Box 2029   Ph: (209)441-0862
Fresno, CA 93718   Fax: (209)441-1372
E-mail: frhistsoc@aol.com
URL: http://www.valleyhistory.org

Contact: Zee B. Smith, Exec.Dir.

Desc: Subject: Fresno County history, city and county records. Holdings: 250 manuscript collections of individuals, families, and businesses; 3000 bound city and county records; 30,000 unbound city and county records. Services: Photograph reproduction; copying; archives open to the public by appointment.

1708 ▪ Fresno County Free Library
Special Collections

2420 Mariposa St.   Ph: (209)488-3195
Fresno, CA 93721   Fax: (209)488-1971
URL: http://www.sjvls.lib.ca.us/fresno

Contact: John K. Kallenberg, Libn.

Desc: Subject: Fresno County - local history; California Indians - Mono, Miwok, Yokut. Holdings: 122 bound periodical volumes; 15 linear feet of archival materials; 15,000 microfiche; Fresno newspapers on microfilm (1860 to present). Services: Copying; Library open to the public with restrictions on the Saroyan Collection.

1709 ▪ Fresno Genealogical Society
Library

Box 1429   Ph: (209)488-3236
Fresno, CA 93716
URL: http://www.cybergate.com/libfresl/

Contact: Mary Lou Talens, Libn.

Desc: Subject: Genealogy. Holdings: 2000 books; 1800 periodicals; 43 reels of microfilm and microfiche. Services: Library open to the public.

1710 ▪ Friends of Historic Boonville
Archival Collection

PO Box 1   Ph: (660)882-7977
Boonville, MO 65233 Fax: (660)882-9194
E-mail: friendsart@mid-mo.net

Contact: Judy Shields, Adm.

Desc: Subject: Boonville and Cooper County - history and genealogy. Holdings: 125 books; 110 newspapers; letters; personal papers. Services: Copying; collection open to the public.

1711 ▪ Friends of Historic Meridian
Historical Collection

PO Box 155   Ph: (517)347-7300
Okemos, MI 48805-0155 Fax: (517)347-7300

Contact: Jan Woosley, Village Coord.

Desc: Subject: Local history and genealogy. Holdings: 5 cubic feet of census, tax, cemetery records; 600 photographs. Services: Collection open to the public by appointment; answers mail enquiries.

1712 ▪ Fullerton Arboretum
Heritage House Library
VictorianaLocal History Collection

California State   Ph: (714)278-4792
  University, Fullerton Fax: (714)278-7066
PO Box 34080
Fullerton, CA 92834-6850

Contact: Shirley Fisk, Hd.Libn.

Desc: Subject: Victoriana, local history. Holdings: 200 books, bound periodical volumes, and pamphlets. Services: Copying; collection open to authorized researchers by appointment.

1713 ▪ Fullerton College
William T. Boyce Library

321 E. Chapman Ave. Ph: (714)992-7061
Fullerton, CA 92832-1351 Fax: (714)992-1786

Contact: John L. Ayala, Dean, Lrng.Rscrs.

Desc: Subject: History of Fullerton College and the Fullerton community, 1900 to present. Holdings: 101,086 books; 569 dissertations; 87,726 microforms; 14,336 pamphlets; 4602 maps; 145 linear feet of papers, oral history tapes, transcripts; 3194 photographs; 1135 slides; 1253 videotapes. Services: Interlibrary loan; copying; Library open to the public.

1714 ■ Fullerton Public Library
Local History Collection
Launer Room

353 W. Commonwealth Ave.   Ph: (714)738-6342
Fullerton, CA 92832   Fax: (714)447-3280
URL: http://www.ci.fullerton.ca.us/localhis.htm

Contact: C. Thomas, Cur.

Desc: Subject: Fullerton, California history. Holdings: Books; reports; manuscripts; 200 historic photographs. Services: Library open to the public.

1715 ■ Fulton County Historical and Genealogical Society
Parlin-Ingersoll Library

PO Box 583   Ph: (309)785-8095
Canton, IL 61520

Contact: Anita Thomas, Libn.

Desc: Subject: Fulton County history, genealogy, and literature. Holdings: 800 books; cemetery inscriptions; marriage records; scrapbooks; funeral home records; local newspapers on microfilm. Services: Copying; Library open to the public.

1716 ■ Fulton County Historical Society
Library

Box 115   Ph: (717)294-3369
McConnellsburg, PA 17233

Contact: Hazel Harr, Libn.

Desc: Subject: Local history and genealogy. Holdings: 300 books; microfilm collection; 100 volumes of Pennsylvania Archives. Services: Copying; Library open to the public on a limited schedule.

1717 ■ Fulton County Historical Society
Library

37 E. 375 N   Ph: (219)223-4436
Rochester, IN 46975

Contact: Shirley Willard, Pres.

Desc: Subject: Local history and genealogy, Elmo Lincoln (first movie Tarzan), Potawatomi Indians. Holdings: 4000 books; 20 file cabinets of clippings; 5 file cabinets of documents; 25 films; 25 rooms of archival materials. Services: Copying; Library open to the public for reference use only.

1718 ■ Galesburg Public Library
Special Collections

40 E. Simmons St.   Ph: (309)343-6118
Galesburg, IL 61401   Fax: (309)343-4877
URL: http://www.misslink.net/gplibrary/index.htm/

Contact: Marcia Heise, Spec.Coll.Libn.

Desc: Subject: History - Illinois, Knox County, Galesburg; genealogy; local authors including Carl Sandburg. Holdings: 7510 books and pamphlets; 325 manuscripts; 4310 photographs, slides, negatives; 120 maps; 30 oral history tapes; 15 phonograph records; 14 videotapes; 9 newspapers on microfilm. Services: Copying, SDI; collections open to the public with restrictions.

1719 ■ Gallatin County Historical Society
Library

R.R. 1   Ph: (618)272-7092
Ridgway, IL 62979

Contact: Lucille Lawler, Sec.

ogy. Holdings: Books; county censuses; cemetery records. Services: Library will answer written inquiries; open to the public by appointment.

1720 ■ Gannon University
Nash Library
University Archives

619 Sassafras St.   Ph: (814)871-7348
Erie, PA 16541   Fax: (814)871-5666
E-mail: sparks002@mail1.gannon.edu
URL: http://www.gannon.edu/LIBRARY/library.2htm

Contact: Robert W. Sparks, Archv.Supv.

Desc: Subject: Gannon University history; Erie area history, Erie Diocese history (parish, clergy, religious orders). Holdings: Vertical files; photographs; videotapes; audiocassettes; documents; publications; memorabilia. Services: Copying, Library open to the public.

1721 ■ Garden Grove Historical Society

12174 Euclid St.   Ph: (714)530-8871
PO Box 4297
Garden Grove, CA 92842-4297

Desc: Subject: Local history. Holdings: 200 books. Services: Library not open to the public (requests for information will be directed to curator).

1722 ■ Gardiner Public Library
Community Room

152 Water St.   Ph: (207)582-3312
Gardiner, ME 04345
URL: http://www.gpl.lib.me.us/hist.htm

Contact: Anne Estrada Davis, Lib.Dir.

Desc: Subject: Kennebec Valley history and genealogy. Holdings: Microfilm; vertical files. Services: Illinois; copying; Library open to the public with restrictions.

1723 ■ Garland County Historical Society
Archives

222 McMahan Dr.   Ph: (501)623-6766
Hot Springs, AR 71913   Fax: (501)623-6766
E-mail: bjmclane@prodigy.net

Contact: Bobbie J. McLane, Archv.Ed.

Desc: Subject: Local history, genealogy. Holdings: 150 books; 58 bound periodical volumes; 30 file drawers of subject files; 2000 local newspapers, 1887 to present; ledgers and account books; city and township maps; 10,000 photographs; city directories, 1887 to present; telephone directories, 1903 to present; Sentinel-Record, 1909-1949 (microfilm). Services: Copying, archives open to the public on a limited schedule or by appointment.

1724 ■ Geauga County Historical Society
Shanower Memorial Library

14653 E. Park St.   Ph: (216)834-4012
Box 153
Burton, OH 44021

Contact: Marlene F. Collins, Off.Mgr.

Desc: Subject: Local history. Holdings: 1000 books. Services: Library open to the public by appointment.

1725 ■ Genealogical Center Library

PO Box 71343
Marietta, GA 30007-1343

Contact: Barbara A. Geisert, Dir.

Desc: Subject: Genealogy. Holdings: 6000 regular print books; 9,000 regular print genealogical magazines. Services: Library lends books by mail to the public on fee basis.

1726 ■ Genealogical Forum of Oregon, Inc.
Library

2130 SW 5th Ave., Ste. 220   Ph: (503)227-2398
Portland, OR 97201-4934
URL: http://www.gfo.org

Desc: Subject: Genealogy, history, vital records, census. Holdings: 20,000 books; 5000 vertical files; unbound periodicals. Services: Copying; Library open to the public (fee for non-members).

1727 ■ Genealogical Society of Butler County
Poplar Bluff Library

PO Box 426
Poplar Bluff, MO 63901

Contact: Dewayne Beck Meir

Desc: Subject: Butler County, Southeast Missouri, multistate exchanges. Holdings: 400 books; family histories; city directories and phone books; newspapers, 1893 to present, on microfilm. Services: Copying; Library open to the public with restrictions.

1728 ■ Genealogical Society of Flemish Americans
Library

18740 13 Mile Rd.   Ph: (810)776-9579
Roseville, MI 48066
URL: http://members.xoom.com/GSFA

Contact: Jerry DeFauw, Lib.Comm.Chm.

Desc: Subject: Belgian - history, art, geography; Flemish and Dutch ancestry and genealogy. Holdings: 200 volumes. Services: Genealogical research; translation (Flemish, French, Latin); Library open to the public for reference use only.

1729 ■ Genealogical Society of Linn County, Iowa
Linn County Genealogical Research Center

813 1st Ave., S.E.   Ph: (319)369-0022
Cedar Rapids, IA 52406

Contact: Ron Baty, Pres.

Desc: Subject: Linn County, Iowa, genealogy. Holdings: 10,000 books; 1300 reels of microfilm of marriage, birth and death records, probates, land deeds for Linn County; federal and state census of Linn county. some microfilm for Benton County family history; complete 1790 Federal Census Index; 1925 Linn County census; 1860, 1870, 1880 Iowa Federal Census Index; 1880, 1900, and 1920 Soundex of Iowa; Old Newspapers of Linn County on microfilm. Services: Copying; Library open to the public.

1730 ■ Genealogical Society of New Jersey
Manuscript Collections

Special Collections and   Ph: (732)932-7510
   University Archives   Fax: (732)932-7012
Alexander Library
169 College Ave.
Rutgers University
New Brunswick, NJ
   08901-1163
E-mail: jriemer@rci.rutgers.edu
URL: http://www.libraries.rutgers.edu/rulib/spcol/
   spcol.htm

Contact: Ronald Becker, Hd., Spec.Coll

Desc: Subject: Genealogical records and information pertaining to New Jersey families. Services: Copying; collections open to the public for reference use only.

1731 ■ Genesee County History Department
Research Library

3 W. Main St.   Ph: (716)344-2550
Batavia, NY 14020

Contact: Susan L. Conklin, County Hist.

Desc: Subject: History - local, area (original Genesee County), state; western New York land records and genealogy files; famous people of the area. Holdings: 1460 books; 400 bound periodical volumes; 20 bound atlases; 512 journals; 50 reels of microfilm; 11 bound volumes of Genesee County Federal Census Records, 1810-1880 (indexed); daily indexed newspapers, 1823-1974; VF drawers of people, places, things, organizations, churches, schools, local history; historical society newsletters; genealogical queries and answers; 7000 photographs. Services: Copying; Library open to the public on a limited schedule.

1732 ■ Geneva Historical Society
James D. Luckett Memorial Archives

543 S. Main St.   Ph: (315)789-5151
Geneva, NY 14456   Fax: (315)789-0314
E-mail: genevhst@flare.net

Desc: Subject: Local history, architecture, genealogy. Holdings: 5500 books; 50,000 photograph images; 185 boxes and 20 VF drawers of clippings, manuscripts, pamphlets, documents, diaries; 39 reels of microfilm of 19th century Geneva newspapers; 27 reels of microfilm of federal and state census for Ontario County, NY, 1820-1925; 7 reels of microfilm of early Geneva church records; Sanborn Insurance maps of Geneva, 1867-1925 (on microfilm); local Catholic church records (on microfilm); village minutes, 1812-1920 (on microfilm); 64 cassette tapes of local oral history. Services: Copying; genealogical research; archives open to the public for reference use only.

1733 ■ George S. Patton, Jr. Historical Society
Library

3116 Thorn St. E.   Ph: (619)282-4201
San Diego, CA 92104-4618   Fax: (619)282-1920
E-mail: mike.province@sduniontrib.com
URL: http://members.aol.com/pattonsghq/homeghq.html

Contact: Charles M. Province, Pres.

Desc: Subject: George S. Patton, Jr., Third U.S. Army, military science and history. Holdings: 300 books; 500 bound periodical volumes; videotapes; films. Services: Copying; Library open to the public.

1734 ■ Georgia Historical Society
Library & Archives

501 Whitaker St.   Ph: (912)651-2128
Savannah, GA 31499   Fax: (912)651-2831
URL: http://www.georgiahistory.com

Contact: Frank T. Wheeler, Asst.Dir.

Desc: Subject: Savannah history, Georgia history, genealogy. Holdings: 20,000 books; 1385 feet of manuscripts and private papers; 216 feet of noncurrent Chatham County naturalization and courts records; 966 feet of noncurrent City of Savannah records; Savannah newspapers, 1763 to present, on microfilm; maps of Savannah, Georgia, U.S.; collection of photographs and prints of Savannah and Georgia; federal censuses of Georgia, 1820-1860, on microfilm. Services: Copying; Library open to the public.

1735 ■ Georgia (State) Department of Archives and History
Reference Services

330 Capitol Ave., S.E.   Ph: (404)656-2350
Atlanta, GA 30334   Fax: (404)651-9270
URL: http://www.sos.state.ga.us/archives

Contact: Brenda S. Banks, Dir., Ref.Preservation

Desc: Subject: Georgia, southeastern U.S., genealogy. Holdings: 20,000 volumes; 2000 reels of microfilm of

newspapers; 10,500 maps; 2000 manuscript volumes; 20,000 prints and photographs. Services: Copying; services open to the public.

1736 ■ German Genealogical Society of America
Library

PO Box 517   Ph: (909)593-0509
La Verne, CA 91750-0517
URL: http://feefhs.org

Desc: Subject: German genealogy and ethnic history. Holdings: 3000 volumes; manuscripts; maps; foreign telephone directories; 4,500 family and surname files. Services: Translation; research; Library open to the public and by appointment.

1737 ■ German Historical Institute
Library

1607 New Hampshire Ave., NW   Ph: (202)387-3355
Washington, DC 20009   Fax: (202)483-3430
E-mail: library@ghi-dc.org
URL: http://www.ghi-dc.org

Contact: Monika Hein

Desc: Subject: German history, immigration, political history, emigration, GermanAmerican relations. Holdings: 22,000 books; 2000 bound periodical volumes; reels of microfilm; microfiche; CD-ROMs. Services: Copying; Library open to the public.

1738 ■ Germantown Friends Meeting
Friends Free Library

5418 Germantown Ave.   Ph: (215)951-2355
Philadelphia, PA 19144   Fax: (215)951-2697

Contact: Helen M. Eigabroadt, Dir.

Desc: Holdings: 58,000 books. Services: Interlibrary loan; copying; Library open to the public.

1739 ■ Germantown Historical Society
Library and Archives

5501 Germantown Ave.   Ph: (215)844-0514
Philadelphia, PA 19144-2291   Fax: (215)844-2831
E-mail: ghs@libertynet.org

Contact: Cynthia Gosling, Actg.Dir.

Desc: Subject: History of Germantown, Mt. Airy, Chestnut Hill, and Wissahickon sections of Philadelphia. Holdings: 3200 books; scrapbooks; newspapers published in Germantown, 1830 to present; deeds and briefs of title; local genealogies. Services: Copying; Library and genealogical research available to the public on fee basis.

1740 ■ Glengarry Genealogical Society
Alex W. Fraser Library

RR 1   Ph: (613)347-2363
20342 Arlington Rd.
Lancaster, ON, Canada K0C 1N0
E-mail: jars@glen-net.ca

Contact: Rhonda Ross

Desc: Subject: Genealogy, church records, history, gravestone inscriptions. Holdings: 1000 volumes; 59 reels of microfilm of church records of St. Raphael's, St. Andrew's PresbyterianUnited (Williamstown), and St. Andrew's West Catholic; Glengarry News; Fr. Ewan's MacDonald papers; microfiche of birth, marriage, death records (Scotland); 75 manuscripts on gravestones; 75 binders of clippings of birth, marriage, death records; 22 binders of local church records; 80 binders of family genealogies; 13 Ontario Historical County Atlases.

1741 ■ Glenview Area Historical Society
Hibbard Library

1121 Waukegan Rd.   Ph: (847)724-2235
Glenview, IL 60025

Desc: Subject: Area history - families, buildings, town functions, service clubs, businesses. Holdings: Obituaries; bicentennial collection; photographs; property deeds for early settlers; Northfield township record books, 1850-1910; Services: Copying; Library open to the public by appointment.

1742 ■ Glenville State College
Robert F. Kidd Library
West Virginia Collection

100 High St.   Ph: (304)462-4109
Glenville, WV 26351   Fax: (304)462-4049
URL: http://www.glenville.wvnet.edu/other/rfkidd.htm

Contact: Richard Tubesing, Dir.

Desc: Subject: West Virginia history and genealogy.

1743 ■ Gloucester County Historical Society
Library

17 Hunter St.   Ph: (609)845-4771
Woodbury, NJ 08096-4605   Fax: (609)845-0131
E-mail: gchs@citnet.com
URL: http://www.rootsweb.com/njglouce/gchs/

Contact: Edith E. Hoelle, Lib.Dir.

Desc: Subject: Genealogy, New Jersey and U.S. history. Holdings: 7800 books; 2230 reels of microfilm of documents; 114 bound volumes of newspapers; 55 VF drawers of files of genealogy and history, photographs, typescripts, clippings. Services: Copying; Library open to the public.

1744 ■ Godfrey Memorial Library

134 Newfield St.   Ph: (860)346-4375
Middletown, CT 06457   Fax: (860)347-9874
E-mail: godfrey.@connix.com
URL: http://www.godfrey.org

Contact: Nancy J. Doane, Dir.

Desc: Subject: Genealogy, local history, biography. Holdings: 16,000 books. Services: Copying; genealogical research; Library open to the public.

1745 ■ Golden and District Historical Society
Archives

Box 992   Ph: (250)344-5169
Golden, BC, Canada V0A 1H0   Fax: (250)344-5169
E-mail: colgino@rockies.net

Contact: Colleen Palumbo, Musm.Cur.

Desc: Subject: Local history. Holdings: Golden Star newspapers; 4 reels of microfilm of Donald Truth newspaper; tax assessment rolls; early police diaries. Services: Archives open to the public with restrictions.

1746 ■ Goodhue County Historical Society
Library and Archives

1166 Oak St.   Ph: (651)388-6024
Red Wing, MN 55066   Fax: (651)388-3577
E-mail: research@goodhistory.org
URL: http://www.goodhistory.org

Contact: Heather Craig, Libn.Archv.

Desc: Subject: Goodhue County, local and state history. Holdings: 2100 books; 10,000 clippings and manuscripts; 15,000 photographs; state census records, 1865-1905 (microfilm); school census, 1917 to present; record books for local area organizations and businesses. Services: Copying and photo reproduction; Library open to the public.

1747 ▪ Goshen Historical Society
Library
c/o Terry Hall, Pres.   Ph: (860)491-8612
184 Wellsford Dr.
Goshen, CT 06756

Contact: Hazel Wadhams, Cur.

Desc: Subject: Local history, genealogy. Holdings: 1000 books. Services: Genealogical research; library open to the public on a limited schedule and by appointment.

1748 ▪ Grand Rapids Public Library
Local History Collection
60 Library Plaza, N.E.   Ph: (616)456-3640
Grand Rapids, MI 49503   Fax: (616)456-4577
URL: http://www.grapids.lib.mi.us

Contact: Robert E. Raz

Desc: Subject: Grand Rapids, Michigan, and Old Northwest territory history, genealogy. Holdings: 40,000 books. Services: Copying; collection open to the public for reference use only.

1749 ▪ Grand Traverse Pioneer & Historical
Society
Library
Box 1108
Traverse City, MI 49684

Contact: Steve Harold, Archv.

Desc: Subject: History - homesteading, transportation, Cherry Festival; local family history; local lumbering; historical buildings. Holdings: 100 books, 15 diaries, 2000 photographs; 300 biographies; 1500 negatives; 1500 clippings; 60 oral history tapes; 20 maps. Services: Copying; center open to the public.

1750 ▪ Grant County Historical Society
Library
Hwy. 79E   Ph: (218)685-4864
PO Box 1002
Elbow Lake, MN 56531

Contact: Patricia Benson, Cur.

Desc: Subject: Local and state history, archeology, genealogy. Holdings: 1000 books; Grant County newspapers on microfilm; biographies; 100 tape recordings of local people and events; census records on microfilm, 1875-1920. Services: Copying; Library open to the public.

1751 ▪ Great Falls Genealogy Society
Library
1400 1st Ave., N., Rm. 30   Ph: (406)727-3922
Great Falls, MT 59401-3299
E-mail: eheisel@mcn.net

Contact: Barbara Gillis, Hd.Libn.

Desc: Subject: Family and local history, probates. Holdings: 3600 books; Great Falls, MT obituary file, late 1800s to present; Cascade County marriage file, 1887-1910; birth records (early 1900s); cemetery and mausoleum records. Services: Library open to the public for reference use only.

1752 ▪ Great Lakes Historical Society
Clarence Metcalf Research Library
480 Main St.   Ph: (216)967-3467
PO Box 435   Fax: (216)967-1519
Vermilion, OH 44089
E-mail: GHLS1@aol.com

Contact: William D. Carle, III

Desc: Subject: Great Lakes - history, shipbuilding, shipwrecks, shipping records, battle of Lake Erie in 1812, lighthouses, lifesaving service, ship logbooks. Holdings: 2500 books; 10,000 photographs; records of shipping firms; logbooks. Services: Library open to members only.

1753 ▪ Greater Loveland Historical Society
Museum
C. Roger Nisbet Library
201 Riverside Dr.   Ph: (513)683-5692
Loveland, OH 45140   Fax: (513)683-5692

Contact: Georgia Whitacre, Libn.

Desc: Subject: Genealogy, Civil War, local history, Loveland High School. Holdings: 1000 books; 100 bound periodical volumes; 1000 archival materials; 1000 photographs. Services: Interlibrary loan; copying; Library open to the public.

1754 ▪ Greater West Bloomfield Historical
Society
Museum Library
3951 Orchard Lake Rd.   Ph: (248)682-2279
PO Box 240514
Orchard Lake, MI 48324

Contact: Thad Radzilowski, Pres.

Desc: Subject: Local history - West Bloomfield Township, Orchard Lake, Apple Island; Chief Pontiac. Holdings: 150 books; 30 linear feet of documents; 70 AV programs; 100 manuscripts. Services: Library open to the public with restrictions.

1755 ▪ Greeley County Historical Society
Library
PO Box 231   Ph: (316)376-4996
Tribune, KS 67879

Contact: Nadine Cheney, Cur.

Desc: Subject: Kansas history, genealogy, agriculture, poetry. Holdings: 500 books, maps, newspapers, telephone directories, soldiers enrollments, and obituaries. Services: Copying; Library open to the public.

1756 ▪ Greeley Municipal Archives
Library
919 7th St.   Ph: (970)350-9220
Greeley, CO 80631-3909   Fax: (970)350-9475

Contact: Peggy A. Ford

Desc: Subject: Greeley and Weld County history, biographies of early pioneers, Colorado history. Holdings: 3000 books; 100 bound periodical volumes; Nunn newspaper for 29 years on microfilm; 39 scrapbooks of clippings; 45 VF drawers of manuscripts, clippings, maps, photographs. Services: Copying; Library open to the public with restrictions.

1757 ▪ Greenbrier Historical Society
Archives
301 W. Washington St.   Ph: (304)645-3398
Lewisburg, WV 24901   Fax: (304)645-5201
E-mail: ghs@access.mountain.net
URL: http://access.mountain.net/ghs/ghs.html

Contact: James E. Talbert, Archv.

Desc: Subject: History of Greenbrier Valley area - people, places, events. Holdings: 1373 titles; 23 periodicals; 10 VF drawers of manuscripts, clippings, pamphlets; 2VF drawer of pictures; facsimiles of Harrison-Handley Map of Greenbrier County (1887); Map of Lewisburg (1880); Bicentennial Map of Greenbrier County (1978); annual journals remaining in print for the years 1969, 1973, 1976-1978, 1980-1997; History of Greenbrier County (1986). Services: Archives open to the public on a limited schedule and on a fee basis.

1758 ▪ Greene County Historical Society
Library and Museum
Box 127   Ph: (724)627-3204
Waynesburg, PA 15370   Fax: (724)627-3204
URL: http://www.greenepa.net/museum/

Desc: Subject: Greene County and Western Pennsylvania history; Union and Confederate armies. Holdings: 1500 books. Services: Copying; Library open to the public for reference use only on fee basis and on limited schedule by appointment.

1759 ▪ Greene County Historical Society
Vedder Memorial Library
R.D. 1, Box 10A   Ph: (518)731-1033
Coxsackie, NY 12051

Contact: Raymond Beecher, Libn.

Desc: Subject: Greene County, The Catskills, mid-Hudson River Valley region. Holdings: 1530 manuscript volumes; 29 VF drawers and 175 boxes of manuscripts; county newspapers, 1792 to present; pictorial file. Services: Library open to the public on a limited schedule.

1760 ▪ Greene County Public Library
Greene County Room
76 E. Market St.   Ph: (937)376-4952
Box 520   Fax: (937)372-4673
Xenia, OH 45385
E-mail: gcr@gcpl.lib.oh.us
URL: http://www.gcpl.lib.oh.us

Contact: Deanna Ulvestad, Coord., Local Hist.

Desc: Subject: Genealogy, with emphasis on Ohio and mid-Atlantic states; local history. Holdings: 6600 books; 115 bound periodical volumes; 3000 reels of microfilm; 80 cassette tapes of local history interviews. Services: Copying; room open to the public.

1761 ▪ Greenfield Community College
Pioneer Valley Resource Center
One College Dr.   Ph: (413)775-1831
Greenfield, MA 01301
E-mail: cletson@gcc.mass.edu

Contact: Carol G. Letson, Dir.

Desc: Subject: Pioneer Valley of Western Massachusetts. Holdings: 2840 books; 429 nonprint materials. Services: Interlibrary loan; copying; center open to the public.

1762 ▪ Greenwich Library
Oral History Project
101 W. Putnam Ave.   Ph: (203)622-7945
Greenwich, CT 06830   Fax: (203)622-7939
URL: http://www.greenwich.lib.ct.us/friends/
     oralhist.htm

Contact: Richard Hart, Ref.Libn.

Desc: Subject: Local history. Holdings: 950 oral history cassettes; 355 microfiche of transcriptions. Services: Interlibrary loan (limited); copying; project open to the public with restrictions.

1763 ▪ Greenwood County Historical Society
Library
120 W. 4th St.   Ph: (316)583-6682
Eureka, KS 67045

Contact: Jeff Hokanson, Co-Hd.

Desc: Subject: Kansas - Greenwood County and Eureka town history and genealogy. Holdings: Greenwood County newspapers, from 1868; Greenwood County census records on microfilm (1860-1925); Greenwood county cemetery records; obituary file (1920s to present); family histories. Services: Copying; Library open to the public.

**1764 ▪ Grout Museum of History and Science
Genealogy, Area History Archives and
Reference Library**
503 South St.   Ph: (319)234-6357
Waterloo, IA 50701   Fax: (319)236-0500

Contact: Janice M. Taylor, Archv.

Desc: Subject: Genealogy, area histories. Holdings: 1800
books; 13,000 clippings; 1500 archival materials; 3000
photographs. Services: Copying; Library open to the public for reference use only.

**1765 ▪ Guale Historical Society
Bryan-Lang Historical Library**
PO Box 725   Ph: (912)576-5601
Woodbine, GA 31569

Contact: John H. Christian, Libn.

Desc: Subject: History, genealogy, Camden County,
coastal Georgia. Holdings: 2000 books; 100 documents;
300 nonbook items. Services: Copying; Library open to
the public.

**1766 ▪ Guysborough Historical Society
Archives**
PO Box 232   Ph: (902)533-4008
Guysborough, NS, Canada B0H
   1N0

Contact: Kim Avery, Cur.

Desc: Subject: Local history, genealogy, historical research.
Holdings: Books; reports. Services: Copying; Library open
to members only.

**1767 ▪ Gwinnett Historical Society
Archives**
PO Box 261   Ph: (770)822-5174
Lawrenceville, GA 30046
E-mail: gwhissoc@bellsouth.net
URL: http://www.gwinnetths.org

Desc: Subject: Gwinnett County, Georgia history and
genealogy. Holdings: Papers; records; family histories; ancestor files. Services: Interlibrary loan; copying; Library
open to the public.

**1768 ▪ Hackettstown Historical Society
Museum**
106 Church St.   Ph: (908)852-8797
Hackettstown, NJ 07840

Contact: Helen G. Montfort, Cur.

Desc: Subject: Local history and genealogy. Holdings: 540
books; 700 newspapers, 1874-1975; 325 documents; 96
genealogies; 30 volumes of Warren County cemetery records; 35 oral histories; 2 volumes of historical buildings
in Hackettstown; 5 histories of Hackettstown by local
historians; 50 scrapbooks and 25 volumes of photographs
of historical materials; 158 slides; 10 maps; 12 cuneiform
tablets; 17 quilts, 1870-1930; 15,500 archival materials;
18 VF drawers. Services: Copying; museum open to the
public for reference use only.

**1769 ▪ Hackley Public Library
Special Collections**
316 W. Webster Ave.   Ph: (616)722-7276
Muskegon, MI 49440   Fax: (616)726-5567
E-mail: hplref@muskegon.k12.mi.us
URL: http://www.muskegon.k12.mi.us/hackley/
   library.htm

Contact: Martha Ferriby, Dir.

Desc: Subject: General interest. Holdings: 190,000 books;
15,000 bound periodical volumes. Services: Library open
to the public.

**1770 ▪ Halifax Historical Society, Inc.
Library**
252 S. Beach St.   Ph: (904)255-6976
Daytona Beach, FL 32114-4407   Fax: (904)255-3765

Contact: Cheryl Atwell, Adm.

Desc: Subject: Florida history, automobiles, history, educational institutions. Holdings: 1000 books; 170 bound
periodical volumes; 44 VF drawers of newspaper clippings, 10,000 photographs, scrapbooks, postcards, maps,
slides. Services: Copying; photo reproduction; Library
open to the public for reference use only by appointment.

**1771 ▪ Hall County Museum
Stuhr Museum
Reynolds Research Center**
3133 W. Hwy. 34   Ph: (308)385-5316
Grand Island, NE 68801   Fax: (308)385-5028

Contact: Russ Czaplewski, Hist.

Desc: Subject: Local and state history; building and community development, 1850-1910; German and Danish
ethnic groups. Holdings: 6000 books; U.S. federal census
records, 1860-1910; Nebraska state census records, 1885;
Grand Island newspaper, 1870-1925; 200 cubic feet and
250 boxes of documents, diaries, letters, manuscripts, and
business ledgers; 22,000 photographs; 28,000 glass plates;
land records on microfilm. Services: Copying; center open
to the public.

**1772 ▪ Hamilton City Library
Bluestem Genealogical Society Collection**
21 E. Main   Ph: (316)678-3646
Hamilton, KS 66853
E-mail: hlibrary@cadvantage.com

Contact: Leta Harrell

Desc: Subject: Genealogy - Greenwood County, Kansas,
United States. Holdings: 100 books; 100 bound periodical
volumes; 48 reels of microfilm. Services: Interlibrary loan;
Library open to the public with restrictions.

**1773 ▪ Hammond Public Library
Calumet Room**
564 State St.   Ph: (219)931-5100
Hammond, IN 46320   Fax: (219)931-3474
URL: http://www.hammond.lib.in.us

Contact: Suzanne Long, Libn.

Desc: Subject: History of Hammond and the Calumet
Region. Holdings: 750 books; 18 VF drawers of pamphlets and clippings; 96 VF drawers of newspaper negatives; 45 personal scrapbooks; 180 tapes (Historical Society programs, community events, personal interviews); 6
video cassettes of interviews. Services: Interlibrary loan;
copying; room open to the public with restrictions, for
reference use only, and on a limited schedule.

**1774 ▪ Hampton Historical Society
Tuck Memorial Museum
Library**
Meeting House Green   Ph: (603)929-0781
PO Box 1601
Hampton, NH 03843
URL: http://www.nh.ultranet.com/hhshome.htm

Contact: Susanne Falzone, Pres.

Desc: Subject: History, biography and autobiography, genealogy. Holdings: 300 volumes; newspapers; photographs of Hampton area; scrapbooks; New Hampshire
Marine Memorial Album; Edward Tuck Memorial Album; oil paintings of old Hampton scenes. Services: Library open to the public by appointment.

1775 ▪ Hancock Historical Museum & Archives
422 W. Sandusky St.   Ph: (419)423-4433
Findlay, OH 45840

Contact: Doramae O'Kelley, Musm.Dir.

Desc: Subject: Hancock County history, family history.
Holdings: 1500 books; 360 cubic feet of archival material;
130 reels of microfilm; 12,000 photographic images. Services: Copying; Library open to the public on a limited
schedule.

**1776 ▪ Handley Regional Library
Archives**
100 W. Piccadilly St.   Ph: (540)662-9041
PO Box 58   Fax: (540)722-4769
Winchester, VA 22604
E-mail: handley@shentel.net
URL: http://www.shentel.net/handley-library/
   archives.html

Contact: Rebecca Ebert, Archv.Libn.

Desc: Subject: Lower Shenandoah Valley - people, culture,
history, genealogy; Frederick Douglass; slavery. Holdings:
Books; personal papers; deeds; church records; cemetery
records; family histories; diaries; 500 lin. ft. of manuscripts
and ephemera; 100 maps; 400 photographs; 100 oral
history tapes; account books. Services: Interlibrary loan;
Library open to the public.

**1777 ▪ Har Zion Temple
Ida and Matthew Rudofker Library**
Hagys Ford & Hollow Rds.   Ph: (610)627-5000
Penn Valley, PA 19072

Desc: Subject: Judaica. Holdings: 10,000 books. Services:
Copying (limited); SDI; Library open to members of
congregation, affiliated organizations, and the community.

**1778 ▪ Harper County Genealogical Society
Library**
c/o Harper Public Library
1000 Oak St.
Harper, KS 67058

Contact: Gail Bellar, Pres.Geneal.Soc.

Desc: Subject: Harper County (Kansas) history; Kansas
history; genealogy. Holdings: 400 books; 1 microfiche;
11 reels of microfilm. Services: Library open to the public
for reference use only.

**1779 ▪ Harrisonburg-Rockingham Historical
Society
Library**
382 High St.   Ph: (540)879-2616
Dayton, VA 22821   Fax: (540)879-2616
E-mail: heritag1@shentil.net

Contact: Faye A. Witters, Adm.

Desc: Subject: History and genealogy of Rockingham
County and Harrisonburg. Holdings: 600 books; 4 VF
drawers of genealogical materials; 6 VF drawers of local
newspaper obituaries; 3 VF drawers of miscellany. Services: Copying; Library open to the public for reference
use only.

**1780 ▪ Harrodsburg Historical Society
Morgan Row Museum and Research Center**
PO Box 316   Ph: (606)734-5985
Harrodsburg, KY 40330

Contact: Mildred Ballard

Desc: Subject: Mercer County and Kentucky history; family and land history. Holdings: 1836 books; 17 bound
periodical volumes; 52 bound newspapers; archives; microfiche; microfilm. Services: Library open to the public.

1781 ■ Hartshorn Family Association Clearinghouse
1204 4th St. Dr., SE Ph: (828)464-4981
Conover, NC 28613 Fax: (828)466-0025
E-mail: derick@twave.net
URL: http://homepages.rootsweb.com/hartshrn/

Contact: Derick S. Hartshorn, Pres.

Desc: Subject: Genealogy. Holdings: 624 books; vital records. Services: Library open to the public by appointment.

1782 ■ Haskell County Historical Society
Fairgrounds Ph: (316)675-8344
PO Box 101
Sublette, KS 67877

Contact: Janice McClure, Cur.

Desc: Subject: Local history. Holdings: 59 reels of microfilm; 60 yearbooks. Services: Library open to the public for reference use only.

1783 ■ Haverford Township Historical Society Library
Box 825 Ph: (610)649-4590
Havertown, PA 19083

Contact: Mary Courtney, Cur.

Desc: Subject: History of Haverford Township, Delaware County, and Pennsylvania. Holdings: Glass photoplates. Services: Library open to the public by appointment.

1784 ■ Haverhill Public Library Special Collections Division
99 Main St. Ph: (978)373-1586
Haverhill, MA 01830-5092 Fax: (508)373-8466
URL: http://www.haverhill.com/library

Contact: John Courtney, Dir.

Desc: Subject: Genealogy and local history, John Greenleaf Whittier, art, early children's books. Holdings: 24,000 books; 800 bound periodical volumes; 1000 pamphlets; 4000 manuscripts; 400 broadsides; 250 maps; 1000 reels of microfilm; city documents in manuscript; 15,000 Haverhill photographs; 375 volumes of bound Haverhill newspapers; 200 volumes of clippings; genealogical microfiche. Services: Interlibrary loan; copying; division open to the public.

1785 ■ Hawaiian Historical Society Library
560 Kawaiahao St. Ph: (808)537-6271
Honolulu, HI 96813 Fax: (808)537-6271
E-mail: bcdunn@lava.net
URL: http://www.hawaiianhistory.org

Contact: Barbara E. Dunn, Adm.Dir. & Libn.

Desc: Subject: Pacific and round the world voyages, history of Hawaiian Islands and Polynesia, local biography. Holdings: 12,000 volumes; 2808 pamphlets; 5 VF drawers of manuscripts; 10 VF drawers of clippings; 5 VF drawers of photographs; early newspapers on microfilm; 3 VF drawers of maps; 1 VF drawer of broadsides; 50 photograph albums and scrapbooks. Services: Copying; Library open to the public, but it is primarily for researchers.

1786 ■ Hayner Public Library Illinois Room
401 State St. Ph: (618)462-0651
Alton, IL 62002 Fax: (618)462-0665
URL: http://www.altonweb.com/hayner

Contact: Joyce Reid, Dir.

Desc: Subject: Illinois and Madison County history; Abraham Lincoln, Elijah P. Lovejoy, genealogy, Mississippi River, Robert Wadlow ("The Alton Giant"), local authors. Services: Room open to the public with restrictions.

1787 ■ Heart of America Genealogical Society & Library, Inc.
Kansas City Public Library Ph: (816)701-3445
311 E. 12th St., 3rd. Fl. Fax: (816)421-7484
Kansas City, MO 64106

Contact: C. Novak, Libn.

Desc: Subject: Genealogy. Holdings: 9000 books; 1800 bound periodical volumes; 2500 family histories and genealogies; ancestor charts. Services: Copying; Library open to the public.

1788 ■ Held-Poage Memorial Home & Research Library
603 W. Perkins St. Ph: (707)462-6969
Ukiah, CA 95482-4726

Contact: Lila J. Lee, Dir.Libn.

Desc: Subject: History - Mendocino County, California, U.S., Civil War; Pomo and other Indians. Holdings: 5000 books; 16,000 negatives; photographs; maps; bound county records; clippings; genealogies. Services: Interlibrary loan; copying; Library open to the public on a limited schedule for reference use only, by appointment.

1789 ■ Hennepin History Museum Archives
2303 3rd Ave., S. Ph: (612)870-1329
Minneapolis, MN 55404 Fax: (612)870-1320
E-mail: hhmuseum@mtn.org
URL: http://www.mtn.org/hhmuseum/

Contact: Jack Kabrud, Cur.

Desc: Subject: Local history, lumber and milling industries, genealogy, house history, transportation. Holdings: 2000 books; 551 bound periodical volumes; 5000 photographs; 75 VF drawers of clippings and ephemera; 150 boxes and 20 VF drawers of archives, maps, atlases; 19 volumes of Sanborn Insurance Maps. Services: Copying; archives open to the public for reference use only.

1790 ■ Henry County Historical Society Museum & Library
606 S. 14th St. Ph: (765)529-4028
New Castle, IN 47362
E-mail: hchis@kiva.net

Contact: Joan Paul, Musm. & Lib.Dir.

Desc: Subject: Henry County and Indiana history. Holdings: Manuscripts; letters; photographs; paintings; scrapbooks; county histories; atlases. Services: Library open to the public on a limited schedule.

1791 ■ Heraldry Society of Canada Heraldic Reference Library
PO Box 8128, Sta. B Ph: (613)731-0867
Ottawa, ON, Canada K1P 5P9

Contact: Howard W. Keck

Desc: Subject: Heraldry, coats of arms. Holdings: 500 books; archival material. Services: Interlibrary loan; Library open to the public with restrictions.

1792 ■ Heritage Commission Corporation Library
147 W. Mound St. Ph: (513)462-7277
PO Box 457
South Charleston, OH 45368

Contact: Janice Brubaker, Sec.

Desc: Subject: Local history, genealogy, D.T&I Railroad. Holdings: 100 books; 25 feet of archival material. Services: Interlibrary loan; Library open to the public.

1793 ■ Heritage Museum Association, Inc. Library
115 Westview Ave. Ph: (850)678-2615
PO Box 488 Fax: (850)678-2615
Valparaiso, FL 32580

Contact: Reginald Adams, Libn.

Desc: Subject: Local and Florida history, Civil War, antiques, folk crafts, genealogy. Holdings: 2500 volumes; 125 bound periodical volumes; 58 boxes of letters, clippings, brochures; 49 linear feet of newspapers; 70 oral history tapes; 20 folders of maps. Services: Library open to the public.

1794 ■ Heritage Presbyterian Church Library
140 Airport Rd. Ph: (302)328-3800
New Castle, DE 19720
URL: http://www.dca.net/heritage

Desc: Subject: Religion, Bible, biography, church history. Holdings: 2000 books. Services: Interlibrary loan; Library open to the public.

1795 ■ Heritage Village Pinellas County Historical Museum Library & Archives
11909 125th St., N. Ph: (813)582-2123
Largo, FL 33774 Fax: (813)582-2455
URL: http://www.co.pinellas.fl.us/bcc/heritag.htm

Contact: Donald J. Ivey, Cur. of Coll.

Desc: Subject: History - Florida, Pinellas County; genealogy; historic conservation and preservation; antiques & collectibles. Holdings: 2500 books; 700 periodical volumes; 200 AV programs; 200 county-wide directories; 5400 photographs; 1000 maps; 200 reels of microfilm of newspapers, census returns, microfiche, and other materials. Services: Copying; Library open to the public.

1796 ■ Herkimer County Historical Society Library
A. Walter Ste.r Memorial Bldg. Ph: (315)866-6413
400 Main St.
Herkimer, NY 13350

Contact: Susan R. Perkins, Adm.Dir.

Desc: Subject: Local history, genealogy. Holdings: 4000 volumes. Services: Library open to the public.

1797 ■ Herrick District Library Genealogy Collection
300 River Ave. Ph: (616)355-1400
Holland, MI 49423 Fax: (616)355-1426
E-mail: holrh@lakeland.lib.mi.us
URL: http://www.macatawa.org/herrick/

Desc: Subject: Holland and Michigan genealogy. Holdings: 3300 books; microfiche; microfilm; 20 CD-ROM.

1798 ■ Highland County Historical Society Library
151 E. Main St. Ph: (513)393-3392
Hilliard, OH 45133

Contact: Jean Wallis, Libn.

Desc: Subject: Local history, genealogy, crusade movement, C.S. Bell Company, Caspar Collins. Holdings: 300 books; archival material; photographs. Services: Library open to the public by appointment.

1799 ■ Highland Park Historical Society Library
Box 56 Ph: (847)432-7090
326 Central Ave. Fax: (847)432-7307
Highland Park, IL 60035

E-mail: hphistoricalsociety@worldnet.att.net
URL: http://www.highlandpark.org/histsoc

Contact: Ellingsworth Mills II, Managing Dir.

Desc: Subject: Local history. Holdings: 500 books; 1000 photographs; 2500 35mm slides. Services: Library open to the public by appointment.

1800 ▪ Historic Northampton
Historical Collection

46 Bridge St.   Ph: (413)584-6011
Northampton, MA 01060   Fax: (413)584-7956
E-mail: hstnhamp@Javanet.com
URL: http://www.virtual-valley.com/histnhamp

Contact: Kerry Buckley, Exec.Dir.

Desc: Subject: Local history and biography. Holdings: Documents; letters; diaries; manuscripts; account books; ephemera; photographs; clippings; oral histories, textiles, paintings, furniture. Services: Copying.

1801 ▪ Historic Pensacola Preservation Board
Library

120 Church St.   Ph: (850)595-5985
Pensacola, FL 32501   Fax: (850)595-5989
E-mail: penshpb@mail.dos.state.fl.us
URL: http://www.dos.state.fl.us/dhr/pensacola

Contact: John Daniels, Dir.

Desc: Subject: Historic preservation, Florida and regional history, museum administration, architectural history, antiques. Holdings: 1800 books; 3 scrapbooks; 30 oral history tapes; slide library. Services: Library open to the public for reference use only by written request. Maintained by Florida State Department of State - Division of Historical Resources.

1802 ▪ Historic Preservation Association of
Bourbon County
Old Fort Genealogical Society
Resource Library

117 S. Main St.   Ph: (316)223-6423
Fort Scott, KS 66701

Contact: Don Miller, Pres.

Desc: Subject: Bourbon County history. Holdings: Books; artifacts; photographs. Services: Museum open to public.

1803 ▪ Historical Association of Southern
Florida
Charlton W. Tebeau Library of Florida History

101 W. Flagler St.   Ph: (305)375-1492
Miami, FL 33130   Fax: (305)372-6313
E-mail: archives@historical-museum.org
URL: http://www.historical-museum.org

Contact: Rebecca A. Smith, Cur., Res.Mtls.

Desc: Subject: Florida history and folk life, especially South Florida; Caribbean; Dade County history; Bahamas. Holdings: 6000 books; 300 bound periodical volumes; 1600 maps; 146 reels of microfilm; 40 VF drawers of pamphlets and clippings; 1 million photographs; 400 linear feet of archival materials and manuscripts; 200 oral history tapes and transcripts; 300 sets of architectural drawings. Services: Copying; Library open to the public for research use only.

1804 ▪ Historical and Genealogical Society of
Indiana County
Library and Archives

200 S. 6th St.   Ph: (724)463-9600
Indiana, PA 15701-2999   Fax: (724)463-9899
E-mail: clarkhs@microserve.net

Desc: Subject: Local history, Western Pennsylvania history and genealogy, Pennsylvania regimental histories, historic

preservation, antiques. Holdings: 10,000 books; 150 volumes of newspapers on microfilm; manuscripts; surname vertical files of Indiana County birth and marriage announcements and obituaries; selected federal census schedules on microfilm. Services: Copying; Library open to the public during specified hours.

1805 ▪ Historical and Genealogical Society of
Somerset County
County Historical Library and Research Center

Somerset Historical Center   Ph: (814)445-6077
10649 Somerset Pike   Fax: (814)443-6621
Somerset, PA 15501

Contact: Susan Seese, Res. Aid

Desc: Subject: Somerset County history, genealogy, decorative arts, agricultural history. Holdings: 3000 books; 15 file drawers of source materials on local history and genealogy; films of documents and source material; 500 reels of microfilm. Services: Copying; microfilm printing; Library open to the public.

1806 ▪ Historical Society of Alpine County
Alpine County Museum
Library

PO Box 517   Ph: (530)694-2317
Markleeville, CA 96120   Fax: (530)694-2317

Contact: Richard C. Edwards, Dir.

Desc: Subject: Alpine County history. Holdings: 400 books; 500 documents; photographs; manuscripts. Services: Copying (limited); research facility open to the public by appointment.

1807 ▪ Historical Society of Berks County
Library

940 Centre Ave.   Ph: (610)375-4375
Reading, PA 19601   Fax: (610)375-4376
URL: http://www.berksweb.com/histsoc

Contact: Barbara Gill, Dir.

Desc: Subject: Local history, genealogy, German Americans in Pennsylvania. Holdings: 9000 books; 400 bound periodical volumes; 504 maps; 500 reels of microfilm; documents; letters; diaries; muster rolls. Services: Copying; Library open to the public.

1808 ▪ Historical Society of Carroll County
Research Library

210 E. Main St.   Ph: (410)848-6494
Westminster, MD 21157   Fax: (410)848-3596
E-mail: hscc@carr.org
URL: http://www.carr.org/hscc

Contact: Jay A. Graybeal, Dir.

Desc: Subject: Family and local history. Holdings: 2500 books; 100 bound periodical volumes; 100 AV programs; 10,000 manuscripts; 25 nonbook items. Services: Copying (limited); Library open to the public on a fee basis. Appointments are required for Manuscript Room.

1809 ▪ Historical Society of the Cocalico
Valley
Museum and Library

249 W. Main St.   Ph: (717)733-1616
Box 193
Ephrata, PA 17522

Contact: Cynthia Marquet, Libn.

Desc: Subject: Local history, genealogy, Pennsylvania German culture and art. Holdings: 1600 books; 5300 manuscripts and typescripts; 8550 photographs; 240 tapes and reels of microfilm. Services: Copying; genealogical research; Library open to the public.

1810 ▪ Historical Society of Dauphin County
John HarrisSimon Cameron Mansion
Alexander Family History Library

219 S. Front St.   Ph: (717)233-3462
Harrisburg, PA 17104   Fax: (717)233-6059
URL: http://www.visithhc.com/harrismn.html

Contact: Warren W. Wirebach, Libn.

Desc: Subject: Local history and genealogy. Holdings: 1000 books; 2000 reports; 150 bound periodical volumes; 500 manuscripts; 500 patents. Services: copying; Library open to the public with restrictions.

1811 ▪ Historical Society of Delaware
Library

505 Market St. Mall   Ph: (302)655-7161
Wilmington, DE 19801   Fax: (302)655-7844
E-mail: hsd@dca.net
URL: http://www.hsd.org

Contact: Barbara E. Benson

Desc: Subject: Delaware - history, business, industry; politics and diplomacy; law; religion; genealogy. Holdings: 50,000 books; 10,000 pamphlets; 2 million manuscripts; 53 cubic feet of ephemera; 12 VF drawers and 120 catalog drawers of reference and genealogical files. Services: Interlibrary loan (limited); copying; photograph reproduction; Library open to the public.

1812 ▪ Historical Society of Douglas County
LibraryArchives Center

5730 N. 30th, Bldg. 11-B   Ph: (402)451-1013
Omaha, NE 68111   Fax: (402)451-1394
E-mail: hsdc-lac@radiks.net
URL: http://www.radiks.net/hsdc-lac

Contact: Jeffrey S. Spencer, Dir.

Desc: Subject: History - Douglas County, Omaha; Department of the PlatteFort Omaha; Douglas County authors, overland trails, Missouri Valley exploration and fur trade. Holdings: 1800 books; 850 letters; 6000 photographs; 7500 collected items; diaries; memoirs; scrapbooks; oral history interviews and transcripts; legal documents and business records; documents; artifacts; art work; maps. Services: Copying; photograph duplication; Library open to the public for reference use only.

1813 ▪ Historical Society of Frederick County
Library

24 E. Church St.   Ph: (301)663-1188
Frederick, MD 21701   Fax: (301)663-0526
E-mail: http://www.library@fwp.net

Contact: Marie H. Washburn, Libn.

Desc: Subject: History, genealogy, religion, literature, Frederick County. Holdings: 3500 books; 500 photographs; 70 historic maps; glass negatives; manuscripts. Services: Copying; Library open to the public for reference use only.

1814 ▪ Historical Society of Haddonfield
Library

343 King's Hwy., E.   Ph: (609)429-7375
Haddonfield, NJ 08033

Contact: Katherine M. Tassini, Libn.

Desc: Subject: Local and state history, genealogy. Holdings: 1500 volumes; 3 VF drawers of maps; 15 VF drawers of manuscripts; pamphlets collection; newspapers on microfilm; history recordings. Services: Library open to the public on limited schedule.

1815 ▪ Historical Society of Long Beach
Archives

Box 1869   Ph: (562)495-1210
Long Beach, CA 90801-1869 Fax: (562)495-1281

Contact: Julie Bartolotto, Exec.Dir.

Desc: Subject: Local history. Holdings: 2000 slides; 85 scrapbooks; 16 VF drawers of newspaper clippings; 10 VF drawers of pamphlets and ephemera. Services: Copying; archives open to the public; rotating exhibits.

1816 ▪ Historical Society of Marshall County Research Library

PO Box 304 Ph: (515)752-6664
Marshalltown, IA 50158
URL: http://www.hsmc@mtnia.com

Contact: Mikael W. Vogt, Musm.Dir.

Desc: Subject: Marshall County history, Iowa history. Holdings: City directories; periodicals; agriculture yearbook; early newspapers, public school yearbooks, photo archive; Iowa history texts; local history material. Services: Copying; Library open to the public for reference use only.

1817 ▪ Historical Society of Michigan Center for Teaching Michigan History

2117 Washtenaw Ave. Ph: (734)769-1828
Ann Arbor, MI 48104 Fax: (734)769-4267
E-mail: hsofmich@leslie.k12.mi.us

Contact: Hugh D. Gurney, Dir.

Desc: Subject: Michigan history, teaching. Holdings: 300 books; 50 bound periodical volumes. Services: Copying; open to the public by appointment.

1818 ▪ Historical Society of Moorestown Library

12 High St. Ph: (609)235-0353
Box 477
Moorestown, NJ 08057

Contact: Diane Reid, Pres.

Desc: Subject: Local history, historic clothing, local genealogy. Holdings: 380 books. Services: Library open to the public on a limited schedule.

1819 ▪ Historical Society of Newburgh Bay and the Highlands
Helen V. Gearn Library

189 Montgomery St. Ph: (914)561-2585
Newburgh, NY 12550

Contact: Mary McTamaney, Chm. of Lib.Comm.

Desc: Subject: Local history. Holdings: 3000 books; maps; pictures; city directories; scrapbooks. Services: Library open to the public by appointment.

1820 ▪ Historical Society of Ocean Grove, New Jersey
LibraryArchives

Box 446 Ph: (732)774-1869
Ocean Grove, NJ 07756

Contact: Elsalyn Palmisano, Libn.Archv.

Desc: Subject: Ocean Grove and Victoriana. Holdings: 350 books. Services: Library open to the public.

1821 ▪ Historical Society of Old Newbury Library

Cushing House Museum Ph: (978)462-2681
98 High St. Fax: (978)462-0134
Newburyport, MA 01950

1822 ▪ Historical Society of Old Yarmouth Library

PO Box 11 Ph: (508)362-3021
Yarmouth Port, MA 02675

Contact: Grace T. Hudson, Libn.

Desc: Subject: History - Yarmouth, Cape Cod, Massachusetts; Cape Cod genealogy and literature. Holdings: 100 books; 100 papers of archival material. Services: Copying; Library open to the public for reference use only.

1823 ▪ Historical Society of Palm Beach County
Library

400 N. Dixie Highway Ph: (561)832-4164
West Palm Beach, FL Fax: (561)832-7965
 33401-4210

Contact: Kristen H. Gaspari, Lib.Hd.

Desc: Subject: History of Palm Beach County, local authors, Florida history. Holdings: 5000 books; 160 bound periodical volumes; 100,000 photographs; early slides of Palm Beach County; 25 VF drawers of pamphlets, documents, reports; 10 files of postcards of Florida; 5000 slides of Florida; 2 hurricane films. Services: Copying; Library open to the public.

1824 ▪ Historical Society of Pennsylvania Library

1300 Locust St. Ph: (215)732-6200
Philadelphia, PA 19107-5699 Fax: (215)732-2680
E-mail: hsppr@aol.com
URL: http://www.libertynet.org/pahist

Contact: Cynthia J. Little, VP for Res.Svcs.

Desc: Subject: History - U.S., Colonial, early republic, Revolutionary, Civil War, Pennsylvania; genealogy; Afro-Americana. Holdings: 300,000 volumes; 15 million manuscripts; 2800 microcards; 25,000 microfiche; 16,000 reels of microfilm; maps; prints; drawings; paintings; newspapers; ephemera; artifacts; photographs. Services: Copying; Library open to the public on fee basis.

1825 ▪ Historical Society of Porter County
Old Jail Museum Library

153 Franklin St Ph: (219)465-3595
Valparaiso, IN 46383-5631

Contact: Bonnie Cuson, Cur.

Desc: Subject: Porter County and Indiana history. Holdings: Books; reports; manuscripts. Services: Copying; Library open to the public for reference use only on limited schedule.

1826 ▪ Historical Society of Princeton Library

158 Nassau St. Ph: (609)921-6748
Princeton, NJ 08542 Fax: (609)921-6939
URL: http://www.princetonol.com/groups/histsoc

Contact: Gail Stern, Dir.

Desc: Subject: Princeton and New Jersey history and genealogy. Holdings: 2000 volumes; 500 manuscript collections; 20,000 glass plate negatives; photographs; maps; microfilm; post cards; architectural drawings. Services: Copying (limited); Library open to the public for reference use only on limited schedule.

1827 ▪ Historical Society of Quincy and Adams County
Library

425 S. 12th St. Ph: (217)222-1835
Quincy, IL 62301

Contact: Barbara Lieber

Desc: Subject: History and biography of Illinois, Quincy, and Adams County; history of dolls. Holdings: 1100 volumes; 25 bound periodical volumes; manuscripts. Services: Copying; Library open to the public for reference use only.

1828 ▪ Historical Society of Rockland County
Library

20 Zukor Rd. Ph: (914)634-9629
New City, NY 10956 Fax: (914)634-8690
E-mail: HSRockland@aol.com

Contact: Sarah E. Henrich, Exec.Dir.

Desc: Subject: Local history, genealogy. Holdings: 850 books; 50 manuscripts; 12 VF drawers; 10 boxes of archival material; 20 boxes of family papers; photographs. Services: Copying; Library open to the public by appointment.

1829 ▪ Historical Society of Saratoga Springs Beatrice S. Sweeney Archive and George S. Bolster Photographic Collection

Casino, Congress Park Ph: (518)584-6920
Box 216 Fax: (518)581-1477
Saratoga Springs, NY 12866
E-mail: historicalsociety@juno.com

Desc: Subject: Historical Saratoga Springs, including Saratoga's mineral springs and Saratoga as a 19th-century resort. Holdings: 1800 books; 80 bound periodical volumes; 16 VF drawers of documents, letters, clippings, pamphlets, unbound reports; 70 18th- to 20th-century local maps; 19th- and 20th-century handbills, advertisements, posters; 20 World War I posters; local architectural plans; 75 19th-century historical engravings and lithographs; 300,000 photographic negatives of local architecture, businesses, and people, 1860 to present; 300 local post cards, 1870-1950; local newspapers, 1819-1890; city directories, 1868 to present. Services: Copying; Library open to researchers by appointment.

1830 ▪ Historical Society of Seattle & King County
Sophie Frye Bass Library of Northwest Americana

Museum of History & Industry Ph: (206)324-1126
2700 24th Ave., E. Fax: (206)324-1346
Seattle, WA 98112
URL: http://www.seattlehistory.org

Contact: Mary Montgomery, Libn.

Desc: Subject: History - Seattle, King County, Pacific Northwest, maritime. Holdings: 10,000 books; 200 bound periodical volumes; 500,000 photographs; 1200 maps and charts; 250 linear feet of manuscripts; 250 linear feet of ephemera and clippings. Services: Copying; Library open to the public by appointment.

1831 ▪ Historical Society of the Tarrytowns Library

1 Grove St. Ph: (914)631-8374
Tarrytown, NY 10591

Contact: Sara Mascia, Adm.

Desc: Subject: General history of the communities and the region; capture of Major John Andre at Tarrytown, September 23, 1780, and allied events; Westchester County and New York State history; local genealogy. Holdings: 3000 books; 100 bound periodical volumes; 36 VF drawers of clippings, letters, documents, pictures; 715 cataloged maps, 1785 to present; Civil War manuscripts and records; local weekly newspapers, 1875-1946, on microfilm; microfilm of The Daily News, 1914-1922, 1925-1966; The Argus, 1875-1909. Services: Copying; Library open to the public on limited schedule.

1832 ▪ The Historical Society of the Town of Greenwich, Inc.
William E. Finch, Jr. Archives

39 Strickland Rd. Ph: (203)869-6899
Cos Cob, CT 06807 Fax: (203)869-6727

Contact: Susan Richardson, Archv.

Desc: Subject: Local history, genealogy, 19th century American impressionist art, American decorative art. Holdings: 2000 books; manuscripts; documents; photographs; post cards; ephemera. Services: Library open to the public by appointment.

1833 ▪ Historical Society of Washington, DC Research Collections

1307 New Hampshire Ave. NW   Ph: (202)785-2068
Washington, DC 20036   Fax: (202)887-5785
E-mail: hswlibrary@ibm.net

Contact: Gail R. Redmann, Lib.Dir.

Desc: Subject: Washington, DC history, Washingtoniana. Holdings: 15,000 volumes; 500 manuscripts. Services: copying; photograph reproductions; library open to the public (free to members, fee for non-members).

1834 ▪ Historical Society of Western Pennsylvania
Library & Archives Division

Sen. John Heinz Pittsburgh   Ph: (412)454-6364
   Regional History Center   Fax: (412)454-6028
1212 Smallman St.
Pittsburgh, PA 15222
URL: http://trfn.clpgh.org/hswp

Contact: Dr. Carolyn S. Schumacher, Dir., Lib. & Archv.

Desc: Subject: History of Pittsburgh and Western Pennsylvania, family history, iron and steel, glass manufacturing, French & Indian War, health and medicine, business, ethnic history, women's history, genealogy. Holdings: 40,000 books; 1000 bound periodical volumes; 265 reels of microfilm; 400,000 photographs; 90 boxes of unbound newspapers; 28 VF drawers of pamphlets and clippings; 10,000 linearfeet and 888 bound volumes of manuscripts. Services: Copying; Library open to the public.

1835 ▪ Historical Society of York County
Library and Archives

250 E. Market St.
York, PA 17403   Ph: (717)848-1587
   Fax: (717)848-1589

Contact: June Lloyd, Libn.Archv.

Desc: Subject: York County and city history, York County genealogy, Pennsylvania and American history, fine and decorative arts. Holdings: 25,000 books; 1400 bound periodical volumes; 15,000 York County land records; 18,000 York County tax records, 1762-1900; 1000 linear feet of York County manuscripts, pamphlets, and clippings; 100,000 photographs and negatives of York County; 3100 reels of microfilm of York County newspapers and manuscripts; Dempwolf Architectural Firm architectural drawings (1880-1930); 200 maps; 125 rolls of motion picture film. Services: Copying; limited research by mail; Library open to the public on fee basis.

1836 ▪ History Museum and Historical Society of Southwest Virginia
Library

Box 1904
Roanoke, VA 24008   Ph: (540)342-5770
   Fax: (540)224-1238
E-mail: history@roanoke.infi.net
URL: http://www.historymuseum.org

Contact: Clare White, Hd.Libn.

Desc: Subject: Roanoke and Southwest Virginia history. Holdings: 500 books. Services: Library open to researchers by appointment.

1837 ▪ Hobart Historical Society, Inc.
Mariam J. Pleak Memorial Library and Archive

706 E. 4th St.   Ph: (219)942-0970
Box 24
Hobart, IN 46342

Contact: Elin B. Christianson, Cur.

Desc: Subject: Local history and genealogy. Holdings: 1200 books; 36 VF drawers of archival materials; 50 reels of microfilm of Hobart newspapers. Services: Interlibrary loan; copying; Library open to the public.

1838 ▪ Hodgeman County Historical Society

c/o Mary Ford   Ph: (316)357-8794
Rte. 2
PO Box 115
Jetmore, KS 67854

Contact: Richard Lucas, Cur.

Desc: Subject: Hodgeman County history. Holdings: 50 books; 30 reports. Services: Library not open to the public.

1839 ▪ Holland Society of New York
Library

122 E. 58th St.   Ph: (212)758-1871
New York, NY 10022-1939
E-mail: HollSoc@aol.com

Contact: Linda Rolufs, Libn.

Desc: Subject: Colonial history of the New Netherland Area (New York, New Jersey, Delaware) with emphasis on genealogical sources and cultural history; genealogies of families which settled there prior to 1675. Holdings: 5000 volumes; 300 reels of microfilm. Services: Copying; Library open to the public on a limited schedule.

1840 ▪ Holocaust Center of Northern California

639 14th Ave.   Ph: (415)751-6040
San Francisco, CA 94118   Fax: (415)751-6735
E-mail: library@holocaust-sf.org
URL: http://www.holocaust-sf.org

Contact: David Stein, Ph.D., Exec.Dir.

Desc: Subject: Holocaust, Nazi Germany, modern Europe, World War II, Jews in Europe and North Africa, survivors of concentration camps. Holdings: 13,000 books; 2000 photographs; 700 oral history tapes and transcripts; 400 videotapes; 200 audiotapes of programs on the Holocaust; 50 artifacts of the period. Services: Copying; center open to the public for reference use only.

1841 ▪ Hopkins Historical Society
Library

1010 1st St., S.   Ph: (612)935-5878
Hopkins, MN 55343

Contact: Henry Pokorny, Archv.

Desc: Subject: Hopkins, Minnesota history. Holdings: 741 books (150 in Bohemian language); 6971 pictures; 5855 documents; 6445 newspapers; 1054 artifacts; 1687 magazines; 480 maps; 208 city directories; 45 scrapbooks. Services: Library open to the public by appointment.

1842 ▪ Houghton County Historical Society
Museum

5500 Hwy. M-26, PO Box 127   Ph: (906)296-4121
Lake Linden, MI 49945   Fax: (906)296-9191

Contact: Leo Chaput, Cur.

Desc: Subject: Mining, transportation, engineering, forestry, industry, local history. Holdings: Figures not available. Services: Museum open to the public; research approval from Board of Trustees.

1843 ▪ Houston Public Library
Clayton Library
Center for Genealogical Research

5300 Caroline St.   Ph: (713)284-1999
Houston, TX 77004-6896
URL: http://www.hpl.lib.tx.us

Contact: Margaret J. Harris, Mgr.

Desc: Subject: Genealogy. Holdings: 60,000 books; 3000 bound periodical volumes; 60,000 reels of microfilm; 50,000 microfiche; VF material. Services: Copying; center open to the public.

1844 ▪ Houston Public Library
Houston Metropolitan Research Center

500 McKinney Ave.   Ph: (713)247-2222
Houston, TX 77002   Fax: (713)247-1131
E-mail: archives@hpl.lib.tx.us
URL: http://www.hpl.lib.tx.us

Contact: Louis J. Marchiafava, Ph.D., Archv.

Desc: Subject: Houston - business, politics, architecture, church records, city and county government, agencies. Holdings: 20,000 linear feet of archival material. Services: Copying; center open to the public by appointment.

1845 ▪ Howard University
Moorland-Spingarn Research Center
Manuscript Division

500 Howard Place, NW   Ph: (202)806-7480
Washington, DC 20059   Fax: (202)806-6405
URL: http://www.founders.howard.edu/moorland-spingarn

Contact: Joellen ElBashir, Cur.

Desc: Subject: Afro-Americana, Africana, Caribbeana. Holdings: 2000 linear feet of processed manuscripts; 4800 linear feet of unprocessed manuscripts. Services: Copying; division open to qualified researchers.

1846 ▪ Hoyt Public Library
Eddy Genealogical and Historical Collection

505 Janes Ave.   Ph: (517)755-9827
Saginaw, MI 48607   Fax: (517)755-9829
E-mail: amm@vlc.lib.mi.us
URL: http://www.saginaw.library.lib.mi.us

Contact: Marcia Warner, Br.Hd.

Desc: Subject: Saginaw and Michigan history, genealogy. Holdings: 10,000 books; 1500 bound periodical volumes; 100 feet of manuscripts; 4500 nonbook items. Services: Interlibrary loan (limited); copying; collections open to the public with limited borrowing privileges.

1847 ▪ Hudson Library and Historical Society

22 Aurora St.   Ph: (330)653-6658
Hudson, OH 44236-2947   Fax: (330)650-4693
E-mail: hu3@front1.cpl.org

Contact: E. Leslie Polott, Dir. & Cur.

Desc: Subject: Hudson and Summit County history, Ohio history and genealogy, John Brown. Holdings: 107,418 volumes; 6052 phonograph records; 3105 music CDs; 145 CD-ROMs; 760 reels of microfilm; 3022 microfiche; 1809 slides; 197 boxes of manuscripts; 2684 audiocassettes; 2646 videocassettes. Services: Interlibrary loan; copying; Library open to the public.

1848 ▪ Hugh Moore Historical Park and Museums
National Canal Museum - Archives

30 Centre Sq.   Ph: (610)250-6703
Easton, PA 18042-7743   Fax: (610)559-6690
E-mail: archives@canals.org
URL: http://canals.org

Contact: Tom Heard, Coll.Mgr.

Desc: Subject: Canals; anthracite coal mining; history - iron and steel, railroad, industrial and technological; local history - Pennsylvania Lehigh Valley and anthracite regions, New Jersey. Holdings: 5000 books; 1500 bound periodical volumes; 75 cubic feet of manuscripts and research material; 8000 engineering drawings; 500 maps; 700 films; 200 reels of microfilm 1500 artifacts; 30,000 photographic images (slides, lantern slides, prints, glass plates, negatives). Services: Copying; Library open to the public on a fee basis.

1849 ■ Huguenot Historical Society
Library
88 Huguenot St.   Ph: (914)255-6738
New Paltz, NY 12561   Fax: (914)255-0376
E-mail: hhslib@ix.netcom.com

Contact: Eric J. Roth, Archv.Libn.

Desc: Subject: History of Huguenot religion, demographics and culture; Huguenot genealogy; local and regional history and genealogy - Mid-Hudson Valley, New York. Holdings: 5000 books and manuscripts; 215 reels of microfilm; 64 cubic ft. of vertical files; 26 oversize genealogical charts. Services: Copying; Library open to the public.

1850 ■ Huguenot Society of America
Library
122 E. 58th St.   Ph: (212)755-0592
New York, NY 10022   Fax: (212)317-0676

Contact: Dorothy F. Kimball, Exec.Sec.

Desc: Subject: French Huguenot migration to America, Huguenot history in France and elsewhere, biography, genealogy. Holdings: 2035 volumes; 30 manuscripts; 20 autograph letters. Services: Copying; Library open on a limited schedule.

1851 ■ Huguenot Society of South Carolina
Library
138 Logan St.   Ph: (843)723-3235
Charleston, SC 29401   Fax: (843)853-8476
E-mail: huguenot@cchat.com

Contact: Melissa W. Ballentine, Archv.Libn.

Desc: Subject: Genealogical data on Huguenots and allied families. Holdings: 2000 volumes; 16 VF drawers of genealogical data; microfilm; microfiche; CDs. Services: Library open to the public.

1852 ■ Humboldt State University
Special Collections
Humboldt Room
Rm. 308   Ph: (707)826-4939
Arcata, CA 95521   Fax: (707)826-3440
E-mail: jrb2@axe.humboldt.edu
URL: http://library.humboldt.edu/library

Contact: Joan Berman, Spec.Coll.Libn.

Desc: Subject: Natural resources, native peoples, and primary industries of northwestern California; Humboldt County. Holdings: Books; photographs; pamphlets; maps; manuscripts; newspapers; microfilm; oral history recordings. Services: Copying; Library open to the public.

1853 ■ Hunterdon County Historical Society
Hiram E. Deats Memorial Library
114 Main St.   Ph: (908)782-1091
Flemington, NJ 08822

Contact: Roxanne K. Carkhuff, Lib.Chm.

Desc: Subject: Hunterdon County and New Jersey history and genealogy. Holdings: 5000 books. Services: Copying; genealogical queries answered by mail with SASE; Library open to the public for reference use only.

1854 ■ Huntington Free Library
National Museum of the American Indian
Library
9 Westchester Sq.   Ph: (718)829-7770
Bronx, NY 10461   Fax: (718)829-4875
E-mail: hflib1@metgate.metro.org

Contact: Mary B. Davis, Lib.Dir.

Desc: Subject: Archeology and ethnology of Indians of the Western Hemisphere; linguistics; anthropology; history; current affairs. Holdings: 25,000 volumes; 140 VF drawers; 50 manuscripts. Services: Copying; Library open to the public for reference use only by appointment.

1855 ■ Huntington Historical Society
Library
209 Main St.   Ph: (516)427-7045
Huntington, NY 11743   Fax: (516)427-7056

Contact: Karen Martin, Archv.

Desc: Subject: Local history, genealogy, New York history, American crafts and decorative arts. Holdings: 5000 books; 128 bound periodical volumes; 325 linear feet of manuscripts and archival materials; 20 clipping files; 50,000 photographs; 15,000 slides. Services: Copying; Library open to the public for research only by appointment.

1856 ■ Huxford Genealogical Society, Inc.
Genealogical Library
Corner of Dame & College Sts.   Ph: (912)487-2310
PO Box 595   Fax: (912)487-3881
Homerville, GA 31634
E-mail: hux@planttel.net
URL: http://www.planttel.net/hux

Contact: Violet Bennett, Lib.Mgr.

Desc: Subject: Genealogy Holdings: 2617 volumes (including microfilm); 79 boxes of magazines; 442 boxes of microfilm. Services: Copying; Library open to nonmembers on a fee basis.

1857 ■ Hyde Park Historical Society
Archives
30 Ayles Rd.   Ph: (617)361-4398
Hyde Park, MA 02136   Fax: (617)361-4398
E-mail: nhhlaw@aol.com

Contact: Nancy H. Hannan, Pres.

Desc: Subject: Hyde Park history, Civil War era. Holdings: 1000 books; 400 bound periodical volumes; 100 AV programs; 50 nonbook items. Services: Interlibrary loan; copying; Archives open to the public with restrictions.

1858 ■ Idaho State Historical Society
Library and Archives
450 N. 4th St.   Ph: (208)334-3356
Boise, ID 83702   Fax: (208)334-3198

Contact: Linda Morton-Keithley, Adm.

Desc: Subject: Idaho - state government, irrigation, law, architecture, labor; genealogy; Northwest history. Holdings: 15,000 books; 3800 bound periodical volumes; 8000 cubic feet of manuscripts; 20,000 maps; 10,000 cubic feet of Idaho State archives; 300,000 photographs; 20,500 reels of microfilm; 60 cubic feet of vertical file material. Services: Interlibrary loan (limited to microfilm and oral history); copying; Library and archives open to the public.

1859 ■ Illinois State Data Center
Illinois Bureau of the Budget   Ph: (217)782-1381
605 Stratton Bldg.   Fax: (217)524-4876
Springfield, IL 62706
E-mail: sebetsch@bob084rl.state.il.us

Contact: Sue Ebetsch, Coord.

Desc: Subject: U.S. Census Bureau information. Holdings: 1000 volumes; census maps, 1970-1990; computer tapes; microfiche; CD-ROMs. Services: Copying; center open to the public.

1860 ■ Illinois State Historical Library
Old State Capitol   Ph: (217)524-7216
Springfield, IL 62701-1507   Fax: (217)785-6250

URL: http://www.state.il.us/hpa/lib

Contact: Kathryn M. Harris

Desc: Subject: Illinois history, Lincolniana, Civil War history, Midwest Americana, Mormon history, Indian history, genealogy. Holdings: 172,000 volumes; 10.1 million manuscripts; 76,000 reels of newspapers on microfilm; 3000 maps; 4000 broadsides. Services: Interlibrary loan (limited); copying; Library open to the public.

1861 ■ Illinois State University
Census and Data Users Services
Library
Research Services Bldg., Ste. A   Ph: (309)438-5946
Normal, IL 61790-4950   Fax: (309)438-2898
E-mail: cadus@ilstu.edu

Contact: Roy C. Treadway, Dir.

Desc: Subject: U.S. Census data. Holdings: 600 volumes; 800 computer cartridges; 100 compact discs; 1970, 1980, and 1990 census data and recent economic censuses for Illinois and surrounding states; population projections. Services: Library open to the public.

1862 ■ Independent Community Consultants
Library
Planning and Training Office
PO Box 141
Hampton, AR 71744

Contact: Jerry Cronin, Hd.Libn.

Desc: Subject: Nonprofit organizations - organizational and community problems; statistics on corporate philanthropy, population, and social trends. Holdings: 9000 books, tapes, and microfiche; statistics.

1863 ■ Indian and Colonial Research Center,
Inc.
Eva Butler Library
Box 525   Ph: (860)536-9771
Old Mystic, CT 06372

Contact: Brian Rogers, Cons.

Desc: Subject: Indians, genealogy, colonial history. Holdings: 2000 books; 954 manuscripts; 90 maps and atlases; 2000 early American notebooks; 69 boxes of bulletins and pamphlets; 2000 photographs. Services: Copying; Library open to the public.

1864 ■ Indian Hill Historical Society
Library
8100 Given Rd.   Ph: (513)891-1873
Cincinnati, OH 45243   Fax: (513)891-1873
E-mail: ihhist@one.net
URL: http://www.indianhill.org

Desc: Subject: Indian Hill village, antiques, barns, homes, village family histories, village resident biographical information. Holdings: 150 books; 20 bound periodical volumes; 20 reports; 50 archival materials; files. Services: Library open to the public by appointment for reference use only.

1865 ■ Indiana Historical Society
William Henry Smith Memorial Library
450 W. Ohio St.   Ph: (317)232-1879
Indianapolis, IN 46202   Fax: (317)233-3109
E-mail: bjohnson@indianahistory.org
URL: http://www.indianahistory.org

Contact: Bruce L. Johnson, Dir.

Desc: Subject: History of Indiana and Old Northwest. Holdings: 67,000 books and pamphlets; 573 serial titles held; 5300 manuscript collections; 1000 maps; 1600 reels of microfilm; 2308 artifact items. Services: Limited photocopying; photographic reproductions; preservation consultations; preservation microfilming; Library open to the public.

1866 ■ Indiana Jewish Historical Society Archive

124 W. Wayne St., 216   Ph: (219)422-3862
Fort Wayne, IN 46802-2505   Fax: (219)422-3862

Contact: Eileen F. Baitcher, Exec.Dir.

Desc: Subject: History of Jewish communities, congregations, organizations in Indiana; family and oral histories. Holdings: 6000 items. Services: Archive open to the public by appointment.

1867 ■ Indiana State Library

140 N. Senate Ave.   Ph: (317)232-3675
Indianapolis, IN 46204-2296   Fax: (317)232-3728
URL: http://www.statelib.lib.in.us

Contact: C. Ray Ewick, Dir.

Desc: Subject: Genealogy, Indiana history, federal and state documents, library science. Holdings: 1.6 million items; regional depository for federal documents; state documents. Services: Interlibrary loan; copying; Library open to the public.

1868 ■ Indiana State Library Indiana Division

140 N. Senate Ave.   Ph: (317)232-3670
Indianapolis, IN 46204-2296   Fax: (317)232-3728
URL: http://www.statelib.lib.in.us

Contact: Andrea Bean Hough, Sr.Subj.Spec.

Desc: Subject: Indiana - history, authors, biography, music and composers; local history. Holdings: 70,500 volumes; depository for state documents; 10,900 maps; 50,135 pamphlets; 3.25 million manuscripts; 34 VF drawers of pictures; 40 VF drawers of programs; 2500 broadsides; 2000 reels of microfilm; 72,000 reels of microfilm from newspapers; 395 oral history tapes; 148 VF drawers of clippings. Services: Interlibrary loan; copying (both limited); division open to the public.

1869 ■ Indiana University Oral History Research Center

Ashton-Aley 264   Ph: (812)855-2856
Bloomington, IN 47405   Fax: (812)855-4869
E-mail: ohrc@indiana.edu
URL: http://www.indiana.edu/ohrc

Desc: Subject: Indiana - history, industry, agriculture, politics. Holdings: 60 books; 1700 oral histories; 1 VF drawer; clippings. Services: Copying (limited); Library open to the public for reference use only.

1870 ■ Indiana University-Purdue University at Indianapolis Ruth Lilly Special Collection and Archives

755 W. Michigan St.   Ph: (317)274-0464
Indianapolis, IN 46202   Fax: (317)278-2331
E-mail: tjdaniel@iupui.edu
URL: http://www.ulib.iupui.edu/special

Desc: Subject: History of Indiana University, Purdue University at Indianapolis and its predecessor schools; German-Americana; history of philanthropy. Holdings: 4327 books; 4500 linear feet of archives; 289 reels of microfilm; 5057 audio tapes; 520 visual recordings; 275,000 photographs; 50,400 musical scores; 720 microfiche. Services: Copying; Library open to the public during business hours.

1871 ■ Inner City Cultural Center Langston Hughes Memorial Library

The Ivar Theater   Ph: (323)962-2102
1605 N. Ivar Ave.   Fax: (213)386-9017
Hollywood, CA 90028

Desc: Subject: Ethnic groups, performing and visual arts. Holdings: 6500 uncataloged books; 300 bound periodical volumes; 100 manuscripts; 100 sound recordings and tapes; 250 clippings; 175 reports; 200 photographs. Services: Library not open to the public.

1872 ■ Iowa Genealogical Society Library

6000 Douglas   Ph: (515)276-0287
PO Box 7735
Des Moines, IA 50322-7735
E-mail: igs@digiserve.com
URL: http://www.digiserve.com/igs/igs.htm

Contact: Anne Covino, Libn.

Desc: Subject: Genealogy, local history. Holdings: 166 volumes of D.A.R. lineage books; 69 volumes of Pennsylvania archives; U.S. and foreign genealogy books; 2000 genealogies; 1400 rolls of Iowa courthouse records; 60 volumes of Germans to America books; 50 CD-ROMs. Services: Copying; Library open to the public on fee basis, free to members.

1873 ■ Iron County Museum Raymond Gustafson Archives

Box 272   Ph: (906)265-2617
Caspian, MI 49915

Contact: Marcia Bernhardt, Cur.

Desc: Subject: Local history, lumbering, mining. Holdings: 200 books; 1500 other cataloged items; 8200 underground mining maps; 7500 photographs; 50,000 obituaries; 135 archival boxes. Services: Archives open to researchers by request.

1874 ■ Isaac M. Wise Temple Ralph Cohen Memorial Library

8329 Ridge Rd.   Ph: (513)793-2556
Cincinnati, OH 45236   Fax: (513)793-3322

Contact: Jenny Schaffzin, Libn.

Desc: Subject: Judaica, Holocaust. Holdings: 18,000 books. Services: Library open to the public with restrictions.

1875 ■ Isanti County Historical Society Resource Center

Box 525   Ph: (612)689-4229
Cambridge, MN 55008   Fax: (612)689-5134
E-mail: varrow2@ecenet.com
URL: http://www.Braham.com

Contact: Valorie Stavem Arrowsmith, Dir.

Desc: Subject: Isanti County history, potato history, Swedish immigration. Holdings: 250 books; 400 photographs of rural life, 1890-1930; 3 VF drawers of documents; 30 oral history tapes. Services: Interlibrary loan; copying; center open to the public on a limited schedule and by appointment for reference use.

1876 ■ Itasca County Historical Society Itasca Heritage Center

Central School Bldg.   Ph: (218)326-6431
10 NW Fifth St.
Grand Rapids, MN 55744
E-mail: ichso@northernnet.com

Desc: Subject: Itasca County and Minnesota history. Holdings: Books; photographs; manuscripts; artifacts. Services: Copying; Library open to researchers by appointment.

1877 ■ Jackson County Genealogical Society Library

415 1/2 S. Poplar St.   Ph: (812)358-2118
Brownstown, IN 47220-1939

Desc: Subject: Jackson County, Indiana - genealogy, history. Holdings: 1200 books; 4 microfiche; 14 reels of microfilm; family histories; birth, death, and marriage records; cemetery records. Services: Copying; Library open to the public.

1878 ■ Jackson County Historical Society Archives and Research Library

Independence Square   Ph: (816)252-7454
  Courthouse, Rm. 103   Fax: (816)461-1510
Independence, MO 64050
E-mail: jchsarch@crn.org

Contact: Kelly Chambers, Dir.

Desc: Subject: Local Civil War history, Jackson County history, CaliforniaOregon Trail, William Quantrill, Jesse James, Kansas City and Independence. Holdings: 2000 books; 400 bound periodical volumes; 3000 cubic feet of manuscripts, letters, records; 40 VF drawers of abstracts; clipping file; maps. Services: Copying; center open to the public.

1879 ■ Jackson County Historical Society Library

307 N. Hwy. 86   Ph: (507)662-5505
PO Box 238
Lakefield, MN 56150-0238

Desc: Subject: County history. Holdings: 200 books; 3 dissertations; plat books for county, 1874 to present; county newspapers on microfilm. Services: Library open to the public for reference use only.

1880 ■ Jackson County Public Library Indiana History and Genealogy Collection

303 W. 2nd St.   Ph: (812)522-3412
Seymour, IN 47274   Fax: (812)522-5456
E-mail: erebber@japl.lib.in.us
URL: http://www.seymour.org/jcpl.htm

Contact: Elizabeth Rebber, Staff Genealogy Spec.

Desc: Subject: Indiana - genealogy, history. Holdings: Books; maps; microfiche; microfilm; papers; pictures. Services: Library open to the public.

1881 ■ Jackson State University Information Services Library

3825 Ridgewood Rd.   Ph: (601)982-6313
Jackson, MS 39211   Fax: (601)982-6144

Contact: Dr. Lou H. Sanders, Dir.

Desc: Subject: Census, statistics, Mississippi economic data, business, industrial development. Holdings: 34,000 books; census data. Services: Interlibrary loan; copying; telephone inquiries; Library open to the public with restrictions.

1882 ■ JacksonHinds Library System Eudora Welty Library Special Collections

300 N. State St.   Ph: (601)968-5811
Jackson, MS 39201   Fax: (601)968-5817
URL: http://www.jhls.lib.ms.us

Contact: Carolyn McCallum, Hd.Libn.

Desc: Holdings: 195,569 books; 430 microfilm; 233 general periodicals (on disc); 443 business periodicals (on disc.) Services: Interlibrary loan; copying; collections open to the public.

1883 ▪ Jacksonville Historical Society Archives

Jacksonville University Ph: (904)745-7267
Carl S. Swisher Library
2800 University Blvd. N.
Jacksonville, FL 32211

Contact: Mrs. Gene Cooper

Desc: Subject: Local history. Holdings: 2039 books; 4060 photographs; 300 post cards; 400 slides; 150 tapes; 250 maps; 10 videotapes; 82 artifacts. Services: Copying; Library open to the public by appointment.

1884 ▪ Jacksonville Public Library Florida and Genealogy Collections

122 N. Ocean St. Ph: (904)630-2410
Jacksonville, FL 32202 Fax: (904)630-2431

Contact: Kenneth G. Sivulich, Lib.Dir.

Desc: Subject: Genealogy, especially southeastern United States; Florida and Jacksonville - history, biography, description and travel, politics and government, plants and wildlife, fine arts, economics. Holdings: 19,478 books and cataloged pamphlets; 1096 bound periodical volumes; 8802 reels of microfilm; 12,081 checklisted Florida documents; 60 file boxes and 8042 checklisted copies of Jacksonville documents; 110 file boxes of Florida documents; 11 VF drawers of uncataloged pamphlets; 17 VF drawers of newspaper clippings; 2 VF drawers of photographs; 480 maps; 22,185 microfiche. Services: Copying; collection open to the public for serious research with restrictions.

1885 ▪ The Jacobite Association Athlone Court & Historiographer Royal Research Library

White Rose House
Box 211
Cross River, NY 10518
E-mail: jacobite_party@yahoo.com

Contact: Neil Christopher Bennett, Libn.

Desc: Subject: Jacobites - biography, history, genealogy, peerages; British history and culture. Holdings: 4000 books; 6100 bound periodical volumes; manuscripts and archival papers. Services: Answers questions submitted by mail.

1886 ▪ James A. Garfield Historical Society Library

8107 Main St.
PO Box 144
Garrettsville, OH 44231

Contact: Edith H. Sampson

Desc: Subject: Garrettsville history. Services: Library open to the public with restrictions.

1887 ▪ James E. Whalley Museum and Library

351 Middle St. Ph: (603)436-3943
Portsmouth, NH 03801

Contact: Lynn J. Sanderson, Pres.

Desc: Subject: Freemasonry; genealogy; history - New Hampshire, New Hampshire seacoast, Portsmouth. Holdings: 3600 books; 600 bound periodical volumes; 96 file drawers; 100 boxes; 1000 other cataloged items. Services: Copying; Library open to the public by appointment.

1888 ▪ Jefferson County Historical Society Library

228 Washington St. Ph: (315)782-3491
Watertown, NY 13601 Fax: (315)782-2913
URL: http://nsi.imcnet.net/JCHS/

Contact: Elise Chan, Curator of Collections

Desc: Subject: Watertown and Jefferson County history. Holdings: 750 volumes; pamphlets, ledgers, daybooks, account books, journals of 19th century country stores; 19th century bank record books; boxes of archival materials; current museum periodicals and directories. Services: Copying; Library open to the public for reference use only.

1889 ▪ Jefferson County Historical Society Museum
Richard McCurdy Research Library

892 Worcester St., Ste. 210 Ph: (781)237-5300
Wellesley, MA 02482 Fax: (781)237-1688
E-mail: jai-energy@worldnet.att.com
URL: http://www.olympus.net/arts/jcmuseum/index.html

Contact: Dr. Niki R. Clark, Dir.

Desc: Subject: Jefferson County and regional history; biography; ships and shipping; early Pacific Northwest histories; historic preservation and restoration. Holdings: 400 volumes; 100 maps and nautical charts; 200 manuscript cases of Jefferson County local history and family history; 9000 historical photographs; Genealogical Society records; city, county, school records; bound volumes of the Port Townsend Leader, 1891 to present; Port Townsend Leader, 1889-1904, 1931-1941 on microfilm; Press File. Services: Copying; Library open to the public for reference use only under supervision of research staff.

1890 ▪ Jefferson Historical Society and Museum
Archives

223 Austin St., West Ph: (903)665-2775
Jefferson, TX 75657

Desc: Subject: Local history, Civil War, genealogy. Holdings: Books; bound periodical volumes; 35 manuscripts; 20 notebooks of clippings; several hundred documents; maps. Services: Archives open to the public with restrictions.

1891 ▪ Jekyll Island Authority
Jekyll Island Museum Archives

381 Riverview Dr. Ph: (912)635-2119
Jekyll Island, GA 31527 Fax: (912)635-4420

Contact: Karen McInnis, Chief Cur.

Desc: Subject: Jekyll Island early history and state era. Holdings: 1100 books; 1375 documents; 2000 photographs; 32 manuscripts. Services: Copying; archives open to the public by appointment with restrictions on some holdings.

1892 ▪ Jewish Federation of Nashville and Middle Tennessee
Archives

801 Percy Warner Blvd. Ph: (615)356-3242
Nashville, TN 37205 Fax: (615)352-0056
E-mail: nashfedlib@aol.com

Contact: Lee Haas, Dir.

Desc: Holdings: 3 record groups; 47 manuscript collections; 120 small collections; Jewish newspapers on microfilm. Services: Interlibrary loan; archives open to the public with restrictions.

1893 ▪ Jewish Historical Society of Metrowest
Archives

901 Rte. 10, E. Ph: (973)884-4800
Whippany, NJ 07981-1156 Fax: (973)428-8237
E-mail: jfien@aol.com
URL: http://www.jhsmw.org

Contact: Joseph A. Settanni, Archv.

Desc: Subject: Jewish Historical Society of Metrowest history, cemeteries, Jewish studies, politics, social welfare, education, anti-Semitism, World War II, volunteerism, Holocaust, civil rights movement, church-state issues, childhood studies, women's studies, veterans, labor, philanthropy, public health, cultural affairs, Israel, Middle East, Russia, biographical casefiles, senior citizens, ethnographic subjects, immigration, recreation. Holdings: Maps; memorabilia; institutional records; private manuscripts; photographic collections; audiovisual materials; ephemera; oral histories; videocassettes; microfilm, magnetic electronic media. Services: Archives open to the public.

1894 ▪ Jewish Historical Society of New York, Inc.
Library

8 W. 70th St. Ph: (212)415-5544
New York, NY 10023
E-mail: swsiegel@pipeline.com

Contact: Steven W. Siegel, Sec.

Desc: Subject: American and New York Jewish history, Jewish genealogy. Holdings: Figures not available. Services: Provides telephone and e-mail reference service only.

1895 ▪ The Jewish Museum of Maryland
Archives

15 Lloyd St. Ph: (410)732-6400
Baltimore, MD 21202 Fax: (410)732-6451
E-mail: info@jhsm.org
URL: http://www.jhsm.org

Contact: Virginia R. North, Archv.

Desc: Subject: History of Jews in Maryland, 18th century to present; social welfare history. Holdings: 3000 books; 560 linear feet of manuscripts; genealogical works; listing of local Jewish organizations, members, birth and death records, immigration records, census records; microfiche and microfilm of local Jewish publications; Jewish Chronicle (Vol. 1-2, 1875), Jewish Comment (Vols. 1-51, April 26, 1895 to June 28, 1918), Jewish Exponent (November 25, 1887 to August 31, 1888), Hapisgah (1891-1892), Sinai (1856-1864), Jewish Times (September 24, 1919 to present). Services: Copying; archives open to the public by appointment (Monday through Thursday).

1896 ▪ Johnson County Historical Society
Mary Miller Smiser Heritage Library

300 N. Main St. Ph: (816)747-6480
Warrensburg, MO 64093

Desc: Subject: History of Johnson county townships, genealogy, business, transportation. Holdings: 500 volumes; directories; census records; diaries; cemetery records; documents; manuscripts; marriage records; 75 tapes; 6 cu.ft. of church records; 50 cu.ft. of school records. Services: Copying; Library open to the public for reference use only.

1897 ▪ Johnson County Library
Central Resource Library
Local HistoryGenealogyUrban Reference

9875 W. 87th St. Ph: (913)495-2400
Overland Park, KS 66212
URL: http://www.jcl.lib.ks.us/is/lclhist/loclhist.htm

Contact: Monica Carmack, Libn.

Desc: Subject: History of Kansas, particularly Johnson County; genealogy; Johnson County municipal and county reference. Holdings: 9200 books; 150 bound periodical volumes; 300 microfiche; 300 microfilm; 40 file drawers of subject listed local newspaper clippings; extensive obituary index for Johnson County, 1977-present. Services: Interlibrary loan; copying; SDI (for municipal and county officials); Library open to the public.

1898 ■ Johnstown Historical Society
Library Reference Center
17 N. William St.   Ph: (518)762-7076
Johnstown, NY 12095

Contact: James F. Morrison, Archv.

Desc: Subject: Local history; historical persons associated with Johnstown - Sir William Johnson, Molly Brant, Major Nick Stoner, Captain Silas Talbot, Lafayette, Washington Irving, Aaron Burr, Elizabeth Cady Stanton, Judge Daniel Cady, Governor Enos Throop, E.L. Henry, Brigadier General Edgar S. Dudley, Grace Livingston Hill, Rose M. Knox. Holdings: 1600 books; 52 bound periodical volumes; 400 booklets and pamphlets; 2300 photographs; 1350 documents; 5 files of clippings; 43 old maps; 6 files of old documents; 2 files of genealogical materials; 1100 old newspapers; and 300 old periodicals. Services: Library open to the public.

1899 ■ Joint Free Public Library of
Morristown & Morris Township
Local History and Genealogy Department
1 Miller Rd.   Ph: (973)538-3473
Morristown, NJ 07960   Fax: (973)267-4064
URL: http://www.jfpl.org/gene.htm

Contact: Susan H. Gulick

Desc: Subject: Morristown, Morris Township, and New Jersey history and genealogy. Holdings: Books; manuscripts; family histories; genealogical records and indexes; 1000 maps and land plottings; 50 atlases; 10,000 photographs and postcards. Services: Interlibrary loan.

1900 ■ Jones Library, Inc.
Special Collections
43 Amity St.   Ph: (413)256-4090
Amherst, MA 01002   Fax: (413)256-4096
URL: http://www.gazettenet.com/joneslibrary/

Contact: Bonnie J. Isman, Lib.Dir.

Desc: Subject: Local and regional history, Amherst authors, genealogy. Holdings: 15,000 books; 50,000 historical photographs; 20,000 other cataloged items; 240 reels of microfilm. Services: Copying; collections open to the public.

1901 ■ Jones Memorial Library
2311 Memorial Ave.   Ph: (804)846-0501
Lynchburg, VA 24501   Fax: (804)846-0501
URL: http://www.jmlibrary.org

Contact: Phillip W. Rhodes, Dir.

Desc: Subject: Genealogy, architectural drawings, local history, family histories. Holdings: 20,000 books; 5000 bound periodical volumes; 500 boxes of archival items; 3500 reels of microfilm; 12,000 drawings. Services: Copying; Library open to the public.

1902 ■ Josephine County Historical Society
Research Library
512 S.W. 5th St.   Ph: (503)479-7827
Grants Pass, OR 97526
URL: http://www.webtail.com/jchs

Contact: Rose M. Scott, Exec.Dir.

Desc: Subject: History - Josephine County, southern Oregon. Holdings: 755 books; 156 bound periodical volumes; 10 VF drawers of clippings; 4 VF drawers of photographs; 2000 slides; 106 boxes of manuscripts; 21 oral history tapes; unbound periodicals; maps. Services: Copying; Library open to the public.

1903 ■ Joy Reisinger Genealogical Collection
1020 Central Ave.   Ph: (608)269-6361
Sparta, WI 54656   Fax: (608)269-6929
E-mail: joycgrs@centuryinter.net

Contact: Joy Reisinger, Owner

Desc: Subject: Genealogy, Canadian history, Quebec and Ontario history, Wisconsin History. Holdings: 270 linear feet of shelves. Services: Copying; Library open to the public by appointment.

1904 ■ Judah L. Magnes Memorial Museum
Western Jewish History Center
2911 Russell St.   Ph: (510)549-6956
Berkeley, CA 94705   Fax: (510)849-3673

Contact: Kim Klausner, Archv.

Desc: Subject: History of Jews in the Western United States; memoirs, oral histories, genealogy of Western Jews. Holdings: 1500 books; 50 bound periodical volumes; 10 unbound 19th century periodicals; 653 linear feet and 34 5 archival collections; 115 oral histories; 80 titles on microfilm; 14 VF drawers of pamphlets, family biographies, ephemera; 10,000 photographs; 320 tapes and cassettes. Services: Interlibrary loan; copying (both limited); center open to the public.

1905 ■ Kamloops Museum and Archives
Library
207 Seymour St.   Ph: (250)828-3576
Kamloops, BC, Canada V2C   Fax: (250)314-2016
2E7

Contact: Elisabeth Duckworth, Cur.Archv.

Desc: Subject: Fur trade, biography, history - natural, regional, social. Holdings: 1800 books; 3000 bound periodical volumes; 50,000 archival items; 20,000 microfiche; 2600 reels of microfilm; original documents, maps, and photographs; out-of-print books and journals; old telephone directories, newspapers, magazines, and newsletters, phonograph records, and tapes. Services: Copying; Library open to the public (no lending).

1906 ■ Kanabec County Historical Society
Kanabec History Center
805 W. Forest Ave.   Ph: (320)679-1665
PO Box 113   Fax: (320)679-1673
Mora, MN 55051
E-mail: kanabechistory@ncis.com
URL: http://www.kanabechistory.com

Contact: Edna Cole, Exec.Dir.

Desc: Subject: Kanabec County, Minnesota, Minnesota counties, Native Americans, farming, ethnic groups, local authors. Holdings: 196 books; 148 bound periodical volumes; 117 nonbook items. Services: Copying; Center open to the public for reference use only on a fee basis.

1907 ■ Kandiyohi County Historical Society
Victor E. Lawson Research Library
610 N.E. Hwy. 71   Ph: (320)235-1881
Willmar, MN 56201
E-mail: kandhist@wechet.com

Contact: Mona Nelson-Balcer, Dir.

Desc: Subject: History - local, state, U.S. Holdings: 1100 books; 500 bound periodical volumes; 297 volumes and 67 linear feet of archival material and manuscripts. Services: Copying; Library open to the public by appointment.

1908 ■ Kankakee County Historical Society
Museum
801 S. 8th Ave.   Ph: (815)932-5279
Kankakee, IL 60901   Fax: (815)932-5204
E-mail: museum@daily-journal.com

Contact: Anne L. Chandler, Dir.

Desc: Subject: County and state history, Civil War. Holdings: 4000 books; genealogies; city directories; manuscripts; documents; clippings; Civil War volumes. Services: Copying; research.

1909 ■ Kansas City Public Library
Special Collections
311 E. 12th St.   Ph: (816)701-3400
Kansas City, MO 64106   Fax: (816)701-3401
E-mail: lhistory@kcpl.lib.mo.us
URL: http://www.kcpl.lib.mo.us

Contact: Katherine Long, Dept.Mgr.

Desc: Subject: Local history, genealogy, Trans-Mississippi West, Civil War. Holdings: 43,192 titles; 1000 bound periodical volumes; 2800 reels of microfilm; 15,000 photographs; 25,000 postcards; advertising cards; maps. Services: Copying; room open to the public.

1910 ■ Kansas State Historical Society
Library & Archives Division
Center for Historical Research   Ph: (785)272-8681
6425 SW 6th St.   Fax: (785)272-8682
Topeka, KS 66615-1099
E-mail: referenc@hspo.wpo.state.ks.us
URL: http://.www.kshs.org

Contact: Patricia A. Michaelis, Div.Dir.

Desc: Subject: Kansas history, local history of Kansas and other states, genealogy, American Indians, the West, American biography, Civil War, Kansas government records and publications. Holdings: 83,441 books; 54,303 general pamphlets; 9465 volumes and 45,915 pamphlets of Kansas state publications; 32,000 cubic ft. of state archives and local government records; 7763 cubic ft. of manuscripts; 500,000 photographs; over one million feet of films, videotapes, and audiotapes; 25,200 maps, blueprints, and drawings; 75,000 reels of microfilm. Services: Interlibrary loan; copying (limited); Library & archives open to the public.

1911 ■ Kansas State Library
Capitol Building   Ph: (785)296-3296
300 SW 10th Ave., Rm. 343   Fax: (785)296-6650
Topeka, KS 66612-1593
URL: http://www.skyways.lib.ks.us/kansas/

Contact: Duane Johnson, State Libn.

Desc: Subject: Public administration, census, Kansas government and legislation. Holdings: 65,000 books; 10,000 periodical volumes; 60,000 other cataloged items. Services: Interlibrary loan; copying; Library open to the public.

1912 ■ Kansas State University
Minority Resource Research Center
Hale Library   Ph: (913)532-7470
Manhattan, KS 66506   Fax: (913)532-6144
E-mail: mroyse@ksu.edu
URL: http://www.lib.ksu.edu

Contact: Molly Royse

Desc: Subject: African-American history and literature, American ethnic studies, Kansas minority groups, Native American archeology, 20th century Native American sociology, Chicano studies. Holdings: 5000 volumes; 147 microfiche; 388 reels of microfilm; 15 VF drawers of reports; 4 VF drawers of archives; 732 AV programs. Services: Interlibrary loan; copying; Library open to the public.

1913 ■ Kansas State University
Population Research Laboratory
Library
204 Waters Hall   Ph: (785)532-4962
Manhattan, KS 66506-4003   Fax: (785)532-6978

Contact: Leonard Bloomquist, Dir.

Desc: Subject: Demography - community, rural, developing countries. Holdings: 600 books; 50 other cataloged items; Census of Population, 1920-1990; Census of Agriculture, 1930, 1950-1960, 1969, 1974, 1978, 1982, 1987, 1992. Services: Data and analysis provided to the public upon request.

1914 ■ Kellogg, Iowa Historical Museum Library
218 High St., Box 295   Ph: (515)526-3430
Kellogg, IA 50135-0295

Desc: Subject: Kellogg, Iowa history, genealogy, and culture. Holdings: Photographs; scrapbooks; books. Services: Copying; Library open to the public with restrictions.

1915 ■ Keneseth Israel Synagogue Library
2227 West Chew St.   Ph: (610)435-9074
Allentown, PA 18104

Contact: Anne Stakelon, Libn.

Desc: Subject: Judaica, religion, Biblical history, literature. Holdings: 5000 books; recordings. Services: Library open to the public.

1916 ■ Kenilworth Historical Society Library
415 Kenilworth Ave.   Ph: (847)251-2565
Box 181
Kenilworth, IL 60043-1134

Contact: Patricia McClaren Babb, Pres.

Desc: Subject: Local history; area authors. Holdings: 500 books; archives. Services: Copying; Library open to the public for reference use only.

1917 ■ Kennebunkport Historical Society Library
PO Box 1173   Ph: (207)967-2751
Kennebunkport, ME 04046   Fax: (207)967-1205
E-mail: kporths@gwi.net
URL: http://www.kporthistory.org

Contact: Ellen Moy, Dir.

Desc: Subject: Kennebunkport history, local authors. Holdings: Documents; manuscripts; artifacts; photographs. Services: Copying; research assistance; Library open to the public.

1918 ■ Kenosha County Historical Society & Museum Historical Research Library
6300 3rd Ave.   Ph: (414)654-5770
Kenosha, WI 53143   Fax: (414)654-1730

Contact: Robert Fuhrman, Exec.Dir.

Desc: Subject: Local, regional, state history; genealogy; iconography. Holdings: 1500 books; 250 bound periodical volumes; local newspapers; 9 VF drawers of documents and clippings; maps, 1837-1920s; 5000 photographic images; 100 manuscripts, diaries, ledgers; file of death notices. Services: Copying; Library open to the public.

1919 ■ Kent Historical Society Library
116 Macedonia Brook Rd.   Ph: (203)927-3055
Kent, CT 06757

Desc: Subject: Local history, settlement, development; Scaticook Indians; iron industry; genealogy. Holdings: 20 VF drawers; ledgers. Services: Library open to the public.

1920 ■ Kent Memorial Library Historical Room
50 N. Main St.   Ph: (860)668-3896
Suffield, CT 06078   Fax: (860)668-3895
E-mail: director@suffield-library.org
URL: http://www.suffield-library.org

Contact: Joseph J. Cadieux, Dir.

Desc: Subject: Local history, genealogy. Holdings: 1000 books; 50 bound periodical volumes; 100 diaries; 125 account books on microfilm; 35,000 manuscripts, letters; 1000 photographs; photograph albums; scrapbooks of clippings, 1898 to present; newspapers. Services: Copying; room open to the public by appointment.

1921 ■ Kenton County Public Library Kentucky & Local History Collection
5th & Scott Sts.   Ph: (606)491-7610
Covington, KY 41011   Fax: (606)655-7956
E-mail: cking@kenton.lib.ky.us
URL: http://www.kenton.lib.ky.us

Contact: Charles King, Local Hist.Libn.

Desc: Subject: Kentucky genealogy, local history. Holdings: 4300 books; 200 bound periodical volumes; 6000 reels of microfilm; 1500 local history files; 600 family files; 2000 titles of microfiche; 1200 maps. Services: Interlibrary loan; copying; collection open to the public for reference use only.

1922 ■ Kentucky Historical Society KHS Library
Old Capitol Annex   Ph: (502)564-3016
300 W. Broadway   Fax: (502)564-4701
Box 1792
Frankfort, KY 40602-1792
URL: http://www.kyhistory.org

Contact: Anne McDonnell, Lib.Dir.

Desc: Subject: Kentucky history, genealogy, history. Holdings: 80,000 books; 15,000 bound periodical volumes; 10,000 reels of microfilm; 1000 cubic feet of manuscripts; 125 cubic feet of maps; 75,000 photographs. Services: Copying; Library open to the public.

1923 ■ Kentucky (State) Department for Libraries & Archives Public Records Division
PO Box 537   Ph: (502)564-8300
Frankfort, KY 40602   Fax: (502)564-5773
URL: http://www.kdla.state.ky.us/

Contact: Richard N. Belding, Dir.State Archv.

Desc: Subject: Kentucky - history, genealogy, government, politics, health services. Holdings: 96,000 cubic feet of state and local government records, including those of the judicial and legislative branches; 45,000 reels of microfilm; 1000 microfiche; 100 videocassettes; 200 audiocassettes; 25,000 photographic negatives. Services: Copying; archives open to the public.

1924 ■ Kern County Museum Library
3801 Chester Ave.   Ph: (661)852-5000
Bakersfield, CA 93301   Fax: (661)322-6415
URL: http://www.KCMuseum.org

Contact: Jeff Nickell

Desc: Subject: Local history. Holdings: 2400 volumes; 1000 periodicals; approximately 250,000 photograph archive. Services: Copying and photograph reproductions; Library open to staff and researchers.

1925 ■ Kesher Zion Synagogue and Sisterhood Library
1245 Perkiomen Ave.   Ph: (610)374-1763
Reading, PA 19602-1399   Fax: (610)375-1352

Contact: Rachel Yaffee, Libn.

Desc: Subject: Judaica. Holdings: 2500 books. Services: Library open to the public with restrictions.

1926 ■ Kewanee Historical Society Library
211 N. Chestnut St.   Ph: (309)854-9701
Kewanee, IL 61443
URL: http://www.intelcities.com/summit

Contact: Marcella Richards, Cur.

Desc: Subject: Local history - Kewanee, factory, business, people. Holdings: 200 scrap books. Services: Library open to the public.

1927 ■ Kilby Store and Farm Heritage Branch Library
PO Box 84   Ph: (604)796-3859
Harrison Mills, BC, Canada   Fax: (604)796-8341
  V0M 1L0
E-mail: bchlma@uniserv.com

Contact: Bob Parliament, Area Mgr.

Desc: Subject: Kilby family and farm, Harrison Mills history, Milk Shippers Association, the 1920s, museology. Holdings: 500 books; archival items (100 ft.) Services: Library open to the public by appointment.

1928 ■ Kingsborough Community College of City University of New York Kingsborough Historical Society Library
2001 Oriental Blvd.   Ph: (718)368-5259
Brooklyn, NY 11235   Fax: (718)368-5481

Contact: John B. Manbeck, Archv.

Desc: Subject: Brooklyn, New York history. Holdings: 100 books; photographs; clippings; newspapers; pamphlets; color slides; films; music. Services: Interlibrary loan; Library open to the public.

1929 ■ Kinsey's On The Move Family Archives
775 S. 13th Ave.   Ph: (303)659-4232
Brighton, CO 80601

Contact: Judy Kinsey Brookes, Ed.

Desc: Subject: Genealogy. Holdings: 200 volumes; family group files; photographs; maps; journals; area histories. Services: Copying; Library open by appointment only for genealogists.

1930 ■ Kittochtinny Historical Society Library
175 E. King St.   Ph: (717)264-1667
Chambersburg, PA 17201

Contact: Lillian F. Colletta, Pres.

Desc: Subject: History, genealogy. Holdings: Books; manuscripts; newspapers (microfilm, hard copy); cemetery records; funeral directors' records; abstracts of wills; family files; historical files; historical photographs. Services: Library open to the public on a limited schedule.

1931 ■ K.K. Bene IsraelRockdale Temple Sidney G. Rose Memorial Library
8501 Ridge Rd.   Ph: (513)891-9900
Cincinnati, OH 45236   Fax: (513)891-0515

Contact: Ellen Dunsker, Libn.

Desc: Subject: Judaica. Holdings: 8000 books. Services: Library open to the public with restrictions.

1932 ▪ Knox County Historical Society Library
Ph: (816)397-2349
rs>Edina, MO 63537
Fax: (660)397-3331

Contact: Brenton Karhoff, Pres.

Desc: Subject: Local and state history, genealogy. Holdings: 120 books; 50 bound periodical volumes; 7 scrapbooks; clippings. Services: Copying; Library open to the public with restrictions.

1933 ▪ Knox County Public Library System McClung Historical Collection
500 W. Church Ave.
Ph: (423)544-5744
Knoxville, TN 37902-2505

Contact: Steve Cotham, Mgr.

Desc: Subject: History and genealogy of Knoxville, Knox County, Tennessee, and other southeastern states. Holdings: 44,872 books; 5320 bound periodical volumes; 1 million manuscripts; 1369 maps; 10,615 reels of microfilm; 34,456 microfiche; 135 VF drawers of photographs and clippings. Services: Copying; collection open to the public for reference use only.

1934 ▪ Koochiching County Historical Society Museum
Smokey Bear Park
Ph: (218)283-4316
214 6th St.
International Falls, MN 56649

Contact: Edgar S. Oericheauer, Exec.Dir.

Desc: Subject: History - Koochiching County, Boise Cascade, personal; logging. Holdings: 600 volumes; 21 VF drawers and 15 boxes of records and manuscripts; 15 VF drawers of photographs. Services: Copying; museum open to the public.

1935 ▪ Kootenay Lake Archives
Box 537
Ph: (250)353-9633
Kaslo, BC, Canada V0G 1M0
Fax: (250)353-2525
E-mail: archives@pop.kin.bc.ca
URL: http://www.kin.bc.ca/archives/klhs/archives.html

Contact: Elizabeth Scarlett, Archv.

Desc: Subject: Local history, 1891 to present. Holdings: Books; society records; journals; newspapers; photographs; personal papers; audiocassettes; videocassettes. Services: Copying; archives open to the public for reference use only.

1936 ▪ Kootenay Museum Association and Historical Society Nelson Museum Archives
402 Anderson St.
Ph: (604)352-9813
Nelson, BC, Canada V1L 3Y3
Fax: (604)352-5721

Contact: Alan R. Ramsden, Pres.

Desc: Subject: Local history, west Kootenays. Holdings: Photographs; West Kootenay archival material; assessment rolls; NDV-DTVC archival collection. Services: Copying (limited); archives open to the public on a limited schedule when staff member is present.

1937 ▪ Kosciusko County Historical Society Genealogy Section Jail Museum Genealogy Library
PO Box 1071
Ph: (219)269-1078
Warsaw, IN 46581-1071
URL: http://culture.kconline.com/kchs

Contact: Caroline Fawley, Libn.

Desc: Subject: Kosciusko County. Holdings: 1000 books; 200 reels of microfilm; 200 family histories; county courthouse records; cemetery and plat books; tax records, 1843-1969, on microfilm; censuses, 1840-1920; newspapers on microfilm; family histories; city directories; school yearbooks; obituary abstracts. Services: Copying; Library open to the public on a limited schedule.

1938 ▪ Lac Qui Parle County Historical Society Museum Library
250 8th Ave. South
Ph: (320)598-7678
Madison, MN 56256

Desc: Subject: State and local history, Indian history and artifacts, genealogy. Holdings: 1600 books; 100 bound periodical volumes; 50 old and rare books; 50 other cataloged items; 15 binders of obituaries, 1964-1989; newspaper file; scrapbooks; pioneer stories; city, county, territorial, statehood centennials. Services: Library open to the public for reference use only.

1939 ▪ Lackawanna Historical Society Catlin House Library and Archives
232 Monroe Ave.
Ph: (717)344-3841
Scranton, PA 18510
Fax: (717)344-3815

Contact: Mary Ann Moran, Exec.Dir.

Desc: Subject: Local history and literature, genealogy, ethnic studies, architecture. Holdings: 3220 volumes; 54 VF drawers of manuscripts, maps, blueprints. Services: Copying; Library open to the public on fee basis.

1940 ▪ Ladson Genealogical Library
c/o Ohoopee Regional
Ph: (912)537-8186
   Library System
Fax: (912)537-8186
610 Jackson St.
Vidalia, GA 30474
E-mail: ladson@mail.toombs.public.lib.ga.us

Contact: Emily Hartz, Branch Mgr.

Desc: Subject: Eastern Seaboard genealogy, particularly Georgia. Holdings: Family and county histories; cemetery listings; marriage records; census records. Services: Copying; Library open to the public.

1941 ▪ Lake County Historical Society Research Library
8610 King Memorial Rd.
Ph: (440)255-8979
Mentor, OH 44060-8207
Fax: (216)255-8980

Contact: Karon Tomlinson, Res.Libn.Cur.

Desc: Subject: Local history and genealogy, President James A. Garfield. Holdings: 2500 books; manuscripts; clippings; Painesville Telegraph on microfilm 1822-1924; 11 reels of microfilm of Federal Census, 1820-1910; Lake County and Geauga County marriages to 1900; Common Pleas, probate court, and deeds to 1840; obituaries to 1900. Services: Copying; Library open to older students and adults.

1942 ▪ Lake County Historical Society, Inc. Library
PO Box 7800
Ph: (352)343-9890
Tavares, FL 32778-7800
Fax: (352)343-9814
E-mail: histryrus@aol.com

Contact: Donna Jean Hayes, Sec.Libn.

Desc: Subject: Local history and affairs. Holdings: Newspaper articles, 1880 to present; cassette tapes; survey maps; courthouse records; photographs; several volumes of Pioneers. Services: Copying; Library open to the public.

1943 ▪ Lake Erie Islands Historical Society Library
PO Box 25
Ph: (419)285-2804
441 Catawba Ave.
Fax: (419)285-3814
Put-in-Bay, OH 43456

Contact: Edwin Isaly, Cur.

Desc: Subject: Battle of Lake Erie, early trimotor aviation, Lake Erie western basin history, John Brown Jr., Put-in-Bay and Lake Erie steamships. Holdings: 800 books; reports; 3500 archival materials. Services: Copying; Library open to the public at librarian's discretion.

1944 ▪ Lake Tahoe Historical Society Lake Tahoe Museum Library
PO Box 404
Ph: (530)541-5458
South Lake Tahoe, CA 96156

Desc: Subject: Lake Tahoe and Sierra Nevada history, California and Nevada Indians. Holdings: 50 books; 150 documents; 4 AV programs; 15 nonbook items; 50 manuscripts. Services: Library open to the public by appointment.

1945 ▪ Lake of the Woods County Historical Society Museum LibraryArchives
8th Ave., S.E.
Ph: (218)634-1200
Baudette, MN 56623

Contact: Marlys Hirst, Cur.

Desc: Subject: County and state history, local natural history. Holdings: 400 books; 15 manuscripts; 3 VF drawers of documents and reports; 60 reels of microfilm of local and regional newspapers, 1897-1985. Services: Copying; Library open to the public.

1946 ▪ Lakewood Historical Society Library
14710 Lake Ave.
Ph: (216)221-7343
Lakewood, OH 44107

Contact: Mazie M. Adams, Exec.Dir.

Desc: Subject: Lakewood and Rockport Twp. Holdings: 400 books. Services: Library open to the public by appointment.

1947 ▪ Lakewood's Heritage Center Archives
797 S. Wadsworth Blvd.
Ph: (303)987-7850
Lakewood, CO 80226
Fax: (303)987-7851

Contact: Kristen Anderson, Coll.Cur.

Desc: Subject: 20th Century Colorado and Western history, arts and crafts of the past, U.S. transportation history, farming history, Lakewood history. Holdings: 2500 books; 5 AV programs; 6500 photographs; 182 linear feet of manuscripts. Services: Archives open to the public by appointment.

1948 ▪ Lancaster County Historical Society Library
Willson Bldg.
Ph: (717)392-4633
230 N. President Ave.
Fax: (717)293-2735
Lancaster, PA 17603
URL: http://www.lanclio.org

Contact: Mary Virginia Shelley

Desc: Subject: History of Southeastern Pennsylvania and Lancaster County. Holdings: 10,300 books; 1500 bound periodical volumes; 740 bound newspaper volumes; 200 manuscript groups and document collection. Services: Copying; Library open to the public.

1949 ■ Lancaster Historical Commission Document Collection

Town Hall, Thayer Dr. Ph: (508)368-4355
PO Box 351
Lancaster, MA 01523

Contact: Anne Androski, Ch.

Desc: Subject: History of Lancaster and central Massachusetts. Holdings: 150 books; 45 reels of microfilm; 3 VF drawers of manuscripts; military history records; letters; and other archival materials. Services: Copying; Library open to the public on a limited schedule.

1950 ■ Lancaster Mennonite Historical Society Library

2215 Millstream Rd. Ph: (717)393-9745
Lancaster, PA 17602-1499 Fax: (717)393-8751

Contact: Carolyn C. Wenger, Dir.

Desc: Subject: Local, denominational, and Reformation history; genealogy, especially Pennsylvania German names; theology; Pennsylvania German dialect; arts and culture. Holdings: 26,000 titles; 3000 archive boxes; 220,000 vital statistics cards; 200 maps; 420 reels of microfilm. Services: Translation; copying; Library open to the public (fee for non-members).

1951 ■ Landis Valley Museum Library

2451 Kissel Hill Rd. Ph: (717)569-0401
Lancaster, PA 17601 Fax: (717)560-2147

Contact: Dr. Carolyn Stuckert, Mus.Dir.

Desc: Subject: History, Pennsylvania German culture, crafts, folklore, agriculture, cooking, decorative arts and crafts. Holdings: 7000 volumes. Services: Library open to the public by appointment only.

1952 ■ Lapeer County Genealogy Society Marguerite deAngeli Library

921 W. Nepessing St. Ph: (810)664-6971
Lapeer, MI 48446
URL: http://www.lapeer.lib.mi.us/Library/Genealogy/Index.html

Contact: Keitha VerPlanck, Libn.

Desc: Subject: Lapeer, Michigan genealogy. Holdings: Books; family histories; cemetery records; genealogical resources. Services: Library open to the public with restrictions.

1953 ■ Latah County Historical Society Research Library

327 E. 2nd Ph: (208)882-1004
Moscow, ID 83843 Fax: (208)882-0759
E-mail: lchlibrary@moscow.com

Contact: Joann Jones

Desc: Subject: Latah County authors and history. Holdings: 400 books; 400 feet of boxes of manuscripts; 23 boxes of pamphlets; 25 reels of microfilm; 3 file drawers of clippings and ephemera; 9500 photographs. Services: Copying; Library open to the public for reference use only.

1954 ■ Lawrence County Museum Lawrence County Historical Society Library

PO Box 73 Ph: (614)532-1222
Ironton, OH 45638

Contact: Sharon Kouns, Trustee

Desc: Subject: Hanging Rock iron region, Lawrence County, local military, ironmasters. Holdings: 300 books; 25 bound periodical volumes. Services: Library open to the public for reference use only.

1955 ■ Laws Railroad Museum and Historical Site Library

Library & Arts Bldg. Ph: (760)873-5950
Silver Canyon Rd.
PO Box 363
Bishop, CA 93515

Desc: Subject: History - California, Western, U.S.; railroads; technology; science; poetry; prose; art. Holdings: 3800 books; 200 bound periodical volumes; antique books. Services: Copying; Library open to the public for reference use only.

1956 ■ Lawton Public Library Family History Room

110 SW Fourth St. Ph: (580)581-3450
Lawton, OK 73501 Fax: (580)248-0243
URL: http://www.cityoflawton.ok.us/library/

Desc: Subject: Oklahoma history, genealogy, people, and culture. Holdings: 6000 books and periodicals; 150,000 microfiche; 3000 reels of microfilm; records; family histories. Services: Library open to the public.

1957 ■ Layland Museum Padon Research Library & Archives

201 N. Caddo St. Ph: (817)645-0940
Cleburne, TX 76031 Fax: (817)645-0926

Contact: Julie Baker, Dir.Cur.

Desc: Subject: American material culture; American social history; local and state history. Holdings: Books; photographs; slides; scrapbooks; letters; periodicals; newspapers. Services: Copying.

1958 ■ Le Roy House Museum and Historical Society Library

23 E. Main St. Ph: (716)768-7433
Box 176 Fax: (716)768-7579
Le Roy, NY 14482
URL: http://www.iinc.com/jello

Desc: Subject: Local history and genealogy. Holdings: 900 books; 10 bound periodical volumes; 20 VF drawers of reports, clippings, and scrapbooks; family photographs; local family manuscripts; local photographs and newspapers, 1826 to present. Services: Copying; Library open to the public on a limited schedule.

1959 ■ Le Sueur County Historical Society Museum Library

Box 240 Ph: (507)267-4620
Elysian, MN 56028
E-mail: museum@lchs.mus.mn.us
URL: http://www.lchs.mus.mn.us

Contact: Shirley Zimprich, Geneal.

Desc: Subject: Local and state history. Holdings: 1405 volumes; 60 interview tapes of older citizens; 700 reels of microfilm of newspapers; 40 volumes of obituary clippings, county church records, state laws and statistics, county cemetery records, local store ledgers, and county tax receipts. Services: Genealogy open to the public for reference use only.

1960 ■ Leavenworth County Genealogical Society Library

PO Box 362 Ph: (913)682-8181
Leavenworth, KS 66048
E-mail: greyink@idir.net

Contact: Nettie Graden, Bk.Comm.Ch.

Desc: Subject: Genealogy - Leavenworth County, Kansas, Missouri. Holdings: 2000 books; 1100 bound periodical volumes; 50 reports; 175 microfiche; 250 reels of microfilm. Services: Copying; Library open to the public.

1961 ■ Leavenworth County Historical Society and Museum Library

1128 5th Ave. Ph: (913)682-7759
Leavenworth, KS 66048 Fax: (913)682-2089
URL: http://leavenworth-net.com/LCHS/

Contact: Mark Bureman, Musm.Adm.

Desc: Subject: Leavenworth County history, genealogy. Holdings: 1000 books; 10,000 archival materials. Services: Copying; Library open to the public.

1962 ■ Lebanon County Historical Society Library

924 Cumberland St. Ph: (717)272-1473
Lebanon, PA 17042 Fax: (717)272-7474
URL: http://www.leba.net/history2

Contact: Christine L. Mason, Asst. to Exec.Dir.

Desc: Subject: History of Lebanon County and Pennsylvania, local genealogy, Germans in Pennsylvania. Holdings: 3000 pictures; 3000 files; 1000 deeds; 700 reels of microfilm; archives. Services: Copying; genealogical searching (fee); Library open to the public with restrictions.

1963 ■ Lecompton Historical Society Territorial Capitol - Lane Museum

609 Woodson St. Ph: (913)887-6275
Lecompton, KS 66050 Fax: (913)887-6148
URL: http://www.lecomptonkansas.com

Contact: Paul Bahnmaier, Pres.

Desc: Subject: Territorial Kansas, Lane University. Holdings: 2500 books. Services: Museum open to the public.

1964 ■ Lee County Historical Society Research Center

113 Madison Ave. Ph: (815)284-1134
PO Box 58
Dixon, IL 61021-0058
E-mail: lchs1@cin.net
URL: http://www.lchs.cin.net

Desc: Subject: Lee County, Illinois. Holdings: Books; church records. Services: Library open to the public by appointment.

1965 ■ Lee County Iowa Historical Society Samuel F. Miller House Museum Library

PO Box 125 Ph: (319)524-7283
Keokuk, IA 52632

Contact: Linda Bradley, Pres.

Desc: Subject: Lee County - economic development, early city government, local authors. Holdings: 200 books; 1000 manuscripts. Services: Copying; Library open to the public with restrictions.

1966 ■ Leelanau Historical Museum Archives

203 E. Cedar St. Ph: (616)256-7475
Leland, MI 49654 Fax: (616)256-7650
E-mail: ljgleemusc@traverse.com
URL: http://www.leelanau.com/history/

Contact: Laura Quackenbush, Cur.

Desc: Subject: Leelanau County history. Holdings: 500 books. Services: Copying; archives open to the public by appointment.

1967 ■ Lehigh County Historical Society
Scott Andrew Trexler II Memorial Library
Old Court House   Ph: (610)435-1072
5th & Hamilton Sts.   Fax: (610)435-9812
Box 1548
Allentown, PA 18105
E-mail: upsoc@voicenet.com
URL: http://www.voicenet.com/vpsoc.lchs

Contact: Twyla J. Thompson, Libn.Archv.

Desc: Subject: Pennsylvania and Lehigh County history, genealogy. Holdings: 1000 books; 200 newspaper volumes; 2000 pamphlets; 50,000 photographs and negatives; 200 manuscriptts, archives, records of local families and businesses; deeds; maps; church records. Services: Copying; Library open to the public on fee basis.

1968 ■ Lennox and Addington County Museum
Library & Archives
97 Thomas St., E.   Ph: (613)354-3027
Postal Bag 1000   Fax: (613)354-3112
Napanee, ON, Canada K7R 3S9
E-mail: museum@fox.nstn.ca
URL: http://fox.nstn.ca/museum/

Contact: Jane Foster, Mgr.

Desc: Subject: Local history and genealogy. Holdings: 300 linear feet of bound volumes; 340 linear feet of manuscripts and miscellanea; 80 linear feet of newspapers; 27 linear feet of photographs. Services: Genealogical research; copying; Library open to the public.

1969 ■ Lesbian Herstory Educational
Foundation, Inc.
Lesbian Herstory Archives
PO Box 1258   Ph: (718)768-3953
New York, NY 10116   Fax: (718)768-4663
URL: http://www.datalounge.net/lha/

Desc: Subject: Lesbian history and culture, women's history. Holdings: 20,000 books; 30 bound periodical volumes; 500 unbound periodical volumes; 800 audiocassettes; 200 videotapes; 1500 subject files; dissertations. Services: Copying; archives open to the public by appointment.

1970 ■ Lewis & Clark Public Library
Lewis & Clark County Genealogical Society
Library
PO Box 5313   Ph: (406)447-1690
Helena, MT 59604   Fax: (406)447-1687
URL: http://www.mth.mtlib.org/LCLGnuPage/
     LibraryBoard/HoursServices/Services/
     Genealogical_Soc.html

Contact: Deborah Schlesinger, Dir.

Desc: Subject: Lewis & Clark County, Montana, genealogy. Holdings: Figures not available. Services: Interlibrary loan; Library open to the public.

1971 ■ Lewis County Historical Museum
Library
599 NW Front Way   Ph: (360)748-0831
Chehalis, WA 98532   Fax: (360)740-5646
E-mail: lchm@myhome.net

Contact: Karla Clark

Desc: Subject: History of Lewis County, Chehalis Indians, genealogy. Holdings: 15,000 photographs; 400 oral history cassette tapes; 36 feet of archival papers and newspaper clippings; 15 feet of family histories; 200 maps. Services: Family research upon request; copies and transcripts of oral history tapes; Library open to the public - must have staff present.

1972 ■ Lewiston Public Library
Lewiston History Collection
200 Lisbon St.   Ph: (207)784-0135
Lewiston, ME 04240   Fax: (207)784-3011
E-mail: rspeer@lpl.avcnet.org
URL: http://www.avcnet.org/LPL/

Contact: Richard A. Speer, Dir.

Desc: Subject: Lewiston, Androscoggin County, and Maine history and genealogy. Holdings: City directories; scrapbooks; personal accounts; reports; records of organizations.

1973 ■ Lewistown Genealogy Society, Inc.
Library
701 W. Main St.   Ph: (406)538-5212
Lewistown, MT 59457

Contact: Rachel Eide, Pres.

Desc: Subject: Genealogy, local history. Holdings: 750 books. Services: Copying; Library open to the public.

1974 ■ Lexington Historical Society, Inc.
LibraryArchives
Box 514   Ph: (781)862-1703
Lexington, MA 02173   Fax: (781)862-4920
URL: http://www.lexingtonma.org/LexHistSoc/

Desc: Subject: Lexington history. Holdings: 500 books; 50 hours of oral history tapes; documents; manuscripts; photographs. Services: Library open to the public by appointment.

1975 ■ Lexington Public Library
Central Library
Kentucky Room
140 E. Main St.   Ph: (606)231-5520
Lexington, KY 40507   Fax: (606)231-5545
URL: http://www.lexpublib.org/reference/kyroom.html

Contact: Ronald P. Steensland, Lib.Dir.

Desc: Subject: Kentucky - history, genealogy, government. Services: Interlibrary loan.

1976 ■ Library of Congress
American Folklife Center
Thomas Jefferson Bldg.   Ph: (202)707-5510
Washington, DC 20540-8100   Fax: (202)707-2076
E-mail: folklife@loc.gov
URL: http://lcweb.loc.gov/folklife

Contact: Margaret Bulger

Desc: Subject: American folklife with emphasis on research, public programs, and technical assistance; folksong; folk music; folklife; ethnomusicology; oral history. Holdings: 4000 books; 1000 serial titles; 45,000 hours of unpublished field recordings; manuscript collection (700,000 pages); results of current research projects including fieldnotes, sound recordings, photographs, and videotapes; 200,000 ephemera; 400,000 photographs. Services: Copying (limited); reading room open to the public; listening by appointment; correspondence, e-mail, and telephone inquiries; an intern program for interested students.

1977 ■ Library of Congress
Humanities and Social Sciences Division
Local History & Genealogy Reading Room
Thomas Jefferson Bldg.,   Ph: (202)707-5522
   Rm. G42   Fax: (202)707-1957
Washington, DC 20540-4664
URL: http://lcweb.loc.gov/rr/genealogy

Contact: Judith P. Reid, Team Hd.

Desc: Subject: U.S. local history; genealogy - international in scope. Services: Copying; section open to adults only.

1978 ■ Licking County Genealogical Society
Library
743 E. Main St.   Ph: (740)345-3571
Box 4037
Newark, OH 43058-4037
E-mail: lcgs1@juno.com
URL: http://mocin.licking.on.us/libraries/lcgs/
     index.html

Contact: Mrs. G.R. Rose, Libn.

Desc: Subject: Genealogy. Services: Copying; Library open to the public for reference use only.

1979 ■ Licking County Historical Society
Library
PO Box 785   Ph: (740)345-4898
Newark, OH 43058   Fax: (740)345-2983

Contact: Karen Dickman, Libn.

Desc: Subject: Licking County history, Wherle Stove Company, early transportation, Civil War. Holdings: 2500 books; 5000 archival materials; photographs. Services: Interlibrary loan; copying; Library open to the public.

1980 ■ Limestone County Archives
310 W. Washington St.   Ph: (205)233-6404
Athens, AL 35611   Fax: (205)233-6403
URL: http://fly.hiwaay.net/gbf

Contact: Philip W. Reyer, Archv.

Desc: Holdings: Books; 99 bound periodical volumes; 537 reels of microfilm; 3500 manuscripts and public records; 82 cubic ft of papers; 4000 photographs. Services: Copying; archives open to the public.

1981 ■ Lincoln County Historical Society
Library
545 S.W. 9th   Ph: (541)265-7509
Newport, OR 97365   Fax: (541)265-3992
E-mail: coasthistory@newportnet.com
URL: http://www.newportnet.com/coasthistory//
     home.htm

Contact: Loretta Harrison, Exec.Dir.

Desc: Subject: Lincoln County and Oregon history, local Indian reference material. Holdings: 220 volumes and manuscripts. Services: Copying, photo reproductions; Library open to the public for reference use only.

1982 ■ Lincoln Library
Sangamon Valley Collection
326 S. 7th St.   Ph: (217)753-4910
Springfield, IL 62701

Contact: Edward J. Russo, City Hist.

Desc: Subject: Local history, genealogy, current area information. Holdings: 8000 books; 200 bound periodical volumes; 30,000 local photographs. Services: Interlibrary loan; copying; collection open to the public.

1983 ■ Linn County Historical Society
Library
Box 137   Ph: (913)352-8739
Pleasanton, KS 66075

Contact: Ola May Earnest, Pres.

Desc: Subject: Local history and genealogy, county history. Holdings: 600 books; 30 manuscripts; 8 drawers; newspapers and census on microfilm. Services: Copying; genealogical research; Library open to the public for reference use only.

1984 ■ Litchfield Historical Society
Ingraham Library
Box 385   Ph: (860)567-4501
Litchfield, CT 06759   Fax: (860)567-3565

Contact: Catherine Keene Fields, Dir.

Desc: Subject: Local history, genealogy, early American legal and female education. Holdings: 10,000 volumes; 600 linear feet of manuscripts. Services: Copying; genealogical research; Library open to the public.

1985 ■ Literary and Historical Society of Quebec
Library
44 St. Stanislas St.   Ph: (418)694-9147
Quebec, PQ, Canada G1R 4H3

Contact: Sylviane Dubois, Archv.

Desc: Subject: Quebec history. Holdings: 30,000 books. Services: Library open to the public with restrictions.

1986 ■ Logan County Genealogical Society
Library
PO Box 36   Ph: (937)593-7811
Bellefontaine, OH 43311
E-mail: logan.county.ogs@logan.net

Contact: Lucy Rose, Libn.

Desc: Subject: Genealogy. Holdings: 1000 books; 150 reels of microfilm; microfiche IGI index; compact discs. Services: Copying; Library open to the public.

1987 ■ Lombard Historical Society
Library
23 W. Maple St.   Ph: (630)629-1885
Lombard, IL 60148   Fax: (630)629-9927

Contact: Joel Van Haaften, Dir.

Desc: Subject: Lombard - history, people, buildings, authors; Victorian era; Du Page history. Holdings: 276 books; documents; manuscripts. Services: Library open to the public for reference use only.

1988 ■ London Public Libraries
London Room
305 Queens Ave.   Ph: (519)661-5125
London, ON, Canada N6B 3L7

Contact: W. Glen Curnoe, Libn.

Desc: Subject: London and London area - history, family genealogy, local architecture; London Public Library history. Holdings: Books; newspapers; reels of microfilm; unbound reports; scrapbooks; family manuscripts; oral history tapes; pictures; clippings, 1940 to present; documents, including municipal documents. Services: Copying; room open to the public for reference use only.

1989 ■ Long Beach Public Library
Literature and History Department
101 Pacific Ave.   Ph: (562)570-7500
Long Beach, CA 90822   Fax: (562)570-6956

Contact: Claudine Burnett, Lit. & Hist.Libn.

Desc: Subject: Fiction, literature, foreign languages, travel, biography, history. Holdings: 78,500 books; 70 VF drawers. Services: Interlibrary loan.

1990 ■ Lorain County Historical Society
Gerald Hicks Memorial Library
509 Washington Ave.   Ph: (440)322-3341
Elyria, OH 44035   Fax: (440)322-2817

Desc: Subject: Local, state, national history; genealogy. Holdings: 623 volumes. Services: Library open to the public on a limited schedule for reference use only.

1991 ■ Los Alamos Historical Museum Archives
PO Box 43   Ph: (505)662-6272
Los Alamos, NM 87544   Fax: (505)662-6312
URL: http://www.losalamos.com/lahistory

Contact: Patricia F. Goulding, Archv.

Desc: Subject: Los Alamos history, Northern New Mexico's history and archeology. Holdings: 800 books; 92 serial titles, including local newspapers and Los Alamos National Laboratory publications; 271 oral history audiocassettes; 125 linear feet of archival and manuscripts collections; 254 maps; 8000 photographs; 1500 slides; 18 linear feet of photograph albums; 250 films and videotapes. Services: Copying; photo print copies of archival photographs; archives open to the public by appointment.

1992 ■ Los Angeles Harbor College
Library
Archives
1111 Figueroa Pl.   Ph: (310)522-8292
Wilmington, CA 90744   Fax: (310)522-8435
E-mail: campbel@smtplink.laccd.edu
URL: http://www.lahc.cc.ca.us

Contact: Elisabeth Campbell, Libn.

Desc: Holdings: Pamphlets, clippings, photographs. Services: Archives open to the public by appointment only.

1993 ■ Los Angeles Public Library
History and Genealogy Department
630 W. 5th St.   Ph: (213)228-7400
Los Angeles, CA 90071   Fax: (213)228-7409
E-mail: history@lapl.org
URL: http://www.lapl.org

Contact: Jane Nowak, Dept.Mgr.

Desc: Subject: History, travel, biography, Californiana, genealogy, local history, heraldry, newspapers. Holdings: 268,000 volumes; 91,000 maps; 2.7 million photographs; 800 historical specimen newspapers; 25,000 reels of microfilm of newspapers, U.S. city directories; census records. Services: Interlibrary loan; copying (limited).

1994 ■ Los Angeles Public Library
Social Sciences, Philosophy and Religion Department
630 W. 5th St.   Ph: (213)228-7300
Los Angeles, CA 90071   Fax: (213)228-7309
E-mail: social@lapl.org
URL: http://www.lapl.org

Contact: Jane Nowak, Dept.Mgr.

Desc: Subject: Philosophy, religion, psychology, social problems, government, foreign affairs, international relations, law, criminology, education, women's movements, family relations, ethnic groups, interpersonal relations. Holdings: 324,000 volumes; CD-ROMs. Services: Interlibrary loan; copying; department open to the public.

1995 ■ (Louisiana) State Library of Louisiana
PO Box 131   Ph: (225)342-4913
Baton Rouge, LA 70821   Fax: (225)219-4804
E-mail: tjaques@pelican.state.lib.la.us
URL: http://smt.state.lib.la.us/

Contact: Thomas F. Jaques, State Libn.

Desc: Holdings: 427,806 volumes; 4211 maps; 10,000 photographs; 21,754 reels of microfilm. Services: Interlibrary loan; copying; Library open to the public.

1996 ■ Louisiana (State) Office of the Secretary of State
Division of Archives, Records Management, and History
Box 94125   Ph: (504)922-1206
Baton Rouge, LA 70804   Fax: (504)925-4726

Contact: Dr. Donald J. Lemieux, State Archv.Dir.

Desc: Subject: State and local government records, Louisiana history, genealogy. Holdings: 11,100 books; 30,000 cubic feet of archival government records; 53,400 reels of microfilm. Services: Copying; microfilming conservation laboratory; division open to the public.

1997 ■ Lowndes County Historical Society
Archives
305 W. Central Ave.   Ph: (912)247-4780
PO Box 434   Fax: (912)247-2840
Valdosta, GA 31603
E-mail: lownhist@surfsouth.com

Contact: Albert S. Pendleton, Cur.

Desc: Subject: History and genealogy of Valdosta and Lowndes County, 1860 to present. Holdings: 700 photographs; letters; biographical sketches; organization and county government records; genealogical materials. Services: Archives open to the public on a limited schedule and by appointment to special groups.

1998 ■ Lycoming County Historical Society
Museum
Library
858 W. 4th St.   Ph: (570)326-3326
Williamsport, PA 17701-5824 Fax: (570)326-3689
E-mail: lchsmuse@csrlink.net

Desc: Subject: Genealogy; local history. Holdings: 3000 books; periodicals; pamphlets; archival materials; county naturalization papers; Grit newspaper files; tax records; cemetery records; genealogical information. Services: Copying; Library open to the public by appointment.

1999 ■ Lyme Historical Society, Inc.
Archives
96 Lyme St.   Ph: (860)434-5542
Old Lyme, CT 06371   Fax: (860)434-6259
E-mail: flogris@connux.com
URL: http://www.flogris.org

Contact: Laurie Bradt, Register

Desc: Subject: Local history and art. Holdings: 20,000 manuscripts and documents; 1200 photographs; 6 boxes of clippings. Services: Copying; archives open to the public by appointment.

2000 ■ Lynn Museum
Library
125 Green St.   Ph: (781)592-2465
Lynn, MA 01902   Fax: (617)592-0012

Contact: Diane Shephard, Libn.

Desc: Subject: Lynn and Essex County history, genealogy. Holdings: 3000 books; 20,000 photographs; 37 VF drawers and 50 feet of unbound books, manuscripts, clippings, records; newspapers. Services: Copying; Library open to the public.

2001 ■ Lyons Historical Society
Lyons Redstone Museum
Library
340 High   Ph: (303)823-6692
Box 9   Fax: (303)823-8257
Lyons, CO 80540

Contact: LaVern M. Johnson, Pres.

Desc: Subject: Lyons area history. Holdings: 15 volumes; 20 reels of microfilm; 1 AV program; obituary files; resident name files; business files; town newspapers, 1927-1941 and 1968-1989. Services: Copying; Library open to the public for reference use only (June through September).

2002 ■ Macculloch Hall Historical Museum
Macculloch Hall Archives
45 Macculloch Ave.   Ph: (973)538-2404
Morristown, NJ 07960   Fax: (973)538-9428
E-mail: macchall@aol.com
URL: http://www.machall.org

Contact: Jane R. Odenweller, Archv.

Desc: Subject: Macculloch-Miller family, Thomas Nast, whig political party, Morris Canal. Holdings: 1000 books; 100 documents; 2000 manuscripts; 1000 photographs; 2000 prints and drawings. Services: Copying; archives open to the public by appointment.

2003 ■ Macomb County Historical Society
Crocker House Museum
Sabin and Lena Crocker Library
15 Union St.   Ph: (810)465-2488
Mt. Clemens, MI 48043

Contact: Betty Lou Morris

Desc: Subject: Local history, Crocker family genealogy, Victorian literature. Holdings: City directories; atlases; scrapbooks; pamphlet file. Services: Library open to the public by appointment.

2004 ■ Madawaska Historical Society
Madawaska Public Library Research Center
Main St.   Ph: (207)728-4272
Madawaska, ME 04756

Contact: Patsy Theriault

Desc: Subject: Madawaska area history, genealogy, folk tales. Holdings: Photographs; microfilm; microfiche. Services: Copying; Center open to the public for reference use only.

2005 ■ Madera County Historical Society
MuseumLibrary
Old County Courthouse   Ph: (209)673-0291
210 W. Yosemite Ave.
Box 478
Madera, CA 93639

Desc: Subject: History - Madera County, California, school, pioneer families, San Joaquin valley. Holdings: Photographs; diaries; clippings; maps; charts; documents; scrapbooks. Services: Copying; Library open to the public for reference use only with member present.

2006 ■ Madison County Historical Society
PO Box 124   Ph: (740)852-2977
London, OH 43140

Contact: Gretchen Green, Musm.Dir.

Desc: Subject: Madison County history. Holdings: 2000 books. Services: Library open to the public.

2007 ■ Madison County Historical Society
Library
435 Main St.   Ph: (315)363-4136
Box 415
Oneida, NY 13421

Contact: Mary King, Libn.

Desc: Subject: Local history, genealogy, traditional crafts. Holdings: 1850 books; 150 bound periodical volumes; 650 pamphlets, brochures, 19th & 20th century newspapers, maps, broadsides; 90 tapes; 54 films; 13 VF drawers of slides. Services: Copying; Library open to the public with restrictions.

2008 ■ Madison County Historical Society
Museum Library
715 N. Main St.   Ph: (618)656-7562
Edwardsville, IL 62025

Contact: Marion Sperling, Libn.

Desc: Subject: Illinois and Madison County history; genealogical history of residents of Madison County. Holdings: 2479 books; 27 filing drawers and 50 feet of library shelves of manuscripts, documents, diaries, secretarial books, and county papers; 308 reels of microfilm of Madison County newspapers, including 267 rolls of microfilm Edwardsville Intelligencer, 1869-1920, 1988 to present; 4 filing drawers and 7 bins of photographs and portraits; 24 photo albums (late nineteenth and early twentieth century); county cemetery inventories; county marriage records index; maps. Services: Research; copying; Library open to the public for reference use only.

2009 ■ Madison County Historical Society, Inc.
Library
Eastern Kentucky University   Ph: (606)622-1792
Special Collections and Archives   Fax: (606)622-1174
Library 126
Richmond, KY 40475-3121
E-mail: archive@acs.eku.edu

Contact: Charles Hay

Desc: Subject: Local and state history. Holdings: 10 volumes; 2 scrapbooks; 100 newspaper articles; 50 items in Kentucky Bicentennial Series. Services: Library open to the public by appointment.

2010 ■ Madison Historical Society, Inc.
Library
853 Boston Post Rd.   Ph: (203)245-4567
Box 17
Madison, CT 06443
E-mail: achard@c.shore.com

Contact: Mrs. E. Smith

Desc: Subject: Local history, genealogy, religion, arts. Holdings: 850 volumes; 6 VF drawers of manuscripts, sermons, photographs, clippings, reports, pamphlets. Services: Library open to the public by appointment.

2011 ■ Madison Township Historical Society
Thomas Warne Historical Museum and Library
150 Morristown Rd.   Ph: (732)566-0348
Matawan, NJ 07747   Fax: (732)566-6943

Contact: Alvia D. Martin, Cur.

Desc: Subject: Local history, genealogy. Holdings: 1233 books; postcards; newspapers; pamphlets; phonograph records; maps. Services: Library open to the public for reference use only.

2012 ■ Mahaffie Stagecoach and Farm
Library
1100 Kansas City Rd.   Ph: (913)782-6972
Olathe, KS 66061   Fax: (913)397-5114

Contact: Jack Tinnell, Pres.Dir.

Desc: Subject: Santa Fe Trail, local and state history, 19th Century clothing, Oregon Trail, 19th-century decorative arts, museum administration. Holdings: 500 volumes; 50 bound periodical volumes; 200 reports; 100 archive items. Services: Copying; SDI; Library open to the public.

2013 ■ Mahaska County Historical Society
Irma Glatty Library
PO Box 578   Ph: (515)672-2989
Oskaloosa, IA 52577

Contact: Dolly BeDillon, Libn.

Desc: Subject: Local history, military history. Holdings: 350 books; bound periodical volumes; documents; city directories; family histories; maps; plat books; nonbook items. Services: Copying; Library open to the public.

2014 ■ Mahoning Valley Historical Society and Arms Family Museum of Local History and Archival Library
648 Wick Ave.   Ph: (330)743-2589
Youngstown, OH 44502   Fax: (330)743-7210

Contact: H. William Lawson, Dir.

Desc: Subject: Mahoning Valley Region, Youngstown, Mahoning County, steel industry, immigration, genealogy. Holdings: 300 cubic feet of books; 25 cubic feet of bound periodical volumes; 2500 cubic feet of archival material; 2 cubic feet of microfilm; 400 cubic feet of photographs. Services: Copying; photograph duplication; Library open to the public.

2015 ■ Main Line Reform Temple
Library
410 Montgomery Ave.   Ph: (610)649-7800
Wynnewood, PA 19096

Contact: Betty Graboyes, Libn.

Desc: Subject: Judaica. Holdings: 8000 items. Services: Library open to the public with special permission.

2016 ■ Maine Historical Society
Library
485 Congress St.   Ph: (207)774-1822
Portland, ME 04101   Fax: (207)775-4301
E-mail: nnayes@mainehistory.org
URL: http://www.mainehistory.org

Contact: Nicholas Noyes, Libn.

Desc: Subject: Maine history and biography, New England history and genealogy. Holdings: 100,000 books; newspapers; documents; records; manuscripts; artifacts; photographs; maps. Services: Copying; Library open to the public on fee basis.

2017 ■ Maine Maritime Museum
LibraryArchives
243 Washington St.   Ph: (207)443-1316
Bath, ME 04530   Fax: (207)443-1665
E-mail: lipfert@bathmaine.com
URL: http://www.bathmaine.com

Contact: Nathan Lipfert, Lib.Dir.

Desc: Subject: Maine and American maritime history, shipbuilding in Maine, local history and genealogy. Holdings: 8000 books; 800 bound periodical volumes; 1000 pamphlets; 400 navigation charts; 20 unbound journals; 25,000 photographs; 30,000 ship plans; 1000 ships' logs, account books, ledgers; 250 document boxes. Services: Copying; Library open to the public.

2018 ■ Maine State Library
LMA Bldg.   Ph: (207)287-5600
State House Sta. 64   Fax: (207)287-5615
Augusta, ME 04333
E-mail: reference.desk@state.me.us
URL: http://www.state.me.us/msl/mslhome.htm

Contact: J. Gary Nichols, State Libn.

Desc: Subject: Maine - history, genealogy, state, county, and local histories. Holdings: 400,000 volumes; federal and state government documents. Services: Interlibrary loan; copying; Library open to the public.

2019 ■ Malden Historical Society
Library
Malden Public Library   Ph: (617)324-0220
36 Salem St.
Malden, MA 02148

Contact: John Tramondozzi, Cur.

Desc: Subject: Maldeniana. Holdings: 2000 books. Services: Library not open to the public.

2020 ■ Manchester City Library
New Hampshire Room

405 Pine St.   Ph: (603)624-6550
Manchester, NH 03104-6199   Fax: (603)624-6559
URL: http://www.manchester.lib.nh.us

Contact: Cynthia O'Neil, Libn.

Desc: Subject: New Hampshire - state and local history, biography, genealogy; history of Amoskeag Corporation. Holdings: 5800 books; 752 bound periodical volumes; 140 microfilm of scrapbooks of Manchester news clippings, 1840-1942; photographs of Amoskeag mills and millyards; Manchester Union Leader subject clipping file; 29 microfilm Manchester Vital Records in public domain. Services: Limited copying; genealogical and state historical research and reference; room open to the public for reference use only, on a limited schedule.

2021 ■ Manchester Historical Society
Library

10 Union St.   Ph: (978)526-7230
Manchester-by-the-Sea, MA
  01944

Contact: Esther M. Proctor, Libn.

Desc: Subject: Local history. Holdings: 400 books; 15 bound periodical volumes; 4 drawers of photographs of local homes and people; old local maps; genealogy manuscripts. Services: Copying; Library open to the public with restrictions.

2022 ■ Manitoba Genealogical Society Inc.
Library

E-1045 St. James St.   Ph: (204)783-9139
Winnipeg, MB, Canada R3H   Fax: (204)783-0190
  1B1
E-mail: mgs@mbnet.mb.ca
URL: http://www.freenet.mbnet.mb/mgs

Contact: Louisa Shermerhorn, Libn.

Desc: Subject: Manitoba genealogical information, genealogy, biography, family history. Holdings: 4000 volumes; genealogical resource periodicals; area directories. Services: Copying; Library open to the public with restrictions.

2023 ■ Mansfield Historical Society
Edith Mason Library

954 Storrs Rd.   Ph: (860)429-6575
Box 145
Storrs, CT 06268-2285
E-mail: info@mansfield-history.org
URL: http://www.mansfield-history.org

Contact: Richard Schimmelpfeng, Libn.

Desc: Subject: Local Mansfield history. Holdings: 451 books; 3000 photographs; 2950 manuscripts, account books, scrapbooks, diaries. Services: Genealogical searching (limited); Library open to the public with restrictions from May to October.

2024 ■ Marblehead Historical Society
Jeremiah Lee Mansion

161 Washington St.   Ph: (781)631-1768
PO Box 1048
Marblehead, MA 01945
E-mail: macin@greennet.net

Contact: Karen MacInnis

Desc: Subject: Local history and genealogy, deeds, ships' logs. Holdings: Books; bound periodical volumes. Services: Library open to the public.

2025 ■ Marin County Historical Society
Museum & Library

1125 B St.   Ph: (415)454-8538
San Rafael, CA 94901
URL: http://www.marinwebcom/marinhistory/

Contact: Jocelyn A. Moss, Libn.Cur.

Desc: Subject: History of Marin County and California, history of coastal Indians. Holdings: 1000 volumes; 100 bound manuscripts and studies. Services: Copying; Library open to the public for reference use only.

2026 ■ Marin County Library
Anne Kent California Room

Administration Bldg.   Ph: (415)499-7419
Civic Center   Fax: (415)499-3017
San Rafael, CA 94903
URL: http://www.co.marin.ca.us/libs/

Contact: Carol Starr

Desc: Subject: Marin County local history, California history, Frank Lloyd Wright, San Francisco and Bay area, San Quentin Prison. Holdings: 2500 books; 40 bound periodical volumes; 600 reports; 36 boxes of archival materials; 1726 microfiche; 3 drawers of photographs. Services: Copying; Library open to the public.

2027 ■ Marion Area Genealogical Society
Library

PO Box 844   Ph: (740)387-4255
Marion, OH 43301
URL: http://128.146.189.6/Local/Marion.html

Desc: Subject: Marion County history, Ohio history, genealogy, Marion city history. Holdings: 250 books; 100 bound periodical volumes; 50 reports. Services: Copying; Library open to the public.

2028 ■ Marissa Historical & Genealogical
Society
Library

PO Box 47   Ph: (618)295-2562
Marissa, IL 62257-0047

Contact: Elda L. Jones, Pres.

Desc: Subject: Genealogy, local history. Holdings: Scrapbooks; area histories; rare books; ledgers; autographs; cemetery records; court records; census records; coal-related articles; microfilm; microfiche. Services: Copying; Library open to the public with restrictions.

2029 ■ Marquette County Historical Society
J.M. Longyear Research Library

213 N. Front St.   Ph: (906)226-3571
Marquette, MI 49855
E-mail: mqtcohis@uproc.lib.mi.us

Contact: Linda K. Panian, Libn.

Desc: Subject: History of Great Lakes area and Michigan - shipping, railroads, industries, ethnic groups, mining (copper, gold, silver, and iron). Holdings: 8000 books; 2000 pamphlets; 35 VF drawers of letters, manuscripts, maps, photographs, documents; all known copies of local newspaper, Lake Superior Journal, Lake Superior News, and Mining Journal, July 1846 to present, on microfilm. Services: Library open to the public.

2030 ■ Mars Hill College
Renfro Library
Appalachian Room Special Collections

     Ph: (704)689-1394
rs>Mars Hill, NC 28754   Fax: (704)689-1474
E-mail: PHarmon@mhc.edu
URL: http://www.mhc.edu

Contact: Peggy Harmon, Spec.Coll.Supv.

Desc: Subject: Appalachian life and culture, ballads, country music, Southern Baptists, genealogy, college history. Holdings: 6700 books; 240 linear feet of manuscripts; 238 reels of microfilm. Services: Copying (limited); collections open to the public.

2031 ■ Marshall County Historical Society
Library

PO Box 123   Ph: (309)246-2349
Lacon, IL 61540

Contact: Eleanor Bussell, Cur.

Desc: Subject: History - Marshall and Putnam counties, Illinois, United States; Abraham Lincoln; antiques; early church and school books. Holdings: 780 books; 15 manuscripts; magazines. Services: Copying; Library open to the public.

2032 ■ Marshall County Historical Society
Museum
Library

123 N. Michigan St.   Ph: (219)936-2306
Plymouth, IN 46563

Contact: Linda Rippy, Dir.

Desc: Subject: Marshall County and Indiana history, genealogy. Holdings: 600 books; 734 reels of microfilm of Marshall County newspapers; 15 oral history tapes. Services: Copying; performs research; Library open to the public.

2033 ■ Marshall Historical Society & Honolulu
House Museum
Archives

Box 68   Ph: (616)781-8544
Marshall, MI 49068   Free: 800-877-5763
     Fax: (616)781-8544

Desc: Subject: Marshall history, pioneers, homes, views; Calhoun County history; railroads. Holdings: 300 books; 9 boxes of photographs; 28 boxes of manuscripts and documents; 30 boxes of clippings and unbound periodicals; 4 boxes of maps. Services: Copying; answers public inquiries by mail; archives open to the public by appointment.

2034 ■ Marshall University
James E. Morrow Library
Special Collections

400 Hal Greer Blvd.   Ph: (304)696-2343
Huntington, WV 25755   Fax: (304)696-5858
E-mail: brown@marshall.edu
URL: http://www.marshall.edu/speccoll/

Contact: Lisle G. Brown, Cur.

Desc: Subject: West Virginiana, Civil War, Appalachian studies, history of medicine. Holdings: 18,400 books; 400 bound periodical volumes; 1479 linear feet of manuscripts; 25,200 West Virginia state documents; 600 cubic feet of university archives; 30 linear feet of miscellanea. Services: Interlibrary loan; copying; collections open to the public.

2035 ■ Martha's Vineyard Historical Society
Vineyard Museum
Gale Huntington Library of History

59 School St.   Ph: (508)627-4441
PO Box 827   Fax: (508)627-4436
Edgartown, MA 02539
E-mail: mvhist@vineyard.net

Contact: Peter Van Tassel, Libn.

Desc: Subject: History of Martha's Vineyard, genealogy, whaling history, shipping, maritime history, history of Island Indians, literature by Island authors. Holdings: 33,000 items, including 3000 volumes; 225 boxes of archival material; customs office account books; records; deeds; correspondence; manuscripts; photographs; oral histories; videotapes; maps and charts. Services: Copying; Library open to the public for reference use only.

2036 ▪ Martin County Historical Society, Inc.
Pioneer Museum
Library
304 E. Blue Earth Ave.   Ph: (507)235-5178
Fairmont, MN 56031

Contact: Helen Simon, Cur.

Desc: Subject: American Indian, Civil War, Minnesota history. Holdings: 612 bound periodical volumes; 476 reels of microfilm of Martin County newspapers. Services: Copying; Library open to the public for reference use only.

2037 ▪ Mary B. Cunningham Historical
Resource Center
Penniman Genealogical Library
31 Tenney Rd.   Ph: (617)848-1640
Braintree, MA 02184-6512   Fax: (617)380-0731

Contact: Marjorie Maxham, Lib.Archv.

Desc: Subject: Local history and genealogy. Holdings: 1000 volumes. Services: Copying; Library open to the public by appointment.

2038 ▪ Mary Ball Washington Museum Family
Research Center
Box 97   Ph: (804)462-7280
Lancaster, VA 22503-0097   Fax: (804)462-6107

Contact: Christine C. Townley, Exec.Dir.

Desc: Subject: U.S. and Virginia history; county histories; genealogy; family history. Holdings: 6500 books; 200 bound periodical volumes; historical research and family papers. Services: Interlibrary loan; copying; research service; library open to the public.

2039 ▪ Mary Holmes College
Learning Resources Center
Oral History Collection
Hwy. 50, W.   Ph: (601)494-6820
Box 1257   Fax: (601)494-5319
West Point, MS 39773
E-mail: mprice@ramsstate.edu

Contact: Marty Price, Dir.

Desc: Subject: History, sociology, folklore. Holdings: 26,000 volumes. Services: Interlibrary loan; copying; collection open to the public for reference use only.

2040 ▪ Maryland Historical Society
Library
201 W. Monument St.   Ph: (410)685-3750
Baltimore, MD 21201   Fax: (410)385-2105
E-mail: pcatzen@mdhs.org
URL: http://www.mdhs.org

Contact: David DeLorenzo, Lib.Dir.

Desc: Subject: Maryland and regional history and genealogy, United States history. Holdings: 55,000 books; 1500 newspaper volumes; 3 million manuscripts; 10,000 pamphlets; 1700 reels of microfilm; 5000 prints; 250,000 photographs; 3000 maps; 26 VF drawers of clippings; 1 million pcs. printed ephemera. Services: Copying; Library open to the public with fee for nonmembers.

2041 ▪ Maryland State Archives
Library
350 Rowe Blvd.   Ph: (410)260-6400
Annapolis, MD 21401   Fax: (410)974-3895
E-mail: archives@mdarchives.state.md.us
URL: http://www.mdarchives.state.md.us

Contact: Christine E. Alvey, Libn.

Desc: Subject: History - Maryland, American, African American, other states; genealogy; biography. Holdings: 16,000 books; 450 bound periodical volumes; reports; manuscripts; archives. Services: Copying; Library open to the public for reference use only.

2042 ▪ Maryland State Law Library
Courts of Appeal Bldg.   Ph: (410)260-1430
361 Rowe Blvd.   Fax: (410)974-2063
Annapolis, MD 21401
E-mail: mike.miller@courts.state.md.us
URL: http://www.lawlib.state.md.us

Contact: Michael S. Miller, Dir.

Desc: Subject: Law, Marylandia, genealogy. Holdings: 380,000 books; 13,000 bound periodical volumes; newspapers; 6000 reels of microfilm; selected U.S. Government documents depository. Services: Interlibrary loan; copying; Library open to the public.

2043 ▪ Mason County Historical Society
Research Library
White Pine Village   Ph: (616)843-4808
1687 S. Lakeshore Dr.   Fax: (616)843-7089
Ludington, MI 49431-2166
E-mail: whitepine@masoncounty.net
URL: http://www.lumanet.org/whitepine

Contact: Ronald M. Wood, Dir., Hist.Soc.

Desc: Subject: History - Mason County, Native American, marine, lumbering, businesses, industries; biography. Holdings: 500 books; 20 VF drawers of clippings, photographs, legal documents, brochures, newspapers; local newspapers on microfilm. Services: Copying; Library open to the public.

2044 ▪ Massachusetts Historical Society
Library
1154 Boylston St.   Ph: (617)536-1608
Boston, MA 02215   Fax: (617)859-0074
URL: http://www.masshist.org

Contact: Peter Drummey, Libn.

Desc: Subject: History - Massachusetts, New England, U.S. Holdings: 200,000 books; maps; prints; photographs, newspapers. Services: Copying; Library open to qualified researchers.

2045 ▪ Massachusetts Institute of Technology
Institute Archives and Special Collections
Hayden Library, Rm. 14N-118   Ph: (617)253-5690
77 Massachusetts Ave.   Fax: (617)258-7305
Cambridge, MA 02139-4307
URL: http://libraries.mit.edu/archives/

Contact: Megan Sniffin-Marinoff, Inst.Archv.

Desc: Subject: Archival and manuscript collections concerning M.I.T. and science and technology in the 19th and 20th centuries. Holdings: 48,601 books; 1409 bound periodical volumes; 2629 bound serial volumes; 163,169 microforms; 200 photographs; 4595 technical reports; 13,000 cubic feet of manuscripts and archival materials; 84,335 theses; 3 scores. Services: Copying.

2046 ▪ Maui Historical Society
Library
2375-A Main St.   Ph: (808)244-3326
Wailuku, HI 96793   Fax: (808)244-3920
URL: http://www.mauimuseum

Desc: Subject: Hawaii, Maui. Holdings: 600 books; 6 VF drawers of mounted clippings; 10 VF drawers of photographs; 1 drawer of slides; 8 VF drawers of historical files by subject; 5 VF drawers of archeological files; 22.5 linear feet of archives and manuscripts. Services: Copying.

2047 ▪ McAllen Genealogical Society
Library
601 N. Main   Ph: (956)682-4531
McAllen, TX 78501
E-mail: librarian@mcallen.lib.tx.us
URL: http://www.mcallen.lib.tx.us/

Contact: Janette Josserand, Geneal.Libn.

Desc: Subject: Genealogy. Holdings: 4900 books; 590 bound periodical volumes. Services: Copying; Library open to the public.

2048 ▪ McKinley Museum of History, Science,
and Industry
Ramsayer Research Library
PO Box 20070   Ph: (330)455-7043
Canton, OH 44701   Fax: (330)455-1137
E-mail: mmuseum@neo.lrun.com

Contact: W.J. Weber, Libn.

Desc: Subject: President William McKinley and family, Stark County history and industry, local family histories. Holdings: 3200 books; 4000 other cataloged items; 27 reels of microfilm of McKinley papers and McKinleyana. Services: Library open to the public for reference use only on a limited schedule.

2049 ▪ McKinney Job Corps
Library
1701 N. Church St.   Ph: (972)542-2623
PO Box 8003   Fax: (972)542-8870
McKinney, TX 75069

Contact: K.D. McCleskey, Libn.

Desc: Subject: Ethnic history, special education, self-improvement, psychology, careers, guidance and counseling. Holdings: 10,500 books; 390 phonograph records. Services: Library not open to the public.

2050 ▪ McLean County Historical Society
Stevenson-Ives Library
200 N. Main St.   Ph: (309)827-0428
Bloomington, IL 61701   Fax: (309)827-0100
E-mail: mch@darkstar.rsa.lib.il.us

Contact: Patricia A. Hamilton, Libn.Archv.

Desc: Subject: History - McLean County, Central Illinois, Illinois; Civil War; genealogy. Holdings: 8000 books; 200 historical journals; 197 bound newspaper volumes; 40 CD-ROMs; papers of locally and militarily important people and local organizations; 250 linear feet of archives. Services: Copying; Library open to the public for reference use only.

2051 ▪ McPherson County Historical Society
Library
540 E. Hill St.   Ph: (316)241-2699
McPherson, KS 67460

Contact: L. Peterson, Pres.

Desc: Subject: McPherson County, Kansas.

2052 ▪ McPherson County Old Mill Museum
and Park
120 Mill St.   Ph: (785)227-3595
PO Box 94   Fax: (785)227-2810
Lindsborg, KS 67456
URL: http://www.chamber@lindsborg.org

Contact: Lenora Lynam, Archv.

Desc: Subject: McPherson County history. Holdings: 100 books; 40 bound periodical volumes; 2500 archival materials. Services: Copying; Library open to the public.

2053 ■ Medfield Historical Society Library

6 Pleasant St.   Ph: (508)359-4773
Box 233
Medfield, MA 02052
E-mail: peakfield@aol.com

Contact: Richard DeSorgher, Pres.

Desc: Subject: Local history and genealogy. Holdings: Books, bound periodical volumes, reports, manuscripts, archives, photographs. Figures not available. Services: Library open to the public by permission.

2054 ■ Medford Historical Society Library

153 Brooks St.   Ph: (781)396-9032
Medford, MA 02155

Contact: Michael Bradford, Cur.-Libn.

Desc: Subject: Local history. Holdings: Books; manuscripts; letters; archives of local newspapers (to 1930) and early Boston newspapers (early 19th century). Services: Library open to the public for reference use only.

2055 ■ Medford Mail Tribune Library

PO Box 1108
Medford, OR 97501   Ph: (541)776-4411
    Fax: (541)776-4376

Contact: Pamela S. Sieg, Libn.

Desc: Subject: Southern Oregon topics and personalities; local history. Holdings: 1000 volumes; 34 LF drawers of clippings, photographs, and maps. Services: Library open to the public by appointment.

2056 ■ Memorial Foundation of the Germanna Colonies in Virginia Archives

PO Box 693   Ph: (540)825-1496
Culpeper, VA 22701-0693   Fax: (540)825-6572
E-mail: office@germanna.org
URL: http://www.germanna.org

Contact: Rose Marie Martin, Ed.

Desc: Subject: Germanna Colonies in Virginia. Holdings: Books; photographs; family histories. Services: Archives open to the public.

2057 ■ Memorial Presbyterian Church Greenhoe Library

1310 Ashman St.   Ph: (517)835-6759
Midland, MI 48640

Contact: Esther Frost, Libn.

Desc: Subject: Bible interpretation, church history, Christian education, prayer, peace, justice. Holdings: 5000 books; periodicals; archival materials; tapes; videotapes; compact discs. Services: Library open to the public; theological reference section open to Midland community clergy..

2058 ■ Memorial University of Newfoundland Folklore and Language Archive

    Ph: (709)737-8401
rs>St. John's, NF, Canada A1B   Fax: (709)737-4718
    3X8
E-mail: MUNFLA@morgan.UCS.MUN.CA

Contact: Dr. Martin J. Lovelace, Dir.

Desc: Subject: Newfoundland, Labrador, the Maritime Provinces - folklore, folklife, language, oral history, popular culture. Holdings: 14,000 manuscripts; 120,000 5x8 Folklore Survey Cards; 25,000 tape recordings; 12,000 photographs. Services: Copying (limited); archive open for scholarly research.

2059 ■ MemphisShelby County Public Library & Information Center
Memphis Room Collections

1850 Peabody Ave.   Ph: (901)725-8821
Memphis, TN 38104   Fax: (901)725-8814
URL: http://www.memphislibrary.lib.tn.us

Contact: Judith A. Drescher, Lib.Dir.

Desc: Subject: MemphisShelby County, genealogy, Mardi GrasCotton Carnival, yellow fever, Blues and Beale Street, Mississippi steamboats. Holdings: 11,120 books; 1250 bound periodical volumes; 1200 maps; 500,000 newspaper clippings; 11,000 photographs; 3000 pages of oral history transcripts; 250 manuscript collections; 7500 reels of microfilm. Services: Interlibrary loan; copying; collections open to the public.

2060 ■ Mendocino Historical Research, Inc.
Lemos Library

45007 Albion St.   Ph: (707)937-5791
PO Box 922   Fax: (707)937-4233
Mendocino, CA 95460

Contact: Katherine Bicknell, Exec.Dir.

Desc: Subject: Town of Mendocino, Mendocino County coast. Holdings: 500 books; 100 documents; 15,000 vintage photographs; nonbook items. Services: Copying; Library open to the public by appointment.

2061 ■ Mennonite Historians of Eastern Pennsylvania (MHEP)
Mennonite Historical Library & Archives

Mennonite Heritage Center   Ph: (215)256-3020
Box 82, 565 Yoder   Fax: (215)256-3023
Harleysville, PA 19438
E-mail: info@mhep.org
URL: http://www.mhep.org/Page5.html

Contact: Joel D. Alderfer, Libn.

Desc: Subject: History - Mennonite church, Anabaptist, local; genealogy; folklore; church music; Pennsylvania Germans; peace and non-resistance. Holdings: 6050 books; 716 bound periodical volumes; 315 manuscript collections; 537 bound church bulletins; 186 reels of microfilm; 1860 audiocassettes; 50 maps; 2000 photographs; 118 archival collections; 36 videotapes; 350 broadsides, posters, and prints; 425 vertical and genealogical files; 175 transcripts (church and cemetery records, diaries, account books). Services: Copying; Library open to the public.

2062 ■ Mennonite Historical Library

Goshen College   Ph: (219)535-7418
Goshen, IN 46526   Fax: (219)535-7438
E-mail: mhl@goshen.edu
URL: http://www.goshen.edu

Contact: John D. Roth, Dir.

Desc: Subject: Anabaptist, Mennonite, Amish, and Hutterian Brethren writings and history; genealogy; limited materials relating to the Church of the Brethren, the Society of Friends, and regional history. Holdings: 50,000 books; 10,500 bound periodical volumes; 105 VF drawers of unpublished treatises, archival materials, pamphlets, folders, maps, photographs, photocopies; microforms; phonograph records. Services: Interlibrary loan; copying; Library open to the public.

2063 ■ Merced County Library
Special Collections

2100 "O" St.   Ph: (209)385-7643
Merced, CA 95340   Fax: (209)726-7912
E-mail: li05@co.merced.ca.us
URL: http://library.co.merced.ca.us

Contact: Charleen Renteria, County Libn.

Desc: Subject: Federal, state, and local documents; state and local history; genealogy; maps. Holdings: 358,686 books; 935 U.S. documents; 616 Merced County documents; 689 maps. Services: Collections open to the public.

2064 ■ Mercer County Historical Society Library and Archives

119 S. Pitt St.   Ph: (724)662-3490
Mercer, PA 16137
URL: http://www.pathway.net/mchs

Contact: William Philson, Exec.Dir.

Desc: Subject: Mercer County history. Holdings: 2500 books; 200 bound periodical volumes; newspapers; maps; surveys; microfilm; manuscript materials. Services: Copying; mail research requests accepted; Library open to the public.

2065 ■ Mercer University
Georgia Baptist History Depository

Main Library   Ph: (912)752-2968
1300 Edgewood Ave.   Fax: (912)752-2111
Macon, GA 31207-0001
E-mail: broome_sg@mercer.edu
URL: http://www.cdsearch.mercer.edu/mainlib/
    special_collections/default.htm

Contact: Susan G. Broome, Hd., Spec.Coll.

Desc: Subject: History - Georgia Baptist, Mercer University, Tift College, Cooperative Baptist Fellowship, local. Holdings: 300 microfiche; 900 reels of microfilm. Services: Copying; Library open to the public.

2066 ■ Mercyhurst College
Sr. Mary Lawrence Franklin Archival Center

501 E. 38th St.   Ph: (814)824-2190
Erie, PA 16546   Fax: (814)824-2219
E-mail: eglaser@mercyhurst.edu

Contact: Earleen Glaser, Ref.Libn. & Archv.

Desc: Subject: Mercyhurst College Archives; Erie County - societies, organizations, women's groups, history, churches; ethnic studies. Holdings: 1806 books; 363 accessions; 6 files of oversize maps, charts, blueprints; 269 reels of microfilm; 2952 slides; 57 16mm films; 115 videotapes; 24 magnetic tapes; 254 film work cores. Services: Interlibrary loan (limited); archives open to the public by appointment.

2067 ■ Mesa Family History Center Library

41 S. Hobson   Ph: (602)964-1200
Mesa, AZ 85204   Fax: (602)964-7137

Contact: Glenn E. Scott, Dir.

Desc: Subject: Genealogy, history. Holdings: 16,000 books; 45,000 microfiche; 63,000 reels of microfilm. Services: Copying; Library open to the public.

2068 ■ Mesquite Public Library
Genealogy Collection

300 W. Grubb Dr.   Ph: (972)216-6229
Mesquite, TX 75149

Desc: Subject: Mesquite, Texas history and genealogy. Holdings: Census records (microfilm); journals; family histories, genealogical research materials.

2069 ■ Metropolitan Toronto Reference Library
Special Collections Centre

789 Yonge St.   Ph: (416)393-7153
4th Floor   Fax: (416)393-7229
Toronto, ON, Canada M4W
    2G8

Contact: David Kotin, Team Ldr.

Desc: Services: Interlibrary loan; Library open to the public for reference use only.

2070 ■ Miami County Genealogy Society
Library
North Side of Square   Ph: (913)294-4940
PO Box 123
Paola, KS 66071

Contact: Betty Bendorf

Desc: Subject: Genealogy, research in Miami County. Holdings: 200 books; quarterlies; family histories; 80 reels of microfilm. Services: Copying; Library open to the public.

2071 ■ Miami County Museum
Hal C. Phelps Archives
51 N. Broadway   Ph: (765)473-9183
Peru, IN 46970   Fax: (765)473-3880
E-mail: mchs@netusa1.net
URL: http://www.netusa1.net/mchs

Contact: Joyce Miller, Archv.Dir.

Desc: Subject: Miami County history, Miami Indians, circus, Cole Porter. Holdings: 1000 books; 250 bound periodical volumes; 10 AV programs. Services: Copying.

2072 ■ Miami-Dade Public Library
Federal Documents Division
101 W. Flagler St.   Ph: (305)375-5575
Miami, FL 33130-1523   Fax: (305)375-3048
E-mail: d009410c@dc.seflin.org

Contact: Mary Garcia, Libn. II

Desc: Subject: Legislation, census, U.S. treaties. Holdings: 170,000 U.S. Government publications (selective depository); legislative documents. Services: Collection open to the public.

2073 ■ Miami-Dade Public Library
Genealogy Collection
101 W. Flagler St.   Ph: (305)375-5580
Miami, FL 33130   Fax: (305)375-3048
URL: http://www.mdpls.org

Contact: Renee Pierce, Geneal.Libn. III

Desc: Subject: Genealogy. Holdings: 13,800 volumes; 14,100 reels of microfilm of census; 3100 reels of microfilm of directories, 1861-1935; 1647 American directories, through 1860, on microfiche; 3600 microfiche; 1500 reels of miscellaneous microfilm. Services: Copying; room open to the public.

2074 ■ Michigan City Public Library
Indiana Room
One Library Plaza   Ph: (219)873-3044
Michigan City, IN 46360
E-mail: reference@mclib.org
URL: http://www.mclib.org/

Contact: Rose Chenoweth, Lib.Dir.

Desc: Subject: Michigan City, LaPorte County, and Indiana history and genealogy. Holdings: Pamphlet files; census holdings; family histories; microfiche histories; obituary file; county history holdings; oral history cassettes; cemetery lists; photographs; slides.

2075 ■ Middle Georgia Historical Society
Archives
935 High St.   Ph: (912)743-3851
Macon, GA 31201   Fax: (912)745-3132

Contact: Katherine C. Oliver, Exec.Dir.

Desc: Subject: Sidney Lanier, Macon, Georgia history. Holdings: Books. Services: Copying; archives open to the public for reference use only.

2076 ■ Middlebury Historical Society
Middlebury Academy Museum Library
22 S. Academy St.   Ph: (716)495-6692
PO Box 198
Wyoming, NY 14591-0198

Contact: Mary Lester, Cur.

Desc: Subject: Middlebury Academy. Holdings: 920 volumes, maps, documents. Services: Library open to the public on a limited schedule.

2077 ■ Middlesex County Historical Society
Library
151 Main St.   Ph: (860)346-0746
Middletown, CT 06457   Fax: (860)346-0746

Contact: Dione Longley, Dir.

Desc: Subject: Connecticut history, genealogy, town histories. Holdings: archives; manuscripts; letters; notebooks; records. Services: Library open to the public by appointment only.

2078 ■ (Midland) City of Midland
Grace A. Dow Memorial Library
Special Collections
1710 W. St. Andrews Dr.   Ph: (517)837-3430
Midland, MI 48640-2698   Fax: (517)837-3468
E-mail: jalsip@vlc.lib.mi.us

Contact: James B. Alsip, Lib.Dir.

Desc: Subject: Local history. Holdings: 233,951 books; 150 bound periodical volumes; 1000 reports; 65,300 microfiche; 1800 reels of microfilm. Services: Interlibrary loan; copying; collections open to the public.

2079 ■ Midland County Historical Society
Archives
1801 W. St. Andrews   Ph: (517)835-7401
Midland, MI 48640

Contact: Gary F. Skory, Dir.

Desc: Subject: Midland, Michigan history and genealogy. Holdings: 1000 books; local newspapers, 1870 to present, on microfilm; maps; slides; pictures. Services: Copying; archives open to the public by appointment.

2080 ■ Midwest Historical & Genealogical Society, Inc.
Library
Box 1121   Ph: (316)264-3611
Wichita, KS 67201

Contact: Jerry Stout, Libn.

Desc: Subject: Genealogy, local history. Holdings: 10,000 books; 700 bound periodical volumes; 150 Kansas cemetery references; 100 scrapbooks of obituaries and golden anniversaries; 600 reels of microfilm; 24 VF drawers. Services: Copying; Library open to the public with restrictions.

2081 ■ Mifflin County Historical Society
Library
1 W. Market St., Ste. 1   Ph: (717)242-1022
Lewistown, PA 17044-2128

Contact: Jean A. Suloff, Libn.

Desc: Subject: History of central Pennsylvania and Mifflin County. Holdings: 1000 books; manuscripts; maps; pictures. Services: Library open to the public with restrictions.

2082 ■ Milan Public Library
Special Collections
151 Wabash St.   Ph: (734)439-1240
Milan, MI 48160   Fax: (734)439-5625
E-mail: milan@monroe.lib.mi.us

URL: http://cwic1.jackson.lib.mi.us/milan

Contact: Gail Hardenbergh, Lib.Dir.

Desc: Subject: Milan, Michigan history, culture, and people; business. Holdings: Books; records; microfiche; microfilm; pictures. Services: Interlibrary loan; copying; Library open to the public.

2083 ■ Milford Area Historical Society
Library
906 Main St.   Ph: (513)248-0324
Milford, OH 45150

Contact: Maxine Van Aken, Libn.

Desc: Subject: Local history, genealogy. Holdings: 200 books; 30 bound periodical volumes; 100 archival items. Services: Copying; Library open to the public.

2084 ■ Milford Historical Society
Historical Museum Reference Room
124 E. Commerce St.   Ph: (248)685-7308
Milford, MI 48381

Contact: Mary Lou Gharrity, Musm.Dir.

Desc: Subject: Milford genealogy and history. Holdings: Oak Grove Cemetery records; early family genealogies; Civil War records. Services: Copying; room open to the public with restrictions.

2085 ■ Millicent Library
Archives Department
Fairhaven, MA 02719
URL: http://www.tiac.net/users/millie/archives.htm

Contact: Debbie Charpentier, Archv.

Desc: Subject: Fairhaven, Massachusetts - history, genealogy, culture, authors. Services: Archives open to the public with restrictions.

2086 ■ Milwaukee County Historical Society
Library and Archives
910 N. Old World Third St.   Ph: (414)273-8288
Milwaukee, WI 53203
URL: http://www.milwaukeecountyhistsoc.org

Contact: Steve Daily, Cur., Res.Coll.

Desc: Subject: History of Milwaukee County, history of socialist movements, Germans and other immigrant groups. Holdings: 5200 books; 75 bound periodical volumes; 60 bound volumes of government proceedings; manuscript collections; iconographic material maps. Services: Copying; Library open to the public on a fee basis.

2087 ■ Milwaukee Public Library
Humanities Division
Special Collections
814 W. Wisconsin Ave.   Ph: (414)286-3000
Milwaukee, WI 53233-2385   Fax: (414)286-2137

Contact: Virginia Schwartz, Coord.

Desc: Subject: History - local, Great Lakes, Wisconsin, surrounding states; genealogy; Milwaukee; regional transportation. Holdings: 30,000 books; 1200 bound periodical volumes; theses; 165 boxes of pamphlets; 40,000 photographs; 500 linear feet of manuscripts; 2500 maps and lake charts; 300 atlases; railroad photos and technical drawings. Services: Interlibrary loan; copying (limited); collections open to nonresident public for reference use.

2088 ■ Mineral County Museum & Historical Society
Library
PO Box 533   Ph: (406)822-4626
Superior, MT 59872

Contact: Deborah J. Davis, Cur.

Desc: Subject: History - Montana, local, regional, Western; mining. Holdings: 500 books; unbound periodical volumes; documents; 24 manuscripts; nonbook items (including historic photographs). Services: Interlibrary loan; copying; Library open to the public.

2089 ■ Mineral Point Historical Society Archives

Orchard Lawn - Jos.   Ph: (608)987-2884
  Gundry House
234 Madison St.
Mineral Point, WI 53565

Contact: Dean Connors, Pres.

Desc: Subject: Victorian houses and minerals and rocks. Holdings: 350 legal documents; papers of pioneers; account books and records of local firms; Civil War diaries; maps. Services: Archives open to the public with permission from the board of directors.

2090 ■ Minisink Valley Historical Society Library

138 Pike St.   Ph: (914)856-2375
PO Box 659   Fax: (914)856-1049
Port Jervis, NY 12771-0659
E-mail: mvhs1889@magiccarpet.com
URL: http://www.minisink.org

Contact: Peter Osborne, III, Exec.Dir.

Desc: Subject: Local history and genealogy. Holdings: 10,000 manuscripts and archival materials; 10,000 photographs, genealogical records, and Works Progress Administration files. Services: Copying; genealogical research; Library open to the public on a limited schedule.

**2091 ■ Minneapolis Public Library
Humanities Division
History Department**

300 Nicollet Mall   Ph: (612)630-6080
Minneapolis, MN 55401
URL: http://www.mpls.lib.mn.us

Contact: Betsy Williams, Div.Mgr.

Desc: Subject: History, travel, geography, government, politics, biography, genealogy, heraldry, coins, general law. Holdings: 177,800 books; 28,000 bound periodical volumes; 750 other cataloged items; 15,000 reels of microfilm; 1300 audiotapes and books; U.S. Geological Survey maps. Services: Interlibrary loan; copying.

**2092 ■ Minnesota Historical Society
Fort Snelling Branch Library**

Fort Snelling History Center   Ph: (612)726-1171
St. Paul, MN 55111   Fax: (612)725-2429
URL: http://www.mnhs.org

Contact: Stephen E. Osman

Desc: Subject: History - Minnesota, regional, military; American Indians; American and regional archeology; 19th century America. Holdings: 6000 volumes; 1500 other cataloged items. Services: Library open to the public for reference use only.

**2093 ■ Minnesota Historical Society
Library**

345 Kellogg Blvd., W.   Ph: (651)296-2143
St. Paul, MN 55102-1906   Fax: (651)297-7436
E-mail: Reference@mnhs.org
URL: http://www.mnhs.org

Contact: Denise Carlson, Hd., Ref.

Desc: Subject: Minnesota and Upper Midwest: genealogy, Scandinavians in North America, ethnic groups, transportation, agriculture, arts, commerce, family life, industry, Indians, political life. Holdings: 500,000 monographs, government documents, and microform volumes; 100

VF drawers; 500,000 photographs; 35,000 maps; 1300 atlases; 4.5 million issues of 3000 titles of newspaper volumes; 37,000 cubic feet of manuscripts; 45,000 cubic feet of Minnesota government records. Services: Interlibrary loan; copying; Library open to the public for reference use only.

**2094 ■ (Minnesota) State Department of
Planning
DATANET**

330 Centennial Office Bldg.   Ph: (612)296-6866
658 Cedar St.   Fax: (612)296-1212
St. Paul, MN 55155

Contact: Richard Fong, Info.Spec.

Desc: Subject: Minnesota and the United States - 1990 demographics, economic indicators, agriculture, state and county rankings, adolescent health, business patterns, natural resources, state grants and loans, Gross State Product data for all 50 states. Holdings: 90 megabytes of summary statistical databases on hard disc.

**2095 ■ Minnesota (State) Iron Range Research
Center
State Government Library**

Hwy. West 169   Ph: (218)254-3325
PO Box 392   Fax: (218)254-4938
Chisholm, MN 55719
E-mail: dcb@ironworld.com
URL: http://www.ironworld.com

Contact: Debra L. Fena

Desc: Subject: Minnesota Mesabi, Vermilion, and Cuyuna Iron Ranges - mining, labor, local, lumbering and oral histories; local government; genealogy. Holdings: 3600 books; 188 bound periodical volumes; more than 5000 reels of microfilm; more than 100,000 accessioned photographs; 1250 oral history tapes; 2253 linear feet of government records; 885.75 linear feet of manuscripts; 70 theses and dissertations. Services: Research services; Interlibrary loan;census microfilm rental; Library open to the public.

**2096 ■ Minnesota State University, Mankato
Memorial Library
M. J. Lass Center for Minnesota Studies**

PO Box 8419   Ph: (507)389-5949
Mankato, MN 56002-8419   Fax: (507)389-5155
E-mail: tim.smith@mankato.msus.edu

Contact: Dr. Sylverna Ford, Dean, Lib.Svcs.

Desc: Subject: Minnesota. Holdings: Minnesota State document depository collection. Services: Interlibrary loan; copying; Center open to the public.

2097 ■ Mission Community Archives

33215 Second Ave.   Ph: (604)820-2621
PO Box 3522   Fax: (604)820-2621
Mission, BC, Canada V2V 4L1
E-mail: mca@city.mission.bc.ca

Contact: Valerie Billesberger, Archv.

Desc: Subject: Mission, British Columbia area - social, economic, and political development; local history; genealogy; archives administration. Holdings: 446 linear feet of archival material; books; pamphlets; clippings. Services: Copying; archives open to the public by appointment.

**2098 ■ Missisquoi Historical Society
Missisquoi Museum
Reference Library & Archives**

Box 186   Ph: (450)248-3153
Stanbridge East, PQ, Canada J0J Fax: (450)248-0420
2H0
E-mail: sochm@globetrotter.net
URL: http://www.geocities.com/Heartland/lake/8392

Contact: Judy Antle, Archv.

Desc: Subject: Eastern Townships of Quebec - genealogy, history, biography, geography; Canadiana; antiques. Holdings: 4000 books; 50 bound periodical volumes; 693 reports, manuscripts, clippings, documents, maps, oral history tapes. Services: Interlibrary loan; copying; library open to the public for reference use only.

**2099 ■ Mississippi (State) Department of
Archives and History
Archives and Library Division**

PO Box 571   Ph: (601)359-6850
Jackson, MS 39205   Fax: (601)359-6964

Contact: H.T. Holmes, Div.Dir.

Desc: Subject: Mississippiana, genealogy, Confederate history, colonial history of Southeast United States. Holdings: 58,000 volumes; 17,000 cubic feet of official state archives; 2000 manuscript collections; 24,000 nonbook items; 6000 cubic feet of manuscripts; 7095 maps; 18,000 reels of microfilm; 200,000 photographs; 3 million feet of newsfilm; 2203 architectural drawings; 158 VF drawers. Services: Copying; Library open to the public for reference use only.

**2100 ■ Missouri Historical Society
Archives**

Library and Research Center   Ph: (314)746-5410
PO Box 11940   Fax: (314)746-4548
St. Louis, MO 63112-0040

Contact: Chuck Hill, Archv.

Desc: Subject: St. Louis history and culture, Missouri, Mississippi Valley, American West. Holdings: 6000 linear feet of archival materials. Services: Copying; archives open to the public.

**2101 ■ Missouri Historical Society
Library**

PO Box 11940   Ph: (314)746-4500
St. Louis, MO 63112-0040

Contact: Emily Miller, Libn.

Desc: Subject: History - St. Louis, Missouri, Western United States, Missouri and Mississippi Rivers; fur trade; biography; genealogy; theater; Thomas Jefferson; early Mississippi travel; steamboats; Lewis and Clark expedition; American Indians. Holdings: 75,000 book, pamphlet, and periodical titles; 2000 bound newspaper volumes; 2500 maps. Services: Copying; Library open to the public.

**2102 ■ Missouri Historical Society
Photograph & Prints Collection**

PO Box 11940   Ph: (314)746-4511
St. Louis, MO 63112   Fax: (314)746-4548

Contact: Duane Sneddeker, Cur.

Desc: Subject: St. Louis and Missouri and Western life - buildings, street scenes, Indians, theater, music, transportation, valentines, steamboats, aviation, Lindbergh pictures. Holdings: 500,000 photographs, postcards, prints, daguerreotypes, tintypes, ambrotypes, advertising materials. Services: Print and reproduction services available on fee basis; use of archives for reference may be requested.

2103 ■ Missouri State Archives

600 W. Main   Ph: (573)751-3280
PO Box 778   Fax: (573)526-7333
Jefferson City, MO 65102
E-mail: archref@mail.sos.state.mo.us
URL: http://mosl.sos.state.mo.us

Contact: Kenneth H. Winn, State Archv.

Desc: Subject: Missouri history, genealogy. Holdings: 1400 linear feet of books; 110,000 cubic feet of archival material; 65,000 microfiche; 51,600 reels of microfilm. Services: Copying; Library open to the public.

2104 ▪ Mitchell County Historical Society Library
Box 52 Ph: (515)732-4047
Osage, IA 50461-0052

Contact: Karen Hemrich, Cur.

Desc: Subject: Local history. Holdings: 100 books; 3 AV programs; 250 nonbook items; newspaper clippings; school and church records. Services: Library open during summer weekends only.

2105 ▪ Mobile Public Library
Local History and Genealogy Division
701 Government St. Ph: (334)208-7093
Mobile, AL 36602 Fax: (334)208-5866
URL: http://www.acan.net/library

Contact: Charlotte Chamberlain, Div.Mgr.

Desc: Subject: Local history, genealogy. Holdings: 15,112 books; 1700 bound periodical volumes; 1871 reels of microfilm of Mobile newspapers; 6900 reels of microfilm of federal census records; 56 reels of microfilm of French and Spanish colonial records; 206 reels of microfilm on miscellaneous subjects. Services: Library open to the public for reference use only.

2106 ▪ Monmouth County Historical Association
Library and Archives
70 Court St. Ph: (732)462-1466
Freehold, NJ 07728 Fax: (732)462-8346
E-mail: mchalib@cjrlc.org
URL: http://www.monmouth.com/mcha/

Contact: Carla Z. Tobias, Libn.Archv.

Desc: Subject: Monmouth County history and genealogy, church and Bible records. Holdings: 7000 books; 870 bound periodical volumes; VF drawers of newspaper clippings; pamphlets; programs; manuscript collections; microfilm; photographs; maps; broadsides; extensive newspaper collection. Services: Copying; Library open to the public.

2107 ▪ Monroe County Genealogical Society
Carnegie-Evans Library
Rte. 3, Box 215 Ph: (515)932-2593
Albia, IA 52531-9550

Contact: Sarah Hindman, Correspondence Sec.

Desc: Subject: State, regional, local history and genealogy. Holdings: Cemetery, land, marriage, family, and school records and histories; maps and plot books; veteran material; newspapers; newsletters. Services: Interlibrary loan (limited); copying; Library open to the public.

2108 ▪ Monroe County Historical Association
Elizabeth Dimmick Walters Library
Stroud Community House Ph: (717)421-7703
900 Main St. Fax: (717)421-9199
Stroudsburg, PA 18360
E-mail: mcha@ptdprolog.net

Contact: Candace McGreevy, Exec.Dir.

Desc: Subject: Monroe County history and genealogy. Holdings: 1200 books; 100 bound periodical volumes; 300 reports; 2000 archival items; 500 reels of microfilm; 45 cubic feet of documents and manuscripts; newspapers; clippings; maps. Services: Copying; Library open to the public.

2109 ▪ Monroe County Historical Society Library
PO Box 538 Ph: (740)472-1933
Woodsfield, OH 43793 Fax: (740)472-5156

Contact: Mitchell Schumacher, Pres.

Desc: Subject: Monroe County and Ohio history, genealogy. Holdings: Archival materials; microfiche; reels of microfilm. Services: Copying; query research; Library open to the public.

2110 ▪ Monroe County Local History Room & Library
200 W. Main Ph: (608)269-8680
PO Box 419 Fax: (608)269-8921
Sparta, WI 54656
E-mail: mclhr@centuryinter.net

Contact: Audrey Johnson, County Hist.Libn.

Desc: Subject: Local history, genealogy. Holdings: 800 books; 400 reels of microfilm; 14 VF drawers of cemetery records; 12,000 documents; 5000 photographs. Services: Interlibrary loan; copying; Library open to the public.

2111 ▪ Montana Historical Society LibraryArchives
225 N. Roberts Ph: (406)444-2681
PO Box 201201 Fax: (406)444-2696
Helena, MT 59620
E-mail: mthislib@mcn.net
URL: http://www.his.mt.gov

Contact: Robert M. Clark, Hd., Lib. & Archv.Div.

Desc: Subject: Lewis and Clark Expedition; George Armstrong Custer; Charles M. Russell; military history of the Montana Indians; Montana biographygenealogy; mining; cattle and range; homesteading. Holdings: 50,000 books; 5000 bound periodical volumes; 50,000 state publications; 6500 cubic feet of private papers; 200,000 photographs; 14,000 reels of microfilm of Montana and other newspapers; 16,000 maps; 4000 broadsides and ephemera; 1500 oral history interviews. Services: Interlibrary loan; copying (both limited); Library open to the public for research and reference use only.

2112 ▪ Montana (State) Department of Commerce
Census & Economic Information Center
1424 9th Ave. Ph: (406)444-2896
Helena, MT 59620-0505 Fax: (406)444-1518
E-mail: ceic@state.mt.us
URL: http://commerce.state.mt.us/ceic

Contact: Patricia A.B. Roberts, Prog.Mgr.

Desc: Subject: Montana - demography, census, economics. Holdings: 4000 documents; census maps; CD-ROMs; microfiche; magnetic tapes. Services: Copying; SDI; center open to the public for reference use only.

2113 ▪ Montana State Library
1515 E. 6th Ave. Ph: (406)444-3004
Helena, MT 59620 Fax: (406)444-5612
E-mail: kstrege@mst.state.mt.us
URL: http://msl.state.mt.us

Contact: Karen Strege, State Libn.

Desc: Subject: General collection. Holdings: 60,725 books; 527 periodical titles; 28,988 state publications; 345,058 federal publications. Services: Interlibrary loan; copying; Library open to the public.

2114 ▪ Montgomery County Department of History and Archives
Old Court House Ph: (518)853-8186
Fonda, NY 12068 Fax: (518)853-8392
E-mail: histarch@superior.net

Contact: Jacqueline Murphy, County Hist.Rec.Mgmt.Off.

Desc: Subject: Local and state history, genealogy, county archives. Holdings: 9350 books; 100 bound periodical volumes; 1200 maps; 800 genealogies; county documents; will abstracts; deeds; church and cemetery records. Services: Copying; Library open to the public.

2115 ▪ Montgomery County Genealogy Society Library
Coffeyville Public Library Ph: (316)251-1370
PO Box 444 Fax: (316)251-1512
311 West 10th St.
Coffeyville, KS 67337-0444

Contact: Karyl Buffington

Desc: Subject: Genealogy. Holdings: Archival materials; microfiche; reels of microfilm. Services: Interlibrary loan; copying; Library open to the public.

2116 ▪ Montgomery County Historical Society Library
7 N. Main St. Ph: (937)228-6271
Dayton, OH 45402 Fax: (937)331-7160

Contact: Mary Oliver, Cur., Hist. & Coll.

Desc: Subject: Local history, Montgomery County history. Holdings: 2500 books; 2000 archival materials. Services: Copying; photo reprints; Library open to the public by appointment.

2117 ▪ Montgomery County Historical Society Library
103 W. Montgomery Ave. Ph: (301)340-2974
Rockville, MD 20850 Fax: (301)340-2871
E-mail: mchistory@mindspring.com
URL: http://www.montgomeryhistory.org

Contact: Jane C. Sween, Libn.

Desc: Subject: History, biography, genealogy. Holdings: 3000 books; information files on history of Montgomery County, Maryland; photographs; plats; card files of early court records; church records; marriage records. Services: Copying; Library open to the public on fee basis.

2118 ▪ Montgomery's Inn Museum Archives
4709 Dundas St. W Ph: (416)394-8113
Etobicoke, ON, Canada M9A Fax: (416)394-6027
1A8

Contact: Randall Reid

Desc: Subject: Decorative arts, local history, genealogy. Holdings: 1000 books. Services: Library open to the public for reference use only.

2119 ▪ Moraga Historical Society Archives
Moraga Public Library Ph: (510)376-6852
1500 St. Mary's Rd. Fax: (925)376-3034
Moraga, CA 94556

Contact: Margaret Skinner, Archv.

Desc: Subject: Moraga Rancho area history, including the town of Moraga; Moraga family history and genealogy 1835 to present; history of communities of Orinda, Lafayette, and Canyon; history of Rancho Laguna de los Palos Colorados. Holdings: 725 books; 260 oral history tapes; 30 VF drawers of clippings and documents; minutes of the meetings of the Moraga Company (1912-1953); 6 volumes of land title abstracts; 164 files of court cases, 1850-1940; 800 photographs; 390 maps; 60 reels of microfilm of documents, letters, dissertations, parish records to 1900; California mission records; tax assessor's records.

Services: Copying; photograph reproduction; archives open to the public for reference use only on a limited schedule.

2120 ▪ Moravian Historical Society
Museum and Library
214 E. Center St.   Ph: (610)759-5070
Nazareth, PA 18064   Fax: (610)759-5070

Contact: Susan Dreydoppel, Exec.Dir.

Desc: Subject: Moravian church history and biography, Pennsylvania history, genealogy. Holdings: 5000 books; 1000 bound periodical volumes; 1000 archives. Services: Copying; Library open to the public with restrictions.

2121 ▪ Morgan County Historical Society
Library
210 N. Monroe St.   Ph: (573)369-2555
Versailles, MO 65084

Contact: Calvin A. Draegert, Cur.

Desc: Subject: Local history. Holdings: Cemetery records; 1850, 1860, 1870 census records; family history records; marriage books. Services: Library open to the public on a limited schedule.

2122 ▪ Morris County Historical Society
Archives
303 W. Main St.   Ph: (316)767-5716
Council Grove, KS 66846
E-mail: annetcg@midusa.net

Contact: Bonnie McClintock, Archv.

Desc: Subject: Morris County, family history. Holdings: 175 books; bound periodical volumes. Services: Library open to the public.

2123 ▪ Morris County Historical Society
Victorian Resource Library
68 Morris Ave.   Ph: (973)267-3465
Morristown, NJ 07960-4212   Fax: (973)267-8773

Desc: Subject: Local social and cultural history of the Victorian-Edwardian periods. Holdings: 1300 books; 150 bound periodical volumes; 100 boxes of county and individual interest; 900 photographs. Services: Library open to the public by appointment.

2124 ▪ Morris County Library
New Jersey Collection
30 E. Hanover Ave.   Ph: (973)285-6974
Whippany, NJ 07981   Fax: (973)285-6982
E-mail: heagney@main.morris.org
URL: http://www.gti.net/mocolib1.mcl.html

Contact: Marie Heagney, Prin.Libn.

Desc: Subject: State and local history, genealogy. Holdings: 4000 books; 90 bound periodical volumes; 19 VF drawers; 675 reels of microfilm. Services: Copying; collection open to the public.

2125 ▪ Morrow Memorial United Methodist
Church
Adult Library and Media Center
600 Ridgewood Rd.   Ph: (973)763-7676
Maplewood, NJ 07040   Fax: (973)763-6798

Contact: Kathy Finch, Adult Libn.

Desc: Subject: Bible translations and commentaries, Christian beliefs and living, death and dying, family issues, marriage, parenting, aging, divorce, bereavement, religious art, social issues, devotional aids, church history, ecumenicism, world order, missions, travel, poetry and drama, biography, fiction. Holdings: 1800 books; 160

filmstrips; 550 audio cassettes of Sunday services; 36 videotapes; slides; picture files. Services: Library open to the public.

2126 ▪ Morton County Historical Museum
PO Box 1248 (Highway 56)   Ph: (316)697-2833
Elkhart, KS 67950   Fax: (316)697-4390

Contact: Helen C. Brown, Dir.Cur.

Desc: Subject: Morton County history, Santa Fe Trail, family history. Holdings: Figures not available. Services: Interlibrary loan; copying; Library open to the public.

2127 ▪ Moultrie County Historical &
Genealogical Society
Moultrie County Heritage Center
117 E. Harrison St.   Ph: (217)728-4085
Box 588
Sullivan, IL 61951-0588

Contact: Mary L. Storm, Libn.

Desc: Subject: Local history and genealogy. Holdings: 695 books; 8 VF drawers of family surname folders; 10 VF drawers of official county records; 72 reels of microfilm of newspapers and census. Services: Center open to the public on a limited schedule; will answer mail inquiries.

2128 ▪ Mount Clemens Public Library
Genealogy Collection
150 Cass Ave.   Ph: (810)469-6200
Mt. Clemens, MI 48043   Fax: (810)469-6668
URL: http://www.libcoop.net/mountclemens

Contact: Donald E. Worrell, Jr.

Desc: Subject: Mount Clemens, Michigan genealogy. Holdings: 3000 books; records; county histories; atlases; microfilm.

2129 ▪ Mount Zion Hebrew Congregation
Temple Library
1300 Summit Ave.   Ph: (612)698-3881
St. Paul, MN 55105   Fax: (612)698-1263

Contact: Robert A. Epstein, Libn.

Desc: Subject: Jews, history, religion, literature, biography, philosophy; Israel. Holdings: 9250 books; 125 phonograph records; 25 cassette tapes; 100 videotapes. Services: Copying; Library open to the public with restrictions.

2130 ▪ Mountain View Public Library
History Center Collection
585 Franklin St.   Ph: (650)903-6337
Mountain View, CA 94041   Fax: (650)903-0358
URL: http://www.ci.mtnview.ca.us/newlibrary/
        history.html

Desc: Subject: Mountain View history and culture. Holdings: Books; maps; pictures; manuscripts; audiovisual materials; handwritten and drawn artifacts; city documents. Services: copying; Library open to the public.

2131 ▪ Multnomah County Library
Humanities Section
801 SW Tenth Ave.   Ph: (503)248-5123
Portland, OR 97205-2597   Fax: (503)248-5226
E-mail: jeanb@nethost.multomah.lib.or.us
URL: http://www.multnomah.lib.or.us/lib/

Contact: Jean Barnett, Assoc. Central Lib.Dir.

Desc: Subject: Philosophy, psychology, religion, foreign languages, theater, literature, literary criticism, geography, library science, travel, history, biography, general works, genealogy, antiques, architecture, costume, dance, fine arts, handicrafts, interior decorating, motion pictures, music, photography. Holdings: 240,000 volumes; 59,000

maps; 38,000 music scores; 18,000 musical compact discs; 6000 musical audiocassettes; 7000 audiocassettes (humanities subjects); 10 drawers of genealogy microfiche. Services: Interlibrary loan; copying; section open to the public.

2132 ▪ Muncy Historical Society and Museum
of History
Historical Library
Muncy Public Library   Ph: (717)546-5014
108 S. Main St.
Muncy, PA 17756

Contact: Laurie Bay, Libn.

Desc: Subject: Local history. Holdings: 1000 books. Services: Copying; collections may be consulted by appointment.

2133 ▪ Museum of Western Colorado
Research Center & Special Library
233 S 5th St.   Ph: (970)242-0971
PO Box 20000-5020   Fax: (970)242-3960
Grand Junction, CO
    81502-5020
E-mail: judypa@colosys.net
URL: http://www.colosys.net/uranium

Contact: Judy Prosser-Armstrong, Libn.Archv.

Desc: Subject: Western Colorado, Mesa County, and Grand Junction history; genealogy; paleontology; geology; anthropology. Holdings: 3500 books and monographs; 18,000 historical and aerial photographs; 2200 audiocassettes; maps and verticle files; institutional archives; reels of microfilm; National Park Service publications on historic preservation; site inventories. Services: Interlibrary loan; copying; photographic reproduction (including scanning); Center open to the public.

2134 ▪ Muskegon County Museum
Archives
430 W. Clay Ave.   Ph: (616)722-0278
Muskegon, MI 49440   Free: 888-843-5661
                                     Fax: (616)728-4119
E-mail: baabmaat@aol.com

Contact: John McGarry, Dir.

Desc: Subject: Muskegon County history, Woodland Indians, lumbering, natural history, Michigan history, museum operations, maritime history. Holdings: 2000 books; 9000 photographs; 2000 postcards. Services: Copying; Library open to the public for reference use only.

2135 ▪ Mystic River Historical Society
William A. Downes Building Library
74 High St.   Ph: (860)536-4779
PO Box 245
Mystic, CT 06355
E-mail: mrhs5@juno.com

Contact: Helen Keith, Cur.

Desc: Subject: Local history and genealogy. Holdings: 600 books; 1000 manuscripts; 4000 photographs. Services: Copying; library and photo collections open to the public.

2136 ▪ Nanaimo & District Museum Society
100 Cameron Rd.   Ph: (250)753-1821
Nanaimo, BC, Canada V9R 2X1   Fax: (250)753-1777
E-mail: ndmuseum@island.net

Desc: Subject: History - local Native Canadian groups, coal mining, Nanaimo area, fishing and logging industries. Holdings: 1000 volumes; 4000 photographs; 150 maps; 8000 archival materials. Services: Copying; archives open to the public for reference use only with supervision.

2137 ■ Napa County Historical Society
Library
Goodman Library Bldg.   Ph: (707)224-1739
1219 1st St.   Fax: (707)224-5933
Napa, CA 94559

Contact: Diane S. Ballard, Exec.Dir.

Desc: Subject: Napa County history. Holdings: 3500
books; 3500 pictures; 210 boxes of newspaper clippings
and ephemera; 50 linear feet of scrapbooks, diaries, manuscripts; artifacts and tools; Napa Register, 1954 to present;
Napa Journal, 1890-1960; St. Helena Star, 1975 to present; Napa Valley Times, 1985-1989. Services: Copying;
Library open to the public.

2138 ■ Napa Valley Genealogical &
Biographical Society
Library
1701 Menlo Ave.   Ph: (707)252-2252
Napa, CA 94558
E-mail: nvgbs@napanet.net
URL: http://www.napanet.net/nvgbs/

Contact: Dolores Hibbert, Libn.

Desc: Subject: Genealogy. Holdings: 6000 books; Hartford Times; family and surname files. Services: Copying;
Library open to the public on fee basis.

2139 ■ Nashua Public Library
Chandler Memorial Library and Ethnic Center
257 Main St.   Ph: (603)594-3415
Nashua, NH 03060

Contact: Margaret Merrigan, Libn.

Desc: Subject: Ethnic groups in the U.S., foreign languages. Holdings: 7000 books. Services: Interlibrary loan;
center open to the public.

2140 ■ Natick Historical Society
Library
Bacon Free Library Bldg.   Ph: (508)647-4841
58 Eliot St.   Fax: (508)651-7013
South Natick, MA 01760
E-mail: elliot@ma.ultranet.com
URL: http://www.ultranet.com/elliot

Contact: Anne K. Schaller, Dir.

Desc: Subject: Local history, vital records of Massachusetts
towns. Holdings: 900 books. Services: Copying; Library
open to the public for reference use only.

2141 ■ National Archives & Records
Administration
National Archives
Pacific Alaska Region
6125 Sand Point Way, NE   Ph: (206)526-6507
Seattle, WA 98115-7999   Fax: (206)526-6545
E-mail: archives@seattle.nara.gov
URL: http://www.nara.gov

Contact: Susan H. Karren, Archv.Oper.Coord.

Desc: Subject: Historical records of agencies of the Federal
Government for Washington, Oregon, Montana, and
Idaho; Bureau of Customs; Bureau of Land Management;
Bureau of Indian Affairs; U.S. Army Corps of Engineers;
U.S. District Courts; Bonneville Power Administration.
Holdings: 30,000 cubic feet of records; 60,000 reels of
microfilm. Services: Copying; branch open to the public
with restrictions.

2142 ■ National Archives & Records
Administration
National Archives
Southwest Region
501 Felix at Hemphill, Bldg. 1   Ph: (817)334-5525
Box 6216   Fax: (817)334-5621
Fort Worth, TX 76115

E-mail: archives@ftworth.nara.gov
URL: http://www.nara.gov

Contact: Kent Carter, Dir., Regional Adm.

Desc: Subject: Inactive records of U.S. government agencies in Texas, Oklahoma, Arkansas, Louisiana. Holdings:
68,000 cubic feet of records; 70,000 reels of microfilm.
Services: Copying; archives open to the public except for
restricted records.

2143 ■ National Archives & Records
Administration
National Archives at College Park
Office of the Archivist of the   Ph: (301)713-6779
   United States   Fax: (301)713-6497
8601 Adelphi Rd.
College Park, MD 20740-6001
E-mail: inquire@arch2.nara.gov
URL: http://www.nara.gov

Contact: John W. Carlin, Archv. of the United States

Desc: Subject: United States history, archives and manuscripts, genealogical research, government publications,
United States politics and government. Holdings: 1.9
million cubic feet of textual, cartographic, audiovisual,
and machine readable records, 1774 to present; more
than 4 billion government documents; 276,000 reels of
microfilm; 113,000 other microforms; 126,000 reels of
motion picture film; 182,000 sound recordings; 1.1 million still pictures; 2.6 million maps and charts; 2.8 million
architectural and engineering plans; 15.9 million aerial
photographs; 11,940 magnetic computer electronic data
sets. Services: Copying; archives open to the public.

2144 ■ National Archives & Records
Administration
Pacific Region
1000 Commodore Dr.   Ph: (650)876-9009
San Bruno, CA 94066-2350   Fax: (650)876-9233
E-mail: archives@sanbruno.nara.gov
URL: http://www.nara.gov/regional/sanfranc.html

Contact: Daniel Nealand, Dir.

Desc: Subject: Archival records of the Federal Government
in Nevada (except Clark County), Northern California,
Hawaii, American Samoa, Guam, the Trust Territory of
the Pacific Islands. Holdings: 50,000 cubic feet of original
records; 55,000 reels of microfilm. Services: Copying;
genealogy workshops; branch open to the public.

2145 ■ National Archives & Records
Administration
Silvio O. Conte Branch
10 Conte Dr.   Ph: (413)445-6885
Pittsfield, MA 01201   Fax: (413)445-7599
URL: http://www.nara.gov

Contact: Jean Nudd

Desc: Subject: United States census (all states 1790-1920);
Federal records (Revolutionary and Civil War, pensions,
naturalization data, immigration passenger manifests, diverse ethnic origins). Holdings: Microfilm.

2146 ■ National Genealogical Society
Library
4527 17th St., N.   Ph: (703)525-0050
Arlington, VA 22207-2399   Free: 800-473-0060
                                         Fax: (703)525-0052
E-mail: library@ngsgenealogy.org
URL: http://ngsgenealogy.org

Contact: Dereka Smith, Libn.

Desc: Subject: Genealogy, local history, bibliography.
Holdings: 30,000 books; 5000 bound periodical volumes;
300 boxes of manuscript materials; 40 VF drawers of

documents, clippings, pamphlets; microfilm; microfiche.
Services: Copying; Library open to the public; daily use
fee for non-members.

2147 ■ National Guard Educational Foundation
Library of the National Guard
1 Massachusetts Ave., NW   Ph: (202)789-0031
Washington, DC 20001   Fax: (202)682-9358
URL: http://www.ngaus.org

Contact: Col. Donald R. Perkins, (Ret.) Lib.Cons.

Desc: Holdings: Military histories, including the National
Guard and state militia archives; Adjutants General Reports. Services: Copying; Library open to the public.

2148 ■ National Society, Daughters of the
American Revolution
Aloha Chapter
DAR Memorial Library
1914 Makiki Heights Dr.   Ph: (808)949-7256
Honolulu, HI 96822

Contact: Mary L. Cloyd, Libn.

Desc: Subject: Family genealogies, state and regional history, colonial genealogy. Holdings: 3500 books; 350
bound periodical volumes. Services: Copying; Library
open to the public.

2149 ■ National Society, Daughters of the
American Revolution
Library
1776 D St., NW   Ph: (202)879-3229
Washington, DC 20006-5392   Fax: (202)879-3227
URL: http://www.dar.org

Contact: Eric G. Grundset, Lib.Dir.

Desc: Subject: Genealogy, U.S. local history, U.S. history,
American Indian history, American women's history.
Holdings: 150,000 books; 14,000 bound periodical volumes; 53,000 microforms; 300,000 files of manuscript
material, genealogical records, pamphlets. Services: Copying; Library open to the public on a fee basis.

2150 ■ National Society of the Sons of the
American Revolution
Genealogy Library
1000 S. 4th St.   Ph: (502)589-1776
Louisville, KY 40203

Contact: Michael A. Christian, Libn.

Desc: Subject: American history and genealogy, Revolutionary War, Colonial America. Holdings: 38,000 books;
2800 volumes periodicals; 15,000 microforms; 173 compact discs. Services: Copying; Library open to the public
on a fee basis.

2151 ■ National Society of the Sons of the
American Revolution
New Jersey Society
S.A.R. Library
101 W. 9th Ave.   Ph: (908)245-1777
Roselle, NJ 07203

Contact: Howard W. Wiseman, Libn.

Desc: Subject: Genealogy, Revolutionary War history and
biography, local history, patriotic organizations. Holdings: 2000 books; 1000 bound periodical volumes; 1000
other cataloged items. Services: Copying; Library open
to the public on a limited schedule.

2152 ■ National Society of the Sons of Utah
Pioneers
Library
3301 E. 2920, S.   Ph: (801)484-4441
Salt Lake City, UT 84109   Fax: (801)484-4442

Desc: Subject: Genealogy, pioneer history. Holdings: 5000 books; 5000 personal pioneer histories; articles; family histories; old photographs; genealogical histories; magazines; microfiche; films. Services: Library open to the public for reference use only.

2153 ■ Nebraska State Historical Society
Fort Robinson Museum
Library
Box 304   Ph: (308)665-2919
Crawford, NE 69339   Fax: (308)665-2917

Contact: Tom Buecker, Cur.

Desc: Subject: Fort Robinson history. Holdings: Fort Robinson records on microfilm; Red Cloud and Spotted Tail Agency records; diaries and interview manuscripts; newspapers of Crawford and Chadron, Nebraska. Services: Library open to the public by appointment.

2154 ■ Nebraska State Historical Society
John G. Neihardt State Historic Site
Research Library
Elm and Washington Sts.   Ph: (402)648-3388
Box 344   Free: 888-777-4667
Bancroft, NE 68004   Fax: (402)648-3388
E-mail: neihardt@gpcom.net

Contact: Charles Trimble, Dir.

Desc: Subject: John G. Neihardt; American Indian culture and religion; Missouri River; fur trade; Nebraska and Plains history. Holdings: 202 books; 74 bound periodical volumes; 100 audiotapes and transcripts; 1 VF drawer of pamphlets and photographs; 3 dissertations; clipping files. Services: Library open to the public for reference use only.

2155 ■ Nebraska State Historical Society
Library Archives Division
1500 R St.   Ph: (402)471-4771
Box 82554   Fax: (402)471-8922
Lincoln, NE 68501

Contact: Andrea I. Faling, Assoc.Dir., Lib.Archv.

Desc: Subject: Nebraska - history, politics, agriculture; Indians of the Great Plains, archeology, Great Plains history, genealogy. Holdings: 80,000 volumes; 563 sets of Sanborn Fire Insurance maps of Nebraska; 2000 maps and 400 atlases relating to Nebraska, 1854 to present; 2500 photographs in Solomon D. Butcher Photograph Collection of Sod Houses; 465 photographs in John A. Anderson Photograph Collection of Brule Sioux; 247,000 other photographs; Nebraska state government publications repository, 1905 to present; 10,000 volumes of genealogical materials; 15,000 cubic feet of state and local archival materials; 8000 cubic feet of manuscripts; 28,000 reels of microfilm of newspapers, 1854-1991. Services: Interlibrary loan (of microfilm); copying; Library/archives open to the public.

2156 ■ Neshaminy-Warwick Presbyterian
Church
Library
1401 Meetinghouse Rd.   Ph: (215)343-6060
Warminster, PA 18974

Contact: Bernard E. Deitrick, Libn.

Desc: Subject: Religion, local history. Holdings: 6650 books; cassette tapes; videocassettes; phonograph records; filmstrips. Services: Library open to the public on a limited schedule.

2157 ■ Ness County Historical Society
Library
123 N. Pennsylvania   Ph: (785)798-3298
Ness City, KS 67560

Contact: Margery Frusher, Pres.

Desc: Subject: History of Ness County, Kansas; antiques; cemetary information. Holdings: 500 books; 100 bound periodical volumes; microfilm; artifacts. Services: Copying; Library open to the public for reference use only.

2158 ■ Nevada County Historical Society
Searls Historical Library
214 Church St.   Ph: (530)265-5910
Nevada City, CA 95959

Contact: Edwin L. Tyson, Libn.

Desc: Subject: Nevada County history. Holdings: 3480 books; 50 bound periodical volumes; 350,000 documents, pamphlets, vertical file materials; 240 maps and charts; 50 tape recordings; 2500 photographs. Services: Copying; Library open to the public with restrictions.

2159 ■ Nevada Historical Society
Library
1650 N. Virginia St.   Ph: (702)688-1190
Reno, NV 89503-1799   Fax: (702)688-2917
E-mail: www@clan.lib.nv.us
URL: http://www.clan.lib.NV.US/museums/hist/hissoc.htm

Contact: Peter L. Bandurraga, Dir.

Desc: Subject: Nevada history, mining, Indians, agriculture, water, gambling, transportation and communication. Holdings: 40,000 books; 5000 bound periodical volumes; 3200 manuscript collections, 7500 reels of microfilm; 300,000 photographs; 55,000 maps; government documents. Services: Copying; limited written research by mail; Library open to the public.

2160 ■ Neville Public Museum
Photograph & Film Collection
210 Museum Pl.   Ph: (920)448-4460
Green Bay, WI 54303   Fax: (920)448-4459

Contact: Mary K. Huelsbeck

Desc: Subject: Art, earth sciences, museum studies, history and anthropology with regional and state emphasis. Holdings: 4500 bound materials; 1.5 million negatives and prints; 4.5 million feet of local news film. Services: Copying; Library open to the public by appointment for reference use only.

2161 ■ New Canaan Historical Society
Library
13 Oenoke Ridge   Ph: (203)966-1776
New Canaan, CT 06840   Fax: (203)972-5917
URL: http://darien.and.newcanaan/nchistorysociety

Contact: Sharon L. Turo, Libn.

Desc: Subject: Genealogy; history - local, state, New England. Holdings: 4000 books; 300 bound periodical volumes; local newspapers, 1868 to present, on microfilm; 4000 biography cards; 915 manuscripts; 30 videocassettes. Services: Copying; Library open to the public.

2162 ■ New Castle Public Library
Pennsylvania History Room
207 E. North St.   Ph: (724)658-6659
New Castle, PA 16101   Fax: (412)658-9012

Contact: Susan Walls, Dir.

Desc: Subject: Pennsylvania history and genealogy. Holdings: 6763 volumes. Services: Interlibrary loan; copying; room open to the public with identification.

2163 ■ New England Historic Genealogical
Society
Library
101 Newbury St.   Ph: (617)536-5740
Boston, MA 02116-3007   Fax: (617)536-7307

URL: http://www.nehgs.org

Contact: Thomas J. Kemp, Dir. of Lib. User Svcs.

Desc: Subject: Genealogy and family history, local history, vital records, heraldry. Holdings: 235,000 volumes; 13,250 reels of microfilm; 130,000 microfiche; 3500 linear feet of manuscripts; city directories; vital records; diaries; regimental histories; church histories. Services: Copying; research; lectures and seminars; Library open to the public on a fee basis.

2164 ■ New Hampshire Historical Society
Tuck Library
30 Park St.   Ph: (603)225-3381
Concord, NH 03301   Fax: (603)224-0463
E-mail: nhhslib@aol.com
URL: http://www.nhhistory.org

Contact: William Copeley, Libn.

Desc: Subject: New Hampshire art and history, New England history and genealogy, architecture and decorative arts of New England. Holdings: 50,000 volumes; 2000 volumes of early New Hampshire newspapers; 200,000 photographs of New Hampshire towns and people; 500 reels of microfilm; 1.5 million pages of manuscripts; 1000 maps. Services: Interlibrary loan (limited); copying; research; Library open to the public.

2165 ■ New Hampshire State Library
20 Park St.   Ph: (603)271-2144
Concord, NH 03301-6314   Fax: (603)271-2205
URL: http://www.state.nh.us/nhsl

Contact: Michael York, Supv.Lib.& Archv.

Desc: Subject: New Hampshire - history, government, political science, law. Holdings: 450,100 books; 16,011 manuscripts; 5271 scores; 12,500 reels of microfilm; 71,770 microcards; 114,000 microfiche; 653 motion pictures; 500 sound recordings. Services: Interlibrary loan; copying; Library open to the public.

2166 ■ New Hanover County Public Library
North Carolina Collection
201 Chestnut St.   Ph: (910)341-4394
Wilmington, NC 28401   Fax: (910)341-4357
E-mail: btetterton@co.new-hanover.nc.us
URL: http://www.co.new-hanover.nc.us/lib/localhis.htm

Contact: North Carolina - history, genealogy, culture. Holdings: Books; pamphlets; maps; vertical files; microfilm; newspapers; photographs. Services: Library open to the public for reference use only.

2167 ■ New Haven Colony Historical Society
Whitney Library
114 Whitney Ave.   Ph: (203)562-4183
New Haven, CT 06510-1025   Fax: (203)562-2002
E-mail: jcampbell@csunet.ctstateu.edu

Contact: James W. Campbell, Libn. and Cur. of Mss.

Desc: Subject: Local history and genealogy. Holdings: 30,000 volumes; 500 maps; 4800 architectural drawings; 260 processed manuscript collection including New Haven County Superior Court documents, 1789-1905; New Haven Clock Company papers, 1853-1946; New Haven Water Company papers, 1820-1895; United Church papers, 1742-1970; Woman's Seamen's Friend Society of Connecticut records, 1859-1968; papers of the Ingersoll, Morris, and Twining families; New Haven city and county documents, 1648-1900; New Haven Board of Education records, 1799-1970; school records, 1715-1963; New Haven YWCA records, 1880 to present; Maritime Collection, 1721-1887; Harbor Collection, 1750-1925; Military Collection, 1737-1945; Civil War Collection, 1861-1931; family papers; corporate records; national and local historic figures A-Z, 1638-1976. Services: Copying; Library open to adults for research only (non-members on a fee basis).

2168 ■ New Jersey Historical Society Library

52 Park Pl.   Ph: (973)596-8500
Newark, NJ 07102   Fax: (973)621-9412

Contact: James A. Kaser, Ph.D., Dir.

Desc: Subject: New Jersey history, genealogy of New Jersey. Holdings: 70,000 books; 3000 bound periodical volumes; 2000 manuscript groups; 400 newspaper titles; 100,000 photographs; 2000 maps. Services: Copying; Library open to the public for reference use only.

2169 ■ New Jersey State Library

PO Box 520   Ph: (609)292-6220
Trenton, NJ 08625-0520   Fax: (609)292-2746
E-mail: jlivingstone@njstatelib.org
URL: http://www.njstatelib.org

Contact: John H. Livingstone, State Libn.

Desc: Subject: Law, New Jersey history and newspapers, political science, public administration, genealogy, social science, library science. Holdings: 750,000 volumes; 35 file cabinets of clippings and pamphlets; 730,000 microforms. Services: Interlibrary loan; copying; consultant services and grant administration for libraries; Library open to the public.

2170 ■ New London County Historical Society Library

11 Blinman St.   Ph: (860)443-1209
New London, CT 06320

Contact: Alice D. Sheriff, Adm.

Desc: Subject: Local history and genealogy. Holdings: 5000 books; 400 antique newspapers; 50 early town and county records; 3000 pieces of family correspondence; 15 ships' logs; 50 feet of manuscripts; 25 early account books. Services: Copying; Library open to the public by appointment.

2171 ■ New Orleans Public Library Louisiana Division

219 Loyola Ave.   Ph: (504)596-2610
New Orleans, LA 70112-2044   Fax: (504)596-2609
E-mail: nopl@gnofn.org
URL: http://www.gnofn.org/nopl

Contact: Collin B. Hamer, Jr., Div.Hd.

Desc: Subject: New Orleans archives, 1769 to present; New Orleans newspapers, 1802 to present; Louisiana state documents; books by Louisianians; books on Louisiana subjects. Holdings: 33,250 books; 2200 newspapers; 14,000 reels of microfilm; 3000 maps; 46,700 Louisiana and New Orleans photographs; 49,935 Louisiana state documents; 6300 newsreels from WVUE-TV. Services: Interlibrary loan; copying; microfilming; division open to the public with restrictions.

2172 ■ New Providence Historical Society Memorial Library Archival Room/Mason Room

Elkwood Ave.   Ph: (908)464-0163
New Providence, NJ 07974

Contact: Ann Chovan, Dir.

Desc: Subject: Local history and current events. Holdings: 197 loose-leaf binders; 40 loose-leaf photograph albums; 86 oral history tapes with 53 transcriptions; VF drawers. Services: Library open to the public.

2173 ■ New York Genealogical and Biographical Society Library

122 E. 58th St., 4th Fl.   Ph: (212)755-8532
New York, NY 10022-1939   Fax: (212)754-4218
URL: http://www.nygbs.org

Contact: Joy Rich, Dir.

Desc: Subject: Genealogy, biography, U.S. and local history. Holdings: 75,000 volumes; 4000 bound periodical volumes; 30,000 manuscripts; 7000 reels of microfilm; 9000 microfiche; 150 CDs; 73 audiocassettes. Services: Copying by mail; Library searches by mail; Library open to the public with restrictions.

2174 ■ New York Historical Society Library

170 Central Park, W.   Ph: (212)873-3400
New York, NY 10024   Fax: (212)875-1591
URL: http://metro.org/members/nyhs.html

Contact: Margaret Heilbrun, Lib.Dir.

Desc: Subject: American history and history of New York City and state, naval history. Holdings: 635,000 books; 2 million manuscripts; 150,000 pamphlets; 25,000 broadsides; 30,000 maps. Services: Copying; Library open to the public.

2175 ■ New York Public Library Belmont Regional Library Enrico Fermi Cultural Center - Italian Heritage Collection

610 E. 186th St.   Ph: (718)933-6410
Bronx, NY 10458   Fax: (718)365-8756
URL: http://www.nypl.org

Contact: Marisa L. Parish, Reg.Libn.

Desc: Holdings: 48,707 books; 2045 nonprint items (videotapes, audio recordings). Services: Center open to the public; reference assistance available on-site only.

2176 ■ New York Public Library Center for Humanities United States History, Local History and Genealogy Division

Fifth Ave. & 42nd St., Rm. 315S   Ph: (212)930-0828
New York, NY 10018
E-mail: histref@nypl.org
URL: http://www.nypl.org

Contact: Ruth A. Carr, Chf.

Desc: Subject: U.S. history; county, city, town histories of the United States; European and American genealogy and heraldry; works on names and flags of the world. Holdings: 215,000 volumes. Services: Copying; division open to the public.

2177 ■ New York Public Library The Research Libraries Science, Industry and Business Library

188 Madison Ave.   Ph: (212)592-7000
New York, NY 10016-4314   Fax: (212)592-7082
E-mail: bbentley@nypl.org
URL: http://www.nypl.org

Contact: Kristin McDonough, Dir.

Desc: Subject: Advertising, astronomy, banks and banking, biotechnology, business and commerce, chemistry, computers and computer science, earth sciences, economics, engineering, environmental science, finance, food science and technology, general science, history of science, industrial relations, insurance, international trade, management, marketing, materials science, mathematics, patents and trademarks, personnel management, public administration, real estate, robotics, small business, statistics, textile industry, trade and technologies, transportation,

union, urban affairs. Holdings: 1.2 million volumes; 127,000 reels of microfilm; 40,000 volume science and business collection (including CD-ROMs and videocassettes). Services: Library open to the public.

2178 ■ New York Public Library The Research Libraries Slavic and Baltic Division

Fifth Ave. & 42nd St., Rm. 217   Ph: (212)930-0714
New York, NY 10018-2788   Fax: (212)930-0693
E-mail: rdavis@nypl.org
URL: http://www.nypl.org

Contact: Edward Kasinec, Chf.

Desc: Subject: Slavic and Baltic literature and linguistics; history (especially Russian Imperial regimental histories and history of Russian revolutionary movements, history of Alaska and her peoples); economics and political science; philosophy; archeology; folklore; art and architecture; ethnology of Baltic, Slavic, and Soviet Central Asian peoples. Holdings: 415,000 volumes; 21,000 microforms. Services: Copying; replies to written and telephone inquiries; division open to the public for reference use only.

2179 ■ New York State Historical Association Research Library

W. Lake Rd.   Ph: (607)547-1470
PO Box 800   Fax: (607)547-1405
Cooperstown, NY 13326
E-mail: nyshalib@telenet.net

Contact: Wayne Wright, Assoc.Dir.

Desc: Subject: New York State history, central New York genealogy, American social history and art, agricultural history. Holdings: 72,183 books; 12,712 bound periodical volumes; 1042 linear feet of manuscripts; 85 sets of microfiche; 4685 reels of microfilm. Services: Interlibrary loan; copying; Library open to the public (fee for nonmembers); collections open to the public for reference use only.

2180 ■ New York State Library

Cultural Education Center   Ph: (518)474-7646
Empire State Plaza   Fax: (518)474-5786
Albany, NY 12230

Contact: Liz Lane, Dir.

Desc: Subject: Education, science, technology, art, architecture, economics, sociology, current affairs, bibliography, New York State documents, New York State newspapers, law, medicine, state and local history, genealogy, heraldry. Holdings: 9 million books, bound periodical volumes, manuscripts, pamphlets; patents; microfilm; microcards; pictures; maps. Services: Interlibrary loan; copying; Library open to the public.

2181 ■ New York State Library Core Reference Services

Cultural Education Center   Ph: (518)474-5355
Empire State Plaza   Fax: (518)474-5786
Albany, NY 12230
E-mail: refserv@unix2.nysed.gov
URL: http://www.nysl.nysed.gov

Contact: Lee Stanton, Prin.Libn.

Desc: Subject: New York State and North American history; bibliography; biography; literature; language; fine and applied arts; library science; genealogy; philosophy; religion; grantsmanship; law - federal, state, foreign; political science; public administration; legislative organization; intergovernmental relations; state and regional planning; education; science; medicine and allied health sciences; technology. Holdings: 2.4 million books; 6.6 million microforms. Services: Interlibrary loan; copying; reference services and borrowing priviledges extended to New York

State government and legislative personnel, physicians and attorneys practicing in New York State, and New York State municipal historians; open to the public.

2182 ■ Newark Public Library
New Jersey Information Center

5 Washington St.   Ph: (973)733-7776
Box 630   Fax: (973)733-5648
Newark, NJ 07101-0630
URL: http://www.npl.org

Contact: Charles F. Cummings, Asst.Dir.

Desc: Subject: New Jersey, Newark, Essex County history and laws; current affairs; travel and description; biography. Holdings: 24,000 books; 1300 bound periodical volumes; 1400 unbound periodical volumes; 5400 reels of microfilm of New Jersey newspapers; 55 VF drawers of clippings in 4000 subject folders; 42,000 documents; 3600 maps. Services: Interlibrary loan (limited); copying (hardcopy and microfilm); copies of prints owned by institution; division open to the public.

2183 ■ Newark United Methodist Church
Bunting Library

69 E. Main St.   Ph: (302)368-8774
Newark, DE 19711-4645

Contact: Marietta J. Garrett, Libn.

Desc: Subject: Religion, Methodist Church history, children's and family-oriented books. Holdings: 4000 books; recordings; filmstrips; videotapes; audiocassettes. Services: Library not open to the public.

2184 ■ (Newfoundland) Provincial Archives of
Newfoundland and Labrador

Colonial Bldg.   Ph: (709)729-3065
Military Rd.   Fax: (709)729-0578
St. John's, NF, Canada A1C
  2C9
E-mail: pan1@mail.gov.nf.ca

Contact: Shelley Smith, Prov.Archv.

Desc: Subject: Newfoundland history, economic history, folklore, sociology, geography, genealogy. Holdings: 180 linear feet of books and booklets; 1200 bound periodical volumes; 11,480 linear feet of archival materials (manuscripts, maps, government documents); 300,000 photographs; films; moving images. Services: Copying; archives open to the public.

2185 ■ Newmarket Historical Society
Stone School Museum Collections

Granite St.   Ph: (603)659-3652
Newmarket, NH 03857

Contact: Sylvia Fitts Getchell, Cur.

Desc: Subject: Newmarket history, textile mills, shoe shops. Holdings: 200 books; 50 old mill and store ledgers; hotel registers; surveying notebooks; 10 AV programs; photographs. Services: Library open to the public.

2186 ■ Newport Historical Society
Library

82 Touro St.   Ph: (401)846-0813
Newport, RI 02840   Fax: (401)846-1853

Contact: Bertram Lippincott, III, Geneal.Libn.

Desc: Subject: Newport and Rhode Island history and genealogy, architecture, decorative arts, religion, gilded age cottages and families. Holdings: 14,000 books; 200 boxes of manuscripts; 100 scrapbooks; newspapers on microfilm. Services: Interlibrary loan (limited); copying; Library open to the public.

2187 ■ Niagara County Historical Society
Library

215 Niagara St.   Ph: (716)434-7433
Lockport, NY 14094   Fax: (716)434-7433

Desc: Subject: Niagara County history and artifacts from 1800s to 1940s. Holdings: 100 volumes; 25 VF drawers of clippings, pamphlets, ephemera, ledgers, family papers. Services: Copying; Library open to the public.

2188 ■ Nicodemus Historical Society

R.R. 2, Box 139   Ph: (913)839-4280
Bogue, KS 67625

Contact: Angela Bates-Tompkins

Desc: Subject: Nicodemus, Kansas; Black women; Emancipation celebrations; Black western history; Black migration. Holdings: Figures not available. Services: Copying; Library open to the public.

2189 ■ Nicola Valley Museum
Archives

PO Box 1262   Ph: (250)378-4145
Merritt, BC, Canada V1K 1B8   Fax: (250)378-4145

Desc: Subject: Nicola Valley; Merritt, British Columbia. Holdings: Figures not available. Services: Archives open to the public.

2190 ■ Nicollet County Historical Society
Treaty Site History Center

1851 N. Minnesota Ave.   Ph: (507)931-2160
St. Peter, MN 56082   Fax: (507)931-0172

Contact: Wayne E. Allen, Ph.D.

Desc: Subject: County and town history, genealogy. Holdings: 500 books; 30 bound periodical volumes; 300 manuscripts; 2500 photographs; 50 other cataloged items; dissertations. Services: Interlibrary loan; copying; museum open to the public.

2191 ■ 92nd Street Young Men's and Young
Women's Hebrew Association
Archives

1395 Lexington Ave.   Ph: (212)415-5542
New York, NY 10128   Fax: (212)427-6119
E-mail: swsiegel@pipeline.com

Contact: Steven W. Siegel, Dir.

Desc: Subject: American Jewish history, Jewish social welfare, performing arts history, amateur athletics, poetry and literature, philanthropy. Holdings: 1500 cubic feet of records; 3000 sound recordings; 500 video recordings. Services: Copying; archives open to the public for reference use only.

2192 ■ Nixon Family Association
Clearinghouse

5817 144 St. E.   Ph: (253)537-8288
Puyallup, WA 98375-5221
E-mail: janetgb@worldnet.att.net

Contact: Janet G. Baccus, Owner

Desc: Subject: Genealogy. Holdings: 1200 volumes; microfiche; film. Services: Copying.

2193 ■ No Man's Land Historical Museum
Archives

207 W. Sewell St.   Ph: (580)349-2670
Box 278   Fax: (405)349-2670
Goodwell, OK 73939

Contact: Dr. Kenneth R. Turner, Cur.

Desc: Subject: Western history, No Man's Land, Panhandle State University history, area newspapers, Dust Bowl,

genealogy. Holdings: 3000 books; 2000 bound periodical volumes; 2000 other cataloged items. Services: Copying; Library open to the public with restrictions.

2194 ■ Noah Webster HouseMuseum of West
Hartford History
Library

227 S. Main St.   Ph: (860)521-5362
West Hartford, CT 06107

Contact: Sally Whipple, Dir.

Desc: Subject: Noah Webster, local history, local architecture and preservation, Connecticut colonial life and culture. Holdings: 800 books; 10 VF drawers of West Hartford social history archives; tax records; microfilm (early issues of CT Courant); West Hartford county land reports; probate records from the 18th and 19th century; 6 VF drawers of pictures, clippings, scrapbooks, letters. Services: Library open to the public by appointment.

2195 ■ Nobleboro Historical Society
Historical Center

PO Box 122   Ph: (207)563-5874
Nobleboro, ME 04555

Contact: Dr. George F. Dow, Cur.

Desc: Subject: Genealogy, local history. Holdings: 100 books; 50 bound periodical volumes; 2000 documents; war, cemetery, and town records. Services: Copying; center open to the public by appointment.

2196 ■ Nodaway County Genealogical Society
Library

417 S. Walnut   Ph: (660)562-3556
Maryville, MO 64468-2464
E-mail: mowry@msc-net

Contact: Letha Marie Mowry, Files Sec.

Desc: Subject: Genealogy. Holdings: 100,000 file cards. Services: Library not open to the public.

2197 ■ Nome LibraryKegoayah Kozga Public
Library

200 Front St.   Ph: (907)443-6627
Box 1168   Fax: (907)443-3762
Nome, AK 99762

Contact: Susan Metsker, Libn.

Desc: Subject: Alaska, Eskimo and Gold Rush artifacts. Holdings: 14,000 books; 1200 audiovisual programs; oral history materials. Services: Interlibrary loan; copying; Library open to the public.

2198 ■ Nordic Heritage Museum
Walter Johnson Library

3014 NW 67th St.   Ph: (206)789-5707
Seattle, WA 98117   Fax: (206)789-3271
E-mail: nordic@intelistep.com

Contact: Marianne Forssblad, Dir.

Desc: Subject: Nordic immigrant history, history, literature, cookery, topography, folk art. Holdings: 10,000 books; 200 bound periodical volumes; 350 Nordic historical magazines; 275 Bibles and religious books; musical recordings; language tapes. Services: Library open to the public by appointment, for reference use only.

2199 ■ Norfolk Historical Society
Archives

Eva Brook Donly Museum   Ph: (519)426-1583
109 Norfolk St. S   Fax: (519)426-1584
Simcoe, ON, Canada N3Y 2W3
E-mail: office@norfolklore.com
URL: http://www.kwic.com/nhs/

Contact: William Yeager, Cur.

Desc: Subject: History - local, Ontario, United States, Europe; census; vital statistics; cemeteries; churches. Holdings: 4000 books; 3000 bound periodical volumes; 1000 microfiche; 2000 reels of microfilm. Services: Copying; Library open to non-members for a fee.

2200 ■ Norfolk Public Library
Sargeant Memorial Room
301 E. City Hall Ave.   Ph: (757)664-7323
Norfolk, VA 23510   Fax: (757)664-7321
URL: http://www.whro.org/cl/npl

Contact: Peggy Haile

Desc: Subject: Norfolk and Virginia history and genealogy. Holdings: 15,975 books; 1036 bound periodical volumes; 63 drawers of newspaper articles, original manuscripts, 19th century local business ledgers, letters, autographs, rare pamphlets; 3215 reels of microfilm of local newspapers, census records, cemetery and church records; 1280 postcards; 19,000 photographs; 1698 topographic and historic maps. Services: Copying; room open to the public on a limited schedule.

2201 ■ North Andover Historical Society
Library
153 Academy Rd.   Ph: (508)686-4035
North Andover, MA 01845

Contact: Carol J. Majahad, Dir.

Desc: Subject: Local history and architecture, genealogy. Holdings: 1200 books; manuscripts; prints; photographs. Services: Copying; Library open to the public for reference use only.

2202 ■ North Central Baptist Church
Media Library
518 NW 14th Ave.   Ph: (352)373-3341
Gainesville, FL 32601

Contact: Lena M. Bush, Media Lib.Dir.

Desc: Subject: Religion, Christian life, children's literature, biography, fiction, crafts, family. Holdings: 15,000 books; 100 vertical files; 350 filmstrips. Services: Interlibrary loan; copying; Library open to the public with restrictions.

2203 ■ North Central Nevada Historical Society
Humboldt Museum
Research Department
PO Box 819   Ph: (702)623-2912
Maple Ave. & Jungo Rd.   Fax: (702)623-5640
Winnemucca, NV 89446

Contact: Pansilee Larson, Director

Desc: Subject: History, genealogy. Holdings: Figures not available.

2204 ■ North Oakland Genealogical Society
Library
Orion Township Public Library   Ph: (248)693-3000
825 Joslyn Rd.   Fax: (248)693-3009
Lake Orion, MI 48362
URL: http://www.orion.lib.mi.us

Contact: Linda Sickles, Dir.

Desc: Subject: Local history, genealogy. Holdings: 1200 books; microfiche; members' ancestral charts; census records; tax records; cemetery documentation. Services: Copying; Library open to the public.

2205 ■ North Olympic Library System
Port Angeles Branch
Pacific Northwest Room
2210 S. Peabody   Ph: (360)452-9253
Port Angeles, WA 98362   Fax: (360)457-2581
E-mail: nolsparf@nols.lib.wa.us

URL: http://www.nols.org

Contact: Susan Skaggs, Br.Mgr.

Desc: Subject: Local history. Holdings: 80 books; 960 bound newspaper volumes, 1916 to present; 584 reels of microfilm; miscellaneous issues on microfilm; several newspapers dating back to 1889. Services: Room open to the public.

2206 ■ North Park Baptist Church
Library
2605 Rex Cruse Dr.   Ph: (903)892-8429
Sherman, TX 75090

Contact: Mrs. Jack Raidt, Dir. of Lib.Svc.

Desc: Subject: Bible, Baptist doctrine, Christian life, missions, history, recreation, travel, literatue. Holdings: 4925 books; recordings; filmstrips; slides; VF materials; 8 mm and 16mm movies; 40 cassette tapes; 18 videotapes. Services: Interlibrary loan; copying; Library open to the public.

2207 ■ North Peace Historical Society
Archives
9323 100th St.   Ph: (250)787-0430
Fort St. John, BC, Canada V1J   Fax: (250)787-0405
4N4
E-mail: fsjnpmuseum@ocol.com
URL: http://www.schoolnet.ca/collections/north_peace

Contact: Donna Redpath, Musm.Cur.

Desc: Subject: Fur trade, early forts, expeditions, city development, local people, First Nations. Holdings: 400 books; 20 reports; 64 feet of archival material. Services: Copying; Library open to the public.

2208 ■ North Queens Heritage Society
Library
Caledonia Sta.   Ph: (902)682-2989
Queens County, NS, Canada
B0T 1B0

Contact: Sandra Rowter

Desc: Subject: North Queens - genealogy, industries, local histories. Holdings: Figures not available. Services: Library open to the public for reference use only.

2209 ■ North St. Paul Historical Society
Museum Library
2666 E. 7th Ave.   Ph: (651)779-6402
North St. Paul, MN 55109

Contact: Betty Lyon, Cur.

Desc: Subject: North St. Paul - history, residents and families, businesses, homes, schools, churches. Holdings: Reports; manuscripts; archives; local newspapers. Services: Library open to the public.

2210 ■ North Shore Congregation Israel
Romanek Cultural Center
Oscar Hillel Plotkin Adult Library
1185 Sheridan Rd.   Ph: (847)835-0724
Glencoe, IL 60022   Fax: (847)835-5613

Contact: Janice B. Footlik, M.A.

Desc: Subject: Religions, philosophy and ethics, the Bible, Apocrypha, sociology, rabbinic literature, music, history of the Jews, Yiddish and Hebrew languages, Jewish biography, Jewish fiction, Zionism and Israel. Holdings: 17,850 books; 150 bound periodical volumes; tapes; film; scripts; pamphlets; clippings; archives; video cassettes. Services: Library open to the public.

2211 ■ North Shore Synagogue
Charles Cohn Memorial Library
83 Muttontown Rd.   Ph: (516)921-2282
Syosset, NY 11791-2400   Fax: (516)921-2393

Desc: Subject: Jewish history, religion, and culture. Holdings: 4000 volumes; phonograph records; 100 sound filmstrips; 150 silent filmstrips; VF drawers. Services: Library not open to the public.

2212 ■ North Suburban Synagogue Beth El
Joseph and Mae Gray Cultural Learning Center
Maxwell Abbell Library
1175 Sheridan Rd.   Ph: (847)432-8900
Highland Park, IL 60035   Fax: (847)432-9242
E-mail: nssbe@nslsilus.org

Contact: Cheryl Banks, Dir.

Desc: Subject: Judaica. Holdings: 16,000 books; 100 bound periodical volumes; 350 phonograph records; 3 VF drawers of pamphlets; 150 filmstrips; 550 videotapes; 300 audiotapes. Services: Interlibrary loan; Library open to the public.

2213 ■ North Vancouver Museum and Archives
209 W. 4th St.   Ph: (604)987-5618
North Vancouver, BC, Canada   Fax: (604)987-5609
V7M 1H8
E-mail: NVMchin@island.net
URL: http://www.district.north-van.bc.ca/nvma

Contact: Robin Inglis, Dir.

Desc: Subject: North Vancouver history. Holdings: 200 books; 1200 archival materials; 18,000 photographs. Services: Copying; archives open to the public.

2214 ■ North York Central Library
Gladys Allison Canadiana Room
5120 Yonge St.   Ph: (416)395-5623
North York, ON, Canada M2N
5N9
URL: http://www.tpl.toronto.on.ca

Contact: Debra Stevens, Mgr.

Desc: Subject: North York history, genealogy, local history of Ontario and historical Canadiana. Holdings: 125,000 monographs. Services: Copying; collection open to the public for reference use only.

2215 ■ Northampton County Historical and
Genealogical Society
Mary Illick Memorial Library
107 S. 4th St.   Ph: (610)253-1222
Easton, PA 18042-4505
URL: http://www.northamptonctymuseum.org

Contact: Paul A. Goudy, Exec.Dir.

Desc: Subject: Local history and genealogy. Holdings: 5000 books; 6000 genealogical files; 6000 postal cards; 1000 deeds; manuscripts; letters. Services: Copying; genealogical research (fee); historical and historic preservation research (fee); Library open to the public on limited schedule for reference use only.

2216 ■ Northborough Historical Society, Inc.
Library
52 Main St.   Ph: (508)393-6298
Box 661
Northborough, MA 01532

Contact: Robert P. Ellis, Hist.

Desc: Subject: Local history. Holdings: Diaries, deeds, genealogical records, records of town organizations, and business ledgers. Services: Library open to the public by appointment.

2217 ▪ Northeast Minnesota Historical Center
Archives
Library 375　　　　　　　　Ph: (218)726-8526
University of Minnesota, Duluth
Duluth, MN 55812
E-mail: pmaus@d.umn.edu
URL: http://www.d.umn.edu/lib/collections/nemn.html

Contact: Patricia Maus, Adm.Cur. of Mss.

Desc: Subject: Regional history, transportation, iron mining technology, environmental issues, social service and civic agencies and organizations, business and industry, women. Holdings: 2500 books; 2000 linear feet of manuscripts; clippings; oral history tapes; 53,000 photographs; blueprints; maps. Services: Copying; Library open to the public.

2218 ▪ Northeastern Illinois Planning
Commission
Library
222 S. Riverside Plaza, Ste. 1800　Ph: (312)454-0400
Chicago, IL 60606-6001　　　　Fax: (312)454-0411
E-mail: tomasso@nipc.org
URL: http://www.nipc.cog.il.us

Contact: Mary Cele Smith, Sr.Plan.

Desc: Subject: Planning, census, transportation, ecology, forecast. Holdings: 1000 books; 20 periodical titles; 15 VF drawers of planning materials; government documents; newsletters. Services: Copying; Library open to the public for reference use only by appointment.

2219 ▪ Northeastern Nevada Museum
Library
1515 Idaho St.　　　　　　　Ph: (702)738-3418
Elko, NV 89801　　　　　　　Fax: (702)778-9318

Contact: Lisa A. Seymour, Dir.

Desc: Subject: Northeastern Nevada, Nevada, pioneers, antiques. Holdings: 3000 books; 30,000 photographs and negatives; 350 unpublished manuscripts; area newspapers on microfilm; maps; vertical files. Services: Copying; research facilities; Library open to the public.

2220 ▪ Northern Arizona University
Cline Library
Special Collections and Archives Department
Box 6022　　　　　　　　　Ph: (520)523-5551
Flagstaff, AZ 86011-6022　　　Fax: (520)523-3770
E-mail: In%karen.underhill@nau.edu
URL: http://www.nau.edu/library/speccoll/

Contact: Karen J. Underhill, Dept.Hd.

Desc: Subject: Arizona, Southwestern U.S., Colorado River and Plateau, Grand Canyon, Navajo, Havasupai, and Hopi Indians. Holdings: 33,000 books; 3189 bound periodical volumes; 3000 linear feet of manuscripts, records, and archival materials; 3500 pamphlets; 850 oral history tapes; 700,000 photographs; 4344 reels of microfilm; 3545 regional historical maps. Services: Copying; collections open to the public with restrictions.

2221 ▪ Northern Illinois University
Regional History Center
　　　　　　　　　　　　　Ph: (815)753-1779
rs>DeKalb, IL 60115

Contact: Glen A. Gildemeister, Dir.

Desc: Subject: Local history - Northern Illinois University, religion, business, rural; agriculture. Holdings: 3047 books; 8335 microforms; 5698 linear feet of manuscripts; government records (naturalization, civil war, election, school, tax, court). Services: Copying; center open to the public.

2222 ▪ Northern Indiana Historical Society
Library
808 W. Washington　　　　　Ph: (219)235-9664
South Bend, IN 46601　　　　Fax: (219)235-9059
URL: http://business.michiana.org/nich

Contact: Mary Renshaw, Archv.

Desc: Subject: Native American history and language; Indiana history; French, Indian, English, and American occupations of Saint Joseph River Valley region; All-American Girls Professional Baseball League; pioneer life; Schuyler Colfax. Holdings: 7500 books; 1500 pamphlets; 10,000 photographs; bound newspapers, 1831-1964; 300 boxes of archival manuscripts, dissertations, documents; clipping files; oral history tapes; videotapes. Services: Library open to the public by appointment for reference use only.

2223 ▪ Northern Virginia Community College at
Annandale
Library
Special Collections
8333 Little River Tpke.　　　Ph: (703)323-3000
Annandale, VA 22003-3796　　Fax: (703)323-3005
URL: http://www.nv.cc.va.us/library/

Contact: Ms. Carol Sinwell

Desc: Subject: Northern Virginia - history, genealogy. Holdings: Figures not available.

2224 ▪ Northminster Presbyterian Church
Library
703 Compton Rd.　　　　　　Ph: (513)931-0243
Cincinnati, OH 45231　　　　Fax: (513)931-0260

Desc: Subject: Bible, religion, family life, children's literature. Holdings: 500 books. Services: Library open to the public.

2225 ▪ Northminster Presbyterian Church
Library
2434 Wilmington Rd.　　　　Ph: (724)658-9051
New Castle, PA 16105

Contact: Susan Dexter, Church Libn.

Desc: Subject: Religion. Holdings: 4400 books. Services: Library open to the public with restrictions.

2226 ▪ Northport Historical Society Museum
Library
215 Main St.　　　　　　　　Ph: (516)757-9859
Box 545
Northport, NY 11768-0545

Contact: Stephanie Fortunato, Libn.Cur.

Desc: Subject: Northport history. Holdings: 300 books; 100 reports; 2000 photographs and negatives. Services: Library open to the public.

2227 ▪ Northville Historical Society
Archives
PO Box 71　　　　　　　　　Ph: (248)348-1845
Northville, MI 48167　　　　Fax: (248)348-0056

Desc: Subject: Architecture, historic preservation. Holdings: 300 books; archival materials. Services: Library open to the public by appointment.

2228 ▪ Northwest Minnesota Historical Center
Library
Moorhead State　　　　　　　Ph: (218)236-2343
　University Library　　　　　Fax: (218)299-5924
1104 7th Ave., S.
Moorhead, MN 56563
E-mail: shoptaug@mhd1.moorhead.msus.edu
URL: http://www.moorhead.msus.edu.archives

Contact: Terry L. Shoptaugh, Dir.

Desc: Subject: Ethnicity in Northwest Minnesota, social welfare, American Indians, politics, government, business, church history, oral history, women's organizations. Holdings: 945 linear feet of local history materials; photographs; microfilm; slides. Services: Copying; Library open to the public.

2229 ▪ Northwest Territory Canadian & French
Heritage Center
Minnesota Genealogical Society Library
PO Box 29397
Brooklyn Center, MN 55429

Contact: Jean Jensen, Libn.

Desc: Subject: Quebec, Canada, Canadians in the U.S., Metis Indians, Franco-Americans. Holdings: 2000 books; 100 bound periodical volumes; 1600 microforms; 100 manuscripts; 30 AV programs. Services: Library open to the public.

2230 ▪ Norwegian-American Historical
Association
Archives
St. Olaf College　　　　　　Ph: (507)646 3221
1510 St. Olaf Ave.　　　　　Fax: (507)646 3734
Northfield, MN 55057
URL: http://www.stolaf.edu/stolaf/other/naha/
　　naha.html

Contact: Forrest E. Brown, Cur. of Archv.

Desc: Subject: Norwegian-American history and genealogy. Holdings: 8000 books; 1500 bound periodical volumes; 500 other volumes; newspapers; scrapbooks; correspondence; clippings; diaries; records; manuscripts. Services: Interlibrary loan (through St. Olaf College Library; PALS); archives open to the public.

2231 ▪ Norwich and District Historical Society
Archives
R.R. 3　　　　　　　　　　　Ph: (519)863-3638
Norwich, ON, Canada N0J 1P0　Fax: (519)863-3638

Contact: Lisa Miettinen, Archv.Adm.

Desc: Holdings: 500 books; 5 bound periodical volumes; 200 cubic feet of archival material; 2000 microfiche; 200 reels of microfilm. Services: Copying; conservation; archives open to the public by appointment.

2232 ▪ Nutley Historical Society Museum
Alice J. Bickers Library
65 Church St.　　　　　　　Ph: (973)667-1528
Nutley, NJ 07110
E-mail: nhsmuseum@aol.com

Contact: David Tiene, Pres.

Desc: Subject: New Jersey and local history. Holdings: 200 volumes. Services: Interlibrary loan; Library open to the public by appointment.

2233 ▪ Oak Grove Lutheran Church
The Juanita Carpenter Library
7045 Lyndale Ave., S.　　　Ph: (612)869-4917
Richfield, MN 55423　　　　Fax: (612)798-0492

Contact: Juanita Carpenter, Libn.

Desc: Subject: Bible reference, devotional and inspirational reading, church history, religious education, family life, children's literature, biography, social concerns, world religions, religious fiction. Holdings: 5000 books; tape cassettes; religious periodicals; videotapes. Services: Library open to the public.

2234 ■ Oak Lawn Public Library
Local History Area
9427 S. Raymond Ave.   Ph: (708)422-4990
Oak Lawn, IL 60453-2434   Fax: (708)422-5061
URL: http://www.lib.oak-lawn.il.us

Contact: William D. Goodfellow, Hd.Ref.Serv.

Desc: Subject: Oak Lawn, IL; local history. Holdings: 400 books; 2000 photographs; 75 files of clippings; 20 boxes of local government records. Services: Library open to the public.

2235 ■ Oakland County Pioneer and Historical
Society
Library & Archives
405 Oakland Ave.   Ph: (248)338-6732
Pontiac, MI 48342   Fax: (248)338-6731

Contact: Charles Martinez, Oper.Mgr.

Desc: Subject: Local, state, family histories; early Oakland County medical history; genealogy; archeology; architecture. Holdings: 2500 books; 1500 bound periodical volumes; 20 volumes of carbons of historical material; 12 VF drawers of photographs; oral histories; clippings; manuscripts; diaries; scrapbooks; maps; newspapers; slides. Services: Copying; Library open to the public for reference use only.

2236 ■ Oakland Public Library
History, Literature and Oakland History Room
125 14th St.   Ph: (510)238-3136
Oakland, CA 94612   Fax: (510)238-2125
E-mail: langm<crs>jl@oak2.ci.oakland.ca.us
URL: http://oak2.ci.oakland.ca.us

Contact: Jean Lanqniun, Sr.Libn.

Desc: Subject: History, travel, biography, English and foreign languages and literature, genealogy, maps. Holdings: 100,663 books; genealogy microfilms. Services: Interlibrary loan; copying; room open to the public.

2237 ■ Ocean County Historical Society
Richard Lee Strickler Center
26 Hadley Ave.   Ph: (732)341-1880
CN 2191   Fax: (732)341-4372
Toms River, NJ 08754

Contact: Richard L. Strickler, Libn.

Desc: Subject: Ocean County history and genealogy, New Jersey history, United States antiques. Holdings: 8000 books; 100 bound periodical volumes; 100 documents; 150 AV programs; 100 manuscripts; 100 nonbook items. Services: Copying; Center open on a fee basis, by appointment and for reference use only.

2238 ■ Ohev Shalom Synagogue
Ray Doblitz Memorial Library
2 Chester Rd.   Ph: (610)874-1465
Wallingford, PA 19086

Contact: Ed Welsh, Libn.

Desc: Subject: Judaica. Holdings: 6000 books; pamphlets; 500 video cassettes on Jewish subjects. Services: Library open to the public with references.

2239 ■ Ohio Genealogical Society
Coshocton County Chapter
Library
PO Box 128   Ph: (740)545-6223
Coshocton, OH 43812-0128   Fax: (740)545-6223
URL: http://www.pe.net/sharyn

Contact: Ellen Pickrell, Pres.

Desc: Subject: Genealogy. Holdings: Figures not available.

2240 ■ Ohio Genealogical Society
Library
713 S. Main St.   Ph: (419)756-7244
Mansfield, OH 44907-1644   Fax: (419)756-7294
E-mail: ogs@ogs.org
URL: http://www.ogs.org

Desc: Subject: Genealogy and history. Holdings: 15,000 books; census for all Ohio counties, 1820-1920 (microfilm); original Ohio 1880 census volumes; 24 file drawers of "First Families of Ohio" applications; 46 drawers of unpublished family history manuscripts; I.G.I. World; Society of Civil War Families of Ohio. Services: Copying; Library open to the public for a fee.

2241 ■ Ohio Genealogical Society
Muskingum County Genealogical Society
Library
Box 2427   Ph: (740)453-8231
Zanesville, OH 43702-2427
E-mail: hyinger@msmisp.com

Contact: Hilda E. Yinger, Lib.Comm.Chm.

Desc: Subject: Genealogy, history. Holdings: 3500 books; 400 bound periodical volumes; township, county, and church registers; tombstone inscriptions; Bible records; atlases; genealogical lessons, lectures, and guides on tape; directories; court records and local newspapers on microfilm; family histories; microfiche. Services: Copying; Library open to the public.

2242 ■ Ohio Genealogical Society
Perry County, Ohio Chapter (OGS)
Library
PO Box 275   Ph: (740)987-7646
Junction City, OH 43748-0275 Fax: (740)987-7646

Contact: Sue Saylor

Desc: Subject: Genealogy. Holdings: 2000 books; 100 bound periodical volumes; 100 manuscripts; 100 microfiche; 25 microfilm. Services: Copying.

2243 ■ Ohio Historical Society
Archives Library Division
1982 Velma Ave.   Ph: (614)297-2510
Columbus, OH 43211-2497   Fax: (614)297-2546
E-mail: gparkinson@ohiohistory.org
URL: http://www.ohiohistory.org

Contact: George Parkinson, Div.Chf.

Desc: Subject: Ohio history, genealogy, archaeology, natural history. Holdings: 140,461 books; 10,500 microfiche; 88,192 reels of microfilm; 20,000 newspaper volumes. Services: Interlibrary loan; copying; Library open to the public.

2244 ■ Ohr Kodesh Sisterhood Library
8402 Freyman Dr.   Ph: (301)589-3880
Chevy Chase, MD 20815-3897

Contact: Leonard G. Rosenberg, Libn.

Desc: Subject: Judaica. Holdings: 3000 books. Services: Library open to the public for reference use only.

2245 ■ Oklahoma Historical Society
Archives and Manuscript Division
2100 N. Lincoln Blvd.   Ph: (405)522-5209
Oklahoma City, OK 73105   Fax: (405)521-2492
URL: http://www.ok-history.mus.ok.us

Contact: William D. Welge, Dir.

Desc: Subject: Oklahoma and Indian territories, Indian tribes of Oklahoma, pioneer life, missionaries, territorial court records, explorers. Holdings: 3000 reels of microfilm of Indian and Oklahoma affairs; 745,000 historical photo-

graphs; 30,000 reels of microfilm of newspapers; 6000 oral history tapes. Services: Copying; archives open to the public.

2246 ■ Oklahoma Historical Society
Division of Library Resources
2100 N. Lincoln Blvd.   Ph: (405)521-2491
Oklahoma City, OK 73105   Fax: (405)521-2492
URL: http://www.ok-history.mus.ok.us

Contact: Edward Connie Shoemaker, Lib.Dir.

Desc: Subject: Oklahoma and American Indian history, American west, Oklahoma genealogy. Holdings: 62,593 books; 10,600 reels of microfilm of U.S. Census, 1790-1920; 25,000 reels of microfilm of Oklahoma newspapers, 1893 to present. Services: Copying; Library open to the public for research use only.

2247 ■ Oklahoma Historical Society
Museum of the Western Prairie
Bernice Ford Price Reference Library
1100 Memorial Dr.   Ph: (580)482-1044
Box 574   Fax: (580)482-0128
Altus, OK 73522-0574
E-mail: muswestpr@ok-history.mus.ok.us
URL: http://www.ok-history.museum.ok.us

Contact: Burna Cole, Libn.

Desc: Subject: History of southwest Oklahoma, pioneer families, Plains Indians, cowboys, early settlers. Holdings: 1500 books; 100 bound periodical volumes; documents; oral history tapes; archival collections; photographs. Services: Copying; Library open to the public by appointment.

2248 ■ Old Brutus Historical Society, Inc.
Library
516 N. Seneca St.   Ph: (315)834-9342
Weedsport, NY 13166

Contact: Jeanne Baker, Hist.

Desc: Subject: Genealogy, local history. Holdings: 2000 books; 2000 photographs; 50,000 genealogy sheets; 2000 agricultural and household artifacts. Services: Library and museum open to the public; Genealogy open to the public on a limited schedule and by appointment.

2249 ■ Old Charles Town Library, Inc.
200 E. Washington St.   Ph: (304)725-2208
Charles Town, WV 25414   Fax: (304)725-6618

Contact: Marcia Lance, Actg.Libn.

Desc: Subject: Local history, genealogy, West Virginia history. Holdings: 65,000 books; 1034 bound periodical volumes. Services: Copying; Library open to the public.

2250 ■ Old Colony Historical Society
Museum & Library
66 Church Green   Ph: (508)822-1622
Taunton, MA 02780

Contact: Katheryn P. Viens, Dir.

Desc: Subject: Local and military history, decorative arts, genealogy. Holdings: 7000 books; other cataloged items. Services: Copying; museum and Library open to the public for reference use only.

2251 ■ Old Fort Genealogical Society of
Southeastern Kansas
Library
502 S. National Ave.   Ph: (316)223-3300
Fort Scott, KS 66701

Contact: Virginia Brown, Libn.

Desc: Subject: Bourbon County and regional history, genealogy. Holdings: 500 books; 150 reports; 50 microfiche; 200 reels of microfilm; 25 CD-ROMs. Services: Library open to the public.

2252 ▪ Old Kings Courthouse Museum Library

37 Cornwallis St.   Ph: (902)678-6237
Kentville, NS, Canada B4N 2E2   Fax: (902)679-0066
E-mail: khs@glinx.com
URL: http://www.go.ednet.ns.ca/ip96003/

Contact: Bria Stokesbury, Cur.

Desc: Subject: Genealogy, local history, school textbooks. Holdings: 300 books; 2000 archival materials; 100 microfiche; 200 reels of microfilm. Services: Copying; Library open to the public for a fee.

2253 ▪ Old Saybrook Historical Society Archives

PO Box 4
Old Saybrook, CT 06475
URL: http://oldsaybrook.com/History/society.htm

Desc: Subject: Old Saybrook history. Holdings: 1000 books; maps; ledgers; photographs; papers. Services: Archives open to the public by appointment.

2254 ▪ Old Woodbury Historical Society Library

PO Box 705, Hurd House   Ph: (203)263-2696
Main St.
Woodbury, CT 06798

Contact: Vera T. Elsenboss

Desc: Subject: History of Woodbury. Holdings: Figures not available. Services: Library not open to the public.

2255 ▪ Old York Historical Society Library

207 York St   Ph: (207)363-4974
PO Box 312   Fax: (207)363-4021
York, ME 03909
URL: http://www.nentug.org/museums/oldyork

Contact: Virginia S. Spiller, Libn.Genel.

Desc: Subject: Local history, decorative arts, genealogy, Maine history, architecture. Holdings: 3000 books; 200 bound periodical volumes; 55 feet of manuscripts and archives; 3000 microfiche; 50 reels of microfilm; 4 VF drawers. Services: Copying; Library open to the public for reference use only on limited schedule.

2256 ▪ Old York Road Historical Society Archives

Jenkintown Library   Ph: (215)886-8590
York and Vista Rds.   Fax: (215)884-2243
Jenkintown, PA 19046

Contact: Joyce H. Root, Archv.

Desc: Subject: Local history and genealogy. Holdings: Books; newspapers; pamphlets; clippings; photographs; maps; deeds. Services: Archives open to the public for reference.

2257 ▪ Old York Road Temple Beth Am Library

971 Old York Rd   Ph: (215)886-8000
Abington, PA 19001   Fax: (215)886-8320

Desc: Subject: Religion, Judaica. Holdings: 5000 books. Services: Library not open to the public.

2258 ▪ Olmsted County Historical Society Archives

1195 County Rd. 22, S.W.   Ph: (507)282-9447
Rochester, MN 55902   Fax: (507)289-5481

E-mail: sweetman@millcom.com
URL: http://www.selco.lib.mn.us/ochs/index.htm

Contact: Sherry Sweetman, Archv.Libn.

Desc: Subject: Olmsted County history, Minnesota history, genealogy, 19th century farming. Holdings: 6000 books; 400 bound periodical volumes; 1000 reels of microfilm of Olmsted County newspapers, 1859 to present; 100 VF drawers of documents, pamphlets, photographs; Minnesota census records through 1920. Services: Copying; photo reproduction; archives open to the public (fees charged for staff research).

2259 ▪ Oneida County Historical Society Colonel Tharratt Gilbert Best Library

1608 Genesee St.   Ph: (315)735-3642
Utica, NY 13502-5425   Fax: (315)732-0806

Contact: Richard Aust, Cur.

Desc: Subject: History - Oneida County, Utica, Mohawk Valley. Holdings: 2200 volumes; 3500 pamphlets; 250,000 manuscript pieces. Services: Copying; Library open to the public.

2260 ▪ Onondaga County Public Library Local History/Genealogy

Galleries of Syracuse   Ph: (315)435-1800
447 S. Salina St.   Fax: (315)435-8533
Syracuse, NY 13202-2494
URL: http://www.co.onondaga.ny.us/ocpl/index.html

Contact: Lawrence J. Frank, Exec.Dir.

Desc: Subject: Genealogy; history - Syracuse, Onondaga County, northeastern U.S. Holdings: 37,000 volumes; 40 VF drawers of clippings; 17 VF drawers of genealogical notes; 360 maps; 15,000 reels of microfilm; 26 drawers of microfiche. Services: Copying; collections open to the public.

2261 ▪ Ontario County Historical Society Research Center

55 N. Main St.   Ph: (716)394-4975
Canandaigua, NY 14424   Fax: (716)394-9356
E-mail: ochs@eznet.net
URL: http://www.ochs.org

Contact: Edward Varno, Exec.Dir.

Desc: Subject: New York early land dealings, Civil War, history of Ontario County and western New York. Holdings: 4000 books; bound Ontario County newspapers, 1803-1968; 500 maps; 40,000 manuscripts; 250 volumes in Manchester Library Collection; 6500 pieces of ephemera; 25,000 photographs and negatives; censuses on microfilm. Services: Copying; archives open to the public for use on premises with staff assistance.

2262 ▪ Ontario Genealogical Society Library

c/o Canadiana Department,   Ph: (416)395-5624
   North York Central Library
North York Centre, 6th Fl.
5120 Yonge St.
Toronto, ON, Canada M2N
   5N9
URL: http://www.ogs.on.ca

Contact: Jean Bircham, Coord., Lib.Div.

Desc: Subject: Genealogy and family history, heraldry, local history, biography. Holdings: 4500 books; 45 bound periodical volumes; 1500 family histories. Services: Interlibrary loan (limited); copying; Library open to the public for reference use only.

2263 ▪ Ontario Genealogical Society, Kingston Branch

Box 1394   Ph: (613)549-8888
Kingston, ON, Canada K7L 5C6
URL: http://post.queensu.ca/murducKb/Kgbrogs.htm

Contact: Beverly Harris, Br.Libn.

Desc: Subject: Genealogy, genealogical research, local history. Holdings: 750 books; 200 bound periodical volumes; 12 VF drawers of genealogical information; transcribed cemetery stones; transcribed census; bibliographies. Services: Copying; Library open to the public.

2264 ▪ Orange County Library System Genealogy Department

101 E. Central Blvd.   Ph: (407)425-4694
Orlando, FL 32801   Fax: (407)425-6779
URL: http://www.ocls.lib.fl.us

Contact: Gregg B. Gronlund, Hd.

Desc: Subject: Genealogy, family history, heraldry, surnames. Holdings: 25,000 books; 2400 bound periodical volumes; 8 VF drawers of the papers of Beatrice Brown Commander; 14 VF drawers of miscellaneous family papers; 100 exchange periodicals. Services: Interlibrary loan (limited); copying (limited); department open to the public.

2265 ▪ Orleans County Historical Society Old Shone House Museum Library

Cyrus Eaton House   Ph: (802)754-2022
RR 1, Box 500
Orleans, VT 05860
E-mail: osh@together.net

Desc: Subject: History - Vermont, Orleans County (late 18th century to present), 19th-century America. Holdings: 1500 books; documents (deeds, marriage records, postal records); maps; atlases; manuscripts; diaries; 2000 photographs; 12 films and videos; sound recordings. Services: Copying; Library open to the public by appointment.

2266 ▪ Orphan Voyage Kammandale Library of Concerned United Birth Parents

57 N. Dale   Ph: (651)224-5160
St. Paul, MN 55102

Contact: Jeanette G. Kamman, Dir.

Desc: Subject: Local history, genealogy, grapho analysis - orphan histories. Holdings: 50,000 books; 5000 periodical volumes; pamphlets; maps. Services: Library open to the public by appointment.

2267 ▪ Orthodox Church in America Department of History and Archives

Box 675   Ph: (516)922-0550
Syosset, NY 11791   Fax: (516)922-0954

Contact: Alexis Liberovsky, Archv.

Desc: Subject: American Orthodox Church history - Carpatho-Russian, Greek; immigration history - Russian, Syrian, Albanian. Holdings: 270 linear feet of administrative archival materials; 240 linear feet of personal papers and collections; 200 linear feet of books, periodicals, photos, and other cataloged items. Services: Copying; archives open to the public at librarian's discretion.

2268 ▪ Oshawa Community Archives

1450 Simcoe St., S.   Ph: (905)436-7624
Oshawa, ON, Canada L1H 8S8   Fax: (905)436-7625

Contact: Tammy Robinson, Archv.

Desc: Subject: Oshawa history. Holdings: Family histories; manuscripts; microfilm; maps; photographs. Services: Copying; archives open to the public.

2269 ■ Ossining Historical Society Museum Library

196 Croton Ave.   Ph: (914)941-0001
Ossining, NY 10562   Fax: (914)941-0001
E-mail: ohsm@aol.com

Contact: Roberta Y. Arminio, Info.Dir.

Desc: Subject: Local history and genealogy. Holdings: 1100 books; 122 bound periodical volumes; 390 volumes of newspapers; 10 VF drawers of manuscripts, pamphlets, clippings, documents, and reports; 300 maps; 1000 photographs. Services: Interlibrary loan; copying; Library open to the public.

2270 ■ Ottawa Jewish Historical Society Archives

151 Chapel St.   Ph: (613)789-7306
Ottawa, ON, Canada K1N 7Y2   Fax: (613)789-4593

Contact: Shirley Berman, Archv.

Desc: Subject: Jewish community of Ottawa. Holdings: 100 books; 500 reports; 55 linear meters of archival materials; 20 reels of microfilm; 1000 photographs; 150 sound recordings. Services: Copying; archives open to the public.

2271 ■ Ottawa Public Library Ottawa Room

120 Metcalfe St., 3rd Fl.   Ph: (613)236-0301
Ottawa, ON, Canada K1P 5M2   Fax: (613)236-0732
URL: http://www.opl.ottawa.on.ca

Contact: Thomas Rooney, Libn.

Desc: Subject: Ottawa - history, municipal affairs, authors, genealogy, imprints; Ottawa Valley. Holdings: 22,798 books; 104 boxes of archival records; 103 boxes of Annual reports; 604 periodicals and city and telephone directories; 45 cassettes; 2 videocassettes; 88 microfiche; 21 reels of microfilm; 1312 vertical files; 13 volumes of Ottawa history scrapbooks; 2 volumes of Ottawa schools' scrapbooks; 39 linear feet of uncataloged municipal documents; 244 rare books; 1292 maps. Services: Copying; room open to the public for reference use only.

2272 ■ Otter Tail County Historical Society E.T. Barnad Library

1110 Lincoln Ave., W.   Ph: (218)736-6038
Fergus Falls, MN 56537   Fax: (218)739-3075

Desc: Subject: Local history. Holdings: 500 books; 200 bound periodical volumes; manuscripts; business records; oral histories; records and newspapers on microfilm; slides; dissertations; maps; photographs. Services: Library open to the public with restrictions.

2273 ■ Our Lady of Sorrows Basilica Archives

3121 W. Jackson Blvd.   Ph: (773)638-5800
Chicago, IL 60612

Contact: Rev. Conrad Borntrager, O.S.M., Archv.

Desc: Subject: Parish archives. Holdings: 66 bound periodical volumes; 78 linear feet of archives; 2 filing drawers of photographs; 56 blueprints. Services: Archives open to the public with restrictions.

2274 ■ Our Redeemers Lutheran Church Library

800 10th St. South   Ph: (612)843-3151
Benson, MN 56215

Contact: Marlene Skold, Libn.

Desc: Subject: Theology, devotional material. Holdings: 2000 books; pamphlets; filmstrips. Services: Library open to the public with restrictions.

2275 ■ Outaouais Genealogical Society Library

BP 2025, Succ. B   Ph: (819)243-5536
Hull, PQ, Canada J8X 3Z2   Fax: (819)682-3252
E-mail: sgo@bvx.ca

Contact: Jean de Chantal, Libn.

Desc: Subject: Genealogy, history, census reports. Holdings: 1500 books; 100 microfiche; 175 microfilm. Services: Copying; library open to the public for reference use only.

2276 ■ Owyhee County Historical Complex Helen Nettleton Library

Box 67   Ph: (208)495-2319
Murphy, ID 83650

Contact: Glenda R. Bean, Cur.

Desc: Subject: Owyhee County history, mining, agriculture, Indians, ranching, transportation. Holdings: 1100 books; 10 boxes of reports and manuscripts; 8 VF drawers of clippings and pictures; 20 boxes of archival materials; 1 drawer of microfilm; 50 oral history tapes. Services: Copying; Library open to the public with restrictions.

2277 ■ Oyster Bay Historical Society Research Library

20 Summit St.   Ph: (516)922-5032
Box 297   Fax: (516)922-6892
Oyster Bay, NY 11771-0297
E-mail: obhistory@aol.com

Contact: Thomas A. Kuehhas, Dir.Libn.

Desc: Subject: Long Island - revolutionary, colonial, 17th-20th century history and genealogy; Oyster Bay history. Holdings: 1050 books; 26 bound periodical volumes; 50 filing boxes of letters and manuscripts; 1000 photographs; 60 maps and atlases; original deeds, letters, documents. Services: Copying; Library open to the public for reference use only.

2278 ■ Oysterponds Historical Society, Inc. OHS Research Library

Village Lane   Ph: (516)323-2480
PO Box 844
Orient, NY 11957

Contact: Courtney Burns, Dir.

Desc: Subject: Local history. Holdings: 1350 volumes; 3000 documents and records; 12 VF drawers; 3500 glass plates; 19th century diaries, ship logs, business papers, 1848-1852; postcards; local wills and papers. Services: Library open to the public by appointment.

2279 ■ Ozarks Genealogical Society Library

534 W. Catalpa
Springfield, MO 65807
E-mail: osociety@mail.orion.org

Desc: Subject: Southwest Missouri history and genealogy. Holdings: 2750 books; microfilm; microfiche; manuscripts. Services: Library open to the public.

2280 ■ Palm Springs Desert Museum Toor Library & Hoover Natural Science Library

101 Museum Dr.   Ph: (760)325-7186
PO Box 2310   Fax: (760)327-5069
Palm Springs, CA 92263
E-mail: psmuseum@aol.com

Contact: Sidney Williams, Dir.Educ.Prog.

Desc: Subject: Art, natural science, local history, state history. Holdings: 8000 books; 20 bound periodical volumes. Services: Libraries not open to the public.

2281 ■ Park Avenue Synagogue Edmond de Rothschild Library

50 E. 87th St.   Ph: (212)369-2600
New York, NY 10128

Contact: Susan Vogelstein, Head Libn.

Desc: Subject: Judaica - adult, juvenile. Holdings: 9000 books. Services: Library open to the public with special permission only.

2282 ■ Park College McAfee Memorial Library Special Collections

8700 River Park   Ph: (816)741-2000
Parkville, MO 64152-3795   Fax: (816)741-4911
E-mail: aschultis@mail.park.edu

Contact: Ann Schultis, Dir. of Lib.Sys.

Desc: Subject: Park College history. Holdings: 132,000 books; 5000 bound periodical volumes. Services: Interlibrary loan; copying; Library open to the public.

2283 ■ Park Forest Public Library Park Forest Local History Collection

400 Lakewood Blvd.   Ph: (708)748-3731
Park Forest, IL 60466   Fax: (708)748-8829
URL: http://www.lincolnnet.net/users/lrpfhs/

Contact: Barbara Flynn, Hd.Libn.

Desc: Subject: Park Forest - history (1946 to present), architecture, shopping centers, government. Holdings: 45 boxes of archival materials; 26 boxes and 103 reels of microfilm of Park Forest newspapers, 1949 to present; 127 videocassettes; 231 mounted photographs; 2274 photographs; 491 slides; 16 audiotapes; scrapbooks; 7 VF drawers of local government documents; 4 VF drawers of local history materials; 2 oversize packets; 1 document box for oversize materials. Services: Interlibrary loan (limited); copying; collection open to the public.

2284 ■ Park Synagogue Library

3300 Mayfield Rd.   Ph: (216)371-2244
Cleveland Heights, OH 44118 Fax: (216)321-0639
E-mail: sarajane@parksyn.org
URL: http://www.parksyn.org

Contact: Sarajane Dolinsky, Libn.

Desc: Subject: Judaica, Jewish history. Holdings: 15,000 books; 100 bound periodical volumes. Services: Interlibrary loan; Library open to the public for reference use only.

2285 ■ Parma Area Historical Society Library

PO Box 29002   Ph: (440)886-1931
Parma, OH 44129

Contact: Robert Horley, Dir.

Desc: Subject: History of Parma, Ohio. Holdings: 400 books; 100 reports. Services: Library not open to the public.

2286 ■ Pasadena Historical Museum Research Library & Archives

470 W. Walnut St.   Ph: (626)577-1660
Pasadena, CA 91103-3594   Fax: (626)577-1662

Contact: Tania Rizzo, Archv.

Desc: Subject: History of the Pasadena area. Holdings: 1500 books; pamphlets; clippings; albums; diaries; maps;

documents; periodicals; manuscripts; ephemera. Services: Copying; photo reproductions; Library and archives open to the public for research only.

2287 ■ Pasadena Public Library
Pasadena Centennial Room
285 E. Walnut St. Ph: (626)744-4052
Pasadena, CA 91101 Fax: (626)796-3818
URL: http://www.ci.pasadena.ca.us

Contact: Luis Herrara

Desc: Subject: California and Pasadena local history, genealogy. Holdings: 5200 books; 183 periodicals and newsletters; 4000 Pasadena photographs; 240 Pasadena scrapbooks; 1800 Pasadena documents; 90 linear feet of Pasadena ephemera and clippings; 22 linear feet of pamphlets; 20 16mm films; 165 videocassettes; 1600 reels of microfilm of Pasadena newspapers; 200 architectural drawings. Services: Interlibrary loan, copying, division open to the public.

2288 ■ Passaic County Historical Society
Local History and Genealogy Library
Lambert Castle Ph: (973)881-2761
Valley Rd. Fax: (973)357-1070
Paterson, NJ 07503

Contact: Andrew Shick, Dir.

Desc: Subject: Genealogy, local history. Holdings: 4000 books. Services: Copying; Library open to the public by appointment.

2289 ■ Patten Free Library
Sagadahoc History and Genealogy Room
33 Summer St. Ph: (207)443-5141
Bath, ME 04530 Fax: (207)443-3514
E-mail: pfl@patten.lib.me.us
URL: http://www.patten.lib.me.us/

Contact: Denise R. Larson, Mgr.

Desc: Subject: Sagadahoc County, Maine history, genealogy, and culture. Holdings: 1000 books; 10 ft. of microfiche; 450 rolls of microfilm; 2500 photographs. Services: Library open to the public.

2290 ■ Peabody Essex Museum
Phillips Library
East India Square Ph: (978)745-9500
Salem, MA 01970 Fax: (978)741-9012
E-mail: pem@pem.org

Desc: Subject: Essex County history, New England maritime history and culture, early American history, genealogy, ethnology, archaeology, natural history. Holdings: 400,000 books; bound periodical volumes; early American printed material; directories; newspapers (complete for Salem); 5200 linear feet of manuscript business records and personal papers of merchants and families; logbooks; journals; diaries; manuscripts of American literary figures; maps; photographs. Services: Copying; photographic orders; Library open to the public on fee basis.

2291 ■ Pejepscot Historical Society
Library
159 Park Row Ph: (207)729-6606
Brunswick, ME 04011 Fax: (207)729-6012
E-mail: pejepscot@curtislibrary.com
URL: http://www.curtislibrary.com/pejepscot.htm

Contact: Deborah Smith, Dir.

Desc: Subject: Joshua Lawrence Chamberlain, local history. Holdings: 700 volumes. Services: Copying; Library open to the public.

2292 ■ Pendleton District Historical, Recreational and Tourism Commission
Reference Library
125 E. Queen St. Ph: (864)646-3782
PO Box 565 Fax: (864)646-2506
Pendleton, SC 29670
E-mail: pendtour@innova.net

Contact: Hurley E. Badders, Exec.Dir.

Desc: Subject: History - Pendleton district, South Carolina, U.S.; genealogy; church history; travel, tourism, and recreation; antiques and historic preservation; archeology. Holdings: 1500 books; 200 boxes of clippings, unbound reports, other cataloged items; 90 books and documents on microfilm; 10 drawers of photographs; 4 drawers of family histories; 75 maps; 90 ledgers. Services: Copying; Library open to the public.

2293 ■ Peninsula Library and Historical Society
6105 Riverview Rd. Ph: (330)657-2665
PO Box 236 Fax: (330)657-2311
Peninsula, OH 44264-0236

Contact: Edith M. Minns, Libn.Dir.

Desc: Subject: History, biography, literature, arts. Holdings: 35,000 books; 162 bound periodical volumes; 2500 AV programs; 24 VF drawers of pamphlets and clippings; 150 maps. Services: Interlibrary loan; copying; Library open to the public.

2294 ■ Peninsula Temple Beth El
Library
1700 Alameda de Las Pulgas Ph: (650)341-7701
San Mateo, CA 94403 Fax: (650)570-7183

Contact: Elayne L. Kane, Lib.Chm.

Desc: Subject: Philosophy of Judaism; history of Judaism and the Jewish religion; fiction of Jewish content or by Jewish authors; Jewish publications; Israel - description and travel; history of the Jews in the U.S. Holdings: 7500 books; periodicals; cassettes; records. Services: Library open to the public.

2295 ■ Pennsylvania Dutch Folk Culture Society
Heritage Library
PO Box 306 Ph: (610)683-1589
Kutztown, PA 19530

Contact: Anna R. Stein, Ex.Dir.

Desc: Subject: Pennsylvania genealogy, language, churches, and folklore. Holdings: Photographs; archival items. Services: Copying; Library open to the public.

2296 ■ Penobscot Marine Museum
Stephen Phillips Memorial Library
Church St. Ph: (207)548-2529
PO Box 498 Fax: (207)548-2520
Searsport, ME 04974-0498
E-mail: pmmlib@acadia.net
URL: http://www.acadia.net/pmmuseum

Contact: John G. Arrison, Libn.Archv.

Desc: Subject: Maritime history, genealogy, marine history, biography of mariners. Holdings: 12,000 volumes; archival materials; clippings; 3000 navigational charts; manuscripts; photographs; vital records and census data of Knox, Waldo, Hancock counties on microfilm. Services: Copying; Library open to the public.

2297 ■ Pensacola Historical Society
Lelia Abercrombie Historical Library
117 E. Gov. St. Ph: (850)434-5455
Pensacola, FL 32501

Contact: Sandra L. Johnson, Cur.

Desc: Holdings: 1500 books; 180 microfilm; 26 paintings; 212 linear feet of photographs; 87 linear feet of plans and drawings; 32 linear feet of VF drawers; 20 linear feet of Pensacola directories; 7 linear feet of ephemera; 26 linear feet of genealogical materials; 77 linear feet of historical and genealogical writings; 10 linear feet of finding aids; 52 linear feet of newspapers, drawings, artwork, and scrapbooks; 93 linear feet of manuscripts. Services: Copying; Library open to the public with restrictions.

2298 ■ (Penticton) R. N. Atkinson Museum and Archives
785 Main St. Ph: (250)490-2451
Penticton, BC, Canada V2A Fax: (250)492-0440
5E3
E-mail: museum@city.penteton.be.ca

Contact: Randall Manuel, Dir.Cur.

Desc: Subject: Local and regional governments, pioneers, military history, historic transportation, aboriginal history, rails, ship, mines, pioneers, ranching. Holdings: 300 books; 30 linear meters of bound periodical volumes; 3 meters of reports; 350 square meters of archival material; 30,000 photographs. Services: Library open to the public for reference use only.

2299 ■ Peoria Historical Society
Library
Bradley University Library Ph: (309)677-2822
Peoria, IL 61625 Fax: (309)677-2558
E-mail: frey@bradley.bradley.edu
URL: http://www.bradley.edu/itr/lib/

Contact: Charles J. Frey, Spec.Coll.Libn.

Desc: Subject: Peoria - pictures, biographies, churches, schools, business and industry, authors. Holdings: 1800 books; 102 LF VF drawers; 20,000 photographic images. Services: Copying; Library open to the public.

2300 ■ Perry Historians
Library
PO Box 73 Ph: (717)582-4896
New Bloomfield, PA 17074

Contact: Fae Cupp

Desc: Subject: Genealogy, local history. Holdings: 5000 books; 400 reels of microfilm; 1000 land drafts; 4500 family surname files; 500,000 index cards. Services: Copying; Library open to the public on a limited schedule; provides research services.

2301 ■ Peterborough Historical Society
Library
Grove St. Ph: (603)924-3235
Box 58
Peterborough, NH 03458

Contact: Ellen Derby, Exec.Dir.

Desc: Subject: History of Peterborough and New Hampshire, antiques. Holdings: 1000 books; tax records; clippings; early mill account books; maps; letters; early deeds; scrapbooks. Services: Library open to the public.

2302 ■ Petersham Historical Society, Inc.
Library
Main St. Ph: (508)724-3380
Petersham, MA 01366

Contact: Delight Gale Haines, Libn.Cur.

Desc: Subject: Petersham history and genealogy. Holdings: 800 books; 600 pamphlets and reports; 15 VF drawers of documents, diaries, pictures; 8 VF drawers of clippings and manuscripts; 20 maps. Services: Library open to the public with restrictions.

2303 ▪ Pettaquamscutt Historical Society
Library
2636 Kingstown Rd.   Ph: (401)783-1328
Kingston, RI 02881

Contact: Elizabeth R. Albro, Cur.

Desc: Subject: Local history and genealogy, Rhode Island history. Holdings: 1000 books; manuscripts. Services: Library open to the public on a limited schedule.

2304 ▪ P.H. Sullivan Foundation
Museum & Genealogy Library
225 W. Hawthorne St.   Ph: (317)873-4900
PO Box 182   Fax: (317)873-4047
Zionsville, IN 46077

Contact: Edie Kellar Mahaney, Exec.Dir.

Desc: Subject: Boone County, Indiana history and genealogy, U.S. genealogy. Holdings: 6000 books; 500 reels of microfilm. Services: Copying; Library open to the public for reference use only.

2305 ▪ Piatt County Historical & Genealogical
Society
Resource Center
PO Box 111   Ph: (217)762-2442
Monticello, IL 61856
URL: http://www.monticello.com

Contact: Linda Redmond, Libn.

Desc: Subject: Genealogy. Holdings: 500 books. Services: Copying; Center open on a limited schedule and by appointment.

2306 ▪ Pickaway County Historical Society
Library
PO Box 85   Ph: (740)474-9144
Circleville, OH 43113

Contact: Darlene Weaver, Lib.Dir.

Desc: Subject: Local history, genealogy. Holdings: 2000 books; 500 archival items; microfiche; 100 reels of microfilm. Services: Copying; Library open to the public.

2307 ▪ Pilgrim Congregational Church
Library
2310 E. 4th St.   Ph: (218)724-8503
Duluth, MN 55812

Contact: Jody Ondich, Assoc. Minister

Desc: Subject: Bible, liberal theology, church and social action, United Church of Christ and Congregational history, social issues, meditation and prayer. Holdings: 1800 books. Services: Library open to church members.

2308 ▪ Pilgrim Society
Pilgrim Hall Museum
75 Court St.   Ph: (508)746-1620
Plymouth, MA 02360-3891   Fax: (508)747-4228
E-mail: pegbaker@ici.net

Contact: Peggy M. Baker, Dir.

Desc: Subject: Pilgrim history, Plymouth, Massachusetts and Plymouth Colony, 1620-1692. Holdings: 6000 books; 800 bound periodical volumes; 4000 photographs; 12,000 manuscripts, maps, prints, charts, ephemera. Services: Copying; Library open to researchers by appointment.

2309 ▪ Pinal County Historical Society, Inc.
Library
715 S. Main St.   Ph: (520)868-4382
Box 851
Florence, AZ 85232

Contact: Mary A. Faul, Libn.

Desc: Subject: Arizona and Southwest history, Pinal County. Holdings: 650 books; 75 bound periodical volumes; clippings and pictures of local county history. Services: Library open to researchers on a limited schedule.

2310 ▪ Pioneer Historical Society
Library
242 E. John St.   Ph: (814)623-2011
Bedford, PA 15522   Fax: (814)623-2011

Contact: Kay Williams, Libn.

Desc: Subject: Bedford County history, genealogy. Holdings: 1570 items. Services: Copying; Library open to the public.

2311 ▪ Pipestone County Historical Society
Research Library
113 S. Hiawatha   Ph: (507)825-2563
Pipestone, MN 56164   Fax: (507)825-2563
E-mail: pipctymu@rconnect.com
URL: http://www.pipestone.mn.us/Museum/
      Homepa1.HTM

Contact: Chris Roelfsemanhumme, Musm.Dir.

Desc: Subject: Local, county, and state history. Holdings: 500 books; 150 bound periodical volumes; 212 reels of microfilm; oral history transcripts; county newspapers. Services: Library open to the public with restrictions; research requests necessary by mail or e-mail.

2312 ▪ Plainfield Public Library
Guilford Township Historical Collection
1120 Stafford Rd.   Ph: (317)839-6602
Plainfield, IN 46168-2230   Fax: (317)839-4044
E-mail: scarter@plainfield.lib.in.us
URL: http://www.plainfield.lib.in.us/history/
      history.html-ssi

Contact: Susan Miller Carter, Dept.Hd.

Desc: Subject: History and genealogy - Plainfield, Hendricks, Marion, Morgan, Montgomery, Putnam, and Boone counties; Virginia, North Carolina, Tennessee, Kentucky, Ohio genealogy; Society of Friends Western Yearly Meeting; local authors; Indianapolis city directories, 1880-1940. Holdings: 14,937 books; 202 bound periodical volumes; 145 bound newspaper volumes; 28 oral history tapes and transcripts; 8 file drawers of photographs; 34 file drawers of clippings and pamphlets; 376 boxes of manuscripts; obituary file; 1132 audiovisual materials; 764 reels of microfilm and 566 microfiche of local newspapers, census data, and local history materials. Services: Copying; collection open to the public, (call for hours and information); limited research for mail requests - send SASE.

2313 ▪ Platte County Historical & Genealogical
Society
Ben Ferrel Platte County Museum Library
3rd and Ferrel St.   Ph: (816)431-5121
PO Box 103
Platte City, MO 64079

Contact: Fran Bohachick, Hd.Libn.

Desc: Subject: Platte County, genealogy, county history, county architecture. Holdings: 300 books; 200 bound periodical volumes; 2 file cabinets of family group sheets; 2000 nonbook items. Services: Library open to the public on a limited schedule or by appointment.

2314 ▪ Plumas County Museum
Library
500 Jackson St.   Ph: (530)283-6320
PO Box 10776   Fax: (530)283-6415
Quincy, CA 95971
E-mail: pcmuseum@psln.com

Contact: Scott Lawson, Dir.

Desc: Subject: Plumas county history, agricultural history, Maidu Indians, mining history, logging and lumber. Holdings: 1000 books; 150 taped interviews; 100 manuscripts; bound periodical volumes; letters; government documents; other cataloged items; historic photographs. Services: Copying (limited); Library open to the public by appointment.

2315 ▪ Plymouth Historical Society Museum
Library & Archives
155 S. Main St.   Ph: (313)455-8940
Plymouth, MI 48170   Fax: (313)455-7797
E-mail: stew03@juno.com

Contact: Beth A. Stewart, Dir.

Desc: Subject: Plymouth history, genealogy, Michigan history, Michigan in the Civil War, Civil War history. Holdings: 500 books; 1000 documents; 1000 photographs; Plymouth newspapers, 1878-1956 on microfilm; census records; marriage and cemetery records, 1840-1950. Services: Interlibrary loan; copying; Library open to the public for reference use only.

2316 ▪ Polish Institute of Arts and Sciences of
America, Inc.
Alfred Jurzykawski Memorial Library
208 E. 30th St.   Ph: (212)686-4164
New York, NY 10016   Fax: (212)545-1130
E-mail: piasa@worldnet.att.net
URL: http://home.att.net/piasa/

Contact: Krystyna Baron, Chf.Libn.

Desc: Subject: Poland - humanities, social sciences, ethnicity, Polish America. Holdings: 25,000 books; 500 periodical titles; newspapers on microfilm; maps. Services: Copying; Library open to the public on a limited schedule.

2317 ▪ Polish Nobility Association Foundation
Leonard J. Suligowski Reference Library
529 Dunkirk Rd.   Fax: (410)377-4352
Anneslie, MD 21212-2014
URL: http://www.geocities.com/athens/olympus/8691/
      tpna.htm

Contact: Leonard Suligowski

Desc: Subject: Polish history, heraldry, nobility. Holdings: 500 books; 100 other cataloged items.

2318 ▪ Polk County Historical and Genealogical
Library
100 E. Main St.   Ph: (941)534-4380
Bartow, FL 33830   Fax: (941)534-4382

Contact: Joseph E. Spann, Mgr.

Desc: Subject: History - Polk County, Florida, Southeastern United States; genealogies of Southeastern United States families. Holdings: 12,000 books; 610 bound periodical volumes; 1200 family histories; 4103 reels of microfilm of census reports; 600 reels of microfilm including census reports, newspapers, county records. Services: Copying; Library open to the public.

2319 ▪ Pollard Memorial Library
Local History Collection
401 Merrimack St.   Ph: (508)970-4120
Lowell, MA 01852   Fax: (508)970-4117
URL: http://www.uml.edu/Lowell/library.html

Desc: Subject: Lowell, Massachusetts - history, genealogy, authors, artists. Services: Interlibrary loan; copying; Library open to the public.

2320 ▪ Pomona Public Library
Special Collections Department

625 S. Garey Ave.　　　　　Ph: (909)620-2026
Box 2271　　　　　　　　Fax: (909)620-3713
Pomona, CA 91766-2271
E-mail: pomref@tstonramp.com

Contact: Bruce Guter, Supv.

Desc: Holdings: 10,297 books. Services: Interlibrary loan; copying; department open to the public.

2321 ▪ Pope County Museum and Archives

809 S. Lakeshore Dr.　　　　Ph: (320)634-3293
Glenwood, MN 56334
E-mail: pcmuseum@runestone.net

Contact: Merlin Peterson, Cur.

Desc: Subject: History local, business, personal; genealogy. Holdings: 1343 volumes. Services: Copying; Library open to the public for reference use only.

2322 ▪ Population and Development Program Research
Library

Cornell University　　　　　Ph: (607)255-4924
B-12 Warren Hall　　　　　Fax: (607)254-2896
Ithaca, NY 14853-7801
E-mail: bj11@cornell.edu

Contact: Linda Pope, Libn.

Desc: Subject: Population, social science. Holdings: 10,000 books. Services: Library not open to the public.

2323 ▪ Population Reference Bureau, Inc.
LibraryInformation Service

1875 Connecticut Ave., NW,　　Ph: (202)483-1100
Ste. 520　　　　　　　　Fax: (202)328-3937
Washington, DC 20009
E-mail: zuali@prb.org
URL: http://www.prb.org

Contact: Zuali Malsawma, Libn.

Desc: Subject: Demography, U.S. census, family planning, migration, environment, population policy. Holdings: 14,000 books; 2500 reprints and papers, 15 VF drawers of pamphlets, clippings, reprints. Services: Interlibrary loan; copying; Library open to the public.

2324 ▪ Portage County Historical Society
Library and Museum

65491 N. Chestnut St.　　　　Ph: (330)296-3523
Ravenna, OH 44266
URL: http://www2.clearlight.com/pchs

Contact: Raymond Wilson, Pres.

Desc: Subject: County history - families, industries, organizations, genealogy. Holdings: Family histories; early tax records; county records, documents, atlas; cemetery records; official roster of Ohio soldiers, sailors, and Marines in the Spanish War and World War I; military and presidential histories; local directors; census records (1820-1920) on microfilm; Ohio histories. Services: Copying; Library open to the public for reference use only.

2325 ▪ Portsmouth Athenaeum
Library and Museum

6-8 Market Sq.　　　　　　Ph: (603)431-2538
Box 848　　　　　　　　Fax: (603)431-7180
Portsmouth, NH 03802-0848
E-mail: athenaeum@juno.com

Contact: Richard G. Adams

Desc: Subject: Portsmouth - local history and genealogy; local and New England maritime, military, and cultural history; 19th century travel and description, biography; art; architecture; decorative arts; resources document en-

tire Piscataqua area, including southern Maine. Holdings: 35,000 books; 350 bound volumes of New Hampshire newspapers; 260 linear feet of manuscripts; 250 linear feet of rare books; 12,000 photographs. Services: Library open to the public three days a week or by appointment.

2326 ▪ Portsmouth Public Library
Local History Room

601 Court St.　　　　　　Ph: (757)393-8501
Portsmouth, VA 23704　　　　Fax: (804)393-5107

Contact: Barnabas W. Baker, Lib.Asst.

Desc: Subject: Local history, lighthouses and lightships, genealogy. Holdings: 4000 books; 200 bound periodical volumes; 70 maps; 350 documents; 21,400 photographs; Norfolk County and Portsmouth wills and deeds, 1637-1820. Services: Interlibrary loan; copying; room open to the public.

2327 ▪ Prairie Trails Museum Library of Wayne County, Iowa

Hwy. 2　　　　　　　　Ph: (515)872-2211
E. Jefferson St.
Corydon, IA 50060
E-mail: vmay@geneseo.net
URL: http://www.roots.web.com/iawayne/vm2

Contact: Wilma West, Libn.

Desc: Subject: History, genealogy. Holdings: Books; family files; microforms, school records. Services: Library open to the public on a limited schedule or by appointment; answers mail queries.

2328 ▪ Preble County District Library
Preble County Room

450 S. Barron St.　　　　　Ph: (937)456-4970
Eaton, OH 45320　　　　　Fax: (937)456-6092
E-mail: pcroom@infinet.com
URL: http://www.pcdl.lib.oh.us/

Contact: Susan H. Kendall, Dir.

Desc: Subject: Preble County and Miami Valley - history, genealogy. Holdings: 5000 books; 75 bound periodical volumes; 1750 reels of microfilm and microfiche; 2000 court records. Services: Copying; Library open to the public.

2329 ▪ Prince Rupert City and Regional Archives

PO Box 1093　　　　　　Ph: (250)624-3326
Prince Rupert, BC, Canada V8J　Fax: (250)624-3706
　4H6
E-mail: archives@citytel.net

Contact: Barbara Sheppard, Archv.

Desc: Subject: Prince Rupert, British Columbia. Holdings: 600 books. Services: Archives open to the public.

2330 ▪ Princeton University
Office of Population Research
Library

21 Prospect Ave.　　　　　Ph: (609)258-4874
Princeton, NJ 08544　　　　Fax: (609)258-1150
E-mail: belanger@opr.princeton.edu
URL: http://opr.princeton.edu

Contact: Maryann Belanger, Dir.

Desc: Subject: Population studies, demography (emphasis on methodology), fertility, mortality, census, vital statistics. Holdings: 34,000 volumes; 12,000 reprints; 14,000 manuscripts and pamphlets; 3500 reels of microfilm. Services: Interlibrary loan; copying; Library open to the public for reference use only.

2331 ▪ Prowers County Historical Society
Big Timbers Museum
Library

North Santa Fe Trail　　　　Ph: (719)336-2472
Box 362
Lamar, CO 81052

Contact: Jeanne Clark, Cur.

Desc: Subject: Local history. Holdings: 200 books; Prowers County newspapers. Services: Library open to the public for reference use only.

2332 ▪ Public Library of Anniston & Calhoun County
Alabama Room

108 E. 10th St.　　　　　Ph: (256)237-8501
Box 308
Anniston, AL 36202

Contact: Thomas B. Mullins, Dept.Hd.

Desc: Subject: History - Anniston, Calhoun County, Alabama, and southeastern states; genealogy. Holdings: 9000 books; 400 bound periodical volumes; 9500 microfilm-smicrofiche; manuscripts. Services: Copying; room open to the public.

2333 ▪ Public Library of Cincinnati and Hamilton County
History and Genealogy Department

800 Vine St.　　　　　　Ph: (513)369-6905
Cincinnati, OH 45202-2071　　Fax: (513)369-4599
E-mail: historystaff@plch.lib.oh.us
URL: http://plch.lib.oh.us

Contact: Patricia Van Skaik, Hd.

Desc: Subject: History, genealogy, maps, bibliography, geography, travel. Holdings: 270,574 books; 10,785 bound periodical volumes and newspapers; 43,940 reels of microfilm; 236,043 microfiche; 40,085 maps; 2390 atlases; 480 gazetteers; 255 carto-bibliographies; 444 reels of microfilm of maps; 6505 maps on microfiche; 21 globes. Services: Interlibrary loan; copying; faxing; open to the public.

2334 ▪ Public Library of Nashville and Davidson County
The Nashville Room

225 Polk Ave.　　　　　　Ph: (615)862-5783
Nashville, TN 37203-3585　　Fax: (615)862-5884
E-mail: mhearne@waldo.nashv.lib.tn.us
URL: http://www.nashv.lib.tn.us

Contact: Donna Nicely, Lib.Dir.

Desc: Subject: History and genealogy of Nashville and its residents, 1779 to present. Holdings: 13,000 books; scrapbooks; school diaries of the 1890s; 12 file drawers of census microfilm; manuscripts of local authors; interviews with local authors; Nashville obituaries (online); Nashville movies; photographs; slides; oral history tapes. Services: Copying; room open to the public.

2335 ▪ Pulaski County Historical Society
Library

Public Library Bldg.　　　　Ph: (606)678-8401
PO Box 36
Somerset, KY 42502

Contact: Jerri Brown, Pres.

Desc: Subject: Genealogy; history - local, regional, state. Holdings: Genealogical books and family files; census, marriage, birth, death, and cemetery records. Services: Copying; Library open to the public.

2336 ▪ Putnam County Historical Society and Foundry School Museum
Reference Library
63 Chestnut St.　　　　　Ph: (914)265-4010
Cold Spring, NY 10516　　Fax: (914)265-2884
E-mail: PCHS@highlands.com

Contact: Elaine Baldwin, Libn.

Desc: Subject: Genealogy; Putnam, Westchester, and Dutchess County history; West Point; American Revolution; Hudson River; West Point Foundry; the Civil War. Holdings: 1200 volumes; 2 VF drawers of clippings and newspapers; 30 boxes of archival materials and letters; 2 VF drawers of maps; manuscripts; microfiche. Services: Library open to the public on a limited schedule.

2337 ▪ Putnam County Public Library
Putnam County Historical Society Collection
103 E. Poplar St.　　　　Ph: (765)653-2755
Greencastle, IN 46135　　Fax: (765)653-2756

Contact: Ellen Sedlack, Dir.

Desc: Subject: County history and genealogy. Holdings: Books; clippings; letters; diaries; scrapbooks; microfilm; tape recordings; movies. Services: Copying; genealogical inquiries answered.

2338 ▪ Quaco Historical Society
Library
　　　　　　　　　　　　Ph: (506)833-4740
rs>St. Martins, NB, Canada E0G
2Z0

Contact: Elizabeth Thibodeau, Libn.

Desc: Subject: Atlantic maritime history, wooden shipbuilding, local history. Holdings: 5000 books. Services: Copying; Library open to the public.

2339 ▪ (Quebec Province) Archives Nationales du Quebec
Bibliotheque
1210 avenue du Seminaire
C.P. 10450　　　　　　　Ph: (418)644-4797
Ste. Foy, PQ, Canada G1V 4N1　Fax: (418)646-0868
URL: http://www.anq.gouv.qa.ca

Contact: Renald Lessard, Hd. of Dept.

Desc: Subject: Genealogy; government institutions; archives management and the administration of documents; history of French America. Holdings: 30,786 books; 1802 bound periodical volumes; 382 reels of microfilm of journals; 482 reels of microfilm; 2166 serials on microfiche. Services: Interlibrary loan; copying; Library open to the public.

2340 ▪ Quebec Province Ministere des Ministere des Relations avec les citizens et de l'Immigration
Centre de Documentation
360, rue McGill　　　　　Ph: (514)873-3263
Montreal, PQ, Canada H2Y 2E9　Fax: (514)864-2468
E-mail: http://www.mrci.gouv.gc.ca

Contact: Denis Robichaud, Chf.

Desc: Subject: Immigration, demography, population, ethnicity, minorities, refugees, civic relations, citizenship. Holdings: 21,000 books; 2000 bound periodical volumes; 100,000 newspaper clippings on immigration. Services: Interlibrary loan; copying; center open to the public by appointment.

2341 ▪ Queens Borough Public Library
Long Island Division
89-11 Merrick Blvd.　　　Ph: (718)990-0770
Jamaica, NY 11432　　　　Fax: (718)658-8342
URL: http://www.queenslibrary.com

Contact: Judith Box, Div.Mgr.

Desc: Subject: Long Island local history, genealogy, and memorabilia. Holdings: 32,150 books; 2177 bound periodical volumes; 360 running feet of clipping files; 6121 maps; 240,000 manuscripts; 8100 reels of microfilm; 72,000 pictures, prints, photographs, postcards, glass plate negatives. Services: Interlibrary loan; copying; division open to the public.

2342 ▪ Queens College of City University of New York
Ethnic Materials Information Exchange Collection
Benyam Dosenthal Library　Ph: (718)997-3626
65-30 Kissena Blvd.　　　Fax: (718)997-3753
Flushing, NY 11367

Contact: David Cohen, Prog.Dir.

Desc: Subject: Ethnic studies resources, minority groups in America, multicultural librarianship. Holdings: 1000 volumes; 40 filmstrips; 10 tapes; 250 pamphlets; curriculum materials; vertical file of clippings for each group and information area. Services: Center not open to the public.

2343 ▪ Quincy Historical Society
Wirtanen Library
Adams Academy Bldg.　　Ph: (617)773-1144
8 Adams St.　　　　　　Fax: (617)472-4990
Quincy, MA 02169

Contact: Dr. Edward Fitzgerald, Dir.

Desc: Subject: Quincy area history and genealogy. Holdings: 4000 books; 5000 pamphlets; 4000 photographs; 100 cubic feet of manuscripts. Services: Copying; Library open to the public with restrictions.

2344 ▪ Racine Heritage Museum
Archives
S. 701 Main St.　　　　　Ph: (414)636-3926
Racine, WI 53403　　　　Fax: (414)636-3940

Contact: Dr. Mary Ellen Conaway, Dir.

Desc: Subject: Local history, Racine County, corporate business histories, military history, genealogy. Holdings: 1500 books; 12 four-drawer vertical files of clippings and pamphlets. Services: Copying; Library open to the public on a limited schedule.

2345 ▪ Radcliffe College
Arthur and Elizabeth Schlesinger Library on the History of Women in America
10 Garden St.　　　　　Ph: (617)495-8647
Cambridge, MA 02138　　Fax: (617)496-8340
E-mail: s_mcdowell@radcliffe.edu
URL: http://Hplus.harvard.edu

Contact: Dr. Mary Maples Dunn, Dir.

Desc: Subject: Women - suffrage, medicine, education, law, social service, labor, family, organizations; history of American women in all phases of public and private life. Holdings: 65,000 volumes; 3000 bound periodical volumes; 1000 major collections of papers on individual American women, families, women's organizations; 9550 reels of microfilm; 2250 magnetic tapes; 464 oral history transcripts; 70 VF drawers; 4000 reels of audio- and videotapes; 7777 linear feet of manuscripts; 100,000 photographs. Services: Interlibrary loan; copying; Library open to the public.

2346 ▪ Radnor Historical Society
Research Library and Museum
Finley House　　　　　　Ph: (610)688-2668
113 W. Beech Tree Ln.
Wayne, PA 19087

Contact: J. Bennett Hill, Jr., Pres.

Desc: Subject: Local and Pennsylvania history. Holdings: 300 volumes; 4 boxes of genealogical papers; 4 drawers of maps; 4 boxes of photographs, 1880 to present. Services: Library open to the public.

2347 ▪ Ramsey County Historical Society
Research Center
Library
75 W. 5th St., Rm. 323　Ph: (612)222-0701
St. Paul, MN 55102　　　Fax: (612)223-8539
E-mail: mollie@rchs.com

Contact: Mollie A. Spillman, Cur.Archv.

Desc: Subject: Local history. Holdings: 1500 books; maps; pamphlets; documents; pictures. Services: Library open to the public for reference use only.

2348 ▪ Rawlins County Genealogical Society
PO Box 203　　　　　　Ph: (785)626-3805
Atwood, KS 67730　　　Fax: (785)626-3670

Contact: Delores Luedke, Res.

Desc: Subject: Genealogy. Holdings: Figures not available. Services: Library open to the public for reference use only.

2349 ▪ Ray County Historical Society and Museum
Museum Library
PO Box 2　　　　　　　Ph: (816)776-2305
Richmond, MO 64085

Contact: Norma Edson, Libn.

Desc: Subject: Genealogy, history. Holdings: 1550 books; 55 bound periodical volumes; 371 nonbook items; manuscripts; newspapers and census and probate records on microfilm. Services: Copying; Library open to the public.

2350 ▪ Reform Congregation Keneseth Israel
Meyers Library
8339 Old York Rd.　　　Ph: (215)887-8700
Elkins Park, PA 19027　Fax: (215)877-1070

Contact: Sidney August, Libn.

Desc: Subject: Judaica. Holdings: 10,200 books; 200 bound periodical volumes. Services: Interlibrary loan; Library open to the public with permission.

2351 ▪ Rensselaer County Historical Society
Library
59 Second St.　　　　　Ph: (518)272-7232
Troy, NY 12180　　　　Fax: (518)273-1264
E-mail: rchs@crisny.org
URL: http://www.crisny.org/not-for-profit/rchs

Contact: Stacy P. Draper, Cur.

Desc: Subject: Rensselaer County history. Holdings: 2500 books; letters; local business daybooks; maps and atlases; diaries; pamphlets; scrapbooks; tradecards; postcards. Services: Copying; Library open to the public for reference use only.

2352 ▪ Research Center for Beaver County and Local History
1301 7th Ave.　　　　　Ph: (724)846-4340
Beaver Falls, PA 15010　Fax: (412)846-0370

Desc: Subject: Local history, genealogy. Holdings: 3000 books; marriage and death notices; cemetery listings; census microfilm; Pennsylvania archives; Daughters of the American Revolution lineage materials. Services: Copying; center open to the public for reference use only.

2353 ▪ Research Foundation for Jewish Immigration, Inc.
Archives

570 7th Ave., Rm. 1106   Ph: (212)921-3871
New York, NY 10018   Fax: (212)575-1918

Contact: Dennis E. Rohrbaugh, Archv.

Desc: Subject: Biography, bibliography, oral history. Holdings: 300 transcriptions of oral history interviews with German-Jewish emigres in the United States. Services: Archives open to the public by appointment; telephone and written inquiries accepted.

2354 ▪ Reveille United Methodist Church
Reveille Memorial Library

4200 Cary Street Rd.   Ph: (804)359-6041
Richmond, VA 23221   Fax: (804)359-6090

Contact: Mary F. Guthrie, Adult Libn.

Desc: Subject: Bible studies, devotions, travel, art, philosophy, psychology, fiction. Holdings: 8459 books; tapes; pictures; slides; films; 4 VF drawers. Services: Interlibrary loan; Library open to the public.

2355 ▪ Revelstoke Museum and Archives

315 1st St. W   Ph: (250)837-3067
PO Box 1908   Fax: (250)837-3094
Revelstoke, BC, Canada V0E
2S0
E-mail: rm_chin@junction.net

Contact: Catherine English, Cur.Archv.

Desc: Subject: Local history, local rail transportation, local National Parks history. Holdings: 2000 archival collections; 12 reels of microfilm. Services: Copying; archives open to the public for reference use only.

2356 ▪ Rhode Island Historical Society
Library

121 Hope St.   Ph: (401)331-8575
Providence, RI 02906   Fax: (401)751-7930

Contact: Allison Cywin, Lib.Dir.

Desc: Subject: Rhode Island history, New England genealogy, local history. Holdings: 150,000 volumes; 2000 linear feet of manuscripts; 12,000 reels of microfilm of newspapers. Services: Copying; Library open to the public for reference use only.

2357 ▪ Rhode Island Jewish Historical Association
Library and Archives

130 Sessions St.   Ph: (401)331-1360
Providence, RI 02906   Fax: (401)272-6729
E-mail: rijhistory@aol.com
URL: http://www.dowtech.com.rijha/

Contact: Eleanor F. Horvitz, Libn.Archv.

Desc: Subject: History of Rhode Island Jews, Jews in the United States. Holdings: 114 square feet of books. Services: Library open to the public in presence of librarian.

2358 ▪ Rhode Island (State) Department of Administration
Office of Municipal Affairs
Office of Planning and Library Services

1 Capitol Hill   Ph: (401)277-3975
Providence, RI 02908-5893

Contact: Patricia Chorney, Supv., Res.

Desc: Subject: Planning, U.S. census, public administration and finance, transportation, economics, human services, land use, zoning. Holdings: 4000 volumes. Services: Library open to the public by appointment.

2359 ▪ Rice County Museum & Library

1814 2nd Ave. NW   Ph: (507)332-2121
Faribault, MN 55021

Desc: Subject: Rice County, Minnesota. Holdings: 800 books; 500 manuscripts; 250 magazines and scrapbooks. Services: Copying; archives open to the public with restrictions.

2360 ▪ Richfield Historical Society
Library

PO Box 215   Ph: (440)659-6451
Richfield, OH 44286

Contact: Virginia Baumgardner, Cur.

Desc: Subject: Richfield Township, Richfield Village, schools, churches, century homes, Farnham Home. Holdings: Books. Services: Library open to the public on a limited schedule.

2361 ▪ Richmond Museum of History
Library

400 Nevin Ave.   Ph: (510)235-7387
PO Box 1267   Fax: (510)235-4345
Richmond, CA 94802

Contact: Kathleen Rupley, Adm.Cur.

Desc: Subject: Richmond history. Holdings: 640 volumes; 1500 photographs; archival material. Services: Library open to the public for reference use only by appointment.

2362 ▪ Riley County Genealogical Society
Library

2005 Claflin Rd.   Ph: (913)565-6495
Manhattan, KS 66502-3415
E-mail: RCGS@flinthills.com
URL: http://www.flinthills.com/rcgs

Contact: Jane Brown, Pres.

Desc: Subject: Genealogy, state and local history. Holdings: 3800 books; 600 bound periodical volumes; 3 VF drawers of original biographies; 1 VF drawer and 13 card file drawers of genealogical charts of society members' ancestors; 250 reels of microfilm of census materials; 6 card drawers of microfiche of genealogical and land records. Services: Copying; SDI; Library open to the public.

2363 ▪ Riley County Historical Society
Seaton Memorial Library
Taylor and Charlson Archives

2309 Claflin Rd.   Ph: (785)565-6490
Manhattan, KS 66502

Contact: Jeanne C. Mithen, Libn.Archv.

Desc: Subject: History of Manhattan City and Riley County, Kansas; Kansas State University. Holdings: 4500 books; 400 bound periodical volumes; 250 scrapbooks; 6000 local photographs; 2 architect's filing cabinets of maps, documents, newspaper tear sheets and special issues; 2230 cubic feet of manuscripts and archival records; 20 oral history tapes; 30 videocassettes. Services: Copying; Library open to the public for reference use only.

2364 ▪ Riverside Presbyterian Church
Jean Miller Library

849 Park St.   Ph: (904)355-4585
Jacksonville, FL 32204

Contact: Evelyn Parker, Libn.

Desc: Subject: Religion, general subjects. Holdings: 2500 books. Services: Library not open to the public.

2365 ▪ Rochester Historical Society
Library

485 East Ave.   Ph: (716)271-2705
Rochester, NY 14607

Desc: Subject: Local history. Holdings: 10,000 titles; 200 periodical titles; 25 volumes of RHS publications; manuscript and archival material; photographs; maps; genealogical material; complete file of Rochester directories, 1827 to present. Services: Library open to the public with restrictions.

2366 ▪ Rochester Public Library
Local History and Genealogy Division

115 South Ave.   Ph: (716)428-8370
Rochester, NY 14604   Fax: (716)428-7313
URL: http://www.rochester.lib.ny.us

Contact: Wayne Arnold, Hd.

Desc: Subject: History of Rochester and Genesee area, genealogy (primarily New York and New England). Holdings: 25,000 books; 15 cases and 400 volumes of manuscripts; 1800 maps; 500 scrapbooks; 145 VF drawers of newspaper clippings; 80 VF drawers of pamphlets and ephemera; 20 VF drawers of pictures; 12 drawers of postcards; 638 reels of microfilm; 120 films. Services: Copying (limited).

2367 ▪ Rock County Historical Society
Archives of Rock County History

10 S. High   Ph: (608)756-4509
PO Box 8096   Fax: (608)756-3036
Janesville, WI 53547

Contact: Maurice J. Montgomery, Archv.

Desc: Subject: Rock County local history; land speculation. Holdings: 11,892 bound volumes; 40 VF drawers of manuscripts and photocopies of clippings; 500 volumes of school records, business records, diaries; 4 boxes and 15 cubic feet of maps; 50 drawers of cataloged photographs and other miscellaneous items; 4000 abstracts of title of Rock County Lands; 17,000 probate records, 1839-1930. Services: Copying; archives open to the public on a limited schedule.

2368 ▪ Rockefeller University
Rockefeller Archive Center

15 Dayton Ave.   Ph: (914)631-4505
Sleepy Hollow, NY 10591-1598   Fax: (914)631-6017
E-mail: archive@rockvax.rockefeller.edu
URL: http://www.rockefeller.edu/archive.ctr/

Contact: Dr. Darwin H. Stapleton, Dir.

Desc: Subject: African-American history; agriculture; American philanthropy; arts; economic development; education; humanities; international relations; labor; medicine; physical, natural, and social sciences; politics; population; public health; religion; social welfare; women's history. Holdings: 30,000 cubic feet of archival and manuscript collections; 500,000 photographs; 4000 microfiche; 2000 films. Services: Copying; scholarships for research related to archives holdings; conferences and seminars on topics related to archives holdings; center open to scholars by appointment.

2369 ▪ Rockingham Society of Genealogists
Library

Exeter Public Library   Ph: (603)436-5824
Box 81
Exeter, NH 03833
E-mail: path3242@aol.com

Contact: Marilyn Berridge, Libn.

Desc: Subject: Genealogy, biography, history. Holdings: 40 books. Services: Library open to the public.

2370 ■ Rockville Public Library
RockvilleVernon Local History Collection

52 Union St.	Ph: (860)875-5892
PO Box 1320	Fax: (860)875-9795
Vernon, CT 06066	

Contact: P. Ciparelli, Lib.Dir.

Desc: Subject: Local history. Services: Interlibrary loan; copying; Library open to the public.

2371 ■ Rocky Mount Historical Association
LibraryMuseum

200 Hyder Hill Rd.	Ph: (423)538-7396
Rocky Mount Pkwy.	Fax: (423)538-5983
Piney Flats, TN 37686-4630	

Contact: Norman O. Burns, II, Exec.Dir.

Desc: Subject: Local and regional history, Southwest Territory history, genealogy, technology, biography. Holdings: 1000 books; 1000 bound periodical volumes; 7 VF drawers of clippings; 2 VF drawers and 2 boxes of manuscripts; photographs. Services: Copying; Library open to the public for reference use only by appointment.

2372 ■ Rocky Mountain Jewish Historical Society
Ira M. Beck Memorial Archives

Center for Judaic Studies	Ph: (303)871-3016
University of Denver	Fax: (303)871-3037
Denver, CO 80208	

Contact: Dr. Jeanne Abrams, Archv.

Desc: Subject: Jewish history of region. Holdings: 8000 linear feet of microfilm, manuscripts, original records, and oral history tapes; 5000 photographs. Services: Copying; Library open to the public.

2373 ■ Roman Catholic Archdiocese of Toronto
Archives

1155 Yonge St., Ste. 505	Ph: (416)934-0606
Toronto, ON, Canada M4T	Fax: (416)934-3444
1W2	

Contact: Marc Lerman, Archv.

Desc: Subject: Toronto Catholic history, diocesan administrative history, genealogy, parish history. Holdings: 1600 linear ft. of archival items; 500 reels of microfilm. Services: Copying; Library open to the public on a limited schedule.

2374 ■ Rome Historical Society
William E. Scripture Memorial Library

200 Church St.	Ph: (315)336-5870
Rome, NY 13440	Fax: (315)336-5912

Contact: Kathleen Hynes-Bouska, Cur.

Desc: Subject: Rome and Oneida County, genealogy, Civil War, American Revolution, social history, industrial history. Holdings: 2500 books; 500 bound periodical volumes; 3000 archival documents; La Vita (Italian language newspaper), 1918-1945, on microfilm; historical documents on microfilm. Services: Copying; Library open to the public (appointment recommended; fee for non-members; advance appointment necessary for Rome Turney Radiator Records Collection).

2375 ■ Roosevelt University
Oral History Project in Labor History

430 S. Michigan Ave.	Ph: (312)341-3643
Chicago, IL 60605	Fax: (312)341-2425
URL: http://www.roosevelt.edu/library	

Contact: Mary Beth Riedner, Actg.Dir.

Desc: Subject: Oral histories in labor history. Holdings: 246 hours of taped interviews. Services: Copying. The oral history transcripts are held in the Roosevelt University library where they may be read but not checked out.

2376 ■ Roscoe Village Foundation
Library

381 Hill St.	Ph: (740)623-6567
Coshocton, OH 43812	
E-mail: RVHistorian@Coshocton.com	

Contact: Wilma Hunt, Hist.

Desc: Subject: Canals, local history. Holdings: 150 books. Services: Library open to the public by appointment.

2377 ■ Ross County Genealogical Society
Library

PO Box 6352	Ph: (740)773-2715
Chillicothe, OH 45601	

Contact: Grace Baer, Libn.

Desc: Subject: Genealogy. Holdings: Books; microfiche; reels of microfilm. Services: Copying; Library open to the public.

2378 ■ Ross County Historical Society
Library

45 W. 5th	Ph: (740)773-1896
Chillicothe, OH 45601	

Contact: Evelyn Walker, Libn.

Desc: Subject: History; children's literature. Holdings: 12,000 books; 250 bound periodical volumes; 20,000 archival materials; 200 reels of microfilm. Services: Copying; Library open to the public.

2379 ■ Rowan Public Library
Edith M. Clark History Room

201 W. Fisher St.	Ph: (704)638-3020
PO Box 4039	Fax: (704)638-3013
Salisbury, NC 28144-4039	
E-mail: cherryk@co.rowan.nc.us	
URL: http://www.lib.co.rowan.nc.us	

Contact: Kevin Cherry, Local Hist., Geneal.Libn.

Desc: Subject: Local and regional history and genealogy. Holdings: 12,000 books; 226 bound periodical volumes; 2200 reels of microfilm; 700 microfiche; 125 linear feet of documents; 300 maps. Services: Copying; room open to the public.

2380 ■ Rowan University
Rowan University Library
Stewart Room

201 Mullica Hill Rd.	Ph: (609)256-4967
Glassboro, NJ 08028-1701	Fax: (609)256-4924
E-mail: garrabrant@library.rowan.edu	
URL: http://www.rowan.edu	

Contact: William A. Garrabrant, Spec.Coll.

Desc: Subject: New Jersey history, early religious history, genealogy, Indians of North America, Revolutionary War, War of 1812, Grinnell Arctic expedition. Holdings: 16,300 books; 422 bound periodical volumes; 5000 manuscripts; 13 VF drawers of college archives; 4200 volumes of masters' theses; rare books; deeds; surveys; marriage licenses; acts of assembly. Services: Copying (limited); room open to the public for reference use only.

2381 ■ Rowland E. Robinson Memorial Association
Rokeby Museum
Library

4334 Rte. 7	Ph: (802)877-3406
Ferrisburg, VT 05456	

Contact: Jane Williamson, Musm.Dir.

Desc: Subject: Family history, abolition, reform, agriculture, Quakerism. Holdings: 2000 books; 30 cubic feet of archival materials; 60 reels of microfilm; 1000 unbound periodicals. Services: Library open to the public by appointment.

2382 ■ Rushville Public Library
Indiana Room

130 W. 3rd St.	Ph: (765)932-3496
Rushville, IN 46173	Fax: (765)932-4528
E-mail: rushlib@comsys.net	
URL: http://www.comsys.net/rushlib/index.html	

Contact: Sue Otte, Dir.

Desc: Subject: Genealogy, history, Indiana nature and people, Civil War, Daughters of the American Revolution, Wendell Willkie. Holdings: Books; records; audiocassettes. Services: Interlibrary loan; copying; Library open to the public.

2383 ■ Russell County Historical Society
Library

331 Kansas St.	Ph: (785)483-3637
PO Box 245	
Russell, KS 67665	
E-mail: rchs@russellks.net	

Contact: Jeff McCoy, Dir.

Desc: Subject: Genealogy; history - county and general. Holdings: 300 books; 750 archival items; 3000 microfiche. Services: copying; Library open to the public.

2384 ■ Rutherford B. Hayes Presidential Center
Library

Spiegel Grove	Ph: (419)332-2081
Fremont, OH 43420-2796	Fax: (419)332-4952
E-mail: hayeslib@rbhayes.org	
URL: http://www.rbhayes.org	

Contact: Roger D. Bridges, Dir.

Desc: Subject: Rutherford B. Hayes library and papers; Hayes family papers and papers of many of the President's contemporaries, including William M. Evarts; Civil War and Reconstruction in the South; American railroads; the American presidency and its development; U.S. political and economic history; American biography; American letters; Ohio history; Sandusky River Valley history; genealogy. Holdings: 75,000 volumes; 1 million manuscripts; 75,000 photographs; 6200 reels of microfilm of census, manuscripts, newspapers; 6100 bound newspaper volumes. Services: Interlibrary loan; copying; Library open to the public.

2385 ■ Rutland Free Library
Vermont Historical Collection

10 Court St.	Ph: (802)773-1860
Rutland, VT 05701-4058	Fax: (802)773-1825
URL: http://www.rutlandhs.k12.vt.us/rutlandfree/	
rfhome.htm	

Desc: Subject: Rutland, Vermont - history, genealogy. Holdings: 4000 books; microfilm; documents; federal censuses; county business patterns; maps; atlases; cemetery records; vertical files. Services: Copying; collection open to the public.

2386 ■ Rye Historical Society
Library

One Purchase St.	Ph: (914)967-7588
Rye, NY 10580	Fax: (914)967-6253
E-mail: Ryehistory@aol.com	

Desc: Subject: Local history, local family genealogy. Holdings: 1500 books; 20 bound periodical volumes; 30 linear feet of manuscripts; 750 maps; 100 oral history audiotapes; 105 almanacs. Services: Copying; Library open to the public.

2387 ▪ Sacramento Area Council of Governments
Library
3000 S St., Ste. 300   Ph: (916)457-2264
Sacramento, CA 95816   Fax: (916)457-3299
E-mail: data_center@sacog.org
URL: http://www.sacog.org

Contact: Rhonda R. Egan, Libn.

Desc: Subject: Planning, transportation planning, census. Holdings: 3900 cataloged items; Federal census materials. Services: Interlibrary loan; copying; Library open to the public for reference use only.

2388 ▪ Sacramento History & Science Division
Sacramento Archives & Museum Collection
Center
551 Sequoia Pacific Blvd.   Ph: (916)264-7072
Sacramento, CA 95814-0229   Fax: (916)264-7582
E-mail: jhenley@sacto.org

Contact: James E. Henley, Mgr.

Desc: Subject: Regional history, printing, theater, ethnic history, photography. Holdings: 5000 books; 3 million photographs; 5600 linear feet of government records; 150 VF drawers of regional maps; lithographs; 10 million feet of local NBC TV affilliate news film, 1958-1982; 1600 linear feet of personal and business records; 19th-century newspapers. Services: Copying; archives open to the public by appointment.

2389 ▪ St. Augustine Historical Society
Library
271 Charlotte St.   Ph: (904)825-2333
St. Augustine, FL 32084   Fax: (904)824-2569
E-mail: sahs@aug.com

Contact: Taryn Rodriguez-Boette, Lib.Dir.

Desc: Subject: History of St. Augustine and environs, history of Florida, genealogy. Holdings: 10,000 books; photocopies; manuscripts; documents; microfilm; 10,000 photographs; 5000 maps; pictures; card calendar of Spanish documents, 1512-1821; card index of St. Augustine people, 1594 to present. Services: Copying; Library open to the public for reference use only.

2390 ▪ St. Catharines Museum
LibraryArchives
1932 Government Rd.   Ph: (905)984-8880
PO Box 3012   Fax: (905)984-6910
St. Catharines, ON, Canada
L2R 7C2
E-mail: stcmchin@niagara.com

Contact: Arden Phair, Cur. of Coll.

Desc: Subject: History - St. Catharines, Welland Canal, shipping. Holdings: 1600 books; 2000 maps and plans; 350 pamphlets and leaflets; 210 unbound periodicals; 187 reels of microfilm; 79 street directories; 5 drawers of documents; 3400 historical photographs. Services: Copying; Library open to the public.

2391 ▪ St. Charles County Historical Society
Archives
101 S. Main St.   Ph: (314)946-9828
St. Charles, MO 63301

Contact: Carol Wilkins, Archv.

Desc: Subject: St. Charles County and Missouri history; genealogy. Holdings: Figures not available for books; 12 VF drawers of court records; 7 VF drawers of miscellanea; 4 VF drawers of photographs; 161 reels of microfilm; deeds; cemetery records; school records. Services: Copying; archives open to the public on fee basis.

2392 ▪ St. Clair Shores Public Library
Local History Collection
22500 Eleven Mile Rd.   Ph: (810)771-9020
St. Clair Shores, MI 48081
URL: http://www.macomb.lib.mi.us/stclairshores/

Contact: Arthur M. Woodford, Dir.

Desc: Subject: Michigan history and genealogy. Holdings: Books; periodicals. Services: Library open to the public.

2393 ▪ St. Lawrence County Historical
Association
Archives
3 E. Main St.   Ph: (315)386-8133
Box 8   Fax: (315)386-8134
Canton, NY 13617
E-mail: slcha@northnet.org
URL: http://www.slcha.org

Contact: Trent Trulock, Dir.

Desc: Subject: St. Lawrence County history. Holdings: 1500 books; 150 bound periodical volumes; 4000 maps, clippings, pamphlets, documents. Services: Copying; archives open to the public.

2394 ▪ St. Louis Comptrollers Office
Microfilm Department
1200 Market St., Rm. 1   Ph: (314)622-4274
St. Louis, MO 63103

Contact: Edward J. Machowski, Mgr.

Desc: Subject: St. Louis, Missouri; genealogy. Holdings: 60,000 reels of microfilm of fiscal records, vital statistics, building and tax records. Services: Copying; department open to the public.

2395 ▪ St. Louis Genealogical Society
Library
PO Box 43010   Ph: (314)968-2763
St. Louis, MO 63143-0010
E-mail: stlgsmail@primary.net
URL: http://www.rootsweb.com/~mostlogs/
    STINDEX.HTM

Contact: Mary T. Berthold

Desc: Subject: Genealogy, family histories. Holdings: 40,000 volumes; 500 reels of microfilm; 250 microfiche; 100 cassette tapes. Services: Copying; limited genealogical research (fee based); Library open to the public.

2396 ▪ St. Louis Public Library
History and Genealogy Department
Central Library   Ph: (314)539-0385
1301 Olive St.   Fax: (314)539-0393
St. Louis, MO 63103-2389
URL: http://www.slpl.lib.mo.us

Contact: Joseph M. Winkler, Mgr. of Res.Coll.

Desc: Subject: U.S. history; general history; archaelogy; travel; St. Louis area history; genealogy of Missouri, Illinois, and most states east of the Mississippi River; heraldry; maps. Holdings: 24,000 volumes; 14,000 microforms, 110,000 maps; 30,000 vertical files. Services: Interlibrary loan; copying; department open to the public.

2397 ▪ St. Lucie County Historical Museum
Library
414 Seaway Dr.   Ph: (561)462-1795
Fort Pierce, FL 34949   Fax: (561)462-1877

Contact: DeeDee Roberts, Supv.

Desc: Subject: History of Indian River area; national, state, and local history; genealogy and archives of early families. Holdings: 650 volumes. Services: Library open to the public by appointment for reference use only.

2398 ▪ St. Paul's Church
Archives
605 Reynolds St.   Ph: (706)724-2485
Augusta, GA 30901   Fax: (706)722-0904

Desc: Subject: St. Paul's Church history, 1750 to present. Holdings: Church bulletins, meetings minutes, correspondence of church officers, church registers, and marriage, baptism, and communicant records. Services: Archives open to the public.

2399 ▪ St. Paul's Episcopal Church
Library
1066 Washington Rd.   Ph: (412)531-7153
Pittsburgh, PA 15228   Fax: (412)531-9820

Contact: Charla Wilbur, Parish Admin.

Desc: Subject: Church and local history. Holdings: 2000 books; tapes. Services: Copying; Library open to the public.

2400 ▪ St. Petersburg Museum of History
Archives
335 Second Ave., NE   Ph: (813)894-1052
St. Petersburg, FL 33701   Fax: (813)823-7276
E-mail: spmh@ij.net
URL: http://www.ij.net/SPMH/

Contact: Midge Laughlin, Archv.

Desc: Subject: St. Petersburg history; Florida history, Pinellas history, local aviation history. Holdings: 5000 books, manuscripts, documents, and records. Services: Copying; lectures; photographic copies; archives open to the public for reference use only.

2401 ▪ Salem County Historical Society
Josephine Jaquett Memorial Library
79-83 Market St.   Ph: (609)935-5004
Salem, NJ 08079   Fax: (609)935-0728
URL: http://www.salemcounty.com/
    historicalsociety.index/html

Contact: Alice G. Diggs, Libn./Sec.

Desc: Subject: Genealogy and history of Salem County. Holdings: Business records; church and cemetery records; government records; local histories; legal documents; personal and family papers and collections, 17th-20th centuries; school records; voluntary association, organization and club records; maps and surveys; genealogies; Biblerecords; directories and almanacs; Salem County newspapers, 1817-present; oral histories; photographs; broadsides; scrapbooks; prints and paintings; reference and rare book collection. Services: Copying; research assistance; microfilm reader; Library open to the public for reference use only during restricted hours.

2402 ▪ The Salisbury Association
History Room
c/o Scoville Memorial Library   Ph: (860)435-2838
Main St.   Fax: (860)435-8136
Salisbury, CT 06068

Contact: Virginia F. Moskowitz, History Room

Desc: Subject: Iron, railroads, genealogy. Holdings: Archives; microfilm. Services: Copying; room open to the public for reference use only.

2403 ▪ Salisbury Historical Society
Archives
67 Warner Rd.   Ph: (603)648-2774
Salisbury, NH 03268

Contact: Dennis Melchin, Pres.

Desc: Subject: Local history, genealogy. Holdings: 50 books; manuscripts and original documents pertaining to Salisbury. Services: Genealogical research; archives open to the public on a limited schedule.

2404 ■ Salmon Brook Historical Society
Reference and Educational Center
208 Salmon Brook St.   Ph: (860)653-9713
Granby, CT 06035
URL: http://www.harborside.com/home/plp2241/
    sbhs.html

Contact: Carol Laun, Cur.

Desc: Subject: Local and area history, genealogy, religion, agriculture and industry, military history. Holdings: 1500 books; 50 bound periodical volumes; 250 other cataloged items; 9 VF drawers of original documents; 22 VF drawers of research information and clippings; 20 boxes of pamphlets, booklets, newspapers; 300 deeds; 150 account books; 5 VF drawers of genealogy materials; 30 boxes of genealogy materials. Services: Center open to the public by appointment.

2405 ■ Samford University
Samford University Library
Special Collections
800 Lakeshore Dr.   Ph: (205)870-2749
Birmingham, AL 35229   Fax: (205)870-2642
E-mail: ecwells@samford.edu
URL: http://www.davisweb.samford.edu

Contact: Elizabeth C. Wells, Spec.Coll.Libn.

Desc: Subject: Alabama history, literature, and imprints; Early Southeast - Indians, travel, law; genealogical source records; Southern Reconstruction; Irish history and genealogy. Holdings: 25,653 books; 2562 bound periodical volumes; 806 microcards; 349 phonograph records; 2725 maps; 1477 linear feet of manuscripts; 7739 reels of microfilm; 7828 prints and photographs; 3113 microfiche; 150 oral histories; 37 atlases; 1 globe; 60 relief models. Services: Interlibrary loan; copying; collections open to the public.

2406 ■ San Antonio Public Library
TexanaGenealogy Department
600 Soledad   Ph: (210)207-2500
San Antonio, TX 78205-1208   Fax: (210)207-2558
URL: http://www.sat.lib.tx.us

Contact: Josephine Myler

Desc: Subject: Texana, genealogy. Holdings: 28,625 books; 25,052 reels of microfilm; 21,928 microfiche; San Antonio and Texas vertical file. Services: Interlibrary loan.

2407 ■ San Bernardino County Archives
777 E. Rialto Ave.   Ph: (909)387-2030
San Bernardino, CA   Fax: (909)387-2232
   92415-0795

Contact: James D. Hofer, Archv.

Desc: Subject: County government records. Holdings: 200 books; county maps; early newspapers; government documents; scrapbooks. Services: Copying; archives open to the public.

2408 ■ San Diego Historical Society
Research Archives
Box 81825   Ph: (619)232-6203
San Diego, CA 92138   Fax: (619)232-6297
URL: http://edweb.sdsu.edu/SDHS/

Contact: Richard W. Crawford, Archv.Dir.

Desc: Subject: History - San Diego County, California, Baja California. Holdings: 9500 volumes; 4500 bound periodical volumes; 500 photostats of documents in the Archivo General, Cuidad de Mejico Collection, 1769-1840; 5500 feet of local public records; business ledgers

and reports; census reports; maps; architectural records; 2 million photographs; newspapers on microfilm. Services: Copying; archives open to the public with restrictions.

2409 ■ San Diego Historical Society
Research Archives
Photograph Collection
PO Box 81825   Ph: (619)232-6203
San Diego, CA 92138   Fax: (619)232-6297
URL: http://edweb.sdsu.edu/sdhs/

Contact: Greg Williams, Cur. of Photo.

Desc: Subject: San Diego city and county, 1867-1990; Baja California and Southwestern Native American photographs. Holdings: 2.1 million large format professional glass plate and film negatives, vintage prints, and reference prints; slides; films. Services: Collection open to the public on a limited schedule; photographs available for research, display, publication, and advertising on fee basis.

2410 ■ San Diego Public Library
Special Collections
Genealogy Room
820 E St.   Ph: (619)236-5834
San Diego, CA 92101-6478   Fax: (619)236-5811
URL: http://www.ci.san-diego.ca.us/public-library/

Contact: Jane Selvar, Supv.

Desc: Subject: General genealogy. Holdings: 4870 books; 314 reels of microfilm. Services: Copying; room open to the public for reference use only.

2411 ■ San Juan County Historical Society
Archive
PO Box 154   Ph: (970)387-5838
Silverton, CO 81433

Contact: Allen Nossaman, Archv.Dir.

Desc: Subject: San Juan County and Colorado history. Holdings: 100 books; 5000 photographs; 36 reels of microfilm; 120 oral history tapes; 25 video tapes; 600 cubic feet of maps, slides, correspondence, records. Services: Archive open to the public by appointment or Monday and Wednesday, 1pm - 6pm.

2412 ■ San Mateo County Historical Association
Library
College of San Mateo Campus   Ph: (650)574-6441
777 Hamilton St.   Fax: (650)299-0141
Redwood City, CA 94063

Contact: Carol Peterson, Archv.

Desc: Subject: San Mateo County history. Holdings: 1200 books; 3052 pamphlets; 38,418 photographs; 355 manuscripts; 440 student monographs; 908 documents, including assessment books, diaries, municipal and county records. Services: Copying; Library open to the public.

2413 ■ Sandy Bay Historical Society and Museums
Library
Box 63   Ph: (508)546-9533
Rockport, MA 01966-0063

Contact: Cynthia A. Peckham, Cur.

Desc: Subject: History of Rockport (Sandy Bay), Cape Ann, Essex County; Rockport families. Holdings: 500 books; 750 manuscripts. Services: Copying; Library open to qualified researchers.

2414 ■ Sandy Spring Museum
Library
17901 Bentley Rd.   Ph: (301)774-0022
Sandy Spring, MD 20860-1001   Fax: (301)774-8149

E-mail: ssmfp@worldnet.att.net

Contact: Fran Parker, Dir.

Desc: Subject: Local history and genealogy. Holdings: 1700 books; 735 documents; 2015 manuscripts. Services: Copying; Library open to the public.

2415 ■ Santa Barbara County Genealogical Society
Library
Box 1303   Ph: (805)884-9909
Goleta, CA 93116-1303
E-mail: sbcgs@juno.com
URL: http://www.compuology.com/sbarbara/

Contact: Marion D. Denniston

Desc: Subject: Genealogy. Holdings: 5000 books; 500 periodical volumes; family histories; ancestral charts. Services: Copying; Library open to the public.

2416 ■ Santa Barbara Historical Museums
Gledhill Library
136 E. De La Guerra St.   Ph: (805)966-1601
Box 578   Fax: (805)966-1603
Santa Barbara, CA 93102-0578

Contact: Michael Redmon, Dir. of Res. & Pub.

Desc: Subject: Local history and genealogy. Holdings: 5000 books; 42,000 photographs; 425 oral history tapes. Services: Copying; photograph reproduction; Library open to the public on a fee basis (waived for museum members and students).

2417 ■ Santa Ynez Valley Historical Society
Ellen Gleason Library
Box 181   Ph: (805)688-7889
Santa Ynez, CA 93460   Fax: (805)688-7889

Contact: Phil Lockwood, Cur.

Desc: Subject: History of Santa Ynez Valley, Santa Barbara County, early California. Holdings: 1000 books. Services: Library open to the public for reference use only by appointment.

2418 ■ Sara Hightower - Regional Library
Special Collections
205 Riverside Pkwy.   Ph: (706)236-4607
Rome, GA 30161   Fax: (706)236-4605
E-mail: gentryt@mail.floyd.public.lib.ga.us
URL: http://www.floyd.public.lib.ga.us/sara.htm

Contact: Teresa A. Gentry, Libn.Cur.

Desc: Subject: Cherokee Indians, Georgia and local history, genealogy, Southern history, Civil War. Holdings: 14,000 books; 64 VF drawers; 350 maps; 8000 microforms; 600 unbound periodicals. Services: Interlibrary loan; copying; collections open to the public with restrictions.

2419 ■ Saratoga County Historical Society
Brookside History Center
6 Charlton St.   Ph: (518)885-4000
Ballston Spa, NY 12020   Fax: (518)885-7085
E-mail: info@brooksidemuseum.org
URL: http://www.brooksidemuseum.org

Desc: Subject: Saratoga County, New York. Holdings: 1500 volumes; manuscripts; photographs; genealogy materials. Services: Copying; Library open to the public.

2420 ■ Saskatchewan Genealogical Society
Library
1870 Lorne St.   Ph: (306)780-9207
Regina, SK, Canada S4P 2L7   Fax: (306)781-6021
URL: http://www.saskgenealogy.com

Contact: Laura M. Hanowski, Libn.

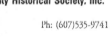

Desc: Subject: Genealogy, local and family history. Holdings: 17,000 books; 265 bound periodical volumes; 32,000 microfiche; 1150 reels of microfilm; 8 videotapes. Services: Interlibrary loan; copying; Library open to the public for reference use only. Performs searches.

2421 ■ Saskatoon Public Library
Local History Room
311 23rd St., E.   Ph: (306)975-7578
Saskatoon, SK, Canada S7K 0J6   Fax: (306)975-7542
E-mail: lhstaff@charly.publib.saskatoon.sk.ca
URL: http://www.publib.saskatoon.sk.ca

Contact: Ruth Millar, Local Hist.Hd.

Desc: Subject: History - local biographies, architecture, Riel Rebellion, prairie, fur trade. Holdings: 7191 books. Services: Library open to the public.

2422 ■ Sauk County Historical Society, Inc.
Historical Museum Library
531 4th Ave.   Ph: (608)356-1001
Baraboo, WI 53913
URL: http://www.saukcounty.com/schs

Contact: Kathy Waddell, Cur.

Desc: Subject: Local history, Indian ethnology, genealogy. Holdings: 2000 books; 2000 newspaper clippings. Services: Copying; Library open to the public by appointment; genealogy research (fee).

2423 ■ Saybrook Colony Founders Association, Inc.
Library and Archives
PO Box 1635   Ph: (860)395-1635
Old Saybrook, CT 06475-1000
E-mail: scfainc@snet.net
URL: http://oldsaybrook.com/History/society.htm

Contact: Elaine F. Staplins, Charter Pres.

Desc: Subject: Saybrook County - history, genealogy; English settlers. Holdings: Books, maps, ledgers, photographs; papers. Services: Library and archives open to the public by appointment, and every Thursday 9 am to noon.

2424 ■ Scarborough Historical Society
Scarborough Archives
730 Scarborough Golf Club Rd.   Ph: (416)396-6930
PO Box 593, Sta. A   Fax: (416)282-9482
Scarborough, ON, Canada
  M1G 1H7
E-mail: shs@interlog.com

Contact: Rick Schofield

Desc: Subject: History, genealogy. Holdings: 500 books; 200 reels of microfilm. Services: Copying; archives open to the public at librarian's discretion.

2425 ■ Schenectady County Historical Society
Grems - Doolittle Library
32 Washington Ave.   Ph: (518)374-0263
Schenectady, NY 12305

Contact: Elsie M. Maddaus, Archv.Libn.

Desc: Subject: Schenectady County and New York State history, genealogy. Holdings: 3500 volumes; clippings; manuscripts; pamphlets; documents; slides; pictures; maps. Services: Copying; family research (fee); research by mail (fee); Library open to the public on fee basis.

2426 ■ Schoharie County Historical Society
Reference Library
Old Stone Fort Museum   Ph: (518)295-7192
N. Main St.
R.D. 2, Box 30A
Schoharie, NY 12157

Contact: Christine Palmatier, Libn.Archv.

Desc: Subject: Schoharie County history and genealogy, regional and New York State history. Holdings: 2000 books; 500 pamphlets; 12,000 documents, letters, indentures, manuscripts, maps; scrapbooks; pictures. Services: Copying; Library open to the public for reference use only on a fee basis (free to Schoharie County residents and SCHS members).

2427 ■ School of American Research
Library
Box 2188   Ph: (505)982-3583
Santa Fe, NM 87504-2188   Fax: (505)989-9809
E-mail: JaneG@SARSF.org

Desc: Subject: Anthropology, archeology, ethnology, Southwest Indian arts. Holdings: 6000 books; 300 bound periodical volumes. Services: Interlibrary loan; Library not open to the public.

2428 ■ Schuyler County Genealogical Center and Historical Museum
Genealogy Library
200 S. Congress   Ph: (217)322-6975
Rushville, IL 62681

Contact: Judy Ward, Libn.

Desc: Subject: Genealogy. Holdings: 2000 books. Services: Library open to the public.

2429 ■ Schuyler County Historical Society, Inc.
Research Library
108 N. Catharine St.   Ph: (607)535-9741
PO Box 651
Montour Falls, NY 14865

Contact: Doris Gauvin, Musm.Dir.

Desc: Subject: Schuyler County history, the society. Holdings: 500 books; 220 bound periodical volumes; 300 cemetery records; 5000 clippings; 100 manuscripts; 20 maps; 36 diaries; old local newspapers. Services: Copying; Library open with staff supervision.

2430 ■ Scituate Historical Society
Library
43 Cudworth Rd.   Ph: (781)545-1083
Scituate, MA 02066
URL: http://www.ziplink.net/history

Contact: Virginia Heffernan, Libn.

Desc: Subject: Local history, genealogy. Holdings: 600 books. Services: Library open to the public.

2431 ■ Scotch-Irish Society
Library
PO Box 181
Bryn Mawr, PA 19010

Desc: Subject: History and culture of Scotch-Irish people in Scotland, Ireland, and the U.S. Services: Library open to the public with restrictions.

2432 ■ Scott County Iowa Genealogical Society
Special Collection
PO Box 3132   Ph: (319)326-7902
Davenport, IA 52808-3132

Contact: Gaycha Mayhew, Soc.Libn.

Desc: Subject: Scott County, genealogy. Holdings: Books; microfilm; microfiche; vital records. Services: Copying; collection open to the public.

2433 ■ Seattle Genealogical Society
Genealogical Library
PO Box 75388   Ph: (206)522-8658
Seattle, WA 98125-0388

Desc: Subject: Genealogy, family history, Washington state history. Holdings: 6000 books; 1000 bound periodical volumes microfilm; microfiche. Services: Copying; Library open to non-members on a fee basis.

2434 ■ Seneca Falls Historical Society
Jessie Beach Watkins Memorial Library
55 Cayuga St.   Ph: (315)568-8412
Seneca Falls, NY 13148   Fax: (315)568-8426
E-mail: sfhs@flarenet

Contact: Frances Barbieri, Exec.Dir.

Desc: Subject: Area history, Victoriana, Civil War. Holdings: 1500 books; 4 VF drawers; local newspaper, 1839 to present, on microfilm; manuscripts. Services: Copying; Library open to the public on a fee basis; free to members.

2435 ■ Seventh-Day Baptist Historical Society
Library
3120 Kennedy Rd.   Ph: (608)752-5055
Box 1678   Fax: (608)752-7711
Janesville, WI 53547
E-mail: sdbhist@inwave.com
URL: http://www.seventhdaybaptist.org

Contact: Don A. Sanford, Hist.

Desc: Subject: Seventh Day Baptist history; Sabbatarian literature, church history, religion; New England history; genealogy. Holdings: 2500 books; 500 bound and indexed periodical volumes; 250 society record books; tracts; reports; church records; letters; manuscripts. Services: Library open to the public (appointment suggested). Research available on church history and genealogy.

2436 ■ Seymour Public Library District
Special Collections
176 Genesee St.   Ph: (315)252-2571
Auburn, NY 13021   Fax: (315)252-7985

Contact: Stephen C. Erskine, Dir.

Desc: Holdings: 2700 books; 150 bound periodical volumes; 137 reports; 330 bound newspapers. Services: Library open to the public.

2437 ■ Sharlot Hall Museum
Archives & Library
415 W. Gurley St.   Ph: (520)445-3122
Prescott, AZ 86301   Fax: (520)776-9053
E-mail: sharlot@sharlothall.lib.az.us
URL: http://sharlothall.lib.az.us

Contact: Michael Wurtz, Archv.

Desc: Subject: Anglo and Indian history of the Southwest, especially Arizona; Arizona history and mining. Holdings: 9000 volumes; 250 linear feet of uncataloged items; 200 oral historyfolklore tapes; 93,000 photographs; manuscripts; diaries; artifacts; letters. Services: copying; Libraryarchives open to the public.

2438 ■ Shasta Historical Society Research
Library
1449 Market St.   Ph: (530)243-3720
Redding, CA 96001   Fax: (530)246-3708
URL: http://www.shastahistory.org

Desc: Subject: Local history, pioneer genealogy. Holdings: 1100 books, 6 bound periodical volumes, 10,000 photos on CD-ROM. Services: Copying; Library open to the public.

2439 ■ Sheboygan County Historical Research
Center
518 Water St.   Ph: (920)467-4667
Sheboygan Falls, WI 53085   Fax: (920)467-1395
E-mail: schrc@execpc.com

Contact: Janice Hildebrand, Libn.

Desc: Subject: County history and genealogy. Holdings: 5000 books; historic photographs; 100,000 negatives and prints; county land records. Services: Copying; center open to the public for reference use only.

2440 ■ Sheldon Museum & Cultural Center

Box 269   Ph: (907)766-2366
Haines, AK 99827   Fax: (907)766-2368
E-mail: sheldmus@seaknet.alaska.edu
URL: http://seaknet.alaska.edu/sheldmus/

Contact: Cynthia L. Jones

Desc: Subject: Tlingit art and culture, Alaskan history. Holdings: 1150 books; 5600 feet of home movies; Haines and Skagway newspapers on microfilm; AV programs on historical and resource subjects; photographs, 1897 to present; autographed correspondence; journals, manuscripts, deeds from circa 1900; maps; charts. Services: Center open to the public for reference use only.

2441 ■ Shelter Island Historical Society
Havens House Museum
Archives

PO Box 847   Ph: (516)749-0025
Shelter Island, NY 11964-0847   Fax: (516)749-1825

Contact: Peggy Dickerson, Dir.

Desc: Subject: Local history. Holdings: 200 books; 25 bound periodical volumes; 200 postcards; 400 literary documents; 100 financial documents; 30 maps; 1600 clippings; 425 photographs; genealogical material. Services: Copying; archives open to the public for reference use only.

2442 ■ Shenandoah County Library
Local History and Genealogy Collection

800 E. Broad St.   Ph: (804)692-3500
Richmond, VA 23219-1905
URL: http://www.shenandoah.co.lib.va.us/
    genealogy.htm

Desc: Subject: Shenandoah County and the Shenandoah Valley history and genealogy; Civil War; Pennsylvania; Maryland; West Virginia; Virginia. Holdings: Books; microforms; records; photographs; archival materials; Civil War materials. Services: Copying; Library open to the public.

2443 ■ Sheridan County Historical Society, Inc.
Agnes & Clarence Benschoter Memorial Library

Box 274   Ph: (308)327-2917
Rushville, NE 69360   Fax: (308)327-2166
E-mail: rwbuchan@gpcom.net

Contact: Robert W. Buchan, Cur.

Desc: Subject: Western and Nebraska history; military; genealogy. Holdings: 700 books; 100 bound periodical volumes; clippings; manuscripts; albums. Services: Copying; Library open to the public by appointment.

2444 ■ Sherman Research Library

614 Dahlia Ave.   Ph: (949)673-1880
Corona Del Mar, CA 92625

Contact: Dr. William O. Hendricks, Dir.

Desc: Subject: Pacific Southwest history, 1870 to present - economic development, land and water, transportation, immigration. Holdings: 20,000 books; 400 bound periodical volumes; 2500 pamphlets; 375 document boxes of business papers; 1475 reels of microfilm of newspapers; 200 theses and dissertations on microfilm; 2000 maps. Services: Interlibrary loan; Library open to the public.

2445 ■ Shiloh Baptist Church
Susie E. Miles Library

1510 9th St.   Ph: (202)232-4200
Washington, DC 20001   Fax: (202)234-6235

Contact: Vera G. Hunter, Dir.

Desc: Subject: Bible, African-Americans, church history, religion. Holdings: 6000 books; 115 videocassettes; 20 transparencies; 10 filmstrips; 50 audiocassettes. Services: Library open to the public on a limited schedule.

2446 ■ Shiloh Museum of Ozark History
Library

118 W. Johnson Ave.   Ph: (501)750-8165
Springdale, AR 72764   Fax: (501)750-8171
E-mail: shiloh@caven.uark.edu
URL: http://www.uark.edu/ALADDIN/shiloh

Contact: Bob Besom, Dir.

Desc: Subject: Northwest Arkansas - history, authors; antiques; archeology; anthropology. Holdings: 800 books; 26 AV programs; 150,000 photographic images; 30 VF drawers; archival material. Services: Research; copying; Library open to the public by appointment.

2447 ■ Shippensburg Historical Society
Archives

52 W. King St.   Ph: (717)532-6727
Shippensburg, PA 17257

Contact: Helen L. Hunsecker, Libn.

Desc: Holdings: Figures not available. Services: Archives open to the public by appointment.

2448 ■ Siloam Springs Museum
Museum Archives

112 N. Maxwell   Ph: (501)524-4011
PO Box 1164
Siloam Springs, AR 72761
E-mail: ssmuseum@bstream.com

Contact: Don Warden, Musm.Dir.

Desc: Subject: Siloam Springs area history. Holdings: 10,000 books, periodicals, local documents, manuscripts, newspapers, photographs, and post cards. Services: Copying; archives maintains closed stacks.

2449 ■ Simcoe County Archives

R.R. 2   Ph: (705)726-9331
Minesing, ON, Canada L0L 1Y0   Fax: (705)725-5341
E-mail: archives@bar.imag.net
URL: http://www.county.simcoe.on.cal

Contact: Bruce J. Beacock, Archv.

Desc: Subject: Simcoe County history, business, and genealogy; cartography; lumbering history. Holdings: 1500 books; 500 bound periodical volumes; 70 Women's Institute histories; 1000 county assessment rolls; 2700 feet of Simcoe County municipal records; 150 magnetic tapes; 50 feet of Georgian Bay Lumber Company papers; 500 maps; 12,000 photographs; census records on microfilm. Services: Copying; scanning; archives open to the public.

2450 ■ Simcoe Public Library
History/Genealogy Department

46 Colborne St., S.   Ph: (519)426-3506
Simcoe, ON, Canada N3Y 4H3   Fax: (519)426-0657
E-mail: spl@kwic.com
URL: http://www.spl.kwic.com/spl.html/

Contact: Autar Ganju

Desc: Subject: Simcoe, Ontario history and culture. Holdings: Books; family history books and files; local newspapers, 1840 to present (microfilm); census records on mi-

crofilm; genealogy records; Ontario Genealogical Society (Norfolk Branch) Collection. Services: Interlibrary loan; copying; Library open to the public.

2451 ■ Simi Valley Historical Society
Archives

R.P. Strathearn Historical Park Ph: (805)526-6453
137 Strathearn Place   Fax: (805)526-6462
Box 940461
Simi Valley, CA 93094-0461

Desc: Subject: Simi Valley history, 1874-1960. Holdings: 500 letters and archival materials. Services: Archives open to the public by appointment.

2452 ■ Simsbury Historical Society
Blanche C. Skoglund Memorial Library

800 Hopmeadow St.   Ph: (860)658-2500
Box 2
Simsbury, CT 06070

Contact: Stephen Eric Simon, Libn.

Desc: Subject: Simsbury and vicinity genealogy and history. Holdings: 2000 books, pamphlets, and serials; 300 reels of microfilm; photographs; slides; maps. Services: Library open to the public by appointment.

2453 ■ Siouxland Heritage Museums
Library

200 W. 6th St.   Ph: (605)367-7097
Sioux Falls, SD 57104   Fax: (605)367-6004

Contact: William J. Hoskins, Director

Desc: Subject: South Dakota history; U.S. history - silver question; 19th century works on ethnology and natural science; Indians. Holdings: 9000 books; 200 bound periodical volumes; 100 maps; 150 linear feet of manuscripts; 10,000 photographs. Services: Copying; Library open to the public.

2454 ■ Siskiyou County Museum
Library

910 S. Main St.   Ph: (530)842-3836
Yreka, CA 96097

Contact: Michael Hendryx, Musm.Dir.

Desc: Subject: History of Siskiyou County. Holdings: 1000 books; 250 ledgers and account books; 2500 documents; 19,000 photographs; 275 bound volumes of county newspapers, 1862-1980; voter registers. Services: Library open to the public by appointment.

2455 ■ Skagit County Historical Museum
Historical Reference Library

501 S. 4th St.   Ph: (360)466-3365
PO Box 818   Fax: (360)466-1611
La Conner, WA 98257
E-mail: marid@co.skagit.wa.us

Contact: Mari Anderson Densmore, Libn.

Desc: Subject: Skagit County - history, statistics, demographics, industry, social, economic, community life, transportation; pioneer family genealogies; local Indian histories. Holdings: 1500 books; 308 bound periodical volumes; 10,000 photographs; 700 newspapers; 700 business documents; 200 letters; 200 district school accountsrecords; 100 maps; 700 clippings and clipping scrapbooks; 300 programsannouncements; 80 pioneer diaries; 220 oral history tapes with transcripts; American popular music, 1866-1954; local newspapers, 1900 to present. Services: Copying; microfilm reading and printing; research by appointment.

2456 ▪ Smith County Historical Society
Library
213 Parliament St.
Smith Center, KS 66967-2914

Contact: Donna Martin, Pres.

Desc: Subject: Smith County, Kansas.

2457 ▪ Smithtown Historical Society
Library
Box 69   Ph: (516)265-6768
Smithtown, NY 11787   Fax: (516)265-6768

Contact: Louise P. Hall, Dir.

Desc: Subject: Local history and genealogy. Holdings: 1000 books; 300 bound periodical volumes; 5000 deeds, ledgers, documents, letters, surveys. Services: Copying; Library open to the public.

2458 ▪ Smoky Hill Museum
Library
211 W. Iron Ave.   Ph: (785)826-7460
PO Box 101   Fax: (785)826-7444
Salina, KS 67402

Contact: Ann Deegan, Cur. of Coll.

Desc: Subject: History - Salina, Kansas; Saline County, Kansas; Smoky Hill region, Kansas. Holdings: 700 books; 38 bound periodical volumes; 60 linear feet of archival material; 45 flat files of archival material; 2000 photographs. Services: Copying; Library open to the public by appointment.

2459 ▪ Snake River Heritage Center
Library
2295 Paddock Ave.   Ph: (208)549-0205
PO Box 307
Weiser, ID 83672

Contact: Carol Odoms, Mgr.

Desc: Subject: Snake River Country, Intermountain Institute, local authors. Holdings: Figures not available. Services: Library open to the public during museum hours.

2460 ▪ Snyder County Historical Society
Library
30 E. Market St.   Ph: (570)837-6191
Box 276   Fax: (570)837-4282
Middleburg, PA 17842

Contact: Emily C. Rahter, Libn.

Desc: Subject: Local history, Pennsylvania history, Pennsylvania military history, genealogy. Holdings: 3000 volumes; 1000 historical bulletins; early land grants, warrants, deeds. Services: Copying; Library open to the public with permission.

2461 ▪ Societe d'Histoire et d'Archeologie des Monts
Bibliotheque
675 Chemin du Roy, Rte. 132   Ph: (418)763-7871
CP 1192
Ste. Anna-des-Monts, PQ,
    Canada G0E 2G0

Desc: Subject: Local history, genealogy, ethnography, Canadiana, archeology. Holdings: 40,000 books; 200 bound periodical volumes; 4 archive collections. Services: Library open to the public by appointment.

2462 ▪ Societe d'Histoire de Sherbrooke
Bibliotheque
275, rue Dufferin   Ph: (819)821-5406
Sherbrooke, PQ, Canada J1H   Fax: (819)821-5417
    4M5

Contact: Helene Liard, Archv.

Desc: Subject: Local and regional history of the Eastern Townships. Holdings: 7300 volumes; 40,000 photographs; 700 maps; archives. Services: Bibliotheque open to the public.

2463 ▪ Societe de Genealogie de Quebec
Library
C.P. 9066   Ph: (418)651-9127
Ste. Foy, PQ, Canada G1V 4A8   Fax: (418)651-2643
URL: http://www.total.net/sgq

Contact: Serge Goudreau, Libn.

Desc: Subject: Genealogy. Holdings: 3000 books; microfiche. Services: Copying; Library open to the public (4 fee for non-members).

2464 ▪ Societe Genealogique de l'Est du Quebec
Bibliotheque
110, rue de l'eveche Est   Ph: (418)724-3242
Rimouski, PQ, Canada G5L   Fax: (418)724-3242
    1X9
E-mail: sgeq@quebectel.com
URL: http://www.genealogie.org

Contact: Bernard Rioux

Desc: Subject: Genealogy, history. Holdings: 7500 books, microfiche, microfilm. Services: Library open to non-members for 2day fee; members free; repertories of birth, marriage, and death for sale.

2465 ▪ Societe Historique-de-la-Cote-du-Sud
Bibliotheque
C.P. 937   Ph: (418)856-2104
La Pocatiere, PQ, Canada G0R   Fax: (418)856 2104
    1Z0
E-mail: archsud@globetrotter.qc.ca

Contact: Elphege Levesque, Pres.

Desc: Subject: History - regional, church, Canada, Quebec; genealogy. Holdings: 1500 books; 500 bound periodical volumes; 1500 archival boxes; 400 pamphlets. Services: Genealogical searches; Library open to the public.

2466 ▪ Societe Historique du Saguenay
Bibliotheque
C.P. 456   Ph: (418)549-2805
Chicoutimi, PQ, Canada G7H
    5C8

Contact: Roland Belanger, Archv.

Desc: Subject: Regional history and geography, genealogy, oral history, folklore. Holdings: 18,000 books; 200 bound periodical volumes; 300,000 photographs; 65,000 negatives; 1500 maps. Services: Copying; Library open to the public for reference use only.

2467 ▪ Somers Historical Museum - Archives
11 Battle St.   Ph: (860)749-6505
Somers, CT 06071   Fax: (860)749-5879
E-mail: genialgeni@aol.com

Contact: Jeanne De Bell

Desc: Subject: Local and state history, genealogy. Holdings: 200 books; 1 VF drawer of local history material; 1 box of early deeds and letters, 1730-1865. Services: Archives open to the public with restrictions.

2468 ▪ Somers Historical Society
Dr. Hugh Grant Rowell Circus Library Collection
Elephant Hotel   Ph: (914)277-4977
Box 336
Somers, NY 10589

Contact: Francis Billingsley, Pres.

Desc: Subject: Circus, genealogy. Holdings: 600 books; 4 VF drawers of uncatalogued pamphlets and manuscripts; 10 maps; 1000 circus-related materials. Services: Collection open to the public for reference use only by appointment.

2469 ▪ Sons of the Revolution in the State of California
Library
600 S. Central Ave.   Ph: (818)240-1775
Glendale, CA 91204
E-mail: sr@walika.com
URL: http://www.walika.com/sr.htm

Contact: Edwin W. Coles, Lib.Dir.

Desc: Subject: Genealogy, military history, colonial American history, history. Holdings: 35,000 volumes; 2000 bound periodical volumes; 2500 family genealogies. Services: Copying; genealogical research; Library open to the public.

2470 ▪ Sourisseau Academy
Library
History Department   Ph: (408)924-6510
San Jose State University
San Jose, CA 95192-0147
E-mail: glaffey@isc.sjsu.edu
URL: http://web.sjsu.edu/glaffey/sourisseau.html

Contact: Glory Anne Laffey

Desc: Subject: History - San Jose, Santa Clara County, California. Holdings: 28 linear feet of books; 5 linear feet of manuscripts; photographs; ephemera. Services: Library open to the public by appointment.

2471 ▪ South Carolina Historical Society
Library
Fireproof Bldg.   Ph: (843)723-3225
100 Meeting St.   Fax: (843)723-8584
Charleston, SC 29401
URL: http://www.schistory.org

Contact: Dr. David O. Percy, Exec.Dir.

Desc: Subject: South Carolina history, architecture, literature, slavery, politics, economy, genealogy. Holdings: 35,000 books and bound periodical volumes; 10,000 pamphlets; 3000 linear feet of manuscripts; microfiche; 2000 architectural drawings; 2500 photographs; ephemera. Services: Copying; Library open to the public on fee basis.

2472 ▪ South Pasadena Public Library
Local History Collection
1100 Oxley St.   Ph: (626)403-7333
South Pasadena, CA 91030   Fax: (626)403-7331
E-mail: sppladmin@south-pasadena.gov
URL: http://www.mcls.org/bin/entity/60

Contact: Terri Maguire, Dir.

Desc: Subject: South Pasadena history. Holdings: Photographs; historical documents; directories, 1895 to present.

2473 ▪ South Suburban Genealogical & Historical Society
Library
Box 96   Ph: (708)333-9474
South Holland, IL 60473-0096
E-mail: ssghs@hotmail.com
URL: http://www.rootsweb.com/ssghs/ssghs.htm

Contact: Alice DeBoer, Hd.Libn.

Desc: Subject: Genealogy, local history. Holdings: 6900 books; 450 bound periodical volumes; 300 reels of microfilm; federal census; land records; indexed wills; Bible records; obituaries; family work sheet files; local church records; local township records; local newspapers; local telephone directories; local cemetery records. Services: Copying; Library open to the public.

2474 ▪ Southern California Genealogical Society
Family Research Library

417 Irving Dr.   Ph: (818)843-7247
Burbank, CA 91504-2408   Fax: (818)843-7267
E-mail: scgs@keyconnect.com
URL: http://www.scgsgenealogy.com

Contact: Doug Miller, Pres.

Desc: Subject: State and local history, family history. Holdings: 15,000 books; 2500 bound periodical volumes; 15 file drawers of maps; 40 drawers of manuscripts. Services: Copying; computer usage; Library open to the public.

2475 ▪ Southern Lorain County Historical Society

PO Box 76   Ph: (440)647-4367
Wellington, OH 44090

Contact: Michael Giar, Pres.

Desc: Subject: Local history. Holdings: 100 books. Services: Library open to the public on a limited schedule.

2476 ▪ Southern Maryland Studies Center Library

8730 Mitchell Rd.   Ph: (301)934-2251
PO Box 910   Fax: (301)934-7699
La Plata, MD 20646-0910
E-mail: smsc@charles.cc.md.us
URL: http://www.charles.cc.md.us/librarycccc

Contact: Sarah L. Barley, Coord.

Desc: Subject: Southern Maryland - history, culture, development; genealogy. Holdings: 2040 books; 130 bound periodical volumes; 502 reels of microfilm; 30 AV programs; 334 oral history audiotapes; 209 manuscript collections. Services: Interlibrary loan; copying; Center open to the public for reference use only.

2477 ▪ Southern Ohio Genealogical Society Reference Library

Box 414
Hillsboro, OH 45133

Desc: Subject: Genealogy, local history. Holdings: 1200 books; 250 bound periodical volumes; 100 family files; 85 family history files; 3700 burial records of veterans buried in Highland County, OH; 83 volumes of published family histories; 75 family history manuscripts; census maps; passenger and immigration records.

2478 ▪ Southern Oregon Historical Society Research Library

106 N. Central Ave.   Ph: (541)773-6536
Medford, OR 97501-5926   Fax: (541)776-7994
URL: http://www.sohs.org

Contact: Jacquelyn Sundstrand, Lib.Archv.Coord.

Desc: Subject: Jackson County and southern Oregon history, historic preservation, museum techniques. Holdings: 4900 books; 100 bound periodical volumes; 800 manuscript collections; 350 oral histories; 300 maps; architectural drawings. Services: Interlibrary loan (limited); copying; Library open to the public.

2479 ▪ Southern Utah University Gerald R. Sherratt Library Special Collections Department

351 W. Center St.   Ph: (435)586-7945
Cedar City, UT 84720   Fax: (435)865-8152
E-mail: nickerson@suu.edu

URL: http://www.li.suu.edu

Contact: Matthew Nickerson, Spec.Coll.Libn.

Desc: Subject: Southern Paiute Indian history, local history, University archives, Shakespeare. Holdings: 7000 volumes; 925 oral history tapes; 457 phonograph records; 1445 linear feet of manuscript collections; 51,000 photographs and negatives; 804 linear feet of archives; 1743 maps. Services: Interlibrary loan; copying; department open to the public for reference use only.

2480 ▪ Southold Historical Society Museum Library

54325 Main Rd.   Ph: (516)765-5500
PO Box 1   Fax: (516)765-5500
Southold, NY 11971

Desc: Subject: Local and state history, genealogy, local fishing and farming, early textbooks, decorative arts. Holdings: 300 books; pamphlets; ledgers; ships log. Services: Library open to the public by appointment.

2481 ▪ Southwest Minnesota Historical Center

Southwest State University   Ph: (507)537-7373
Marshall, MN 56258   Fax: (507)537-6115
E-mail: louwagie@ssu.southwest.msus.edu

Contact: Jan Louwagie, Coord.

Desc: Subject: Local history, church histories, Iceland, agricultural history, genealogy. Holdings: 150 books; records; 200 oral history interviews. Services: Copying; center open to the public (by appointment only in July and August).

2482 ▪ Spotsylvania Historical Association, Inc. Frances L.N. Waller Research Museum and Library

PO Box 64   Ph: (540)582-7167
Spotsylvania, VA 22553

Contact: Martha C. Carter

Desc: Subject: Spotsylvania County history, Civil War battlefields, colonial settlers and forts since 1671, genealogy statistics, Lafayette's campaign through Spotsylvania County 1781. Holdings: 2500 books; 100 bound periodical volumes; 800 booklets; 1 bookcase of Ohio and Virginia historical reports; 4 VF drawers of local manuscripts; maps; tapes; photostats; slides; film; reprints. Services: Copying; Library open to the public for reference use only.

2483 ▪ Stafford County Historical & Genealogical Society Library

100 S. Main St.
PO Box 249
Stafford, KS 67578

Desc: Subject: Stafford County history. Holdings: 200 books; 21 reels of microfilm. Services: Library open to the public by appointment.

2484 ▪ Stamford Historical Society Library

1508 High Ridge Rd.   Ph: (203)329-1183
Stamford, CT 06903-4107   Fax: (203)322-1607
URL: http://www.cslnet.ctstate.edu/STAMFORD/
      INDEX.html

Contact: Ronald Marcus, Libn.

Desc: Subject: History - Stamford, Fairfield County, State of Connecticut. Holdings: 7800 books and pamphlets; 65 Stamford tax lists manuscripts, 1712-1876; 136 Stamford Revolutionary War damage claims manuscripts, 1776-1783; 300 Stamford newspapers, 1829-1925; 2000 Stamford pictures, 1870-1940; 1000 Stamford slides, 1870-1920; 25 Stamford maps, 1800-1961; 65 Stamford account books manuscripts, 1787-1941; 12 Stamford dia-

ries, 1850-1929; 16 VF drawers of documents and clippings. Services: Copying; Library open to the public on a limited schedule.

2485 ▪ Stark County Historical Society Library

PO Box 20070   Ph: (330)455-7043
Canton, OH 44701   Fax: (330)455-1137
E-mail: museum@neo.lrun.com
URL: http://www.mckinleymuseum.org

Contact: Wilbur Weber, Res.Libn.

Desc: Subject: William McKinley, Canton, Stark County. Holdings: 4000 books; reports; archival materials. Services: Interlibrary loan; copying; Library open to the public.

2486 ▪ State Historical Society of Iowa Library Archives

402 Iowa Ave.   Ph: (319)335-3916
Iowa City, IA 52240-1806   Fax: (319)335-3935
URL: http://www.state.ia.us/government/dca/shsi

Contact: Shaner Magalhaes, Bureau Chf.

Desc: Subject: History - Iowa, the frontier, agriculture, railroad, women, education in Iowa, Indians of the region; genealogy. Holdings: 140,000 books; 12,000 bound periodical volumes; 16,000 pamphlets; 24,000 reels of microfilm; 10,000 bound newspapers; 25 VF drawers of newspaper clippings; 1800 oral history interviews; 4000 linear feet of manuscripts. Services: Interlibrary loan; copying; Library open to the public.

2487 ▪ State Historical Society of Iowa Library and Archives Bureau

600 E. Locust   Ph: (515)281-6200
Des Moines, IA 50319   Fax: (515)282-0502
URL: http://www.uiowa.edu/shsi/library/library.htm

Contact: Ruth Bartels

Desc: Subject: History - Iowa, agriculture, railroad, regional Indians; historic preservation; genealogy. Holdings: 75,350 books; 2500 linear feet of manuscripts; 35,000 reels of microfilm; 64 VF drawers of pamphlets and clippings. Services: Interlibrary loan; copying; Library open to the public.

2488 ▪ State Historical Society of Missouri Library

1020 Lowry St.   Ph: (573)882-7083
Columbia, MO 65201-7298   Fax: (573)884-4950
E-mail: shsofmo@umsystem.edu
URL: http://www.system.missouri.edu/shs

Contact: James W. Goodrich, Exec.Dir.

Desc: Subject: Missouri and midwestern history, works by and about Missourians. Holdings: 452,000 volumes; 1278 bound volumes of newspapers; 2775 maps; 46,079 reels of microfilm of Missouri newspapers; 100,000 photographs; 6726 reels of microfilm of census records. Services: Interlibrary loan of microfilmed newspapers; copying; Library open to the public.

2489 ▪ State Historical Society of North Dakota State Archives and Historical Research Library

Heritage Center   Ph: (701)328-2668
612 East Blvd.   Fax: (701)328-3710
Bismarck, ND 58505
URL: http://www.state.nd.us/hist

Contact: Gerald Newborg, State Archv.Div.Dir

Desc: Subject: North Dakota and Dakota Territory; social, cultural, economic, and political history; early exploration and travel; fur trade; plains military history; Northern Plains region - archeology, prehistory, ethnology, ethnohistory; historic preservation; genealogy. Holdings:

100,400 volumes; 2198 cubic feet of manuscripts; 11,740 cubic feet of state and county archives; 100,000 photographs; 12,500 reels of microfilm of microfilm of manuscripts, records and newspapers; 1421 titles of North Dakota newspapers; 2100 titles of periodicals; 1843 oral history interviews; sound recordings; maps; videotapes; motion pictures; newsfilm archives. Services: Interlibrary loan (limited); copying; Library open to the public for reference use only.

2490 ▪ State Historical Society of Wisconsin Library

816 State St.   Ph: (608)264-6534
Madison, WI 53706-1482   Fax: (608)264-6520
E-mail: shswlib@ccmail.adp.wisc.edu
URL: http://www.wisc.edu/shs-library/index.html

Contact: J. Kevin Graffagnino, Dir.

Desc: Subject: History - American, Canadian, Wisconsin, local, labor; radicalreform movements and groups in the U.S. and Canada; ethnic and minority groups in North America; genealogy; women's history; military history; religious history. Holdings: 1.6 million books and bound periodical volumes; 100,000 cubic feet of archives; 1.5 million microfiche and reels of microfilm. Services: Interlibrary loan; copying; Library open to the public.

2491 ▪ State Library of Ohio

PER Division/Darla Cottrill   Ph: (614)644-7061
65 S. Front St., Rm. 506   Fax: (614)728-2788
Columbus, OH 43215-4163
E-mail: dcottril@mail.slonet.ohio.gov
URL: http://winslo.ohio.gov

Contact: Michael Lucas

Desc: Subject: Management, social sciences, education, public administration, Ohio history. Holdings: 626,377 books; 601,330 microforms; CD-ROMs. Services: Interlibrary loan; copying; faxing; Library open to the public.

2492 ▪ Staten Island Historical Society Library

441 Clarke Ave.   Ph: (718)351-1611
Staten Island, NY 10306   Fax: (718)351-6057

Contact: Maxine Friedman, Chf.Cur.

Desc: Subject: History of Staten Island and neighboring communities, U.S. history. Holdings: 5000 books; 350 bound periodical volumes; 30 VF drawers of Staten Island history; 8 VF drawers of Staten Island genealogies; 110 reels of microfilm; 1200 cubic feet of manuscripts; 9000 uncataloged items; 75 audiotapes; 30 videotapes; 320 bound volumes of newspapers. Services: Copying; Library open to the public by appointment only.

2493 ▪ Stearns History Museum Research Center & Archives

235 33rd Ave., S.   Ph: (320)253-3752
St. Cloud, MN 56301-0702   Fax: (320)253-2172
E-mail: info@stearns-museum
URL: http://www.stearns-museum.org

Contact: John W. Decker, Asst.Dir. - Archv.

Desc: Subject: Genealogy, county history, Luxembourg immigration, architecture, agriculture, granite industry. Holdings: 2000 books; 1100 bound periodical volumes; 18 VF drawers of biographical and family files (15,000 names); 1800 oral history tapes, 1975 1988; 1225 reels of microfilm of Stearns County newspapers; 18,500 photographs and slides; 22 reels of microfilm of Stearns County naturalization records, 1852-1954; 7 reels of microfilm of Stearns County Land Office tract index records, 1853-1910; St. Cloud city directories, 1888-1998; Stearns County birth and death records, 1946-1982, and marriage records, 1916-1980; Minneapolis Irish Standard, 1886-1920, reels of microfilm; Meyer's Ort German Empire

Gazetteer, 1912; Austro-Hungarian Empire Gazetteer, 1845; Germans to America, 1850-1890; Trier Emigrant by Joseph Mergen, vols. 1-8. Services: Copying; center open to the public.

2494 ▪ Steele County Historical Society Archives

PO Box 144   Ph: (701)945-2394
Hope, ND 58046-0144

Contact: Russell Ford-Dunker, Musm.Dir.

Desc: Subject: Local history. Holdings: Oral history tapes; photograph collection; town and school records; church and county records; manuscripts; Hope Pioneer Newspaper, 1883-1957. Services: Archives open to the public with restrictions.

2495 ▪ Stephen Wise Free Synagogue Rabbi Edward E. Klein Memorial Library

30 W. 68th St.   Ph: (212)877-4050
New York, NY 10023   Fax: (212)787-7108

Contact: Helen Singer, Dir.

Desc: Subject: Judaica. Holdings: 4300 books; 50 linear feet of archival materials; 175 videocassettes. Services: Interlibrary loan; copying; Library open to the public for reference use only.

2496 ▪ Stonington Historical Society Richard W. Woolworth Library

Box 103   Ph: (860)535-1131
Stonington, CT 06378

Contact: Mary M. Thacher, Libn.

Desc: Subject: Genealogy, local history, biography. Holdings: 1400 books; 35 feet of manuscripts; photographs; ships' logs; biographies; maps; newspaper clippings; memorabilia. Services: Copying; Library open to the public by appointment.

2497 ▪ Stratford Historical Society Library

Box 382   Ph: (203)378-0630
Stratford, CT 06615-0382

Contact: Joyce Bradbury

Desc: Subject: Stratford history and family genealogy. Holdings: 800 volumes; genealogical records and documents. Services: Library open to the public.

2498 ▪ Struthers Historical Society Library

50 Terrace St.   Ph: (330)750-1766
Struthers, OH 44471

Contact: Marian Kutlesa

Desc: Subject: Local history. Holdings: 100 books; 65 bound periodical volumes. Services: Library open to the public by appointment.

2499 ▪ Sturgis Library

Main St.   Ph: (508)362-6636
Box 606   Fax: (508)362-5467
Barnstable, MA 02630
E-mail: sturgis@capecod.net
URL: http://www.capecod.net/sturgis

Contact: Christopher J. Lindquist, Chf.Libn.

Desc: Subject: Genealogy, Barnstable County history, maritime history, 19th century English and American literature. Holdings: 61,902 books; 200 bound periodical volumes; 663 sound recordings, tapes, and cassettes; 125 reels of microfilm; 60 flat pictures; 1500 land deeds; 25 maps and charts. Services: Interlibrary loan; copying;

service to homebound and institutionalized; Library open to the public; special collections accessible only on fee basis.

2500 ▪ Suburban Temple Gries Library

22401 Chagrin Blvd.   Ph: (216)991-0700
Beachwood, OH 44122   Fax: (216)991-0705

Contact: Claudia Z. Fechter, Libn.

Desc: Subject: Judaica. Holdings: 6000 books; 100 phonograph records; 4 VF drawers. Services: Interlibrary loan; copying; Library open to the public by appointment.

2501 ▪ Suffolk County Historical Society Library

300 W. Main St.   Ph: (516)727-2881
Riverhead, NY 11901

Contact: David Kerkhof, Libn.

Desc: Subject: Suffolk County and Long Island history and genealogy. Holdings: 15,000 volumes; microfilm; manuscripts; clippings; records; documents; photographs; fiber swatch-books. Services: Copying; Library open to the public with restrictions.

2502 ▪ Sul Ross State University Division of the Library and Information Technologies

Bryan Wildenthal   Ph: (915)837-8123
   Memorial Library
East Hwy. 90
PO Box C-114
Alpine, TX 79832
URL: http://www.sulross.edu/library/

Desc: Subject: General educational and reference resources, publications of the State of Texas, Texas geography and cartography, Texas history. Holdings: 215,000 books; 464,000 microforms; 25,000 photographs; 5000 maps, pictures, and charts; 2600 videocassettes and films; 2000 audio recordings. Services: Interlibrary loan; copying; Library open to the public.

2503 ▪ Sumner County Historical Society Archives

c/o Ruth Swan, President   Ph: (316)777-1434
Chisholm Trail Museum
PO Box 213
Mulvane, KS 67110

Contact: Anita Busch, Dir.

Desc: Subject: Genealogy, local history. Holdings: Archival material. Services: Library open to the public on a limited schedule.

2504 ▪ Susquehanna County Historical Society and Free Library Association

2 Monument Sq.   Ph: (717)278-1881
Montrose, PA 18801   Fax: (717)278-9336
URL: http://www.epix.net/suspulib

Contact: Susan Stone, Dir.

Desc: Subject: Genealogy, natural science, art, music, humanities, religion. Holdings: 75,105 volumes; 475 genealogical items. Services: Interlibrary loan; copying; Library open to the public with restrictions.

2505 ▪ Sussex County Historical Society Library and Museum

82 Main St.   Ph: (973)383-6010
Box 913
Newton, NJ 07860

Contact: Barbara Lewis Waskowich, Cur.Sec.

Desc: Subject: New Jersey and Sussex County history, archeology, genealogy, antiques. Holdings: 2000 books; 300 genealogical files. Services: Library open to the public on a limited schedule.

2506 ▪ Swedish-American Historical Society
Swedish-American Archives of Greater Chicago

5125 N. Spaulding Ave.   Ph: (773)583-5722
Chicago, IL 60625   Fax: (773)267-2362
E-mail: kanders3@northpark.edu

Desc: Subject: Swedish settlement in the U.S., Swedish culture, Swedish-American organizations, Swedish contributions to development of the U.S., outstanding Swedish-Americans, Swedish Immigration to Chicago. Holdings: 3000 books (largely in Swedish); 400 archive boxes of records; Swedish newspapers printed in Chicago, 1871-1981. Services: Copying; translations; archives open to the public by appointment.

2507 ▪ Swenson Swedish Immigration
Research Center

Augustana College   Ph: (309)794-7204
639 38th St.   Fax: (309)794-7443
Rock Island, IL 61201-2296
E-mail: sag@augustana.edu
URL: http://www.augustana.edu/administration/
    swenson/

Contact: Dag Blanck, Dir.

Desc: Subject: Swedish immigration to the U.S., Swedish-American life and culture, biography of Swedes in the U.S. Holdings: 12,500 books; 1000 bound periodical volumes; 200 uncataloged periodicals; 5.5 linear feet of Scandinavian-American Picture Collection; 200 linear feet of manuscripts; 8 linear feet of Oliver A. Linder clipping files; 1560 reels of microfilm of Swedish-American newspapers; 2000 reels of microfilm of Swedish-American church records; 412 reels of microfilm of records and papers of Swedish-American benevolent, fraternal, and cultural organizations and their institutions; 59 reels of microfilm of personal and professional papers of immigrants; 89 reels of microfilm and 6 loose-leaf volumes of name indexes to Swedish port of embarkation records: Gothenburg, 1869-1930, Malmo, 1874-1895, Stockholm 1869-1920; Norrkoping 1860-1920; Gavle, 1846-1858, Kalmar, 1880-1893; and Ockelbo, 1864-1894; other Swedish emigrant lists, 1817-1861; 14 reels of microfilm of name indexes to Norwegian ports of embarkation: Bergen, 1874-1924, Kristiania (Oslo), 1871-1902, and Trondheim, 1867-1890. Services: Copying; center open to the public by appointment.

2508 ▪ Tacoma Public Library
Special Collections

1102 Tacoma Ave., S.   Ph: (253)591-5622
Tacoma, WA 98402   Fax: (206)591-5470
URL: http://www.tpl.lib.wa.us

Contact: Susan H. Hardie, Dir.

Desc: Subject: Pacific Northwest and Washington state history. Holdings: 40,000 books; 3000 bound periodical volumes; 800 linear feet of manuscripts; 750 linear feet of local government archives; 30,000 slides; 35,000 maps; 80 VF drawers of clippings; 90 drawers of microforms. Services: Interlibrary loan; copying; collections open to the public.

2509 ▪ Talbot County Free Library
Maryland Room

100 W. Dover St.   Ph: (410)822-1626
Easton, MD 21601   Fax: (410)820-8217
E-mail: jerry@esrl.libmd.us

Desc: Subject: History - local and state, with emphasis on Talbot County and other locations on the eastern

shore; genealogy. Holdings: 4337 books; unbound periodicals; 18 VF drawers; 63 boxes of manuscripts and ephemera; 157 boxes and bound volumes of newspapers; 200 reels of microfilm of newspapers; 32 reels of microfilm of census data; 30 reels of microfilm of church records; 6 reels of microfilm of tax lists; 2 reels of microfilm of dissertations; 900 photographs; 369 maps. Services: Copying; room open to the public for reference use only.

2510 ▪ Tallmadge Historical Society
Library & Archives

PO Box 25   Ph: (330)633-2217
Tallmadge, OH 44278

Contact: Tobi Battista, Archv.

Desc: Subject: History - Tallmadge, Summit County, Ohio. Holdings: 250 books; 100 bound periodical volumes; 300 manuscripts. Services: Library open to the public by appointment.

2511 ▪ Tama County Historical Society
Museum Library

200 N. Broadway   Ph: (515)484-6767
Toledo, IA 52342

Contact: Joan Bidwell, V.P.

Desc: Subject: Genealogy, local history. Holdings: Books; microforms. Services: Copying; Library open to the public for reference use only.

2512 ▪ Tampa Hillsborough County Public
Library
Special Collections

900 N. Ashley St.   Ph: (813)273-3652
Tampa, FL 33602   Fax: (813)273-3641
E-mail: spcuser@scfn.thpl.lib.fl.us
URL: http://scfn.thpl.lib.fl.us/thpl/main/spc.htm

Contact: Joe R. Stines, Dir. of Libs.

Desc: Subject: Genealogy; government documents - U.S., state, local; Florida history; Foundation Center affiliate library. Holdings: 20,000 books; 500 bound periodical volumes; 170,000 documents; 323,000 pieces of microfiche; 11,535 reels of microfilm. Services: Interlibrary loan; Library open to the public.

2513 ▪ Teaneck Public Library
Oral and Local History Project

840 Teaneck Rd.   Ph: (201)837-4171
Teaneck, NJ 07666   Fax: (201)837-0410
URL: http://www.teaneck.org

Contact: Michael McCue, Dir.

Desc: Subject: Local history, early families, Jewish community, black community. Holdings: 100 cassettes; 4 notebooks; 1000 index cards; photographs; transcriptions; documentary film; historical exhibits; slidetape show. Services: Copying; project open to the public by appointment.

2514 ▪ Temple Adath Israel
Ruben Library

270 Highland Ave.   Ph: (610)664-5150
Merion, PA 19066   Fax: (610)664-0959

Contact: Fred Kazan, Rabbi

Desc: Subject: Judaica. Holdings: 2500 books. Services: Interlibrary loan; Library open to area college students or by member sponsorship.

2515 ▪ Temple Ahavath Sholom
Rabbi A. Alan Steinbach Library

1906 Ave. V   Ph: (718)769-5350
Brooklyn, NY 11229-4506

Contact: Penny Klein, Libn.

Desc: Subject: Jewish ethics, history, music; theology; comparative religion; biography; fiction (Jewish content). Holdings: 4500 books; Rabbi Steinbach's manuscripts; Jewish antiquities. Services: Library open to the public with restrictions.

2516 ▪ Temple Beth-El
Billie Davis Rodenberg Memorial Library

1351 S. 14th Ave.   Ph: (954)920-8225
Hollywood, FL 33020   Fax: (954)920-7026

Contact: Roslyn Kurland, Libn.

Desc: Subject: Judaica. Holdings: 8500 volumes. Services: Interlibrary loan; copying; library open for reference use only.

2517 ▪ Temple Beth-El
Library

139 Winton Rd., S.   Ph: (716)473-1770
Rochester, NY 14610   Fax: (716)473-2689

Contact: Anne Kirshenbaum, Libn.

Desc: Subject: Judaica - religion, philosophy, social science, history, art, literature, language, fiction, biography for adults and juveniles. Holdings: 6325 books; 7 file drawers of pamphlets and clippings. Services: Interlibrary loan; Library open to the public with special permission.

2518 ▪ Temple Beth-El
William G. Braude Library

70 Orchard Ave.   Ph: (401)331-6070
Providence, RI 02906   Fax: (401)331-8068

Contact: Reini Silverman, Libn.

Desc: Subject: Judaica, Hebraica, Yiddish, Biblical studies, Holocaust, philosophy, folklore, music, rabbinics, anti-Semitism, Latin American Jewry. Holdings: 25,000 books; 258 bound periodical volumes; 432 pamphlets; clippings; programs of interest to Rhode Island Jews; Yiddish and Hebrew books. Services: Interlibrary loan; Library open to the public.

2519 ▪ Temple Beth-El
Ziskind Memorial Library

385 High St.   Ph: (508)674-3529
Fall River, MA 02720   Fax: (508)674-3058

Desc: Subject: English Judaica. Holdings: 6000 volumes; 200 phonograph records; 300 pamphlets and clippings. Services: Library open to the public.

2520 ▪ Temple Beth-El of Great Neck
Hattie & Albert Grauer
Library

5 Old Mill Rd.   Ph: (516)487-0900
Great Neck, NY 11023

Contact: Dorothy Zimbalist, Libn.

Desc: Subject: Judaica - history, Holocaust, literature, biography, Israel. Holdings: 10,000 books; records; reference books. Services: Interlibrary loan; Library open to the public with restrictions.

2521 ▪ Temple Beth El of Greater Buffalo
Library

2368 Eggert Rd.   Ph: (716)836-3762
Tonawanda, NY 14150

Contact: Sandra Freed Gralnik, Libn.

Desc: Subject: Judaica. Holdings: 5000 books; phonograph records; tapes; videotapes. Services: Library open to the public.

2522 ■ Temple Beth Israel Library
10460 N. 56th St.　　　　Ph: (602)951-0323
Scottsdale, AZ 85253-1133　　Fax: (602)951-7150
URL: http://www.templebethisrael.com

Contact: Norma D. Sadick, Lib.Dir.

Desc: Subject: Jewish history, Bible, literature, Jewish genealogy, rabbinics, biography, art, music. Holdings: 17,541 books; 26 VF drawers of pamphlets, clippings, and maps; 470 audiocassettes. Services: Interlibrary loan; Library open to the public.

2523 ■ Temple Beth Joseph Rose Basloe Library
N. Prospect St.　　　　Ph: (315)866-4270
Herkimer, NY 13350

Desc: Subject: Judaica. Holdings: 3500 books. Services: Library open to the public.

2524 ■ Temple Beth Sholom Herbert Goldberg Memorial Library
1901 Kresson Rd.　　　　Ph: (609)547-6113
Cherry Hill, NJ 08003

Contact: Doris Corman, Libn.

Desc: Subject: Judaica. Holdings: 3000 books.

2525 ■ Temple Beth Sholom Library
4144 Chase Ave.　　　　Ph: (305)538-7231
Miami Beach, FL 33140　　Fax: (305)531-5428

Contact: Leslie Harris, Libn. & Educ. Media Spec.

Desc: Subject: Judaica (adult and juvenile), rabbinics. Holdings: 5000 books. Services: Interlibrary loan; copying; Library open to the public with restrictions.

2526 ■ Temple Beth Zion Suburban Library
700 Sweet Home Rd.　　　Ph: (716)886-7150
Amherst, NY 14226　　　Fax: (716)886-7152

Contact: Madeline Davis, Libn.

Desc: Subject: Jewish religion, history, literature, art. Holdings: 13,000 books; 250 filmstrips and slides; 200 records and cassettes; video cassettes. Services: Interlibrary loan; Library open to the public.

2527 ■ Temple B'nai Israel Lasker Memorial Library
3008 Ave. O　　　　　Ph: (409)765-5796
Galveston, TX 77550　　　Fax: (409)765-8302

Contact: Sophie Nussenblatt, Libn.

Desc: Subject: Judaism, Jewish history, biblical history, Bible commentaries. Holdings: 2000 books. Services: Library open to the public.

2528 ■ Temple B'rith Kodesh Library
2131 Elmwood Ave.　　　Ph: (716)244-7060
Rochester, NY 14618　　　Fax: (716)244-0557

Contact: Annette Sheiman, Libn.

Desc: Subject: Judaica. Holdings: 8000 books. Services: Library open to members of local congregations and students of local colleges and universities.

2529 ■ Temple Emanu-El Congregational Library
99 Taft Ave.　　　　　Ph: (401)331-1616
Providence, RI 02906　　　Fax: (401)421-9279

Contact: Mara Sokolsky, Libn.

Desc: Subject: Judaica, comparative religion. Holdings: 9000 books. Services: Interlibrary loan; copying; Library open to the public with deposit.

2530 ■ Temple Emanu-El Davis Library
225 N. Country Club Rd.　　Ph: (520)327-4501
Tucson, AZ 85716

Desc: Subject: Judaica. Holdings: 8000 books; 150 phonograph records; 50 filmstrips; 50 videotapes; 20 audiotapes. Services: Copying; Library open to the public for reference use only.

2531 ■ Temple Emanu-El Ivan M. Stettenheim Library
1 E. 65th St.　　　　Ph: (212)744-1400
New York, NY 10021-6596

Desc: Subject: Judaica. Holdings: 20,000 books. Services: Library open to the public.

2532 ■ Temple Emanu-El Library
1701 Washington Ave.　　Ph: (305)538-2503
Miami Beach, FL 33139　　Fax: (305)535-3122

Contact: Ruth M. Abelow, Libn.

Desc: Subject: Judaica including religion, Bible, Israel, biography, literature, history, sociology, and education. Holdings: 8500 books; 55 cataloged periodicals; 270 pamphlets; 40 pamphlet boxes of uncataloged pamphlets on Israel and religion; 8 books of clippings. Services: Library open to the public with refundable deposit.

2533 ■ Temple Emanu-El Sonahend Family Library
455 Neptune Blvd.　　　Ph: (516)431-4060
Long Beach, NY 11561

Desc: Subject: Jewish religion and literature; Bible; Hebraica; current events in Israel. Holdings: 6000 books; 90 bound periodical volumes; 50 VF drawers; 110 videotapes; audiotapes; filmstrips; sound recordings. Services: Library open to members.

2534 ■ Temple Emanu-El William P. Engel Library
2100 Highland Ave.　　　Ph: (205)933-8037
Birmingham, AL 35255
E-mail: elinorsue@aol.com

Contact: Elinor Sue Staff, Libn.

Desc: Subject: Judaica, religion, culture. Holdings: 3500 books. Services: Interlibrary loan; copying; Library open to the public.

2535 ■ Temple Emanuel Library
1101 Springdale Rd.　　　Ph: (609)489-0029
Cherry Hill, NJ 08003　　Fax: (609)489-0032
URL: http://www.templeemanuel.org

Contact: Rene Batterman, Libn.

Desc: Subject: Judaism. Holdings: 5000 books; records; tapes. Services: Copying; Library open to the public with restrictions.

2536 ■ Temple Emanuel Library
150 Derby Ave.　　　　Ph: (203)397-3000
PO Box 897
Orange, CT 06477

Contact: Meryl Farber, Chm., Lib.Comm.

Desc: Subject: Judaica. Holdings: 1200 books; 25 phonograph records. Services: Library open to the public with permission.

2537 ■ Temple de Hirsch Sinai Library
1511 E. Pike　　　　　Ph: (206)323-8486
Seattle, WA 98122-4199　　Fax: (206)324-6772

Contact: Rebecca Alexander, Libn.

Desc: Subject: Judaism, Jewish history, literature, biography, Holocaust, children's literature. Holdings: 8500 books. Services: Interlibrary loan; copying (limited); Library open to the public.

2538 ■ Temple Israel Libraries and Media Center
5725 Walnut Lake Rd.　　Ph: (248)661-5700
West Bloomfield, MI 48323　Fax: (248)661-1302
E-mail: tilibrary@aol.com

Contact: Rachel Erlich, Dir.

Desc: Subject: Judaism - history, biography, literature, arts, children's literature; Holocaust; Bible study; Israel. Holdings: 12,000 books; 8 VF drawers of clippings and pamphlets, video cassettes, CD-ROMs. Services: Library open to the public.

2539 ■ Temple Israel Library
2324 Emerson Ave., S.　　Ph: (612)377-8680
Minneapolis, MN 55405　　Fax: (612)377-6630
E-mail: gkalman@templeisrael.com

Contact: Georgia Kalman, Libn.

Desc: Subject: Judaica, Jewish religion, philosophy. Holdings: 6000 books. Services: Library open to the public.

2540 ■ Temple Israel Library
140 Central Ave.　　　　Ph: (516)239-1140
Lawrence, NY 11559　　　Fax: (516)239-0859

Desc: Subject: Judaica and allied subjects. Holdings: 5100 books; 20 bound periodical volumes; 225 filmstrips; 10 cassettes. Services: Library open to the public with permission.

2541 ■ Temple Israel Library
1901 N. Flagler Dr.　　　Ph: (561)833-8421
West Palm Beach, FL 33407　Fax: (407)833-0571
URL: http://www.temple-israel.com

Contact: Elsie Leviton, Chm., Lib.Comm.

Desc: Subject: Judaica - history, literature, sociology, arts. Holdings: 7000 books; 12 bound periodical volumes; 1000 pamphlets, bibliographies, archives, clippings; 8 VF drawers; phonograph records; filmstrips. Services: Library open to residents of Palm Beach County.

2542 ■ Temple Israel Library
Longwood Ave. & Plymouth St.　Ph: (617)566-3960
Boston, MA 02215　　　Fax: (617)731-3711
E-mail: aabrams@tisrael.org

Contact: Ann Carol Abrams, Libn.

Desc: Subject: Judaica. Holdings: 15,000 books. Services: Library open to the public for reference use only.

2543 ■ Temple Israel Neipris Library
125 Pond St.　　　　　Ph: (781)784-3986
PO Box 377　　　　　Fax: (781)784-0719
Sharon, MA 02067

Contact: Florette Brill

Desc: Subject: Jewish religion, philosophy, history; American Jewish life; Israel and Zionism; Hebrew. Holdings: 3250 books; 65 tapes; videos; games. Services: Interlibrary loan; Library open to the public with restrictions.

2544 ■ Temple Israel
Paul Peltason Library
No. 1 Rabbi Alvan D. Rubin Dr.   Ph: (314)432-8050
Creve Coeur, MO 63141   Fax: (314)432-8053
E-mail: eli@ti-stl.org

Contact: Rabbi Mark L. Shook

Desc: Subject: Judaica. Holdings: 4000 books. Services: Library open to the public with restrictions.

2545 ■ Temple Israel
Rabbi Louis Witt Memorial Library
1 Riverbend   Ph: (937)496-0050
Dayton, OH 45405   Fax: (937)496-0060

Contact: Julie Orenstein, Ch., Lib.Comm.

Desc: Subject: Judaica. Holdings: Figures not available. Services: Library open to the public with restrictions.

2546 ■ Temple Israel of Greater Miami
Library
137 N.E. 19th St.   Ph: (305)573-5900
Miami, FL 33132   Fax: (305)573-5904

Desc: Subject: Judaica, the Bible, philosophy, Israel. Holdings: 11,000 books; pamphlets; American Jewish Archives; Near East reports; records; tapes; slides. Services: Interlibrary loan; copying; Library open to the public for reference use only.

2547 ■ Temple Judea
Mel Harrison Memorial Library
5500 Granada Blvd.
Coral Gables, FL 33146

Contact: Zelda Harrison, Chf.Libn.

Desc: Subject: Judaica. Holdings: 6000 books. Services: Library not open to the public.

2548 ■ Temple Judea Mizpah
Library
8610 Niles Center Rd.   Ph: (847)676-1566
Skokie, IL 60077   Fax: (847)676-1579

Contact: Judy Duesenberg, Lib.Chm.

Desc: Subject: Judaica. Holdings: 4000 books; 20 bound periodical volumes. Services: Copying; Library open to the public with restrictions.

2549 ■ Temple Ohabai Shalom
Library
5015 Harding Rd.   Ph: (615)352-7620
Nashville, TN 37205   Fax: (615)352-9365

Contact: Lee Haas

Desc: Subject: Bible commentary, Jewish history, children's literature, Judaica. Holdings: 8275 books. Services: Interlibrary loan; copying; Library open to the public.

2550 ■ Temple Ohabei Shalom
Sisterhood Library
1187 Beacon St.   Ph: (617)277-6610
Brookline, MA 02146   Fax: (617)277-7881

Contact: Janice Adler, Libn.

Desc: Subject: Bible, Judaism, biography, history, Israel, religion, theology, Jewish literature. Holdings: 3500 books. Services: Library open to the public with restrictions.

2551 ■ Temple Shaarey Zedek
Rabbi Isaac Klein Library
621 Getzville Rd.   Ph: (716)838-3232
Amherst, NY 14226   Fax: (716)835-6154
E-mail: tsz@wzrd.com

Contact: Judith E. Carrel, Libn.

Desc: Subject: Judaica. Holdings: 6500 volumes. Services: Library open to the public.

2552 ■ Temple Sharey Tefilo-Israel
Echikson, Ehrenkrantz, Abelson Library
432 Scotland Rd.   Ph: (973)763-4116
South Orange, NJ 07079   Fax: (973)763-3941

Contact: H. Linda Trope, Exec.Dir.

Desc: Subject: Bible; Judaism - religion, history, customs, ceremonies, holidays, practices, theology, philosophy, social sciences; fiction; Holocaust; women's issues. Holdings: 4755 volumes. Services: Library open to the public for reference use only.

2553 ■ Temple Sholom of Broomall
Library
55 N. Church Lane   Ph: (610)356-5165
Broomall, PA 19008

Contact: Barbara Clarke, Libn.

Desc: Subject: Judaica. Holdings: 2400 books. Services: Interlibrary loan; Library not open to the public.

2554 ■ Temple Sinai
Dr. Alex Morrison Library
50 Alberta Dr.   Ph: (716)834-0708
Buffalo, NY 14226   Fax: (716)834-0708

Desc: Subject: Judaica, Holocaust. Holdings: 3008 volumes. Services: Library open to the public.

2555 ■ Temple Sinai
Jack Balaban Memorial Library
New Albany Rd.   Ph: (609)829-0658
Cinnaminson, NJ 08077   Fax: (609)829-0310

Contact: Marilyn Prant, Libn.

Desc: Subject: Holocaust; Jewish history, religion, holidays, authors. Holdings: 1500 books; videos. Services: Interlibrary loan; Library open to the public with restrictions.

2556 ■ Temple Sinai
Library
3100 Military Rd., NW   Ph: (202)363-6394
Washington, DC 20015

Contact: Margaret Mallett Chachkin, Libn.

Desc: Subject: Judaism - philosophy, history; Bible; theology; Jews in the United States; Jewish rituals, traditions, folklore, art, literature, and music; Israeli history; Holocaust. Holdings: 8000 volumes; 2 VF drawers of clippings. Services: Library open to the public.

2557 ■ Temple Sinai Religious School
Library
50 Sewall Ave.   Ph: (617)277-5888
Brookline, MA 02446   Fax: (617)277-5842
E-mail: whe_waldorf@flo.org

Contact: Leeann Shamash, Prin., Rel.Sch.

Desc: Subject: Judaica, religion, Bible, Talmud. Holdings: 2200 books. Services: Library not open to the public.

2558 ■ Temple Tifereth Israel
Lee and Dolores Hartzmark Library
26000 Shaker Blvd.   Ph: (216)831-3233
Beachwood, OH 44122   Fax: (216)831-4216

E-mail: makeck@hotmail.com
URL: http://HTTwww.TTTI.org

Desc: Subject: Judaica, a children's collection, adult fiction, holocaust material. Holdings: 20,000 books; audiovisual materials. Services: Interlibrary loan; copying; Library open to the public.

2559 ■ Tennessee (State) Department of State
Tennessee State Library and Archives
403 7th Ave., N.   Ph: (615)741-2764
Nashville, TN 37243-0312   Fax: (615)741-6471
E-mail: egleaves@mail.state.tn.us
URL: http://www.state.tn.us/sos/statelib/tslahome.htm

Contact: Edwin S. Gleaves, Ph.D., Libn. & Archv.

Desc: Subject: Tennesseana, U.S. and local history, state and local government, law and public administration, genealogy. Holdings: 631,604 books; 5279 cubic feet manuscript items; 27,916 cubic feet archival documents; 137,337 reels of microfilm; 312,434 sheets of microfiche; 40,760 audiotapes; 106,664 photographs. Services: Interlibrary loan; copying; Library open to the public.

2560 ■ Tennessee Western History Association
Library
PO Box 111864   Ph: (615)834-5069
Nashville, TN 37222   Fax: (615)832-9128

Contact: Steve Eng, Cur.

Desc: Subject: Tennessee and the Old West, Jesse and Frank James, the Seventh Cavalry (at Nashville), Ned Buntline, Clay Allison, Aaron Burr, Nat Love (black cowboy), Tennesseans in Texas, J. Frank Dalton (Jesse James imposter), John Joel Glanton, John Wilkes Booth, Knights of the Golden Circle, filibusters, Western music. Holdings: 200 books; 100 letters; 300 magazines; 300 miscellaneous items; articles and news clippings; photographs; affidavits; artifacts; maps. Services: Copying; research (both limited); Library open to serious scholars by appointment.

2561 ■ Texarkana Museums System
Library
219 State Line Ave.   Ph: (903)793-4831
Box 2343   Fax: (903)793-7108
Texarkana, TX 75504

Desc: Subject: Local history. Holdings: 1800 books; 20 scrapbooks of early residents; 40 Texarkana city directories; 46 annuals of local high schools. Services: Copying; Library open to the public by appointment; fee charged; call for information.

2562 ■ Texas A&M University
Cushing Library
PO Box 5000   Ph: (409)845-1951
College Station, TX   Fax: (409)862-4761
  77843-5000
E-mail: stevensmith@tamu.edu
URL: http://www.tamu.edu/library/cushing/
  cushing.html

Contact: Dr. Donald H. Dyal, Dir.

Desc: Subject: Military history, science fiction, range livestock industry, 19th- and 20th-century illustration, Texas A&M University, Texas agriculture, 20th-century Texas politics, technology, 16th- to 19th-century naval architecture; sea fiction authors, including Bill Owens, J. Frank Dobie, P.G. Wodehouse, W. Somerset Maugham, Matthew Arnold, Rudyard Kipling, Roy Fuller, A.E. Coppard; science fiction and fantasy authors, including Ray Bradbury, Michael Moorcock, John Sladek, and Robert Heinlein. Holdings: 77,300 books; 26,575 linear feet of records and manuscripts; 8000 bound periodical volumes. Services: Copying; photographic reproduction.

2563 ▪ Texas A&M University Oral History Program

James Gilliam Gee Library   Ph: (903)886-5737
Texas A&M University   Fax: (903)886-5723
- Commerce
PO Box 3011
Commerce, TX 75429-3011
E-mail: conrad@bois.darc.tamu-commerce.edu
URL: http://www.tamu-commerce.edu/library

Contact: Dr. James H. Conrad, Coord. of Oral Hist.

Desc: Subject: History of East Texas - railroad, cotton, blacks, medicine; Texas social work; institutional history. Holdings: 350 volumes; 925 cassette tapes of interviews. Services: Copying; program open to the public with restrictions.

2564 ▪ Texas Catholic Conference Catholic Archives of Texas

1600 N. Congress   Ph: (512)476-6296
PO Box 13124   Fax: (512)476-3715
Austin, TX 78711
E-mail: cat@onr.com
URL: http://www.onr.com/user/cat

Contact: Kinga L. Perzynska, Archv.

Desc: Subject: Spanish exploration and missionary period (1519-1836), Catholic Church history in Texas, immigration and emigration, colonization. Holdings: 1500 volumes; 70,000 pages of Spanish and Mexican documents, 1519-1890; 270 document cases of ecclesiastical records; 40 document cases of private collections; 170 reels of microfilm of Catholic newspapers; 15,000 photographs. Services: Copying; Library open to the public.

2565 ▪ Texas State Library and Archives Commission

1201 Brazos   Ph: (512)463-5455
PO Box 12927   Fax: (512)463-5436
Austin, TX 78711-2927
E-mail: pio@tsl.state.tx.us
URL: http://www.tsl.state.tx.us

Contact: Peggy D. Rudd, Dir. & Libn.

Desc: Subject: Texas history and government, genealogy, librarianship. Holdings: 1.4 million books and bound periodical volumes; 336,184 microforms of newspapers and tax records. Services: Interlibrary loan; copying; Library open to the public with restrictions.

2566 ▪ Thayer County Museum Historical & Genealogical Library

PO Box 387   Ph: (402)768-7313
Belvidere, NE 68315
E-mail: kjwmson@navix.net

Contact: Jacqueline J. Williamson, Musm. Co-Cur.

Desc: Subject: Thayer County history, past and present residents, Thayer family genealogies. Services: Copying; Library open to the public at librarian's discretion on a seasonally variable schedule or by appointment.

2567 ▪ Thetford Historical Society Library

PO Box 33   Ph: (802)785-2068
Thetford, VT 05074

Contact: Charles Latham, Jr.

Desc: Subject: Thetford history, local crafts and manufacturing, Vermont history. Holdings: 4000 books; 400 bound periodical volumes; 150 linear feet of archival materials. Services: Copying; Library open to the public.

2568 ▪ Thomas Balch Library

208 W. Market St.   Ph: (703)779-1328
Leesburg, VA 20176   Fax: (703)779-7363

E-mail: janetbl@erols.com
URL: http://www.leesburgva.com/library/balch.html

Desc: Subject: Loudoun County, Virginia - history, genealogy, religion, culture; African American history - slavery, religion, education. Holdings: Books; letters; diaries; personal histories; records; maps; VF drawers; deeds; microfilm. Services: Copying; Library open to the public.

2569 ▪ Thomas County Historical Society Library

1905 S. Franklin, Box 465   Ph: (785)462-4590
Colby, KS 67701   Fax: (785)462-4592
E-mail: prairie@colby.ixks.com

Contact: Sue Ellen Taylor, Dir.

Desc: Subject: Local history. Holdings: 500 linear feet of microfilm, manuscripts, books, archives, photographs, slides, clippings, cassettes. Services: Copying; Library open to the public for reference use only.

2570 ▪ Thomas Raddall Research Centre Archives

PO Box 1078   Ph: (902)354-4058
Liverpool, NS, Canada B0T 1K0   Fax: (902)354-2050
E-mail: linda.rafuse@ns.sympatico.ca

Contact: Linda Rafuse, Dir.

Desc: Subject: Genealogy, local history, businesses, shipping. Holdings: 100 books; 100 bound periodical volumes; 600 archival files; 2500 microfiche; 300 reels of microfilm. Services: Copying; Library open to the public.

2571 ▪ Thunder Bay Historical Museum Library

425 Donald St., E.   Ph: (807)623-0801
Thunder Bay, ON, Canada P7E   Fax: (807)622-6880
5V1
E-mail: tbhm@tbaytel.net
URL: http://www.tbaytel.net/tbhms

Contact: Tory Tronrud, Cur.Archv.

Desc: Subject: History - northwestern Ontario, Canada, material. Holdings: 2500 books; 100 bound periodical volumes; 400 feet of archival material; 150,000 images. Services: Copying; Library open to the public by appointment.

2572 ▪ Ticonderoga Historical Society Library

Hancock House   Ph: (518)585-7868
Moses Circle
Ticonderoga, NY 12883

Desc: Subject: Local and area history, 1609 to present. Holdings: 10,000 volumes; correspondence; diaries; journals; logbooks; account books; business records; financial records; genealogical materials; public documents; maps; photographs. Services: Library open to the public.

2573 ▪ Tillamook County Pioneer Museum Library

2106 Second St.   Ph: (503)842-4553
Tillamook, OR 97141   Fax: (503)842-4553

Contact: M. Wayne Jensen, Jr., Dir.

Desc: Subject: Northwest history and natural history, local history, genealogy. Holdings: Genealogy and county records; reference books; Tillamook Indian material; Tillamook County cemetery records; county newspapers; Naval Air Station Collection (Blimp Base WWII). Services: Copying; Library open to the public during museum hours.

2574 ▪ Tioga County Historical Society Museum Library

110-112 Front St.   Ph: (607)687-2460
Owego, NY 13827   Fax: (607)687-7788
E-mail: tiogamus@clarityconnect.com

Desc: Subject: Tioga County, Owego, and Southern Tier (New York) history and genealogy. Holdings: 5000 books; archives (30 cubic feet); 200 microfilm. Services: Copying; Library open to the public; small fee for non-members.

2575 ▪ Tippecanoe County Historical Association Alameda McCollough Research & Genealogy Library

1001 South St.   Ph: (765)476-8420
Lafayette, IN 47901   Fax: (765)476-8414
E-mail: library@tcha.mus.in.us
URL: http://www.tcha.mus.in.us

Contact: Paul J. Schueler, Coll.Mgr.

Desc: Subject: Genealogy; Indiana; Tippecanoe County and local history. Holdings: 7000 books; 150 bound periodical volumes; 125 VF drawers of manuscripts and clippings; 40 scrapbooks; 575 reels of microfilm; 10,000 negatives; 2000 photographs. Services: Copying; Library open to the public.

2576 ▪ Toledo-Lucas County Public Library Local History & Genealogy Department

325 Michigan St.   Ph: (419)259-5233
Toledo, OH 43624   Fax: (419)255-1334

Contact: James C. Marshall, Dept.Mgr.

Desc: Subject: Genealogy, local history, regional materials - Ohio, Indiana, Michigan, Illinois, Kentucky and original 13 colonies. Holdings: 30,000 books; 1000 bound periodical volumes; 600 reels of microfilm; 3100 microfiche; 500 scrapbooks relating to the local area; 800 reels of microfilm of Ohio census, at ten-year intervals, 1820-1880, 1900, 1910, 1920; 1200 reels of microfilm of Ohio Soundex census index, 1880, 1900, 1910, 1920; 284 reels of microfilm of Michigan census, at 10-year intervals, 1820-1880, 1900, 1910, 1920; 780 reels of microfilm of Michigan census index, 1880, 1900, 1910, 1920; 255 reels of microfilm of Kentucky census, at ten-year intervals, 1810-1880; 88 reels of microfilm of Kentucky census index, 1880; 465 reels of microfilm of Toledo Blade, 1835 to present; 381 reels of microfilm of Toledo Times, 1900-1975; Toledo City Council and Committee Minutes, 1837-1899; 41 reels of microfilm of probate court records, 1835-1990; 125 reels of microfilm of Common Pleas Civil Journals, 1835-1940; 20 reels of microfilm of birth and death records, 1858-1990; 36 reels of microfilm of city police department jail registrations, 1872-1921; 30 reels of microfilm of Lucas County naturalization records, 1853-1929. Services: Copying; department open to the public.

2577 ▪ Tongass Historical Museum Library

629 Dock St.   Ph: (907)225-5600
Ketchikan, AK 99901   Fax: (907)225-5602

Contact: Michael Naab, Musm.Dir.

Desc: Subject: Alaska - forestry, mining, fishing, Indians. Holdings: 500 books; 700 cubic feet of regional archives. Services: Copying; Library open to the public for reference use only.

2578 ▪ Topeka Genealogical Society Library

PO Box 4048   Ph: (913)233-5762
Topeka, KS 66604-0048
E-mail: TGS@networksplus.net
URL: http://www.networksplus.net/donno/

Contact: Katy Matthews, Libn.

Desc: Subject: Genealogy, history. Holdings: 5000 books; 630 periodical titles; 520 holding boxes; Shawnee County Kansas burial records file; Shawnee Co. naturalizations; city directories; surname reference file. Services: Copying; Library open to the public with restrictions.

2579 ■ Topeka High School Historical Society

800 W. 10th St.   Ph: (913)575-6252
Topeka, KS 66612

Desc: Subject: Topeka High School history. Holdings: Figures not available. Services: Library open to the public.

2580 ■ Torrington Historical Society, Inc.
John H. Thompson Memorial Library

192 Main St.   Ph: (860)482-8260
Torrington, CT 06790

Contact: Mark McEachern, Exec.Dir.

Desc: Subject: History - Torrington, Litchfield County, Connecticut. Holdings: 5000 volumes; 200 boxes of microfilm; 800 sets of local architectural drawings. Services: Copying; library open to the public for reference use only.

2581 ■ Trenton Public Library
Trentoniana Collection

120 Academy St.   Ph: (609)392-7188
Trenton, NJ 08608   Fax: (609)396-7655
E-mail: tpl_nj@hslc.org

Contact: Robert E. Coumbe, Dir.

Desc: Subject: Local history, genealogy. Holdings: 5000 books; 403 bound periodical volumes; 45,000 photographs; 34 VF drawers; 300 maps and atlases; manuscripts (18 linear ft.); 28 reels of film; 35 audiotapes; 47 oral histories; Trenton newspapers on microfilm; 5 pieces of Lenox china; 3 VF drawers of memorabilia; 30 boxes of unspecified materials. Services: Copying; collection open to the public.

2582 ■ Tri-Cities Historical Society Museum
Library

1 N. Harbor Dr.   Ph: (616)842-0700
PO Box 234   Fax: (616)842-3698
Grand Haven, MI 49417
E-mail: temuseum@grandhaven.com
URL: http://www.grandhaven.com/museum

Contact: Elizabeth Kammeraad, Musm.Dir.

Desc: Subject: Local history - Grand Haven, Spring Lake, Ferrysburg, and North Ottawa County, Michigan. Holdings: 1000 books; 10 AV programs; manuscripts; prints. Services: Copying; Library open to the public by appointment.

2583 ■ Tri-County Heritage Society
Reference Library

PO Box 352   Ph: (610)286-7477
Morgantown, PA 19543   Fax: (610)286-6588
E-mail: tchslibrary@juno.com

Contact: Janet Lahr, Libn.

Desc: Subject: History - state, local; architectural research; genealogy. Holdings: 1000 books; 500 bound periodical volumes; 60 cubic feet archival materials; 25 reels of microfilm; maps; warrants; surveys. Services: Copying; Library open to the public for reference use only.

2584 ■ Troy Public Library
Special Collections

510 W. Big Beaver Rd.   Ph: (248)524-3538
Troy, MI 48084-5289   Fax: (248)524-0112
E-mail: stoutenb@lcm.macomb.lib.mi.us
URL: http://web.macomb.lib.mi.us/troy

Contact: Brian H. Stoutenburg, Dir.

Desc: Holdings: 222,230 books; 205,781 microfiche; 4333 reels of microfilm. Services: Interlibrary loan; copying; collections open to the public with restrictions.

2585 ■ Tucson Family History Center

500 S. Langley   Ph: (520)298-0905
Tucson, AZ 85710   Fax: (520)298-2339
E-mail: kcwebb@gci-net.com

Contact: Kimber C. Webb, Dir.

Desc: Subject: Genealogy. Holdings: 10,000 books; bound periodical volumes; microfiche; 3000 reels of microfilm. Services: Copying; microform loans.

2586 ■ Tulane University
Howard-Tilton Memorial Library
Louisiana Collection

    Ph: (504)865-5643
rs>New Orleans, LA 70118   Fax: (504)865-6773
URL: http://www.tulane.edu/lmiller/
    SpecCollHomePage.html

Contact: Joan G. Caldwell, Hd.

Desc: Subject: Louisiana - history and politics, art and architecture, literature, genealogy. Holdings: 40,000 books and bound periodical volumes; 99 VF drawers of clippings, pamphlets, and other material; 29 VF drawers of pictures, portraits; 11 cases of maps; 54 boxes of Louisiana sheet music. Services: Copying; collection open to the public with restrictions.

2587 ■ Tulare Public Library
Inez L. Hyde Memorial Collection

113 North F. St.   Ph: (209)685-2342
Tulare, CA 93274   Fax: (209)685-2345

Contact: Michael C. Stowell

Desc: Subject: Genealogy, local history. Holdings: 4509 volumes; 3640 reels of microfilm; 3095 titles on 17,335 microfiche. Services: Genealogy Room open to the public with restrictions.

2588 ■ Tulsa Historical Society
Library

Box 27303   Ph: (918)596-1350
Tulsa, OK 74149-0303   Fax: (918)596-1353

Contact: Robert Powers, Cur.

Desc: Subject: Local and state history. Holdings: 600 cubic feet of reminiscences of pioneers, oral history tapes, diaries, business records, public documents, manuscript maps, and photographs. Services: Copying; Library open to the public for reference use only.

2589 ■ Tuolumne County Genealogical Society
Library

158 W. Bradford Ave.   Ph: (209)532-1317
Box 3956
Sonora, CA 95370

Contact: Louise Leedy, Lib.Coord.

Desc: Subject: Genealogy, county and state history (includes books on all states). Holdings: 1000 books; 80 reels of microfilm; 1000 microfiche; 550 fiche; 5000 unbound periodicals. Services: Copying; answers research queries; Library open to the public.

2590 ■ Tuscarawas County Genealogical
Society
Library

PO Box 141   Ph: (216)922-0531
New Philadelphia, OH 44663

Contact: Keith Schaar, Geneal.Soc.Pres.

Desc: Subject: Genealogy, local history. Holdings: 357 books; 346 bound periodical volumes; 92 genealogical newsletters; 352 family histories; 85 cemetery records; 24 local histories; 22 city directories; 10 passenger and ship records; 39 state histories; 18 court records; 60 war records; 69 research guides; 88 church and sect histories; 259 city and county histories; 27 colonial records; 4 alien country histories; 29 land records and atlases; 25 printed census records; 27 phone books; 119 vital statistics records; 149 reels of microfilm of probate, census, war, marriage, birth, and death records. Services: Copying; Library open to the public on a limited schedule.

2591 ■ Ukrainian Cultural and Educational
Centre
Library

184 Alexander Ave., E.   Ph: (204)942-0218
Winnipeg, MB, Canada R3B   Fax: (204)943-2857
0L6
E-mail: ucec@mb.sympatico.ca

Contact: Larissa Tolchinsky, Libn.

Desc: Subject: Ukrainian history, literature, language, art, ethnography; Ukrainian settlement in Canada. Holdings: 41,500 books; 31,000 periodicals; 300 scores; 2000 slides. Services: Copying; Library open to the public for reference use only.

2592 ■ Ukrainian Genealogical and Historical
Society of Canada
Library

R.R. 2   Ph: (402)932-6811
Cochrane, AB, Canada T0L 0W0
URL: http://www.feefhs.org/ca/frgughsc.html

Desc: Subject: Ukrainian culture, genealogy, and history. Holdings: Books; family histories; memorabilia; maps. Services: Library open to the public by appointment.

2593 ■ Ukrainian Museum-Archives, Inc.

1202 Kenilworth Ave.   Ph: (216)781-4329
Cleveland, OH 44113-4424

Contact: Andrew Fedynsky, Dir.

Desc: Subject: Ukrainian Revolution, post World War II immigration of Ukrainians, religion, linguistics. Holdings: 16,000 books; 800 bound periodical volumes; 1250 unbound periodicals; 300 photographs; archival materials in Ukrainian. Services: Copying; archives open to the public for reference use only.

2594 ■ Union County Historical Society
Library

Union County Courthouse   Ph: (570)524-8666
S. Second St.   Fax: (570)524-8743
Lewisburg, PA 17837
E-mail: hstoricl@ptd.net
URL: http://www.rootsweb.com/paunion/society.html

Contact: Gary W. Slear, Chm., Archv. & Musm.

Desc: Subject: Local history, genealogy. Holdings: 260 books; 250 bound periodical volumes; 40 cubic feet of clippings; tax records on microfilm. Services: Copying; Library open to the public.

2595 ■ United Church of Christ First
Congregational Church of Woodstock
John Eliot Library

Rte. 169   Ph: (860)928-7405
Woodstock, CT 06281

Contact: Cheryl R. Wakely, Libn.

Desc: Subject: Religion, children's literature, philosophy, psychology, parenting, self-help, literature, biography.

Holdings: 2000 books; 3 bound periodical volumes; 10 reports; 2000 archival items; 60 AV items. Services: Library open to the public.

2596 ■ United Empire Loyalists' Association of Canada
National Headquarters
National Loyalist Reference Library
50 Baldwin St., Ste. 202   Ph: (416)591-1783
Toronto, ON, Canada M5T   Fax: (416)591-7506
  1L4
E-mail: uela@npiec.on.ca
URL: http://www.npiec.on.ca/uela/uela1.htm

Desc: Subject: Loyalist history, history of Loyalist families, genealogy, education. Holdings: 1000 books. Services: Library not open to the public.

2597 ■ United Methodist Church
Armstrong Chapel
Church Library
5125 Drake Rd.   Ph: (513)561-4220
Cincinnati, OH 45243   Fax: (513)561-3062

Contact: Michell Terry

Desc: Subject: Theology; Bible - study, history; Christianity - education, life, practice; healing ministry; poetry; literature; biography. Holdings: 3000 books; 240 videotapes. Services: Copying; Library open to the public.

2598 ■ United Methodist Church
South Georgia Conference - Commission on Archives and History
Arthur J. Moore Methodist Museum - Library
Epworth-by-the-Sea   Ph: (912)638-4050
PO Box 20407
St. Simons Island, GA 31522
E-mail: methmuse@juno.com

Contact: Mary Vice, Dir.Cur.

Desc: Holdings: 5000 volumes; 150 bound periodical volumes; 20 documents; 6 AV programs. Services: Copying; Library open to the public for reference use only.

2599 ■ United Methodist Commission on Archives & History
South Carolina Conference
Historical Society - Sandor Teszler Library
Wofford College   Ph: (864)597-4309
429 N. Church St.   Fax: (864)597-4329
Spartanburg, SC 29303-3663
E-mail: stonerp@wofford.edu

Contact: R. Phillip Stone, Archv.

Desc: Subject: Methodist history with particular reference to South Carolina Methodism. Holdings: 2000 books and bound periodical volumes; minutes of the South Carolina conference; letters; notes; manuscripts; records of some South Carolina churches. Services: Library open to the public for reference use only.

2600 ■ United Methodist Historical Society
Baltimore-Washington Annual Conference
Lovely Lane Museum Library
2200 St. Paul St.   Ph: (410)889-4458
Baltimore, MD 21218-5897

Contact: Rev. Edwin Schell, Exec.Sec.Libn.

Desc: Subject: Religion, Wesleyana, American church history, higher education, Methodism. Holdings: 5000 books; 280 bound periodical volumes; 18,000 reports, personal papers, church histories, clippings. Services: Interlibrary loan; copying; Library open to qualified researchers.

2601 ■ U.S. Army Military History Institute
22 Ashburn Dr.   Ph: (717)245-3611
Carlisle Barracks   Fax: (717)245-4370
Carlisle, PA 17013-5008
E-mail: awcc-dmh@awc.carlisle.army.mil
URL: http://carlisle-www.army.mil/usamhi/

Contact: Nancy L. Gilbert, Asst.Dir., Lib.Svc.

Desc: Subject: Military history, U.S. and foreign history. Holdings: 292,000 books; 9000 bound periodical volumes; 247,000 military publications; 6800 military unit histories; 3050 hours of taped oral history interviews; 7 million manuscripts; 1,250,000 photographs; 15,000 reels of microfilm. Services: Interlibrary loan; copying; institute open to the public.

2602 ■ U.S. Army - Total Army Personnel Center
Personnel Service Support Directorate
The Institute of Heraldry - Library
Fort Belvoir, Bldg. 1466   Ph: (703)806-4967
Fort Belvoir, VA 22060-5579   Fax: (703)806-4964

Contact: Roy Ellis Cornwell, Libn.

Desc: Subject: Heraldry, arts, colors, flags, lettering and decorations, history, medals, military history (chiefly U.S.), military insignia, military uniforms, seals, signs, symbolisms, weapons. Holdings: 22,600 volumes; 15 VF drawers. Services: Library open to the public by appointment.

2603 ■ U.S. Bureau of the Census
Information Services Program
Atlanta Regional Office - Library
101 Marietta St. NW, Ste. 3200   Ph: (404)730-3833
Atlanta, GA 30303-2700   Fax: (404)730-3964
E-mail: atlanta.regional.office@ccmail.census.gov
URL: http://www.census.gov

Desc: Subject: U.S. census reports. Holdings: 15,000 books; 4500 microfiche; 260 CD-ROMs. Services: Office open to the public.

2604 ■ U.S. Bureau of the Census
Information Services Program
Boston Regional Office - Library
2 Copley Pl., Ste. 301   Ph: (617)424-0510
PO Box 9108   Fax: (617)424-0547
Boston, MA 02117-9108
URL: http://www.census.gov/robos/www

Contact: Arthur G. Dukakis, Reg.Dir.

Desc: Subject: U.S. census reports. Holdings: 4000 books; 8 VF drawers; 1992 economic censuses, 1990 census reports (hard copy CD-ROM); census maps. Services: Copying; Library open to the public; CD-ROM by appointment.

2605 ■ U.S. Bureau of the Census
Information Services Program
Census Publication Center
6900 W. Jefferson Ave.   Ph: (303)969-7750
Lakewood, CO 80235   Fax: (303)969-6777
E-mail: gerald.l.odonnell@ccmail.census.gov
URL: http://www.census.gov

Contact: Pat Rodriguez

Desc: Subject: U.S. census reports. Holdings: Figures not available. Services: Copying; statistical assistance; Center open to the public.

2606 ■ U.S. Bureau of the Census
Information Services Program
Charlotte Regional Office - Library
901 Center Park Dr., Ste. 106   Ph: (704)344-6144
Charlotte, NC 28217-2935   Fax: (704)344-6549

E-mail: W_K_Wright@ccmail.census.gov
  Jacquelyn_K_Billings@ccMail.Census
URL: http://www.census.gov/FTP/Pub/rocha/www/

Contact: Susan B. Hardy, Reg.Dir.

Desc: Subject: U.S. census reports. Holdings: 4000 books; 6 drawers of microfiche. Services: Copying; Library open to the public for reference use only.

2607 ■ U.S. Bureau of the Census
Information Services Program
Chicago Regional Office - Census Data Resource Center
2255 Enterprise Dr., Ste. 5501   Ph: (312)353-9747
Westchester, IL 60154-5800   Fax: (312)353-9114
URL: http://www.census.gov

Contact: Stanley D. Moore, Reg.Dir.

Desc: Subject: U.S. census - population, housing, manufacturers, retail trade, agriculture, wholesaleservice trades. Holdings: 3500 books; 350 bound periodical volumes; 200 series; Census Bureau computer tape technical documentation; 1990 census tract maps; 1980 census tract maps for Chicago region. Services: Copying (limited); assistance with census data through telephone access services; free census data access and use workshops; consultations; center open to the public.

2608 ■ U.S. Bureau of the Census
Information Services Program
Dallas Regional Census Center - Library
8700 Stemmons Fwy., Ste. 300   Ph: (214)665-3050
Dallas, TX 75247   Fax: (214)655-3081
E-mail: Paula.K.Wright@ccmail.census.gov
URL: http://www.census.gov

Desc: Subject: U.S. census reports. Holdings: 3500 volumes; 1960, 1970, 1980, and 1990 census reports (hard copy and CD-ROM); Current Survey and Economic Census Reports. Services: Copying (limited); Library open to the public.

2609 ■ U.S. Bureau of the Census
Information Services Program
Detroit Regional Office - Information Center
1395 Brewery Park Blvd.   Ph: (313)259-1875
PO Box 33405   Fax: (313)259-5971
Detroit, MI 48232
URL: http://www.census.gov

Contact: Barbara Clayton, Info.Serv.Spec.

Desc: Subject: U.S. census reports. Holdings: 5000 volumes; federal and state publications. Services: Copying; center open to the public.

2610 ■ U.S. Bureau of the Census
Information Services Program
Kansas City Office - Library
II Gateway Center, Ste.600   Ph: (913)551-6711
400 State Ave.   Fax: (913)551-6789
Kansas City, KS 66101-2410
URL: http://www.census.gov

Contact: Henry L. Palacios, Reg.Dir.

Desc: Subject: U.S. census reports - population, demographics. Holdings: 1000 books; 800 bound periodical volumes; reports; archives; microfiche. Services: Copying; Library open to the public.

2611 ■ U.S. Bureau of the Census
Information Services Program
Los Angeles Regional Office - Library
15350 Sherman Way, Ste. 310   Ph: (818)904-6339
Van Nuys, CA 91406

Contact: Larry Hugg, Info.Spec.

Desc: Subject: U.S. census and survey reports - population, housing, economic, construction, agriculture, retail trade, manufactures, foreign trade. Holdings: Figures not available. Services: Library open to the public.

2612 ■ U.S. Bureau of the Census
Information Services Program
New York Regional Office - Library

26 Federal Plaza, Rm. 37-100   Ph: (212)264-4730
New York, NY 10278   Fax: (212)264-6549
E-mail: ny.isp@ccmail.census.gov
URL: http://www.census.gov

Contact: Fernando Armstrong, Asst.Reg.Dir.

Desc: Subject: U.S. census data reports. Holdings: 15,000 volumes; CD-ROMs. Services: SDI (limited); Library open to the public.

2613 ■ U.S. Bureau of the Census
Information Services Program
Philadelphia Regional Office - Reference Center

1601 Market St., 21st Fl.   Ph: (215)656-7580
Philadelphia, PA 19103-2395   Fax: (215)656-7575
URL: http://www.census.gov

Contact: David E. Kearney, Info.Svcs.Spec.

Desc: Subject: U.S. census reports. Holdings: Census publications; 1990 census for Delaware, Maryland, New Jersey, District of Columbia, and Pennsylvania on CD-ROM. Services: Data training activities; reference center open to the public.

2614 ■ U.S. Bureau of the Census
Information Services Program
Seattle Regional Office - Library

700 5th Ave., Ste. 5100   Ph: (206)533-5835
Seattle, WA 98104   Fax: (206)533-5857
E-mail: mcintosh@census.gov
URL: http://www.census.gov/ftp/pub/rosea/www/
   isp.html

Contact: Cam McIntosh

Desc: Subject: U.S. decennial census reports, economic and agricultural census reports, current population and economic reports. Holdings: 5000 documents; maps; CD-ROMs. Services: Copying; Library open to the public.

2615 ■ U.S. National Park Service
Effigy Mounds National Monument Library

151 Hwy 76   Ph: (319)873-3491
Harpers Ferry, IA 52146   Fax: (319)873-3743

Contact: Kate Miller, Supt.

Desc: Subject: Archeology, anthropology, ethnology, local history, natural sciences. Holdings: 2600 books. Services: Library open to the public for reference use only.

2616 ■ U.S. National Park Service
Gettysburg National Military Park
Cyclorama Center Library

97 Taneytown Rd.   Ph: (717)334-1124
Gettysburg, PA 17325   Fax: (717)334-1997
E-mail: scott_hartwig@NPS.gov
URL: http://www.nps.gov/gett/

Contact: D. Scott Hartwig

Desc: Subject: Battle of Gettysburg, Civil War, Lincoln, 19th century life, environment. Holdings: 5000 books; 25 VF drawers; 1700 maps and plans; 180 reels of microfilm. Services: Library open to the public by appointment.

2617 ■ U.S. National Park Service
Hubbell Trading Post - National Historic Site Library

PO Box 150   Ph: (520)755-3475
Ganado, AZ 86505
E-mail: mary_furney@nps.gov

Contact: Mary Furney

Desc: Subject: Navajo history and culture, trading posts, Southwestern history. Holdings: 550 books; 1500 microfiche. Services: Library open to the public by appointment.

2618 ■ U.S. National Park Service
Lyndon B. Johnson National Historical Park Library

Box 329/100 Ladybird Ln.   Ph: (830)868-7128
Johnson City, TX 78636   Fax: (830)868-7863

Contact: John T. Tiff, Hist.

Desc: Subject: Lyndon B. Johnson and his family, Texas hill country history, local natural history. Holdings: 3605 books; 750 slides; 20 VF drawers of pamphlets; artifacts; 125 reels of 35mm microfilm of historic newspapers. Services: Copying (limited); Library open to the public for reference use only for approved research.

2619 ■ U.S. National Park Service
Ocmulgee National Monument Library

1207 Emery Hwy.   Ph: (912)752-8257
Macon, GA 31217-4399   Fax: (912)752-8259

Contact: Sylvia Flowers, Cultural Rsrc.Spec.

Desc: Subject: American archeology, American ethnology, Native American studies. Holdings: 5000 books; 300 bound periodical volumes; 100 reports; 50 archival items Services: Copying; Library open to the public by appointment.

2620 ■ U.S. National Park Service
Statue of Liberty-Ellis Island Library

Statue of Liberty   Ph: (212)363-6307
   National Monument   Fax: (212)363-6302
Liberty Island
New York, NY 10004
URL: http://www.nps.gov/stli

Desc: Subject: Statue of Liberty and Ellis Island history, immigrationemigration, ethnic culture, National Park Service. Holdings: 4000 books; 7000 photographs; 2200 negatives; 17,000 slides; 3300 aperture cards; 185 microfiche; 100 reports; 400 manuscripts; 80 films; 3 VF drawers of research papers; 650 videotapes. Services: Interlibrary loan; copying; tape and photograph duplication; Library open to the public by appointment.

2621 ■ U.S. Navy
Naval Historical Center
Operational Archives Branch

Washington Navy Yard   Ph: (202)433-7164
901 M St., SE   Fax: (202)433-2833
Washington, DC 20374-5060
URL: http://www.history.navy.mil

Contact: Bernard F. Cavalcante, Br.Hd.

Desc: Subject: U.S. Naval history, naval operations, naval archives, naval biography. Holdings: 10,000 feet of records and documents, including 500 feet of action and operational reports, 1946-1953; 150 feet of naval command war diaries, 1946-1953; 570 feet of miscellaneous records and publications, 1931-1973. Services: Copying (limited); reading room open to the public.

2622 ■ U.S. Navy
Naval Institute
History, Reference & Preservation Library

    Ph: (410)295-1023
rs>Annapolis, MD 21402   Fax: (410)269-7940

E-mail: dstitzel@usni.org
URL: http://www.usni.org

Contact: Dawn Stitzel

Desc: Subject: U.S. and foreign Navy photographs - ships, aircraft, personalities, weapons; naval biography; Coast Guard biography; naval aviation; American Revolution; Civil War; World War I; World War II; Korean War; Vietnam War; Desert Storm. Holdings: 5500 books; 200 bound volumes containing 90,000 pages of transcripts; 450,000 U.S. and foreign naval and maritime photographs; 390 oral history materials; more than 100 years of bound volumes of Proceedings and Naval History magazines. Services: Library open to the public.

2623 ■ U.S. Presidential Libraries
John F. Kennedy Library

Columbia Point   Ph: (617)929-4500
Boston, MA 02125   Fax: (617)929-4538
E-mail: library@kennedy.nara.gov
URL: http://www.cs.umb.edu/jfklibrary

Contact: Bradley S. Gerratt

Desc: Subject: John F. Kennedy and his administration, mid-20th century American politics and government. Holdings: 35,000 volumes; 34 million manuscript pages; 2.2 million pages of records of the Democratic National Committee; 500,000 pages of collections of personal papers; 40,000 pages of oral history interviews; 12,500 museum objects; 2500 reels of records and papers; 150,000 photographs; 5400 hours of sound recordings; 6.5 million feet of motion picture film. Services: Interlibrary loan; copying; Library open to the public.

2624 ■ U.S. Presidential Libraries
Lyndon Baines Johnson Library and Museum

2313 Red River St.   Ph: (512)916-5137
Austin, TX 78705   Fax: (512)916-5171
E-mail: library@johnson.nara.gov
URL: http://www.lbjlib.utexas.edu

Contact: Harry J. Middleton, Dir.

Desc: Subject: Lyndon B. Johnson - career, administration, family, papers; U.S. Presidency; American political, social, and economic history, 1937 to present. Holdings: 17,072 books; 5138 unbound periodicals; 45 million archives-manuscript pages; 622,136 photographs; 8395 video recordings; 13,803 sound recordings; 37,101 museum items; 824,777 feet of motion picture film; 14 VF drawers of periodical articles; 5 VF drawers of papers and dissertations; 9 VF drawers of newspaper clippings. Services: Interlibrary loan (limited); copying; Library open to the public.

2625 ■ Universite Laval
Bibliotheque Generale

Cite Universitaire   Ph: (418)656-2131
Quebec, PQ, Canada G1K 7P4   Fax: (418)656-3048
E-mail: alain.bourque@bibl.ulaval.ca
URL: http://www.bibl.ulaval.ca

Contact: Alain Bourque, Lib.Hd.

Desc: Subject: Humanities, art, law, social sciences, French Canadian and Quebec studies, French Canadian folklore, Quebec geography, French and French Canadian literature, 19th-century French musical press, philosophy of science; philosophy - Aristotelian, Thomist, and French modern. Holdings: 1.5 million books; 230,240 bound periodical volumes; 1,125,120 microfiche; 106,134 microfilm; 125,468 maps; 12,900 films & videotapes. Services: Interlibrary loan; copying; SDI; Library open to the public for reference use only.

2626 ■ Universite de Moncton
Centre d'etudes acadiennes

    Ph: (506)858-4085
rs>Moncton, NB, Canada E1A   Fax: (506)858-4530
   3E9

URL: http://www.umoncton.ca/etudeacadiennes/centre/cea.html

Contact: Maurice Basque, Dir.

Desc: Subject: Acadian history, genealogy, and folklore. Holdings: 12,300 books and pamphlets; 3240 reels of microfilm; 3307 feet of manuscripts; 3435 reels of magnetic tape of Acadian folk tales and songs. Services: Interlibrary loan (limited); copying; center open to the public.

2627 ▪ Universite de Montreal
Departement de Demographie
Centre de Documentation

C.P. 6128,   Ph: (514)343-6111
  Succ. "Centre-ville"   Fax: (514)343-2309
Montreal, PQ, Canada H3C 3J7
E-mail: frechetm@ere.umontreal.ca

Contact: Micheline Frechette, Doc.

Desc: Subject: Census, vital statistics, mortality, marriages, fertility, population theory and policy, migration, geographical distribution and ethnic groups, historical demography, aging, health, linguistic groups, demography of the Third World. Holdings: 5000 books; 3000 bound periodical volumes; 4200 reprints, dissertations, and unbound reports. Services: Interlibrary loan; copying; center open to the public.

2628 ▪ Universite Sainte-Anne
Archives du Centre acadien

Church Point, NS, Canada B0W 1M0
E-mail: Cacadien@ustanne.ednet.ns.ca
URL: http://www.shelburne.nscc.ns.ca/nsgna/arcca/index.html

Desc: Subject: Acadian life in Nova Scotia, Canadian history and genealogy, religious history. Holdings: 6000 volumes; 200 lin. ft. of documents; 5000 photographs; church records. Services: Archives open to the public for 5 daily fee or 25 Annual fee.

2629 ▪ University of Alabama
William Stanley Hoole Special Collections
Library

Box 870266   Ph: (205)348-0500
Tuscaloosa, AL 35487-0266   Fax: (205)348-1699
E-mail: egarriso@bama.ua.edu
URL: http://www.lib.ua.edu/hoole

Contact: Ellen Garrison, Cur.

Desc: Subject: Alabamiana, travels in the South East, southern Americana, early imprints, state documents. Holdings: 78,144 books; 12,500 theses, dissertations, and pamphlets, 10,000 phono recordings, 5000 pieces of sheet music. Services: Copying; Library open to the public.

2630 ▪ University of Alberta
Bibliotheque Saint-Jean

8406 Rue Marie-Anne   Ph: (403)465-8711
  Gaboury (91e)   Fax: (403)468-2550
Edmonton, AB, Canada T6C
  4G9
E-mail: Juliette.Henley@ualberta.ca

Contact: Juliette J. Henley, Hd.Libn.

Desc: Subject: French-Canadian and Western Canadian history, ethnology, French and French-Canadian literature, French language resources in education, arts, humanities, social sciences, and science. Holdings: 180,000 items (mainly in French); 5200 bound periodical volumes; 24,000 microforms; 6000 audiovisuals. Services: Interlibrary loan; Library open to the public.

2631 ▪ University of Arkansas at Little Rock
Institute for Economic Advancement (IEA)
Research Library

2801 S. University, Rm 541   Ph: (501)569-8521
Little Rock, AR 72204   Fax: (501)569-8555

E-mail: dabullwinkle@ualr.edu
URL: http://www.aiea.ualr.edu

Contact: Davis A. Bullwinkle, Res.Libn.

Desc: Subject: Business and economics, industrial development, labor, demographics, government and taxes, census, banking, agriculture, labor law, management, education, energy, transportation, tourism. Holdings: 6500 books; census data for U.S. and Arkansas, 1900 to present. Services: Copying; Library open to the public for reference use only.

2632 ▪ University of Arkansas at Pine Bluff
John Brown Watson Memorial Library
Learning and Instructional Resources Centers

1200 N. University Dr.   Ph: (870)543-8411
PO Box 4930   Fax: (870)543-8440
Pine Bluff, AR 71611

Contact: E.J. Fontenette, Libn.

Desc: Subject: History and biography, emigration, sociology, literature, slavery and emancipation, education, music, religion, economics. Holdings: 214,977 volumes (microform and bound periodicals). Services: Interlibrary loan; copying; Library open to the public.

2633 ▪ University of California, Berkeley
Ethnic Studies Library

30 Stephens Hall, No. 2360   Ph: (510)643-1234
Berkeley, CA 94720-2360   Fax: (510)643-8433
E-mail: csl@library.berkeley.edu
URL: http://cslibrary.berkeley.edu

Contact: Lillian Castillo-Speed, Lib.Coord., Chicano Col l.Spec.

Desc: Subject: Chicano, Mexican American, Spanish speakingsurname people in U.S.; Raza; farmworkers; bilingual and biculturalgroups; Native Americans; Asians in the U.S., past and present. Holdings: 68,579 volumes; 150 bound periodical volumes; 30,000 other cataloged items; 1500 microforms; 550 audiotapes, 206 videotapes, 31 16mm films; 5000 slides; 20 maps; 1000 noncurrent journal titles; 150 linear feet of archives, 150 phonograph records. Services: Interlibrary loan; Library open to the public.

2634 ▪ University of California, Davis
Michael and Margaret B. Harrison Western
Research Center

Department of   Ph: (530)752-1621
  Special Collections   Fax: (530)752-3148
Shields Library
Davis, CA 95616

Contact: John Skarstad, Hd., Spec.Coll.

Desc: Subject: History and development of the trans-Mississippi West, mid-19th century to present; American Indians; ethnic studies; military, local, and economic history; sociology; folklore; exploration and travel; geography; religious studies, especially the Catholic and Mormon churches; literature; art and architecture; history of printing. Holdings: 20,710 volumes. Services: Center open to the public by appointment only.

2635 ▪ University of California, Irvine
Main Library
Southeast Asian Archive

Rm. 360   Ph: (949)824-4968
PO Box 19557   Fax: (949)824-5740
Irvine, CA 92623-9557
E-mail: afrank@uci.edu
URL: http://www.lib.uci.edu/rrsc/sasian.html

Contact: Anne Frank, Lib.Hd.

Desc: Subject: Post-1975 exodus and resettlement of refugees and immigrants from Cambodia, Laos, Vietnam;

Cambodian, Hmong, Laotian, and Vietnamese culture and history; Southeast Asians in Orange County and Southern California. Holdings: 1955 books and reports; 288 dissertations and theses; 48 videocassettes; 12 audiocassettes; 609 periodical titles; newspaper clippings; journal articles; conference papers; refugee orientation materials; ephemera. Services: Interlibrary loan; copying; Library open to the public.

2636 ▪ University of California, Los Angeles
Chicano Studies Research Library

58 Haines Hall, Box 951380   Ph: (310)206-6052
Los Angeles, CA 90095-1380
URL: http://www.sscnet.ucla.edu/csrc/library

Contact: Judith Herschman, Actg. Chicano Stud.Libn.

Desc: Subject: Immigration, labor, higher education, school desegregation, Raza women, Chicano literature, U.S.-Mexico relations. Holdings: 15,000 books; 174 bound periodical volumes; 254 manuscripts; 1850 theses and dissertations; 114 16mm films and videotapes; 10,464 clippings and pamphlets; 100 student papers; 2231 reels of microfilm; 136 posters; 3 multimedia kits; 319 pictorial items; 135 sound recordings; 229 videocassettes; 707 audiotapes; 8 filmstrips; 830 volumes of newspapers; 22 realia; 34 maps; 342 slides. Services: Copying; Library open to the public for reference use only.

2637 ▪ University of Central Arkansas
Torreyson Library
Archives & Special Collections

                                 Ph: (501)450-3418
Conway, AR 72035   Fax: (501)450-5208
E-mail: jimmyb@mail.uca.edu
URL: http://Library.uca.edu

Contact: Jimmy Bryant, Dir., Archv.

Desc: Subject: Arkansas - history, culture, literature, geography. Holdings: 15,000 books; 150 manuscripts; 25,000 photographic images; 5200 pamphlets; 1200 maps. Services: Copying; topical bibliographies available for a fee; collections open to the public with restrictions.

2638 ▪ University College of Cape Breton
Beaton Institute
Eachdraidh Archives

Box 5300   Ph: (902)563-1329
Sydney, NS, Canada B1P 6L2   Fax: (902)562-8899
E-mail: rmorgan@caper2.uccb.ns.ca
URL: http://www.uccb.ns.ca

Contact: Dr. R.J. Morgan, Dir.

Desc: Subject: Cape Breton Island - history, labor history, Gaelic literature, folklore, political history, industrial history; traditional Scottish music of Cape Breton Island; genealogy. Holdings: 5000 books; 200 bound periodical volumes; 300 unbound reports; 50,000 photographs; 1000 maps; 200 meters of manuscripts; 5 VF drawers of clippings; 600 reels of microfilm; 200 large scrapbooks; 3500 tapes; 600 slides; 100 videotapes. Services: Copying; archives open to the public.

2639 ▪ University of Florida
Samuel Proctor Oral History Program
Library

104 Anderson Hall   Ph: (352)392-7168
PO Box 115215   Fax: (352)846-1983
Gainesville, FL 32611-5215
E-mail: jpleasan@history.ufl.edu
URL: http://www.clas.ufl.edu/history/oral

Contact: Dr. Julian M. Pleasants

Desc: Subject: Southern history, southeastern Indians, political leaders, Florida newspapers, Florida history. Holdings: 3200 cassette interviews. Services: Library open to the public for reference use only.

2640 ▪ University of Hawaii at Manoa
Archives
2550 The Mall   Ph: (808)956-8264
Honolulu, HI 96822
URL: http://www2/hawaii/edu/speccoll/arch/

Desc: Subject: Hawaii - ethnic relations, labor history, World War II, war records; British Navy history; Fulbright Foundation; Joseph Grew (ambassador to Japan, 1941); Socialist movements in the U.S. (20th century), United States Advisory Commission on International Education and Cultural Affairs; William Allen White. Holdings: Books; manuscripts; photographs; periodicals; audiovisuals; personal papers. Services: Library open to the public by appointment.

2641 ▪ University of Illinois
Illinois Historical Survey
346 Main Library   Ph: (217)333-1777
1408 W. Gregory Dr.   Fax: (217)333-2214
Urbana, IL 61801

Contact: John Hoffmann, Libn.

Desc: Subject: Illinois history. Holdings: 14,000 volumes; 1750 maps; 1000 linear feet of archives and manuscripts; 700 reels of microfilm of manuscripts; 3500 VF items. Services: Copying; Library open to the public for reference and research only.

2642 ▪ University of Kansas
Government Documents and Map Library
6001 Malott Hall   Ph: (785)864-4662
Lawrence, KS 66045-2800   Fax: (785)864-5154
E-mail: dkoepp@ukans.edu
URL: http://kuhttp.cc.ukans.edu/cwis/units/kulib/docs/ govdocs.html

Contact: Donna Koepp, Doc.Libn.

Desc: Subject: Census, U.S. legislative history, British parliamentary history. Holdings: 1,060,370 documents; 10,310 microforms. Services: Interlibrary loan; copying; collection open to the public.

2643 ▪ University of Kansas
Institute for Public Policy and Business Research
607 Blake Hall   Ph: (913)864-3701
Lawrence, KS 66045-2960   Fax: (913)864-3683
E-mail: t-helyar@ukans.edu
URL: http://www.ukans.edu/cwis/units/ippbr

Contact: Thelma Helyar, Libn.

Desc: Subject: Survey research; economic indicators; economic, community, and rural development; census data; data processing; econometric models; demographics; statistics; business; forecasting. Holdings: 8000 volumes. Services: Interlibrary loan; copying; institute open to the public.

2644 ▪ University of Louisville
University Archives and Records Center
Oral History Center
Ekstrom Library   Ph: (502)852-6674
Louisville, KY 40292   Fax: (502)852-6673
E-mail: ARCHIVES@louisville.edu
URL: http://www.louisville.edu/library/uarc

Contact: William J. Morison, Dir.Univ.Archv.

Desc: Subject: History of Louisville, Kentucky, including the Louisville Orchestra; prominent citizens; university history; the Louisville and Nashville Railroad; photography; Jewish history; local government; African American history; Kentucky distilling industry; Bernheim Forest. Holdings: 1300 interviews. Services: Copying; copies of tapes, finding aids, and selected transcripts available; center open to the public.

2645 ▪ University of Maine
Maine Folklife Center
Dept. of Anthropology   Ph: (207)581-1891
5773 S. Stevens Hall   Fax: (207)581-1823
Orono, ME 04469-5773
E-mail: folklife@maine.edu
URL: http://www.umaine.edu/folklife

Contact: Edward D. Ives, Dir.

Desc: Subject: Folklore, oral history. Holdings: 2566 cataloged accessions; 8000 photographs of lumbering and other aspects of folklife; 2500 slides; 400 LP recordings; 150 videotapes. Services: Copying; archives open to the public.

2646 ▪ University of Massachusetts at Boston, Harbor Campus
Joseph P. Healey Library - Dept. of Archives and Special Collections
     Ph: (617)287-5944
rs>Boston, MA 02125   Fax: (617)287-5950
E-mail: elizabeth@delphinus.lib.umb.edu
URL: http://www.lib.umb.edu

Contact: Sharon Bostick, Dir.

Desc: Subject: Local urban history, peace and social protest, social welfare institutions, Dorchester local history, community action, Vietnam War. Holdings: 6000 books; 200 bound periodical volumes; 3000 feet of archival material. Services: Copying; Library open to the public.

2647 ▪ University of Massachusetts at Lowell
Center for Lowell History
40 French St.   Ph: (508)934-4997
Lowell, MA 01852   Fax: (978)934-4995
E-mail: mayo@libvax.uml.edu
URL: http://www.libvax.uml.edu/

Contact: Martha Mayo, Dir.

Desc: Subject: Middlesex Canal; Lowell, Massachusetts; hydraulics; women in industry; textile manufacturing; immigrants; Warren H. Manning. Holdings: 28,000 volumes; records and manscripts; 6000 maps and plans; 1000 hours of oral histories; 40,000 photographs; 25 paintings; 2000 reels of microfilm. Services: Copying; photographic reproduction; collections open to the public.

2648 ▪ University of Memphis
Chucalissa Museum Library
1987 Indian Village Dr.   Ph: (901)785-3160
Memphis, TN 38109   Fax: (901)785-0519
URL: http://msuvx2.memphis.edu/anthropology/ cnuc.html

Desc: Subject: Eastern North American archeology and ethnology; museum studies; geology of southeastern United States. Holdings: 2000 books. Services: Library open to the public for reference use only.

2649 ▪ University of Memphis
Libraries
Special Collections Department
Campus Box 526500   Ph: (901)678-2210
Memphis, TN 38152-6500
URL: http://www.lib.memphis.edu

Contact: Ed Frank, Cur.

Desc: Subject: Lower Mississippi Valley - history, culture, literature. Holdings: 36,078 volumes; 8.7 million manuscript items, including photographs and sheet music; 830 maps; 3271 oral histories on audiotape; 507 videotapes; 228 reels of 16mm film; 86 records. Services: Copying; collections open to the public.

2650 ▪ University of Minnesota
Immigration History Research Center
826 Berry St.   Ph: (612)627-4208
St. Paul, MN 55114   Fax: (612)627-4190
E-mail: wurlx001@tc.umn.edu
URL: http://www.umn.edu/ihrc

Contact: Joel Wurl, Cur.

Desc: Subject: East, Central, and South European and Near Eastern immigration and ethnic groups in the United States, 1880 to present, with emphasis on Finns, Italians, and Slavic peoples; ethnic labor and political movements; ethnic churches, presses, and fraternal organizations; resettlement of refugees after World War II; immigrant welfare agencies; Ukraine and Ukrainians. Holdings: 46,800 volumes, including 3000 serial titles and files of 900 newspapers; 1685 AV programs; 65 maps; 5000 feet of manuscripts; 5403 microforms. Services: Interlibrary loan (microfilm only); copying (limited); collection open for research upon application.

2651 ▪ University of Nebraska--Lincoln
University Archives and Special Collections
308 Love Library   Ph: (402)472-2531
Lincoln, NE 68588-0410   Fax: (402)472-5131
E-mail: michelef@unllib.unl.edu
URL: http://iris.unl.edu

Contact: Michele Fagan

Desc: Subject: Nebraskana, World Wars I and II, ethnicity, French Revolution, railroads, American folklore, university archives. Holdings: 44,000 books; 1000 bound periodical volumes; 5000 cubic feet of university archives; 20,000 volumes of university theses and dissertations; 20 linear feet of manuscripts; 20 linear feet of glass negative plates and prints. Services: Copying; collections open to the public.

2652 ▪ University of New Mexico
Bureau of Business & Economic Research Data Bank
1920 Lomas Blvd., N.E.   Ph: (505)277-6626
Albuquerque, NM 87131-6021   Fax: (505)277-2773
URL: http://www.unm.edu/bber

Contact: Kevin Kargacin, Sr. Economist

Desc: Subject: New Mexico - economics, income, employment, demographics, census. Holdings: 14,000 cataloged publications. Services: Copying; mail-out and fax serivce; census computer tape processing; bureau open to the public.

2653 ▪ University of New Mexico
Center for Southwest Research
General Library   Ph: (505)277-8726
Albuquerque, NM 87131   Fax: (505)277-6019
E-mail: cswrref@unm.edu
URL: http://www.unm.edu/cswrref

Contact: Marilyn Fletcher, Spec.Coll.

Desc: Subject: History of the American West, New Mexico history and culture, history and culture of Mexico and Latin America, Indians of the Southwest, southwestern architectural history, Hispanic and Native American studies. Holdings: 38,500 volumes; 2100 tape recordings; 3150 linear feet of manuscript material; 80,000 photographs; 250 videocassettes. Services: Copying.

2654 ▪ University of North Dakota
Elwyn B. Robinson Department of Special Collections
Chester Fritz Library   Ph: (701)777-4625
Box 9000   Fax: (701)777-3319
Grand Forks, ND 58202-9000
E-mail: slater@plains.nodak.edu

URL: http://www.und.nodak.edu/dept/library/index.html

Contact: Sandra Slater, Hd., Archv. & Spec.Coll.

Desc: Subject: History - North and South Dakota, Northern Great Plains, Plains Indian, environmental, agrarian radicalism; Nonpartisan League (North Dakota); genealogy; oral history; ethnic heritage and family history (North Dakota); Norwegian local history. Holdings: 37,673 books; 14,914 linear feet of manuscript material; 4325 reels of microfilm; 49,511 photographs; 4234 AV items; 7440 theses and dissertations. Services: Copying; department open to the public for reference use only.

2655 ■ University of North Texas Libraries
Oral History Program
University Sta., Box 311214 Ph: (940)565-2549
Denton, TX 76203 Fax: (940)565-2599
E-mail: ii50@jove.acs.unt.edu
URL: http://www.library.unt.edu/

Contact: Dr. Ronald E. Marcello, Dir.

Desc: Subject: World War II, New Deal, integration, business history, institutional history, Holocaust; Texas political history, Vietnam War. Holdings: 1400 transcripts and oral history tapes. Services: Copying; program open to the public with restrictions.

2656 ■ University of Oklahoma
Western History Collections
630 Parrington Oval, Rm. 452 Ph: (405)325-3641
Norman, OK 73019 Fax: (405)325-2943
URL: http://www.ou.edu/libraries/

Contact: Donald L. DeWitt, Cur.

Desc: Subject: American Indian, Oklahoma, American Southwest, American Trans-Mississippi West, recent U.S. history. Holdings: 65,000 books; 13,000 linear feet of manuscripts; 250,000 items in photographic archives; 20,000 microforms; 3600 maps; 1400 transcripts, tapes, and discs of oral history; 5000 pamphlets and documents; 1500 linear feet of University of Oklahoma archives; newspapers, posters, broadsides. Services: Copying (limited); collections open to the public.

2657 ■ University of Pennsylvania
Population Studies Center
Demography Library
3718 Locust Walk Ph: (215)898-5375
Philadelphia, PA 19104-6298 Fax: (215)898-2124
E-mail: lnewman@pop.upenn.edu
URL: http://www.pop.upenn.edu/library/demlib.html

Contact: Lisa A. Newman, Libn.

Desc: Subject: Foreign and United States census, population organizations, demographic surveys, statistics. Holdings: 28,000 books; 750 bound periodical volumes; reprints; dissertations. Services: Interlibrary loan; Library not open to the public but special requests will be taken from related interest institutions.

2658 ■ University of Rhode Island
Rhode Island Oral History Collection
Library - Special Collections Ph: (401)874-2594
Kingston, RI 02881 Fax: (401)874-4608
URL: http://www.library.uri.edu

Contact: David C. Maslyn, Hd., Spec.Coll.

Desc: Subject: Millworkers of Rhode Island and their social milieu, 1900 to present; Narragansett Indians; university history; local Franco-American community; state jewelry industry; Rhode Island's Islands (Block, Prudence, Conanicut); Galilee fisherman; immigrants; women's suffrage; town government (Yankee ingenuity). Holdings: 400

tapes of interviews; 70 tapes and transcripts of interviews on 1938 hurricane; typescripts of taped interviews of mill workers. Services: Collection open to the public.

2659 ■ University of Rochester
Government Documents and Microtext Center
Rush Rhees Library Ph: (716)275-4484
Wilson Blvd. Fax: (716)473-1906
Rochester, NY 14627-0055
E-mail: chansen@rcl.lib.rochester.edu
URL: http://rodent.lib.rochester.edu/doc

Contact: Catherine Hansen, Libn.

Desc: Subject: U.S. Congress, U.S. Bureau of the Census, New York State, women's studies, black studies, North American Indians, American and British literature. Holdings: 590,000 government documents in paper; 4 million microform - government documents and other; CD-ROMs. Services: Interlibrary loan; copying; Center open to the public.

2660 ■ University of South Florida at Saint Petersburg
Nelson Poynter Memorial Library
Special Collections
140 7th Ave. S. Ph: (727)553-3404
St. Petersburg, FL 33701 Fax: (727)553-1196
E-mail: arsenaul@nelson.usf.edu

Contact: F. Landon Greaves, Lib.Dir.

Desc: Subject: Marine science, local and regional history, oral history, journalism, campus archives, ethics. Holdings: 3650 books; 150 bound periodical volumes, 100 reports; 500 linear feet of archival material; 880 audiovisual materials. Services: Copying; Library open to the public.

2661 ■ University of Southern California
Population Research Laboratory
Library
University Park, 730 Ph: (213)740 6265
  Childs Way Fax: (213)740-6003
Los Angeles, CA 90089-0377
E-mail: Heer@usc.edu
URL: http://www.usc.edu/dept/pop/

Contact: Prof. David M. Heer, Dir.

Desc: Subject: Population, demography, census, human ecology, urban sociology. Holdings: 6000 U.S. Bureau of Census reports, vital statistics reports, United Nations reports, maps, computer tapes, journals, books, reprints, dissertations, newsletters, pamphlets, bibliographies. Services: Library open to the public upon request.

2662 ■ University of Southern Mississippi
McCain Library and Archives
Box 5148 Ph: (601)266-4345
Hattiesburg, MS 39406-5148 Fax: (601)266-6269
E-mail: Toby.Graham@usm.edu
URL: http://www.lib.usm.edu/

Contact: Kay L. Wall, Dir.

Desc: Subject: Mississippiana, genealogy, Civil War, Confederate States of America, children's literature, British and American literary criticism, political cartoons. Holdings: 73,000 volumes; 7500 linear feet of manuscripts and illustrations. Services: Copying (limited); Library open to the public for reference use only.

2663 ■ University of Southwestern Louisiana
Jefferson Caffery Louisiana Room
Southwestern Archives and Manuscripts
Collection
Dupre Library Ph: (318)482-6031
302 E. St. Mary Blvd. Fax: (318)482-5841
Lafayette, LA 70503

E-mail: BTurner@ucs.usl.edu
URL: http://www.usl.edu/Departments/Library/

Contact: Dr. I. Bruce Turner, Hd., Archv. & Spec.Coll.

Desc: Subject: Cajun and Creole culture; history - state, local, university; horticulture; Louisiana politics; agriculture; literature; petroleum; genealogy. Holdings: 25,000 volumes; 36 VF drawers of clippings and pamphlets; 1900 theses; 250 manuscript collections (2000 linear feet); 1000 audiotapes; microforms. Services: Copying; microfilming; collection open to the public.

2664 ■ University of Texas at Austin
Center for American History
SRH 2.101 Ph: (512)495-4515
Austin, TX 78712 Fax: (512)495-4532
URL: http://www.lib.utexas.edu/Libs/CAH/cah.html

Contact: Dr. Don E. Carleton, Dir.

Desc: Subject: Texas history, literature, and folklore; University of Texas publications and history; Southern and Western history; select U.S. history topics. Holdings: 154,801 volumes; 3000 linear feet of university records; 60,000 linear feet of manuscripts and archives; 36,677 maps; 3850 titles of historic Texas and Southern newspapers; 1.2 million photographs; 48,000 slides; 100 VF drawers of clippings; 1525 scrapbooks; 24,815 reels of microfilm; 1582 microfiche; 4293 tapes of oral recordings; Sound Archives (45,896 audiocasettes, phonograph records, audiotapes). Services: Interlibrary loan (copies only); copying; center open to the public.

2665 ■ University of Texas at El Paso
Institute of Oral History
Liberal Arts 334 Ph: (915)747 7052
El Paso, TX 79968 Fax: (915)747-5905

Desc: Subject: History - El Paso and Ciudad Juarez, Chihuahua, University of Texas, El Paso; Mexican Americans; the Border, Mexican Revolution; Border Labor History. Holdings: 905 interviews. Services: Institute not open to the public.

2666 ■ University of Texas at El Paso
Library
C.L. Sonnichsen Special Collections Department
  Ph: (915)747-5697
rs>El Paso, TX 79968-0582 Fax: (915)747-5327
E-mail: crivers@utep.edu/library/special.html

Contact: Claudia Rivers

Desc: Subject: Southwestern U.S., Northern Mexico, U.S.-Mexico border, Chicano studies, military, Judaica, printing arts. Holdings: 53,500 books. Services: Copying; collections open to the public.

2667 ■ University of Virginia
Special Collections Department
University of Virginia Library Ph: (804)924-3025
Charlottesville, VA 22903-2498 Fax: (804)924-3143
E-mail: mssbks@virginia.edu
URL: http://www.lib.virginia.edu/speccol

Contact: Michael Plunkett, Dir.

Desc: Subject: American history and literature; Virginia history and literature. Holdings: 227,000 books; 8056 reels of microfilm; 105 drawers of maps; 65 oversized boxes of broadsides; 120,000 photographs and prints; 981 phonodiscs; 727 reel-to-reel tapes; 65 cassette tapes; 349 motion picture films; 176 videotapes; 7966 microfiche; 11.6 million cataloged manuscript and archival items. Services: Interlibrary loan (limited); copying; Library open to the public.

2668 ■ University of Washington
Center for Studies in Demography and Ecology
Library
109 Savery Hall
Box 353340
Seattle, WA 98195
Ph: (206)543-9525
Fax: (206)543-2516
E-mail: nmorrow@u.washington.edu

Contact: Nancy Morrow, CSDE Libn.

Desc: Subject: Census, vital statistics, demography, ecology, Southeast Asia. Holdings: 4000 books; 4400 government documents; 2200 other publications and papers. Services: Library open to the public.

2669 ■ University of Wisconsin--Eau Claire
Special Collections
Area Research Center, University Archives,
Rare Books
McIntyre Library
Eau Claire, WI 54702
Ph: (715)836-2739
Fax: (715)836-2949
E-mail: library.archives@uwec.edu
URL: http://www.uwec.edu/Admin/Library/
    speccoll.html

Contact: Lawrence D. Lynch, Archv.

Desc: Subject: History of western Wisconsin, lumbering history, genealogy, university history. Holdings: 1605 linear feet and 854 reels of microfilm of historical manuscripts and local public records; 417 maps and atlases; 1583 linear feet and 883 reels of microfilm of university records; 4482 photographic prints; 169,400 university-related negative frames. Services: Copying; center open to the public for reference use only.

2670 ■ University of Wisconsin--Green Bay
Area Research Center
2420 Nicolet Dr.
Green Bay, WI 54311-7001
Ph: (920)465-2539
E-mail: speccoll@gbms01.uwgb.edu

Contact: Debra Anderson, Archv.

Desc: Subject: Local history, genealogy, Belgian Americans. Holdings: 7900 books; 7000 linear feet of local governmental records and private papers; University of Wisconsin - Green Bay, University Archives. Services: Interlibrary loan; copying; center open to the public; answers telephone, email, and mail reference questions on a limited basis.

2671 ■ University of Wisconsin--Madison
Center for Demography
Library
4471 Social Science Bldg.
1180 Observatory Dr.
Madison, WI 53706
Ph: (608)263-6372
Fax: (608)262-8400
E-mail: brand@ssc.wisc.edu
URL: http://www.ssc.wisc.edu/cde/library

Contact: Wendy Brand, Spec.Libn.

Desc: Subject: Demography. Holdings: 12,000 books; U.S. census reports; international population censuses, 1945-1967 (microfilm); reprints; documents. Services: Library open to the public with restrictions.

2672 ■ University of Wisconsin--Madison
Data and Program Library Service
3308 Social Science Bldg.
Madison, WI 53706
Ph: (608)262-7962
Fax: (608)262-9711
E-mail: DPLS@DPLS.DACC.WISC.EDU
URL: http://dpls.dacc.wisc.edu/archive.html

Contact: Cindy Severt, Hd.

Desc: Subject: Political science, sociology, economics, history, censusdemography. Holdings: 300 books; 5000 data files; 80 bound periodical volumes; 3000 codebooks for data; 70 guides to data archival holdings; 3000 electronic media materials.

2673 ■ University of Wisconsin--Madison
Department of Rural Sociology
Applied Population Laboratory - Reference
Service
1450 Linden Dr.
308 Agriculture Hall
Madison, WI 53706
Ph: (608)262-1515
Fax: (608)262-6022
URL: http://www.ssc.wisc.edu/poplab

Contact: David Mohn

Desc: Subject: Demographic material; decennial census, economic census, and census material. Holdings: 2000 books; 24 VF drawers of pamphlets. Services: Copying; Library open to the public by appointment.

2674 ■ University of Wisconsin--Oshkosh
Information Technology Division - Polk Library
Special Collections
800 Algoma Blvd.
Oshkosh, WI 54901
Ph: (920)424-3334
Fax: (920)424-7338
E-mail: watkins@uwosh.edu
URL: http://www.uwosh.edu/departments/llr/

Contact: Dr. John Berens, Asst. Vice Chancellor, Tech.

Desc: Subject: Local history, county records, manuscripts. Holdings: Government documents (640,890 paper and 921,826 microfiche); 31,314 maps; 2240 linear feet of manuscripts, archives, and closed stack books. Services: Interlibrary loan; copying; collections open to the public for reference use only.

2675 ■ University of Wisconsin--Parkside
University Archives and Area Research Center
900 Wood Rd., Box 2000
Kenosha, WI 53141-2000
Ph: (414)595-2411
Fax: (414)595-2545
URL: http://www.uwp.edu/info-services/library

Contact: Ellen J. Pedraza, Archv.

Desc: Subject: History - local, state, university; genealogy. Holdings: 1323 titles; 3834 linear feet of manuscripts and archives; 1178 reels of microfilm of censuses. Services: Copying; archives open to the public.

2676 ■ University of Wisconsin--Platteville
Karrmann Library
Southwest Wisconsin Room
1 University Plaza
Platteville, WI 53818
Ph: (608)342-1719
Fax: (608)342-1645
E-mail: freymiller@uwplatt.edu
URL: http://vms.www.uwplatt.edu/library/

Contact: Paul V. Moriarty, Interim Asst., Info.Svcs.

Desc: Subject: History - local, state, university; genealogy; mining. Holdings: 2803 linear feet of unbound reports, manuscripts, and county documents; 32,174 photographs, plus 7.8 linear feet unprocessed; 2352 microresources; 730 magnetic tapes; 415 filmsvideotapes (archives); 171 maps; 964 blueprints; 192 museum objects. Services: Interlibrary loan; copying; collections open to the public.

2677 ■ University of Wisconsin--River Falls
Area Research Center
Chalmer Davee Library
410 S. 3rd St.
River Falls, WI 54022
Ph: (715)425-3567
E-mail: susan.g.watson@uwrf.edu

Contact: Susan Ginter Watson, Dir.

Desc: Subject: History of northwestern Wisconsin (Pierce, Polk, St. Croix, and Burnett Counties); Civil War history; genealogy; university history. Holdings: 2500 books; 2000 linear feet of manuscript collections; 2600 reels of microfilm; 800 pamphlets; 10,000 photographs; maps; newspaper collection. Services: Interlibrary loan; copying; center open to the public for reference use only.

2678 ■ Upland Public Library
Local History Collection
450 N. Euclid Ave.
Upland, CA 91786
Ph: (909)931-4200
URL: http://uplandpl.lib.ca.us/

Desc: Subject: Upland, California history. Holdings: Books; oral history tapes; newspaper articles; photographs; slides.

2679 ■ Upper Snake River Valley Historical
Society
Library
51 North Center
Box 244
Rexburg, ID 83440
Ph: (208)356-9101

Contact: Cleo Johnson, Libn.

Desc: Subject: Idaho history. Holdings: 3000 books; 650 tapes; 25 videotapes; 15 maps. Services: Copying; Library open to the public by appointment.

2680 ■ USCCCN Masters of Philanthropy
Library
Box 863
Millburn, NJ 07041
Ph: (732)549-2599
Fax: (732)549-2599
E-mail: uscccn@juno.com

Contact: Dr. A. Herbert Peterson, Pres.

Desc: Subject: Philanthropy, Satanism, the occult, Afro-Carribean studies, cults and intervention, business. Holdings: 3000 books; continuously updated reports, publications, videos, and training manuals (intervention and prevention guides). Services: Library open to the public by appointment.

2681 ■ Utah History
Information Center
300 Rio Grande
Salt Lake City, UT 84101-1182
Ph: (801)533-3535
Fax: (801)533-3504
E-mail: cehistry.uhic@email.state.ut.us
URL: http://www.history.utah.org

Desc: Subject: History - Utah, Mormon, Western, Indian. Holdings: 25,000 books; 50,000 bound periodical volumes; 500,000 photographs; 22,000 pamphlets; 33,000 maps; 1500 oral history tapes; 3500 linear feet of manuscripts; 6000 reels of microfilm; 160 feet of clippings files; 5500 museum objects. Services: Copying; Library open to the public.

2682 ■ Uxbridge-Scott Museum
Archives & Research Center
Box 1301
Uxbridge, ON, Canada L9P 1N5
Ph: (905)852-5854
E-mail: museum@uxbridge.com

Desc: Subject: Uxbridge-Scott history, genealogy, and culture. Holdings: Birth and death records; census records; deeds; maps; marriage records; photographs; scrapbooks. Services: Library open to the public.

2683 ■ Van Alstyne Public Library
Van Alstyne Genealogy Society
117 N. Waco
PO Box 629
Van Alstyne, TX 75495
Ph: (903)482-5991
E-mail: vanalstynepl@texoma.net
URL: http://www.texoma.net/vanalstynepl/
    welcome.html

Contact: Juanita Hazelton, Dir.

Desc: Subject: Van Alstyne area genealogy and history. Holdings: Books; audiocassettes; videotapes; local family files; obituary files; local history files; family histories; cemetery records. Services: Interlibrary loan; copying; Library open to the public.

2684 ■ Van Buren County Historical Society
Van Buren Historical Library
PO Box 452   Ph: (616)621-2188
Hartford, MI 49057

Contact: Vivian Hutchins

Desc: Subject: History of Van Buren County and Michigan. Holdings: Books on Van Buren County; family pictures; family histories; oral histories; newspaper clippings; obituaries; township records; cemetery records; photographs. Services: Library open to the public with restrictions.

2685 ■ Van Wyck Homestead Museum
Library
PO Box 133   Ph: (914)896-9560
Fishkill, NY 12524

Contact: Patricia McGurk

Desc: Subject: Local and American history, early American crafts, genealogy, American Indian, biography. Holdings: 700 books; 80 bound periodical volumes; 100 early military documents; clippings and early local newspapers; early business ledgers and schoolbooks; local diaries. Services: Library open to the public by appointment.

2686 ■ Vancouver Museum
Library and Resource Centre
1100 Chestnut St.   Ph: (604)736-4431
Vancouver, BC, Canada V6J 3J9 Fax: (604)736-5417

Contact: Lynn Maranda, Cur. of Anthropology

Desc: Subject: Local history, decorative arts, anthropology, ethnology, archaeology, museology, Asian studies, natural history. Holdings: 15,000 volumes. Services: Library not open to the public.

2687 ■ Vandalia Historical Society
James Hall Library
307 North 6th St.   Ph: (618)283-0024
Vandalia, IL 62471

Contact: Mary Burtschi, Dir.

Desc: Subject: Illinois and local history. Holdings: 100 books; photographs; manuscripts; reports; letters; scrapbooks. Services: Library open to the public by appointment.

2688 ■ Venango County Genealogical Club
Library
2 Central Ave.   Ph: (814)678-3077
Oil City, PA 16301-3122   Fax: (814)676-8028
E-mail: oclibrary@mail.usachoice.net
URL: http://www.usachoice.net/oclibrary/

Contact: K.D. Kelly, Pres.

Desc: Subject: Oil City, Pennsylvania - history, genealogy. Holdings: 1000 books; 100 archives; 200 manuscripts; 25 microfiche; 100 reels of microfilm. Services: Library open to the public.

2689 ■ Ventura County Museum of History and
Art
Library & Archives
100 E. Main St.   Ph: (805)653-0323
Ventura, CA 93001   Fax: (805)653-5267
E-mail: library@vcmha.org
URL: http://www.vcmha.org

Contact: Charles N. Johnson, Libn.

Desc: Subject: Local history. Holdings: 5000 books; 32,000 photographs; 40,000 negatives; 250 oral histories; 15,000 manuscripts; 400 maps; 750 architectural plans and drawings. Services: Copying; photograph reproduction; Library open to the public for reference use only.

2690 ■ Vermont Folklife Center
Archive
PO Box 442   Ph: (802)388-4964
Middlebury, VT 05753   Fax: (802)388-1844
E-mail: mtaft@sover.net
URL: http://www.vermontfolklifecenter.org

Contact: Michael Taft

Desc: Subject: Vermont history - social, cultural, economic, folk art. Holdings: audiocassettes; videocassettes; photographs; slides; family histories; diaries; letters. Services: Copying; archives open to the public.

2691 ■ Vermont Historical Society
Library
Pavilion Office Bldg.   Ph: (802)828-2291
109 State St.   Fax: (802)828-3638
Montpelier, VT 05609-0901
E-mail: vhs@vhs.state.vt.us
URL: http://www.state.vt.us/vhs

Contact: Paul A. Carnahan, Libn.

Desc: Subject: Vermont history and Vermontiana, New England state and local history, genealogy. Holdings: 40,000 books and bound periodical volumes; 1000 maps; 30,000 photographs; 200 reels of microfilm; 1057 cubic feet of manuscripts; pamphlets; 7000 broadsides. Services: Interlibrary loan (limited); copying; Library open to the public.

2692 ■ Vesterheim, Norwegian-American
Museum
Reference Library
502 W. Water St.   Ph: (319)382-9681
Decorah, IA 52101   Fax: (319)382-8828
E-mail: vesterheim@vesterheim.org

Contact: Carol A. Hasvold, Libn.

Desc: Subject: Norwegian-American history, genealogy, folk arts, antiques. Holdings: 10,000 books. Services: Library open to the public for reference use only.

2693 ■ Vicksburg & Warren County Historical
Society
McCardle Library
Old Court House Museum   Ph: (601)636-0741
Vicksburg, MS 39183

Contact: Blanche Terry, Res.Dir.

Desc: Subject: Confederacy, local history, genealogy. Holdings: 2000 volumes. Services: Copying; Library open to the public with restrictions.

2694 ■ Vietnam Refugee Fund
Library
6433 Nothana Dr.   Ph: (703)971-9178
Springfield, VA 22150

Contact: Dr. Dao Thi Hoi

Desc: Subject: Vietnam, Asia, resettlement of Vietnamese refugees into the U.S. Holdings: 3000 volumes.

2695 ■ Vigo County Public Library
Special Collections
One Library Sq.   Ph: (812)232-1113
Terre Haute, IN 47807   Fax: (812)234-2899
URL: http://vax1.vigo.lib.in.us

Contact: Betty Martin, Dir.

Desc: Subject: State and local history, genealogy. Holdings: 8560 books; 1799 bound periodical volumes; 455 maps and charts; 275 archival collections; 4080 reels of microfilm. Services: Copying; collections open to the public for reference use only.

2696 ■ Vincennes University
Byron R. Lewis Historical Library
LRC 22   Ph: (812)888-4330
Vincennes, IN 47591   Fax: (812)888-5471
E-mail: gstevens@vunet.vinu.edu

Contact: Robert R. Stevens, Dir.

Desc: Subject: Political, social, economic and general history of Lower Wabash Valley; university archives; oral history of Depression Era; genealogy. Holdings: 7500 volumes; manuscripts; photographs; maps; broadsides; newspapers; pamphlets. Services: Limited area and genealogical research; Library open to the public.

2697 ■ Vineland Historical and Antiquarian
Society
Library
108 S. 7th St.   Ph: (609)691-1111
PO Box 35
Vineland, NJ 08362

Contact: Charles J. Girard, Actg.Libn.

Desc: Subject: Genealogy and local history, Americana, antiques. Holdings: 5000 books; bound local newspapers, 1861-1935; pamphlets and documents; census material on microfilm. Services: Copying; Library open to the public on a limited schedule.

2698 ■ Virginia Baptist Historical Society
Library
University of Richmond   Ph: (804)289-8434
Box 34
Richmond, VA 23173

Contact: Fred Anderson, Exec.Dir.

Desc: Subject: History - Virginia Baptist, Baptist, religious, church, Virginia State Confederate, Colonial Virginia. Holdings: 18,000 books; 650 bound periodical volumes; 95 VF drawers of manuscripts, documents, papers, diaries, journals. Services: Copying; Library open to the public by appointment.

2699 ■ Virginia Historical Society
Library and Museum
428 North Blvd.   Ph: (804)358-4901
Box 7311   Fax: (804)355-2399
Richmond, VA 23221
URL: http://www.vahistorical.org

Contact: Charles F. Bryan, Jr., Dir.

Desc: Subject: Virginiana, Americana. Holdings: 135,000 volumes; 7 million manuscripts; prints and engravings; maps and printed ephemera; sheet music; newspapers; paintings. Services: Copying; Library open to the public.

2700 ■ Virginia (State) Library of Virginia
800 E. Broad St.   Ph: (804)692-3500
Richmond, VA 23219-1905
URL: http://vsla.edu

Contact: Nolan T. Yelich, State Libn.

Desc: Subject: Virginiana, Southern and Confederate history, genealogy, social sciences, U.S. colonial history. Holdings: 717,052 volumes, serials, bound periodical volumes; 66,517 maps; 55,323 cubic feet of manuscripts; 362,497 reels of microfilm, compact discs, videocassettes, and microfiche. Services: Interlibrary loan; copying; Library open to the public.

2701 ■ W.A. Rankin Memorial Library
502 Indiana St.　　　　　Ph: (316)325-3275
Neodesha, KS 66757　　　Fax: (316)325-3275
URL: http://www.neodesha.k12.ks.us/neodesha/
　　aup.html

Contact: Barbara Shoop, Libn.

Desc: Subject: Local history, family genealogies. Holdings: 20,000 books; 200 reels of microfilm. Services: Interlibrary loan; copying; Library open to the public.

2702 ■ Waco-McLennan County Library
Genealogy Department
1717 Austin Ave.　　　　Ph: (254)750-5945
Waco, TX 76701　　　　 Fax: (254)750-5940
URL: http://www.waco-texas.com

Contact: William Buckner, Ref.Svcs.Mgr.

Desc: Subject: Genealogy. Holdings: 14,103 books; 15,298 bound periodical volumes; 7502 reels of microfilm; 105 titles on microfiche. Services: Copying; department open to the public.

2703 ■ Wakarusa Public Library
Special Collections
124 N. Elkhart St.　　　　Ph: (219)862-2465
PO Box 485　　　　　　　Fax: (219)862-4156
Wakarusa, IN 46573
E-mail: wakalib@serv1.wakarusa-olive.lib.in.us

Contact: Jody O'Neill

Desc: Subject: Local history, family history, genealogy. Holdings: Photographs; news clippings; microfilm; bound geneologies and newspapers; historic journals and ledgers. Services: Copying; collections open to the public.

2704 ■ Wallingford Historical Society, Inc.
Library
180 S. Main St.　　　　　Ph: (203)294-1996
Box 73
Wallingford, CT 06492

Contact: Robert Beaumont, Pres.

Desc: Subject: Local history, genealogy. Holdings: 450 books. Services: Library not open to the public.

2705 ■ Wallisville Heritage Park
Library
PO Box 16　　　　　　　Ph: (409)389-2252
Wallisville, TX 77597-0016　Fax: (409)389-2466
E-mail: wallisvilleheritagepark@juno.com

Contact: Kevin Ladd, Dir.

Desc: Subject: Chambers County, TX - history, genealogy. Holdings: 2000 books; 1000 bound periodical volumes; 300 microfilm; 10,000 negatives; archival materials; vertical files. Services: Library open to the public.

2706 ■ Walnut Creek Historical Society
Sherwood D. Burgess History Room
2660 Ygnacio Valley Rd.　　Ph: (925)935-7871
Walnut Creek, CA 94598　　Fax: (925)935-7871

Contact: Jerry Loucks, Libn.Archv.

Desc: Subject: Walnut Creek history. Holdings: 500 books; 62 bound periodical volumes; 6 VF drawers of maps, manuscripts, files, records; 1300 photographs; 25 tapes; 120 unbound newspapers. Services: History room open to the public by appointment and on a limited schedule.

2707 ■ Warren County Genealogical Society
Library
PO Box 296　　　　　　　Ph: (513)932-8886
Lebanon, OH 45036-0296

Contact: Chester Dunn, Pres.

Desc: Subject: Genealogy. Holdings: 3000 volumes; microfiche; microfilm. Services: Copying; Library open to the public on a limited schedule.

2708 ■ Warren County Historical Society
Library and Archives
210 Fourth Ave.　　　　　Ph: (814)723-1795
PO Box 427　　　　　　　Fax: (814)728-3479
Warren, PA 16365
E-mail: warrenhistory@allegany.com
URL: http://nathan.allegany.com/warrenhistory/

Desc: Subject: History - local, state, Indian; genealogy; Quaker records; local authors. Holdings: 2000 books; 700 archival boxes of material from local and area families and businesses; 250 boxes of magnetic tapes. Services: Copying; Library open to the public with restrictions.

2709 ■ Warren County Historical Society
Museum and Library
105 S. Broadway　　　　　Ph: (513)932-1817
Lebanon, OH 45036-0223
E-mail: WCHS@compuserve.com

Contact: Mary Payne, Dir.

Desc: Subject: Local history, genealogy, archeology, Warren County, Shaker records, agriculture, textiles. Holdings: 3000 volumes; 1600 family files; 600 general county information files; 75,000 index cards of county residents; 350 reels of microfilm of court records, church census, newspapers, school records; 24 volumes of cemetery, marriage, and birth records; 87 bound copies of Ohio Historical Society quarterlies; Warren County court, census, school, and church records. Services: Copying; genealogy research; Library open to the public.

2710 ■ Warren County Historical Society
Warren County Museum and Historical Library
Market and Walton
PO Box 12
Warrenton, MO 63383

Contact: William Frick, Dir.

Desc: Subject: History - Warren County, family, Missouri, Central Wesleyan College. Holdings: Church and school records; microfilm of Warren County newspapers and early Warren County newspapers; family histories; obituary files. Services: Copying; Library open to the public by appointment.

2711 ■ Warsaw Historical Society
Library
15 Perry Ave.　　　　　　Ph: (716)786-2030
Warsaw, NY 14569

Contact: D.M. Lane, Pres.

Desc: Subject: Civil War and Wyoming County history. Holdings: 500 books; 100 years of local newspapers bound by years; local publications. Services: Library open to the public by appointment.

2712 ■ Waseca County Historical Society
Research Library
315 2nd Ave., N.E.　　　　Ph: (507)835-7700
Box 314
Waseca, MN 56093
E-mail: wchs@platecnet
URL: http://www.platec.net/wchs/index.html

Contact: Margaret Sinn, Exec.Dir.

Desc: Subject: County, community; history; genealogy. Holdings: 1000 books; 750 unbound documents; 140 reels of microfilm. Services: Copying; Library open to the public with restrictions.

2713 ■ Washington County Historical
Association
Library
104 S. 14th St.　　　　　Ph: (402)468-5740
Ft. Calhoun, NE 68023
URL: http://www.newashcohist.org

Contact: Agnes L. Smith, Libn.Cur.

Desc: Subject: Genealogy; local and state history; military history. Holdings: 800 photographs; 60 bound periodical volumes; 140 maps and atlases; 84 manuscripts of letters, genealogies, pioneer reminiscences, and other items; 3000 photographs; 23 photograph albums; 4250 clippings. Services: Library open to the public for reference use only.

2714 ■ Washington County Historical &
Genealogical Society
Library
PO Box 31　　　　　　　Ph: (785)325-2198
Washington, KS 66968

Contact: Jack Barley, Pres.

Desc: Subject: Washington County history, Washington County genealogy. Holdings: Microfilm. Services: Copying; Library open to the public.

2715 ■ Washington County Historical Society
Jamieson Memorial Library
135 W. Washington St.　　Ph: (301)797-8782
PO Box 1281
Hagerstown, MD 21741

Contact: Mary J. Rogers

Desc: Subject: Washington County and Western Maryland - history, genealogy. Holdings: 1000 books; 30 business ledgers; 1000 files; vertical files; photograph files. Services: Copying; Library open to the public by appointment.

2716 ■ Washington County Historical Society
Library
Stevens Memorial Museum　Ph: (812)883-6495
307 E. Market St.
Salem, IN 47167

Contact: Martha Bowers, Libn.

Desc: Subject: Genealogy, history, religion, biography, antiques. Holdings: 8000 books; 75 records; 255 genealogies; 36 cemetery record books; 80 church histories; 1340 family files; 206 reels of microfilm; 45 state histories; 60 Daughters of the American Revolution and Colonial Dames records; 400 files of general historical data; 2 Justice of Peace books; 13 records of 1923 survey of Washington County; 25 files of marriage affidavits, applications, and certificates; 1 file of deeds; booklets of clubs and lodges; 61 diaries; 34 account books; 34 township books; war and school records; census records for Indiana (1820-1920). Services: Copying; Library open to the public on fee basis.

2717 ■ Washington County Historical Society
Warden's Home Museum
Library
602 N. Main St.　　　　　Ph: (612)439-5956
Stillwater, MN 55082
E-mail: btp2001@aol.com

Contact: Brent T. Peterson, Res.Assoc.

Desc: Subject: History - Washington County, Minnesota, St. Croix River Valley. Holdings: 300 volumes. Services: Library open to the public for reference use only.

2718 ■ Washington County Historical Society
and Le Moyne House Museum
Library
49 E. Maiden St.　　　　　Ph: (724)225-6740
Washington, PA 15301　　Fax: (724)225-8495

Contact: Helen B. Miller, Libn.

Desc: Subject: Southwestern Pennsylvania history and biography, with emphasis on Washington County. Holdings: 1600 titles; old newspapers. Services: Library open to the public on a limited schedule for reference use only; research service for mailed inquiries.

2719 ■ Washington and Lee University
Special Collections Department

James G. Leyburn Library	Ph: (540)463-8663
Lexington, VA 24450	Fax: (540)463-8964
E-mail: stanley.v@wlu.edu	

URL: http://www.wlu.edu/vstanley/speccoll.html

Contact: C. Vaughan Stanley, Spec.Coll.Libn.

Desc: Subject: Local history, genealogy, university history, Civil War, Robert E. Lee. Holdings: 29,000 rare books, 1900 linear feet of manuscripts. Services: Copying; department open to the public.

2720 ■ Washington Memorial Library
Genealogy Department
Middle Georgia Archives

1180 Washington Ave.	Ph: (912)744-0821
PO Box 6334	Fax: (912)742-3161
Macon, GA 31208 6334	

Contact: Willard L. Rocker, Chf.Geneal.

Desc: Subject: Genealogy, history, county histories, heraldry, British genealogies. Holdings: 23,454 books; 65 bound periodical titles; 133 city directories; 9686 of microfilm, 7329 microfiche; 239 maps; 26 drawers of architectural drawings; 61 boxes of county and family histories; 84 CD-ROMs. Services: Copying; archives open to the public for reference use only.

2721 ■ Washington State University
Manuscripts, Archives & Special Collections

PO Box 645610	Ph: (509)335-6691
Pullman, WA 99164-5610	Fax: (509)335-6721
E-mail: mascref@wsu.edu	

URL: http://www.wsulibs.wsu.edu/holland/masc/masc.htm

Contact: Laila Miletic-Vejzovic, Hd.

Desc: Subject: History - Pacific Northwest, agriculture, veterinary history; 20th-century British literature; wildlife and outdoor recreation; ethnic history. Holdings: 23,000 volumes; manuscripts; photographs; audiotapes; videotapes; phonograph records; maps; broadsides; theses and dissertations. Services: Copying.

2722 ■ Washington Township Historical
Society
Library

6 Fairview Ave.	Ph: (908)876-9696
PO Box 189	
Long Valley, NJ 07853	

Desc: Subject: Washington Township, genealogy. Holdings: Figures not available. Services: Library open to the public for reference use only.

2723 ■ Washtenaw County Metropolitan
Planning Commission
Library

110 N. Fourth Ave.	Ph: (734)994-2435
PO Box 8645	Fax: (734)994-8284
Ann Arbor, MI 48107	

URL: http://www.co.washtenaw.mi.us/DEPTS/PLAN

Desc: Subject: Planning, census of population and housing, recreation, statistics, transportation, water sewage and drainage, conservation, urban growth and renewal, zoning ordinances, land use plans, development plans, subdivi-

sion ordinances. Holdings: 5000 books, reports, and bound periodical volumes. Services: Copying; Library open to the public at librarian's discretion.

2724 ■ Waterloo Historical Society
Grace Schmidt Room of Local History

85 Queen St., N.	Ph: (519)743-0271
Kitchener, ON, Canada N2H 2H1	Fax: (519)570-1360

E-mail: shoffman@kpl.org
URL: http://www.dcs.uwaterloo.ca/marj/history/whs.html

Contact: Susan Hoffman, Local Hist.Libn. & Archv.

Desc: Subject: History - Kitchener, Waterloo County, general. Holdings: 500 books. Services: Interlibrary loan; copying; Library open to the public.

2725 ■ Waterloo Library and Historical Society

31 E. Williams St.	Ph: (315)539-3313
Waterloo, NY 13165	Fax: (315)539-7798
E-mail: ssnyder@lakenet.org	

URL: http://207.111.4.79/waterloo/home.htm

Contact: Sandra J. Snyder

Desc: Subject: Local history, antiques. Holdings: 30,000 books; pictures; maps; diaries; letters; organization minute books; 1000 town and county records. Services: Interlibrary loan; copying; Library open to the public with restrictions.

2726 ■ Watertown Historical Society
Archives

919 Charles St.	Ph: (920)261-2796
Watertown, WI 53094	

Contact: Linda Werth, Octagon House Mgr.

Desc: Subject: First kindergarten in America, Margarethe Meyer Schurz, Carl Schurz, Octagon House, local history. Holdings: 100 volumes; photographs; clippings. Services: Archives open to the public.

2727 ■ Watertown Historical Society
Library

22 DeForest St.	Ph: (860)274-8777
Watertown, CT 06795	
E-mail: faite@juno.com	

Contact: Florence Crowell, Cur.

Desc: Subject: Genealogy, local and state history, local authors. Holdings: 1200 books. Services: Library open to the public with permission required for circulation.

2728 ■ Waterville Historical Society
Library and Archives

64 Silver St.	Ph: (207)872-9439
Waterville, ME 04901	

Contact: Caroline Waldman, Lib.Hd.

Desc: Subject: History - local, regional, state; Civil War. Holdings: 1520 books; local newspaper, 1853-1906; early account books; old documents and letters; maps; old photographs. Services: Archives open to the public with restrictions.

2729 ■ Waukegan Historical Society
John Raymond Memorial Library

1917 N. Sheridan Rd.	Ph: (847)360-4772
Waukegan, IL 60087	Fax: (847)662-0952

Desc: Subject: Environmental history; local history. Holdings: 1600 books; 10 bound newspapers; 18 VF drawers of pamphlets; 4 drawer case of slides; 1 cabinet of maps and posters; 4 portfolios of old newspapers; 10 VF drawers

of photographs; 1 VF drawer of material on landmark buildings; 8 VF drawers of ephemera. Services: Copying; Library open to the public for reference use only.

2730 ■ Waukesha County Museum
Research Center

101 W. Main St.	Ph: (414)548-7186
Waukesha, WI 53186	Fax: (414)896-6862

Contact: Terry Becker, Archv.

Desc: Subject: Local history and genealogy. Holdings: 7000 books; 87 bound periodical volumes; 1 VF drawer of cemetery records; 1 VF drawer of census records; 40 VF drawers of newspaper clippings; 14,000 photographs; 10,000 negatives; 1800 slides; archival material. Services: Copying; center open for reference use only.

2731 ■ Wayne County Department of History
Library

9 Pearl St.	Ph: (315)946-5470
PO Box 131	Fax: (315)946-5978
Lyons, NY 14489	

E-mail: wchist@redsuspenders.com
URL: http://www.waynecountyny.org

Contact: Deborah J. Ferrell, County Hist.

Desc: Subject: Wayne County history and genealogy, western New York history. Holdings: 1800 volumes; 20 VF drawers of clippings, archives, pictures, pamphlets, scrapbooks, newspapers. Services: Copying (limited); Library open to the public for reference use only.

2732 ■ Wayne Historical Museum
Historical Commission Archives

1 Town Square	Ph: (734)722-0113
Wayne, MI 48184	

Contact: Virginia Preston, Dir.

Desc: Subject: Local history. Holdings: Clippings; manuscripts, documents; maps; genealogical material; cemetery inscriptions; church, school, and local government records; local biographies; photographs. Services: Archives open to the public.

2733 ■ Webster Groves Historical Society
History Center

1155 S. Rock Hill Rd.	Ph: (314)968-1857
Webster Groves, MO 63119-3956	

Contact: John Dalzell

Desc: Subject: Webster Groves history. Holdings: 50 books; 27 volumes of local newspapers; 80 lateral file drawers of records and papers. Services: Copying; Center open to the public by appointment.

2734 ■ Weld Library District
Lincoln Park Branch Library
Special Collections

919 7th St.	Ph: (970)350-9210
Greeley, CO 80631	Fax: (970)350-9215

Contact: Charlene Parker, Br.Supv.

Desc: Subject: Germans from Russia - history, genealogy, personal reminiscences; history and genealogy - Greeley, Weld County, Colorado. Holdings: 1450 books; 33 bound periodical volumes. Services: Interlibrary loan; copying; collections open to the public.

2735 ■ Wellington County Museum
Archives

R.R. 1	Ph: (519)846-0916
Fergus, ON, Canada N1M 2W3	Fax: (519)846-9630
E-mail: wcmchin@sentex.net	

Contact: Karen Wagner, Archv.

Desc: Subject: Municipal records, genealogy, maps and plans. Holdings: 2300 books; 750 linear feet of municipal records and manuscripts; 11,000 photographs; 850 maps; 600 reels of microfilm of newspapers, land abstracts, municipal records, and other items. Services: Copying; Library open to the public.

2736 ▪ Wellsville Historical Society Library

PO Box 13   Ph: (330)532-1018
Wellsville, OH 43968

Contact: Mary Clark, Geneal.

Desc: Subject: Local history, tri-state area history, genealogy. Holdings: Figures not available.

2737 ▪ West Central Minnesota Historical Center
Research Center

University of Minnesota, Morris   Ph: (320)589-6172
600 E. Fourth St.   Fax: (320)589-6117
Morris, MN 56267

Contact: Wilbert H. Ahern, Dir.

Desc: Subject: Ethnicity in west central Minnesota, agribusiness, Minnesota politics and government, oral history, church history. Holdings: 650 linear feet of local history materials; oral history cassettes; microfilm. Services: Copying; Library open to the public.

2738 ▪ West End Synagogue
Library

3810 West End Ave.   Ph: (615)269-4592
Nashville, TN 37205   Fax: (615)269-4695

Contact: Lee Haas

Desc: Subject: Judaica, children's literature, Yiddish. Holdings: 9500 books. Services: Interlibrary loan; copying; Library open to the public.

2739 ▪ West Florida Regional Library

200 W. Gregory   Ph: (850)435-1760
Pensacola, FL 32501   Fax: (904)435-1739
E-mail: wfrl04@pcola.gulf.net
URL: http://www.virtualpcola.com/WFRL

Contact: Eugene Fischer, Superintendent

Desc: Subject: Genealogy. Holdings: 1200 books; 1000 microfiche; 1500 microfilm; 65 CD-ROMs. Services: Copying; Library open to the public.

2740 ▪ West Georgia Regional Library
Genealogy Collection

710 Rome St.   Ph: (770)836-6711
Carrollton, GA 30117   Fax: (770)836-4787
E-mail: willisr@mail.carroll.public.lib.ga.us

Contact: James P. Cooper, Dir.

Desc: Subject: Genealogy, local history, family history. Holdings: 3000 books; 2000 nonbook items. Services: Copying; collection open to the public.

2741 ▪ West Hants Historical Society
Genealogies Collections

281 King St.   Ph: (902)798-4706
PO Box 2335
Windsor, NS, Canada B0N 2T0
E-mail: dyer@glinx.com
URL: http://www.glinx.com/users/whhs

Contact: Susan Dyer, Geneal.

Desc: Subject: Genealogy, local history. Holdings: 400 books; 12 reels of microfilm; maps. Services: Copying; Library open to the public on a limited schedule and by appointment.

2742 ▪ West Tennessee Historical Society
Library

University of Memphis   Ph: (901)678-2210
McWherter Library,   Fax: (901)678-8218
  Special Collections
Memphis, TN 38152
E-mail: efrank@cc.memphis.edu

Contact: Edwin G. Frank

Desc: Subject: Western Tennessee, Memphis and regional history. Holdings: 1000 books; 80 cubic feet of 19th and early 20th century manuscripts, scrapbooks, and articles including archives of the society and its predecessor organizations, 1857 to present. Services: Copying; Library open to the public.

2743 ▪ West Virginia (State) Department of Education and the Arts
Division of Culture and History
Archives and History Library

1900 Kanawha Blvd., E.   Ph: (304)558-0230
Charleston, WV 25305-0300   Fax: (304)558-2779
URL: http://www.wvlc.edu/history/historyw.html

Contact: Fredrick H. Armstrong, Dir.

Desc: Subject: West Virginia archives, genealogy; history - U.S., Civil War, colonial, military. Holdings: 39,000 books; 5400 bound periodical volumes; 7200 linear feet of state archives; 200 linear feet of special collections; 30,562 reels of microfilm; 79,000 photographs; 76,500 stories on newsfilm and videotape from four West Virginia television stations, 1954-1993; 6250 maps; 7500 architectural drawings; 24 VF drawers of clippings. Services: Copying; Library open to the public for reference use only.

2744 ▪ West Virginia University
Office of Health Services Research
Library

WVU Health Sciences Center   Ph: (304)293-1086
PO Box 9145   Fax: (304)293-6685
Morgantown, WV 26506-9145
E-mail: alubman@wvuohsr1.hsc.wvu.edu

Contact: Alex Lubman, Program Mgr.

Desc: Subject: Census and vital statistics, hospital discharges, Medicaid and Medicare, employment-related health insurance, small computer systems development, adolescent pregnancy. Holdings: Books; reports; census documents for West Virginia and contiguous states; tape files of vital statistics for West Virginia; census tape files for West Virginia. Services: Copying; Library open to the public by appointment.

2745 ▪ West Virginia University
West Virginia and Regional History Collection

WVU Libraries   Ph: (304)293-3536
Colson Hall   Fax: (304)293-3981
PO Box 6464
Morgantown, WV 26506
E-mail: wiseref@wvnvm.wvnet.edu
URL: http://gopher.wvnet.edu

Contact: John A. Cuthbert, Cur.

Desc: Subject: Appalachian, regional, state, and local history, literature, arts, and genealogy. Holdings: 35,000 volumes; 27,400 reels of microfilm; 18,000 linear feet of manuscripts and archives; 1200 newspapers; 100,000 photographs; oral histories; folk music; university archives. Services: Copying; Library open to the public.

2746 ▪ Westchester County Department of Parks, Recreation and Conservation
Trailside Nature Museum

Ward Pound Ridge Reservation   Ph: (914)763-3993
Cross River, NY 10518   Fax: (914)773-2429
E-mail: trailsid@bestweb.net

Contact: Beth Herr, Cur.

Desc: Subject: Delaware culture, Native American herbalism, Algonkian tribes of the Eastern United States, Algonkian linguistics, Northeastern United States archeology, tribes of the greater New York area. Holdings: 1000 books; 500 bound periodical volumes; 10 file boxes of unbound material. Services: Copying; center open to the public by appointment for reference use only.

2747 ▪ Westchester County Historical Society
Library

2199 Saw Mill River Rd.   Ph: (914)592-4323
Elmsford, NY 10523   Fax: (914)592-6481

Contact: Elizabeth G. Fuller, Libn.

Desc: Subject: Genealogy and history of Westchester County and New York State, history of New York City. Holdings: 5000 books; 350 bound periodical volumes; 8 VF drawers of manuscripts; 6 VF drawers of photographs; 12 VF drawers of clippings; 10 drawers of maps. Services: Copying; Library open to the public.

2748 ▪ Western Hennepin County Pioneer Association, Inc.
Avery Stubbs Memorial Archives
Library

1953 W. Wayzata Blvd.   Ph: (612)473-6557
Box 332
Long Lake, MN 55356

Contact: Tom Turnham

Desc: Subject: Local and family history. Holdings: 2000 books; 25 bound periodical volumes; 1200 family histories; 15 municipal histories; vital records; 7 rolls of microfilm of newspapers; 800 cataloged portraits and photographs; church and business histories; maps. Services: Copying; photograph reproduction; Library open to the public on a fee basis.

2749 ▪ Western Historical Manuscript Collection

Thomas Jefferson Library   Ph: (314)516-5143
University of Missouri, St. Louis
8001 Natural Bridge Rd.
St. Louis, MO 63121
E-mail: whmc@umsl.edu
URL: http://www.umsl.edu/whmc

Contact: Ann Morris, Assoc.Dir.

Desc: Subject: History - state and local, women's, Afro-American, ethnic, education, immigration; socialism; 19th-century science; environment; peace; religion; Missouri politics; social reform and welfare; photography; journalism; business; labor. Holdings: 12,000 linear feet of manuscripts, photographs, oral history tapes, and university archives. Services: Interlibrary loan (limited); copying of manuscripts and photographs; Library open to the public with restricted circulation.

2750 ▪ Western Kentucky University
Department of Special Library Collections
Manuscripts and Archives

The Kentucky Bldg.   Ph: (502)745-6434
Bowling Green, KY 42101   Fax: (502)745-4878
URL: http://www2.wku.edu/www/library/d1sc/

Contact: Riley Handy, Hd., Spec.Coll.Dept.

Desc: Subject: Rare Kentuckiana, Mammoth Cave, Kentucky writers, Civil War, Shakers, Ohio Valley, Western Kentucky University, Folklore, Regional oral history, traditional arts, folk songs and music. Holdings: 6275 cubic feet; 22 VF drawers; 1600 photographs; 400 land grants; 4700 cassettes and tapes; 2250 folklore manuscripts; collections of folk songs, beliefs, speech, correspondence. Services: Copying (limited); archives open to the public for research and reference.

2751 ■ Western Lake Erie Historical Society Library
PO Box 5311   Ph: (419)865-0326
Toledo, OH 43611

Contact: Harry Archer, Actg.Lib.Hd.

Desc: Subject: Great Lakes - maritime history, boats, people, communities, wars. Holdings: Books; bound periodical volumes; archival materials; 5000 ship photographs.

2752 ■ Western Michigan University Archives and Regional History Collections
East Hall, Rm. 111   Ph: (616)387-8490
Kalamazoo, MI 49008-5081   Fax: (616)387-8484
E-mail: sharon.carlson@wmich.edu
URL: http://www.wmich.edu/library/archives.html

Contact: Sharon Carlson, Dir.

Desc: Subject: Local and regional history, genealogy, history of Western Michigan University. Holdings: 13,508 books; 16,728 linear feet of manuscripts; 3545 reels of microfilm, photographs, selected governmental records, and other archival materials. Services: Copying; collection open to the public.

2753 ■ Western New York Genealogical Society, Inc. Library
PO Box 338   Ph: (716)655-1299
Hamburg, NY 14075

Desc: Subject: Genealogy and local history. Holdings: 2150 books; 4400 unbound periodicals; 350 pamphlets, paperbacks, manuscripts, articles; genealogical society publications; 315 reels of microfilm. Services: Copying; Library open to the public.

2754 ■ Western Pennsylvania Genealogical Society Library
4400 Forbes Ave.   Ph: (412)687-6811
Pittsburgh, PA 15213-4080

Contact: Marilyn Holt, Libn.

Desc: Subject: Genealogy, local history. Holdings: 8000 volumes; 1 VF drawer of cemetery information; 3 VF drawers of family files; 45 feet of newsletters; 1 VF drawer of church information. Services: Copying; Library open to the public.

2755 ■ Western Reserve Historical Society Library
10825 East Blvd.   Ph: (216)721-5722
Cleveland, OH 44106   Fax: (216)721-5702
E-mail: pomerleau@whrs.org
URL: http://www.wrhs.org

Contact: Kermit J. Pike, Dir.

Desc: Subject: Ohio history, American genealogy, Civil War, slavery and abolitionism, ethnic history, African Americans. Holdings: 239,000 books; 26,250 volumes of newspapers; 50,500 pamphlets; 20 million manuscripts; 40,250 reels of microfilm. Services: Interlibrary loan; copying; Library open to the public.

2756 ■ Westerville Public Library Local History Resource Center
126 S. State St.   Ph: (614)882-8277
Westerville, OH 45787
E-mail: history@wpl.lib.oh.us
URL: http://www.wpl.lib.oh.us/library

Desc: Subject: Ohio history; Westerville genealogical resources. Holdings: 1500 photographs; diaries; high school year books; documents. Services: Library open to the public.

2757 ■ Westminster Historical Society Library
110 Main St.   Ph: (508)874-5569
Box 177
Westminster, MA 01473

Contact: Betsy Hannula, Cur.

Desc: Subject: Westminster history. Holdings: 200 books; 200 bound periodical volumes; 20 manuscripts. Services: Copying; Library open to the public.

2758 ■ Westminster Presbyterian Church Library
2040 Washington Rd.   Ph: (412)835-6630
Pittsburgh, PA 15241   Fax: (412)835-5690

Contact: Tom Sandes, Lib.Dir.

Desc: Subject: Religion, West Pennsylvania history. Holdings: 5000 books. Services: Library open to the public.

2759 ■ Westminster Presbyterian Church Library
4400 N. Shartel   Ph: (405)524-2204
Oklahoma City, OK 73118   Fax: (405)524-4740

Contact: J. Richard Hershberger, Assoc. Minister

Desc: Subject: Religion, church history, biography. Holdings: 1200 volumes. Services: Library open to the public with restrictions.

2760 ■ Westmoreland County Historical Society Calvin E. Pollins Memorial Library
951 Old Salem Rd.   Ph: (412)836-1800
Greensburg, PA 15601-1352

Contact: Jane Maina, Libn.

Desc: Subject: Local history, genealogy, fine and decorative arts, archeology. Holdings: 1500 books; 12 VF drawers; 56 bound volumes of local newspapers; 12,000 documents; 50 reels of microfilm; 500 slides; 400 architectural drawings of Westmoreland County. Services: Copying; Library open to the public on a fee basis.

2761 ■ Weston County Museum District Anna Miller Museum
Box 698   Ph: (307)746-4188
Newcastle, WY 82701   Fax: (307)746-4188
E-mail: annamm@trib.com

Desc: Subject: Weston County; Wyoming and Western history. Holdings: 50 bound periodical volumes; periodicals, 1860 to present; local history, clippings, pamphlets, booklets, manuscripts; 92,000 local history photographs. Services: Copying, educational programs, Library open to the public for reference use only.

2762 ■ Westport Historical Society Library
PO Box 3031   Ph: (508)636-6011
Westport, MA 02790-0700

Contact: Lincoln S. Tripp

Desc: Subject: Westport and New Bedford, Massachusetts history. Holdings: 300 books; documents. Services: Copying; Library open to the public with restrictions.

2763 ■ Westwood First Presbyterian Church Walter Lorenz Memorial Library
3011 Harrison Ave.   Ph: (513)661-6846
Cincinnati, OH 45211   Fax: (513)389-3681

Contact: Marian B. McNair, Libn.

Desc: Subject: Religion, curriculum materials, children's books, fiction, biography, bible reference. Holdings: 3906 books; 1 VF drawer; 85 videotapes; audiovisual materials; Presbyterian College bulletins. Services: Interlibrary loan; Library open to the public.

2764 ■ Wethersfield Historical Society Old Academy Library
150 Main St.   Ph: (860)529-7656
Wethersfield, CT 06109   Fax: (860)529-1905
E-mail: director@wethhist.org
URL: http://www.wethhist.org

Contact: Brenda Milkofsky, Dir.

Desc: Subject: Wethersfield history, genealogy, maritime history. Holdings: 1000 books; 2000 photographs; 75 linear feet of account books, ship logs, letters, broadsides, maps, sermons, wallpaper, diaries, manuscripts. Services: Copying; Library open to the public.

2765 ■ Wheat Ridge Historical Society Library
PO Box 1833   Ph: (303)421-9111
Wheat Ridge, CO 80034   Fax: (303)467-2539

Contact: Claudia Worth, Pres.

Desc: Subject: Wheat Ridge history, local government, arts, crafts, tuberculosis sanitariums. Holdings: 675 books; 25 bound periodical volumes; 50 audiovisual programs; 30 manuscript collections; 25 VHS units; 60 audio records. Services: Library open to the public.

2766 ■ White River Valley Historical Society Museum Library
918 H St., S.E.   Ph: (253)939-2783
Auburn, WA 98002   Fax: (253)939-4523

Contact: Patricia Cosgrove

Desc: Subject: Local Northwest history and genealogy, history of local industries. Holdings: 2000 volumes; 25 boxes of pamphlets; 250 maps; 25 cassette tapes. Services: Library open to the public for reference use only.

2767 ■ Whitfield-Murray Historical Society Crown Gardens and Archives
715 Chattanooga Ave.   Ph: (706)278-0217
Dalton, GA 30720

Contact: Marcelle White, Exec.Sec.

Desc: Subject: Local history and genealogy. Holdings: 500 books; 4500 nonbook items. Services: Copying; archives open to the public.

2768 ■ Whiting-Robertsdale Historical Society Historical Museum
1610 119th St.   Ph: (219)659-1432
Whiting, IN 46394-1702

Contact: Elizabeth L. Gehrke, Cur.

Desc: Subject: Local history. Holdings: Documents; papers; records; pictures; artifacts; maps; real estate abstracts; local newspapers, 1894 to present. Services: Library open to the public for reference use only.

2769 ■ Wichita Genealogical Society
PO Box 3705
Wichita, KS 67201-3705
URL: http://history.cc.ukans.edu/kansas/wgs/wgs.html

Contact: Diane Scannell

Desc: Subject: Genealogy, local history. Holdings: Figures not available.

2770 ■ Wicomico County Free Library
Maryland Room and Genealogy Collection
122-126 S. Division St.   Ph: (410)749-5171
Salisbury, MD 21801   Fax: (410)548-2968
URL: http://www.co.wicomico.md.us/library/info.html

Desc: Subject: Maryland and DelMarVa Peninsula history, folklore, religion and genealogy. Holdings: Books; wills; church records; land grants; muster rolls; pension files; ship passenger lists; family histories; microfilm; census records. Services: Interlibrary loan; copying; Library open to the public.

2771 ■ Wilkin County Historical Society
Library
704 Nebraska Ave.   Ph: (218)643-1303
Breckenridge, MN 56520

Desc: Subject: Local history. Holdings: 258 books. Services: Library open to the public.

2772 ■ Will County Historical Society
Archives
803 S. State St.   Ph: (815)838-5080
Lockport, IL 60441

Contact: Rose Bucciferro, Dir.

Desc: Subject: History of Will County, Illinois, and the Illinois and Michigan Canal, 1830-1935; genealogy. Holdings: 400,000 archival materials, including property records, surname files, biographies, cemetery records. Services: Archives not open to the public; written requests will be answered by mail.

2773 ■ Willa Cather State Historic Site
Archives
326 N. Webster St.   Ph: (402)746-2653
Red Cloud, NE 68970   Fax: (402)746-2652
URL: http://www.willacather.org

Desc: Subject: Willa Cather's life and art, the lives of real people who are prototypes of Cather's characters. Holdings: 400 books; 20 bound periodical volumes; 200 periodicals containing articles dealing with Cather and her works; 250 letters; 1900 photographs; 700 pages of clippings; 175 reels of microfilm. Services: Copying (limited); archives open to the public.

2774 ■ Willard Library of Evansville
Special Collections Department
21 1st Ave.   Ph: (812)425-4309
Evansville, IN 47710   Fax: (812)425-4303

Contact: Lyn Martin, Spec.Coll.Libn.

Desc: Subject: History and genealogy of Evansville, Vanderburgh County, and the surrounding areas in Indiana, Illinois, and Kentucky, 1800 to present. Holdings: 9500 books; 1300 microforms; 3000 linear feet of personal papers, city, township, and county records. Services: Interlibrary loan; copying (both limited); department open to the public.

2775 ■ Willard Public Library
Local History and Genealogy Collection
7 W. Van Buren St.   Ph: (616)968-8166
Battle Creek, MI 49017   Fax: (616)968-3284
E-mail: rhulsey@willard.lib.mi.us
URL: http://www.willard.lib.mi.us/localhis.htm

Contact: Richard A. Hulsey, Dir.

Desc: Subject: Battle Creek and Michigan history and genealogy. Holdings: 5000 monographs and bound journals; photographs. Services: Interlibrary loan; copying; Library open to the public.

2776 ■ Williamstown House of Local History
Library
1095 Main St.   Ph: (413)458-2160
Williamstown, MA 01267-2637

Contact: Nancy Burstein, Cur.

Desc: Subject: Williamstown history. Holdings: Books; documents; photographs; newspapers, artifacts. Services: Library open to the public.

2777 ■ Wilshire Boulevard Temple
Sigmund Hecht Library
3663 Wilshire Blvd.   Ph: (213)388-2401
Los Angeles, CA 90010   Fax: (213)388-2595

Desc: Subject: Judaica, Bible, philosophy, religion, Jewish history, education, language and literature, arts, sociology. Holdings: 17,000 volumes; 100 pamphlets; 12 VF drawers of uncataloged pamphlets; 100 filmstrips. Services: Interlibrary loan; Library open to the public for reference use only.

2778 ■ Wilson County Historical Society
Museum Library
420 N. 7th   Ph: (316)378-3965
Fredonia, KS 66736

Contact: C. Jean Vorhees

Desc: Subject: The West; Kansas; pioneer life; plains agriculture - tools, equipment, facilities. Holdings: 400 books; 300 bound periodical volumes; 1050 indexed pictures; 68 indexed notebooks of clippings; 15 notebooks of clipped obituaries from last 40 years in Wilson County; books of grade school local history essays, 1983-1984; 50 genealogies. Services: Copying; Library open to the public for reference use only.

2779 ■ Wilson Czech Opera House Corporation
Foundation Museum
"House of Memories"
415 27th St., Hwy. 40   Ph: (913)658-3343
PO Box 271
Wilson, KS 67490

Contact: Jean Kingston, Dir.

Desc: Subject: Family history, local history. Holdings: 100 books; 4 bound periodical volumes; reports; archival materials; pictures; glass slides; handbills; other cataloged items. Services: Museum open to the public.

2780 ■ Wilton Historical Society, Inc.
Library
249 Danbury Rd.   Ph: (203)762-7257
Wilton, CT 06897   Fax: (203)762-3297
URL: http://www.wiltonlibrary.org

Contact: Marilyn Gould, Dir.

Desc: Subject: Connecticut and Wilton history and genealogy. Holdings: 500 volumes; manuscripts; genealogy; maps. Services: Copying; Library open to the public for reference use only. Library housed at the Wilton Public Library.

2781 ■ Winchester Historical Society
Solomon Rockwell House
Archive
225 Prospect St.   Ph: (860)379-8433
PO Box 206   Fax: (860)379-1614
Winsted, CT 06098
E-mail: MWH345@aol.com

Contact: Frank Smith, Pres.

Desc: Subject: Local history. Holdings: Books; photographs; maps; documents; 5000 glassplate negatives. Services: Archive open to the public by appointment.

2782 ■ Windsor Historical Society, Inc.
Library
96 Palisado Ave.   Ph: (860)688-3813
Windsor, CT 06095

Contact: Robert T. Silliman, Dir.

Desc: Subject: Genealogy, local history, biography. Holdings: 3500 books; bound Windsor periodicals; 3000 school books, almanacs, early photographs, lantern slides concerning Windsor and its people, and other cataloged items. Services: Copying; Library open to the public for reference use only.

2783 ■ Wise County Historical Society, Inc.
Wise County Historical Commission Archive
1602 S. Trinity   Ph: (940)627-3732
Box 427
Decatur, TX 76234

Contact: Rosalie Gregg, Exec.Dir.

Desc: Subject: Wise County history, family histories, cemetery records, census. Holdings: Books; microfiche; Wise County birth, marriage, and death records. Services: Copying; archive open to the public for reference use only; will answer mail inquiries (must enclose self-addressed, legal-sized stamped envelope).

2784 ■ Withlacoochee Regional Planning
Council
Library
1241 S.W. 10th St.   Ph: (352)732-1315
Ocala, FL 34474-2798   Fax: (352)732-1319
E-mail: wrpc@atlantic.net

Contact: Vivian A. Whittier, Info.Spec.

Desc: Subject: Statistics, planning, land use, water, energy, census data, hazardous materials. Holdings: 6000 bound periodical volumes; maps; technical reports. Services: Copying; Library open to the public with restrictions on lending.

2785 ■ Wolfeboro Historical Society
Library
233 S. Main St.   Ph: (603)569-4997
Box 1066
Wolfeboro, NH 03894

Contact: Dianne Rogers, Pres.

Desc: Subject: Local history and genealogy, 19th century fire engines. Holdings: Books; maps; scrapbooks of local events; town reports; old school records. Services: Library open to the public on a limited schedule.

2786 ■ Woodson County Historical Society
Rte. 1   Ph: (316)625-2371
Yates Center, KS 66783
E-mail: lgcall@sekansas

Contact: Linda Call, Treas.

Desc: Subject: Woodson County history, genealogy. Holdings: 20 bound periodical volumes. Services: Library open to the public by appointment.

2787 ■ Woodstock Historical Society, Inc.
John Cotton Dana Library
26 Elm St.   Ph: (802)457-1822
Woodstock, VT 05091   Fax: (802)457-2811

Contact: Marie McAndrew-Taylor, Libn. & Archv.

Desc: Subject: Woodstock history, antiques, Vermont history, Woodstock genealogy. Holdings: 1500 books; 51 bound periodical volumes; 500 pamphlets; 42 maps; 300 VF folders of papers and manuscripts; account books and records of Woodstock merchants. Services: Library open to the public.

2788 ■ Worcester County Library
307 N. Washington St.   Ph: (410)632-2600
Snow Hill, MD 21863   Fax: (410)632-1159
E-mail: worc@dmv.com
URL: http://www.worc.lib.md.us

Contact: Stewart Wells, Dir.

Desc: Subject: Worcester County - history, genealogy. Holdings: 400 books; 97 bound periodical volumes; 200 documents; 7 AV programs; 50 manuscripts; 95 nonbook items; Worcester County land records. Services: Interlibrary loan; copying; Library open to the public.

2789 ■ Worcester Historical Museum
Library
30 Elm St.   Ph: (508)753-8278
Worcester, MA 01609   Fax: (508)753-9070

Contact: Theresa Davitt, Libn.

Desc: Subject: Worcester history. Holdings: 20,000 volumes; photographs; maps; manuscripts; graphics; newspapers; ephemera. Services: Copying; Library open to the public for research.

2790 ■ World Jewish Genealogy Organization
Library
1605 48th St.   Ph: (718)435-4400
Brooklyn, NY 11219-0009   Fax: (718)633-7050

Contact: Rabbi N. Halberstam, Libn.

Desc: Subject: Judaica. Holdings: 10,000 books. Services: Library not open to the public.

2781 ■ Worthington Historical Society
Lillian Skeele Library
50 W. New England Ave.   Ph: (614)885-1247
Worthington, OH 43085   Fax: (614)436-1620

Desc: Subject: Local history and genealogy, historic preservation, decorative arts, pioneer crafts, dolls, lace-making, architecture. Holdings: 875 books. Services: Interlibrary loan; copying; Library open to the public by appointment.

2792 ■ Wright Information Center
Clearinghouse
1511 S.W. 65th Terrace   Ph: (561)402-7502
Boca Raton, FL 33428-7819

Contact: Phyllis M. Heiss, Pres.

Desc: Subject: Genealogy. Holdings: 675 volumes. Services: Library not open to the public.

2793 ■ Wright State University
Special Collections & Archives
Paul Laurence Dunbar Library
                              Ph: (937)775-2092
rs>Dayton, OH 45435   Fax: (937)775-4109
E-mail: archive@library.wright.edu
URL: http://130.108.121.217/staff/Dunbar/arch/
       schome.htm

Contact: Dawne Dewey, Hd., Spec.Coll. & Archv.

Desc: Subject: Aeronautics history, Wright Brothers, Ohio and local history, genealogy, Arthur Rackham. Holdings: 12,000 books and bound periodical volumes; 30 linear feet of Wright Brothers Papers; 24 linear feet of James M. Cox Papers; 20 linear feet of labor union records; 200 linear feet of local business records; 100 linear feet of local church records; Wright Brothers photographs (1600 on CD-ROM); microfilm. Services: Copying; microfilming; collections open to the public.

2794 ■ Wyandot County Historical Society
Wyandot Museum
Library
130 S. 7th St.   Ph: (419)294-3857
PO Box 372
Upper Sandusky, OH 43351

Desc: Subject: Wyandot Mission, Indian artifacts. Holdings: 500 books. Services: Library open to the public for reference use only.

2795 ■ Wyandotte County Historical Society
and Museum
Harry M. Trowbridge Research Library
631 N. 126th St.   Ph: (913)721-1078
Bonner Springs, KS 66012   Fax: (913)721-1394
E-mail: wycomus@toto.net

Contact: John R. Nichols, Archv.

Desc: Subject: Wyandotte County and Kansas City history; Wyandot, Shawnee, and Delaware Indians. Holdings: 4000 books; 1000 bound periodical volumes; clippings; 539 reels of microfilm; 6000 photographs; maps. Services: Copying; Library open to the public with restrictions.

2796 ■ Wyandotte Historical Museum
2610 Biddle Ave.   Ph: (734)324-7297
Wyandotte, MI 48192   Fax: (734)324-7283
E-mail: wymuseum@ili.net

Contact: Marc M. Partin, Dir.

Desc: Subject: Wyandotte history, early local industries, local businesses, shipbuilding, Wyandot Indians, Victorian era. Holdings: 1000 books; 10,000 archival items; 25 reels of reels of microfilm. Services: Copying; Library open to the public by appointment.

2797 ■ Wyoming Historical and Geological
Society
Bishop Memorial Library
49 S. Franklin St.   Ph: (570)823-6244
Wilkes-Barre, PA 18701   Fax: (570)823-9011
URL: http://www.whgs.org

Contact: Jesse Teitelbaum, Libn.Archv.

Desc: Subject: Wyoming Valley and Pennsylvania history. Holdings: 7000 books; 500 bound periodical volumes; 1000 reels of microfilm of Wilkes Barre newspapers 1797-1950; 9000 photographs. Services: Copying; Library open to the public on a limited schedule.

2798 ■ Wyoming Pioneer Home
Library
141 Pioneer Home Dr.   Ph: (307)864-3151
Thermopolis, WY 82443

Contact: Julie Miller

Desc: Subject: History, general. Holdings: 4500 books. Services: Interlibrary loan; Library not open to the public.

2799 ■ Wyoming (State) Department of State
Parks and Cultural Resources
State Archives
Barrett Bldg.,   Ph: (307)777-7826
2301 Central   Fax: (307)777-7044
Cheyenne, WY 82002
E-mail: wyarchive@missc.state.wy.us
URL: http://commerce.state.wy.us/cr/archives/
       index.htm

Contact: Tony Adams, State Archv.Dir., WY Archv.

Desc: Subject: Wyoming and Western history. Holdings: 6500 volumes; 29,000 cubic feet of archival materials; 84,000 reels of microfilm; scrapbooks; manuscripts; maps and plats; documents; letters; ledgers; diaries; research collections; census records; oral histories; folklore; AV programs; territorial and state government records. Services: Copying; department open to the public.

2800 ■ Wytheville Community College
Kegley Library
1000 E. Main St.   Ph: (540)223-4742
Wytheville, VA 24382   Fax: (540)223-4745

Contact: Anna Ray Roberts, Coord., Lib.Svcs.

Desc: Subject: Southwest Virginia history and genealogy. Holdings: 800 books; 86 bound periodical volumes; 323 historical maps; 500 oral history interviews; data on 252 local cemeteries; 20 VF drawers; 200 volumes of family history; 300 volumes of local history; 216 reels of microfilm. Services: Copying; collections open to the public.

2801 ■ Yadkin County Public Library
Paul Price Davis History Room
233 E. Main St.   Ph: (336)679-8792
Box 607   Fax: (336)679-4625
Yadkinville, NC 27055

Contact: Malinda Sells, Br.Libn.

Desc: Subject: Local and North Carolina history. Holdings: 700 volumes; 50 reels of microfilm of census data, marriage records, wills, deeds, estates, court minutes of county, 1851-1950; 16 drawers of family genealogies, local history; The Yadkin Ripple, 1893 to present, 59 reels of microfilm; The Enterprise and The Tribune, both 1981 to present. Services: Interlibrary loan; Copying; room open to the public for reference use only.

2802 ■ Yakima Valley Genealogical Society
Library
Box 445   Ph: (509)248-1328
Yakima, WA 98907
URL: http://www.rootsweb.com/wayvgs/

Contact: Ellen Brzoska, Libn.

Desc: Subject: Genealogy, family, Yakima County, central Washington history. Holdings: 2000 volumes; 3000 bound periodical volumes; 100,000 card Yakima County cemetery file; 50,000 card Klickitat and Kittitas Counties cemetery file; 8 VF drawers of reports, clippings, pamphlets, and documents; 200 reels of microfilm and cassette tapes; 100 family history interview sheets. Services: Interlibrary loan; copying; Library open to the public for reference use only.

2803 ■ Yarmouth County Museum
Research Library and Archives
22 Collins St.   Ph: (902)742-5539
Yarmouth, NS, Canada B5A   Fax: (902)749-1120
3C8
E-mail: ycn0056@ycn.library.ns.ca
URL: http://www.ycn.library.ns.ca/museum/
       yarcomus.htm

Contact: Laura Bradley, Libn.Archv.

Desc: Subject: Local history and genealogy, shipping. Holdings: 1300 books; local newspapers, 1833-1990s; 2 VF drawers and 20 shelves of archival materials; manuscripts; maps; charts; clippings; pictures; genealogy records. Services: Copying; Library open to the public; genealogy research conducted.

2804 ■ Yivo Institute for Jewish Research
Library and Archives
15 W. 16th St.   Ph: (212)246-6080
New York, NY 10011   Fax: (212)292-1892
E-mail: yivo1@metgate.metro.org
URL: http://www.baruch.cuny.edu/yivo/

Contact: Zachary Baker, Hd.Libn.

Desc: Subject: Yiddish language, literature, drama, folklore; East European Jewry; European Jewry in the 19th and 20th centuries; Jewish history; Jewish immigration to the U.S.; Jews under Nazi rule. Holdings: 350,000 volumes; 12,000 linear feet of manuscript collections, records of institutions, individual collections, general records of the Yivo archives, photograph collections, art collections; 30 linear feet of tapes and recordings; 6000 reels of microfilm. Services: Interlibrary loan; copying; Library open to the public.

2805 ■ Yonkers Historical Society Library

City Hall, Rm. 415A   Ph: (914)965-0401
Yonkers, NY 10701   Fax: (914)865-0401
URL: http://www.yonkershistory.org

Contact: Marianne Winstanley, Dir.

Desc: Subject: History - Yonkers, NY, Westchester County, NY, Hudson River; local authors. Holdings: 400 books; manuscripts; documents. Services: Library open to the public for reference use by appointment only.

2806 ■ Young Historical Library

201 Main St.   Ph: (316)897-6236
PO Box 55
Little River, KS 67457-0055

Contact: Doris Cory, Libn.

Desc: Subject: Genealogy. Holdings: Figures not available. Services: Library open to the public on a limited schedule or by appointment.

2807 ■ Zion Mennonite Church Library

149 Cherry Ln.   Ph: (215)723-3592
PO Box 495
Souderton, PA 18964
URL: http://www.zionmennonite.org

Contact: Gwen N. Hartzel, Libn.

Desc: Subject: Bible, Mennonite Church history, books for children and young people. Holdings: 5000 books. Services: Interlibrary loan; Library open to the public.

Publishers

2808 ■ ABK Publications

3 Lakeview Dr.   Ph: (603)448-1780
Hanover, NH 03755

Contact: Agnes Kurtz, Owner-Pub.

Desc: Publishes on sports and genealogy. Presently inactive.

2809 ■ ABP Abstracts

PO Box 815
Whitakers, NC 27891

Contact: A. B. Pruitt.

Desc: Publishes books on land records in North Carolina. Offers genealogical research.

2810 ■ Acadian Genealogy Exchange

863 Wayman Branch Rd.   Ph: (606)356-9825
Covington, KY 41015-2201   Fax: (606)356-9825
URL: http://www.acadiangenexch.com

Contact: Janet Jehn, Ed. & Pub.

Desc: Publishes Acadian genealogical material. Offers a quarterly newsletter, Acadian Genealogy Exchange. Accepts unsolicited manuscripts; must pertain to Acadian, Cajun or French-Canadian genealogy. Distributes Editions Lemeac.

2811 ■ ACETO Bookmen

5721 Antietam Dr.   Ph: (941)924-9170
Sarasota, FL 34231

Contact: Charles D. Townsend, Owner.

Desc: Publishes genealogical material.

2812 ■ Advance Business Systems

PO Box 127   Ph: (508)394-4479
Osterville, MA 02655   Fax: (508)220-1886
URL: http://emcee.com/lrsears

Contact: L. Ray Sears, III, Owner; Vickie J. Sears, Sec.-Treas.

Desc: Publishes genealogy.

2813 ■ AGLL, Inc./Heritage Quest

PO Box 329   Ph: (801)298-5358
Bountiful, UT 84011-0329   Free: 800-760-AGLL
    Fax: (801)298-5468
E-mail: sales@heritagequest.com

Contact: Raeone C. Steuart, Dir. of Operations; Bradley W. Steuart, Pres./CEO.

Desc: Publishes indexes of tax lists, census records, ship passenger lists, mortality records, birth records, and other miscellaneous records. Publications are available in print, microform, and other electronic media. Accepts unsolicited manuscripts, query first.

2814 ■ Aldergrove Publishing Co.

3207-275A St.   Ph: (604)856-1192
Aldergrove, BC, Canada V4W   Fax: (604)856-1192
3J5

Contact: A. Patricia Stanyer, Pres., Ed., & Pub.; Kathleen Paulson, VP.

Desc: Publishes Canadian folklore and novels with Canadian background.

2815 ■ Allegany County Historical Society

218 Washington St.   Ph: (301)777-8678
Cumberland, MD 21502   Fax: (301)777-8678

Contact: Sharon Nealij, Dir.; Lee Dewitt, Pres.

Desc: Publishes an original Civil War diary to honor Maryland's 350th birthday. Also offers a quarterly newsletter.

2816 ■ Alligator Book Co.

314 Seabrook Dr.   Ph: (803)689-2655
Hilton Head Island, SC 29926   Fax: (803)681-3568

Contact: A.S. Winston, III, Owner.

Desc: Publishes family genealogies and fiction. Does not accept unsolicited manuscripts.

2817 ■ American Artist Publishing Co.

PO Box 12   Ph: (502)249-3685
Dixon, KY 42409   Fax: (502)249-8147

Contact: Ernest W. Johnston, Pub.

Desc: Publishes books on genealogy, bible study, and accounting. Offers newsletters.

2818 ■ American Association for State & Local History/AASLH

1717 Church St.   Ph: (615)320-3203
Nashville, TN 37203-2991   Fax: (615)327-9013
E-mail: history@aaslh.org
URL: http://www.aaslh.org

Contact: Terry Davis, Exec. Dir.; Natalie Norris, Dir., Marketing.

Desc: Nonprofit organization established to promote, educate, and preserve history in North America. Publishes books on collections, how-to, preservation, administration, oral history, reference, etc. Also publishes periodicals, technical leaflets, and reports. Offers a monthly newsletter, and a quarterly magazine. Accepts unsolicited manuscripts from authors who have queried first.

2819 ■ American College of Heraldry, Inc.

PO Box 710
Cottondale, AL 35453
E-mail: acainfo@acaresourcecenter.org

Contact: David Pittman Johnson, Pres.

Desc: Offers a quarterly, The Armiger's News. Does not accept unsolicited manuscripts.

2820 ■ American Family Records Association

PO Box 15505   Ph: (816)252-0950
Kansas City, MO 64106
E-mail: amfamrecord@aol.com

Contact: Ann Reinert, Pres.

Desc: A nonprofit association promoting genealogical research. Publishes a periodical and associated booklets. Offers a quarterly journal, Family Records Today..

2821 ■ American Genealogical Lending Library

PO Box 329   Ph: (801)298-5358
Bountiful, UT 84011-0329   Free: 800-658-7755
    Fax: (801)298-5468
E-mail: www.heritagequest.com
URL: http://www.heritagequest.com

Contact: Brad Steuart, Pres.; Raeone C. Steuart, VP & Dir. of Operation; Bradley Steuart, Dir. of Mktg., Sec. & Treas.

Desc: Publishes books for historians and genealogists. Offers Heritage Quest Magazine and publications on microfilm and microfiche. Accepts unsolicited manuscripts. Distributes for Heritage Books Ancestry and Genealogical Publishing Co.

2822 ■ American Impressions

1903 12th Ave. NE   Fax: (704)322-3138
Hickory, NC 28601

Contact: Marilyn A. Childers, Pres.; Dixie Ingram, VP.

Desc: Subjects include How-to, self-help, genealogy, inspirational, success, motivation. Publishes and markets through mail order select types of materials.

2823 ■ American Jewish Committee

165 E. 56th St.   Ph: (212)751-4000
New York, NY 10022   Free: 800-551-3252
    Fax: (212)751-4017
E-mail: info@ajc.org
URL: http://www.ajc.org

Contact: David A. Harris, Exec. Dir.; Robert S. Rifkind, Pres.

Desc: Resource for human-relations agencies, schools, churches, synagogues, civic organizations, and individuals concerned with intergroup understanding and support for Israel. Offers American Jewish Year Book, Commentary Magazine, Common Quest Magazine, research studies, other pulications, and newsletters.

2824 ■ Amherst Township Historical Society

150 Church St.   Ph: (902)667-2561
Amherst, NS, Canada B4H 3C3

Contact: Kim M. Gorveatt, Dir. & Curator; Carol Corney, Pres.; Vicki Randall, Sec.; Clare Fraser, VP; Evelyn Lane, Treas.

Desc: Publishes on local history and genealogy. Also publishes a newsletter and offers a calendar.

2825 ■ M. Frederick Amos

352 Blythewood Rd.   Ph: (905)632-6656
Burlington, ON, Canada L7L 2G8
E-mail: amos@spectranet.ca

Desc: Publishes family genealogies.

2826 ■ Ancestor Publishers
6166 Janice Way   Ph: (303)420-3460
Arvada, CO 80001
E-mail: info@ancestorspy.com
URL: http://www.ancestorspy.com

Contact: Donna Clark, Owner.

Desc: Publishes genealogical records on microfiche.

2827 ■ Ancestral Historian Society
Postal Unit 529
Evans, GA 30809

Contact: J. Stewart, Dir.; Angie Dorrill, Office Mgr.

2828 ■ Ancestry Inc.
PO Box 990   Ph: (801)426-3500
Orem, UT 84059-0990   Free: 800-262-3787
     Fax: (801)426-3501
E-mail: abrummer@ancestry.com
URL: http://www.ancestry.com

Contact: Paul Allen; Dan Taggart.

Desc: Publishes genealogical reference books, CD-ROMs, and magazines. Does not accept unsolicited manuscripts.

2829 ■ Mrs. Daniel A. Arbuckle
883 Mountain View Ave.   Ph: (613)596-1132
Ottawa, ON, Canada K2B 5G1

Contact: Mrs. Daniel A. Arbuckle, Author.

Desc: Local and family history.

2830 ■ Arkansas Ancestors
222 McMahan Dr.   Ph: (501)623-6766
Hot Springs National Park, AR   Fax: (501)623-6766
  71913

Contact: Bobbie J. McLane, Pub.

Desc: Publishes historical and genealogical research materials of Arkansas and Alabama.

2831 ■ Arkansas Genealogical Society, Inc.
1411 Shady Grove Rd.   Ph: (501)262-4513
PO Box 908   Fax: (501)262-4513
Hot Springs, AR 71902-0908
URL: http://www.rootsweb.com/args

Contact: Margaret Harrison Hubbard, Ed.

Desc: Publishes on Arkansas genealogical research. Offers a resource directory, microfiche, research aids, and The Arkansas Family Historian publication for members. Accepts unsolicited manuscripts.

2832 ■ Arkansas Research
PO Box 303   Ph: (501)470-1120
Conway, AR 72033   Fax: (501)470-1120
URL: http://biz.ipa.net/arkresearch

Contact: Desmond Walls Allen, Owner.

Desc: Publishes genealogical and historical research source materials, specializing in Arkansas. Publishes Arkansas Historical and Genealogical Magazines.

2833 ■ Association for Gravestone Studies
278 Main St., Ste. 207   Ph: (413)772-0836
Greenfield, MA 01301-3230
E-mail: ags@javanet.com
URL: http://www.berkshire.net/ags

Contact: Rosalee Oakley, Acting Admin.; Denise R. Webb, Administrator.

Desc: Nonprofit organization devoted to the study and preservation of gravestones. Offers a newsletter and an annual journal, Markers. Accepts unsolicited manuscripts.

2834 ■ Association of Professional Genealogists (APG)
PO Box 40393
Denver, CO 80204-0393
URL: http://www.apgen.org/

Contact: Shirley Langdon Wilcox, Pres.; Marie V. Melchiori, VP.

Desc: Publishes on genealogy. Offers APG Quarterly..

2835 ■ Mary D. Atkinson
RFD 1, Box 275   Ph: (304)628-3573
Cairo, WV 26337-0223

Contact: Mary D. Atkinson, Pub.

Desc: Biography, genealogy, history.

2836 ■ Augury Press/Hereditary Register of the U.S.A.
PO Box 40355
Phoenix, AZ 85067-0355

Contact: Ralph M. Pabst, Pres.

2837 ■ Augustana Historical Society
Augustana College   Ph: (309)794-7266
Rock Island, IL 61201   Fax: (309)794-7230

Contact: Keith Johnson, Pres.

Desc: Aims to help preserve the historical record of the Swedish immigrants and their church, and to encourage historical research by publication. Publishes on Swedish-American history and culture.

2838 ■ Automated Archives Inc.
1160 S. State St., Ste. 250   Ph: (801)226-6066
Orem, UT 84058   Fax: (801)224-0449

Contact: Paul R. Derby, Pres.; Jay E. Potter, VP; Lyman D. Platt, VP.

Desc: Produces genealogical information on CD-ROM. Accepts unsolicited manuscripts.

2839 ■ Avotaynu, Inc.
155 N. Washington Ave.   Ph: (201)387-7200
Bergenfield, NJ 07621   Free: 800-286-8296
     Fax: (201)387-2855
E-mail: info@avotaynu.com
URL: http://www.avotaynu.com

Contact: Gary Mokotoff, Pub.; Sallyann Amdur Sack, Ed.

Desc: Publishes on genealogy.

2840 ■ Nancy Chappelear Baird
1285 Shank Dr., No. 219   Ph: (540)564-6513
Harrisonburg, VA 22802

Contact: Nancy Chappelear Baird, Owner.

Desc: Self-publisher of historical and genealogical reference books.

2841 ■ Louise M. Bamford
65 Lawson Ct.   Ph: (506)472-8202
Fredericton, NB, Canada E3A
  5G3

Desc: Publishes on genealogy.

2842 ■ Banner Press, Inc.
PO Box 660180   Ph: (205)822-4783
Birmingham, AL 35266

Contact: Neola W. Helmbold, Pres. & Dir.

Desc: Publishes books, genealogy charts, and census extracts.

2843 ■ Barn Hill
Rittenhouse Claridge, Ste. 201   Ph: (215)732-7680
Philadelphia, PA 19103-5919   Fax: (215)732-2829

Contact: Helen Estes Seltzer, Owner.

Desc: Genealogy. Does not accept unsolicited manuscripts.

2844 ■ C. Virginia Barnes
2 5th Ave., 16M   Ph: (212)227-4714
New York, NY 10011   Fax: (212)732-9453

Contact: C. Virginia Barnes, Owner.

Desc: Genealogy, magic, music. Does not accept unsolicited manuscripts.

2845 ■ Lucille Basler
50 N. 5th   Ph: (573)883-3134
Sainte Genevieve, MO 63670

Contact: Lucille Basler, Author.

Desc: Publishes on the history of Ste. Genevieve.

2846 ■ R. W. Beatty, Academic Publisher
PO Box 26   Ph: (540)338-4034
Arlington, VA 22210

Contact: Richard W. Beatty, Pres.

Desc: Subjects include: Health, K-12 school, history, music, genealogy. Publishes educational textbooks for all levels. Offers monographs, training materials, catalogs, and prints, among others. Accepts unsolicited manuscripts.

2847 ■ Bell Books
10460 N. Palmyra Rd.   Ph: (330)538-2046
North Jackson, OH 44451-9793

Contact: Carol Willsey Bell, Owner & Pub.

Desc: Publishes on Ohio genealogy.

2848 ■ Belle Publications
172 Pathway Ln.   Ph: (765)463-6361
West Lafayette, IN 47906

Contact: I. Belle Schalliol, Owner & Ed.; Willis Lee Schalliol, Assoc. Ed./Bus. Mgr.

Desc: Publishes on history and genealogy.

2849 ■ Tom & Genevieve H. Bellis
2606 S. Troy St.
Arlington, VA 22206

Desc: Subject: Genealogy.

2850 ■ Berrien County Genealogical Society
PO Box 8808   Ph: (616)944-0278
Benton Harbor, MI 49023-8808
E-mail: bcgensoc@aol.com
URL: http://www.qtm.net/bcgensoc

Contact: Paula Jorgensen, VP; Patsy Pullins, Treas.; Brenda Sears, Pres.

Desc: Genealogical society. Members receive quarterly, the Pastfinder. Accepts unsolicited manuscripts.

2851 ■ The Bibliographer
14 Ponderosa Ave.   Ph: (603)883-9188
Nashua, NH 03062-1018   Fax: (603)623-4412

Contact: Helen F. Evans, Owner.

Desc: Publishes materials on American women and early New Hampshire legal records.

2852 ▪ Big Barn Press

608 N. Cleveland St.　　　　　Ph: (903)813-2357
Sherman, TX 75090　　　　　Fax: (903)813-2368
E-mail: jlincecum@austinc.edu

Contact: Jerry B. Lincecum, Pres.; Peggy A. Redshaw, VP.

Desc: Publishes autobiography, family history, and humor.

2853 ▪ Blair County Genealogical Society, Inc.

431 Scotch Valley Rd.　　　　Ph: (814)696-3492
Hollidaysburg, PA 16648

Contact: Robert Hewitt, Pres.; Ray Beck, VP; Jennie Amrhein, Corresponding Sec.; Penny Knisely, Treas.; Addie Beck, Research Sec.

Desc: Publishes genealogical data such as cemetery records, church records, funeral home records, tax records, and any other material that gives information to persons tracing their family trees. Also offers a quarterly newsletter.

2854 ▪ Bluffton Historical Preservation Society, Inc.

PO Box 742　　　　　　　　Ph: (803)757-3650
Bluffton, SC 29910　　　　　Fax: (803)757-6604

Contact: J. H. Harrison, Jr., Pres.; J. Moultrie Lee, VP; Ann Elliott, Treas./Sec.; Dorothy Smith, Corresponding Sec.

Desc: Does not accept unsolicited manuscripts.

2855 ▪ Ima Gene Boyd

370 E. Archwood Ave.　　　　Ph: (330)773-1757
Akron, OH 44301-2157

Contact: Ima Gene Boyd, Compiler & Pub.

Desc: Self-publisher of family history.

2856 ▪ Margie M. Boyd

PO Box 248　　　　　　　　Ph: (409)423-3298
Kirbyville, TX 75956-0248

Desc: Publishes on the history of the Rigsby, Lawson, and Foster families.

2857 ▪ Carl Boyer III

PO Box 220333　　　　　　　Ph: (805)259-3154
Santa Clarita, CA 91322-0333
E-mail: cboyer@sosinet.net

Contact: Carl Boyer, III, Proprietor.

Desc: Subject: Genealogy. Does not accept unsolicited manuscripts.

2858 ▪ Brigance Publishing

278 Royal Oaks Dr.　　　　　Ph: (423)982-0223
Maryville, TN 37801
E-mail: brigance@worldnet.att.net

Contact: Albert H. Brigance, Owner.

Desc: Publishes books on genealogy. Books contain student skill text for teaching reading and building reading skills.

2859 ▪ British Columbia Genealogical Society

PO Box 88054　　　　　　　Ph: (604)325-0374
Richmond, BC, Canada V6X
　3T6
URL: http://www.npsnet.com/bcgs

Desc: Publishes on genealogy in British Columbia, Canada. Accepts unsolicited manuscripts. Distributes for Federation of Family Hisotry Societies Publications.

2860 ▪ Brooks Enterprises

10717 Sunset Blvd.　　　　　Ph: (405)748-7474
Oklahoma City, OK 73120-2437

Contact: Clifton R. Brooks, Proprietor.

Desc: Publishes a one-name family quarterly journal.

2861 ▪ Brossart Publishing

20715 Viento Valle　　　　　Ph: (760)741-3255
Escondido, CA 92025　　　　Fax: (760)741-9517

Contact: Marlin W. Brossart, Owner.

Desc: Subject: Genealogy. Self-publisher. Does not accept unsolicited manuscripts.

2862 ▪ Bryn Ffyliaid Publications

300 Lake Marina Dr.,　　　　Ph: (504)288-7956
　Unit 16BW　　　　　　　Fax: (504)288-7956
New Orleans, LA 70124-1676

Contact: June Banks Evans, Pub.

Desc: Publishes on genealogy and teacher education.

2863 ▪ Bucks County Genealogical Society

PO Box 1092　　　　　　　Ph: (215)230-9410
Doylestown, PA 18901

Contact: Audrey Wolfinger, Pres.; Peggy H. Adams, VP; Marilyn Becker, Sec.; Laura Hager, Treas.

Desc: Publishes genealogical and historical information on Bucks County, Pennsylvania. Offers a quarterly newsletter. Accepts unsolicited manuscripts related to Bucks County research.

2864 ▪ Bullbrier Press

RR 1 Box 332　　　　　　　Ph: (717)769-7345
Jersey Shore, PA 17740　　　Fax: (717)769-7345
E-mail: bullb@cub.kcnet.org

Contact: Joanna M. K. Smith, Proprietor.

Desc: Publishes on plants, art, engineering, and genealogy.

2865 ▪ William Burns Association

15202 Crescent St.　　　　　Ph: (703)670-4742
Dale City, VA 22193

Contact: John Thomas Reynolds, Dir.

Desc: Publishes genealogical research on William Burns and associated families.

2866 ▪ C & L Historical Publications

PO Box 703
Toast, NC 27049

Contact: Carol Leonard Snow, Owner.

Desc: Publishes genealogical and historical information pertaining to Surry County, North Carolina. Does not accept unsolicited manuscripts.

2867 ▪ Robert Campbell

2084 Naskapi Dr.　　　　　Ph: (613)745-3323
Ottawa, ON, Canada K1J 8M3

Contact: Robert B. Campbell, Pres.

Desc: Publishes family history.

2868 ▪ Cap K Publications

358 S. Bentley Ave.　　　　　Ph: (310)472-9206
Los Angeles, CA 90049
URL: http://www.lacspc.org/kiermeet

Contact: Cap Kieruluff, Owner.

Desc: Publishes on genealogy.

2869 ▪ Carroll County Genealogical Society

59 3rd St. NE　　　　　　　Ph: (330)627-2094
Carrollton, OH 44615

Contact: Sara Finnicum, Pres.; Marguerite Finnicum, VP; Judy Van Horne, Corresponding Sec.; Shirley Anderson, Recording Sec.; Pauline Davis, Treas.

Desc: Publishes on history and genealogy of families associated with Carroll County, Ohio.

2870 ▪ Center for Life Stories Preservation

137 Bates Ave.　　　　　　Ph: (651)774-5015
St. Paul, MN 55106
URL: http://www.storypreservation.com/who.html

Desc: Publishes a book on how to preserve family history.

2871 ▪ Central New York Genealogical Society, Inc.

PO Box 104, Colvin Sta.
Syracuse, NY 13205

Contact: Joan Green, Chrmn.; Charles E. Browne, Ed.; Harold Witter, Treas.

Desc: Promotes the study of genealogy in New York State. Offers Tree Talks quarterly. Does not accept unsolicited manuscripts.

2872 ▪ Centre d'Etudes Acadiennes

Universite de Moncton　　　　Ph: (506)858-4085
Moncton, NB, Canada E1A 3E9　Fax: (506)858-4086
URL: http://www.umoncton.ca/etudeacadiennes/centre/
　cea.html

Contact: Maurice Basque, Dir.; Ginette Leger, Sec.

Desc: Publishes on the Acadians. Most publications are in French.

2873 ▪ Cheshire Cat Press/Iron Gate Publishing

PO Box 2611　　　　　　　Ph: (519)472-5572
Sarnia, ON, Canada N7T 7V8

Contact: Glen C. Phillips, Proprietor.

Desc: Publishes specialized historical reference and genealogy books, plus local and Canadian history. Also offers posters and prints, historical research services, and photo sales. Accepts unsolicited manuscripts related to what we public.

2874 ▪ Chippewa Heritage Publications

PO Box 16736　　　　　　　Ph: (218)878-3449
Duluth, MN 55816-0736

Contact: Michael D. Munnell, Pub. & Author.

Desc: Publishes genealogical information relating to the Great Lakes region American Indians, with emphasis on Chippewa, Ojiwe, and Anishinabe Tribal people.

2875 ▪ Aldene and Les Church

15 Lorne St. N.　　　　　　Ph: (613)432-8986
Renfrew, ON, Canada K7V 1K8
E-mail: a&lchurch@renfrew.net

Contact: H. L. Church; A. R. Church.

Desc: Publishes genealogical reference books.

2876 ▪ Church and Synagogue Library Association

PO Box 19357　　　　　　　Ph: (503)244-6919
Portland, OR 97280-0357　　Free: 800-542-2752
　　　　　　　　　　　　Fax: (503)977-3734
E-mail: csla@worldaccessnet.com
URL: http://www.worldaccessnet.com/csla

Contact: Judy Janzen, Administrator; Karen Bota, Publications Ed.

Desc: Provides guides and bibliographies useful in the establishment and maintenance of library services in churches and synagogues. Also publishes a journal. Does not accept unsolicited manuscripts.

2877 ▪ Ciga Press
PO Box 654
Fallbrook, CA 92088

Ph: (619)728-9308
Fax: (619)728-9308

Contact: Ruth Blake, Man. Ed.; Louis F. Burns, Ed.

Desc: Publishes some genealogical materials, but mostly publishes Osage Indian materials.

2878 ▪ Laura M. Clarenbach
5009 Risser Rd.
Madison, WI 53705-1366

Desc: Nonprofit self-publisher of a family history.

2879 ▪ Clark County Genealogical Society
1511 Main St.
PO Box 2728
Vancouver, WA 98668

Contact: Jerri St. John, Pres.; Roy Katschke, VP; Jennifer Warren, Sec.; Mary Katschke, VP; Rose Marie Harshman, Publications Mgr.

Desc: Publishes genealogical information for Clark and Skamania County, Washington. Does not accept unsolicited manuscripts.

2880 ▪ Clearfield Co.
200 E. Eager St.
Baltimore, MD 21202

Ph: (410)625-9004
Fax: (410)752-8492

Contact: Roger Sherr, Pres.

Desc: Publishes original works and discount reprints in the field of genealogy. Distributes other publisher's overruns and remainders. Accepts unsolicited manuscripts.

2881 ▪ William L. Clink
148 Finch Ave. W.
Willowdale, ON, Canada M2N 2J2

Ph: (416)221-5645

Contact: William L. Clink.

Desc: Selected histories and family genealogies. Publishes nonfiction.

2882 ▪ Closson Press
1935 Sampson Dr.
Apollo, PA 15613-9208
E-mail: rclosson@nb.net
URL: http://www.clossonpress.com

Ph: (724)337-4482
Fax: (724)337-9484

Contact: Marietta Closson, Proprietor; Mary Closson, GM.

Desc: Publishes specialty genealogical and historical publications. Accepts unsolicited manuscripts; genealogy & history only.

2883 ▪ Colchester Historical Museum
29 Young St.
PO Box 412
Truro, NS, Canada B2N 5C5
E-mail: chmusarc@auracom.com

Ph: (902)895-6284
Fax: (902)895-9530

Contact: Edith Patterson, Pres.; Terence White, Museum Board Chrmn.; Penny Lighthall; Nan Harvey, Archivist.

Desc: Publishes on local history and genealogy. Also publishes a newsletter. Does not accept unsolicited manuscripts

2884 ▪ Andrew Cook Genealogical Society Inc.
46 King St.
Tillsonburg, ON, Canada N4G 3E7

Ph: (519)842-9433
Fax: (519)842-4604

Contact: Kathryn Cook, Pres.; Dianne Cook, VP.

Desc: Nonprofit publisher of genealogy. Also offers a semi-annual newsletter.

2885 ▪ Helen C. Cooper
2308 Lillooet Crescent
Kelowna, BC, Canada V1V 1T1
E-mail: helen_cooper.bc.sympatico.ca

Ph: (250)860-4936

Desc: Subjects include: Canadian military, genealogy. Self publisher. Does not accept unsolicited manuscripts.

2886 ▪ A. Maxim Coppage
653 Pershing Dr.
Walnut Creek, CA 94596

Ph: (510)938-9248

Desc: Publishes books on southern genealogy and history and the quarterly Virginia Settlers..

2887 ▪ Coralex Publisher
PO Box 2011
Calgary Pl. Postal Outlet
Calgary, AB, Canada T2P 4T2

Ph: (403)288-8834
Fax: (403)241-1244

Contact: Alex Cheung, Mktg. Mgr.

Desc: Publishes educational books for immigrants to the United States who speak English as a second language.

2888 ▪ Corporation of the County of Huron
County Court House
Goderich, ON, Canada N7A 1M2

Ph: (519)524-8394
Fax: (519)524-2044

Desc: Publishes on life in Huron County, with maps and histories of its municipalities, names of residents, and stories of families, churches, organizations, and businesses.

2889 ▪ Cottontail Publications
79 Drakes Ridge
Bennington, IN 47011-1802

Ph: (812)427-3921
Fax: (812)427-3921

Contact: Ellyn R. Kern, Pub.

Desc: Desires to publish books and reports on presidential history, local history and genealogy, and alternative life styles. Publishes newsletter The Presidents' Journal..

2890 ▪ Cottonwood County Historical Society
812 4th Ave.
Windom, MN 56101

Ph: (507)831-1134

Contact: Lowell Tjentland, Pres.; Garnet Bodze, 1st VP; Marilyn Erickson, Sec.; Margaret McDonald, Treas.

Desc: A historical museum which publishes materials related to history, historical collections, exhibits, interpretation and preservation of artifacts, genealogy and genealogical research.

2891 ▪ Margaret M. Cowart
7801 Tea Garden Rd. SE
Huntsville, AL 35802

Ph: (205)881-2097

Desc: Publishes genealogical resource books, specializing in early land records.

2892 ▪ Helen W. Crawford
509 Nacoqdoches
Jacksonville, TX 75766

Ph: (903)586-2942

Desc: Publishes on Cherokee County, Texas records for use in doing family and historical research.

2893 ▪ John R. Crossman
2907 S. 46th St.
Milwaukee, WI 53219-3427

Ph: (414)421-5637

Contact: John R. Crossman, Pres.

Desc: Publishes genealogies. Does not accept unsolicited manuscripts. Presently inactive.

2894 ▪ Crowder Enterprises
22 Canter Blvd.
Nepean, ON, Canada K2G 2M2

Ph: (613)224-2880

E-mail: ahoo9@freenet.carleton.ca

Contact: Norman Kenneth Crowder, Proprietor.

Desc: Publishes historical and genealogical works and research aids. Offers genealogical research services.

2895 ▪ A. Eileen Smith Cunningham
Rte. 2, Box 10
Carrollton, IL 62016

Ph: (217)942-3868

Contact: A. Eileen Cunningham.

Desc: Publishes on local and family history. Offers black and white art prints. Does not accept unsolicited manuscripts.

2896 ▪ Curtis Media Inc.
4102 Inwood Ln.
Colleyville, TX 76034-3851

Ph: (817)285-7091
Fax: (817)285-0176

Contact: Ray Wantuchowicz, Pres.; Pete Willson, Operations Dir.; Paula Oates, Mktg. Dir.

Desc: Publishes local histories including family histories.

2897 ▪ Lena V. D'Agostino
4728 190th St.
Flushing, NY 11358

Ph: (607)278-5808

Desc: Subjects include genealogy and family life.

2898 ▪ Danbury House Books
PO Box 253
Oakland, ME 04963-0253

Ph: (207)465-2610

Contact: Michael J. Denis, Owner; Jeanine Denis, Co-Owner.

Desc: Reprints out-of-print historical/genealogical works, mostly excerpted from New England works. Distributes for Genealogical Publishing Co., Everton, and Heritage Books.

2899 ▪ Judith M. Darby
1 Cartbridge Rd.
Weston, CT 06883

Ph: (203)222-1727
Fax: (203)222-1261

Contact: Judith M. Darby, Owner.

Desc: Publishes family genealogies. Also offers information on historical homes.

2900 ▪ Virginia Carlisle d'Armand
3636 Taliluna Ave., No. 235
Knoxville, TN 37919

Ph: (423)522-3147

Contact: Virginia Carlisle d'Armand.

Desc: Publishes family and regional history.

2901 ▪ James Doyle Davison
PO Box 1092
Wolfville, NS, Canada B0P 1X0

Ph: (902)542-3088

Desc: Publishes regional history and biographies.

2902 ▪ W. S. Dawson Co.
801 Cathedral Dr.
Virginia Beach, VA 23455
E-mail: n2504@cxis.net

Ph: (757)490-2504
Fax: (757)490-3494

Contact: C. W. Tazewell, Pub.

Desc: Publishes history of Eastern Virginia, genealogy, biography, and reprints of rare books. Also publishes The Tazewell Quandary and Goode Goodies newsletters. Does not accept unsolicited manuscripts. Offers software, online services, and CD-ROM formats. Distributes for University Press of Virginia, Fred B. Rothman Co., Norfolk Historical Society, et al.

2903 ■ George P. De Kay
RR 1
Hyde Park, ON, Canada N0M 1Z0

Contact: George P. De Kay.

Desc: Publishes genealogy.

2904 ■ Dean Publications
2204 El Canto Circle   Ph: (916)366-0100
Rancho Cordova, CA
95670-3120

Contact: Mary Dean Alsworth, Owner.

Desc: Subjects: Genealogy, local history.

2905 ■ Decatur Genealogical Society
PO Box 1548   Ph: (217)429-0135
Decatur, IL 62525-1548

Contact: Jean Fox, Pres.; Sue Bergandine, 1st VP; Ann
Irwin, 2nd VP; Cheri Hunter, Librarian; Linda Williams, Treas.

Desc: Preserves and publishes material of historical and
genealogical nature for central Illinois, including a
monthly newsletter, quarterlies, books, and maps. Accepts
unsolicited manuscripts for review.

2906 ■ Dedham Historical Society
PO Box 215   Ph: (781)326-1385
Dedham, MA 02027-0215   Fax: (781)326-5762
E-mail: dhs@dedham.com
URL: http://www.dedham.com/dhs

Contact: Ronald F. Frazier, Exec. Dir. & CEO.

Desc: Publishes books on Dedham history. Also offers
postcards and copies of genealogical and collection manuscripts.

2907 ■ Delaware County Historical Alliance
120 E. Washington St.   Ph: (765)282-1550
Muncie, IN 47305-1734   Fax: (765)282-1058
E-mail: dcha@iquest.net
URL: http://www.iguest.net/dcha/

Contact: Jackie Stuart, Administrative Asst.

Desc: Publishes historical and genealogical information
about Muncie County, Indiana. Does not accept unsolicited manuscripts.

2908 ■ L. George Dewar
PO Box 100   Ph: (902)859-2424
O'Leary, PE, Canada C0B 1V0

Desc: Local and family history. Accepts unsolicited manuscripts.

2909 ■ Dream Weavers Publishing
7530 W. 10th St., No. 305   Ph: (303)237-4561
Lakewood, CO 80215   Fax: (303)232-5958

Contact: Sandra Talkington, Owner & Ed.

Desc: Subjects include: New age, Native American history,
humor, genealogy. Publishes fiction and non-fiction. Accepts unsolicited manuscripts; send the first chapter, dou-
ble spaced.

2910 ■ Richard H. Driessel
301 Barbie Dr.   Ph: (414)335-3956
West Bend, WI 53090

Contact: Richard H. Driessel, Pres.; Margaret L.
Driessel, VP.

Desc: Local Wisconsin history, genealogy.

2911 ■ Dubois County Historical Society
737 W. 8th St.   Ph: (812)482-3074
Jasper, IN 47546

Contact: Mary Ann Hayes, Pres.

Desc: .

2912 ■ Duplechain Publishing
108 Louisa St.   Ph: (318)837-6711
Broussard, LA 70518

Contact: Maxine Duplechain Duhon.

Desc: Publishes genealogical materials.

2913 ■ Dyck Family History Book Committee
PO Box 1053   Ph: (204)325-8757
Winkler, MB, Canada R6W 4B1
E-mail: joyeck@freemet.mbca

Contact: Jacob Dyck, Chrmn.

Desc: Publishes a family history book about the descendants of Jacob Dyck and Elizabeth Jaeger.

2914 ■ Douglas Eaton Eagles
923 Wedgewood Ave.   Ph: (519)344-6430
Sarnia, ON, Canada N7V 3E8

Contact: Douglas Eaton Eagles.

Desc: Subject: Genealogy.

2915 ■ Eastern Townships Research Centre
Faculty Box 132   Ph: (819)822-9600
Lennoxville, PQ, Canada J1M   Fax: (819)822-9661
1Z7

Contact: Dr. Melissa Clark-James, Chair; Rina Kampeas,
Exec. Dir.; Sylvie Cote, Archivist.

Desc: Publishes bibliographies. Offers two periodicals,in-
cluding the Journal of Eastern Townships Studies..

2916 ■ Effingham County Genealogical Society
PO Box 1166
Effingham, IL 62401

Contact: Arnetia Osborn, Pres.

Desc: Publishes genealogy information on Effingham
county. Offers a newsletter. Accepts unsolicited manuscripts.

2917 ■ Egeon Enterprises
PO Box 146153   Ph: (415)826-3387
San Francisco, CA 94114

Contact: Pamela Miller, Partner; Richard Rees, Partner.

Desc: Publishes on genealogy. Accepts unsolicited manuscripts.

2918 ■ Earle W. Elliott
85 Humewood Dr.   Ph: (613)968-7281
Belleville, ON, Canada K8N 4E3

Contact: Earle W. Elliott.

Desc: Self-publisher of family history and genealogy. Presently inactive.

2919 ■ Ericson Books
1614 Redbud St.   Ph: (409)564-3625
Nacogdoches, TX 75961   Fax: (409)552-8999

Contact: Carolyn Ericson, Owner; Kathryn Davis,
Exec. Asst.

Desc: Publishes regional history and genealogical titles.
Distributes for Dietz Press and GPC Southern History
Press.

2920 ■ Erin Go Braugh Books
4629 E. Earll Dr.   Ph: (602)952-0779
Phoenix, AZ 85018

Contact: Joseph L. Grady, Pres. & Ed.-in-Chief; Emma
R. Grady, Sec.-Treas.

Desc: Publishes a family history and sociological study of
Irish-American immigrants.

2921 ■ The Eschenbachs
8206 Baring Ave.   Ph: (219)322-5433
Munster, IN 46321-1409

Contact: Virginia S. Eschenbach, Owner; Robert Eschenbach, Owner.

Desc: Publishes a handbook for both beginning and experienced German genealogists.

**2922 ■ Norma Pontiff Evans, Genealogical
Services**
515 20th St.   Ph: (409)835-7175
Beaumont, TX 77706

Contact: Norma Pontiff Evans, Owner.

2923 ■ Everton Publishers, Inc.
PO Box 368   Ph: (435)752-6022
Logan, UT 84323-0368   Free: 800-443-6325
Fax: (435)752-0425

Contact: A. Lee Everton, Jr., Pres. & Pub.; Bob Arbon,
VP; Valarie N. Chambers, Ed.; Richard Singleton, Book
Review Ed.; Sandra Hall, Book Review Ed.

Desc: Publishes books pertaining to genealogy and history.
Accepts unsolicited manuscripts.

2924 ■ Excelsior Cee Publishing
PO Box 5861   Ph: (405)329-3909
Norman, OK 73070   Fax: (405)329-6886
E-mail: ecp@oecadvantage.net

Contact: J.C. Marshall, Pres.; Clyde Marshall.

Desc: Subjects include: How-to, writing, inspiration, genealogy, decorating, education, nostalgia, Americana, family
history, humor. Publishes nonfiction and educational
books. Accepts unsolicited manuscripts.

**2925 ■ Fairfield County Chapter of the Ohio
Genealogical Society**
PO Box 1470   Ph: (740)653-2745
Lancaster, OH 43130-0570
E-mail: chapter@fairfieldgenealogy.org
URL: http://www.fairfieldgenealogy.org

Contact: Patsy Kishler, Pres.; Carol Swinehart, VP; Joan
Odell, Treas.; Karen Smith, Corresponding Sec.; Marvene
Judy, Recording Sec.

Desc: Publishes records of Fairfield County, Ohio ancestors. Publications are intended for use by genealogists.
Offers the quarterly newsletter Fairfield Trace..

2926 ■ Fairfield House
3 Fairfield Dr.   Ph: (410)747-6590
Baltimore, MD 21228

Contact: Richard M. Byers, Owner.

Desc: Subjects include genealogy and fiction. Does not
accept unsolicited manuscripts.

2927 ■ Family History Library
Family History Department   Ph: (801)240-2331
35 North West Temple   Free: 800-453-3860
Salt Lake City, UT 84150-3400   Fax: (801)240-5551
E-mail: fhl@ldschurch.org

Contact: Jimmy Parker, Mgr.

Desc: Publishes instructional booklets and genealogy software package for personal computer use. Also produces microfiche indexes of the library's computer files.

2928 ▪ Family History World
PO Box 129   Fax: (801)250-6717
Tremonton, UT 84337
E-mail: genealogy@utahlinx.com

Contact: Arlene H. Eakle, Owner & Pres.; Alma D. Eakle, Jr., General Mgr.; Afton Reintjes, Dir. of Research.

Desc: Distributor.

2929 ▪ Family Tree Press
Rte He2, Box 180V   Ph: (520)478-4012
Payson, AZ 85541

Contact: Fay Dearden, Owner; Douglas Dearden, Partner.

Desc: Publishes German genealogical self-help and instructional materials.

2930 ▪ Fawcett History Book Club
PO Box 1
Fawcett, AB, Canada T0G 0Y0

Contact: Marianne Cochrane, Ed., Treas., & Sales; Elwood Boyd, Ed. & Sales; Germaine McCann, Sec.

Desc: Publishes family history evolving around area of Fawcett.

2931 ▪ Federation of Genealogical Societies
PO Box 3385   Ph: (801)422-9688
Salt Lake City, UT 84110-3385   Fax: (801)422-9688

Contact: Curt B. Witcher, Pres., Administration; Ruth Keys Clark, VP, Membership Services; Gary Mokotoff, VP, External Affairs.

Desc: Publishes family history research books. Offers a quarterly FGS Forum..

2932 ▪ Fisher House Publishers
10907-34 A Ave.   Ph: (403)435-2320
Edmonton, AB, Canada T6J   Fax: (403)468-2058
2T9
E-mail: fisher@ocii.com
URL: http://www.ocii.com/fisher

Contact: John R. Fisher, Pres.

Desc: Publishes education materials, biographies and family histories. Offers electronic services. Accepts unsolicited manuscripts; send resume.

2933 ▪ Fitzwilliam Enterprises
352 Imperial Rd. S.
Guelph, ON, Canada N1K 1L8

Desc: Subjects include: Heraldry, genealogy. Presently inactive.

2934 ▪ Florentine Press
PO Box 705   Ph: (904)358-2736
Jacksonville, FL 32201

Contact: Evelyn McDaniel Frazier Bryan, Owner.

Desc: Publishes historical and genealogical books pertaining mainly to South Carolina.

2935 ▪ Fort Worth Genealogical Society
PO Box 9767
Fort Worth, TX 76147

Contact: Jari Emmons, Pres.; Pat Gordon, 1st VP; Martha Ann Past, 2nd VP; Jerry Grant, 3rd VP.

Desc: Preserves county records, early family histories, and historical information. Publishes a quarterly journal, Footprints..

2936 ▪ Shirley Phillips Friel
1104 Crestview Dr.   Ph: (219)665-5720
Angola, IN 46703
E-mail: pfriel2@juno.com

Contact: Shirley Phillips Friel, Author.

Desc: Publishes on the Phillips family.

2937 ▪ Fulton County Historical Society, Inc.
PO Box 115
McConnellsburg, PA 17233

Contact: Daniel Swain, Pres.; Hazel Harr, Librarian; Todd Hoffner, Sec.

Desc: Publishes local histories and resource materials of Fulton County, Pennsylvania. Provides genealogical research. Accepts unsolicited manuscripts.

2938 ▪ Bertha L. Gable, Author and Publisher
506 N. Walnut
Clarksville, TX 75426

Contact: Bertha L. Gable, Owner.

Desc: Self-publishes genealogical research on Red River County, Texas.

2939 ▪ Ganymede Press
64 Jarrow Rd.   Ph: (905)934-1744
St. Catharines, ON, Canada
L2M 1B6
E-mail: brianfinn@hotmail.com

Contact: Brian Narhi, Prop.

Desc: Publishes on history and genealogy. Offers diskettes. Accepts unsolicited manuscripts.

2940 ▪ GE Publications
1707 Laurel
Odessa, TX 79761

Contact: James F. Gammon, Owner.

Desc: Publishes genealogical books; also offers consulting services on Texas genealogical research.

2941 ▪ Genco Publishers
45 Sharon Ave.   Ph: (416)385-0900
Hamilton, ON, Canada L8T 1E2

Contact: Ida Crozier, Chrmn.; Murray Crozier, Vice-Chrmn., Sec.-Treas.

Desc: Publishes genealogies for the recording of individual family histories.

2942 ▪ Genealogical Data Services
3106 Northbrook Dr.   Ph: (608)245-9597
Middleton, WI 53562-1641   Fax: (608)245-0279

Contact: Joseph Pasowicz, Jr., Partner; Joan A. Pasowier, Partner.

Desc: Publishes genealogical compilations for researchers.

2943 ▪ Genealogical Enterprises
1140 Windsong Ln.   Ph: (941)534-4380
Siesta Key
Sarasota, FL 34242

Contact: Bernard J. Diedrich, Pres.; Marjorie H. Diedrich, Author & Researcher.

Desc: Publishes genealogy and family histories.

2944 ▪ Genealogical Institute
PO Box 129   Free: 800-377-6058
Tremonton, UT 84337   Fax: (801)250-6717
E-mail: genealogy@utahlinx.com

Contact: Arlene H. Eakle, Education & Research Division.

Desc: Publishes on family history, research methods and options, and local history. Offers two newsletters.

2945 ▪ Genealogical Publishing Co., Inc.
1001 N. Calvert St.   Ph: (410)037-8271
Baltimore, MD 21202   Free: 800-296-6687
    Fax: (410)752-8492
E-mail: orders@genealogical.com

Contact: Barry Chodak, Pres.; Michael Tepper, VP & Ed.-in-Chief; Joseph Garonzik, Mktg. Dir.

Desc: Publishes reference books on genealogy, local history, immigration, and family matters. Offers a videotape. Accepts unsolicited manuscripts.

2946 ▪ Genealogical Sources, Unltd.
407 Ascot Ct.   Ph: (423)690-7831
Knoxville, TN 37923-5807

Contact: George K. Schweitzer, Proprietor.

Desc: Publishes genealogical guidebooks. Does not accept unsolicited manuscripts.

2947 ▪ General Society of Mayflower Descendants
PO Box 3297   Ph: (508)746-5058
Plymouth, MA 02361

Contact: Caroline L. Kardell, Historian General; Richard H. Maxwell, Governor General.

Desc: Does not accept unsolicited manuscripts.

2948 ▪ Clara Sesler Genther
3352 Gano Ave.   Ph: (513)221-3908
Cincinnati, OH 45220

Contact: Clara Sesler Genther.

Desc: Publishes a family history.

2949 ▪ Georgia Department of Archives and History
330 Capitol Ave. SE   Ph: (404)656-2393
Atlanta, GA 30334   Fax: (404)657-8427

Contact: Edward Weldon, Dir.; Steven W. Engerrand, Asst. Dir.

Desc: Publishes research materials about the state of Georgia, records management materials, and the Georgia Official and Statistical Register. Offers microform copies of official records.

2950 ▪ Georgia Pioneers Publications
1510 N. Cleveland St., No. A
Albany, GA 31701-1527

Contact: Mary Carter, Owner.

Desc: Publishes genealogical records abstracted from county courthouses and state archives.

2951 ▪ German-Texan Heritage Society
507 E. 10th St.   Ph: (512)482-0927
PO Box 684171   Fax: (512)482-8809
Austin, TX 78768
URL: http://www.main.org/germantxn

Contact: Rodney C. Koenig, Pres.; Karl Micklitz, VP; Arliss Treybig, Sec.; Teresa Schwqusch Chavez, Exec. Dir.

Desc: Publishes reprints of German-Texana. Also publishes a journal three times a year. Accepts unsolicited manuscripts.

2952 ▪ S. F. Getchell
51 N. Main St.   Ph: (603)659-3652
Newmarket, NH 03857
E-mail: sfgetch@nh.ultranet.com

Contact: Sylvia Fitts Getchell, Owner.

Desc: Publishes historical and genealogical works.

2953 ▪ Gloucester County Historical Society

17 Hunter St.   Ph: (609)845-4771
Woodbury, NJ 08096-4605 Fax: (609)845-0131
E-mail: gchs@citnet.com

Contact: Janet Burr, Publications Chrmn.; J. Laughlin, Bulletin Ed.; Richard M. Burr, Pres.; Dorothy Range, VP; Robert Boakes, Second VP.

Desc: Publishes on the history of southern New Jersey, Delaware, and southern Pennsylvania area, as well as genealogies of families living within same geographical perimeter. Also offers society newsletters, genealogical charts, family group sheets, and miscellaneous aids to help the genealogist. Accepts unsolicited manuscripts; publication depends on committee.

2954 ▪ Godfrey Memorial Library

134 Newfield St.   Ph: (203)346-4375
Middletown, CT 06457   Fax: (203)347-9874
E-mail: godfrey@connix.com
URL: http://www.godfrey.org

Contact: Nancy Doane, Dir.

Desc: A genealogical library that publishes a biographical index. Offers limited family research and provides photocopies from specified genealogies or histories. Accepts unsolicited manuscripts for use by the library's patrons; not for publishing.

2955 ▪ Golden Gambit Books

76 Wheaton Dr.   Ph: (508)222-0176
Attleboro, MA 02703
URL: http://www.efbaasp.net

Contact: R. Moisan, Ed.

Desc: American historical fiction, American Indian culture and history, military autobiographies, oldtime prizefighting. Publishes fiction and nonfiction.

2956 ▪ Goodhue County Historical Society & Museum

1166 Oak St.   Ph: (651)388-6024
Red Wing, MN 55066   Fax: (651)388-3577

Contact: Char Henn, Curator; Charles Richardson, Pres.

Desc: Offers audio-visual programs of ethnic immigration into Goodhue County and a book on the history of Red Wing, an American Indian. Also offers yearly directories for genealogy research and libraries. Publishes Historical New Bulletin and Museum Briefs, each three times a year. A historical bus tour is offered annually.

2957 ▪ Winifred M. Gourley

Satilla Regional Library   Ph: (912)384-6450
Genealogy Department   Fax: (912)384-5365
201 S. Coffee Ave.
Douglas, GA 31533

Contact: Betty Schild, Library Dir.; Winifred Merier-Gourley, Genealogy Researcher.

Desc: Publishes on family and local history.

2958 ▪ Green Creek Publishing Co.

2251 Van Antwerp Rd.
Schenectady, NY 12309

Contact: W. V. Ligon, Pres.

Desc: Publishes genealogy and local history.

2959 ▪ Greenbrier Historical Society

301 W. Washington St.   Ph: (304)645-3398
Lewisburg, WV 24901   Fax: (304)645-5201

E-mail: ghs@access.mountain.net
URL: http://www.mountain.net/ghs/ghs.html

Contact: John Garnett, Pres.; James Talbert, Archivist; Harry McFarlane, Treas.; Joyce Mott, Museum Dir.

Desc: Publishes an annual journal and other historical material on Greenbrier County. Offers a regional map and a facsimile document. Accepts unsolicited manuscripts.

2960 ▪ Gregath Publishing Co.

PO Box 505   Ph: (918)542-4148
Wyandotte, OK 74370   Free: 800-955-5232
                         Fax: (918)542-4148
E-mail: gregath@galstar.com
URL: http://www.gregathcompany.com

Contact: Ann Gregath, Eastern Div. Pres.; Fredrea Gregath Cook, Midwest Div. Pres.; Carrie Ann Cook, Midwest Div. VP.

Desc: Specializes in genealogy and regional history materials. offers textbooks.

2961 ▪ Griepp Publishing

3505 Coolheights Dr.   Ph: (310)541-6334
Rancho Palos Verdes, CA 90275 Fax: (310)541-3669
E-mail: fgriepp@earthlink.net

Contact: Frank R. Griepp, Pres.; Muriel H. Griepp, VP.

Desc: Publishes on family history, genealogy, and military history.

2962 ▪ J. B. Griffith

16 Greens Lake Rd.   Ph: (706)866-7056
Rossville, GA 30741

Desc: Publishes books about the genealogy and history of various counties in Georgia. Accepts unsolicited manuscripts for research projects.

2963 ▪ Guild Bindery Press, Inc.

PO Box 120969   Ph: (615)292-2033
Nashville, TN 37212   Fax: (615)292-2037
E-mail: guildmedia@aol.com

Contact: Randall J. Bedwell, Pres.

Desc: Publishes historical genealogy books.

2964 ▪ W. C. Hall

427 6th St.   Ph: (515)382-6457
Nevada, IA 50201

Contact: W. C. Hall.

Desc: Subject: Genealogy.

2965 ▪ G. P. Hammond Publishing

PO Box 546   Ph: (540)465-8447
Strasburg, VA 22657-0546

Contact: Gene Paige Hammond, Pres. & CEO; Evelyn E. Hammond, VP; Eric P. Hammond, Jr., Accountant & Treas.; Rachel W. Hammond, Ed.; Paul F. Wilson.

Desc: Publishes historical and genealogical books and maps. Does not accept unsolicited manuscripts.

2966 ▪ Hampton House

PO Box 21482   Ph: (614)457-6703
Columbus, OH 43221   Fax: (614)457-6730

Contact: Joy Wade Moulton, Pres.; Edward Q. Moulton, VP.

Desc: Publishes books on genealogical research in England and the U.S.

2967 ▪ Phyllis Hapner

1019 N. Long St.   Ph: (217)774-3036
Shelbyville, IL 62565   Fax: (217)774-3036

Contact: Phyllis Hapner.

Desc: Publishes genealogical material pertaining to Shelby County, IL.

2968 ▪ Mary M. Harper

2558 Cherrywood Ln.   Ph: (407)267-1037
Titusville, FL 32780
E-mail: maryharp99@aol.com

Contact: Mary M. Harper.

Desc: Texas genealogy.

2969 ▪ Gloria C. Hartzell

1449 Yoder Ave.   Ph: (215)367-8769
Gilbertsville, PA 19525 Fax: (610)367-8769

Desc: Publishes genealogy books. Also offers coats of arms and pedigree charts.

2970 ▪ Hastings County Historical Society

PO Box 1418   Ph: (613)968-5023
Belleville, ON, Canada K8N 5J1

Contact: Gerald E. Boyce, Sales Mgr.

Desc: Offers publications relating to the Belleville-Hastings County-Bay of Quinte area of Ontario. Offers a monthly newsletter and genealogical research relating to Hastings County, Ontario.

2971 ▪ Heart of the Lakes Publishing

2989 Lodi Rd.   Ph: (607)532-4997
PO Box 299   Fax: (607)532-4684
Interlaken, NY 14847-0299
E-mail: hlpbooks@aol.com

Contact: Walter W. Steesy, Partner; Mary A. Steesy, Partner.

Desc: Publishes New York local history and genealogical books. Offers book production services for authors and small publishers.

2972 ▪ Hearthside Press

5735-A Telegraph Rd.   Ph: (703)960-0086
Alexandria, VA 22303   Fax: (703)960-0087
E-mail: info@hearthstonebooks.com

Contact: Stuart Nixon, Proprietor.

Desc: Publishes on genealogy. Does not accept unsolicited manuscripts.

2973 ▪ Hebert Publications

PO Box 147   Ph: (318)873-6574
Rayne, LA 70578-0147

Contact: Donald J. Hebert.

Desc: Publishes genealogical and historical works on Louisiana. Accepts unsolicited manuscripts.

2974 ▪ Hendricks Books

2110 Elm   Ph: (816)584-8500
Higginsville, MO 64037-1436

Contact: James Duncan, Owner; C.E. Hendricks, Co-owner.

Desc: Publishes books on area history, military histories, genealogical information, and local directories. Does not accept unsolicited manuscripts.

2975 ▪ M. Hepburn & Associates Inc.

181 Beaver Point Rd.   Ph: (250)653-4250
Saltspring Island, BC, Canada Free: 800-990-4250
   V8K 1Y8   Fax: (250)653-4291
URL: http://www/saltspring.com/mha

Contact: Mhora Hepburn, Prop.

Desc: Publishes on family history and biography. Accepts unsolicited manuscripts.

2976 ■ The Heraldry Society of Canada
PO Box 8128, Terminal T
Ottawa, ON, Canada K1G 3H9

Contact: Jean Matheson, Pres.; Howard Keck, Treas.; John J. Kennedy, Ed.

Desc: Publishes on heraldry, genealogy, flags and history. Also publishes a quarterly journal, a quarterly newsletter, Heraldry in Canada, and the newsletter The Gonfannon. Offers maps. Accepts unsolicited manuscripts.

2977 ■ Heritage Books, Inc.
1540-E Pointer Ridge Pl.   Ph: (301)390-7709
Bowie, MD 20716   Free: 800-398-7709
                              Fax: (301)390-7153
E-mail: heritagebooks@pipeline.com
URL: http://www.heritagebooks.com

Contact: Leslie K. Towle, Pres.

Desc: Publishes books on history, genealogy, and Americana with emphasis on genealogies and genealogical reference works.

2978 ■ Heritage House
9605 Vandergriff Rd.   Ph: (317)862-3330
PO Box 39128   Free: 800-419-0200
Indianapolis, IN 46239   Fax: (317)862-2599

Contact: Patricia Gooldy, Pres.; Ray Gooldy, Pub.; Walter R. Gooldy, CEO.

Desc: Publishes on genealogy.

2979 ■ Virginia Sharpe Hershey
5325 Wikiup Bridgeway
Santa Rosa, CA 95404

Desc: Family history.

2980 ■ Higginson Book Co.
148 Washington St.   Ph: (978)745-7170
PO Box 778   Fax: (978)745-8025
Salem, MA 01970
E-mail: higginsn@cove.com
URL: http://www.higginsonbooks.com

Contact: Robert Murphy, Owner & Pres.; Laura Bjorklund, VP & General Mgr.

Desc: Publishes on genealogy and history. Also publishes reprints. Does not accept unsolicited manuscripts. Distributes for Everton Publishers.

2981 ■ Highland Heritage/Glengarry Genealogical Society
RR 1   Ph: (613)347-2363
Lancaster, ON, Canada K0C
   1N0

Contact: Alex W. Fraser, Mgr.; Rhoda Ross, Asst.

Desc: Publishes local family histories and genealogies. Also publishes a bimonthly newsletter, Bridging the Gap, and offers maps. Accepts unsolicited manuscripts relating to Glengarry County. Alternate telephone number: (613)347-3180.

2982 ■ Isabel Louise Hill
363 University Ave.   Ph: (506)455-3883
Fredericton, NB, Canada E3B
   4H9

Desc: Geneology, local history, heritage.

2983 ■ Hillsboro Adobe House Museum
501 S. Ash St.   Ph: (316)947-3775
Hillsboro, KS 67063

Contact: David F. Wiebe, Dir.

Desc: Local history, religious history, genealogy. Publishes nonfiction.

2984 ■ Allan Hins, Publisher
5963 Chase Ave.
Downers Grove, IL 60516

Contact: Allan G. Hins, Ed. & Pub.

Desc: Publishes historical and genealogical information on Germans from Russia who now live in the United States, with an emphasis on the families from Bessarabia.

2985 ■ Historical Society of Carroll County
210 E. Main St.   Ph: (410)848-6494
Westminster, MD 21157
E-mail: hscc@carr.org

Contact: Jay Graybeal, Exec. Dir.

Desc: Publishes local history and genealogical materials on central Maryland.

2986 ■ Margaret M. Hofmann Genealogical & Historical Research
PO Box 446   Ph: (919)536-4304
Roanoke Rapids, NC 27870   Free: 800-455-8891

Contact: Margaret M. Hofmann.

Desc: Publishes North Carolina records as genealogical and local history source material.

2987 ■ Holbrook Research Institute
4 Mayfair Circle   Ph: (508)987-0881
Oxford, MA 01540-2272
URL: http://www.archivepublishing.com

Contact: Jay Mack Holbrook, Owner; Delene Holbrook, Office Mgr.

Desc: Publishes reference volumes of early American records for use by historians, demographers, and genealogists. Also supplies microfiches of early Massachusetts vital records.

2988 ■ Holland House Inc.
PO Box 7045, Sta. A   Ph: (506)693-8739
St. John, NB, Canada E2L 4S4 Fax: (506)693-8739
E-mail: global@spectranet.ca
URL: http://www.spectranet.com/global/ca

Contact: Mrs. B. Holt, Pres.; Sharon Hanlon, VP; Mrs. E.A.D. Hanlon, Sec. & Treas.

Desc: Publishes books on social history, genealogy, and social anthropology.

2989 ■ Hood County Genealogical Society
PO Box 1623   Ph: (817)573-2557
Granbury, TX 76048-8623
E-mail: ancestor@hcnews.com
URL: http://www.hcnews.com/ancestor

Contact: Wayne Moyers, Pres.; Jack Hughes, 1st VP; Karen Nace, 2nd VP; Janie Hall, Rec. Sec.; Frances Aderhold, Treas.; Roy Malone, Quarterly Newsletter; Frank Saffarrans, Internet Web Page Editor.

Desc: Aim is to preserve the history of Hood County and to aid those persons doing family research by holding educational seminars on genealogical research. Offers a quarterly newsletter.

2990 ■ Hopkins County Genealogical Society, Inc.
PO Box 51
Madisonville, KY 42431-0051

Contact: D.W. Dockrey, Pres.; Cindy Kington, Corresponding Sec.; Wanda Adams, Ed.; Lana Arnold, Treas.; Wanda Adams, Ed.

Desc: Publishes materials for genealogists researching Hopkins County and other counties in Kentucky. Accepts unsolicited manuscripts.

2991 ■ Vicki Bidinger Horton
HC86, Box 50B   Ph: (304)492-5994
Green Spring, WV 26722   Free: 800-822-4487

Contact: Vicki Horton, Owner.

Desc: Publishes genealogy books concerning Hampshire County, West Virginia. Does not accept unsolicited manuscripts.

2992 ■ Hosmer Heritage
PO Box 7086   Ph: (530)541-3562
South Lake Tahoe, CA
   96158-0086

Contact: Ronald L. Roberts, Pub. & Author.

Desc: Self-publisher of genealogical material.

2993 ■ House of Airlie
20 Kimdale St.   Ph: (613)226-8404
Nepean, ON, Canada K2G 0W9

Contact: Garfield Ogilvie, Author-Pub.

Desc: Publishes on local history and genealogy.

2994 ■ House of York
2035 Smokey Dr.   Ph: (209)826-6506
Los Banos, CA 93635   Fax: (209)827-4516

Contact: Courtney G. York, Owner.

Desc: Genealogy.

2995 ■ Eric E. Hovemeyer
8775 Mockingbird Ln.   Ph: (513)931-7269
Cincinnati, OH 45231
E-mail: ausberry@tso.cin.ix.net

Contact: Eric E. Hovemeyer, Author & Compiler; Gretchen A. Hovemeyer, Ed. & Production Mgr.; Stephen G. Hovemeyer, Printer.

Desc: Publishes genealogical and historical information. Does not accept unsolicited manuscripts.

2996 ■ Ella B. Hughes
22526 Peaceful Pines Rd.   Ph: (504)748-8261
Husser, LA 70442

Contact: Ella B. Hughes.

Desc: Publishes family history and genealogy.

2997 ■ Huguenot Historical Society
18 Broadhead Ave.   Ph: (914)255-1660
New Paltz, NY 12561   Fax: (914)255-0376

Contact: Timothy F. Harley, Dir.

Desc: Publishes genealogies, history, and cookbooks of the Huguenots, as well as publications about the surrounding areas.

2998 ■ Huguenot Society of America
122 E. 58th St.   Ph: (212)755-0592
New York, NY 10022   Fax: (212)317-0676

Contact: Courtney A. Haff, Pres.; Dorothy F. Kimball, Exec. Sec.

Desc: Accepts unsolicited manuscripts.

2999 ■ Hunterdon House
38 Swan St.   Ph: (609)397-2523
Lambertville, NJ 08530

Contact: Thomas B. Wilson.

Desc: Publishes on genealogy, particularly vital records of use to genealogists.

3000 ■ Iberian Publishing Co.
548 Cedar Creek Dr.   Ph: (706)546-6740
Athens, GA 30605-3408   Free: 800-394-8634
                      Fax: (706)546-6740
E-mail: iberian@iberian.com
URL: http://www.iberian.com

Contact: John Vogt, Owner; Sheryl B. Vogt, Treas.; Dorothy Bryant, Sec.; Chris Alexander, Ed./SYSOP.

Desc: Publishes Virginia public records prior to 1850.

3001 ■ Illiana Genealogical & Historical Society
PO Box 207   Ph: (217)431-8733
Danville, IL 61834-0207
E-mail: ighs@danville.net

Contact: Sally Powell, Pres.; Floyd Martin, VP; Dale Hoover, Treas.; Phylis Snider, Rec. Sec.; Betti Meinart, Corresponding Sec.

Desc: Promotes and maintains an interest in history and genealogy. Offers an 1850 map of Vermilion County. Accepts unsolicited manuscripts.

3002 ■ Illinois State Genealogical Society
PO Box 10195   Ph: (217)789-1968
Springfield, IL 62791-0195

Contact: George Wylder, 1st VP; Sharon Stenzel, Pres.; Charles Dirst, Treas.

Desc: Publishes genealogy books on Illinois residents. Also publishes four quarterlies and six newsletters for members. Offers a spring workshop and a fall conference; developed a marriage product database. Accepts unsolicited manuscripts.

3003 ■ Immigration History Research Center
826 Berry St.   Ph: (612)627-4208
St. Paul, MN 55114   Fax: (612)627-4190
E-mail: ihrc@gold.tc.umn.edu
URL: http://www.umn.edu/ihrc

Contact: Rudolph J. Vecoli, Dir.; Joel Wurl, Curator & Asst. Dir.; Judith Rosenblatt, PR.

Desc: Fosters the study of human migration, particularly the immigration to the U.S. from eastern, central, and southern Europe and the Near East. Offers a newsletter, IHRC News, a periodical, Spectrum, and the IHRC Annual Report. Also offers audio cassettes. Does not accept unsolicited manuscripts.

3004 ■ Immigration and Refugee Services of America (IRSA)
U.S. Committee for Refugees (USCR)
1717 Massachusetts Ave. NW,   Ph: (202)797-2105
Ste. 701   Fax: (202)797-2363
Washington, DC 20036
E-mail: irsa@irsa-uscr.org

Contact: Roger P. Winter, Exec. Dir. (IRSA); James L. Aldrich, Assoc. Dir.; Roger P. Winter, Dir. U.S. Committee for Refugees (USCR); Ginny Hamilton, Ed. (USCR); Adrian T. Paul, Communications Assoc.

Desc: "Immigration and Refugee Services of America (IRSA) is a national, nonprofit organization concerned with people in either forced or voluntary migration and the issues faced by individuals or groups as a result of their migration." The U.S. Committee for Refugees (USCR) is program of IRSA and serves as the research arm, providing publications, videos, and expert testimony to assist and protect refugees and displaced persons worldwide. Publications include the World Refugee Survey and the Refugee Report..

3005 ■ Institute of Family History & Genealogy
21 Hanson Ave.
Somerville, MA 02143-3714

Contact: Joseph M. Glynn, Jr., Dir. & Librarian.

Desc: Publishes genealogical guides.

3006 ■ Irish Family Names Society
2345 Ashley Park Dr.
Plano, TX 75074

Contact: William P. Durning, Dir.

Desc: Publishes materials on origins of Scottish and Irish family names.

3007 ■ Irish Genealogical Foundation
PO Box 7575   Ph: (816)454-2410
Kansas City, MO 64116   Fax: (816)454-2410
URL: http://www.irishroots.com

Contact: Michael C. O'Laughlin, Pres.; April O'Neilan, Mgr.; Patricia Donahue, Archives; Russell O'Laughlin, Archives.

Desc: Publishes on Irish-American heritage and genealogy, classical works on old Ireland, and original works on Irish-American settlement. Publishes O'Lochlain's Journal of Irish Families, published monthly. Also publishes a monthly newsletter on the internet. Produces surname maps.

3008 ■ Irish Genealogical Society
21 Hanson Ave.   Ph: (617)237-1570
Somerville, MA 02143-3714

Contact: Joseph M. Glynn, Jr., Dir. & Librarian.

Desc: Publishes a manual.

3009 ■ Iron County Museum
Box 272   Ph: (906)265-2617
Caspian, MI 49915

Contact: Harold Bernhardt, Pres.; Marcia Bernhardt, Curator; Shirley Carlson, Treas.; Audrey Ridolphi, Programs Dir.; Beverly Gustafson, Sec.

Desc: Publishes oral history and research projects. Offers a annual newsletter, Past Present Prints..

3010 ■ Iron Gate Publishing
PO Box 999   Ph: (303)530-2551
Niwot, CO 80544   Fax: (303)530-5273
E-mail: irongate@estreet.com
URL: http://www.irongate.com

Contact: Dina C. Carson, Pub.

Desc: Publishes materials aiding genealogists in the areas of self-publishing, video production, and seminar presentation. Accepts unsolicited manuscripts; query first with letter.

3011 ■ Iroquois County Genealogical Society
103 W. Cherry St.   Ph: (815)432-2215
Watseka, IL 60970-1524   Fax: (815)432-3730
E-mail: iroqgene@techinter.com
URL: http://www.rootsweb.com/ilicgs/index.htm

Desc: Publishes genealogical research. Also offers a quarterly periodical, The Iroquois Stalker. Accepts unsolicited manuscripts.

3012 ■ ISC Publications
PO Box 10192
Costa Mesa, CA 92627

Contact: Pat Sanders, Dir.

Desc: Publishes on adoption/genealogy search.

3013 ■ Jackson County Historical Society
PO Box 7   Ph: (618)684-3455
Murphysboro, IL 62966

Contact: Kenneth Cochran, Pres.; Ellen Gates, Treas.

Desc: Publishes materials of historical and genealogical significance to Jackson County, Illinois. Offers The Jacksonian Ventilator, a quarterly newsletter.

3014 ■ Martha Werst Jackson
509 Pea Ridge Rd.   Ph: (502)622-7374
Scottsville, KY 42164

Contact: Martha Werst Jackson, Genealogist & Author.

Desc: Publishes genealogical books to preserve old records.

3015 ■ Janova Press, Inc.
2412 Ingleside, 1C   Ph: (513)861-0511
Cincinnati, OH 45206   Fax: (513)961-8616

Contact: Rita M. Edlin, Sec.

Desc: Memoirs, autobiographies, and literature of immigrant Jews before 1920. Publishes nonfiction. Does not accept unsolicited manuscripts.

3016 ■ Hazel Wright Reynolds Jasper
5925 Terrace Park Dr. N.   Ph: (813)541-5095
106 ARL
St. Petersburg, FL 33709

Contact: Hazel W. Jasper, Author & Pub.

Desc: Publishes a local history of Kent County, Delaware, featuring the town of Magnolia.

3017 ■ Jewish Genealogical Society of Illinois
PO Box 515   Ph: (708)509-0201
Northbrook, IL 60065-0515

Contact: Scott E. Meyer, Pres.; Alan Spencer, Ed.

Desc: Promotes genealogical research through publications and meetings. Also serves as a repository for materials to assist researchers. Offers Morasha, a monthly newsletter and Search, a quarterly journal.

3018 ■ Daniel F. Johnson
PO Box 26025   Ph: (506)696-7429
St. John, NB, Canada E2J 4M3

Desc: Publishes genealogical materials.

3019 ■ David E. Johnson
175 Locke St. N.   Ph: (416)526-1494
Hamilton, ON, Canada L8R 3B1

Contact: David E. Johnson, Pub.

Desc: Genealogy of the Johnson family in Ontario.

3020 ■ Jordan Valley Heritage House, Inc.
PO Box 99   Ph: (503)859-3144
Stayton, OR 97383

Desc: In addition to publishing books, sells supplies for tracing a family tree.

3021 ■ Junius, Inc.
842 Lombard St.   Ph: (215)627-8298
Philadelphia, PA 19147-1317

Contact: Richard J. Alperin, Pres.; Norman Alperin, VP; Dorothy E. Alperin, Sec.

Desc: Publishes on Jewish genealogy and art. Does not accept unsolicited manuscripts.

3022 ■ Kallam Cemetery Compiling Co.

146 Kallam Rd. Ph: (336)374-4146
Mount Airy, NC 27030

Contact: Wallace Kallam.

Desc: Compiles and publishes historic information from cemeteries of Virginia and North Carolina for families and genealogists.

3023 ■ Kanen-Smith & Carter

525 Ontario St. Ph: (905)937-2132
St. Catharines, ON, Canada L2N 6P5
E-mail: skanen@vaxxine.com

Desc: Self-publishes on genealogy.

3024 ■ Kansas Genealogical Society

Village Square Mall Ph: (316)225-1951
2601 Central
PO Box 103
Dodge City, KS 67801

Desc: Publishes on genealogy. Also publishes The Treesearcher quarterly.

3025 ■ Betty Robertson Kaufman

2117 S. Harlan St. Ph: (303)985-9437
Denver, CO 80227-3617

Desc: Genealogy.

3026 ■ Kearney Publishing Co.

2515 Peachtree Ln. Ph: (847)753-9546
Northbrook, IL 60062-3432

Contact: Michael J. Kearney, Pres.

Desc: Publishes historical information on families from Ireland, Germany, Switzerland and Belgium that settled in Iowa, Missouri, South Dakota and Ohio in the mid 19th century. Does not accept unsolicited manuscripts.

3027 ■ Kelley Publications

PO Box 208 Ph: (937)386-2375
Seaman, OH 45679

Contact: Stephen Kelley, Pres.

Desc: Publishes on the history and genealogy of Adams County, Ohio. Also produces art prints of historical sites.

3028 ■ Arthur R. Kilner

173 Ridgebury Dr. Ph: (513)372-0783
Xenia, OH 45385 Fax: (513)372-1698

Contact: Arthur R. Kilner, Author & Pub.

Desc: Publishes historical and genealogical reference materials to inform the professional researcher. Offers photographs or slides of historical and nature sites.

3029 ■ Kingston Literacy

88 Wright Crescent Ph: (613)547-2012
Kingston, ON, Canada K7L Fax: (613)547-2024
4T9
E-mail: kinglit@kos.net

Contact: Carynne Arnold, Exec. Dir.; Rose Strohmaier, Oral History Coord.; Martha Rudden, Office Coord.

Desc: Publishes oral history books for adult new readers. Also provides tutoring in reading, writing, and math to adults. Does not accept unsolicited manuscripts.

3030 ■ Kinseeker Publications

PO Box 184 Ph: (616)276-7653
Grawn, MI 49637

E-mail: kinseeker6@aol.com
URL: http://www.angelfire.com/biz/kinseeker/index.html

Contact: Victoria Wilson, Owner.

Desc: Publishes books on genealogy. Offers 25 genealogical newsletters for the surnames of Arnold, Carroll, Ewing, Ferguson, Gibson, Norton, Wolf, Zingsheim, and others. Also offers genealogical charts, forms, stationary, bookmarks, and cards. Accepts unsolicited manuscripts.

3031 ■ Kinship

60 Cedar Heights Rd. Ph: (914)876-4592
Rhinebeck, NY 12572
E-mail: 71045.1516@compuserve.com

Contact: Nancy V. Kelly, Owner.

Desc: Provides source material and vital records for genealogists and local historians.

3032 ■ Kintracers

Box 48271, Midlake RPO
Calgary, AB, Canada T2X 3C7

Contact: Neil Broadhurst.

Desc: Publishes reference books. Accepts unsolicited manuscripts pertaining to Canadian genealogy.

3033 ■ Clyde and Alna Kiser

Courtland Ter. Ph: (704)834-4967
2300 Aberdeen Blvd.
Gastonia, NC 28054

Contact: Clyde V. Kiser, Ed. & Pub.; Alna L. Kiser, Ed.

Desc: Publishes a book about the ancestry and descendants of the Larkin Kiser and Sylvanus Carpenter families.

3034 ■ Kitchen Table: Women of Color Press

PO Box 40-4920 Ph: (718)935-1082
Brooklyn, NY 11240-4920 Fax: (718)935-1107

Contact: Andrea Lockett, Pub.; Carolyn Antonio, Office Mgr.

Desc: "The first publisher in North America with a commitment to publishing and distributing the work of First and Third World women of all racial/cultural heritages, sexualities, and classes." Accepts unsolicited manuscripts.

3035 ■ Edward Kryder

2502 Lisbon Ln. Ph: (703)765-9065
Alexandria, VA 22306 Fax: (703)370-6234
E-mail: ekryder@vts.edu

Desc: Genealogy.

3036 ■ Land Yacht Press

PO Box 210262 Ph: (615)646-2186
Nashville, TN 37221-0262 Fax: (615)646-2186
E-mail: landyachtpress@juno.com

Contact: John-Paul Richiuso, Pres.

Desc: Publishes how-to and reference books on local history, genealogy and museums for a professional and general audience. Offers audio and video cassettes. Accepts unsolicited manuscripts.

3037 ■ The N. W. Lapin Press

105 Surrey Rd. Ph: (804)296-8669
Charlottesville, VA 22901-2223

Contact: Joanne Lovelace Nance, Pub.; Margaret Barringer Weems, Ed.-in-Chief.

Desc: Publishes genealogical and historical reference books for adult audience. Also offers research services for individuals, professional researchers, and authors. Accepts unsolicited manuscripts.

3038 ■ Largy Books

PO Box 6023 Ph: (780)791-1750
Fort McMurray, AB, Canada Fax: (780)791-1750
T9H 4W1
E-mail: largyboo@incentre.net
URL: http://www.atech.ab.ca/largybooks

Contact: Linda K. Meehan.

Desc: Publishes an index on the 1901 Irish census. Offers microform and diskettes. Does not accept unsolicited manuscripts.

3039 ■ Latah County Historical Society

327 E. 2nd Ph: (208)882-1004
Moscow, ID 83843
E-mail: lchs@moscow.co

Contact: Mary Reed, Dir.; Joann Jones, Curator; Dick Beck, Pres.

Desc: Publishes on local and regional history. Also offers a semi-annual journal, Latah Legacy..

3040 ■ L'Avant Studios

PO Box 1711 Ph: (904)576-1327
Tallahassee, FL 32302 Fax: (904)576-1327

Contact: David A. Avant, Jr., Partner; George D. Avant, Jr., Partner.

Desc: Subjects include: History, genealogy, hunting. Publishes nonfiction.

3041 ■ Lawrence Publishing

264 S. Willo-Esque Ph: (316)943-2325
Wichita, KS 67209

Contact: Robert D. Lawrence.

Desc: Publishes family genealogies and local histories for families, researchers, and historians.

3042 ■ Gwen Lefton

2 Leamont Terr. Ph: (902)466-5559
Dartmouth, NS, Canada B2Y 1V2

Desc: Publishes on genealogy and family history of New England's settlers. Does not accept unsolicited manuscripts.

3043 ■ Leon County Genealogical Society, Inc.

PO Box 400 Ph: (409)396-6283
Centerville, TX 75833

Contact: Emma Bass, Board; Ruby Johnson, VP; Clara Goodsell, Pres.

Desc: Nonprofit publisher of genealogical and historical records of Leon County. Accepts unsolicited manuscripts.

3044 ■ Les Editions Laplante-Agnew

1404 Lands End Rd. Ph: (250)656-5714
North Saanich, BC, Canada V8L 5K1
E-mail: laurette@IslandNet.com

Contact: Laurette Agnew, Pres.

Desc: Publishes on history and genealogy. Does not accept unsolicited manuscripts.

3045 ■ Liberty Bell Associates

PO Box 51
Franklin Park, NJ 08823

Contact: Maryly B. Penrose, Pres.; Thomas F. Penrose, VP.

Desc: History, genealogy.

3046 ■ Libra Publications
5179 Perry Rd.   Ph: (410)875-2824
Mount Airy, MD 21771   Fax: (410)875-0180

Contact: Mary K. Meyer, Proprietor.

Desc: Publishes genealogical source records. Also produces a lineage chart and provides mailing list. Distributed by Baker & Taylor.

3047 ■ Linden Tree
1204 W. Prospect   Ph: (218)879-5727
Cloquet, MN 55720

Contact: Marilyn Lind.

Desc: Publishes genealogical research and family history.

3048 ■ Links Genealogy Publications
8125 Arroyo Vista Dr.   Ph: (916)682-3381
Sacramento, CA 95823-5935   Fax: (916)682-6720

Contact: Iris Carter Jones, Owner.

Desc: Publishes family history and genealogical information. Offers a quarterly newsletter, The Fountain and Krefeld Immigrants & Their Descendants..

3049 ■ Jo White Linn
PO Box 1948   Ph: (704)633-3575
Salisbury, NC 28145-1948
E-mail: jowlinn@juno.com

Contact: Jo White Linn, Pres.

Desc: Publishes on North Carolina history, genealogy, and law. Offers Rowan County Register, a genealogical periodical.

3050 ■ Lionside Business Services, Inc.
R.R. 2   Ph: (207)457-1482
PO Box 726
Lebanon, ME 04027

Contact: Donald E. Pray, Pres.

Desc: Publishes genealogical and historical books on Lebanon, Maine.

3051 ■ The Lisi Press
460 S. Woodlands Dr.   Ph: (813)789-5674
Oldsmar, FL 34677-2313
E-mail: lisipress@juno.com
URL: http://www.lisi.press.com

Contact: Thomas J. Laforest, Pres.; J. M. Laforest, VP; Edie K. Laforest, Sec.-Treas.

Desc: Publishes on the history, genealogy, and social development of the French-Canadian culture in North America as it developed from 1608 until the conquest in 1763. Series complete with volume 30.

3052 ■ Lithuanian Research & Studies Center, Inc.
5620 S. Claremont Ave.   Ph: (773)434-4545
Chicago, IL 60636-1039   Fax: (773)434-9363
E-mail: lrsc@mcs.net

Contact: John A. Rackauskas, Pres.; Robert A. Vitas, Exec. VP; Kazys Ambrozaitis, MD, Board Chrmn.; Jonas Dainauskas, Corporate Sec.

Desc: Sponsors and publishes original research on Lithuanian and Lithuanian-American subjects. Reprints significant periodical volumes and documents. Also represents Lithuanian publishers in the U.S. Accepts unsolicited manuscripts; query first.

3053 ■ Livres Carraig Books, Inc.
PO Box 8733   Ph: (418)651-5918
Ste. Foy, PQ, Canada G1V 4N6
E-mail: carraig@total.net

Contact: Marianna O'Gallagher, Owner & Mgr.

Desc: Publishes on the history of the Irish in the province of Quebec. Offers some genealogical reference letters. Distributes for Celtic Arts Toronto and New Ireland Press.

3054 ■ Alison Lobb
RR 2   Ph: (519)482-7167
Clinton, ON, Canada N0M 1L0   Fax: (519)482-7167

Contact: Alison Lobb.

Desc: Publishes history related to Goderich Township. Presently inactive.

3055 ■ Log Cabin Publishing
244 Maple Leaf Ave. N., R.R.   Ph: (905)894-2134
No. 2
Ridgeway, ON, Canada L0S 1N0

Contact: R. Robert Mutrie, Proprietor.

Desc: Publishes on pre-confederation Ontario and colonial New York history for reading, reference, and family genealogies. Does not accept unsolicited manuscripts.

3056 ■ Lost in Canada?
1020 Central Ave.   Ph: (608)269-6361
Sparta, WI 54656   Fax: (608)269-6929

Contact: Joy Reisinger, Owner.

Desc: Publishes on Canadian genealogy.

3057 ■ Carol Loudermilk-Edwards
8040 Raleigh Pl.   Ph: (303)429-3310
Westminster, CO 80030

Contact: Carol A. Edwards, Owner.

Desc: Publishes historical and genealogical records.

3058 ■ JWC Low Co.
PO Box 472012   Ph: (415)665-2934
San Francisco, CA 94147   Fax: (415)665-2934
E-mail: yonus-low@worldnet.att.net

Contact: Jeanie W.C. Low.

Desc: Publishes books researching Chinese American families. Does not accept unsolicited manuscripts.

3059 ■ Lynn Michael-John Associates
80 Roser Crescent   Ph: (905)623-9147
Bowmanville, ON, Canada L1C   Fax: (905)623-9147
3N9
E-mail: lmjassoc@durham.net
URL: http://www.durham.net/lmjassoc

Contact: Sherrell Branton Leetooze, Prop.; Roger Michael Leetooze, VP.

Desc: Publishes on local and family history and biographies for Canadians. Does not accept unsolicited manuscripts.

3060 ■ Lyon Press
PO Box 50741   Ph: (505)299-1598
Albuquerque, NM 87181-0741

Contact: Donald Ray Barnes, Owner.

Desc: Publishes on genealogy. Offers research services. Accepts unsolicited manuscripts.

3061 ■ Eswyn Lyster
349 Poplar Ave.   Ph: (250)752-9723
Qualicum Beach, BC, Canada
V9K 1J7

Contact: Eswyn Lyster.

Desc: Self-publisher of family history.

3062 ■ M B Publications
1608 Ontario St.   Ph: (819)563-2709
Sherbrooke, PQ, Canada J1J 3S9

Contact: Michael Benazon.

Desc: Publishes Canadian short stories and Jewish genealogy. Does not accept unsolicited manuscripts.

3063 ■ Mahoning County Chapter of the Ohio Genealogical Society
PO Box 9333   Ph: (330)793-4726
Boardman, OH 44513-9333
E-mail: jocelynf@cisnet.com

Desc: Gathers and publishes genealogical material from various sources including courthouses, family records, cemeteries, etc.

3064 ■ Madeline Malott
391 County Rd. 20   Ph: (519)733-2785
Kingsville, ON, Canada N9Y
2K3

Contact: Madeline Malott, Pub.

Desc: Publishes a book on local history and genealogy. Does not accept unsolicited manuscripts.

3065 ■ Manitoba Genealogical Society, Inc.
Unit E, 1045 St. James St.   Ph: (204)783-9139
Winnipeg, MB, Canada R3H   Fax: (204)783-0190
1B1
E-mail: mgs@mbnet.mb.ca
URL: http://www.mbnet.mb.ca/mgs

Contact: Louisa Shermerhorn, Librarian.

Desc: A nonprofit organization that promotes and encourages an interest in genealogy and family history in Manitoba. Publishes a quarterly journal, Generations, as well as directories and pedigree charts. Offers seminars and work shops, genealogical research, and a resource center of books and microform publications open for use by the public. Does not accept unsolicited manuscripts.

3066 ■ Mar-Cro Publications
1630 Victor Way   Ph: (209)523-7683
Modesto, CA 95351

Contact: Vera N. Marlett; Edgar E. Marlett.

Desc: Publishes family histories.

3067 ■ Marietta Publishing Co.
2115 N. Denair Ave.   Ph: (209)634-9473
Turlock, CA 95382

Contact: Janet G. Parker, Pub.; J. Carlyle Parker, Ed.

Desc: Publishes genealogy and library reference materials for genealogists and librarians. Offers microfiche of out-of-print titles.

3068 ■ Market Fact Finders, Inc.
Rames 1, Ste. 132   Ph: (605)387-5336
Olivet, SD 57052

Contact: Arlo Auch, Pres.; Judith Auch, Mgr.; Heather Westendorf, Product Development; Heidi Haro, Mktg. Dir.; Holly Auch, Sales.

Desc: Publishes family histories and travel guides. Offers travel calendars and two newspapers, River Valley Voice and Life of Leisure. Accepts unsolicited manuscripts; include a self-addressed, stamped envelope.

3069 ■ Martin County Historical Society
PO Box 468   Ph: (919)795-3374
Williamston, NC 27892

Contact: Doris L. Wilson, Chrmn., Library Committee.

Desc: Publishes on history and genealogy. Does not accept unsolicited manuscripts.

3070 ■ Maryland Genealogical Society, Inc.

201 W. Monument St.   Ph: (410)685-3750
Baltimore, MD 21201
E-mail: pdanders@MdHs.org

Contact: Jon Harlan Livezey, Pres.; Helyn H. Collison, Recording Sec.

Desc: Accepts unsolicited manuscripts.

3071 ■ James H. Mason

195 Tierra Rejada Rd., No. 13   Ph: (805)584-0132
Simi Valley, CA 93065-0854
E-mail: jhmason@juno.com

Contact: James H. Mason, Pres.

Desc: Purpose is to compile Dudley family genealogies.

3072 ■ McClain Printing Co.

PO Box 403   Ph: (304)478-2881
Parsons, WV 26287   Free: 800-654-7179
     Fax: (304)478-4658
URL: http://www.wvweb.com/mpc

Contact: Ken Smith, VP.

Desc: Subjects include: History, poetry, genealogy. Book distributor. Also distributes brochures, magazines, pamphlets, newsletters, flyers, and posters.

3073 ■ McFarlan Family Enterprises

12837 76th Ave.   Ph: (604)596-7699
Surrey, BC, Canada V3W 2V3

Contact: J. Robert Dahling, Pub.

Desc: Publishes family genealogies. Also offers a quarterly newsletter.

3074 ■ Molodija Books

PO Box 689   Ph: (410)374-3117
Hampstead, MD 21074   Fax: (410)374-3569
E-mail: books@molodija.com
URL: http://www.molodija.com

Contact: Raimonda Mikatavage, Pub.

Desc: Publishes educational books for U.S. immigrants and refugees. Does not accept unsolicited manuscripts.

3075 ■ Meridional Publications

7101 Winding Way   Ph: (919)556-2940
Wake Forest, NC 27587

Contact: Robert Reckenbeil, Pub.

Desc: Subjects include: Local color, genealogy, poetry. Publishes nonfiction books. Also offers microform and electronic formats.

3076 ■ Merritt Genealogical Publications

1686 E. Ardenwood Ct.   Ph: (510)685-3414
Concord, CA 94521

Contact: Dee Merritt, Author & Pub.

Desc: Publishes genealogical materials, historical documents, family histories for county historians and amateur and professional genealogists.

3077 ■ Microform Books

4 Mayfair Circle   Ph: (508)987-0881
Oxford, MA 01540-2722
URL: http://www.archivepublishing.com

Contact: Jay M. Holbrook, Owner; DeLene C. Holbrook, Office Mgr.

Desc: Publishes microfiches of out-of-publication Massachusetts Vital Records to 1850, and The Mayflower Descendants. Does not accept unsolicited manuscripts.

3078 ■ Mid-West Tennessee Genealogical Society

PO Box 3343
Jackson, TN 38303-0343

Contact: Jewel Wilkins, Pres.; Lyda Kowalski, VP.

3079 ■ Lois N. Miller Genealogical Publications

1018 Sunset Dr.   Ph: (501)443-2666
Fayetteville, AR 72701

Contact: Lois N. Miller.

Desc: Publishes a compilation of court records.

3080 ■ Mills Historical Press

1732 Ridgedale Dr.   Ph: (205)752-4031
Tuscaloosa, AL 35406   Fax: (205)752-5979

Contact: Elizabeth Shown Mills, Pres.; Gary B. Mills, VP; Donna Rachal Mills, Sec.

Desc: Publishes genealogical and historical reference works.

3081 ■ Missouri State Library

600 W. Main   Ph: (314)751-3615
PO Box 387   Fax: (314)751-3612
Jefferson City, MO 65102
E-mail: libref@mail.more.net
URL: http://www.mosl.sos.state.mo.us/lib-ser/libser.html

Contact: Sara Parker, State Lbn.; Frank Pascoe, Reference; Beth Eckles, Wolner Library for the Blind/Handicapped; Barbara Reading, Library Dev.; Madeline Matson, Pub./Spec. Proj.

Desc: Publishes CD-ROMs containing bibliographic records from all libraries in Missouri, as well as legal, historical, genealogical, horticultural, economical, maps, census, and other data about Missouri.

3082 ■ Clifford Moase

11 Nicole Ct.   Ph: (902)466-3401
Dartmouth, NS, Canada B2Y 4P3

Contact: Clifford Moase, Pub.

Desc: Publishes on the genealogy of the Moase family. Does not accept unsolicited manuscripts.

3083 ■ Modlin's Ancestral Treesearch

118 Weaver Dr.   Ph: (252)792-5472
Williamston, NC 27892-1849
E-mail: shepji@coastalnet.com

Contact: Jennifer M. Sheppard, Owner.

Desc: Publishes on genealogy.

3084 ■ Andrew J. Morris

PO Box 535
Farmington, MI 48332
E-mail: ajmorris@mich.com
URL: http://genealogy.org/ajmorris/

Contact: Andrew J. Morris, Proprietor.

Desc: Reprints out-of-print histories and genealogies in microform for genealogists and historians.

3085 ■ Morten Publishing Co., Inc.

136 Wedgewood   Ph: (708)381-1440
Barrington, IL 60010

Contact: Sue Morten O'Brien, Pres.; Judith G. O'Brien, Sec.; James J. O'Brien, VP.

Desc: Publishes a genealogical reference of lineages of Americans of all ethnic backgrounds.

3086 ■ Mountain Empire Genealogical Quarterly

PO Box 628   Ph: (540)796-5233
Pound, VA 24279

Contact: Gregory L. Vanover, Ed. & Pub.; Joan S. Vanover, Ed.

Desc: Promotes genealogy and assists genealogists in their search.

3087 ■ Mountain Press

PO Box 400   Ph: (423)886-6369
Signal Mountain, TN 37377   Fax: (423)886-5312

Contact: James L. Douthat, Ed.

Desc: Publishes materials of a historical and genealogical nature for eastern Tennessee and southwestern Virginia.

3088 ■ Multicultural History Society of Ontario

43 Queen's Park Crescent E.   Ph: (416)979-2973
Toronto, ON, Canada M5S   Fax: (416)979-7947
2C3
E-mail: mhso.mail@utoronto.ca
URL: http://www.utoronto.ca/mhso

Contact: Prof. Paul Robert Magocsi, CEO.

Desc: Publishes on history, immigration and multiculturalism. Also publishes a newsletter. Offers microform publications. Does not accept unsolicited manuscripts.

3089 ■ Museum of Jewish Heritage

1 Battery Park Plz.   Ph: (212)968-1800
New York, NY 10004   Fax: (212)968-1368

Contact: Dr. David Altshuler, Dir.

Desc: Publishes a newsletter, distributes a bibliography of Holocaust titles, and a series of oral history books and a poster series based on material in their archives. Provides reference services.

3090 ■ Muskingum County Footprints

2740 Adamsville Rd.   Ph: (614)453-8231
Zanesville, OH 43701

Contact: Hilda E. Yinger, Sylvia Hargrove, Owners & Pubs.

Desc: Publishes a series of records and indexes relating to the people and events of Muskingum County, Ohio. Accepts unsolicited manuscripts; must be related to Muskingum County, Ohio.

3091 ■ Albert E. Myers

900 S. Arlington Ave., Rm. 100   Ph: (717)545-4761
Harrisburg, PA 17109-5089   Fax: (717)545-4765

Contact: Albert E. Myers, Pub.

Desc: Ancestry, genealogy.

3092 ■ National Archives and Records Administration

Publications Division   Ph: (202)763-1896
7th St. & Pennsylvania Ave. NW   Free: 800-788-6282
Washington, DC 20408   Fax: (202)763-6025

Contact: Trudy H. Peterson, Acting Archivist; Linda Brown, Asst. Archivist, Public Programs; Sandra Glasser, Dir., Mktg. & Product Development.

Desc: Publishes reference aids including guides and catalogs for archivists, librarians, historians, biographers, and genealogists. Also publishes general interest books about the National Archives and its holdings. Offers posters. Alternate telephone number: (202) 724-0085.

3093 ■ National Directory of Local Researchers
450 Potter St.   Ph: (419)335-6485
Wauseon, OH 43567

Contact: Howard V. Fausey, Ed. & Pub.

Desc: Publishes a listing of genealogical researchers and local and state genealogical societies. Publishes Barnes Family Digest. Also of ancestor charts and family group sheets.

3094 ■ National Genealogical Society
4527 17th St. N.   Ph: (703)525-0050
Arlington, VA 22207-2399   Free: 800-473-0060
              Fax: (703)525-0052

E-mail: ngs@ngsgenealogy.org

Contact: Shirley L. Wilcox, Pres.; Francis J. Shane, Exec. Dir.; Russell L. Henderson, Publications Mgr.

3095 ■ National Historical Publishing Co.
830 Greeson Hollow Rd.   Ph: (931)722-5706
PO Box 539   Free: 800-729-3885
Waynesboro, TN 38485   Fax: (931)722-7293

Contact: Virgil D. White, Owner.

Desc: Publishes books for historical and genealogical research. Does not accept unsolicited manuscripts.

3096 ■ Nebraska State Genealogical Society
PO Box 5608
Lincoln, NE 68505

Contact: Carole Blaser, Pres.; Trish Collister, VP; Michelle Hansen, Sec.; Marcia A. Buescher, Treas.; Patricia A. Wagner, Publications Dir.

Desc: Publishes genealogical information on Nebraska. Offers an interlibrary loan program that includes microfilm to members. Inquire with Publications Director regarding unsolicited manuscripts.

3097 ■ Barbara Nethercott
1310 Brydges St.   Ph: (519)451-7594
London, ON, Canada N5W   Fax: (519)451-7594
    2C4
E-mail: 76032.2577@compuserve.com

Contact: Barbara Balch.

Desc: Publishes a family history and a biannual Dadswell Family Bulletin..

3098 ■ New Brunswick Genealogical Society
Box 3235, Sta. B   Ph: (506)755-6800
Fredericton, NB, Canada E3A
    5G9
URL: http://www.bitheads.com/nbgs/

Contact: C. L. Craig, Pres.; Ivan Edgett, Treas.

Desc: Publishes material of interest to genealogical researchers. Offers a quarterly newsletter/magazine, Generations. Accepts unsolicited manuscripts.

3099 ■ New Canaan Historical Society
13 Oenoke Ridge   Ph: (203)966-1776
New Canaan, CT 06840   Fax: (203)972-5917
E-mail: newcanaan.historical@snet.net

Contact: William H. Kirby, Pres.; Sharon Turo, Librarian; Janet Lindstrom, Exec. Dir.

Desc: Produces material related to individuals, businesses, buildings, and historical events which involve local history of the town of New Canaan. Offers video cassettes and postcards.

3100 ■ New England Historic Genealogical Society
101 Newbury St.   Ph: (617)536-5740
Boston, MA 02116-3007   Fax: (617)536-7307
E-mail: anovick@nehgs.org
URL: http://www.nehgs.org

Contact: Ralph J. Crandall, Exec. Dir.; Sue Moran, Dir. of Mktg.; Jane Fiske, Dir. of Pub.

Desc: Publishes primary records for the genealogical and historical community. Also publishes bibliographical aids and reference works with an emphasis on New England. Offers a quarterly journal, a bimonthly newsletter, microfilm, forms, and charts. Distributes for Ancestry, Inc., Heritage Books, Picton Press, Boyer, and G.P.C.

3101 ■ New Haven Colony Historical Society
114 Whitney Ave.   Ph: (203)562-4183
New Haven, CT 06510   Fax: (203)562-2002

Contact: David Carter, Pres.; Gilbert Kenna, VP; Marvin S. Arons, VP; Hannah Smith, Asst. to Exec. Dir.

Desc: Publishes on genealogy and the history of New Haven and the New Haven area. The nonprofit society offers the Journal of The New Haven Colony Historical Society, and maintains a museum, research library, teaching center, and historic house.

3102 ■ New Roots Press
3-83 Trunk Rd.   Ph: (604)748-3112
Duncan, BC, Canada V9L 2N7   Fax: (604)748-1335

Contact: Mary Beth Small, Pres.; Hazura Sangha, VP; Hortensia Houle, Exec. Dir.

Desc: Publishes fund-raising materials for the Cowichan Valley Intercultural and Immigrant Aid Society, a nonprofit organization that provides immigrant settlement services and multicultural awareness programs. Also offers a newsletter, video cassettes and a television program. Does not accept unsolicited manuscripts.

3103 ■ New Testament Christian Press
PO Box 1694   Ph: (610)544-2871
Media, PA 19063

Contact: Jody L. Apple, Owner & Pub.

Desc: A publishing company devoted to the distribution of religious and philosophical works among the churches of Christ and the religious world at large, as well as scholarly and popular circles.

3104 ■ New Trails
PO Box 766   Ph: (802)229-0648
Montpelier, VT 05602

Contact: Alice Eichholz, Proprietor.

Desc: Publishes research guides and source material on family history.

3105 ■ Next Decade, Inc.
39 Old Farmstead Rd.   Ph: (908)879-6625
Chester, NJ 07930   Free: 800-595-5440
              Fax: (908)879-6625

E-mail: nexdec@aol.com

Contact: Barbara Brooks Kimmel, Pres.; Carol E. Rose, Mktg. Mgr.

Desc: Subjects: Reference, immigration, citizenship, investment. Publishes nonfiction reference books. Accepts unsolicited manuscripts. Distributes for several other publishers.

3106 ■ Sylvia Nimmo
6201 Kentucky Rd.   Ph: (402)331-2384
Omaha, NE 68133

Contact: Sylvia Nimmo.

Desc: Publishes genealogical and historical research aids and source materials.

3107 ■ North Carolina Genealogical Society
PO Box 1492   Ph: (252)752-0944
Raleigh, NC 27602
E-mail: ncgs@earthlink.net
URL: http://www.ncgenealogy.org

Contact: John H. Oden, III, Pres.; Elliott Futrell, 2nd VP; Crestena Oakley, Sec.; Judith G. Hinton, Treas.

Desc: Publishes on North Carolina history and genealogy. Offers North Carolina Genealogical Journal and NCGS Newsletter quarterly. Accepts unsolicited manuscripts; query first.

3108 ■ Northwest Georgia Historical & Genealogical Society, Inc.
PO Box 5063   Ph: (706)234-2110
Rome, GA 30162-5063
URL: http://www.rootsweb.com/ganwhags/index.html

Contact: Patricia A. Millican, Pres.; Sandra L. Ballard, Treas.

Desc: A nonprofit organization specializing in the preservation of historical and genealogical data from northwest Georgia. Publishes a quarterly journal and one book, available direct from the Society.

3109 ■ Notation Press
47 Lee Rd., No. 428   Ph: (205)887-5948
Auburn, AL 36830   Fax: (205)887-3289

Contact: Nell Esslinger, Owner; Raymond G. Miller, Inspector & Artist; Doyle DePriest, Printer.

Desc: Publishes on music and genealogy. Presently inactive.

3110 ■ T. J. Obal
739 Hillsdale Ave.   Ph: (201)664-7836
Hillsdale, NJ 07642-2515

Contact: Thaddeus J. Obal, Author.

Desc: Publishes a compilation of surnames of Polish ancestry.

3111 ■ Ohio Genealogical Society
713 S. Main St.   Ph: (419)756-7294
Mansfield, OH 44907-1644   Fax: (419)756-8681
E-mail: ogs@ogs.org
URL: http://www.ogs.org

Contact: Fred Mayer, Pres.; Dianne Young, VP; Ted Minier, Treas.; Thomas Neel, Mgr.

Desc: Publishes material to promote genealogical and historical research and to aid in publication, preservation, and safeguarding of genealogical material pertaining to Ohio.

3112 ■ Oklahoma Genealogical Society
PO Box 12986   Ph: (405)751-1979
Oklahoma City, OK 73157

Contact: Mary Jackson Duffe, Pres.; Ruth Eager Moran, 1st VP; Nancy Colvin Cotton, 2nd VP; Geneva Lumley Coates, Treas.

3113 ■ Oldbuck Press, Inc.
1025 Watkins   Ph: (501)336-8184
Conway, AR 72032
E-mail: obsales@aol.com

Contact: Joe Goss, Owner; Phillip A. Sperry, Operations Mgr.

Desc: Publishes historical and genealogical books. Accepts unsolicited manuscripts. Distributes for University of Arkansas Press, Louisiana State University Press, and Ark Research.

3114 ■ Onion Creek Press
PO Box 100   Ph: (210)966-3567
Utopia, TX 78884

Desc: Publishes an oral history book.

3115 ■ Oral History Association
Dickinson College   Ph: (717)245-1036
PO Box 1773   Fax: (717)245-1046
Carlisle, PA 17013
E-mail: oha@dickinson.edu
URL: http://www.dickinson.edu/oha

Contact: Howard Green, Pres.; Laurie Mercier, VP; Madelyn Campbell, Exec. Sec.

Desc: Publishes on oral history. Offers Oral History Review, Oral History Association Newsletter, and Annual Report and Membership Directory. Accepts unsolicited manuscripts.

3116 ■ Orange County Genealogical Society
Historic 1841 Courthouse   Ph: (914)342-1190
101 Main St.
Goshen, NY 10924-1917

Contact: Patricia P. Thomas, Pres.; Marilyn Terry, 1st VP; Genie Shorter, 2nd VP; Jeanne Krish, Treas.; Joyce Weissen, Correspondence Sec.

Desc: Publishes to encourage genealogical research. Collects and preserves family and genealogical records and papers and makes them available for study. Offers maps.

3117 ■ Osgoode Township Historical Society
7814 Rideau St.   Ph: (613)821-4062
Vernon, ON, Canada K0A 3J0

Contact: Doug Hughes, Pres.; Anne Leighton-Kyle, Treas.; Donna Bowen, Archivist.

Desc: Publishes history of Osgoode township written by local people.

3118 ■ Phyllis Smith Oyer
263 Bakerdale Rd.   Ph: (716)663-1735
Rochester, NY 14616-3654

Desc: Publishes books on genealogy. Does not accept unsolicited manuscripts.

3119 ■ Ozarks Genealogical Society, Inc.
PO Box 3945, Glenstone Sta.   Ph: (417)831-2773
Springfield, MO 65808
E-mail: ososiety@mail.orion.org
URL: http://www.rootsweb.com/ozarksgs

Contact: Patsy L. McHaffie, Pres.; Lynn Shelley, 1st VP; Fannie Frank, 2nd VP; Wm. Bill Wood, Business Mgr.; Hazel Voris, Publications Chrmn.

Desc: Publishes genealogical material pertaining to the Missouri Ozarks. Also publishes a newsletter and Ozar'kin, a quarterly journal. Offers study groups, maps, and a genealogy library. Accepts unsolicited manuscripts.

3120 ■ Jerome S. Ozer, Publisher
340 Tenafly Rd.   Ph: (201)567-7040
Englewood, NJ 07631   Fax: (201)567-8134

Contact: Jerome S. Ozer, Pres.; Harriet Ozer, Treas.

Desc: Publishes library reference books and college textbooks in ethnic studies, American history, the performing arts, psychology, and psychiatry. Distributes for Center for Migration Studies and Creative Therapeutics.

3121 ■ Bonnie Page Publications
PO Box 70   Ph: (423)426-2338
Lake City, TN 37769

Desc: Publishes books of local history.

3122 ■ Park Genealogical Books
PO Box 130968   Ph: (651)488-4416
Roseville, MN 55113-0968   Fax: (651)488-2653
URL: http://www.parkbooks.com

Contact: Mary Hawker Bakeman, Owner.

Desc: Publishes on genealogy.

3123 ■ Past to Present
700 St. Clair Pkwy.   Ph: (519)862-1644
Corunna, ON, Canada N0N
  1G0

Contact: Donald Carpenter.

Desc: Publishes genealogical and historical books on the U.S. and Canada.

3124 ■ Pavilion Press
453 Amity   Ph: (616)857-2781
PO Box 250
Douglas, MI 49406

Contact: Arthur L. Lane, Jr., Pres. & Treas.; Kathryn B. Lane, Mgr.

Desc: Publishes on Michigan history and travel. Offers a series of guidebooks for tourists to other countries. Distributes for the Glenn Sesquecentennial Committee and the Allegan County Historical Society.

3125 ■ Peabody Essex Museum
East India Sq.   Ph: (978)745-9500
Salem, MA 01970   Free: 800-745-4054
    Fax: (978)741-9012
E-mail: pem@pem.org

Contact: William T. La Moy, Ed., Peabody Essex Museum Collections; Lynne Francis-Lunn, Dir., Licensing & Product Development; Daniele Lambrechts, Peabody Essex Museum Shop Mgr.; Donald Marshall, Pub., The American Neptune.

Desc: Publishes works on the history of Essex County, Massachusetts, and New England. Offers maps and photographic slides.

3126 ■ P.E.M. Publishing
37-9012 Walnut Grove Dr.   Ph: (604)888-3623
Langley, BC, Canada V1M 2K3   Fax: (604)888-3623

Contact: Elaine Mitten.

Desc: Publishes on local and family history. Does not accept unsolicited manuscripts.

3127 ■ Bonnie Peters
3212 Curtis Ln.   Ph: (423)687-3842
Knoxville, TN 37918-4003

Contact: Bonnie Peters, Historian.

Desc: Publishes pictorial histories with genealogical sketches pertaining to Union County, Tennessee. Does not accept unsolicited manuscripts.

3128 ■ Picton Press
PO Box 250   Ph: (207)236-6565
Rockport, ME 04856-0250   Fax: (207)236-6713
E-mail: sales@pictonpress.com
URL: http://www.pictonpress.com

Contact: Lewis Bunker Rohrbach, Pres.; Candy McMahan, Office Mgr.; Marlene Groves, Shipping.

Desc: Subjects include History, geneaology, children's stories. Publishes nonfiction and children's books. Accepts unsolicited manuscripts.

3129 ■ Pipe Creek Publications
5179 Perry Rd.   Ph: (410)875-2824
Mount Airy, MD 21771   Fax: (410)875-0150

Contact: Mary K. Meyer, Mgr.

Desc: Publishes on genealogy. Offers mailing lists of genealogical societies and libraries. Accepts genealogical source records of Mid-Atlantic states. Distributes for Libra Publications.

3130 ■ Piscator Publications
908 N. Madison
Jackson, MS 39202

Contact: James S. Fisher.

Desc: Publishes genealogy books.

3131 ■ Planning Services Public Advisory Committee
PO Box 1030   Ph: (902)542-3232
Wolfville, NS, Canada B0P 1X0   Fax: (902)542-5066

Desc: Publishes on local history and genealogy.

3132 ■ Jacques Plante
3023 St. Marle   Ph: (514)474-4713
Mascouche, PQ, Canada J7K   Fax: (514)522-9811
  1P2

Contact: Jacques Plante, Pres.

Desc: Publishes on genealogy.

3133 ■ Plymouth Rock Foundation, Inc.
Fisk Mill   Ph: (603)876-4685
PO Box 577   Free: 800-210-1620
Marlborough, NH 03455-0577   Fax: (603)876-4120
E-mail: plyrock@top.monad.net
URL: http://www.plymrock.org

Contact: John G. Talcott, Jr., Pres.; Rus Walton, Exec. Dir.

Desc: Provides Christian high schools and universities, churches, and families with material on Biblical principles of government and America's Christian history. Coordinates activities of local Christian Committees of Correspondence nationwide. Also publishes a monthly newsletter and offers audio and video tapes.

3134 ■ Polish Genealogical Society of America, Inc.
984 N. Milwaukee Ave.   Ph: (773)776-5551
Chicago, IL 60622
E-mail: pgsamerica@aol.com
URL: http://www.pgsa.org

Contact: Paul S. Valasek, Pres.

Desc: Publishes Polish genealogical reference books in English. Offers an ancestor index card file and website. Accepts unsolicited manuscripts.

3135 ■ Polish Genealogical Society of Connecticut
8 Lyle Rd.   Ph: (860)223-5596
New Britain, CT 06053
E-mail: pgsne2@aol.com

Contact: Jonathan Shea, Pres.; Joseph Maciora, VP; Constance Ochnio, Treas.

Desc: Publications are of interest to genealogists whose roots are in Poland and the Northeastern U.S.; offers translations, language manuals, cemetery inscriptions, indices, and a database search for surnames in ancestry file. Also publishes Pathways and Passages, a newsletter and maintains the archive and resource center.

3136 ■ Benoit Pontbriand
2390 Marie-Victorin
Sillery, PQ, Canada G1T 1K1

Contact: B. Pontbriand, Pub.

Desc: Publishes marriage records, by parish or county, for genealogical research.

3137 ■ Porter Publications International
PO Box 7533   Ph: (813)324-7367
Winter Haven, FL 33883   Fax: (813)324-7367

Contact: Howard Leonard Porter, Pres.

Desc: Publishes on genealogy and family histories, especially migrational histories. Also offers audio and video cassettes.

3138 ■ Portola Press
PO Box 1225   Ph: (805)965-1924
Santa Barbara, CA 93102

Contact: Philip O'Faolain, Pres. & Owner; Jenny Kelly O'Ceallaig.

Desc: Publishes Irish-American history and genealogy, dating from the early 1600's concentrating on the homelands of the first Irish to come to America and the contributions to American development.

3139 ■ Posey Publications
635 S. 560 E.
Orem, UT 84058-6327

Contact: Joanna W. Posey, Mktg. & Research.

Desc: Publishes genealogical research and historical writing.

3140 ■ Prince George's County Genealogical Society, Inc.
PO Box 819   Ph: (301)855-8655
Bowie, MD 20718-0819
E-mail: pgcgs@juno.com

Contact: Daniel M. LaRue, Pres.; Diane Stultz, Special Publications Chrmn.; Karen Duffy Miles, Archivist; Mary Frazer, Ed.

Desc: Publishes books to support genealogical research and methodology. Also offers a newsletter. Accepts unsolicited manuscripts.

3141 ■ Pro Familia Publishing
128 Gilmour Ave.   Ph: (416)767-2804
Toronto, ON, Canada M6P   Fax: (416)767-7398
    3B3

Contact: Peter Bela Merey, Pub.

Desc: Publishes manuscripts on history, genealogy, and heraldry. Directly involved in the editing and typesetting of manuscripts and the advising of clients on the propriety of the contents in an effort to produce works at a scholarly level. Also offers family charts, maps, and mount illustrations. Accepts unsolicited manuscripts.

3142 ■ Publishers of Beaver County Records
851 Route 68   Ph: (412)843-5314
New Brighton, PA 15066

Contact: Helen G. Clear; Mae H. Winne.

Desc: Purpose of publications is to make available to genealogical researchers indices of Beaver County court house records.

3143 ■ Quinsept, Inc.
20 Grassland St.   Ph: (781)641-2930
Lexington, MA 02421-7922   Free: 800-637-7668
    Fax: (781)641-1080

Contact: Stephen C. Vorenberg, Pres.; Patricia J. Vorenberg, VP.

Desc: Publishes computer software on genealogy.

3144 ■ Ragusan Press
2527 San Carlos Ave.   Ph: (415)592-1190
San Carlos, CA 94070   Fax: (415)592-1526

Contact: Adam S. Eterovich, Pres.

Desc: Publishes on Croations. Also produces maps, cassettes, guides, research aids, translations, and family coats of arms.

3145 ■ Read Publishing
1181 Deer Park Rd.   Ph: (613)225-7425
Nepean, ON, Canada K2E 6H4
E-mail: ap357@ncf.ca

Contact: Donald E. Read, Pub.

Desc: Genealogy, family history, parish registers, local history. Does not accept unsolicited manuscripts.

3146 ■ Lee Fleming Reese
4872 Old Cliffs Rd.   Ph: (619)583-8348
San Diego, CA 92120-1144

Contact: Lee Fleming Reese.

Desc: Genealogy, autobiographies.

3147 ■ Reprint Co. Publishers
PO Box 5401   Ph: (864)579-4433
Spartanburg, SC 29304

Contact: Thomas E. Smith, Owner & Pub.

Desc: Publishes reprints and selected originals in areas of local history and genealogical source material for southeastern states. Also assists individuals and organizations wishing to self-publish.

3148 ■ Research Foundation for Jewish Immigration
570 7th Ave., Rm. 1106   Ph: (212)921-3871
New York, NY 10018   Fax: (212)575-1918

Contact: Curt C. Silberman, Pres.; Herbert A. Strauss, Sec. & Coordinator of Research.

Desc: Researches and publishes studies related to the migration and acculturation of German-speaking, Central European, non-Jewish and Jewish Nazi persecutees in various resettlement countries. Publications include a three-volume dictionary of emigres, annotated source guides to archival and research materials, and monographs of conferences.

3149 ■ Rhode Island Genealogical Society
128 Massasoit Dr.
Warwick, RI 02888

Contact: Ruth Wilder Sherman, Production Ed.; John D. Bacon, Treas.

Desc: A nonprofit genealogical society which publishes books and a magazine on Rhode Island historical and genealogical interests.

3150 ■ RMB Services
251 Second St.   Ph: (905)640-7391
Stouffville, ON, Canada L4A   Fax: (905)640-9359
    1B9

Contact: R. Burkholder, Contact.

Desc: Publishes genealogical materials. Does not accept unsolicited manuscripts.

3151 ■ Ruth Flesher Robb
9295-101 Lake Park Dr. SW   Ph: (941)433-5372
Fort Myers, FL 33919-4822

Contact: Ruth Flesher Robb.

Desc: Publishes census records and indexes of Illinois, West Virginia, and Virginia.

3152 ■ Rocky Ridge Press
807 Lindsay Ct.   Ph: (804)288-0680
Richmond, VA 23229-6823

Contact: Benjamin B. Weisiger, III, Proprietor.

Desc: Publishes abstracts of Virginia county records for genealogical research.

3153 ■ Rose Family Association
1474 Montelegre Dr.   Ph: (408)268-2137
San Jose, CA 95120   Fax: (408)268-2165
URL: http://www.ourworld.compuserve.com/
    homepages/christiner

Contact: Christine Rose, Ed.

Desc: Publishes materials regarding various Rose families who are not necessarily related to each other and are of different nationalities. Also publishes two quarterlies, Rose Family Bulletin and Association Newsletter..

3154 ■ Clara Mae Ross
PO Box 203   Ph: (336)993-8208
Colfax, NC 27235

Desc: Publishes genealogical research materials for Virginia.

3155 ■ Ralph Rowland
418 Hillsboro Dr.   Ph: (301)593-1571
Silver Spring, MD 20902
E-mail: rowlandw@wam.umd.edu

Contact: Ralph W. Rowland, Pres.

Desc: Publishes books on family history.

3156 ■ Saga Publications & Research
PO Box 925   Ph: (204)378-2758
Arborg, MB, Canada R0C 0A0   Fax: (204)378-2758

Contact: Nelson S. Gerrard.

Desc: Publishes historical and genealogical works for North Americans of Icelandic heritage. Offers Icelandic genealogical research services and maps of Iceland.

3157 ■ St. Joseph History Book Project
131 Sunset Dr.   Ph: (814)226-9281
Lucinda, PA 16235

Contact: Margaret O. Wolbert, Coordinator.

Desc: Publishes on the local history and genealogy of Lucinda, Pennsylvania.

3158 ■ St. Louis Public Library
1301 Olive St.   Ph: (314)241-2288
St. Louis, MO 63103   Fax: (314)241-3840

Contact: Glen E. Holt, Exec. Dir.; Waller McGuire, Dep. Dir.; William Jackson, CFO; Diane Freiermuth, Dir., Public Svcs.; Leslie Holt, Dir., Youth Svcs./Family Literacy; Judith E. Simms, Dir., Development; Gerald S. Brooks, Dir., Mktg./Community Relations; Barry V. Berry, HR/Support Svcs.

Desc: Provides the library community and clientele with research tools not available elsewhere. Also offers a calendar and Intercom, a newsletter.

3159 ■ Saline County History and Heritage Society, Inc.
PO Box 221   Ph: (501)778-3770
Bryant, AR 72089-0221

Contact: Shirlene Chilton, Pres.; Steve Perdue, VP; Gail Blackburn, Sec.; Carolyn Earle Billingsley, Treas.

Desc: Publishes county government records and genealogy of Saline County, Arkansas. Offers a quarterly The Saline..

3160 ■ Saline Research
2301 Billingsley Ln.   Ph: (501)847-0402
Alexander, AR 72002-2802   Fax: (501)847-0402

Contact: Carolyn Earle Billingsley, Owner.

Desc: Publishes source records for genealogists. Also reprints out-of-print genealogy material, Offers professional genealogical research.

3161 ■ San Bernardino Valley Genealogical Society
PO Box 2220
San Bernardino, CA 92406

Contact: Marcia Patrick, Pres.; Lyndon Davis, VP; Myrl A. Swanson, Recording Sec.

Desc: Publishes a quarterly magazine for members, subscribers, and for exchange with like organizations. Contains San Bernardino County vital records, other local records of genealogical and historical interest, biography, and society news.

3162 ■ San Francisco Historic Records
1204 Nimitz Dr.   Ph: (415)755-2204
Daly City, CA 94015-3621

Contact: Louis J. Rasmussen, Pub.

Desc: Publishes lists of passengers on ships, trains, and covered wagons in the 1800's.

3163 ■ Faye Sea Sanders
311 Sage Rd.   Ph: (502)897-1245
Louisville, KY 40207

Contact: Faye Sea Sanders.

Desc: Publishes materials for Kentucky genealogical research.

3164 ■ Sasco Associates
PO Box 335   Ph: (203)255-4768
Southport, CT 06490   Fax: (203)255-4768

Contact: Kay Jackson, Mgr.; Dorchester L. Horne, Subsidiary & Reprint Rights.

Desc: Genealogy, music, radio, and television history.

3165 ■ Saskatchewan Genealogical Society
PO Box 1894   Ph: (306)780-9207
Regina, SK, Canada S4P 3E1   Fax: (306)781-6021
URL: http://www2.regina.smica/sys/; http://www.saskgenealogy.com

Contact: Janis Bohlken, Pres.; Laura M. Hanowski, Librarian; Marge Thomas, Exec. Dir.

Desc: Promotes the study of family history. Provides research services for those searching in Saskatchewan. Offers a quarterly journal, publications, and material on microforms.

3166 ■ S.C. Department of Archives and History
8301 Parklane Rd.   Ph: (803)896-6100
Columbia, SC 29223   Fax: (803)896-6167
URL: http://www.state.sc.us/scdah

Contact: Rodger Stroup, Dir.; Alexia J. Helsley, Dir., Education; Judith M. Andrews, Supervisor, Editing & Production; Carrie W. Bassett, Publications, Sales & Mktg.

Desc: Publishes popular, documentary, historical booklets, and letter press volumes on South Carolina history. Also publishes curriculum support materials for the teaching of South Carolina history. Publications available in microform.

3167 ■ William R. Scaife, Publisher
PO Box 98094   Ph: (770)987-2863
Atlanta, GA 30359   Fax: (404)634-3067

Contact: William R. Scaife, Owner.

Desc: Publishes books on the American Civil War. Also publishes genealogies. Offers maps.

3168 ■ Roger F. Scherger
2005 Wilshire Dr.   Ph: (937)773-7484
Piqua, OH 45356

Desc: Publishes genealogical research and family histories. Offers a quarterly newsletter.

3169 ■ Scott Barker
PO Box 417   Ph: (801)531-9297
Salt Lake City, UT 84110   Free: 800-643-4303
                             Fax: (801)531-6819
E mail: sbarker@atsbci.net

Contact: Johni Cerry, Pres.; Paula Biesinger, VP.

Desc: Publishes family history books and monographs. Accepts unsolicited manuscripts; returned if postage paid.

3170 ■ Scribe Write Books
102 Rolling Green Pl.   Ph: (406)721-1424
Missoula, MT 59803

Contact: Alan Wiener, CEO.

Desc: Publishes family heritage and diet control/support books.

3171 ■ Scroll Publishing Co
9465 County Rd. 487   Ph: (903)597-8023
PO Box 6175   Fax: (903)597-4176
Tyler, TX 75706
E-mail: scroll@earlychurch.com
URL: http://www.earlychurch.com

Contact: David W. Bercot, Pub.; Dean Taylor, General Mgr.

Desc: Publishes books on early Christianity and on the history of churches.

3172 ■ Beatrice West Seitz
2608 E. Racine St., Apt. 11 Ph: (608)754-6175
Janesville, WI 53545-5227

Contact: Beatrice West Seitz, Owner & Author.

Desc: Publishes on family history.

3173 ■ Frank Sellers
Crane Brook Rd.   Ph: (603)835-2331
Alstead, NH 03602   Fax: (603)835-2863

Contact: F. M. Sellers, Owner.

Desc: Self-publisher of books on guns and genealogy. Does not accept unsolicited manuscripts.

3174 ■ SFK Genealogy
12 Dell Pl.   Ph: (706)295-2228
Rome, GA 30161-7006

Contact: Shirley F. Kinney, Owner & Pub.; James P. Kinney, VP.

Desc: A historical and genealogical researcher; abstracts and transcribes official county records, newspapers, and census records and compiles family genealogies. Books are sold direct only.

3175 ■ Shelby County Historical and Genealogical Society
PO Box 286   Ph: (217)774-2260
Shelbyville, IL 62565
E-mail: shgensoc@bmmhnet.com

Contact: Jim Graven, Pres.; June McCain, VP; Denna Lupton, Treas.

Desc: Publishes aids to persons in historical and genealogical research.

3176 ■ Walter Lee Sheppard, Jr.
923 Old Manoa Rd.   Ph: (610)449-2167
Havertown, PA 19083

Contact: Walter Lee Sheppard, Jr., Owner/Pres.

Desc: Primarily short-run publisher of technical and genealogy books. Offers microfilm.

3177 ■ Sherwood House Publishing
13837 115th Ave.   Ph: (604)588-8647
Surrey, BC, Canada V3R 5Y3   Fax: (604)588-8647

Contact: Ted Staunton, Owner.

Desc: Publishes on history and genealogy. Also offers newsletters and magazines. Does not accept unsolicited manuscripts.

3178 ■ Mary Jo Davis Shoaf
5140 Hackney Ln., SW   Ph: (540)774-2667
Roanoke, VA 24018-2240

Contact: Mary Jo Davis Shoaf, Pub.

Desc: Publishes history and genealogy books.

3179 ■ Byron Sistler & Associates, Inc.
1712 Natchez Trace   Ph: (615)297-3085
PO Box 120934   Free: 800-578-9475
Nashville, TN 37212   Fax: (615)298-2807
E-mail: sistler@nash.mindspring.com

Contact: Barbara J. Sistler, Pres.; George A. Cook, VP; Byron Sistler, Sec.-Treas.

Desc: Originally a hobby, became full-time business in 1978. Publishes and indexes Tennessee genealogical materials. Distributes for Southern Historical Press, Ingmire Publications, Genealogical Publishing Co., Iberian Pub., Heritage Books, Inc., and Ye Olde Genealogie Shoppe.

3180 ■ Sleeper Co.
PO Box 10570
Alexandria, VA 22310-0570

Contact: Laura Hulslander, Owner.

Desc: Publishes genealogical material on Washington County, New York. Accepts unsolicited manuscripts. Distributes for Heritage Books, Clearfield Press, and Genealogical Publishing Co.

3181 ■ Alma A. Smith
554 Anna May Dr.   Ph: (513)528-1840
Cincinnati, OH 45244

Contact: Alma Aicholtz Smith, Owner.

Desc: Local history and genealogy. Self-publisher.

3182 ■ Society for German-American Studies
St. Olaf College   Ph: (507)646-3233
Northfield, MN 55057-1098   Fax: (507)646-3732
E-mail: rippleyl@stolaf.edu
URL: http://www.lib.iupui.edu/kade/

Contact: Don H. Tolzmann, Pres.; Volker Schmeissner, 1st VP; Dolores Hoyt, 2nd VP; William Roba, Treas.; Frances Ott Allen, Sec.-Membership.

Desc: Encourages scholarly research into the migration of Germans and German-speaking people to the North American continent. Also publishes a quarterly newsletter. Accepts unsolicited manuscripts.

3183 ■ Society of Mayflower Descendants in the State of Rhode Island and Providence Plantations

128 Massasoit Dr.   Ph: (401)781-6759
Warwick, RI 02888

Contact: Ruth Wilder Sherman, Production Ed.; Elsie B. Williams, Sec.

Desc: A nonprofit historical and educational group that publishes books about the Pilgrims and their descendants. Also known as Rhode Island Mayflower Society/Descendants.

3184 ■ South Carolina Magazine of Ancestral Research

PO Box 21766   Ph: (803)772-6919
Columbia, SC 29210
E-mail: scmar@juno.com

Contact: Brent H. Holcomb, Ed.

Desc: Publishes on South Carolina genealogy. Back issues of magazine available in bound volumes.

3185 ■ South Central Pennsylvania Genealogical Society, Inc.

PO Box 1824   Ph: (717)843-6169
York, PA 17405-1824

Contact: Margaret Barg, Pres.; Richard Konkel, VP; Barbara Rudy, Recording Sec.; Jean Robinson, Corresponding Sec.; Pat Gross, Membership.

Desc: Publishes on the genealogy of York County, Pennsylvania. Offers a newsletter Our Name's the Game..

3186 ■ Southeast Texas Genealogical and Historical Society

c/o Tyrrell Historical Library   Ph: (409)833-2759
PO Box 3827   Fax: (409)833-5828
Beaumont, TX 77704-3827

Contact: Charles J. Beaugh; Jennifer D. Hudson; Becky LaVera Caruthers; Kay Barnes; John L. Mikeska; Yvonne Sutherlin; Shirley White; Bill Windle; Kerry Girolamo.

Desc: Publishes to promote the study of family history. Accepts material and manuscripts for publication. Offers a quarterly Yellowed Pages to members.

3187 ■ Southern Genealogist's Exchange Society, Inc.

PO Box 2801   Ph: (904)387-9142
Jacksonville, FL 32203
E-mail: jbilly@freewwweb.com
URL: http://www.angelfire.com/fl/sges

Contact: Perry N. Medlock, Pres.; Doris Wilson, 2nd VP.

Desc: Publishes volumes of the U.S. 1850 census of the state of Florida. Also publishes The Exchange quarterly.

3188 ■ Southern Historical Press, Inc.

375 W. Broad St.   Ph: (803)233-2346
PO Box 1267   Fax: (803)233-2349
Greenville, SC 29601

Contact: Labruce Lucas, Jr., Pres.

Desc: Publishes on the history and genealogy of the South. Distributor for The Reprint Co., Genealogical Publishing Co., and Byron Sistler and Associates.

3189 ■ Southwest Pennsylvania Genealogical Services

PO Box 253   Ph: (412)238-3176
Laughlintown, PA 15655

Contact: William L. Iscrupe, Pub.; Shirley Iscrupe, Assoc. Ed.

Desc: Publishes reprints of old Pennsylvania county histories, atlases, and biographical books. Also offers new Pennsylvania genealogical reference books and five quarterly magazines. Accepts unsolicited manuscripts; send detailed proposal first.

3190 ■ Southwest Polonia Press

3308 Nairn St.   Ph: (915)598-7194
El Paso, TX 79925

Contact: Francis C. Kajencki, Pres.; Anthony Szafranski, Ed. & Mgr.

Desc: Publishes on American history.

3191 ■ Sowa Books

9637 Huntress Ln.
San Antonio, TX 78255

Contact: Janet Dawson Ebrom, Partner; Richard Allan Sowa, Partner.

Desc: Publishes a comprehensive family history.

3192 ■ Spindrift Publishing

PO Box 50   Ph: (902)637-2569
Barrington, NS, Canada B0W   Fax: (902)667-2324
1E0

Contact: Hattie A. Perry, Author & Pub.

Desc: Self-publisher on local history and genealogy.

3193 ■ Spinner Publications, Inc.

164 William St.   Ph: (508)994-4564
PO Box 1801   Free: 800-292-6062
New Bedford, MA 02740   Fax: (508)994-6925
E-mail: spinner@ultranet.com
URL: http://www.ultranet.com/spinner/

Contact: Joseph D. Thomas, Pub.; Milton P. George, Pres.

Desc: Nonprofit press; publishes regional history on people and culture of southeastern Massachusetts. Conducts local history and oral history curriculum in elementary schools. Also offers pictorial calendars. Accepts unsolicited manuscripts either typewritten or on a wordprocessing diskette.

3194 ■ Stagecoach Library

1840 S. Wolcott Ct.   Ph: (303)922-8856
Denver, CO 80219

Contact: D. J. Porter, Owner.

Desc: Offers materials for genealogical research. Presently inactive.

3195 ■ Stamford Genealogical Society, Inc.

PO Box 249
Stamford, CT 06904-0249

Contact: Thomas J. Kemp, Ed.

Desc: Publishes material in the fields of genealogy and local history. Publishes Connecticut Ancestry quarterly.

3196 ■ Stanly County Genealogical Society

PO Box 31
Albemarle, NC 28002-0031

Contact: Quentin Smith, Pres.; James Russell, VP; Eloise M. Ausband, Dir.; Coy Hatley, Dir.; George Hahn, Dir.

Desc: Publishes on genealogy. Offers a quarterly, Journal..

3197 ■ Stemmons Publishing

PO Box 612   Ph: (801)254-2152
West Jordan, UT 84084

Contact: John D. Stemmons, Pub.

Desc: Publishes of genealogy reprints and microfiche of newspaper indexes. Does not accept unsolicited manuscripts.

3198 ■ Stewart University Press

350 County Rd. No. 175   Ph: (205)447-2939
Piedmont, AL 36272

Contact: Mrs. Frank Ross Stewart, Pres.

Desc: Nonprofit publisher of county, church, family, and other histories. Accepts unsolicited manuscripts.

3199 ■ Helen S. Stinson

Rte. 1, Box 78
Statts Mills, WV 25279

Contact: Helen S. Stinson.

Desc: Publishes genealogical resource materials, primarily on West Virginia, but some family histories of other areas.

3200 ■ Stephen J. Stokes

Rte. 10, Box 413J14
Winston-Salem, NC 27127

Contact: Violet M. Sink Stokes.

Desc: Genealogy.

3201 ■ Stoneycroft Publishing

RR 1, Box 1710   Ph: (902)742-2667
Yarmouth, NS, Canada B5A 4A5
E-mail: nstn1873@fox.nstn.ca

Contact: Gwen Guiou Trask, Ed.; F. Stuart Trask, Mgr.

Desc: Publishes local history, genealogy, and biographies. Offers generation "FAN CHARTS.".

3202 ■ William N. Stryker

3804 Adrienne Dr.
Alexandria, VA 22309

Desc: Genealogy of Stryker and Striker families.

3203 ■ D. A. Sturgill

15 Smithwood Ln.   Ph: (336)359-2280
Piney Creek, NC 28663
E-mail: tdunino@aol.com
URL: http://www.businesson.com/careerd/
hanksfam.htm

Desc: Publishes on genealogy. Does not accept unsolicited manuscripts.

3204 ■ William S. Sullwold, Publishing

18 Pearl St.   Ph: (508)823-0924
Taunton, MA 02780   Fax: (508)823-0924

Contact: William S. Sullwold, Owner.

Desc: Publishes books on regional history, geneaology, and collectibles; limited editions for societies and individuals. Does not accept unsolicited manuscripts.

3205 ■ Summit County Genealogical Society

PO Box 2232   Ph: (330)733-6185
Akron, OH 44309
E-mail: summit0gs@acorn.net

Contact: Howard Hill, Pres.; Rodger Marble, VP; Judy Davis, Treas.; Louise Royce, Recording Sec.; Dorothy Briggs, Corresponding Sec.

Desc: Publishes on genealogy. Also produces a monthly newsletter, The Highpoint..

Master Index

3206 ▪ Summit Publications
PO Box 39128
Indianapolis, IN 46239
Ph: (317)862-3330
Free: 800-419-0200
Fax: (317)862-2599

Contact: Patricia Gooldy, Pres.; Ray Gooldy, Pub.

Desc: Publishes genealogical books on local history records.

3207 ▪ Richard Sunbury
4702 Richmond Ave.
Austin, TX 78745
Ph: (512)444-6838

Contact: Richard Sunbury, Owner; Ann Sunbury, Mgr.

Desc: Publishes the Sunbury family history.

3208 ▪ Surname Searches
1110 W. 16th St.
Stuttgart, AR 72160-5735
Ph: (870)673-1455

Contact: Jane Whiteman.

3209 ▪ Polly Rachel McGaughey Sutton
2700 NW 61st St.
Oklahoma City, OK 73112
Ph: (405)842-4149

Contact: Polly Rachel McGaughey Sutton, Pub.

Desc: Publishes a family history.

3210 ▪ Tangled Roots Press
3561 W. 27th Ave.
Vancouver, BC, Canada V6S 1P9
Ph: (604)734-8551

Contact: William S. Hoar, Owner & Operator.

Desc: Publishes books of family history.

3211 ▪ TCI Genealogical Resources
PO Box 15839
San Luis Obispo, CA
93406-5839
Ph: (805)550-3551
E-mail: tcigen@worldnet.att.net
URL: http://www.tcigenealogy.com

Contact: Peter E. Carr, Pres.

Desc: Publishes genealogical journals and books. Does not accept unsolicited manuscripts.

3212 ▪ Tecumseth and West Gwillimbury Historical Society
RR 3
Tottenham, ON, Canada L0G
1W0
Ph: (905)936-2789

Contact: Betty Anderson, Pres.; Adeline Rogers, VP; Jean Smith, Sec.; Cathy Black, Treas.; Franz Aschwanden, Past Pres.

Desc: Researches, records, and preserves the history of Tecumseth and West Gwillimbury townships.

3213 ▪ Tennessee Valley Publishing
5320 Yosemite Trail
Box 52527
Knoxville, TN 37909
Ph: (423)584-5235
Free: 800-762-7079
Fax: (423)584-5395
E-mail: tvp1@ix.netcom.com

Contact: Margaret Kitchell, Owner.

Desc: Publishes family histories for clients nationwide. Also publishes books on general topics including poetry, religion, cookbooks, and materials on the history and genealogy of eastern Tennessee.

3214 ▪ Thode Translations
RR 7, Box 306
Marietta, OH 45750-9437
Ph: (740)373-3728

Contact: Ernest Thode, Owner.

Desc: Publishes on Germanic genealogy and maps of central Europe. Does not accept unsolicited manuscripts.

3215 ▪ Joe C. Tinney
800 Lake Air Dr.
Waco, TX 76710
Ph: (817)776-8763

Desc: Genealogy.

3216 ▪ TLC Genealogy
PO Box 403369
Miami Beach, FL 33140-1369
Free: 800-858-8558
Fax: (305)531-1158
E-mail: staff@tlc-gen.com
URL: http://www.tlc-gen.com

Desc: Publishes books on genealogy. Also provides search services. Does not accept unsolicited manuscripts.

3217 ▪ Topeka Genealogical Society, Inc.
PO Box 4048
Topeka, KS 66604-0048
Ph: (785)233-5762
E-mail: tgs@networksplus.net
URL: http://www.networksplus.net/donno/

Contact: Pat Thomas, Pres.; Shirley O'Toole, Publications Mgr.; Betty Wood, Corresponding Sec.; Shirley Warden, Quarterly Ed.

Desc: Publishes Kansas genealogical material, with special emphasis on the eastern portion of the state. Also publishes a quarterly newsletter. Does not accept unsolicited manuscripts.

3218 ▪ Topp-of-the-Line
W. 1304 Cliffwood Ct.
Spokane, WA 99218-2917
Ph: (509)467-2299
E-mail: toppline@cet.com
URL: http://www.cet.com/toppline/

Contact: Bette Butcher Topp, Owner.

Desc: Genealogy. Accepts unsolicited manuscripts.

3219 ▪ Triadoption Publications
PO Box 638
Westminster, CA 92684
Ph: (714)892-4098
Fax: (714)892-4098

Contact: Mary Jo Rillera, Pres.; Dave Dir., Ronnie Endo, Treas.; Diane Leach, VP; Charlene Emerson, Sec.

Desc: A nonprofit corporation tracing families separated by adoption. Also offers tapes, pamphlets, and booklets.

3220 ▪ Tulsa Genealogical Society
PO Box 585
Tulsa, OK 74101-0585
Ph: (918)742-3893

Contact: Fran Frame, Pres.

Desc: Publishes local genealogical materials. Offers Tulsa Annals three times a year. Accepts unsolicited manuscripts pertaining to genealogy.

3221 ▪ Carol Mund Twardzik
PO Box 61
Spy Hill, SK, Canada S0A 3W0
Ph: (306)745-3838

Desc: Publishes on genealogy.

3222 ▪ Hazle A. Tyler
2258 S. Virginia Ave.
Springfield, MO 65807

Contact: Hazle A. Tyler, Owner.

Desc: Publishes genealogical and historical records.

3223 ▪ Uhl's Publishing Co.
289 Fisher Settlement
Spencer, NY 14883
Ph: (607)589-6594

Contact: Laura C. Uhl, Pub. & Owner.

Desc: Publishes on genealogy and history of Spencer, NY and Spencer schools. Does not accept unsolicited manuscripts.

3224 ▪ United Empire Loyalists' Association of Canada, Toronto Branch
234 Eglinton Ave. E., Ste. 406
Toronto, ON, Canada M4P
1K5
Ph: (416)489-1783
Fax: (416)489-3664

Contact: John D. Warburton, Pres.; Kathie Orr, Past-Pres.; Mark Lathem, Treas.; Ed Cass, Pub. Comm.

Desc: Publishes a book on history of Canadian Loyalists and a genealogy of association members.

3225 ▪ Elizabeth Starr Versailles
42 Nash Hill Rd.
Williamsburg, MA 01096
Ph: (413)268-7576

Desc: Genealogy.

3226 ▪ Virginia Book Co.
PO Box 431
114 S. Church St.
Berryville, VA 22611
Ph: (540)955-1428

Contact: Lorraine F. Myers, Mgr.

Desc: Publishes original works and reprints on Virginia local history and genealogy.

3227 ▪ Virginia Genealogical Society
5001 W. Broad St., Ste. 115
Richmond, VA 23230
Ph: (804)285-8954
Fax: (804)285-0394
URL: http://www.vgs.org

Contact: Wesley Pippenger, Pres.; J. Richard Morris, Treas.

Desc: Publishes genealogical source records of Virginia. Accepts unsolicited manuscripts.

3228 ▪ VKM Publishing Co.
Rte. 1, Box 169
Rayville, MO 64084

Contact: Sharon R. Bright, Office Mgr.

Desc: Publishes historical and genealogical works.

3229 ▪ Betty Jean Walte
702-520 Wellington St.
London, ON, Canada N6A 3R2
Ph: (519)434-1676

Desc: Ontario genealogy and history.

3230 ▪ Walden Press
34 Walden St.
PO Box 127
Concord, MA 01742
Ph: (508)369-4888

Contact: William Spencer Jarnigan, CEO.

Desc: Publishes genealogical books on the Jarnagin family and related namesakes. Also offers videos, as a companion to the books, and genealogical display charts.

3231 ▪ Margaret Waring
PO Box 753
Comanche, TX 76442
Ph: (915)356-3428

Contact: Margaret Waring, Owner.

Desc: Publishes local history and genealogy for Comanche County, Texas.

3232 ▪ Washington County Historical Society, Inc.
118 E. Dickson St.
Fayetteville, AR 72701-5612
Ph: (501)521-2970
URL: http://biz.ipa.net/wchs

Contact: Charles Stewart, Pres.; Robert McKinney, VP; Don Schaefer, Ed.; Babette Goodman, Sec.; Dan Grubb, Treas.

Desc: Publishes on the history of Washington County, Arkansas. Accepts unsolicited manuscripts.

3233 ■ Wayne County Historical Society and Museum
E. Hwy. 2   Ph: (515)872-2483
316 NE St.
Corydon, IA 50060

Contact: Janet Fry Winslow, Pres.; Harold Greenlee, VP; Verlin Akers, Treas.; Neva Trumbo, Curator; Wilma S. West, Librarian.

Desc: Publishes historical and genealogical publications on Wayne County, Iowa. Offers an alternate telephone number: (515)872-2211.

3234 ■ Matilda Jenkins Webb
261 Zaks Way   Ph: (423)623-6641
Newport, TN 37821

Desc: Genealogy.

3235 ■ William G. Weger
425 N. Green, Apt. 5   Ph: (515)583-3014
PO Box 976
Ottumwa, IA 52501

Contact: William G. Weger, Pres.

Desc: Genealogy. Presently inactive.

3236 ■ Maralyn A. Wellauer
2845 North 72 St.   Ph: (414)778-1224
Milwaukee, WI 53210   Fax: (414)778-2109
E-mail: swissmis@interserv.com
URL: http://www.execpc.com/fhea

Desc: Publishes materials on foreign genealogical research in particular Switzerland. Does not accept unsolicited manuscripts.

3237 ■ J. L. Wells
Rte. 1, Box 2770   Ph: (904)935-1531
O Brien, FL 32071

Contact: John Lamar Wells, Owner.

Desc: Publishes on genealogy.

3238 ■ Wells, Phillips & Leonard, Genealogical Publications
521 N. Franklin Rd.   Ph: (910)786-2992
Mount Airy, NC 27030

Contact: Virginia G. Phillips, Partner; Carol J. Leonard, Partner; Agnes M. Wells, Partner.

3239 ■ West Augusta Historical & Genealogical Society
2515 10th Ave.   Ph: (304)422-1774
Parkersburg, WV 26101-5829

Contact: Wes Cochran, Ed.

Desc: Publishes censuses for the state of Ohio. Does not accept unsolicited manuscripts.

3240 ■ West-Central Kentucky Family Research Association
PO Box 1932   Ph: (502)684-4150
Owensboro, KY 42302

Contact: Mrs. Margarte Alford, Jr., Bulletin Ed.; Dot Smithson, Ky Family Records Editor; Norma E. Williams, Corresponding Sec.

3241 ■ West Central Missouri Genealogical Society and Library, Inc.
705 Broad St.   Ph: (660)747-6264
Warrensburg, MO 64093-2032
E-mail: yunguns@iland.net

Contact: J. Eldon Yung, Publication Coordinator.

Desc: Publishes local genealogical material. Accepts unsolicited manuscripts.

3242 ■ Westchester County Historical Society
2199 Saw Mill River Rd.   Ph: (914)592-4323
Elmsford, NY 10523   Fax: (914)592-6481

Contact: Elizabeth Fuller, Librarian.

Desc: Publishes on the history and genealogy of Westchester County. Offers a quarterly journal and a newsletter. Accepts unsolicited manuscripts.

3243 ■ Western Pennsylvania Genealogical Society
4400 Forbes Ave.   Ph: (412)622-3154
Pittsburgh, PA 15213-4080

Contact: Jean S. Morris, Quarterly Ed.

Desc: Publishes books on western Pennsylvania history and genealogy. Does not accept unsolicited manuscripts.

3244 ■ Westland Publications
PO Box 820   Ph: (520)762-1920
Vail, AZ 85641
E-mail: westlandpubn@The River.com

Contact: Helen Smith Barrette.

Desc: Publishes mainly genealogical reference works, particularly immigration to the New World from Europe.

3245 ■ Wheatfield Press
506 King Edward St.
Winnipeg, MB, Canada R3J 1L8

Contact: Eric Jonasson, Pub.

Desc: Publishes material on Canadian genealogy in particular and genealogy in general. Are also publishing consultants and printing representatives.

3246 ■ Whitfield Books
1841 Pleasant Hill Rd.   Ph: (510)938-6759
Pleasant Hill, CA 94523

Contact: Vallie Jo Whitfield, Pub. & Writer; Joanne Whitfield, Ed.

Desc: Offers genealogy assistance on the surname Whitfield. Also offers newsletters.

3247 ■ Who's Who in Genealogy & Heraldry
PO Box 413   Ph: (301)725-0222
Savage, MD 20763

Contact: P. W. Filby, Author.

Desc: Publishes on genealogists.

3248 ■ Willow Bend Books & Family Line Publications
65 E. Main St.   Ph: (410)876-6101
Westminster, MD 21157   Free: 800-876-6103
    Fax: (410)876-6101
E-mail: willowbend@mediasoft.net

Contact: Craig R. Scott, Owner; Sallie Mallick, Office Mgr.

Desc: Publishes genealogical source books. Offers computer software. Career books for Genealogical Publishing Co., Heritage Books, Hearthstone Books, Southern Historical Press, and 100 other publishers.

3249 ■ Wilson County Genealogical Society
PO Box 802   Ph: (919)237-1258
Wilson, NC 27894   Fax: (919)237-3392
E-mail: ancestor@sprintmail.com

Contact: Sue E. Powell, Pres.; Carroll Arthur, VP; Henry Powell, Treas.; Carol Forbes, Sec.

Desc: Publishes genealogical research data on Wilson County, North Carolina.

3250 ■ J. Floyd Wine
924 Woodland Ave.   Ph: (540)662-5735
Winchester, VA 22601-5824

Desc: Genealogy, history.

3251 ■ Winnebago & Boone Counties Genealogical Society
PO Box 10166   Ph: (815)226-4884
Loves Park, IL 61131-0166

Contact: Ann Brubaker, Pres.; Virginia Skoglund, VP; Ruth Lunde, Corresponding Sec.; Betty Jane Lagerquist, Recording Sec.; Shirl D. Reed, Treas.

Desc: Publishes genealogical reference works on specific locations in Illinois. Offers a bimonthly newsletter to society members.

3252 ■ Winter Soldier Archive
2490 Chaning Way   Ph: (510)527-0616
Berkeley, CA 94704

Contact: Clark C. Smith, Dir.

Desc: Publishes oral history and other documentation of the Vietnam War experience.

3253 ■ Wisconsin State Genealogical Society, Inc.
2109 20th Ave.   Ph: (608)325-2609
Monroe, WI 53566
URL: http://www.rootsweb.com/wsgs

Contact: John A. Brissee, Pres.; Roland Littlewood, VP; Ruth Steffen, Sec.; Virginia V. Irvin, Treas.

Desc: Publishes materials related to the genealogy of Wisconsin. Offers a quarterly, WSGS Newsletter. Accepts unsolicited manuscripts for newsletter.

3254 ■ Woods Hole Historical Collection
PO Box 185   Ph: (508)548-7270
Woods Hole, MA 02543   Fax: (508)540-1969
URL: http://www.photoark.com/wdshole.html

Contact: Jane McLaughlin, Publications Committee Chrmn.

Desc: Publishes books related to the history and life of the seashore scientific community of Woods Hole, Massachusetts. Offers history archive of documents, photos, diaries, and oral history tapes. Also offers a biannual journal, Spritsail. .

3255 ■ Mildred S. Wright
140 Briggs   Ph: (409)832-2308
Beaumont, TX 77707-2329

Contact: Mildred S. Wright.

Desc: Publishes family histories, genealogical research aids (e.g. cemetery inventories and court house record transcriptions).

3256 ■ Yakima Valley Genealogical Society
PO Box 445   Ph: (509)248-1328
Yakima, WA 98907-0445

Desc: Compiles, prepares, preserves, and indexes genealogical and historical records of local interest and of interest to its members.

3257 ■ Yates Publishing
PO Box 67   Ph: (406)777-3797
Stevensville, MT 59870   Fax: (406)777-1012

Contact: William A. Yates, Owner.

Desc: Publishes files of information on surnames.

3258 ■ Ye Olde Genealogie Shoppe
9605 Vandergriff Rd.   Ph: (317)862-3330
PO Box 39128   Free: 800-419-0200
Indianapolis, IN 46239   Fax: (317)862-2599
URL: http://www.yogs.com

Contact: Walter R. Gooldy, Owner; Patricia A. Gooldy, Owner.

Desc: Publishes indexes to census, birth, marriage, and death records, will abstracts, indexes to county histories, etc. for use in genealogical research. Publishes microform publications, charts, and forms for same audience.

3259 ■ Dena Lynn Winslow York
1005 Mapleton Rd.   Ph: (207)764-4264
Mapleton, ME 04757

Contact: Dena Lynn Winslow York, Author.

Desc: Publishes genealogical and historical books.

3260 ■ Gloryann Young
Rte. 3, Box 55   Ph: (918)655-3126
Wister, OK 74966

Contact: Gloryann Young, Pub.

Desc: Publishes genealogical studies.

Research Centers

3261 ■ Alabama Archives and History Department
624 Washington Ave.   Ph: (334)242-4435
PO Box 300100   Fax: (334)240-3433
Montgomery, AL 36130-0100
URL: http://www.archives.state.al.us

Contact: Edwin C. Bridges, Dir.

Desc: Integral unit of state government of Alabama. Research: Archives and history.

3262 ■ American International College Oral History Center
James J. Shea Memorial Library   Ph: (413)747-6225
1000 State St.   Fax: (413)737-2803
Springfield, MA 01109-3189
E-mail: kutley@cwmars.org
URL: http://www.aic.edu

Contact: Dr. F. Knowlton Utley, Lib.Dir.

Desc: Integral unit of James J. Shea Memorial Library, American International College. Research: Western Massachusetts and Connecticut Valley oral history.

3263 ■ Artesia Historical Museum and Art Center Research Facility
505 W Richardson   Ph: (505)748-2390
Artesia, NM 88210   Fax: (505)746-3880

Contact: Nancy Dunn, Mus.Dir.

Desc: Independent, nonprofit organization. Research: Artesia area history, farming, ranching, and genealogy.

3264 ■ Balch Institute for Ethnic Studies
18 S 7th St.   Ph: (215)925-8090
Philadelphia, PA 19106   Fax: (215)925-4392
E-mail: balchlib@balchinstitute.org
URL: http://libertynet.org/balch

Contact: Dr. John Tenhula, Pres.

Desc: Independent, nonprofit research, educational, and public service museum. Research: Immigration, race, and ethnicity. Activities focus on documenting and interpreting the American multicultural experience.

3265 ■ Baylor University Institute for Oral History
PO Box 97271   Ph: (254)710-3437
Waco, TX 76798-7271   Fax: (254)710-1571
E-mail: rebecca_sharpless@baylor.edu
URL: http://www.baylor.edu/oral_history

Contact: Dr. M. Rebecca Sharpless, Dir.

Desc: Integral unit of Baylor University. Research: Gathering, transcribing, editing, and preserving audio and video tape-recorded oral history memoirs in fields of religion, music, law, business, university history, women's history, Texas history, and numerous special areas.

3266 ■ Bowling Green State University Center for Archival Collections
Jerome Library, 5th Fl.   Ph: (419)372-2411
Bowling Green, OH 43403   Fax: (419)372-0155
E-mail: pyon@bgnet.bgsu.edu
URL: http://www.bgsu.edu/colleges/library/cac.html

Contact: Paul D. Yon, Dir.

Desc: Integral unit of College of Learning Resources at Bowling Green State University. Research: Regional, state, and local history and related fields, with emphasis on material in county and municipal governmental records, local newspapers, and manuscripts. Utilizes 20,000 volumes of court records, vital statistics, tax records, institutional records, official reports, minutes of municipal and village councils, and official correspondence and papers of prominent groups and citizens. Research strengths include women's history, Civil War, Great Lakes history, agricultural history, church, and genealogy. Responsible for care and preservation of University records, rare books, and special collections.

3267 ■ Brazorial County Historical Museum Research Center
100 E Cedar   Ph: (409)864-1208
Angleton, TX 77515   Fax: (409)864-1217
E-mail: jmurray@bchm.org
URL: http://www.bchm.org

Contact: Robert Handy, Dir.

Desc: Independent, nonprofit organization. Research: Brazoria County and Texas history, families of Brazoria County, and oral history.

3268 ■ Bureau of the Census
     Ph: (301)457-2135
rs>Washington, DC 20233   Fax: (301)457-3761

Contact: Kenneth Prewitt, Dir.

Desc: Research: Collects, tabulates, and publishes a wide variety of statistical data on the population and economy of the nation. Data are available to government and public users for the development and evaluation of economic and social programs. Activities of the Bureau include: decennial censuses of population and housing; quinquennial censuses of agriculture, state and local governments, manufacturers, mineral industries, distributive trades, construction industries, service industries, and transportation; current surveys which provide information on many of the subjects covered in the censuses at monthly, quarterly, annual, or other intervals; compilation of current Research: statistics on U.S. foreign trade, including data on imports, exports, and shipping; special censuses as requested and financed by state and local governments; publication of population estimates and projections; cur-

rent data on population and housing characteristics; and current reports on manufacturing, retail and wholesale trade, services, construction, imports and exports, state and local government finances and employment, and other subjects.

3269 ■ Bureau of the Census--Demographic Programs Population Division International Programs Center Eurasia Branch
Washington Plaza II, Rm. 117   Ph: (202)457-1362
U.S. Bureau of Census   Fax: (202)457-1539
Washington, DC 20233
E-mail: jdunlop@ccmail.census.gov
URL: http://www.census.gov/ipc/www/

Contact: John Dunlop, Contact

Desc: Research: Responsible for conducting economic and demographic research on all countries in Europe and Asia. Most research is focused on the newly independent states of the former Soviet Union (NISFSU), former communist countries of Eastern Europe, and China. Activities involve: data collection and analysis of all European and Asian countries' economic and demographic statistics; and research on NISFSU's and China's population, labor force, input-output, national accounts, and industry. Current industry studies cover the fuel, chemical, and machine-building sectors.

3270 ■ Canadian Mennonite Brethren Conference Board of Communications Centre for Mennonite Brethren Studies
1-169 Riverton Ave.   Ph: (204)669-6575
Winnipeg, MB, Canada R2L   Fax: (204)654-1865
2E5
E-mail: CmbsArchives@CdnMBConf.ca
URL: http://www.concordcollege.mb.ca/concord/
    cmbs.htm

Contact: Abe Dueck, Dir.

Desc: Integral unit of the Canadian Mennonite Brethren Conference Board of Communications, located at Concord College. Research: Mennonite history and theology, focusing on collecting and preserving historical Mennonite records.

3271 ■ Carpatho-Rusyn Research Center
Box 131-B
Orwell, VT 05760

Contact: Paul R. Magocsi, Pres.

Desc: Independent, nonprofit organization. Research: History, language, and culture of the Carpatho-Rusyns in Europe (including Slovakia, Poland, Ukraine, and Yugoslavia) and the immigrants and descendants of the ethnic group in the United States. Provides research fellowships and project funding.

3272 ■ Center for Immigration Research
Balch Institute of Ethnic Studies   Ph: (215)922-3454
18 S 7th St.   Fax: (215)922-3201
Philadelphia, PA 19106
E-mail: v5043e@vm.temple.edu

Contact: Prof. Ira A. Glazier, Dir.

Desc: Unit of Temple University and Balch Institute of Ethnic Studies, an independent, nonprofit organization. Research: International migration, including family history and demographic and socioeconomic studies of migration to the U.S.

3273 ■ Center for Migration Studies
209 Flagg Pl.   Ph: (718)351-8800
Staten Island, NY 10304-1199   Fax: (718)667-4598

E-mail: cmslft@aol.com
URL: http://www.cmsny.org

Contact: Dr. Lydio F. Tomasi, Exec.Dir.

Desc: Independent, nonprofit research organization. Research: Sociodemographic, economic, political, historical, legislative, and pastoral aspects of human migration and refugee movements and ethnic group relations.

3274 ■ Center for Southern Folklore

209 Beale St.   Ph: (901)525-FOLK
PO Box 226   Fax: (901)525-3945
Memphis, TN 38103
E-mail: queenbee@southernfolklore.com
URL: http://www.southernfolklore.com

Contact: Judy Peiser, Exec.Dir.

Desc: Independent, nonprofit organization. Research: Folk and ethnic cultures of the South, including studies in folklore, music, arts, and crafts. Current projects focus on cultural tourism and an interpretive study of social history and folk culture in three downtown Memphis areas: Beale Street, Cotton Row, and the Mississippi Riverfront. Also investigates the folklife and social history of the ethnic communities of Memphis and the Mid-South.

3275 ■ Center for the Study of Aging, Inc.

706 Madison Ave.   Ph: (518)465-6927
Albany, NY 12208-3604   Fax: (518)462-1339
E-mail: iapaas@aol.com
URL: http://members.aol.com/iapaas

Contact: Sara Harris, Exec.Dir.

Desc: Independent, nonprofit educational and research foundation. Research: Social and medical research on aging, including physical activity and aging, housing for the elderly, geriatric cardiology, nutrition, mental health, oral history, public policy, caregiving, prevention and respite care for the frail elderly.

3276 ■ Charles County Community College Southern Maryland Studies Center

8730 Mitchell Rd.   Ph: (301)934-2251
PO Box 910   Fax: (301)934-7699
La Plata, MD 20646-0910
E-mail: smsc@charles.cc.md.us
URL: http://www.charles.cc.md.us

Contact: Sarah L. Barley, Coord.

Desc: Integral unit of Charles County Community College. Research: Southern Maryland, including history, culture, development, and genealogy.

3277 ■ Cherokee County Historical Society Research Center

PO Box 247   Ph: (712)436-2624
Cleghorn, IA 51014

Contact: Anne Wilberding, Pres.

Desc: Independent, nonprofit organization. Research: Cherokee County history and genealogy.

3278 ■ Clayton Library Center for Genealogical Research

5300 Caroline   Ph: (713)284-1999
Houston, TX 77004-6896
URL: http://www.hpl.lib.tx.us/clayton/

Contact: Margaret J. Harris, Mgr.

Desc: Integral unit of Houston Public Library. Research: Genealogy. Provides research assistance for inquiries into personal genealogical history.

3279 ■ Columbia University East Asian Institute

420 W 118th St.   Ph: (212)854-2592
New York, NY 10027   Fax: (212)749-1497
E-mail: nlc3@columbia.edu
URL: http://www.columbia.edu/cu/sipa/regional/eai

Contact: Madeleine Zelin, Dir.

Desc: Integral unit of Columbia University. Research: Modern and contemporary conditions in east and southeast Asia, with emphasis on social sciences, including China, Japan, Korea, the Pacific Basin, and United States-East Asian relations.

3280 ■ Columbia University Oral History Research Office

Butler Library, Box 20   Ph: (212)854-2273
New York, NY 10027   Fax: (212)854-5378
E-mail: rjg5@columbia.ed
URL: http://www.columbia.edu/cu/libraries/indiv/oral/

Contact: Dr. Ronald J. Grele, Dir.

Desc: Research unit of Columbia University. Research: History, political science, social action, business, law, medicine, social work, labor, journalism, international affairs, fine arts, civil liberties, social security and unemployment, popular arts, naval history, black history, and pure science. Creates source materials by conducting interviews with persons who, as participants or observers, have acquired experience that merits preservation.

3281 ■ Fred Roberts Crawford Witness to the Holocaust Project

Emory University   Ph: (404)329-6428
Atlanta, GA 30322

Contact: Prof. Deborah Lipstadt, Dir.

Desc: Separate department at Emory University operated under primary control of the Department of Religion. Research: Records testimonies of World War II military personnel, witnessed the liberation of the concentration camps; collects photographs, diaries, and maps of Holocaust period; records and collects survivor testimonies; develops methodology for computer information retrieval of transcripts and interviews; and abstracts and indexes transcripts, video tapes, and photographs.

3282 ■ Harrison County Research Center

Harrison County   Ph: (903)938-2680
 History Museum   Fax: (903)935-4379
Peter Whetstone Sq.
Marshall, TX 75670
E-mail: museum@prysm.net
URL: http://www.cets.stasu.edu/Harrison/

Contact: Gwen Nolan, Off.Mgr.

Desc: Integral unit of Harrison County Historical Museum. Research: U.S. history, the Civil War, state and local history of Texas, world history, genealogy, railroads, and music.

3283 ■ Hawaii Chinese History Center

111 N King St., Ste. 410   Ph: (808)521-5948
Honolulu, HI 96817-4703

Contact: Roger Liu, Contact

Desc: Independent, nonprofit organization. Research: History of the Chinese in Hawaii, including genealogy, traditions, historic sites, and biographies of early and contemporary leaders.

3284 ■ Hiram College Northwoods Field Station

PO Box 123   Ph: (906)569-5331
Wetmore, MI 49895   Fax: (906)569-5449

Contact: Prof. Hale Chatfield, Dir.

Desc: Integral unit of Hiram College and located in Hiawatha National Forest twelve miles from Lake Superior in Michigan's Upper Peninsula. Research: Field biology, geology, environmental studies, natural history, and local oral history and folklore. Station is surrounded by federal lands of hardwood and conifer forests, meadows, bogs, a river, and over a dozen undeveloped lakes.

3285 ■ Historic Annapolis Foundation Research Center

18 Pinkney St.   Ph: (410)267-7619
Annapolis, MD 21401   Fax: (410)267-6189
URL: http://www.annapolis.org

Contact: Ann Fligstein, Pres.

Desc: Independent, nonprofit organization. Research: State and local history, historic preservation, urban planning, and decorative arts.

3286 ■ Idaho State Historical Society

1109 Main, Ste. 250   Ph: (208)334-2682
Boise, ID 83702-5642   Fax: (208)334-2774
E-mail: sguerber@ishs.state.id.us
URL: http://www.state.id.us/ishs/index.html

Contact: Steve Guerber, Dir.

Desc: Integral unit of state of Idaho. Research: History of Idaho and the Pacific Northwest. Compiles inventories of historical sites and archaeological and architectural resources, researches and nominates sites to the National Register of Historic Places, maintains site records, and conducts surveys and excavations of historic and prehistoric sites. Collects and maintains oral histories of Idahoans.

3287 ■ Indian and Colonial Research Center

Eva Butler Library   Ph: (203)536-9771
Main St.
PO Box 525
Old Mystic, CT 06372

Contact: Joan Cohn, Pres.

Desc: Independent, nonprofit organization. Research: Native American Indians, including the lifestyle and culture of the Pequots, Narragansetts, and Nehantics; and local history, including genealogy, oral history, old homes, and early American school books, maps, and photographs.

3288 ■ Indiana University Bloomington Oral History Research Center

Memorial Hall W, Rm. 401   Ph: (812)855-2856
Bloomington, IN 47405   Fax: (812)855-4869
E-mail: ohrc@indiana.edu
URL: http://www.indiana.edu/ohrc

Contact: Dr. John Bodnar, Dir.

Desc: Integral unit of Indiana University Bloomington. Research: Recent history of the Midwest, economic and labor history of Indiana, and Indiana community histories. Projects include historic preservation, the auto industry in Indiana, economic development, ethnicity, and the people of Indianapolis.

3289 ■ Institute for Central European Research

2910 Warrensville Center Rd.   Ph: (216)752-9927
Shaker Heights, OH 44122

Contact: Baron W.K. von Uhlenhorst-Ziechmann, Dir.

Desc: Independent, nonprofit organization. Research: Central European and diplomatic history, horticulture, genealogy and heraldry, and general culture.

3290 ▪ Institute for Public Affairs

11 Broadway, 14th Fl. Ph: (212)563-4000
New York, NY 10004 Fax: (212)564-9058
E-mail: ndiament@ou.org
URL: http://www.ou.org

Contact: Nathan Diament, Exec.Dir.

Desc: Integral unit of Union of Orthodox Jewish Congregations of America. Research: Middle East peace, education, energy, civil rights, religious accommodation, the welfare of Israel, and legislative issues of importance to the traditional Jewish community in America with emphasis on Jewish survival, assimilation, anti-semitism, Soviet-Jewry, and ethnic and civil concerns in America.

3291 ▪ John Carroll University
Community Research Center

Sociology Department Ph: (216)397-4381
University Heights, OH 44118 Fax: (216)397-4376
E-mail: dukes@jcvaxa.jcu.edu

Contact: Duane Dukes, Dir.

Desc: Integral unit of John Carroll University. Research: Public opinion, organizational, and political analyses; assessment of neighborhood and community issues; compilation of demographics and crime statistics; and program evaluations in law enforcement, juvenile delinquency, education, and environmental areas.

3292 ▪ Johns Hopkins University
Institute for Global Studies in Culture, Power and History

404 Macaulay Hall Ph: (410)516-7794
3400 N Charles St. Fax: (410)516-6080
Baltimore, MD 21218-2684
E-mail: iscph@jhuvms.hcf.jhu.edu
URL: http://www.jhu.edu/igscph

Contact: Giovanni Arrighi, Dir.

Desc: Integral unit of Johns Hopkins University. Research: Center focuses on history, culture, and ethnicity of societies world-wide, with an emphasis on local-level culture history. Sponsors programs in African American studies, women's studies, and Atlantic history, culture, and society.

3293 ▪ Latino Institute

36 S Wabash Ave., Ste. 1226 Ph: (312)214-4272
Chicago, IL 60603 Fax: (312)214-4273
E-mail: latinos1@aol.com

Contact: Sylvia Puente, Dir.

Desc: Independent, nonprofit organization. Research: Current projects include analyzing census data on Latinos in Chicago, Latino workforce development, immigration, and education. Topics of study have included the empowerment of Chicago's Latino electorate, housing and employment for Latinos in Chicago.

3294 ▪ Lyon College
Regional Studies Center

Mabee Simpson Library Ph: (870)698-4330
2300 Highland Ave. Fax: (870)698-4279
Batesville, AR 72501
E-mail: ghyde@lyon.edu

Contact: Gene Hyde, Mgr.

Desc: Integral unit of Mabee Library, Lyon College. Research: Arkansas history, Arkansas folklore, Ozark folk music, local genealogy, and the American Civil War.

3295 ▪ Mankato State University
Southern Minnesota Historical Center

PO Box 8419 Ph: (507)389-1029
Mankato, MN 56001 Fax: (507)389-5155
E-mail: daardi.sizemore@mankato.msus.edu

Contact: Daardi Sizemore, Contact

Desc: Integral unit of Mankato State University. Research: Mankato civic affairs, Minnesota politics and government, business, oral history, and education in Southern Minnesota.

3296 ▪ MARC Research Services

600 Broadway, Ste. 300 Ph: (816)474-4240
Kansas City, MO 64105 Fax: (816)421-7758
E-mail: mtrillo@marc.org
URL: http://www.marc.org

Contact: Manny Trillo, Mgr.

Desc: Division of the Mid-America Regional Council (MARC), a voluntary association of local governments in the Kansas City area. Research: Provides demographic and economic information on the Kansas City region to assist local governments and the business community. Areas of specialization include forecasting, regional census statistics, information systems, market research, environmental management, housing and urban planning, and transportation planning and management. Provides aerial photography, a wide selection of regional base maps, and custom computer generated maps.

3297 ▪ Memorial University of Newfoundland
Folklore and Language Archive

G.A. Hickman Bldg., Ph: (709)737-8401
Rm. E4038 Fax: (709)737-4718
St. John's, NF, Canada A1B 3X8
E-mail: munfla@morgan.ucs.mun.ca

Contact: Dr. Philip Hiscock, PhD, Arch.

Desc: Integral unit of Memorial University of Newfoundland. Research: Conducts and supports research on the folklore, folklife, language, oral history, and popular culture of Newfoundland, Labrador, and the Maritime Provinces. Collects, organizes, and preserves manuscripts (including student research essays, songs, letters, and diaries), audio tapes, photographs, videotapes, printed documents, and artifacts of the region. Also collects local radio broadcast materials and compiles discographies and folklore bibliographies.

3298 ▪ Michigan State University
University Archives and Historical Collections

101 Conrad Hall Ph: (517)355-2330
East Lansing, MI 48824-1327 Fax: (517)353-9319
E-mail: honhart@pilot.msu.edu
URL: http://pilot.msu.edu/unit/msuarhc

Contact: Dr. Frederick L. Honhart, Dir.

Desc: Integral unit of Michigan State University. Research: Collects, preserves, and makes available historical materials relating to local and regional history and national and international topics, including manuscripts, diaries, letters, account books, and records of individuals, families, businesses, and organizations. The collection houses microfilm copies of letters, speeches, and papers of prominent men in Congress connected with the land-grant movement and oral history and pictorial records relating to transportation, agriculture, industry, lumbering, and other topics. Maintains all permanent records of the University.

3299 ▪ Moorhead State University
Northwest Minnesota Historical Center

Livingston Lord Library Ph: (218)236-2343
Moorhead, MN 56563 Fax: (218)299-5924
E-mail: shoptaug@mhd1.moorhead.msus.edu
URL: http://www.moorhead.msus.edu/library/archives

Contact: Terry L. Shoptaugh, Dir.

Desc: Integral unit of Moorhead State University. Research: Ethnicity in Northwest Minnesota, social welfare,

Native Americans, politics, government, business, church history, oral history, agriculture, and women's organizations.

3300 ▪ Mountain Press Research Center

PO Box 400 Ph: (423)886-6369
Signal Mountain, TN Free: 800-856-4713
37377-0400 Fax: (423)886-5312
E-mail: jimd@mountainpress.com
URL: http://www.mountainpress.com

Contact: James L. Douthat, Contact

Desc: Independent, nonprofit research center. Research: Geneological and historical research in the mid-Atlantic and Southeastern regions of the U.S.

3301 ▪ Multicultural History Centre

43 Queen's Pk. Cres. E Ph: (416)979-2973
Toronto, ON, Canada M5S Fax: (416)979-7947
2C3

Contact: Prof. William Dunphy, Chm./CEO

Desc: Independent, nonprofit organization. Research: History of ethnic groups, with special emphasis on Ontario.

3302 ▪ National Council of La Raza
Policy Analysis Center

1111 19th St., Ste. 1000 Ph: (202)785-1670
Washington, DC 20036 Free: 800-332-6257
Fax: (202)776-1792
URL: http://www.nclr.org

Contact: Charles Kamasaki, Sr.VP

Desc: Research, policy analysis, and advocacy component administered by the Office of Research, Advocacy, and Legislation of the National Council of La Raza, a nonprofit organization. Research: Research and policy analysis from a Hispanic perspective, including studies on education, employment and training, immigration, civil rights enforcement, housing and community development, Hispanic poverty, the elderly, business and economic development, language issues, substance abuse, and AIDS. Prepares demographic analyses of Hispanic Americans. Provides technical assistance to Hispanic community-based organizations, answers inquiries, and makes referrals.

3303 ▪ Our Lady of the Lake University of San Antonio
International Center

411 SW 24th St. Ph: (210)431-3918
San Antonio, TX 78207-4619 Fax: (210)436-0824
E-mail: nagym@lake.ollusa.edu
URL: http://www.ollusa.edu

Contact: Dr. Margit Nagy

Desc: Academic, research, and outreach unit of Our Lady of the Lake University of San Antonio. Research: Modern Japanese social history, history of Japanese in Texas, and Hungarian immigration history. Coordinates intercultural programs for faculty, staff, and students.

3304 ▪ Panhandle-Plains Historical Museum
Research Center

Box 967, WTAMU Sta. Ph: (806)651-2261
Canyon, TX 79016 Fax: (806)651-2250
E-mail: Lisa.Lambert@wtamu.edu
URL: http://www.wtamu.edu/museum/home.html

Contact: Lisa S. Lambert, Archv./Libn.

Desc: Independent, nonprofit organization. Research: Texas and Southwest history, ranching, Indians of the Great Plains, archeology of Texas Panhandle, ethnology, clothing and textiles, fine arts, antiques, and museum science.

3305 ▪ Pennsylvania Ethnic Heritage Studies Center

1228 Cathedral of Learning
Pittsburgh, PA 15260
Ph: (412)648-7390
Fax: (412)648-1168

Desc: Separately incorporated unit affiliated with Center for International Studies at University of Pittsburgh. Research: Immigration and ethnicity in Pennsylvania, including development of curriculum materials for public and private schools, archival acquisition, and a mini-grant program.

3306 ▪ Pennsylvania State University Population Research Institute

601 Oswald Tower
University Park, PA 16802
Ph: (814)865-0486
Fax: (814)863-8342
E-mail: pri.info@pop.psu.edu
URL: http://www.pop.psu.edu

Contact: Dr. Daniel T. Lichter, Dir.

Desc: Integral unit of Intercollege Research Programs, Pennsylvania State University. Research: Demography and population, including labor; population redistribution, migration, and immigration; population growth and characteristics; population development and policies; determinants and consequences of fertility; population genetics, morbidity, and mortality; and demographic change, public policy intervention, rural and agricultural advancements in developing countries, applications of GIS to demography and biodemography.

3307 ▪ Princeton University Office of Population Research

21 Prospect Ave.
Princeton, NJ 08544-4870
Ph: (609)258-4870
Fax: (609)258-1039
E-mail: opr@opr.princeton.edu
URL: http://opr.princeton.edu

Contact: Dr. Marta Tienda, Dir.

Desc: Integral unit of Princeton University. Research: Mathematical and statistical demography, population policy, economic demography, historical and environmental demography, population and development, immigration, fertility, mortality, migration, international health policy, contraceptive technology, reproductive health, marriage and the family, and demographic modeling.

3308 ▪ Research Centre for Canadian Ethnic Studies

University of Calgary
Calgary, AB, Canada T2N 1N4
Ph: (403)220-5720
Fax: (403)282-9298

Contact: Dr. Madeline A. Kalbach, Dir. & Ch. of Ethnic Stud.

Desc: Separately incorporated institute under the responsibility of the Dean of Faculty of Social Sciences, University of Calgary. Research: Canadian ethnic groups, with emphasis on their cultural, historical, and literary contributions to Canadian identity. Attempts to stimulate and coordinate research of this type conducted elsewhere in Canada and abroad.

3309 ▪ Resource and Research Center for Beaver County and Local History

Carnegie Free Library
1301 7th Ave., 2nd Fl.
Beaver Falls, PA 15010-4217
Ph: (724)846-4340
Fax: (724)846-0370

Contact: Dr. William E. Irion, Dir.

Desc: Independent, nonprofit organization sponsored by Beaver County Commissioners. Research: The history of Beaver County, Pennsylvania and surrounding counties and states. Interests include ethnic history, genealogy, county planning and engineering, North American Indians, and the War of the Rebellion.

3310 ▪ Edgar and Frances Reynolds Research Center

Stuhr Museum of the
Prairie Pioneer
3133 W Hwy. 34
Grand Island, NE 68801
Fax: (308)385-5028

Contact: Sandi Yoder, Exec.Dir. Mus.

Desc: Integral unit of Stuhr Museum. Research: Local and state history; town building and community development from 1840 to 1920; genealogy.

3311 ▪ Rockefeller University Rockefeller Archive Center

Pocantico Hills
15 Dayton Ave.
North Tarrytown, NY
10591-1598
Ph: (914)631-4505
Fax: (914)631-6017
E-mail: archive@rockvax.rockefeller.edu
URL: http://rockefeller.edu/arc-cent/arc-cent.html

Contact: Dr. Darwin H. Stapleton, Dir.

Desc: Integral unit of Rockefeller University. Research: Fosters research related to holdings at the Center, which include records and papers of the Rockefeller Foundation, the Rockefeller University, the Rockefeller Family, the Rockefeller Brothers Fund, the Commonwealth Fund, the Russell Sage Foundation, the Markle Foundation, and other individuals and organizations.

3312 ▪ Rutgers University Institute of Jazz Studies

Dana Library, 4th Fl.
Newark, NJ 07102
Ph: (973)353-5595
Fax: (973)353-5944

Contact: Dan Morgenstern, Dir.

Desc: Integral unit of John Cotton Dana Library at Rutgers University, with its own advisory board. Research: Jazz and related music, oral history, ethnomusicology, Afro-American history, and sound documentation.

3313 ▪ Samford University Institute of Genealogy and Historical Research

Samford University Library
Birmingham, AL 35229-7008
Ph: (205)870-2780
Fax: (205)870-2642
E-mail: mbthomas@samford.edu
URL: http://www.samford.edu/schools/ighr/ighr.html

Contact: Jean Thomason, Dir.

Desc: Integral unit of Samford University. Research: Genealogy studies.

3314 ▪ San Juan County Archaeological Research Center and Library

PO Box 125
Bloomfield, NM 87413
Ph: (505)632-2013
Fax: (505)632-1707
URL: http://www.more2it.com/salmon

Contact: Larry L. Baker, Exec.Dir.

Desc: Integral unit of San Juan County Museum Association, an independent, nonprofit organization. Research: Southwest archaeology, history, anthropology, oral history, Native Americans, and natural science.

3315 ▪ Santa Barbara Museum of Natural History

2559 Puesta del Sol Rd.
Santa Barbara, CA 93105
Ph: (805)682-4711
Fax: (805)569-3170
E-mail: brapp@sbnature2.org
URL: http://www.sbnature2.org

Contact: F. Brian Rapp, Interim Exec.Dir.

Desc: Independent, nonprofit organization. Research: Anthropology, including ethnobotany, and genealogy and culture of the Chumash Indians. Natural history investigations center on systematics and biology of mollusks and parasites of marine animals; invertebrate zoology, especially the land snails of the California Islands; marine mammals; and birds of the region.

3316 ▪ Dr. William M. Scholl Center for Family and Community History

60 W Walton
Chicago, IL 60610
Ph: (312)255-3535
E-mail: scholl@newberry.org
URL: http://www.newberry.org/nl/scholl/L3rscholl.html

Desc: Research unit of the Newberry Library. Research: American social history, urban history, Chicago history, community studies, social and geographic mobility, and labor history.

3317 ▪ Sheboygan County Historical Research Center, Inc.

518 Water St.
Sheboygan Falls, WI 53085
Ph: (920)467-4667
Fax: (920)467-1395
E-mail: Schrc@execpc.com
URL: http://www.schrc.org

Contact: Rose M. Rumpff, Exec.Dir.

Desc: Independent, nonprofit organization established through the merger of the Sheboygan County Historical Society, Sheboygan Genealogy Society, and Landmarks Limited. Research: Maintains collection of historical and genealogical materials on Sheboygan County, Wisconsin.

3318 ▪ Smithsonian Institution Archives Office

2135 Arts and Industries Bldg.,
MRC 414
900 Jefferson Dr., S.W.
Washington, DC 20560
Ph: (202)357-1420
Fax: (202)357-2395
E-mail: SIAEMOO1@SIVM.SI.EDU

Contact: Ethel W. Hedlin, Dir.

Desc: Research: Archives preserve, organize, and provide access to papers and documents of historical value relating to the Smithsonian and the history of 19th and 20th century American science, culture, and the arts. Other fields of interest are 19th and 20th century American natural history; Western exploration in the 19th century; and American art and biography. Collections include official records of the Smithsonian; private papers that document the Smithsonian's role through the lives of eminent scholars; oral histories; and records of projects once connected with the Smithsonian. The Archives are open to all qualified researchers. Institutional History Division conducts research and oral history Research: interviews on history of the Smithsonian Institution and publishes The Papers of Joseph Henry, first secretary of the Smithsonian. National Collections Program monitors and provides advice on collections management policies for museums.

3319 ▪ Somerset Historical Center Historical and Genealogical Society of Somerset County

10649 Somerset Pke.
Somerset, PA 15501
Ph: (814)445-6077
Fax: (814)443-6621

Contact: Charles Fox, Admin.

Desc: Integral unit of Somerset Historical Center, an independent, nonprofit organization. Research: Somerset County, Pennsylvania, history, agriculture, crafts and trades, vernacular archiecture concentrations, genealogy, and decorative arts.

3320 ▪ South Dakota Oral History Center

Dakota Hall, Rm. 12
414 E Clark St.
Vermillion, SD 57069
Ph: (605)677-5209
Fax: (605)677-6525
E-mail: iais@usd.edu

URL: http://www.usd.edu/iais

Contact: Leonard R. Bruguier, Dir.

Desc: Integral unit of Institute of American Indian Studies, University of South Dakota. Research: Collects and preserves South Dakota and American Indian oral histories.

3321 ▪ South Dakota State University
Census Data Center

| | Ph: (605)688-4132 |
| rs>Brookings, SD 57007 | Fax: (605)688-6354 |

E-mail: satterlj@mg.sdstate.edu
URL: http://web.sdstate.edu/departments/soc

Contact: Dr. James Satterlee, Dir.

Desc: Integral unit of South Dakota State University. Research: Population census, agriculture census, minorities, and migration. The Center responds to out-state needs of public and private agencies for census data and is a repository for all census data for South Dakota. Participates in the U.S. Census Bureau State Data Center program.

3322 ▪ Southern Illinois University at
Carbondale
University Museum

| MC 4508 | Ph: (618)453-5388 |
| Carbondale, IL 62901 | Fax: (618)453-7409 |

E-mail: museum@siu.edu
URL: http://www.museum.siu.edu

Contact: Dr. John J. Whitlock, Dir.

Desc: Integral unit of Southern Illinois University at Carbondale. Research: Art, anthropology, geology, history, museology, ethnology, and oral history.

3323 ▪ Southwest State University
Southwest Minnesota Historical Center

Social Science, Rm. 141	Ph: (507)537-7373
1501 State St.	Fax: (507)537-6115
Marshall, MN 56258	

E-mail: louwagie@ssu.southwest.msus.edu
URL: http://www.southwest.msus.edu

Contact: Jan Louwagie, Coord.

Desc: Integral unit of Southwest State University. Research: Local history, church histories, Iceland, agricultural history, and genealogy.

3324 ▪ Starsmore Center for Local History

Colorado Springs	Ph: (719)578-6650
Pioneers Museum	Fax: (719)578-6718
215 S Tejon St.	
Colorado Springs, CO 80903	

E-mail: lwitherow@ci.colospgs.co.us

Contact: Leah Davis Witherow, Archv.

Desc: Integral unit of Colorado Springs Pioneers Museum, an independent, nonprofit organization. Research: Colorado history, local history, and genealogy.

3325 ▪ State Historical Society of Wisconsin
Archives Division

| 816 State St. | Ph: (608)264-6460 |
| Madison, WI 53706 | Fax: (608)264-6472 |

E-mail: archives.reference@ccmail.adp.wisc.edu
URL: http://www.shsw.wisc.edu/archives/

Contact: Robert Granflater, Contact

Desc: Integral unit of State Historical Society of Wisconsin, operating cooperatively with a network of research centers at the Superior Public Library (WI), and components of the University of Wisconsin system. Research: Social, economic, and cultural history of Wisconsin and the U.S., including the development of labor, civil rights, and other social reform movements and the modern his-

tory of mass communications, film, and theater in America. Identifies, collects, and maintains personal papers, organization and business records, genealogies and local histories, maps, oral histories, photographs, and Wisconsin state and local government and court records.

3326 ▪ State University of New York at Buffalo
Center for Studies in American Culture

Department of English	Ph: (716)645-2560
306 Samuel Clemens Hall	Fax: (716)645-5980
Buffalo, NY 14260	

E-mail: csac@acsu.buffalo.edu

Contact: Prof. Diane Christian, Co-Dir.

Desc: Integral unit of State University of New York at Buffalo. Research: Folklore, plus oral, film, and political history. Acts as a funding agent and administers postgraduate work for students in several linked departments.

3327 ▪ Stearns History Museum

| 235 33rd Ave. S | Ph: (320)253-8424 |
| St. Cloud, MN 56301-3752 | Fax: (320)253-2172 |

E-mail: info@stearns-museum.org
URL: http://www.stearns-museum.org

Contact: John W. Decker, Archv.

Desc: Independent, nonprofit organization. Research: Genealogy, county history, architecture, agriculture, Luxembourg immigration, and granite industry.

3328 ▪ Suomi College
Finnish-American Heritage Center

| 601 Quincy St. | Ph: (906)487-7347 |
| Hancock, MI 49930-1882 | Fax: (906)487-7300 |

URL: http://www.suomi.gdu.com

Contact: E. Olaf Rankinen, Archv. Emeritus

Desc: Integral unit of Suomi College. Research: Suomi Synod and Finnish-American church history, Finnish-Americans, temperance, mutual benefit societies, Finns, and Finland.

3329 ▪ Texas A&M University
Real Estate Center

Wehner Bldg., Rm. 314	Ph: (409)845-2031
College Station, TX	Free: 800-244-2144
77843-2115	Fax: (409)845-0460

E-mail: rmalcolm@tamu.edu
URL: http://recenter.tamu.edu

Contact: Dr. Malcolm Richards, Dir.

Desc: Research activity at Texas A&M University, operating under a nine-member advisory committee appointed by the governor of Texas. Research: Real estate, including appraisal, brokerage, computer software, demography, development, economics education, financing, home buying and selling, investment, law, marketing, mineral leasing, mortgage instruments, multifamily housing, reference materials, rural properties, and tax. Assists real estate professionals, educators, and consumers by providing information on the economy, taxation, law, finance, population, and households.

3330 ▪ University of Arkansas at Little Rock
Institute for Economic Advancement

| 2801 S University, Rm. 541 | Ph: (501)569-8521 |
| Little Rock, AR 72204 | Fax: (501)569-8538 |

E-mail: dabullwinkle@ualr.edu
URL: http://www.aiea.ualr.edu/depts/rsch.ub/
    default.html

Contact: Davis A. Bullwinkle, Res.Libn.

Desc: Integral unit of University of Arkansas at Little Rock. Research: Business and economics, industrial development, labor statistics, demographics, government and taxes, economic development and U.S. census.

3331 ▪ University of California at Berkeley
Regional Oral History Office

| 486 Bancroft Library | Ph: (510)642-7395 |
| Berkeley, CA 94720-6000 | Fax: (510)642-7589 |

E-mail: roho@library.berkeley.edu
URL: http://www.lib.berkeley.edu/BANC/ROHO

Contact: Willa K. Baum, Dir.

Desc: Integral unit of Bancroft Library, University of California at Berkeley. Research: Conducts researched oral history interviews with persons who were leading figures or well-placed witnesses to major events or trends in California and western U.S. history. Subjects of research include agriculture; water resources and land use; the arts, including interviews with artists, writers, printers, photographers, and architects; business and labor, particularly California wine industry; conservation, Sierra Club, and forest history; legal history; political history, including suffragists, women political leaders, and Warren, Knight-Brown, and Reagan administrations; social history, including Jewish community and Russian emigres; science and technology; higher Research: education, particularly University of California; mining; and medical history, the AIDS epidemic, molecular biology and biotechnology industry, disabled persons independence movement, and HMOs.

3332 ▪ University of California, Davis
Michael and Margaret B. Harrison Western
Research Center

Department of	Ph: (530)752-1621
Special Collections	Fax: (530)752-3148
Shields Library	
100 North West Quad	
Davis, CA 95616-5292	

E-mail: jlskarstad@ucdavis.edu

Contact: John Skarstad, Hd., Spec.Colls.

Desc: Integral unit of University of California, Davis. Research: History and development of the trans-Mississippi West, from the mid-19th century to the present; American Indians; ethnic studies; military, local, and economic history; sociology; folklore; religious studies, especially the Catholic and Mormon churches; geography; exploration and travel literature; art and architecture; and history of printing.

3333 ▪ University of California, Los Angeles
Harbor-UCLA Medical Center
Research and Education Institute

| 1124 W Carson St., B-4 South | Ph: (310)222-4266 |
| Torrance, CA 90502 | Fax: (310)222-4264 |

E-mail: linkeh@harbor2.humc.edu
URL: http://www.humc.edu/rei

Contact: Prof. Keh-Ming Lin, MD, Dir.

Desc: Integral unit of University of California, Los Angeles School of Medicine and Department of Psychiatry at Harbor-UCLA Medical Center. Research: Role of ethnicity (including culture) and biological variables in the mental health of ethnic minority populations. Conducts studies using pharmacokinetic, pharmacodynamic, and pharmacogenetic research techniques to examine ethnic and individual differences in responses to psychotropic drugs.

3334 ▪ University of Cincinnati
Institute for Policy Research

| Mail Location 0132 | Ph: (513)556-5028 |
| Cincinnati, OH 45221 | Fax: (513)556-9023 |

E-mail: alfred.tuchfarber@uc.edu
URL: http://www.ipr.uc.edu

Contact: Dr. Alfred J. Tuchfarber, Dir.

Desc: Umbrella organization for the Survey Research Center; the Southwest Ohio Regional Data Center; the Social,

Behavioral, and Health Sciences Data Archive; and the Center for Neighborhood & Community Studies, University of Cincinnati. Research: Demographic analysis, survey research, evaluation research, economic studies, planning studies, policy analysis, systems analysis, historical studies, regional analysis, community studies, needs assessment, information systems, and census data archiving and dissemination. Operates the omnibus Greater Cincinnati Survey and the omnibus Ohio Poll.

3335 ■ University of Cincinnati
Southwest Ohio Regional Data Center

Mail Location 132   Ph: (513)556-5077
Cincinnati, OH 45221   Fax: (513)556-9023
E-mail: mark.carrozza@uc.edu
URL: http://www.ipr.uc.edu/SORDC/index.htm

Contact: Mark A. Carrozza, Dir.

Desc: Research center of the Institute for Policy Research, University of Cincinnati. Research: Maintains a complete archive of data and products from the Bureau of the Census, including a collection of machine-readable files (tapes and cd-roms) of 1970, 1980, and 1990 censuses of population and housing for Ohio, Kentucky, and Indiana, as well as regional demographic and economic data. Also maintains a social science data archive with information on community and urban studies; conflict, terrorism, and war; economic indicators; education; energy; health; international systems; legal systems; political indicators and electoral behavior; and social indicators and quality of life.

3336 ■ University College of Cape Breton
Beaton Institute

Box 5300   Ph: (902)563-1329
Sydney, NS, Canada B1P 6L2   Fax: (902)562-8899
E-mail: rmorgan@caper2.uccB.NS.CA
URL: http://www.uccb.ns.ca/beaton

Contact: Dr. R.J. Morgan, Dir.

Desc: Integral unit of University College of Cape Breton. Research: Cape Breton Island, including its history, labor history, Gaelic literature, folklore, political and industrial history, traditional Scottish music, genealogy, and Mikmaq history.

3337 ■ University of Colorado at Boulder
Center for Comparative Politics

Department of Political Science,   Ph: (303)492-1738
     Campus Box 333   Fax: (303)492-0978
Boulder, CO 80309
E-mail: christian.davenport@colorado.edu

Contact: Dr. Christian Davenport, Dir.

Desc: Integral unit of Department of Political Science at University of Colorado at Boulder; operating under its own board of control. Research: Ethnic and class-based groups, social and economic policies, growth of state powers and resources, ethnic conflicts, political terrorism and revolution, political institutions, nationalism, citizenship, politics of language, immigration, and group-institution relationships in democratic, authoritarian, and revolutionary situations. Projects conducted on the global level, including areas of western Europe, eastern Europe, Latin America, and Africa, as well as human rights.

3338 ■ University of Connecticut
Center for Oral History

405 Babbidge Rd., Box U-205   Ph: (860)486-5245
Storrs, CT 06269-1205   Fax: (860)486-4582
E-mail: Stave@uconnvm.uconn.edu
URL: http://www.oralhistory.uconn

Contact: Prof. Bruce M. Stave, Dir.

Desc: Integral unit of University of Connecticut. Research: History and development of Connecticut, the University of Connecticut, and other related subjects, including projects on the political activities of fully enfranchised Connecticut women, Holocaust survivors in the Connecticut region, the ethnic peoples of Connecticut, Connecticut workers and a half century of technological change (1930-1980), a photographic history of northeast Connecticut, and a volume on European immigration to America; home of the Oral History Review. Recent projects include "Witnesses to Nuremberg," an oral history of American participants at the war crimes trials, and an oral history of the Connecticut General Assembly.

3339 ■ University of Denver
Center for Judaic Studies
Holocaust Awareness Institute

2199 S University Blvd.   Ph: (303)871-3020
Denver, CO 80208   Fax: (303)871-3037
E-mail: sauger@du.edu

Contact: Stephanie Auger, Dir.

Desc: Integral unit of Center for Judaic Studies, University of Denver. Research: Collects oral histories of survivors of the Holocaust.

3340 ■ University of Hawaii at Manoa
Center for Oral History

Social Science Bldg., Rm. 724   Ph: (808)956-6259
Social Science Research Institute   Fax: (808)956-9794
2424 Maile Way
Honolulu, HI 96822
E-mail: wnishimo@hawaii.edu
URL: http://www2.soc.hawaii.edu/css/oral_hist/
     index.html

Contact: Warren S. Nishimoto, Dir.

Desc: Integral unit of Social Science Research Institute of University of Hawaii at Manoa. Research: Records and preserves through oral interviews the recollections of Hawaii's people. Transcript topics include life histories of native Hawaiians, perspectives on Hawaii's statehood, and social and labor history. Serves as a resource center for researchers, students, and the general community.

3341 ■ University of Louisville
Oral History Center

University Archives and   Ph: (502)852-6674
     Records Center   Fax: (502)852-6673
Ekstrom Library
Louisville, KY 40292
E-mail: archives@louisville.edu
URL: http://www.louisville.edu/library/uarc/

Contact: Mary Margaret Bell, Co-Dir.

Desc: Integral unit of University Archives and Records Center, University of Louisville. Research: History of Louisville, Kentucky, including the Louisville Orchestra, prominent citizens, university history, the Louisville and Nashville Railroad, photography, Jewish history, local government, African American history, Kentucky distilling industry, and Bernheim forest.

3342 ■ University of Louisville
University Archives and Records Center

Ekstrom Library   Ph: (502)852-6674
Louisville, KY 40292   Fax: (502)852-6673
E-mail: archives@louisville.edu
URL: http://www.louisville.edu/library/uarc

Contact: Dr. William J. Morison, Dir. & Univ.Archiv.

Desc: Integral unit of University of Louisville. Research: History of the University and the Louisville region. Administers oral history and records management programs at the University.

3343 ■ University of Louisville
Urban Studies Institute
Kentucky State Data Center

426 W Bloom St.   Ph: (502)852-7990
Louisville, KY 40208   Fax: (502)852-7386
E-mail: sdcenter@ulkyvm.louisville.edu
URL: http://www.louisville.edu/cbpa/sdc

Contact: Ron Crouch, Dir.

Desc: Integral unit of Center for Urban and Economic Research, University of Louisville, established as a result of an agreement between the commonwealth and the U.S. Census Bureau. Research: Provides state census data and information through a network of 62 centers distributed throughout Kentucky. Serves as a clearinghouse for census materials.

3344 ■ University of Maine
Maine Folklife Center

5773 S Stevens Hall   Ph: (207)581-1891
Orono, ME 04469   Fax: (207)581-1823
E-mail:
     pauleena_macdougall@voyager.umeres.maine.edu
URL: http://www.ume.maine.edu/researchpublic.html

Contact: Edward D. Ives, Dir.

Desc: Integral unit of Department of Anthropology, University of Maine. Research: Folklore and oral history of Maine and the Northeast U.S., including local history, lumbering, and river-driving.

3345 ■ University of Massachusetts at Amherst
Social and Demographic Research Institute

Machmer Hall   Ph: (413)545-3416
PO Box 34830   Fax: (413)545-0746
Amherst, MA 01003-4830
E-mail: dla@sadri.umass.edu

Contact: Dr. Douglas L. Anderton, Dir.

Desc: Integral unit of Department of Sociology, University of Massachusetts at Amherst. Research: Sociology and demography, including the estimations on the size of homeless populations, demographics of hazardous waste sites, sociology of 19th century America, social stratification, effects of natural disasters, rehabilitation of released felons, medical care for the homeless and mentally ill, relations between parents and their adult children, social networks, Political Action Committees, and crime decision making. Evaluates social programs and develops survey research methods, encompassing interests of affiliated departments of the University.

3346 ■ University of Memphis
Oral History Research Office

CB 526121   Ph: (901)678-2524
Memphis, TN 38152-6121   Fax: (901)678-2720
E-mail: cwcrwfrd@.memphis.edu

Contact: Dr. Charles W. Crawford, Dir.

Desc: Integral unit of University of Memphis. Research: Preserves and studies memoirs of men and women who have made significant contributions to society, especially those related to Tennessee Valley Authority, southern writers, Memphis jazz and blues, development of hardwood-lumber industry, Memphis events of 1968, garbage strikes, boycotts, demonstrations, riots, Martin Luther King, Jr. assassination, Memphis Jewish community, organization of labor in Memphis, folk-culture of Central Ozarks, history of Fayette County, Tennessee, Winfield Dunn gubernatorial administration, Southern Tenant Farmers Union, unidentified flying object sightings, Robert Church family of Memphis, Memphis during Crump era, oral history of American Research: Alliance of Health, physical education, recreation and dance leaders, and presidents and award recipients.

3347 ■ University of Michigan
Detroit Area Study
3528 LS&A Bldg.   Ph: (734)764-4435
500 S State St.   Fax: (734)763-6887
Ann Arbor, MI 48109
URL: http://www.unich.edu

Contact: Peter Miller, Div.

Desc: Integral unit of Department of Sociology at University of Michigan, under primary control of Department of Sociology. Research: Collects demographic, socioeconomic, and attitudinal data on social science issues and their significance in the Detroit area. Serves as a major resource for basic research by social scientists at the University and provides graduate training in survey research.

3348 ■ University of Michigan
Population Studies Center
1225 S University Ave.   Ph: (734)998-7275
Ann Arbor, MI 48104-2590   Fax: (734)998-7415
E-mail: davidl@psc.lsa.umich.edu
URL: http://www.psc.lsa.umich.edu

Contact: Dr. David Lam, Dir.

Desc: Integral unit of University of Michigan. Research: Basic demographic research to assist national family planning programs in developing countries. Provides facilities for professional staff and doctoral candidate research in population and human ecology, including studies on economic, historical, and social demography, fertility, the family, aging, mortality, migration, racial stratification, poverty, labor force issues, ethnicity, statistical methodology, and social change and development.

3349 ■ University of Minnesota
Center for Population Analysis and Policy
Humphrey Institute of   Ph: (612)625-0669
 Public Affairs   Fax: (612)625-6351
301 19th Ave. S, Rm. 267
Minneapolis, MN 55455
E-mail: dlevison@hhp.umn.edu
URL: http://www.hhh.umn.edu

Contact: John Bradl, Interim Dean

Desc: Research activity of Hubert H. Humphrey Institute of Public Affairs at University of Minnesota. Research: Interdisciplinary studies in population analysis and policy, including policy analysis, demography, epidemiology, population history, and labor market analysis.

3350 ■ University of Minnesota
Immigration History Research Center
826 Berry St.   Ph: (612)627-4208
St. Paul, MN 55114   Fax: (612)627-4190
E-mail: ihrc@tc.umn.edu
URL: http://www.umn.edu/ihrc

Contact: Prof. Rudolph J. Vecoli, Dir.

Desc: Integral unit of University of Minnesota. Research: Immigration to America, focusing on ethnic groups primarily originating in eastern, central, and southern Europe and the Near East, including history of these groups from time of immigration to present day. The Center also fosters study of immigration policy, immigrant politics, gender, religion, radical movements, and ethnic contributions to the arts.

3351 ■ University of Minnesota
Social Welfare History Archives Center
320 Andersen Library   Ph: (612)624-6394
222 21st Ave. S   Fax: (612)625-5525
Minneapolis, MN 55455-0439
E-mail: d-klaa@tc.umn.edu
URL: http://www.lib.umn.edu/swha.htm

Contact: Prof. David J. Klaassen, Archv.

Desc: Integral unit of University of Minnesota. Research: History of professional social work and social welfare, particularly in U.S. and in twentieth century. Develops manuscript and archival collections that are made available to scholars for research use at the Center.

3352 ■ University of Minnesota, Duluth
Northeast Minnesota Historical Center
Library 375   Ph: (218)726-8526
Duluth, MN 55812   Fax: (218)726-6205
E-mail: pmaus@d.umn.edu

Contact: Pat Maus, Admin.

Desc: Integral unit of University of Minnesota, Duluth and St. Louis County Historical Society. Research: Regional history, transportation, iron mining technology, environmental issues, social service and civic agencies and organizations, business and industry, and women.

3353 ■ University of Minnesota, Morris
West Central Minnesota Historical Center
                            Ph: (612)589-6172
rs>Morris, MN 56267   Fax: (612)589-3811
E-mail: ahernwh@t4.mrs.umn.edu

Contact: Wilbert H. Ahern, Dir.

Desc: Integral unit of University of Minnesota, Morris. Research: Minnesota, focusing on ethnicity of west central Minnesota, politics and government, agribusiness, and history, including oral history, church history, the Great Depression, and World War II.

3354 ■ University of Missouri--Columbia
Center for Studies in Oral Tradition
316 Hillcrest Hall   Ph: (573)882-9720
Columbia, MO 65211   Fax: (573)884-5306
E-mail: csottime@showme.missouri.edu
URL: http://www.missouri.edu/csottime/index.html

Contact: John Miles Foley, Dir.

Desc: Integral unit of University of Missouri--Columbia. Research: Oral tradition, including literary studies, anthropology, folklore, linguistics, and language.

3355 ■ University of Missouri--Columbia
Office of Social and Economic Data Analysis
602 Clark Hall   Ph: (573)882-7396
Columbia, MO 65211   Fax: (573)884-4635
E-mail: hobbsd@umsystem.edu
URL: http://www.oseda.missouri.edu

Contact: Dr. Daryl Hobbs, Dir.

Desc: Integral unit of University of Missouri--Columbia. Research: Maintains census and other databases to assist in the support of research, grant proposals, etc.

3356 ■ University of Moncton
Centre for the Study of Acadians
                            Ph: (506)858-4085
rs>Moncton, NB, Canada E1A Fax: (506)858-4530
 3E9
E-mail: basquem@umoncton.ca
URL: http://www.umoncton.ca/etudeacadiennes/centre/
 cea.html

Contact: Maurice Basque, Dir.

Desc: Integral unit of University of Moncton. Research: Acadian history, genealogy, and folklore.

3357 ■ University of Montana
Center for Population Research
Department of Sociology   Ph: (406)243-5281
Missoula, MT 59812-1047   Fax: (406)243-5951

Contact: Dr. Fred W. Reed, Dir.

Desc: Interdisciplinary research unit at University of Montana. Research: Sociology and demography, with an emphasis on state and local evaluation, assessment, and prediction problems, including population forecasting, population mobility, and methodological assistance to public and private agencies.

3358 ■ University of Montreal
Research Group on Quebec Demography
PO Box 6128, Downtown Sta.   Ph: (514)343-5870
Montreal, PQ, Canada H3C 3J7   Fax: (514)343-2309
E-mail: robert.bourbeau@umontreal.ca
URL: http://www.fas.umontreal.ca/DEMO/

Contact: Robert Bourbeau, Dir.

Desc: Integral unit of University of Montreal, but with its own board of control. Research: Quebec population, including past and recent evolution, historical demography, fertility and the family, sterilization, cost of child rearing, population aging, small populations and subpopulations, and health indicators and mortality.

3359 ■ University of New Mexico
Southwest Hispanic Research Institute/Chicano Studies
1829 Sigma Chi   Ph: (505)277-2965
Albuquerque, NM 87131   Fax: (505)277-3343
E-mail: gonzales@unm.edu

Contact: Dr. Felipe Gonzales, Dir.

Desc: Integral unit of University of New Mexico. Research: Supports, encourages, coordinates, and conducts interdisciplinary research on topics having a Southwestern, Chicano/Hispanic, and U.S.-Mexico border focus, including an oral history project in Roswell, New Mexico; a study of water use and ditch association; and a study of Hispanic working families in the Southwest.

3360 ■ University of North Carolina at Chapel Hill
Carolina Population Center
CB 8120   Ph: (919)966-1710
University Sq.   Fax: (919)966-6638
123 W Franklin St
Chapel Hill, NC 27516-3997
E-mail: amy_tsui@unc.edu
URL: http://www.cpc.unc.edu

Contact: Dr. Amy Ong Tsui, Dir.

Desc: Integral unit of University of North Carolina at Chapel Hill, operating under a University-wide advisory and policymaking board. Research: Coordinates on a University-wide basis, an interdisciplinary program in population research and research training. Activities encompass social, behavioral and health sciences, including anthropology, biostatistics, city and regional planning, economics, epidemiology, family medicine, geography, health behavior and education, maternal and child health, nutrition, obstetrics and gynecology, political science, psychology, health policy and administration, sociology and demography, and public health nursing. Serves as a link between the University and related institutions and agencies in the U.S. and abroad.

3361 ■ University of Pennsylvania
Population Studies Center
3718 Locust Walk   Ph: (215)898-6441
Philadelphia, PA 19104-6298   Fax: (215)898-2124
E-mail: jere behrman@pop.upenn.edu
URL: http://lexis.pop.upenn.edu/welcome.html

Contact: Dr. Jere R. Behrman, Dir.

Desc: Integral unit of School of Arts and Sciences at University of Pennsylvania. Research: Demography, particularly interrelations of economic and social factors, fertility, mortality, and migration. Interests include health and population, aging, historical demography, population and development, international and internal migration, adolescent fertility, population policy, research methods, education, AIDS, health communication, design and evaluation of family planning programs, and racial and ethnic differentials. Demography of Africa and South Asia is emphasized.

3362 ■ University of Puerto Rico
Social Science Research Center
Faculty of Social Science	Ph: (787)764-2511
Rio Piedras, PR 00931	Fax: (787)764-3625

Contact: Mariano Negron Portellno, Dir.

Desc: Integral unit of College of Social Science at University of Puerto Rico. Research: Puerto Rican population, economic development, social structure, migration, social history, sex discrimination, politics, folklore, family, cultural patterns, industrialization, international relations of Puerto Rico and the Caribbean, women's studies, and education. Undertakes scientific research on basic problems as well as on structure of Puerto Rican society. Encourages and trains research scholars to provide material for better policy discussions by the general public, educational institutions, and government.

3363 ■ University of Quebec
INRS-Culture and Society
Bureau B-10	Ph: (514)841-4000
306, Place d'Youville	Fax: (514)841-4015
Montreal, PQ, Canada H2Y	
2B6	

E-mail: frederic_lesemann@INRS-culture.uquebec.ca

Contact: Fr<eacute>d<eacute>ric Lesemann

Desc: Integral unit of the University of Quebec. Research: Family, women, generational studies, ethnic communities, regional history, cultural diffusion, and sociocultural tendencies.

3364 ■ University of South Dakota
Institute of American Indian Studies
Dakota Hall, Rm. 12	Ph: (605)677-5209
414 E Clark St.	Fax: (605)677-6525
Vermillion, SD 57069	

E-mail: lals@usd.edu
URL: http://www.usd.edu/iais

Contact: Leonard R. Bruguier, Dir.

Desc: Integral unit of University of South Dakota. Research: Indians and their affairs, including study of Dakota/Lakota/Nakota languages.

3365 ■ University of Southern California
Population Research Laboratory
3716 S Hope St., Ste. 385	Ph: (213)743-2950
Los Angeles, CA 90007-4377	Fax: (213)743-2460

E-mail: heer@mizar.usc.edu
URL: http://www.usc.edu/dept/pop

Contact: Dr. David Heer, Jr., Contact

Desc: Integral unit of Department of Sociology, University of Southern California. Research: Population and demography, with emphasis on the U.S., Asia, and the Middle East. Studies include fertility and family planning, migration and residential mobility, urbanization and environmental demography, demography of the family and the life cycle, female labor force, status and social economic attainment, morbidity and mortality, demography of social disorganization, historical demography, and demography of aging.

3366 ■ University of Texas at Austin
Center for Intercultural Studies in Folklore and
Ethnomusicology
GRG 220	Ph: (512)471-5689
Austin, TX 78712	Fax: (512)471-5049

E-mail: ayft@utxdp.dp.utexas.edu

Contact: Dr. Deborah Kapchan, Dir.

Desc: Integral unit of University of Texas at Austin. Research: Folklore, popular culture, and ethnomusicology; folk, traditional, and popular music; and legend and reminiscence as oral history.

3367 ■ University of Texas at Austin
Population Research Center
1800 Main Bldg.	Ph: (512)471-5514
Austin, TX 78712	Fax: (512)471-4886

E-mail: fdb@prc.utexas.eduu
URL: http://www.prc.utexas.edu

Contact: Dr. Frank D. Bean, Dir.

Desc: Integral unit of College of Liberal Arts at University of Texas at Austin. Research: Population dynamics and redistribution, demography of inequality, Mexican-American population, family and fertility, mortality, aging and health, utilization of labor and basic demographic processes, including cross-national and cross-cultural studies, especially of Latin America and minorities. Serves as major facility for research in demography and human ecology at the University.

3368 ■ University of Texas at El Paso
Institute of Oral History
Liberal Arts Bldg., 336	Ph: (915)747-7052
El Paso, TX 79968	Fax: (915)747-5948

URL: http://www.utep.edu

Contact: Prof. Margo McBane, Dir.

Desc: Integral unit of Department of History, University of Texas at El Paso. Research: Over 900 oral history interviews and related materials on U.S.-Mexico border history, El Paso and Cuidad Juarez history, and University of Texas at El Paso history. The Institute also holds materials on the labor, ethnic, and women's history of these areas.

3369 ■ University of Utah
American West Center
1901 E South Campus Dr.,	Ph: (801)581-7611
Rm. 1023	Fax: (801)581-7612
Salt Lake City, UT 84112	

E-mail: dan.mccool@poli-sci.utah.edu

Contact: Daniel McCool, PhD, Dir.

Desc: Integral unit of University of Utah. Research: Political, social, economic, and cultural studies of the North American West, American Indian history and traditions, other ethnic groups, oral history, and various related research projects under government and foundation grants.

3370 ■ University of Washington
Center for Studies in Demography and Ecology
PO Box 353340	Ph: (206)543-5412
Seattle, WA 98195-3340	Fax: (206)616-2093

E-mail: plotnick@u.washington.edu
URL: http://csde.washington.edu

Contact: Robert Plotnick, Dir.

Desc: Interdisciplinary research and training unit within College of Arts & Sciences at University of Washington. Research: Demography and human ecology, with emphasis on fertility, mortality, migration, family structure and stratification.

3371 ■ University of Western Ontario
Population Studies Centre
	Ph: (519)661-3819
rs>London, ON, Canada N6A	
5C2	

E-mail: julian@uwo.ca
URL: http://www.sscl.uwo.ca/sociology/popstudies/

Contact: Dr. O.E. Ebanks, Dir.

Desc: Integral unit of University of Western Ontario. Research: Provides facilities and services to faculty and students conducting population-related research.

3372 ■ University of Wisconsin--Eau Claire
Area Research Center
McIntyre Library	Ph: (715)836-2739
Eau Claire, WI 54702	Fax: (715)836-2949

E-mail: library.archives@uwec.edu
URL: http://www.uwec.edu/Admin/Library/
speccoll.html

Contact: Lawrence D. Lynch, Archv.

Desc: Integral unit of University of Wisconsin--Eau Claire. Research: History of western Wisconsin, lumbering history, genealogy, and university history.

3373 ■ University of Wisconsin--Green Bay
Area Research Center
2420 Nicolet Dr.	Ph: (920)465-2539
Green Bay, WI 54311-7001	Fax: (920)465-2388

E-mail: speccoll@mail.uwgb.edu
URL: http://www.wwgb.edu/library/dept/spc.html

Contact: Debra Anderson, Archv.

Desc: Integral unit of University of Wisconsin--Green Bay. Research: Local history and genealogy, Northeastern Wisconsin, Belgian Americans, and University records.

3374 ■ University of Wisconsin--Madison
Applied Population Laboratory
1450 Linden Dr., Rm. 316	Ph: (608)262-1515
Madison, WI 53706	Fax: (608)262-6022

E-mail: voss@ssc.wisc.edu
URL: http://www.ssc.wisc.edu/poplab

Contact: Dr. Paul R. Voss, Dir.

Desc: Research activity of Department of Rural Sociology at University of Wisconsin--Madison. Research: Demographic characteristics of Wisconsin, particularly migration, population estimates and projections, minority populations, and trends.

3375 ■ University of Wisconsin--Madison
Center for Demography and Ecology
4412 Social Science	Ph: (608)262-2182
1180 Observatory Dr.	Fax: (608)262-8400
Madison, WI 53706-1393	

E-mail: wilson@ssc.wisc.edu
URL: http://www.ssc.wisc.edu/cde

Contact: Franklin D. Wilson, Dir.

Desc: Integral unit of Department of Sociology at University of Wisconsin--Madison. Research: Human demography, human ecology, and sociology. Research includes demography of life cycle, family formation and dissolution, fertility, labor force behavior, achievement and housing patterns, spatial distribution of human populations, residential segregation, migration, population redistribution, social problems and policy related to population, legislative behavior concerning population policy, and effects of negative income tax experiments on demographic behavior and residential segregation. Develops demographic methodology and formal models, including applications of general linear model to demographic processes, decomposition of rates and means, analysis of social change Research: by separation of cohort, period, and age effects, estimation of small area population size, and mathematical modelling of population phenomena.

3376 ■ University of Wisconsin--Madison
Data and Computation Center
3313 Social Science Bldg.	Ph: (608)262-7962
1180 Observatory Dr.	Fax: (608)262-9711
Madison, WI 53706	

E-mail: dpls@dpls.dacc.wisc.edu
URL: http://dpls.dacc.wisc.edu

Contact: Cindy Severt, Libn.

Desc: Integral unit of University of Wisconsin--Madison. Research: Demography, economics, social sciences, health sciences, and education.

3377 ▪ University of Wisconsin--Parkside University Archives and Area Research Center
900 Wood Rd. Ph: (414)595-2411
PO Box 2000 Fax: (414)595-2545
Kenosha, WI 53141-2000
E-mail: ellen.pedraza@uwp.edu
URL: http://www.uwp.edu/info-services/library

Contact: Ellen J. Pedraza, Archv./Ref.Libr.

Desc: Integral unit of University of Wisconsin--Parkside. Research: State and local history and genealogy.

3378 ▪ University of Wisconsin--River Falls Area Research Center
Chalmer Davee Library Ph: (715)425-3567
River Falls, WI 54022 Fax: (715)425-3590
E-mail: susan.g.watson@uwrf.edu
URL: http://www.uwrf.edu

Contact: Susan Ginter Watson, Dir.

Desc: Integral unit of University of Wisconsin--River Falls. Research: History of northwestern Wisconsin, including Pierce, Polk, St. Croix, Washburn, and Burnett counties; Civil War, university, oral history and genealogy.

3379 ▪ Waukesha County Historical Museum Research Center
101 W Main St. Ph: (414)548-7188
Waukesha, WI 53186 Fax: (414)896-6862

Contact: Terry Biwer Becker, Archv.

Desc: Integral unit of Waukesha County Historical Museum, an independent, nonprofit organization. Research: Local history and genealogy of Waukesha County.

3380 ▪ Wayne State University Center for Peace and Conflict Studies
2320 Ph: (313)577-3453
Faculty-Administration Bldg. Fax: (313)577-8269
Detroit, MI 48202
E-mail: ab3440@wayne.edu

URL: http://www.pcs.wayne.edu

Contact: Dr. Frederic S. Pearson, Dir.

Desc: Integral unit of Wayne State University, responsible to the Dean of Urban, Labor, and Metropolitan Affairs. In 1991, the Center became part of the Wayne State Hewlett Foundation Program on Mediating Theory and Democratic Systems. Research: Domestic and international conflict and conflict resolution based on the view that war and violence are generally dysfunctional to conflict resolution. Also studies ethnicity and gender issues and develops curriculum strategies, conferences and seminars, and resources for peace education and dispute resolution in domestic and international conflict. Community training in these fields.

3381 ▪ Western Carolina University Mountain Heritage Center
 Ph: (828)227-7129
rs>Cullowhee, NC 28723
URL: http://www.wcu.edu/mhc

Contact: Dr. H. Tyler Blethen, Dir.

Desc: Integral unit of Western Carolina University. Research: History, culture, and natural history of the southern Appalachia region, focusing on the migration of Scotch-Irish settlers, oral histories, and folklore of western North Carolina.

3382 ▪ Western Jewish History Center
Judah L. Magnes Ph: (510)549-6932
 Memorial Museum Fax: (510)849-3673
2911 Russell St.
Berkeley, CA 94705

Contact: Dr. Moses Rischin, Dir.

Desc: Integral unit of Judah L. Magnes Memorial Museum, an independent, nonprofit organization. Research: History of the Jews in the Western U.S., including manuscripts, visual material, geneaology, oral histories, and secondary material.

3383 ▪ Woodrow Wilson International Center for Scholars
1 Woodrow Wilson Plz. Ph: (202)691-4000
1300 Pennsylvania Ave. NW Fax: (202)691-4001
Washington, DC 20523
E-mail: deanwand@wwic.si.edu
URL: http://wwics.si.edu

Contact: Dean W. Anderson, Actg.Dir.

Desc: Separately incorporated, nonprofit, nonpartisan research organization chartered by the U.S. Congress as the nation's official memorial to President Woodrow Wilson. Research: Studies on Russia/the former Soviet Union, East and West Europe, Latan America, Asia, the United States, international issues, and historical, cultural, and literary studies. Specific research projects include ethnicity, urban studies, and governance. Research projects conducted by Fellows selected in an open international competition.

3384 ▪ Winedale Historical Center
PO Box 11 Ph: (409)278-3530
Round Top, TX 78954 Fax: (409)278-3531
E-mail: hwgj@vt.xdp.dp.vtexas.edu

Contact: Dr. Don E. Carleton, Dir.

Desc: Independent, nonprofit center controlled by the University of Texas at Austin. Research: Ethnic cultures of central Texas, including architecture, German culture, folklife, and documentation of nineteenth-century buildings, particularly those located at the Center.

3385 ▪ World Jewish Genealogy Organization
PO Box 190420 Ph: (718)435-4400
Brooklyn, NY 11219-0009 Fax: (718)633-7050

Contact: Rabbi N. Halberstam, Pres.

Desc: Independent, nonprofit international membership organization of rabbinical scholars and historians. Research: Genealogical research is conducted by the members.

3386 ▪ York University Institute for Social Research
4700 Keele St. Ph: (416)736-5061
Toronto, ON, Canada M3J 1P3 Fax: (416)736-5749
E-mail: isrnews@yorku.ca
URL: http://www.isr.yorku.ca/ISR/

Contact: Dr. J. Paul Grayson, Dir.

Desc: Organized research unit of York University. Research: Institute conducts studies for academic researchers, government agencies, public organizations and the private sector in such fields as housing, health, the environmment, gender issues, quality of life, ethnicity and immigration, education, politics, social interaction, law, policy and program evaluation, and methodological research.

Directories

3387 ▪ Address Book for Germanic Genealogy
Genealogical Publishing Co., Inc.
1001 N. Calvert St.   Ph: (410)037-8271
Baltimore, MD 21202   Free: 800-296-6687
                       Fax: (410)752-8492
E-mail: orders@genealogical.com

Contact: Ernest Thode, Editor.

Desc: Covers: over 2,700 sources useful for genealogical researchers with interest in Germany, Austria, Switzerland, and other German-speaking areas; includes about 275 European genealogical societies, 282 European governmental archives, 194 American societies, 380 European religious archives, 175 American religious archives, 770 European municipal archives, 254 genealogists, and numerous libraries, publishers, museums, organizations, etc. Entries include: Name of source, address, brief description. *Freq:* Irregular, previous edition October 1991; 6th ed. January 1997. *Price:* $24.95, plus $3.50 shipping.

3388 ▪ Adoption Searchbook: Techniques for Tracing People
Triadoption Publications
PO Box 638   Ph: (714)892-4098
Westminster, CA 92684   Fax: (714)892-4098

Contact: Mary Jo Rillera, Editor.

Desc: Publication includes: List of sources of information for families separated by adoption searching for information on their kin. Entries include: Source name, address, cost. *Freq:* Irregular, latest edition 1993. *Price:* $18.95.

3389 ▪ African American Historic Places
John Wiley and Sons, Inc.
605 3rd Ave.   Ph: (212)850-6000
New York, NY 10158   Free: 800-225-5945
                      Fax: (212)850-6049
E-mail: subinfo@wiley.com

Contact: Beth L. Savage, Editor.

Desc: Covers: Approximately 800 public and private historic sites of African America importance in 42 U.S. state and two territories. Entries include: Site name as it appears in the National Register, address, description, identification number, listing date. *Price:* $25.95.

3390 ▪ AIA Guide to Boston
Globe Pequot Press, Inc.
6 Business Park Rd.   Ph: (860)395-0440
PO Box 833   Free: 800-243-0495
Old Saybrook, CT 06475   Fax: 800-820-2329
URL: http://www.globe-pequot.com

Contact: Susan Southworth, Editor; Michael Southworth, Editor.

Desc: Covers: over 500 buildings in Boston selected by the editors as being architecturally and historically interesting, including Paul Revere's house, Quincy Market, and others designed by such architects as Charles Bulfinch, I. M. Pei, and others. Entries include: Building name, location, architect's name, description. *Freq:* Irregular. *Price:* $19.95.

3391 ▪ Alabama's Black Heritage: A Tour of Historic Sites
Alabama Bureau of Tourism & Travel
PO Box 4927
Montgomery, AL 36103
E-mail: group@touralabama.org

Contact: Frances Smiley, Editor.

Desc: Covers: sites of significance in Black American history in Alabama. *Price:* $9.50.

3392 ▪ American & British Genealogy & Heraldry
New England Historic Genealogical Society
101 Newbury St.   Ph: (617)536-5740
Boston, MA 02116-3007   Fax: (617)536-7307
E-mail: anovick@nehgs.org
URL: http://www.nehgs.org

Contact: P. William Filby, Editor.

Desc: Description: Not a directory, but the principal bibliographical guide in its field to more than 9,800 selected publications of use in genealogical and heraldic research; includes numerous older books; worldwide scope. For all books still in print publisher name given, with addresses for small or private publishers. *Freq:* Irregular, previous edition 1976; latest edition 1983; supplement 1987. *Price:* $15, base edition, plus $3.50 shipping; $5, supplement, plus $3.50 shipping.

3393 ▪ American Military Cemeteries
McFarland & Co., Inc., Publishers
960 Hwy. 88 W   Ph: (336)246-4460
Box 611   Free: 800-253-2187
Jefferson, NC 28640   Fax: (336)246-5018
E-mail: mcfarland@skybest.com
URL: http://www.mcfarlandpub.com

Contact: Dean W. Holt, Editor.

Desc: Covers: national cemeteries administered by the Department of the Army and by the National Park Service, American Battle Monuments Commission cemeteries and monuments, and state veterans cemeteries. Entries include: Cemetery name, address, location, description including history, types of graves, list of former superin-

tendents and directors; prominent persons interred in cemetery (Medal of Honor recipients, presidents, astronauts). *Freq:* Published 1992. *Price:* $75, plus $4.00 shipping.

3394 ▪ Ancestry's Red Book: American State, County and Town Sources
Ancestry, Inc.
PO Box 990   Ph: (801)426-3500
Orem, UT 84057   Free: 800-262-3787
                  Fax: (801)426-3501
E-mail: support@ancestry-inc.com

Contact: Alice Eichholz, Editor.

Desc: Covers: genealogical information sources available at the regional, state, and county level. Entries include: For regions—General overview. For states—Historical summary, addresses for obtaining each type of record. For counties—County seat address, date county was formed, years for which specific records are available. *Alt. Fmts:* CD-ROM. *Freq:* Irregular, previous edition 1989; latest edition January 1992. *Price:* $49.95, plus $5.50 shipping.

3395 ▪ Asian American Genealogical Sourcebook
Gale Group Inc.
27500 Drake Rd.   Ph: (248)699-4253
Farmington Hills, MI   Free: 800-877-GALE
48331-3535   Fax: (248)699-8070
E-mail: galeord@galegroup.com
URL: http://www.galegroup.com

Contact: Paula K. Byers, Editor.

Desc: Publication includes: Information sources on Asian American genealogy. Entries include: Source name, address, phone. Principal content of publication is background essays and indexes. *Price:* $69.

3396 ▪ Association for Preservation Technology—International Membership Directory and Resource Guide
Association for Preservation Technology
PO Box 3511   Ph: (703)373-1621
Williamsburg, VA 23187   Fax: (804)220-7787

Contact: Susan Ford Johnson, Editor.

Desc: Covers: About 2,000 persons, corporations, and government agencies involved in historic preservation; related libraries and educational programs. Entries include: Name, address, phone, name and title of contact, description of projects or services. *Alt. Fmts:* diskette; mailing labels. *Freq:* Latest edition 1993. *Price:* $25.

3397 ▪ California Historical Landmarks
California State Parks
PO Box 942896   Ph: (916)653-8855
Sacramento, CA 94296-0001   Fax: (916)654-8928

Contact: Pat McLatchey, Editor.

Desc: Number of listings: Over 1,070. Entries include: Site location, site number, county, description of landmark's significance. *Freq:* Every five years. *Price:* $11.95.

3398 ■ Cemeteries Directory

infoUSA

5711 S. 86th Circle   Ph: (402)593-4600
PO Box 27347   Free: 800-555-6124
Omaha, NE 68127   Fax: (402)331-5481
E-mail: internet@infousa.com
URL: http://www.abii.com

Desc: Number of listings: 6,255. Entries include: Cemetery name, address, phone (including area code), size of advertisement, year first in "Yellow Pages". Compiled from telephone company "Yellow Pages," nationwide. *Available:* Online. *Alt. Fmts:* 3x5 cards; diskette; magnetic tape; mailing labels. *Freq:* Annual. *Price:* Please inquire.

3399 ■ Cemeteries of the U.S.

Gale Group Inc.

27500 Drake Rd.   Ph: (248)699-4253
Farmington Hills, MI   Free: 800-877-GALE
  48331-3535   Fax: (248)699-8070
E-mail: galeord@galegroup.com
URL: http://www.galegroup.com

Contact: Deborah M. Burek, Editor.

Desc: Covers: Over 22,800 operating and closed cemeteries; state and local historical and genealogical associations, agencies, and publications able to provide information on cemeteries and records. Entries include: For cemeteries—Name, address, phone, years of operation, ownership, affiliations, facilities and services, records available. For associations and agencies—Name, address, phone. For publications—Title, author, publisher, publication date; publisher's address given in appendix. *Freq:* First edition January 1994. *Price:* $149.95.

3400 ■ Census Catalog and Guide

Customer Services Center

Bureau of the Census   Ph: (301)457-1225
Washington, DC 20233   Fax: (301)457-4714
URL: http://www.census.gov

Contact: Barbara Aldrich, Editor.

Desc: Publication includes: The 1998 Catalog includes a section designed to acquaint the user with Census Bureau Internet web sites. Designed as a companion to the Sources of Assistance found in the 1997 Catalog and Guide, this section provides a selective overview of the sources of data and assistance that are online. The 1998 Catalog leads users through the Census Bureau Internet programs and services and provides web site addresses for regional offices; state data centers; depository libraries; web sites for other government organizations; as well as experts throughout the agency. Entries include: For sources—Name, address, phone. For specialists—Name, address, phone, subject specialty. Principal content is catalog with descriptive listings of documents, reports, computer tapes, CD-ROM's, and other materials issued by the Bureau of the Census. Available in Portable Document Format (PDF). *Freq:* Annual. *Price:* $5, (1998 edition).

3401 ■ The Center: A Guide to Genealogical Research in the National Capital

Genealogical Publishing Co., Inc.

1001 N. Calvert St.   Ph: (410)037-8271
Baltimore, MD 21202   Free: 800-296-6687
                                       Fax: (410)752-8492
E-mail: orders@genealogical.com

Contact: Christina K. Schaefer, Editor, Author.

Desc: Covers: 145 facilities available for genealogical research in the Washington, D.C. metro area, primarily at various units of the National Archives and the Library of Congress, and the libraries of the Daughters of the American Revolution and the National Genealogical Society. Entries include: Facility or unit name, address, phone, hours, types of material available, and, in separate sections, detailed information on what materials are available, where and how to secure access, and notes on scope, content, limitations of the materials. *Freq:* Irregular, previous edition 1992; latest edition 1997. *Price:* $19.95, plus $3.50 p/h.

3402 ■ Chicago's Famous Buildings

University of Chicago Press

5720 S. Woodlawn Ave.   Ph: (773)702-7600
Chicago, IL 60637   Fax: (773)702-0172

Contact: Franz Schulze, Editor; Kevin Harrington, Editor.

Desc: Covers: about 200 architectural landmarks in Chicago, both old and new. Entries include: Building name, address, date built, architects, description, photo. *Freq:* Irregular, latest edition 1980. *Price:* $19.95, cloth; $9.95, paper.

3403 ■ China in Oregon: A Resource Directory

Continuing Education Publications

1633 SW Park   Ph: (503)725-4891
Portland, OR 97207   Free: 800-547-8887
                                       Fax: (503)725-4840

Contact: Jeffrey Barlow, Editor; Christine Richardson, Editor; Jane Leung Larson, Editor.

Desc: Covers: about 475 organizations, companies, educational institutions, museums, and libraries, primarily in Oregon, that provide information about China trade, travel, education, culture, history, and recreation. Entries include: Organization, company, or institution name, address, phone, telex, names and titles of key personnel, subsidiary and branch names and locations, description of projects, products and services. *Freq:* Biennial, even years. *Price:* $15.95, plus $4.00 shipping.

3404 ■ Civil War Genealogical Research

George K. Schweitzer

407 Ascot   Ph: (615)690-7831
Knoxville, TN 37923

Contact: George K. Schweitzer, Editor.

Desc: Publication includes: Lists of state archives, libraries, museums, veterans and other organizations, and other sources of information on persons who served in the Civil War. Entries include: Name, address, some entries include kind and scope of records, etc. *Freq:* Annual, October. *Price:* $12, postpaid, payment with order.

3405 ■ Council on East Asian Libraries— Directory

University of Chicago
East Asian Library

5801 South Ellis   Ph: (773)702-1234
Chicago, IL 60637   Fax: (773)702-6623

Contact: Tai-loi Ma, Editor, President, Curator.

Desc: Covers: About 150 library collections concerned with China, Japan, and Korea. Entries include: Collection name, institution name, address, names and titles of personnel, phone, fax, e-mail address. *Freq:* Irregular, previous edition 1994; latest edition 1996. *Price:* $10, postpaid; included in subscription to "Bulletin".

3406 ■ County Courthouse Book

Genealogical Publishing Co., Inc.

1001 N. Calvert St.   Ph: (410)037-8271
Baltimore, MD 21202   Free: 800-296-6687
                                       Fax: (410)752-8492

E-mail: orders@genealogical.com

Contact: Elizabeth Petty Bentley, Editor.

Desc: Covers: over 3,125 county jurisdictions and 1,577 New England towns and independent VA cities. Entries include: Name, address, phone, date of organization. *Freq:* latest edition 1996; previous edition 1990. *Price:* $34.95, plus $3.50 p/h.

3407 ■ County Reference Guide

Heritage Quest
A Division of American Genealogical Lending Library (AGLL)

PO Box 329   Ph: (801)298-5358
Bountiful, UT 84011-0329   Free: 800-658-7755
                                       Fax: (801)298-5468

E-mail: sales@heritagequest.com
URL: http://www.heritagequest.com

Desc: Covers: Every county in the United States, including those no longer in existence. Entries include: County name, county seat, founding date, parent county or territory, brief notes on vital records available for a given county. *Alt. Fmts:* diskette. *Freq:* As needed. *Price:* Please inquire.

3408 ■ Cumulative List of Organizations

Field Systems Branch
Internal Revenue Service

1111 Constitution Ave. NW   Ph: (202)622-7977
Washington, DC 20224   Fax: (202)622-8026
URL: http://www.irs.ustreas.gov

Desc: Description: Complete title is, "Cumulative List of Organizations Described in Section 170 (c) of the Internal Revenue Code of 1986" (i.e., organizations to which contributions have been determined by the Internal Revenue Service to be deductible from income for federal tax purposes). About 457,000 such organizations are listed in two volumes; individual religious congregations or other subordinate groups under a central organization holding an exemption letter are not listed separately. Entries include: Organization name, city, state; may also include a code indicating that the group listed is a central organization, a private foundation, or other group with limited deductibility. *Freq:* Annual, October; with three quarterly supplements. *Price:* $92, per year, including supplements.

3409 ■ Directory of Affiliated Societies

American Historical Association

400 A St. SE   Ph: (202)544-2422
Washington, DC 20003-3889   Fax: (202)544-8307
E-mail: aha@theaha.org; rtownsend@theaha.org
URL: http://www.theaha.org

Desc: Covers: 100 specialized historical societies affiliated with the American Historical Association. Entries include: Society name, names and titles of key personnel, activities, publications. *Freq:* Annual, fall. *Price:* $10.

3410 ■ Directory of American Libraries with Genealogy or Local History Collections

Scholarly Resources, Inc.

104 Greenhill Ave.   Ph: (302)654-7713
Wilmington, DE 19805-1897   Free: 800-772-8937
                                       Fax: (302)654-3871
E-mail: sales@scholarly.com; sr@scholarly.com
URL: http://www.scholarly.com

Contact: P. William Filby, Editor.

Desc: Covers: nearly 1,600 U.S. and Canadian libraries with collections of genealogical or local history materials. Entries include: Institution name, address, phone, hours of operation, names and titles of key personnel, geographical area served, description of holdings and of additional services offered, if any. *Freq:* Irregular, latest edition 1988. *Price:* $75.

3411 ■ Directory to Canadian Studies in Canada

Association for Canadian Studies
C. P. 8888, Succ. Centre-ville   Ph: (514)987-7784
Montreal, PQ, Canada H3C   Fax: (514)987-3481
  3P8
E-mail: acs-aec@uqam.ca
URL: http://www.er.ugam.ca/nobel/c1015

Contact: Gregory Slogar, Editor.

Desc: Covers: Canadian studies programs, multidisciplinary programs, research centers, journals, academic societies and awards. Entries include: Name and contact information. *Freq:* Irregular, previous edition 1984, latest edition 1993. *Price:* C$10, free to members.

3412 ■ Directory of Caribbean Historians

Association of Caribbean Historians
c/o T. Martinez-Vergne   Ph: (612)696-6488
Dept. of History   Fax: (612)696-6689
Macalester College
St. Paul, MN 55105

Contact: Teresita Martinez-Vergne, Editor.

Desc: Covers: professional historians interested in the history of the Caribbean. Entries include: Personal name and address, research interests. *Freq:* Irregular. *Price:* Free, to ACH members; $10, to nonmembers.

3413 ■ Directory of Family Associations

Genealogical Publishing Co., Inc.
1001 N. Calvert St.   Ph: (410)037-8271
Baltimore, MD 21202   Free: 800-296-6687
          Fax: (410)752-8492
E-mail: orders@genealogical.com

Contact: Elizabeth Petty Bentley, Editor.

Desc: Covers: over 6,500 organizations, each devoted to the study of a family name. Entries include: Family name, related family names, organization name, address, phone, contact name, publications. *Freq:* Irregular, latest edition 3rd ed. 1996. *Price:* $34.95, plus $3.50 p/h.

3414 ■ Directory of Family One-Name Periodicals

Ye Olde Genealogie Shoppe
PO Box 39128   Ph: (317)862-3330
Indianapolis, IN 46239   Free: 800-419-0200
          Fax: (317)862-2599

Contact: John Konrad, Editor.

Desc: Covers: over 1,600 periodicals each devoted to genealogical research on a single family name; most are published by family associations. Entries include: Publication name, address. *Freq:* Formerly annual; latest edition 1993; new edition expected 1995. *Price:* $10, plus $4.00 shipping.

3415 ■ Directory of Federal Historical Programs and Activities

American Historical Association
400 A St. SE   Ph: (202)544-2422
Washington, DC 20003-3889   Fax: (202)544-8307
E-mail: aha@theaha.org

Desc: Covers: about 1,700 federally employed historians and federal government agencies operating historical programs. Entries include: For historians—Name, phone, area of expertise, historical program. For programs—

Name, address, functions of historians. *Freq:* Triennial, previous edition 1990; latest edition December 1993. *Price:* $10.

3416 ■ Directory of Historical and Genealogical Societies, Museums, and Cultural Organizations in Kansas

Kansas State Historical Society
6425 SW 6th Ave.   Ph: (785)272-8681
Topeka, KS 66615-1099   Fax: (785)272-8683
E-mail: snovak@kshs.org
URL: http://www.kshs.org

Contact: Susan S. Novak, Editor, Education/Outreach Div.

Desc: Covers: about 350 historical and genealogical societies, museums, and cultural organizations in Kansas. Entries include: Name, address, phone, description of collections or holdings. *Freq:* Irregular, latest edition spring 1995. *Price:* $5, 1995 edition.

3417 ■ Directory of Historical Organizations in Ohio

Ohio Association of Historical Societies and Museums
c/o Local History Office   Ph: (614)297-2340
Ohio Historical Society   Fax: (614)297-2318
1982 Velma Ave.
Columbus, OH 43211-2497

Contact: Bonnie Such, Editor.

Desc: Covers: over 900 organizations dedicated to preserving, collecting, and interpreting Ohio's state and local history. Entries include: Organization name, address, phone, fax number, name and title of contact, scope and activities, number of members, year established, publication, museum (if any), major programs, days and hours of operation. *Freq:* Triennial, latest edition early 1999. *Price:* $16.50, members, plus $1.50 shipping; $18.50, nonmembers, plus $1.50 shipping.

3418 ■ Directory of Historical Societies, Agencies, and Commissions in Michigan

Historical Society of Michigan
2117 Washtenaw Ave.   Ph: (734)769-1828
Ann Arbor, MI 48104   Fax: (734)769-4267
E-mail: hsofmich@leslie.k12.mi.us

Contact: Matty Raiti, Editor.

Desc: Covers: over 300 statewide and local historical agencies, societies, and historic district commissions in Michigan. Entries include: Organization name, address, phone, contact name, hours of operation, publications, major activities. *Freq:* Previous edition 1993; latest edition July 1998. *Price:* $10.

3419 ■ Directory of History Departments and Organizations in the United States and Canada

American Historical Association
400 A St. SE   Ph: (202)544-2422
Washington, DC 20003-3889   Fax: (202)544-8307
E-mail: aha@theaha.org
URL: http://web.gmu.edu/chnm/aha

Contact: Cecelia J. Dadianr, Editor; Vernon Horn, Editor.

Desc: Covers: over 780 history departments in two- and four-year colleges and universities; historical organizations in the United States and Canada; over 14,000 historians. Entries include: Institution name, address, phone, names of faculty members and their areas of specialization, tuition, application information, enrollment, research facilities and educational programs. *Freq:* Annual, October. *Price:* $70, plus $4.00 shipping, payment with order.

3420 ■ Directory of Professional Genealogists

Association of Professional Genealogists (APG)
PO Box 40393
Denver, CO 80204-0393
E-mail: apg-admin@genealogy.org

Contact: Elizabeth Kelly Kerstens, Editor.

Desc: Covers: member genealogists and related research services. Entries include: Genealogist's name or company name, address; many listings include phone. Has been published as a special issue of the association's newsletter. *Freq:* Biennial, latest edition 1997-98; new edition expected 1999-2000. *Price:* $15, postpaid.

3421 ■ Directory of Resources for Australian Studies in North America

Australia-New Zealand Studies Center
Pennsylvania State University
427 Boucke Bldg.   Ph: (814)863-1603
University Park, PA 16802   Fax: (814)865-3336

Contact: Dr. Nan Bowman Albinski, Editor.

Desc: Covers: over 200 major collections in North American libraries and museums that are relevant to Australian studies. Entries include: Name, address, phone, days and hours of operation, admission requirements, description of holdings, available catalog. *Freq:* Published 1992. *Price:* $15, plus $2.00 shipping.

3422 ■ Directory of South Carolina Historical Organizations

Public Programs Division
South Carolina Department of Archives and History
6301 Parklane Rd.   Ph: (803)734-8577
Columbia, SC 29223-4905   Fax: (803)734-8820
E-mail: hornsby@history.scdan.sc.edu
URL: http://www.scdan.sc.edu/homepage.htm

Contact: Judith M. Andrews, Editor; Ben Hornsby, Editor.

Desc: Covers: about 170 organizations interested in history and historical preservation in South Carolina. Entries include: Organization name, address, phone, names and titles of key personnel. *Freq:* Annual. *Price:* Free.

3423 ■ Directory of Women Historians

American Historical Association
400 A St. SE   Ph: (202)544-2422
Washington, DC 20003   Fax: (202)544-8307
E-mail: aha@h-net.msu.edu

Desc: Covers: Over 1,300 women historians. Entries include: Name, work address, specializations, rank, number of articles and books published. *Freq:* Irregular. *Price:* $7, members; $10, nonmembers.

3424 ■ Discovering Multicultural America

Gale Group Inc.
27500 Drake Rd.   Ph: (248)699-4253
Farmington Hills, MI   Free: 800-877-GALE
  48331-3535   Fax: (248)699-8070
E-mail: galeord@galegroup.com
URL: http://www.galegroup.com.; http://www.gale.com

Desc: Covers: America's largest ethnic groups: African Americans, Asian Americans, Hispanic Americans, and Native North Americans. Information includes 2,000 biographical profiles, 2,500 historical and topical essays, 500 overviews of ethnic landmarks, 350 significant documents, 3,100 timeline events, 5,000 contact organizations, 500 full-text articles. *Available:* Online: GaleNet. *Alt. Fmts:* CD-ROM. *Freq:* Produced 1996. *Price:* $500, Windows stand-alone version.

3425 ▪ Dutch Genealogical Research

Ye Olde Genealogie Shoppe
PO Box 39128   Ph: (317)862-3330
Indianapolis, IN 46239   Free: 800-419-0200
                                Fax: (317)862-2599

Contact: Charles M. Franklin, Editor.

Desc: Publication includes: Lists of United States and Dutch vital statistics offices, periodical publishers, libraries, and genealogical societies of assistance in Dutch genealogical research. Entries include: Generally, listings show organization, agency, or other name, address. *Freq:* Irregular, previous edition 1982; latest edition January 1994. *Price:* $15, plus $4.00 s/h.

3426 ▪ Encyclopedia of American Religions

Gale Group Inc.
27500 Drake Rd.   Ph: (248)699-4253
Farmington Hills, MI   Free: 800-877-GALE
48331-3535   Fax: (248)699-8070
E-mail: galeord@galegroup.com
URL: http://www.galegroup.com.; http://www.gale.com

Contact: J. Gordon Melton, Editor.

Desc: Covers: Approximately 2,300 religious and spiritual groups in the United States and Canada, including Roman Catholic, Judaic, Protestant, Eastern, and Middle Eastern religions, and other beliefs and practices, such as occultism, magick, Satanism, and communes. Contains an essay on the development of religion in the U.S. and Canada; historical essays discussing the development of the 24 major religious families and traditions; and directory sections listing individual churches and groups constituting the religious families discussed in the historical essays (with two additional sections for churches and groups not belonging to one of the religious families). Entries include: Group name, address (if group is still active); description of group's history, beliefs, organization, and leaders; membership data, educational facilities, periodicals, bibliography of sources of additional information. *Alt. Fmts:* CD-ROM; diskette; magnetic tape. *Freq:* Irregular, previous edition 1996, latest edition 1998. *Price:* $205.

3427 ▪ Ethnic Genealogy: A Research Guide

Greenwood Publishing Group, Inc.
88 Post Rd. W.   Ph: (203)226-3571
PO Box 5007   Free: 800-225-5800
Westport, CT 06881-5007   Fax: (203)226-6009
E-mail: prices@greenwood.com
URL: http://www.greenwood.com

Contact: Jessie Carney Smith, Editor.

Desc: Covers: genealogical organizations and societies, and libraries and historical societies with significant collections for research in genealogy of Native Americans, Asian Americans, African Americans, Hispanic Americans, and other ethnic groups. *Freq:* Published 1983. *Price:* $75, individuals, payment must accompany order.

3428 ▪ Family Associations, Societies and Reunions

Ye Olde Genealogie Shoppe
PO Box 39128   Ph: (317)862-3330
Indianapolis, IN 46239   Free: 800-419-0200
                                Fax: (317)862-2599

Contact: Ray Gooldy, Editor.

Desc: Covers: about 2,000 family associations, societies, and regularly scheduled reunions; includes Scottish clan associations; coverage includes Canada. Entries include: Group name, address of contact, variant names. *Freq:* Annual. *Price:* $10, plus $4.00 shipping.

3429 ▪ Family Records, TODAY—Membership Directory Issue

American Family Records Association
PO Box 15505   Ph: (816)252-0950
Kansas City, MO 64106
E-mail: amfamrecord@aol.com

Contact: Nita Neblock, Editor.

Desc: Publication includes: List of about 300 members of the American Family Records Association. Entries include: Member's name, address, member number. Principal content of publication is genealogical research information and source data for a wide range of ethnic cultures. *Freq:* Annual, June/July issue. *Price:* Included in membership; $22, per year.

3430 ▪ French and French-Canadian Family Research

Ye Olde Genealogie Shoppe
PO Box 39128   Ph: (317)862-3330
Indianapolis, IN 46239   Free: 800-419-0200
                                Fax: (317)862-2599

Contact: J. Konrad, Editor.

Desc: Publication includes: List of French and French Canadian genealogical societies and provincial archives in French and French Canadian provinces. Entries include: Institution name, and address. *Freq:* Irregular, previous edition 1993; latest edition 1998. *Price:* $10, plus $4 shipping.

3431 ▪ Genealogical Computing

Ancestry, Inc.
PO Box 990   Ph: (801)426-3500
Orem, UT 84057   Free: 800-262-3787
                                Fax: (801)426-3501
E-mail: support@ancestry-inc.com

Contact: Matthew Helm, Editor; April Lelsh-Helm, Senior Editor.

Desc: Covers: genealogical computer databases, bulletin boards, and interest groups in the United States, Australia, and Great Britain. Entries include: Company name, address, phone, requirements for membership, and description of service. *Available:* Online. *Freq:* Quarterly. *Price:* $8.50, per issue; $25, per year.

3432 ▪ Genealogical Helper—Bureau of Missing Ancestors Section

Everton Publishers, Inc.
PO Box 368   Ph: (435)752-6022
Logan, UT 84323-0368   Free: 800-443-6325
                                Fax: (435)752-0425

Desc: Covers: about 1,000 amateur and professional genealogists who are researching family names; listings are paid. Entries include: Researcher's name, address, status (whether amateur, family genealogist, or professional), county of residence of researcher, and information on families and surnames being researched. *Freq:* Feature appears in each bimonthly issue. *Price:* $6.95, per issue; $24, per year.

3433 ▪ Genealogical Helper—Directory of Genealogical Societies, Libraries, and Periodicals Issue

Everton Publishers, Inc.
PO Box 368   Ph: (435)752-6022
Logan, UT 84323-0368   Free: 800-443-6325
                                Fax: (435)752-0425

Contact: George B. Everton, Jr., Editor.

Desc: Publication includes: Lists of genealogical societies, libraries, and periodicals throughout the world. Entries include: All entries include organization or individual

name and address; periodical listings include frequency and price. *Freq:* Annual, July-August issue. *Price:* $6.95, postpaid, payment with order.

3434 ▪ Genealogical Helper—Directory of Professional Researchers Issue

Everton Publishers, Inc.
PO Box 368   Ph: (435)752-6022
Logan, UT 84323-0368   Free: 800-443-6325
                                Fax: (435)752-0425

Contact: George B. Everton, Jr., Editor.

Desc: Publication includes: List of professional genealogical researchers, worldwide; a listing fee is charged. Entries include: Researcher name, address, specialties; some listings may include additional detail. *Freq:* Annual, September/October. *Price:* $6.95, postpaid, payment with order.

3435 ▪ Genealogical Helper—Genealogy and the Public Library Issue

Everton Publishers, Inc.
PO Box 368   Ph: (435)752-6022
Logan, UT 84323-0368   Free: 800-443-6325
                                Fax: (435)752-0425

Contact: Valarie Chambers, Editor.

Desc: Covers: more than 200 public libraries nationwide which have separate genealogical collections or a special interest in such materials. Entries include: Library name, address. *Freq:* Annual. *Price:* $6.95, postpaid, payment with order.

3436 ▪ Genealogical and Local History Books in Print

Genealogical Publishing Co., Inc.
1001 N. Calvert St.   Ph: (410)037-8271
Baltimore, MD 21202   Free: 800-296-6687
                                Fax: (410)752-8492
E-mail: orders@genealogical.com

Contact: Marian Hoffman, Editor.

Desc: Publication includes: List of over 4,600 suppliers of genealogical books, microform, and computer software in four volumes. Entries include: Organization or personal name, address, name and title of contact, product. Principal content is a description of genealogical and local history books, reprints, microform collections, and specific surname publications, with ordering information. *Freq:* Every 10 yrs.-latest edition 1996; reprint 1997. *Price:* $25, per volume, plus $3.50 s/h.

3437 ▪ Genealogical Periodical Annual Index

Heritage Books, Inc.
1540-E Pointer Ridge Pl.   Ph: (301)390-7709
Bowie, MD 20716   Free: 800-398-7709
                                Fax: (301)390-7153
E-mail: heritagebooks@pipeline.com
URL: http://www.heritagebooks.com

Contact: Leslie K. Towle, Editor; Laird C. Towle, Editor; Anna Lisa Fielding, Editor.

Desc: Publication includes: contact information for about 330 periodicals published by genealogical societies and genealogists and used in indexing surnames, place names, and related topics for this book. Entries include: Name of publication, name of publisher, address, issues indexed, title abbreviation used in book. Publication mainly consists of an idex containing 14,000 genealogical citations (surnames, place names, etc.). *Freq:* Annual, August. *Price:* $32.

3438 ▪ Genealogical Records in Texas

Genealogical Publishing Co., Inc.
1001 N. Calvert St.   Ph: (410)037-8271
Baltimore, MD 21202   Free: 800-296-6687
                                Fax: (410)752-8492

Master Index

E-mail: orders@genealogical.com

Contact: Imogene Kennedy, Editor; Leon Kennedy, Editor.

Desc: Covers: Texas genealogical records created by successive governments for almost 200 years. Includes information on what records can found and where they can be located. *Freq:* Irregular, latest edition 1992; previous edition 1987. *Price:* $35, plus $3.50 p/h.

3439 ▪ Genealogical Research and Resources: A Guide for Library Use

American Library Association (ALA)
50 E. Huron St.   Ph: (312)280-5038
Chicago, IL 60611   Free: 800-545-2433
                         Fax: (312)280-5033
URL: http://www.ala.org/editions
Contact: Lois C. Gilmer, Editor.

Desc: Publication includes: List of genealogical organizations and societies. Principal content of publication is information on genealogical research publications. *Freq:* Latest edition 1988. *Price:* $18; $16.20, for ALA members.

3440 ▪ Genealogical Resources in Southern New Jersey

Gloucester County Historical Society
17 Hunter St.   Ph: (609)845-4771
Woodbury, NJ 08096-4605 Fax: (609)845-0131
E-mail: gchs@citnet.com
Contact: Edith Hoelle, Editor.

Desc: Covers: historical societies, public libraries, colleges, and other sources of records and information for genealogical research. Entries include: Name, address, phone, description of collection/records available, contact name, hours and days open, whether fee is charged, whether copier is available. *Freq:* Irregular, previous edition 1994 edition, latest edition 1999. *Price:* $12.50, postpaid.

3441 ▪ Genealogical Societies and Historical Societies in the United States

Ye Olde Genealogie Shoppe
PO Box 39128   Ph: (317)862-3330
Indianapolis, IN 46239   Free: 800-419-0200
                         Fax: (317)862-2599
Contact: John Konrad, Editor.

Desc: Covers: about 3,000 groups in the United States. Entries include: Society name, address. *Freq:* Annual. *Price:* $10, plus $4.00 shipping.

3442 ▪ The Genealogist's Address Book

Genealogical Publishing Co., Inc.
1001 N. Calvert St.   Ph: (410)037-8271
Baltimore, MD 21202   Free: 800-296-6687
                         Fax: (410)752-8492
E-mail: orders@genealogical.com
Contact: Elizabeth Petty Bentley, Editor.

Desc: Covers: archives, historical societies, libraries, and genealogical societies; religious and ethnic organizations, research centers, surname registries, hereditary societies, and other groups useful to persons doing genealogical research. Entries include: Name, address, phone, name and title of contact. *Freq:* Biennial, latest edition 1998. *Price:* $39.95.

3443 ▪ Genealogy: A Practical Research Guide

RSG Publishing
217 County Hwy.1   Ph: (607)563-9000
Bainbridge, NY 13733-9307
URL: http://www.rsgpublishing.com
Contact: Shirley B. Goerlich, Editor.

Desc: Publication includes: about 25 sources of genealogical materials, primarily firms and agencies that supply forms and information. Entries include: Name, address, type of service provided. Principal content of publication is editorial matter on family research procedures, organization of materials, and advice and description of vital records' sources. Book includes samples of genealogically useful papers, charts, application forms, etc. *Freq:* Irregular, latest edition 1994, previous edition July 1984. *Price:* $38, shipped, soft cover; $48, shipped, hard cover.

3444 ▪ German Family Research Made Simple

Ye Olde Genealogie Shoppe
PO Box 39128   Ph: (317)862-3330
Indianapolis, IN 46239   Free: 800-419-0200
                         Fax: (317)862-2599
Contact: John Konrad, Editor.

Desc: Publication includes: Lists with addresses of archives, periodicals, professional researchers, and publishers of maps likely to be helpful to genealogists; covers each state within Germany. Entries include: Name, address. *Freq:* Latest edition 1992. *Price:* $12, plus $4.00 shipping.

3445 ▪ Guide to Information Resources in Ethnic Museum, Library, and Archival Collections in the United States

Greenwood Publishing Group, Inc.
88 Post Rd. W.   Ph: (203)226-3571
PO Box 5007   Free: 800-225-5800
Westport, CT 06881-5007 Fax: (203)226-6009
E-mail: prices@greenwood.com
URL: http://www.greenwood.com
Contact: Lois J. Buttlar, Editor; Lubomyr R. Wynar, Editor.

Desc: Covers: Several hundred ethnic collections in the United States. Entries include: Name, address, phone, fax, brief description of the scope, size, and accessibility of the collection. *Freq:* Published 1996. *Price:* $79.50.

3446 ▪ Guide to Research Collections of Former United States Senators 1789-1995

Historical Office
United States Senate
                         Ph: (202)224-6900
rs>Washington, DC 20510
URL: http://bioguide.congress.gov
Contact: Karen Dawley Paul, Editor-in-Chief.

Desc: Covers: repositories for collections of papers, letters, photographs, oral histories and similar items written by or relating to former United States senators. Entries include: Senator name, state represented, location and description of holdings, whether open to the public. *Freq:* Irregular, Previous edition 1987; latest edition 1995. *Price:* Free.

3447 ▪ Guidebook to Historic Western Pennsylvania

University of Pittsburgh Press
3347 Forbes Ave.   Ph: (412)383-2456
Pittsburgh, PA 15261   Free: 800-666-2211
                         Fax: (412)383-2466
E-mail: press@pitt.edu
Contact: George Swetnam, Editor; Helene Smith, Editor.

Desc: Covers: 1,300 historical sites in 26 counties of western Pennsylvania, including homes, churches, forts, manufacturing plants, bridges, etc., both preserved sites and ruins; includes some twentieth-century sites. Entries include: Site name, location, address (if applicable), description and explanation of significance, other details as relevant. *Freq:* Irregular, First edition 1976; latest edition 1991. *Price:* $19.95, paper.

3448 ▪ Handbook of Genealogical Sources

George K. Schweitzer
407 Ascot   Ph: (615)690-7831
Knoxville, TN 37923
Contact: George K. Schweitzer, Editor.

Desc: Covers: about 750 libraries, repositories, archives, court houses, etc., with detailed instructions for obtaining genealogical information from them. Entries include: Source name, address, types of data available. *Freq:* Irregular, previous edition 1988; latest edition 1995. *Price:* $15, postpaid, payment with order.

3449 ▪ Handy Book for Genealogists

Everton Publishers, Inc.
PO Box 368   Ph: (435)752-6022
Logan, UT 84323-0368   Free: 800-443-6325
                         Fax: (435)752-0425
Contact: A. Lee Everton, Editor.

Desc: Publication includes: List of associations, societies, libraries, archives, and other organizations and institutions that provide genealogical information. *Freq:* Irregular, latest edition 1999. *Price:* $34.95, plus $2.95 shipping.

3450 ▪ Historic Homes of Florida

Pineapple Press
PO Box 3899   Ph: (941)359-0886
Sarasota, FL 34230-3899 Free: 800-746-3275
                         Fax: (941)351-9988
E-mail: info@pineapplepress.com
URL: http://www.pineapplepress.com
Contact: Susanne Hupp, Editor; H. Patrick Reed, Editor.

Desc: Covers: Approximately 70 restored historic residences in Florida. Entries include: Contact and visiting information. *Price:* $14.95.

3451 ▪ Historic Indiana

Division of Historic Preservation & Archaeology
Indiana Department of Natural Resources
402 W. Washington St.,   Ph: (317)232-1646
Rm. W274   Fax: (317)232-0693
Indianapolis, IN 46204
E-mail: dhpq_at_dnrlan@ima.isd.in.us
Contact: Paul C. Diebold, Editor.

Desc: Covers: about 1,400 public buildings, churches, homes of famous persons; other structures such as bridges, barns, etc; and over 100 districts in Indiana which are listed in The National Register of Historic Places through the United States Department of the Interior. Entries include: Name of structure or area, address or location, date included in the National Register; designation of NHL (National Historic Landmark), HABS (Historic American Buildings Survey), HAER (Historic American Engineering Record), or HABSI (Historic American Buildings Survey Inventory), and/or if property has received a matching grant-in-aid from the Department of Interior. *Freq:* Biennial, current issue 1997-98. *Price:* Free, per single copy.

3452 ▪ Historic Landmarks of Black America

Gale Group Inc.
27500 Drake Rd.   Ph: (248)699-4253
Farmington Hills, MI   Free: 800-877-GALE
  48331-3535   Fax: (248)699-8070
E-mail: galeord@galegroup.com
URL: http://www.galegroup.com
Contact: George Cantor, Editor.

Desc: Covers: 300 sites significant in African-American history. Entries include: Name, location, mailing address, phone, season, days and hours of operation, discussion of site and its significance, admission fees, accessibility to handicapped, exhibits and facilities, special programs. *Freq:* Published May 1991. *Price:* $45.

3453 ■ Historical and Cultural Agencies and Museums in Illinois

Illinois State Historical Society
1 Old State Capitol Plaza   Ph: (217)782-2635
Springfield, IL 62701-1507   Fax: (217)524-8042
E-mail: ishs@eosinc.com
URL: http://www.prairienet.org/ishs

Contact: Jon Austin, Editor, Executive Director.

Desc: Covers: about 1,000 museums, genealogical and historical societies, and other cultural agencies in Illinois. Entries include: Agency or museum name, address, phone, name of contact, hours of operation, program emphasis. *Alt. Fmts:* mailing labels. *Freq:* Biennial, odd years. *Price:* Free, to members, of Th Assoc. of Ill. & Historical Soc.

3454 ■ Historical Documentary Editions

National Historical Publications and Records Commission
U.S. National Archives and Records Administration
8th St. & Pennsylvania Ave. NW   Ph: (202)501-5600
Washington, DC 20408   Fax: (202)501-5601
E-mail: nhprc@arch1.nara.gov

Contact: Timothy D. W. Connelly, Editor, Dir. for Publications.

Desc: Covers: approximately 250 book, microfilm, and microfiche editions from 110 university presses, societies, institutions, and other publishers of the papers of historically significant people and organizations. Entries include: Title, editor, publisher, brief description of edition, format, price; separate section lists publisher name, address, phone. *Freq:* Irregular, previous edition 1988; latest edition 1993. *Price:* Free.

3455 ■ The History Highway: a Guide to Internet Resources

M.E. Sharpe, Inc.
80 Business Park Dr.   Ph: (914)273-1800
Armonk, NY 10504-1715   Free: 800-541-6563
    Fax: (914)273-2106
E-mail: mes@usa.net

Contact: Dennis A. Trinkle, Editor; Dorothy Auchter, Editor; Scott A. Merriman, Editor; Todd E. Larson, Editor.

Desc: Covers: Over 1,000 web sites of history sources, including sources for maps, electronic texts, discussion groups, newsgroups, journals, organizations, etc. Entries include: URL. *Freq:* Published November 1996. *Price:* $62.95.

3456 ■ How and Where to Research Your Ethnic-American Cultural Heritage

R & E Publishers
2132 Otoole Ave.   Ph: (408)432-3443
San Jose, CA 95131   Fax: (408)432-9221

Contact: Diane Parker, Editor.

Desc: Covers: historical societies, cultural institutes, libraries, archives, publishers, and other sources for genealogical research into German, Russian, Native American, Polish, African, Japanese, Jewish, Irish, Mexican, Italian, Chinese, Hungarian, Austrian, Croatian, Vietnamese, Dutch, English, French, Spanish, Filipino, Puerto Rican, Portuguese, Cuban, and Scandinavian backgrounds; 24 separate volumes cover each ethnic group. Entries include: Institution name, address, phone. *Freq:* Most volumes first published 1979; latest editions September 1994. *Price:* $4.50, plus $1.50 shipping per volume.

3457 ■ In Search of Your British & Irish Roots

Macmillan Canada
CDG Books
99 Yorkville Ave.   Ph: (416)963-8830
Toronto, ON, Canada M4W   Fax: (416)923-4821
2E4

Contact: Angus Baxter, Author.

Desc: Publication includes: Lists of historical societies, records offices, parish registers, archives, and other sources of genealogical information in the United Kingdom and Ireland. Entries include: Source name, address. *Freq:* Latest edition 1994. *Price:* C$18.95.

3458 ■ In Search of Your German Roots: A Complete Guide to Tracing Your Ancestors in the Germanic Areas of Europe

Genealogical Publishing Co., Inc.
1001 N. Calvert St.   Ph: (410)037-8271
Baltimore, MD 21202   Free: 800-296-6687
    Fax: (410)752-8492
E-mail: orders@genealogical.com

Contact: Angus Baxter, Editor.

Desc: Publication includes: Lists of genealogical associations in Germany and German genealogical societies in the United States. Entries include: Association name and address, names and titles of key personnel, and description of services provided. Principal content of publication is researching techniques for genealogists. *Freq:* Irregular, latest edition July 1996 (third edition); reprint 1997. *Price:* $11.95, plus $3.50 p/h.

3459 ■ Indexes to Ontario Census Records

N. K. Crowder
22 Canter Blvd.   Ph: (613)224-2880
Nepean, ON, Canada K2G 2M2
E-mail: ah009@freenet.carleton.ca

Contact: Norman Kenneth Crowder, Editor.

Desc: Covers: nearly 250 publishers and sources of indexed censuses of 473 Ontario municipalities from the early 1800s up to 1891. Entries include: Publisher name, address, description of material. *Freq:* Irregular, Previous edition 1987; supplement 1988; latest edition 1992. *Price:* C$12, postpaid.

3460 ■ International Association of Hispanists—List of Members

International Association of Hispanists (AIH)
c/o Department of Spanish   Ph: (603)646-2140
   and Portuguese   Fax: (603)646-3695
Dartmouth College
6072 Dartmouth Hall
Hanover, NH 03755-3511

Desc: Covers: 1,500 college and university professors, scholars, writers, and others engaged in Hispanic studies including literature, language, history, and culture of Spain and Spanish America. Entries include: Name, address. *Freq:* Triennial, latest edition 1995. *Price:* $50.

3461 ■ International Cemetary & Funeral Association—Membership Directory and Buyers Guide

International Cemetery and Funeral Association
1895 Preston White Dr.,   Ph: (703)391-8400
   No. 220   Free: 800-645-7700
Reston, VA 20191   Fax: (703)391-8416
E-mail: joeb@icfa.org

Contact: Joe Budzinski, Editor.

Desc: Covers: 4,700 funeral homes and cemeteries of all types, except government; individual members of the association; suppliers of products, equipment, and materials to the industry. Entries include: For cemeteries—Name,

address, phone, names and titles of key officials, facilities. For individuals—Name, address. For suppliers—Name, address, phone, products, contact. For funeral homes—name, address, phone, key contact. *Freq:* Annual, July. *Price:* $75, payment with order.

3462 ■ International Vital Records Handbook

Genealogical Publishing Co., Inc.
1001 N. Calvert St.   Ph: (410)037-8271
Baltimore, MD 21202   Free: 800-296-6687
    Fax: (410)752-8492
E-mail: orders@genealogical.com

Contact: Thomas Jay Kemp, Editor.

Desc: Covers: vital records offices for 67 countries and territories in North America, the British Isles and other English-speaking countries, and Europe. Entries include: Office name, address, phone, application fees, method of payment, description of holdings, actual application forms to use in obtaining copies of records, and alternative record locations. *Freq:* Triennial, Reprinted 1996. *Price:* $29.95, plus $3.50 p/h.

3463 ■ The Internet for Genealogists

Betterway Books
1507 Dana Ave.   Ph: (513)531-2690
Cincinnati, OH 45207   Free: 800-289-0963
    Fax: (513)531-4082

Contact: Barbara Renick, Editor, Author; Richard S. Wilson, Editor, Author.

Desc: Covers: Computer hardware and software and Internet resources designed for genealogists. Publication includes: Internet addresses for more than 200 genealogy megasites, libraries, catalogs, maps, gazetteers, bookstores, publishers, online databases and living persons directories. *Freq:* Published June 1998. *Price:* $16.99, paperback; C$23.99, paperback.

3464 ■ Iowa Catalog: Historic American Buildings Survey

University of Iowa Press
100 Kuhl House   Ph: (319)335-2000
Iowa City, IA 52242   Free: 800-621-2736
    Fax: (319)335-2055
URL: http://www.uiowa.edu/uipress

Contact: Wesley I. Shank, Editor.

Desc: Covers: about 100 historical buildings. Entries include: Name of site, location, name of architect, name of builder, name of owner, description, including special architectural features, history, date of construction. *Freq:* Published 1979. *Price:* $14.95, paper.

3465 ■ Irish Family Research Made Simple

Ye Olde Genealogie Shoppe
PO Box 39128   Ph: (317)862-3330
Indianapolis, IN 46239   Free: 800-419-0200
    Fax: (317)862-2599

Contact: E. J. Collins, Editor.

Desc: Publication includes: Lists of societies, organizations, archives, etc., in the United States and Ireland useful in research into Gaelic ancestry. Entries include: Name, address. *Freq:* Irregular, previous edition 1993; latest edition 1998. *Price:* $10, plus $4.00 shipping.

3466 ■ Irish Records: Sources for Family and Local History

Ancestry, Inc.
PO Box 990   Ph: (801)426-3500
Orem, UT 84057   Free: 800-262-3787
    Fax: (801)426-3501
E-mail: support@ancestry-inc.com

Contact: James G. Ryan, PhD., Editor.

Desc: Publication includes: Listings of genealogical resources, such as record custodians and clergy, in Ireland. Entries include: Name of source, address, geographical area served. *Freq:* latest edition 1997. *Price:* $49.95, plus $5.50 shipping.

3467 ■ Kansas City: A Place in Time
Landmarks Commission of Kansas City
City Hall, 26th Fl. E.   Ph: (816)274-2555
Kansas City, MO 64106   Fax: (816)274-1840

Desc: Covers: historic structures in Kansas City built in the 1930s or earlier and still in existence; illustrated. Entries include: Text provides detailed information for each building on location, architect, builders, construction, etc., and present status. *Freq:* Irregular, previous edition 1977; latest edition September 1983. *Price:* $6.

3468 ■ Landmark Yellow Pages: All the Names, Addresses, Facts and Figures You Need in Preservation
John Wiley & Sons
605 3rd Ave.   Ph: (212)850-6000
New York, NY 10158-0012   Free: 800-225-5945
                           Fax: (908)302-2300

Desc: Publication includes: Listing of approximately 3,500 local agencies, statewide organizations, and offices of national agencies dedicated to the preservation of old buildings that have historical and/or architectural significance. Entries include: Organization name, address, phone. Part 1 of publication lists reference sources and information on the preservation process. *Freq:* Irregular, previous edition spring 1993, latest edition June 1997. *Price:* $24.95.

3469 ■ Landmarks of American Presidents
Gale Group Inc.
27500 Drake Rd.   Ph: (248)699-4253
Farmington Hills, MI   Free: 800-877-GALE
48331-3535   Fax: (248)699-8070
E-mail: galeord@galegroup.com
URL: http://www.galegroup.com

Contact: Dr. Carl Wheeless, Editor.

Desc: Covers: Historic sites associated with the 41 U.S. presidents. Entries include: Introduction to the president and landmarks, including birthplace, education institutions, homes and lodgings, work, burial place, addresses, background data, current condition of the site, visitation information. *Freq:* Published 1996.

3470 ■ Libraries and Archives in France
Council for European Studies
808-809 International   Ph: (212)854-4172
  Affairs Bldg.   Fax: (212)854-8808
Columbia University
New York, NY 10027
E-mail: ces@columbia.edu

Contact: Erwin K. Welsch, Editor.

Desc: Covers: social science and humanities libraries and archives in France. *Freq:* Irregular, latest edition 1991. *Price:* $25, plus $1.00 shipping.

3471 ■ Libraries and Archives in Italy
Council for European Studies
808-809 International   Ph: (212)854-4172
  Affairs Bldg.   Fax: (212)854-8808
Columbia University
New York, NY 10027
E-mail: ces@columbia.edu

Contact: Rudolph J. Lewanski, Editor; Richard C. Lewanski, Editor.

Desc: Covers: Italian libraries and archives. *Price:* $6, plus $1.00 shipping.

3472 ■ Libraries and Archives in a New Germany
Council for European Studies
808-809 International   Ph: (212)854-4172
  Affairs Bldg.   Fax: (212)854-8808
Columbia University
New York, NY 10027
E-mail: ces@columbia.edu

Contact: Erwin K. Welsch, Editor.

Desc: Covers: German libraries and archives. Entries include: Description of holdings, rules governing access and use, and a bibliography listing collection surveys. *Freq:* Irregular, new edition published June 1994. *Price:* $35.

3473 ■ Maywood Chamber of Commerce—Community Guide
Maywood Chamber of Commerce
411 Madison   Ph: (708)345-1100
Maywood, IL 60153   Fax: (708)345-9701

Desc: Covers: businesses, churches, schools, and civic and social organizations in Maywood, Illinois. *Freq:* Annual, June. *Price:* Free.

3474 ■ Mexican and Spanish Family Research
Ye Olde Genealogie Shoppe
PO Box 39128   Ph: (317)862-3330
Indianapolis, IN 46239   Free: 800-419-0200
                           Fax: (317)862-2599

Contact: J. Konrad, Editor.

Desc: Covers: Organizations with genealogical information on families from Mexico and Spain. Entries include: Organization name and address. *Freq:* Published 1989. *Price:* $10, plus $4.00 shipping.

3475 ■ Meyer's Directory of Genealogical Societies in the U.S.A. and Canada
Mary Keysor Meyer/Libra Publications
5179 Perry Rd.   Ph: (410)875-2824
Mt. Airy, MD 21771   Fax: (410)875-1080

Contact: Mary Keysor Meyer, Editor.

Desc: Covers: Approximately 2,400 genealogical societies and 250 genealogical periodicals in the U.S. and Canada. Entries include: For societies—Name, phone, and location of society, holdings and service information. For periodicals—Periodical name, publisher. *Alt. Fmts:* mailing labels. *Freq:* Biennial, even years. *Price:* $30.

3476 ■ Midwest Archives Conference—Membership Directory
Midwest Archives Conference
c/o Barbara L. Floyd   Ph: (419)530-2170
University Archives   Fax: (419)530-2726
University of Toledo
2801 W. Bancroft
Toledo, OH 43606

Contact: Barbara L. Floyd, Editor, Secretary.

Desc: Covers: more than 1,000 individual and institutional members, largely librarians, archivists, records managers, manuscripts curators, historians, and museum and historical society personnel; about 25 archival associations in the Midwest. Entries include: For institutions—Name of archives, parent organization, address, phone. For individuals—Name, title, business address, phone. *Freq:* Annual. *Price:* $4, postpaid.

3477 ■ Monuments Directory
infoUSA
5711 S. 86th Circle   Ph: (402)593-4600
PO Box 27347   Free: 800-555-6124
Omaha, NE 68127   Fax: (402)331-5481
E-mail: internet@infousa.com
URL: http://www.abii.com

Desc: Number of listings: 8,079. Entries include: Name, address, phone (including area code), size of advertisement, year first in "Yellow Pages," name of owner or manager, number of employees. Compiled from telephone company "Yellow Pages," nationwide. *Available:* Online. *Alt. Fmts:* 3x5 cards; diskette; magnetic tape; mailing labels. *Freq:* Annual. *Price:* Please inquire.

3478 ■ Museum Companion to Los Angeles
Museon Publishing
PO Box 17095   Ph: (310)788-0228
Beverly Hills, CA 90209-2095   Fax: (310)788-0228

Contact: Borislav Stanic, Editor, Publisher.

Desc: Covers: 260 museums, historic houses, libraries with special collections, botanical gardens, and zoos in Los Angeles County, CA. Entries include: Name, address, phone, description, hours and days of operation, membership, publications, facilities, activities/programs, governing authority. *Freq:* Biennial, even years. *Price:* $19.95.

3479 ■ National Association of Canadians of Origins in India—Directory
National Association of Canadians of Origins in India (NACOI)
PO Box 2308, Sta. D   Ph: (613)235-7343
Ottawa, ON, Canada K1P 5W5   Fax: (613)567-0655

Contact: B. Gill, Editor.

Desc: Covers: East Indian community organizations in Canada. *Freq:* Quarterly, with annual edition. *Price:* Free.

3480 ■ National Directory of Researchers
Family Tree Genealogical Society
450 Potter St.   Ph: (419)335-6485
Wauseon, OH 43567

Contact: Howard V. Fausey, Editor.

Desc: Covers: persons who do genealogical research primarily in their own city, county, or adjoining county area. Entries include: For individuals—Researcher name, address, type and area of research done. For state genealogical societies—Name, address. *Freq:* Annual, April. *Price:* $12, per year, included in subscription; $15, Canada, per year, included in subscription.

3481 ■ National Register of Historic Places: Cumulative List
John Wiley and Sons, Inc.
605 3rd Ave.   Ph: (212)850-6000
New York, NY 10158   Free: 800-225-5945
                           Fax: (212)850-6049
E-mail: subinfo@wiley.com

Desc: Covers: 62,000 properties (sites, buildings, districts, structures, etc.) of local, state, or national significance in American history, architecture, archeology, or culture; includes registrations through 1994. Entries include: Name and location of property; significant dates; description and statement of significance; ownership; accessibility; and available survey information. Updated by "National Register of Historic Places Annual Listing of Historic Properties," reprints of the Federal Register. *Freq:* Irregular. *Price:* $98.

3482 ■ National Register of Historic Places—1966 to 1993
John Wiley and Sons, Inc.
605 3rd Ave.   Ph: (212)850-6000
New York, NY 10158   Free: 800-225-5945
                           Fax: (212)850-6049

E-mail: subinfo@wiley.com

Desc: Covers: More than 62,000 historically significant places in the United States. Entries include: Name, address, criteria for listing, listing date, listing number. *Price:* $98.

3483 ▪ The National Yellow Book of Funeral Directors

Nomis Publications, Inc.
PO Box 5122   Ph: (330)788-9608
Youngstown, OH 44514   Free: 800-321-7479
                               Fax: (330)788-1112
E-mail: info@yelobk.com; info@yelobk.com
URL: http://www.yelobk.com; http://www.yelobk.com

Contact: Lucille A. McGuire, Editor, Owner and Publisher.

Desc: Covers: 20,000 United States and Canadian funeral homes; Veteran's Administration hospitals and regional offices; major hospitals; foreign consulates and branch offices; daily papers; mortuary colleges. Entries include: Name of home, address, phone, code for shipping points, city code for daily papers available for obituaries. *Alt. Fmts:* cheshire labels; computer printout; pressure-sensitive labels. *Freq:* Annual, November. *Price:* $75, standard edition; $50, pocket edition.

3484 ▪ Nebraska Local History and Genealogy Reference Guide

Sylvia Nimmo, Publisher
6201 Kentucky Rd.   Ph: (402)331-2384
Papillion, NE 68133

Contact: Sylvia Nimmo, Editor; Mary Cutter, Editor.

Desc: Publication includes: Lists of about 450 genealogical archives and societies, libraries, and museums for genealogists in Nebraska. Entries include: Name, address or location. Principal content includes citations to vital records, directories, historical publications, and other sources useful to Nebraska genealogists. *Freq:* Published December 1986. *Price:* $35, postpaid.

3485 ▪ Newsletter—Society for Historical Archaeology Membership Directory Issue

Society for Historical Archaeology
PO Box 30446   Ph: (520)886-8006
Tucson, AZ 85751-0446   Fax: (520)886-0182
E-mail: sha@azstarnet.com

Contact: Norman F. Barka, Editor.

Desc: Publication includes: List of about 2,100 member archaeologists, historians, anthropologists, and ethnohistorians, and other individuals and institutions having an interest in historical archeology or allied fields. Entries include: Name, address. *Alt. Fmts:* mailing labels. *Freq:* Annual, June. *Price:* Available to members only.

3486 ▪ North American Indian Landmarks—A Traveler's Guide

Gale Group Inc.
27500 Drake Rd.   Ph: (248)699-4253
Farmington Hills, MI   Free: 800-877-GALE
  48331-3535   Fax: (248)699-8070
E-mail: galeord@galegroup.com
URL: http://www.galegroup.com

Contact: George Cantor, Editor.

Desc: Covers: Approximately 340 sites in the U.S. and Canada significant to Native North American history, including historical, tribal, and art museums, monuments, plaques, parks, reservations, birthplaces, grave sites, battlefields. Entries include: Site name, description, location, days and hours of operation, admission fee, phone. Paper-

back edition published by Visible Ink Press, an imprint of Gale Research. *Freq:* Published 1993. *Price:* $34.95, cloth; $17.95, paper.

3487 ▪ Ohio Genealogical Guide

Carol Willsey Bell, C.G.
10460 N. Palmyra Rd.   Ph: (330)538-2046
North Jackson, OH 44451-9793

Contact: Carol Willsey Bell, Editor.

Desc: Covers: location, content, etc., of land, tax, census, church, military, and other records in Ohio; includes lists of libraries, periodicals, etc. Entries include: Name of source, address, description of holdings. *Freq:* Irregular, latest edition 1995 (6th edition). *Price:* $16.75, postpaid.

3488 ▪ Oral History Index: An International Directory of Oral History Interviews

Meckler Publishing
20 Ketchum St   Ph: (203)226-6967
Westport, CT 06880   Free: 800-632-5597
                               Fax: (203)454-5840
E-mail: info@mecklermedia.com

Desc: Covers: 30,000 transcripts of oral history interviews held at 400 organizations and institutions in the U.S., Canada, Great Britain, and Israel. Entries include: Interviewee name, date, subject, code indicating holding institution. A separate listing gives institution's address, phone, and contact name. *Freq:* First edition 1990. *Price:* $145.

3489 ▪ The Order of Americans of Armorial Ancestry—Lineage of Members

Order of Americans of Armorial Ancestry
c/o Mrs. George William
Hallgren,   Sr.,   President
General
PO Box 453
Abingdon, MD 21009-0453
E-mail: ahallgren@yahoo.com

Contact: Arthur Louis Finnell, Editor, Compiler.

Desc: Covers: Americans descended from an immigrant ancestor in colonial America whose forebears in Great Britain or continental Europe had the right to bear arms. Entries include: Name and address of member, and ancestor *Freq:* Irregular, previous edition 1995; latest edition 1997. *Price:* $26.50.

3490 ▪ Peace Archives: A Guide to Library Collections

World Without War Council
1730 Martin Luther King,   Ph: (510)845-1992
  Jr. Way   Fax: (510)845-5721
Berkeley, CA 94709
E-mail: wwwc@wwwc.com

Contact: Marguerite Green, Editor, Former Director, Historian Project.

Desc: Covers: about 30 libraries and archives with paper and manuscript collections of organizations and individuals active in the public effort for peace; about 70 individual collections located in other libraries or archives. Entries include: For libraries—Name, address, phone, director name, description of collection and services. For individual collections—Personal name, library or archive name, location, type of collection, years covered, biographical data. *Price:* $7.

3491 ▪ Pelican Guide to Historic Homes and Sites of Revolutionary America—Volume 1: New England

Pelican Publishing Co.
1101 Monroe St.   Ph: (504)368-1175
PO Box 3110   Free: 800-843-1724
Gretna, LA 70054   Fax: (504)368-1195

E-mail: sales@pelicanpub.com
URL: http://www.pelicanpub.com/

Contact: Adelaide Hechtlinger, Editor.

Desc: Publication includes: Directory of 500 historic locations in Revolutionary New England. Entries include: Home or site name, address. *Freq:* Irregular, latest edition 1976. *Price:* $7.95.

3492 ▪ Pelican Guide to Old Homes of Mississippi

Pelican Publishing Co.
1101 Monroe St.   Ph: (504)368-1175
PO Box 3110   Free: 800-843-1724
Gretna, LA 70054   Fax: (504)368-1195
E-mail: sales@pelicanpub.com
URL: http://www.pelicanpub.com/

Contact: Helen Kerr Kempe, Editor.

Desc: Covers: about 500 architecturally and historically significant houses in Mississippi. Volume one covers Natchez and the southern part of the state; volume two features Columbus and the northern half. Entries include: Name of house, address, brief history, hours open, and admission fees. *Freq:* Volume 1 published 1977; volume 2 published 1984. *Price:* $9.95, plus $1.75 shipping, per volume.

3493 ▪ Pelican Guide to Plantation Homes of Louisiana

Pelican Publishing Co.
1101 Monroe St.   Ph: (504)368-1175
PO Box 3110   Free: 800-843-1724
Gretna, LA 70054   Fax: (504)368-1195
E-mail: sales@pelicanpub.com
URL: http://www.pelicanpub.com/

Contact: Susan Cole Dore, Editor.

Desc: Covers: 240 architecturally and historically significant homes, many of them dating from the early nineteenth century, including private residences as well as houses open to the public. Entries include: Name of home, address, brief history, hours open, admission fees. *Freq:* Irregular, previous edition January 1984; latest edition December 1988. *Price:* $7.95, plus $1.75 shipping.

3494 ▪ Polish Family Tree Surnames

Thaddeus J. Obal
739 Hillsdale Ave.   Ph: (201)664-7836
Hillsdale, NJ 07642-2515

Contact: Thaddeus J. Obal, Editor.

Desc: Covers: more than 1,830 persons doing genealogical research on surnames of Polish ancestry. Entries include: Surname of researchers, address, names in which interested. *Freq:* Biennial, odd years. *Price:* $10.

3495 ▪ Records of Genealogical Value for

Family History Library
Family History Department   Ph: (801)240-2331
35 North West Temple   Free: 800-453-3860
Salt Lake City, UT 84150-3400 Fax: (801)240-5551
E-mail: fhl@ldschurch.org

Desc: Description: The Family History Library is "the world's leading genealogical research library, with over 280,000 volumes, 2,000,000 rolls of microfilm, and 700,000 microfiche that can be loaned to over 3,400 Family History Centers." The library publishes a series of 8-50 page research outlines for numerous countries, provinces, and states. Each research outline describes the types of records available, time period these records cover, contents of the records, and how to obtain them. Outlines emphasize records available at the Family History Library, and include addresses and descriptions of records at other archives and repositories. The outlines sell for $.50 to

$1.00 and are available from the library and at the family history centers. *Alt. Fmts:* CD-ROM; diskette. *Freq:* Irregular.

3496 ■ Research Guide to Libraries and Archives in the Low Countries
Greenwood Publishing Group, Inc.
88 Post Rd. W.   Ph: (203)226-3571
PO Box 5007   Free: 800-225-5800
Westport, CT 06881-5007   Fax: (203)226-6009
E-mail: prices@greenwood.com
URL: http://www.greenwood.com

Contact: Martha L. Brogan, Editor.

Desc: Covers: libraries and archives in Belgium, the Netherlands, and Luxembourg. Entries include: Name, address, phone, history, present holdings, days and hours of operation, publications. *Freq:* Published 1991. *Price:* $99.50.

3497 ■ Researching Arkansas History
Rose Publishing Co., Inc.
2723 Foxcroft Rd., Ste. 208   Ph: (501)227-8104
Little Rock, AR 72227   Fax: (501)224-4442

Contact: Tom W. Dillard, Editor; Valeria Thwing, Editor.

Desc: Publication includes: List of archives, libraries, government offices, and other repositories which hold materials significant in the study of Arkansas history and genealogy; includes sources for Black history and genealogy. Entries include: Institution or department name, address. *Freq:* Published 1979. *Price:* $5, postpaid.

3498 ■ Revolutionary War Genealogy
George K. Schweitzer
407 Ascot   Ph: (615)690-7831
Knoxville, TN 37923

Contact: Dr. George K. Schweitzer, Editor.

Desc: Publication includes: Lists of state archives, libraries, museums, veterans and other organizations, and other sources of information on persons who served in the Revolutionary War. Entries include: Name, address; some entries include kind and scope of records, etc. *Freq:* Annual. *Price:* $12, payment must accompany order.

3499 ■ St. Louis Connections—Free or Inexpensive Research Aids
St. Louis Genealogical Society
4 Sunnen Dr., Ste. 140   Ph: (314)647-8547
St. Louis, MO 63143   Fax: (314)647-8548
E-mail: stlgsmail@primary.net
URL: http://www.rootsweb.com/mostlogs/stindex.htm

Desc: Covers: sources of free or low cost genealogical research publications; patriotic organizations; emphasis on the midwestern U.S. Entries include: Organization or publisher name, address; publication listings. *Freq:* Annual, June. *Price:* $7.50, plus postage.

3500 ■ Scotch-Irish Family Research Made Simple
Ye Olde Genealogie Shoppe
PO Box 39128   Ph: (317)862-3330
Indianapolis, IN 46239   Free: 800-419-0200
                                  Fax: (317)862-2599

Contact: R. G. Campbell, Editor.

Desc: Publication includes: List of government offices, archives, etc., in Scotland and Northern Ireland which are of value to the genealogist. *Freq:* Irregular, previous edition 1992; latest edition 1998. *Price:* $10, plus $4.00 shipping.

3501 ■ Society of American Archivists Directory of Individual and Institutional Members
Society of American Archivists
527 S. Wells St., 5th Fl.   Ph: (312)922-0140
Chicago, IL 60617 3922   Fax: (312)347-1452
E-mail: info@archivists.org

Contact: Teresa M. Brinati, Editor, Dir. of Publications.

Desc: Covers: 4,600 individual and institutional members concerned with management and custody of current and historical records, and with archival administration. Entries include: Member name, company or institution where member works, address, phone, fax, computer network names and identification. *Alt. Fmts:* mailing labels. *Freq:* Biennial, latest edition 1998-99. *Price:* $50, plus $5.00 shipping.

3502 ■ Society for Historians of American Foreign Relations—Roster and Current Research Projects
Society for Historians of American Foreign Relations
c/o David L. Anderson   Ph: (317)788-3264
Department of History   Fax: (317)788-3569
University of Indianapolis
Indianapolis, IN 46227
URL: http://www.ohiou.edu/shafr/shafr.htm

Contact: David L. Anderson, Editor.

Desc: Covers: about 1,800 members and 1,400 research projects. Entries include: For members—Name, mailing address, institutional affiliations, codes indicating major research interest and where projects can be located in research inventory. *Freq:* Biennial, fall of even years. *Price:* Available to members only.

3503 ■ The Source: A Guidebook of American Genealogy
Ancestry, Inc.
PO Box 990   Ph: (801)426-3500
Orem, UT 84057   Free: 800-262-3787
                                  Fax: (801)426-3501
E-mail: support@ancestry-inc.com
URL: http://www.ancestry.com

Contact: Loretto Dennis Szucs, Editor; Sandra Hargreaves Luebking, Editor.

Desc: Publication includes: Lists of federal archives, record centers, state archives, and historical societies, research libraries, heraldry and lineage societies, genealogy publications and publishers, sources of business records, and fraternal organizations. Entries include: Name of the genealogical source, location, contents of the record, means of access, use in research or family history. Main content of the publication is discussion of records useful for research in American genealogy, including Native Americans, Jewish Americans, and African Americans. *Alt. Fmts:* CD-ROM. *Freq:* Irregular, latest edition 1997. *Price:* $49.95, plus $5.50 shipping.

3504 ■ SPNEA Guide
Society for the Preservation of New England Antiquities (SPNEA)
141 Cambridge St.   Ph: (617)227-3956
Boston, MA 02114
URL: http://www.spnea.org

Contact: Nancy Curtis, Editor, Publications Manager.

Desc: Covers: about 35 historic house museums in five New England states. Entries include: Museum name, address, phone, driving directions, hours and days opened, admission cost, photograph, description of museum. *Freq:* Annual, May. *Price:* Free.

3505 ■ State Data Center Program—State Coordinating Organizations Address List
U.S. Bureau of the Census
Customer Services   Ph: (301)457-1171
Washington, DC 20233   Fax: (301)457-4707
URL: http://www.census.gov/sdc/www/

Desc: Covers: over 215 state government agencies, universities, and state libraries that hold Census Bureau reports, maps, and documents and provide reference, training, and consulting services to census data users. Entries include: Agency, university, or library name, address, phone, name of contact. *Freq:* Irregular, latest edition June 1997. *Price:* Free.

3506 ■ Susan B. Anthony Slept Here: A Guide to American Women's Landmarks
Times Books
201 E. 50th St.   Ph: (212)751-2600
New York, NY 10022   Free: 800-726-0600
                                  Fax: (212)572-8797

Desc: Covers: Over 2,000 sites significant to American women's history. Entries include: Site name, address, description. *Freq:* Irregular, previous edition 1976; latest edition 1994. *Price:* $18.

3507 ■ Tracing Your Ancestors in Canada
National Archives of Canada
395 Wellington St.   Ph: (613)996-7458
Ottawa, ON, Canada K1A 0N3   Fax: (613)995-6274
URL: http://www.archives.ca

Contact: Lorraine St. Louis Harrison, Editor; Mary Munk, Editor.

Desc: Publication includes: Provincial and federal offices and archives where records of births, deaths, marriages, and immigration, land titles, and estate documents may be obtained; also includes principal archives of each province. Entries include: Office name, address; archives listings include phone. *Freq:* Irregular, previous edition 1993; latest edition 1997. *Price:* Free.

3508 ■ U.S. Census Bureau—Telephone Contacts for Data Users
U.S. Census Bureau
Public Information Office
Rm: 2705-FB-3   Ph: (301)457-2822
Washington, DC 20233   Fax: (301)457-3670

Contact: Mary G. Thomas, Editor.

Desc: Covers: key personnel of the Bureau of the Census and State Data Centers. Entries include: Function/subject expertise, name, office name, phone. 1991 and 1993 editions were published in their respective March issues of "Census and You." *Freq:* Biennial, odd years. *Price:* Free.

3509 ■ Vermont: A Guide to Its Historic Sites
Vermont Division for Historic Preservation
National Life Bldg.   Ph: (802)828-3051
Montpelier, VT 05620-0501   Fax: (802)828-3206
URL: http://www.state.vt.us/dca/historic/hp-sites.htm

Contact: John P. Dumville, Editor.

Desc: Covers: 14 state-owned historical buildings and sites in Vermont that are open to the public. Entries include: Site name, location, and description. *Freq:* Irregular, latest edition 1999. *Price:* Free.

3510 ■ Virginia Landmarks of Black History
University Press of Virginia
Box 3608, University Sta.   Ph: (804)924-6064
Charlottesville, VA 22903-0608   Free: 800-831-3406
                                  Fax: (804)982-2655
E-mail: upressva@virginia.edu

Contact: Calder Loth, Editor.

Desc: Covers: 64 sites in Virginia with African American historical significance. Entries include: Name, location, historical significance. *Price:* $18.95, paper; $40, cloth.

3511 ■ Visiting the Midwest's Historic Preservation Sites
Jameson Books, Inc.
722 Columbus St.　　　　　Ph: (815)434-7905
Ottawa, IL 61350　　　　　Free: 800-426-1357
　　　　　　　　　　　　　Fax: (815)434-7907
E-mail: 72557.3635@compuserve.com

Contact: Marjory Grannis, Editor; Uri Grannis, Editor; Rosemary Hale, Editor; George Hale, Editor.

Freq: Irregular. *Price:* $14.95.

3512 ■ Where to Write for Vital Records: Births, Deaths, Marriages and Divorces
National Center for Health Statistics
6525 Belcrest Rd., No. 1064　　Ph: (301)436-8500
Hyattsville, MD 20782-2003
URL: http://www.cdc.gov/nchsww; http://
　　www.cdc.gov/nchswww

Contact: Elizabeth Wadda, Editor, Public Affairs Specialist.

Desc: Covers: vital statistics offices in each state. Entries include: Name and address of office, cost of full copy, cost of short form, any special requirements, dates of records held. *Alt. Fmts:* CD-ROM. *Freq:* Irregular, previous edition April 1991; latest edition 1993. *Price:* $2.25.

3513 ■ Women Remembered: A Guide to Landmarks of Women's History
Greenwood Publishing Group, Inc.
88 Post Rd. W.　　　　　Ph: (203)226-3571
PO Box 5007　　　　　Free: 800-225-5800
Westport, CT 06881-5007　Fax: (203)226-6009
E-mail: prices@greenwood.com
URL: http://www.greenwood.com

Contact: Marion Tinling, Editor.

Desc: Covers: over 2,000 historic sites, monuments, statues, and other historical markers documenting the role of women in American history. Basis of selection for the directory includes one of the following: the women made significant contributions to society (as determined by the editors), performed a documented heroic act, or were documented participants in a historic event. In addition, sites must be open to the public; markers for only local significance are omitted. Does not include sites for living women, spouses or daughters of commemorated men, sites closed to the public, or gravesites. Entries include: Name of site or marker, name of woman commemorated, location, type of landmark, hours open, description of historical event. *Freq:* Published 1986. *Price:* $89.50.

Newsletters

3514 ■ AAFA Action
The Alford American Family Association (AAFA)
PO Box 1586　　　　　Ph: (314)831-8648
Florissant, MO 63031-1586
E-mail: 72154.1610@compuserve.com

Contact: Pamela Alford Thompson, Editor.

Desc: Records, preserves, and disseminates biographical and historical information on the Alford family, including spellings and variations—Allford, Alvord, Alfred, etc. Recurring features include news of research, reports of meetings, obituaries, Alford sports, business, queries, and census reports. *Freq:* Quarterly. *Price:* Included in membership.

3515 ■ The Abbey Newsletter
Abbey Publications, Inc.
7105 Geneva Dr.　　　　Ph: (512)929-3992
Austin, TX 78723-1510　　Fax: (512)929-3995
E-mail: abbeypub@flash.net
URL: http://www.palimpsest.stanford.edu/byorg/
　　abbey/; http://www.palimpsest.stanford.edu/byorg/
　　abbey

Contact: Ellen R. McCrady, Editor.

Desc: Encourages the development of library and archival conservation, particularly technical advances and cross-disciplinary research in the field. Covers book repair and the conservation of books, papers, photographs, and non-paper materials. Recurring features include book reviews, news of research, job listings, convention reports, a calendar of events, and an occasional column about equipment and supplies. *Freq:* 8/year. *Price:* $45/year for individual; $55/year for institution.

3516 ■ ACA Bulletin
Association of Canadian Archivists (ACA)
Box 2596, Sta. D　　　　Ph: (613)445-4564
Ottawa, ON, Canada K1P 5W6　Free: 888-445-4565
　　　　　　　　　　　　　Fax: (613)445-4563
E-mail: aca@magmacom.com

Contact: John Macleod, Editor.

Desc: Functions as a forum for all persons who are engaged in the discipline and practice of archival science. Publishes brief articles on archives and activities of archivists and the Association. Recurring features include news of research, a calendar of events, notices of publications available, job listings, meeting reports, and notices of educational opportunities available. *Freq:* 6/year. *Price:* Included in membership.

3517 ■ Acadian Genealogy Exchange
Janet B. Jehn
863 Wayman Branch Rd.　　Ph: (606)356-9825
Covington, KY 41015　　　Fax: (606)356-9825

Contact: Janet B. Jehn, Editor.

Desc: Devoted to the Acadians, French Canadian families sent into exile in 1755. Carries family genealogies, historical notes, cemetery lists, census records, and church and civil registers. Recurring features include inquiries and answers, book reviews, and news of research. *Freq:* Semiannual. *Price:* $17.

3518 ■ ACDA Bulletin
Association of Catholic Diocesan Archivists (ACDA)
711 W. Monroe St.　　　　Ph: (773)736-5150
Chicago, IL 60661-3515

Contact: Christine Taylor, Editor.

Desc: Recurring features include reports of meetings, news of educational opportunities, job listings, book reviews, and notices of publications available. *Freq:* 3/year. *Price:* Included in membership.

3519 ■ Acorns to Oaks
Oakland County Genealogical Society
Box 1094
Birmingham, MI 48012-1094

Contact: Pamela Epple, Editor.

Desc: Publishes public and private genealogical records, primarily relating to Oakland County, Michigan. Recurring features include news of research, a calendar of events, reports of meetings, news of educational opportunities, book reviews, notices of publications available, and columns titled Michigan Genealogical Council News, Begin-

ner's Tip, 100 Years Ago in Oakland County. *Freq:* Quarterly. *Price:* Included in membership; $15, individuals; $16, Canada; $18, elsewhere.

3520 ■ Adams Addenda-II
Adams Addenda Association
218 Kickapoo Forest　　　Ph: (815)756-5760
Onalaska, TX 77360
E-mail: adad@syslink.mcs.com

Contact: Robert Adams Gaebler, Pub. and Man. Ed.

Desc: Provides information for people researching the Adams family. Recurring features include feature articles, Bible and public records, family group sheets, the James Taylor Adams collection, and a section about using the internet for genealogical research. *Freq:* Semiannual, as needed. *Price:* $18, Included in membership.

3521 ■ Adams County Trumpeter
Adams County, Indiana, Historical Society
Box 262　　　　　　　　Ph: (219)724-3482
Decatur, IN 46733

Contact: Dianne Linn, Editor.

Desc: Contains information on the Society's activities. *Freq:* Quarterly. *Price:* Included in membership.

3522 ■ The Adams Family Chronicle
Adams Family Association, Inc.
946 Morgan Ave.　　　　Ph: (904)663-4507
Chattahoochee, FL 32324

Contact: Lowell F. Adams, Editor.

Desc: Provides members of the Association with historical and genealogical information as well as news of the family. Recurring features include news of research, a calendar of events, reports of meetings, book reviews, and notices of publications available. *Freq:* Quarterly. *Price:* Included in membership.

3523 ■ African America News
Charles H. Wright Museum of African American History
315 Warren Ave.　　　　Ph: (313)494-5800
Detroit, MI 48201-1443　　Fax: (313)494-5855

Contact: Carla Glamo, Editor.

Desc: Describes and carries interpretive articles on the Museum's exhibits and acquisitions. Recurring features include listings of workshops, seminars, and lecture series conducted by the Museum. *Freq:* Quarterly. *Price:* Included in membership.

3524 ■ AGS Quarterly
Association for Gravestone Studies
278 Main St., Ste. 207　　Ph: (413)772-0836
Greenfield, MA 01301-3230
E-mail: ags@javanet.com
URL: http://www.berkshire.net/ags

Contact: Rosalee Oakley, Editor.

Desc: Concerned with the study and preservation of national and international gravestones: folk art carvings, lettering, epitaphs, shapes, materials used, and symbolism. Recurring features include articles on conservation procedures, Association news, book reviews, news of research, and regional news. *Freq:* Quarterly. *Price:* Included in membership.

3525 ■ Alabama Archivist
University of South Alabama Archives
USA Springhill, Rm. 0722　Ph: (334)434-3800
Mobile, AL 36688　　　　Fax: (334)434-3622

Contact: Elisa Baldwin, Editor.

Desc: Provides news of archival activities in Alabama, covering archival repositories and significant historical collections, special work by archivists, legislative matters relating to historical records, and general information concerning the archival profession and standards. Recurring features include Society reports, news of research, and a calendar of events. *Freq:* Semiannual. *Price:* Included in membership; $10/year for nonmembers.

3526 ■ Alberta History
Alberta History
PO Box 4035, Sta. C   Ph: (403)261-3662
Calgary, AB, Canada T2T 5M9 Fax: (403)269-6029

Contact: Hugh A. Dempsey, Editor.

Desc: Features historical information about Alberta. *Alt. Fmts:* microform. *Freq:* Quarterly. *Price:* C$25, individuals.

3527 ■ ALCTS Network News
Association for Library Collections and Technical Services (ALCTS)
50 E. Huron St.   Ph: (312)944-6780
Chicago, IL 60611   Free: 800-545-2433
                         Fax: (312)280-5033
E-mail: alcts@ala.org

Contact: Karen Muller, Editor.

Desc: Contains advance copy of articles and features that will appear later in the print publication ALCTS Newsletter (see separate listing). Features current legislative news, news from the library technical services and publishing world, and ALCTS candidates for office and election results, as well as conference schedules (including meeting room locations) and reports shortly after the conference of major actions and events. *Available:* Online. *Freq:* Irregular.

3528 ■ Allen County/Fort Wayne Historical Society—Bulletin
Allen County/Fort Wayne Historical Society
302 E. Berry St.   Ph: (219)426-2882
Fort Wayne, IN 46802   Fax: (219)424-4419

Contact: Linda Miller, Editor.

Desc: Provides Historical Society members with news of coming events, exhibitions, and lectures. Features information on the permanent archives and historical texts collection of the Old City Hall Historical Museum. Recurring features include news of research, reports of meetings, and a calendar of events. *Freq:* Quarterly. *Price:* Included in membership.

3529 ■ Allen Family Circle
Allen Family Circle
4906 Ridgeway   Ph: (816)353-4976
Kansas City, MO 64133-2545

Contact: Lois T. Allen, Editor.

Desc: Contains genealogical information on the Allen surname. Recurring features include news of research, notices of publications available, and queries. *Freq:* Annual. *Price:* $2.50.

3530 ■ American-Canadian Genealogist
American-Canadian Genealogical Society
PO Box 6478   Ph: (603)622-1554
Manchester, NH 03108-6478 Fax: (603)626-9812

Contact: Anne-Marie Perrault, Editor.

Desc: Genealogies of French Canadians and Franco Americans. Contains queries, genealogies, and family histories. Recurring features include book reviews, news of research, statistics, and family associations. *Freq:* Quarterly. *Price:* Included in membership.

3531 ■ American Veterans Committee Bulletin
American Veterans Committee, Inc.
6309 Bannockburn Dr.   Ph: (301)320-6490
Bethesda, MD 20817   Fax: (301)320-6490

Contact: Gus Tyler, Chrm.; June Willenz, Exec.Dir.

Desc: Newsletter of the American Veterans Committee. Includes membership activities and information and news of interest to American veterans.

3532 ■ AMIA Newsletter
Association of Moving Image Archivists (AMIA)
8949 Wilshire Blvd.   Ph: (310)550-1300
Beverly Hills, CA 90211 Fax: (310)550-1363
E-mail: amia@ix.netcom.com; glukow@pacbell.net

Contact: Sally Hubbard.

Desc: Presents information on the preservation of film and video materials, and the moving image archival profession. REC news of research, a calendar of events, reports of meetings, job listings, book reviews, and notices of publications available. *Freq:* Quarterly. *Price:* Included in membership; $35/year for students and libraries.

3533 ■ Among the Coles
Coles County, Illinois, Genealogical Society
PO Box 592
Charleston, IL 61920-0592

Contact: Max Sweeney, Editor.

Desc: Provides news for families tracing their family histories in Coles County, Illinois. *Freq:* Bimonthly. *Price:* Included in membership.

3534 ■ An Drochaid
Clans & Scottish Societies of Canada
c/o St. Andrews Church   Ph: (416)593-0518
73 Simcoe St.
Toronto, ON, Canada M5J 1W9

Contact: Alene M. McNeill.

Desc: Serves as a means of communication among various clans and Scottish societies in Canada. Contains reports from member societies and news items of Scottish or Celtic interest. Recurring features include a calendar of events. *Freq:* 5/year. *Price:* C$12, Canada, year; C$15, U.S.

3535 ■ Ancestor Hunt
Ashtabula County Genealogical Society, OGS No. 83
860 Sherman St.   Ph: (216)466-4521
c/o Geneva Library
Geneva, OH 44041
E-mail: acgs@interlaced.net

Contact: Marlon (Mayes) Holmes, Editor.

Desc: Focuses on historical and genealogical information on individuals who lived in Astabula County, Ohio. Tracks queries, research articles, and reviews. Recurring features include news of research, a calendar of events, reports of meetings, notices of publications available, and columns titled Observation from the President, ACGS in Review, and Lost Lambs, plus computerized genealogy and support group information. *Alt. Fmts:* microfiche. *Freq:* Quarterly. *Price:* Included in membership.

3536 ■ Ancestor Update
Genealogical Society of Henry and Clayton Counties, Inc.
PO Box 1296   Ph: (770)954-1301
McDonough, GA 30253

Contact: William H. Tanksley, Jr., Editor.

Desc: Covers the genealogy and history of Georgia's Henry and Clayton Counties. Recurring features include news of research, a calendar of events, reports of meetings, news of educational opportunities, notices of publications available, book reviews, and queries on family and area history. Remarks: Incorporates the former Henry County, Georgia Update, and Ancestors Unlimited. *Freq:* Quarterly. *Price:* Included in membership.

3537 ■ Ancestry Trails
Trumbull County Chapter Ohio Genealogical Society
PO Box 309   Ph: (330)889-2249
Warren, OH 44482-0309

Contact: Barbara Layfield, Editor; Mitzie Fenstermaker, Editor.

Desc: Provides chapter news and articles concerning genealogical research. Recurring features include letters to the editor, news of research, a calendar of events, reports of meetings, book reviews, notices of publications available, queries, and news of new members and families being researched. *Freq:* Monthly. *Price:* $10/year.

3538 ■ ANERA Newsletter
American Near East Refugee Aid (ANERA)
1522 K St. NW, Ste. 202 Ph: (202)347-2558
Washington, DC 20005   Fax: (202)682-1637
E-mail: gubser@access.digex.net

Contact: Doris Warrell, Editor.

Desc: Provides information on economic, cultural, and social aspects of the Middle East, as well as reports on the organization's development and relief projects in the area. *Freq:* Quarterly. *Price:* Free.

3539 ■ ANLA Newsletter
Association Newfoundland & Labrador Archives (ANLA)
Colonial Bldg., Military Rd. Ph: (709)726-2869
St. Johns, NF, Canada A1C 2C9 Fax: (709)729-0578

Contact: Joe Le Clair, Editor.

Desc: Concerned with the activities of archives and archivists in the province and generally. Recurring features include calendar of events, reports of meetings, book reviews, notices of publications available, and column titled Preservation Pickles. *Freq:* Quarterly. *Price:* C$15, individuals, Canada; C$30, institutions, Canada.

3540 ■ APG Quarterly
Association of Professional Genealogists (APG)
PO Box 40393
Denver, CO 80204-0393
E-mail: apg-admin@genealogy.org

Contact: Elizabeth Kelley Kerstens, Editor.

Desc: Provides professional genealogists with information on bibliography, business management, marketing, records preservation, genealogical research, and teaching family history. Features includes Association news, book reviews, news of research, and columns titled Question of the Quarter, Profile of a Professional, Small Business Squibes, and Internet News. *Freq:* Quarterly. *Price:* Included in membership; $35, U.S.; $40, Canada; $55, elsewhere.

3541 ■ Appler Family Newsletter
Charles R. Appler
10417 New Bedford Ct. SE Ph: (941)368-6373
Lehigh Acres, FL 33936-7253

Contact: Charles R. Appler, Editor.

Desc: Reports on genealogical research concerning the Appler family. Notes achievements of Appler descendants as well as births, deaths, and marriages. Recurring features include reports of meetings and an Open Letter to All Appler Cousins. Alternate address from May 31 to October 31: PO Box 1897, Hillsboro, NH 03244-1897; phone (603)478-3357. *Freq:* 4/year. *Price:* $7.

3542 ▪ Archibald Clan Newsletter
Clan Archibald Family Association
302 S. Wilson
Hillsboro, KS 67063

Contact: Peggy Goertzen, Editor.

Desc: Concerned with preserving Archibald family history, facilitating the exchange of information about the family, and locating family members. Recurring features include news of members, news of research, letters to the editor, book reviews, and a calendar of events. *Freq:* Quarterly. *Price:* $10/year, U.S. and Canada; $15 elsewhere.

3543 ▪ Archival Outlook
Society of American Archivists
527 S. Wells St., 5th Fl.   Ph: (312)922-0140
Chicago, IL 60617-3922   Fax: (312)347-1452
E-mail: info@archivists.org

Contact: Teresa Brinati, Editor.

Desc: Publishes news of relevance to the professional archival community. Recurring features include a calendar of events, quick tips feature, news from constituent groups, news of educational opportunities, and job listings. *Freq:* Bimonthly. *Price:* Included in membership.

3544 ▪ Archives Society of Alberta Newsletter
Archives Society of Alberta (ASA)
PO Box 21080   Ph: (403)228-0827
Dominion Postal Outlet   Fax: (403)244-5173
Calgary, AB, Canada T2P 4H5
URL: http://www.glenbow.org/asa/newslet/
    welcome.htm

Contact: Jim Bowman, Editor.

Desc: Designed to serve the interests of the professional archival community in Alberta by publishing news of the profession and the Society's activities. Provides a forum for member discussion and debate. Recurring features include a and calendar of events, reports of meetings. *Freq:* Quarterly. *Price:* Included in membership.

3545 ▪ Arenac County Historical Society Newsletter
Arenac County Historical Society
PO Box 272   Ph: (517)876-6399
Au Gres, MI 48703

Desc: Recurring features include a calendar of events. *Price:* Included in membership.

3546 ▪ Arkansas Family Historian
Arkansas Genealogical Society, Inc.
1411 Shady Grove Rd.   Ph: (501)262-4513
PO Box 908   Fax: (501)262-4513
Hot Springs, AR 71902-0908
URL: http://www.rootsweb.com/args

Contact: Margaret Harrison Hubbard, Editor.

Desc: Offers genealogical information on citizens of Arkansas. Contains primary and secondary source materials and family data. Recurring features include news of research. *Freq:* Quarterly. *Price:* $20, Included in membership.

3547 ▪ The Armiger's News
American College of Heraldry, Inc.
PO Box 710
Cottondale, AL 35453

E-mail: acainfo@acaresourcecenter.org

Contact: David Robert Wooten, Editor.

Desc: Focuses on activities of the College and general news related to heraldry and genealogy. Presents coats of arms borne in the Americas and abroad, and describes the specific individuals, families, and corporate bodies bearing the arms. Recurring features include book reviews and biographies. *Freq:* Quarterly. *Price:* Included in membership; $25/year for nonmembers; $10/year for libraries.

3548 ▪ Army Families
Army Family Liaison Office, Department of the Army
DAIM-ZAF, Rm. 2D665   Ph: (703)695-7714
Washington, DC 20310-0600   Fax: (703)693-2587

Contact: Joe Wasserman, Editor.

Desc: Directed toward army families and provides tips and policy on jobs, benefits, education, finances, and government programs. Recurring features include news of educational opportunities and book reviews. columns titled Guard/Reserve, Money Savers, Health, and News Roundup. *Freq:* Quarterly. *Price:* Free.

3549 ▪ Augustana Historical Society Newsletter
Augustana Historical Society
Augustana College Library   Ph: (309)794-7317
Rock Island, IL 61201
E-mail: alijb@augustana.edu; hicaldwell@augustana.edu

Contact: Judy Belan, Editor; John Caldwell, Editor.

Desc: Presents articles and notes on the history of Augustana College and the Augustana Lutheran Church. Provides news of activities and publications of the Society. *Freq:* Semiannual. *Price:* Free.

3550 ▪ Austins of America
Austins of America Genealogical Society
23 Allen Farm Ln.   Ph: (978)369-8591
Concord, MA 01742-2202
E-mail: anft78a@prodigy.com; AOAGS@alum.mit.edu
URL: http://www.aoags.org

Contact: Dr. Michael E. Austin, Editor.

Freq: Semiannual. *Price:* $9; $17, two years.

3551 ▪ Autrey, Autry, Autery Bulletin
Autrey Family Association, AFA-199
17570 Al Hwy. 10   Ph: (205)385-2503
Thomasville, AL 36784

Contact: Robert M. Autry, Editor.

Freq: Quarterly. *Price:* $25.

3552 ▪ The Avery Advocate
Stephanie Lantiere
53 Manila St.   Ph: (860)274-6115
Oakville, CT 06779   Fax: (860)945-3439
E-mail: averyadvoc@aol.com
URL: http://www.members.aol.com/averyadvoc/
    averyweb.htm

Contact: Joseph Lantiere, Editor.

Desc: Directed toward the Avery family, including feature stories about family members, births, and deaths. Recurring features include interviews, news of research, reports of meetings, book reviews, and notices of publications available. *Freq:* Quarterly. *Price:* $10, individuals, and institutions in the U.S.;; $15, individuals, and institutions in Canada.

3553 ▪ Baby House Voices
Windsor's Community Museum
254 Pitt St. West   Ph: (519)253-1812
Windsor, ON, Canada N9A   Fax: (519)253-0919
    5L5
E-mail: wcmchin@mnsi.net

Contact: Janet Cobban, Editor; Hugh Barrett, Coord.

Desc: Provides information on Windsor's Community Museum.

3554 ▪ Band of Botsford Bulletin
Botsford Family Historical Association, Inc.
215 Buckingham Ave.   Ph: (203)878-4444
Milford, CT 06460

Desc: Contains genealogical information on the Botsford surname. Recurring features include letters to the editor, news of research, a calendar of events, reports of meetings, and notices of publications available. *Freq:* 2-4/year. *Price:* Included in membership; $10/year for nonmembers.

3555 ▪ The Barnett Banner
BARNETT BANNER
3025 Princess Ln.   Ph: (972)422-4103
Plano, TX 75074   Free: 800-769-5528
          Fax: (972)578-9437
E-mail: 2034440@mcimail.com

Contact: Dawn Barnett, Editor.

Desc: Covers family histories and news of the Barnett family across the U.S. *Price:* $15, U.S., monthly; $5, single issue.

3556 ▪ Barney Family News
Barney Family Historical Association
7503 Ridgebrook Dr.   Ph: (703)451-3916
Springfield, VA 22153-1931   Fax: (703)451-2814
E-mail: bfha@aol.com

Contact: William C. Barney, Editor.

Desc: Features genealogical information and family history of the surname Barney. Recurring features include letters to the editor, news of research, reports of meetings, and notices of publications available. *Freq:* Quarterly. *Price:* $10.

3557 ▪ Barthmes Family Newsletter
Barthmes Family Association, Inc.
6460 N. Richardson Rd.   Ph: (812)339-2763
Unionville, IN 47468-9704

Contact: Mita W. Glass, Editor.

Desc: Provides genealogical information and history on the Barthmes family. *Freq:* Quarterly. *Price:* $7, family.

3558 ▪ Bell Chimes
Clan Bell Descendants
79 Elm Hill St.   Ph: (802)885-3151
Springfield, VT 05156-2420

Contact: Irving Bell, Editor.

Desc: Features information on the descendants of the Bell surname, especially descendants of persons born in the United Kingdom and Scotland. Recurring features include letters to the editor, interviews, news of research, reports of meetings, book reviews, and columns titled The Bells Are Ringing, The Bells of St. Andrews, What Bells Are Doing, History of the Border Bells, and Cities That Ring. *Freq:* Bimonthly. *Price:* $25.

3559 ▪ Bennett Exchange Newsletter
Beverly Baumann
17 Breeman St.   Ph: (518)869-5260
Albany, NY 12205-4928

Contact: Beverly Bennett Baumann, Editor.

Desc: Carries family charts, histories, census reports, and various records of genealogical pertinence to the surname Bennett. *Freq:* Quarterly. *Price:* $12, U.S. and Canada, plus 4 .55 stamps; $15, other countries, plus SASE.

3560 ■ Bethel Courier

Bethel Historical Society, Inc.
14 Broad St.   Ph: (207)824-2908
PO Box 12
Bethel, ME 04217
E-mail: history@bdc.bethel.me.us

Contact: Stanley Russell Howe, Ph.D., Editor.

Desc: Contains information on the Bethel Historical Society. Includes historical articles and book reviews. *Freq:* Quarterly. *Price:* Included in membership.

3561 ■ Bits of Our Heritage

Brown County Ohio Historical Society
PO Box 238   Ph: (937)444-3521
Georgetown, OH 45121

Contact: Dorothy Helton, Editor.

Desc: Discusses society news and Brown County, Ohio history. Recurring features include a calendar of events, reports of meetings, and essays from 8th grade students on county history. *Alt. Fmts:* mailing labels. *Freq:* Quarterly. *Price:* Included in membership.

3562 ■ Blue Grass Roots

Kentucky Genealogical Society, Inc.
PO Box 153   Ph: (502)875-4452
Frankfort, KY 40602
E-mail: bdharney2@aol.com
URL: http://members.aol.com/bdharney2

Contact: Landon Wills, Editor; Ilene Wills, Editor.

Desc: Publishes transcriptions, abstractions, and annotations of Kentucky public records of genealogical research value, as well as information on research sources, tips, and techniques. Remarks: Also available in microform. Cumulative index (1973-1984) is available for $15. Original issues (1973-1984) available on a roll of microfilm for $15. *Alt. Fmts:* microform. *Freq:* 4/year. *Price:* Included in membership.

3563 ■ Boone County Genealogical Society Newsletter

Boone County Genealogical Society
PO Box 453
Boone, IA 50036

Contact: Doris Eschliman, Editor.

Desc: Covers history in Iowa, genealogical records (births, marriages, deaths, cemeteries, etc.), membership news, and family charts. Recurring features include news of research, a calendar of events, reports of meetings, news of educational opportunities, and notices of publications available. *Price:* Included in membership.

3564 ■ Boone Genealogical Quarterly

Boone County Genealogical Society
PO Box 306   Ph: (304)369-2769
Madison, WV 25130-0306

Contact: Janet Barket Hager, Editor.

Desc: Provides genealogical information pertinent to Boone County, West Virginia. Includes cemetary listings and Society news. Features notices of publications available, queries, and news of related organizations. *Freq:* Quarterly. *Price:* Included in membership.

3565 ■ Born Young

Young Family Association
347 12th Ave. N.   Ph: (612)455-3626
South St. Paul, MN 55075-1957   Fax: (612)455-2897

Contact: Vicki Young Albu, Editor.

Desc: Focuses on genealogical information on the Young, Jung, and Yonge surnames. Features articles of historical interest and transcripts of revolutionary war pension applications. Recurring features include news of research, book reviews, notices of publications available, and a column titled Free Queries. *Freq:* 4/year. *Price:* $15.

3566 ■ Bourland Bulletin

Bourland Society
Rte. 3, Box 5206   Ph: (417)538-4133
Galena, MO 65656

Contact: Madeline Huff, President.

Desc: Functions as a supplement to the genealogical works "The Bourlands in America" and "The Loving Family in America." Lists births, deaths, and marriages among the ancestors and current members of the Bourland and Loving/Lovan/Lovvorn families. *Freq:* Quarterly. *Price:* $15/year.

3567 ■ Bozarth Beacon

Gayle Rose Mark
3743 S. E St.   Ph: (541)746-9736
Springfield, OR 97478

Contact: Gayle (Rose) Mark, Editor.

Desc: Furnishes information on the Bozarth family, including Bible, census, birth, marriage and death records. Provides human interest stories, news clips, family group records, ancestor charts, obituaries, and queries pertaining to Bozarth surnames. Serves as a national clearinghouse for Bozarth data. Seeks to learn more about Bozarth ancestors and preserve the history and genealogy of the family. Recurring features include book reviews. *Freq:* 4/year. *Price:* $10/year.

3568 ■ Bradford Compact Newsletter

Governor William Bradford Compact
5204 Kenwood Ave.   Ph: (301)654-7233
Chevy Chase, MD 20815-6604

Contact: John Marshall Pogue, M.D., Editor.

Desc: Directed toward the descendants of Governor Bradford. Aims to establish a record of the accomplishments of his descendants. Also contains information on events, members, and projects. Recurring features include a calendar of events, reports of meetings, essays, book reviews, and notices of publications available. *Freq:* Annual. *Price:* Included in membership.

3569 ■ Branching Out from St. Clair County Illinois

Marissa Historical & Genealogical Society
PO Box 47   Ph: (618)295-2562
Marissa, IL 62257-0047

Contact: Eloise Triefenbach, Editor; Elda Jones, Editor.

Desc: Presents historical and genealogical information, family charts, and cemetery, birth, and marriage records. *Freq:* Quarterly. *Price:* $15/year.

3570 ■ BR(E)ASHE(A)R(S) Family Branches

Arzella Brashear Spear
3110 NE 11th St.   Ph: (817)268-1581
Mineral Wells, TX 76067-4128

Contact: Arzella Brashear Spear, Editor.

Desc: Features genealogical records of the Brashear surname and its variations. Recurring features include letters to the editor and news of research. *Freq:* Monthly. *Price:* $20, U.S., Free, sample copy.

3571 ■ A Brief Relation

Friends of Historic St. Mary's City
Box 24   Ph: (301)862-0991
St. Marys City, MD 20686   Fax: (301)862-0968

Contact: Candace T. Matelic, Exec. Dir.; Jeanne Chandler, President; Karin Stanford, Editor; Muffin Padukiewicz, Circulation Mgr.

Desc: Educates on events and history of St. Mary's City, a living history museum. Recurring features include a calendar of events and news of members. *Freq:* Quarterly. *Price:* Included in membership.

3572 ■ British Columbia Genealogist—Quarterly

British Columbia Genealogical Society
PO Box 88054   Ph: (604)325-0374
Richmond, BC, Canada V6X
3T6
URL: http://www.npsnet.com/bcgs; http://www.npsnet.com/bcgs/

Contact: Maureen Hyde; Esther Perry.

Desc: Provides genealogical and historical information. Recurring features include letters to the editor, news of research, reports of meetings, and book reviews. *Freq:* Quarterly. *Price:* $30/year.

3573 ■ Broyles Family Newsletter

John K. Broyles Sr.
302 Woodland Hills Rd.   Ph: (423)457-5866
Clinton, TN 37716-5934
E-mail: jkbroyles@icx.net

Contact: John K. Broyles, Sr., Editor.

Desc: Provides census, marriage, death, and cemetery records on the Broyles family. Recurring features include letters to the editor, news of research, reports of meetings, book reviews, and notices of publications available. *Freq:* Bimonthly. *Price:* $12.50/year, $22/2 years.

3574 ■ Bryan County Heritage—Quarterly

Bryan County Heritage Association
PO Box 153   Ph: (405)434-5848
Calera, OK 74730

Contact: Wanda Shelton, Editor.

Desc: Gives genealogical information on individuals (including Indians) who resided in Bryan County, Oklahoma. *Freq:* Quarterly. *Price:* $15.

3575 ■ Bucks County Genealogical Society Newsletter

Bucks County Genealogical Society
PO Box 1092   Ph: (215)230-9410
Doylestown, PA 18901

Contact: Donna Humphrey, President, part of staff; Audrey Wolfinger, Editor.

Desc: Contains news of Society programs and activities, as well as genealogical information. Recurring features include news of research, a calendar of events, notices of publications available, and queries. *Freq:* 4/year. *Price:* Included in membership; $15, nonmembers.

3576 ■ Buffalo Chips

Fort Kearney Genealogical Society
PO Box 22
Kearney, NE 68848

Contact: Mardi Anderson, Editor.

Desc: Covers records and related information from Buffalo County, NE. *Freq:* Quarterly. *Price:* Included in membership.

3577 ▪ Bunker Banner

Bunker Family Association of America
9 Sommerset Rd.   Ph: (609)589-6140
Turnersville, NJ 08012-2122
E-mail: mary-gene.page@omnibbs.com

Contact: Carole R., Editor; Gil Bunker, Editor.

Desc: Provides genealogical information, stories, and articles by or about the Bunker family. Publicizes events and reunions. Recurring features include news of research, reports of meetings, and documentation of births, deaths, and marriages. *Freq:* 4/year. *Price:* Included in membership.

3578 ▪ Burbank Banner

John R. Burbank
80 East St.
Bristol, VT 05443

Contact: John R. Burbank, Editor.

Desc: Provides information and data on the Burbank/ Burbanck family. Includes news of research, articles on genealogy, family anecdotes, and revisions of the 1928 Genealogy by George Burbank Sedgley. *Freq:* Occasional. *Price:* $6 for 4 issues.

3579 ▪ Burnett Family Newsletter

Burnett Family Genealogical Association
3891 Commander Dr.   Ph: (770)455-6445
Chamblee, GA 30341-0016

Contact: Thomas Robley Burnett, Editor.

Desc: Contains genealogical information on for the Burnett surname. Recurring features include reports of meetings. *Freq:* 4/year. *Price:* Included in membership.

3580 ▪ Bush-Meeting Dutch

Dr. David Koss
Illinois College   Ph: (217)245-3460
Jacksonville, IL 62650

Contact: Dr. David H. Koss, Editor.

Desc: Recurring features include news of research, book reviews, reprinted Civil War letters, early conference records of denominations, and obituaries from church papers. *Freq:* Quarterly. *Price:* $5/year.

3581 ▪ Cahokian

Cahokia Mounds Museum Society
30 Ramey St.   Ph: (618)344-7316
Collinsville, IL 62234   Fax: (618)346-5162

Contact: Chris Pallozola, Editor.

Desc: Covers the activities of the Cahokia Mounds State Historic Site and related archeological topics. Recurring features include interviews, news of research, a calendar of events, reports of meetings, and columns titled Museum Shop and From the Executive Director. *Freq:* Quarterly. *Price:* Included in membership.

3582 ▪ Calhoun County Lines and Links

Calhoun County Historical and Genealogical Society
PO Box 242
Grantsville, WV 26147

Contact: Norma K. Shaffer, Editor.

Desc: Contains genealogical charts and historical articles. Recurring features include reports of meetings and notices of publications available. *Freq:* 3/year. *Price:* Included in membership.

3583 ▪ California Genealogical Society Newsletter

California Genealogical Society
1611 Telegraph Ave., Ste. 200   Ph: (510)663-1358
Oakland, CA 94612-2152   Fax: (510)663-1596
E-mail: calgensoc@aol.com

Desc: Provides information to the genealogy community of the greater San Francisco Bay area and nationwide events. *Freq:* Bimonthly. *Price:* Included in membership.

3584 ▪ Calvert County Maryland Genealogy Newsletter

Calvert County Genealogy Society
c/o Jerry and Mildred   Ph: (410)535-0839
  Bowen O'Brien
PO Box 9
Sunderland, MD 20689

Contact: Jerry O'Brien, Editor; Mildred Bowen O'Brien, Editor.

Desc: Provides information on the early families of Calvert County and the surrounding counties. Endeavors to make difficult data accessible. Recurring features include news of research and notices of publications available. *Freq:* Monthly. *Price:* $15.

3585 ▪ Camden County Historical Society— Bulletin

Camden County Historical Society
Park Blvd. & Euclid Ave.   Ph: (609)964-3333
Camden, NJ 08103

Contact: David C. Munn, Editor.

Desc: Features genealogical information on individuals who lived in Camden County, NJ or subjects related to Camden County History. *Freq:* Annual.

3586 ▪ Canada's Immigration & Citizenship Bulletin

Canada Law Book, Inc.
240 Edward St.   Ph: (905)841-6472
Aurora, ON, Canada L4G 3S9   Free: 800-263-3269
                                Fax: (905)841-5085
E-mail: webmaster@canadalawbook.ca
URL: http://www.canadalawbook.ca

Contact: Frank N. Marrocco, Editor; Henry M. Goslett, Editor; Gary W. Moore, Editor.

Desc: Addresses topics in immigration and citizenship law and policy, including problems facing entrepreneur and investor immigrants, effects of new immigration regulations, new refugee determination procedures, and Free Trade Agreement issues. Remarks: Alternate toll-free telephone number: 800-263-3269 (in Canada only). *Freq:* 10/year. *Price:* C$166, Canada.

3587 ▪ Canadian Museum of Flight Newsletter

Canadian Museum of Flight
5333 216th St., No. 200   Ph: (604)532-0035
Langley Airport   Fax: (604)532-0056
Langley, BC, Canada V2Y 2N3
E-mail: museum@canadianflight.org

Contact: C.R. Goguillot, Editor.

Desc: Focuses on the displays, collection, and aircraft preservation and restoration activities of the Museum. Promotes the preservation of aviation history. Contains articles on types of civilian, military, experimental, and prototype aircraft, from the pre-World War I era to present day aviation. Recurring features include reports of meetings, job listings, lists of new members, book reviews, letters to the editor, interviews, news of research, a calendar of events, notices of publications available, and col-

umns titled New Members, Members Forum, Obituaries, and Donations. *Freq:* Quarterly. *Price:* Included in membership.

3588 ▪ Canfield Family Association—Quarterly

Canfield Family Association
1144 N. Gordon   Ph: (316)942-7120
Wichita, KS 67203-6611

Contact: Genevieve (Canfield) Martinson, Editor.

Desc: Features genealogical and historical information on the Canfield surname. Covers census and Bible records, queries, and lineage of family members. Recurring features include news of research and book reviews of Canfields, anywhere, any time period. *Freq:* Quarterly. *Price:* $8, U.S.; $4, libraries; $14, elsewhere.

3589 ▪ Cape Breton Genealogical Society Newsletter

Cape Breton Genealogical Society
PO Box 53
Sydney, NS, Canada B1P 6G9

Contact: Mildred Howard, Editor.

Desc: Provides genealogical documentation on the counties of Cape Breton. Presents information on ancestorial lineage, land grant papers, news clippings from The Sydney Post, coal claims, lists of teachers, cemetery documentations, marriages, estate documents, and queries. *Freq:* Semiannual. *Price:* Included in membership.

3590 ▪ Carroll Cousins

Carroll County Genealogical Society
59 3rd St. NE   Ph: (330)627-2094
Carrollton, OH 44615
E-mail: ohcarrol@cannet.com

Contact: Linda Houyouse, Editor; Lois J. Hemming, Editor.

Desc: Provides genealogical information on families from Carrollton, Ohio. Includes census, church, veteran, school, day book records, and membership news. Recurring features include a calendar of events, notices of publications available, and a column titled Lines from Lois. *Freq:* Quarterly. *Price:* $7, U.S.; $8, Canada, Free, to libraries or in exchange with other societies.

3591 ▪ Census and You

Public Information Office
Bureau of the Census
U.S. Department of Commerce   Ph: (301)457-3042
Washington, DC 20233   Fax: (301)457-3670
URL: http://www.census.gov/prod/www/abs/
  msgen.html

Contact: Neil Fillman, Editor.

Desc: Informs users about new data products and plans for upcoming censuses and surveys. Describes various types of statistical reports and series available. Good guide to Census Bureau's data on the Internet. *Freq:* Bimonthly. *Price:* $21/year, U.S.; $26.25 elsewhere.

3592 ▪ Center for Migration Studies Newsletter

Center for Migration Studies of New York, Inc.
209 Flagg Pl.   Ph: (718)351-8800
Staten Island, NY 10304   Fax: (718)667-4598
E-mail: cmslft@aol.com
URL: http://www.cmsny.org

Contact: Lydio F. Tomasi, Editor.

Desc: Reports on conferences, publications, documentations and research projects, and library/archives activities of the Center. *Freq:* Semiannual. *Price:* Free.

3593 ■ Chester District Genealogical Society—Bulletin

Chester District Genealogical Society
PO Box 336
Richburg, SC 29729-0336

Contact: Jean Nichols, Editor.

Desc: Features historical and genealogical information on individuals who lived in Chester, Lancaster Union, York, and Fairfield City in South Carolina. Recurring features include news of research, book reviews, and notices of publications available. *Freq:* Quarterly. *Price:* $16, individuals, year; $7, institutions.

3594 ■ The Chestnut Tree

Pierre Chastain Family Association, Inc.
4830 Worchester Pl.   Ph: (919)854-5998
Jamestown, NC 27282

Contact: Loyce Coolidge, Editor.

Desc: Features genealogical data on the surname Chastain and related families. Recurring features include letters to the editor, news of research, a calendar of events, reports of meetings, news of educational opportunities, and notices of publications available. Remarks: Editor's address is 1912 Green Mountain, No. 201K, Little Rock, AR 72212; (501) 223-2114. *Freq:* Quarterly. *Price:* $12/year.

3595 ■ CIR Reports

Center for Immigrants' Rights (CIR)
48 St. Marks Place   Ph: (212)505-6890
New York, NY 10003

Desc: Furnishes information on immigrants' rights and policy initiatives. Recurring features include interviews, news of research, and reports of meetings. *Freq:* 2/year. *Price:* Included in membership; $35/year for non members.

3596 ■ Clan Matheson Society Newsletter

Clan Matheson Society
c/o Malcolm Matheson, III   Ph: (703)771-7171
PO Box 307   Fax: (703)777-3608
The Plains, VA 20198-0307
E-mail: clanmathsn@aol.com

Contact: Major Sir Fergus Matheson, BT, Editor.

Desc: Provides historical and genealogical information pertaining to the Matheson family. Seeks to promote interest and research in family history by publicizing research findings and encouraging individual contributions of pertinent information. Recurring features include letters to the editor, interviews, news of research, reports of meetings, book reviews, and a calendar of events. Remarks: Newsletter is written at The Old Rectory, Hedenham, Bungay Norfolk NR35 2LD, England *Freq:* Annual. *Price:* Included in membership.

3597 ■ Clan McCullough/McCulloch Newsletter

Betty K. Summers
PO Box 271759   Ph: (970)223-5874
Fort Collins, CO 80527-1759

Contact: Betty K. Summers, Editor.

Desc: Compiles information and data pertaining to the surnames McCullogh/McCulloch/McCully, including all variations. Publishes material from government, census, marriage, and other records. Recurring features include queries from readers and notices of publications available. *Freq:* 4/year. *Price:* Free, to libraries; $15, nonmembers.

3598 ■ The Clark Clarion

The Clark Clarion
633 E. 13th St.
Bowling Green, KY 42101-2531

Contact: Ruth Lanphear, Editor.

Desc: Publishes marriage and legal records, obituaries, biographies, family genealogies, and other information related to the Clark and Clarke families. Recurring features include news of research, book reviews, and genealogical queries. Remarks: Also available in book format (four years to a volume). *Freq:* Quarterly. *Price:* $8/year.

3599 ■ Clark County Genealogical Society Newsletter

Clark County Genealogical Society
1511 Main St.
PO Box 2728
Vancouver, WA 98668
E-mail: katschke@worldaccess.com

Contact: Lois Kullberg, Editor.

Desc: Provides a means of communication among Society members; covers Society activities and other genealogical events. Recurring features include a calendar of events, reports of meetings, notices of publications available, committee reports and notices, and research instructions. *Available:* Online. *Freq:* Monthly. *Price:* Included in membership.

3600 ■ Clark House News

Historical and Genealogical Society of Indiana County
Silas M. Clark House   Ph: (412)463-9600
200 S. 6th St.
Indiana, PA 15701-2999

Contact: Silas M. Clark House, Editor.

Desc: Publishes news and activities of the Historical and Genealogical Society of Indiana County, Pennsylvania. *Price:* Included in membership.

3601 ■ Clay County Researcher

Clay County Genealogical Society, Inc.
PO Box 56   Ph: (812)835-2321
Centerpoint, IN 47840
E-mail: ccgslib@ticz.com
URL: http://www.ticz.com/ccgslib/

Contact: Pat Wilkinson, Editor.

Desc: Carries genealogical information on the families of early Clay County, Indiana. Recurring features include excerpts for early Clay Co. newspapers; new in the library, notices of publications available, reports of meetings, a calendar of events, and queries. *Freq:* 4/year. *Price:* Included in membership; $3.75/issue for nonmembers.

3602 ■ CMS Newsletter

Center for Migration Studies of New York, Inc.
209 Flagg Pl.   Ph: (718)351-8800
Staten Island, NY 10304   Fax: (718)667-4598
E-mail: cmslft@aol.com; sales@cms.org
URL: http://www.cmsny.org

Contact: Lydio F. Tomasi, Editor.

Desc: Reports on the publishing, documentation, and research carried on at the Center. Reference is to international emigration and immigration, group and individual, rather than to internal movements of the shifting of the labor pool. Covers significant conferences and speeches. Recurring features include accounts of awards and grants, announcements of articles on migration in other periodical publications, news of research, book reviews, a calendar of events, and columns titled CMS People and Events, Visitors, and CMS Archives and Library. *Freq:* Biennial. *Price:* Free.

3603 ■ Coffey Cousin's Clearinghouse

Bonnie Culley
1416 Green Berry Rd.   Ph: (573)635-9057
Jefferson City, MO 65101-3620

Contact: Bonnie Culley, Editor.

Desc: Disseminates genealogical information and data on descendants of Coffee/Coffey families in the U.S. Carries queries from readers, introductions of members, and information about the annual convention. *Freq:* Quarterly. *Price:* $8; $10, elsewhere.

3604 ■ Conference of Intermountain Archivists (CIMA) Newsletter

Conference of Intermountain Archivists (CIMA)
PO Box 2048   Ph: (801)975-4023
Salt Lake City, UT 84114-2048   Fax: (801)974-0336
URL: http://www.lib.utah.edu/cima

Contact: Glen Fairclough, Editor; Jeff Kintop, Assistant Editor.

Desc: Concerned with the preservation and use of archival and manuscript materials in the Intermountain West and adjacent areas. Disseminates information on research materials and archival methodology; provides a forum for the discussion of common concerns; and cooperates with similar cultural and educational organizations. Recurring features include news of research, preservation, members, and job openings. *Freq:* Quarterly. *Price:* Included in membership.

3605 ■ Conger Confab

J.C. Conger
428 W. Vine St.   Ph: (217)544-6122
Springfield, IL 62704-2933
E-mail: writer@eosinc.com

Contact: Jon C. Conger, IV, Editor.

Desc: Published to promote Conger family unity, to encourage area reunions, and to foster awareness that all Congers are cousins. Contains items and reprinted newspaper articles on Conger family members and family letters. Remarks: Cumulation covering 1974 through 1993 available in hardcover edition with index. *Freq:* Quarterly. *Price:* $8/yr; $15/two years.

3606 ■ The Connector

Hamilton National Genealogical Society, Inc.
215 S.W. 20th Ter.   Ph: (816)690-7768
Oak Grove, MO 64075-9648
E-mail: hamgen@qnl.com
URL: http://www.qni.com/hamgen/index.html

Contact: Larry M. Hamilton, Editor.

Desc: Contains genealogical information on individuals with the surname Hamilton. Lists available data from primary and secondary sources, original writings by Hamiltons, and announcements of births and deaths. Recurring features include genealogical queries, census readings, obituaries, ahnentafel charts, and genealogies. *Freq:* Monthly. *Price:* $20, U.S.; $28, Canada.

3607 ■ ConservatioNews

Arizona State University Libraries
Department of Archives and Manuscripts
Box 871006   Ph: (602)965-3145
Tempe, AZ 85287-1006   Fax: (602)965-9169
E-mail: iacrps@asuvm.inre.asu.edu

Contact: Robert P. Spinder, Editor; Heather McIntyre, Editor.

Desc: Concerned with the preservation of paper documents, magnetic media, published materials, photographs, and film. Carries articles on the theory and practice of conservation, questions and answers to specific problems, and product news. Recurring features include news of members, book reviews, and a calendar of events. *Freq:* Quarterly. *Price:* Included in membership.

3608 ▪ The Coordinator

Genealogical Council of Maryland
c/o Richard G. Schmidt
1209 Finneans Run
Arnold, MD 21012
E-mail: mailgcm@aol.com

Contact: Richard G. Schmidt, Editor.

Desc: Provides details of Council meetings and committee activities as well as financial reports. Includes news of related organizations, notices of conferences and workshops, and articles on historical and genealogical topics. *Freq:* Quarterly. *Price:* Included in membership.

3609 ▪ Copeland Cuzzins

Olsen Enterprises
3931 S. 238th St.   Fax: (206)878-4267
Kent, WA 98032
E-mail: carlcindy2

Contact: Lucinda Olsen, Editor.

Desc: Devoted to the surname Copeland and other variant spellings. Subscription includes free queries. *Freq:* Quarterly. *Price:* $15, individuals, U.S.

3610 ▪ Cornsilk

DeKalb County Historical & Genealogical Society
PO Box 295   Ph: (815)784-2015
Sycamore, IL 60178

Contact: Florence E. Marshall, Editor; Phyllis Kelley, Editor.

Desc: Tracks activities of the Society. Contains information on the location and availability of genealogical research resources such as cemetary and church records, obituaries and burial locations of DeKalb County veterans, and old newspaper articles. Recurring features include columns titled Queries and the President's Message. *Freq:* Quarterly. *Price:* Included in membership, $15.00.

3611 ▪ Corral Dust

Panhandle Plains Historical Society
WTAMU Box 60967   Ph: (806)656-2244
Canyon, TX 79016   Fax: (806)656-2250
E-mail: museum@wtamu.edu
URL: http://www.wtamu.edu/museum; http://
      www.wtamu.edu/museum

Contact: Linda J. Moreland, Editor.

Desc: Supplies information on the activities, acquisitions, and collections of the Society, which exhibits, studies, and preserves objects relating to the history of the plains and the Texas Panhandle. Recurring features include editorials, news of research, news of members, a calendar of events, and the column Director's Desk. *Freq:* Quarterly. *Price:* Included in membership.

3612 ▪ Coryell Newsletter

N. Burr Coryell
PO Box 662   Ph: (805)965-3749
Santa Barbara, CA 93102-0662

Contact: N. Burr Coryell, Editor.

Desc: Carries items concerning members of the Coryell family, including family group sheets, family narratives, and obituaries. Offers tips on source documents for genealogical research. *Freq:* Periodic. *Price:* Donation requested; free to institutions.

3613 ▪ The Coward Family Newsletter

Coward Family Reunion
2140 Marion St.   Ph: (205)822-2446
Birmingham, AL 35226-3012

Contact: Trudy Adams, Editor.

Desc: Provides news of current and historical Coward family activities, tracing the lineage of James Coward of Rutherford County, North Carolina, and his descendants and others of the same surname. *Alt. Fmts:* microfilm. *Freq:* Semiannual. *Price:* Donation requested.

3614 ▪ Craig-Links

Ann Burton
43799 Valley Rd.   Ph: (616)423-8639
Decatur, MI 49045

Contact: Ann Burton, Editor; Conrad Burton, Editor.

Desc: Provides a forum for the exchange of genealogical research on families with the surname Craig. Features family narratives, diary excerpts, and genealogical records. Recurring features include book reviews, genealogical queries, letters to the editor, and a portrait registry. Yearly index. *Freq:* Quarterly. *Price:* $20, U.S. and Canada.

3615 ▪ Crane Flock Newsletter

Edith C. Breker
21 Poinsettia Dr.   Ph: (941)693-2343
Ft. Myers, FL 33905

Contact: Edith Breker, Editor.

Desc: Contains genealogical information on the Crane surname. Recurring features include news of research and queries. *Freq:* Quarterly. *Price:* $8/year for individuals; free for institutions.

3616 ▪ The Crawford Exchange

Seafog Publishers
PO Box 671   Ph: (916)253-3489
Janesville, CA 96114

Contact: June Crawford Sanders, Editor.

Desc: Carries family lineages, histories, census reports, and various records of genealogical interest for those researching the surname Crawford, and variant spellings. Recurring features include queries, biographic abstracts, book reviews, and potpourrie. *Alt. Fmts:* large-print. *Freq:* Semiannual. *Price:* $15.00/year, U. S.; $19 elsewhere.

3617 ▪ Crowl Connections

Crowl Family Association
9603 Bel Glade St.   Ph: (703)281-9562
Fairfax, VA 22031-1105

Contact: Gail Komar, Editor.

Desc: Contains genealogical information on the Crowl surname. Recurring features include news of research, a calendar of events, and notices of publications available. *Freq:* Quarterly. *Price:* $12/year for individuals; $6 for libraries, $22/2 years.

3618 ▪ The Crown and Eagle

The Hereditary Order of Descendants of the Loyalists and Patriots of the American Revolution
c/o Mrs. Donald C. Tralenger
Ottawa Hill Rte. 1
Box 154
Miami, OK 74354-9370

Contact: Patricia Tralenger, Editor.

Desc: Carries news of the Order, which works to replace lost or destroyed historical and lineage records of members. Includes items on both loyalist and patriot ancestry, news of members, and events of the Order. *Freq:* Semiannual. *Price:* Included in membership.

3619 ▪ The Cunningham Lair

The Cunningham Lair
Box 225   Ph: (408)462-2175
Ben Lomond, CA 95005   Fax: (408)462-3851

Contact: Nona Williams, Editor and Publisher.

Desc: Provides genealogical research and information on the Cunningham family. *Freq:* Quarterly. *Price:* $15, individuals; $4, single issue.

3620 ▪ Dadswell Family Bulletin

Allison and Busby
c/o Schocken Books
200 Madison Ave.
New York, NY 10016

Contact: Barbara Balch Nethercott, Editor.

Desc: Features information on the Dadswell surname. Covers recent births, marriages, and deaths. *Freq:* 2/year. *Price:* $6/2 yrs., Canada, $7/2 yrs. overseas.

3621 ▪ Dean & Creech Annual Newsletter

Lloyd Dean
6770 US 60 E.   Ph: (606)784-9145
Morehead, KY 40351

Contact: Lloyd Dean, Editor.

Desc: Provides information on the annual Dean and Creech family reunion. Contains news of genealogical research. Includes a calendar of events. *Freq:* Annual. *Price:* Free.

3622 ▪ Descendants of Daniel Cole Society Newsletter

Descendants of Daniel Cole Society
PO Box 367   Ph: (914)628-0912
Mahopac Falls, NY 10542

Contact: Dorothy E. Kelsey, Editor.

Desc: Presents information on the genealogical history of Daniel Cole. Recurring features include letters to the editor, news of research, and news of educational opportunities. *Freq:* 4/year. *Price:* Included in membership; $10, nonmembers.

3623 ▪ Descendants of Peter Shaklee (1756-1834) Newsletter

Peter Shaklee Family Organization
14901 N. Pennsylvania, Apt. 369   Ph: (405)372-0484
Oklahoma City, OK 73134-6072

Contact: William E. Shaklee, Editor.

Desc: Concerned with the genealogy of Peter Shaklee. Contains family stories and current news about his descendants. Recurring features include news of research, a calendar of events, and reports of meetings. *Freq:* Quarterly. *Price:* $7/year.

3624 ▪ Diablo Descendants Newsletter

Contra Costa County Genealogical Society
PO Box 910   Ph: (510)376-6124
Concord, CA 94522-0910

Contact: Karen Wetherall, Asst. Editor.

Desc: Features items of interest to geneaologists. *Freq:* Monthly. *Price:* Included in membership; free to libraries.

3625 ▪ The Dinghy

Pentref Press
PO Box 2782   Ph: (207)255-4114
Kennebunkport, ME
   04046-2782

Contact: Rosemary Bachelor, Editor.

Desc: Concerned with genealogical data on Colonial era American families. Remarks: Acts as a supplement to The Second Boat (see separate entry). *Available:* Online. *Freq:* Bimonthly. *Price:* $25/year.

3626 ■ Disa and Data Letter

McConnaughey Society of America

5410 S. Meridian St.   Ph: (317)786-4363
PO Box 47051   Free: (317)786-8380
Indianapolis, IN 46247-0051   Fax: (317)782-1821

Contact: Pat McConnaughay Gregory, Editor.

Desc: Offers members current news of genealogical research findings about all spellings of the McConnaughey surname. Publishes letters and contributed data from other researchers, including original records and biographical sketches. Includes news of members and family happenings of interest. Recurring features include letters, reports of meetings, notices of publications available, and queries. *Available:* Online. *Freq:* Monthly, occasionally bimonthly (two months combined into one issue). *Price:* Included in membership.

3627 ■ Disbrow Family Newsletter

Cassius L. Disbrow

435 N. Franklin   Ph: (605)334-6280
Sioux Falls, SD 57103   Fax: (605)334-6280
E-mail: siouxcash2@aol.com

Contact: Cassius L. Disbrow, Editor.

Desc: Contains genealogical and historical information relating to families with variations on the Disbrow surname in the U.S. Lists census indexes, family Bible records, and other sources of genealogical records. Recurring features include news of research and reports of meetings. *Freq:* Quarterly. *Price:* $10.

3628 ■ Dobie Connection

Dobie Clan of North America

17154 Valley Creek Dr.   Ph: (440)572-4172
Cleveland, OH 44136-4407

Contact: George N. Dobie, II, Editor.

Desc: Contains genealogical information on the Dobie family as well as news on current family members. Recurring features include news of research, a calendar of events, reports of meetings, news of scholarships, and columns titled Kith 'n' Kin, Recording History, Prize Winning Essays, and Scotlinks. *Freq:* Semiannual. *Price:* Included in membership; $5, nonmembers, U.S.; $6.50, nonmembers, Canada.

3629 ■ Dorot

Jewish Genealogical Society

PO Box 6398   Ph: (212)330-8257
New York, NY 10128   Fax: (212)787-9552
E-mail: jgsny@aol.com

Contact: Alex E. Friedlander, Editor.

Desc: Covers pertinent genealogical research, and carries a random bibliography. Recurring features include information on programs and events. *Freq:* Quarterly. *Price:* Included in membership.

3630 ■ The Doughty Tree

Doughty Family Association

209 Farragut Ave.   Ph: (609)625-7561
Mays Landing, NJ 08330-1716

Contact: Clarence Doughty, Editor.

Desc: Covers genealogical information on families with the surname Doughty or its variations. Lists court records, obituaries, census reports, family bible records, and compiled family histories. Recurring features include letters to the editor, news of research, a calendar of events, and

a column titled Branches of the Doughty Tree. *Alt. Fmts:* Braille; microfilm. *Freq:* 4/year. *Price:* $10/year, U.S. and Canada; $12 elsewhere.

3631 ■ Douglas Trails & Traces

Douglas County Genealogical Society

PO Box 113
Tuscola, IL 61953

Contact: M. Tracy Carpenter, Editor.

Desc: Focuses on county court minutes, queries, newspaper articles, and historical stories concerning individuals of Douglas County. Recurring features include news of research, and notices of publications available. *Freq:* Quarterly. *Price:* $6.50, charter members; $7.50, individuals; $8.50, families.

3632 ■ Durch Die Fensterscheibe

BGM Publications

28635 Old Hideaway Rd.   Ph: (708)639-2400
Cary, IL 60013

Contact: Betty G. Massman, Editor.

Desc: Gives genealogical data for the surname Scheib, Shipe, Shive, and other variations. Provides wills, deeds, Bible records, church records, and other related material. Recurring features include news of research, obituaries, marriages, births, given name index, and an inquiries column. *Alt. Fmts:* microform. *Freq:* Quarterly. *Price:* $18/year, U.S.; $25, elsewhere.

3633 ■ Dusty Shelf

Kansas City Area Archivists
The Nazarene Archives

6401 The Paseo   Ph: (816)333-7000
Kansas City, MO 64131
URL: http://cctr.umkc.edu/WHMCKC/KCAA/
      KCAAHOME.HTM

Contact: Stan Ingersol, Editor.

Desc: Contains essays and editorials on local and national archives. Recurring features include a calendar of events, reports of meetings, news of educational opportunities, job listings, notices of publications available, and a column titled Conservation Notes. *Freq:* 3/year. *Price:* Included in membership.

3634 ■ Eastern Nebraska Genealogical Society Newsletter

Eastern Nebraska Genealogical Society

PO Box 541   Ph: (402)721-9553
Fremont, NE 68026-0541
E-mail: usacrs.com/museum.htm

Contact: Claire Mares, Editor.

Desc: Reports news, activities, and events of the society. Contains historical newspaper clippings and other genealogical information. Recurring features include news of research, a calendar of events, and reports of meetings. *Available:* Online: American Online. *Freq:* Monthly. *Price:* Included in membership.

3635 ■ Eastern Washington Genealogical Society—Bulletin

Eastern Washington Genealogical Society (EWGS)

PO Box 1826   Ph: (509)456-7553
Spokane, WA 99210-1826
URL: http://www.onlinepub.net/ewgs

Contact: Doris J. Woodward, Editor.

Desc: Publishes articles of genealogical interest to members. Recurring features include news of research, book reviews, vital records, notices of publications available, and

columns titled Hotlines, EWGS Surnames, and Library Acquisitions & Newspaper Extractions. *Freq:* Quarterly. *Price:* $20, U.S., with membership.

3636 ■ Easy Access

Oregon Historical Society Press

1200 Park Ave. SW   Ph: (503)222-1741
Portland, OR 97205   Fax: (503)221-2035

Contact: M.C. Cuthill, Editor; Kris White, Editor.

Desc: Reports news for archival professionals. Recurring features include letters to the editor, news of research, a calendar of events, reports of meetings, news of educational opportunities, job listings, book reviews, and notices of publications available. *Freq:* Quarterly. *Price:* $10/year.

3637 ■ Eells Family Association—Bulletin

Eells Family Association

35 Townsend St.   Ph: (607)865-5686
Walton, NY 13856

Contact: Dr. Walter E. Eells, Editor.

Desc: Contains news of the Eells family, including births, deaths, and historical items. Recurring features include letters to the editor, news of research, reports of meetings, and news of members. *Freq:* Quarterly. *Price:* $15/year, $150 for lifetime membership.

3638 ■ 1812 War Cry

General Society of the War of 1812

c/o Dennis F. Blizzard
805 Kellogg Rd.
Lutherville, MD 21093

Contact: Dennis Blizzard, Editor.

Desc: Promotes the aims of the Society, which are "to perpetuate the memory and victories of the War of 1812; encourage research and publication of historical data; and cherish, maintain, and extend the institution of American freedom and foster the patriotism and love of the country." *Freq:* Quarterly. *Price:* Free.

3639 ■ The Ellis Cousins Newsletter

Ellis Cousins Nationwide

1201 Maple St.   Ph: (806)247-3053
Friona, TX 79035   Fax: (806)247-2211

Contact: Bill Ellis, Editor; Carol Ellis, Editor.

Desc: Compiles family historical articles and information relating to individuals with the Ellis surname. Lists family Bible records, marriages and obituaries, reunion announcements, and genealogical queries. Recurring features include letters to the editor, news of research, book reviews, notices of publications available, and columns titled Dear Cousin and Ellis Menagerie. *Freq:* Quarterly. *Price:* $15/year, U.S.; $19, Canada.

3640 ■ Encampment Newsletter

Society of the Descendants of Washington's Army at Valley Forge

PO Box 915
Valley Forge, PA 19482-0915

Contact: Betty Brown Miller, Editor.

Desc: Helps to coordinate the activities of the Society, whose members are direct descendants (over 18 years old) of soldiers who served in the Continental Army at Valley Forge under the command of George Washington (December 19, 1777 to June 19, 1778). Publishes incidents of the encampment and other historical news. Recurring features include Society news and announcements of awards. *Freq:* Quarterly. *Price:* Included in membership.

3641 ▪ Estes Trails

Historic Trails Library
RR 2, Box 288
Collinsville, MS 39325-9429

Contact: Mary Estes Beckham, Editor.

Desc: Reprints data from birth, marriage, death, and Bible records pertaining to members of the Estes family. Also publishes results of genealogical research and various biographical data of interest to family researchers. Recurring features include queries, book reviews, notices of publications available, interviews, letters to the editor, reports of meetings, and a calendar of events. *Freq:* Quarterly. *Price:* $15/year, U.S.; $20 elsewhere.

3642 ▪ Evangeline Genealogical & Historical Society Newsletter

Evangeline Genealogical & Historical Society
PO Box 664
Ville Platte, LA 70586

Contact: John A. Young, Editor.

Desc: Provides Society members with information on genealogical seminars and workshops, meetings, library acquisitions, ongoing and new projects. Recurring features include news of research, a calendar of events, reports of meetings, and notices of publications available. *Freq:* Quarterly. *Price:* $10, U.S. and Canada, year.

3643 ▪ Factfinder for the Nation

Customer Services Center
Bureau of the Census
U.S. Department of Commerce   Ph: (301)457-4100
Washington, DC 20233   Fax: (301)457-4714

Desc: Consists of 22 individual publications, each of which is updated variably (as often as every two or three years). Provides those using census information in the analysis of historical trends concise and informative explanations of various Census Bureau programs. Included in the Factfinder series is each of the following titles: Statistics on Race and Ethnicity, Availability of Census Records About Individuals, Agriculture Statistics, History and Organization, Reference Sources, Housing Statistics, Population Statistics, Census Geography—Concepts and Products, Construction Statistics, Retail Trade Statistics, Wholesale Trade Statistics, Statistics on Service Industries, Transportation, Communications, & Utilities Statistics, Foreign Trade Statistics, Statistics on Manufactures, Statistics on Mineral Industries, Statistics on Governments, Census Bureau Programs and Products, Enterprise Statistics, Energy and Related Statistics, International Programs, and Data for Communities. Recurring features include a brief history of each Census Bureau program. Transporation, Communications, & Utilities Statistics. *Freq:* Irregular. *Price:* $.25 to $1.00/issue.

3644 ▪ FAIR/Immigration Report

Federation for American Immigration Reform (FAIR)
1666 Connecticut NW, Ste. 400   Ph: (202)328-7004
Washington, DC 20009   Free: 800-395-0890
                                 Fax: (202)387-3447
E-mail: fair@fairus.org

Contact: Scipio Garling, Editor.

Desc: Reports on political, social, demographic, and economic implications of immigration law and policy. Recurring features include statistics, book reviews, and news of research. *Freq:* Monthly. *Price:* Included in membership.

3645 ▪ Fairfield Trace

Fairfield County Chapter of the Ohio Genealogical Society
PO Box 1470   Ph: (740)653-2745
Lancaster, OH 43130-0570

E-mail: chapter@fairfieldgenealogy.org
URL: http://www.fairfieldgenealogy.org

Contact: Carol Swinehart.

Desc: Features news of research, notices of publications available, and columns titled Queries, First Families of Fairfield County, Surname Search, and Pastors and Churches. *Freq:* Quarterly. *Price:* Included in membership.

3646 ▪ Family Findings

White Publishing Co.
Box 3343
Jackson, TN 38303-0343

Desc: Consists of genealogical news. *Freq:* Quarterly. *Price:* $15, individuals; $4, single issue.

3647 ▪ Family Ties

Holland Genealogical Society
300 River Ave.   Ph: (616)394-1400
Holland, MI 49423

Contact: Alma Jean Steketee, Editor.

Desc: Contains genealogical and historical information for Holland, Michigan. Recurring features include news of research and reports of meetings. *Freq:* 3/year. *Price:* Included in membership.

3648 ▪ Fisk/Fiske Family Association Newsletter

Fisk/Fiske Family Association
343 N. 1st St.
Lindsborg, KS 67456-2004

Contact: Irwin Wesley Fisk, Editor.

Desc: Features articles for persons interested in genealogical data and historical articles on persons with the surname Fisk or Fiske. Recurring features include news of research, book reviews, and queries. *Available:* Online: America Online. *Alt. Fmts:* database. *Freq:* Annual. *Price:* $9/year for individuals; free to institutions.

3649 ▪ Flipping Flippins

Flippin Family Association
12206 Brisbane Ave.   Ph: (972)241-2739
Dallas, TX 75234   Fax: (972)620-1416

Contact: Nova A. Lemons, Editor.

Desc: Gathers genealogical information on the Flippen, Flippin, and Flipping surname. Recurring features include letters to the editor, news of research, calendar of events, book reviews, and notices of publications available. *Freq:* Quarterly. *Price:* Included in membership.

3650 ▪ Foothills Genealogical Society Newsletter

Foothills Genealogical Society of Colorado, Inc.
PO Box 150382   Ph: (303)232-1483
Lakewood, CO 80215-0382

Contact: Patricia A. Kemper, Editor.

Desc: Features news of research, a calendar of events, reports of meetings, news of educational opportunities, book reviews, and notices of publications available. *Freq:* Bimonthly. *Price:* Included in membership.

3651 ▪ Footprints in Time

Annette Williams
PO Box 584   Ph: (704)827-6437
Mt. Holly, NC 28120

Contact: Annette Williams, Editor.

Desc: Provides genealogical and historical information. Recurring features include letters to the editor, interviews, reports of meetings, book reviews, and notices of publications available. *Price:* Included in membership.

3652 ▪ For the Record. . .

Lower Cape Fear Historical Society
126 S. 3rd St.   Ph: (910)762-0492
Wilmington, NC 28401   Fax: (910)763-5869
E-mail: latimer@wilmington.net

Contact: Blonnie Bunn Wyche, Editor.

Desc: Seeks to preserve the past of Lower Cape Fear in North Carolina. Reports on news of the Society, including events and announcements. Recurring features include a collection, book reviews, and columns titled President's Corner and From the Archives. *Freq:* Quarterly. *Price:* Included in membership.

3653 ▪ Forecast

American Demographics
PO Box 4949   Ph: (203)358-9900
Stamford, CT 06907   Free: 800-828-1133
                                 Fax: (203)358-5833
E-mail: editors@demographics.com;
    forecast@demographics.com
URL: http://www.demographics.com

Contact: Shannon Dortch, Editor.

Desc: Analyzes consumer trends, reports on projections of consumer markets, and forecasts demand for products. Covers news of the producers and suppliers of demographic data, demographic trends, and new data products. *Available:* Online: LEXIS-NEXIS. *Freq:* Monthly. *Price:* $199/year.

3654 ▪ The Forkner Clan Newsletter

The Forkner Clan Newsletter
2610 Yadon Rd.   Ph: (406)284-3396
Manhattan, MT 59741-8020

Contact: Mona Forkner Paulas, Editor.

Desc: Attempts to reach genealogists and family researchers throughout the U.S. who are interested in the Forkner surname. Shares results of genealogical research and announcements of births, marriages, and deaths among Forkners and related family members. Recurring features include letters to the editor and genealogical queries. *Freq:* Quarterly. *Price:* $15/year.

3655 ▪ Fort Belknap Genealogical Association Newsletter

Fort Belknap Genealogical Association
Fort Belknap Historical Society
Box 409   Ph: (940)549-1856
Graham, TX 76450

Desc: Reports on genealogical information and news of the historical society. *Freq:* Annual. *Price:* Included in membership.

3656 ▪ Fort Concho Guidon

Fort Concho National Historic Landmark
630 S. Oakes   Ph: (915)481-2646
San Angelo, TX 76903-7013   Fax: (915)657-4540
E-mail: hqtrs@fortconcho.com

Contact: Evelyn Lemons, Editor.

Desc: Presents news concerning the programs and activities of the Fort Concho Museum, a historical museum displaying artifacts and clothing dating from the period when Fort Concho functioned as a military outpost. Provides updates on Museum collections, library acquisitions, and membership drives, and reports on local cultural associations affiliated with the Museum. Recurring features include notices of publications available, a calendar of events, and news of educational opportunities. *Available:* Online. *Freq:* Quarterly. *Price:* Included in membership.

3657 ■ Fox Tales

Fox Valley Genealogical Society
PO Box 5435   Ph: (630)369-0744
Naperville, IL 60567-5435
E-mail: fvgs1@aol.com

Contact: Michael R. Fichtel, Editor.

Desc: Provides genealogical and historical information focusing on DuPage, Kane, Kendall, and Will Counties in Illinois, as well as other areas. Features Queries—persons seeking genealogical information about ancestors. Recurring features include letters to the editor, news of research, a collection, reports of meetings, news of educational opportunities, book reviews, and notices of publications available. *Freq:* Bimonthly. *Price:* Included in membership.

3658 ■ Franklin County Tennessee Tidings

Franklin County Tennessee Tidings
PO Box 130   Ph: (615)962-1476
Winchester, TN 37398   Fax: (615)962-1477

Contact: Jerry T. Limbaugh, Editor.

Desc: Recurring features include a calendar of events, reports of meetings, notices of publications available, queries, family charts, and indexes to records including index to Loose Court papers and index to brides names in surviving bonds, etc. *Freq:* Quarterly. *Price:* Included in membership; $20, nonmembers.

3659 ■ The FRANKLINTONIAN

Franklin County Genealogical Society
PO Box 44309   Ph: (614)469-1300
Columbus, OH 43204-0309   Fax: (614)274-1946

Contact: Jennie Spring-Starr, Editor.

Desc: Features genealogical information from ancestor charts, newspapers, Bible and court records, research suggestions, and the location of genealogical materials in Franklin County, Ohio. Recurring features include news of research, a calendar of events, book reviews, and notices of publications available. *Freq:* 6/year. *Price:* Included in membership.

3660 ■ Frary Family Newsletter

Frary Family Association
12 Lohmann Pl.   Ph: (201)384-2111
Dumont, NJ 07628

Contact: Grace Frary, Editor.

Desc: Contains news of individuals with the Frary surname. Reports on family reunions and family history. Recurring features include editorials, news of members, and a calendar of events. *Freq:* Semiannual. *Price:* Included in membership.

3661 ■ Frederick Findings

Lineage Search Associates
7315 Colts Neck Rd.   Ph: (804)730-7414
Mechanicsville, VA 23111-4233   Fax: (804)730-7414

Contact: Michael E. Pollock, Editor.

Desc: Contains genealogical and historical information on Frederick County, Virginia and surrounding areas. *Freq:* Quarterly. *Price:* $25, individuals; $21, libraries; $21, institutions.

3662 ■ French Canadian/Acadian Genealogists of Wisconsin—Quarterly

French Canadian/Acadian Genealogists of Wisconsin
PO Box 414   Ph: (414)541-8820
Hales Corners, WI 53130-0414

URL: http://www.execpc.com/lkboyea/index.html

Contact: Joyce Banachowski, Contact.

Desc: Covers the history of French Canadian/Acadian persons. Provides information on available means of genealogical research and on genealogy publishing. Recurring features include news of research, a calendar of events, reports of meetings, news of educational opportunities, book reviews, notices of publications available, biographical sketches, and extracts of association records. *Freq:* Quarterly. *Price:* Included in membership.

3663 ■ The Frenchline

French Family Association
521 River View Dr.   Ph: (408)227-4411
San Jose, CA 95111
E-mail: frenchfamilyassociation@compuserve.com

Contact: Mara T. French, Editor.

Desc: Created to "promote interest and research in the French family" and to "publish results of French family research including pedigree charts." Recurring features include listings of books, letters, and photos from the Association's library on the French family. Also includes columns titled From the President, The French Potpourri, Ffrench Ffotos, The French Connection, The Royal Southern French, From the Shoebox, Line by Line, The Boston Transcript, Short Charts, Early Generations Long Charts, Ye Olde World News, and What's Coming Up! *Freq:* Quarterly. *Price:* Included in membership.

3664 ■ Fretzletter

Fretz Family Association
c/o Rockhill   Ph: (215)257-4635
   Mennonite Community
3250 State Rd., No. 263
Sellersville, PA 18960

Contact: Mary Fretz Shively, Editor; Lottie K. Diehl, typist.

Desc: Carries genealogical information of interest to Fretz family members. Monitors family activities, births, deaths, and marriages. Recurring features include news of research, letters to the editor, book reviews, and a calendar of events. *Freq:* Quarterly. *Price:* Donation requested.

3665 ■ Friends of Mamie's Birthplace Newsletter

Mamie Doud Eisenhower Birthplace Foundation, Inc.
PO Box 55   Ph: (515)432-1896
Boone, IA 50036   Fax: (515)432-2571

Contact: Larry Adams, Editor.

Desc: Devoted to the preservation of the birthplace and memory of Mamie Doud Eisenhower (1896-1979), former First Lady to President Dwight D. Eisenhower. Includes announcements of activities, programs, deaths; member profiles; and quizzes. *Freq:* Semiannual. *Price:* Included in membership.

3666 ■ Frisbie-Frisbee Family Association of America—Bulletin

Frisbie-Frisbee Family Association
16 Bingham Rd.   Ph: (909)626-5898
Owego, NY 13827-3345

Contact: Linda Frisbie, Editor.

Desc: Contains notices of births, deaths, marriages, and other family news for those with the surname Frisbie (variously spelled) or of Frisbie descent. Profiles noteworthy Frisbies, past and present. *Freq:* Quarterly. *Price:* Included in membership.

3667 ■ Fulton County Folk Finder

Fulton County Historical Society, Inc.
37 East 375 North   Ph: (219)223-4436
Rochester, IN 46975-8384
URL: http://ics.net/fchs

Contact: Shirley Willard, Editor.

Desc: Provides information on Society activities and resources. Contains genealogical information and queries, family group sheets, and Civil War veterans records. *Freq:* Semiannual. *Price:* Included in membership; $6, individuals; $8, organization or family.

3668 ■ Fulton County Historical Society Newsletter

Fulton County Historical Society, Inc.
37 East 375 North   Ph: (219)223-4436
Rochester, IN 46975-8384
URL: http://icss.net/fchs

Contact: Shirley Willard, Editor.

Desc: Reports on Society exhibits, its living-history village, festivals, publications, and other activities. Features articles on County history. Includes death notices and newspaper clippings. *Freq:* Semiannual. *Price:* $15/year.

3669 ■ Gage Family Newsletter

John A. Gage
29 Seminole Ct.   Ph: (813)294-2496
Winter Haven, FL 33881
E-mail: winhavgage@yahoo.com

Contact: John A. Gage, Editor.

Desc: Compiles genealogical data regarding the Gage surname. Recurring features include queries. *Freq:* Quarterly. *Price:* $8/year, U.S.; $14 elsewhere.

3670 ■ Gathering Gibsons

Kinseeker Publications
PO Box 184   Ph: (616)276-7653
Grawn, MI 49637
E-mail: kinseeker6@aol.com
URL: http://www.angelfire.com/biz/kinseeker/index.html

Contact: V. Wilson, Editor.

Desc: Provides genealogical information on the surname Gibson. *Freq:* Quarterly.

3671 ■ Gebhart Society of America Newsletter

Gebhart Society of America
PO Box 142   Ph: (301)241-3312
Sabillasville, MD 21780-0142

Contact: Victor Gebhart, Editor.

Desc: Features historical and genealogical information on the Gebhard/Gebhart surnames. Recurring features include news of research, reports of meetings, and notices of publications available. *Freq:* 4/year. *Price:* $6.50.

3672 ■ Genealogical Computing

Ancestry, Inc.
PO Box 990   Ph: (801)426-3500
Orem, UT 84057   Free: 800-262-3787
            Fax: (801)426-3501
E-mail: support@ancestry-inc.com; gceditor@ancestry-inc.com
URL: http://www.ancestry.com

Contact: Matthew Helm, Editor; April Helm, Editor.

Desc: Focuses on the uses of personal computers for genealogical records management. Reviews and discusses the applications of various computer software and offers how-to articles and tips from users. Recurring features include program directories, survey results, letters to the editor, and interest group directories. *Freq:* Quarterly. *Price:* $25, U.S.; $30, Canada; $35, elsewhere.

3673 ▪ Genealogical Gems
Fox Valley Genealogical Society
PO Box 1592   Ph: (414)733-5358
Appleton, WI 54913-1592

Contact: Mary E. Klein, Editor.

Desc: Presents current Society activities, new acquisitions, research tips, a surname file, queries, and previously unpublished materials of local, state, and national genealogical and historical value. Recurring features include news of research, a calendar of events, reports of meetings, queries, and book reviews. *Freq:* Quarterly. *Price:* Included in membership; $10/year for nonmember individuals; $5 for nonmember institutions.

3674 ▪ The Genealogical Journal
Genealogical Society of Davidson County
PO Box 1665
Lexington, NC 27293-1665

Contact: Marie L. Hinson, Editor; Kathleen M. Craver, Editor.

Desc: Provides historical and genealogical information on Davidson County, North Carolina. Recurring features include book reviews, notices of publications available, and columns titled Death Certificates, Minutes of the Court, News from the Dispatch, Division of Land, and Queries. *Freq:* Quarterly. *Price:* Included in membership.

3675 ▪ Genealogical Society of Flemish Americans Newsletter
Genealogical Society of Flemish Americans
18740 13 Mile Rd.   Ph: (810)776-9579
Roseville, MI 48066

Contact: Margaret Roets, Editor.

Desc: Concerned with tracing the family history of Flemish Americans. Contains announcements for classes, awards, name changes, resources, and special events. *Freq:* Semiannual. *Price:* Included in membership.

3676 ▪ Genealogical Society of New Jersey Newsletter
Genealogical Society of New Jersey
c/o Joseph Klett
7 Mercer St.
Hopewell, NJ 08525

Contact: Joseph R. Klett, Editor.

Desc: Contains program announcements, news of New Jersey research facilities, genealogies in progress, news from family associations, queries, lists of new members, book reviews. *Freq:* Semiannual. *Price:* Included in membership; $15.

3677 ▪ Genealogical Society of Old Tyron County—Bulletin
Genealogical Society of Old Tyron County
PO Box 938
Forest City, NC 28043

Contact: Miles Philbeck, Jr., Editor.

Desc: Covers genealogy and history of Old Tyron County, North Carolina. *Freq:* Quarterly. *Price:* Included in membership; $17.50/year for nonmembers.

3678 ▪ German Genealogical Society of America Newsletter
German Genealogical Society of America
PO Box 517   Ph: (909)593-0509
La Verne, CA 91750-0517

Contact: Anne Larkin, Editor.

Freq: 5/year. *Price:* Included in membership.

3679 ▪ Germans from Russia Heritage Society Newsletter
Germans from Russia Heritage Society
1008 E. Central Ave.   Ph: (701)223-6167
Bismarck, ND 58501   Fax: (701)223-4421
E-mail: grhs@btigate.com
URL: http://www.grhs.com

Contact: Randy Heinz, Editor.

Desc: Spotlights genealogical and historical information on individuals of German-Russian descent. Recurring features include news of research, a calendar of events, and reports of meetings. *Freq:* Quarterly. *Price:* Free, with members.

3680 ▪ Gila Heritage
Northern Gila County Genealogical Society, Inc.
Box 952
Payson, AZ 85547-0952

Contact: Opal Follin, Editor.

Desc: Contains local historical and genealogical information.

3681 ▪ Gillespie Clan Newsletter
Dennis F. Gillespie
116 Ula La Cumbre
Greenbrae, CA 94904-1333

Desc: Provides genealogical information on the Gillespie family. Recurring features include letters to the editor and news of research. *Freq:* Quarterly. *Price:* $24.

3682 ▪ Gilmer County Historical Society Newsletter
Gilmer County Historical Society
214 Walnut St.   Ph: (304)462-5620
Glenville, WV 26351   Fax: (304)462-5620

Contact: Ron Miller, Editor.

Desc: Provides news of the Society; carries queries and historical information on one-room schools according to the West Virginia Census of 1900, 1910 and 1920. *Freq:* Quarterly. *Price:* $10/year.

3683 ▪ Gilmore Genealogical Newsletter
Gilmore Genealogical Newsletter
3522 Twin City Hwy.
Groves, TX 77619

Desc: Compiles information on Gilmore family, including genealogical chart updates, historical news, and family reunion notices. *Freq:* Annual. *Price:* $34.95.

3684 ▪ The Goddard Newsletter
Goddard Association of America
118 S. Volustia   Ph: (316)682-4942
Wichita, KS 67211

Contact: Kathryn Goddard Meyer, Editor; V.G. Johnson, Editor.

Desc: Contains genealogical and historical information concerning Goddard and Goddard-related families. Recurring features include news of research, news of the Association, interviews, and a column titled Climbing Our Family Trees. *Freq:* 4/year. *Price:* Included in membership.

3685 ▪ Gold Star Wives of America Newsletter
Gold Star Wives of America, Inc.
PO Box 361986
Birmingham, AL 35236-1986

Contact: Lavone Tueting, Editor.

Desc: Serves as a medium of communication for widows of military servicemen or of men who died of a service-related condition. Publishes information on social security benefits, activities of members, and pending legislation. Recurring features include national convention news, obituaries, news of members, Service Corner, and President's Message, and information on VA benefits. *Freq:* Quarterly. *Price:* Included in membership.

3686 ▪ Goodenows' Ghosts
Goodenow Family Association
Rte. 2, Box 718   Ph: (304)876-2008
Shepherdstown, WV 25443

Contact: William S. Groenier, Editor; Janet Groenier, Editor.

Desc: Carries genealogical information on the Goodenough/Goodnow/Goodenow/Goodno surname. Provides historical information, biographies, obituaries, public and Bible records, lineage charts, and queries. Recurring features include reports on family reunions and index. *Freq:* Quarterly. *Price:* Included in membership; $20, annum.

3687 ▪ Goodwin News
Goodwin Family Organization
39 Lost Trail Rd.   Ph: (505)625-0961
Roswell, NM 88201-9509

Contact: Alice B. Sharp, Editor.

Desc: Contains genealogical and current information on members of the Goodwin family. Recurring features include letters to the editor, a calendar of events, reports of meetings, book reviews, and notices of publications available. *Freq:* 2/year. *Price:* $18, members, in U.S.; $22, members, in Canada and Mexico; $25, members, elsewhere.

3688 ▪ Government Affairs Bulletin
NAFSA: Association of International Educators
1875 Connecticut Ave. NW,   Ph: (202)462-4811
   Ste. 1000   Free: 800-836-4994
Washington, DC 20009-5728   Fax: (202)667-3419
E-mail: inbox@nafsa.org
URL: http://www.nafsa.org

Contact: Andrea Prazuch, Editor.

Desc: Reports on government activities in international educational exchange, including pending legislation affecting immigration, grant announcements, and exchange programs. Remarks: NAFSA is an acronym for National Association for Foreign Student Affairs, the organization's former name. *Freq:* 8/year. *Price:* $45, members; $75, nonmembers.

3689 ▪ Grapevine
Paul Sniffen
PO Box 124   Ph: (908)741-9560
Red Bank, NJ 07701   Fax: (908)530-2065

Contact: Paul Sniffen, Editor.

Desc: Features genealogical information and news of reunions on the Kniffin-Sniffen family. Recurring features include a calendar of events. *Available:* Online: Reunions USA. *Alt. Fmts:* diskette. *Freq:* Semiannual. *Price:* Free.

3690 ▪ Green Country Quarterly
Broken Arrow Genealogical Society
Box 1244   Ph: (918)455-8619
Broken Arrow, OK 74013-1244

Contact: Marmie Apsley, Editor.

Desc: Provides ancestor charts, family group records, ahnentafels, cemetary surveys, excerpts from the 1910 census of Broken Arrow, Bible data, and library acquisitions. Recurring features include a calendar of events, reports of meetings. *Freq:* 4/year. *Price:* $10/year.

3691 ■ Griswold Family Association of America Newsletter

Griswold Family Association of America, Inc.
116 Garden St.   Ph: (203)529-4264
Wethersfield, CT 06109

Contact: Richard-Evelyn Griswold, Editor.

Desc: Provides genealogical and historical information relating to the Griswold family. Describes current activities of the Association, including news of ongoing research and Association-sponsored events such as tours and reunions. Recurring features include reports of meetings, notices of publications available, and a calendar of events. *Freq:* Quarterly. *Price:* Included in membership.

3692 ■ Guilford Genealogist

Guilford County Genealogical Society
Box 9693
Greensboro, NC 27429-0693

Contact: Mary A. Browning, Editor.

Desc: Abstracts public records, brief family genealogies, Bible records, cemetery records, and other matters of genealogical interest to those researching Guilford County, North Carolina families. Recurring features include letters to the editor, news of research, book reviews and information and inquiries on Guilford families, tombstones, and court records. *Freq:* Quarterly. *Price:* Included in membership; $20/year for nonmembers.

3693 ■ Halfyard Heritage Newsletter

R.R. Halfyard
9 Frontenac Dr.   Ph: (905)934-3651
St. Catharines, ON, Canada
L2M 2E1

Contact: Robert R. Halfyard, Editor.

Desc: Features historical and genealogical information on the Halfyard surname. Recurring features include news of research and columns News of Family. *Freq:* Quarterly. *Price:* $10/year, U.S. and Canada.

3694 ■ Hancock Heritage

Hancock County Chapter
Ohio Genealogical Society
PO Box 672
Findlay, OH 45839-0672

Contact: Bev Kelly, Editor; Anita Rush, Editor.

Desc: Furnishes genealogical information relating to Hancock County, Ohio. Provides genealogical charts, Supreme Court district journals, wills, and queries. Recurring features include reports of meetings and news of research. *Freq:* Quarterly. *Price:* Included in membership.

3695 ■ Hart County Historical Society Quarterly

Hart County Historical Society
Box 606
Munfordville, KY 42765

Contact: Susan Craddock Lafferty, Contact.

Desc: Compiles and disseminates historical and genealogical facts on Hart County, Kentucky. *Freq:* Quarterly. *Price:* $12, members.

3696 ■ Hawaii Bottle Museum—News

Hawaii Bottle Museum
PO Box 1635   Ph: (808)775-0411
Honokaa, HI 96727-1635

Contact: Sue Loewenhardt, Editor.

Desc: Reflects the Museum's interest in bottles and the glass industry as they relate to the history of Hawaii and the various groups of people who live in Hawaii. Reports on Museum exhibits and upcoming events. Recurring features include historical trivia, news of research, news of members, and a calendar of events. *Freq:* Semiannual. *Price:* Included in membership; $3/year for nonmembers, U.S. and Canada; $5 elsewhere.

3697 ■ Hazelrigg Family Newsletter

Hazelrigg Family Association
1708 N. Trail Ridge   Ph: (816)252-7303
Independence, MO 64056

Contact: Michael Hazelrigg, Editor.

Desc: Serves as the official publication of the Association, promoting its interest in drawing closer ties between Hazelrigg descendants and furthering genealogical research on the family. Recurring features include letters to the editor, news of research, and notices of upcoming family events and reunions. *Price:* Included in membership.

3698 ■ Heartlines

Heart of America Genealogical Society
Kansas City Public Library, 3rd   Ph: (816)701-3445
Fl., Gen. Rm.
311 E. 12th St.
Kansas City, MO 64106

Contact: Marilyn R. Finke, President.

Desc: Supplies information on genealogical research resources, news of the Society and its library, news of other genealogical societies, and a list of library acquisitions. *Freq:* 4/year. *Price:* Included in membership.

3699 ■ The Heller Helper

BGM Publications
28635 Old Hideaway Rd.   Ph: (708)639-2400
Cary, IL 60013

Contact: Betty G. Massman, Editor; Gayle J. Larson, Editor.

Desc: Functions as a research aid for genealogists seeking their Heller roots, and as a means for bringing together Heller cousins and family members. Publishes primary and secondary resources, family Bible records, and other information on the Heller surname. Includes notices of births, deaths, and weddings. *Freq:* Quarterly. *Price:* $18/year.

3700 ■ The Heritage Dispatch

Haileybury Heritage Museum
451 Meridian Ave.   Ph: (705)672-1922
PO Box 911   Fax: (705)672-3200
Haileybury, ON, Canada P0J
1K0

Contact: Brian Dobbs, Editor.

Desc: Provides information about the Haileybury Heritage Museum in Ontario, Canada. Recurring features include a calendar of events.

3701 ■ Herlacher Herald

RHC Enterprises, Inc.
19341 Knotty Pine Way   Ph: (303)481-2875
Monument, CO 80132

Contact: Ruth Herlacher Christian, Editor.

Desc: Concerned with current activities of the Horlacher family and with their ancestors. Carries genealogical research information and birth, death, and marriage announcements. Recurring features include a query column. *Freq:* Quarterly. *Price:* $6/year, U.S.

3702 ■ HIAS Headlines & Highlights

Hebrew Immigrant Aid Society (HIAS)
333 7th Ave.   Ph: (212)613-1351
New York, NY 10001-5004   Fax: (212)967-4483

Contact: Kara Larson, Editor.

Desc: Reports on HIAS activities and information regarding refugee migration and resettlement in the United States and around the world. *Freq:* Quarterly. *Price:* Included in membership.

3703 ■ The Highpoint

Summit County Genealogical Society
PO Box 2232   Ph: (330)733-6185
Akron, OH 44309
E-mail: summit0gs@acorn.net

Contact: Howard Hill, Editor.

Desc: Provides genealogical information such as cemetery records, vital statistics, and newspaper excerpts. Announces chapter meetings and seminars. Allows free queries. Recurring features include news of research, reports of meetings, news of educational opportunities, and notices of publications available. *Freq:* 10/year. *Price:* Included in membership.

3704 ■ Hinman Heritage

Hinman Family Association (HFA)
c/o Milton E. Hinman   Ph: (602)890-2827
2263 E. Leonora St.
Mesa, AZ 85213-2259

Contact: Milton E. Hinman, Editor.

Desc: Concentrates on providing historical information on the Hinman family, including birth, marriage, and death notices, articles from newspapers, wills, and census and war records. Recurring features include letters to the editor, queries, a calendar of events, and a column titled Letter From the President of the HFA. *Freq:* Quarterly. *Price:* Included in membership.

3705 ■ Historic Kern

Kern County Historical Society
PO Box 141   Ph: (805)322-4962
Bakersfield, CA 93302

Contact: Curtis Darling, Editor.

Desc: Consists of the Society's news and local historical information on Kern County, California. *Freq:* Quarterly. *Price:* $3.50, individuals; $1, single issue.

3706 ■ Historic New Orleans Collection Quarterly

Historic New Orleans Collection
533 Royal St.   Ph: (504)523-4662
New Orleans, LA 70130   Fax: (504)598-7104
URL: http://www.hnoc.org

Contact: Patricia Brady, Editor; Louise C. Hoffman, Editor.

Desc: Features articles relating to New Orleans history and to the projects, activities, and acquisitions of the Historic New Orleans Collection, which is a history museum of New Orleans and the Gulf South. Recurring features include news of research, meeting reports, and notices of publications available. Also carries staff profiles and a column from the Director. *Freq:* Quarterly. *Price:* Free.

3707 ■ Historical Footnotes

Concordia Historical Institute
801 DeMun Ave.   Ph: (314)505-7900
St. Louis, MO 63105   Fax: (314)505-7901
E-mail: chi@chi.lcms.org

URL: http://chi.lcms.org/; http://chi.lcms.org/
    publications/histfoot.htm

Contact: Marvin Huggins, Editor.

Desc: Provides information on activities, programs, and collections of the Institute. Relates news of Lutheran Church history and archives in North America. Recurring features include news of research and reports of meetings. *Freq:* 4/year. *Price:* Included in membership.

3708 ■ Historical and Genealogical Society of Indiana County Newsletter

Historical and Genealogical Society of Indiana County
Silas M. Clark House   Ph: (412)463-9600
200 S. 6th St.
Indiana, PA 15701-2999

Desc: Covers Society meetings and activities. Contains announcements, notices of publications available, news of members, a calendar of events, and a list of monetary and material donations. *Price:* Included in membership.

3709 ■ History Center News

Historical Society of Rockland County
20 Zukor Rd.   Ph: (914)634-9629
New City, NY 10956   Fax: (914)634-8690
E-mail: hsrockland@aol.com

Contact: Sarah E. Henrich, Director.

Desc: Provides information on the historical society's activities, events, exhibits, and volunteer programs. Also contains history and news on Rockland County, New York. *Freq:* Quarterly. *Price:* $30, family; $25, individuals.

3710 ■ Hogan Family Association—Research Quarterly

Terry M. Hogan
2647 Willow Lake Dr.
Greenwood, IN 46143

Contact: Terry M. Hogan, Editor.

Desc: Contains historical and genealogical information on the Hogan family. Concentrates on research, including findings and research tips along with information on genealogical services available. Recurring features include notices of publications available. *Freq:* Semiannual. *Price:* Included in membership.

3711 ■ Hollowell Heritage

Palouse Publications
310 SE Camino   Ph: (509)334-1732
Pullman, WA 99163-2206

Contact: Janet Margolis Damm, Editor.

Desc: Provides a network for Hollowell family researchers. Recurring features include news of educational opportunities, a calendar of events, reports of meetings, book reviews, and notices of publications available. *Freq:* Irregular. *Price:* $6.50/issue.

3712 ■ Hoopes Family Organization Newsletter

Hoopes Family Organization, Inc.
910 Delaware   Ph: (415)841-7713
Berkeley, CA 94710

Contact: Zan H. Turner, Editor.

Desc: Updates the three completed volumes of the Hoopes Family Record with additions and corrections to the research already completed. Also carries reprints of relevant news articles and personal letters of interest to the extended Hoopes family. Recurring features include news of members. *Freq:* Semiannual. *Price:* Included in membership; $12/year for nonmembers, U.S. and Canada; free to institutions.

3713 ■ Hoosier Genealogist

Indiana Historical Society
315 W. Ohio St.   Ph: (317)232-1882
Indianapolis, IN 46202-3299   Free: 800-447-1830
                              Fax: (317)233-3109
URL: http://www.indianahistory.org/

Contact: Ruth Dorrel, Editor.

Desc: Contains local historical and genealogical information. *Freq:* Quarterly. *Price:* $30, members.

3714 ■ Hubbell Family Historical Society—Annual

Hubbell Family Historical Society
2051 E. McDaniel St.
PO Box 3813 GS
Springfield, MO 65808-3813

Contact: Robert L. Hubbell, Editor.

Desc: Distributed by the Society to inform members of updated genealogical information on the Hubbell, Hubbel, Hubble, Huble, and Hubel family. Contains items of biographical and historical interest and Society news. Recurring features include membership list, obituaries, and queries. *Freq:* Annual. *Price:* Included in membership.

3715 ■ Hubbell Family History Society—Family Notes

Hubbell Family Historical Society
2051 E. McDaniel St.
PO Box 3813 GS
Springfield, MO 65808-3813

Contact: John A. Hubbell, Editor.

Desc: Informs members about personal news items, accomplishments of family members, society projects and events. *Freq:* Semiannual. *Price:* Included in membership.

3716 ■ Humphrey Family Quarterly

Robert L. Humphrey
701 Mountain Trail   Ph: (205)647-3485
Warrior, AL 35180

Contact: Robert Llewellyn Humphrey, Editor.

Desc: Seeks to be a continuing resource for Humphrey family researchers and those interested in family history in general. Recurring features include genealogical charts, research queries, newspaper clippings, reproduced source documents, biographical sketches, and notices of publications available. Also contains letters to the editor and news of family reunions and other events of interest. *Freq:* Quarterly. *Price:* Included in membership.

3717 ■ Hunterdon Historical Newsletter

Hunterdon County Historical Society
114 Main St.   Ph: (908)782-1091
Flemington, NJ 08822

Contact: Roxanne K. Charkhuff, Editorial Chair.

Desc: Publishes local history and genealogy articles, as well as Society news. Recurring features include a collection, book reviews, and Notes and Queries, Acquisitions, and Family Associations. *Price:* $15, individuals; $25, institutions.

3718 ■ The Hyden Families

Hyden Families Association
PO Box 6575   Ph: (504)834-3632
New Orleans, LA 70174

Contact: Gene Hyden, Editor.

Desc: Seeks to provide genealogical and historical information concerning Hiden and Hyden surnames. Reprints out-of-print research works and publishes original source materials, including biographical sketches of ancestors.

Encourages contributions of historical records to aid in genealogical research and provides a forum for presenting research queries. Publishes occasional special issues focusing on a specific state or country. Recurring features include columns titled Feedback and Missing Cousins. *Freq:* Quarterly. *Price:* $15/year, U.S. and Canada.

3719 ■ Idol Family Newsletter

John L. Idol
PO Box 413   Ph: (919)644-0445
Hillsborough, NC 27278
E-mail: balder@mindspring.com

Contact: John L. Idol, Editor.

Desc: Carries news and information on the Idol family. Recurring features include interviews, a calendar of events, reports of meetings, old family letters, deeds, and a column titled Idol Chatter. *Freq:* Annual. *Price:* $1.50.

3720 ■ IHRC News

Immigration History Research Center
University of Minnesota
826 Berry St.   Ph: (612)627-4208
St. Paul, MN 55114   Fax: (612)627-4190
E-mail: ihrc@gold.tc.umn.edu
URL: http://www.umn.edu/ihrc

Contact: Judith Rosenblatt, Editor.

Desc: Covers Center and Friends of IHRC activities. Details acquisitions of manuscript collections and print materials. Recurring features include interviews, news of research, and notices of publications available. *Freq:* 3/year. *Price:* Free.

3721 ■ Immigrant Genealogical Society Newsletter

Immigrant Genealogical Society
PO Box 7369   Ph: (818)848-3122
Burbank, CA 91510-7369
URL: http://fweeths.org/igs/trgigs.html

Contact: Jean Nepsund, Editor.

Desc: Covers Society business and programs. Contains suggestions for conducting genealogical research. Recurring features include a calendar of events, reports of meetings, news of educational opportunities, book reviews, notices of publications available, news of research, and notices of library acquisitions. *Freq:* Monthly. *Price:* $20, U.S.; $35, foreign.

3722 ■ Immigration Briefings

Federal Publications
1120 20 St. NW   Ph: (202)337-7000
Washington, DC 20036   Free: 800-922-4330
                              Fax: (202)659-2233

Contact: Patricia Mariani, Editor.

Desc: Covers topics in immigration and nationality law. Each issue is a monograph written by an expert in the field. *Alt. Fmts:* CD-ROM. *Freq:* 12/year. *Price:* $366.

3723 ■ Immigration Digest

Family History World
Genealogical Institute
PO Box 22045   Ph: (801)250-6717
Salt Lake City, UT 84122

Contact: Arlene H. Eakle, PhD, Editor.

Desc: Reports on new resources to link immigrant ancestors with their origins. Includes analytical reviews of source books and passenger lists. *Available:* Online. *Freq:* Irregular. *Price:* $16.50, single issue.

3724 ■ Immigration Newsletter

National Immigration Project of the National Lawyers Guild, Inc.
14 Beacon St., Ste. 506   Ph: (617)227-9727
Boston, MA 02108   Fax: (617)227-5495
E-mail: nipdan@nlg.org

Contact: Gail Pendleton, Editor; Dan Kesselbrenner, Editor.

Desc: Discusses immigration issues from the legal viewpoint. Concerned with the protection of civil rights and liberties, the elimination of racism, and the extension of the rights of workers, women, farmers, and minority groups. Recurring features include a listing of available publications, accounts of recent cases, and a column titled Brief Bank. *Freq:* 2-3/year. *Price:* $50, individuals, for four issues; $75, institutions, U.S., for four issues; $100, institutions, elsewhere, for four issues.

3725 ■ Imprints

Genealogical Society of Broward County, Inc.
Box 485   Ph: (954)463-8834
Ft. Lauderdale, FL 33302

Contact: Lillian Trubey, Editor.

Desc: Contains articles, reprints, queries, and local records on genealogical information from Broward County, Florida. *Freq:* Quarterly. *Price:* $12, individuals; $3, single issue.

3726 ■ Infinity

Preservation Section
Society of American Archivists (SAA)
527 S. Wells St., 5th Fl.   Ph: (312)922-0140
Chicago, IL 60607   Fax: (312)347-1452
E-mail: info@archivists.org

Desc: Informs members of Society and archives news and events. Recurring features include news of research, a calendar of events, reports of meetings, news of educational opportunities, book reviews, notices of publications available, and a column titled From the Chair. *Freq:* Quarterly. *Price:* Included in membership.

3727 ■ INS Communique

Immigration and Naturalization Service
U.S. Department of Justice
Chester A. Arthur Bldg.   Ph: (202)514-2648
425 Eye St., N.W.
Washington, DC 20536

Contact: Richard L. Kenney, Editor; Mitchell J. Katz, Associate Editor.

Desc: Provides news and information on the activities of the U.S. Immigration and Naturalization Service and its employees. *Freq:* Monthly. *Price:* free to employees.

3728 ■ The Institute for Southern Studies Newsletter

Institute for Southern Studies
University of South Carolina   Ph: (803)777-2340
Columbia, SC 29208   Fax: (803)777-8987

Contact: Jeannie Weingarth, Editor.

Desc: Examines the lifestyle and culture of the South. Recurring features include notices of publications available. *Freq:* Quarterly. *Price:* Free.

3729 ■ International Newsletter on Migration

Center for Migration Studies of New York, Inc.
209 Flagg Pl.   Ph: (718)351-8800
Staten Island, NY 10304   Fax: (718)667-4598
E-mail: cmslft@aol.com; sales@cms.org
URL: http://www.cmsny.org

Contact: Catherine Wihtol de Wenden, Editor; Lydio F. Tomasi, Ph.D., Editor.

Desc: Reports on conferences, publications, research projects, and other developments concerning international immigration and refugees. *Freq:* Quarterly. *Price:* $29.50, individuals; $64, institutions; $38.50, other countries; $73, institutions, other countries.

3730 ■ International Society for British Genealogy and Family History Newsletter

International Society for British Genealogy and Family History (ISBGFH)
PO Box 3115   Ph: (801)272-2178
Salt Lake City, UT 84110-3115

Contact: Sherry Irvine, Editor.

Desc: Contains feature articles on British and Irish genealogical research. Includes queries from members, news items, and reviews of new publications. *Freq:* Quarterly. *Price:* Included in membership.

3731 ■ Interpreter Releases

Federal Publications
1120 20 St. NW   Ph: (202)337-7000
Washington, DC 20036   Free: 800-922-4330
      Fax: (202)659-2233
URL: http://www.fedpub.com/immigration/

Contact: Maurice A. Roberts, Editor Emeritus; Juan P. Osuna, Managing Editor; Danielle M. Polen, Editor; Patricia Mariani, Editor.

Desc: Covers immigration and nationality law: legislative developments, amendments to regulations, statistical data, and digests of court and administrative agency decisions. Recurring features include articles by experts in the field. *Alt. Fmts:* CD-ROM. *Freq:* 48/year. *Price:* $522; $422, universities, public libraries.

3732 ■ Iowa Genealogical Society Newsletter

Iowa Genealogical Society
Box 7735   Ph: (515)276-0287
Des Moines, IA 50322-7735
E-mail: igs@digiserve.com
URL: http://www.digiserve.com/igs/igs.htm

Contact: George Giesler, Editor.

Desc: Updates society activities and current events. Recurring features include news of research, a calendar of events, reports of meetings, news of educational opportunities, and notices of publications available. *Freq:* Bimonthly. *Price:* Included in membership; $25, individuals; $29, Family.

3733 ■ Ireton Newsletter

Family History & Genealogy Center
1300 E. 109th St.   Ph: (816)942-5497
Kansas City, MO 64131   Fax: (816)943-0477

Contact: La Roux Gillespie, Editor.

Desc: Provides genealogy and history on families with the surname Ireton/Irton/Urton. Recurring features include letters to the editor and interviews. *Freq:* Quarterly. *Price:* $12.

3734 ■ Irish Families

Irish Genealogical Foundation
PO Box 7575   Ph: (816)454-2410
Kansas City, MO 64116   Fax: (816)454-2410
URL: http://www.irishroots.com; http://www.irishroots.com

Contact: Michael C. O'Laughline, Owner.

Desc: Promotes research on Irish heritage and genealogy. Recurring features include letters to the editor, news of

members, a calendar of events, news of research, and notices of publications available. *Freq:* 12/year. *Price:* $54, 6/year; $104, 12/year.

3735 ■ ISGS Newsletter

Illinois State Genealogical Society
PO Box 10195   Ph: (217)789-1968
Springfield, IL 62791-0195

Desc: Keeps members abreast of what is going on in Illinois and surrounding areas in genealogy. Recurring features include a question and answer column. *Freq:* Quarterly. *Price:* Included in membership.

3736 ■ Jackson County History

Jackson County Historical Society
PO Box 22   Ph: (304)372-2541
Ripley, WV 25271-0022

Contact: Carolyn T. Miihlbach, Editor.

Desc: Presents historical articles on those individuals who resided in Jackson County, West Virginia. Includes marriage, death, and war documents. *Freq:* Quarterly. *Price:* Included in membership; $14/year for nonmembers.

3737 ■ Jacob's Ladder

Christlieb-Chrislip-Crislip Family Association
693 Ridge Rd.   Ph: (518)793-6869
Queensbury, NY 12804-6901

Contact: Ned Crislip, Editor.

Desc: Promotes family unity among those with the surname Christlieb, Chrislip, or Crislip. Supplies updates on Association activities and publishes various biographical and genealogical data on family members. Recurring features include letters to the editor, notices of publications available, book reviews, meeting reports, poetry, and columns titled A Few Minutes With Our President, Sunshine and Sorrow, and Bits and Pieces. *Freq:* 4/year. *Price:* Included in membership; free to libraries and historical societies.

3738 ■ Janney Journal

Sue Wight
PO Box 413   Ph: (801)738-2705
Duchesne, UT 84021

Contact: Susan J. Wight, Editor.

Desc: Compiles genealogical information on the Janney surname. Discusses current news of living family members. Recurring features include letters to the editor, news of genealogical research, a calendar of events, and reports of meetings. *Freq:* Quarterly. *Price:* $10/year, U.S. and Canada.

3739 ■ The John and Mable Ringling Museum of Art Newsletter

John and Mable Ringling Museum of Art
5401 Bay Shore Rd.   Ph: (941)359-5700
Sarasota, FL 34243   Fax: (941)359-5745

Contact: Barbara Linick, Editor.

Desc: Provides news and information concerning activities of the Museum. Recognizes new members and volunteers. Publicizes support from grants, corporations, endowments, and contributions. Features art from the collection and works of historical significance. *Freq:* 4/year. *Price:* Included in membership.

3740 ■ Johnson Reporter

Johnson Family Niagra Peninsula Region
504 Kilman Rd., RR 1   Ph: (905)892-2390
Ridgeville, ON, Canada L0S 1M0

Contact: Roy Johnson, Editor; David Johnson, Editor.

Desc: Provides genealogical information on the Johnson family and others. *Freq:* Biennial. *Price:* C$10.

3741 ■ Journal of the Lancaster County Historical Society

Lancaster County Historical Society
230 N. President Ave.   Ph: (717)392-4633
Lancaster, PA 17603-3125

Contact: John W. W. Loose, Editor.

Desc: Covers local history and genealogy. *Freq:* Quarterly. *Price:* Free to members; $5, single issue.

3742 ■ J.W. Dawes Family Newletter

Ardath Dawes
259 East Ave.   Ph: (412)588-5153
Greenville, PA 16125

Contact: Ardath Dawes, Editor.

Desc: Provides genealogical and historical information relating to descendants of J.W. Dawes. Contains current research, including notices of births, marriages, and deaths. Publishes information sent by correspondents of interest to readers. Recurring features include reports of annual meetings and columns titled Presidential Message, From the Editor, Yesterdays Memories, Writing Your Memories, and Chart of J.W. Dawes Descendants. *Available:* Online. *Freq:* 3/year. *Price:* $12.

3743 ■ The Kansas City Genealogist

Heart of America Genealogical Society
Kansas City Public Library, 3rd   Ph: (816)701-3445
   Fl., Gen. Rm.
311 E. 12th St.
Kansas City, MO 64106

Contact: Joanne C. Eakin, Editor.

Desc: Carries historical articles about Missouri and surrounding environs, especially Jackson County, Missouri. Publishes bible records, court records, cemetery listings, and related material. Recurring features include queries, a calendar of events, news of research, book reviews, and a column titled My Favorite Ancestor. *Freq:* Quarterly. *Price:* $15/year.

3744 ■ Kansas Review

Kansas Council Genealogical Societies Inc.
PO Box 3858   Ph: (913)774-4411
Topeka, KS 66604-6858

Contact: Ruth Sanderson, Editor.

Desc: Features news of the Society, historical and genealogical records, and publications relating to the state of Kansas and its residents. Recurring features include news of research, calendar of events, reports of meetings, book reviews, and notices of publications available. *Remarks:* Alternate phone numbers are (785)272-7550 and (913)962-2669. *Freq:* Quarterly. *Price:* Included in membership; $10/year for nonmembers.

3745 ■ Keeping a "Lowe" Profile

Brenda Lowe-Acquaviva
4801 Woodhall   Ph: (313)640-8030
Detroit, MI 48224-2226
E-mail: tombston@ix.netcom.com
URL: http://www.geocities.com/Heartland/Plains/2684

Contact: Brenda Lowe-Acquaviva, Editor; Carol Nowak, Co-Editor; Anne Hood, Contributing Editor.

Desc: Devoted to the Lowe surname and its variants, including Low, Law, Lough, Loe, and others. *Freq:* 3/year. *Price:* $17, per year for three issues.

3746 ■ Kennedy—Gazette

Kennedy Society of America, Inc.
520 Harrison Ave.   Ph: (740)432-6263
Cambridge, OH 43725

Contact: Donald G. Canaday, Editor.

Desc: Provides news and activities of the Society and articles of the Scottish Kennedy Clan. Features information on highland games. Recurring features include letters to the editor, a calendar of events, reports of meetings, listings of new members, and columns titled Miscellany, Genealogy, and News from the Family. *Freq:* Quarterly. *Price:* Included in membership.

3747 ■ Kershner Kinfolk

Kershner Family Association
1449 Fox Run Dr.   Ph: (704)535-6025
Charlotte, NC 28212   Fax: (704)535-8345

Contact: William E. Kershner, Jr., Editor.

Desc: Presents articles on the history and genealogy of the Kershner family (including those with the surnames Kirschner, Kerschner, Karshner, Karschner, and Cashner). Relates Kershner family activities, publishes results of research, and reprints official records of interest. Recurring features include notices of publications available, letters to the editor, and columns titled Queries and Vital Statistics. *Freq:* Quarterly. *Price:* Included in membership; $14, annually.

3748 ■ Kingston Relations

Kingston Branch
Ontario Genealogical Society
Box 1394
Kingston, ON, Canada K7L 5C6

Contact: Dawn Broughton, Editor.

Desc: Discusses genealogy. Recurring features include news of research, a calendar of events, reports of meetings, notices of publications available, and a column titled Surname Search. *Freq:* 5/year. *Price:* Included in membership.

3749 ■ Kinship Kronicle

Rockingham Society of Genealogists
PO Box 81   Ph: (603)436-5824
Exeter, NH 03833-0081

Contact: Carl W. Brage, Editor.

Desc: Offers information on genealogical materials and queries. *Freq:* Quarterly. *Price:* $6.50/year, U.S.; $8, Canada; $10 elsewhere.

3750 ■ KWM Newsletter

Kendall Whaling Museum
PO Box 297   Ph: (781)784-5642
Sharon, MA 02067   Fax: (781)784-0451
URL: http://www.kwm.org

Contact: Elisabeth J. McGregor, Editor.

Desc: Disseminates news of collections and programs of the Kendall Whaling Museum, which is concerned with the history of whaling, marine art, maritime history, enthnology, natural history, and cetology. Recurring features include research news, a calendar of events, reports of meetings, reviews and notices of publications, and columns titled Recent Acquisitions, Looking Back, Speaking Frankly, Gems from the Library, Gems from the manuscript collection. *Freq:* Quarterly. *Price:* Included in membership.

3751 ■ Lasater Lineage's

Olsen Enterprises
3931 S. 238th St.   Fax: (206)878-4267
Kent, WA 98032

Desc: Designed to help families with the surname Lasater (and its variant spellings) to find ancestors, missing relatives, and learn about other Lasater's in both the past and present. Also contains handwriting analysis. *Freq:* Quarterly. *Price:* $15, U.S.

3752 ■ Latin American Jewish Studies

Latin American Jewish Studies Association (LAJSA)
Dept. of Modern Languages   Ph: (610)328-8682
   and Literatures   Fax: (610)328-7769
Swarthmore College
500 College Ave.
Swarthmore, PA 19081
E-mail: jfriedm1@swarthmore.edu

Contact: Joan Esther Friedman, Editor.

Desc: Supports an information network among scholars studying Latin American Jewry. Recurring features include book reviews, current bibliography, conference news, letters to the editor, job listings, and interviews. *Alt. Fmts:* mailing lists. *Freq:* Semiannual. *Price:* $30, individuals; $41, institutions; $13, students.

3753 ■ The Laughlin Eagle

The Laughlin Eagle
1270 63rd Terrace So.   Ph: (813)867-3982
St. Petersburg, FL 33705   Fax: (813)867-5002

Contact: Richard G. Racheter, Editor.

Desc: Concerned with Homer Laughlin. *Freq:* Quarterly. *Price:* $18, individuals, U.S.

3754 ■ Lawton Issue

Tony Fusco
159 Linwood Ave.
Buffalo, NY 14209-2003

Desc: Dedicated to the surname of Lawton, including variant spellings. Covers records, histories, and free queries. *Freq:* Quarterly. *Price:* $16, individuals, U.S.

3755 ■ Leavenworth County Historical Society Gazette

Leavenworth County Historical Society
1128 5th Ave.   Ph: (913)682-7759
Leavenworth, KS 66048-3213   Fax: (913)682-2089
URL: http://leavenworth-net.com/lchs

Contact: Robert A. Holt, Editor.

Desc: Provides news and information for members of the Society. Also contains history on Leavenworth County. *Freq:* Quarterly. *Price:* $10, individuals; $2.50, single issue.

3756 ■ Lehmer-Leamer-Lamer Newsletter

Laurence E. Leamer
221 Torrance Ave.   Ph: (607)748-6021
Vestal, NY 13850

Contact: Laurence E. Leamer, Editor.

Desc: Carries current family news and genealogical information concerning descendants and in-laws of Johannes and Wilhelm Lehmer, who came to York County, Pennsylvania, from Stammheim, Germany, in 1750. Publishes historical items and listings of family births, deaths, and marriages. Recurring features include news of research, letters to the editor, reports of meetings, book reviews and notices of publications available, and a calendar of events. Also includes columns titled Arrivals, Departures, Recruits, and Additions and Updates. *Freq:* Semiannual. *Price:* $3/year.

3757 ▪ Lennox and Addington Historical Society Newsletter

Lenjalin Publications
1330 Terrace Park Dr.   Ph: (319)359-7220
Bettendorf, IA 52722-0816

Contact: Sharon Milrey, Editor.

Freq: 9/year.

3758 ▪ Library & Museums Quarterly

Springfield Library & Museums
220 State St.   Ph: (413)263-6800
Springfield, MA 01103-1772   Fax: (413)263-6807
E-mail: jhanna@spfldlibmus.org

Contact: Marianne Gambaro, Director of Public Relations.

Desc: Lists exhibitions, activities, courses, and other information about the Springfield Library & Museums. Recurring features include articles on collections and donor information. *Freq:* Quarterly. *Price:* Included in membership.

3759 ▪ LIRS Bulletin

Lutheran Immigration and Refugee Service (LIRS)
390 Park Ave. S.   Ph: (212)532-6350
New York, NY 10016-8803   Fax: (212)683-1329

Contact: Benjamin Bankson, Editor.

Desc: Provides human interest stories, commentaries, and updates about U.S. refugee resettlement and advocacy relating to the Lutheran network. Reports news on LIRS activities, developments in U.S. immigration policy, and the availability of new LIRS materials. *Freq:* 2/year. *Price:* Free.

3760 ▪ Livesay Bulletin

Livesay Historical Society
c/o Virginia Smith   Ph: (717)328-3810
104 Linden Ave.
Mercersburg, PA 17236

Contact: Virginia Smith, Editor.

Desc: Compiles genealogical information on the Lievsay/Levesey/Livesey/Leausay family and promotes fellowship among family members. Publishes historical background on ancestors in England and carries census records, will, old letters, military and cemetery records, and other items of interest. Recurring features include Society news, notices of publications available, meeting reports, and a calendar of events. *Freq:* 4/year. *Price:* $20.

3761 ▪ The Locke Sickle & Sword

Locke Family Association
102 Crooked Spring Rd.   Ph: (617)251-4804
North Chelmsford, MA 01863
URL: http://people.ne.mediaone.net/ddhayes

Contact: Donald P. Hayes, Editor.

Desc: Reports on activities of the Association, a genealogical organization interested in descendants of John Locke and Nathaniel Locke of New Hampshire and William Locke of Massachusetts. Contains news of research and queries. Recurring features include interviews, meeting reports, notices of publications available, and a calendar of events. *Freq:* 4/year. *Price:* Included in membership.

3762 ▪ Long Island Archives Conference Newsletter

Long Island Archives Conference
History Department   Ph: (718)990-6229
St. John's University   Fax: (718)380-0353
Jamaica, NY 11439

Contact: Richard Harmond, Editor.

Desc: Covers upcoming events and acquisitions of the Department, including national and state government and nongovernment archives. Recurring features include reports of meetings, job listings, and columns titled President's Column and What's New. *Freq:* 3/year. *Price:* Free.

3763 ▪ Lookin' for Lockes

Orella Chadwick
7650 Fairview Rd.   Ph: (503)842-6036
Tillamook, OR 97141

Contact: Orella Chadwick, Editor.

Desc: Provides genealogical information, charts, and data on Locke descendants outside of Massachusetts and New Hampshire. Publishes census and Bible records, deeds, wills, and other items of interest. Recurring features include queries from researchers. *Freq:* Quarterly. *Price:* $15, individuals.

3764 ▪ Los Meganos

East Contra Costa Historical Society & Museum
PO Box 547   Ph: (510)684-2117
Bethel Island, CA 94511   Fax: (510)684-9610

Contact: Robert D. Gromm, Editor.

Desc: Provides information on East Contra Costa Historical Society meetings, and historical information. Recurring features include pioneer family profiles. *Freq:* 4/year. *Price:* Included in membership, Free, school and county libraries.

3765 ▪ Lower Cape Fear Historical Society Newsletter

Lower Cape Fear Historical Society
126 S. 3rd St.   Ph: (910)762-0492
Wilmington, NC 28401   Fax: (910)763-5869
E-mail: latimer@wilmington.net

Contact: Blonnie Wyche, Editor.

Desc: Contains news of the Society and coverage of speeches by members. *Freq:* Quarterly. *Price:* Included in membership.

3766 ▪ The Luptonian

David Walker Lupton
PO Box 443   Ph: (252)745-7037
Bayboro, NC 28515-0443
E-mail: cn3038@coastalnet.com

Contact: David Walker Lupton, Editor.

Desc: Presents articles, family histories, genealogical listings, and queries pertaining to individuals with the Lupton surname. Recurring features include news of research, letters to the editor, news of members, and book reviews. *Freq:* Irregular. *Price:* Free.

3767 ▪ Lybarger Linkages

Lybarger Memorial Association
PO Box 611
Delaware, OH 43015-0611
E-mail: lybarger@midohio.net

Contact: Lee H. Lybarger, Contact.

Desc: Provides family history and genealogical information on the Lybargers. *Freq:* Semiannual.

3768 ▪ Mac Dhubhaich

Clan MacDuff Society of America
8278 Longford Dr.   Ph: (817)244-2049
Fort Worth, TX 76116
E-mail: bmcduff@aol.com

Contact: Noliah McDuff, Editor.

Desc: Includes material on Clan MacDuff Society activities, as well as information about Scottish games, historical

articles, genealogical queries, and related resources. Recurring features include a calendar of events, a Covener's column, a Regional Covener's column, and a Genealogist's column. *Freq:* Quarterly. *Price:* Included in membership; $15, nonmembers; $15, institutions.

3769 ▪ Madden Family Newsletter

Mariam W. Schaefer
1101 Wilmington Ave., Apt. A   Ph: (513)293-0779
Dayton, OH 45420
E-mail: 105367.634@compuserve.com

Contact: Marian W. Schaefer, Editor.

Desc: Compiles genealogical information and data on the Madden family and descendants in the U.S., Canada, Great Britain, Ireland, and elsewhere. Carries census, land, marriage, cemetary, and other records. Recurring features include queries and news of members. *Freq:* Quarterly. *Price:* $15/year, U.S.; $20 elsewhere.

3770 ▪ Magny Families Association Newsletter

Magny Families Association
56 Remington Rd.   Ph: (203)683-8943
Windsor, CT 06095

Contact: Dorothy Many, Editor.

Desc: Serves as an information exchange for the Association, which is devoted to helping members "establish and document family lines of descent, both male and female, from any Manee/Maney/Manny/Manney/Many/etc." Provides lineage charts, census data, excerpts from diaries, puzzles, births/deaths/marriages of members, information about family reunions. *Freq:* Semiannual. *Price:* $15/year.

3771 ▪ MAHD Bulletin

Museums, Arts, and Humanities Division (MAHD)
Special Libraries Association (SLA)
c/o Eliza Robertson   Ph: (919)549-0661
National Humanities Center   Fax: (919)990-8535
7 Alexander Dr.
Research Triangle Park, NC
  27709

Contact: Eliza Robertson, Editor.

Desc: Discusses pertinent events, issues, and publications concerning special libraries. Recurring features include interviews, news of research, a calendar of events, reports of meetings, news of educational opportunities, book reviews, notices of publications available, and a column titled On My Mind. *Freq:* 4/year. *Price:* Included in membership.

3772 ▪ Manley Family Newsletter

Trudi Manley
171 Nathan Dr.   Ph: (516)567-0386
Bohemia, NY 11716

Contact: Trudi Manley, Editor.

Desc: "Dedicated to preserving history, informing Manley/Manly descendants of their heritage, and acquainting family members with other living relatives." Carries lineage charts and data, photographs, biographies of Manley/Manly ancestors and living descendants, researched historical genealogical articles, and family reunion news. Recurring features include queries and research information from readers, interviews, Manley/Manly business and place names, current family news and activities. *Freq:* Semiannual. *Price:* $15/year.

3773 ▪ Manuscript Society—News

The Manuscript Society
350 N. Niagara St.
Burbank, CA 91505
E-mail: manuscrip@aol.com

Contact: S.L. Carson, Editor.

Desc: Examines news regarding location and collection of handwritten documents, letters, and autographs of historic value. Carries news on preservation, thefts, forgeries, exhibits, and discoveries. Reports current chapter and Society news. Recurring features include news of members, personal profiles, annual meetings, notices of sale and trade opportunities, announcements of auctions, and a column from the president on the collection of historic documents. *Freq:* Quarterly. *Price:* Included in membership.

3774 ■ The Maple Leaflet

French-Canadian Genealogical Society of Connecticut, Inc.
Box 928   Ph: (860)872-2597
Tolland, CT 06084-0928

Contact: Paul Labossiere, Editor.

Desc: Contains articles on French-Canadian Genealogical Society of Connecticut's library events and new acquisitions. *Freq:* Quarterly. *Price:* $20, members.

3775 ■ Maryland Genealogical Society Newsletter

Maryland Genealogical Society, Inc.
201 W. Monument St.   Ph: (410)685-3750
Baltimore, MD 21201
E-mail: pdanders@MdHs.org; pdanders@mdhs.org

Contact: Ella Rowe, Editor.

Desc: Publishes news of the Society, its members, and its activities. Contains information on the location and availability of genealogical research resources such as tombstone inscriptions, wills, marriage records, and materials available in specific collections or regions of the U.S. Recurring features include News of other genealogical societies. *Freq:* 4/year. *Price:* Included in membership.

3776 ■ Maryland's Colonial Families Newsletter

Charla Ann Marchione
28 Park Circle
Cherry Hill, NJ 08034-2614

Contact: Charla Ann Marchione, Editor.

Desc: Concerned with Maryland ancestors, including surnames such as Beall, Brewer, Butler, Carmack, Crist, Crockett, Duvall, Edmundson, Friend, Gist, Gorsuch, Hedges, Julian, Morgan, Norris, Odell, Ogden, Owens, Prather, Ray, Ridenour, Swearinen, Thomas, Van Meter, Walling, and Williams. Searches for ancestors and publishes findings in the newsletter. Also contains militia lists, church records, and other information. Accepts free queries from subscribers. *Freq:* Quarterly. *Price:* $12, individuals, U.S.; $3, single issue.

3777 ■ Mason Family Newsletter

Compu-Chart
363 S. Park Victoria Dr.   Ph: (408)262-1051
Milpitas, CA 95035-5708
E-mail: 103137.3321@compuserve.com

Contact: Paula Perkins Mortensen, Editor.

Desc: Contains genealogical information on the Mason surname. *Freq:* Quarterly. *Price:* $10/year, U.S.; $15 elsewhere.

3778 ■ McCord

McCord Museum of Canadian History
690 Sherbrooke St. W.   Ph: (514)398-7100
Montreal, PQ, Canada H3A   Fax: (514)398-5045
   1E9

Contact: Wanda Palma, Editor.

Desc: Informs the public of the Museum's activities and collections. Describes exhibitions, special events, announcements, sponsorships, upcoming projects, programs, and publications. Recurring features include news of research, a calendar of events, and columns titled "Profile" and "Interview". Remarks: English and French versions available. *Freq:* 3/year. *Price:* Included in membership.

3779 ■ Member News

Minnesota Historical Society
345 Kellogg Blvd. W.   Ph: (651)297-5774
St. Paul, MN 55102-1906   Fax: (651)297-2967

Contact: Laurie Brickley, Editor; Elizabeth Sagisser Turichin, Editor; Therese Downey, Editor.

Desc: Informs members of Society activities and events, with features on exhibits at the Society's Historic Sites and the Minnesota History Center. Focuses on the Society's collections of art, photographs, manuscripts, artifacts, books, and maps. Covers the historic preservation movement in Minnesota. projects, historic sites, and museums. Recurring features include publications and acquisitions, a calendar of events, and columns titled Exhibits on the Road, Ask An Expert, News Notes, and Classes and Workshops. *Freq:* Bimonthly. *Price:* Included in membership.

3780 ■ Mercer County Heritage

Mercer County Historical Society
119 S. Pitt St.
Mercer, PA 16137

Contact: William Philson, Editor.

Desc: Updates members on the Mercer County Historical Society's events and news. Includes local history information. *Freq:* Quarterly. *Price:* Free, for members.

3781 ■ Meriwether Connections

Meriwether Society
PO Box 19967
San Diego, CA 92159
E-mail: TMSIMC@aol.com

Contact: Joe M. Oglesby, Editor.

Desc: Covers the family history and genealogy of individuals with the surname Meriwether. Contains genealogical queries and news of interest to the Society. *Freq:* Quarterly. *Price:* Included in membership; $15/year for nonmembers; free to institutions.

3782 ■ MHEP Quarterly

Mennonite Historians of Eastern Pennsylvania (MHEP)
Box 82   Ph: (215)256-3020
565 Yoder Rd.   Fax: (215)256-3023
Harleysville, PA 19438
E-mail: info@mhep.org

Contact: Beth Rice Imchen, Editor.

Desc: Contains articles on area Mennonite history and family genealogy. Serves as a communications vehicle to members. Recurring features include a calendar of events, reports of meetings, news of research, and notices of publications available. *Freq:* Bimonthly. *Price:* Included in membership; $25, individuals; $35, institutions, U.S.; $31, individuals; $41, institutions, Canada.

3783 ■ Mid-Atlantic Archivist

Mid-Atlantic Regional Archives Conference
c/o George   Ph: (202)994-7283
   Washington University   Fax: (202)463-6205
The Gelman Library
2130 H St. NW
Washington, DC 20052

Contact: G. David Anderson, Editor.

Desc: Contains news and information for and about members of the Conference. Seeks exchange of information between colleagues, improvement of competence among archivists, and encourages professional involvement of persons actively engaged in the preservation and use of historical research materials. Recurring features include letters to the editor, news of members, book reviews, a calendar of events, and columns titled Preservation News, Reference Shelf, Session Abstracts, Software News, and Employment Opportunities. Remarks: Alternate fax number is (202) 994-1340. *Freq:* Quarterly. *Price:* Included in membership; $10/year for nonmembers.

3784 ■ Milestones

Miles Merwin (1623-1697) Association, Inc.
1733 Blue Bell Rd.   Ph: (215)646-0231
Blue Bell, PA 19422-2117

Contact: Merwyn R. Buchanan, Editor.

Desc: Contains genealogical information relating to the descendants of Miles Merwin (1623-1697). Gives notice of Association events and research findings. Recurring features include news of members, reports of meetings, book reviews, notices of publications available, and a calendar of events. *Freq:* 3/year. *Price:* $12.50/year.

3785 ■ Mill Race Quarterly

Northville Historical Society
PO Box 71   Ph: (810)348-1845
Northville, MI 48167   Fax: (248)348-0056

Contact: Sandra Basse, Editor.

Desc: Contains historical articles and features of events at the Village. Recurring features include a collection. *Freq:* Quarterly. *Price:* $10.

3786 ■ Minerva

Linda Grant DePauw
20 Granada Rd.   Ph: (410)437-5379
Pasadena, MD 21122-2708

Contact: Linda Grant DePauw, Editor.

Desc: Provides information about women and the military. Topics include women in the military and military wives. Recurring features include letters to the editor and news. *Freq:* Quarterly. *Price:* $50, individuals; $75, institutions; $12.95, single issue.

3787 ■ Monroe County Genealogical Society Newsletter

Monroe County Genealogical Society
Albia Public Library   Ph: (515)932-2593
203 Benton Ave. E
Albia, IA 52531

Contact: Vivian Shelquist, Editor.

Desc: Contains local genealogical material and data. Recurring features include queries, letters to the editor, news of research, and notices of publications available. *Freq:* Quarterly. *Price:* Included in membership.

3788 ■ Monroe County Historical Society Newsletter

Monroe County Historical Society, Inc.
PO Box 422   Ph: (608)272-3266
Sparta, WI 54656   Fax: (608)272-3266
E-mail: mchlr@centuryinter.net;
   raildoll@centuryinter.net

Contact: Jim Brown, Editor.

Desc: Provides news of the Society, which seeks to advance, disseminate, and preserve the knowledge of the history of Monroe County. Recurring features include news of research, a calendar of events, reports of meetings, news of educational opportunities, and articles on the history of Monroe County. *Freq:* 4/year. *Price:* Included in membership.

3789 ■ Monroe, Juneau, Jackson County Genealogy Workshop Newsletter

Carolyn Habelman
1488 Aqua Rd.   Ph: (608)378-4388
Black River Falls, WI   Fax: (608)378-3006
  54615-7609

Contact: Carolyn Habelman, Editor.

Desc: Provides genealogy data from Monroe, Juneau, and Jackson counties in Wisconsin. Includes listings of area high school alumni and pensioners, and cemetery markers from late 19th and early 20th centuries. Recurring features include news of research, a calendar of events, news of educational opportunities, book reviews, notices of publications available, and a column titled Surname Queries. *Freq:* Quarterly. *Price:* $7, U.S.; $10, elsewhere.

3790 ■ Monthly Product Announcement

U.S. Department of Commerce
Customer Service
Bureau of the Census
                                      Ph: (301)457-4501
rs>Washington, DC 20233   Fax: (301)457-4714
E-mail: majordomo@scensus.gov
URL: http://www.ccnsus.gov/mp/www/mpa.htmlmpa

Contact: Mary Kilbride, Editor.

Desc: Provides listings of all new Census Bureau products, primarily publications and data files, and includes ordering information and order forms. Covers demographic, geographic, and economic subjects derived from census and survey information, and estimates and projections programs. *Freq:* Monthly. *Price:* Free.

3791 ■ The Morgan Link

Morgan County Chapter
Ohio Genealogical Society
PO Box 418   Ph: (614)962-3816
McConnelsville, OH
  43756-0418

Contact: Cris Reed, Editor.

Desc: Contains genealogical data, articles, and queries concerning Morgan County, Ohio. Covers chapter activities and acquisitions. Recurring features include notices of publications available, a calendar of events, and a column titled News from the Past. *Freq:* Quarterly. *Price:* Included in membership.

3792 ■ Morgan Migrations

Lineage Search Associates
7315 Colts Neck Rd.   Ph: (804)730-7414
Mechanicsville, VA 23111-4233   Fax: (804)730-7414

Contact: Michael E. Pollock, Editor.

Desc: Features genealogical and historical research on the surname Morgan and variations of this last name. *Freq:* 3/year. *Price:* $18, individuals.

3793 ■ The Moriarty Clan

James Moriarty
4314 S. Oak Park Ave.   Ph: (708)484-7951
Stickney, IL 60402

Contact: James Moriarty, Editor.

Desc: Contains stories of people in the U.S. and abroad with the surname Moriarty. Assists in genealogical searches. Recurring features include letters to the editor, news of research, and interviews. *Freq:* Semiannual.

3794 ■ MTM News

MTM News
PO Box 491   Ph: (252)223-0298
Newport, NC 28570

Contact: Heather Donova, Editor.

Desc: Contains information for military families and serves as a correspondence/pen pal newsletter. *Freq:* Monthly. *Price:* $12, U.S.; $20, elsewhere.

3795 ■ Museum Archivist

Museum Archives Section
Society of American Archivists
c/o Amon Carter Museum   Ph: (817)738-1933
3501 Camp Bowie Blvd.   Fax: (817)738-4066
Fort Worth, TX 76107-2695
URL: http://www.chin.gc.ca/Resoures/Forum/
  e_forum.html

Contact: Paula Stewart, Editor.

Desc: Provides news of Society and Section activities, meetings, symposia, educational programs, project research, repository reports, notes, and announcements. Recurring features include letters to the editor, news of research, reports of meetings, and news of educational opportunities. *Freq:* 2/year. *Price:* Free.

3796 ■ Museum of the Great Plains Newsletter

Institute of the Great Plains
Elmer Thomas Park   Ph: (405)581-3460
601 Ferris   Fax: (405)581-3458
P.O. Box 68
Lawton, OK 73502

Contact: Steve Wilson, Editor.

Desc: Reports on the exhibits, educational programming, museum activities, and archival collections of the Museum, which is concerned with the history, archeology, and natural history of the Great Plains of North America. Recurring features include acquisitions news. *Freq:* Annual. *Price:* Incl. in subscription to the Great Plains Journal.

3797 ■ Museum Notes

Eastern Washington State Historical Society
Cheney Cowles Museum   Ph: (509)456-3931
2316 W. 1st Ave.   Fax: (509)456-7690
Spokane, WA 99204

Contact: Glenn Mason, Director, Cheney Cowles Museum.

Desc: Provides information about exhibits, educational programs, research, staff, and special events at the Cheney Cowles Museum. Reviews status major policy and legislation at federal, state, and local levels. Recurring features include news of research, a calendar of events, reports of meetings, and news of educational opportunities. *Freq:* Quarterly. *Price:* Included in membership.

3798 ■ Museum Notes

Iroquois Indian Museum
PO Box 7   Ph: (518)296-8949
Howes Cave, NY 12092   Fax: (518)296-8955
E-mail: iroquois@telenet.net

Desc: Consists information on the Iroquois Indian Museum. Includes news on museum collections, activities, acquisitions, and volunteers.

3799 ■ Museum Record

Bay County Historical Society
321 Washington Ave.   Ph: (517)893-5733
Bay City, MI 48708   Fax: (517)893-5741

Contact: Claire O'Laughlin, Editor.

Desc: Provides news and activities of the Society and information on the history of Bay County. *Freq:* Bimonthly. *Price:* $15; $10, retiree copies.

3800 ■ The Mustard Seed

Jesuit Refugee Service
1616 P St. NW, Ste. 400   Ph: (202)462-0400
Washington, DC 20036   Fax: (202)328-9212
E-mail: jesuitusa@igc.apc.org

Contact: Laurie E. O'Bryon, Editor.

Desc: Covers the activities of the Jesuit Refugee Service, providing information on and analysis of refugee and human rights issues. Encourages promotion of refugee services and increased refugee awareness. Recurring features include resources available and an announcement page. *Freq:* 3/year. *Price:* Free.

3801 ■ Nash Notations

Kimberly Straight
PO Box 49535   Ph: (719)532-0038
Colorado Springs, CO
  80949-9535
E-mail: nashnotations@usa.net

Contact: Kimberly Straight, Editor.

Desc: Presents genealogical research on the surname Nash (all spellings). Provides census information and listings of births, deaths, and marriages in the Nash family. Recurring features include notices of publications available, photos, free unlimited queries for subscribers. *Freq:* Quarterly. *Price:* $14, U.S.; $16, Canada.

3802 ■ National Military Family Association Public Relations & Marketing

National Military Family Association, Inc.
6000 Stevenson Ave., Ste. 304   Ph: (703)823-6632
Alexandria, VA 22304-3526   Fax: (703)751-4857
E-mail: families@nmfa.org
URL: http://www.nmfa.org

Contact: Patty Engelen, Editor; Donna Clodfelter, Director; Claire Lyn Saxon, Assoc. Dir.

Desc: Reports on current and proposed legislation affecting military families, quality of military life, and problems facing military families. Covers topics such as health care, relocation and housing, spouse employment, education, and retirement and survivor benefits. Recurring features include Association news and legislative updates. *Freq:* Monthly. *Price:* Included in membership.

3803 ■ Nevada State Museum Newsletter

Nevada State Museum Docent Council
Nevada State Museum   Ph: (702)687-4810
600 N. Carson St.
Carson City, NV 89701

Contact: Jack Gibson, Editor.

Desc: Provides information on the activities, programs, exhibitions, and events of the Nevada State Museum. Recurring features include interviews, news of research, a calendar of events, reports of meetings, book reviews, and columns titled The Docent File, Nevada Minerals, Views of the Past, In and about the Museum, and Jan's Boutique. *Freq:* Bimonthly. *Price:* Included in membership.

3804 ■ New Baltimore Historical Society Newsletter

New Baltimore Historical Society
51065 Washington   Ph: (810)725-4755
New Baltimore, MI 48047

Contact: Loretta L. Anne.

Desc: Carries information of interest to those concerned with the history and genealogy of New Baltimore, Michigan. *Freq:* Monthly.

3805 ■ New Brunswick Historical Society Newsletter

New Brunswick Historical Society
120 Union St.   Ph: (506)652-3590
Saint John, NB, Canada E2L 1A3

Contact: Cathy Wilson, Editor.

Desc: Features articles relating to New Brunswick history. Recurring features include interviews, news of research, a calendar of events, reports of meetings, and book reviews. *Freq:* 8/year (monthly except June, July, August, and December). *Price:* Included in membership.

3806 ■ New England Archivists Newsletter

New England Archivists
Massachusetts Archives   Ph: (617)727-2816
220 Morrissey Blvd.
Boston, MA 02125

Contact: Elizabeth Andrews, Editor; Judy Farrar, Editor; Elisabeth Kaplan, Editor; Jean Berry, Editor.

Desc: Contains regional archival news and announcements. Recurring features include a calendar of events, reports of meetings, job listings, book reviews, workshops, reports on repositories, and feature articles on archival subjects. Remarks: 20-year accumulative index available. *Freq:* Quarterly. *Price:* Included in membership.

3807 ■ New England Connexion

New England Connexion
PO Box 621   Ph: (914)294-6867
Goshen, NY 10924   Fax: (914)291-7114
E-mail: nhsip@frontiernet.net;
    nhsip@ny.frontiercomm.net

Contact: Nancy H. Smit, Editor.

Desc: Covers New England genealogy. *Freq:* Quarterly. *Price:* $10, U.S.; $13, Canada; $2.50, single issue.

3808 ■ New Hampshire Historical Society Newsletter

New Hampshire Historical Society
30 Park St.   Ph: (603)225-3381
Concord, NH 03301   Fax: (603)224-0463
E-mail: nhhsadmin@aol.com

Contact: Joan Desmarais, Editor.

Desc: Provides information on Society exhibits, current research conducted by staff, special programs, and new acquisitions by the Society museum and library. Recurring features include news of research, a calendar of events, and member news. *Freq:* Semiannual. *Price:* Included in membership; free to visitors.

3809 ■ New York Pedigrees

Family Tree
Box 4311   Ph: (208)939-7141
Boise, ID 83711
E-mail: familytree@aol.com

Contact: Patricia R. James, Editor; Anna Nasman, Circulation Mgr.; Lenora. Hansen, Circulation Mgr.

Desc: Contains, in each issue, information on 100 pedigrees from various areas of New York. *Freq:* Periodic. *Price:* $7, single issue.

3810 ■ Newsletter of the Multicultural History Society of Ontario

Multicultural History Society of Ontario
43 Queen's Park Crescent E.   Ph: (416)979-2973
Toronto, ON, Canada M5S   Fax: (416)979-7947
    2C3

E-mail: mhso.mail@utoronto.ca
URL: http://www.utoronto.ca/mhso

Contact: Dr. Lillian Petroff, Editor.

Desc: Features news of research, a calendar of events, reports of meetings, news of educational opportunities, and notices of publications available. *Freq:* Annual. *Price:* Free.

3811 ■ Newsletter of the S.L.A. Marshall Military History Collection

The Library of The University of Texas at El Paso
University of Texas at El Paso
El Paso, TX 79968-0582

Contact: Thomas F. Burdett, Editor.

Desc: Provides information on the University of Texas at El Paso's Marshall military history collection. Includes news on acquisitions related to the Marshall collection and other military history collections of the library.

3812 ■ Newsletter of the Society of Maine Archivists

Society of Maine Archivists
The Edmund S. Muskie Archives
Bates College   Ph: (207)786-6354
70 Campus Ave.   Fax: (207)786-6035
Lewiston, ME 04240
E-mail: muskie@abacus.bates.edu

Contact: Chris Beam, Editor.

Desc: Reports on acquisitions, events relating to historical documentation, and grant information. Recurring features include a calendar of events, letters to the editor, news of research, reports of meetings and columns titled From the SMA President, From the Editor, and Tips for Archivists. *Freq:* Quarterly. *Price:* Included in membership.

3813 ■ NGS Newsletter

National Genealogical Society
4527 17th St. N.   Ph: (703)525-0050
Arlington, VA 22207-2399   Free: 800-473-0060
                                    Fax: (703)525-0052
E-mail: ngs@ngsgenealogy.org;
    newsletter@ngsgenealogy.org
URL: http://www.ngsgenealogy.org/

Contact: Russ Henderson, Editor.

Desc: Features news of the Society and the genealogical community, articles on genealogical methods, sources, repositories, and NGS's library acquisitions; and members' queries. Recurring features include a calendar of events. *Freq:* Bimonthly. *Price:* Included in membership.

3814 ■ Nichols Nostalgia

Jean Gordon Vaughan
PO Box 365   Ph: (310)634-6466
Byron, CA 94514-0365

Contact: Jean Gordon Vaughan, Editor.

Desc: Presents genealogical records (census, Bible, birth, marriage, death, and cemetery) on the Nichols, Nickells, Nicholas surname. Preserves family history and records. Recurring features include letters to the editor, news of research, reports of meetings, book reviews, and notices of publications available. *Freq:* Quarterly. *Price:* $18/year, U.S.; $20, elsewhere.

3815 ■ Nicola Valley Historical Quarterly

Nicola Valley Museum Archives Association
2202 Jackon Ave.   Ph: (250)378-4145
PO Box 1262   Fax: (250)378-4145
Merritt, BC, Canada V1K 1B8

Contact: Ken Moyes, Editor; Sigurd Teit, Editor; Bette Sulz, Editor; Barb Watson, Editor.

Desc: Covers various subjects related to Nicola Valley, British Columbia. Recurring features include letters to the editor. *Price:* Included in membership; issue price depending on number of pages.

3816 ■ North American Manx Association— Bulletin

North American Manx Association
24 NW 8th Ave.   Ph: (309)932-8272
Galva, IL 61434

Contact: Michelle Smith, Editor; Sally Dahlquist, Editor.

Desc: Intended for descendants of families from the Isle of Man. Works to establish a closer union of all Manx people and to stimulate ties with the Isle of Man through the World Manx Association. Covers the Association and regional clubs' activities undertaken to preserve Manx culture and tradition. Recurring features include historical and genealogical information, a calendar of events, letters to the editor, reports of meetings, and obituaries. *Available:* Online. *Freq:* Quarterly. *Price:* Included in membership; $15, individuals; $20, for families.

3817 ■ North Carolina State Planning Newsletter

Office of State Planning
Governor's Office of North Carolina
116 W. Jones St.   Ph: (919)733-4131
Raleigh, NC 27603-8005   Fax: (919)715-3562
E-mail: g1sp047@ospl.state.nc.us
URL: http://www.ospl.state.nc.us/ospl/

Contact: Sheila White Chavis, Editor.

Desc: Provides information about state planning activities, such as performance/program budgeting. Publicizes census, demographic, social, and economic data available for the state and its component geographic areas. Includes data on state and local government, businesses, and the general public. Recurring features include news of research and notices of publications available. *Freq:* 4/year. *Price:* Free.

3818 ■ North Suburban Genealogical Society Newsletter

North Suburban Genealogical Society
c/o Winnetka Public Library   Ph: (708)446-7220
768 Oak St.
Winnetka, IL 60093

Contact: David Denis, Editor.

Desc: Presents news of the Society; lists new acquisitions. Recurring features include interviews, news of research, a calendar of events, reports of meetings, and book reviews. *Freq:* Bimonthly. *Price:* Included in membership.

3819 ■ Northern Arizona Genealogical Society Bulletin

Northern Arizona Genealogical Society
Box 695
Prescott, AZ 86302

Contact: J.C. Paulsen, Editor.

Desc: Focuses on the Society's activities and provides genealogical information. *Freq:* Quarterly.

3820 ■ Norwegian Tracks

Vesterheim Norwegian-American Museum
PO Box 379   Ph: (319)382-9681
Decorah, IA 52101   Fax: (319)382-8828
E-mail: vesterheim@vesterheim.org

Contact: Blaine Hedberg, Editor.

Desc: Reports on the activities of the Center, which promotes the study of Norwegian heritage and ethnic background and provides for the search of genealogical inquiries. Includes information on ethnic customs; lists cemetery, church, and census reports; and describes methods of researching descendants. Updates genealogical queries. *Freq:* Quarterly. *Price:* Included in membership.

3821 ▪ Nuggets from Paradise

Paradise Genealogical Society, Inc.
PO Box 460   Ph: (530)877-2330
Paradise, CA 95967-0460
E-mail: pargenso@jps.net
URL: http://www.jps.net/pargenso

Desc: Contains genealogical news. Recurring features include research tips, notices of publications available, a calendar of events, reports of meetings and other events, interviews, and news of educational opportunities. *Freq:* Monthly. *Price:* Included in membership.

3822 ▪ O'Dell's Lost & Found

O'Dell's Lost & Found
718 Summerland Dr.   Ph: (702)564-6452
Henderson, NV 89015-8135

Contact: Judy Hanson, Editor.

Desc: Presents genealogical records (census, Bible, birth, marriage, death, and cemetery) on the O'Dell/Odell/Odle surname. Preserves family history and records. Recurring features include letters to the editor, news of research, reports of meetings, book reviews, and notices of publications available. *Freq:* Quarterly. *Price:* $20/year, U.S.; $24 Canada.

3823 ▪ Odiorne Newsletter

Barbara O. Kerr
896 B5 Quinnipiac Ave.
New Haven, CT 06513

Contact: Barbara O. Kerr, Editor.

Desc: Publishes news about the Odiorne family around the U.S. and Canada, including historical anecdotes and family reunions. *Freq:* 3a/yr. *Price:* $3.

3824 ▪ Ogle County Links

Ogle County Genealogical Society
PO Box 251
Oregon, IL 61061

Contact: Viola Myers, Editor.

Desc: Seeks to provide genealogical and historical information concerning Ogle County. Recurring features include news of research, a calendar of events, and reports of meetings. *Freq:* 4/year. *Price:* Included in membership.

3825 ▪ Ohio Genealogical Society Newsletter

Ohio Genealogical Society
713 S. Main St.   Ph: (419)756-7294
Mansfield, OH 44907-1644   Fax: (419)756-8681
E-mail: ogs@ogs.org
URL: http://www.ogs.org

Contact: Synda Peters, Editor.

Desc: Fosters interest in people who helped to establish and perpetuate the state of Ohio. Connects the Society's 6,800 members and 100 chapters. Acts as a clearinghouse for genealogical information on Ohio families. Recurring features include news of research, a calendar of events, reports of meetings, news of educational opportunities, and notices of publications available. Also includes financial reports, listings of library acquisitions, computer genealogy articles, chapter addresses, and queries. *Freq:* Monthly. *Price:* $27/year, U.S.; $37 elsewhere.

3826 ▪ Ohio's Last Frontier

Williams County Genealogical Society
Box 293
Bryan, OH 43506

Contact: Marlene Smith, Editor.

Desc: Covers Society projects and activities. Contains local genealogical information. Recurring features include news of research, reports of meetings, notices of publications available, and queries. *Freq:* Monthly. *Price:* Included in membership.

3827 ▪ OHS Bulletin

The Ontario Historical Society
34 Parkview Ave.   Ph: (416)226-9011
Willowdale, ON, Canada M2N   Fax: (416)226-2740
3Y2

Contact: Meribeth Clow, Editor.

Desc: Focuses on the Ontario heritage field, including articles on museums, local historical societies, architectural preservation, folklore, and government grants and programs related to Ontario heritage. Recurring features include a calendar of events, reports of meetings, news of educational opportunities, book reviews, and notices of publications available. *Freq:* 6/year. *Price:* Included in membership.

3828 ▪ Okeechobee Genealogist

Genealogical Society of Okeechobee
PO Box 371
Okeechobee, FL 34973

Contact: Barbara Parker, Editor.

Desc: Supports genealogical research and the preservation of genealogical, biographical, and historical records. *Freq:* Quarterly. *Price:* Included in membership.

3829 ▪ Oklahoma Genealogical Society Quarterly

Oklahoma Genealogical Society
PO Box 12986   Ph: (405)751-1979
Oklahoma City, OK 73157

Desc: Features information pertaining to local genealogy and history. *Freq:* Quarterly. *Price:* $15, single issue; $18, family.

3830 ▪ Old Sturbridge Visitor

Old Sturbridge, Inc.
1 Old Sturbridge Village Rd.   Ph: (508)347-3362
Sturbridge, MA 01566-1198   Fax: (508)347-0377
E-mail: langdon@osv.org
URL: http://www.osv.org

Contact: Alberta Sebolt George, President; Jack Larkin, Senior Editor.

Desc: Provides news of the museum. *Freq:* Quarterly. *Price:* $12, nonmembers.

3831 ▪ On Board

Board for Certification of Genealogists
PO Box 14291
Washington, DC 20044

Contact: Liz Kelly Kerstens, Editor.

Desc: Educates the public on genealogical research, methodology, and professional ethics. *Freq:* 3/year. *Price:* $15.

3832 ▪ Ontario Genealogy Society—NewsLeaf

Ontario Genealogical Society
40 Orchard View Blvd., Ste. 102   Ph: (416)489-0734
Toronto, ON, Canada M4R   Fax: (416)489-9803
1B9

Contact: David Caron, Editor.

Desc: Covers genealogy in Ontario, Canada. News notice of events and meetings, branch notes, obituaries, notices of publications available, and a president's message. *Price:* Free, to members.

3833 ▪ Oral History Association Newsletter

Oral History Association (OHA)
c/o Mary K. Quinlan   Ph: (402)420-1473
7524 S. 35th St.   Fax: (402)420-1770
Lincoln, NE 68516

Contact: Mary K. Quinlan, Editor.

Desc: Provides news of this Association, which deals with American and international oral history. Recurring features include news of research and of members, grant information, a calendar of events, and a column titled From the President. *Freq:* 3/year. *Price:* Included in membership.

3834 ▪ Oral History Research Center Newsletter

Oral History Research Center
Indiana University
Ashton-Aley 264   Ph: (812)855-2856
Bloomington, IN 47405   Fax: (812)855-4869
E-mail: ohrc@indiana.edu
URL: http://www.indiana.edu/ohrc

Contact: Professor John E. Bodnar, Editor.

Desc: Informs of the activities and projects of the Center. Recurring features include news of research. *Freq:* Annual. *Price:* Free.

3835 ▪ Orange County Genealogical Society Quarterly

Orange County Genealogical Society
Historic 1841 Courthouse   Ph: (914)342-1190
101 Main St.
Goshen, NY 10924-1917
E-mail: nhslp@ny.frontiernet.net

Contact: Nancy H. Smit, Editor.

Desc: Covers genealogy-related topics, particularly for Orange County, New York, and surrounding area. *Freq:* Quarterly. *Price:* Included in membership.

3836 ▪ Orangeburg German-Swiss Newsletter

Orangeburgh German Swiss Genealogical Society
PO Box 974
Orangeburg, SC 29116-0974

Contact: Beverly Shuler, Editor.

Desc: Provides genealogical information on German-Swiss heritage, cemetery records, and family Bible data of Orangeburgh Township. Recurring features include letters to the editor, a calendar of events, news of members, queries, and a column titled the President's Report. *Freq:* Quarterly. *Price:* Included in membership.

3837 ▪ Oregon Genealogical Society Quarterly

Oregon Genealogical Society, Inc.
Box 10306   Ph: (541)484-5939
Eugene, OR 97440-2306

Contact: Betty Marx, Editor.

Desc: Contains information on the Society's activities, Oregon history, and genealogical research. *Freq:* Quarterly. *Price:* $22, individuals; $3, single issue.

3838 ▪ Ott Family Newsletter

Ott Family Newsletter
310 Franklin St., No. 148
Boston, MA 02110-3100
E-mail: ArocMac@aol.com

Contact: Cora Ott, Editor.

Desc: Designed to assist the various Ott families (Ott, Otte, Otto, Utt, etc.) in researching their families. Freq: 3/year. Price: $8.

3839 ■ Our Heritage

Genealogical Society of Van Zandt County
Box 716
Canton, TX 75103-0716

Contact: Jane Gamon, Contact.

Desc: Furnishes genealogical information pertaining to Van Zandt County, Texas. Freq: Quarterly. Price: $10, individuals; $12, family.

3840 ■ Our Missing Links

Kosciusko County Historical Society
Box 1071
Warsaw, IN 46580

Contact: Sue Zellers, Contact.

Desc: Reports on Kosciusko County's genealogical and historical information Freq: Quarterly. Price: $10.

3841 ■ Overholser Family Association—Bulletin

Overholser Family Association
313 Henry Ln.   Ph: (610)566-4888
Wallingford, PA 19086

Contact: Barbara B. Ford, Editor.

Desc: Presents genealogical information on the surnames Overholser and Oberholtzer. Recurring features include news of research and a calendar of events. Freq: Semi-annual.

3842 ■ Past, Present, and Future

La Crosse County Historical Society, Inc.
Box 7272
La Crosse, WI 54602-7272

Contact: Teresa Uhls, Editor.

Desc: Contains articles on local history. Freq: Bimonthly. Price: $25, individuals.

3843 ■ Pea River Trails

Pea River Historical and Genealogical Society
Box 810628
Enterprise, AL 36331-0628

Contact: Clayton G. Metcalf, Editor.

Desc: Contains genealogical and historical news. Freq: Quarterly. Price: $15, individuals.

3844 ■ Pennsylvania Minuteman

Pennsylvania Society
Sons of the American Revolution
2203 Walch St.
Monongahela, PA 15063

Contact: R. Steven Houtz, Editor.

Desc: Publicizes the Society's activities. Discusses membership, finances, awards, and upcoming meetings. Recurring features include a calendar of events, reports of meetings, editorials, and a column titled President's Message. Freq: Quarterly. Price: Included in membership; $4/year for nonmembers.

3845 ■ Peoria County Genealogical Society Newsletter

Peoria Genealogical Society
PO Box 1489   Ph: (309)692-4500
Peoria, IL 61655-1489
URL: http://www.rootsweb.com/ilpeoria/pcqs.htm

Contact: Jeff Schlatter, Editor.

Desc: Contains genealogical information pertaining to Peoria County, Illinois. Recurring features include news of research, reports of meetings, news of educational opportunities, book reviews, and columns titled Queries, and From the President. Freq: 9-12/year. Price: Included in membership.

3846 ■ Perkins Family Newsletter

Compu-Chart
363 S. Park Victoria Dr.   Ph: (408)262-1051
Milpitas, CA 95035-5708
E-mail: 103137.3321@compuserve.com

Contact: Paula Merkins Mortensen, Editor.

Desc: Contains genealogical news on the Perkins surname. Freq: Quarterly. Price: $10/year, U.S.; $15 elsewhere.

3847 ■ Phelps Connections

Phelps Connections
Beryl Phelps Keegan
104 S. Cove Rd.
Williamsburg, VA 23188-9325
E-mail: jjkeegan@erols.com
URL: http://phelps-connections.org

Contact: Deborah Lee Rothery, Editor.

Desc: Deals with Phelps family genealogists. Provides vital records, such as land, census, military, probate, and Bible records, along with lineages, queries, and researched articles. Recurring features include news of research, news of educational opportunities, and notices of publications available. Includes a column titled Area Coordinators. Freq: Quarterly. Price: Included in membership.

3848 ■ Piatt County Historical & Genealogical Society Newsletter

Piatt County Historical & Genealogical Society
PO Box 111   Ph: (217)762-4676
Monticello, IL 61856

Contact: Lisa Winters, Editor.

Desc: Contains information of interest to genealogists and historians on Piatt County, Illinois. Recurring features include reports of meetings, book reviews, news of research, and notices of publications available. Freq: Quarterly. Price: $8/year for individuals, $9 for institutions, U.S.; $10 and $11.

3849 ■ Pied Cow

Chadbourne Family Association
HCR 77, Box 8350   Ph: (207)284-6484
North Waterboro, ME 04061

Contact: Elaine Chadbourne Bacon, Editor.

Desc: Contains historical and contemporary genealogical items on the Chadbourne surname. Notes births, deaths, and marriages. Recurring features include interviews, news of research, a calendar of events, reports of meetings and reunions, and news of members. Freq: Semiannual. Price: Included in membership.

3850 ■ Pioneer Branches

Northeast Washington Genealogical Society
c/o Colville Publishing Library
195 S. Oak
Colville, WA 99114

Contact: Doris Kilcup Winskie, Editor; Donna Speed Husby, Editor.

Desc: Contains genealogical articles of broad and local interest, and coverage of local and regional & historical materials. Recurring features include Queries, news of research, a calendar of events, reports of meetings, book reviews, and notices of publications available. Freq: Quarterly. Price: Included in membership; free to libraries; $15, single; $18, couple.

3851 ■ The Pipings

Clan Gillean U.S.A.
PO Box 4061   Ph: (713)581-2845
Alvin, TX 77512-4061

Contact: Lawrence M. Rankin, Editor.

Desc: Provides genealogical exchange for those with the surname MacLean, Maclaine and related families. Covers pipe and harp music, clan and family history, and poetry. Recurring features include letters to the editor, a calendar of events, reports of meetings, and book reviews. Freq: Quarterly. Price: $15/year.

3852 ■ Polish Genealogical Society—Bulletin & Journal

Polish Genealogical Society of America, Inc.
984 N. Milwaukee Ave.   Ph: (773)776-5551
Chicago, IL 60622
E-mail: pgsamerica@aol.com
URL: http://www.pgsa.org

Contact: William F. Hoffman, Editor.

Desc: Promotes research in Polish genealogies and heraldry. Carries information on research methodology, geographic locations, bibliographies, and selected histories. Recurring features include original material by professional genealogists and personal accounts by amateurs, letters to the editor, book reviews, news of research, an information-exchange section, and a question-and-answer column. Freq: Quarterly. Price: $15/year.

3853 ■ Pollock Potpourri

Lineage Search Associates
7315 Colts Neck Rd.   Ph: (804)730-7414
Mechanicsville, VA 23111-4233   Fax: (804)730-7414

Contact: Michael E. Pollock, Editor.

Desc: Devoted to genealogical and historical research on the surname Pollock and alternate spellings such as Polk and Poague. Freq: Quarterly. Price: $12, individuals.

3854 ■ Pony Express Mail

Pony Express Historical Association
12th & Penn Box 1022   Ph: (816)232-8206
St. Joseph, MO 64502

Contact: Gary Chilcote, Editor; Carolyn Chilcote, Publisher.

Desc: Provides information on the Patee House Museum, a national landmark which served as headquarters for the Pony Express in 1860, and the Jesse James Home, the site where the outlaw was killed. Researches history of the Pony Express and Jesse James (1847-82). Freq: 10/year. Price: $10, U.S.; $15, other countries.

3855 ■ Poplar Row

Jackson Chapter of Ohio Genealogical Society
PO Box 807
Jackson, OH 45640-0807

Desc: Reports genealogical information, including news clips from the Jackson Standard Journal. Recurring features include book reviews, notices of publications available, queries, reports of meetings, and queries. Freq: Quarterly. Price: $8/year.

3856 ■ Population Studies

Bureau of Economic and Business Research
College of Business Administration
University of Florida
221 Matherly Hall   Ph: (904)392-0171
PO Box 117145   Fax: (904)392-4739
Gainesville, FL 32611-7145

E-mail: bebr@bebr.cba.ufl.edu

Contact: Dr. Stanley Smith, Editor.

Desc: Carries a signed article in each issue which focuses on an aspect of Florida population estimation, including projections and age, race, and sex breakdowns by county, household number, and size. *Alt. Fmts:* microform. *Freq:* 3/year. *Price:* $35.

3857 ▪ Population Studies Centre Newsletter

Population Studies Centre
University of Western Ontario   Ph: (519)661-3819
London, ON, Canada N6A 5C2

Contact: Suzanne Shiel, Editor.

Desc: Describes ongoing research and activities at the Centre. *Freq:* Semiannual. *Price:* Free.

3858 ▪ Post Scripts

Bourne Historical Society, Inc.
Box 3095   Ph: (508)759-9487
Bourne, MA 02532-0795

Contact: Bruce D. Cody, Editor.

Desc: Provides news of the Society, which collects, preserves, and disseminates research and materials concerning the history of the town of Bourne, Cape Cod, and southeastern Massachusetts. Features news of the Bourne Historical Society and Museum, archaeological finds, historic preservation projects, and articles concerning area history. Includes news of research, a calendar of events, news of members, and a column titled Curator's Corner. *Freq:* 4/year. *Price:* Included in membership.

3859 ▪ Potter County Historical Society Quarterly Bulletin

Potter County Historical Society
308 N. Main St., Box 605   Ph: (814)274-8124
Coudersport, PA 16915

Contact: Robert K. Currin, Contact.

Desc: Provides information on local history and news of Potter County, Pennsylvania. *Freq:* Quarterly. *Price:* $0.50, single issue. Included in membership.

3860 ▪ Poweshiek County Iowa Searcher

Poweshiek County Historical & Genealogical Society
206 N. Mill St.   Ph: (515)623-3322
Box 280
Montezuma, IA 50171

Contact: Ferne Norris, Editor.

Desc: Covers activities of the Society, which seeks to "kindle and keep alive an active interest in state, county, and local history." Recurring features include genealogical queries, research tips, news of meetings and conferences, and items of trivia and local history. *Freq:* Quarterly. *Price:* Included in membership.

3861 ▪ Prairie Gleaner

West Central Missouri Genealogical Society and Library, Inc.
705 Broad St.   Ph: (660)747-6264
Warrensburg, MO 64093-2032
E-mail: yunguns@iland.net

Contact: A.J. Heck, Editor; J. Eldon Yung, Publications.

Desc: Provides genealogical information on Bates, Benton, Cass, Henry, Jackson, Johnson, Lafayette, Pettis, St. Clair, and Saline Counties in Missouri. *Freq:* Quarterly. *Price:* $12, individuals.

3862 ▪ Preservation Tips

Chicora Foundation, Inc.
PO Box 8664   Ph: (803)787-6910
Columbia, SC 29202-8664   Fax: (803)787-6910
E-mail: chicora1@aol.com

Contact: Michael Trinkley, Director.

Desc: Provides the latest research and technology on preserving articles for use in museums, libraries, archives, and personal collections. Discussion of preservation ranges from certain types of adhesives to disaster preparedness. Recurring features include news of research, a calendar of events, news of educational opportunities, and notices of publications available. *Freq:* Quarterly. *Price:* $10.

3863 ▪ Presidential Families Gazette

Presidential Families of America
608 S. Conway Rd., Ste. G
Orlando, FL 32807-1044

Contact: Dr. Lawrence Kent, Founder & Editor.

Desc: Publishes general Society news and on subjects relating to Presidents of the U.S. and to their kin who are PFA members. *Freq:* 3/year. *Price:* Included in membership, Must send self addressed stamped envelope.

3864 ▪ The Primary Source

Society of Mississippi Archivists
PO Box 1151   Ph: (601)359-6889
Jackson, MS 39215-1151   Fax: (601)359-6964
E-mail: sboyd@mdah.state.ms.us;
    irmgard.wolfe@usm.edu

Contact: Mattie Sink, Editor.

Desc: Focuses on activities and trends in the archival and library community both regionally and nationally. Includes information on conservation and articles on state repositories and their holdings. Recurring features include news of research, book reviews, and a calendar of events. *Freq:* Quarterly. *Price:* $7.50, individuals; $15, institutions.

3865 ▪ Prince Edward Island Museum and Heritage Foundation Newsletter

Prince Edward Island Museum and Heritage Foundation
2 Kent St.   Ph: (902)368-6600
Charlottetown, PE, Canada   Fax: (902)368-6608
C1A 1M6
E-mail: peimuse@psi.net; peimuse@bud.peinet.pc.ca

Contact: Christopher Severance, Editor.

Desc: Serves to update members on the activities of the Museum, including system's programming, exhibitions, and collections. Includes board news and site reports. *Freq:* Quarterly. *Price:* Included in membership.

3866 ▪ Prince George's County Genealogical Society—Bulletin

Prince George's County Genealogical Society, Inc.
PO Box 819   Ph: (301)855-8655
Bowie, MD 20718-0819
E-mail: pgcgs@juno.com

Contact: Philip F. Brown, Editor.

Desc: Publishes Society news and notices of activities, meeting minutes, and genealogical information from local sources. Recurring features include news of research, a calendar of events, reports of meetings, news of educational opportunities, and book reviews. *Freq:* 10/year. *Price:* Included in membership; $12/year for nonmembers.

3867 ▪ PSDC News

Pennsylvania State Data Center
Penn State Harrisburg   Ph: (717)948-6336
777 W. Harrisburg Pike   Fax: (717)948-6754
Middletown, PA 17057-4897
E-mail: psdc@psu.edu
URL: http://www.hbg.psu.edu/psdc

Contact: Diane E. Shoop, Editor.

Desc: Contains information on PSDC products, services, and projects. Covers data and publications released by the U.S. Census Bureau, Pennsylvania state agencies, and the PSDC, as well as tips on using available data and resources. Recurring features include a calendar of events, news of conferences, and notices of publications available, survey analysis from Center for Survey Research, and economic development news from Economic Development Research and Training Center. *Freq:* 3/year. *Price:* $15.

3868 ▪ The Public Historian

University of California Press/Journals
2120 Berkeley Way   Ph: (510)643-7154
Berkeley, CA 94720-0001   Fax: (510)642-9917
E-mail: journal@ucop.edu

Contact: Shelley Bookspan, Editor; Lindsey Reed, Contact.

Desc: Covers public history. Remarks: Subscription includes membership in the National Council on Public History, and their newsletter, Public History News. *Freq:* Quarterly. *Price:* $47; $21, students; $69, institutions.

3869 ▪ Putman County Heritage

Putnam County Historical Society
201 E. Main St.   Ph: (419)532-3008
Box 264
Kalida, OH 45853-0264

Contact: Edward A. Rieman, Editor.

Desc: Traces the history of Putnam County, Ohio, with past news items and stories of residents. Covers Society activities. Recurring features include news of research, a calendar of events, reports of meetings, and notices of publications available, and all other programs of the Society. *Freq:* Quarterly. *Price:* Included in membership; $8/year for others; free to institutions.

3870 ▪ Putnam County Genealogical Society Newsletter

Putnam County Genealogical Society
PO Box 2354   Ph: (904)325-7107
Palatka, FL 32178

Contact: Mary E. Murphy-Hoffman, Editor.

Desc: Provides information on events and meetings, as well as tips and hints on genealogical research. Recurring features include news of research, a calendar of events, reports of meetings, news of educational opportunities, and a column titled From Your President. *Freq:* Monthly.

3871 ▪ Quarterdeck

Columbia River Maritime Museum, Inc.
1792 Marine Dr.   Ph: (503)325-2323
Astoria, OR 97103   Fax: (503)325-2331
E-mail: columbia@seasurf.com

Contact: Karen Carpenter, Editor.

Desc: Features events, activities, and news of the Columbia River Maritime Museum. Details an historical event or story in each issue. Recurring features include a calendar of events, news of educational opportunities, book reviews, and listings of exhibits and lectures. *Freq:* Quarterly. *Price:* Included in membership.

3872 ■ Rainey Times

Rainey Times
Rte. 4, Box 56
Sulphur Springs, TX 75482

Ph: (903)439-1081
Fax: (903)439-1081

Contact: Marynell Bryant, Editor.

Desc: Provides genealogical information on the surname Rainey and all spelling variations such as Raney and Ranney. *Freq:* Annual. *Price:* $20, individuals.

3873 ■ Ramey Ramblings

Gary and Melinda Ramey
1160 E. Ave. J-12
Lancaster, CA 93535
E-mail: RameyRamblings@huges.net

Ph: (805)942-8762

Contact: Gary Ramey, Editor; Melinda Ramey, Editor.

Desc: Reports on genealogical research on the surnames Ramey, Remy, and Rhamy. Lists vital statistics, subscribers pedigree charts. Recurring features include genealogical queries. *Freq:* Annual. *Price:* $7.

3874 ■ Rampant Lion

Scottish Historic & Research Society of the Delaware Valley, Inc.
102 St. Pauls Rd.
Ardmore, PA 19003-2811

Ph: (610)649-4144

Contact: Blair C. Stonier, Editor; Penelope J. Stonier, Editor.

Desc: Features articles on Scottish history and genealogy. Recurring features include a calendar of events, reports of meetings, news of educational opportunities and members, book reviews, and notices of publications available. *Freq:* 11/year. *Price:* Included in membership; $20, family; $15, regular.

3875 ■ RCGS Newsletter

Ross County Genealogical Society
Ohio Genealogical Society
PO Box 6352
Chillicothe, OH 45601

Ph: (614)773-2715

Contact: Joanne Johnson, Editor.

Desc: Presents historical and genealogical information on individuals who lived in Ross County, Ohio. Recurring features include news of research, a calendar of events, reports of meetings, notices of publications available, queries, library acquisitions, and committee reports. *Freq:* Quarterly. *Price:* Included in membership.

3876 ■ RCHA News

Regional Council of Historical Agencies
PO Box 28
Cooperstown, NY 13326

Free: 800-895-1648

Contact: Linda Norris, Editor.

Desc: Newsletter of the Regional Council of Historical Agencies. Contains information on historical museums, sites, collections, and activities. Recurring features include news of members and news of research. *Freq:* Quarterly.

3877 ■ The Record

National Archive and Records Administration
National Archive at College Park
8601 Adelphi Rd.
College Park, MD 20740-6001

Ph: (301)713-6000

Contact: Roger A. Bruns, Editor.

Desc: Describes the activities and issues surrounding the National Archive and Records Administration, and serves to promote discussion and dialogue among its constituents. Provides information on preservations, Archive issues, the electronic documentary highway, teaching ap-

proaches, and family and genealogical history. Recurring features include news of research, reports of meetings, and notices of publications available. *Freq:* 5/year. *Price:* Free.

3878 ■ Red Tower

Clan Galbraith Association of North America
c/o Tressie Nealy
509 S.E. 70th
Oklahoma City, OK 73149-2601

Contact: Barbara Patterson, Editor; Tressie Nealy, Librarian; Frances Williams.

Desc: Contains news and information on the Galbraith surname and Scottish genealogy. Recurring features include letters to the editor, news of research, a calendar of events, reports of meetings, news of educational opportunities, notices of publications available, and information on the Galbraith Castle in Scotland. Also surnames Calbreath, Culbreath, Galbreath, Gilbreath, Gilrenth, Kilbreath, Kulbreath, etc. *Freq:* 4/year. *Price:* Included in membership.

3879 ■ Research News

Family History World
Genealogical Institute
PO Box 22045
Salt Lake City, UT 84122

Ph: (801)250-6717

Contact: Arlene H. Eakle, PhD, Editor.

Desc: Carries practical information on genealogical research. Identifies new research methods, tools, and publications. Recurring features include statistics, book reviews, and news of research. *Available:* Online. *Freq:* Irregular. *Price:* $5.50, single issue.

3880 ■ Richardson Family Researcher & Historical News

Richardson Heritage Society
PO Box 123
Broken Bow, NE 68822

Ph: (308)872-2167

Contact: Harry M. Richardson, Editor.

Desc: Concerned with news and information relating to the Richardson and Moore families. Publishes genealogical research queries, letters to the editor, and news of Society and family activities. Recurring features include news of research, news of members, and notices of publications available. Remarks: Incorporates the former Moore Family Inquirer. *Freq:* Quarterly. *Price:* $10/year.

3881 ■ Robert McKay Clan Newsletter

Robert McKay Clan
5319 Manning Pl. NW
Washington, DC 20016

Ph: (202)363-3663

Contact: Wallace Shipp, Editor; Dorothy Shipp, Editor.

Desc: Compiles news of births, deaths, marriages, and activities of McKay family members. Also promotes the annual gathering of McKays. Recurring features include letters to the editor and reprinted articles on McKays. *Freq:* Annual. *Price:* Donation.

3882 ■ The Root Digger

Solano County Genealogical Society, Inc.
Box 2494
Fairfield, CA 94533
E-mail: nmorebeck@jps.net

Ph: (707)446-6869

Contact: Kathleen Carroll, Editor.

Desc: Presents articles on genealogy and news of the Society. Recurring features include news of research, a calendar of events, and reports of meetings. Remarks: Quarterly issue includes Solano and California Sections. *Freq:* Monthly, (except July and August). *Price:* $15, individuals; $18, for families.

3883 ■ Rose Family Association Newsletter

Rose Family Association
1474 Montelegre Dr.
San Jose, CA 95120
URL: http://www.ourworld.compuserve.com/
    homepages/christiner

Ph: (408)268-2137
Fax: (408)268-2165

Contact: Christine Rose, Editor.

Desc: Provides data on the Rose family. Recurring features include news of research, genealogical data, news of family reunions and other Rose family events, newspaper items, membership lists, and queries. *Freq:* Quarterly. *Price:* $13/year, U.S., $15, Canada.

3884 ■ The R's Relatives

Robert D. Gromm
PO Box 547
Bethel Island, CA 94511

Ph: (510)684-2117
Fax: (510)684-9610

Contact: Robert D. "Bob" Gromm, Editor.

Desc: Concerned with the family surnames of Robison, Robinson, Robson, Robertson, Roberson, Roberts, Robbins, Robb, and others. Subscription includes free queries. *Freq:* Quarterly. *Price:* $12, individuals, U.S.; $14, Canada, /year.

3885 ■ St. Louis Genealogical Society—News 'N' Notes

St. Louis Genealogical Society
4 Sunnen Dr., Ste. 140
St. Louis, MO 63143
E-mail: stlgsmail@primary.net
URL: http://www.rootsweb.com/

Ph: (314)647-8547
Fax: (314)647-8548

Contact: Charlene F. Fagyal, Editor.

Desc: Contains news of Society activities, members, and related organizations. Details available resources, such as archives, census information, libraries, and publications. *Freq:* Monthly. *Price:* Included in membership.

3886 ■ Sans Tache

Clan Npier in North America, Kilmahew
Rte. 2, Box 614
Ramer, AL 36069-9245

Ph: (334)281-0505

Contact: Brig.Gen. John H. Napier, III, Editor.

Desc: Contains genealogical and family history on the Napier clan in North America. *Freq:* Annual. *Price:* Free, members.

3887 ■ Saskatchewan Genealogical Society—Bulletin

Saskatchewan Genealogical Society
PO Box 1894
Regina, SK, Canada S4P 3E1
E-mail: margethomas.sgs@cableregina.com
URL: http://www2.regina.smica/sys/; http://
    www.saskgenealogy.com

Ph: (306)780-9207
Fax: (306)781-6021

Desc: Promotes and provides information on family history. *Freq:* Quarterly. *Price:* Included in membership.

3888 ■ SCAN

Simcoe County Branch
Ontario Genealogical Society
Box 892
Barrie, ON, Canada L4M 4Y6

Contact: Sandra Beatty, Editor.

Desc: Provides information on genealogical and historical research in Simcoe County. Recurring features include a calendar of events, reports of meetings, book reviews, queries, and articles concerning family histories. *Freq:* Quarterly. *Price:* Included in membership.

3889 ▪ Schale (Westfalen) Newsletter

Dr. David Koss
Illinois College   Ph: (217)245-3460
Jacksonville, IL 62650

Contact: Dr. David Koss, Editor.

Desc: Provides historical and genealogical information on families from Schale (Westphalia), Germany and their American descendants. Recurring features include news of research and book reviews. *Freq:* Quarterly. *Price:* $5/year.

3890 ▪ Schneider Connections

BGM Publications
28635 Old Hideaway Rd.   Ph: (708)639-2400
Cary, IL 60013

Contact: Betty G. Massman, Editor.

Desc: Gives genealogical data for the surname Schneider and its variations. Provides wills, deeds, Bible records, church records, and other related material. Recurring features include news of research, obituaries, marriages, births, given name index, and a queries column. Remarks: Also available in microform. Publication suspended as of January 2000. *Freq:* Quarterly. *Price:* $18/yr., U.S.; $25 elsewhere.

3891 ▪ SCWH Newsletter

University of Arkansas
Department of History
Old Main 416
Fayetteville, AR 72701

Contact: Dr. Anne J. Bailey, Editor.

Desc: Informs members of the association's activities. Aims to advance the professional development of historians of the American Civil War in all areas—military, political, social, and others. Recurring features include short articles, book reviews, current events, calls for papers, and notices of conferences. *Freq:* Quarterly. *Price:* Included in membership.

3892 ▪ Search Light

Betty M. Light Behr
RD 8
Carmel, NY 10512-9808

Contact: Betty M. Light Behr, Editor.

Desc: Carries archival material and genealogical/biographical data pertaining to members of the Light (with variant spellings) family. Prints unpublished manuscripts and genealogies; immigration, naturalization, and passenger lists; and articles on ethnic history relating to the family. Recurring features include vital records, queries, and notices of family reunions; birth, death, and marriage announcements; notices of publications and resources available; and columns titled Spot Light On, Dear Kin, and Sparks. *Freq:* Quarterly. *Price:* $7.50, U.S.; $12.50, elsewhere.

3893 ▪ The Searcher

Southern California Genealogical Society
417 Irving Dr.   Ph: (818)843-7247
Burbank, CA 91504
URL: http://www.cwire.com/scgs/

Contact: Al Lewis, Editor.

Desc: Contains articles and news pertaining to genealogical research. Recurring features include genealogical records; listings of the Society's library acquisitions; news of members; editorials; book reviews; a calendar of events; letters to the editor; notices of seminars, workshops, and conferences; and columns titled Periodical News and Queries. *Freq:* Monthly. *Price:* Included in membership.

3894 ▪ The Second Boat

Pentref Press
PO Box 2782   Ph: (207)255-4114
Kennebunkport, ME
  04046-2782

Contact: Rosemary Bachelor, Editor.

Desc: Concerned with genealogical data on Colonial era American families. Publishes family genealogies covering the 1600's and 1700's, lineage summaries, ancestor charts, public and Bible records, and old letters and photographs. Recurring features include genealogical queries and columns titled Looking for Lost Ladies and Second Boat Ancestor Lists. *Available:* Online. *Freq:* Bimonthly. *Price:* $25/year.

3895 ▪ Seneca Searchers

Seneca County Genealogical Society
PO Box 157   Ph: (419)447-5303
Tiffin, OH 44883-0157

Contact: Don Rogier, Editor; Joan Dysinger, Editor.

Desc: Presents genealogical information on individuals from Seneca County, Ohio. Recurring features include news of research, a calendar of events, reports of meetings, notices of publications available, and columns titled At Our Meeting, History of Seneca Co., Queries, and New at TSPL. *Freq:* Bimonthly. *Price:* $10/year.

3896 ▪ Shelby Exchange

Judith Trolenger
Hunt Star Rt, Box 234   Ph: (830)238-4750
Ingram, TX 78025-9704
E mail: hoberta@hilconet.com

Contact: Mrs. Judith A. Trolinger, Editor.

Desc: Serves as a genealogical information exchange for persons interested in the Shelby families. Publishes census, military service, land purchase, marriage, and death records, focusing on all areas in the U.S. in each issue. Recurring features include queries from readers, Free queries and submissions; annually, 2nd issue-Focus on "Shelby Ladies". *Freq:* Quarterly. *Price:* $12.50/yr.

3897 ▪ Shem Tov

Jewish Genealogical Society of Canada (Toronto)
PO Box 446, Sta. A   Ph: (416)638-3280
Willowdale, ON, Canada M2N
  5T1
E-mail: henry_wellisch@tvo.org

Desc: Provides genealogical research information and techniques for those of Jewish descent. Recurring features include interviews, news of research, a calendar of events, reports of meetings, news of educational opportunities, and book reviews. *Freq:* Quarterly. *Price:* Included in membership; $30/year for nonmembers.

3898 ▪ The Sims Seeker

BGM Publications
28635 Old Hideaway Rd.   Ph: (708)639-2400
Cary, IL 60013

Contact: Betty G. Massman, Editor.

Desc: Gives genealogical data for the surname Sims and its variations. Provides wills, deeds, Bible records, and other related materials. Recurring features include news of research, obituaries, marriages, births, given name index, and a queries column. *Freq:* Quarterly. *Price:* $18/year.

3899 ▪ SITREP

Royal Canadian Military Institute
426 University Ave.   Ph: (416)597-0286
Toronto, ON, Canada M5G   Fax: (416)597-6919
  1S9

Contact: Capt. Mihail Murgoci, Editor.

Desc: Provides a SITREP (Situation Report) on the institute as well as some news on the Canadian military. Recounts military history of interest or import to members past and present of the Canadian military establishment. Recurring features include letters to the editor, function announcements, military history articles on military badges and medals and book reviews. *Freq:* Monthly. *Price:* Included in membership.

3900 ▪ SLA Marshall Military History Collection Newsletter

SLA Marshall Military History Collection
Library   Ph: (915)747-5697
University of Texas at El Paso
El Paso, TX 79968-0582

Contact: Thomas F. Burdett, Editor.

Desc: Announces acquisitions and developments in the Collection, providing background information on the new acquisitions. Focuses on military history with special emphasis on the military career and correspondence of General Samuel Lyman Atwood Marshall (1900-1977). Recurring features include book reviews. *Freq:* Irregular. *Price:* Free.

3901 ▪ Smith Families of England & New England

Olsen Enterprises
3931 S. 238th St.   Fax: (206)878-4267
Kent, WA 98032

Desc: Designed to aid families of the Smith line with research of their family history and acts as a forum to exchange information. Also contains handwriting analysis. *Freq:* Quarterly. *Price:* $15, U.S.; $17, elsewhere.

3902 ▪ Snake River Heritage Center Newsletter

Snake River Heritage Center
2295 Paddock Ave   Ph: (208)549-0205
PO Box 307
Weiser, ID 83672

Contact: Carol Odoms, Editor.

Desc: Announces Museum activities. Contains news of members, notices of publications available, and historical notes on the Snake River country. *Freq:* Quarterly. *Price:* Included in membership.

3903 ▪ Societe Genealogique Canadienne-Francaise Memoires

Societe Genealogique Canadienne Francaise
CP 335, St. Place d'Armes   Ph: (514)729-8366
Montreal, PQ, Canada H2Y   Fax: (514)729-1170
  3H1
URL: http://www.sgcf.com

Contact: Normand Robert, President.

Desc: Contains genealogical and historical articles. *Freq:* Quarterly. *Price:* C$30, individuals; C$7, single issue.

3904 ▪ Society of Descendants of Johannes de la Montagne—News Letter

Society of Descendants of Johannes de la Montagne
3657 W. Nichols   Ph: (417)831-6140
Springfield, MO 65803

Contact: Lois Stewart, Editor.

Desc: Features genealogical, historical, and biographical articles on proved or possible descendants of Dr. Jean de la Montagne, Huguenot physician in New Amsterdam and Vice-Director of the colony under Peter Stuyvesant. Seeks to facilitate the exchange of accurate information held by descendants and to stimulate interest and research in de la Montagne family history. Contains articles on genealogical research techniques and problems and publishes records from Bibles, letters, census reports, archives, and other documents. Recurring features include biographies of descendants, letters to the editor, interviews, news of research, and an editor's column. *Freq:* Quarterly. *Price:* Included in membership; $10/year for non-members.

3905 ■ Society for German-American Studies Newsletter

Society for German-American Studies
St. Olaf College   Ph: (507)646-3233
Northfield, MN 55057-1098   Fax: (507)646-3732
E-mail: rippleyl@stolaf.edu
URL: http://www-lib.iupui.edu/kade/

Contact: LaVern J. Rippley, Editor.

Desc: Focuses on German immigration and settlements in the U.S. and on German-American history and culture. Recurring features include notices of publications of interest, book reviews, and news of research. *Freq:* Quarterly. *Price:* Included in membership.

3906 ■ South Dakota Hall of Fame Newsletter

South Dakota Hall of Fame
PO Box 180   Ph: (605)734-4216
Chamberlain, SD 57325-0180   Free: 800-697-3130

Contact: Chad E. Mutziger, Editor.

Desc: Features historical information of South Dakota. *Freq:* Quarterly. *Price:* $37.50; $4.50, single issue.

3907 ■ South End

Wayne State University
Reuther Library
5401 Cass Ave.   Ph: (313)577-4024
Detroit, MI 48202   Fax: (313)577-4300

Contact: William R. Gulley, Editor.

Desc: Reports Association news and news from national archives and repositories in Michigan. Carries feature items of interest to archivists. Recurring features include book reviews, listings of training and job opportunities, and a calendar of events. *Freq:* 2/year. *Price:* Included in membership.

3908 ■ Southern Demographic News

Southern Demographic Association
Department of Sociology   Ph: (601)266-5339
   and Anthropology
Box 5074
University of
   Southern Mississippi
Hattiesburg, MS 39406-5074

Contact: Jerry McKibben, Editor; Kimberly Faust, Editor.

Desc: Contains short items of news and information on population research. Discusses Association activities and research. Recurring features include a calendar of events and news of educational opportunities. *Freq:* Quarterly. *Price:* $30/year.

3909 ■ Southern Roots & Shoots

Delta Genealogical Society
c/o Rossville Public Library   Ph: (423)886-6369
504 McFarland Ave.
Rossville, GA 30741

Desc: Provides historical and genealogical information concerning Tennessee, Alabama, and Georgia. Recurring features include news of research, a calendar of events, book reviews, notices of publications available, queries and pedigree charts, name index, and columns by the

editors for Tennessee, Georgia, and Alabama. *Available:* Online: Company N.A. *Freq:* 3/year. *Price:* $12/year to individuals; $15 to others.

3910 ■ The Southwestern Archivist

Society of Southwest Archivists (SSA)
c/o Glenn L. McMullen   Ph: (504)388-6501
Louisiana State University   Fax: (504)334-1695
Hill Memorial Library
Special Collections
Baton Rouge, LA 70803
URL: http://www.tulane.edu//miller/
    speccoghomepage.html

Contact: Glenn L. McMullen, Editor.

Desc: Supports the aims of the Society, which include: "to provide a means for effective cooperation among people concerned with the documentation of human experience," and "to promote the adoption of sound principles and standards for the preservation and administration of records." Recurring features include news of research, news of members, and a calendar of events. *Freq:* Quarterly. *Price:* $10/year for membership; $25 for institutions.

3911 ■ Spectrum

Immigration History Research Center
University of Minnesota
826 Berry St.   Ph: (612)627-4208
St. Paul, MN 55114   Fax: (612)627-4190
E-mail: ihrc@gold.tc.umn.edu

Contact: Rudolph J. Vecoli, Editor; Joel Wurl, Editor; Judith Rosenblatt, Editor.

Desc: Objective is "to create better understanding and appreciation of the role ethnicity and immigration played in shaping the culture of this country." Contains research articles based on the IHRC's collections or its conferences and seminars. *Freq:* Irregular. *Price:* $8.50, single issue.

3912 ■ Speegle Family Newsletter

Ima Gene Boyd
370 E. Archwood Ave.   Ph: (330)773-1757
Akron, OH 44301-2157

Contact: Ima Gene (Guthery) Boyd, Editor.

Desc: Provides genealogical information on the Speegle family. *Freq:* Quarterly. *Price:* $7.

3913 ■ SSGHS News

South Suburban Genealogical and Historical Society
PO Box 96   Ph: (708)333-9474
South Holland, IL 60473-0096

Contact: Deborah J. Somerville, Editor.

Desc: Presents news of the Society. Recurring features include news of research, a calendar of events, news of educational opportunities, reports of meetings, and notices of publications available. *Freq:* Monthly. *Price:* Included in membership.

3914 ■ State Data Center Newsletter

Tennessee State Data Center
University of Tennessee at Knoxville
Center for Business and   Ph: (615)974-5441
   Economic Research
Glocker Business Bldg., Ste. 100
Knoxville, TN 37996-4170

Contact: Betty B. Vickers, Editor.

Desc: Informs data users on surveys, censuses, and publications of the U.S. Department of Commerce and Bureau of the Census. Recurring features include news of research, calendar of events, reports of meetings, and notices of publications available. *Freq:* Semiannual. *Price:* Free.

3915 ■ Strawbery Banke Newsletter

Strawbery Banke Museum
PO Box 300   Ph: (603)433-1100
Portsmouth, NH 03802-0300   Fax: (603)433-1129

Desc: Provides news of the Museum and the activities it sponsors. Describes recent museum acquisitions and exhibits. Reports on the progress of the restoration of various sites and on current archeological excavations. Recurring features include news of research, announcements of new staff members, a list of seasonal highlights, and a calendar of events. *Freq:* Quarterly. *Price:* Included in membership.

3916 ■ Studebaker Family

Studebaker Family National Association
6555 S. State, Rte. 202   Ph: (937)667-4451
Tipp City, OH 45371   Fax: (937)667-4798

Contact: Sara Studebaker, Editor.

Desc: Contains information and research on the Studebaker family. Recurring features include news of research, a calendar of events, and reports of meetings. *Freq:* Quarterly. *Price:* Included in membership; $15/year for non-members.

3917 ■ Surnames Beginning with Van, Vander & Vanden

Olsen Enterprises
3931 S. 238th St.   Fax: (206)878-4267
Kent, WA 98032

Contact: Lucinda Olsen, Editor.

Desc: Designed to aid those who are researching any family line beginning with the surname of Van, Vander or Vanden. Also contains handwriting analysis. *Freq:* Quarterly. *Price:* $15, U.S.

3918 ■ Taylor County in Profile

Taylor County Historical and Genealogical Society, Inc.
PO Box 522
Grafton, WV 26354

Contact: Geneva M. Phelps, Editor; Betty Nettoe, Editor.

Desc: Publishes genealogical information concerning Taylor County families, which includes obituaries, birth and death records, and diary excerpts. Recurring features include news of Society activities and research. *Freq:* 4/year. *Price:* Included in membership.

3919 ■ Tennessee Archivist

Society of Tennessee Archivists
c/o Tennessee State Library   Ph: (615)741-2561
   & Archives   Fax: (615)741-6471
403 Seventh Ave. N.
Nashville, TN 37243-0312
E-mail: dmartinson@juno.com
URL: http://www.arkay.net/tnarchivist/

Contact: David R. Sowell, Editor.

Desc: Provides information on state and national archival activities. Announces professional meetings and workshops, archival job openings, and new collections. Features articles on archives and records repositories in Tennessee. Recurring features include a calendar of events, reports of meetings, news of educational opportunities, job listings, notices of publications available, and columns titled Editorial, Message from the President, and Committee Reports. *Freq:* Quarterly. *Price:* Included in membership; Free in exchange with other archival organizations.

3920 ■ Terrebonne Life Lines

Terrebonne Genealogical Society
Box 295, Sta. 2
Houma, LA 70360

Contact: Audrey Westerman, Editor.

Desc: Presents genealogical information on families related to the parishes of Assumption, LaFourche, and Terrebonne, Louisiana. Recurring features include book reviews. *Freq:* Quarterly. *Price:* Included in membership.

3921 ■ Think On

Clan Maclellan in America, Inc.
8636 Don Carol Dr.   Ph: (510)527-6867
El Cerrito, CA 94530

Contact: A. L. McClellan, Editor.

Desc: Covers the genealogy and experiences of MacLellans (any spelling) and Gillilands in America and Scotland. Recurring features include a calendar of events, reports of meetings, book reviews, and geneological queries. *Freq:* Quarterly. *Price:* Included in membership; $15.

3922 ■ Timmons Family Newsletter

Bunnie Timmons Runman
PO Box 262   Ph: (612)675-3457
Montrose, MN 55363

Contact: Bunnie Runman, Editor.

Desc: Provides genealogical information on the Timmons surname and its various spellings. Contains birth, marriage, and death records; wills; census results; biographies; and queries. Recurring features include news of research, a calendar of events, and notices of publications available. *Freq:* Quarterly. *Price:* Free; funded by donations.

3923 ■ Tolstoy Foundation Update

Tolstoy Foundation, Inc.
104 Lake Rd.   Ph: (914)268-6722
Valley Cottage, NY 10989-2459   Fax: (914)268-6937

Desc: Features news of the Foundation. Focuses on assistance of refugees and immigrants, the plight of the former Soviet Union's social and economic problems, and Foundation programs.

3924 ■ Topics

George C. Marshall Foundation
PO Drawer 1600   Ph: (703)463-7103
Lexington, VA 24450   Fax: (703)464-5229
E-mail: marshall@vmi.edu

Contact: Joellen K. Bland, Editor.

Desc: Covers current events at Marshall Foundation, developments affecting the Foundation, and the history of George C. Marshall. Lists Associate and Society members occasionally. *Freq:* 4/year. *Price:* Free.

3925 ■ Townsend Missing Links

Townsend Family Missing Links Association
5712 Antietam Dr.   Ph: (941)924-9170
Sarasota, FL 34231-4903

Contact: Charles Townsend, Editor.

Desc: Covers information on the Townsend family from the earliest date in America to the 1850s. Assists in the search for ancestors. *Price:* $15, U.S.; $20, Canada; $30, elsewhere.

3926 ■ Traces

South Central Kentucky Historical & Genealogical Society
PO Box 157
Glasgow, KY 42142-0157
E-mail: sckhgs@glasgow-ky.com

Contact: Martha P. Harrison, Editor.

Desc: Focuses on south central Kentucky history and genealogy. Recurring features include letters to the editor, a calendar of events, reports of meetings, book reviews, and notices of publications available. *Freq:* Quarterly. *Price:* $12/year.

3927 ■ Tracks & Traces

Union County Genealogical
c/o Barton Library   Ph: (501)863-5447
200 E. 5th St.   Fax: (501)862-3944
El Dorado, AR 71730-3897

Contact: Dorathy Boulden, Editor.

Desc: Disseminates genealogical and historical information on Union County, Arkansas. Features census information, family information, queries, and news of members. Recurring features include a column titled From the President. *Freq:* Semiannual, May and November. *Price:* Included in membership.

3928 ■ Tree Talks

Central New York Genealogical Society, Inc.
PO Box 104, Colvin Sta.
Syracuse, NY 13205

Desc: Publishes scholarly articles on genealogy and related subjects, with an emphasis on New York state history prior to 1850. Includes portions of wills, administrative deeds, account books, church and cemetery records, tax lists, vital records, and unpublished Bible records. Recurring features include book reviews and a query column. *Freq:* Quarterly. *Price:* Included in membership.

3929 ■ The Treesearcher

Kansas Genealogical Society
Village Square Mall   Ph: (316)225-1951
2601 Central
PO Box 103
Dodge City, KS 67801

Contact: Mr. Rooney, Editor.

Desc: Publishes prime source records submitted by members: Bible, cemetery, and early newspaper extractions; court and other records. Recurring features include news of members, book reviews, a calendar of events, and columns titled Trading Post (queries) and Tips (on which research), and Tumbleweeds (tips for Kansas genealogical research). *Freq:* Quarterly. *Price:* $15, individuals; $20, for families; $12, libraries.

3930 ■ Tri-City Genealogical Society Bulletin

Tri-City Genealogical Society
Box 1410
Richland, WA 99352-1410

Contact: Leona George, Contact.

Desc: Reports on the Society's activities and genealogical news and research. *Freq:* Semiannual. *Price:* $10, individuals, Free to qualified subscribers, genealogical societies and libraries.

3931 ■ Under Construction

Mendocino Coast Genealogical Society
PO Box 762   Ph: (707)937-5482
Fort Bragg, CA 95437

Contact: Alice Holmes, Editor.

Desc: Provides news and information concerning the Society, which provides assistance to individuals interested in genealogy, sponsors programs of a genealogical nature, collects and preserves genealogical material, and supplies research materials and books to the Fort Bragg Branch of the Mendocino County Library. Recurring features include news of research, a calendar of events, reports of meetings, notices of publications available, information on other societies, and a column titled the President's Message. *Freq:* 4/year. *Price:* Included in membership; $7.50/year for nonmembers.

3932 ■ Valentine News

The Valentine Museum
The Museum of the Life and History of Richmond
1015 E. Clay St.   Ph: (804)649-0711
Richmond, VA 23219-1590   Fax: (804)643-3510
E-mail: valmus@mindspring.com

Contact: Margaret J. Tinsley, Editor.

Desc: Describes the museum's exhibitions, public programs, and projects. Recurring features include a calendar of events and news of educational opportunities. *Freq:* Quarterly. *Price:* Free, w/membership.

3933 ■ Virginia Genealogical Society Newsletter

Virginia Genealogical Society
5001 W. Broad St., Ste. 115   Ph: (804)285-8954
Richmond, VA 23230   Fax: (804)285-0394
URL: http://www.vgs.org

Contact: Barbara Vires Little, Editor.

Desc: Includes news of research, a calendar of events, news of educational opportunities, book reviews, notices of publications available, queries, and a column titled Acquisitions at the Virginia State Archives. *Freq:* Bimonthly. *Price:* Included in membership, $26.

3934 ■ War Stories

Historical Preservation Association
7229 Park West Circle, No. 103   Ph: (817)551-2816
Fort Worth, TX 76134

Contact: David B. Miller, Historian.

Desc: Shares and preserves events and stories that involved American Service members during wars and conflicts. *Freq:* Quarterly. *Price:* $20, individuals.

3935 ■ Washington

Washington County Chapter of the Ohio Genealogical Society
PO Box 2174   Ph: (740)373-1641
Marietta, OH 45750-2174

Contact: Sharon Cory Gardner, Editor.

Desc: Offers genealogical information on Washington County, OH. Contains queries, cemetery readings, and Bible and church records. Recurring features include news of research, a calendar of events, book reviews, notices of publications available, and news of the past. *Freq:* Quarterly. *Price:* Included in membership.

3936 ■ Webster's Wagon Wheel

Webster County Historical and Genealogical Society
Box 215   Ph: (502)639-5170
Dixon, KY 42409

Contact: Betty J. Branson, Editor.

Desc: Contains historical and genealogical information. *Freq:* Quarterly. *Price:* $10, individuals; $2.50, single issue.

3937 ■ Weimer Genealogical Center Newsletter

Weimer Genealogical Center
11207 Morris Pl. NE   Ph: (505)299-6117
Albuquerque, NM 87112

Contact: Ellen Weimer, Editor.

Desc: Contains research of the Weimer surname and its variants. Includes obituaries, family lists, and letters from current family members. *Freq:* Quarterly. *Price:* $25/year.

3938 ▪ West-Central Kentucky Family Research Association—Bulletin

West-Central Kentucky Family Research Association
PO Box 1932
Owensboro, KY 42302   Ph: (502)684-4150

Contact: Margaret Alford, Editor.

Desc: Supplies genealogical information on the west-central area of Kentucky. Recurring features include news of research, a calendar of events, queries, reports of meetings, news of educational opportunities, book reviews, and notices of publications available. *Freq:* Quarterly. *Price:* Included in membership; $15/year.

3939 ▪ Western Reserve Historical Society Genealogical Committee—Bulletin

Western Reserve Historical Society
10825 East Blvd.   Ph: (216)721-5722
Cleveland, OH 44106   Fax: (216)721-0645

Contact: Sue Bennett, Editor.

Desc: Provides articles on genealogical research, recent accessions of the WRHS library, and research methods. Recurring features include a calendar of events, book reviews, a listing of special holdings for manuscripts research, and new acquisitions to the collection. *Freq:* Quarterly. *Price:* $5/year.

3940 ▪ Where the Trails Cross

South Suburban Genealogical and Historical Society
PO Box 96   Ph: (708)333-9474
South Holland, IL 60473-0096

Contact: Janice Helge, Editor.

Desc: Supplies local historical information on topics such as land, obituaries, churches, cemetery readings, and school records. *Alt. Fmts:* microfilm. *Freq:* Quarterly. *Price:* $15, Included in membership.

3941 ▪ White Eagle

Polish Nobility Association
529 Dunkirk Rd.   Ph: (301)377-4352
Baltimore, MD 21212

Contact: Leonard Suligowski, Editor.

Desc: Carries news of the Association, which promotes the study and preservation of Polish history, chivalry, heraldry, and genealogy among descendants of titled aristocrats and members of the nobility. Recurring features include genealogical and heraldic information, letters to the editor, and member news. *Freq:* Semiannual. *Price:* Included in membership, varies, $15 minimum.

3942 ▪ Whitman County Genealogical Society—News Letter

Whitman County Genealogical Society
PO Box 393   Ph: (509)332-2386
Pullman, WA 99163-0393

Contact: Judy Standar McMurray, Editor.

Desc: Publishes local and non-local genealogical materials. Updates news on historical museums; marriage records, birth records, death records, census records, extracts of probate reports, and other statistical records; the Society's library; officials and members; and activities and events. Lists electronic library holdings. Recurring features include reports of meetings and notices of publications available. *Freq:* 10/year. *Price:* $20/year.

3943 ▪ Wilson Museum Bulletin

Castine Scientific Society
Wilson Museum
PO Box 196   Ph: (207)326-8545
Castine, ME 04421-0796

Contact: Patricia Hutchins, Curator.

Desc: Disseminates information and research on the museum collection and local history. *Freq:* 3/year. *Price:* $5, members, Free, upon request.

3944 ▪ Wisconsin State Genealogical Society Newsletter

Wisconsin State Genealogical Society, Inc.
2109 20th Ave.   Ph: (608)325-2609
Monroe, WI 53566
URL: http://www.rootsweb.com/wsgs

Contact: Virginia Irvin, Editor.

Desc: Provides readers with Wisconsin genealogical material. Contains cemetery records, obituaries, passenger lists, and marriage and other vital records. Publishes reminiscences and articles on family reunions, and a query column for members. *Freq:* 4/year. *Price:* Included in membership.

3945 ▪ Wood County Chapter Ohio Genealogical Society Newsletter

Wood County Chapter Ohio Genealogical Society
PO Box 722
Bowling Green, OH 43402-0722

Contact: Lolita Guthrie, Editor.

Desc: Covers Society activities and contains genealogical information. Recurring features include letters to the editor, news of research, a calendar of events, reports of meetings, notices of publications available, and queries. *Freq:* Bimonthly. *Price:* $8 for individuals and $10 for families.

3946 ▪ Wyandot Tracers

Ohio Genealogical Society
PO Box 414
Upper Sandusky, OH 43351-0414

Contact: Nira Beaschler, Editor.

Desc: Provides historical and genealogical information on individuals who lived in Wyandot County, Ohio. Recurring features include news of research, a calendar of events, and notices of publications available. *Freq:* Bimonthly. *Price:* Included in membership.

3947 ▪ WyMonDak Messenger

Tri-State Genealogical Society
c/o Public Library   Ph: (605)892-4407
905 5th Ave.
Belle Fourche, SD 57717-1702

Contact: Pat Engebretson, Editor.

Desc: Contains genealogical material of interest to those searching for ancestors from Crook County, Wyoming; Carter County, Montana; Butte and Harding counties in South Dakota, and parts of Perkins, Meade, and Lawrence counties. *Price:* $5/year.

3948 ▪ York County Genealogical Society Newsletter

York County Genealogical Society
82 Damon Ave.   Ph: (781)665-4664
Melrose, MA 02176

Contact: Theodore S. Bond, Editor.

Desc: Provides articles and discussion on genealogical information. *Freq:* Semiannual. *Price:* $15, individuals, includes 4 journals; $10, institutions, includes 4 journals.

Periodicals

3949 ▪ Acadiensis

University of New Brunswick
Department of History   Ph: (506)453-4978
Fredericton, NB, Canada E3B
  5A3
E-mail: acadnsis@unb.ca

Desc: Journal covering the regional history of Atlantic Canada. *Freq:* Semiannual. *Price:* C$21, individuals; C$10.65, single issue.

3950 ▪ Accounting Historians Journal

Academy of Accounting Historians
c/o William D. Samson   Ph: (205)348-2903
Culverhouse School   Fax: (205)348-8453
  of Accounting
University of Alabama
Tuscaloosa, AL 35401

Contact: Dick Fleischman, Journal Editor; Elliot Slocum, Notebook Editor.

Desc: Professional journal for accounting historians. *Freq:* Semiannual. *Price:* $40, individuals; $50, institutions.

3951 ▪ Alabama Heritage

Alabama Heritage
University of Alabama   Ph: (205)348-7467
Box 870342   Fax: (205)348-7473
Tuscaloosa, AL 35487-0342

Contact: Suzanne R. Wolfe, Editor; Sara Martin, Director.

Desc: Historical magazine for the general public. Covers cultural heritage of Alabama and the South. *Freq:* Quarterly. *Price:* $16.95, individuals; $28.95, two years; $38.95, Three Years.

3952 ▪ Alliance

John W. Yopp Publications, Inc.
803 Port Republic St.   Ph: (843)521-0239
PO Box 1147   Free: 800-849-9677
Beaufort, SC 29902   Fax: (843)521-1398

Contact: Mary Y. Cronley, Editor and Publisher; Joseph Cronley, Research Editor; Jean Herrington, Accounts/Classifieds; Sondra Kreger, Asst. Editor/Circulation Mgr.

Desc: Trade magazine for the funeral and cemetery industry. *Freq:* 6/year. *Price:* $30, individuals; $3, single issue.

3953 ▪ Almanac

Society for Pacific Coast Native Iris
c/o Terri   Ph: (707)964-3907
  Hudson, Sec.-Treasurer   Fax: (707)964-3907
33450 Little Valley Rd.
Fort Bragg, CA 95437
E-mail: irishud@mcn.org

Contact: Lewis Lawyer, Editor/Circulation Mgr.

Desc: Journal covering hybrid and species Pacific Coast native iris, their care, locations and events. *Alt. Contact:* 4333 Oak Hill Rd., Oakland, CA 94605. *Freq:* Semiannual. *Price:* $4, individuals.

3954 ▪ The American Archivist

Society of American Archivists
527 S. Wells St., 5th Fl.   Ph: (312)922-0140
Chicago, IL 60617-3922   Fax: (312)347-1452
E-mail: info@archivists.org

Contact: Philip B. Eppard, Editor; Teresa M. Brinati, Dir. Pub.

Desc: Journal for the North American archival profession discussing trends in archival theory and practice and also featuring book reviews. *Alt. Fmts:* microfilm. *Freq:* Semiannual. *Price:* $85, individuals; $100, out of country.

3955 ▪ The American Genealogist

The American Genealogist
PO Box 398   Ph: (706)865-6440
Demorest, GA 30535-0398   Fax: (706)865-6440
E-mail: amgen@stc.net

Contact: David L. Greene, Editor and Publisher; Robert
C. Anderson, Editor; A. Jane McFerrin, Managing Editor.

Desc: Scholarly genealogy journal. *Alt. Fmts:* microform.
Freq: Quarterly. *Price:* $25, individuals; $48, two years;
$70, for 3 years; $7, single issue.

3956 ▪ American Heritage

American Heritage
60 5th Ave.   Ph: (212)206-5500
New York, NY 10011-8882   Fax: (212)620-2332
E-mail: mail@americanheritage.com
URL: http://www.americanheritage.com

Contact: Richard F. Snow, Editor; Edward Z. Hughes,
Publisher.

Desc: Magazine on the political, cultural, and social aspects
of American history. *Freq:* 8/year. *Price:* $32, individuals;
$4.95, single issue.

3957 ▪ The American Historical Review

American Historical Association
400 A St. SE   Ph: (202)544-2422
Washington, DC 20003-3889   Fax: (202)544-8307
E-mail: aha@theaha.org; amhrev@indiana.edu

Contact: Michael Grossberg, Editor.

Desc: Scholarly journal. *Alt. Contact:* American Historical
Review 914 Atwater Ave., Bloomington, IN 47401; telephone: (812)855-7609; fax: (812)855-5827. *Freq:* 5/year.
Price: individuals, sliding scale from $30-$120; $65, indi-
viduals, average.

3958 ▪ American Jewish Archives

American Jewish Archives
3101 Clifton Ave.   Ph: (513)221-1875
Cincinnati, OH 45220   Fax: (513)221-7812
E-mail: gzola@cn.huc.edu
URL: http://www.huc.edu/aja

Contact: Dr. Gary P. Zola, Editor

Desc: Scholarly journal covering American Jewish history.
Freq: Semiannual.

3959 ▪ American Jewish History

American Jewish Historical Society
2 Thornton Rd.   Ph: (617)891-8110
Waltham, MA 02154   Fax: (617)899-9208
E-mail: ajhs@ajhs.org

Contact: Marc Lee Raphael, Editor; Michael Feldberg,
Exec. Dir.

Desc: Journal on American Jewish history. *Alt. Fmts:* microfilm; microform. *Freq:* Quarterly. *Price:* $50, individu-
als; $69, libraries; $15, single issue.

3960 ▪ Ancestors West

Santa Barbara County Genealogical Society
Box 1303
Goleta, CA 93116

Contact: Lesley Fagan, Contact.

Desc: Journal covering genealogy and local history. *Freq:*
Quarterly. *Price:* $15, individuals; $3, single issue.

3961 ▪ Ancestry

Palm Beach County Genealogical Society, Inc.
Box 1746
West Palm Beach, FL 33402-1746

Contact: Jane M. Allen, Circulation.

Desc: Genealogical magazine. *Freq:* Quarterly. *Price:* $15,
individuals; $2.50, single issue.

3962 ▪ Annals of Iowa

State Historical Society of Iowa
402 Iowa Ave.   Ph: (319)335-3912
Iowa City, IA 52240   Fax: (319)335-3935

Contact: Marvin Bergman, Editor.

Desc: State historical journal. *Alt. Contact:* , 402 Iowa
Ave., Iowa City, IA 52240; telephone: (319)335-3931;
fax: (319)335-3935. *Freq:* Quarterly. *Price:* $20, individu-
als; $6, single issue.

3963 ▪ Arizona Highways

Arizona Highways
2039 W. Lewis Ave.   Ph: (602)258-6641
Phoenix, AZ 85009   Free: 800-543-5432
                                   Fax: (602)254-4505
URL: http://www.arizhwys.com/

Contact: Robert J. Early, Editor; Rebecca Mong, Managing Editor; Nina LaFrance, Publisher.

Desc: Travel magazine covering regional history, natural
science, folklore, and natural history. *Alt. Contact:* 2039
W. Lewis Ave., Phoenix, AZ 85009. *Freq:* Monthly. *Price:*
$19, individuals; $2.99, out of area, single issue.

3964 ▪ Arkansas Family Historian

Arkansas Genealogical Society, Inc.
1411 Shady Grove Rd.   Ph: (501)262-4513
PO Box 908   Fax: (501)262-4513
Hot Springs, AR 71902-0908
URL: http://www.rootsweb.com/args

Desc: Journal covering genealogy and history in Arkansas.
Freq: Quarterly. *Price:* $20, individuals.

3965 ▪ Arkansas Historical Quarterly

Arkansas Historical Association
University of Arkansas   Ph: (501)575-5884
History Dept., 416 Old Main   Fax: (501)575-2642
Fayetteville, AR 72701

Contact: Jeanne M. Whayne, Editor; Gretchen Gearhart,
Assistant Editor; Patrick Williams, Assoc. Editor; Rhonda
Hukill, Business Mgr.

Desc: Historical magazine. *Freq:* Quarterly. *Price:* $16,
individuals; $24, other countries; $4.50, single issue.

3966 ▪ Arlington Historical Magazine

Arlington Historical Society, Inc.
PO Box 402   Ph: (703)892-4204
Arlington, VA 22210-0402

Contact: Karl VanNewkirk, Editor.

Desc: Magazine covering local history. *Freq:* Annual. *Price:*
$9.75, individuals.

3967 ▪ Atlanta History

Atlanta Historical Society, Inc.
130 W. Paces Ferry Rd.   Ph: (404)814-4085
Atlanta, GA 30305   Fax: (404)814-2041

Contact: Kim Blass, Managing Editor; Brad Rice, Editor;
Andy Ambrose, Assoc. Editor.

Desc: Journal covering local history. *Freq:* Quarterly. *Price:*
$20, individuals; $5, single issue.

3968 ▪ Augusta Historical Bulletin

Augusta Historical Bulletin
PO Box 686
Staunton, VA 24402

Contact: Katharine Brown, Editor; Nancy Sorrells, Editor.

Desc: Journal covering local history and genealogy. *Freq:*
Semiannual. *Price:* $15, individuals.

3969 ▪ Avotaynu

Avotaynu, Inc.
155 N. Washington Ave.   Ph: (201)387-7200
Bergenfield, NJ 07621   Free: 800-286-8296
                                   Fax: (201)387-2855
E-mail: info@avotaynu.com
URL: http://www.avotaynu.com

Contact: Sallyann Amdur Sack, Editor.

Desc: Journal covering Jewish genealogy. *Alt. Fmts:* CD-
ROM. *Freq:* Quarterly. *Price:* $32, individuals; $10, single issue.

3970 ▪ Backtracker

Northwest Arkansas Genealogical Society
Box 796   Ph: (501)273-3890
Rogers, AR 72757-0796

Contact: George Crabtree, Editor.

Desc: Genealogical journal of Northwest Arkansas. *Freq:*
Quarterly. *Price:* $12.50, individuals; $3.50, single issue.

3971 ▪ Bedford Historical Quarterly

Bedford County Historical Society
250 Riverbend Rd.
Shelbyville, TN 37160-7217

Contact: Roy Turrentine, Editor.

Desc: Historical and genealogical publication. *Alt. Contact:*
c/o Roy Turrentine, 339 Rippy Ridge Rd., Normandy,
TN 37360; telephone: (931)857-9341. *Freq:* Quarterly.
Price: $12.50, individuals; $3.25, single issue.

3972 ▪ Berks County Genealogical Society Journal

Berks County Genealogical Society
Box 305
Kutztown, PA 19530-0305

Contact: Lois Ann Mast, Editor.

Desc: Historical and genealogical magazine. *Freq:* Quarterly.

3973 ▪ Biography Index

The H.W. Wilson Co.
950 University Ave.   Ph: (718)588-8400
Bronx, NY 10452   Free: 800-367-6770
                                   Fax: 800-590-1617
E-mail: custserv@hwwilson.com

Contact: Charles R. Cornell, Editor.

Desc: Quarterly index of biographical material in books
and magazines. *Available:* Online: Dialog. *Freq:* Quarterly. *Price:* $160, U.S. and Canada; $180, other countries

3974 ▪ British Columbia Genealogist

British Columbia Genealogical Society
PO Box 88054   Ph: (604)325-0374
Richmond, BC, Canada V6X
  3T6
URL: http://www.npsnet.com/bcgs; http://
  www.nps.net/bcgs

Desc: Journal covering local genealogy. *Freq:* Quarterly.
Price: C$30, Canada.

3975 ▪ Bushong Bulletin

Carol Willsey Bell
10460 N. Palmyra Rd.   Ph: (330)538-2046
North Jackson, OH 44451-9793

Contact: Carol Willsey Bell, Editor.

Desc: Periodical covering genealogy of the Bushong family. *Freq:* Quarterly. *Price:* $10, individuals.

3976 ■ Camden Fifth Series

Cambridge University Press
40 W. 20th St.   Ph: (212)924-3900
New York, NY 10011-4211   Free: 800-221-4512
                                 Fax: (212)691-3239

Desc: Journal published on behalf of the Royal Historical Society. *Freq:* Semiannual.

3977 ■ Canfield Family Association

Canfield Family Association
1144 N. Gordon   Ph: (316)942-7120
Wichita, KS 67203-6611

Contact: Genevieve (Canfield) Martinson, Editor.

Desc: Genealogical publication covering information about Canfield, Camfield, and Campfield names. *Freq:* Quarterly. *Price:* $8, individuals; $14, out of country.

3978 ■ Catholic Cemetery

National Catholic Cemetery Conference
710 N. River Rd.   Ph: (847)824-8131
Des Plaines, IL 60016   Fax: (847)824-9608

Contact: Irene K. Pesce, Editor.

Desc: Magazine on cemetery administration, maintenance, and equipment. *Freq:* Monthly. *Price:* $35, individuals.

3979 ■ Central Kentucky Researcher

Taylor County Historical Society
Box 14   Ph: (502)465-7033
Campbellsville, KY 42719

Contact: Aileen McKinley, Editor/Circulation Mgr.

Desc: Local historical magazine. *Freq:* Quarterly. *Price:* Free to qualified subscribers.

3980 ■ Centre County Heritage

Centre County Historical Society
1001 E. College Ave.   Ph: (814)234-4779
State College, PA 16801   Fax: (814)234-1694
E-mail: cchs@csrlink.net

Contact: W. Douglas Macneal, Editor.

Desc: Scholarly journal covering local history. *Freq:* Semiannual. *Price:* $10, individuals; $5, single issue.

3981 ■ Champaign County Genealogical Society Quarterly

Champaign County Genealogical Society
c/o Champaign County   Ph: (217)367-4025
   Historical Archives   Fax: (217)367-4061
201 S. Race St.
Urbana, IL 61801-3283

Contact: Joan Black Lund, Editor.

Desc: Genealogical publication. *Freq:* Quarterly. *Price:* $15, individuals; $3.50, single issue.

3982 ■ Chicago History

Chicago Historical Society
Clark St. at North Ave.   Ph: (312)642-4600
Chicago, IL 60614   Fax: (312)266-2077
URL: http://www.chicagohistory.org

Contact: Rosemary K. Adams, Editor.

Desc: Magazine containing articles and photos about Chicago and American history. *Freq:* 3/year. *Price:* $30, individuals.

3983 ■ Chips from Many Trees and Growing Roots

ACETO Bookmen
5721 Antietam Dr.   Ph: (941)924-9170
Sarasota, FL 34231

Contact: Charles D. Townsend, Editor/Manager.

Desc: Genealogical magazine covering families in Canada and the U.S. *Freq:* Quarterly. *Price:* $20, individuals; $25, Canada; $30, elsewhere.

3984 ■ The Christian Civic League Record

Christian Civic League
PO Box 5459   Ph: (207)622-7634
Augusta, ME 04332   Free: 800-769-4132
                                 Fax: (207)621-0035
E-mail: email@cclmaine.org

Contact: Cynthia Randall, Editor.

Desc: Magazine on civic action. *Freq:* Monthly. *Price:* $10, individuals.

3985 ■ The Columbia

Valley Quarterlies
60 Cedar Heights Rd.   Ph: (914)876-4592
Rhinebeck, NY 12572

Contact: Arthur Kelly, Editor.

Desc: Journal covering local history and genealogy. *Freq:* Annual. *Price:* $16, individuals; $4.50, single issue.

3986 ■ Connecticut Maple Leaf

French-Canadian Genealogical Society of Connecticut, Inc.
Box 928   Ph: (860)872-2597
Tolland, CT 06084-0928

Contact: Albert J. Marceau, Editor.

Desc: Journal covering French-Canadian genealogy in Connecticut. *Alt. Fmts:* microfiche. *Freq:* Semiannual. *Price:* Free to qualified subscribers.

3987 ■ Cow Neck Peninsula Historical Society Journal

Cow Neck Peninsula Historical Society
336 Port Washington Blvd.   Ph: (516)365-9074
Port Washington, NY 11050

Contact: Mildred G. Lee, Publicity Chairor.

Desc: Journal covering local history. *Freq:* Annual. *Price:* $3, single issue.

3988 ■ Dallas Journal

Dallas Genealogical Society
Box 12446   Ph: (214)670-7932
Dallas, TX 75225-0446
E-mail: dgs@chrysalis.org
URL: http://www.dallasgenealogy.org

Desc: Journal covering history and genealogy of Dallas County, Texas for members. *Freq:* Annual. *Price:* Free to qualified subscribers.

3989 ■ Daughters of the American Revolution Magazine

National Society Daughters of the American Revolution
1776 D St. NW   Ph: (202)879-3286
Washington, DC 20006-5392   Fax: (202)879-3283

Contact: Mary Rose Hall, Editor; Mary Rose Hall, Editor.

Desc: Official magazine of the DAR. *Alt. Fmts:* microform. *Freq:* 10/year. *Price:* $12, individuals.

3990 ■ de Halve Maen

Holland Society of New York
122 E. 58th St.
New York, NY 10022

Contact: Dr. David William Voorhees, Editor.

Desc: Scholarly journal covering the Nieuw Netherland Colony and genealogy relating to families arriving in the Colony prior to 1675. *Freq:* Quarterly. *Price:* $28.50, individuals; $32.50, out of country; $7.50, single issue.

3991 ■ Delaware Genealogical Society Journal

Delaware Genealogical Society
505 Market St. Mall
Wilmington, DE 19801
URL: http://www.delgensoc.org

Contact: Mary Fallon Richards, Editor; John C. Richards, Pub. Coordinator; Edward E. Gray, Business Mgr.

Desc: Journal covering genealogy. *Freq:* Semiannual. *Price:* Free to qualified subscribers; $4, single issue, (back issues); $14.50, others (vol. of 4 issues).

3992 ■ Detroit Society for Genealogical Research Magazine

Detroit Society for Genealogical Research, Inc.
The Burton Historical Collection   Ph: (313)833-1480
Detroit Public Library
5201 Woodward Ave. & Kirby
Detroit, MI 48202-4093
URL: http://dsgr.org

Contact: Patricia Ibbotson, Editor.

Desc: Genealogy magazine. *Freq:* Quarterly. *Price:* $20, individuals.

3993 ■ Dewitt County Genealogical Society Quarterly

Dewitt County Genealogical Society
Box 632   Ph: (217)935-3493
Clinton, IL 61727-0632

Contact: Betty Adcock, Editor.

Desc: Genealogical magazine. *Freq:* Quarterly. *Price:* $15, individuals; $4, single issue.

3994 ■ East Texas Historical Journal

East Texas Historical Association
Box 6223, SFA Sta.   Ph: (409)468-2407
Nacogdoches, TX 75962   Fax: (409)468-2190

Contact: Archie P. McDonald, Editor.

Desc: Journal covering local history in Texas. *Freq:* Semiannual. *Price:* $25, individuals; $7.50, single issue.

3995 ■ Elk Horn

Elk County Historical Society
PO Box 361
Ridgway, PA 15853

Contact: Iva A. Fay, Editor.

Desc: Magazine covering local history. *Freq:* Triennial. *Price:* Free to qualified subscribers; $1, single issue.

3996 ■ Essex Genealogist

Essex Society of Genealogists
Box 313   Ph: (978)664-9279
Lynnfield, MA 01940-0313
E-mail: essexsoc@aol.com

Contact: Marcia Lindberg, Editor; Nancy Hayward, Managing Editor.

Desc: Genealogical magazine covering Essex County, Massachusetts. *Freq:* Quarterly. *Price:* $18, individuals; $5, single issue.

3997 ■ Eswau Huppeday

Broad River Genealogical Society, Inc.
Box 2261
Shelby, NC 28151-2261
URL: http://www.rootsweb.comorcclevel/brgs.htm

Contact: JoAnn Freeman Surratt, Editor; Ned Cash, Chief of Publications.

Desc: Genealogical journal. *Freq:* Quarterly. *Price:* $15, individuals.

3998 ■ Everton's Genealogical Helper

Everton Publishers, Inc.
PO Box 368   Ph: (435)752-6022
Logan, UT 84323-0368   Free: 800-443-6325
                                        Fax: (435)752-0425
E-mail: adrate@everton.com; bas@evcalon.com

Contact: Valerie N. Chambers, Editor; A. Lee Eventon, Publisher.

Desc: Genealogy magazine. *Alt. Contact:* 3223 S. Main, Nibley, UT 84321. *Freq:* Bimonthly. *Price:* $24, individuals.

3999 ■ Families

Ontario Genealogical Society
40 Orchard View Blvd., Ste. 102   Ph: (416)489-0734
Toronto, ON, Canada M4R   Fax: (416)489-9803
1B9

Contact: Hal Courchesne, Editor.

Desc: Journal covering genealogy and family history. *Freq:* Quarterly. *Price:* C$45, individuals.

4000 ■ Family Chronicle

Moorshead Magazines Ltd.
10 Gateway Blvd., Ste. 490   Ph: (416)696-5488
North York, ON, Canada M3C   Free: 888-326-2476
3T4   Fax: (416)696-7395
E-mail: famchron@moorshead.com

Contact: Halvor Moorshead, Publisher; Jeff Chapman, Editor.

Desc: Consumer magazine covering genealogy. *Freq:* Bimonthly. *Price:* C$21, individuals; C$24.95, Canada; C$3.95, single issue, Canada; C$4.95, Canada.

4001 ■ Family Records TODAY

American Family Records Association
PO Box 15505   Ph: (816)252-0950
Kansas City, MO 64106
E-mail: amfamrecord@aol.com

Contact: Nita Neblock, Editor.

Desc: Journal. *Freq:* Quarterly.

4002 ■ Flashback

Washington County Historical Society, Inc.
118 E. Dickson St.   Ph: (501)521-2970
Fayetteville, AR 72701-5612
URL: http://biz.ipa.net/wchs

Contact: Don E. Schaefer, Editor.

Desc: Magazine covering local history. *Freq:* Quarterly. *Price:* $15, members, individual; $25, members, family; $4, single issue.

4003 ■ Flipping Flippins

Nova A. Lemons
12206 Brisbane Ave.   Fax: (972)620-1416
Dallas, TX 75234-6528
E-mail: lemstar@juno.com

Desc: Genealogical journal for Flippen, Flippin, Flipping, etc., surnames. *Freq:* Quarterly. *Price:* $15, individuals.

4004 ■ Flower of the Forest Black Genealogical Journal

Mullac Publishing
1364 Walker Ave.   Ph: (410)323 3883
Baltimore, MD 21239

Desc: Journal covering Black genealogical and historical issues. *Freq:* Annual. *Price:* $7, individuals.

4005 ■ Footprints in Time

Gaston-Lincoln Genealogical Society
Box 584
Mount Holly, NC 28120

Desc: Genealogical magazine.

4006 ■ Fort Smith Historical Society Journal

Fort Smith Historical Society, Inc.
c/o Fort Smith Public Library   Ph: (501)783-0229
61 S. 8th St.
Fort Smith, AR 72901

Contact: Amelia Martin, Editor.

Desc: Journal covering local history and genealogy. *Alt. Contact:* 2121 Wolfe Ln., Fort Smith, AR 72901-6243; telephone: (501)783-1237; fax: (501)782-0649. *Freq:* Semiannual, April and Sept. *Price:* $15, individuals; $7.50, single issue.

4007 ■ Fulton County Images

Fulton County Historical Society, Inc.
37 East 375 North   Ph: (219)223-4436
Rochester, IN 46975-8384

Contact: Shirley Willard, Editor.

Desc: Journal covering local history. *Freq:* Annual. *Price:* $15, individuals; $25, family or group.

4008 ■ Genealogical Computing

Ancestry, Inc.
PO Box 990   Ph: (801)426-3500
Orem, UT 84057   Free: 800-262-3787
                                           Fax: (801)426-3501
E-mail: support@ancestry-inc.com

Contact: Jake Gearing, Managing Editor; Matt Grove, Associate Editor; Lynda Angelastro, Associate Editor.

Desc: Magazine covering use of computers in genealogy. *Freq:* Quarterly.

4009 ■ Genealogical Goldmine

Paradise Genealogical Society, Inc.
PO Box 460   Ph: (530)877-2330
Paradise, CA 95967-0460
E-mail: pargenso@jps.net

Desc: Genealogical journal covering local and general family histories. *Freq:* Semiannual. *Price:* Free to qualified subscribers.

4010 ■ Genealogical Helper

Everton Publishers, Inc.
PO Box 368   Ph: (435)752-6022
Logan, UT 84323-0368   Free: 800-443-6325
                                           Fax: (435)752-0425

Contact: Valerie Chambers, Editor; Lee A. Everton, Publisher; Bob Arbor, Manager.

Desc: Genealogical publication. *Price:* $24, individuals; $26.10, out of country; $6.95, single issue; $8.95, elsewhere.

4011 ■ Genealogical Journal of Jefferson County, New York

The Family Tree
PO Box 4311   Ph: (208)939-9141
Boise, ID 83711

E-mail: familytre@aol.com

Contact: Pat James, Contact; Anna Nasman, Contact.

Desc: Journal of genealogical information. *Freq:* Annual. *Price:* $17.50, individuals.

4012 ■ Genealogical Journal of Oneida County, New York

The Family Tree
PO Box 4311   Ph: (208)939-9141
Boise, ID 83711
E-mail: familytre@aol.com

Contact: Patricia James, Contact; Anna Nasman, Contact.

Desc: Genealogical journal of Oneida County, New York. *Freq:* Annual. *Price:* $17.50, individuals.

4013 ■ Genealogy Bulletin

AGLL, Inc./Heritage Quest
PO Box 329   Ph: (801)298-5358
Bountiful, UT 84011-0329   Free: 800-760-AGLL
                                           Fax: (801)298-5468
E-mail: sales@heritagequest.com
URL: http://www.agll.com

Contact: William Dollarhide, Managing Editor.

Desc: Bi-monthly newsletter which features articles on pursuing your genealogical research. Eac issue contains 3,000 name-date-place queries and keeps you current on what's happening in the field of genealogy. *Available:* Online: AGLL BBS. *Alt. Contact:* PO Box 329, Bountiful, UT 84011-0329. *Alt. Fmts:* microfiche. *Freq:* Bimonthly. *Price:* $18, individuals; $40, other countries.

4014 ■ Generations

Manitoba Genealogical Society, Inc.
Unit E, 1045 St. James St.   Ph: (204)783-9139
Winnipeg, MB, Canada R3H   Fax: (204)783-0190
1B1
E-mail: mgs@mbnet.mb.ca
URL: http://www.mbnet.mb.ca/mgs

Contact: Joyce Elias, Editor.

Desc: Genealogical journal. *Freq:* Quarterly. *Price:* C$25, individuals.

4015 ■ Georgia Historical Quarterly

Georgia Historical Quarterly
301 LeConte Hall   Ph: (706)542-6300
University of Georgia   Fax: (706)542-2455
Athens, GA 30602

Contact: John C. Inscoe, Editor.

Desc: Historical magazine. *Freq:* Quarterly. *Price:* $35, individuals.

4016 ■ Goldenseal

The Cultural Center
Division of Culture and History
1900 Kanawha Blvd. E.   Ph: (304)558-0220
Charleston, WV 25305-0300   Fax: (304)558-2779
E-mail: lilly-jo@wvlc.wvnet.edu
URL: http://www.wvlc.wvnet.edu/culture/goldensl/html

Desc: Consumer magazine covering local history. *Freq:* Quarterly. *Price:* $16, individuals; $20, out of country; $4.95, single issue.

4017 ■ Greenbrier Historical Society Journal

Greenbrier Historical Society
301 W. Washington St.   Ph: (304)645-3398
Lewisburg, WV 24901   Fax: (304)645-5201
E-mail: ghs@access.mountain.net
URL: http://www.mountain.net/ghs/ghs.html

Contact: Joyce Mott.

Desc: Journal covering history and genealogy. *Freq:* Annual. *Price:* $10.50, members; $25, institutions, member; $16.50, nonmembers.

4018 ▪ Hawkeye Heritage
Iowa Genealogical Society
Box 7735
Des Moines, IA 50322-7735
E-mail: igs@digiserve.com
Ph: (515)276-0287

Contact: Rhonda Q. Riordan, Exec.Dir.

Desc: Journal covering genealogy in Iowa. *Freq:* Quarterly. *Price:* $25, members; $5, single issue.

4019 ▪ Heritage
New York State Historical Association
PO Box 800
Cooperstown, NY 13326
Ph: (607)547-1400
Fax: (607)547-1404

Contact: Paul S. D'ambrosio, Editor.

Desc: Magazine of the New York Historical Association. *Freq:* Quarterly. *Price:* $4.95, single issue; $16, individuals.

4020 ▪ Heritage Quest Magazine
AGLL, Inc./Heritage Quest
PO Box 329
Bountiful, UT 84011-0329
Ph: (801)298-5358
Free: 800-760-AGLL
Fax: (801)298-5468
E-mail: sales@heritagequest.com
URL: http://www.heritagequest.com

Contact: Leland K. Meitzler.

Desc: Magazine on genealogy. *Alt. Contact:* PO Box 40, Orting, WA 98360-0040; telephone: (253)770-0551; fax: (253)770-0551. *Freq:* Bimonthly. *Price:* $28, individuals.

4021 ▪ Heritage of Vermilion County
Vermillion County Museum Society
116 N. Gilbert St.
Danville, IL 61832
Ph: (217)442-2922

Contact: Donald G. Richter; Susan E. Richter.

Desc: Journal covering local history in Illinois. *Freq:* Quarterly. *Price:* $10, individuals; $2.50, single issue.

4022 ▪ Hidden Valley Journal
Escondido Genealogical Society
Box 2190
Escondido, CA 92033-2190

Contact: Sandy Sneider, Editor.

Desc: Magazine covering local and family history and genealogy. *Alt. Contact:* 1750 W. Citracado Pkwy., Spc. 47, Escondido, CA 92029-4127; fax: (760)741-4030. *Freq:* Annual. *Price:* $10, single issue.

4023 ▪ Historic Kern
Kern County Historical Society
PO Box 141
Bakersfield, CA 93302
Ph: (805)322-4962

Contact: Curtis Darling, Editor.

Desc: Journal covering local history. *Freq:* Quarterly. *Price:* $3.50, individuals; $10, members; $1, single issue.

4024 ▪ Historic Madison
Historic Madison, Inc. of Wisconsin
Box 2721
Madison, WI 53701-2721
Ph: (608)249-7920
URL: http://www.danenet.org/hmi

Contact: Tess Mulrooney, President/Editor.

Desc: Local historical society magazine. *Freq:* Annual. *Price:* $6.50, single issue.

4025 ▪ Historic Morris Emporium
Emporium Production Center
3117 Rte. 10 E.
Denville, NJ 07834
Ph: (973)899-9092
Fax: (973)366-6815

Contact: Bruce Spicer, Circulation Mgr.

Desc: Consumer magazine covering local history. *Freq:* Quarterly. *Price:* $6, individuals.

4026 ▪ Historic Preservation Forum
National Trust for Historic Preservation
1785 Massachusetts Ave. NW
Washington, DC 20036-2117
Ph: (202)588-6296
Free: 800-944-6847
Fax: (202)588-6223
E-mail: forum@nthp.org
URL: http://www.nationaltrust.org

Contact: Byrd Wood.

Desc: Journal covering historic preservation. *Freq:* Quarterly. *Price:* $110, individuals.

4027 ▪ Historic Traveler
Cowles History Group
6405 Flank Dr.
Harrisburg, PA 17112
Ph: (203)321-1781
Fax: (203)322-0302

Contact: Tom Huntington, Editor; Peter Lenahan, Publisher; Suzanne Kradel, Advertising Dir.

Desc: Consumer magazine covering travel to historic sites. *Freq:* Bimonthly. *Price:* $11.97, individuals; $16.95, Canada; $35.97, other countries; $3.99, single issue.

4028 ▪ The Historical Messenger
Historical Society, Illinois Great Rivers Conference, United Methodist Church
Box 515
Bloomington, IL 61702-0515
Ph: (309)828-5092
Fax: (309)829-4820

Contact: Vera Swantner, Editor.

Desc: Religious and historical publication. *Freq:* Quarterly. *Price:* $10, individuals.

4029 ▪ Historical Methods
Heldref Publications
Helen Dwight Reid
  Educational Foundation
1319 18th St. NW
Washington, DC 20036-1802
Ph: (202)296-6267
Free: 800-365-9753
Fax: (202)296-5149
E-mail: revu@heldref.org; hm@heldref.org
URL: http://www.heldref.org/

Contact: Grant Williams, Advertising Mgr.; Douglas J. Kirkpatrick, Director; Fred Huber, Circulation Mgr.; Gwen Arnold, Marketing Dir.; Barbara Kahn, Managing Editor.

Desc: Journal on quantitative methods for historical research. *Available:* Online: EBSCO; Infonautics; Information Access; Inst. Scient. Info.; UMI. *Alt. Fmts:* CD-ROM. *Freq:* Quarterly. *Price:* $43, individuals; $94, institutions, add $13 for postage outside the United States.

4030 ▪ History News
American Association for State & Local History/ AASLH
1717 Church St.
Nashville, TN 37203-2991
Ph: (615)320-3203
Fax: (615)327-9013
E-mail: history@aaslh.org
URL: http://www.aaslh.org; http://www.nashville.net/
  aaslh

Contact: Lauren Batte, Editor; Natalie Norris, Dir., Mktg.

Desc: Magazine for employees of historic sites, museums, and public history agencies. Coverage includes museum education programs and techniques for working with volunteers. *Freq:* Quarterly.

4031 ▪ Independent Republic Quarterly
Horry County Historical Society
PO Box 2025
Conway, SC 29528

Contact: Christopher C. Boyle, Editor.

Desc: Local historical journal. *Freq:* Quarterly. *Price:* $25, individuals.

4032 ▪ Iowa Heritage Illustrated
State Historical Society of Iowa
402 Iowa Ave.
Iowa City, IA 52240
Ph: (319)335-3912
Fax: (319)335-3935

Contact: Ginalie Swaim, Editor.

Desc: State history magazine. *Freq:* Quarterly. *Price:* $19.95, individuals; $6, single issue.

4033 ▪ Irish Family Journal
Irish Genealogical Foundation
PO Box 7575
Kansas City, MO 64116
Ph: (816)454-2410
Fax: (816)454-2410
URL: http://www.irishroots.com; http://
  www.irishroots.com

Contact: Michael C. O'Laughlin, Editor.

Desc: Journal of Irish family history and research. *Freq:* Monthly. *Price:* $104; $54, 6 issues/yr.

4034 ▪ Jackson County Chronicles
Jackson County, Alabama Historical Association
435 Barbee Ln.
Scottsboro, AL 35769-3745
Ph: (256)259-5286

Contact: Ann B. Chambless, Editor.

Desc: Journal covering local history. *Freq:* Quarterly. *Price:* $10, individuals; $3.50, single issue.

4035 ▪ Je Me Souviens
American-French Genealogical Society
Box 2113
Pawtucket, RI 02861-0113
Ph: (401)765-6141
Fax: (401)765-6141
E-mail: afgs@ids.net

Contact: Paul P. Delisle, Editor.

Desc: Genealogical journal. *Alt. Contact:* PO Box 171, Millville, MA 01529; telephone: (508)885-4316. *Freq:* Semiannual. *Price:* $30, individuals.

4036 ▪ Jonathan
Jonathan Club
545 S. Figueroa St.
Los Angeles, CA 90071-1704
Ph: (213)624-0881
Fax: (213)488-1425

Contact: Edward Rivers, Editor.

Desc: Club magazine featuring California art, member news, and social activities. *Freq:* Monthly. *Price:* $24, other countries.

4037 ▪ Journal of African American Men
Transaction Publishers
35 Berrue Cir.
Piscataway, NJ 08854
Ph: (732)445-2280
Free: 888-999-6778
Fax: (732)445-3138
E-mail: trans@transactionpub.com
URL: http://www.transactionpub.com

Contact: Gary A. Sailes, Editor; Richard Majors, Deputy Editor.

Desc: Journal that serves as a forum for social scientists engaged in the analysis of the unique struggles and triumphs of black males. *Freq:* Quarterly. *Price:* $40, individuals; $72, two years; $96, institutions.

4038 ▪ The Journal of Afro-Latin American Studies and Literatures
Department of Language and Modern Literature
18525 Tarragon Way   Ph: (301)946-9503
Germantown, MD 20874-2026

Contact: Rosangela Maria Vieira, Editor; Kathleen Palombo King, Editor.

Desc: Publication that examines the contributions of African decendants to the development of the U.S. *Freq:* 2/year.

4039 ▪ Journal of Aging and Ethnicity
Springer Publishing Co.
536 Broadway   Ph: (212)431-4370
New York, NY 10012   Fax: (212)941-7842
E-mail: springer@springerpub.com

Contact: Donald E. Gelfand, Ph.D., Editor; Rafael Ortiz, Advertising Mgr.; Cory Sklaire, Circulation Mgr.; Matt Fenton, Production Mgr.

Desc: Scholarly journal for researchers and professionals in gerontology and geriatrics, emphasizing the ethnic population of North America. *Alt. Contact:* c/o Donald E. Gelfand, Ph. D., Editor, Department of Sociology, 2228 F/AB Wayne State University, Detroit, MI 48202; telephone: (313)577-0774; fax: (313)577 2735. *Price:* $26, individuals; $62, two years; $49, individuals, out of country; $74, two years, out of country; $70, institutions; $105, institutions, two years; $79, institutions, out of country; $119, institutions, two years out of country; $15, single issue.

4040 ▪ Journal of American Ethnic History
Transaction Publishers
35 Berrue Cir.   Ph: (732)445-2280
Piscataway, NJ 08854   Free: 888-999-6778
                              Fax: (732)445-3138
E-mail: trans@transactionpub.com
URL: http://www.transactionpub.com

Contact: Ronald H. Bayor, Editor.

Desc: Journal addressing various aspects of American immigration and ethnic history including background of emigration, ethnic and racial groups, native Americans, and immigration policies. *Alt. Contact:* School of History, Technology and Society, Georgia Institute of Technology, 250 North Ave., Atlanta, GA 30332; telephone: (404)894 6834; fax: (404)894-0535. *Alt. Frnts:* Braille. *Freq:* Quarterly. *Price:* $30, individuals; $62, other countries, individuals; $15, students; $72, institutions; $104, other countries, institutions; $55, two years, individuals; $138, two years, institutions.

4041 ▪ The Journal of American History
Organization of American Historians (OAH)
112 N. Bryan Ave.   Ph: (812)855-7312
Bloomington, IN 47408-4199   Fax: (812)855-0696
E-mail: oah@oah.indiana.edu

Contact: Prof. David Thelen, Editor.

Desc: History journal. *Alt. Contact:* 1125 E. Atwater Ave., Bloomington, IN 47401; telephone: (812)855-2816; fax: (812)855-9939. *Freq:* Quarterly.

4042 ▪ Journal of the Early Republic
Society for Historians of the Early American Republic
1358 University Hall   Ph: (765)494-4135
Department of History   Fax: (765)496-1755
Purdue University
West Lafayette, IN 47907-1358
E-mail: jer@sla.purdue.edu

Contact: John L. Larson, Editor; Michael A. Morrison, Editor.

Desc: Journal covering history of the Early American Republic for members. *Freq:* Quarterly. *Price:* Free to qualified subscribers.

4043 ▪ Journal of Negro History
Association for the Study of Afro-American Life and History
1407 14th St. NW   Ph: (202)667-2822
Washington, DC 20005-3704   Fax: (202)387-9802

Contact: Dr. Alton Hornsby, Jr., Editor.

Desc: Afro-American history journal. *Alt. Contact:* Morehouse College, Box 20, Atlanta, GA 30314; telephone: (404)215-2620; fax: (404)215-2715; Morehouse College, Box 20, Atlanta, GA 30314; telephone: (404)681-2650; fax: (404)215-2715. *Freq:* Quarterly. *Price:* $30, individuals; $6.50, single issue.

4044 ▪ Kansas City Genealogist
Heart of America Genealogical Society
Kansas City Public Library, 3rd   Ph: (816)701-3445
   Fl., Gen. Rm.
311 E. 12th St.
Kansas City, MO 64106

Contact: Joanne Chiles Eakin, Editor.

Desc: Genealogical society journal prints unpublished records for genealogists and family historians. *Freq:* Quarterly.

4045 ▪ Kentucky Ancestors
Kentucky Historical Society
100 W. Broadway   Ph: (502)564-3016
PO Box 1792   Fax: (502)564-4701
Frankfort, KY 40602-1792
E-mail: tom.stephens@mail.state.ky.us
URL: http://www.kyhistory.org

Contact: Thomas E. Stephens, Editor.

Desc: Journal featuring Kentucky family history. *Freq:* Quarterly.

4046 ▪ Latah Legacy
Latah County Historical Society
327 E. Second   Ph: (208)882-1004
Moscow, ID 83843   Fax: (208)882-0759
E-mail: lcha@moscow.com

Contact: Mary Reed, Editor.

Desc: Scholarly journal covering local history. *Freq:* Semiannual. *Price:* $4, single issue.

4047 ▪ Le Pasquin
Association des Familles Paquin Inc.
41, des Cantons   Ph: (418)849-4501
Charlesbourg, PQ, Canada G1H
   7B1

Desc: Local genealogical magazine. *Freq:* Quarterly. *Price:* C$15, individuals.

4048 ▪ Lewis County Historical Society Journal
Lewis County Historical Society
High St.   Ph: (315)348-8089
Box 277
Lyons Falls, NY 13368

Contact: Charlotte, Beagle, ED; Lisa Becker, Museum Dir.

Desc: Journal covering local history. *Freq:* Annual. *Price:* $5, single issue, plus S&H.

4049 ▪ Long Island Forum
Friends for Long Island's Heritage
1864 Muttontown Rd.   Ph: (516)571-7600
Syosset, NY 11791   Fax: (516)571-7623

E-mail: info@fflih.org

Contact: Richard F. Welch, Editor.

Desc: Magazine on Long Island history and folklore. *Alt. Contact:* PO Box 277, Woodbury, NY 11797. *Freq:* Quarterly.

4050 ▪ A Lot of Bunkum
Old Buncombe County Geological Society
Box 2122   Ph: (828)293-1894
Asheville, NC 28802
URL: http://www.main.nc.us/OBCGS; http://
   www.main.nc.us/OBCGS

Contact: Hank Muller, Editor.

Desc: Journal covering local genealogy. *Freq:* Quarterly. *Price:* Free to qualified subscribers.

4051 ▪ Louisiana History
Louisiana Historical Association
PO Box 42808   Ph: (318)482-6029
Lafayette, LA 70504   Fax: (318)482-6028
E-mail: rrml554@usl.edu

Contact: Carl Brasseaux, Managing Editor.

Desc: History magazine. *Alt. Contact:* PO Box 40831, Lafayette, LA 70504-0831; telephone: (318)482-6871; fax: (318)482-6028. *Freq:* Quarterly. *Price:* $25, institutions.

4052 ▪ Loyalist Gazette
United Empire Loyalists' Association of Canada
Dominion Office, The George   Ph: (416)591-1783
   Brown House   Fax: (416)591-7506
50 Baldwin St., Ste. 202
Toronto, ON, Canada M5T
   1L4
E-mail: uela@npiec.on.ca

Contact: Peter Johnson, Editor.

Desc: Scholarly journal covering history and genealogy related to the United Empire Loyalists and The Revolutionary War period. *Freq:* Semiannual. *Price:* C$15, individuals; C$7.50, single issue.

4053 ▪ Lynn—Linn Lineage Quarterly
Phyllis J. Bauer, Editor and Publisher
3510 Turnberry Dr.   Ph: (815)385-9626
Mc Henry, IL 60050-7557
E-mail: pjbauer@mc.net

Contact: Pyhllis J. Bauer, Editor and Publisher.

Desc: Trade publication covering genealogy. *Freq:* Quarterly. *Price:* $22, individuals.

4054 ▪ Magazine of Virginia Genealogy
Virginia Genealogical Society
5001 W. Broad St., Ste. 115   Ph: (804)285-8954
Richmond, VA 23230   Fax: (804)285-0394
URL: http://www.vgs.org

Contact: Barbara Vines Little, Editor.

Desc: Journal covering genealogy in Virginia. *Freq:* Quarterly. *Price:* $26, individuals.

4055 ▪ Maine Genealogist
Maine Genealogical Society
Box 221
Farmington, ME 04938-0221

Contact: Lois W. Thurston, Editor.

Desc: Trade journal covering history and genealogy in Maine. *Freq:* Quarterly. *Price:* $20, members.

4056 ▪ Maine History

Maine Historical Society
485 Congress St.   Ph: (207)774-1822
Portland, ME 04101   Fax: (207)775-4301
URL: http://mainehistory.org

Contact: Richard Judd, Editor.

Desc: Scholarly journal covering local history. *Freq:* Semi-annual. *Price:* $20, individuals.

4057 ▪ Markers

Association for Gravestone Studies
278 Main St., Ste. 207   Ph: (413)772-0836
Greenfield, MA 01301-3230
E-mail: ags@javanet.com
URL: http://www.berkshire.net/ags

Contact: Richard E. Meyer.

Desc: Scholarly journal covering gravestone history, art and folklore. *Freq:* Annual. *Price:* $37, single issue.

4058 ▪ Maryland Historical Magazine

Maryland Historical Society
201 W. Monument St.   Ph: (410)685-3750
Baltimore, MD 21201   Fax: (410)385-2105
URL: http://www.mdhs.org

Contact: Robert I. Cottom, Jr., Editor; Donna Shear, Managing Editor.

Desc: Magazine on Maryland history and culture. *Freq:* Quarterly. *Price:* Free, to members; $6, single issue; $30, institutions.

4059 ▪ The Mayflower Quarterly

General Society of Mayflower Descendants
PO Box 3297   Ph: (508)746-5058
Plymouth, MA 02361

Contact: Alice C. Teal, Editor.

Desc: Magazine on Pilgrim history in colonial New England. *Alt. Contact:* 224 North Shore Rd., Marmora, NJ 08223; telephone: (609)390-1491; fax: (609)390-2743. *Freq:* Quarterly. *Price:* Included in membership; $10, nonmembers; $15, out of country; $7, to libraries.

4060 ▪ Mid-America (Chicago)

Loyola University of Chicago
Department of History
6525 Sheridan Rd.
Chicago, IL 60626

Contact: Maryann Spiller, Copy Editor.

Desc: Historical journal. *Freq:* Triennial. *Price:* $15, individuals; $16, out of country.

4061 ▪ Missouri State Genealogical Association Journal

Missouri State Genealogical Association
Box 833   Ph: (573)442-2387
Columbia, MO 65205-0833

Contact: Robert M. Doerr, Editor; Jerry R. Ennis, Editorial Dir.

Desc: Journal covering genealogy in Missouri. *Freq:* Quarterly. *Price:* $15, individuals.

4062 ▪ The Mohawk

Valley Quarterlies
60 Cedar Heights Rd.   Ph: (914)876-4592
Rhinebeck, NY 12572
E-mail: kelly@kinsh.pny.com

Contact: Arthur Kelly, Editor.

Desc: Journal covering local history and genealogy. *Freq:* Annual. *Price:* $16, individuals; $4.50, single issue.

4063 ▪ NABJ Journal

National Association of Black Journalists
8701A Adelphi Rd.   Ph: (301)445-7100
Adelphi, MD 20783-1716   Fax: (301)445-7101
URL: http://www.nabj.org

Contact: Yvette Walker, Editor; Debbie R. Chase, Managing Editor; Gerry Van Treek, Advertising Rep.

Desc: Professional magazine covering journalism trends and their impact on Afro-American reporters. *Freq:* Quarterly. *Price:* $9, individuals; $1.50, single issue.

4064 ▪ National Genealogical Society Quarterly

National Genealogical Society
4527 17th St. N.   Ph: (703)525-0050
Arlington, VA 22207-2399   Free: 800-473-0060
                                    Fax: (703)525-0052
E-mail: ngs@ngsgenealogy.org

Contact: Elizabeth Shown Mills, Editor; Gary B. Mills, Coeditor.

Desc: Genealogy journal. *Alt. Contact:* Dept of History, Univ. of Alabama, Box 870212, Tuscaloosa, AL 35487-0212; telephone: (205)752-4031; fax: (205)752-5979. *Alt. Fmts:* CD-ROM; microform. *Freq:* Quarterly. *Price:* $40, institutions, and libraries; $40, individuals, and libraries.

4065 ▪ Negro History Bulletin

Association for the Study of Afro-American Life and History
1407 14th St. NW   Ph: (202)667-2822
Washington, DC 20005-3704   Fax: (202)387-9802

Contact: Dr. Cynthia Neverdon-Morton, Editor.

Desc: Magazine profiling black history through feature articles and biographies. *Freq:* Quarterly, or Bi-annually. *Price:* $25, individuals.

4066 ▪ New England Historical and Genealogical Register

New England Historic Genealogical Society
101 Newbury St.   Ph: (617)536-5740
Boston, MA 02116-3007   Fax: (617)536-7307
E-mail: anovick@nehgs.org
URL: http://www.nehgs.org

Contact: Jane F. Fiske, Editor; Aileen Novick, Assistant.

Desc: Scholarly journal focusing on genealogy and history. *Alt. Fmts:* CD-ROM. *Freq:* Quarterly. *Price:* Free to qualified subscribers; $40, institutions.

4067 ▪ New Jersey History

New Jersey Historical Society
52 Park Place   Ph: (973)596-8500
Newark, NJ 07102   Fax: (973)596-6957

Contact: Nikki Shepardson, Managing Editor.

Desc: Scholarly journal covering local history. *Freq:* Semi-annual. *Price:* $15, individuals, subscription; $30, libraries.

4068 ▪ New Mexico Historical Review

University of New Mexico
1013 Mesa Vista Hall   Ph: (505)277-5839
Albuquerque, NM 87131-1186   Fax: (505)277-6023
E-mail: nmhr@unm.edu

Contact: Robert Himmerich y Valencia, Editor.

Desc: Magazine publishing historical essays and documents. *Alt. Fmts:* microfilm. *Freq:* Quarterly. *Price:* $26, individuals; $36, institutions, foreign add $4; $6, single issue, plus shipping & handling; $40, other countries, institutions.

4069 ▪ The New York Genealogical and Biographical Record

New York Genealogical and Biographical Society
122 E. 58th St.   Ph: (212)755-8532
New York, NY 10022-1939   Fax: (212)754-4218
E-mail: nygbs@sprynet.com

Contact: Henry B. Hoff, Consulting Editor; Harry Macy, Editor.

Desc: Genealogical magazine focusing on New York State. *Freq:* Quarterly.

4070 ▪ Newport History

Newport Historical Society
82 Touro St.   Ph: (401)846-0813
Newport, RI 02840   Fax: (401)846-1853
E-mail: newporthistorical@juno.com

Contact: Ron M. Potvin, Editor.

Desc: Scholarly journal covering local history. *Freq:* Quarterly. *Price:* $30, individuals; $7, single issue.

4071 ▪ North Carolina Genealogical Society Journal

North Carolina Genealogical Society
PO Box 1492   Ph: (252)752-0944
Raleigh, NC 27602
E-mail: ncgs@earthlink.net
URL: http://www.ncgenealogy.org; http://
    www.ncgenealogy.org

Contact: Raymond Winslow, Jr., Editor.

Desc: Journal covering genealogy in North Carolina. *Freq:* Quarterly. *Price:* $30, individuals.

4072 ▪ North Louisiana Historical Association Journal

North Louisiana Historical Association
Box 6701   Ph: (318)797-5355
Shreveport, LA 71136   Fax: (318)797-5122

Contact: Alan S. Thompson, Editor.

Desc: Journal covering local history. *Freq:* Triennial. *Price:* $13, individuals; $3, single issue.

4073 ▪ Northeast African Studies

Michigan State University Press
1405 S. Harrison Rd., Ste. 25   Ph: (517)355-9543
East Lansing, MI 48823-5202   Fax: 800-678-2120
E-mail: ethiopia@hs7.hst.msu.edu
URL: http://www.pilot.msul.edu/unit/msupress/
    index.html

Contact: Harold G. Marcus, Editor.

Desc: Scholarly journal covering Northeast African studies. *Alt. Contact:* Michigan State University, 319 Morrill Hall, East Lansing, MI 48824-1036. *Freq:* Triennial. *Price:* $30, individuals; $48, out of country.

4074 ▪ Northeast Mississippi Historical and Genealogical Society Quarterly

Northeast Mississippi Historical and Genealogical Society
Box 434
Tupelo, MS 38802-0434

Contact: Martis D. Ramage, Jr., Editor.

Desc: Genealogical and historical journal covering Northeast Mississippi. *Freq:* Quarterly. *Price:* $15, individuals.

4075 ▪ Northwest Trail Tracer

Northwest Territory Genealogical Society
Lewis Historical Library, LRC 22
Vincennes University
                                    Ph: (812)888-4330
rs>Vincennes, IN 47591

Contact: Donna Beeson, Editor.

Desc: Journal covering genealogy. *Freq:* Quarterly. *Price:* $12, individuals.

4076 ■ Nuestras Raices/Our Roots

Genealogical Society of Hispanic America
Box 9606   Ph: (720)564-0631
Denver, CO 80209-0606   Fax: (720)202-1151
E-mail: escritorio@compuserve.com;
    wrtrconsult@earthlink.net

Contact: Maryellen Nead Salazar.

Desc: Journal covering Hispanic genealogy and history in the Southwestern U.S. and Mexico. *Freq:* Quarterly. *Price:* $20, individuals.

4077 ■ The Nugget

California Genealogical Society
1611 Telegraph Ave., Ste. 200   Ph: (510)663-1358
Oakland, CA 94612-2152   Fax: (510)663-1596
E-mail: calgensoc@aol.com

Contact: Marje Kelt.

Desc: Journal covering genealogy. *Freq:* Quarterly. *Price:* Free to qualified subscribers.

4078 ■ Ohio Genealogical Society Report

Ohio Genealogical Society
713 S. Main St.   Ph: (419)756-7294
Mansfield, OH 44907-1644   Fax: (419)756-8681
E-mail: ogs@ogs.org
URL: http://www.ogs.org

Contact: Jean Nathan, Editor.

Desc: Journal covering genealogy and family history in Ohio. *Alt. Contact:* 3803 MacNicholas Ave., Cincinnati, OH 45236. *Freq:* Quarterly. *Price:* $27, individuals.

4079 ■ Ohio History

Ohio Historical Society
1982 Velma Ave.   Ph: (614)297-2360
Columbus, OH 43211-2497   Fax: (614)297-2367
E-mail: ohiohistory@ohiohistory.org

Contact: Dr. Robert L. Daugherty, Editor; Laura A. Russell, Assoc. Editor.

Desc: Journal covering history in Ohio and the Middle West U.S. *Alt. Contact:* telephone: (614)297-2363; fax: (614)297-2367. *Freq:* Semiannual. *Price:* $6, members; $18, nonmembers; $30, institutions.

4080 ■ Ohio Records & Pioneer Families

Ohio Genealogical Society
713 S. Main St.   Ph: (419)756-7294
Mansfield, OH 44907-1644   Fax: (419)756-8681
E-mail: ogs@ogs.org
URL: http://www.ogs.org

Contact: Susan Dunlap Lee, Editor.

Desc: Professional journal covering Ohio genealogy and history. *Freq:* Quarterly. *Price:* $18, individuals.

4081 ■ O'Lochlainn's Personal Journal of Irish Families

Irish Families
Box 7575   Ph: (816)454-2410
Kansas City, MO 64116   Fax: (816)454-2410
E-mail: mike@irishroots.com
URL: http://www.irishroots.com

Desc: Illustrated magazine tracing Irish families and Irish heritage worldwide. *Freq:* Monthly. *Price:* $54, individuals.

4082 ■ Olympia Genealogical Society Quarterly

Olympia Genealogical Society
Box 1313
Olympia, WA 98507-1313

Contact: Jerri McCoy, Editor.

Desc: Magazine covering local genealogy and society information. *Freq:* Quarterly. *Price:* $15, individuals; $18, family.

4083 ■ Onomastica Canadiana

Canadian Society for the Study of Names
c/o Prof. W. Ahrens   Ph: (416)736-5016
Dept. of Languages, Literatures,   Fax: (905)264-7517
    and Linguistics
York University
Toronto, ON, Canada M3J 1P3

Contact: Wolfgang, Ahrens, ED; Andre Lapierre, Assoc. Editor.

Desc: Scholarly journal covering all aspects of names and linguistics. *Freq:* Semiannual. *Price:* C$20, individuals.

4084 ■ Owen County History & Genealogy

Owen County Historical and Genealogical Society
PO Box 569   Ph: (812)829-4466
Spencer, IN 47460

Contact: Vivian Zollinger, Editor; Roger Peterson, Publications.

Desc: Journal covering history and genealogy of Owen County, Indiana. *Alt. Contact:* c/o Vivian Zollinger, RR 2, Box 49, Gosport, IN 47433; telephone: (812)829-4466. *Freq:* Quarterly. *Price:* $10, individuals; $2.50, single issue.

4085 ■ Pacific Historical Review

University of California Press/Journals
2120 Berkeley Way   Ph: (510)643-7154
Berkeley, CA 94720-0001   Fax: (510)642-9917
E-mail: journal@ucop.edu
URL: http://library.berkeley.edu:8080/ucalpress/
    journals

Contact: David Johnson, Editor; Carl Abbott, Editor.

Desc: Journal covering the history of American expansionism to the Pacific. *Freq:* Quarterly. *Price:* $28, individuals; $19, students; $24, other countries; $69, institutions; $58, institutions, other countries; $16, students, other countries; $9, single issue; $16, single issue, institutions.

4086 ■ Pennsylvania Heritage

Pennsylvania Historical and Museum Commission
3rd & North Sts.   Ph: (717)783 2618
PO Box 1026   Free: 800 747 7790
Harrisburg, PA 17108-1026   Fax: (717)787-8312
URL: http://www.phmc.state.pa.us; http://
    www.paheritage.org

Contact: Michael J. O'Malley, III, Editor.

Desc: Journal focusing on Pennsylvania history, culture, and art and the Pennsylvania Heritage Society. *Freq:* Quarterly. *Price:* $20, yearly; $35, two years; $5, single issue.

4087 ■ Pennsylvania Magazine of History and Biography

Historical Society of Pennsylvania
1300 Locust St.   Ph: (215)732-6200
Philadelphia, PA 19107-5699   Fax: (215)732-2680
E-mail: pmhb@aol.com
URL: http://www.libertynet.org/pahist

Contact: Jill Garner, Asst. Editor; Ian M.G. Quimby, Editor.

Desc: Journal covering the history, literature, and culture of the Mid-Atlantic states from settlement to the present. *Alt. Fmts:* microform. *Freq:* 3/year.

4088 ■ Pensacola History Illustrated

Pensacola Historical Society
117 E. Government St.   Ph: (850)434-5455
Pensacola, FL 32501
E-mail: phstaff@freent.com

Contact: Virginia Parks, Editor; Sandra Johnson, Editor.

Desc: Journal covering local history. *Freq:* Semiannual. *Price:* $25, individuals.

4089 ■ Pharmacy in History

American Institute of the History of Pharmacy
University of Wisconsin   Ph: (608)262-5378
School of Pharmacy
425 N. Charter St.
Madison, WI 53706
E-mail: aihp@macc.wisc.edu

Contact: Gregory J. Higby, Editor.

Desc: Journal focusing on the history of pharmacy. *Freq:* Quarterly. *Price:* $50, individuals.

4090 ■ Phelps County Genealogical Society Quarterly

Phelps County Genealogical Society
Box 571
Rolla, MO 65402-0571

Contact: Marguerite Mason, Editor.

Desc: Genealogical magazine. *Freq:* Quarterly. *Price:* $18, individuals.

4091 ■ Phillips County Historical Review

Phillips County Historical Review
623 Pecan St.   Ph: (870)338-3271
Helena, AR 72342

Contact: Ivey S. Gladin, Editor.

Desc: Periodical covering local history. *Price:* $10, individuals; $5, single issue.

4092 ■ Pine, The Plow and the Pioneer

Three Lakes Historical Society
Box 250
Three Lakes, WI 54562
URL: http://www.newnorth.net/robwack/museum.htm

Contact: Betty Karow, Editor.

Desc: Journal covering local family history. *Alt. Contact:* 7270 Father Williams Rd., Three Lakes, WI 54562; telephone: (715)546-2621.

4093 ■ The Plantagenet Connection

HT Communications
Box 1401   Ph: (303)657-2723
Arvada, CO 80001   Fax: (303)773-8962
E-mail: khf333@aol.com

Contact: Kenneth Harper Finton, Editor and Publisher.

Desc: Journal covering history and genealogy. *Available:* Online. *Freq:* Semiannual. *Price:* $24, individuals; $26, Canada; $32, other countries.

4094 ■ Prologue

National Archives and Records Administration
8601 Adelphi Rd.   Ph: (301)713-7360
College Park, MD 20740-6001   Fax: (301)713-7270
E-mail: inquire@nara.gov

URL: http://www.nara.gov/publications/prologue/
prologue.html

Contact: Mary Ryan, Managing Editor; Olivia Hylton,
Subscriptions.

Desc: Periodical covering historical articles based on research in the National Archives and Presidential libraries.
Freq: Quarterly. *Price:* $16, individuals; $4, single issue.

4095 ■ Quaker Queries
Ruby Simonson McNeill
PO Box 779   Ph: (206)262-3300
Napavine, WA 98565-0779
E-mail: rubym@localaccess.com
URL: http://www.localaccess.com/rubym/quakerqu.htm

Desc: Magazine covering Quaker issues, reviews, and genealogy. *Freq:* Irregular. *Price:* $7.75, single issue.

4096 ■ The Quarterly
St. Lawrence County Historical Association
PO Box 8   Ph: (315)386-8133
Canton, NY 13617   Fax: (315)386-8134
E-mail: slcha@northnet.org

Contact: Rebecca Thompson, Editor; Trent Trulock,
Editor.

Desc: Magazine for members of the historical association.
Freq: Quarterly. *Price:* $25; $4, single issue, plus $2
postage.

4097 ■ Queen City Heritage
Cincinnati Museum Center
1301 Western Ave.   Ph: (513)287-7058
Cincinnati, OH 45203-1129   Fax: (513)287-7095

Contact: Dottie L. Lewis, Editor.

Desc: Journal covering local history in Cincinnati, Ohio.
Freq: Quarterly. *Price:* $27, individuals; $5, single issue.

4098 ■ Register of Kentucky Historical Society
Kentucky Historical Society
100 W. Broadway   Ph: (502)564-3016
PO Box 1792   Fax: (502)564-4701
Frankfort, KY 40602-1792
URL: http://www.kyhistory.org

Contact: Dr. Thomas H. Appleton, Jr., Editor.

Desc: Historical magazine. *Freq:* Quarterly. *Price:* $25,
individuals; $35, institutions.

4099 ■ Reminisce
Reiman Publications, LLC
5400 S. 60th St.   Ph: (414)423-0100
Greendale, WI 53129-1404   Free: 800-682-9019
                                 Fax: (414)423-8463

Desc: Magazine featuring vintage photos and recollections
of events in the 20's, 30's, 40's, and 50's. *Freq:* Monthly.

4100 ■ Rochester History
Office of the City Historian
Rochester Public Library
115 South Ave.   Ph: (716)428-8095
Rochester, NY 14604-1896   Fax: (716)428-8098

Contact: Ruth Rosenberg-Naparsteck, Editor; Carol Fede,
Circulation Mgr.

Desc: Scholarly journal covering local history. *Freq:* Quarterly. *Price:* $8, individuals; $3, single issue.

4101 ■ Rogue Digger
Rogue Valley Genealogical Society, Inc.
133 S. Central Ave.   Ph: (541)770-5848
Medford, OR 97501
E-mail: rugs@grrtech.com

Contact: Jean E. Maack, Editor; Joyce Chase Jarvis, President.

Desc: Journal covering genealogy and history. *Freq:* Quarterly. *Price:* $25, individuals.

4102 ■ ROTA.GENE
Print Shack
499 Federal Rd.   Ph: (203)775-4515
Brookfield, CT 06804   Fax: (203)775-0180

Contact: James R. High, Editor.

Desc: Genealogical and historical magazine printed for
the International Fellowship of Rotarians *Freq:* Quarterly.
Price: $20, individuals.

4103 ■ Royal Historical Society Transactions
Cambridge University Press
40 W. 20th St.   Ph: (212)924-3900
New York, NY 10011-4211   Free: 800-221-4512
                                 Fax: (212)691-3239

Desc: Journal containing articles of historical research.
Freq: Annual. *Price:* $56, annual.

4104 ■ The SAR Magazine
*National Society Sons of the American Revo-
lution*
1000 S. 4th St.   Ph: (502)589-1776
Louisville, KY 40203   Fax: (502)589-1671
E-mail: nssar@sar.org

Contact: Winston C. Williams, Editor; Wayne R. Wied-
man, Advertising Mgr.

Desc: Magazine reporting on Society activities at the national, state, and local levels. Includes sources for genealogical research. *Alt. Contact:* PO Box 26595, Milwaukee,
WI 53226; telephone: (414)782-9410; fax: (414)782-
6645. *Freq:* Quarterly. *Price:* $10, individuals; $2.50, single issue.

4105 ■ The Saratoga
Valley Quarterlies
60 Cedar Heights Rd.   Ph: (914)876-4592
Rhinebeck, NY 12572

Contact: Arthur Kelly, Editor.

Desc: Journal covering local history and genealogy. *Freq:*
Annual. *Price:* $16, individuals; $4.50, single issue.

4106 ■ Saskatchewan Genealogical Society
Saskatchewan Genealogical Society
PO Box 1894   Ph: (306)780-9207
Regina, SK, Canada S4P 3E1   Fax: (306)781-6021
URL: http://www2.regina.smica/sys/; http://
         www.saskgenealogy.com

Contact: Marge Thomas, Exec. Dir.

Desc: Journal covering history and genealogy. *Freq:* Quarterly.

4107 ■ Scandinavian Review
American-Scandinavian Foundation
15 E. 65th St.   Ph: (212)879-9779
New York, NY 10021   Fax: (212)249-3444

Desc: Journal covering people, politics and lifestyles and
cultures of all five Nordic countries. *Freq:* Triennial. *Price:*
$15, individuals; $13, institutions; $5, single issue.

4108 ■ Sea Classics
Challenge Publications, Inc.
7950 Deering Ave.   Ph: (818)887-0550
Canoga Park, CA 91304-5063   Fax: (818)884-1343
E-mail: mail@challengeweb.com

Contact: Ed Schnepf, Editor; Belinda Henderson, Advertising Mgr.; Susan Duprey, Circulation Mgr.

Desc: Consumer magazine covering current and historical
maritime and naval events. *Freq:* Monthly. *Price:* $29.95,
individuals; $4.50, single issue.

4109 ■ Skinner Kinsmen Update
Brandywine Press
Box 2594
Rancho Cucamonga, CA 91729
E-mail: skinner.kinsmen@usa.net
URL: http://www.dc.smu.edu/Skinner/SPA/
         SkinnerFamAssoc.htm

Contact: Gregg Legutki, Editor.

Desc: Journal covering genealogy of the Skinner family.
Freq: Quarterly. *Price:* $16.50, individuals.

4110 ■ Smoky Mountain Historical Society Journal
Smoky Mountain Historical Society
Box 5078
Sevierville, TN 37864
URL: http://www.smokykin.com/smhs

Desc: Journal covering local history. *Freq:* Quarterly. *Price:*
$10, individuals; $4, single issue.

4111 ■ The Sons of Norway Viking
Sons of Norway
1455 W. Lake St.   Ph: (612)827-3611
Minneapolis, MN 55408   Fax: (612)827-0658
URL: http://www.sofn.com

Contact: Martha Parsons, Editor; Kathy Rumpza, Advertising Contact; Terri Purcell, Art Dir.; Suzy Vescio, Production Mgr.

Desc: Official Sons of Norway magazine reporting on
fraternal society's programs and activities. It also features
Norwegian and Norwegian-American history and culture.
Freq: Monthly.

4112 ■ Southern California Quarterly
Historical Society of Southern California
200 East Ave., 43   Ph: (213)222-0546
Los Angeles, CA 90031-1304
E-mail: hssc@idt.net

Contact: Doyce B. Nunis, Jr., Editor.

Desc: Scholarly journal covering local history. *Freq:* Quarterly. *Price:* Free to qualified subscribers.

4113 ■ Southern Genealogists Exchange Quarterly
Southern Genealogist's Exchange Society, Inc.
PO Box 2801   Ph: (904)387-9142
Jacksonville, FL 32203
E-mail: jbilly@freewwweb.com
URL: http://www.angelfire.com/fl/sges

Contact: Mary-Louise Howard, Editor; Richard B. Cardell, President; Doris R. Wilson, Corresponding Secretary.

Desc: Genealogical and historical magazine. *Freq:* Quarterly. *Price:* $20, individuals; $6, single issue.

4114 ■ Speculum, A Journal of Medieval Studies
Medieval Academy of America
1430 Massachusetts Ave.   Ph: (617)491-1622
Cambridge, MA 02138   Fax: (617)492-3303
E-mail: maa@fas.harvard.edu
URL: http://www.georgetown.edu/MedievalAcademy/

Contact: Luke Wenger, Editor.

Desc: Scholarly journal containing reviews and articles pertaining to all disciplines of medieval studies. *Freq:* Quarterly. *Price:* $55, individuals; $80, institutions, libraries; $20, single issue.

4115 ■ Stanstead Historical Society Journal
Societe Historique de Stanstead-Stanstead Historical Society
Box 268, 35 Dufferin Rd.　　　Ph: (819)876-7322
Stanstead, PQ, Canada J0B 3E0　Fax: (819)876-7936
E mail: mccrcip@interlinx.qc.ca

Desc: Local historical journal. *Freq:* Biennial.

4116 ■ Stepping Stones
Warren County Historical Society
210 Fourth Ave.　　　Ph: (814)723-1795
Box 427
Warren, PA 16365

Contact: Chase Putnam, Editor.

Desc: Journal covering local history. *Freq:* Triennial. *Price:* $10, individuals; Free to qualified subscribers.

4117 ■ Swedish American Genealogist
Swenson Swedish Immigration Research Center Augustana College
639 38th St.　　　Ph: (309)794-7204
Rock Island, IL 61201-2273　Fax: (309)794-7443
E-mail: sag@augustana.edu

Contact: Dr. James E. Erickson, Editor; Jill Seaholm, Circulation Mgr.

Desc: Professional journal covering Swedish American genealogy, biography, and personal history. *Alt. Contact:* c/o Dr. James E. Erickson, 7008 Bristol Blvd., Edina, MN 55435-4108; telephone: (612)925-1008. *Freq:* Quarterly. *Price:* $25, individuals.

4118 ■ Tequesta
Historical Association of Southern Florida
101 W. Flagler St.　　　Ph: (305)375-1492
Miami, FL 33130　　　Fax: (305)375-1609
E-mail: publications@historical-museum.org

Contact: Paul George, Ph.D., Editor; Jamie Welch, Managing Editor.

Desc: Journal covering local history. *Freq:* Annual. *Price:* Free to qualified subscribers; $5, single issue.

4119 ■ Timeline
Ohio Historical Society
1982 Velma Ave.　　　Ph: (614)297-2360
Columbus, OH 43211-2497　Fax: (614)297-2367
E-mail: timeline@ohiohistory.org

Contact: Christopher S. Duckworth, Editor and Publisher.

Desc: Magazine covering history, archaeology, natural science, and the arts especially of Ohio. *Freq:* Bimonthly. *Price:* $27, individuals, included in membership fee; $6, single issue.

4120 ■ The Tombstone Epitaph
Tombstone Epitaph Corp.
Box 1880　　　Ph: (602)457-2211
Tombstone, AZ 85638

Contact: Dean Prichard, Editor.

Desc: Journal featuring articles by contemporary historians and archival material concerning 19th century western history. *Freq:* Monthly. *Price:* $15, individuals; $20, other countries; $18; $25, outside U.S.

4121 ■ Topeka Genealogical Society Quarterly
Topeka Genealogical Society, Inc.
PO Box 4048　　　Ph: (785)233-5762
Topeka, KS 66604-0048
E-mail: tgs@networksplus.net
URL: http://www.networksplus.net/donno/

Contact: Marsha Neiswender, Editor; Helen L. King, Editor.

Desc: Journal covering local genealogy. *Alt. Fmts:* microfilm. *Freq:* Quarterly. *Price:* $15, individuals; $20, other countries.

4122 ■ The Torch
Nationwide Promotion Ltd.
12 Dawn Dr.　　　Ph: (902)468-5709
Dartmouth, NS, Canada B3B　Free: 888-468-5141
1H9　　　Fax: (902)468-5697

Desc: Periodical for the Royal Canadian Legion. *Freq:* Quarterly. *Price:* Free to qualified subscribers.

4123 ■ Tree Tracers
Southwest Oklahoma Genealogical Society Tree Tracers Committee
Box 148　　　Ph: (580)581-3450
Lawton, OK 73502-1048　Fax: (580)248-0243
E-mail: lawtonlib@cityof.lawton.ok.us

Contact: Donna Irwin, Editor.

Desc: Journal covering local history and genealogy. *Freq:* Quarterly. *Price:* $15, individuals; $4.50, single issue. Free to qualified subscribers.

4124 ■ UDC Magazine
Acron Publishing Inc.
1306 Gaskins Rd.　　　Ph: (804)754-2101
Richmond, VA 23409　　Free: 800-360-8517
　　　Fax: (804)754-1534

Contact: Mrs. William Wills, Editor-in-Chief; Mrs. John G. Williams, Sr., Chairman; Kristin Jannett, Circulation Mgr.

Desc: Membership magazine covering historical information. *Alt. Contact:* UDC Business Office, 328 North Blvd., Richmond, VA 23220-4057; telephone: (804)355-1636; fax: (804)353-1396. *Freq:* Monthly, 11 months (June-July combined). *Price:* $12, individuals; $2.50, single issue.

4125 ■ Utah Genealogical Association
Utah Genealogical Association
Box 1144　　　Free: 888-463-6842
Salt Lake City, UT 84110
URL: http://www.infouga.org

Contact: George Ryskamp; Peggy Ryskamp.

Desc: Journal covering methods and resources for researching family history. *Price:* $35, individuals.

4126 ■ The Virginia Genealogist
The Virginia Genealogist
Box 5860　　　Ph: (703)371-9115
Falmouth, VA 22405-5860　Fax: (703)374-9264

Contact: John Frederick Dorman, Editor and Publisher.

Desc: Genealogy magazine. *Freq:* Quarterly. *Price:* $25, individuals.

4127 ■ Washington History
Historical Society of Washington, D.C.
1307 New Hampshire NW　Ph: (202)785-2068
Washington, DC 20036-1507　Fax: (202)887-5785

Contact: Jane Freundel Levey, Editor.

Desc: Historical journal covering local history. *Freq:* Semi-annual. *Price:* $30, individuals; $7, single issue.

4128 ■ Westchester Historian
Westchester County Historical Society
2199 Saw Mill River Rd.　Ph: (914)592-4323
Elmsford, NY 10523　　Fax: (914)592-6481

Contact: Elisabeth Fuller, Editor.

Desc: Scholarly journal covering local history. *Freq:* Quarterly.

4129 ■ Western Kentucky Journal
Brenda Joyce Jerome
PO Box 325　　　Ph: (812)853-8092
Newburgh, IN 47629-0325

Contact: Brenda Joyce Jerome, Editor and Publisher.

Desc: Genealogical publication. *Freq:* Quarterly. *Price:* $22, individuals.

4130 ■ Western Maryland Genealogy
GenLaw Resources
PO Box 9187　　　Ph: (301)947-5572
Gaithersburg, MD 20898-9187　Fax: (301)977-8062
E-mail: genlaw@mindspring.com

Contact: Donna Valley Russell, Contributing Editor; Patricia Abelard Andersen, Editor and Publisher.

Desc: Trade journal covering local genealogy. *Freq:* Quarterly. *Price:* $20, individuals; $30, Canada.

4131 ■ Yesterday and Today in Lawrence County
Lawrence County Historical Society
PO Box 431　　　Ph: (931)762-2249
Lawrenceburg, TN 38464　Fax: (931)762-2240

Desc: Journal covering history and genealogy for society members. *Freq:* Quarterly. *Price:* Included in membership.

4132 ■ York Pioneer
York Pioneer and Historical Society
2482 Yonge St.　　　Fax: (416)231-1829
Toronto, ON, Canada M4P
2H5

Contact: Jeanine Cameron Avigdor, Editor.

Desc: Journal covering local history in Canada. *Freq:* Annual. *Price:* C$13, individuals.

CD-ROMs

4133 ▪ Ancestral File
35 NW Temple   Ph: (801)240-2309
Salt Lake City, UT 84150
E-mail: fhl@lds.org

Desc: Contains approximately 30 million names of interest of genealogists. Includes links to other names, including those of persons submitting information to the database. *Database type:* directory.

4134 ▪ The Asian-American Experience
27500 Drake Rd.   Ph: (248)699-4253
Farmington Hills, MI   Free: 800-347-4253
    48331-3535   Fax: (248)699-8069
URL: http://www.galegroup.com

Desc: Tells the history of Asian Americans from their perspective and in their own words. Treats Asian migration to North America, the Chinese exclusion of the 19th century, and the Japanese internment in the 1940s. *Database type:* full text; audio; image.

4135 ▪ CACI's Gold Standard Solution with Scan/US
1100 N. Glebe Rd., Ste. 200   Ph: (703)841-7977
Arlington, VA 22201-4714   Free: 800-292-2224
                       Fax: (703)243-6272
E-mail: cthompson@caci.com
URL: http://www.caci.com

Desc: Includes data for the United States and its population for more than 200 demographic variables based on 1994 population statistics, 1995 forecasts, year 2000 projections, and 1990 census data. Based on this data, enables the user to create customized demographic maps for counties, states, ZIP codes, Areas of Dominant Influence (ADI), Designated Market Areas (DMAs), Metropolitan Statistical Areas (MSAs), and custom regions. *Database type:* statistical; image.

4136 ▪ California As I Saw It: First Person Narratives of California's Early Years, 1849-1900
2809 Main St.   Ph: (714)756-9500
Irvine, CA 92614   Free: 800-922-7979
                   Fax: (714)769-6943
E-mail: info@zbw.ifw-kiel.de

Desc: Features a collection of contents from 192 books, of recollections of early California, all digitized by the World Library's American Memory Project. *Database type:* full text.

4137 ▪ Canada 1991 Census Profiles
Statistical Reference Center   Ph: (613)951-8116
National Capitol Region   Free: 800-263-1136
R.H. Coats Bldg., Lobby   Fax: (613)951-0581
Holland Ave.
Ottawa, ON, Canada K1A 0T6

E-mail: infostats@statcan.ca
URL: http://www.statcan.ca/start.html

Desc: Contains detailed census information corresponding to the 1991 National Canadian census. Provides Station overviews of geographic areas, incorporating hundreds of cultural, demographic, housing, family, and economic characteristics of the Canadian population. *Database type:* statistical.

4138 ▪ CD-ROM Index to NIDS
1101 King St.   Ph: (703)683-4890
Alexandria, VA 22314   Free: 800-752-0515
                   Fax: (703)683-7589
E-mail: info@chadwyck.com
URL: http://www.chadwyck.com

Desc: Contains citations to the National Inventory of Documentary Sources in the United Kingdom and Ireland (NIDS UK and Ireland) and the National Inventory of Documentary Sources in the United States (NIDS US). Provides access by titles of collections within a repository, names, and subjects. *Database type:* bibliographic.

4139 ▪ Census '90
1301 Pennsylvania Ave., N.W.,   Ph: (202)393-2666
Ste. 522   Fax: (202)638-2248
Washington, DC 20004-1701
E-mail: slaterco@netcom.com

Desc: Contains more than 275 data tables for every item covered in the census. Covers the United States, states, counties, cities, places with a population of 10,000 or more, minor civil divisions, census regions, and metro and urbanized areas. *Database type:* statistical.

4140 ▪ Census '90 Rural
1301 Pennsylvania Ave., N.W.,   Ph: (202)393-2666
Ste. 522   Fax: (202)638-2248
Washington, DC 20004-1701
E-mail: slaterco@netcom.com

Desc: Contains 1990 Census data for the rural and nonrural areas of each county in the United States. *Database type:* statistical.

4141 ▪ Census '90 Zip
1301 Pennsylvania Ave., N.W.,   Ph: (202)393-2666
Ste. 522   Fax: (202)638-2248
Washington, DC 20004-1701
E-mail: slaterco@netcom.com

Desc: Contains more than 1500 data items from the 1990 Census covering all 29,000 residential ZIP codes. *Database type:* statistical.

4142 ▪ Census of Population and Housing, 1990: Equal Employment Opportunity File
Suitland Federal Center   Ph: (301)457-4100
Washington, DC 20233-8300   Fax: (301)457-4714

URL: http://www.census.gov

Desc: Contains statistics from the 1990 U.S. Census of Population and Housing on the U.S. *Database type:* statistical.

4143 ▪ Census USA
5711 S. 86th Circle   Ph: (402)593-4593
P.O. Box 27347   Free: 800-321-0869
Omaha, NE 68127   Fax: (402)537-6065
E-mail: internet@infousa.com
URL: http://www.infousa.com

Desc: Contains census information on U.S. households. *Database type:* full text; numeric.

4144 ▪ CensusCD
PO Box 10   Ph: (732)651-2000
East Brunswick, NJ 08816   Free: 800-577-6717
                   Fax: (732)651-2721
E-mail: info@geolytics.com
URL: http://www.geolytics.com

Desc: Contains the complete 1990 United States census. Provides more than 3,500 variables for 16 levels of United States geography, from block-group-level up. *Database type:* statistical; full text.

4145 ▪ Civil War: America's Epic Struggle
244 North Ave.   Ph: (914)235-4340
New Rochelle, NY 10801-6402   Fax: (914)235-4367
URL: http://www.mutied.com

Desc: Contains a compendium of material on the American Civil War. Includes thousands of photos, more than 100 maps (many animated), diary entries and personal accounts of Grant, Lee, Lincoln, and many other participants. *Database type:* full text; image.

4146 ▪ European Monarchs on CD-ROM
1313 Fifth St. S.E., Suite 223A
Minneapolis, MN 55414

Desc: Contains information on early European kings and queens as well as the most of the current royal families. For each individual, provides name, date of birth, date of death, date of coronation, date of abdication, marriages, number of children, parentage, and interesting facts about the king's or queen's reign. *Database type:* full text; image.

4147 ▪ Family History Library Catalog
35 NW Temple   Ph: (801)240-2309
Salt Lake City, UT 84150
E-mail: fhl@lds.org

Desc: Provides information on the holdings of the Family History Library, including I.D. or call number, source information, keywords, and locality. *Database type:* bibliographic.

4148 ■ Family Tree Maker Birth Records

PO Box 6125　　　　　Ph: (415)382-4400
Novato, CA 94948　　　Free: 800-474-8696
　　　　　　　　　　　Fax: (415)382-4419
URL: http://www.familytreemaker.com

Desc: Provides an alphabetical listing combining birth information from six different CDs. Each record contains an individual's first and last name, date and state or country of birth, and number of original CD. *Database type:* directory.

4149 ■ Family Tree Maker CD-ROM

PO Box 6125　　　　　Ph: (415)382-4400
Novato, CA 94948　　　Free: 800-474-8696
　　　　　　　　　　　Fax: (415)382-4419
URL: http://www.familytreemaker.com

Contact: Christine Lang, Customer Service Representative.

Desc: Contains a listing of the names of more than 750 million people from World Family Tree CD-ROMs, U.S. Census records indexes of the 1700s to 1900s, selected state marriage records indexes, and Social Security death benefits records. *Database type:* full text; directory.

4150 ■ Family Tree Maker Family History Collection

PO Box 6125　　　　　Ph: (415)382-4400
Novato, CA 94948　　　Free: 800-474-8696
　　　　　　　　　　　Fax: (415)382-4419
URL: http://www.familytreemaker.com

Desc: Contains information on family geneologies researched and compiled by a variety of sources. Corresponds to Family Tree Maker's Family Archives CDs collection. *Database type:* directory.

4151 ■ Family Tree Maker Family Pedigrees

PO Box 6125　　　　　Ph: (415)382-4400
Novato, CA 94948　　　Free: 800-474-8696
　　　　　　　　　　　Fax: (415)382-4419
URL: http://www.familytreemaker.com

Desc: Contains researched family trees compiled by different research firms. Corresponds to Family Tree Maker's Family Archives CDs collection. *Database type:* directory.

4152 ■ Family Tree Maker Ireland Census Records

PO Box 6125　　　　　Ph: (415)382-4400
Novato, CA 94948　　　Free: 800-474-8696
　　　　　　　　　　　Fax: (415)382-4419
URL: http://www.familytreemaker.com

Desc: Contains Ireland Census data from two counties, County Londonderry (1831) and County Cavan (1841). Includes head of household's first and last name, Soundex code, township, and microfilm page number. *Database type:* directory.

4153 ■ Family Tree Maker Land Records

PO Box 6125　　　　　Ph: (415)382-4400
Novato, CA 94948　　　Free: 800-474-8696
　　　　　　　　　　　Fax: (415)382-4419
URL: http://www.familytreemaker.com

Desc: Contains information from federal government land transactions, including individual's name, Soundex code, date of transaction, and name of land office, statuatory reference number, entry classification, accession number, image number, and title transfer authority code. Corresponds to the Family Tree Maker's Family Archives CDs collection. *Database type:* directory.

4154 ■ Family Tree Maker Marriage Records Indexes

PO Box 6125　　　　　Ph: (415)382-4400
Novato, CA 94948　　　Free: 800-474-8696
　　　　　　　　　　　Fax: (415)382-4419
URL: http://www.familytreemaker.com

Desc: Contains indexes to marriage records, including name and Soundex code of each spouse, marriage date, and county in which the marriage was recorded. Corresponds to the Family Tree Maker's Family Archives CDs collection. *Database type:* directory.

4155 ■ Family Tree Maker Military Records

PO Box 6125　　　　　Ph: (415)382-4400
Novato, CA 94948　　　Free: 800-474-8696
　　　　　　　　　　　Fax: (415)382-4419
URL: http://www.familytreemaker.com

Desc: Contains images of military service records, showing name, state or territory of service, rank, and unit. Corresponds to Family Tree Maker's Family Archives CDs collection. *Database type:* directory; image.

4156 ■ Family Tree Maker Mortality Index

PO Box 6125　　　　　Ph: (415)382-4400
Novato, CA 94948　　　Free: 800-474-8696
　　　　　　　　　　　Fax: (415)382-4419
URL: http://www.familytreemaker.com

Desc: Contains indexes of mortality records of several states. Includes full name, Soundex code, sex, occupation, state of birth, and age at death. *Database type:* directory.

4157 ■ Family Tree Maker Social Security Death Benefits Records: United States, 1937-1996

PO Box 6125　　　　　Ph: (415)382-4400
Novato, CA 94948　　　Free: 800-474-8696
　　　　　　　　　　　Fax: (415)382-4419
URL: http://www.familytreemaker.com

Desc: Contains Social Security death benefit information, including individual's first and last name, dates of birth and death, Social Security number, issuing state, state of residence at death, ZIP code of last known residence, ZIP code of address where death payment was sent, and Soundex code for last name. Corresponds to Family Tree Maker's Family Archives CDs collection. *Database type:* directory.

4158 ■ Family Tree Maker United States Census Indexes

PO Box 6125　　　　　Ph: (415)382-4400
Novato, CA 94948　　　Free: 800-474-8696
　　　　　　　　　　　Fax: (415)382-4419
URL: http://www.familytreemaker.com

Desc: Contains indexes to United States Census records, including individual's first and last name, Soundex code, state and county census, and microfilm page number. Corresponds to Family Tree Maker's Family Archives CDs collection. *Database type:* directory.

4159 ■ FamilySearch

35 NW Temple　　　　Ph: (801)240-2309
Salt Lake City, UT 84150
E-mail: fhl@lds.org

Desc: Contains the International Genealogical Index (IGI), Ancestral File (AF), U.S. Social Security Death Index, Military Index, and Family History Library Catalog databases, as well as the Personal Ancestral File (PAF) genealogy program. *Database type:* full text; directory; bibliographic.

4160 ■ Fast Reference Facts CD-ROM

27500 Drake Rd.　　　　Ph: (248)699-4253
Farmington Hills, MI　　Free: 800-347-4253
　48331-3535　　　　　Fax: (248)699-8069
URL: http://www.galegroup.com

Desc: Contains more than 5000 facts taken from the ready reference files of libraries covering frequently asked and difficult-to-answer reference desk questions. Includes 350 charts, graphs, and line drawings as well as bibliographic citations. *Database type:* full text; bibliographic; image.

4161 ■ GeoRef, 1996 Census

Statistical Reference Center　　Ph: (613)951-8116
National Capitol Region　　　Free: 800-263-1136
R.H. Coats Bldg., Lobby　　　Fax: (613)951-0581
Holland Ave.
Ottawa, ON, Canada K1A 0T6
E-mail: infostats@statcan.ca
URL: http://www.statcan.ca/start.html

Contact: GEO-Help.

Desc: Enables users to explore the links among all standard levels of geography and to determine geographic codes and names, and population and dwelling counts. Also provides enumeration area (EA) correspondence data for 1996 EAs and 1991 Census EAs. *Database type:* statistical.

4162 ■ Her Heritage: A Biographical Encyclopedia of Famous American Women

955 Massachusetts Ave.　　Ph: (617)964-9996
Cambridge, MA 02139　　Free: 800-99-PLGRM
　　　　　　　　　　　Fax: (617)491-6415
E-mail: info@PLGRM.com
URL: http://www.PLGRM.com

Desc: Provides biographies of more than 1000 famous American women, both past and present from all fields of endeavor. Covers the arts, science, health, law, politics, religion, and social reform. *Database type:* full text; image; video; audio.

4163 ■ ImmForms Plus

620 Opperman Dr.　　　Ph: (651)687-7000
St. Paul, MN 55164-0526　Free: 800-328-9352
　　　　　　　　　　　Fax: (651)687-5827
URL: http://www.westgroup.com

Contact: Reference Attorney.

Desc: Contains exact duplicates of more than 85 immigration-related forms that can be filled in on screen and printed out for submission, including forms for the Immigration and Naturalization Service, the U.S. Department of Labor, and the U.S. *Database type:* full text.

4164 ■ The Immigrant Experience

27500 Drake Rd.　　　　Ph: (248)699-4253
Farmington Hills, MI　　Free: 800-347-4253
　48331-3535　　　　　Fax: (248)699-8069
URL: http://www.galegroup.com

Desc: Presents the stories of America's immigrants, including Native American migrations, European immigrants, Asian migrations of the 19th century, the incorporation of Hispanic peoples as the United States expanded westward, and African Americans' 20th century exodus to Northern cities. Covers efforts to "Americanize" immigrants and Native Americans and the status of immigrants in the context of the current multicultural debate. *Database type:* full text; audio; image.

4165 ■ Income by Age

5375 Mira Sorrento Place,　　Ph: (619)622-0800
　Ste. 400　　　　　　　Free: 800-866-6510
San Diego, CA 92121　　Fax: (619)550-5800
URL: http://www.natdecsys.com

Contact: Robert Galvin, Production Mgr.

Desc: Contains demographic cross-tabulations of household income by age of head of household. Includes 1980 and 1990 census data, current-year estimates, and 5-year projections for 7 age groups and 8 income ranges. *Database type:* numeric.

4166 ■ LDS Historical Library CD

2405 W. Orton Circle   Free: 800-908-3400
West Valley City, UT 84119
URL: http://www.infobase.ldsworld.com

Desc: Contains 150 personal journals and writings of early Church of Jesus Christ of Latter-Day Saints members who witnessed the Restoration first-hand, accompanied by their black and white photographs. Includes the complete text of the following writings: LDS Scripture, Church Chronology (1805-1913) by Andrew Jensen, History of the Church (7 volumes) by Joseph Smith, Latter-Day Saint Biographical Encyclopedia, Excerpts by Andrew Jensen, Comprehensive History of the Church (6 volumes) by B.H. *Database type:* image; full text.

4167 ■ MarketBase

53 Brown Rd   Free: 800-633-9568
Ithaca, NY 14850-1262

Contact: Eric Cohen, Vice President.

Desc: Contains data from the 1970, 1980, and 1990 U.S. Census of Population and Housing, current-year estimates, and 5-year and 10-year projections of selected demographic characteristics. *Database type:* statistical.

4168 ■ Military Index

35 NW Temple   Ph: (801)240-2309
Salt Lake City, UT 84150
E-mail: fhl@lds.org

Desc: Lists approximately 100,000 U.S. servicemen who died in the Korean and Vietnam wars. *Database type:* directory.

4169 ■ N.Y. State Births and Deaths 1800-1988; NY PA NJ Marriage 1790-1900

1623 West 3640 South
St. George, UT 84770
URL: http://www.gencd.com

Desc: Contains information on state births and deaths between 1839 and 1890 for New York, Pennsylvania, and New Jersey. *Database type:* statistical.

4170 ■ 1981 Census - Small Area Statistics for England, Scotland and Wales

1101 King St.   Ph: (703)683-4890
Alexandria, VA 22314   Free: 800-752-0515
    Fax: (703)683-7589
E-mail: info@chadwyck.com
URL: http://www.chadwyck.com

Desc: Contains small area statistics from the United Kingdom census of 1981, with boundary mapping to the ward level in England and Wales, and to the postcode sector in Scotland. Enables users to analyze data as displayed, as tables, and as charts and choropeth and centroid maps. *Database type:* full text; bibliographic; directory.

4171 ■ ONSITE

53 Brown Rd   Free: 800-633-9568
Ithaca, NY 14850-1262

Contact: John Hobson.

Desc: Contains more than 4000 items of demographic data and more than 50 demographic report formats summarized from the U.S. Census of Population and Housing

(1970 and 1980), plus current-year estimates and 5 to 10-year projections produced by Urban Decision Systems, Inc. *Database type:* statistical.

4172 ■ PCensus-USA

3873 Airport Way   Ph. (360)734-3318
P.O. Box 9754   Free: 800-663-1334
Bellingham, WA 98227-9754   Fax: (360)734-4005
E-mail: info@tetrad.com
URL: http://www.tetrad.com

Desc: Provides demographic information on 3141 counties in 50 states in the United States. Enables the user to make site selections or market analyses by defining a specific geographic area, including block groups, place names, census tracts, or counties. *Database type:* image; statistical.

4173 ■ Population Statistics

1301 Pennsylvania Ave., N.W.,   Ph: (202)393-2666
Ste. 522   Fax: (202)638-2248
Washington, DC 20004-1701
E-mail: slaterco@netcom.com

Contact: George E. Hall.

Desc: Contains complete demographic and housing data from the 1980 U.S. Census of Population and Housing for the United States as a whole, all states, Metropolitan Statistical Areas (MSAs), counties, cities and places with a population of 10,000 or more persons. *Database type:* statistical.

4174 ■ Postal Codes Counts

Statistical Reference Center   Ph. (613)951-8116
National Capitol Region   Free: 800-263-1136
R.H. Coats Bldg., Lobby   Fax: (613)951-0581
Holland Ave,
Ottawa, ON, Canada K1A 0T6
E-mail: infostats@statcan.ca
URL: http://www.statcan.ca/start.html

Desc: Contains population and dwelling counts for all six-character postal codes reported by respondents in the 1996 census. Counts are provided by individual postal code, by forward sortation area, and by province or territory. *Database type:* statistical.

4175 ■ The Story of Civilization

2809 Main St.   Ph: (714)756-9500
Irvine, CA 92614   Free: 800-922-7979
    Fax: (714)769-6943
E-mail: info@zbw.ifw-kiel.de

Desc: Surveys the history and culture of ancient civilizations worldwide from the beginning of history in Egypt and the Near East, through the Origins of Christianity, the Dark Ages, Italian Renaissance, the debate between faith and reason, and the age of Napoleon. Contains the complete text of the 11 volume print set as well as original illustrations, video, and footnotes. *Database type:* full text; image.

4176 ■ Surname Reference CD

1300 E. Woodfield   Ph: (847)995-9222
Ste. 506   Fax: (847)995-9290
Schaumburg, IL 60173
E-mail: DJHAY@geusource.com

Contact: Daniel J. Hay, Publisher.

Desc: Contains more than 504,000 surnames, indexed alphabetically and by Soundex, Diatch-Mokotoff, and SimDex codes used to identify names by variant spellings. *Database type:* directory.

4177 ■ U.S. Social Security Death Index

35 NW Temple   Ph: (801)240-2309
Salt Lake City, UT 84150

E-mail: fhl@lds.org

Desc: Contains information on persons whose deaths were reported to the Social Security Administration from 1962 to 1993, as well as a few records of deaths before 1962. Includes birth and death dates and the person's last place of residence, state where the person lived when they were issued a Social Security number, and the actual Social Security number and the place where death payment was sent. *Database type:* directory.

4178 ■ UXL Biographies 2.0

27500 Drake Rd.   Ph: (248)699-4253
Farmington Hills, MI   Free: 800-347-4253
   48331-3535   Fax: (248)699-8069
URL: http://www.galegroup.com

Contact: Customer Service. Toll-free: 800-877-GALE.

Desc: Contains the complete text of more than 2500 biographies of popular and historic figures, written for students. Includes more than 3000 illustrations, including portraits, of the biographees. *Database type:* full text; image.

Online

4179 ■ Alberta Statistical Information System

Rm. 259 Terrace Bldg   Ph: (403)427-3099
9515 107th St.   Fax: (403)427-0409
Edmonton, AB, Canada T5K
   2C3

Contact: Wayne Blumstengel, Project Coordinator.

Desc: Contains more than 80,000 monthly, quarterly, and annual current and historical time series of socio-economic data for the Canadian province of Alberta and its census divisions and municipalities. Covers economic accounts, including provincial gross domestic product, and government, personal, and business income and outlay; population estimates and projections, vital statistics, and migration; building permits, housing starts, and apartment rental and vacancy rates; manufacturing, retail, and agriculture industries; business and commerce, including bankruptcies, foreclosures, and real estate sales; and social welfare caseloads, crime and traffic offenses, and labor force activity. *Available:* Alberta Treasury, Statistics. *Database type:* time series.

4180 ■ The American Civil War, 1861-1865: World Wide Web Information Archive

One DIGEX Plaza   Ph: (301)847-5000
Beltsville, MD 20705
E-mail: server@digex.net
URL: http://www.access.digex.net/bdboyle/cw.html

Contact: Bryan Boyle.

Desc: This site, created and maintained by Civil War buff Bryan Boyle, is an excellent gateway to the study of this landmark American historical event. Boyle's site offers a staggering list of links to Civil War-related resources on the Internet. These links are divided into less than a dozen categories, including Documents, Books, and Other Info; Reenactment and Living History Web; Regimental History Web; Regimental Histories; Civil War Collections; and Battle Summaries. *Database type:* image; directory; full-text.

4181 ■ American Historical Association

400 A St. SE   Ph: (202)544-2422
Washington, DC 20003-3889   Fax: (202)544-8307
E-mail: aha@theaha.org
URL: http://chnm.gmu.edu/aha/index.html

Desc: Web site covers issues and activities of the organization. Users may also order publications, become a member, and find other related organizations all online. *Database type:* full-text; directory.

4182 ■ American Statistics Index
4520 East-West Hwy., Suite 800   Ph: (301)654-1550
Bethesda, MD 20814-3389   Free: 800-638-8380
                                 Fax: (301)654-4033
E-mail: 12425 (DIALMAIL)
URL: http://www.cispubs.com

Desc: Contains more than 142,000 citations, with abstracts, to publications containing social, economic, demographic, and other statistical data collected and analyzed by the U.S. government. *Available:* The Dialog Corporation, DIALOG. *Database type:* bibliographic.

4183 ■ Annual Demographic Update
53 Brown Rd.   Ph: (607)257-0567
Ithaca, NY 14850   Free: 800-234-5997
                                 Fax: (607)266-0425
URL: http://www.claritas.com

Contact: Bob Kreutter.

Desc: Contains 1990 data, current-year estimates, and five-year projections of key demographics, including data on households, populations, families, income, age, and race. *Available:* Claritas Data Services. *Database type:* statistical.

4184 ■ Biography Master Index
27500 Drake Rd.   Ph: (248)699-4253
Farmington Hills, MI   Free: 800-347-4253
48331-3535   Fax: (248)699-8069
URL: http://www.galegroup.com

Contact: Customer Service. Toll-free: 800-877-GALE.

Desc: Contains more than 10.6 million citations to biographical information appearing in more than 2300 editions and volumes of more than 700 source publications, including English-language general and geographical Who's Who-type publications, major biographical dictionaries, handbooks, and directories. Covers more than 4 million current and historical persons. *Available:* The Dialog Corporation, DIALOG; The Gale Group, GaleNet. *Database type:* bibliographic.

4185 ■ CANSIM Census Summary Data Service
Statistical Reference Center   Ph: (613)951-8116
National Capitol Region   Free: 800-263-1136
R.H. Coats Bldg., Lobby   Fax: (613)951-0581
Holland Ave.
Ottawa, ON, Canada K1A 0T6
E-mail: infostats@statcan.ca
URL: http://www.statcan.ca/start.html

Desc: Covers census data for Canada and its provinces, providing coverage of 50,000 geographic areas. Contains more than 1000 tables of census data, including main enumeration areas, urban census tracts, federal electoral districts, municipalities, counties and regional municipalities, and metropolitan areas. *Available:* Statistics Canada. *Database type:* statistical.

4186 ■ CENDATA
Suitland Federal Center   Ph: (301)457-4100
Washington, DC 20233-8300   Fax: (301)457-4714
URL: http://www.census.gov

Desc: Contains selected text and numeric data from Census Bureau economic and demographic reports, press releases, and new product announcements. Economic and demographic reports cover agriculture, business, construction and housing, foreign trade, government, manufactur-

ing, and selected data from Current Population Reports, and the 1990 U.S. *Available:* CompuServe Information Service. *Database type:* full text; numeric.

4187 ■ County and Court Records
Marquis One Tower, Ste. 1400   Ph: (404)479-6500
245 Peachtree Center Ave.   Free: 800-235-4008
Atlanta, GA 30303   Fax: (404)479-6700
URL: http://www.infoam.com

Desc: Contains key public records for selected counties in the states of California, Georgia, Pennsylvania, and Texas. Covers tax liens, trade names, grantor/grantee, judgments, limited partnerships, UCC filings, lis pendens, and assumed names. *Available:* Information America (IA). *Database type:* directory.

4188 ■ County Personal Income, Population, and Employment
1110 Vermont Ave., NW   Ph: (202)775-0610
Washington, DC 20005   Fax: (202)833-3673
URL: http://www.fdic.gov

Desc: Contains approximately 180,000 annual time series from the Bureau of Economic Analysis for all U.S. counties. *Available:* The WEFA Group. *Database type:* time series.

4189 ■ DISCovering World History
27500 Drake Rd.   Ph: (248)699-4253
Farmington Hills, MI   Free: 800-347-4253
48331-3535   Fax: (248)699-8069
URL: http://www.galegroup.com

Contact: Customer Service. Toll-free: 800-877-GALE.

Desc: Contains essays on frequently studied historical periods, social movements, significant individuals, and key events within specific disciplines worldwide. Entries are hyperlinked, enabling the user to cross historical periods for purposes of comparison. *Available:* The Gale Group, GaleNet. *Database type:* full text; image.

4190 ■ EEO Data
53 Brown Rd.   Ph: (607)257-0567
Ithaca, NY 14850   Free: 800-234-5997
                                 Fax: (607)266-0425
URL: http://www.claritas.com

Desc: Contains occupational information derived from the U.S. Census of Population and Housing. *Available:* Claritas Data Services. *Database type:* statistical.

4191 ■ Genealogy Forum
5000 Arlington Centre Blvd.   Ph: (614)457-8600
P.O. Box 20212   Free: 800-848-8990
Columbus, OH 43220   Fax: (614)457-0348
E-mail: webmaster@compuserve.com
URL: http://www.compuserve.com

Desc: Provides text files equipped with appropriate information on starting or continuing a family history search. Includes shareware programs to help trace birthdates, baptismal records, and marriages. *Available:* CompuServe Information Service. *Database type:* bulletin board.

4192 ■ The Genealogy Home Page
University Park, PA
URL: http://www.genhomepage.com/

Contact: Stephen Wood.

Desc: The Genealogy Home Page provides information for those interested in tracking their family history. Links include Genealogy help and guides, Newsgroups and mailing list, and Genealogy Societies. The FTP site contains a wealth of free and shareware genealogy software. *Database type:* full-text; directory.

4193 ■ Genealogy Toolbox
URL: http://genealogy.tbox.com

Contact: Matthew Helm, Exec. V-P.

Desc: Whether you're a full-time genealogist or setting out for the first time to try to trace your family tree, the resources offered by the Geneaology Toolbox will come in handy. Genealogy SiteFinder is undoubtedly the centerpiece of this valuable site, offering annotated, cross-indexed links to more than 45,000 genealogy-related sites on the Internet. *Database type:* directory; full-text.

4194 ■ Hiscabeq
75, de Port-Royal Est,   Ph: (514)382-0895
  Bureau 300   Fax: (514)384-9139
Montreal, PQ, Canada H3L
  3T1
E-mail: info@sdm.qc.ca
URL: http://www.sdm.qc.ca

Desc: Contains approximately 30,000 records of monographs, theses, and articles from more than 700 periodicals on the history of Quebec and Canada. Covers prehistory, ethnohistory, explorations, genealogies, and cultural, economic, political, religious, and social history. *Available:* Services Documentaires Multimedia Inc. (SDM). *Database type:* bibliographic.

4195 ■ Historical Text Archive
PO Box 5325
Mississippi State, MS 39762
E-mail: msuinfo@ur.msstate.edu
URL: http://www.msstate.edu/Archives/History/

Contact: Prof. Don Mabry, Assoc. Dean, College of Arts & Sciences.

Desc: An incredible resource for the historian or researcher, this site makes available hundreds of historical documents in several formats. In the United States section, for example, you can read transcriptions of the full text of the documents on this site, or you can view electronic images of the original documents, often in the handwriting of the historical figure who wrote them. *Database type:* full-text; image; bibliographic.

4196 ■ Illinois in the Civil War
218 S. Mechanic   Ph: (309)836-3706
Macomb, IL 61455   Fax: (309)833-3905
E-mail: webmaster@outfitters.com
URL: http://www.outfitters.com/illinois/history/civil

Desc: The Illinois in the Civil War site supplies information on individuals and their outfits from Illinois whom served during the Civil War. Data is grouped in easy to find sections and covers such topics as Civil War sites in Illinois, Illinois women in the Civil War, medal of honor recipients, and other historical data. *Database type:* bibliographic; full-text; image.

4197 ■ International Genealogical Index
35 NW Temple   Ph: (801)240-2309
Salt Lake City, UT 84150
E-mail: fhl@lds.org

Desc: Indexes more than 280 million birth, christening, and marriage records. Available as part of the FamilySearch series. *Available:* Church of Jesus Christ of Latter Day Saints, Family History Library. *Database type:* directory.

4198 ■ LEXIS Immigration Library
9443 Springboro Pike   Ph: (937)865-6800
PO Box 933   Free: 800-227-4908
Dayton, OH 45401-0933   Fax: (937)865-6909
URL: http://www.lex-nexis.com

Desc: Provides specific federal case law and agency materials, as well as secondary research materials, focusing on federal immigration matters. *Available:* LEXIS-NEXIS, LEXIS. *Database type:* full text.

4199 ▪ Living History Forum
5000 Arlington Centre Blvd. Ph: (614)457-8600
P.O. Box 20212 Free: 800-848-8990
Columbus, OH 43220 Fax: (614)457-0348
E-mail: webmaster@compuserve.com
URL: http://www.compuserve.com

Desc: A forum for the discussion of historical reenactments. Contains information on artifacts and props, costumes, museums, living history groups, Renaissance festivals, archaeology, and related activities and events. *Available:* CompuServe Information Service. *Database type:* full text.

4200 ▪ New York City Public Records
38 E. 29th St., 8th Fl. Ph: (212)519-3063
New York, NY 10016-7911 Fax: (212)519-3067
URL: http://www.pdcny.com

Contact: Harold G. Free, President.

Desc: Contains public record information for various sections of New York City. Comprises the following 6 files: Mortgage/Deed Indices–contains records for the boroughs of Manhattan, Brooklyn, Queens, and the Bronx. *Available:* Public Data Corporation. *Database type:* bibliographic.

4201 ▪ Ohio in the Civil War
960 Kingsmill Pkwy., Ste. 101 Free: 800-848-4638
Columbus, OH 43229
E-mail: support@infinet.com
URL: http://www.infinet.com/lstevens/a/civil.html

Desc: The history of Ohio in the Civil War is recorded on this site. Resources include a bibliography, war stories, detailed data about various divisions, prison camps, links to research sites, and more. *Database type:* bibliographic; directory.

4202 ▪ Online Genealogy Library at Ancestry.com
PO Box 990
Orem, UT 84059-0990 Ph: (801)426-3500
E-mail: techmail@ancestry-inc.com Fax: (801)426-3501
URL: http://www.ancestry.com/ancestry/search.asp

Desc: Ancestry.com, which calls itself "the largest online genealogy search engine," has considerable resources available on-site to back up that claim. It makes available several free databases for the genealogy researcher, including the Social Security Death Index (updated to June 1998), the Ancestry World Tree (which contains over 7 million names), and a selection of other databases such as The Source, A Guidebook for Genealogy; WWI Civilian Draft Registrations; and 50,000 Bibliographic Sources from the Library of Congress. *Database type:* full-text; directory; numeric; statistical.

4203 ▪ People Finder
Marquis One Tower, Ste. 1400 Ph: (404)479-6500
245 Peachtree Center Ave. Free: 800-235-4008
Atlanta, GA 30303 Fax: (404)479-6700
URL: http://www.infoam.com

Contact: Customer Support.

Desc: Contains profiles of 160 million individuals, 92 million households, and 71 million telephone numbers in the United States. For each household, provides family name, current address, telephone number, social security numbers, previous addresses and records for deceased individuals date of birth, residence type, length of residence,

family members, their dates of birth, and up to ten neighbors with addresses and telephone numbers. *Available:* Information America (IA). *Database type:* directory.

4204 ▪ POPLINE
8600 Rockville Pike Ph: (301)496-3147
Bethesda, MD 20894 Free: 800-638-8480
Fax: (301)480-3537
URL: http://www.sis.nlm.nih.gov/dirline

Desc: Contains approximately 251,000 citations, with abstracts, to the worldwide literature on family planning and population. Includes research in human fertility, contraceptive methods, maternal and child health care, family planning services, AIDS in developing countries, program operations and evaluations, community issues, demography, censuses, vital statistics, and related health, law, and policy issues. *Available:* U.S. National Library of Medicine (NLM), TOXNET; National Information Services Corporation (NISC), BiblioLine. *Database type:* bibliographic.

4205 ▪ Population of States and Counties of the United States: 1790 to 1990
Suitland Federal Center Ph: (301)457-4100
Washington, DC 20233-8300 Fax: (301)457-4714
URL: http://www.census.gov

Desc: Provides comprehensive census data on the population of the States, Territories and counties. Includes data from 21 decennial censuses. *Available:* U.S. Bureau of the Census. *Database type:* statistical.

4206 ▪ RAND Genealogy Club
1700 Main St. Ph: (310)393-0411
PO Box 2138 Fax: (310)393-4818
Santa Monica, CA 90407-2138
E-mail: pboren@rand.org
URL: http://www.rand.org/personal/Genea

Desc: The RAND Genealogy site provides information learned by the RAND employees in tracing their own heritage. The site is a database designed to offer insight for the person searching for their roots and provides numerous resources such as location lists, historical data, and links to other sites concerning genealogy. *Database type:* directory; full-text.

4207 ▪ Senior Life
53 Brown Rd. Ph: (607)257-0567
Ithaca, NY 14850 Free: 800-234-5997
Fax: (607)266-0425
URL: http://www.claritas.com

Contact: Bob Kreutter.

Desc: Contains data from the U.S. Census of Population and Housing, current-year estimates, and 5-year forecasts on persons aged 55 and older. *Available:* Claritas Data Services. *Database type:* statistical.

4208 ▪ State and Metropolitan Area Data Book
Suitland Federal Center Ph: (301)457-4100
Washington, DC 20233-8300 Fax: (301)457-4714
URL: http://www.census.gov

Desc: Provides data from censuses and surveys. Includes information from more than 60 government agencies and private sources. *Available:* U.S. Bureau of the Census. *Database type:* statistical.

4209 ▪ The USGenWeb Project
PO Box 6798
Frazier Park, CA 93222-6798
URL: http://www.usgenweb.org

Contact: Nancy Trice, National Coordinator.

Desc: This expansive and ambitious web site is an absolute wealth of information for genealogists, roots tracers, and anyone interested in the history and development of the United States. You can begin your search with extensive information for researchers, includes FAQs, hints, lists, and other information you can put to use immediately. *Database type:* full-text; image; directory.

4210 ▪ WellCount
601 Dempsey Rd. Ph: (614)882-8179
Westerville, OH 43081-8978 Free: 800-332-2104
Fax: (614)898-7786
E-mail: h20-ngwa@h20-ngna.org
URL: http://www.ngwa.org

Desc: Contains approximately 40,000 records of 1990 U.S. census data providing counts of U.S. *Available:* National Ground Water Information Center (NGWIC), Ground Water Network. *Database type:* statistical.

Other formats

4211 ▪ Block-face Data File
Statistical Reference Center Ph: (613)951-8116
National Capitol Region Free: 800-263-1136
R.H. Coats Bldg., Lobby Fax: (613)951-0581
Holland Ave.
Ottawa, ON, Canada K1A 0T6
E-mail: infostats@statcan.ca
URL: http://www.statcan.ca/start.html

Contact: Geo-help.

Desc: Format: diskette. Contains 1996 census population and dwelling counts for block-faces in urban centers covered by the Street Network Files. Links the block-face to all other levels of standard geography through geographic codes. *Database type:* statistical; directory.

4212 ▪ The Blue Disk - Genealogy Societies
1300 E. Woodfield Ph: (847)995-9222
Ste. 506 Fax: (847)995-9290
Schaumburg, IL 60173
E-mail: DJHAY@geosource.com

Desc: Format: diskette. Contains listing of more than 2,160 geneological societies in the United States and Canada. *Database type:* directory.

4213 ▪ CANSIM Census Data on Magnetic Tapes
Statistical Reference Center Ph: (613)951-8116
National Capitol Region Free: 800-263-1136
R.H. Coats Bldg., Lobby Fax: (613)951-0581
Holland Ave.
Ottawa, ON, Canada K1A 0T6
E-mail: infostats@statcan.ca
URL: http://www.statcan.ca/start.html

Desc: Format: magnetic tape. Contains Canadian census data. Corresponds in part to the CANSIM online database. *Database type:* statistical.

4214 ▪ CANSIM Census Profile Data on Diskettes
Statistical Reference Center Ph: (613)951-8116
National Capitol Region Free: 800-263-1136
R.H. Coats Bldg., Lobby Fax: (613)951-0581
Holland Ave.
Ottawa, ON, Canada K1A 0T6
E-mail: infostats@statcan.ca
URL: http://www.statcan.ca/start.html

Desc: Format: diskette. Provides census profiles covering data on population, families, labor force, households, and dwellings for numerous standard national, provincial, and regional geographic areas in Canada. Source of data is the Census of Population and Housing for 1981 and 1986. *Database type:* statistical.

4215 ▪ Death Certificates and Social Security Applications: Two Genealogical Sources

1300 E. Woodfield   Ph: (847)995-9222
Ste. 506   Fax: (847)995-9290
Schaumburg, IL 60173
E-mail: DJHAY@geusource.com

Desc: Format: Diskette. Contains the complete text of Death Certificates and Social Security Applications, for use in family history research. *Database type:* full text.

4216 ▪ GenDisk Magazine

1300 E. Woodfield   Ph: (847)995-9222
Ste. 506   Fax: (847)995-9290
Schaumburg, IL 60173
E-mail: DJHAY@geusource.com

Desc: Format: Diskette. An electronic magazine intended for genealogists who utilize a computer in their research. Contains articles dealing with genealogy, columns, reviews, editorials, specials, a calendar of events, and limited advertisements. *Database type:* full text.

4217 ▪ LC MARC: National Union Catalog of Manuscript Collections

101 Independence Ave., S.E.   Ph: (202)707-6100
Washington, DC 20541-4912   Free: 800-255-3666
    Fax: (202)707-1334
E-mail: cdsinfo@loc.gov
URL: http://www.lcweb/loc.gov/cds

Contact: Customer Service Unit.

Desc: Format: magnetic tape. Contains full bibliographic descriptions and cataloging information for approximately 6000 collections of personal and family papers, business records, and other manuscripts of historical and research importance that are cataloged by the Library of Congress. Includes information on the location of collections. *Database type:* bibliographic.

4218 ▪ Marriage Laws in the United States, 1887-1906

1300 E. Woodfield   Ph: (847)995-9222
Ste. 506   Fax: (847)995-9290
Schaumburg, IL 60173
E-mail: DJHAY@geusource.com

Desc: Format: Diskette. Contains the complete text of Marriage Laws in the United States, 1887-1906, by Desmond Walls Allen. Provides insights into the legal structure and social guides of marriage requirements in the United States during this time period. *Database type:* full text.

4219 ▪ Marriage Records

P.O. Box 329   Ph: (801)298-5446
593 W. 100 North   Free: 800-658-7758
Bountiful, UT 84011-0329   Fax: (801)298-5468
E-mail: sales@heritagequest.com
URL: http://www.heritagequest.com

Contact: Raeone Steuart.

Desc: Format: Diskette. Contains information indexed by state on marriage records. Provides cross-indexed bride and groom names and original record type. *Database type:* bibliographic.

4220 ▪ 1890 Civil War Veterans and Widows Special Census

P.O. Box 329   Ph: (801)298-5446
593 W. 100 North   Free: 800-658-7758
Bountiful, UT 84011-0329   Fax: (801)298-5468
E-mail: sales@heritagequest.com
URL: http://www.heritagequest.com

Contact: Raeone Steuart.

Desc: Format: Diskette. Contains information from the 1890 census conducted by the U.S. federal government covering Civil War veterans and their widows. *Database type:* statistical.

4221 ▪ 1870 Federal Census

P.O. Box 329   Ph: (801)298-5446
593 W. 100 North   Free: 800-658-7758
Bountiful, UT 84011-0329   Fax: (801)298-5468
E-mail: sales@heritagequest.com
URL: http://www.heritagequest.com

Contact: Raeone Steuart.

Desc: Format: Diskette. Provides information from the 1870 census conducted by the U.S. federal government in the cities or states of Georgia; Chicago, Illinois; St. *Database type:* statistical.

4222 ▪ 1860 Federal Census

P.O. Box 329   Ph: (801)298-5446
593 W. 100 North   Free: 800-658-7758
Bountiful, UT 84011-0329   Fax: (801)298-5468
E-mail: sales@heritagequest.com
URL: http://www.heritagequest.com

Contact: Raeone Steuart.

Desc: Format: Diskette. Contains information from the 1860 census conducted by the U.S. federal government in 1860 in the states of California, Connecticut, Delaware, District of Columbia, Florida, Oregon, and Rhode Island. *Database type:* statistical.

4223 ▪ 1986 Census Final Population and Dwelling Counts on Diskette

Statistical Reference Center   Ph: (613)951-8116
National Capitol Region   Free: 800-263-1136
R.H. Coats Bldg., Lobby   Fax: (613)951-0581
Holland Ave.
Ottawa, ON, Canada K1A 0T6
E-mail: infostats@statcan.ca
URL: http://www.statcan.ca/start.html

Desc: Format: diskette. Contains census data for Canadian regions. Comprises the following 2 files: National Summary Package--contains census data for Canadian provinces, regions, census divisions, census metropolitan areas (CMAs), and census agglomerations. *Database type:* statistical.

4224 ▪ 1790 Federal Census

P.O. Box 329   Ph: (801)298-5446
593 W. 100 North   Free: 800-658-7758
Bountiful, UT 84011-0329   Fax: (801)298-5468
E-mail: sales@heritagequest.com
URL: http://www.heritagequest.com

Contact: Raeone Steuart.

Desc: Format: Diskette. Contains information from the first census conducted by the U.S. federal government in the states of Maine, New Hampshire, New York, North Carolina, Rhode Island, and Vermont. *Database type:* statistical.

4225 ▪ USA GeoGraph II - Spanish Edition

6160 Summit Dr. N   Ph: (612)569-1500
Minneapolis, MN 55430-4003   Free: 800-685-6322
    Fax: (612)569-1548
E-mail: pkallio@learningco.com
URL: http://www.learningco.com

Desc: Format: Diskette. Contains multimedia demographic, social, environmental, economic and 1990 U.S. census data for the United States, including all 50 states, District of Columbia, and 6 territories. *Database type:* image; audio.

4226 ▪ Yellow Disk - Genealogical Vendor Database

1300 E. Woodfield   Ph: (847)995-9222
Ste. 506   Fax: (847)995-9290
Schaumburg, IL 60173
E-mail: DJHAY@geusource.com

Desc: Format: diskette. Contains contact information on genealogical vendors in the United States. For each vendor provides company name, city, telephone, or product type. *Database type:* directory.

Geographic Index

This index provides a geographical listing of all entry names. Index references are to book entry numbers rather than to page numbers.

California

Florida

Georgia

Kansas

Kentucky

Michigan

Rockingham Society of Genealogists (Exeter) .1009
Rockingham Society of Genealogists (Exeter) .2369
Hampton Historical Society (Hampton) 1774
Piscataqua Pioneers (Hampton) 956
ABK Publications (Hanover) 2808
International Association of Hispanists—List
   of Members (Hanover) 3460
Clan Chisholm Society - United States
   Branch (Keene) 210
American-Canadian Genealogical Society
   (Manchester) 43
American-Canadian Genealogical Society, Inc.
   (Manchester) 1262
American-Canadian Genealogist
   (Manchester) 3530
Manchester City Library (Manchester) 2020
Plymouth Rock Foundation, Inc.
   (Marlborough) 3133
The Bibliographer (Nashua) 2851
Nashua Public Library (Nashua) 2139
S. F. Getchell (Newmarket) 2952
Newmarket Historical Society (Newmarket) ..2185
Peterborough Historical Society
   (Peterborough) 2301
James E. Whalley Museum and Library
   (Portsmouth) 1887
Portsmouth Athenaeum (Portsmouth) 2325
Strawbery Banke Newsletter (Portsmouth) ...3915
Salisbury Historical Society (Salisbury) 2403
Wolfeboro Historical Society (Wolfeboro) ...2785

New Jersey
Allaire Village, Inc. (Allaire) 1255
Atlantic City Free Public Library (Atlantic
   City) 1303
Haney Family Association (Belvidere) 508
Avotaynu (Bergenfield) 3969
Avotaynu, Inc. (Bergenfield) 2839
Bridgeton Public Library (Bridgeton) 1369
Burlington County Historical Society
   (Burlington) 1395
Camden County Historical Society
   (Camden) 1419
Camden County Historical Society—Bulletin
   (Camden) 3585
Cape May County Historical & Genealogical
   Society (Cape May Court House) 1432
Congregation Beth Jacob-Beth Israel (Cherry
   Hill) 1553
Maryland's Colonial Families Newsletter
   (Cherry Hill) 3776
Temple Beth Sholom (Cherry Hill) 2524
Temple Emanuel (Cherry Hill) 2535
Next Decade, Inc. (Chester) 3105
Temple Sinai (Cinnaminson) 2555
Cranford Historical Society (Cranford) 1579
Crosswicks Public Library (Crosswicks) 1581
Historic Morris Emporium (Denville) 4025
Frary Family Newsletter (Dumont) 3660
CensusCD (East Brunswick) 4144
Angele Fernande Daniel Family Organization
   (Eatontown) 56
Jerome S. Ozer, Publisher (Englewood) 3120
Hunterdon County Historical Society
   (Flemington) 1853
Hunterdon Historical Newsletter
   (Flemington) 3717
Liberty Bell Associates (Franklin Park) 3045

Monmouth County Genealogy Club
   (Freehold) 780
Monmouth County Historical Association
   (Freehold) 2106
Rowan University (Glassboro) 2380
Cumberland County Historical Society
   (Greenwich) 1584
Bergen County Historical Society
   (Hackensack) 1327
Hackettstown Historical Society
   (Hackettstown) 1768
Historical Society of Haddonfield
   (Haddonfield) 1814
Sons of Union Veterans of the Civil War
   (Hammonton) 1091
T. J. Obal (Hillsdale) 3110
Polish Family Tree Surnames (Hillsdale) 3494
Genealogical Society of New Jersey
   Newsletter (Hopewell) 3676
Flagon and Trencher (Lakewood) 398
Hunterdon House (Lambertville) 2999
Washington Township Historical Society
   (Long Valley) 2722
Historical Society of the United Methodist
   Church (Madison) 544
World Methodist Historical Society
   (Madison) 1229
Morrow Memorial United Methodist Church
   (Maplewood) 2125
Madison Township Historical Society
   (Matawan) 2011
The Doughty Tree (Mays Landing) 3630
Genealogical Society of Bergen County
   (Midland Park) 439
USCCCN Masters of Philanthropy
   (Millburn) 2680
Historical Society of Moorestown
   (Moorestown) 1818
Joint Free Public Library of Morristown &
   Morris Township (Morristown) 1899
Macculloch Hall Historical Museum
   (Morristown) 2002
Morris County Historical Society
   (Morristown) 2123
Genealogical Society of New Jersey (New
   Brunswick) 1730
New Providence Historical Society (New
   Providence) 2172
New Jersey Historical Society (Newark) 2168
New Jersey History (Newark) 4067
Newark Public Library (Newark) 2182
Rutgers University (Newark) 3312
Sussex County Historical Society (Newton) ..2505
Nutley Historical Society Museum (Nutley) ..2232
Historical Society of Ocean Grove, New
   Jersey (Ocean Grove) 1820
Passaic County Historical Society (Paterson) ..2288
Johannes Schwalm Historical Association
   (Pennsauken) 647
Journal of African American Men
   (Piscataway) 4037
Journal of American Ethnic History
   (Piscataway) 4040
African and Caribbean Immigrant Resource
   Center (Plainfield) 16
Historical Society of Princeton (Princeton) ..1826
Princeton University (Princeton) 3307
Princeton University (Princeton) 2330

Grapevine (Red Bank) 3689
Runkle Family Association (Ringoes) 1016
National Society of the Sons of the American
   Revolution (Roselle) 2151
Salem County Historical Society (Salem) 2401
Atlantic County Historical Society (Somers
   Point) 1304
Temple Sharey Tefilo-Israel (South Orange) ..2552
Clan Currie Society (Summit) 214
Fairleigh Dickinson University (Teaneck) 1654
Teaneck Public Library (Teaneck) 2513
Ocean County Historical Society (Toms
   River) 2237
New Jersey State Library (Trenton) 2169
Trenton Public Library (Trenton) 2581
Bunker Banner (Turnersville) 3577
Bunker Family Association of America
   (Turnersville) 146
Beth Israel Congregation (Vineland) 1335
Vineland Historical and Antiquarian Society
   (Vineland) 2697
Genealogical Society of the West Fields
   (Westfield) 462
Jewish Historical Society of Metrowest
   (Whippany) 1893
Morris County Library (Whippany) 2124
Genealogical Resources in Southern New
   Jersey (Woodbury) 3440
Gloucester County Historical Society
   (Woodbury) 2953
Gloucester County Historical Society
   (Woodbury) 1743

New Mexico
Albuquerque Public Library (Albuquerque) ...1252
Church of Jesus Christ of Latter-Day Saints
   (Albuquerque) 1484
Congregation B'nai Israel (Albuquerque) 1554
David Family Organization (Albuquerque) 319
Frederick Wilhelm Haury Family
   Organization (Albuquerque) 407
Lyon Press (Albuquerque) 3060
Mary Ellen Kinney Family Organization
   (Albuquerque) 738
New Mexico Historical Review
   (Albuquerque) 4068
Prall Family Association (Albuquerque) 966
University of New Mexico (Albuquerque) 3359
University of New Mexico (Albuquerque) 2653
University of New Mexico (Albuquerque) 2652
Weimer Genealogical Center Newsletter
   (Albuquerque) 3937
Artesia Historical Museum and Art Center
   (Artesia) 3263
San Juan County Archaeological Research
   Center and Library (Bloomfield) 3314
First United Methodist Church (Deming) ...1676
Caton Family Association (Farmington) 179
Los Alamos Historical Museum Archives (Los
   Alamos) 1991
Chaves County Genealogical Society
   (Roswell) 188
Church of Jesus Christ of Latter-Day Saints
   (Roswell) 1508
Goodwin Family Organization (Roswell) 482
Goodwin News (Roswell) 3687
School of American Research (Santa Fe) 2427

Orangeburg German-Swiss Newsletter
(Orangeburg) 3836
Orangeburgh German Swiss Genealogical
Society (Orangeburg) 916
Pendleton District Historical, Recreational
and Tourism Commission (Pendleton) ... 2292
Chester District Genealogical Society
(Richburg) 192
Chester District Genealogical Society—
Bulletin (Richburg) 3593
Calhoun County Museum (St. Matthews) .. 1404
MacFaddien Family Society (Sardinia) 722
Reprint Co. Publishers (Spartanburg) 3147
United Methodist Commission on
Archives & History (Spartanburg) 2599
Sumter County Genealogical Society
(Sumter) 1124

South Dakota
WyMonDak Messenger (Belle Fourche) 3947
South Dakota State University (Brookings) ... 3321
Lyman-Brule Genealogical Society
(Chamberlain) 720
South Dakota Hall of Fame Newsletter
(Chamberlain) 3906
Coatney/Courtney Family Association
(Freeman) 266
Hyde County Historical and Genealogical
Society (Highmore) 570
Lake County Genealogical Society (Madison) .. 687
Dakota Wesleyan University (Mitchell) 1589
Mitchell Kinship Program (Mitchell) 779
Market Fact Finders, Inc. (Olivet) 3068
Disbrow Family Newsletter (Sioux Falls) 3627
Siouxland Heritage Museums (Sioux Falls) ... 2453
Norbert Barrie Family Organization
(Turton) 844
American Indian Research Project
(Vermillion) 1269
South Dakota Oral History Center
(Vermillion) 3320
University of South Dakota (Vermillion) 3364

Tennessee
Lillard Family Association (Benton) 700
Spurlock Family Association (Blountville) 1106
Tennessee Genealogical Society (Brunswick) .. 1135
Chattanooga-Hamilton County Bicentennial
Library (Chattanooga) 1465
Broyles Family Newsletter (Clinton) 3573
Sons of Confederate Veterans (Columbia) 1087
Lincoln County Genealogical Society
(Fayetteville) 701
Family Findings (Jackson) 3646
Mid-West Tennessee Genealogical Society
(Jackson) 3078
Roane County Genealogical Society
(Kingston) 1004
Civil War Genealogical Research (Knoxville) . 3404
Virginia Carlisle d'Armand (Knoxville) 2900
Genealogical Sources, Unltd. (Knoxville) 2946
Goff/Gough Family Association (Knoxville) ... 480
Handbook of Genealogical Sources
(Knoxville) 3448
Knox County Public Library System
(Knoxville) 1933
Bonnie Peters (Knoxville) 3127
Revolutionary War Genealogy (Knoxville) ... 3498

State Data Center Newsletter (Knoxville) 3914
Tennessee Valley Publishing (Knoxville) 3213
Bonnie Page Publications (Lake City) 3121
Yesterday and Today in Lawrence County
(Lawrenceburg) 4131
Moore County Historical and Genealogical
Society (Lynchburg) 786
Clan McLaren Association of North America
(Madisonville) 243
Weakley County Genealogical Society
(Martin) 1191
Brigance Publishing (Maryville) 2858
Carroll County Historical Society
(McKenzie) 173
Center for Southern Folklore (Memphis) 3274
MemphisShelby County Public Library &
Information Center (Memphis) 2059
University of Memphis (Memphis) 2649
University of Memphis (Memphis) 2648
University of Memphis (Memphis) 3346
West Tennessee Historical Society
(Memphis) 2742
American Association for State & Local
History/AASLH (Nashville) 2818
Association for the Development of Religious
Information Systems (Nashville) 73
Disciples of Christ Historical Society
(Nashville) 337
Disciples of Christ Historical Society
(Nashville) 1615
Fisk University (Nashville) 1677
Guild Bindery Press, Inc. (Nashville) 2963
History News (Nashville) 4030
Jewish Federation of Nashville and Middle
Tennessee (Nashville) 1892
Land Yacht Press (Nashville) 3036
Public Library of Nashville and Davidson
County (Nashville) 2334
Byron Sistler & Associates, Inc. (Nashville) .. 3179
Society of Tennessee Archivists (Nashville) ... 1082
Southern Baptist Hisorical Library and
Archives (Nashville) 1097
Temple Ohabai Shalom (Nashville) 2549
Tennessee Archivist (Nashville) 3919
Tennessee (State) Department of State
(Nashville) 2559
Tennessee Western History Association
(Nashville) 2560
West End Synagogue (Nashville) 2738
Matilda Jenkins Webb (Newport) 3234
Rocky Mount Historical Association (Piney
Flats) 2371
Smoky Mountain Historical Society Journal
(Sevierville) 4110
Bedford Historical Quarterly (Shelbyville) 3971
Mountain Press (Signal Mountain) 3087
Mountain Press Research Center (Signal
Mountain) 794
Mountain Press Research Center (Signal
Mountain) 3300
Van Buren County Historical Society
(Spencer) 1165
Obion County Historical Society (Union
City) 855
Cabbage/Cabage Surname Organization
(Washburn) 150
National Historical Publishing Co.
(Waynesboro) 3095

Franklin County Tennessee Tidings
(Winchester) 3658

Texas
Sul Ross State University (Alpine) 2502
The Pipings (Alvin) 3851
Amarillo Genealogical Library (Amarillo) 1259
Atchley/Harden Family Association
(Amarillo) 80
Brazoria County Historical Museum
(Angleton) 1367
Brazorial County Historical Museum
Research Center (Angleton) 3267
Clan MacDuff Society of America
(Arlington) 230
Cass County Genealogical Society (Atlanta) ... 175
The Abbey Newsletter (Austin) 3515
Austin Genealogical Society (Austin) 85
Clan Scott Society (Austin) 252
Daughters of the Republic of Texas (Austin) .. 317
Federation of Genealogical Societies (Austin) .. 392
German-Texan Heritage Society (Austin) 2951
Historical Society of the Episcopal Church
(Austin) 543
Pierre Bowdoin/Baudoin Family Association
(Austin) 950
Richard Sunbury (Austin) 3207
Texas Catholic Conference (Austin) 2564
Texas State Library and Archives Commission
(Austin) 2565
U.S. Presidential Libraries (Austin) 2624
University of Texas at Austin (Austin) 2664
University of Texas at Austin (Austin) 3366
University of Texas at Austin (Austin) 3367
Matagorda County Genealogical Society (Bay
City) 742
Beaumont Public Library System
(Beaumont) 1316
Norma Pontiff Evans, Genealogical Services
(Beaumont) 2922
Southeast Texas Genealogical and Historical
Society (Beaumont) 3186
Mildred S. Wright (Beaumont) 3255
Mid-Cities Genealogical Society (Bedford) 766
Genealogical Society of Kendall County
(Boerne) 451
Hutchinson County Genealogical Society
(Borger) 569
Fort Clark Historical Society (Brackettville) .. 1691
Stephens County Genealogical Society
(Breckenridge) 1111
Berry Surname Organization (Burkeville) 112
Rogers Clan (Burkeville) 1011
Our Heritage (Canton) 3839
Corral Dust (Canyon) 3611
Panhandle-Plains Historical Museum
(Canyon) 3304
Leon County Genealogical Society, Inc.
(Centerville) 3043
Donley County Genealogical Society
(Clarendon) 343
Bertha L. Gable, Author and Publisher
(Clarksville) 2938
Layland Museum (Cleburne) 1957
Texas A&M University (College Station) 2562
Texas A&M University (College Station) 3329
Curtis Media Inc. (Colleyville) 2896
Margaret Waring (Comanche) 3231

Vermont

Virginia

Wisconsin

Wyoming

Canada

Alberta

Prince Edward Island

Quebec

Saskatchewan

Master Index

This index provides an alphabetical listing of all entry names and important keywords within entry names. Index references are to book entry numbers rather than to page numbers.

Master Index

Master Index

Great Plains Newsletter; Museum of the 3796
Greater Loveland Historical Society Museum. .1753
Greater West Bloomfield Historical Society . . .1754
Greatorex Family Organization; Holmes-. 551
Greeley County Historical Society 1755
Greeley Municipal Archives. 1756
Green Country Quarterly 3690
Green Creek Publishing Co. 2958
Greenbrier Historical Society. 1757,
Greenbrier Historical Society Journal. 4017
Greene County Genealogical Society 493
Greene County Historical and Genealogical
    Society 494
Greene County Historical Society 1758,
Greene County Public Library. 1760
Greene County Room. 1760
Greene-Dunn Family Association; Scully- 1048
Greene Family Organization; Jeremiah. 634
Greenfield Community College. 1761
Greenhoe Library .2057
Greenway Family Association 495
Greenwich Library. 1762
Greenwood County Historical Society 1763
Gregath Publishing Co. 2960
Gregor Society; American Clan 44
Gregor Society of Canada; Clan 222
Gregor Society Pacific Northwest Chapter;
    Clan. 223
Gregson Family Association; John Robinson -
    Ann 655
Grems - Doolittle Library 2425
Griepp Publishing. 2961
Gries Library. 2500
Griesemer Family Association 496
J. B. Griffith. 2962
Grigsby Family Society; National. 812
Grinnell Family Association. 497
Griswold Family Association of America
    Newsletter 3691
Groberg - Holbrook Genealogical
    Organization. 498
Grout Museum of History and Science 1764
Grover Family Organization 499
Guale Historical Society 1765
Guide to Information Resources in Ethnic
    Museum, Library, and Archival
    Collections in the United States 3445
Guide to Research Collections of Former
    United States Senators 1789-1995. 3446
Guidebook to Historic Western Pennsylvania. .3447
Guild Bindery Press, Inc.. 2963
Guilford Genealogist 3692
Guilford Township Historical Collection 2312
Guthrie Family Organization; Thomas. 1143
Guysborough Historical Society. 1766
Gwinnett Historical Society. 1767

H

Hacker's Creek Pioneer Descendants 500
Hackettstown Historical Society. 1768
Hackley Public Library 1769
Hadley - Hawthorne - Dickey - Walden
    Family Reunion Association 501
Hal C. Phelps Archives 2071
Hales Family History Society. 502
Halferty Family Registry 503

Halfyard Heritage Newsletter. 3693
Halifax Historical Society, Inc. 1770
Hall County Museum 1771
Hall of Fame Newsletter; South Dakota 3906
Hall Family Organization; Thomas 1144
Hall and Mary Bates Family Organization;
    John 652
W. C. Hall 2964
Hallam Association .504
Hallockville Museum Farm 505
Hamilton City Library 1772
Hamilton County Genealogical Society 506
Hamilton Hutton, Sr., Family Organization;
    Alexander 28
Hamilton National Genealogical Society 507
Hammond Public Library 1773
G. P. Hammond Publishing 2965
Hampton Historical Society. 1774
Hampton House 2966
Hancock Heritage .3694
Hancock Historical Museum & Archives. 1775
Handbook of Genealogical Sources 3448
Handley Regional Library 1776
Handy Book for Genealogists 3449
Haney Family Association 508
Hans/Henry Segrist Family Organization. 509
Hansen Family Organization; Sophus
    Frederick 1092
Phyllis Hapner 2967
Happy Family Organization; James 626
Har Zion Temple 1777
Harbor-UCLA Medical Center 3333
Harden Family Association; Atchley/ 80
Harden - Hardin - Harding Family
    Association 510
Hardin County Chapter, Ohio Genealogical
    Society 511
Hardin County Historical and Genealogical
    Society 512
Hardin - Harding Family Association;
    Harden - 510
Harding Family Association; Harden -
    Hardin - 510
Harless Family Association. 513
Harper County Genealogical Society 514
Harper County Genealogical Society 1778
Mary M. Harper. 2968
Harrison County Genealogical Society. 515, 5
Harrison County Research Center 3282
Harrison Family Association 517
Michael and Margaret B. Harrison Western
    Research Center 3332
Western Research Center; Michael and
    Margaret B. Harrison 3332
Harrisonburg-Rockingham Historical Society. .1779
Harrodsburg Historical Society 1780
Harry and Anna Feinberg Library 1559
Harry M. Trowbridge Research Library 2795
Harry Simons Library 1330
Hart County Historical Society 518
Hart County Historical Society Quarterly 3695
Harting Family Association 519
Hartshorn Family Association 520
Hartshorn Family Association 1781
Gloria C. Hartzell. .2969
Haskell County Historical Society 1782
Hastings County Historical Society 2970
Hathaway Family Association 521

Hattie & Albert Grauer. 2520
Haury Family Organization; Frederick
    Wilhelm. 407
Havens House Museum 2441
Haverford Township Historical Society 1783
Haverhill Public Library 1784
Haviland Family Organization. 522
Hawaii Bottle Museum—News 3696
Hawaii Chinese History Center 3283
Hawaii Times Photo Archives Foundation 523
Hawaiian Historical Society. 1785
Hawkes Family Association; Adam. 7
Hawkeye Heritage. 4018
Hawkins Association (Descendants of Robert
    and Mary of Massachusetts, Zachariah
    Hawkins of New York, and Joseph
    Hawkins of Connecticut) 524
Haws and Hannah Whitcomb Family
    Organization; Gilberth 475
Hawthorne - Dickey - Walden Family
    Reunion Association; Hadley - 501
Haymore Family Organization. 525
Hayner Public Library. 1786
Hazelbaker Families. 526
Hazelrigg Family Newsletter 3697
Heald Family Association 527
Heart of America Genealogical Society &
    Library, Inc. 1787
Heart of the Lakes Publishing 2971
Hearthside Press 2972
Heartlines. 3698
Hebert Publications. 2973
Heckman Family Organization; William
    Jacob 1215
Hedrick Family Association; Smith-. 1066
Heiney Family Tree .528
Heinlein Family Association; Henlein/ 532
Held-Poage Memorial Home & Research
    Library. 1788
Helen Blau Memorial Library 1452
Helen Nettleton Library 2276
Helen V. Gearn Library 1819
Helena Family History Center. 1498
The Heller Helper. 3699
Hempstead County Genealogical Society 529
Henderson County Genealogical and
    Historical Society 530
Hendricks Books. .2974
Hendricks County Genealogical Society. 531
Henlein/Heinlein Family Association. 532
Hennepin History Museum. 1789
Henry County Genealogical Society. 533
Henry County Historical Society. 1790
Henry Historical and Genealogical Society. . . .534
Henry Segrist Family Organization; Hans/ 509
M. Hepburn & Associates Inc. 2975
Her Heritage: A Biographical Encyclopedia of
    Famous American Women 4162
Heraldic Reference Library 1791
Heraldry; American & British Genealogy &. . .3392
Heraldry; American College of. 45
Heraldry Fellowship of Rotarians;
    International Genealogy and 578
Heraldry Organization; Western 1201
Heraldry Society of Canada. 1791
The Heraldry Society of Canada 2976
Herbert Goldberg Memorial Library 2524

W